PRINCIPLES OF DIGITAL IMAGE SYNTHESIS

THE MORGAN KAUFMANN SERIES IN COMPUTER GRAPHICS AND GEOMETRIC MODELING

Series Editor, Brian A. Barsky

Principles of Digital Image Synthesis
Andrew S. Glassner

Radiosity & Global Illumination
François X. Sillion and Claude Puech

Knotty: A B-Spline Visualization Program
Jonathan Yen

User Interface Management Systems: Models and Algorithms
Dan R. Olsen, Jr.

Making Them Move: Mechanics, Control, and Animation of Articulated Figures
Edited by Norman I. Badler, Brian A. Barsky, and David Zeltzer

Geometric and Solid Modeling: An Introduction
Christoph M. Hoffmann

An Introduction to Splines for Use in Computer Graphics and Geometric Modeling
Richard H. Bartels, John C. Beatty, and Brian A. Barsky

VOLUME TWO

Andrew S. Glassner

PRINCIPLES OF DIGITAL IMAGE SYNTHESIS

MORGAN KAUFMANN PUBLISHERS, INC. SAN FRANCISCO, CALIFORNIA

Sponsoring Editor Michael B. Morgan
Production Manager Yonie Overton
Assistant Editor Douglas Sery
Assistant Production Editor Julie Pabst
Composition Ed Sznyter, Babel Press
Illustration Tech-Graphics
Cover, Text, and Color Insert Design Carron Design
Copyeditor Gary Morris
Indexer Steve Rath
Proofreaders Bill Cassell, Ken DellaPenta, and Mary Gillam
Color Separation Color Tech
Printer Quebecor Printing

Morgan Kaufmann Publishers, Inc.
Editorial and Sales Office
340 Pine Street, Sixth Floor
San Francisco, CA 94104-3205
USA
Telephone 415/392-2665
Facsimile 415/982-2665
Internet mkp@mkp.com

99 98 97 96 95 5 4 3 2 1

Library of Congress Cataloging-in-Publication Data

Glassner, Andrew S.
Principles of digital image synthesis / Andrew S. Glassner.
p. cm.
Includes bibliographical references and index.
ISBN 1-55860-276-3 (v. 2: hardcover)
1. Computer graphics. 2. Image processing–Digital techniques.
I. Title.
T385.G585 1995
006.6–dc20 94-36565

To the inspiration of Leonardo da Vinci

Snow taken from the high peaks of mountains might be carried to hot places and let to fall at festivals in open places at summer time.

Leonardo da Vinci

CONTENTS

Preface xxi

Summary of Useful Notation xxix

VOLUME I (UNITS I AND II)

Color Plates *Following page 322*

I THE HUMAN VISUAL SYSTEM AND COLOR 1

1 The Human Visual System 5
- 1.1 Introduction 5
- 1.2 Structure and Optics of the Human Eye 6
- 1.3 Spectral and Temporal Aspects of the HVS 14
- 1.4 Visual Phenomena 23
  - 1.4.1 Contrast Sensitivity 23
  - 1.4.2 Noise 28
  - 1.4.3 Mach Bands 29
  - 1.4.4 Lightness Contrast and Constancy 31
- 1.5 Depth Perception 33
  - 1.5.1 Oculomotor Depth 34
  - 1.5.2 Binocular Depth 35
  - 1.5.3 Monocular Depth 37
  - 1.5.4 Motion Parallax 41
- 1.6 Color Opponency 42
- 1.7 Perceptual Color Matching: CIE *XYZ* Space 44

1.8 Illusions 51
1.9 Further Reading 55
1.10 Exercises 55

2 Color Spaces 59
2.1 Perceptually Uniform Color Spaces: $L^*u^*v^*$ and $L^*a^*b^*$ 59
2.2 Other Color Systems 66
2.3 Further Reading 68
2.4 Exercises 68

3 Displays 71
3.1 Introduction 71
3.2 CRT Displays 71
3.3 Display Spot Interaction 76
3.3.1 Display Spot Profile 76
3.3.2 Two-Spot Interaction 78
3.3.3 Display Measurement 79
3.3.4 Pattern Description 82
3.3.5 The Uniform Black Field ($\tau = 0$) 85
3.3.6 Clusters of Four ($\tau = .25$) 85
3.3.7 Clusters of Two ($\tau = .5$) 89
3.3.8 The Uniform White Field ($\tau = 1$) 94
3.3.9 Spot Interaction Discussion 97
3.4 Monitors 97
3.5 *RGB* Color Space 100
3.5.1 Converting *XYZ* to Spectra 104
3.6 Gamut Mapping 106
3.7 Further Reading 111
3.8 Exercises 112

II SIGNAL PROCESSING 115

4 Signals and Systems 127
4.1 Introduction 127
4.2 Types of Signals and Systems 127
4.2.1 Continuous-Time (CT) Signals 128
4.2.2 Discrete-Time (DT) Signals 129
4.2.3 Periodic Signals 130
4.2.4 Linear Time-Invariant Systems 132
4.3 Notation 135
4.3.1 The Real Numbers 135
4.3.2 The Integers 136
4.3.3 Intervals 136
4.3.4 Product Spaces 137

4.3.5 The Complex Numbers 138
4.3.6 Assignment and Equality 139
4.3.7 Summation and Integration 140
4.3.8 The Complex Exponentials 140
4.3.9 Braket Notation 143
4.3.10 Spaces 146
4.4 Some Useful Signals 148
4.4.1 The Impulse Signal 148
4.4.2 The Box Signal 153
4.4.3 The Impulse Train 154
4.4.4 The Sinc Signal 155
4.5 Convolution 155
4.5.1 A Physical Example of Convolution 160
4.5.2 The Response of Composite Systems 161
4.5.3 Eigenfunctions and Frequency Response of LTI Systems 163
4.5.4 Discrete-Time Convolution 164
4.6 Two-Dimensional Signals and Systems 165
4.6.1 Linear Systems 165
4.6.2 Two-Dimensional Brakets 166
4.6.3 Convolution 167
4.6.4 Two-Dimensional Impulse Response 168
4.6.5 Eigenfunctions and Frequency Response 168
4.7 Further Reading 169
4.8 Exercises 170

5 Fourier Transforms 173
5.1 Introduction 173
5.2 Basis Functions 175
5.2.1 Projections of Points in Space 175
5.2.2 Projection of Functions 176
5.2.3 Orthogonal Families of Functions 179
5.2.4 The Dual Basis 182
5.2.5 The Complex Exponential Basis 184
5.3 Representation in Bases of Lower Dimension 186
5.4 Continuous-Time Fourier Representations 191
5.5 The Fourier Series 192
5.5.1 Convergence 194
5.6 The Continuous-Time Fourier Transform 197
5.6.1 Fourier Transform of Periodic Signals 201
5.6.2 Parseval's Theorem 203
5.7 Examples 203
5.7.1 The Box Signal 203

5.7.2 The Box Spectrum 206
5.7.3 The Gaussian 208
5.7.4 The Impulse Signal 210
5.7.5 The Impulse Train 211
5.8 Duality 213
5.9 Filtering and Convolution 214
5.9.1 Some Common Filters 219
5.10 The Fourier Transform Table 221
5.11 Discrete-Time Fourier Representations 222
5.11.1 The Discrete-Time Fourier Series 222
5.11.2 The Discrete-Time Fourier Transform 225
5.12 Fourier Series and Transforms Summary 229
5.13 Convolution Revisited 231
5.14 Two-Dimensional Fourier Transforms 234
5.14.1 Continuous-Time 2D Fourier Transforms 234
5.14.2 Discrete-Time 2D Fourier Transforms 238
5.15 Higher-Order Transforms 239
5.16 The Fast Fourier Transform 240
5.17 Further Reading 240
5.18 Exercises 240

6 Wavelet Transforms 243
6.1 Introduction 243
6.2 Short-Time Fourier Transform 246
6.3 Scale and Resolution 252
6.4 The Dilation Equation and the Haar Transform 252
6.5 Decomposition and Reconstruction 263
6.5.1 Building the Operators 267
6.6 Compression 274
6.7 Coefficient Conditions 277
6.8 Multiresolution Analysis 282
6.9 Wavelets in the Fourier Domain 285
6.10 Two-Dimensional Wavelets 291
6.10.1 The Rectangular Wavelet Decomposition 291
6.10.2 The Square Wavelet Decomposition 293
6.11 Further Reading 297
6.12 Exercises 297

7 Monte Carlo Integration 299
7.1 Introduction 299
7.2 Basic Monte Carlo Ideas 300
7.3 Confidence 305
7.4 Blind Monte Carlo 307

7.4.1 Crude Monte Carlo 307
7.4.2 Rejection Monte Carlo 308
7.4.3 Blind Stratified Sampling 309
7.4.4 Quasi Monte Carlo 310
7.4.5 Weighted Monte Carlo 312
7.4.6 Multidimensional Weighted Monte Carlo 315
7.5 Informed Monte Carlo 319
7.5.1 Informed Stratified Sampling 319
7.5.2 Importance Sampling 320
7.5.3 Control Variates 325
7.5.4 Antithetic Variates 326
7.6 Adaptive Sampling 327
7.7 Other Approaches 327
7.8 Summary 327
7.9 Further Reading 329
7.10 Exercises 329

8 Uniform Sampling and Reconstruction 331
8.1 Introduction 331
8.1.1 Sampling: Anti-Aliasing in a Pixel 332
8.1.2 Reconstruction: Evaluating Incident Light at a Point 334
8.1.3 Outline of this Chapter 336
8.1.4 Uniform Sampling and Reconstruction of a 1D Continuous Signal 336
8.1.5 What Signals Are Bandlimited? 340
8.2 Reconstruction 341
8.2.1 Zero-Order Hold Reconstruction 344
8.3 Sampling in Two Dimensions 347
8.4 Two-Dimensional Reconstruction 352
8.5 Reconstruction in Image Space 354
8.5.1 The Box Reconstruction Filter 354
8.5.2 Other Reconstruction Filters 358
8.6 Supersampling 359
8.7 Further Reading 365
8.8 Exercises 366

9 Nonuniform Sampling and Reconstruction 369
9.1 Introduction 369
9.1.1 Variable Sampling Density 369
9.1.2 Trading Aliasing for Noise 371
9.1.3 Summary 375
9.2 Nonuniform Sampling 375
9.2.1 Adaptive Sampling 376

9.2.2 Aperiodic Sampling 381
9.2.3 Sampling Pattern Comparison 386
9.3 Informed Sampling 388
9.4 Stratified Sampling 388
9.4.1 Importance Sampling 392
9.4.2 Importance and Stratified Sampling 395
9.5 Interlude: The Duality of Aliasing and Noise 398
9.6 Nonuniform Reconstruction 404
9.7 Further Reading 404
9.8 Exercises 404

10 Sampling and Reconstruction Techniques 407
10.1 Introduction 407
10.2 General Outline of Signal Estimation 409
10.3 Initial Sampling Patterns 409
10.4 Uniform and Nonuniform Sampling 411
10.5 Initial Sampling 415
10.5.1 Uniform Sampling 415
10.5.2 Rectangular Lattice 417
10.5.3 Hexagonal Lattice 417
10.5.4 Triangular Lattice 420
10.5.5 Diamond Lattice 420
10.5.6 Comparison of Subdivided Hexagonal and Square Lattices 420
10.5.7 Nonuniform Sampling 424
10.5.8 Poisson Sampling 424
10.5.9 N-Rooks Sampling 424
10.5.10 Jitter Distribution 426
10.5.11 Poisson-Disk Pattern 427
10.5.12 Precomputed Poisson-Disk Patterns 427
10.5.13 Multiple-Scale Poisson-Disk Patterns 430
10.5.14 Sampling Tiles 437
10.5.15 Dynamic Poisson-Disk Patterns 440
10.5.16 Importance Sampling 443
10.5.17 Multidimensional Patterns 448
10.5.18 Discussion 455
10.6 Refinement 463
10.6.1 Sample Intensity 464
10.7 Refinement Tests 465
10.7.1 Intensity Comparison Refinement Test 465
10.7.2 Contrast Refinement Test 467
10.7.3 Object-Based Refinement Test 468

10.7.4 Ray-Tree Comparison Refinement Test 472
10.7.5 Intensity Statistics Refinement Test 473
10.8 Refinement Sample Geometry 480
10.9 Refinement Geometry 481
10.9.1 Linear Bisection 481
10.9.2 Area Bisection 485
10.9.3 Nonuniform Geometry 490
10.9.4 Multiple-Level Sampling 490
10.9.5 Tree-Based Sampling 492
10.9.6 Multiple-Scale Template Refinement 497
10.10 Interpolation and Reconstruction 497
10.10.1 Functional Techniques 499
10.10.2 Warping 499
10.10.3 Iteration 503
10.10.4 Piecewise-Continuous Reconstruction 507
10.10.5 Local Filtering 517
10.10.6 Yen's Method 522
10.10.7 Multistep Reconstruction 531
10.11 Further Reading 537
10.12 Exercises 538

Bibliography B-1

Index I-1

VOLUME II (UNITS III, IV, AND V)

Color Plates *Following page 894*

III MATTER AND ENERGY 541

11 Light 545
11.1 Introduction 545
11.2 The Double-Slit Experiment 545
11.3 The Wave Nature of Light 549
11.4 Polarization 554
11.5 The Photoelectric Effect 560
11.6 Particle-Wave Duality 563
11.7 Reflection and Transmission 563
11.8 Index of Refraction 567
11.8.1 Sellmeier's Formula 569
11.8.2 Cauchy's Formula 570
11.9 Computing Specular Vectors 572
11.9.1 The Reflected Vector 573

11.9.2 Total Internal Reflection 574
11.9.3 Transmitted Vector 576
11.10 Further Reading 578
11.11 Exercises 579

12 Energy Transport 581
12.1 Introduction 581
12.2 The Rod Model 582
12.3 Particle Density and Flux 583
12.4 Scattering 584
12.4.1 Counting New Particles 585
12.5 The Scattering-Only Particle Distribution Equations 587
12.6 A More Complete Medium 591
12.6.1 Explicit Flux 593
12.6.2 Implicit Flux 595
12.7 Particle Transport in 3D 596
12.7.1 Points 596
12.7.2 Projected Areas 597
12.7.3 Directions 598
12.7.4 Solid Angles 599
12.7.5 Integrating over Solid Angles 605
12.7.6 Direction Sets 606
12.7.7 Particles 613
12.7.8 Flux 614
12.8 Scattering in 3D 619
12.9 Components of 3D Transport 621
12.9.1 Streaming 622
12.9.2 Emission 623
12.9.3 Absorption 623
12.9.4 Outscattering 624
12.9.5 Inscattering 625
12.9.6 A Complete Transport Model 626
12.9.7 Isotropic Materials 629
12.10 Boundary Conditions 630
12.11 The Integral Form 635
12.11.1 An Example 636
12.11.2 The Integral Form of the Transport Equation 637
12.12 The Light Transport Equation 643
12.13 Further Reading 644
12.14 Exercises 644

13 Radiometry 647
13.1 Introduction 647

13.2 Radiometric Conventions 648
13.3 Notation 648
13.4 Spherical Patches 649
13.5 Radiometric Terms 651
13.6 Radiometric Relations 653
13.6.1 Discussion of Radiance 656
13.6.2 Spectral Radiometry 659
13.6.3 Photometry 660
13.7 Reflectance 661
13.7.1 The BRDF f_r 663
13.7.2 Reflectance ρ 667
13.7.3 Reflectance Factor R 670
13.8 Examples 672
13.8.1 Perfect Diffuse 672
13.8.2 Perfect Specular 673
13.9 Spherical Harmonics 675
13.10 Further Reading 678
13.11 Exercises 678

14 Materials 681
14.1 Introduction 681
14.2 Atomic Structure 682
14.3 Particle Statistics 690
14.3.1 Fermi-Dirac Statistics 691
14.4 Molecular Structure 694
14.4.1 Ionic Bonds 695
14.4.2 Molecular-Orbital Bonds 696
14.5 Radiation 704
14.6 Blackbodies 705
14.6.1 Bose-Einstein Statistics 705
14.7 Blackbody Energy Distribution 708
14.7.1 Constant Index of Refraction 713
14.7.2 Linear Index of Refraction 714
14.7.3 Radiators 715
14.8 Phosphors 715
14.9 Further Reading 718
14.10 Exercises 718

15 Shading 721
15.1 Introduction 721
15.2 Lambert, Phong, and Blinn-Phong Shading Models 726
15.2.1 Diffuse Plus Specular 728
15.3 Cook-Torrance Shading Model 731

15.3.1 Torrance-Sparrow Microfacets 732
15.3.2 Fresnel's Formulas 732
15.3.3 Roughness 737
15.3.4 The Cook-Torrance Model 738
15.3.5 Polarization 739
15.4 Anisotropy 740
15.4.1 The Kajiya Model 741
15.4.2 The Poulin-Fournier Model 742
15.5 The HTSG Model 744
15.6 Empirical Models 747
15.6.1 The Strauss Model 747
15.6.2 The Ward Model 750
15.6.3 The Programmable Model 752
15.7 Precomputed BRDF 753
15.7.1 Sampled Hemispheres 753
15.7.2 Spherical Harmonics 756
15.8 Volume Shading 757
15.8.1 Phase Functions 758
15.8.2 Atmospheric Modeling 764
15.8.3 The Earth's Ocean 769
15.8.4 The Kubelka-Munk Pigment Model 770
15.8.5 The Hanrahan-Krueger Multiple-Layer Model 778
15.9 Texture 780
15.10 Hierarchies of Scale 781
15.11 Color 786
15.12 Further Reading 789
15.13 Exercises 789

16 Integral Equations 791
16.1 Introduction 791
16.2 Types of Integral Equations 792
16.3 Operators 795
16.3.1 Operator Norms 798
16.4 Solution Techniques 798
16.4.1 Residual Minimization 800
16.5 Degenerate Kernels 801
16.6 Symbolic Methods 804
16.6.1 The Fubini Theorem 804
16.6.2 Successive Substitution 805
16.6.3 Neumann Series 806
16.7 Numerical Approximations 808
16.7.1 Numerical Integration (Quadrature) 809

16.7.2 Method of Undetermined Coefficients 810
16.7.3 Quadrature on Expanded Functions 812
16.7.4 Nyström Method 814
16.7.5 Monte Carlo Quadrature 817
16.8 Projection Methods 817
16.8.1 Projection 819
16.8.2 Pictures of the Function Space 819
16.8.3 Polynomial Collocation 825
16.8.4 Tchebyshev Approximation 830
16.8.5 Least Squares 831
16.8.6 Galerkin 833
16.8.7 Wavelets 837
16.8.8 Discussion 839
16.9 Monte Carlo Estimation 840
16.9.1 Random Walks 842
16.9.2 Path Tracing 844
16.9.3 The Importance Function 848
16.10 Singularities 864
16.10.1 Removal 866
16.10.2 Factorization 867
16.10.3 Divide and Conquer 868
16.10.4 Coexistence 868
16.11 Further Reading 868
16.12 Exercises 869

17 The Radiance Equation 871
17.1 Introduction 871
17.2 Forming the Radiance Equation 872
17.2.1 BDF 872
17.2.2 Phosphorescence 873
17.2.3 Fluorescence 874
17.2.4 FRE 875
17.3 TIGRE 877
17.4 VTIGRE 878
17.5 Solving for *L* 880
17.6 Further Reading 882
17.7 Exercises 882

IV RENDERING 883

18 Radiosity 887
18.1 Introduction 887
18.2 Classical Radiosity 888

18.2.1 Collocation Solution 891
18.2.2 Galerkin Solution 892
18.2.3 Classical Radiosity Solution 893
18.2.4 Higher-Order Radiosity 899
18.3 Solving the Matrix Equation 900
18.3.1 Jacobi Iteration 903
18.3.2 Gauss-Seidel Iteration 903
18.3.3 Southwell Iteration 904
18.3.4 Overrelaxation 905
18.4 Solving Radiosity Matrices 906
18.4.1 Jacobi Iteration 907
18.4.2 Gauss-Seidel Iteration 907
18.4.3 Southwell Iteration 909
18.4.4 Progressive Refinement 911
18.4.5 Overrelaxation 913
18.4.6 Comparison 914
18.5 Form Factors 916
18.5.1 Analytic Methods 916
18.5.2 Contour Integration 919
18.5.3 Physical Devices 921
18.5.4 Projection 925
18.5.5 Discussion 937
18.6 Hierarchical Radiosity 937
18.6.1 One Step of HR 954
18.6.2 Adaptive HR 961
18.6.3 Importance HR 964
18.6.4 Discussion 974
18.7 Meshing 974
18.8 Shooting Power 976
18.9 Extensions to Classical Radiosity 979
18.10 Further Reading 982
18.11 Exercises 984

19 Ray Tracing 987
19.1 Introduction 987
19.2 Photon and Visibility Tracing 988
19.3 Visibility Tracing 990
19.3.1 Strata Sets 993
19.3.2 Applying Resolved Strata 999
19.3.3 Direct and Indirect Illumination 1002
19.3.4 Discussion 1035
19.4 Photon Tracing 1037

19.5 Bidirectional Ray-Tracing Methods 1039
19.6 Hybrid Algorithms 1044
19.7 Ray-Tracing Volumes 1049
19.8 Further Reading 1050
19.9 Exercises 1050

20 Rendering and Images 1053
20.1 Introduction 1053
20.2 Postprocessing 1054
20.2.1 A Nonlinear Observer Model 1057
20.2.2 Image-Based Processing 1061
20.2.3 Linear Processing 1063
20.3 Feedback Rendering 1064
20.3.1 Illumination Painting 1066
20.3.2 Subjective Constraints 1067
20.3.3 Device-Directed Rendering 1069
20.4 Further Reading 1072
20.5 Exercise 1072

21 The Future 1073
21.1 Technical Progress 1073
21.1.1 Physical Optics 1074
21.1.2 Volume Rendering 1074
21.1.3 Information Theory 1075
21.1.4 Beyond Photo-Realism: Subjective Rendering 1076
21.2 Other Directions 1077
21.3 Summary 1080

V APPENDICES 1083

A Linear Algebra 1085
A.1 General Notation 1085
A.2 Linear Spaces 1085
A.2.1 Norms 1086
A.2.2 Inf and Sup 1087
A.2.3 Metrics 1087
A.2.4 Completeness 1088
A.2.5 Inner Products 1088
A.3 Function Spaces 1090
A.4 Further Reading 1091

B Probability 1093
B.1 Events and Probability 1093
B.2 Total Probability 1095

B.3 Repeated Trials 1097
B.4 Random Variables 1098
B.5 Measures 1101
B.6 Distributions 1102
B.7 Geometric Series 1103
B.8 Further Reading 1103

C Historical Notes 1105
C.1 Specular Reflection and Transmission 1105
C.1.1 Specular Reflection 1109
C.1.2 Specular Transmission 1110

D Analytic Form Factors 1113
D.1 Differential and Finite Surfaces 1113
D.1.1 Differential to Differential 1113
D.1.2 Differential to Finite 1114
D.1.3 Finite to Finite 1122
D.2 Two Polygons 1132

E Constants and Units 1135

F Luminaire Standards 1139
F.1 Terminology 1139
F.2 Notation 1143
F.3 The IES Standard 1143
F.3.1 The Big Picture 1145
F.3.2 The Tilt Block 1145
F.3.3 The Photometry Block 1149
F.4 The CIE Standard 1152
F.4.1 The Main Block 1154
F.4.2 The Measurement Block 1155
F.4.3 The Photometry Block 1159

G Reference Data 1163
G.1 Material Data 1164
G.2 Human Data 1169
G.3 Light Sources 1172
G.4 Phosphors 1177
G.5 Macbeth ColorChecker 1179
G.6 Real Objects 1191

Bibliography B-1

Index I-1

PREFACE

Inspiration begins with imagination and the spirit to create. Then comes the need to communicate, to share an idea or thought. Grab a pencil and you can make it real: a *picture*, abstraction made concrete, ideas preserved in time. Our hearts and minds are moved to tell stories, to teach what we think and feel to others and learn the same from them.

Of all the visual media, computer graphics is one of the newest. The computer is a powerful amplifier—it can take terse descriptions of the world and create pictures of that world, using any rules you choose. If we choose the classical rules of light, then we can make pictures that can pass for photographs; other rules explore other ways of seeing.

The field of *image synthesis*, also called *rendering*, is a field of transformation: it turns the rules of geometry and physics into pictures that mean something to people. To accomplish this feat, the person who writes the programs needs to understand and weave together a rich variety of knowledge from math, physics, art, psychology, physiology, and computer science. Thrown together, these disciplines seem hardly related. Arranged and orchestrated by the creator of image synthesis programs, they become part of a cohesive, dynamic whole. Like cooperative members of any complex group, these fields interact in our minds in rich and stimulating ways.

I find each of these disciplines inherently interesting; together they are fascinating. Understanding the interplay of such diversity and exploring the connections is exciting, and with the understanding of such elegant ideas comes a deep satisfaction. That's why I love computer graphics: it's stimulating to the intellect and rewarding to the heart.

I couldn't find a book that presented image synthesis as a complete and integrated field of study, encompassing all of the topics I just mentioned. But I love to write. And so this book was born.

The big idea in this book is to lay out the rules that tell a computer how to take 3D shapes and lights and create a picture—one that would pass for a photograph of that scene if it existed. So our driving problem is the simulation of Nature's illumination of a scene, the capturing of that illumination on film, and its presentation to an observer. Sometimes we bypass the film idea and just imagine an observer in the scene. We often make it easy and pretend the observer has only one eye, so we can ask, "Given this scene, what picture do I show to the observer to make her think that she's viewing the real scene?" We use all the disciplines I listed earlier to answer this question, since our goal is not merely to create an image, but to create a perceptual response in the viewer.

It's all a trick! Like any visual medium, computer graphics creates illusions. Fred Brooks [65] has observed that our job as image synthesists is to create an illusion of reality—to make a picture that carries our message, not necessarily one that matches some objective standard. It's a creative job.

This book is not about how to write specific programs, or how to implement particular algorithms. The history of computer graphics is like any discipline of thought: tried-and-true ideas are constantly challenged by new ideas, and sometimes the older ones, once seemingly invulnerable, are found somehow deficient and fade away. So it is with rendering algorithms; our marketplace of ideas is a noisy and bustling place right now.

But there are some ideas that I believe are fundamental, that come from the basis of our discipline and lie at the heart of all we do. Those are the ideas in this book. I have included many examples from current practice, but I rarely go into their details. There are lots of references, and you can find a wealth of implementation information in the literature. My purpose here is to discuss the underlying principles—the ideas that have slowly emerged as the core of our discipline.

There are three such basic fields: human vision, signal processing, and physics. These are not independent disciplines; as I've said, much of the fun of image synthesis is seeing how these fields fit together. But here I have chosen to give each of these topics its own day on the stage, in the form of a unit of the book. The fourth unit pulls the first three topics together and shows how they combine to make rendering algorithms. I look at two of today's most popular techniques, hierarchical radiosity and distribution ray tracing, as examples to illustrate the principles. Finally, the fifth unit contains several appendices with short topic summaries, historical notes, and reference data.

I make a general argument in this book. To design and implement a computer system for creating synthetic digital images for people to view, you need to understand the physics of the world you are simulating, the appropriate methods for simulating those physics in the computer, and the nature of the human visual system that ultimately interprets the image.

The following few paragraphs describe the structure of the book and show how the discussion has been arranged to provide an accumulating body of mathematical, physical, and physiological information that culminates in a modern image rendering system. There's too much information here for a one-semester course on image synthesis. Teachers may choose to present in detail only some of the information in this book, covering the rest at a higher level; deciding where to dig deeply and where to summarize lightly will depend on the instructor, the course, and the students. The only material that ought not be skipped is the section on notation in Chapter 4. With suitable summaries from the instructor to cover the gaps, students can work sequentially, skipping material as desired. Since the book is cumulative, I don't recommend hopping back and forth.

In Volume 1, Unit I covers the human visual system, the effects of displays on images, and the representation of color. The idiosyncrasies of the human visual system are endless; it's a finely tuned physical and neurological system of great complexity, which we are only beginning to understand in a quantified way. But there are some large-scale features that we do understand and that are important to computer graphics: those are the topics I stress in Chapter 1. I discuss some of the ways of representing color in Chapter 2, so that you can write programs that manipulate color information correctly. In addition, Chapter 3 considers the effect of a display on an image, since the transformation of a mathematical ideal into a physical reality inevitably includes a change in the message.

Unit II addresses digital signal processing. In a digital computer, we transform the smooth signals of everyday life into digitized, or sampled, representations. For example, we usually compute the color of an image only at a finite number of points on the display (the pixels), rather than at every infinitely small point on the image. This simple operation has profound repercussions, which often clash with an intuition born of our experience in the physical world. To ignore these effects is to invite a flood of visual and numerical problems, from "jaggies" or stairsteps in an image to an incorrect simulation with splotchy illumination and other ugly artifacts. To understand these issues, Chapter 4 discusses the nature of digital signals, and then Chapter 5 introduces the Fourier transform, which is a mathematical tool that reveals some of the internal structure of a signal. Like listening to an orchestral symphony and then looking at the complete score, taking the Fourier transform of a signal lets us isolate different components of the signal for closer study. A related tool is the wavelet transform, which is presented in Chapter 6. With these tools we can find ways to efficiently and accurately compute the integrals of functions. This is an essential part of image synthesis; in fact, much of image synthesis can be seen as nothing but numerical integration of various types. Chapter 7 covers the basic ideas of Monte Carlo integration, which is a powerful tool for handling this complex type of problem.

With these analytic and comparative tools available to guide the discussion, I turn to more practical issues involved in rendering images. Chapter 8 discusses uniform sampling, which is the process of taking a continuous signal and turning it into a digital representation by taking evenly spaced measurements. This process, though conceptually simple, introduces a Pandora's box of unexpected problems. An alternative is nonuniform sampling, addressed in Chapter 9, which offers a different blend of advantages and disadvantages. Unit II ends with Chapter 10's survey of the signal-processing methods that have proven of most use in image synthesis in recent years.

Unit III, which opens Volume 2, turns to the physics of the real world. We begin with a study of the nature of light in Chapter 11, and then move on in Chapter 12 to quantify the movement of energy through the world using the tools of energy transport. Chapter 13 presents the field of radiometry, which offers us terms and units for discussing the quantities and qualities of light present in different parts of a scene. Chapter 14 covers the physics of materials, so we have some understanding of how they interact with the light striking them. This leads us to Chapter 15's study of the large-scale simulation of light-matter interaction, known in computer graphics as shading. The equations that describe how the shading on one object affects the shading on another involve integrals, so we look at the mathematical methods for manipulating and solving such integral equations in Chapter 16. By Chapter 17, we've learned enough to gather these ideas into a single equation known as the radiance equation, which gives the basic structure for how light moves through an environment. This is the single most important equation in image synthesis, and every digital image based on geometrical optics is always an approximate solution of it.

The presentation of the radiance equation crowns the theoretical development covered in this book. Rendering practice is largely involved with finding ways to accurately and efficiently solve this equation. Because a complete analytic solution appears impossible in any but the most trivial environments, we must cut corners, simplify, and otherwise approximate everything involved in image-making, from the geometry of the scene to the physics of the simulation. The methods of digital signal processing give us the tools to understand which approximations are reasonable and what their effects will be, so we can choose our simplifications in a principled way.

Unit IV demonstrates how the ideas in the first three units may be combined to make a complete rendering algorithm. I present the popular techniques of radiosity and ray tracing in Chapters 18 and 19 by applying different sets of assumptions and simplifications to the radiance equation. Chapter 20 returns to the themes of Unit I and discusses how displays affect the perception of a computed image. I present some ideas for compensating for this distortion. The unit ends with Chapter 21, in which I offer a few opinions about where I think image synthesis is headed.

Unit V consists of seven appendices. Appendices A–D offer reference material on linear algebra and probability, some historical discussion of reflection and refraction, and a catalog of analytic form factors for computing radiation exchange. Appendix E provides a summary of useful constants and units, Appendix F an interpretation of the two most popular standards for describing real physical lighting instruments, and Appendix G measured spectral emission and reflectivity data for a wide variety of materials. For your convenience, the bibliography and index are printed at the end of each volume.

The language of geometry, signals, and physics is largely written in mathematics. So there are mathematics in this book, because that's the best way people have found for expressing clearly, simply, and precisely what are usually very simple and elegant ideas. I've tried to use the most straightforward math possible at all times. This may mean I've used some notation that's unfamiliar to you. It's all explained, and I hope it's not at all tricky. There's lots of discussion about the equations and what they mean, and it builds slowly. If you flip through the book now and something looks daunting, don't be concerned: by the time we reach the complex-looking stuff it won't be complex at all, because you'll know how to read it.

If you know something about linear algebra (vectors and matrices), and you remember the basic ideas of calculus (what integrals and differentials are, even if you're rusty on the mechanics), then you have everything you need to get through this book. There's a short appendix on probability if you're unfamiliar with that field; everything we use in the text is covered there. The occasional forays into other areas of math are well-paved. I encourage you to consult standard math texts when you want to, but I hope that you will infrequently need to.

This book does not consider all of computer graphics—such a book would be a huge undertaking. I address only image synthesis: the job of converting a scene description into a picture. There are many other important subfields in computer graphics, including implicit and explicit modeling, motion control, compositing, lighting, and more. You can find discussions of these topics and pointers to more literature in the general textbooks. A good introductory text is Hearn and Baker [199]. More encyclopedic and detailed discussions are available in Foley et al. [147] and Watt and Watt [473]. A general introduction without math may be found in my book for artists and designers [159].

If you're studying on your own, make use of the references; there's a world of alternate explanations of almost everything in here. If you can study with a friend, I encourage you to do so; it's easier and often much more pleasant than working on your own. I have always learned at least as much from my colleagues as I have from my teachers.

I hope that this book is useful both to the student studying independently and the student in the classroom. There are some exercises at the end of each chapter. These ask mostly for prose descriptions and discussions, rather than mathematical manipulation; the goal is to think about what the math represents, not the mechanics of how it accomplishes the representation. If the ideas are in place, the mechanics will come; going in the other direction is much harder.

I enjoy computer graphics. I like math and I like art, and image synthesis stimulates me analytically and emotionally. This book shares with you what I feel are the most important and rewarding ideas in image synthesis.

Acknowledgments

Nobody can write a book of this magnitude alone. It gives me great pleasure to acknowledge and thank all those people who have generously given to me their time, energy, and support. I cannot list everyone who has helped me; such a list would fill another volume! I have singled out below those people who have been especially helpful over the three years that I have been working on this project.

This book was written while I was a member of the research staff at the Xerox Palo Alto Research Center (PARC), where my colleagues offered me stimulation, encouragement, and support. Lisa Alfke of the PARC Technical Information Center was my librarian *extraordinaire*. She tracked down and obtained hundreds of papers, theses, and reports, many obscure and out of print. My thanks go also to the rest of the helpful and widely resourceful TIC staff. My managers, Eric Bier, Frank Crow, Per-Kristian Halvorsen, and Maureen Stone, all offered a supportive and encouraging atmosphere.

Many members of the Xerox PARC research staff made themselves available for discussions, help, and moral support; I thank Marshall Bern, Dan Bloomberg, Jules Bloomenthal, Ken Fishkin, John Gilbert, Don Kimber, Ralph Merkle, Les Niles, Dan Russel, and Maureen Stone. Kim Brook and Kathleen Dunham provided secretarial support and helped with countless daily tasks. Thanks to Brian Tramontana and Natalie Jerimijenko, photographer and subject, respectively, for Natalie's photograph used in Unit II.

The final stages of the book's production were carried out while I was a Researcher at Microsoft Research. My thanks go to my manager, Dan Ling, and my colleagues at Microsoft for their support.

This book has been brewing for several years. Thanks to Jeff Hultquist for helping to shape the book and to Brian Barsky for getting it on the road to reality. Deep thanks to Mike Morgan for his brave and enthusiastic support of this project through delays and dramatic changes. I appreciate the wind in my sails offered by Jim Arvo, Dan Bloomberg, Eric Braun, Lakshmi Dasari, Eric Haines, Pat Hanrahan, Jeff Hultquist, Mike Morgan, Peter Shirley, and Maureen Stone. They encouraged me, at different times and in different places, to continue with this project when I was ready to quit.

Many computer graphics people generously gave time to answer questions about their work and to provide supplementary materials. Thanks to Rob Cook, Ken Fishkin, Steven Gortler, Eric Haines, Pat Hanrahan, Paul Heckbert, Masa Inakage, Eric Jansen, Jim Kajiya, Jean-Luc Maillot, Don Mitchell, Sumant Pattanaik, Rich Redner, Holly Rushmeier, David Salesin, Peter Schröder, Peter Shirley, François

Sillion, Maureen Stone, Sam Uselton, Greg Ward, and Jack van Wijk. Particular thanks go to Jim Arvo for generously allowing me to use his unpublished notes on integral equations and transport theory.

This manuscript has benefited greatly from the suggestions made by volunteers who reviewed drafts of various chapters. For their advice I thank Dan Bloomberg, Ken Fishkin, Marc Levoy, David Marimont, David Salesin, Peter Schröder, Maureen Stone, Greg Turk, and Greg Ward. In particular, Eric Haines and Peter Shirley have read almost all of the manuscript in some form and some chapters in several forms—surely a Herculean task. Any errors that remain are purely my responsibility.

The production of this book presented many challenges, but it was executed with great skill and cheerfulness by Yonie Overton and Julie Pabst. My thanks to both for their imagination, precision, and, most of all, care for this project.

Where you work affects your mood and influences the final result. Three particularly pleasant places deserve special mention: Farley's in San Francisco, where I developed most of the first half of the book with cups of hot chocolate in hand, and Hobee's and Printers, Inc. in Palo Alto, where almost all of Unit III was developed from behind cups of hot tea.

It would have been easy to get burned out on a project of this size. Gary Marks and Jennifer Youngdahl kept my musical soul alert and creative even when I was too busy to practice. My parents, Bertram and Roberta Glassner, and my siblings, Adriana, Bruce, and Marshall, offered encouragement and support. Eric Braun and Chuck and Pam Mosher helped me stay on the big path. Lakshmi Dasari provided moral support in numerous large and small ways.

To those who are about to learn image synthesis, I extend my hopes that you find the process rewarding and exciting. Image synthesis is a field that can fire the imagination and stimulate the intellect, satisfying heart and mind. I hope you find the journey illuminating.

Andrew S. Glassner
Seattle, Washington

SUMMARY OF USEFUL NOTATION

Notation	Meaning	Section where defined
$\mathcal{R}_\mathcal{V}$	The visual band	1.3
$\mathcal{R}$	The real numbers	4.3.1
$\mathcal{Z}$	The integers	4.3.2
$\mathcal{C}$	The complex numbers	4.3.5
$\bar{z}$	The complex conjugate of z	4.3.5
$\otimes$	Cartesian product	4.3.4
$\oplus$	Cartesian sum	4.3.4
$\sum_k, \sum_{k \in Z}$	Summation over all integers	4.3.7
$\sum_{k \in [N]}$	Summation over $[d, d+N-1]$	4.3.7
$\int dt$	Integration over $[-\infty, \infty]$	4.3.7
$\langle f \| g \rangle$	Inner product of $\overline{f}$ and g	4.3.9
$f * h$	Convolution of f and h	4.5
$H(\omega)$	System response	4.5.3
$\mathcal{F}\{x\}$	Fourier transform	5.12
$\overset{\mathcal{F}}{\longleftrightarrow}$		
$(\mathcal{K}x)(t)$	Kernel integral operator on x	16.3
$(\mathcal{L}x)(t)$	Composite integral operator on x	16.3
$\psi, \psi_k, \psi'_k, \psi_2$	Fourier basis functions	4.3.8
$\delta(t)$	Dirac impulse distribution	4.4.1
$b_W t, b_W[n]$	Box functions	4.4.2
$\mathrm{III}_T(t), \mathrm{III}_T[n]$	Impulse trains	4.4.3
$\mathrm{sinc}(x)$	$\sin(x)/x$	4.4.4
$v(\mathbf{r}, \vec{\omega})$	Visible-surface function	12.12.2
Q	Energy	13.5
Φ	Power (flux)	13.5
I	Intensity	13.5
M, B	Exitance (radiosity)	13.5
E	Irradiance	13.5
L	Radiance	13.5

III

MATTER AND ENERGY

I ask to have this much granted me—to assert that every ray passing through air of equal density throughout, travels in a straight line from its cause to the object or place it falls upon.

Leonardo da Vinci

INTRODUCTION TO UNIT III

In this part of the book we turn our attention to the physical world around us. Each chapter focuses on one part of a discussion that will lead us to the climax of the unit: the *radiance equation*.

We begin with a study of *light* in its many forms. This leads us to *transport theory*, which is a means for quantifying the distribution of energy in an environment; light energy will ultimately be our main concern. To describe this distribution of light, we use ideas drawn from the field of *radiometry*, which provides us terms and units for discussing how much light energy of a particular type is moving from one place to another in a scene. For image synthesis we are quite interested in the interaction of light and a *material*, which is any physical substance that interacts with light. After we discuss the foundations of material structure, we will examine *shading*, which is a class of high-level techniques for modeling the interaction of light and matter. Finally, we observe that the equation that links all of these concepts is an *integral equation*; finding a solution to this type of equation is the goal of image synthesis, so we discuss methods for solving integral equations in some detail.

One way to look at a rendering algorithm is as a *simulation* of some model of the physics of light. We are completely free to choose how the physics will work: the everyday coarse physics of our universe is only one important example. But choosing the natural world as a driving problem has two benefits. The first is that we *know* what the world looks like, so we can use our own visual system and experience to debug our pictures. Computer graphics has benefited from a very high bandwidth channel for communicating the results of potentially millions of runs of our algorithms: a picture. If the picture doesn't look right, we can form theories about our bugs just by looking. This isn't a conclusive test that a program is correct, but it's a great way of spotting many ways in which it may be incorrect.

The second advantage of the natural world as our subject is that it is important in a practical sense, with applications from flight simulation to industrial design. Since the natural world comes from without, we have no more creative freedom when using an accurate simulation model than we would have over materials in the real world. This tends to prevent certain kinds of artistic exploration. Nevertheless, simulations of the real world are more easily debugged and have wider immediate application, so they have become the most popular driving problem for rendering.

Good mathematical treatments of the physics of surfaces and the physics of light have been around for a while; computer graphics has recently started to move deeper into this literature. It seems that the best way to describe how energy bounces around is with an equation that describes the relationship of all the light in the scene at once. This is an integral equation.

Just as a differential equation expresses a function in terms of its derivatives, an integral equation expresses a function in terms of its integrals. Given a scene, we can write down the equation that precisely describes the energy at every point in the scene. To find the light anywhere in the scene, we need only get the value of the light function at that point and in that direction.

Unfortunately, solving for this "radiance equation" analytically seems hopeless. Just as we saw for sampling, when we seek general solutions for complicated functions in multiple dimensions, numerical techniques offer hope where analytic methods fail.

Finding solutions to the indelightradiance equation is what rendering is all about. Almost every rendering algorithm published to date can be thought of as a solution technique for that equation. The recent link between the theory of integral equations and the indelightradiance equation has provided a solid basis of important results to guide our development of new algorithms.

To see how the same function may admit different solutions, we can look at rendering from the point of view of a house painter. The customer has left the following painting instructions in an implicit form: "Place three coats of blue paint on all vertical walls." The house painter has lots of ways to satisfy this requirement (that is, lots of solutions to the equation). For example, she can place blue dots at random all over the walls until statistically the average depth is three coats; she can paint all four walls once and then repeat that action two times; or she can paint each wall three times in a row before moving on. Each of these methods will give a slightly different result, and they offer different advantages; suppose the painter is concerned with the time it takes and the amount of exercise she gets while painting. Painting random dots keeps her moving but it's slow, painting the same wall three times before moving on has little movement but it's fastest; the other method is in between. When we look at solution methods to the indelightradiance equation, we find we are interested in the running time, memory requirements, and generality of the solution, as well as artifacts or restrictions.

This unit gives us the vocabulary for quantifying the distribution of light throughout an environment as it interacts with matter, and the mathematical tools for finding a description of this distribution that may be used for creating images.

It probably doesn't matter if, while trying to be modest and eager watchers of life's many spectacles, we sometimes look clumsy or get dirty or ask stupid questions or reveal our ignorance or say the wrong thing or light up with wonder like the children we all are.

Diane Ackerman
("A Natural History of the Senses," 1990)

11

LIGHT

11.1 Introduction

In image synthesis we are interested in the simulation of *light*. Light has a famous dual nature: in some situations it seems to behave as though it is a stream of particles, and in other situations as though it is a wave. This dual nature leads to phenomena that we see every day, from shiny pieces of metal to the colors in a bird's feathers.

We will briefly discuss both interpretations. In this book we will generally ignore the wave aspect of light, but it is important to justify that decision on physical grounds, and understand what we are giving up by doing so.

11.2 The Double-Slit Experiment

We consider the wave nature of light first. We begin by noting that when waves of any sort pass through a small hole, or around an object with a sharp edge, they always tend to spread out. This physical phenomenon is called *diffraction*. In the 1600s Huygens suggested that when a wave encounters an opaque barrier containing a very small hole, on the other side of the barrier the hole looks like a point source

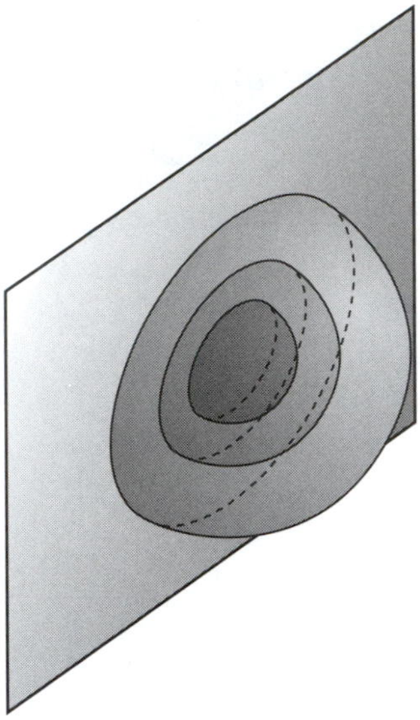

FIGURE 11.1
A small hole acts like a spherical point source of waves.

of spherically symmetric waves, as in Figure 11.1. A single slit in a barrier acts as a source of cylindrical waves, as shown in Figure 11.2. This means that a sharp shadow turns into a fuzzy one some distance from the edge.

In 1801 Thomas Young performed an elegant and influential experiment called the *double-slit experiment*, which argued strongly for the wave interpretation of the nature of light.

Young's experiment is illustrated schematically in Figure 11.3(a). Starting at the left of the experimental setup, sunlight strikes an opaque barrier with a single small vertical slit. At some distance beyond the first barrier is a second, opaque barrier, this time with two parallel slits. Beyond this second barrier sits a sheet of blank paper. When the slits are close together, the pattern of light striking the paper has the form shown in Figure 11.3(b). The remarkable thing about this pattern is that it consists of alternating bright and dark bands. The problem that confronted Young was how to explain this pattern.

This can be done most easily by positing that the light exiting the two slits has a wavelike nature. That is, as light radiates from each slit, its energy at any point may

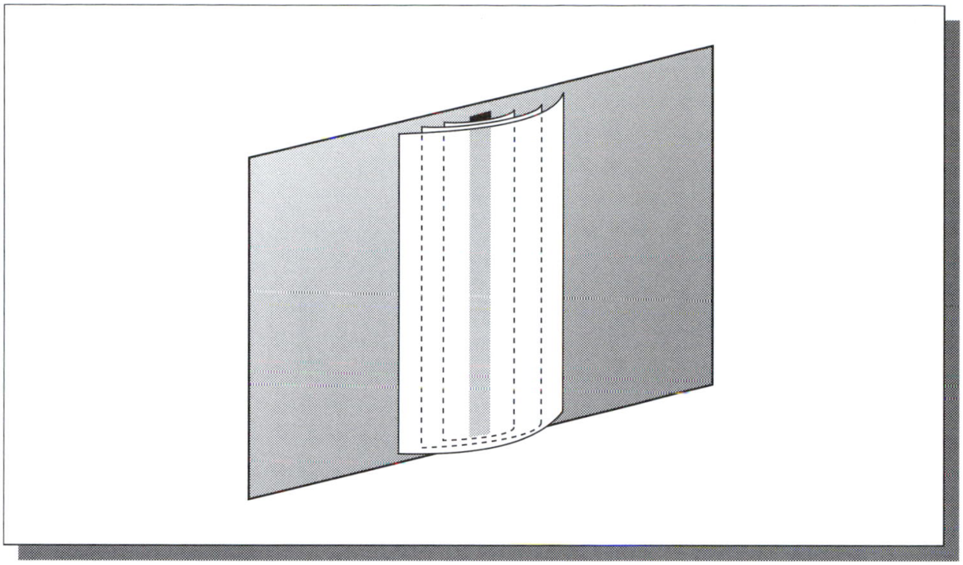

FIGURE 11.2
A small slit acts like a cylindrical source of waves.

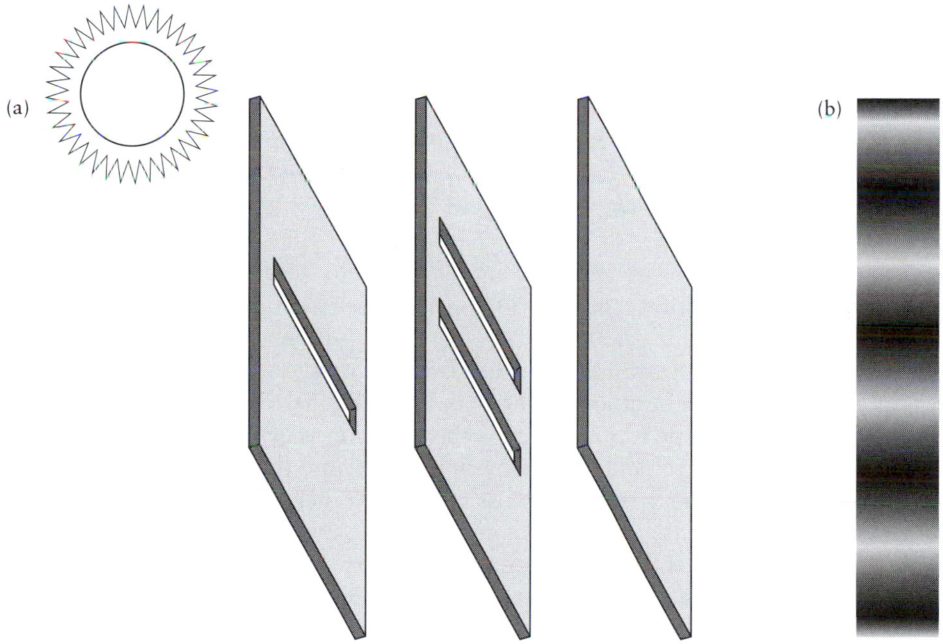

FIGURE 11.3
The double-slit experiment. (a) Experimental setup. (b) Pattern on the recording screen.

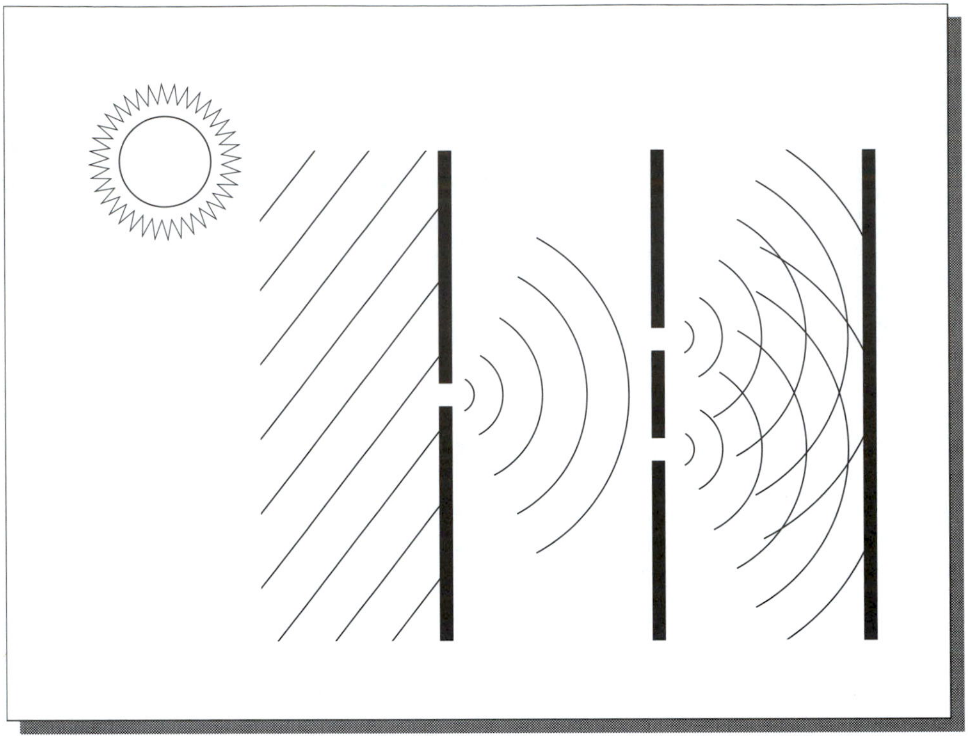

FIGURE 11.4
A slice of the double-slit experiment.

be described by a function that is periodic with time. Let us assume that this is the case.

This assumption suggests there is a periodic function $A(x, t)$ that gives us the energy of a beam of light at any point x and time t. If we fix x, then the function depends only on the time t. Suppose that this function is given by $A(t) = \sin(t)$.

Returning now to the double-slit experiment, because the waves are cylindrically symmetric we can take an arbitrary cross section parallel to the axis of the waves to represent the general case; we do this in Figure 11.4. We set up a coordinate system with the origin between the slits, oriented as shown. The two slits are at positions $(0, S_1)$ and $(0, S_2)$, and we are interested in the combined energy of the waves falling on some point $P = (l, p)$.

The two waves travel distances $||P - S_1||$ and $||P - S_2||$. Now we can see the reason for the single-slit barrier; this sets up the initial wave so that it strikes both slits at the same distance from the first slit, so the waves leaving the double slits have the same phase. In other words, at any time t, the same wave is generated in synchrony at both slits (which act as sources of cylindrical waves).

Since the waves are periodic over distance, then at a given moment if we move along the receiving screen, we will sweep through the wave function, since the distance to the slit will be either smoothly increasing or decreasing depending on where we are and in which direction we're moving. The distances to the two slits are different for every point except the one exactly between them, so we would expect in general that the amplitude of the received waves will vary with position. In fact, at some places the waves both arrive at their maximum amplitude.

Suppose at some point P the distance d_1 to slit 1 is given by $d_1 = k_1 2\pi + \pi/2$ and the distance to slit 2 is given by $d_2 = k_2 2\pi + \pi/2$ for two integers k_1 and k_2. Then at this point the waves *constructively interfere*, since $\sin(d_1) + \sin(d_2) = 1 + 1 = 2$, and we get a bright spot. But suppose at some other point Q one wave arrives at its maximum and the other at its minimum, so $d_1 = k_1 2\pi + \pi/2$ and $d_2 = k_2 2\pi + 3\pi/2$. Then $\sin(d_1) + \sin(d_2) = 1 - 1 = 0$. In this case the waves *destructively interfere* and we get a dark spot. Between these extremes we get different intensities due to different amounts of *interference* between the two waves.

This light-and-dark pattern of *interference fringes* argued strongly that we should interpret light as a wave phenomenon, since the wave theory explains the physical phenomena accurately and elegantly. The study of the wave nature of light is called *physical optics*.

Throughout this book, we will use the symbol ν to refer to the *frequency* of a beam of light (the symbol f is also common for this term, but we reserve that to stand for functions). The distance traveled by a beam during the time it takes to oscillate through one period is the *wavelength* λ. If light has a speed of propagation c in a particular medium, then $c = \lambda\nu$.

11.3 The Wave Nature of Light

We will find it useful to develop a basic understanding of the wave nature of light. This will allow us to understand the phenomenon of *polarization*, and its role in various *shading models* discussed in Chapter 15.

Following the classical approach of Bohren and Huffman [53], we describe light as energy carried by a pair of coupled fields: the *electric field* $\mathbf{E}$ and the *magnetic field* $\mathbf{H}$. In general, both $\mathbf{E}$ and $\mathbf{H}$ are complex-valued functions of space and time. They are described by a set of four famous equations known as *Maxwell's equations*, which lay down the principles for the behavior of electricity and magnetism. Because the two fields are intimately coupled (one never appears without the other), the single term *electromagnetic* is often used to describe this energy. Both the electric and magnetic fields may be modeled as *time-harmonic fields*, that is, periodic functions of time and space. The *Poynting vector* $\mathbf{S} = \mathbf{E} \times \mathbf{H}$ indicates the magnitude and *direction of propagation* of the transfer of electromagnetic energy.

The simplest time-harmonic fields are the *plane waves*, which are nothing but the complex sinusoids from Unit II in a slightly different form:

$$\begin{aligned}\mathbf{E} &= \mathbf{E}_0 e^{-j(\mathbf{k}\cdot\mathbf{x}+\omega t)}\\ \mathbf{H} &= \mathbf{H}_0 e^{-j(\mathbf{k}\cdot\mathbf{x}+\omega t)}\end{aligned} \tag{11.1}$$

Here we have made the exponential depend on a *wave vector* $\mathbf{k}$ that describes the direction of propagation of the wave.

This form of wave has an immediate physical interpretation. The complex exponential sweeps out a coupled set of sine and cosine curves as a function of its argument. Consider for a moment just the first term in the argument $-j(\mathbf{k}\cdot\mathbf{x}+\omega t)$. If this term were only the spatial position $\mathbf{x}$, then the wave would be spherical: at all points the same distance from the origin, the exponent would have the same value. Instead we are using $\mathbf{k}\cdot\mathbf{x}$, which means that the value of the function at each spatial point $\mathbf{x}$ is found by projecting that point perpendicularly onto the direction vector $\mathbf{k}$. In other words, $\mathbf{k}$ is the normal to a plane, and all points on that plane have the same value. The scalar offset for the plane is controlled by the second term, ωt, which simply says that as the time t increases, each plane moves away at a speed ω. Thus this complex exponential creates an endless series of moving planes of constant (complex) value. This is diagrammed in Figure 11.5.

In general, $\mathbf{k}$ may be complex ($\mathbf{k} = \mathbf{k}_r + j\mathbf{k}_i$) for two real vectors $\mathbf{k}_r$ and $\mathbf{k}_i$, so we can expand Equation 11.1 as

$$\begin{aligned}\mathbf{E} &= \mathbf{E}_0 \exp[(\mathbf{k}_i\cdot\mathbf{x}) + j(\mathbf{k}_r\cdot\mathbf{x} - \omega t)]\\ &= \mathbf{E}_0 \exp[\mathbf{k}_i\cdot\mathbf{x}]\exp[j\mathbf{k}_r\cdot\mathbf{x} - j\omega t]\\ \mathbf{H} &= \mathbf{H}_0 \exp[(\mathbf{k}_i\cdot\mathbf{x}) + j(\mathbf{k}_r\cdot\mathbf{x} - \omega t)]\\ &= \mathbf{H}_0 \exp[\mathbf{k}_i\cdot\mathbf{x}]\exp[j\mathbf{k}_r\cdot\mathbf{x} - j\omega t]\end{aligned} \tag{11.2}$$

where $\mathbf{E}_0\exp[\mathbf{k}_i\cdot\mathbf{x}]$ is the *amplitude* of the electric field, and $\phi = \mathbf{k}_r\cdot\mathbf{x} - \omega t$ is the *phase*; the same labels apply to the components of the magnetic field.

Note that $\mathbf{k}_i\cdot\mathbf{x}$ defines a plane with surface normal $\mathbf{k}_i$. Therefore $\mathbf{k}_i$ is perpendicular to *surfaces of constant phase*; that is, all points $\mathbf{x}$ on that plane have the same phase ϕ. Similarly, $\mathbf{k}_r$ is perpendicular to *surfaces of constant amplitude*. When $\mathbf{k}_i$ and $\mathbf{k}_r$ are parallel, we say the waves are *homogeneous*; otherwise they are *inhomogeneous*.

To see how the electromagnetic field moves through space, it is helpful to track a surface of constant phase. This is called a *wavefront*. This is just like watching the high points of the ripples created by a stone thrown into a pond; the top of a ripple forms a circle of constant phase, and following that point tells us something

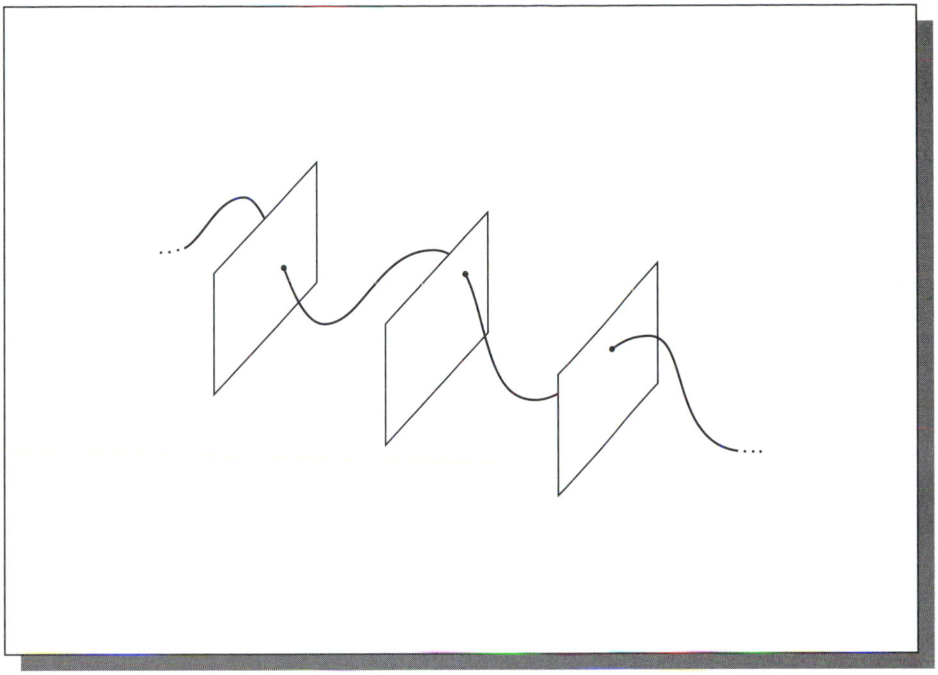

FIGURE 11.5
The geometry of plane waves.

about how fast the wave is traveling. Consider a plane wave moving in a direction parallel to the Z axis (that is, $\mathbf{k}_r = (0, 0, 1)$). At some time t_0, it will have phase $\phi = \mathbf{k}_r z - \omega t$. At some time $t_0 + \Delta t$, it will have moved a distance Δz, but the phase is the same by definition: $\phi = \mathbf{k}_r(z + \Delta z) - \omega(t + \Delta t)$. The *phase velocity* v is the speed of this surface. Equating the two expressions for ϕ, we find

$$v = \frac{\Delta z}{\Delta t} = \frac{\omega}{\mathbf{k}_r} \tag{11.3}$$

which defines the velocity (in direction $\mathbf{k}_r$) of the wavefront.

To proceed, we turn to *Maxwell's equations* [53] for electromagnetic energy. These equations are one of the crown jewels of physics, and represent in a compact and elegant manner important truths about our physical universe. Many different derivations of these equations are available in books on physics, as well as optics, communications, and electronics. Because they are fundamentally based on the wave nature of light, and our concern in this book is almost exclusively on the particle nature of light, we will not see Maxwell's equations again explicitly in this book.

Because this is their only appearance, we will be content to simply state Maxwell's equations here, *in a form specialized for plane waves*, since that's all we care about at the moment. Maxwell's equations for plane waves are four short equalities linking the electric field $\mathbf{E}$, the magnetic field $\mathbf{H}$, the wave vector $\mathbf{k}$, the frequency of radiation ω, and a few physical constants that describe the material (or medium) through which the wave is propagating. These equations are

$$\mathbf{k} \cdot \mathbf{E}_0 = 0 \tag{11.4}$$

$$\mathbf{k} \cdot \mathbf{H}_0 = 0 \tag{11.5}$$

$$\mathbf{k} \times \mathbf{E}_0 = \omega\mu\mathbf{H}_0 \tag{11.6}$$

$$\mathbf{k} \times \mathbf{H}_0 = -\omega\varepsilon\mathbf{E}_0 \tag{11.7}$$

where the *phenomenological material parameters* are as follows:

$$\begin{aligned} &\mu \text{ is the } \textit{permeability} \\ &\sigma \text{ is the } \textit{conductivity} \\ &\chi \text{ is the } \textit{electric susceptibility} \\ \varepsilon = \varepsilon_0(1+\chi) + j\sigma/\omega\ &\text{is the (complex) } \textit{permittivity} \end{aligned} \tag{11.8}$$

The three basic parameters μ, σ, and χ specify the properties of a medium (or material) and characterize how it responds to electromagnetic energy of frequency ω.

Equations 11.4 and 11.5 say that the wave vector $\mathbf{k}$ is perpendicular to both the electric and magnetic fields; such a wave is called *transverse*. They also imply that the electric and magnetic fields are perpendicular to each other (though if they are complex-valued, the interpretation of perpendicular doesn't admit a simple physical picture). When the wave is homogeneous, then the two fields and the wave vector form a set of mutually perpendicular axes in 3D, as shown in Figure 11.6.

We can boil down the material constants into a form that will prove more useful to us in graphics. First cross both sides of Equation 11.6 with the wave vector $\mathbf{k}$:

$$\begin{aligned} \mathbf{k} \times (\mathbf{k} \times \mathbf{E}_0) &= \omega\mu(\mathbf{k} \times \mathbf{H}_0) \\ &= -\omega^2\varepsilon\mu\mathbf{E}_0 \end{aligned} \tag{11.9}$$

where we have applied Equation 11.7. Recalling the vector identity

$$\mathbf{A} \times (\mathbf{B} \times \mathbf{C}) = \mathbf{B}(\mathbf{A} \cdot \mathbf{C}) - \mathbf{C}(\mathbf{A} \cdot \mathbf{B}) \tag{11.10}$$

and applying it to the above,

$$\mathbf{k} \times (\mathbf{k} \times \mathbf{E}_0) = \mathbf{k}(\mathbf{k} \cdot \mathbf{E}_0) - \mathbf{E}_0(\mathbf{k} \cdot \mathbf{k}) \tag{11.11}$$

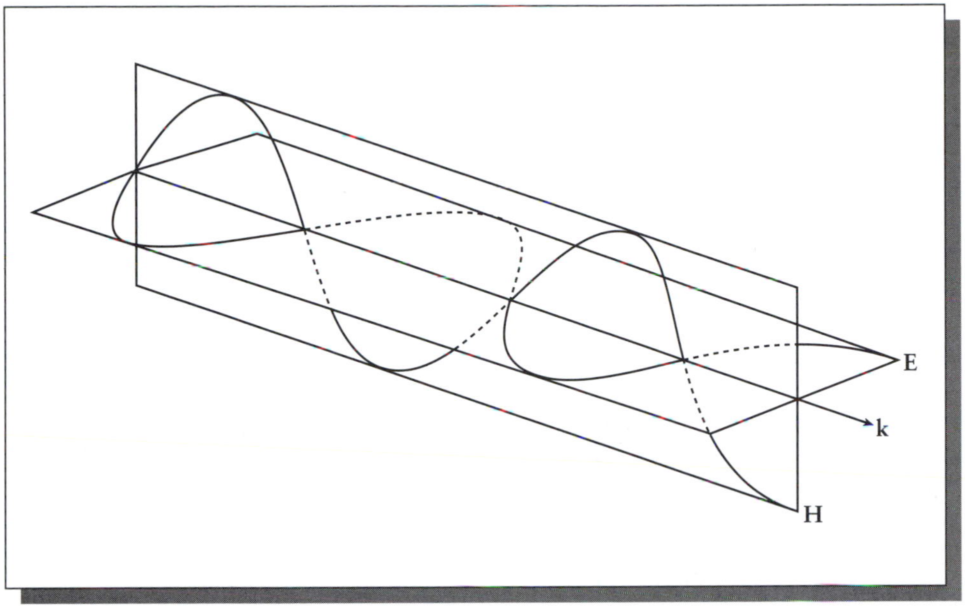

FIGURE 11.6
The wave vector, electric field, and magnetic field are perpendicular.

The first term on the right is 0 from Equation 11.4. Combining Equations 11.11 and 11.9, we find

$$\mathbf{k} \cdot \mathbf{k} = \mathbf{k}_r{}^2 - \mathbf{k}_i{}^2 + 2j\mathbf{k}_r \cdot \mathbf{k}_i = \omega^2 \varepsilon \mu \tag{11.12}$$

This equation tells us that the material properties ε and μ will admit a plane wave with vectors $\mathbf{k}_r$ and $\mathbf{k}_i$, providing they meet a specific condition. The medium does not uniquely specify a particular wave, but it does require that a wave meet this condition.

It is common to rewrite Equation 11.12 as

$$|\mathbf{k}| = |\mathbf{k}_r + j\mathbf{k}_i| = \frac{\omega N}{c} \tag{11.13}$$

where c is the speed of light in a vacuum, and the *complex refractive index* N is given by

$$N = c\sqrt{\varepsilon\mu} = \sqrt{\frac{\varepsilon\mu}{\varepsilon_0\mu_0}} \tag{11.14}$$

where ε_0 and μ_0 are the permittivity and permeability of a vacuum; their values are given in Table E.3. The complex number N is often written

$$N = \eta + j\kappa \tag{11.15}$$

for $\eta, \kappa \geq 0$. The real part of N, often represented by η, is frequently called the *real index of refraction* of the medium. The imaginary part κ is called the *extinction coefficient* and represents how easily a wave can penetrate into the medium. Both of these coefficients are actually functions of wavelength and we will sometimes write them as $\eta(\lambda)$ and $\kappa(\lambda)$ to keep this in mind.

11.4 Polarization

Time-varying electric and magnetic fields need not be radially symmetric around the direction of propagation. For example, Figure 11.7 shows the X and Y components of an electric field propagating in the Z direction. In Figure 11.7(a) the two fields are *in phase*; the peaks and zero-crossings occur at the same location along the X axis. By contrast, in Figure 11.7(b) the two fields are *out of phase*, so that their peaks and zero-crossings are at different places.

Consider just the electric field part of an electromagnetic wave traveling in the Z direction. Expanding out the complex exponential,

$$\mathbf{E} = A\cos(kz - \omega t) - B\sin(kz - \omega t) \tag{11.16}$$

We have seen above that a wavefront of constant phase moves through space; this suggests that if we examine one location in space and measure the field strength over time as it passes by us, it will move through the full cycle. For simplicity, we will look at the field at $z = 0$ [53]:

$$\mathbf{E} = A\cos(\omega t) + B\sin(\omega t) \tag{11.17}$$

Equation 11.17 can be thought of as the curve swept out by the tip of the electric field in the plane $z = 0$ as it moves through space. This curve has the form of an ellipse.

Figure 11.8 shows the variety of curves that can be generated by Equation 11.17. In general, if $A \neq 0, B \neq 0, A \neq B$, then we get an ellipse. An ellipse may be described by three numbers: two axis lengths (a *semi-major axis length* labeled a, and a *semi-minor axis length* labeled b), and an *azimuth angle* labeled ψ (measured with respect to an arbitrary reference axis). If the two axes have equal nonzero lengths, $A = B \neq 0$, then we get a circle. Finally, if $A = 0$ or $B = 0$, the curve degenerates into a line.

Each of these different curves may be swept out by the electric field as it passes through the plane. We use the shape to characterize the light, calling it *elliptically*

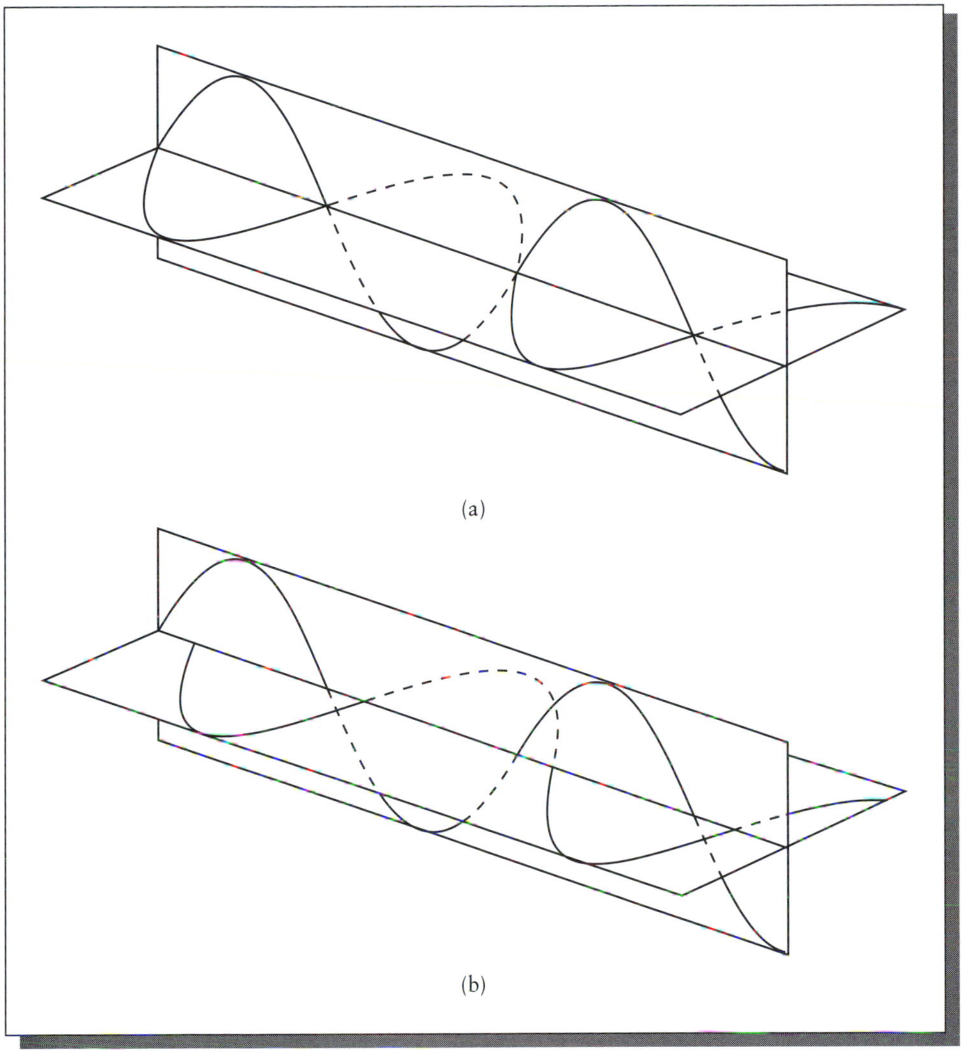

FIGURE 11.7
(a) The two fields are in phase. (b) The two fields are out of phase.

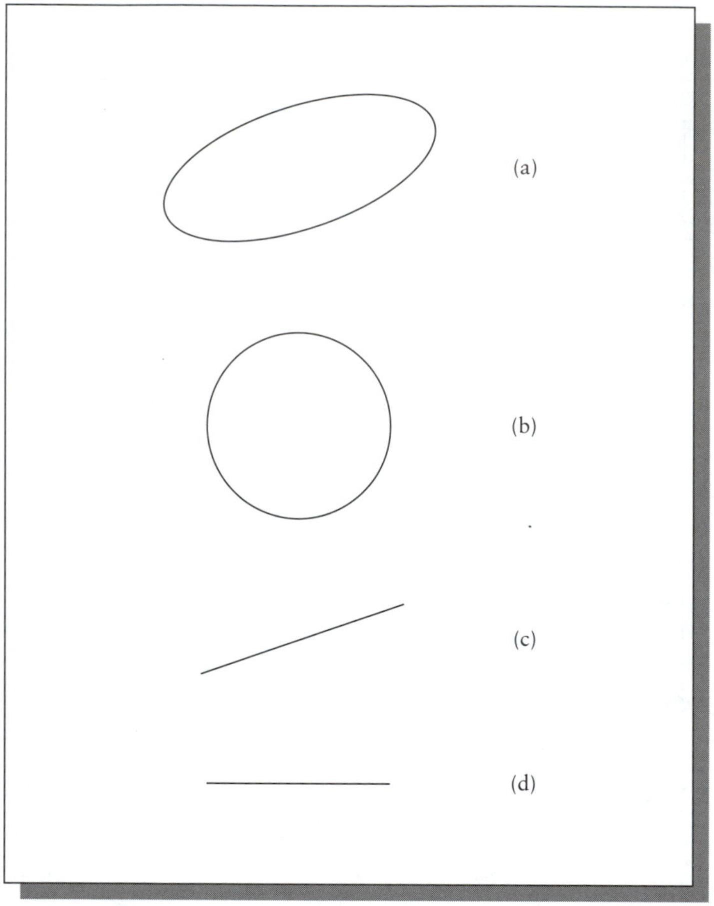

FIGURE 11.8
(a) An ellipse. (b) A circle. (c) A tilted line. (d) An axis-aligned line.

polarized, *circularly polarized* (including *left-* and *right-handed* circular polarization), or *linearly polarized* as appropriate (the term *plane polarized* is a denigrated synonym for linearly polarized [53]). The curve swept out on a stationary plane, regardless of its shape, is called the *vibration ellipse*, and the values (a, b, ψ) are called the *ellipsometric parameters*. The shape and structure of the vibration ellipse reveals the relationship between the phases of different components of the electric field; this relationship is called the *polarization* of the field.

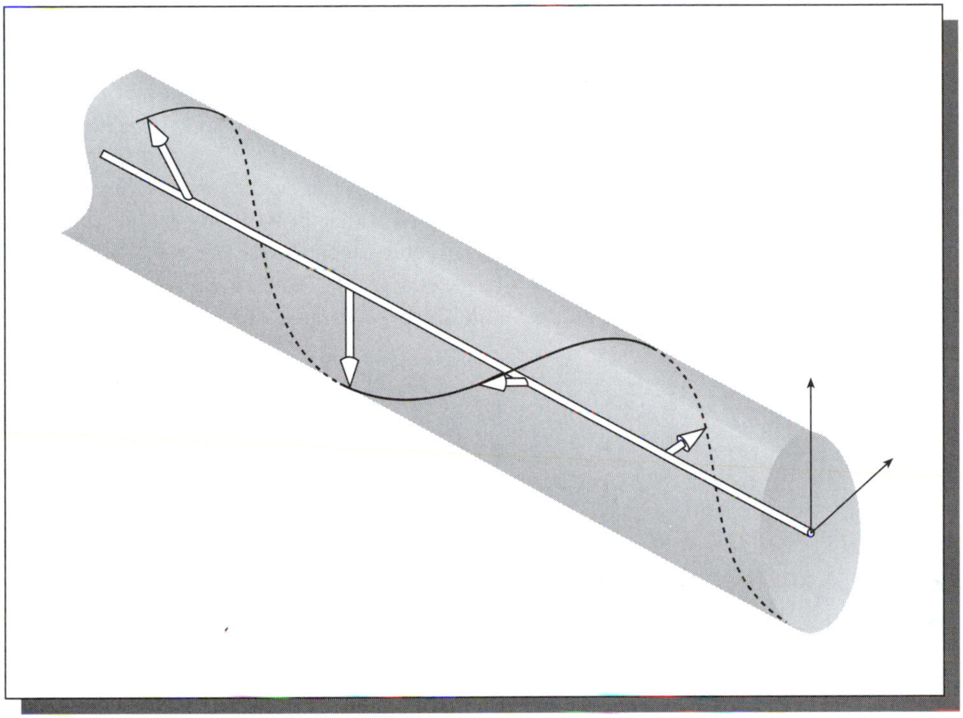

FIGURE 11.9
The two axes for measuring polarization.

Polarization is important to image synthesis because some materials respond differently to light of different polarizations. If the real part η of the complex index of refraction N varies with different forms of linearly polarized light, the material is said to be *linearly birefringent*. If the imaginary part varies, the material is *linearly dichroic*. Similarly, *circularly birefringent* and *circularly dichroic* materials are sensitive to the degree of circular polarization in the incident light.

We typically think of polarization as the projection of the electric field onto two orthogonal vectors lying in the plane perpendicular to the direction of propagation, as in Figure 11.9. Arbitrarily, one of these is called the *parallel axis* and the other the *perpendicular axis* (these axes are also sometimes called *horizontal* and *vertical*). These labels on the axes are relative terms that don't imply an absolute position, just that the axes are mutually perpendicular. Usually when a surface is involved the axes are oriented so that they are parallel and perpendicular to the local tangent plane of the surface at a particular point.

The projection of the field $\mathbf{E}$ onto these axes is written $E_{\parallel}$ and $E_{\perp}$ for the parallel and perpendicular axes, respectively. In general, these will be functions of time. If $E_{\parallel}(t)$ and $E_{\perp}(t)$ are completely correlated over time, the light is said to be *polarized*. If they are completely uncorrelated, the light is *unpolarized*. Light can be *partially polarized*, indicating any amount of coupling between the components (for example, the tip of the field may sweep out an ellipse that rotates slowly over time).

The ellipsometric parameters (a, b, ψ) completely describe the state of polarization of the light. An alternative that is often seen in the literature is a set of four parameters called *Stokes parameters*, which are related to the components of the field as follows [53]:

$$\begin{aligned} I &= E_{\parallel}\overline{E}_{\parallel} + E_{\perp}\overline{E}_{\perp} \\ Q &= E_{\parallel}\overline{E}_{\parallel} - E_{\perp}\overline{E}_{\perp} \\ U &= E_{\parallel}\overline{E}_{\perp} + E_{\perp}\overline{E}_{\parallel} \\ V &= j(E_{\parallel}\overline{E}_{\perp} - E_{\perp}\overline{E}_{\parallel}) \end{aligned} \tag{11.18}$$

(Recall that $\overline{z}$ indicates the complex conjugate of a complex number z.) These are related to the ellipsometric parameters as

$$\begin{aligned} I &= d^2 \\ Q &= d^2 \cos 2\alpha \cos 2\psi \\ U &= d^2 \cos 2\alpha \sin 2\psi \\ V &= d^2 \sin 2\alpha \end{aligned} \tag{11.19}$$

where

$$\begin{aligned} d^2 &= a^2 + b^2 \\ \psi &= \text{azimuth angle}, 0 \leq \psi \leq \pi \\ |\tan \alpha| &= \text{ellipticity} = b/a, \pi/4 \leq \alpha \leq \pi/4 \end{aligned} \tag{11.20}$$

One of the advantages of this form of representation is that we can compute with these parameters more conveniently than with the ellipsometric parameters. The four-vector (I, Q, U, V) can be treated as a column vector that specifies the polarization state of a light beam, which is modified by 4×4 *Mueller matrices* that describe the effect an optical component has on the polarization of light passing through it. To compute the final polarization after a beam has been reflected or transmitted several times, we need only apply the same sequence of matrix transformations to the Stokes parameters.

A simpler computational structure with similar purposes is given by *Jones vectors* and *Jones matrices* [148, 311]. Consider again our wave from above, traveling along the Z axis. We will assume the Y axis is the "perpendicular" direction, so X is the "parallel" direction. We can write the two components of this wave at position z directly:

$$E_x = A_x e^{j(kz-\omega t)} \qquad E_y = A_y e^{j(kz-\omega t+\phi)} \tag{11.21}$$

where we have introduced a phase-retarding factor of ϕ into the Y component. In vector form, we can write these as

$$E_x = \begin{pmatrix} A_x \\ 0 \end{pmatrix} e^{j(kz-\omega t)} \qquad E_y = \begin{pmatrix} 0 \\ A_y \end{pmatrix} e^{j(kz-\omega t+\phi)} = \begin{pmatrix} 0 \\ A_y e^{j\phi} \end{pmatrix} e^{j(kz-\omega t)} \tag{11.22}$$

For polarization, we only care about the phase difference ϕ, so we can ignore the $\exp[j(kz-\omega t)]$ factor common to both components. Since we're only concerned with the phase difference and not the amplitudes, for convenience we will set $A_x = A_y = 1$. The polarization of our light is then described by

$$E_x = \begin{pmatrix} 1 \\ 0 \end{pmatrix} \qquad E_y = \begin{pmatrix} 0 \\ e^{j\phi} \end{pmatrix} \tag{11.23}$$

These are called *Jones vectors.*

These two vectors indicate different polarizations. If a wave is completely characterized by a single Jones vector $(0,1)^t$, then it is linearly polarized. If we take a beam of light linearly polarized in the perpendicular direction (with vector $(1,0)^t$), then adding the two beams corresponds to adding the two vectors, producing linearly light polarized light at a 45-degree angle, $(1,1)^t$. Often Jones vectors are written so that they have unit length, so this vector would be written $(1/\sqrt{2})(1,1)^t$. Left-circularly polarized light with a phase angle of $\pi/2$ would be represented by a Jones vector of $(1/\sqrt{2})(1, e^{j(\pi/2)})^t = (1/\sqrt{2})(1,j)^t$. Similarly, right-circularly polarized light would be $(1/\sqrt{2})(1, e^{j(-\pi/2)})^t = (1/\sqrt{2})(1,-j)^t$. Their sum is $(1/2)(2,0)^t$. There is no Jones vector representation for unpolarized light.

The action of an optical element on a beam of light with a given polarization may be represented by a *Jones matrix*, which is 2×2, and by convention premultiplies the Jones vector (that is, a vector $\mathbf{V}$ is transformed by a matrix $\mathbf{M}$ as $\mathbf{V}' = \mathbf{MV}$). Some examples of Jones matrices are given in Table 11.1. When many optical elements are combined in a series, their combined effect on the polarization of the incident light may be found from the matrix product of the elements, applied to the initial vector in the same order.

For example, suppose we take a beam of light with initial Jones vector $\mathbf{J} = (u,v)^t$ and pass it through a horizontal polarizer $\mathbf{H}$, which removes all but the horizontal component of the energy:

$$\mathbf{J}' = \mathbf{HJ} = \begin{bmatrix} 1 & 0 \\ 0 & 0 \end{bmatrix} \begin{bmatrix} u \\ v \end{bmatrix} = \begin{bmatrix} u \\ 0 \end{bmatrix} \tag{11.24}$$

Horizontal linear polarizer	$\begin{bmatrix} 1 & 0 \\ 0 & 0 \end{bmatrix}$
Vertical linear polarizer	$\begin{bmatrix} 0 & 0 \\ 0 & 1 \end{bmatrix}$
Right-circular polarizer	$\frac{1}{2}\begin{bmatrix} 1 & j \\ -j & 1 \end{bmatrix}$
Left-circular polarizer	$\frac{1}{2}\begin{bmatrix} 1 & -j \\ j & 1 \end{bmatrix}$

TABLE 11.1
Examples of Jones matrices.

The result is a horizontally polarized beam, as we would expect.

If we now add a right-circular polarizer **R** *after* the horizontal polarizer, we find

$$\mathbf{J}' = \mathbf{RHJ} = \begin{bmatrix} 1 & j \\ j & 1 \end{bmatrix} \begin{bmatrix} 1 & 0 \\ 0 & 0 \end{bmatrix} \begin{bmatrix} u \\ v \end{bmatrix} = \begin{bmatrix} 1 & 0 \\ -j & 0 \end{bmatrix} \begin{bmatrix} u \\ v \end{bmatrix} = \begin{bmatrix} u \\ -jv \end{bmatrix} = \begin{bmatrix} 1 \\ -jv/u \end{bmatrix} \tag{11.25}$$

which is a circularly polarized beam. If we reverse the order of the optical apparatus, we get

$$\mathbf{J}' = \mathbf{HRJ} = \begin{bmatrix} 1 & 0 \\ 0 & 0 \end{bmatrix} \begin{bmatrix} 1 & j \\ j & 1 \end{bmatrix} \begin{bmatrix} u \\ v \end{bmatrix} = \begin{bmatrix} 1 & j \\ 0 & 0 \end{bmatrix} \begin{bmatrix} u \\ v \end{bmatrix} = \begin{bmatrix} u + jv \\ 0 \end{bmatrix} \tag{11.26}$$

which is horizontally polarized, albeit with complex amplitude. The fact that optical elements are not commutative is captured by the mathematics, since this property is shared by matrix multiplication.

11.5 The Photoelectric Effect

Another simple experiment can be performed that seems to defy explanation if we think of light as a wave.

Consider the experimental apparatus in Figure 11.10. A beam of light is directed onto a piece of metal (called the *cathode*); located off to one side we have a detection device capable of measuring the energy of any electrons that strike it.

When we shine a beam of light onto the cathode, the detector instantly starts reporting electrons; apparently the light incident on the cathode triggers the expulsion

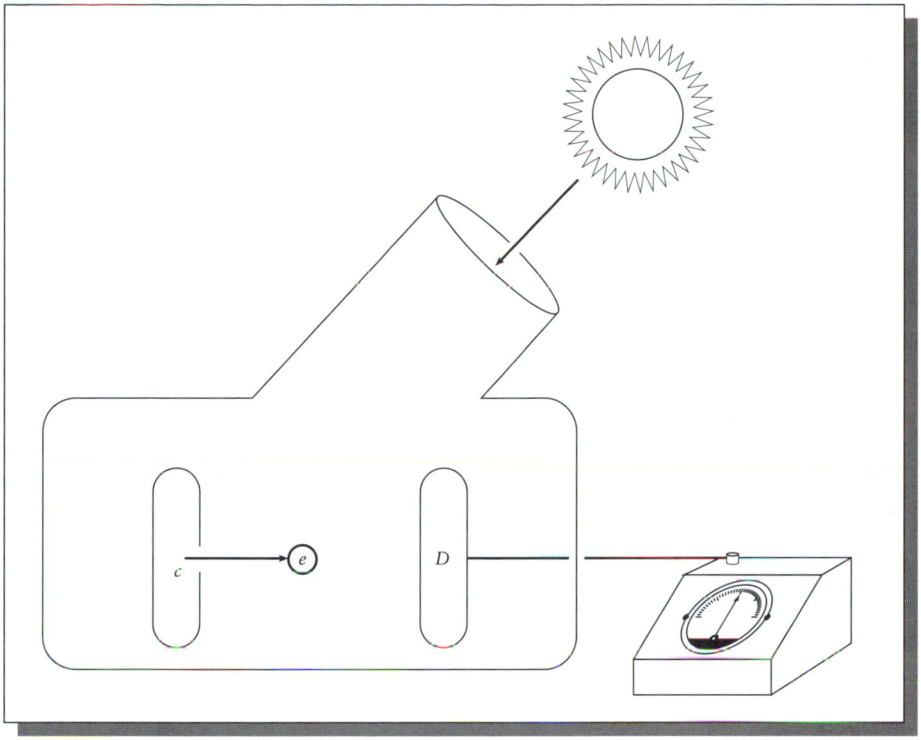

FIGURE 11.10

Apparatus for observing the photoelectric effect. The cathode is c, the detector is D.

of electrons from the metal. For every one of these electrons, we find

$$E = h\nu - p \tag{11.27}$$

where E is the observed energy of the electron, ν is the frequency of the incident energy (interpreted as a wave!), p is a constant characteristic of the metal, and h is a factor that seems constant for all metals and all wavelengths. This expulsion of electrons by light is called the *photoelectric effect*.

If we perform this experiment repeatedly, two important phenomena become clear. First, the energy E of the electrons is independent of the amplitude of the incident beam. In other words, if we illuminate the metal sequentially with a 20-watt light bulb and then an otherwise identical 40-watt light bulb, we get more electrons but their energy does not change. Second, even extremely low amplitudes of light produce some electrons.

The wave theory is unable to account for these phenomena. For the first case, we would expect a stronger wave to impart more energy to the electrons as they are ejected from the metal. Second, if the incident energy is very low, then it would be spread all over the cathode, and nowhere would there be enough energy for an electron to actually manage to get away from the metal (from the above equation, that requires some energy characterized by p).

Einstein postulated that the energy flowing along the incident beam is quantized into small, individual packets called *photons*.[1] When a photon collides with an electron, it transfers its energy to the electron. This transfer cannot happen partially; all of the photon's energy is contained in a single, indivisible packet, which is transferred either in its entirety or not at all.

Since each photon interacts with each electron independently, we can see why increasing the number of photons in the incident beam does not increase the energy of the emitted electrons (though it produces more interactions and thus more electrons). If the energy of a photon is too low, it will be below the threshold energy (call it W_0) required to liberate an electron from the metal. In this case a dense beam of photons of very low energy will not cause the cathode to emit any electrons at all. On the other hand, if each photon has an energy $E > W_0$, then even a very sparse beam will trigger the emission of some electrons, each with an energy $E - W_0$.

We find from the experiment that the energy E of the electrons is related to the frequency ν of the incident energy, again interpreted as a wave. This relationship is simply

$$E = h\nu = hc/\lambda \tag{11.28}$$

The constant h is now known to be one of the fundamental values that determines the structure of our physical universe. Known as *Planck's constant*, it is tabulated in Table E.3 along with the other physical constants used in this book.

We can show that each photon has an *apparent* mass of $m = h\nu/c^2$. But this is not a mass in the conventional sense of something that may be held still and weighed. A photon is a composite entity of motion and energy; there is no such thing as a photon at rest. The photoelectric effect by itself does not prove the existence of photons (the photoelectric effect can be explained just based on the ideas of Planck's constant) and indeed Einstein's paper only discussed the energy of the radiation [427].

Other experimental evidence of the particle nature of light is provided by quantitative photochemistry, the Compton effect, the X-ray absorption edge, the Zeeman effect, and the Raman effect [478].

The study of the particle nature of light is called *geometrical optics*.

---

[1] Einstein's Nobel prize in physics was awarded for his photon theory, not relativity.

11.6 Particle-Wave Duality

Resolution of the dual nature of light is addressed by *quantum optics*. Although we will not go into this subject here, one basic idea is that a photon may be considered a small, physically localized *wave packet*. The packet is a wave but it does not extend infinitely. A highly readable and informative discussion of the resolution of these dual natures of light is given by Feynman in a wonderful little book on quantum electrodynamics [144].

In this book we will limit ourselves to the particle nature of light. The geometrical optics in this chapter will set the stage for this interpretation, and the particle-based transport theory in Chapter 12 will cement it.

What we are excluding by this choice is all hope of cleanly modeling those phenomena of light that are not handled by the particle model, specifically *interference* and *diffraction*. These are not trivial phenomena. Interference accounts for the brilliant colors that we see in thin films, including peacock feathers, oil slicks, and soap bubbles. Diffraction is responsible for some (though not all) soft shadows and light bleeding around the edges of objects.

The advantage of using geometrical optics is that they seem to be more amenable to direct simulation on a computer for the types of complex environments and shading models that we use in computer graphics. A number of reports have been published in the image synthesis literature that use physical optics as an image-formation model [248, 314]. The results of this work have typically required enormous computational resources to produce results of significantly lower fidelity and complexity than those attainable by geometrical optics.

Therefore we make a pragmatic choice, and select the particle model for its simplicity and power. To be blunt, we are simply saying that interference and diffraction are sufficiently infrequent or unimportant that we can afford to ignore them in our general theory.

11.7 Reflection and Transmission

Reflection is the process whereby light of a specific wavelength incident on a material is at least partly propagated outward by the material without change in wavelength. We will have much more to say about reflection in Chapter 13, but for now we will simply discuss some of the larger-scale features of this interaction of light and matter. Most simple models of reflection distinguish a small number of categories that cover the various mechanisms by which light is propagated by a surface. These include

Specular (also called *regular*, or *mirror*) reflection propagates light without scattering, as from the surface of a perfectly smooth mirror, illustrated in Figure 11.11(a).

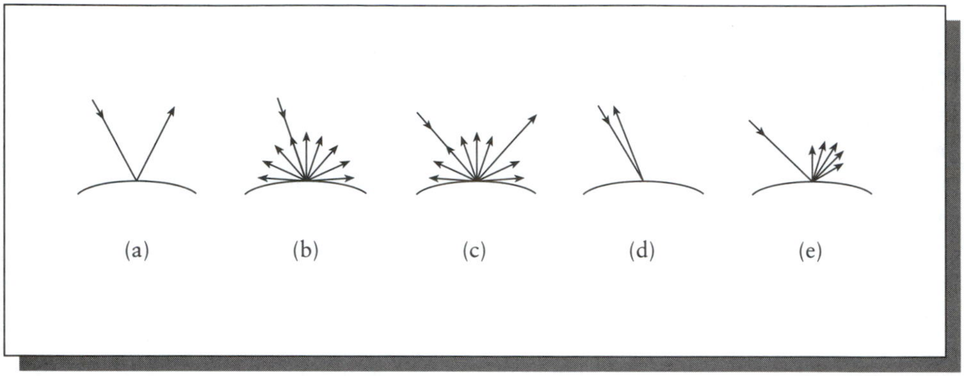

FIGURE 11.11
Different forms of reflection. (a) Specular. (b) Diffuse. (c) Mixed. (d) Retro-reflection. (e) Gloss.

Diffuse reflection sends light in all directions with equal energy; this is illustrated in Figure 11.11(b).

Mixed reflection is a combination of the two types described above. In a material exhibiting mixed reflectance, its overall reflectance is given by a weighted combination of diffuse and specular components. An example is shown in Figure 11.11(c).

Retro-reflection occurs when the incident energy is reflected in directions close to the incident direction, over a wide range of incident directions. Although almost all materials are retro-reflective to some extent, those that retro-reflect most of their incident energy are referred to as *retro-reflectors*. An example retro-reflection profile is shown in Figure 11.11(d).

Gloss is defined as the property of a material surface that involves mixed reflection and is responsible for a mirrorlike appearance of a rough surface. The characteristics of gloss are usually described with the term *glossiness*.

There are five kinds of glossiness, each described by its own scale of degree: *specular*, *sheen*, *contrast*, *directness of image*, and *absence of bloom* [220, 232]. A perfect mirror has unit gloss, and a perfect diffuser (such as that approximated by fine-ground glass) has zero gloss. The different types of gloss are measured by the ratio of reflected to incident light at certain standard angles [232]. Figure 11.12 illustrates the following descriptions of different types of glossiness. In each case the incident and reflected vectors are coplanar but on opposite sides of the normal. The

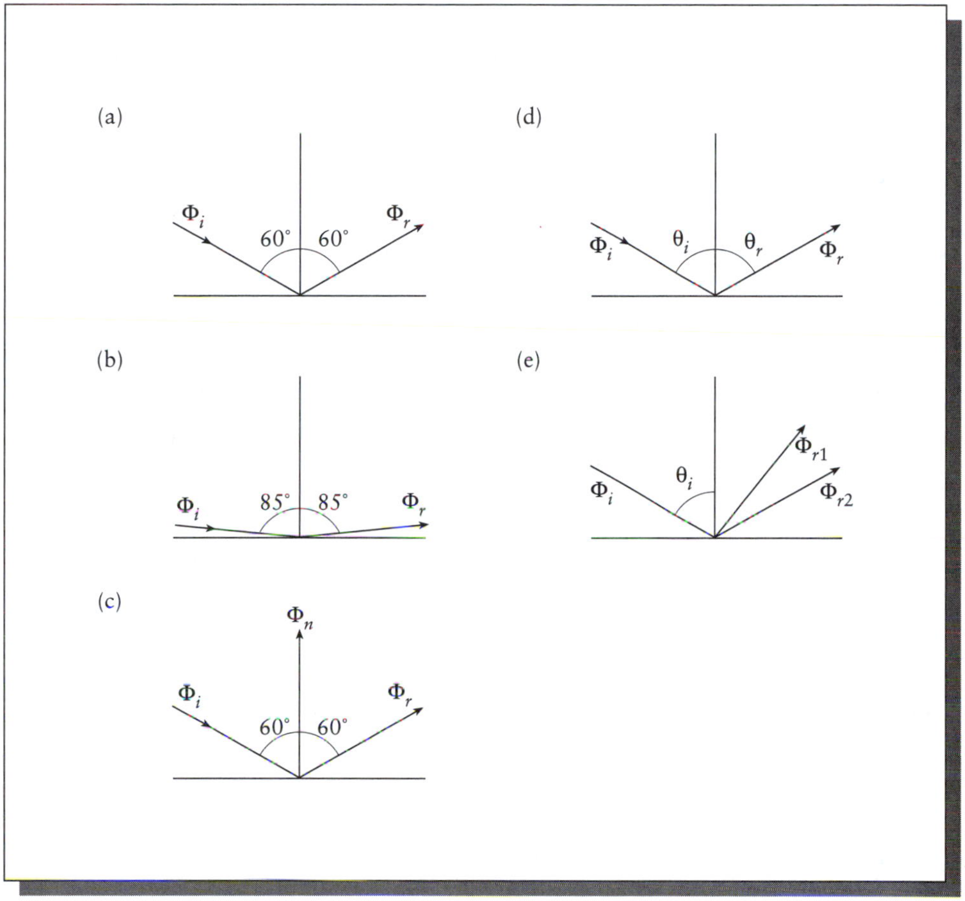

FIGURE 11.12

(a) Specular. (b) Sheen. (c) Contrast. (d) Distinctness of image. (e) Absence of bloom. Redrawn from Judd and Wyszecki, *Color in Business, Science, and Industry*, table 3.1, p. 408.

incident energy is measured as Φ_i and the reflected energy as Φ_r (or Φ_{r1} and Φ_{r2} when necessary). The energy leaving in the direction of the normal is Φ_n.

Specular: This measures the brightness of a highlight. The incident and reflected vectors are set at 60° from the normal. The gloss factor is given by Φ_r/Φ_i.

Sheen: This is the brightness of a highlight at a glancing angle. The incident and reflected vectors are set at 85° from the normal. The gloss factor is given by Φ_r/Φ_i.

Contrast: This is the brightness of a highlight at a glancing angle. The incident and reflected vectors are set at 85° from the normal. The gloss factor is given by Φ_r/Φ_n.

Distinctness of image: This measures the clarity of the highlight or the sharpness of its borders. The incident and reflected vectors are set at angles θ_i and θ_r, which are only a few minutes of arc different with respect to the normal. The gloss factor is given by $d\Phi_r/d\theta_r$, which is the rate of change of the reflected energy with θ_r.

Absence of bloom: This measures the haziness around the highlight. A reflected vector $\mathbf{R}_1$ is set at the reflected direction; the other, $\mathbf{R}_2$, is a few degrees off. The gloss factor is given by Φ_{r2}/Φ_{r1}.

If the reflected light has the same reflectance for all incident azimuth angles ψ, the reflection is termed *isotropic*; otherwise it is *anisotropic*.

Similarly, *transmission* (or *refraction*) is the process whereby light of a specific wavelength incident on the interface (or boundary) between two materials passes (or refracts) through the interface and into the other material without change in wavelength. Like reflection, there are several principal categories of transmission. These include

Specular (or *regular*, or *mirror*) transmission propagates light into the new material without scattering, as when light passes into a clear sheet of glass. This mode is illustrated in Figure 11.13(a).

Diffuse transmission is transmission on a macroscopic scale, without a specular component. As with reflection, diffuse transmission may be isotropic or anisotropic. For example, diffuse transmission is often used for "art glass," to admit light but not permit clear visibility, such as for a shower door. This mode is illustrated in Figure 11.13(b).

Mixed transmission is a combination of diffuse and specular transmission. Most natural materials that admit transmission propagate light with both characteristics. This mode is illustrated in Figure 11.13(c).

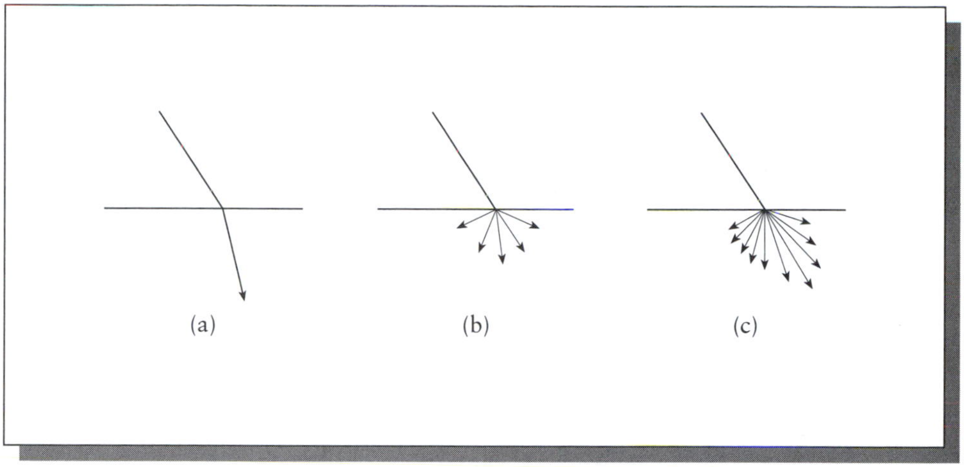

FIGURE 11.13
Different forms of transmission. (a) Specular. (b) Diffuse. (c) Mixed.

Traditional computer graphics rendering systems have emphasized four of these main categories to model surfaces: diffuse and specular reflection, and diffuse and specular transmission. The geometries for these modes are simple and well understood; they are discussed below.

11.8 Index of Refraction

As discussed in Section 11.3, when light moves through a medium denser than a vacuum, its speed decreases. When the extinction coefficient $\kappa = 0$, the ratio of the speed of electromagnetic energy through a medium to its speed in a vacuum is the simple index of refraction $\eta \in \mathcal{R}$ for that material:

$$\eta(\lambda) = \frac{c}{\nu_\lambda} \tag{11.29}$$

where

ν_λ is the velocity of light of wavelength λ in the medium
c is the speed of light in a vacuum

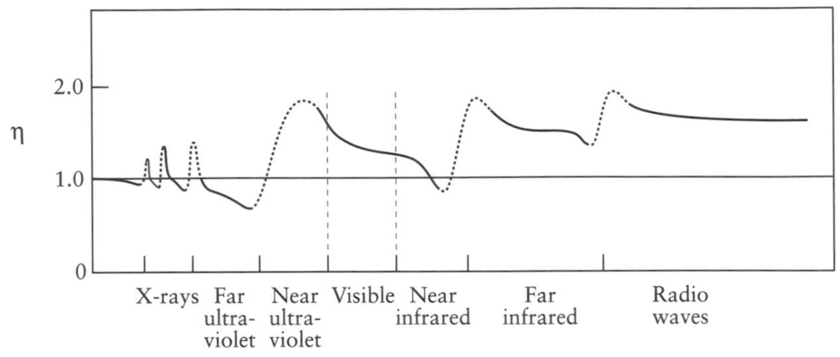

FIGURE 11.14
The index of refraction as a function of wavelength. Redrawn from Jenkins and White, *Fundamentals of Optics*, fig. 23I, p. 478.

Note that the index of refraction is a function of wavelength. Figure 11.14 shows a schematic representation of the index of refraction over a spectrum from the X rays to radio waves.

Note that much of the curve is roughly flat with a downward slope; these are called regions of *normal dispersion*. There are also places where the curve takes a sudden dip and then rises significantly over a short interval before flattening out again; these are regions of so-called *anomalous dispersion*. This latter name comes from the fact that in this region, longer wavelengths are refracted more than shorter ones. However, every substance has such a region at some wavelength, so the phenomenon is actually quite normal [230].

Notice that sometimes the index of refraction dips below 1.0, implying that light of that frequency will move through the medium faster than light in a vacuum. Although this appears to violate a basic principle of relativity, this mathematical oddity doesn't represent an actual transfer of information. Relativity only places an upper limit on the speed with which energy is conveyed from one place to another, and this speed never exceeds the speed of light in the given medium. The essence of the reasoning lies in the concept of the *phase velocity* of superimposed waves. Explanations of anomalous dispersion, indices of refraction below 1, and superluminal phase velocity are not relevant to our needs in this book, since they rarely occur in the visible band. Detailed discussions of these phenomena may be found in the optics texts mentioned in the Further Reading section.

11.8.1 Sellmeier's Formula

A good approximation to the index of refraction curve was given by Sellmeier in 1871 [230]. He proposed that the dip in refractive index was due to selective absorption of particles that vibrate at a certain *natural frequency* ν_0. He suggested that energy passing through a material with such particles might resonate with them, producing both constructive and destructive interference. For a single resonance frequency ν_0, Sellmeier's equation is

$$\eta_\lambda^2 = 1 + \frac{A\lambda^2}{\lambda^2 - {\lambda_0}^2} \tag{11.30}$$

where

λ_0 is the wavelength of light with frequency ν_0: $\lambda_0 = c/\nu_0$

A is a constant for each material

If there are several resonant frequencies, Sellmeier's equation may be written as a summation of resonance terms:

$$\eta_\lambda^2 = 1 + \sum_{i=1}^{n} \frac{A_i\lambda^2}{\lambda^2 - \lambda_i^2} \tag{11.31}$$

We will assume that most optical materials have only one absorption band near the visible region, so we will use the one-term form of Equation 11.30 in the following discussions.

Consider again Figure 11.14. Notice that as $\lambda \to 0, \eta \to 1$; as $\lambda \to \infty, \eta \to 1 + A$. Equation 11.31 agrees exactly with the results of an analysis based on electromagnetic theory with some simplifying assumptions.

Differentiating Equation 11.30 with respect to λ yields

$$\frac{d\eta_\lambda}{d\lambda} = \frac{\dfrac{-2A\lambda^3}{(\lambda^2 - {\lambda_0}^2)^2} + \dfrac{2A\lambda}{\lambda^2 - {\lambda_0}^2}}{2\sqrt{1 + \dfrac{A\lambda^2}{\lambda^2 - {\lambda_0}^2}}} \tag{11.32}$$

Equation 11.32 shows that the change in the index of refraction varies as a function of the third power of wavelength. Thus the index of refraction of a material is a strong function of wavelength and should not be approximated by a single number.

To use Sellmeier's equation, we must obtain values for A and ${\lambda_0}^2$ (note that we never need λ_0 itself, only its squared value). These values can be found by writing Equation 11.30 twice, at two different wavelengths for which the index of refraction is known, and solving simultaneously. We write

$${\eta_1}^2 = 1 + \frac{A{\lambda_1}^2}{{\lambda_1}^2 - {\lambda_0}^2}$$

$$\eta_2{}^2 = 1 + \frac{A\lambda_2{}^2}{\lambda_2{}^2 - \lambda_0{}^2} \tag{11.33}$$

Solving for A and then $\lambda_0{}^2$, we find

$$\begin{aligned} \lambda_0{}^2 &= \frac{S-U}{T-V} \\ A &= \frac{(\eta_1{}^2 - 1)(\lambda_1{}^2 - \lambda_0{}^2)}{\lambda_1{}^2} \end{aligned} \tag{11.34}$$

where

$$\begin{aligned} S &= (\eta_1{}^2 - 1)\lambda_1{}^2\lambda_2{}^2 \\ T &= (\eta_1{}^2 - 1)\lambda_1{}^2 \\ U &= (\eta_1{}^2 - 1)\lambda_1{}^2\lambda_2{}^2 \\ V &= (\eta_1{}^2 - 1)\lambda_2{}^2 \end{aligned} \tag{11.35}$$

The computation of A and $\lambda_0{}^2$ can be made efficient by making use of common subexpressions. Applying Sellmeier's formula is simply an application of Equation 11.30.

Sellmeier's formula is accurate and theoretically justifiable. However, finding η_λ requires a square root. We might be tempted to wonder if there is a good approximation to this formula that avoids the computationally expensive square root. The answer is yes, and it is to be found in *Cauchy's formula.*

11.8.2 Cauchy's Formula

Cauchy's formula is only accurate in regions of normal dispersion. Computer graphics is fortunate that most materials do not have a region of anomalous dispersion near or in the visible band. Figure 11.15 shows the refractive index for several materials in the visible band.

We can simplify Sellmeier's equation to take advantage of the relative flatness of most refractive index curves in the visible band. Rewrite Equation 11.30 as

$$\eta_\lambda{}^2 = 1 + \frac{A}{(1 - \lambda_0{}^2/\lambda^2)} \tag{11.36}$$

Expand Equation 11.36 with the binomial theorem:

$$\eta_\lambda{}^2 = 1 + A\left(1 + \frac{\lambda_0{}^2}{\lambda^2} + \frac{\lambda_0{}^4}{\lambda^4} + \cdots\right) \tag{11.37}$$

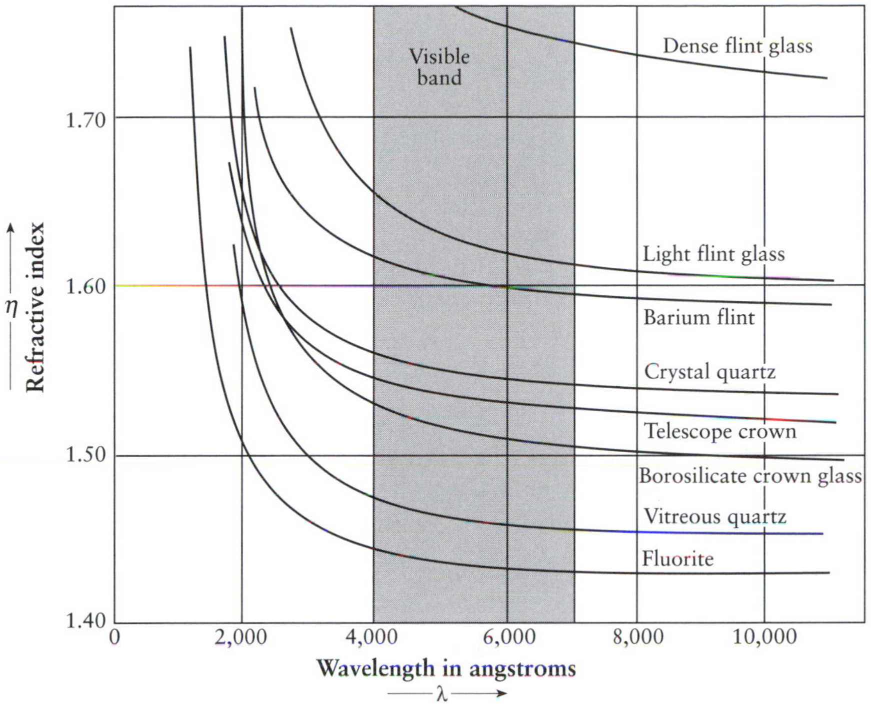

FIGURE 11.15

The refractive index in the visible band for several materials. Redrawn from Jenkins and White, *Fundamentals of Optics*, fig. 23B, p. 466.

When $\lambda \gg \lambda_0$, then $\lambda_0/\lambda \rightarrow 0$, so we may truncate the higher-order terms, leaving

$$\eta_\lambda{}^2 = 1 + A + A\frac{\lambda_0{}^2}{\lambda^2} \tag{11.38}$$

Writing $M = 1 + A$ and $N = A\lambda_0{}^2$,

$$\eta_\lambda = \left(M + N\lambda^{-2}\right)^{\frac{1}{2}} \tag{11.39}$$

Again using the binomial theorem, this expands to

$$\eta_\lambda = M^{\frac{1}{2}} + \frac{N}{2M^{\frac{1}{2}}\lambda^2} + \frac{N^2}{8M^{\frac{3}{2}}\lambda^4} + \cdots \tag{11.40}$$

If we again ignore high-order terms and retain only the first three, we obtain

$$\eta(\lambda) = A + \frac{B}{\lambda^2} + \frac{C}{\lambda^4} \tag{11.41}$$

Equation 11.41 was first given by Cauchy in 1836. It only holds in regions of normal dispersion, and even there it is not as accurate as Sellmeier's equation, but it is a useful approximation [230].

To find the coefficients for Cauchy's equation for some material, select three wavelengths λ_1, λ_2, and λ_3 for which the associated indices of refraction $\eta(\lambda_1) = \eta_1$, $\eta(\lambda_2) = \eta_2$, and $\eta(\lambda_3) = \eta_3$ are known. Then write the three simultaneous linear equations implied by these relations and solve them for A, B, and C:

$$\begin{bmatrix} \eta(\lambda_1) \\ \eta(\lambda_2) \\ \eta(\lambda_3) \end{bmatrix} = \begin{bmatrix} 1 & 1/{\lambda_1}^2 & 1/{\lambda_1}^4 \\ 1 & 1/{\lambda_2}^2 & 1/{\lambda_2}^4 \\ 1 & 1/{\lambda_3}^2 & 1/{\lambda_3}^4 \end{bmatrix} \begin{bmatrix} A \\ B \\ C \end{bmatrix} \tag{11.42}$$

In matrix form, we may write $\mathbf{N} = \mathbf{LA}$, so $\mathbf{A} = \mathbf{L}^{-1}\mathbf{N}$. Inversion of the matrix and expansion gives the following explicit formulas for A, B, and C in terms of the indices of refraction at the selected wavelengths:

$$A = k[\eta_1(sv - tu) + \eta_2(ru - qv) + \eta_3(qt - rs)] \tag{11.43}$$

$$B = k[\eta_1(t - v) + \eta_2(v - r) + \eta_3(r - t)] \tag{11.44}$$

$$C = k[\eta_1(u - s) + \eta_2(q - u) + \eta_3(s - q)] \tag{11.45}$$

where

$$\begin{aligned} q &= 1/{\lambda_1}^2 & r &= 1/{\lambda_1}^4 = q^2 \\ s &= 1/{\lambda_2}^2 & t &= 1/{\lambda_2}^4 = s^2 \\ u &= 1/{\lambda_3}^2 & v &= 1/{\lambda_3}^4 = u^2 \\ k &= \frac{1}{\sqrt{qt - rs + ru - ru - qv + sv}} \end{aligned} \tag{11.46}$$

11.9 Computing Specular Vectors

When a ray of light is specularly reflected from a surface, it leaves the surface in a well-defined direction that is determined by the surface normal and the angle of incidence. Similarly, transmission is defined by the angle of incidence, the normal, and the indices of refraction of the two materials. We will construct these two vectors below.

In this section we will identify vectors of unit length with a hat. So $|\widehat{\mathbf{N}}| = 1$, but $|\mathbf{N}|$ can be any nonzero real number. For convenience, we will draw all vectors as radiating outward from the shading point. This means that the vector $\mathbf{I}$ representing the incident light is drawn pointing toward the source of the light, in exactly the opposite direction of the travel of light itself.

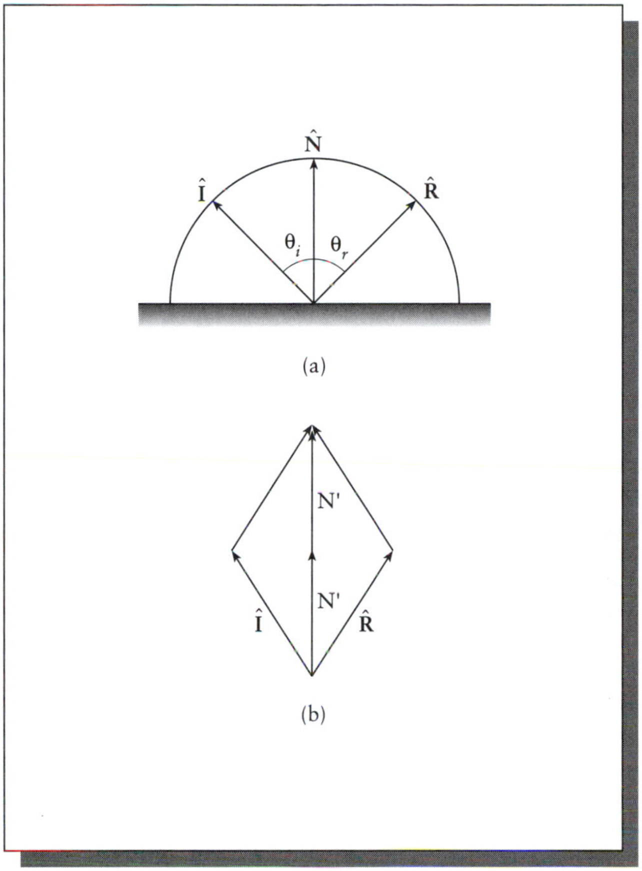

FIGURE 11.16

Geometry of specular reflection. (a) The vectors $\widehat{\mathbf{I}}$, $\widehat{\mathbf{N}}$, and $\widehat{\mathbf{R}}$. (b) The parallelogram formed by $\widehat{\mathbf{I}}$ and $\widehat{\mathbf{R}}$.

11.9.1 The Reflected Vector

The two experimental facts that allow us to construct the specularly reflected vector $\widehat{\mathbf{R}}$ for an incident vector $\widehat{\mathbf{I}}$ and a given normal $\widehat{\mathbf{N}}$ are that the three vectors are all coplanar, and that $\widehat{\mathbf{I}} \cdot \widehat{\mathbf{N}} = \widehat{\mathbf{R}} \cdot \widehat{\mathbf{N}}$. Using these constraints, Figure 11.16(a) shows the three vectors $\widehat{\mathbf{I}}$ representing the incident light direction, $\widehat{\mathbf{N}}$ representing the surface normal, and $\widehat{\mathbf{R}}$ representing the reflected direction. Notice that they all have unit length.

Figure 11.16(b) shows the parallelogram formed by $\widehat{\mathbf{I}}$ and $\widehat{\mathbf{R}}$. The vertical diagonal of this parallelogram is given by $2\mathbf{N}'$, where $\mathbf{N}'$ is a scaled version of the normal vector $\widehat{\mathbf{N}}$: $\mathbf{N}' = \left(\widehat{\mathbf{I}} \cdot \widehat{\mathbf{N}}\right) \widehat{\mathbf{N}}$.

From the parallelogram, we can see that

$$\widehat{\mathbf{R}} + \widehat{\mathbf{I}} = 2\mathbf{N}' \tag{11.47}$$

or

$$\begin{aligned} \widehat{\mathbf{R}} &= 2\mathbf{N}' - \widehat{\mathbf{I}} \\ &= 2\left(\widehat{\mathbf{I}} \cdot \widehat{\mathbf{N}}\right) \widehat{\mathbf{N}} - \widehat{\mathbf{I}} \end{aligned} \tag{11.48}$$

This is the form used by programs.

11.9.2 Total Internal Reflection

When light passes from one medium into a denser medium, its speed decreases. Thus we can never speak of "the speed of light" in the abstract; it must always be with respect to some medium. The most common reference medium is a perfect vacuum, though the speed of light through air is only slightly slower than through a vacuum.

The surface where two media touch is called the *interface*; thus, we see a change in the speed of light at any interface between two materials of different densities. One ramification of the change in speed is that light appears to bend when passing through the interface. The amount of this bending, or *refraction*, is determined by the indices of refraction of the materials on both sides of the interface.

The most basic physical law governing the geometry of refraction was described by Willebrord Snell of the University of Leyden, Holland, in an unpublished paper in 1621 [230]. Descartes later formulated a version of the relation based on the ratio of sines of the involved angles. The law relating the angles is thus variously known as Snell's law and Descartes' law.

This law of refraction may be stated as

$$\eta_i \sin \theta_i = \eta_t \sin \theta_t \tag{11.49}$$

where

θ_i is the angle between an incoming ray and the normal at the interface

θ_t is the angle between the transmitted ray and the reversed normal

η_i is the simple index of refraction for the incident medium

η_t is the simple index of refraction for the medium into which the light is transmitted

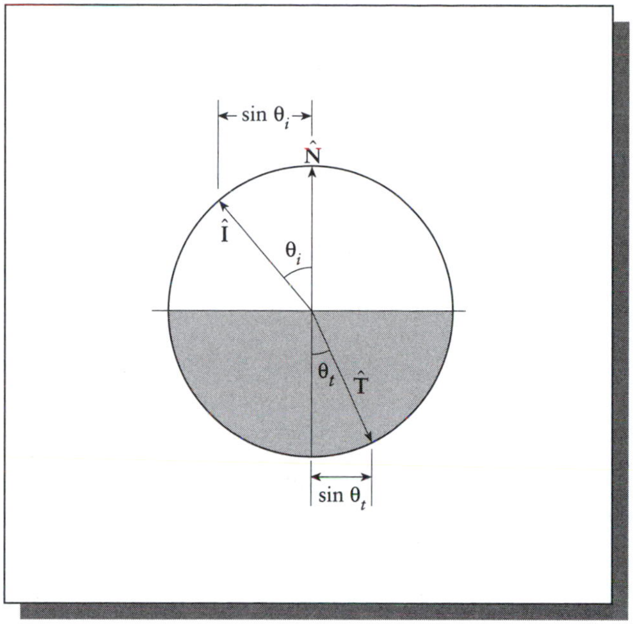

FIGURE 11.17
Snell's law.

The construction for this law is shown in Figure 11.17. The indices of refraction of the media on the incident and transmitted side of the interface are given, respectively, by η_i and η_t.

Figure 11.18(a) shows the result of some rays passing from one medium to a denser medium. In general, the transmitted ray is bent to lie closer to the surface normal than the incident ray.

Figure 11.18(b) shows the path of several rays traveling from a dense material into a less-dense medium. In general, the transmitted ray is bent further from the surface normal than the incident ray. An implication of this statement is that at some angle, called the *critical angle*, the light is bent to lie exactly in the plane perpendicular to the normal at the point where the incident ray strikes the interface. At all angles greater than this the light is reflected back into the original medium. This phenomenon is called *total internal reflection* (TIR). From Snell's law, we find that the critical angle ϕ_c may be found from

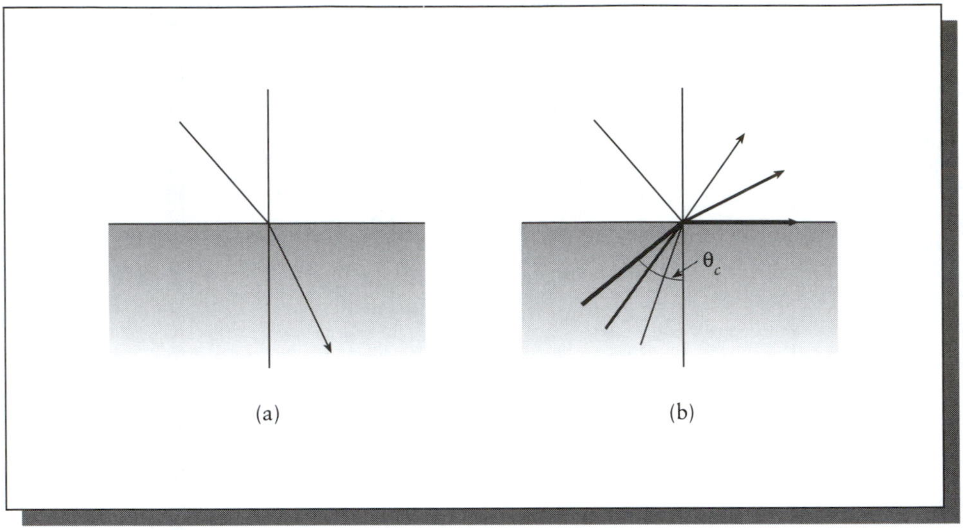

FIGURE 11.18
Refraction. (a) Transmission into a denser medium. (b) Transmission into a rarer medium.

$$\begin{aligned} \eta_i \sin \phi_c &= \eta_t \sin(\pi/2) \\ \sin \phi_c &= \frac{\eta_t}{\eta_i} \end{aligned} \tag{11.50}$$

In words, the critical angle is the smallest angle of incidence, in the denser material, for which light is totally reflected. Correct detection and handling of total internal reflection is critical for creating realistic images of transparent object.

Although Snell's law is typically written as in Equation 11.49, a more precise statement is

$$\eta_i(\lambda) \sin \eta_i = \eta_t(\lambda) \sin \eta_t \tag{11.51}$$

where the dependence of the indices of refraction on wavelength is made explicit.

11.9.3 Transmitted Vector

The graphical construction for the transmitted vector is a bit more complex than that for the reflected vector. Our experimental data is the coplanarity of the incident,

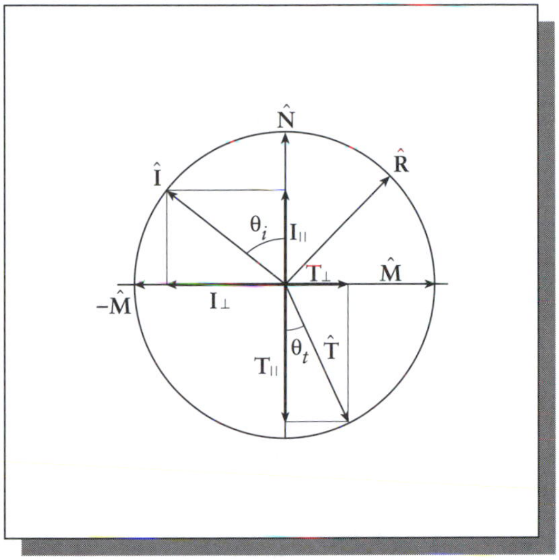

FIGURE 11.19

The geometry of specular transmission.

normal and transmitted vectors, and Snell's law. Our construction of $\widehat{\mathbf{T}}$ is based on the derivation given in Heckbert [209].

Figure 11.19 shows the four vectors $\widehat{\mathbf{I}}$, $\widehat{\mathbf{M}}$, $\widehat{\mathbf{N}}$, and $\widehat{\mathbf{T}}$ where $\widehat{\mathbf{I}}$ and $\widehat{\mathbf{N}}$ are the same as before, $\widehat{\mathbf{T}}$ is the transmitted vector, and $\widehat{\mathbf{M}}$ will be constructed below. Our approach will be to decompose $\widehat{\mathbf{T}}$ into two vectors $\widehat{\mathbf{T}} = \mathbf{T}_\perp + \mathbf{T}_{||}$, which are respectively perpendicular and parallel to the normal.

We begin by constructing the vector $\widehat{\mathbf{M}}$. This is a unit vector in the plane of the interface on the same side of the normal as $\widehat{\mathbf{T}}$. We find $\widehat{\mathbf{M}}$ by first projecting $\mathbf{I}$ into the interface, normalizing the result, and then reflecting it. The projection of $\mathbf{I}$ into the interface gives us the (nonunit) vector $\mathbf{I}_\perp$:

$$\mathbf{I}_\perp = \widehat{\mathbf{I}} - \cos\theta_i \widehat{\mathbf{N}} \tag{11.52}$$

By construction we can see that this vector has length $\sin\theta_i$, so we divide by this magnitude and multiply by -1 to flip it around and get the unit-length vector $\widehat{\mathbf{M}}$:

$$\widehat{\mathbf{M}} = \frac{-1}{\sin\theta_i}(\widehat{\mathbf{I}} - \cos\theta_i \widehat{\mathbf{N}}) \tag{11.53}$$

Now we can see from the construction that $|\mathbf{T}_\perp| = \cos\theta_t$ and $|\mathbf{T}_{||}| = \sin\theta_t$.

Further, $\mathbf{T}_{\|}$ is antiparallel to $\widehat{\mathbf{N}}$ and $\mathbf{T}_{\perp}$ is parallel to $\widehat{\mathbf{M}}$, so

$$\begin{aligned}\widehat{\mathbf{T}} &= \mathbf{T}_{\perp} + \mathbf{T}_{\|} \\ &= \widehat{\mathbf{M}} \sin\theta_t - \widehat{\mathbf{N}} \cos\theta_t \\ &= \frac{-\sin\theta_t}{\sin\theta_i}(\widehat{\mathbf{I}} - \cos\theta_i \widehat{\mathbf{N}}) - \widehat{\mathbf{N}} \cos\theta_t \qquad (11.54)\end{aligned}$$

Equation 11.54 is a perfectly valid expression for $\widehat{\mathbf{T}}$, but it requires us to compute a few sines and cosines we would like to avoid. The only such expression that's computationally convenient is $\cos\theta_i = \widehat{\mathbf{I}} \cdot \widehat{\mathbf{N}}$, so it would be nice to get everything in terms of $\cos\theta_i$.

We begin by noticing that $\sin\theta_t / \sin\theta_i = \eta_i/\eta_t$ from Snell's law, so plugging this in, expanding the terms, and collecting for $\widehat{\mathbf{N}}$, we find

$$\begin{aligned}\widehat{\mathbf{T}} &= -\frac{\eta_i}{\eta_t}(\widehat{\mathbf{I}} - \cos\theta_i \widehat{\mathbf{N}}) - \widehat{\mathbf{N}} \cos\theta_t \\ &= -\frac{\eta_i}{\eta_t}\widehat{\mathbf{I}} + \widehat{\mathbf{N}}\left(\frac{\eta_i}{\eta_t}\cos\theta_i - \cos\theta_t\right) \qquad (11.55)\end{aligned}$$

The only thing left is to express $\cos\theta_t$ in terms of $\cos\theta_i$. We can do this using some trig substitutions:

$$\begin{aligned}\cos\theta_t &= \sqrt{1 - \sin^2\theta_t} \\ &= \sqrt{1 - \left(\frac{\eta_i}{\eta_t}\right)^2 \sin^2\theta_i} \\ &= \sqrt{1 - \left(\frac{\eta_i}{\eta_t}\right)^2 (1 - \cos^2\theta_i)} \qquad (11.56)\end{aligned}$$

Putting this back into the expression for $\widehat{\mathbf{T}}$, we find

$$\widehat{\mathbf{T}} = -\frac{\eta_i}{\eta_t}\widehat{\mathbf{I}} + \widehat{\mathbf{N}}\left(\frac{\eta_i}{\eta_t}\cos\theta_i - \sqrt{1 - \left(\frac{\eta_i}{\eta_t}\right)^2 (1 - \cos^2\theta_i)}\right) \qquad (11.57)$$

Note that $\big(1 - (\eta_i/\eta_t)^2(1 - \cos^2\theta_i)\big)$ may be negative. This is our signal that total internal reflection has occurred.

11.10 Further Reading

The information in this chapter is common to most basic books on optics. Some well-known examples include the books by Born and Wolf [55], Hecht and Zajac [201], Jenkins and White [230], Williams and Becklund [478], and Möller [311].

Review guides such as Hecht's study outline [200] discuss the basic ideas and include worked problem sets with discussion.

A variety of multiple-slit experiments are discussed very nicely by Möller [311]. Feynman has written a highly readable lay account of the dual nature of light in his book *QED* [144], which explains some essential parts of the quantum theory addressing wave/particle duality. Crystals are an especially interesting and useful class of materials; the interaction of light and crystals is discussed at length by Wood [488]. A discussion of light from the viewpoint of modern quantum mechanics may be found in the book by Sudbery [427].

11.11 Exercises

Exercise 11.1

Using only the two formulas $\sin\theta_i = \sin\theta_r$ and $R = aI + bN$, provide an algebraic derivation of the formula for the reflected ray R. (Do not use a geometric construction; you may use trig identities and the basic properties of vectors, though.)

Exercise 11.2

Using only the two formulas $\eta_i \sin\theta_i = \eta_r \sin\theta_r$ and $T = aI + bN$, provide an algebraic derivation of the formula for the refracted ray T. (Do not use a geometric construction; you may use trig identities and the basic properties of vectors, though.) If there are choices to be made at some steps, explain your reasoning.

Exercise 11.3

We assumed in Section 11.8.1 that it was reasonable to use only one term of Sellmeier's formula to compute the index of refraction. It might be argued that the two-term formula is likely to be superior, particularly if it uses one absorption band on each side of the visible region. Do you agree with this argument? Under all circumstances? Assuming finite-precision arithmetic, are there situations when the two-term form is superior? Are there times it doesn't matter? Find expressions for the four constants in the two-part form (advice: use a symbolic math package). How much more computational cost is involved in evaluating this expression for different wavelengths? Is it worth it?

Exercise 11.4

Study the phenomena of magneto-optics and electro-optics. Discuss how you would implement these effects. Are there any applications for this work?

Exercise 11.5

Prove that when the radical in Equation 11.57 is exactly zero, we are at the critical angle $\theta_i = \theta_c$.

I never cared much for moonlit skies,
I never wink back at fireflies;
But now that the stars are in your eyes,
I'm beginning to see the light.

Harry James, Duke Ellington, Johnny Hodges,
and Don George
("I'm Beginning To See the Light," 1944)

12

ENERGY TRANSPORT

12.1 Introduction

In this chapter we look at a method for quantifying the passage of energy through a medium. We will assume that energy is quantized into small, discrete packets, which we will model as particles with particular properties. We will describe the flow of energy through a medium by simply keeping track of the number of particles flowing through each region of the medium. Of course, we will later interpret these particles as light particles (photons), but it takes no more effort to express the theory in general and then later reduce it to that special case.

Techniques for analyzing the flow of moving particles in 3D environments have been developed in great detail in a number of fields. We will base our discussion on an approach known as *transport theory*. This approach has been developed largely for simulating the activity of neutrons in atomic reactors, but is appropriate to such varied phenomena as automobile traffic flow, the configuration of large molecules, gas and plasma dynamics, and (most importantly for us) light.

The purpose of this chapter is to develop a general transport theory that is appropriate for modeling light energy. We will make a few basic assumptions about the properties of the particles and the media that are based on our knowledge of light, but our discussion will be entirely in terms of abstract particles. We will develop a general *transport equation* that describes this energy flow. We will then cast this equation into a form that makes it amenable to solution by computer programs.

This particle-based approach limits our theory to the phenomena described by *geometrical optics*. As mentioned in Chapter 11, by taking a particle theory approach to modeling light, we are excluding the possibility of treating light as a wave, and therefore we will not handle wave phenomena like diffraction and interference.

After we discuss the quantitative measurement of light energy in Chapter 13, we will return to the results developed here to write a general equation that describes the distribution of light in a scene.

The solution to that transport equation is the holy grail of photorealistic image synthesis: for every point in the environment, it completely describes the intensity of light at that point in every direction, wavelength, and polarization. This is the raw energy information that we use to construct a simulated image, because we typically imagine our image as the light distribution that would fall on some piece of film in space. We can simply use the light transport equation to find the description of the light at every point on that film.

We begin our discussion with a very simple transport problem that we can solve analytically to give a general view of what ideas are involved and how they interact. Then we will generalize the problem to the more complex environments used in computer graphics. In general, these more complex problems will require numerical methods to find even approximate solutions.

12.2 The Rod Model

We will begin our discussion of transport theory with a simple model. Even though the geometry will be very restrictive, we will encounter all of the concepts that are important to a complete transport equation. Our presentation follows that of Wing [482].

We will study the flow of particles through a long, narrow, circular rod, as shown in Figure 12.1. The rod has length a and is parameterized by the distance x, such that the left end is $x = 0$ and the right end is $x = a$. The area of a cross section of the rod is A.

We suppose that inside the rod there is only one type of particle, with the following properties:

1 Each particle moves either to the left (parallel to the vector $\mathbf{L}$) or to the right (parallel to the vector $\mathbf{R}$).

2 All particles move with the same speed c.

3 Particles do not interact. Thus, two particles may pass through each other.

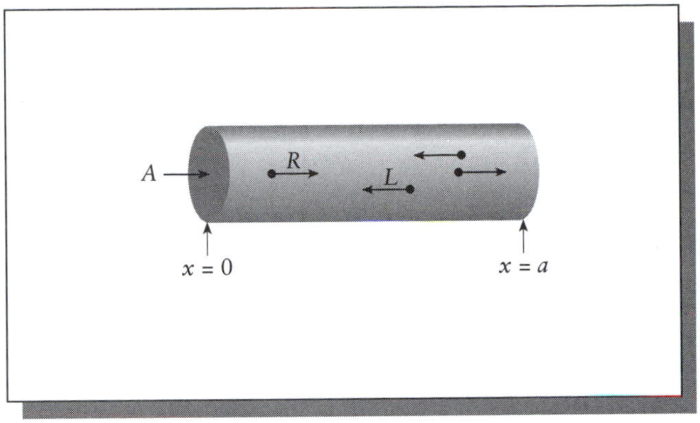

FIGURE 12.1
A rod of length a.

12.3 Particle Density and Flux

We characterize the distribution of particles with two functions, one for each direction of motion. The function $\rho_l(x)$ specifies the *expected density* (the number of particles per unit volume) flowing to the left at point x. Similarly, the function $\rho_r(x)$ specifies the expected density of particles flowing to the right at point x.

We will also find it useful to describe how many particles are flowing through a cross section of the rod per unit time. For example, suppose we wish to know how many right-moving particles pass through the cross section of the rod at $x = x_0$ in a time interval Δt. Since the particles all move at a constant speed c, any particle within a distance of $c\Delta t$ to the left of x_0 will pass through x_0 in this time interval. The subrod over the interval $[x_0 - c\Delta t, x_0]$ has a volume $Ac\Delta t$, as shown in Figure 12.2(a). Since there are $\rho_r(x_0)$ right-moving particles per unit volume at x_0, there are $\rho_r(x_0)Ac\Delta t$ particles in this volume.

Since $\rho_r(x_0)Ac\Delta t$ right-moving particles will pass through the rod at x_0 in time Δt, the number of particles passing through this point per unit time is simply $Ac\rho_r(x_0)$. The same analysis holds for the left-moving particles in the subrod $[x_0, x_0 + c\Delta t]$ illustrated in Figure 12.2(b).

The number of particles per unit time crossing a piece of surface is called the *flux* (Latin for "flow"), usually symbolized by the Greek letter Φ:

$$\begin{aligned}\Phi_R(x) &= Ac\rho_r(x)\\ \Phi_L(x) &= Ac\rho_l(x)\end{aligned} \tag{12.1}$$

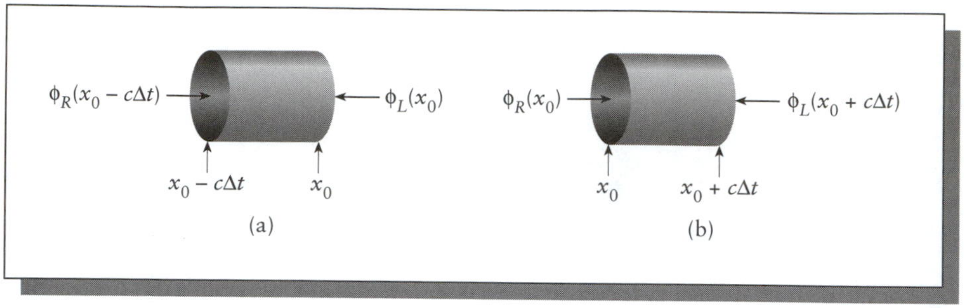

FIGURE 12.2

(a) The subrod to the left of x_0. (b) The subrod to the right of x_0.

12.4 Scattering

If the rod contains nothing (that is, it is internally a perfect vacuum), then any particles injected from either end will flow unimpeded to the other end (recall that by definition our particles pass through each other). However, if the rod contains a material that interacts with the particles, we must consider the results of those interactions.

We will model these interactions statistically. Suppose that the medium consists of dense blobs of material separated by a vacuum. Then some particles will bypass all the blobs, while others will *collide* with one of these pockets of material. We posit a *collision probability*, denoted σ, that specifies the probability that a particle will collide with a blob for each unit of the material traversed. Thus the probability that a right-moving particle injected into the left end of the rod will collide with the medium before it exits at the right end is $a\sigma$; the probability that it will escape without collision is $a(1-\sigma)$. The probability σ is called the *cross section* by physicists; because of the possible confusion of this term with geometric cross sections often discussed in computer graphics, we will not use that name in this book; we call σ the *scattering probability* or the *collision probability*. If the value of σ is the same in all directions (here only two, left and right), the material is said to be *isotropic*; otherwise it is *anisotropic*.

We will assume that when a particle collides with the material in the rod, only one of two basic results can occur. First, the particle can be *absorbed*. In this case, the particle disappears and is converted into some other form of energy, such as heat. Alternatively, the particle may be *scattered*.

What happens when a particle is scattered depends on the medium. In general, one or more particles leave the collision site (or the *event*) in one or more directions.

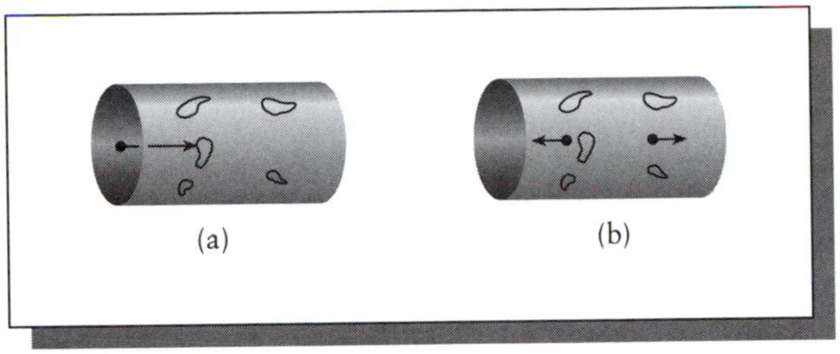

FIGURE 12.3
Our scattering rule results in two particles in opposite directions for each incident particle. (a) A collision: a right-moving particle strikes a blob. (b) The result: one particle in each direction leaves the collision site.

For example, a perfectly elastic scattering event is like the collision of two billiard balls: no new particles are created, and the direction of the scattered particle may be predicted with confidence. Alternatively, the collision of a neutron with an atomic nucleus can result in *fission*, whereby several new neutrons are released in a variety of directions. These are two extremes; the way a material scatters particles is one of the basic parameters that characterizes the appearance of the material, as we will see later when we discuss shading models in Chapter 15.

In the rod model, we will use the following scattering rule for all particles: whenever a particle is scattered, two particles leave the scattering site, one in each direction. This is illustrated in Figure 12.3.

For the time being, we will suppose our medium has no absorption, and only scatters particles.

12.4.1 Counting New Particles

In the next section we will need to discover the probability that a particle entering a subrod $[x_0, x_0 + \Delta x]$ will be scattered. Consider first the right-moving flux at the right end $x_0 + \Delta x$ due to the right-moving particles entering at x_0. Suppose n right-moving particles enter the left end of the subrod at x_0. From the definition of the scattering probability σ, we expect that $n\sigma\Delta x$ particles will be scattered. Since each scattering event produces exactly one right-moving particle, the scattered particles survive in their progeny, and we would expect n right-moving particles to exit the right side of the rod.

Because of scattering, left-moving particles will also contribute to right-moving

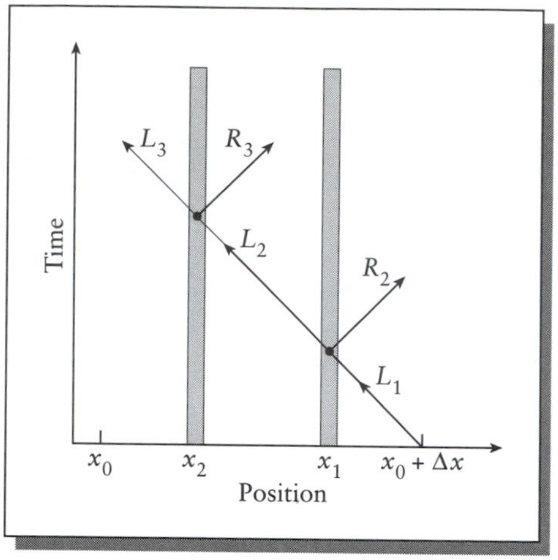

FIGURE 12.4

A space-time diagram of scattering particles. Location is plotted horizontally, time vertically. The vertical stripes represent the location of unmoving blobs in the rod.

flux at $x_0 + \Delta x$. How many right-moving particles will be generated for each left-moving particle?

To answer this question, consider the result of a single collision: one left-moving particle enters the scattering event and two particles come out, one in each direction. If one of those new particles is again scattered, then we will have three particles in the system, and so on. Some of these will emerge at the right end, increasing the number of right-moving particles there. We can account for these higher-order effects with a diagram like Figure 12.4.

In this figure, we plot the location of a particle on the X axis, as time flows along the Y axis. Here we begin with a single particle L_1, entering the rod at $x + \Delta x$, moving to the left with constant speed c. The particle strikes a blob centered at x_1 (notice that since a blob doesn't move over time, it is represented by a vertical stripe in the figure). Call this collision event S_1. The probability $P(S_1)$ of this collision occurring is $P(S_1) = \sigma \Delta x$. The result of the collision is that L_1 is considered to be destroyed and replaced by a new pair of second-generation particles, L_2 and R_2, both leaving the event at constant speed c in opposite directions. This event has increased by one the number of right-moving particles in the system.

We now want to consider what will happen if particle L_2 is itself scattered by striking another blob at $x_2 < x_1$, destroying L_2 and replacing it with two new third-generation particles L_3 and R_3. Call this event S_2. This would add yet another right-moving particle to our system, though there would still be only one left-moving particle. The probability that S_2 will occur, given that S_1 has occurred, is $P(S_2|S_1) = (x_2 - x_1)\sigma\Delta x = \alpha\sigma\Delta x$.

Therefore the total probability $P(S_2)$ of event S_2 occurring is given by the product of S_2 occurring given that S_1 occurred, times the probability of S_1 occurring:

$$P(S_2) = P(S_2|S_1)P(S_1) = (\sigma\Delta x)(\alpha\sigma\Delta x) = (\alpha\sigma^2)(\Delta x)^2 \qquad (12.2)$$

The important thing to notice here is that the probability of a second scattering event is proportional to $(\Delta x)^2$. The probability of a third event would be proportional to $(\Delta x)^3$, and so on.

We don't need to keep explicit track of these higher-order terms. Because the events are separated by space, when the rod becomes small enough (that is, $\Delta x \to 0$), there is only room for one scattering event. Higher-order events are handled in different subrods. So we will abstract away all the higher-order terms into a single composite term $O(\Delta x)$, which represents the probability of multiple collisions in a length Δx of material.

In summary, we can then say that the expected number of right-moving particles produced by a single left-moving particle is $\sigma\Delta x + O(\Delta x)$.

12.5 The Scattering-Only Particle Distribution Equations

We are now ready to start looking at the equations that describe the distribution of particles in the rod.

We begin with a small piece of the rod over the interval $[x_0, x_0 + \Delta x]$. Consider first what happens to the right-moving particles that enter this subrod at x_0. We know that the number of right-moving particles at this point per unit time is given by the flux, $\Phi_R(x_0)$, and we want to find $\Phi_R(x_0 + \Delta x)$.

We find the right-moving flux $\Phi_R(x_0 + \Delta x)$ as the sum of three component fluxes, illustrated in Figure 12.5.

1. ${\Phi_R}^u$: the flux due to right-moving particles that enter from the left per unit time and are *not* scattered, and thus emerge *unscathed*. This is just the probability of a particle not scattering times the expected number of particles per unit time and area. This flux is given by ${\Phi_R}^u = \Phi_R(x_0)(1 - \sigma\Delta x)$.

2. ${\Phi_R}^s$: the flux due to right-moving particles that enter from the left per unit time and *are* scattered, each producing one new right-moving particle. This flux is ${\Phi_R}^s = \Phi_R(x_0)\sigma\Delta x + O(\Delta x)$.

3. ${\Phi_L}^s$: the flux due to left-moving particles that enter from the right per unit time and are scattered, each producing a new right-moving particle. The left-moving flux entering at the right side is $\Phi_L(x + \Delta x)$. We expect the number of

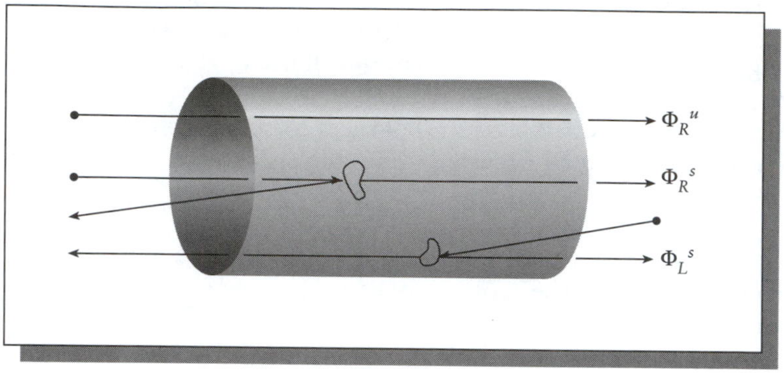

FIGURE 12.5
The three components of flux in the rod.

scattered particles per unit time to then be $\Phi_L{}^s = \Phi_L(x_0+\Delta x)\sigma\Delta x + O(\Delta x)$. Each of these collisions produces exactly one right-moving particle.

Adding these together, we find the flux emerging from the right side of the subrod is

$$\begin{aligned}\Phi_R(x+\Delta x) &= \Phi_R{}^u + \Phi_R{}^s + \Phi_L{}^s \\ &= \Phi_R(x_0)(1-\sigma\Delta x) + \Phi_R(x_0)\sigma\Delta x + O(\Delta x) \\ &\qquad + \Phi_L(x_0+\Delta x)\sigma\Delta x + O(\Delta x) \\ &= \Phi_R(x_0) + \Phi_L(x_0+\Delta x)\sigma\Delta x + O(\Delta x) \qquad (12.3)\end{aligned}$$

where we have rolled together all the higher-order terms into one $O(\Delta x)$ term.

Writing x for x_0, we can now subtract $\Phi_R(x)$ from both sides, divide through by Δx, and take the limit as $\Delta x \to 0$ (we assume that the necessary continuity and limit conditions are satisfied so that this is a well-defined set of operations):

$$\begin{aligned}\lim_{\Delta x\to 0}\frac{\Phi_R(x+\Delta x)-\Phi_R(x)}{\Delta x} &= \lim_{\Delta x\to 0}\left(\frac{\Phi_L(x+\Delta x)\sigma\Delta x}{\Delta x} + O(\Delta x)\right) \\ \frac{d\Phi_R(x)}{dx} &= \sigma\Phi_L(x) \qquad (12.4)\end{aligned}$$

Repeating this process for the left-moving particles emerging at x_0, we find similar results for Φ_L, which differs only by sign:

$$\frac{d\Phi_L(x)}{dx} = -\sigma\Phi_R(x) \qquad (12.5)$$

Equations 12.4 and 12.5 form a pair of differential equations that describe the flux in the rod given that the rod's only effect on the particles is to scatter them.

Our next job is to solve these equations by finding an expression for the unknown flux. We will go after $\Phi_R(x)$ first. We begin by combining these equations into a single second-order differential equation for $\Phi_R(x)$:

$$\frac{d^2\Phi_R(x)}{dx^2} = \frac{d}{dx}\frac{d\Phi_R(x)}{dx} = \frac{d}{dx}(\sigma\Phi_L(x)) = \sigma\frac{d\Phi_L(x)}{dx} = \sigma(-\sigma\Phi_R(x)) = -\sigma^2\Phi_R(x) \tag{12.6}$$

so

$$\frac{d^2\Phi_R(x)}{dx^2} + \sigma^2\Phi_R(x) = 0 \tag{12.7}$$

Because this equation is of second order, we need two constraints to completely define it [60]. It is convenient to provide these constraints as *boundary conditions* that specify the flux at the two ends of the rod. Suppose we inject one left-moving particle per second at the right end and no right-moving particles at the left:

$$\begin{aligned} \Phi_R(0) &= 0 \\ \Phi_L(a) &= 1 \end{aligned} \tag{12.8}$$

Our goal is now to find a solution $\Phi_R(x)$ to Equation 12.7 using the boundary conditions in Equation 12.8. Although they are sometimes easier to specify, boundary condition problems are in general much harder to solve than initial condition problems. Fortunately, Equation 12.4 gives us an easy way to convert Equation 12.8 into initial conditions:

$$\frac{d\Phi_R(a)}{dx} = \sigma\Phi_L(a) = \sigma \tag{12.9}$$

For simplicity, in the next few paragraphs we will write $y(x)$ for $\Phi_R(x)$, and $y'(x)$ and $y''(x)$ for its first and second derivatives. Then our problem may be stated as finding a function $y(x)$ that satisfies

$$\begin{aligned} y''(x) + \sigma^2 y(x) &= 0 \\ y(0) &= 0 \\ y'(a) &= \sigma \end{aligned} \tag{12.10}$$

Equation 12.10 specifies an initial-value problem for a first-order linear homogeneous differential equation with constant coefficients. Therefore we are tempted to try $y(x) = e^{rx}$ as a potential solution [60]. This leads to the trial solution

$$r^2e^{rx} + \sigma^2e^{rx} = 0 \tag{12.11}$$

which, after dividing by $e^{rx} \neq 0$, results in the *characteristic equation* [60]:

$$r^2 + \sigma^2 = 0 \tag{12.12}$$

which has roots $r_1 = j\sigma$, $r_2 = -j\sigma$ (recall that in this book $j = \sqrt{-1}$). So we have found two solutions:

$$\begin{aligned} y_1(x) &= e^{j\sigma x} \\ y_2(x) &= e^{-j\sigma x} \end{aligned} \tag{12.13}$$

These functions contain j, which is rather awkward; we would prefer an equivalent form involving only real numbers. This form is easily found.

We know from the theory of differential equations that all linear combinations of $y_1(x)$ and $y_2(x)$ are also solutions to Equation 12.10. So we create two new functions, $g_1(x)$ and $g_2(x)$, formed from the sum and difference of the previous solutions:

$$\begin{aligned} g_1(x) &= y_1(x) + y_2(x) = e^{j\sigma x} + e^{-j\sigma x} = 2\cos\sigma x \\ g_2(x) &= y_1(x) - y_2(x) = e^{j\sigma x} - e^{-j\sigma x} = 2j\sin\sigma x \end{aligned} \tag{12.14}$$

using Euler's identities for sine and cosine. Our general solution is thus a linear combination of these two solutions:

$$\begin{aligned} y(x) &= c_1 g_1(x) + c_2 g_2(x) \\ &= c_1\cos\sigma x + c_2\sin\sigma x \end{aligned} \tag{12.15}$$

where we have rolled the constants from $g_1(x)$ and $g_2(x)$ into c_1 and c_2.

To find these constants we employ the initial values. First, noting that $y(0) = 0$,

$$\begin{aligned} y(0) &= c_1\cos\sigma 0 + c_2\sin\sigma 0 \\ 0 &= c_1 \end{aligned} \tag{12.16}$$

Second, we use the value of the derivative at a:

$$\begin{aligned} y'(a) &= -c_1\sigma\sin\sigma a + c_2\sigma\cos\sigma a \\ \sigma &= c_2\sigma\cos\sigma a \\ \frac{1}{\cos\sigma a} &= c_2 \end{aligned} \tag{12.17}$$

We now have our complete solution for $y(x) = \Phi_R(x)$:

$$\Phi_R(x) = \frac{\sin\sigma x}{\cos\sigma a} \tag{12.18}$$

Once again we will use Equation 12.4, this time to find $\Phi_L(x)$ from $\Phi_R(x)$:

$$\Phi_L(x) = \frac{1}{\sigma}\frac{d\Phi_R(x)}{dx} = \frac{\cos\sigma x}{\cos\sigma a} \tag{12.19}$$

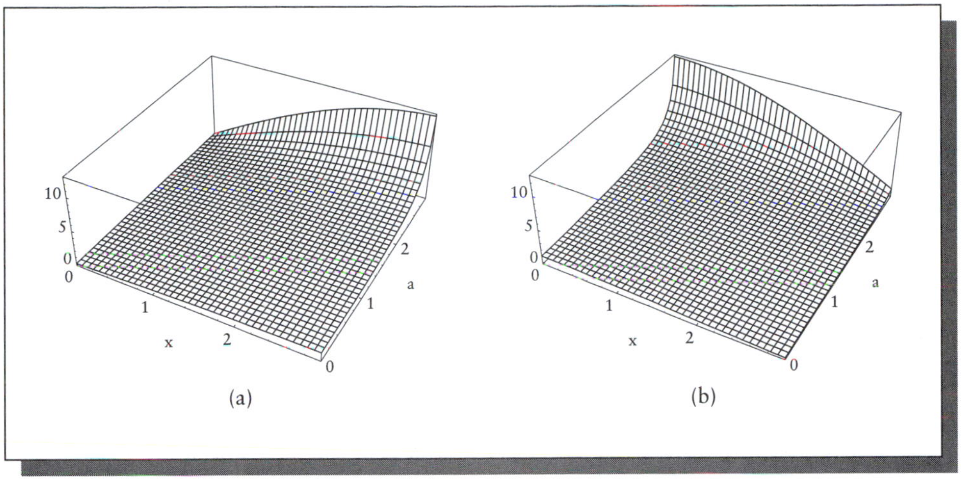

FIGURE 12.6

(a) The flux $\Phi_R(x)$ in the rod for $\sigma = 0.5$ and different values of a. (b) The flux $\Phi_L(x)$ in the rod for $\sigma = 0.5$ and different values of a.

This completes our quest for the flux in the rod given these initial conditions. Figure 12.6 shows plots for this flux along the rod for different values of a.

The solution in Equations 12.18 and 12.19 goes to infinity when $a = \pi/2\sigma$. We say that a rod with these boundary conditions and material is *critical* at this length. If $a > \pi/2\sigma$, the fluxes go negative, which is mathematically well defined but physically meaningless. Thus all rods of length $a < \pi/2\sigma$ can maintain a steady state given this configuration; rods longer than that length are not physically realizable.

Criticality tells us what's happening to the flux in the system over time. If there are more losses than gains, the system is *subcritical*, and eventually the flow will damp out. If gains outnumber losses, then the system will *avalanche* (or experience a *chain reaction*), producing ever more particles until *saturation*; such a system is called *supercritical*. When gains and losses are balanced, then the system is *self-sustaining*, or simply *critical* [431].

12.6 A More Complete Medium

We can generalize the result of the last section to a medium with richer properties. When we move to 3D, we will need to be able to account for particles traveling in

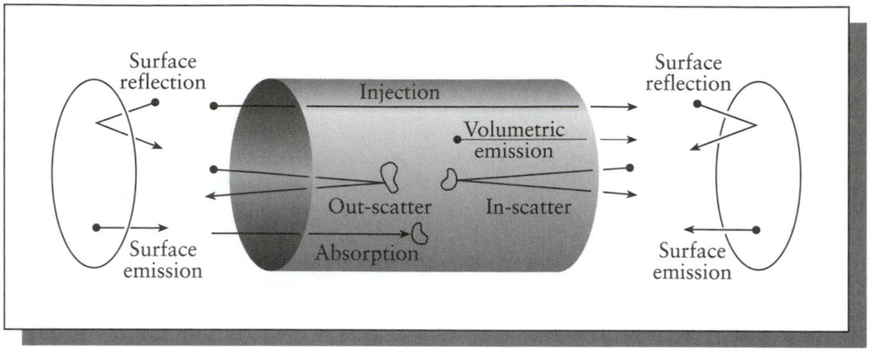

FIGURE 12.7
A subrod in the interval $[x_0, x_0 + \Delta x]$.

any direction. To prepare for that generalization, in this section we will refer to an arbitrary direction $\mathbf{v}$, and some other direction $\mathbf{v}' \neq \mathbf{v}$. In the rod, when $\mathbf{v}$ is equal to $\mathbf{L}$, then $\mathbf{v}'$ is $\mathbf{R}$, and vice versa.

We will characterize the medium by six properties and their effects on the flux. They are illustrated in Figure 12.7.

Reflection $\Phi^r(x, \mathbf{v})$: The ends of the rod may return (or *reflect*) some portion of their incident particles back into the rod. The *albedo*, denoted $0 \leq \beta \leq 1$, describes this percentage. In our model, the ends of the rod have albedos β_0 and β_a. Any particles not returned by the rod ends are assumed to be absorbed. So the left-moving flux reflected back into the rod as right-moving flux at $a = 0$ is $\Phi^r(0, \mathbf{R}) = \beta_0 \Phi(0, \mathbf{L})$, and similarly, $\Phi^r(a, \mathbf{L}) = \beta_a \Phi(a, \mathbf{R})$.

Surface emission $\Phi^s(0, \mathbf{R}), \Phi^s(a, \mathbf{L})$: The end surfaces may emit (or introduce) particles into the rod. The number of particles emitted per unit time is called the *surface* (or *boundary*) *flux*. At the left end ($x = 0$), the emitted particles move to the right and are characterized by $\Phi^s(0, \mathbf{R})$. At the right end ($x = a$), the emitted particles move to the left and are characterized by $\Phi^s(a, \mathbf{L})$.

Absorption $\sigma_a(x, \mathbf{v})$: When particles travel through the rod they may strike some of the rod material and be absorbed. In this case they simply disappear from the system, their energy typically converted into another form (such as heat). The probability of this absorption happening per unit length of the rod at location

x for left-moving particles is given by $\sigma_a(x, \mathbf{L})$. Similarly, the probability of absorption per unit length for right-moving particles is given by $\sigma_a(x, \mathbf{R})$.

Outscatter $\sigma_s(x, \mathbf{v} \to \mathbf{v}')$: When a particle strikes some piece of the material in the rod, it may change direction. We say it is *outscattered*, or *backscattered*. In the rod, this can only mean that the particle is sent back into the direction from which it came. If the particle originally was traveling in the direction $\mathbf{v}$, then after backscattering it is sent away in $\mathbf{v}'$. The probability of this type of scattering per unit length of the rod at location x is given by $\sigma_s(x, \mathbf{v} \to \mathbf{v}')$.

Inscatter $\sigma_s(x, \mathbf{v}' \to \mathbf{v})$: This is the opposite of outscatter. A particle traveling in direction $\mathbf{v}'$ may undergo a collision and be scattered into $\mathbf{v}$. This is called *inscattering*, or *forward-scattering*. The same scattering function is used to characterize this behavior, and only the directions that parameterize it are reversed, so $\sigma_s(x, \mathbf{v}' \to \mathbf{v})$ describes the probability of inscatter per unit distance. If $\sigma_s(x, \mathbf{v} \to \mathbf{v}') = \sigma_s(x, \mathbf{v}' \to \mathbf{v})$ for all $x \in [0, a]$, then the material is said to be *isotropic* with respect to scattering.

Volumetric emission $\epsilon(x, \mathbf{v}), 0 < x < a$: The material may emit particles into the rod by virtue of some internal process. The probability of such an emission in direction $\mathbf{v}$ per unit length of the rod is given by $\epsilon(x, \mathbf{v})$.

Because the scattering functions are defined for an abstract direction $\mathbf{v}$, a particular scattering event can only be characterized as inscatter or outscatter if we specify $\mathbf{v}$. For example, suppose a left-moving particle is scattered and leaves the event by moving to the right. If we are interested in finding the left-moving flux, then this event would be labeled as outscattering; if we were interested in the right-moving flux, it would be inscattering.

There are two general approaches to characterizing the different scattering probabilities. One approach first determines the probability of *any* scattering event and then scales this probability by the relative probabilities of each type of scattering. The other approach simply writes each scattering probability directly, rather than as a fraction of a total scattering probability. We follow the latter approach here.

12.6.1 Explicit Flux

As in the previous section, we will now consider a small subrod and quantify the fluxes inside based on the arriving fluxes and the rod properties. Surface emission and reflection are boundary conditions, so we will not use them here. They will be our principal subject in Section 12.10.

We begin with a small subrod on the interval $[x_0, x_0 + \Delta x]$ illustrated in Figure 12.7. In an internal piece of the rod some number of particles are assumed to be entering from both ends. These are the particles that are absorbed and scattered. The particles that are unaffected are said to *stream* through the volume. Thus the total number of particles exiting the rod is the sum of three positive terms (streaming, volumetric emission, and inscattering) and two negative terms (absorption and outscattering).

For the moment, we will focus explicitly on the expression for the right-moving flux $\Phi(x + \Delta x, \mathbf{R})$ leaving the right side of the tube. That is, $\mathbf{v} = \mathbf{R}$, and $\mathbf{v}' = \mathbf{L}$. So we can write the right-moving flux as a sum of five fluxes, three positive and two negative:

$$\begin{aligned}\Phi(x + \Delta x, \mathbf{R}) &= \text{streaming} + \text{emission} + \text{inscattering} - \text{absorption} - \text{outscattering} \\ &\qquad \Phi_s \quad + \quad \Phi_v \quad + \quad \Phi_i \quad - \quad \Phi_a \quad - \quad \Phi_o\end{aligned} \tag{12.20}$$

We can now fill in each of the five terms in Equation 12.20.

Streaming: This accounts for those particles that arrive at the left side and exit from the right side of the rod without any interaction with the material. We will assume that all such particles pass through and will use the other terms in Equation 12.20 to subtract out those that are absorbed or scattered. So the flux Φ_s due to streaming is just the arriving flux $\Phi(x, \mathbf{R})$:

$$\Phi_s = \Phi(x, \mathbf{R}) \tag{12.21}$$

Emission: The volume emission term is simply the probability of emission per unit volume times the subrod's volume:

$$\Phi_e = \epsilon(x, \mathbf{R})\Delta x + O(\Delta x) \tag{12.22}$$

Inscattering: The inscattered flux is based on the left-moving flux arriving from the right side of the rod at $x + \Delta x$ times the probability that these particles will be inscattered and redirected from moving left into moving right:

$$\Phi_i = \Phi(x + \Delta x, \mathbf{L})\sigma_s(x, \mathbf{L} \to \mathbf{R})\Delta x + O(\Delta x) \tag{12.23}$$

Absorption: The absorbed flux is proportional to the absorption coefficient and the distance traveled by the incident particles:

$$\Phi_a = \Phi(x, \mathbf{R})\sigma_a(x, \mathbf{R})\Delta x + O(\Delta x) \tag{12.24}$$

Outscattering: The outscattered flux is based on the incident flux times the probability that each particle will be scattered from moving right to moving left, times the volume traversed:

$$\Phi_o = \Phi(x, \mathbf{R})\sigma_s(x, \mathbf{R} \to \mathbf{L})\Delta x + O(\Delta x) \tag{12.25}$$

We can now write out Equation 12.20 in detail:

$$\begin{aligned}\Phi(x + \Delta x, \mathbf{R}) &= \Phi_s + \Phi_v + \Phi_i - \Phi_a - \Phi_o \\ &= \Phi(x, \mathbf{R}) + \Delta x \left[\Phi_e(x, \mathbf{R}) + \Phi(x + \Delta x, \mathbf{L})\sigma_s(x, \mathbf{L} \to \mathbf{R})\right] \\ &\quad - \Phi(x, \mathbf{R}) \left[\sigma_a(x, \mathbf{R}) + \sigma_s(x, \mathbf{R} \to \mathbf{L})\right] \\ &\quad + O(\Delta x)\end{aligned} \tag{12.26}$$

We would like to find a solution to Equation 12.26. So, using the same limit argument that we used in the previous section, we subtract $\Phi(x, \mathbf{R})$ from both sides, divide through by Δx, and take the limit as $\Delta x \to 0$:

$$\begin{aligned}\frac{d\Phi(x, \mathbf{R})}{dx} &= \lim_{\Delta x \to 0} \frac{\Phi(x + \Delta x, \mathbf{R}) - \Phi(x, \mathbf{R})}{\Delta x} \\ &= \epsilon(x, \mathbf{R}) + \Phi(x, \mathbf{L})\sigma_s(x, \mathbf{L} \to \mathbf{R}) \\ &\quad - \Phi(x, \mathbf{R}) \left[\sigma_a(x, \mathbf{R}) + \sigma_s(x, \mathbf{R} \to \mathbf{L})\right]\end{aligned} \tag{12.27}$$

We can repeat the whole analysis for the flux arriving at the right end of the subrod and exiting from the left end. This results in

$$-\frac{d\Phi(x, \mathbf{L})}{dx} = \epsilon(x, \mathbf{L}) + \Phi(x, \mathbf{R})\sigma_s(x, \mathbf{R} \to \mathbf{L}) - \Phi(x, \mathbf{L}) \left[\sigma_a(x, \mathbf{L}) + \sigma_s(x, \mathbf{L} \to \mathbf{R})\right] \tag{12.28}$$

Equations 12.27 and 12.28 are too complicated to give us any hope of continuing on along this line of thought. The presence of so many functions that are dependent on x makes it hopeless to search for a general, analytic solution.

12.6.2 Implicit Flux

We have just formed *explicit* expressions for the flux at one location along the rod based on the material properties and the flux at another location. We then saw that it would be very hard to solve the explicit equations. An alternative approach that will be useful in 3D is to find an *implicit* expression for this function.

We posit that the particle flow in the tube has reached a *steady state*. That is, there are still particles moving back and forth, and emission, collisions, and absorption are all occurring, but if we look at the flow through any cross section of the rod, we find that the magnitude of this flow is constant over time. We say that the system is in *equilibrium*, which we express by setting the time derivative of the flux to zero: $\partial\Phi/\partial t = 0$.

When the system is in equilibrium, the gains exactly balance the losses. The gains in a subrod are due to streaming, inscattering, and volumetric emission; losses come from absorption and outscattering. So the equilibrium condition for the rod states that

$$\Phi_s(x, \mathbf{v}) + \Phi_e(x, \mathbf{v}) + \Phi_i(x, \mathbf{v}) = \Phi_o(x, \mathbf{v}) + \Phi_a(x, \mathbf{v}) \tag{12.29}$$

Expanding these terms yields an implicit formula for the flux; that is, the actual flux in the rod is described by a function that satisfies the equality. We won't bother to expand the terms here since the complicated result will not be very intuitive right now. However, we will find that the implicit form is very attractive in 3D, because it may be expressed as an integral equation, which leads to efficient and intuitive solution algorithms.

12.7 Particle Transport in 3D

The rod model of the last section was very simple in many ways. In particular, particles could travel in only two directions, the only surfaces that interacted with the particles were the rod's ends, and these ends were perpendicular to the flow. These conditions allowed us to write explicit expressions for both the left and right flux, and since these two expressions depended only on each other, we could solve them together and (sometimes) find analytic results for both $\Phi(x, \mathbf{R})$ and $\Phi(x, \mathbf{L})$.

In the general 3D case, things are still straightforward, but we lose the geometric simplicity of the rod. In particular, there are an infinite number of directions in which particles can travel, there are a potentially infinite number of surfaces which can interact with particles, and these surfaces can be oriented in any direction.

Although most of the concepts we will cover in 3D were introduced in our discussion of the rod model, the 3D setting requires more bookkeeping than the rod. This translates into a busier mathematical notation.

We begin this section with a discussion of the mathematical ideas that we will need, mostly to allow us to label and selectively gather sets of directions, points, and surfaces. We then use this notation to derive the transport equation in 3D.

12.7.1 Points

We will refer to a generic 3D point in space with the letter $\mathbf{r}$; a point on a *surface* will be denoted $\mathbf{s}$. A particular volume of space will be denoted V. A differential volume in space around $\mathbf{r}$ will generally be referred to as $d\mathbf{r}$. Thus if we have some scalar function $f(\mathbf{r})$, we can find its integral F in a volume V with the expression

$$F = \iiint_V f(\mathbf{r})\, d\mathbf{r} \tag{12.30}$$

This type of triple integral is so common that we will usually simplify the notation by dispensing with the three explicit integral signs, leaving it clear from context that the integral is over a volume of space. Thus we will more often write

$$\int_V f(\mathbf{r})\, d\mathbf{r} \tag{12.31}$$

The domain $\mathcal{R}^3$ stands for all points in all of space. In a similar vein, when we want to integrate over a surface, we will write this as a single integral over the surface (say S), representing a double integral over the surface of S.

The set of all surfaces of the environment is denoted M; each individual surface is an M_i. We will assume that all surfaces are smooth and sufficiently well defined such that every point s on a surface M_i has an associated surface normal $\mathbf{n}(\mathbf{s})$ (recall that all surface normals in this book have unit magnitude, so $|\mathbf{n}(\mathbf{s})| = 1$, $\forall \mathbf{s} \in M$).

12.7.2 Projected Areas

A *projected area* describes how much of a piece of surface area is visible from a particular point of view. Consider a small planar patch of surface A with area $|A|$ and surface normal $\mathbf{N}$, as in Figure 12.8(a). If we project A onto a plane that is perpendicular to its normal, the area of that projection is just the area of A itself. We will often be interested in the area of A when viewed from some other direction, say along a vector $\mathbf{V}$. To find the area of A visible along $\mathbf{V}$, we parallel-project A onto a plane perpendicular to $\mathbf{V}$ and calculate the area of the projection, as in Figure 12.8(b).

The projected area of A in direction $\mathbf{V}$, which we write as $A^{\mathbf{V}}$, is defined as

$$A^{\mathbf{V}} \stackrel{\triangle}{=} A(\mathbf{N} \cdot \mathbf{V}) = A \cos\theta \tag{12.32}$$

To confirm the notation, observe that $A^{\mathbf{N}} = A$.

Much of the published material in the radiometric and other literature simply writes A_p for a projected area (the "p" stands for "projected"), where the reader is expected to figure out or remember what direction the patch is being projected into. Other notation includes the $\cos\theta$ term explicitly in all formulas. I prefer the notation $A^{\mathbf{V}}$ presented here since it explicitly states both the patch and the direction of projection. We will expand the cosine term when it's needed for manipulations.

It is sometimes convenient to think of a projected area as a vector quantity with magnitude and direction corresponding to area and normal, respectively.

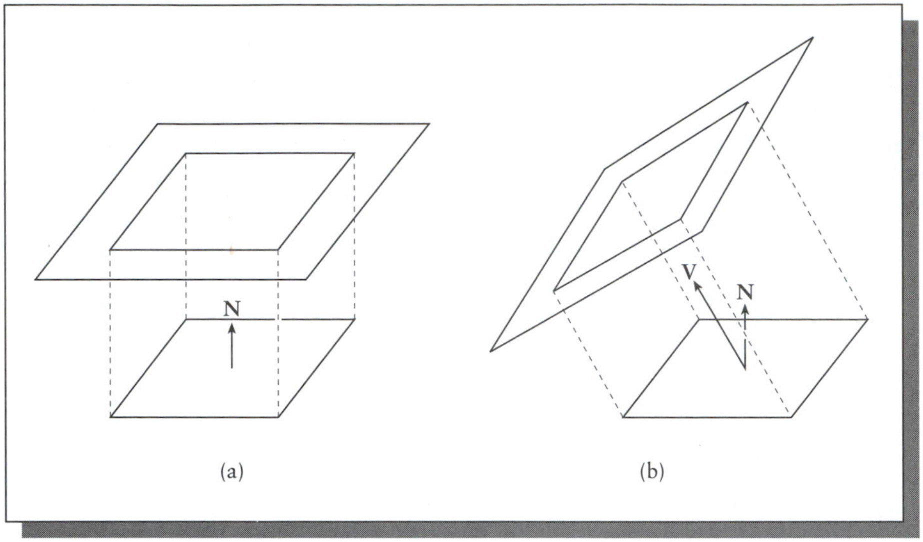

FIGURE 12.8

Projected areas. (a) The area projected onto a plane parallel to itself. (b) When projected onto a nonparallel plane, the projected area diminishes.

12.7.3 Directions

A bold capital roman letter, such as **V**, stands for a vector. We often use vectors to stand for the flow of some material, since they indicate both the direction and magnitude of the flow.

Often we care only about the direction. One approach is to use vector notation with no change. Some authors prefer to place a hat over a vector, such as $\widehat{\mathbf{V}}$, to indicate that a vector has unit length.

A popular alternative, which we adopt, is to use a slightly different notation for unit-length vectors, often called *direction vectors*, or simply *directions*. This notation will generalize below to the idea of a *solid angle*.

We will denote a direction by a vector $\vec{\omega}$. By definition, $|\vec{\omega}| = 1$, so we can think of direction vectors as identifying points on a unit-radius sphere around the origin. For consistency with points, such vectors could be written in bold type, but bold Greek letters are sometimes difficult to distinguish from regular Greek letters. So we will place an arrow above each direction vector to remind us that it is not a scalar.

Figure 12.9 shows a spherical coordinate system for representing directions, and

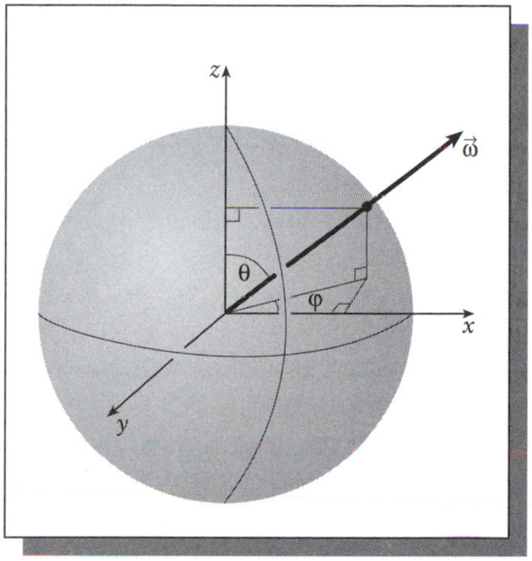

FIGURE 12.9

A spherical coordinate system for locating directions. The angle θ specifies the angle made by a direction $\vec{\omega}$ with the z axis, and ψ specifies the angle made by the projection of $\vec{\omega}$ onto the xy plane with the x axis.

a generic direction vector $\vec{\omega}$. Superimposed on this sphere is a set of left-handed Cartesian coordinates for reference. The angle $\theta \in [0, \pi]$ describes the angle made by $\vec{\omega}$ with the z axis, and the angle $\psi \in [0, 2\pi]$ describes the angle made by the projection of $\vec{\omega}$ onto the xy plane with the x axis. Just as a 3D point may be viewed as a packaging of three scalar components, $\mathbf{r} = (r_x, r_y, r_z)$, so is the direction a combination of two scalars: $\vec{\omega} = (\omega_\theta, \omega_\psi)$. Often it is convenient to think of direction vectors in spherical coordinates, and vectors such as $\mathbf{V}$ in rectilinear coordinates, although of course either form can be expressed in either system.

12.7.4 Solid Angles

A *solid angle* is the 3D analog to the familiar 2D concept of angle. Consider some 2D object viewed from a point. We can draw a circle around that point and then identify the range of the circle isolated by the radial projection of that object, as in Figure 12.10(a). A 2D angle θ may be defined as the ratio of that portion L of the circle's circumference to the radius r of the circle: $\theta = L/r$. If the radius of the circle

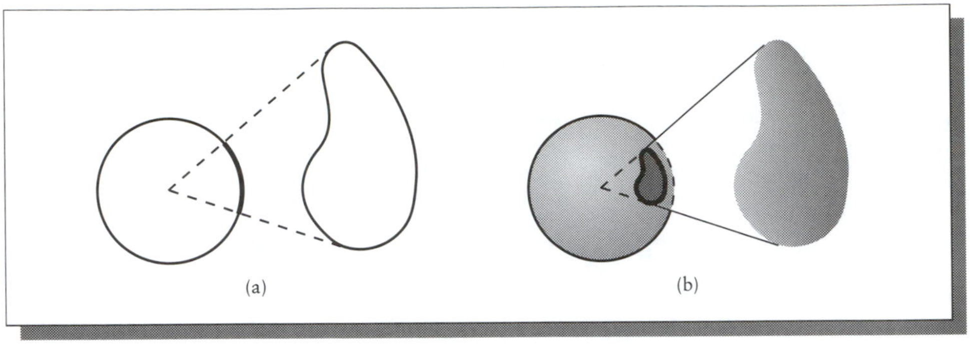

FIGURE 12.10
(a) A 2D angle is formed by the radial projection of an object onto a circle. (b) A 3D solid angle is formed by the radial projection of an object onto a sphere.

is 1, then the angle is simply the indicated length of circumference. For example, one-quarter of any circle of radius r isolates $\theta = (1/4)(2\pi r)/r = \pi/2$ radians.

The solid angle idea generalizes the direction vector $\vec{\omega}$ of the previous section into a whole range of directions. Thinking of a direction vector as a point on a sphere, a differential solid angle indicates a differential region of the sphere. We write a differential solid angle as $d\vec{\omega}$. When the region is of finite size, then we have a finite solid angle, which in this book is represented by a capital Greek letter, typically Λ and Γ.

The directional quantities $\vec{\omega}$, $d\vec{\omega}$, and Γ correspond to the spatial quantities $\mathbf{r}$, $d\mathbf{r}$, and V.

The magnitude of a finite solid angle Γ is the ratio of some portion S of the surface area of a sphere to the squared radius r of the sphere: $\Gamma = S/r^2$. The unit of solid angle is the *steradian* (abbreviated sr), and since the surface area of a sphere is $4\pi r^2$, a full sphere occupies $\Gamma = 4\pi r^2/r^2 = 4\pi$ steradians. The radius of the sphere used for determining the solid angle is immaterial. To see this, if α is the percentage of the surface area of the sphere occupied, then $\Gamma = \alpha(4\pi r^2)/r^2 = \alpha 4\pi$ steradians, so the radius r has dropped out.

It may be helpful to form an intuitive idea of how much of a sphere is subtended by one steradian. The full sphere contains $4\pi \approx 12.566$ radians. The *dodecahedron* is a Platonic solid with twelve equal faces, each a regular pentagon. So one steradian is about equal to the solid angle subtended by one face of a dodecahedron.

It is often useful to find the solid angle subtended by some object as viewed from some point. In this case, the term S may be considered the area of the sphere

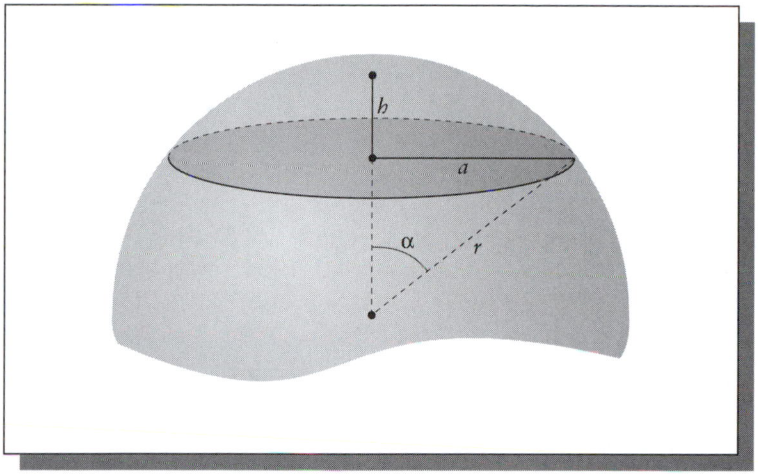

FIGURE 12.11

The geometry of a zone.

intersected by a cone with apex at the center of the sphere, and a cross section formed by the silhouette of the object as seen from the sphere's center, as shown in Figure 12.10(b).

A piece of sphere isolated by a plane is called a *zone*. A zone is characterized by the radius r of the sphere from which it was cut, and its height h. We find h by drawing a radius from the center of the original sphere through the center of the base of the zone; h is the length of this line contained in the zone, as shown in Figure 12.11. The surface area of a zone is given by $S = 2\pi r h$.

The base of a zone is a circle, which we say has radius a, as shown in Figure 12.11. When the radius of the sphere is much greater than the size of the zone (that is, $r \gg a$), we can approximate the area of the zone by the area of this circle. The angle subtended by the zone is labeled in Figure 12.11 as α, so $a = r \sin \alpha$. The radius of this disk is then $\pi a^2 = \pi(r \sin \alpha)^2$. When α is small, $\sin \alpha \approx \alpha$, so the solid angle is simply πa^2.

When the visible surface area of a convex object is small compared to its distance, we can often approximate its solid angle by using a simpler geometric representation for the object. A useful simplification for convex objects is suggested by the observation that a convex body with surface area S, projected onto some random direction, will have an average projected area of $S/4$ [17]. So we can approximate a convex object by a disk with radius $b = \sqrt{S/4\pi}$, oriented orthogonally to the direction of

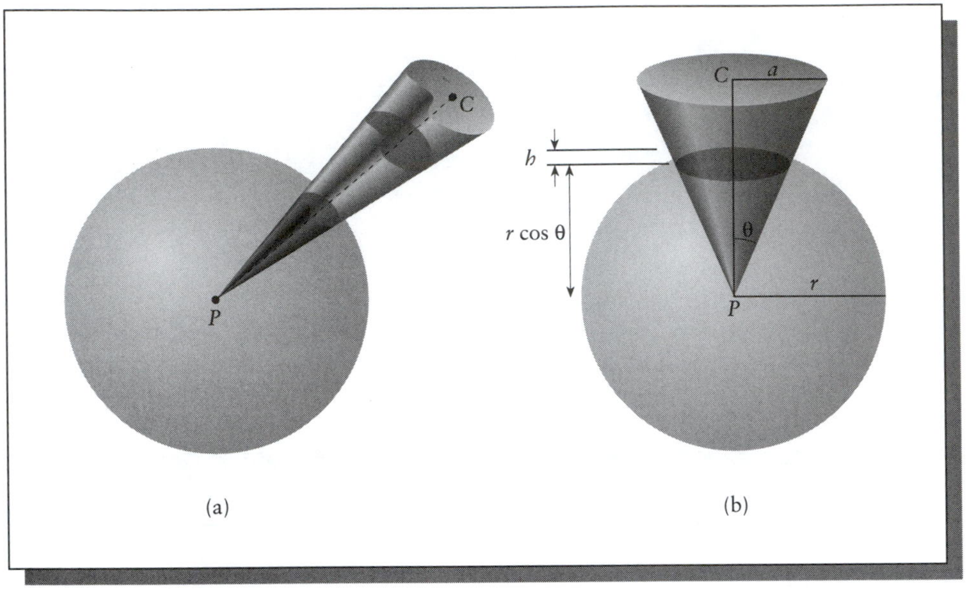

FIGURE 12.12
Solid angle approximation. (a) Approximating the area of a zone by a disk. (b) The geometry of the disk.

view, at the same distance d as the object itself. In Figure 12.12(a), an object viewed from point P has been replaced by a disk of radius b at point C, oriented so that its normal points directly to P.

When this disk is small compared to the distance (that is, $b \gg r$), then we can use the approximation to the zone area discussed above.

To find the zone, consider Figure 12.12(b). The radius of the sphere is $r = |C-P|$. From the diagram, $\theta = \arctan(a/r)$, and $h = r - r\cos\theta = r(1-\cos\theta)$. Thus the actual magnitude of the solid angle is $\Gamma = 2\pi r[r(1-\cos\theta)]/r^2 = 2\pi(1-\cos\theta)$. So we can find the magnitude of the solid angle Γ of a convex object of surface area S at a distance d as

$$\Gamma = 2\pi\left\{1-\cos\left[\tan^{-1}(d/r)\right]\right\} = 2\pi\left[1 - r/\sqrt{(d^2+r^2)}\right] \quad (12.33)$$

where $r = \sqrt{S/4\pi}$. When θ is small, a useful approximation for the cosine is $\cos\theta \approx 1-\theta^2/2$, so we can simplify the solid angle as $\Gamma \approx 2\pi[1-(1-\theta^2/2)] = \pi\theta^2$. The error of this approximation is within 1% for $\theta < 20$ degrees.

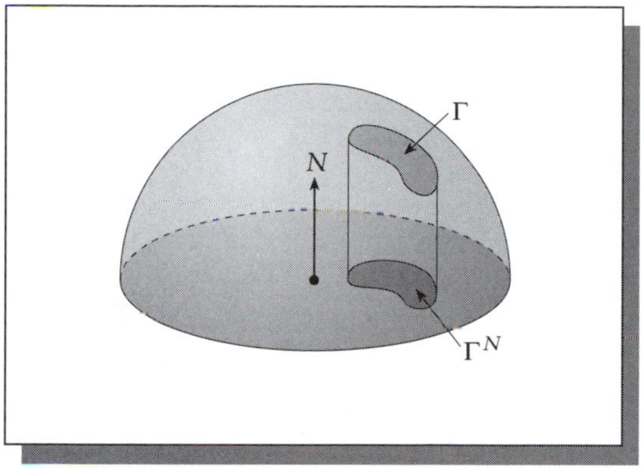

FIGURE 12.13

Projected solid angle.

Just like projected areas, we can find *projected solid angles* by projecting the solid angle onto a plane perpendicular to some direction **V**, as in Figure 12.13. In this book, we write the projected solid angle for the solid angle Γ projected onto direction **V** as $\Gamma^{\mathbf{V}}$, similar to projected area.

Two interesting properties of the solid angle and its computation are worth noting. Figure 12.14 shows that if some object is projected radially onto any surface, then the solid angle occupied by that projection is equal to the solid angle of the original object. This is useful because it is often more convenient to find the solid angles for unusual shapes in two steps, first projecting it onto a simple intermediate surface such as a plane, and then projecting the plane to a hemisphere.

Figure 12.15 shows that the absolute value of the size of the object being projected is not the only thing that matters; two different shapes with the same cross section as seen from a given point can occupy the same solid angle if they are at appropriate distances from the point.

The notation used for solid angles varies a lot from one field to another, and sometimes even within the same field. In particular, in radiometry a capital Greek letter such as Ω often stands for the projected solid angle $\Gamma \cos\theta = \Gamma^{\mathbf{V}}$, and a lowercase Greek letter is used to indicate any type of solid angle, from the infinitely thin direction to finite angles. This variation in notation makes it difficult to recognize even identical equations when written by authors in different fields. In this book, we will find it important to distinguish between directions and solid angles with differential or finite character. Throughout this book we will consistently use arrow-accented lowercase Greek letters such as $\vec{\omega}$ for direction vectors, the notation $d\vec{\omega}$ for

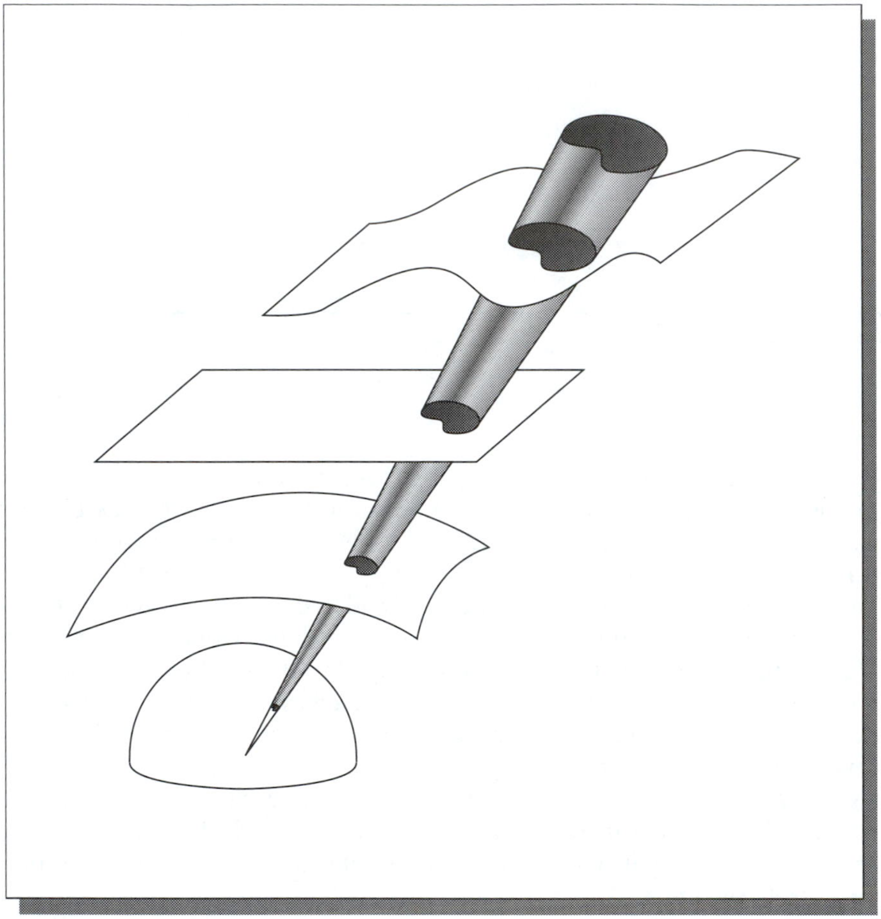

FIGURE 12.14

An object radially projected onto intermediate surfaces. Redrawn from Cohen and Greenberg in *Computer Graphics (Proc. Siggraph '85)*, fig. 4, p. 34.

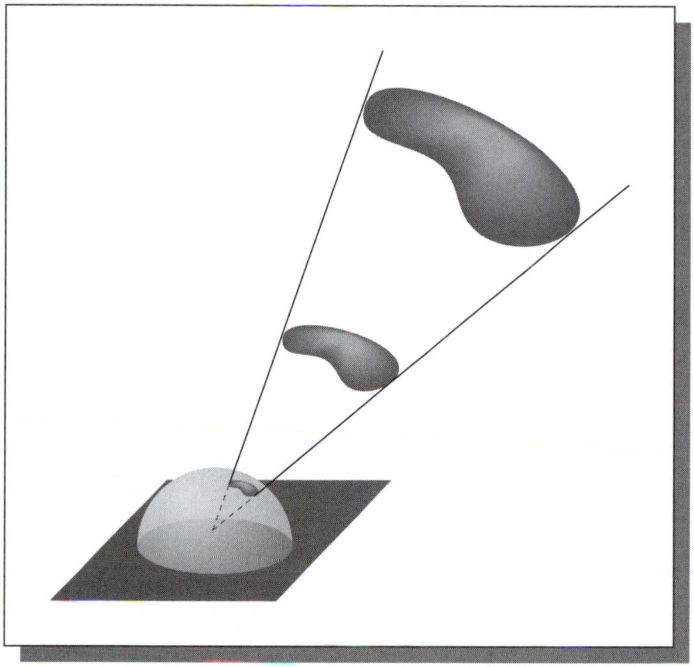

FIGURE 12.15
Two different objects can occupy the same solid angle if they occupy the same cone.

differential solid angles, and capital Greek letters such as Γ for finite solid angles. Compare this to the use of $\mathbf{r}$ for a point, $d\mathbf{r}$ for a differential volume, and V for a finite volume.

12.7.5 Integrating over Solid Angles

We will find it important to integrate functions over solid angles. This is accomplished just by using a finite solid angle as a domain and a differential solid angle in the integral. To show this notation in action, suppose we have a scalar function of direction, $f(\vec{\omega})$, and we wish to integrate this over some finite solid angle (or range of directions) Γ, as in Figure 12.16. We will write this as

$$F = \iiint_{\Gamma} f(\vec{\omega})\, d\vec{\omega} \tag{12.34}$$

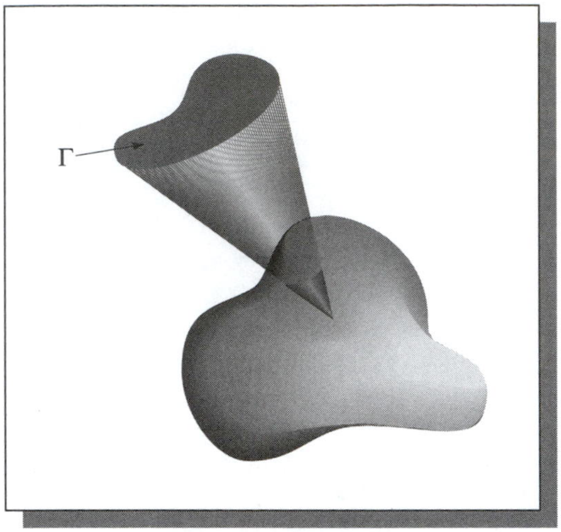

FIGURE 12.16
Integrating a function $F(\vec{\omega})$ over a range Γ.

As with volume integrals, we will usually drop two of the three explicit integral signs and leave it to the domain Γ and differential $d\vec{\omega}$ to reveal that there's a triple integration going on, so we will usually see

$$F = \int_{\Gamma} f(\vec{\omega})\, d\vec{\omega} \tag{12.35}$$

There are three special domains that will prove particularly important to us.

12.7.6 Direction Sets

The first important set is the domain of all possible directions. This is just the 3D sphere, for which we use the topologist's notation $\mathcal{S}^2$ (the 2 in $\mathcal{S}^2$ refers to the 2D surface of the sphere; a circle is $\mathcal{S}^1$).

The other two important special cases arise when we think about the light arriving at a surface point. Consider the normal $\mathbf{N}(s)$ at point s. Any direction $\vec{\omega}$ may be classified into one of four categories, depending on its relationship to the normal and the surface, as illustrated in Figure 12.17.

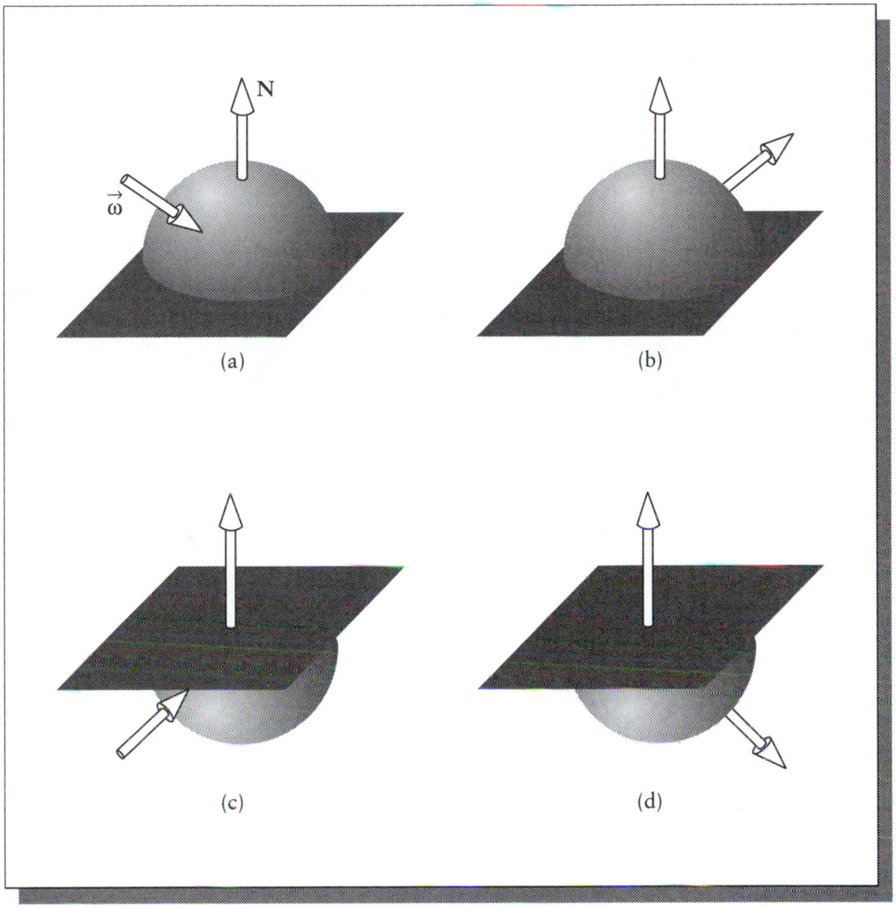

FIGURE 12.17

The directions around a point. (a) Incoming on the front. (b) Outgoing from the front. (c) Incoming on the back. (d) Outgoing from the back.

The surface normal indicates the positive (or front) side of the surface at P; all points Q in space for which $(Q - P) \cdot \mathbf{N} > 0$ are on the positive (or front) side. All vectors arriving at P from the front are gathered together into a hemisphere called Ω_i; this notation is intended to represent the hemisphere above a surface, with the superscript i representing *incoming*, as in Figure 12.17(a). The hemisphere of all directions leaving the point from the front of the surface is written Ω_o, where the o indicates *outgoing*, as in Figure 12.17(b).

Similarly, we write the incoming directions arriving on the back of the surface as $\mho_i$, which is meant to represent the hemisphere below the surface, as in Figure 12.17(c). Finally, the hemisphere of directions departing the back face is written $\mho_o$, illustrated in Figure 12.17(d). The magnitude of each of these hemispherical solid angles is 2π.

We can combine the hemisphere direction sets in sixteen possible ways, as shown in Figure 12.18. Notice that the main diagonal contains identity elements and the matrix is symmetrical. That means there are only six unique new combinations.

Of these six combinations, one represents the set of all incoming directions $(\Omega_i \cup \mho_i)$, one the set of all outgoing directions $(\Omega_o \cup \mho_o)$, and the others mix incoming and outgoing hemispheres. To represent each of these pairs of hemispheres, we use the letter Θ, with superscripts representing the front hemispheres and subscripts representing the back hemispheres. The six combinations may be defined as

$$
\begin{aligned}
\Theta^{io} &\triangleq \Omega_i \cup \Omega_o \cup P^i \\
\Theta^{i}_{i} &\triangleq \Omega_i \cup \mho_i \cup P^i \\
\Theta^{i}_{o} &\triangleq \Omega_i \cup \mho_o \cup P^i \\
\Theta^{o}_{i} &\triangleq \Omega_o \cup \mho_i \cup P^o \\
\Theta^{o}_{o} &\triangleq \Omega_o \cup \mho_o \cup P^o \\
\Theta_{io} &\triangleq \mho_i \cup \mho_o \cup P^i
\end{aligned}
\qquad (12.36)
$$

Notice that when both directions are on the same side, we write the combined term io. These terms are summarized in Table 12.1.

Note that if we had defined Θ^{io} simply as the union of two of the hemispheres, for example, $\Theta^{io} = \Omega_i \cup \Omega_o$, then it would not contain any of the directions in the plane perpendicular to the normal. On surfaces such directions may often be ignored, but in space they are as important as any other direction. Therefore we adopt the convention in Equation 12.36 that each spherical direction set is augmented with a plane of directions, either P^i representing the incoming directions, or P^o representing the outgoing directions. We establish the convention of using the sense of the upper hemisphere if it is used, or the first subscript on the lower hemisphere.

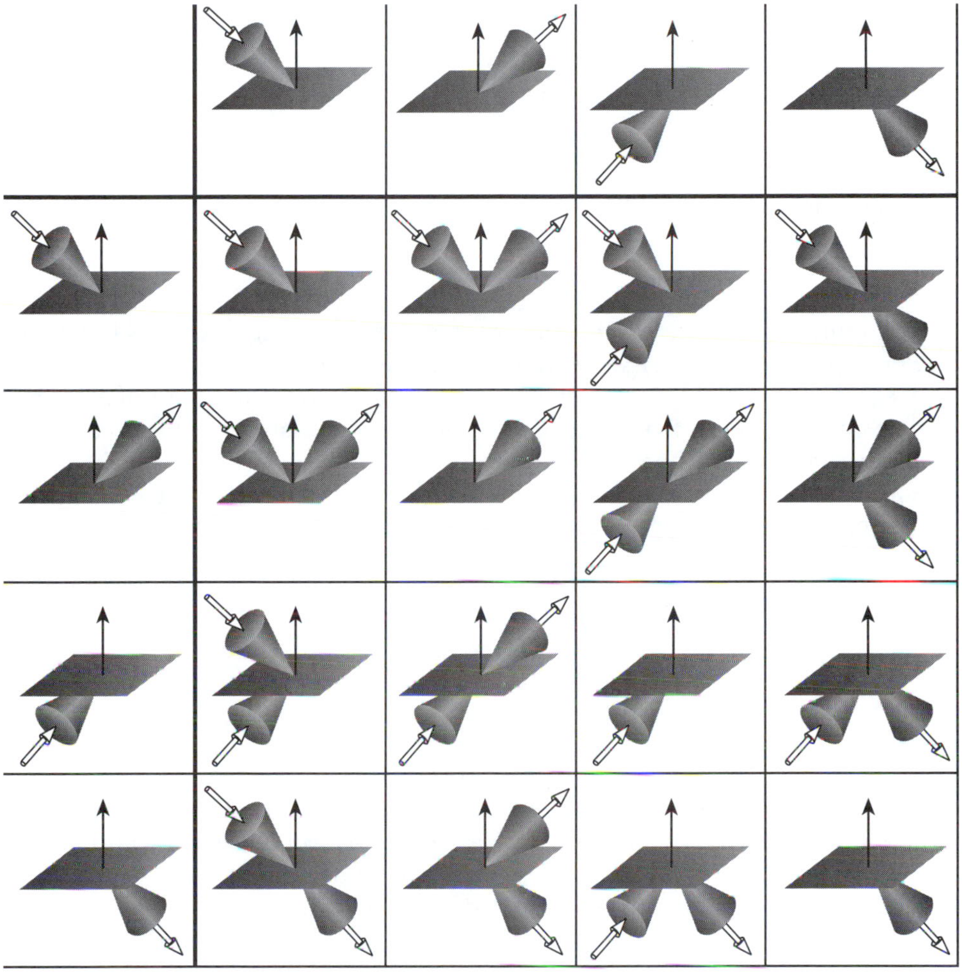

FIGURE 12.18

The sixteen combinations of hemisphere sets.

	Ω_i	Ω_o	$\mho_i$	$\mho_o$
Ω_i	Ω_i	Θ^{io}	Θ^i_i	Θ^i_o
Ω_o	Θ^{io}	Ω_o	Θ^o_i	Θ^o_o
$\mho_i$	Θ^i_i	Θ^o_i	$\mho_i$	Θ_{io}
$\mho_o$	Θ^i_o	Θ^o_o	Θ_{io}	$\mho_o$

TABLE 12.1

Combining direction hemispheres.

With this convention, Θ^i_i represents the set of all incoming directions to a point, and Θ^o_o represents the set of all outgoing directions from a point.

Since there is no surface for a point in space, any convenient vector may be used as the "normal" simply to provide orientation. In most expressions the vector being used as the normal will appear explicitly.

For completeness we can define the four degenerate terms by using a single letter in the appropriate position:

$$\begin{aligned} \Theta^i &= \Omega_i \\ \Theta^o &= \Omega_o \\ \Theta_i &= \mho_i \\ \Theta_o &= \mho_o \end{aligned} \tag{12.37}$$

The meaning of the six different combinations of hemispheres may be made clearer by Figures 12.19 and 12.20. Here we have reduced each hemisphere to a small solid angle. The four combinations show how we can represent the four possibilities of where light comes from and where it goes.

These sets of directions are functions of the point s because they depend on the normal there; different points will partition the sphere of directions differently, as in Figure 12.21. When we need to indicate this dependence, we will write, for example, $\Omega_i(\mathbf{s})$ for Ω_i at point s.

It's important to have a good intuitive feeling for these symbols because they will crop up frequently, and we will generalize this terminology to refer to different measures of light in Chapter 13.

To lock down the four interpretations of the direction hemispheres given above, consider the interaction of a beam of light from the sun arriving at the Earth, as

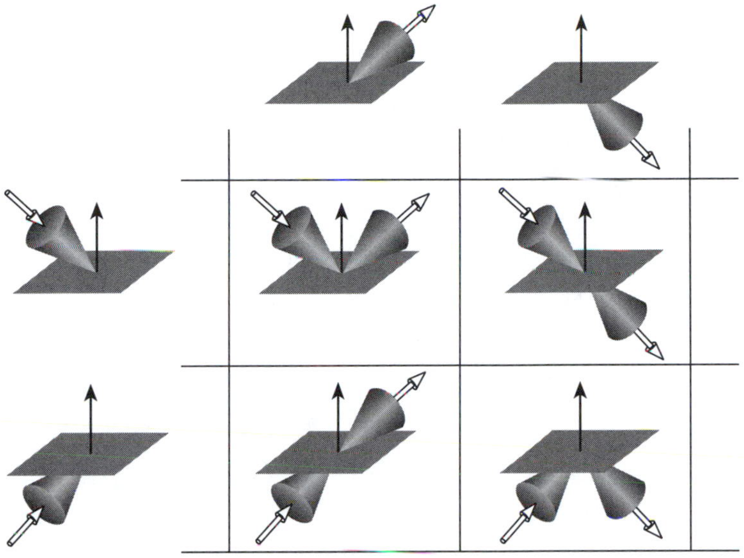

FIGURE 12.19

A grid of the four mixed combinations of hemispheres. Upper left: reflection. Upper right: transmission. Lower left: forward scattering. Lower right: backward scattering.

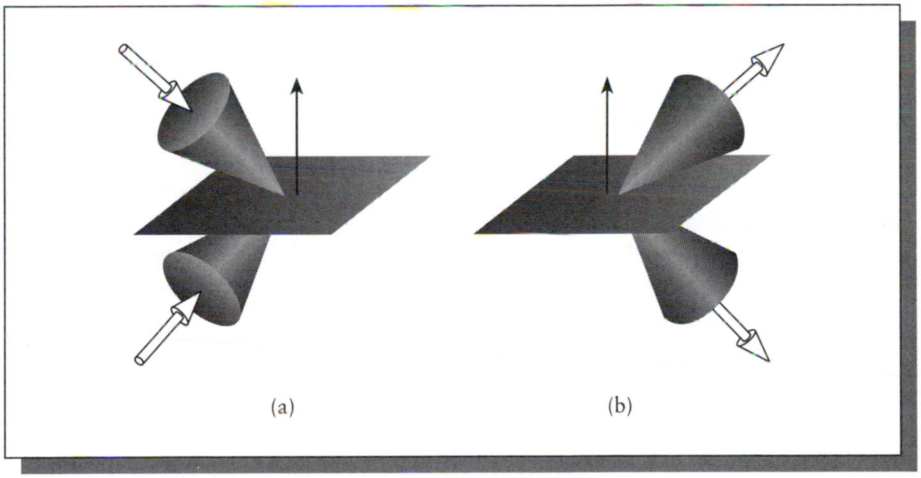

FIGURE 12.20

The two similar combinations of hemispheres. (a) Incoming. (b) Outgoing.

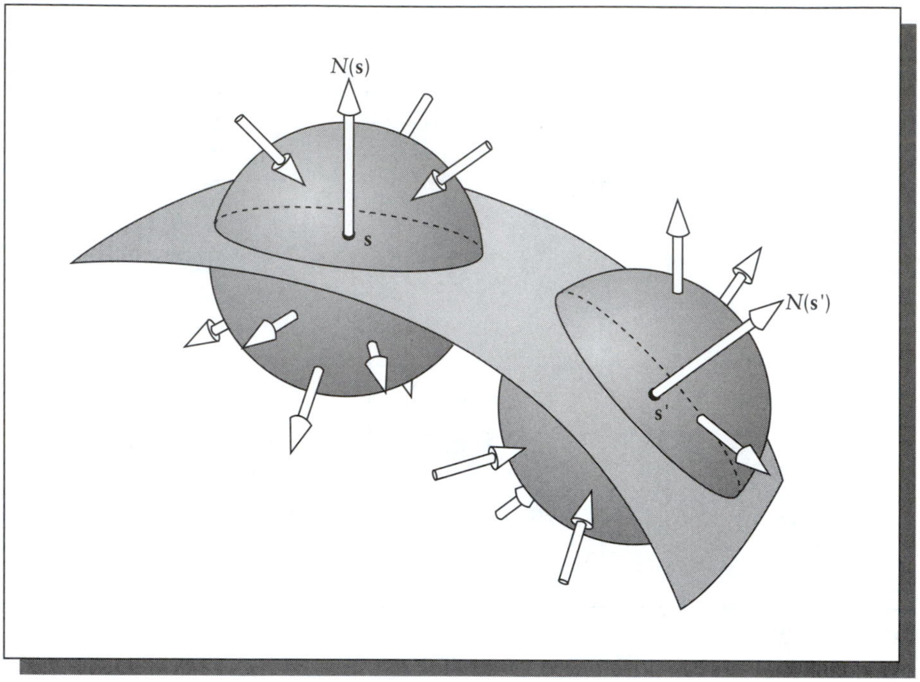

FIGURE 12.21

The orientations of the direction hemispheres depend on the normal at a surface point.

shown in Figure 12.22. For illustration we'll assume that the atmosphere can be represented by a thin spherical shell around the Earth, and that all normals point outward from the Earth's center. The initial ray in direction $\vec{\omega}_1$ arrives from space and strikes a particle in the atmosphere at point **a**, so $\vec{\omega}_1 \in \Omega_i(\mathbf{a})$; that is, it's incident light arriving from outside the surface. If some of the light is reflected back into space in direction $\vec{\omega}_2$, then $\vec{\omega}_2 \in \Omega_o(\mathbf{a})$, since it's departing light leaving the outside of the surface. Some of the light may continue on to the Earth in a new direction $\vec{\omega}_3$, so $\vec{\omega}_3 \in \mho_o(\mathbf{a})$; that is, it's departing light leaving from inside the surface.

Now suppose the light strikes the ground at point **g** and is reflected into direction $\vec{\omega}_4$. From the point of view of **g**, the incident direction $\vec{\omega}_3 \in \Omega_i(\mathbf{g})$ and the reflected direction $\vec{\omega}_4 \in \Omega_o(\mathbf{g})$.

Finally the light strikes another particle in the atmosphere and is deflected before continuing on to space in direction $\vec{\omega}_5$. At this intersection point **b**, the incident direction $\vec{\omega}_4 \in \mho_i(\mathbf{b})$ and the reflected direction $\vec{\omega}_5 \in \Omega_o(\mathbf{b})$.

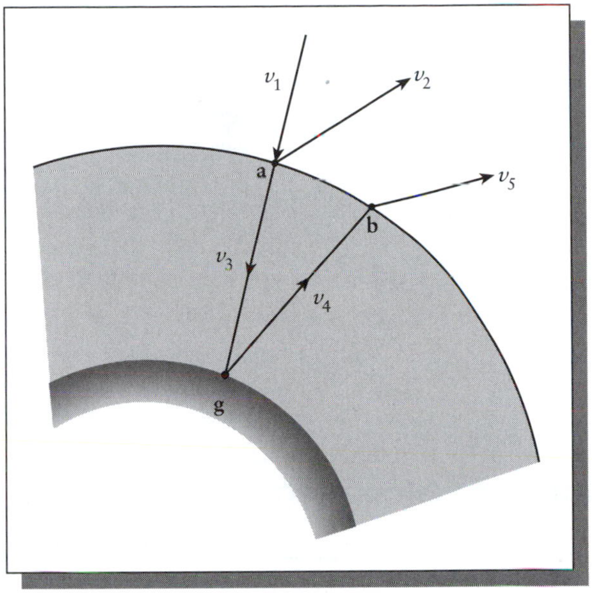

FIGURE 12.22

A ray of light from the sun arriving at the Earth.

12.7.7 Particles

We now turn to characterizing the particles themselves. We will continue to assume particles that have the same properties that they had in the rod model. In 3D, these become simply the following two:

1. All particles move with the same speed c.
2. Particles do not interact. Thus, two particles may pass through each other.

Any particle satisfying these conditions can be completely described by a pair of vectors $(\mathbf{r}, \vec{\omega})$ giving its position and direction of motion (since the speed is always the same). This pair of vectors contains five real scalars: $(\mathbf{r}, \vec{\omega}) = (r_x, r_y, r_z, \omega_\theta, \omega_\psi)$. We may be prompted to think of a five-dimensional Euclidean space $\mathcal{R}^5$, in which each particle is just a point. A better picture is a Cartesian product space of points and directions $\mathcal{R}^3 \otimes \mathcal{S}^2$. This space is called *particle phase space*, or simply the *phase space* for particles.

We define the scalar function $n(\mathbf{r}, \vec{\omega})\colon \mathcal{R}^3 \otimes \mathcal{S}^2 \mapsto \mathcal{R}$ to be the number of particles at the point $(\mathbf{r}, \vec{\omega})$ in phase space (two particles at the same point in phase space are

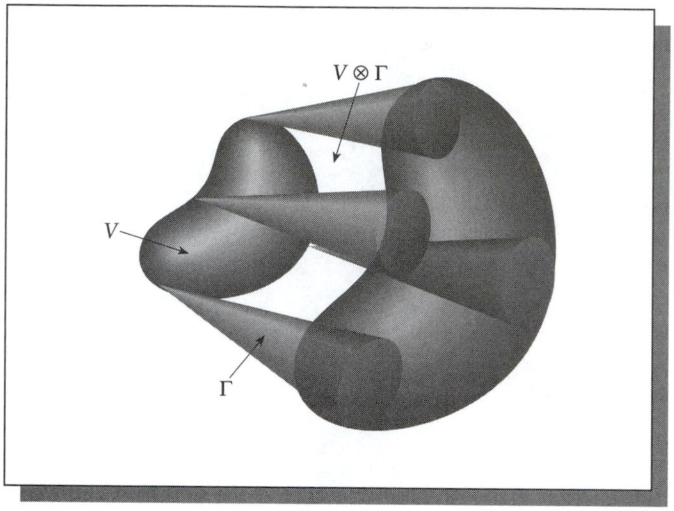

FIGURE 12.23
Counting the number of particles in the region $V \otimes \Gamma$ of phase space.

in the same place, moving in the same direction):

$$n(\mathbf{r}, \vec{\omega}) \triangleq \text{number of particles at } (\mathbf{r}, \vec{\omega}) \tag{12.38}$$

This function is called the *phase space density function.*

We can isolate pieces of phase space by combining a volume V and a range of dimensions Γ, and forming their Cartesian (or direct) product $V \otimes \Gamma$, as shown in Figure 12.23. We can use the phase space density function to find the number of particles in this section of phase space; that is, the number of particles located at any point $\mathbf{r} \in V$ and traveling in any direction $\vec{\omega} \in \Gamma$:

$$N(V, \Gamma) = \int_{\Gamma} \int_{V} n(\mathbf{r}, \vec{\omega})\, d\mathbf{r}\, d\vec{\omega} \tag{12.39}$$

The function $N(V, \Gamma)$ is called the *particle density* in the region $V \otimes \Gamma$.

12.7.8 Flux

It will be useful to us to define the *flux* in 3D; it is based on the same idea as in the rod model but contains an additional bit of geometry.

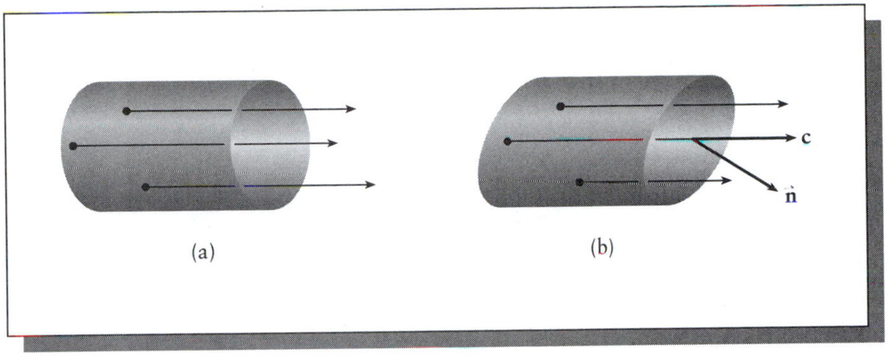

FIGURE 12.24

(a) Particles flowing over a surface element ΔS. (b) The end cap of the tube is tilted relative to the flow.

Suppose that we have isolated some piece of surface ΔS in space, and that there is a flow of particles through it, such that the direction flow is perpendicular to the surface, as in Figure 12.24(a). The particles all have the same vector velocity **c**, and a density ρ (that is, there are ρ particles per unit volume). We want to know the total number of particles flowing over the surface per unit time.

Suppose initially that the velocity is perpendicular to the surface ΔS. Then in the time Δt, the particles that cross ΔS arrive from within a right tube with length $|\mathbf{c}|\Delta t \Delta S$. The density of particles in the tube is given by ρ, so there are $\rho|\mathbf{c}|\Delta t \Delta S$ particles in the tube. The rate of flow per time is found by simply dividing by time, giving Φ, the magnitude of the flux:

$$\Phi = \rho|\mathbf{c}|\Delta S \tag{12.40}$$

Suppose now that the surface is tilted with respect to the flow, so the tube containing the particles is skewed, as in Figure 12.24(b). If the patch has a unit-length surface normal **n**, then the projected area of the patch is $(\mathbf{c} \cdot \mathbf{n})\Delta S$, so the volume of this tube is $(\mathbf{c} \cdot \mathbf{n})\Delta t \Delta S$. As the flow direction **c** strikes the surface less and less head-on, the dot product reduces the size of the tube, until when the flow is perpendicular to the surface (and thus nothing flows through the surface), the tube volume goes to zero. Again, we can find the magnitude of the flux by multiplying by the particle density and dividing through by Δt:

$$\Phi = \rho(\mathbf{c} \cdot \mathbf{n})\Delta S \tag{12.41}$$

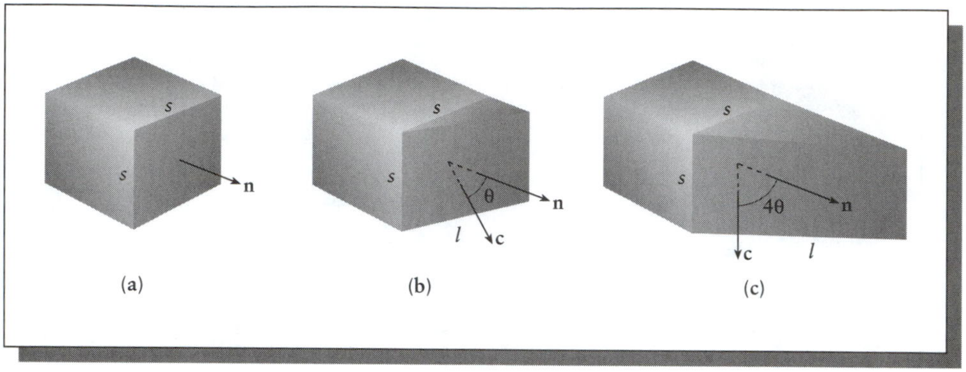

FIGURE 12.25
The cosine term in the flux compensates for the enlarged area of a patch as it turns away from the flow within a fixed tube. (a) $\theta = 0$. (b) $\theta = \theta_0$. (c) $\theta = 4\theta_0$.

It is often useful to treat the flux as a vector quantity:

$$\mathbf{\Phi} = \rho(\mathbf{c} \cdot \mathbf{n})\mathbf{c}\Delta S \tag{12.42}$$

An alternative, more geometrical picture of the origin of the cosine term is given in Figure 12.25. The flux in this figure is flowing through a square tube of side s. In Figure 12.25(a) we see the end of the tube is perpendicular to the flow; that is, $\mathbf{c} \cdot \mathbf{n} = 0$. The area of the end of the tube is s^2, so if there are n particles passing down the tube, the flow per unit area is $\Phi_0 = n/s^2$.

In Figure 12.25(b) the end of the tube now forms an angle of θ_0 with the flow: that is, $\mathbf{c} \cdot \mathbf{n} = \cos(\theta_0)$. The area of the surface through which the particles are flowing is now sl, where $s = l\cos(\theta_0)$. So the total flow passing through this tube per unit area is $\Phi_{\theta_0} = n/(sl) = (n/s^2)\cos(\theta_0) = \Phi_0\cos(\theta_0)$.

Figure 12.25(c) shows a more extreme example: now the flux is $\Phi_{4\theta_0} = n/(sl) = (n/s^2)\cos(4\theta_0) = \Phi_0\cos(4\theta_0)$. So the cosine term (usually represented by a dot product of the flux direction and the normal) is a purely geometric term which we introduce so that we are always talking about flow per unit area. When we discuss flux over a nonplanar surface, we are effectively projecting the entire surface onto a plane perpendicular to the flow, as in Figure 12.26.

We have assumed that the particles are arriving at ΔS along a single direction $\mathbf{c}$. We can easily allow the particles to arrive within a finite solid angle Γ. Recalling

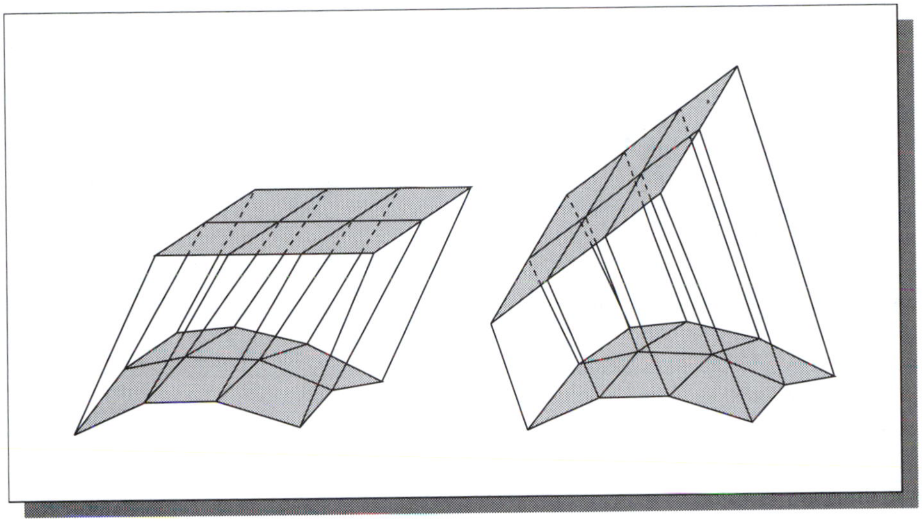

FIGURE 12.26
The flux falling on a surface from two different directions.

that all particles have a common speed c, we can write

$$\Phi(\Delta S, \Gamma) = \int_\Gamma \rho c(\vec{\omega} \cdot \mathbf{n}) \Delta S \, d\vec{\omega} = \rho c \Delta S \int_\Gamma (\vec{\omega} \cdot \mathbf{n}) \, d\vec{\omega} \tag{12.43}$$

The flux has several useful linearity properties, which may be derived either directly from the definition or from experiment [347]. Specifically, the flux is linear with respect to both the size of the area ΔS and the solid angle of the incident flow, Γ, involved in the measurement.

Figure 12.27(a) shows three solid angles, Γ_1, Γ_2, and Γ_3. When we run an experiment where the sizes of the angles and surfaces are large with respect to the wavelength of light, we find

$$\Phi(A, \Gamma_1) + \Phi(A, \Gamma_2) = \Phi(A, \Gamma_1 + \Gamma_2) \tag{12.44}$$

as shown in Figures 12.27(b) and (c). Similarly, if the solid angle shrinks to zero size, so does the flux: $\Phi(A, 0) = 0$.

We can state a similar set of principles with respect to the area under consideration. Figure 12.28 shows two different areas, A_1 and A_2. We find from experiment that

$$\Phi(A_1, \Gamma) + \Phi(A_2, \Gamma) = \Phi(A_1 + A_2, \Gamma) \tag{12.45}$$

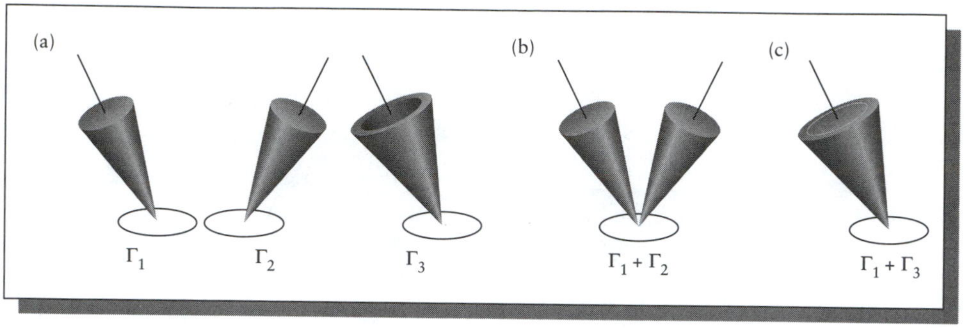

FIGURE 12.27
(a) Solid angles Γ_1, Γ_2, and Γ_3. (b) Solid angle $\Gamma_1 + \Gamma_2$. (c) Solid angle $\Gamma_1 + \Gamma_3$.

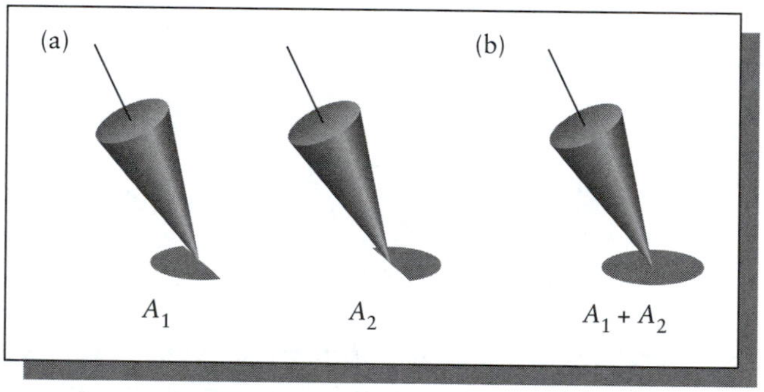

FIGURE 12.28
(a) Surfaces A_1 and A_2. (b) The surface $A_1 + A_2$.

and, as before, $\Phi(0, \Gamma) = 0$.

Although the flux is derived from the particle density and particle motion, our point of view will generally treat the flux as the fundamental description of the particle flow. Most of our discussion will be based on terms that are defined with respect to the flux.

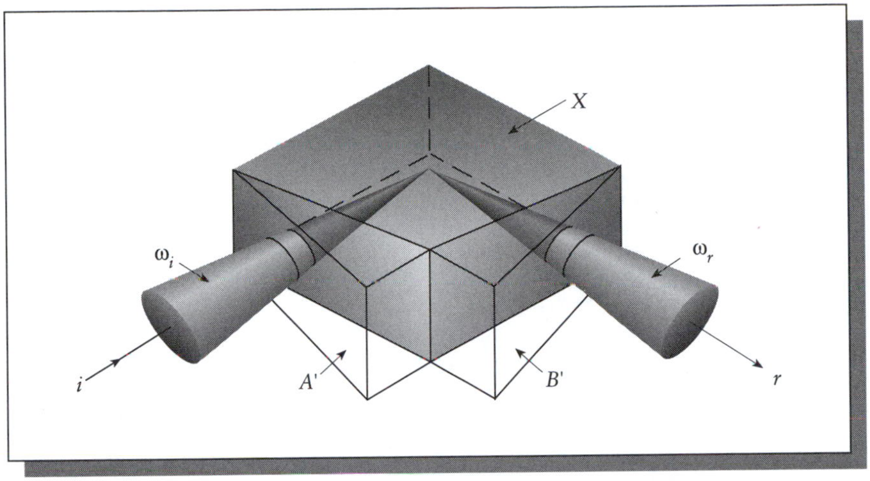

FIGURE 12.29
A scattering volume.

12.8 Scattering in 3D

We can characterize scattering in 3D by what happens to the particles as they pass through a volume, much as we did for the rod model. Presiendorfer [347] carefully describes a set of experiments that can be performed to discover some of the characteristics of volumetric scattering. We summarize those results here.

Figure 12.29 shows a *scattering volume*, denoted X. A scattering volume is defined by two directions, $\vec{\omega}_i$ and $\vec{\omega}_r$, and their associated finite solid angles, Γ_i and Γ_r. Of the twelve edges that make up the volume, four are parallel to $\vec{\omega}_i$, four are parallel to $\vec{\omega}_r$, and the remaining four are perpendicular to the plane spanned by $\vec{\omega}_i$ and $\vec{\omega}_r$. When incident light arriving in direction $\vec{\omega}_i$ enters the volume, we say it does so through face A; the light leaving in direction $\vec{\omega}_r$ exits through face B. Face A (and its opposite face) are parallel to $\vec{\omega}_r$; face B (and its opposite face) are parallel to $\vec{\omega}_i$; In general, face A will not be perpendicular to $\vec{\omega}_i$. As in the figure, we can construct a face A' which shares one edge with A but is perpendicular to $\vec{\omega}_i$; similarly, we can construct a face B' perpendicular to $\vec{\omega}_r$.

We will now summarize the results of three experiments with physical volumes of this type. We are interested in the magnitude of the flux Φ leaving face B for various combinations of incident flux Φ arriving on face A. We will assume that the volume is large with respect to the wavelength of light, and that it is internally uniform (that

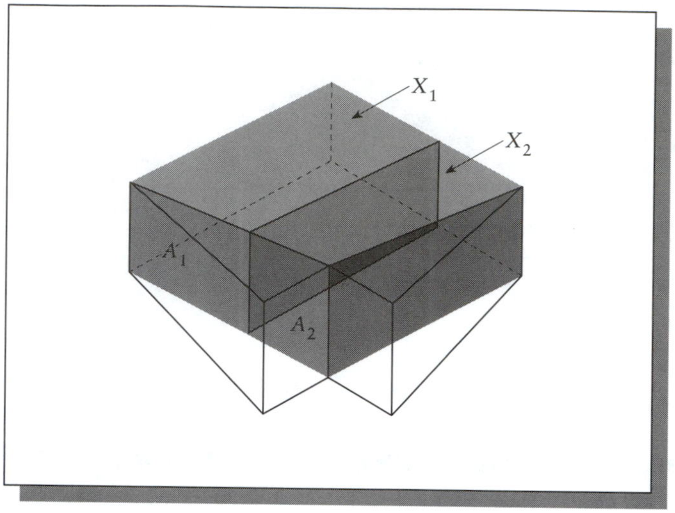

FIGURE 12.30

Splitting the input face into two subfaces.

is, the properties of any small region of the volume are identical to those of any other small region). We will also assume that the volume doesn't generate any flux internally.

In the first experiment we divide the incident face A into two subfaces, A_1 and A_2, which partitions the input flux into two pieces, Φ_{A1} and Φ_{A2}, which induces two corresponding output fluxes, Φ_{B1} and Φ_{B2}. This is illustrated in Figure 12.30. We find from experiment that

$$\Phi_{B1} + \Phi_{B2} = \Phi_B \tag{12.46}$$

In words, this says that the output flux is linear with respect to the area of the input flux.

In the second experiment we divide the input solid angle Γ into two pieces, $\Gamma 1$ and $\Gamma 2$, as in Figure 12.31. Again, each of these solid angles carries its own input flux, which generates a corresponding output flux. From experiment, we find

$$\Phi_{\Gamma 1} + \Phi_{\Gamma 2} = \Phi_\Gamma \tag{12.47}$$

so that the output flux is also linear with respect to the input solid angle.

Finally, we can consider two entirely different scattering volumes, and write the flux that results from two separate input beams. We find once again that the resulting flux is linear with respect to the inputs.

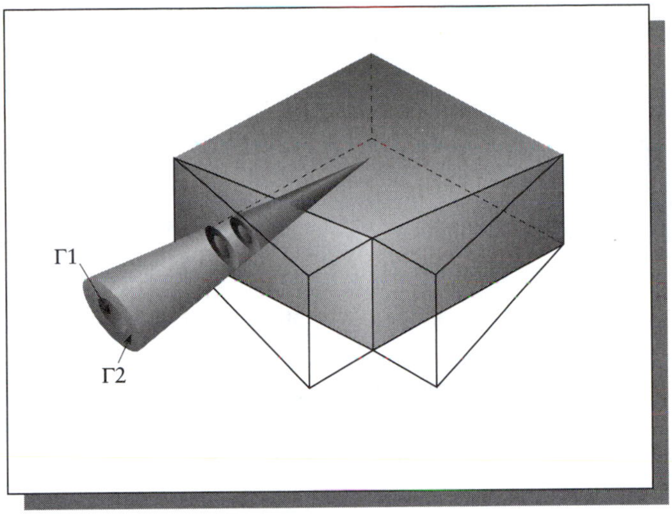

FIGURE 12.31
Splitting the input solid angle into two subsolid angles.

These results can be viewed either as experimental confirmation of the theory, or as the phenomenological basis from which the theory is derived. In either case, most of modern computer graphics is based on these fundamental results.

The essence of these properties is that over most light intensities that we deal with in practice, most materials are *linear*: each packet of light is treated independently of all other packets of light. So if we double the amount of light projected into a volume, we will double the amount that comes out in any given direction.

12.9 Components of 3D Transport

The next few sections follow the presentations by Arvo [15] and Pomraning [342].

Recall our five categories of transport in the rod model from Section 12.6. These are injection (which we will generalize into the term *streaming*), volume emission, and the three types of collisions: inscattering, absorption, and outscattering. These five categories can also be used to characterize particle transport in 3D, although their mathematical expression is more complicated. We will consider each of these categories in turn below.

First, we note two important generalizations that will take us from the rod model

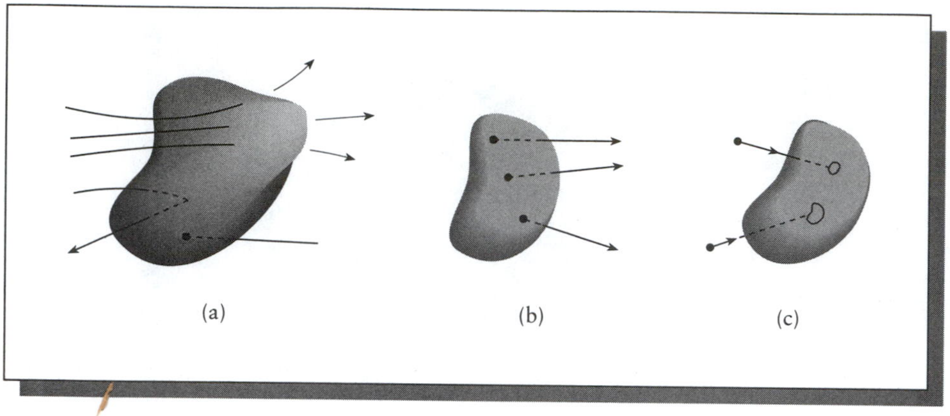

FIGURE 12.32
(a) Streaming. (b) Emission. (c) Absorption.

to 3D. When analyzing the rod model, we isolated a section of the rod and studied the flow into and out of that section. In 3D, we instead use a volume V, which may have any arbitrary shape. The surface of V will be denoted S. In the rod model we were only concerned with two possible directions in which particles could flow (left and right). In 3D, there are an infinite number of directions in which particles can flow. We will typically be concerned with a range of directions, denoted Γ.

In this section we will also concentrate more on flux than on particle densities. This is because we will ultimately be interested in setting the net change of flux within any volume to zero, which is the equilibrium condition of energy, which we assume holds when synthesizing images. We will discuss the equilibrium condition in more detail shortly.

In general, our material functions will depend on both position $\mathbf{r} \in V$ and direction $\vec{\omega} \in \Gamma$, so they vary for every point and every direction in the subspace $V \otimes \Gamma$. We will need to integrate over both domains to find the net results of these functions.

12.9.1 Streaming

We will use the category of *streaming* to describe the *net* flow of particles through a volume V. We begin by finding the net flow of particles through the surface S of V. Because particles can change direction as they move through the volume, we need to account for their changing directions, as in Figure 12.32(a).

We can find this flow easily. Recall the definition of flux from Equation 12.42, which tells us how to find the flux over any small patch ΔS. We can replace the surface S with a polyhedron with many small faces ΔS_i, and then sum together the contributions from each face. The limiting result of this process is the surface integral [378]:

$$\Phi_s = \int_S \Phi(dS)\, dS \tag{12.48}$$

To count all the particles passing through the surface, we need to integrate Equation 12.48 over all the directions Γ in which we are interested, giving us the total flux Φ_s due to streaming:

$$\Phi_s = \int_\Gamma \int_S \Phi(\mathbf{s}, \vec{\omega})\, dS\, d\vec{\omega} \tag{12.49}$$

This quantity will have a positive value when there is a net *loss* of particles through the volume. Note that Φ_s does not measure the *total* number of particles through the volume, but instead cancels those exiting with those arriving, leaving us with a *net* flow.

12.9.2 Emission

To count up the particles emitted inside V, we will posit a *volumetric emission flux* $\epsilon(\mathbf{r}, \vec{\omega})$. This tells us how many particles are emitted per unit time from point $\mathbf{r}$ in the direction $\vec{\omega}$, as shown in Figure 12.32(b).

To find the total flux radiated from the volume in some set of directions due to emission, we can simply integrate this function over all points $\mathbf{r} \in V$ and all directions $\vec{\omega} \in \Gamma$:

$$\Phi_e = \int_\Gamma \int_V \epsilon(\mathbf{r}, \vec{\omega})\, d\mathbf{r}\, d\vec{\omega} \tag{12.50}$$

12.9.3 Absorption

Similarly to emission, we will assume an absorption function $\sigma_a(\mathbf{r}, \vec{\omega})$. This is a scalar value, telling us the expected *percentage* of the flux that will be absorbed as it passes through $\mathbf{r}$ in direction $\vec{\omega}$, as illustrated in Figure 12.32(c).

To find the total absorption in the volume, we simply integrate this percentage weighted by the flux at that point. This gives us an *absorbed flux*, which is the flux that is removed by the material:

$$\Phi_a = \int_\Gamma \int_V \sigma_a(\mathbf{r}, \vec{\omega})\Phi(\mathbf{r}, \vec{\omega})\, d\mathbf{r}\, d\vec{\omega} \tag{12.51}$$

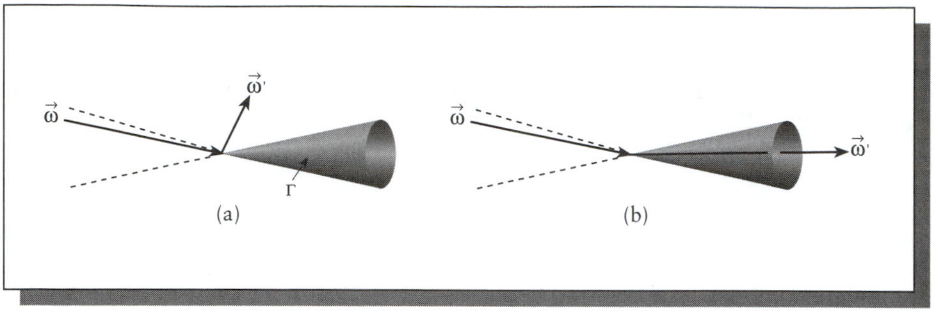

FIGURE 12.33

Outscattering of particles from the beam. (a) Outscatter where the outgoing direction $\vec{\omega}' \notin \Gamma$. (b) Outscatter where the outgoing direction $\vec{\omega}' \in \Gamma$.

12.9.4 Outscattering

Some particles in the stream may interact with the material, but rather than be absorbed, they are deflected and continue on in some new direction. In our case, we are interested in determining the number of particles at a point $\mathbf{r}$ that are deflected from their motion along direction $\vec{\omega}$ into some other direction $\vec{\omega}'$, as shown in Figure 12.33.

As with absorption, we can express this probability with a scalar value that indicates how much of the flux we expect to be scattered this way. The *volume outscattering probability function* $\kappa(\mathbf{r}, \vec{\omega} \to \vec{\omega}')$ specifies the probability that a particle at $\mathbf{r}$ traveling in direction $\vec{\omega}$ will be scattered into any direction $\vec{\omega}'$ per unit distance per unit solid angle. Note that $\vec{\omega}'$ can take on the value of $\vec{\omega}$. The arrow in this notation is useful because it shows the direction of scattering explicitly.

There are at least two ways to specify how a material outscatters: we can measure how many particles that are originally traveling in a direction $\vec{\omega} \in \Gamma$ exit in some other direction $\vec{\omega}' \notin \Gamma$, or we can simply compute the number of particles originally in Γ that are scattered in any direction at all. We will select the latter approach. This means that we will include in our count of scattered particles those that are traveling in directions within Γ both before and after scattering, as in Figure 12.33(b). We will find that this method of accounting works well when combined with our means of counting inscattered particles. In this figure the dashed cone indicates the same directions except with the arrowheads at the scattering event.

With these conditions, the outscattered flux Φ_o is found by integrating over all incident directions $\vec{\omega} \in \Gamma$ at all points $\mathbf{r} \in V$, and by counting the number of particles

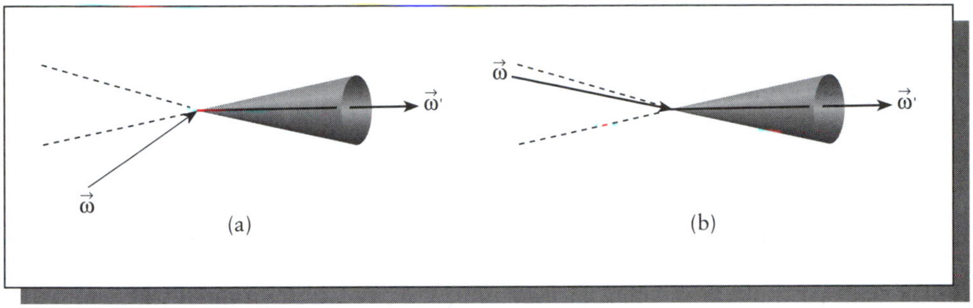

FIGURE 12.34
Inscattering deflects a particle into the range Γ. (a) Inscatter where the incoming direction $\vec{\omega}' \notin \Gamma$. (b) Inscatter where the incoming direction $\vec{\omega}' \in \Gamma$.

deflected into any new direction $\vec{\omega}' \in \mathcal{S}^2$:

$$\Phi_o = \int_\Gamma \int_V \int_{\mathcal{S}^2} \kappa(\mathbf{r}, \vec{\omega} \to \vec{\omega}')\Phi(\mathbf{r}, \vec{\omega})\, d\vec{\omega}'\, d\mathbf{r}\, d\vec{\omega} \tag{12.52}$$

Note that the incident flux $\Phi(\mathbf{r}, \vec{\omega})$ is independent of $\vec{\omega}'$ in the innermost integral. We can then pull it out of that integral and write

$$\Phi_o = \int_\Gamma \int_V \Phi(\mathbf{r}, \vec{\omega}) \int_{\mathcal{S}^2} \kappa(\mathbf{r}, \vec{\omega} \to \vec{\omega}')\, d\vec{\omega}'\, d\mathbf{r}\, d\vec{\omega} \tag{12.53}$$

12.9.5 Inscattering

The category of *inscattering* is closely related to outscattering: it describes when a particle originally arriving at a point **r** along any direction $\vec{\omega}'$ is deflected into a new direction $\vec{\omega} \in \Gamma$, as in Figure 12.34. As with outscattering, we describe the probability of a scattering event occurring with the *volume inscattering probability function*. This is also denoted κ, but the direction of scattering is reversed: $\kappa(\mathbf{r}, \vec{\omega}' \to \vec{\omega})$.

Note that if $\vec{\omega}' \in \Gamma$, then we are counting those particles that are both arriving and departing along a direction in Γ, just as for outscattering.

So the inscattered flux Φ_i is found by integrating over all incident directions $\vec{\omega}' \in \mathcal{S}^2$ at all points $\mathbf{r} \in V$, and by counting the number of particles deflected into any direction $\vec{\omega} \in \Gamma$:

$$\Phi_i = \int_\Gamma \int_V \int_{\mathcal{S}^2} \kappa(\mathbf{r}, \vec{\omega}' \to \vec{\omega})\Phi(\mathbf{r}, \vec{\omega}')\, d\vec{\omega}'\, d\mathbf{r}\, d\vec{\omega} \tag{12.54}$$

Notice that we use the flux coming from $\vec{\omega}'$ rather than $\vec{\omega}$ as in the outscattering case.

12.9.6 A Complete Transport Model

Now that we have an expression for each of the phenomena we want to represent, we are almost ready to combine them into a transport model. What's left are the mechanics of this combination.

The essential observation needed to carry out this combination is that the typical image-synthesis problem addresses a system in *equilibrium*. That is, we assume that the distribution of light in the environment is steady and constant (at least over the time of exposure of the image). This equilibrium usually comes about very quickly because of the great speed of light with respect to the simulated interval over which we estimate the distribution of light in an environment. For example, when we turn on a flashlight in a dark room, the energy from the flashlight first strikes some surfaces, which then reradiate some of the light to other surfaces, and these may in turn reradiate some energy back to the first surfaces. This chain of illumination and reradiation may go very deep, but eventually it settles down into a steady solution where the light energy distribution over time in the room becomes constant. This is obvious to us when we hold the light steady and look around the room: the objects do not periodically grow brighter and dimmer as time goes on. The illumination in the room is then said to be in a steady state, or equilibrium.

This equilibrium condition implies that the change in the flux at every point and every direction in the scene is constant. That is, the time derivative of the flux is zero. In symbols,

$$\frac{\partial \Phi}{\partial t} = 0 \tag{12.55}$$

This does not mean that there is no flow of energy in the scene. Rather, this equilibrium condition says that there is an *active* or *dynamic* equilibrium, in which the flow is constant. We can think of this condition as telling us that the number of particles flowing past any piece of surface (imaginary or real) in the scene per unit time is always constant.

Because this condition holds everywhere in the scene, it also holds over every volume V and every set of directions Γ. Therefore we know that the total gains and losses in our arbitrary volume must total to 0. In symbols, then, we can say that the sum of the two gains (Φ_e due to emission and Φ_i due to inscattering) must equal the sum of the three losses (Φ_s due to streaming, Φ_o due to outscattering, and Φ_a due to absorption).

In symbols,

$$\Phi_e + \Phi_i = \Phi_s + \Phi_o + \Phi_a \tag{12.56}$$

Recall that both Φ_o and Φ_i contain the particles both arriving and departing in direction within Γ. Because they are both positive and on opposite sides of Equation 12.56, these common terms cancel out, leaving us with the net difference, so we truly get the net inscatter and outscatter distributions.

We can now simply plug in our results from above to flesh out this expression:

$$\begin{array}{c} \displaystyle\int_\Gamma \int_V \epsilon(\mathbf{r}, \vec{\omega})\, d\mathbf{r}\, d\vec{\omega} \\ + \\ \displaystyle\int_\Gamma \int_V \int_{S^2} \kappa(\mathbf{r}, \vec{\omega}' \to \vec{\omega}) \Phi(\mathbf{r}, \vec{\omega}')\, d\vec{\omega}'\, d\mathbf{r}\, d\vec{\omega} \end{array} = \begin{array}{c} \displaystyle\int_\Gamma \int_S \Phi(\mathbf{s}, \vec{\omega})\, dS\, d\vec{\omega} \\ + \\ \displaystyle\int_\Gamma \int_V \Phi(\mathbf{r}, \vec{\omega}) \int_{S^2} \kappa(\mathbf{r}, \vec{\omega} \to \vec{\omega}')\, d\vec{\omega}'\, d\mathbf{r}\, d\vec{\omega} \\ + \\ \displaystyle\int_\Gamma \int_V \sigma_a(\mathbf{r}, \vec{\omega}) \Phi(\mathbf{r}, \vec{\omega})\, d\mathbf{r}\, d\vec{\omega} \end{array} \tag{12.57}$$

This equation is much too hard to attempt to solve directly. But notice that four out of five terms in Equation 12.57 have an outermost double integral over the volume V and directions Γ; only the streaming term Φ_s has a different form. We will find that getting everything into the same form will greatly simplify this expression.

Happily, it is easy to convert the streaming term to the same form as the others. Recall the divergence theorem (also known as Gauss's theorem), which states that for a vector function $\mathbf{F}$ and a volume V with surface S, and unit surface normal $\mathbf{n}$ at every point, then

$$\int_S \mathbf{F} \cdot \mathbf{n}\, dS = \int_V \nabla \cdot \mathbf{F}\, dV \tag{12.58}$$

where ∇ is the *del operator*, which in rectilinear Euclidean space is

$$\nabla = \mathbf{i}\frac{\partial}{\partial x} + \mathbf{j}\frac{\partial}{\partial y} + \mathbf{k}\frac{\partial}{\partial z} \tag{12.59}$$

This tells us that the integral of the normal component of the function over the surface is equal to the integral of the divergence of the function throughout the volume. A very readable derivation and discussion of the divergence theorem may be found in Schey [378].

We can use this theorem to rewrite Φ_s in a form that is equivalent to the other terms. First we recall the streaming flux from Equation 12.49. Consider only the inner integral over S, and expand the flux:

$$\int_S \Phi(\mathbf{s}, \vec{\omega})\, dS = \int_S n(\mathbf{r}, \vec{\omega}) \mathbf{c}(\mathbf{r}) \cdot \mathbf{n}(dS)\, dS \tag{12.60}$$

where $n(\vec{\omega}, \mathbf{r})$ is the particle density. From this, we can identify the vector function $\mathbf{F}$ in the divergence theorem as $\mathbf{F}(\vec{\omega}, \mathbf{r}) = n(\vec{\omega}, \mathbf{r})\mathbf{c}(\mathbf{r})$. Then we can rewrite this integral as

$$\int_S n(\mathbf{r}, \vec{\omega}) \mathbf{c}(\mathbf{r}) \cdot \mathbf{n}(dS)\, dS = \int_V \nabla \cdot [n(\mathbf{r}, \vec{\omega})\mathbf{c}(\mathbf{r})]\, dV$$

$$= \int_V \mathbf{c}(\mathbf{r}) \cdot \nabla n(\mathbf{r}, \vec{\omega})\, dV$$
$$= \int_V \vec{\omega} \cdot \nabla \Phi(\mathbf{r}, \vec{\omega})\, dV \tag{12.61}$$

Notice that we have turned a divergence calculation into a gradient, which is then turned into an inner product with respect to the direction of flow.

We can now wrap this result back into the outer integral over Γ to find

$$\Phi_s = \int_\Gamma \int_V \vec{\omega} \cdot \nabla \Phi(\mathbf{r}, \vec{\omega})\, dV\, d\vec{\omega} \tag{12.62}$$

With this change, we can now rewrite Equation 12.57 so that the outermost two integrals on each term are the same:

$$\begin{aligned}&\int_\Gamma \int_V \epsilon(\mathbf{r}, \vec{\omega})\, d\mathbf{r}\, d\vec{\omega} + \int_\Gamma \int_V \int_{\mathcal{S}^2} \kappa(\mathbf{r}, \vec{\omega}' \to \vec{\omega}) \Phi(\mathbf{r}, \vec{\omega}')\, d\vec{\omega}'\, d\mathbf{r}\, d\vec{\omega} \\ &= \int_\Gamma \int_V \vec{\omega} \cdot \nabla \Phi(\mathbf{r}, \vec{\omega})\, dV\, d\vec{\omega} + \int_\Gamma \int_V \Phi(\mathbf{r}, \vec{\omega}) \int_{\mathcal{S}^2} \kappa(\mathbf{r}, \vec{\omega} \to \vec{\omega}')\, d\vec{\omega}'\, d\mathbf{r}\, d\vec{\omega} + \int_\Gamma \int_V \sigma_a(\mathbf{r}, \vec{\omega}) \Phi(\mathbf{r}, \vec{\omega})\, d\mathbf{r}\, d\vec{\omega}\end{aligned} \tag{12.63}$$

The advantage of this form comes when we use the full power of our earlier definition of equilibrium. Recall that when the environment is in equilibrium, there is zero net flux for *every* volume V and set of directions Γ. That means our choice of V and Γ in these derivations don't matter; any choices will do. In other words, we can pick any volume V we want, and any set of directions Γ we want, and we will find that the net flow of particles through the combined phase-space volume defined by these two domains is constant over time. Therefore it must be the case that the equality in Equation 12.63 holds when we replace the integrals just by their integrands. Stripping off the outer two integrals from each term then gives us the *standard one-speed particle transport equation*:

$$\begin{aligned}&\epsilon(\mathbf{r}, \vec{\omega}) + \int_{\mathcal{S}^2} \kappa(\mathbf{r}, \vec{\omega}' \to \vec{\omega}) \Phi(\mathbf{r}, \vec{\omega}')\, d\vec{\omega}' \\ &\quad = \vec{\omega} \cdot \nabla \Phi(\mathbf{r}, \vec{\omega}) + \Phi(\mathbf{r}, \vec{\omega}) \int_{\mathcal{S}^2} \kappa(\mathbf{r}, \vec{\omega} \to \vec{\omega}')\, d\vec{\omega}' + \sigma_a(\mathbf{r}, \vec{\omega}) \Phi(\mathbf{r}, \vec{\omega})\end{aligned} \tag{12.64}$$

Equation 12.64 is known in the physics literature as a *Boltzmann equation* [431]. It tells us that there is a balance of gains and losses at every point in the environment. It

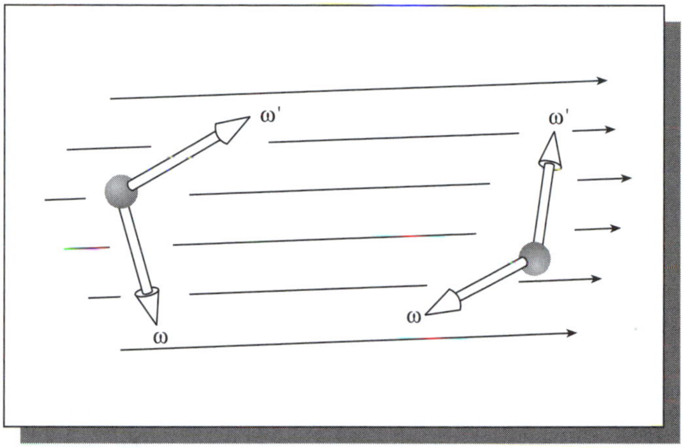

FIGURE 12.35
An isotropic medium; only the angle between the incident and scattered directions matters, not their absolute location.

also gives us a condition on the flux $\Phi(\mathbf{r}, \vec{\omega})$; the flux must be such that Equation 12.64 holds. We say that such a flux is a *solution* of Equation 12.64.

12.9.7 Isotropic Materials

We can simplify Equation 12.64 a bit when the material is *isotropic*. In particular, consider the outscattering term Φ_o.

In an isotropic material, the direction of the incident and scattered directions $\vec{\omega}$ and $\vec{\omega}'$ don't matter; only the angle between them makes a difference. One way to think of this is to imagine two rigid straight sticks, cemented together at one end in fixed position. Label one stick $\vec{\omega}$ and the other $\vec{\omega}'$; no matter how the sticks are moved or rotated in the medium, if it is isotropic, then $\kappa(\mathbf{r}, \vec{\omega} \to \vec{\omega}')$ is a constant. See Figure 12.35. We can indicate this explicitly by writing the function so that it depends only on the dot product between the two vectors: $\kappa(\mathbf{r}, \vec{\omega} \cdot \vec{\omega}')$.

For an isotropic material we can write Φ_o as

$$\begin{aligned} \Phi_o &= \Phi(\mathbf{r}, \vec{\omega}) \int_{S^2} \kappa(\mathbf{r}, \vec{\omega} \cdot \vec{\omega}')\, d\vec{\omega}' \\ &= \Phi(\mathbf{r}, \vec{\omega}) \sigma_{io}(\mathbf{r}) \end{aligned} \tag{12.65}$$

where the *isotropic outscattering coefficient* $\sigma_{io}(\mathbf{r})$ is

$$\sigma_{io}(\mathbf{r}) = \int_{\mathcal{S}^2} \kappa(\mathbf{r}, \vec{\omega}_0 \cdot \vec{\omega}')\, d\vec{\omega}' \tag{12.66}$$

for any choice of $\vec{\omega}_0 \in \mathcal{S}^2$.

We can now roll together the isotropic outscattering coefficient $\sigma_{io}(\mathbf{r})$ and the absorption coefficient $\sigma_a(\mathbf{r})$ into the *isotropic outscattering and absorption coefficient* σ_{ioa}:

$$\sigma_{ioa}(\mathbf{r}) = \sigma_{io}(\mathbf{r}) + \sigma_a(\mathbf{r}) \tag{12.67}$$

and write Equation 12.64 in a simpler form:

$$\epsilon(\mathbf{r}, \vec{\omega}) + \int_{\mathcal{S}^2} \kappa(\mathbf{r}, \vec{\omega}' \to \vec{\omega})\Phi(\mathbf{r}, \vec{\omega}')\, d\vec{\omega}' = \vec{\omega} \cdot \nabla\Phi(\mathbf{r}, \vec{\omega}) + \sigma_{ioa}(\mathbf{r})\Phi(\mathbf{r}, \vec{\omega}) \tag{12.68}$$

Equation 12.68 is the *standard isotropic one-speed particle transport equation*, also called the *standard stationary one-speed particle transport equation.*

12.10 Boundary Conditions

The major result of the previous section was Equation 12.64. Because it contains the del operator ∇, it is at least partly a differential equation. We will concentrate on that nature of the equation for the moment.

We know that all differential equations require boundary conditions in order to be fully specified. In this case, the transport equation describes the transfer of particles through space, so the boundary conditions describe what happens where space "stops"; that is, the surfaces of objects. So we can interpret our boundary conditions as simply a description of what happens to the flux at the surfaces of objects. This boils down to describing how surfaces will reflect (or transmit) the particles striking them.

Following Arvo [15], we will introduce some notation that will help us discuss surfaces and what happens to the flux striking them.

Recall that at each surface point s, the local tangent plane splits the sphere of directions into two hemispherical solid angles. We can think of $\Omega_o(\mathbf{s})$ as representing all the directions in which particles can leave the front of the surface from s, and $\Omega_i(\mathbf{s})$ as containing all directions along which particles can arrive at the outside of $\mathbf{s}$. Our job in finding boundary conditions is to describe the nature of the particles returned to the medium through the directions $\Omega_o(\mathbf{s})$ as a function of the particles arriving from the directions $\Omega_i(\mathbf{s})$.

To facilitate that task, we will generalize the notation to take into account all the points on all the surfaces at once. To motivate this notation, imagine an environment containing exactly three points: $\mathbf{s}_1$, $\mathbf{s}_2$, and $\mathbf{s}_3$. Then we could form the union of the hemispheres of directions leaving the front, to build a subset of $\mathcal{R}^3 \otimes \mathcal{S}^2$:

$$(\mathbf{s}_1 \otimes \Omega_o(\mathbf{s_1})) \cup (\mathbf{s}_2 \otimes \Omega_o(\mathbf{s_2})) \cup (\mathbf{s}_3 \otimes \Omega_o(\mathbf{s_3})) \tag{12.69}$$

This idea generalizes nicely into the situation where we have continuous surfaces made of an infinite number of points. We simply form the collection from all pairs $(\mathbf{s}, \vec{\omega})$ that give a point in space and a direction.

Combining all points with the front outgoing directions Ω_o gives us the set $\mathcal{P}^o$, where the superscript o stands for *outgoing*. Similarly, we get $\mathcal{P}^i$, $\mathcal{P}_o$, and $\mathcal{P}_i$ by combining the set of surface points with the hemispherical sets Ω_i, $\mho_o$, and $\mho_i$:

$$\begin{aligned}
\mathcal{P}^o &\triangleq \{(\mathbf{s}, \vec{\omega}) \in \mathcal{R} \otimes \mathcal{S}^2 : \mathbf{s} \in M, \vec{\omega} \in \Omega_o\} \\
\mathcal{P}^i &\triangleq \{(\mathbf{s}, \vec{\omega}) \in \mathcal{R} \otimes \mathcal{S}^2 : \mathbf{s} \in M, \vec{\omega} \in \Omega_i\} \\
\mathcal{P}_o &\triangleq \{(\mathbf{s}, \vec{\omega}) \in \mathcal{R} \otimes \mathcal{S}^2 : \mathbf{s} \in M, \vec{\omega} \in \mho_o\} \\
\mathcal{P}_i &\triangleq \{(\mathbf{s}, \vec{\omega}) \in \mathcal{R} \otimes \mathcal{S}^2 : \mathbf{s} \in M, \vec{\omega} \in \mho_i\}
\end{aligned} \tag{12.70}$$

So $\mathcal{P}^i$ is the collection of all direction vectors that arrive at a point on M on the same side as the surface normal at that point, and $\mathcal{P}_i$ is the set of all direction vectors that arrive at a point on the side opposite the normal. This interpretation is illustrated in Figure 12.36.

We can form the sixteen combinations of these sets just as we did for the hemispherical sets, producing four mixed-direction sets as before. We define them following the same pattern:

$$\begin{aligned}
\mathcal{P}^{io} &\triangleq \{(\mathbf{s}, \vec{\omega}) \in \mathcal{R} \otimes \mathcal{S}^2 : \mathbf{s} \in M, \vec{\omega} \in \Theta^{io}\} \\
\mathcal{P}^i_o &\triangleq \{(\mathbf{s}, \vec{\omega}) \in \mathcal{R} \otimes \mathcal{S}^2 : \mathbf{s} \in M, \vec{\omega} \in \Theta^i_o\} \\
\mathcal{P}^o_i &\triangleq \{(\mathbf{s}, \vec{\omega}) \in \mathcal{R} \otimes \mathcal{S}^2 : \mathbf{s} \in M, \vec{\omega} \in \Theta^o_i\} \\
\mathcal{P}_{io} &\triangleq \{(\mathbf{s}, \vec{\omega}) \in \mathcal{R} \otimes \mathcal{S}^2 : \mathbf{s} \in M, \vec{\omega} \in \Theta_{io}\}
\end{aligned} \tag{12.71}$$

The two pure incoming and outgoing sets are defined similarly:

$$\begin{aligned}
\mathcal{P}^i_i &\triangleq \{(\mathbf{s}, \vec{\omega}) \in \mathcal{R} \otimes \mathcal{S}^2 : \mathbf{s} \in M, \vec{\omega} \in \Theta^i_i\} \\
\mathcal{P}^o_o &\triangleq \{(\mathbf{s}, \vec{\omega}) \in \mathcal{R} \otimes \mathcal{S}^2 : \mathbf{s} \in M, \vec{\omega} \in \Theta^o_o\}
\end{aligned} \tag{12.72}$$

Our job of specifying boundary conditions now boils down to describing the flux, leaving every point on every surface in terms of the incident flux. In other words, we

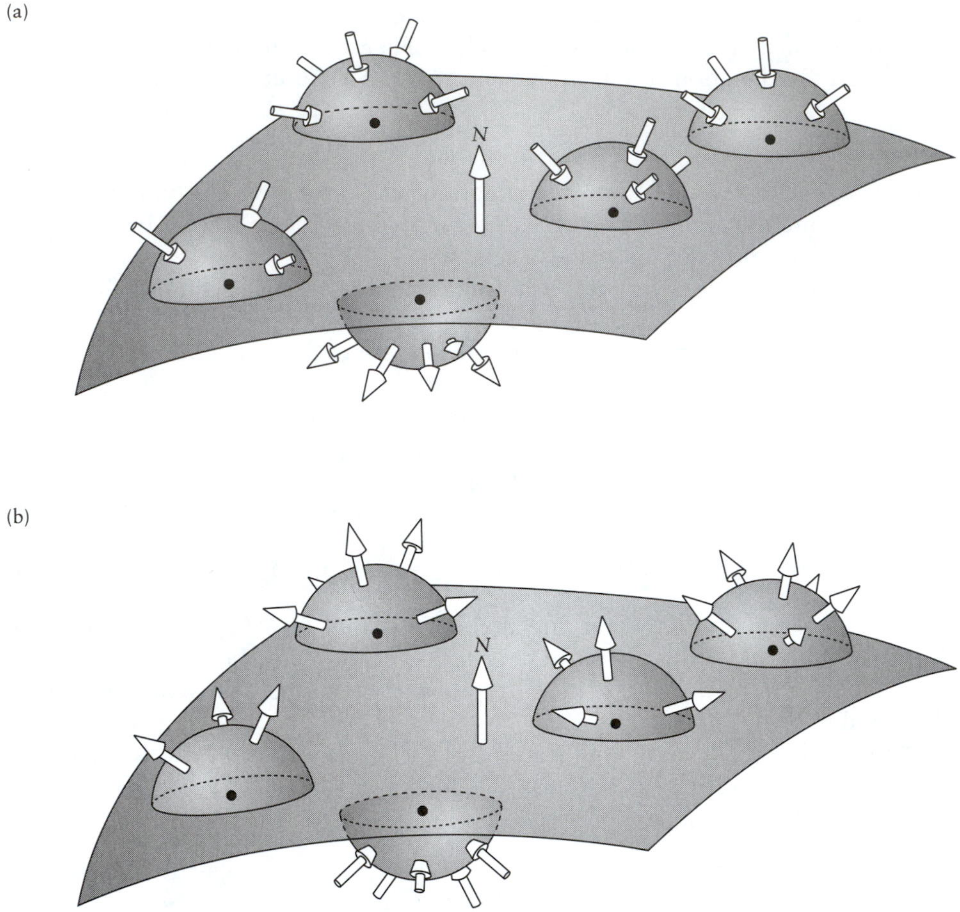

FIGURE 12.36
(a) The set $\mathcal{P}_o^i$. (b) The set $\mathcal{P}_i^o$.

want to describe the flux Φ for all elements of $\mathcal{P}_o^o$ in terms only of Φ for all elements of $\mathcal{P}_i^i$: $\Phi(\mathcal{P}_o^o) = f(\Phi(\mathcal{P}_i^i), E)$, where E encompasses surface emission. The particular choice of f provides the boundary conditions at that point.

There are many ways to specify these boundary conditions, depending on the type of problem at hand and the information that has been given to us. These include the following:

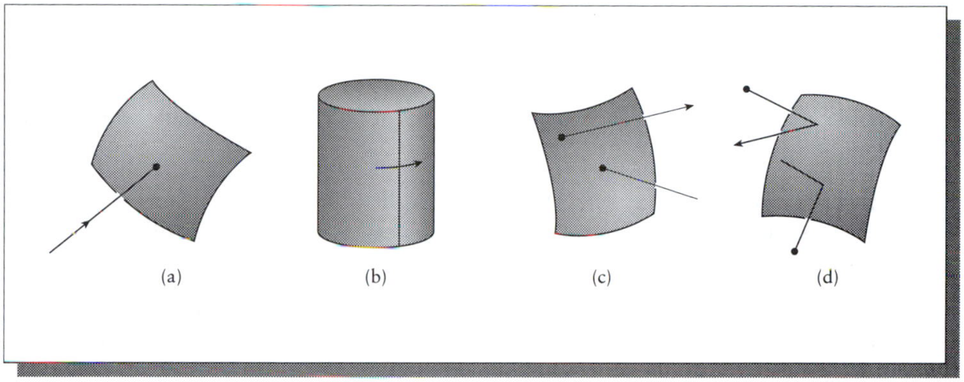

FIGURE 12.37

Different boundary conditions. (a) Free. (b) Periodic. (c) Explicit. (d) Implicit.

Free: When particles can exit the system at a surface but not reenter it, this is called a *free* boundary condition. An example of a free boundary in computer graphics comes from the common practice of surrounding every environment with a large enclosing object, often a perfectly absorbing black sphere. Any energy striking this sphere is simply removed from the system, as in Figure 12.37(a).

Periodic: When a domain is periodic, then the boundary conditions share that property. Periodic conditions are usually involved when several distinct locations in a parameter space map to the same single location in physical space. Periodic conditions can be expressed by constraints like

$$\Phi(\mathbf{s}, \vec{\omega}) = \Phi(\mathbf{s}', \vec{\omega}) \tag{12.73}$$

for two different points $\mathbf{s} \neq \mathbf{s}'$.

For example, one model of the cosmological universe posits that it is *closed*: the universe wraps back upon itself, so that if you go far enough in any direction you'll end up back where you started. A more accessible example is circular travel around the central axis of a right circular cylinder, as in Figure 12.37(b). Here the two ends of the parameter space ($\theta = 0$ and $\theta = 2\pi$) map to the same location in physical space. So $\Phi(s + k\mathbf{v}, \vec{\omega}) = \Phi(s, \vec{\omega})$ where $k \in \mathcal{Z}$ and $\mathbf{v}$ represents a full turn around the cylinder.

Explicit: When the flux leaving a point on a surface is independent of the incident flux, we say that the outgoing flux is specified *explicitly*. This can be expressed with an explicit function:

$$\Phi(\mathbf{s}, \vec{\omega}) = \epsilon_s(\mathbf{s}, \vec{\omega}) \tag{12.74}$$

where ϵ_s is a *surface emission function*. Notice that ϵ_s is independent of the incident flux.

A common use of explicit boundary conditions is to describe a *luminaire*, which emits a fixed pattern of light regardless of what light is falling upon it, as in Figure 12.37(c).

Implicit: When the flux leaving a point on a surface depends on the incident flux, then we specify it with *implicit* or *reflecting* boundary conditions, as in Figure 12.37(d). This is by far the most common type in computer graphics, accounting for most physical surfaces (this class includes transmission of energy through transparent surfaces).

The most general description of an implicit boundary involves an arbitrary function f_s applied to the incident flux to determine the outgoing flux:

$$\begin{aligned} \Phi(\mathbf{s}, \vec{\omega}) &= f_s(\Phi(\mathbf{s}, \vec{\omega}')) \\ \vec{\omega} &\in \Theta_o^o \\ \vec{\omega}' &\in \Theta_i^i \end{aligned} \tag{12.75}$$

where $f_s()$ is a *surface-scattering* function. The function f_s has access to all incident directions $\vec{\omega}'$.

Such a function is more general than we need to simulate real materials. Recall that Section 12.8 showed that volume scattering is linear. Over a very wide range, surface scattering is also linear. Thus the contribution of the incident flux $\Phi(\mathbf{s}, \vec{\omega}_1)$ at point $\mathbf{s}$, along direction $\vec{\omega}_1 \in \mho_i(\mathbf{s})$, is independent of the incident flux $\Phi(\mathbf{s}, \vec{\omega}_2)$ along $\vec{\omega}_2 \in \mho_i(\mathbf{s})$ for $\vec{\omega}_2 \neq \vec{\omega}_1$. This suggests that the surface scattering function f_s above can be rewritten to simply scale the incident flux in each direction, and then sum the scaled fluxes. The amount by which some incident direction $\vec{\omega}'$ is scaled depends only on $\mathbf{s}$ and the outgoing direction $\vec{\omega}$. We can write this as

$$\Phi(\mathbf{s}, \vec{\omega}) = \int_{\mho_i(\mathbf{s})} \kappa_s(\mathbf{s}, \vec{\omega}' \to \vec{\omega}) \Phi(\mathbf{s}, \vec{\omega}')\, d\vec{\omega}' \tag{12.76}$$

where κ_s is the *surface-scattering distribution function*. This gives us the amount contributed to the outgoing flux by the flux in each incident direction $\vec{\omega}' \in \mho_i(\mathbf{s})$. In general, this function can contain distribution functions like the delta function.

In a physical situation, energy must be conserved: that is, no more energy may be sent into $\Theta_o^o(\mathbf{s})$ than arrives along $\Theta_i^i(\mathbf{s})$, and only positive amounts of energy may be radiated:

$$\int_{\Theta_i^i(\mathbf{s})} \kappa_s(\mathbf{s}, \vec{\omega}' \to \vec{\omega})\, d\vec{\omega}' \leq 1 \quad \forall(\mathbf{s}, \vec{\omega}) \in \Theta_o^o(\mathbf{s})$$
$$\kappa_s(\mathbf{s}, \vec{\omega}' \to \vec{\omega}) \geq 0 \quad \forall(\mathbf{s}, \vec{\omega}) \in \Theta_o^o(\mathbf{s}) \tag{12.77}$$

Mixed: The most general boundary conditions are a combination of implicit and explicit; in graphics, this means combining how a surface radiates light with how it reflects it. We can write the boundary conditions at a point $\mathbf{s} \in M$ as

$$\Phi(\mathbf{s}, \vec{\omega}) = \epsilon_s(\mathbf{s}, \vec{\omega}) + \int_{\Theta_i^i(\mathbf{s})} \kappa_s(\mathbf{s}, \vec{\omega}' \to \vec{\omega}) \Phi(\mathbf{s}, \vec{\omega}')\, d\vec{\omega}' \tag{12.78}$$

for all $(\mathbf{s}, \vec{\omega}) \in \mathcal{H}^+$.

When boundary conditions are added to the transport equations 12.64 and 12.68, the result is a complete and well-defined specification for the flux $\Phi(\mathbf{s}, \vec{\omega})$ for every point and direction in the environment. The whole point of most rendering algorithms is to find the function Φ that satisfies that specification.

12.11 The Integral Form

The way we have stated the general transport equation in Equation 12.64 is perfectly valid but inconvenient. Because it contains both an integral and derivative of the unknown quantity Φ, it is called an *ordinary integro-differential equation*. Although solution techniques for integro-differential equations exist [120, 173], the theory for solving this type of equation is not nearly as well developed as the theories for solving partial differential equations [60] and integral equations [251]. Although integral equations are not typically introduced in school to the same extent as differential equations, they have been well studied for a long time [324, 456], and solution techniques for integral equations now appear in standard reference works on numerical methods [348].

To make use of the powerful solution methods for differential or integral equations, we need to convert our transport equation into one of these forms. The usual approach in transport theory is to recast the equation as an integral equation [129], and that is the approach we take here. One of the advantages of the integral equation form is that the boundary conditions are rolled right into the equation, rather than being maintained as a separate set of constraints.

12.11.1 An Example

The process of converting Equation 12.64 into an integral equation requires several steps. These steps involve some new notation and ideas, and you could easily get lost in the clutter. To help keep the forest in sight when walking through the trees, we begin with a simple example that presents the basic steps.

Consider the following integro-differential equation involving an unknown function $f(t)$:

$$\frac{df(t)}{dt} - \lambda \int_a^b K(t, \mu) f(\mu)\, d\mu = g(t) \tag{12.79}$$

where the constraint $g(t)$ and the function $K(t, a)$ are given. When an integral of the type $\int K(t, \mu) f(\mu)\, d\mu$ is used to find f, the function K is called the *kernel* of the integral.

Equation 12.79 contains many of the key features of Equation 12.64, though in a simpler and more abstract form. When $g(t) = 0$, this type of equation is said to be *homogeneous*; otherwise it is *nonhomogeneous*. The function $g(t)$ is variously called the *driving function*, the *forcing function*, or the *input function* in the signal processing and differential equations literatures [60, 151].

Suppose we are also given the initial condition $f(a) = f_a$. Integrating both sides with respect to t yields

$$\begin{aligned} f(t) - \lambda \int_a^b \left(\int_a^t K(\nu, \mu)\, d\nu \right) f(\mu)\, d\mu &= \int_a^t g(\mu)\, d\mu + f_a \\ f(t) - \lambda \int_a^b K^t(t, \mu) f(\mu)\, d\mu &= G(t) + f_a \end{aligned} \tag{12.80}$$

where we have simply collected and renamed some terms in the second line. We now have a completely equivalent representation for the original equation, including the boundary condition.

Because Equation 12.80 expresses the function $f(t)$ only in terms of itself and integrals containing it, an equation of this form is called an *integral equation*. The advantage of this transformation is that we can now use the sophisticated tools of integral equation theory to find $f(t)$.

We will now take this idea and apply it to Equation 12.64 in order to transform it from an integro-differential equation to an integral equation. Most rendering theory is devoted to describing how the theory of integral equations may be used to understand that equation, and the design of algorithms to efficiently solve it for the function Φ, representing the flow of light in a scene.

12.11.2 The Integral Form of the Transport Equation

This section closely follows the derivations presented by Arvo [15] and Pomraning [342].

We start by recapitulating the basic transport equation from Equation 12.64:

$$\begin{aligned}\epsilon(\mathbf{r},\vec{\omega}) &+ \int_{\mathcal{S}^2} \kappa(\mathbf{r},\vec{\omega}' \to \vec{\omega})\Phi(\mathbf{r},\vec{\omega})\, d\vec{\omega}' \\ &= \omega \cdot \nabla\Phi(\mathbf{r},\vec{\omega}) + \Phi(\mathbf{r},\vec{\omega}) \int_{\mathcal{S}^2} \kappa(\mathbf{r},\vec{\omega} \to \vec{\omega}')\, d\vec{\omega}' + \sigma_a(\mathbf{r},\vec{\omega})\Phi(\mathbf{r},\vec{\omega}) \qquad (12.81)\end{aligned}$$

which holds for all $(\mathbf{r},\vec{\omega}) \in (\mathcal{R}^3 - M) \otimes \mathcal{S}^2$.

We remove the differential nature of this equation by converting it to a simple differential equation, and then integrating as in the example in the previous section.

The first step in simplifying Equation 12.81 is to get rid of the del operator and turn the streaming term into a simple derivative. We recall from the definition of the gradient that $\vec{\omega} \cdot \nabla \mathbf{f}$ for any scalar field $\mathbf{f}$ is the directional derivative of $\mathbf{f}$ in the direction of $\vec{\omega}$, since we're projecting the gradient into $\vec{\omega}$ [377]. In other words, $\omega \cdot \nabla\Phi(\mathbf{r},\vec{\omega})$ is just the change in Φ along the direction $\vec{\omega}$. The trick is to notice that we can specify various points along this direction with the expression $\mathbf{r} + \alpha\vec{\omega}$, so that $\alpha = 0$ specifies $\mathbf{r}$, and $\alpha \neq 0$ specifies points along the line parallel to $\vec{\omega}$ passing through $\mathbf{r}$. The directional derivative of Φ onto $\vec{\omega}$ is the derivative of Φ along this line with respect to α:

$$\vec{\omega} \cdot \nabla\Phi(\mathbf{r},\vec{\omega}) = \frac{\partial}{\partial\alpha}\Phi(\mathbf{r} + \alpha\vec{\omega},\vec{\omega})\bigg|_{\alpha=0} \qquad (12.82)$$

Figure 12.38 shows an abstract representation of this operation. Because on the page we can only draw Φ as a function of two variables, this figure shows $\Phi(\mathbf{r},\vec{\omega})$, where $\mathbf{r}$ is a distance.

Looking more closely at Φ around $\mathbf{r}$, we can draw two vectors along the line $\vec{\omega}$, given by $\mathbf{A} = \mathbf{r} + \vec{\omega}$ and $\mathbf{B} = \mathbf{r} - \vec{\omega}$, as in Figure 12.39. The vectors $\mathbf{A}$ and $\mathbf{B}$ are antiparallel, so

$$\begin{gathered}\mathbf{A} = -\mathbf{B} \\ \frac{\partial}{\partial\alpha}\Phi(\mathbf{r} + \alpha\vec{\omega},\vec{\omega}) = -\frac{\partial}{\partial\alpha}\Phi(\mathbf{r} - \alpha\vec{\omega},\vec{\omega}) \qquad (12.83)\end{gathered}$$

This is useful because we would like to look backward along $\vec{\omega}$ and see where the flux is coming from.

The advantage of this approach is that as we look backward from $\mathbf{r}$ along $-\vec{\omega}$, we are simply looking at flux traveling through space. We have just spent a good deal of time describing the scattering, emitting, and absorbing events that can happen as a particle moves through space, so we have a good idea of what's happening to the

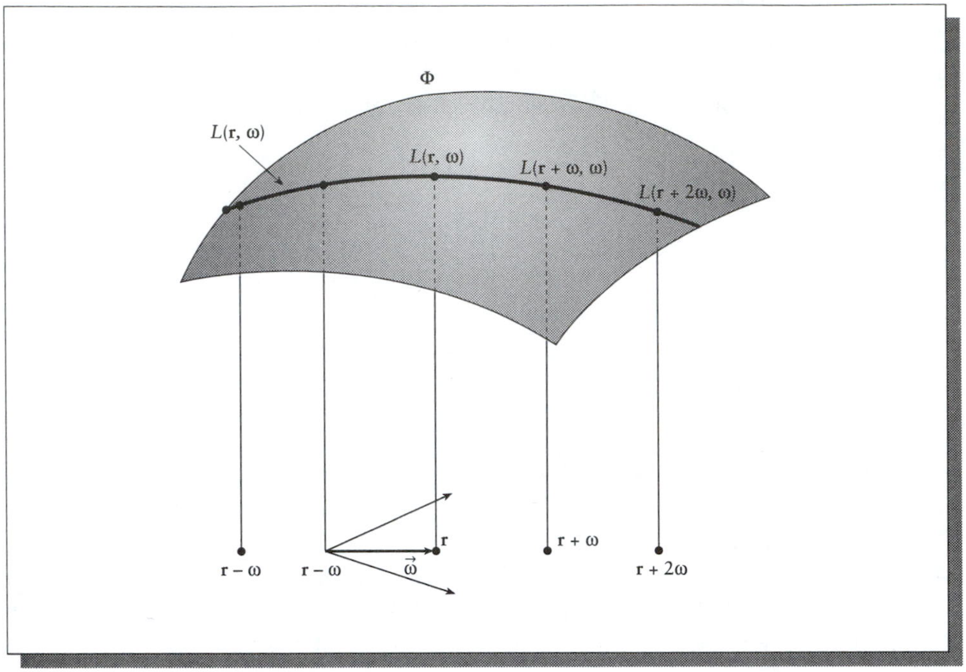

FIGURE 12.38
The function $\Phi(\mathbf{r} + \alpha\vec{\omega}, \vec{\omega})$ as a function of radius $\mathbf{r}$ and direction $\vec{\omega}$.

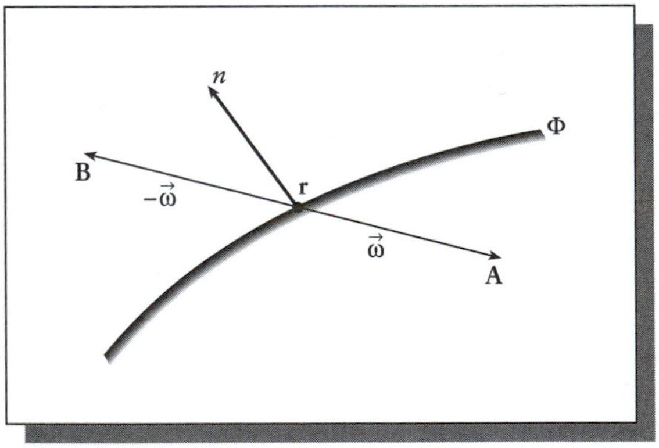

FIGURE 12.39
The vectors $\mathbf{A}$ and $\mathbf{B}$ are antiparallel.

flux at each point along its path along $\vec{\omega}$ from an arbitrary point until it eventually reaches $\mathbf{r}$.

The arbitrary point referred to in the previous sentence will lie either within another bit of volume, or on a surface. If it's on a surface, then we get the flux leaving that point on the surface from the boundary conditions.

This is the essential step in the transformation of Equation 12.64 from an integro-differential equation to an integral equation: by looking far enough backward along the incident direction, we eventually find a surface, and we can find the flux at that point from the boundary conditions. We now turn to phrasing that statement in mathematical terms.

We will need to introduce some new notation, or expressions like Equation 12.64 will start to look simple by comparison.

First we will gather together the positive contributions (or gains) to the flux as it flows through space. We create the *gain function* $G(\mathbf{r}, \vec{\omega})$, which simply combines volumetric emission and inscattering:

$$G(\mathbf{r}, \vec{\omega}) \stackrel{\triangle}{=} \epsilon(\mathbf{r}, \vec{\omega}) + \int_{\mathcal{S}^2} \kappa(\mathbf{r}, \vec{\omega}' \to \vec{\omega})\Phi(\mathbf{r}, \vec{\omega}')\, d\vec{\omega}' \tag{12.84}$$

We will now introduce a whole family of functions derived from those we've seen by placing a hat over them. For any function $f(\mathbf{r}, \vec{\omega})$, the notation $\widehat{f}(\alpha)$ refers to $f(\mathbf{r} - \alpha\vec{\omega}, \vec{\omega})$, so this tells us the value of the function as we walk backward along the direction $-\vec{\omega}$ from the point $\mathbf{r}$ [15].

Using the notation described above, we can write the basic transport equation more succinctly as

$$-\frac{\partial}{\partial\alpha}\widehat{\Phi}(\alpha) + \widehat{\Phi}(\alpha)\int_{\mathcal{S}^2} \kappa(\mathbf{r} - \alpha\vec{\omega}, \vec{\omega} \to \vec{\omega}')\, d\vec{\omega}' = \widehat{G}(\alpha) \tag{12.85}$$

Equation 12.85 looks something like an ordinary differential equation for $\widehat{\Phi}(\alpha)$, but it has two features that seem to prevent it from actually being one. The first is that $\widehat{G}$ seems to depend on $\widehat{\Phi}$, even though the notation hides that dependency. It is true that $\widehat{G}$ does depend on Φ in general, but $\widehat{\Phi}(\alpha)$ is what we're solving for here, and that's an infinitely thin line. In terms of measure theory, $\widehat{\Phi}$ contributes a *set of measure zero* to the integral, and therefore may be safely ignored [425].

The other problem is the unpleasant integral on the left-hand side. But this integral is just a constant with respect to our unknown $\widehat{\Phi}(\alpha)$, so we will write it simply as $\widehat{\sigma}_c(\alpha)$:

$$\widehat{\Phi}(\alpha)\int_{\mathcal{S}^2} \kappa(\mathbf{r} - \alpha\vec{\omega}, \vec{\omega} \to \vec{\omega}')\, d\vec{\omega}' = \widehat{\Phi}(\alpha)\widehat{\sigma}_c(\alpha) \tag{12.86}$$

Multiplying Equation 12.85 by -1 on both sides and substituting the above, we have

$$\frac{\partial}{\partial\alpha}\widehat{\Phi}(\alpha) - \widehat{\Phi}(\alpha)\widehat{\sigma}_c(\alpha) = -\widehat{G}(\alpha) \tag{12.87}$$

This is our first result in this section: it is a linear, first-order differential equation in $\widehat{\Phi}$ with variable coefficients, and even has a first-order coefficient of 1.

This type of equation is easily solved. We digress for a moment to solve it in the general case, and then return to the specifics of Equation 12.87. Consider the following differential equation for $y(x)$, where a derivative is indicated by a prime, as in $y'(x)$:

$$y'(x) + p(x)y(x) = g(x) \tag{12.88}$$

We would like to find $y(x)$. The trick is to look for a function $\mu(x)$ such that when we multiply the left side by $\mu(x)$, the derivative of this product $[\mu(x)y(x)]'$ is equal to the existing left-hand side. Such a function is called an *integrating factor* [60]. Suppose for a moment that we had such a function. Then we can simply multiply everything out and see what $\mu(x)$ would have to be to satisfy these requirements:

$$\begin{aligned} \mu(x)[y'(x) + p(x)y(x)] &= [\mu(x)y(x)]' \\ \mu(x)y'(x) + \mu(x)p(x)y(x) &= \mu(x)y'(x) + \mu'(x)y(x) \end{aligned} \tag{12.89}$$

If we now assume that $\mu(x) \neq 0$,

$$\begin{aligned} \frac{\mu'(x)}{\mu(x)} &= p(x) \\ \ln[\mu(x)] &= \int_0^x p(\tau)\,d\tau \\ \mu(x) &= \exp\left[\int_0^x p(\tau)\,d\tau\right] \end{aligned} \tag{12.90}$$

Note that $\mu(x) > 0$ for all x, so our assumption is fulfilled.

We now return to our problem of solving Equation 12.87. This matches the form of Equation 12.88, with $p(\alpha) = -\widehat{\sigma}(\alpha)_0$. Therefore the integrating factor is

$$\mu(\alpha) = \exp\left[\int_0^\alpha -\widehat{\sigma}_c(\tau)\,d\tau\right] \tag{12.91}$$

Using Equation 12.89 to change the left-hand side, Equation 12.87 becomes

$$\frac{\partial}{\partial\alpha}\left[\mu(\alpha)\widehat{\Phi}(\alpha)\right] = -\mu(\alpha)\widehat{G}(\alpha)$$

$$\int_0^\alpha \frac{\partial}{\partial\tau}\left[\mu(\tau)\widehat{\Phi}(\tau)\right]\,d\tau = \int_0^\alpha -\mu(\tau)\widehat{G}(\tau)\,d\tau$$

$$\mu(\tau)\widehat{\Phi}(\tau)\Big|_{\tau=0}^{\tau=\alpha} = -\int_0^\alpha \mu(\tau)\widehat{G}(\tau)\,d\tau \tag{12.92}$$

Solving for $\widehat{\Phi}(0)$ we find

$$\widehat{\Phi}(0) = \mu(\alpha)\widehat{\Phi}(\alpha) + \int_0^\alpha \mu(\tau)\widehat{G}(\tau)\,d\tau \tag{12.93}$$

Equation 12.93 tells us how to find the flux $\widehat{\Phi}(0) = \Phi(\mathbf{r}, \vec{\omega})$ in terms of the flux arriving along the direction $\vec{\omega}$. As we mentioned before, the purpose of this approach is that we can now look backward along $-\vec{\omega}$ to find a point $\mathbf{s} \in M$; that is, a point on a surface. We use the boundary conditions to find the flux at s directed along $\vec{\omega}$, and then adjust the flux as it travels toward $\mathbf{r}$.

To find this point s, we will create and use the *visible-surface function* (or the *nearest-surface function* or *ray-tracing function*) $\nu(\mathbf{r}, \vec{\omega})\colon \mathcal{R}^3 \otimes \mathcal{S}^2 \mapsto \mathcal{R}$. This takes any point $\mathbf{r}$ and searches along $-\vec{\omega}$ until it finds the nearest point on any surface M_i. This function is the primary object of interest in a ray-tracing program because it is often a very slow operation. But theoretically we have no problem simply defining

$$\nu(\mathbf{r}, \vec{\omega}) \stackrel{\triangle}{=} \inf\{\alpha > 0 : \mathbf{r} - \alpha\vec{\omega} \in M\} \tag{12.94}$$

So $\nu(\mathbf{r}, \vec{\omega})$ is a scalar function that returns the distance from a point $\mathbf{r}$ to the nearest point $\mathbf{s} \in M$. This point is actually given by simply subtracting a vector of length $\alpha\vec{\omega}$ from $\mathbf{r}$:

$$\mathbf{s} = \mathbf{r} - \nu(\mathbf{r}, \vec{\omega})\vec{\omega} \tag{12.95}$$

This function is illustrated in Figure 12.40.

Now that we have a way to identify the surface point s from which flux travels to $\mathbf{r}$ along $\vec{\omega}$, we need to find a description of that flux. This is exactly what is provided by the boundary conditions from Equation 12.78:

$$\Phi(\mathbf{s}, \vec{\omega}) = \varepsilon_s(\mathbf{s}, \vec{\omega}) + \int_{\Theta_i^i(\mathbf{s})} \kappa_s(\mathbf{s}, \vec{\omega}' \to \vec{\omega})\Phi(\mathbf{s}, \vec{\omega}')\,d\vec{\omega}' \tag{12.96}$$

for all $(\mathbf{s}, \vec{\omega}) \in \mathcal{H}^+$.

Combining this with Equation 12.93 and expanding out the "hat" functions, we find

$$\Phi(\mathbf{r}, \vec{\omega}) = \mu(\mathbf{r}, \mathbf{s})\Phi(\mathbf{s}, \vec{\omega}) + \int_0^h \mu(\mathbf{r}, \mathbf{a})G(\mathbf{a}, \vec{\omega})\,d\alpha \tag{12.97}$$

where $\mathbf{a} = \mathbf{r} - \alpha\vec{\omega}$, and $|\vec{\omega}| = 1$.

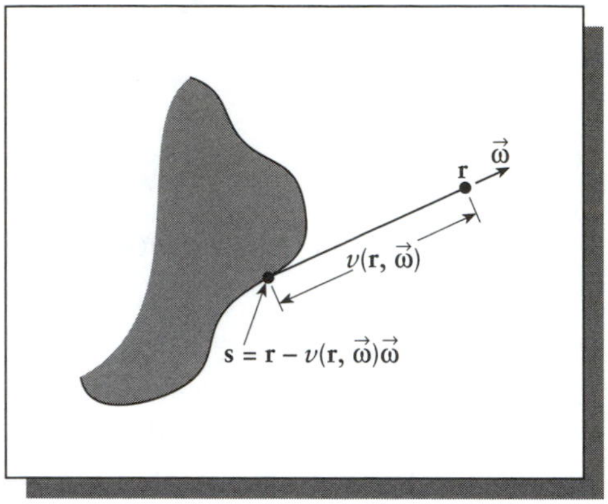

FIGURE 12.40
The visible-surface function.

Expanding out G to see the explicit dependence on Φ, we arrive at our goal in this section: *the integral form of the transport equation*:

$$\begin{aligned}\Phi(\mathbf{r},\vec{\omega}) &= \mu(\mathbf{r},\mathbf{s})\Phi(\mathbf{s},\vec{\omega}) \\ &+ \int_0^h \left[\mu(\mathbf{r},\mathbf{a})\left(\epsilon(\mathbf{a},\vec{\omega}) + \int_{S^2}\kappa(\mathbf{r},\vec{\omega}'\to\vec{\omega})\Phi(\mathbf{a},\vec{\omega}')\,d\vec{\omega}'\right)\right] d\alpha \qquad (12.98)\end{aligned}$$

where

$$\begin{aligned}\mathbf{a} &= \mathbf{r} - \alpha\vec{\omega} \\ h &= \nu(\mathbf{r},\vec{\omega}) \\ \mathbf{s} &= \mathbf{r} - h\vec{\omega} \\ \mu(\mathbf{r},\mathbf{s}) &= \exp\left[\int_0^{||\mathbf{r}-\mathbf{s}||} \sigma_c(\mathbf{r}-\tau\vec{\omega},\vec{\omega})\,d\tau\right] \\ \widehat{\sigma}_c(\mathbf{r},\vec{\omega}) &= \int_{S^2}\kappa(\mathbf{r},\vec{\omega}\to\vec{\omega}')\,d\vec{\omega}' \qquad (12.99)\end{aligned}$$

This equation is a form of a more general relationship called the *Boltzmann equation*, and indeed Equation 12.98 may be derived from the Boltzmann equation along with the boundary conditions [116].

In words, Equation 12.98 says that the flux at a point $\mathbf{r}$, arriving along a direction $\vec{\omega}$, is the sum of two components. The first component is found by searching backward along $-\vec{\omega}$ until we find the nearest point $\mathbf{s}$ on any surface. We find the flux $\Gamma(\mathbf{s}, \vec{\omega})$ leaving that point along $\vec{\omega}$, and adjust its magnitude by the outscattering, emission, and absorption that happen to it along the way from $\mathbf{s}$ to $\mathbf{r}$. The other component is found by looking at every point $\mathbf{r} - \alpha\vec{\omega}$ on the line between $\mathbf{s}$ (where $\alpha = h$) and $\mathbf{r}$ (where $\alpha = 0$). At each point, we combine the volumetric emission at that point with any inscattered flux, and then we adjust the magnitude of that flux by the volumetric effects of outscattering, emission, and absorption as it travels from that point to $\mathbf{r}$. An excellent discussion of the assumptions inherent in any form of transport equation, and this equation in particular, may be found in Pomraning's text [342, pp. 47–49].

This equation really says nothing more nor less than Equation 12.64. The mechanical differences are two: Φ is expressed only in terms of itself and integrals containing it (there are no derivatives containing Φ), and the boundary conditions are contained in the equation itself, rather than as auxiliary constraints. In either case, our goal in image synthesis is to find the function Φ that satisfies the equation and boundary conditions, for that describes the distribution of light in a scene, which is what we need to know to render a picture. In fact, rendering algorithms are nothing but various methods to find approximate descriptions of Φ.

As we mentioned earlier, the integral form of the transport equation is valuable to us because it connects rendering with the deep and well-studied field of integral equations. Stating the transport equation, and establishing its connection to integral equation theory, were the main purposes of this chapter.

12.12 The Light Transport Equation

We have so far computed only "flux," and except for illustrative examples we have not tied down that flux to any particular interpretation. All of the theory in this chapter up to now is equally applicable to any phenomenon that can be modeled by particles that all travel at the same speed, and do not interact with each other. Not too many physical problems satisfy the latter criterion, but if we assume that collisions are very unlikely, then this model can simulate problems from automobile traffic to heat flow, and plasma dynamics to light transport. The last example is of course our primary interest in computer graphics.

All we need in order to tailor the transport equation to computer graphics is to replace the abstract notion of "particle" with the concrete notion of a "photon," and replace the flux with a more convenient term.

That term is the *radiance*, a unit of measurement of light energy. In the next chapter we will discuss the field of *radiometry*, which lays out the definitions for various measurements of light. We will then have the vocabulary to return to the transport equation and express it in terms that will be directly useful for image synthesis.

12.13 Further Reading

Transport theory is essentially a heuristic theory based on common sense and some simple physical observations. The most important of these are the linearity of surface and physical scattering, which are discussed at length by Preisendorfer in his book [347]. He offers an excellent development of the subject in physical terms. An excellent discussion of transport theory for graphics has been presented by Arvo [15]; much of this chapter follows that presentation. Another discussion of the meaning of the transport method is presented by Pomraning in his book [342].

Our rod model followed the presentation in Wing's book [482], which then goes on to develop the method of *invariant embedding*. This is an alternative route to finding the transport equations that has much to offer in terms of conceptual elegance.

Other discussions of transport theory may be found in the fundamental books by Duderstadt and Martin [129], Preisendorfer [347], Tait [431], Wing [482], Williams [481], and Case and Zweifel [75]. Computational methods are discussed in detail by Lenoble [266]. Scattering in particular is discussed in detail in Williams [481].

12.14 Exercises

Exercise 12.1

Derive the left-moving particle flux given by Equation 12.5.

Exercise 12.2

(Use a symbolic math program for this exercise.) If we assume constants for all the material and surface functions in Equations 12.27 and 12.28, then they admit an analytic solution.

(a) Replace all the material functions in Equations 12.27 and 12.28 with constants. Find closed-form expressions for $\Phi(x, \mathbf{L})$ and $\Phi(x, \mathbf{R})$ (don't worry about boundary conditions).

(b) Choose reasonable values for these constants and plot the fluxes as functions of x.

Exercise 12.3

We chose to define inscatter and outscatter by including all directions into which a particle might be scattered. An alternative is to restrict the domains of integration to only those directions not in Γ. Rewrite Equations 12.52 and 12.54 to express this other interpretation. Discuss whether this formulation has any advantage over the form used in the text.

Exercise 12.4

Discuss the physical interpretation of Equations 12.18 and 12.19 for $a = \pi/2\sigma$.

Exercise 12.5

Add an absorption probability σ_a to Equations 12.18 and 12.19. What is the critical value of a as a function of σ_a?

Exercise 12.6

Equation 12.56 contains a balance between the inscattering term Φ_i and the outscattering term Φ_o. When these terms were developed, we noted that they both included scattering events for particles inside the range Γ both before and after scattering. Show explicitly that these particles are not included in Equation 12.56 by writing both as the sum of those events where the particle is in Γ both before and after, and those events where it is not. Show that the common term cancels, and interpret each major step of the math in words.

Exercise 12.7

Equation 12.61 transforms a divergence expression into a gradient expression. The transformation asserts that for a direction $\vec{\omega}$ and vector function $\mathbf{F}$,

$$\nabla \cdot (\vec{\omega}\mathbf{F}) = \vec{\omega} \cdot \nabla\mathbf{F} \tag{12.100}$$

Prove this equality.

Exercise 12.8

There are five *Platonic solids*: these are polyhedra formed by multiple instances of a regular polygon such that every vertex is identical. In these problems, find the solid angle subtended by a single face of each polyhedron.

(a) The tetrahedron: four triangular faces.
(b) The cube: six square faces.
(c) The octahedron: eight triangular faces.
(d) The dodecahedron: twelve pentagonal faces.
(e) The icosahedron: twenty triangular faces.

Difficulties illuminate existence. But they must be fresh, and of high quality.

Tom Robbins
("Even Cowgirls Get the Blues," 1976)

13

RADIOMETRY

13.1 Introduction

The vocabulary of quantified light energy comes from the field of *radiometry*, which gives us the tools we need to tie the abstractions of the transport equation to real, physically measurable phenomena, and the definitions of terms most convenient for discussing that phenomena.

Actually, radiometry was preceded by many years by *photometry*, the study of how a human observer responds to light. As we saw in Unit I, the human visual system has a nonlinear response to light of different frequencies. When we want to discuss light energy in the abstract, we are best off with radiometry, which doesn't drag the human observer into the discussion. We will see that we can always convert a radiometric term to a photometric one when desired.

This chapter is based on the standard reference works by IES [221], Nicodemus et al. [318], and Siegel and Howell [406]. Some material is also based on Hanrahan [188] and Kajiya [235], which discuss radiometry for computer graphics.

13.2 Radiometric Conventions

Radiometric terms describe physical quantities; most radiometric terms can be measured in practice with lab instruments.

Every radiometric term that we will encounter is a function of wavelength, time, position, direction, and polarization, and will vary with each of these dimensions. So any radiometric value g would be fully written as $g(\lambda, t, \mathbf{r}, \vec{\omega}, \gamma)$, which is too bulky to manipulate conveniently. It is traditional in the literature to keep the notation simple and to suppress many of these dependencies. In particular, we will make three standard assumptions, all of which can be relaxed.

First, we will suppress any dependence on polarization.

Second, we will assume (as we did during the development of the transport equation) that energy of different wavelengths is *decoupled*. That is, the energy associated with some region of space, or surface, at wavelength λ_1 is independent of the energy at λ_2. This allows us to set the wavelength parameter to some constant in all of our discussions, so it need not be explicitly present in the equations. This assumption precludes modeling the important phenomenon of *phosphorescence*, where energy is absorbed at one wavelength and reradiated at another.

Third, we will assume that there is no time-dependent behavior in the system. Essentially we are assuming that light travels infinitely fast, and that we are dealing with a stable (or equilibrium) situation. This excludes *luminescence*, which is the phenomenon whereby a material radiates light energy that it absorbed at some previous time.

Although we are excluding phosphorescence and luminescence, it is only for notational simplicity during the development of our energy model. These phenomena will be easily reincorporated into the model in Chapter 17.

These simplifications allow us to get our terms down to five scalar variables, three for position and two for direction, which we can write conveniently as just two vector quantities. So in this chapter we will characterize light in terms of position $\mathbf{r}$ and direction $\vec{\omega}$.

13.3 Notation

The radiometric literature is filled with conflicting and confusing sets of definitions and units for measuring energy. Furthermore, much of that notation has shortcomings. A major disadvantage of the standard notation is that none of the measures are vectors. In fact, we will find some terms that appear identical, yet have different names depending on whether the quantity being measured is flowing toward or away from a surface, a distinction that would be handled easily by vector notation. Worse, this naming is not even consistent, so that even the most important term (radiance) must always be identified (usually by a subscript) as incident, or reflected with respect to a surface. Kajiya has pointed out that *projected areas* and *projected solid angles* are used in radiometry precisely to compensate for the lack of vector dot products [235].

I was very tempted to write the radiometry in this book with vector notation. But that would have only added yet another set of notation incompatible with all the others, and I felt that there were already too many competing standards. Instead, the terms and units in this book follow the conventions adopted by the American National Standards Institute (ANSI) [432] and the Illumination Engineering Society of North America (IES) [221]. The ANSI/IES notation is the closest thing we have to a standard, and familiarity with it allows us to read at least some of the radiometric literature. A complete summary of radiometric terms and units appears in Table 13.1.

This lack of explicit directional terms doesn't remove our need to discuss the direction of flowing energy, it just makes it harder. In this book we will use the bold, uppercase Greek phi ($\mathbf{\Phi}$) to refer to the direction of flowing energy; this reminds us that we are discussing a vector quantity with magnitude given by the flux $\Phi = ||\mathbf{\Phi}||$.

My one bow to notational revision is to avoid the use of conventional terms like A_p for projected area and Ω for projected solid angle, since they leave us completely uninformed about what direction the term is being projected into. Following the terminology of Chapter 12, if any term u is projected into a direction $\mathbf{F}$, we write that as $u^{\mathbf{F}}$. We will also continue to distinguish different types of solid angles as in the last chapter. To recapitulate, directions, differential solid angles, and finite solid angles are represented, respectively, by $\vec{\omega}$, $d\vec{\omega}$, and Γ.

All radiometric terms come in two flavors: *radiometric* and *spectral radiometric*. A *spectral radiometric* term describes some measure of light at a particular wavelength, such as $E(\lambda)$. The regular radiometric terms describe that measure as integrated over all wavelengths: $E = \int_0^\infty E(\lambda)\, d\lambda$. We can also think of each term as a function of an interval of the spectrum, e.g., $E = \int_{\lambda_1}^{\lambda_2} E(\lambda)\, d\lambda$. For simplicity, we will write most of our terms without the specificity of wavelength. Because we are assuming linearity of materials with respect to frequency, any radiometric quantity in this chapter may be interpreted in any of these ways.

13.4 Spherical Patches

We will often project solid angles and spherical patches onto the base of a hemisphere. We will use the vector notation $\mathbf{N}$ to refer to the normal at the base of the hemisphere. So if a patch dA is projected onto the base, we write that as $dA^{\mathbf{N}}$; a projected solid angle is $d\vec{\omega}^{\mathbf{N}}$ or $\Gamma^{\mathbf{N}}$.

We will make extensive use of differential and finite solid angles in this chapter. It will be useful to find the solid angle occupied by a small rectangular patch of

Definition	Name	Unit
Q_e	Radiant energy	joule (J)
Q_v	Luminous energy	talbot
$u_e = dU_e/dV$	Radiant flux density	joule/m^3
$u_v = dU_v/dV$	Luminous flux density	talbot/m^3
$\Phi_e = dU_e/dt$	Radiant power (flux)	watt (W) $\triangleq$ J/sec
$\Phi_v = dU_v/dt$	Luminous power (flux)	lumen (lm) $\triangleq$ talbot/sec
$\Phi_\lambda = d\Phi_e/d\lambda$	Spectral radiant power	W/m
$W_e = d\Phi_e/dA^\Phi$	Radiant power density	W/m^2
$W_v = d\Phi_v/dA^\Phi$	Luminous power density	lm/m^2
$W_\lambda = dW_e/dA^\Phi$	Spectral radiant power density	W/(m$^2 \cdot$ m)
$E_e = d\Phi_e/dA^\Phi$	Irradiance	W/m^2
$E_v = d\Phi_v/dA^\Phi$	Illuminance	lm/m^2
$E_\lambda = dE_e/dA^\Phi$	Spectral irradiance	W/(m$^2 \cdot$ m)
$M_e = d\Phi_e/dA^\Phi$	Radiant exitance	W/m^2
$M_v = d\Phi_v/dA^\Phi$	Luminous exitance	lm/m^2
$M_\lambda = dM_e/dA^\Phi$	Spectral radiant exitance	W/(m$^2 \cdot$ m)
$I_e = d\Phi_e/d\vec{\omega}$	Radiant intensity	W/sr
$I_v = d\Phi_v/d\vec{\omega}$	Luminous intensity	candela (cd) $\triangleq$ lm/sr
$I_\lambda = dI_e/d\vec{\omega}$	Spectral radiant intensity	W/(sr $\cdot$ m)
$L_e = d\Phi_e/(d\vec{\omega}\, dA^\Phi)$	Radiance	W/(sr $\cdot$ m^2)
$L_v = d\Phi_v/(d\vec{\omega}\, dA^\Phi)$	Luminance	lm/(sr $\cdot$ m^2)
$L_\lambda = dL_e\, d\lambda$	Spectral radiance	W/(sr $\cdot$ m^3)

TABLE 13.1
Radiometric, spectral radiometric, and photometric terms.

the sphere. Consider Figure 13.1, where patch dA with dimensions $d\theta$ by $d\psi$ is illustrated. The vertical side of this patch subtends an arc of length $d\theta$ on a great circle of radius r, so its length is $r\,d\theta$. The horizontal side subtends an arc of length $d\psi$, but the radius of that circle is $r \sin\theta$, as shown in the figure. Thus the area of this patch is given by the product

$$dA = (r \sin\theta\, d\psi)(r\, d\theta) = r^2 \sin\theta\, d\theta\, d\psi \tag{13.1}$$

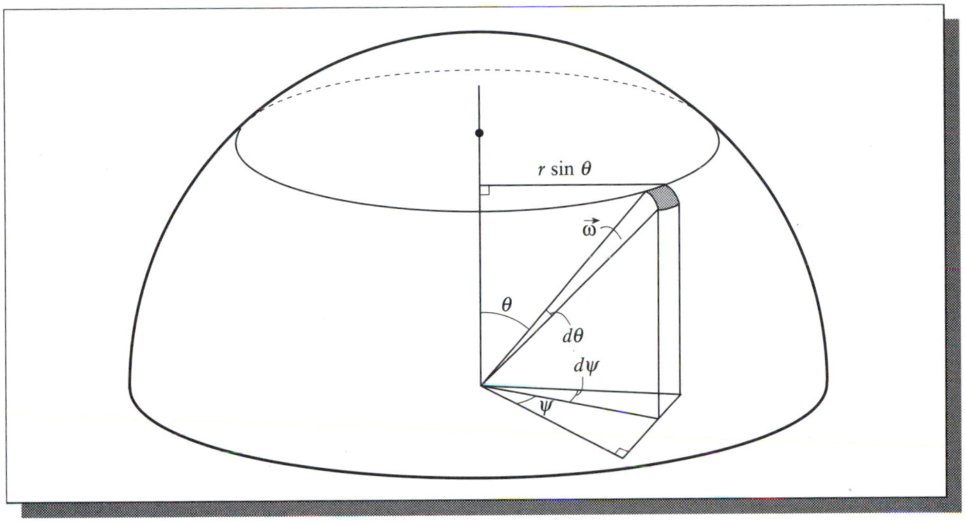

FIGURE 13.1

A differential patch dA and its associated solid angle $\vec{\omega}$.

The differential solid angle associated with this patch is then the area of the patch divided by the sphere's radius:

$$d\vec{\omega} = \frac{dA}{r^2} = \sin\theta \, d\theta \, d\psi \tag{13.2}$$

We can now find the projected differential area and projected differential solid angle of this patch by projecting both quantities onto the plane of the hemisphere (which is parallel to the **N** vector). The projected area $dA^{\mathbf{N}}$ is

$$dA^{\mathbf{N}} = r^2 \, \sin\theta \cos\theta \, d\theta \, d\psi \tag{13.3}$$

and the projected differential solid angle $d\vec{\omega}^{\mathbf{N}}$ is

$$d\vec{\omega}^{\mathbf{N}} = \sin\theta \cos\theta \, d\theta \, d\psi \tag{13.4}$$

13.5 Radiometric Terms

We begin with the basic unit of energy: *radiant energy* is denoted Q, which is measured in *joules* (J). In terms of our particle model, each particle may be thought of as carrying some number of joules of energy.

Recall from Equation 11.28 the basic energy-frequency relationship

$$E = h\nu \qquad [J] \tag{13.5}$$

which specifies an energy E for every frequency ν.

The amount of energy per unit volume may be described by the *radiant energy density* w:

$$w = Q/V \qquad \left[\frac{J}{m^3}\right] \tag{13.6}$$

This can be thought of as the combined energy of each photon in the volume, divided by the size of the volume.

We now turn our attention to measures of *moving* energy. As we saw in the last chapter, the energy flowing through a surface per unit time is called the *flux*. In radiometry, it is called *radiant power* or *radiant flux* Φ at that surface:

$$\Phi = dQ/dt \qquad \left[W = watt \triangleq \frac{J}{s}\right] \tag{13.7}$$

The unit of radiant flux is the *watt* (W), which is one joule per second.

The interaction of radiant energy and matter requires a description of the flow of energy toward or away from a surface. A convenient measure of energy flow is to find the incident or departing flux per unit of surface area. This measure is known as *radiant flux area density* u:

$$u = d\Phi/dA \qquad \left[\frac{W}{m^2}\right] \tag{13.8}$$

The area dA used in the definition of flux density need not be part of an actual surface; indeed, dA can simply be an imaginary 2D surface in space. If the flux over the region is uniform over a finite surface, we may drop the differentials and evaluate $u = \Phi/A$. Note that we have used dA and not its projected area.

Radiant flux density is a useful measure. But because it is a scalar, we don't know whether the flux is arriving at a surface or departing from it. Two terms similar to radiant flux density allow us to make this distinction concrete. If energy is *arriving* at a surface, we call it the *irradiance* E:

$$E = d\Phi/dA \qquad \left[\frac{W}{m^2}\right] \tag{13.9}$$

The measure of flux *leaving* a surface is called the *radiant exitance* M (in computer graphics, this quantity is also called the *radiosity* B):

$$B = M = d\Phi/dA \qquad \left[\frac{W}{m^2}\right] \tag{13.10}$$

The definitions of radiant flux density, irradiance, and radiance were all in terms of a piece of surface area. Our definitions require that the source have some area, differential or finite. When we want to represent a point source, the area goes to zero and we have a problem.

An alternative is to define the ratio of flux with respect to solid angle rather than area; this then works well for describing radiation arriving at or leaving from point sources. We may then define a term corresponding to exitance that finds the rate of change of flux from a point as a function of solid angle. This measure of radiant energy leaving a point, in the direction $\mathbf{\Phi}$, per unit solid angle, is called the *intensity* I:

$$I = d\Phi / d\vec{\omega} \qquad \left[\frac{W}{sr}\right] \tag{13.11}$$

An alternative interpretation of intensity is that it describes the radiant energy leaving a point per unit area at unit distance. Note that the word "intensity" is highly overloaded in computer graphics, used casually to refer to everything from the power of a light source to its perceived brightness.

Finally, we can combine the ideas of solid angle and area into what is perhaps the most important radiometric term. The power arriving at or leaving from a surface, per unit solid angle and per unit projected area, is called the *radiance* L:

$$L = \frac{d^2\Phi}{dA^{\mathbf{\Phi}}\, d\vec{\omega}} = \frac{d^2\Phi}{dA\, d\vec{\omega}^{\mathbf{\Phi}}} \qquad \left[\frac{W}{sr \cdot m^2}\right] \tag{13.12}$$

Notice that we need to use either the projected solid angle or the projected area when working with radiance; in other words, we have introduced a cosine term.

The radiance may alternatively be expressed in terms of the intensity, irradiance, or the exitance:

$$L = \frac{dI}{dA^{\mathbf{\Phi}}} = \frac{dE}{d\vec{\omega}^{\mathbf{\Phi}}} = \frac{dM}{d\vec{\omega}^{\mathbf{\Phi}}} \qquad \left[\frac{W}{sr \cdot m^2}\right] \tag{13.13}$$

When we use the intensity (or irradiance or exitance) to find radiance, we need to use a projected value to get the cosine into the expression. We will see the value of defining radiance in this way in Section 13.6.1.

The radiometric definitions presented here are summarized in Table 13.2.

13.6 Radiometric Relations

The definitions in the previous section may be linked to provide useful relationships between a differential *source* patch dS radiating energy and a differential *receiver* patch dR upon which some of that energy falls, as shown in Figure 13.2. The patches have normals $\mathbf{N}_S$ and $\mathbf{N}_R$, respectively.

Radiant term	Symbol	Definition	Unit
Energy	Q	—	J
Energy density	w	dQ/dV	J/m^3
Power (flux)	Φ	dQ/dt	W
Flux area density	u	$d\Phi/dA$	W/m^2
Intensity	I	$d\Phi/d\vec{\omega}$	W/sr
Exitance (radiosity)	M	$d\Phi/dA$	W/m^2
Irradiance	E	$d\Phi/dA$	W/m^2
Radiance	L	$d^2\Phi/(dA\,d\vec{\omega}\cos\theta)$ $= dI/dA^{\Phi}$ $= dE/d\vec{\omega}^{\Phi}$	$W/(m^2 \cdot sr)$

TABLE 13.2
Radiometric definitions.

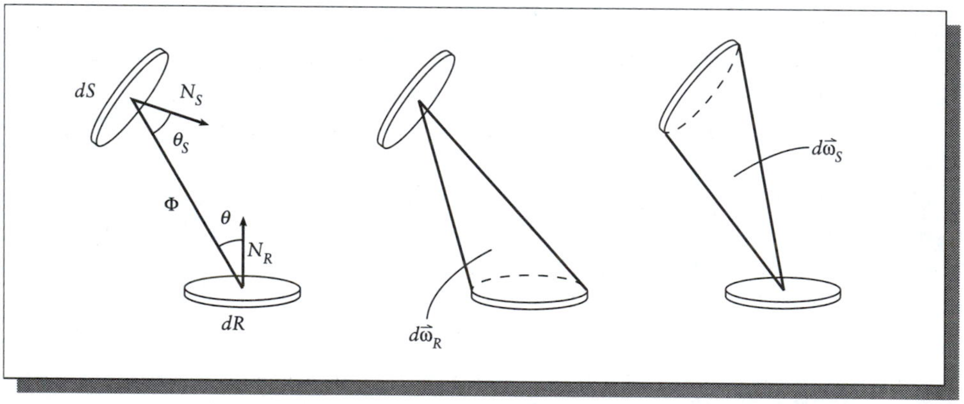

FIGURE 13.2
Patch geometry.

The vector $\mathbf{\Phi}(S, R)$ connects a point $S \in dS$ to a point $R \in dR$. Because both dS and dR are small, the three values $||\mathbf{\Phi}(S, R)||$, $\mathbf{\Phi}(S, R) \cdot \mathbf{N}_S$, and $\mathbf{\Phi}(S, R) \cdot \mathbf{N}_R$ can all be considered constants over all points R and S. So we simply write the vector $\mathbf{\Phi}$ to represent the transfer from S to R. The patch dS presents a projected area $dS^{\mathbf{\Phi}}$ and occupies a solid angle $d\vec{\omega}_S$ from any point $R \in dR$, and similarly for dR.

Consider the term $dA^{\mathbf{\Phi}}\, d\vec{\omega}$ in the definition of radiance in Equation 13.12. In terms of the transfer from dS to dR, we would have $dS^{\mathbf{\Phi}}\, d\vec{\omega}_R$. Let's expand this term, writing $A(dS)$ and $A(dR)$ to refer to the areas of the patches, r to represent the distance between them, and θ_S and θ_R to refer to the angle made by the normal to each patch with the transfer vector $\mathbf{\Phi}$.

$$\begin{aligned} dS^{\mathbf{\Phi}}\, d\vec{\omega}_R &= [A(dS)\cos\theta_S]\left[A(dR)\cos\theta_R/r^2\right] \\ &= \left[A(dS)\cos\theta_S/r^2\right][A(dR)\cos\theta_R] \\ &= dR^{\mathbf{\Phi}}\, d\vec{\omega}_S \end{aligned} \tag{13.14}$$

The substitutions for the solid angles here used the approximation that for a small patch at radius r, the solid angle subtended by the patch is nearly the same as the projected area of the patch divided by r^2. We call Equation 13.14 the *principle of reciprocity of transfer volume*. It says that the product of the size of a projected patch and the solid angle occupied by another patch is the same if the calculation is formed by reversing the labels on the patches.

We can use this principle immediately. From the definition of radiance in Equation 13.12, we can write an expression for the incident radiance L_R falling on dR in terms of the incident flux Φ_R:

$$dL_R = \frac{d\Phi_R}{d\vec{\omega}_R\, dS^{\mathbf{\Phi}}} \tag{13.15}$$

Using the principle of reciprocity of transfer volume, we find

$$d\Phi_R = dL_R\, d\vec{\omega}_R\, dS^{\mathbf{\Phi}} = dL_R\, dR^{\mathbf{\Phi}}\, d\vec{\omega}^S \tag{13.16}$$

Equations 13.16 are called the *flux-radiance relations* [235].

Combining Equation 13.16 with the definition of irradiance in Equation 13.9, we can equate equivalent expressions for $d\Phi$ and solve for the irradiance in terms of the radiance:

$$\begin{aligned} E_R\, dR^{\mathbf{\Phi}} &= d\Phi_R = dL\, dR^{\mathbf{\Phi}}\, d\vec{\omega}_S \\ E_R &= d\vec{\omega}_S\, dL \end{aligned} \tag{13.17}$$

Equation 13.17 is the *irradiance-radiance relation*. It tells us that the irradiance E_R falling on a receiving patch dR due to a source patch dS is equal to the radiance dL of the source times the differential solid angle $d\vec{\omega}_S$ of the source as seen from the receiver. This is an important relationship, because we will find it useful to express the outgoing radiance at a point in terms of the incident irradiance.

13.6.1 Discussion of Radiance

Radiance is a fundamental measure in image synthesis; although it's flux that actually measures the power moving through the environment, many synthesis methods are based on the radiance because it is more convenient. It is important to stop for a moment and lock down the interpretation of radiance.

The definition of radiance is similar in spirit to intensity and irradiance, but it contains an extra cosine term the others do not. To recapitulate, the radiance leaving a point $\mathbf{r}$ on a differential source patch dS into a solid angle $d\vec{\omega}$ around direction $\vec{\omega}$, making an angle θ_s with the source patch, is

$$L(\mathbf{r}, \vec{\omega}) = \frac{d^2\Phi(\mathbf{r}, \vec{\omega})}{d\vec{\omega}\, dS\ cos\theta_s} = \frac{dI(\mathbf{r}, \vec{\omega})}{dS \cos\theta_s} = \frac{dE(\mathbf{r}, \vec{\omega})}{d\vec{\omega} \cos\theta_s} \tag{13.18}$$

To see where the cosine comes from, let's forget about radiance for a moment and imagine a density function of position and direction $P(\mathbf{r}, \vec{\omega})$, defined over the source patch dS. When we integrate this function over some volume of phase space (that is, some combination of source points and directions), we will get the number of photons that will be generated by the surface into that region of phase space. Since we will assume everything is a differential, we can find this total flux by simply scaling the function $P(\mathbf{r}, \vec{\omega})$ by the volume $d\mathbf{r}\, d\vec{\omega}$ of phase space:

$$\Phi(\mathbf{r}, \vec{\omega}) = P(\mathbf{r}, \vec{\omega})\, d\mathbf{r}\, d\vec{\omega} \tag{13.19}$$

Assuming that we know P, all that's left to find the flux is to find an expression for the phase-space volume $d\mathbf{r}\, d\vec{\omega}$. Consider the transmission of flux from a differential source patch dS to a differential receiver patch dR, as shown in Figure 13.3; the vector $\mathbf{V}$ joins the centers of the two patches. The receiver is perpendicular to $\mathbf{V}$, though the source is not. The two patches define a tube in space, which contains the flux. In the figure we see $d\vec{\omega}_s$, the solid angle of the source as seen from the receiver. The flux flows through this solid angle to every point on the receiver; thus, the phase-space volume of the tube is the size of the solid angle times the size of the receiver:

$$d\mathbf{r}\, d\vec{\omega} = dR\, d\vec{\omega}_s \tag{13.20}$$

The total flux is then

$$\Phi(\mathbf{r}, \vec{\omega}) = P(\mathbf{r}, \vec{\omega})\, dR\, d\vec{\omega}_s \tag{13.21}$$

Now suppose that the receiver is replaced by a different receiving patch, dR'. The new patch has the same center point as the old one, so the line $\mathbf{V}'$ joining it to dS is the same as the old $\mathbf{V}$. The new patch makes an angle of $\theta_{R'}$ with this center line, and it has just the right size to fit in the old tube; that is, its projected area is the same as the area of the perpendicular patch: $dR' \cos\theta_{R'} = dR$. In other words, the phase-space volume is conserved:

$$dR\, d\vec{\omega}_s = dR' \cos\theta_{R'}\, d\vec{\omega}_s \tag{13.22}$$

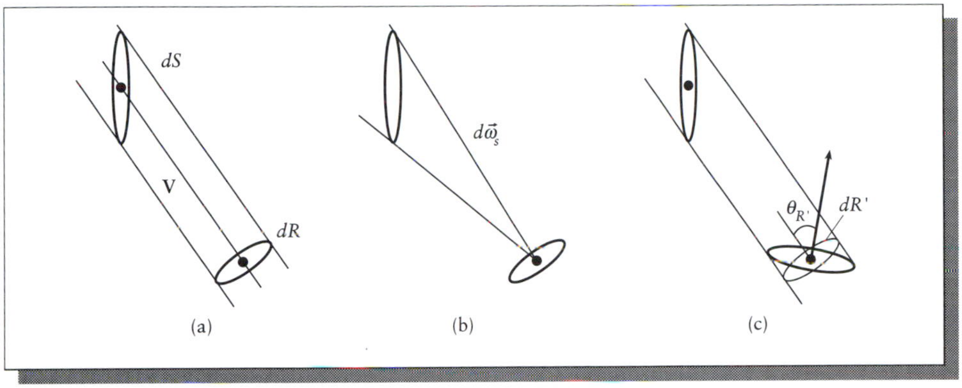

FIGURE 13.3

Transfer of energy from a source to a receiver. (a) The solid containing dS and dR. (b) The solid angle $d\vec{\omega}_s$ occupied by dS as seen from dR. (c) A different receiver dR'.

so we have the satisfying result that the flux traveling down the tube doesn't change just because we've replaced the receiver:

$$\Phi(\mathbf{r},\vec{\omega}) = P(\mathbf{r},\vec{\omega})\, dR' \cos\theta_{R'}\, d\vec{\omega}_s \tag{13.23}$$

In general, then, the density function that we integrate to find the flux traveling from dS to dR is

$$P(\mathbf{r},\vec{\omega}) = \frac{d^2\Phi(\mathbf{r},\vec{\omega})}{(dR\cos\theta_R)\, d\vec{\omega}_s} = \frac{d^2\Phi(\mathbf{r},\vec{\omega})}{dR^{\mathbf{V}}\, d\vec{\omega}_s} \tag{13.24}$$

This is just the radiance L. To see the definition in its traditional form, expand the solid angle and regroup:

$$\begin{aligned} L(\mathbf{r},\vec{\omega}) &= \frac{d^2\Phi(\mathbf{r},\vec{\omega})}{dR^{\mathbf{V}}\, d\vec{\omega}_s} \\ &= \frac{d^2\Phi(\mathbf{r},\vec{\omega})}{(dR\cos\theta_R)(dS\cos\theta_s/|\mathbf{V}|^2)} \\ &= \frac{d^2\Phi(\mathbf{r},\vec{\omega})}{(dS\cos\theta_s)(dR\cos\theta_R/|\mathbf{V}|^2)} \\ &= \frac{d^2\Phi(\mathbf{r},\vec{\omega})}{dS^{\mathbf{V}}\, d\vec{\omega}_r} \end{aligned} \tag{13.25}$$

where $|\mathbf{V}|$ is the length of the line joining the two patches, and $d\vec{\omega}_r$ is the solid angle of the receiver as seen from the patch. This second form involving the projected

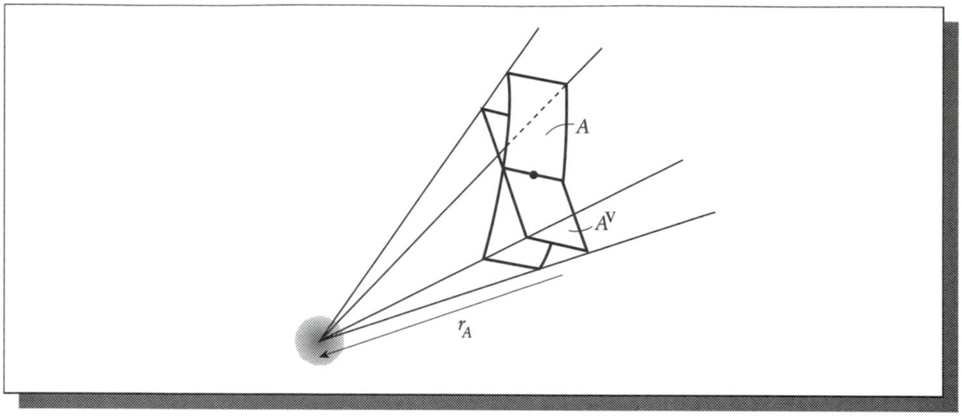

FIGURE 13.4
A patch projected onto a point source.

angle of the source can be a bit confusing, because there doesn't seem to be any reason to project the source patch at all. It's simply the result of an algebraic shuffle; the first form has the geometric interpretation that the radiance is that function of the surface point and direction, which when multiplied by a differential volume of phase space around that point and direction gives the flux emitted into that volume.

We can now make an important observation. We first note that the flux contains an inverse-square term buried within the solid angle, which can be seen from the third line of Equation 13.25:

$$L(\mathbf{r}, \vec{\omega}) = \frac{d^2\Phi(\mathbf{r}, \vec{\omega})r^2}{dR^{\mathbf{V}}\,dS^{\mathbf{V}}} \tag{13.26}$$

where we have renamed the distance $r = |\mathbf{v}|$, and written it in the numerator. The presence of this term is no accident. Consider an isotropic point source of light emitting a total flux Φ_t. Because the source is isotropic, the same flux is distributed equally over the surface of all spheres around the point source. Suppose we have a patch at a distance r_A, and that its projected area onto the source is dA, as in Figure 13.4. Then the flux falling on this patch is $\Phi_t\, dA/r_A^2$ (assuming that the medium is a vacuum). Note that since the radiance $L(\mathbf{r}, \vec{\omega})$ from this source is the same in all directions, and there's only the one point at the source, $L(\mathbf{r}, \vec{\omega}) = L$.

Computing the radiance L from this source, we find

$$\begin{aligned} L &= \frac{(d^2\Phi_t/r_A^2)r_A^2}{dR^{\mathbf{V}}dS^{\mathbf{V}}} \\ &= \frac{d^2\Phi_t}{dR^{\mathbf{V}}dS^{\mathbf{V}}} \end{aligned} \tag{13.27}$$

Notice that the distance term r has dropped out! As the patch recedes, the power it receives falls off with the distance squared, but the definition of radiance compensates exactly. This works fine for any point source, or any differential or finite source far enough away that we can consider it a point.

Although it is flux that is actually transmitted from one patch to another, we know that we can find the flux from the radiance at the source and the geometry of the two patches; therefore, we often sidestep the mechanics and speak of radiance as being transmitted from one patch to another.

The fact that radiance doesn't vary with distance (in a vacuum) is essential to image synthesis; if we didn't have a radiometric quantity with this property we would have had to invent one. Shirley sums up this essential observation in *the ray law* [402]; which we have adapted here:

> **The ray law:** The radiance of a point source onto a patch is invariant as the patch is moved radially with respect to the source.

We will often approximate the flux radiated by a small source patch onto a receiving patch by finding the radiance at a particular point on the source and then multiplying by the volume of phase space defined by the geometry of the two patches. We can find this representative source point by *ray-tracing* (discussed in Chapter 19). If we imagine that the ray is a conduit of information from the source to the receiver, then the information flowing along that ray is radiance. From the radiance at the source and the geometry, we can find the flux arriving at the receiver.

13.6.2 Spectral Radiometry

Recall that each of the radiometric terms introduced in the last section may be evaluated at a specific wavelength. It is sometimes useful to explicitly refer to the value at some particular wavelength λ; thus, irradiance E might actually be written $E(\lambda)$ or E_λ.

When a radiometric term is written at a specific wavelength, it is called a *spectral radiometric term*. Table 13.1 defines each of the spectral radiometric terms. In general, the units of these terms are the units of the radiometric term divided by [m], the unit of length.

13.6.3 Photometry

The human visual system is only responsive to energy in a certain range of the electromagnetic spectrum. Even within that range, the human visual response is not uniform. The concepts of radiometry may be adjusted to represent the perceptions of a statistically standard human observer to objective radiometric quantities; the new terms are described as *photometric* terms, and are distinguished from their radiometric counterparts by appending the subscript v.

Recall from Unit I that the human visual system does not respond equally to all radiation. In particular, the average person is most responsive to signals that arrive in a frequency range from about 380 to 780 nm, sometimes called the *visual band.* This definition includes two approximations. The first is the use of an "average observer," which is a statistical average built from measured data gathered from experiments on human volunteers. Some people are responsive to frequencies outside of this band, and others are not responsive to everything in the band. Nevertheless, the abstraction of an average person is useful in practice. The second approximation is to state that the visual system is "not responsive" outside of these limits. In fact, the response of the visual system tapers toward the edges of this band, and these wavelengths represent somewhat arbitrary cutoff points in the magnitude of the response.

Nevertheless, by international agreement a curve has been defined called the *photopic spectral luminous efficiency* of the human visual system; it is usually written as $V(\lambda)$. This curve is plotted in Figure 13.5, and some values are tabulated in Table G.4 in Appendix G.

By accepting this curve as the response of the human visual system, we can find the perceived brightness by an observer in response to an input signal $S(\lambda)$ by modulating the signal by the response curve and integrating the resulting perceived energy: $\int S(\lambda)V(\lambda)\,d\lambda$.

Modulation of light energy by the spectral response curve forms the basis of a branch of radiometry called *photometry*. Photometric terms are simply radiometric terms weighted by $V(\lambda)$ and then scaled to a new set of units. Each of these terms replaces the word "radiant" with "luminous" in its name, and use the subscript v in its symbol. When radiometric and photometric quantities both appear in an equation, we will label the former with the subscript e.

Luminous energy is denoted Q_v and is measured in *talbots*. For photopic (color) vision, luminous energy is found from the expression

$$Q_v = K_m \int V(\lambda)\, Q_e(\lambda)\, d\lambda \tag{13.28}$$

By international agreement, the conversion factor K_m is defined as 680 lumen/watt (the lumen is defined below as the unit of luminous flux). The density of luminous

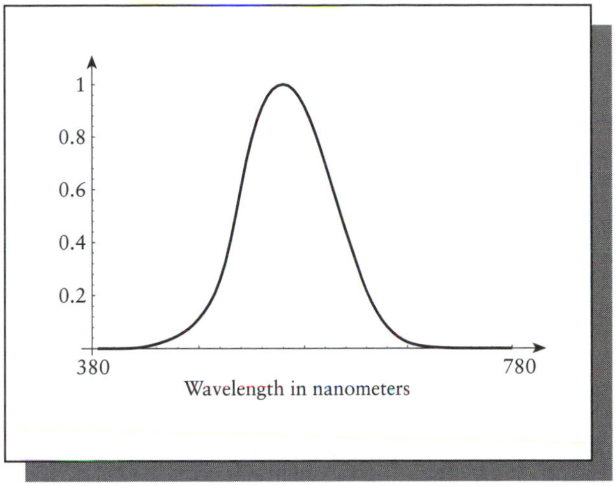

FIGURE 13.5
Spectral efficiency curve.

energy in some volume may be measured by the luminous energy density:

$$w_v = Q_v/V \qquad \left[\frac{\text{talbot}}{m^3}\right] \tag{13.29}$$

The transport of luminous energy over time defines luminous power or luminous flux Φ_v:

$$\Phi_v = dQ_v/dt \qquad \left[\frac{\text{talbot}}{s} \equiv \text{lumen} = \text{lm}\right] \tag{13.30}$$

The unit of radiant flux is the *lumen* (lm), which is one talbot per second.

The other photometric terms parallel the radiometric ones and are summarized in Table 13.1. We have used those terms recommended by the ANSI and IES. Table 13.3 lists some of the other units and their conversion factors to those presented above.

13.7 Reflectance

> *Reflection* is the process by which electromagnetic flux (power), incident on a stationary surface or medium, leaves that surface or medium from the incident side without change in frequency; *reflectance* is the fraction of the incident flux that is reflected. (Nicodemus et al. [318])

Illuminance E_v	$1\ \mathrm{lm/m^2}$	$= 1\ lux(lx) = 9.29 \times 10^{-2}$ foot-candles
		$= 1 \times 10^{-4}$ phot
		$= 1 \times 10^{-1}$ milliphot
		$= 1 \times 10^{3}$ nox
Luminous intensity I_v	$1\ \mathrm{lm/sr}$	= 1 candela (cd) = 1 candle
		= 1.04 carcel
		= 1.11 hefner
Luminance L_v	$1\ \mathrm{cd/m^2}$	= 1 nit
		$= 1 \times 10^{-4}$ stilb
		$= 9.29 \times 10^{-3}$ cd/ft^2
		$= 6.45 \times 10^{-4}$ cd/in^2
		$= \pi$ blondel
		$= \pi$ apostilb
		$= \pi \times 10^{-4}$ lambert
		$= \pi \times 10^{-1}$ millilambert
		$= 2.92 \times 10^{-1}$ foot-lambert
		$= 2.92 \times 10^{-1}$ equivalent foot-candles (eqv)
		$= 3.2 \times 10^{4}$ skot
		$= 2.92 \times 10^{2}$ glim

TABLE 13.3
Other terms used in radiometric literature. *Source:* Data from ANSI [432] and IES [221].

This definition of reflectance makes concrete our intuitive concept of reflection as the percentage of light "bounced" off a surface. Just as with volumes, we say that a surface *scatters* the incident light by changing its direction; in this case, from toward the surface to away from it.

The goal of this section is to define a function that clearly establishes this relationship for different classes of material. The function will return a dimensionless number that relates the output flux to the input flux given the geometry of measurement and the reflectance properties of the surface. The development in this section follows Nicodemus et al. [318]. We will actually derive three functions in this section: the *BRDF* f_r, which describes the ratio of reflected radiance to incident radiance; the *reflectance* ρ, which describes the ratio of reflected flux to incident flux; and the *reflectance factor* R, which describes the reflectance of a material with respect to a

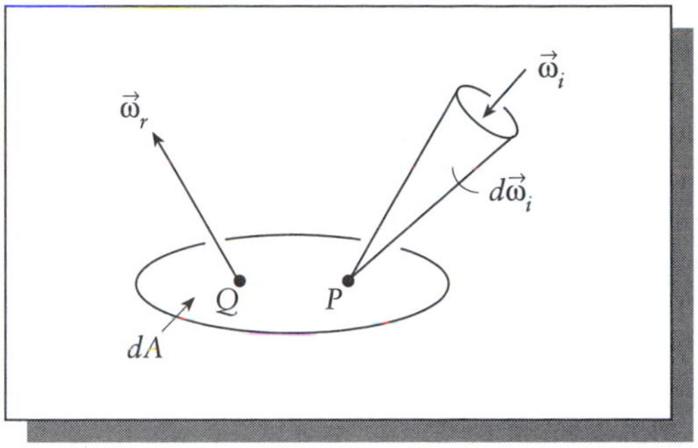

FIGURE 13.6
A simple geometry for deriving reflection.

perfect diffuse reflector. In Chapter 15 we will use these functions to define shading algorithms, which provide the boundary conditions for the light transport equation.

In this chapter we consider only reflectance. When light passes through a material, it is said to be *transmitted*; this effect is called *transmission* of *transmittance*. In general, transmission is very similar to reflectance with a couple of minor additional wrinkles. It is traditional to study reflectance in some detail, and leave transmission out of the discussion entirely until it can be easily included. Here we follow that model and discuss only reflection.

13.7.1 The BRDF f_r

We begin with the diagram of Figure 13.6, which shows some energy arriving at point P on a differential surface dA through an incident differential solid angle $d\vec{\omega}_i$, pointing in direction $\vec{\omega}_i$. We would like to find an expression for the differential radiance dL^r reflected by the surface from point Q into a direction $\vec{\omega}_r$ due to the incident flux $d\Phi_i$ arriving through the differential solid angle $d\vec{\omega}_i$.

In general, the reflected radiance dL^r will be proportional to the incident flux Φ^i:

$$dL^r \propto d\Phi^i \tag{13.31}$$

Spelling out all the dependencies, and naming the proportionality constant S, we find

$$dL^r(d\vec{\omega}_i, P; \vec{\omega}_r, Q) = S(d\vec{\omega}_i, P; \vec{\omega}_r, Q)\, d\Phi^i(d\vec{\omega}_i, P) \tag{13.32}$$

Note that the illumination arrives through a differential solid angle $d\vec{\omega}_i$, but we are measuring the emitted flux only along a direction $\vec{\omega}_r$. Also remember that all of our equations may be interpreted for a specific wavelength, or a finite or half-infinite interval of wavelengths.

The constant of proportionality S depends on the two vectors $\vec{\omega}_i$ and $\vec{\omega}_r$, and the points P and Q of incidence and reflection. The function S is called the *bidirectional scattering-surface reflectance-distribution function*, or BSSRDF [318]. The adjectives refer respectively to the fact that the function depends on both directions, it tells how light is scattered (or reflected) at a surface, and it is a distribution function, in the sense that it may contain distribution (or generalized) functions such as the Dirac delta function $\delta(x)$.

The BSSRDF is a very high-level description of reflection. However, the BSSRDF is a difficult function to measure, store, and compute with, due to its dependence on four vector variables. We will now make some simplifying assumptions about the surface and its illumination that give us a more computationally convenient expression, following Nicodemus [318].

First, we assume that the incident radiance $L^i(\vec{\omega}_i, P)$ has the same cross section over all points on A. That is, for any direction $\vec{\omega} \in d\vec{\omega}_i$, the radiances $L^i(\vec{\omega}_i, P_1)$ and $L^i(\vec{\omega}_i, P_2)$ are the same for every P_1 and P_2. Then we can write the incident radiance from direction $\vec{\omega}$ simply as $L^i(\vec{\omega})$, and leave out the argument P.

It will be useful to express the incident flux Φ in Equation 13.32 in terms of the irradiance E. Here we write the irradiance $E(d\vec{\omega}_i)$ to indicate that it is a function of the incident solid angle. Then we can write the flux as

$$\begin{aligned} d\Phi^i(d\vec{\omega}_i, P) &= dE(d\vec{\omega}_i)\, dA \\ &= L^i(d\vec{\omega}_i)\, d\vec{\omega}_i^{\mathbf{N}}\, dA \end{aligned} \tag{13.33}$$

Since $d\Phi$ strikes each differential area $dA \in A$, the total reflected radiance dL^r comes from integrating $d\Phi^i(d\vec{\omega}_i, P)$ over all points P in A:

$$\begin{aligned} dL^r(d\vec{\omega}_i; \vec{\omega}_r, Q) &= \int_{P\in A} dL^r(d\vec{\omega}_i, P; \vec{\omega}_r, Q) \\ &= \int_{P\in A} S(d\vec{\omega}_i, P; \vec{\omega}_r, Q)\, d\Phi^i(d\vec{\omega}_i, P) \\ &= \int_{P\in A} S(d\vec{\omega}_i, P; \vec{\omega}_r, Q)\, dE(d\vec{\omega}_i)\, dA \\ &= dE(d\vec{\omega}_i) \int_{P\in A} S(d\vec{\omega}_i, P; \vec{\omega}_r, Q)\, dA \end{aligned} \tag{13.34}$$

where we have used the fact that since L^i is independent of position, so is dE.

Now assume that the material is *isotropic*. That is, S depends only on the angle between the incident energy and the normal, so S is rotationally symmetric about the normal. Symbolically, $S(\theta, \psi) = S(\theta, \psi')$ for any ψ', as in Figure 13.7(a).

Furthermore, if the material is *uniform*, then its properties everywhere on A are the same; that is, the position of P doesn't matter. Therefore the only relationship

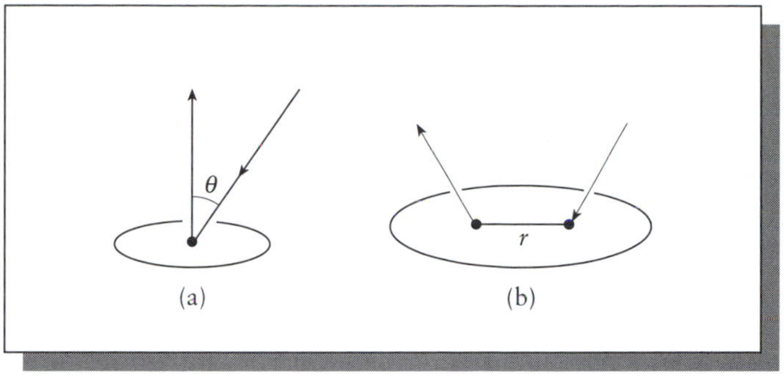

FIGURE 13.7
(a) Isotropy. (b) The distance between P and Q.

between P and Q that matters is the distance r between them, as in Figure 13.7(b). So we can eliminate P and Q from our expressions, leaving only r:

$$\begin{aligned} dL^r(d\vec{\omega}_i, \vec{\omega}_r) &= dE(d\vec{\omega}_i) \int_A S(d\vec{\omega}_i, \vec{\omega}_r, r)\, dA \\ &= dE(d\vec{\omega}_i) f(d\vec{\omega}_i, \vec{\omega}_r, r) \end{aligned} \tag{13.35}$$

where

$$f(d\vec{\omega}_i, \vec{\omega}_r, r) = \int_A S(d\vec{\omega}_i, \vec{\omega}_r, r)\, dA \tag{13.36}$$

for $r = |P - Q|$. The most common notation for this function rolls the r argument into the name of the function, giving us

$$f_r(d\vec{\omega}_i, \vec{\omega}_r) = \int_A S(d\vec{\omega}_i, \vec{\omega}_r, r)\, dA \tag{13.37}$$

If we now allow $\vec{\omega}_r$ to become a differential solid angle $d\vec{\omega}_r$, we can write this function as $f_r(d\vec{\omega}_i \to d\vec{\omega}_r)$. This expresses the proportion of incident flux reflected from $d\vec{\omega}_i$ into $d\vec{\omega}_r$ over all of A. Solving Equation 13.35 for f (now f_r) gives us

$$f_r(d\vec{\omega}_i \to d\vec{\omega}_r) = \frac{dL^r(d\vec{\omega}_i, d\vec{\omega}_r, E)}{dE(d\vec{\omega}_i)} \tag{13.38}$$

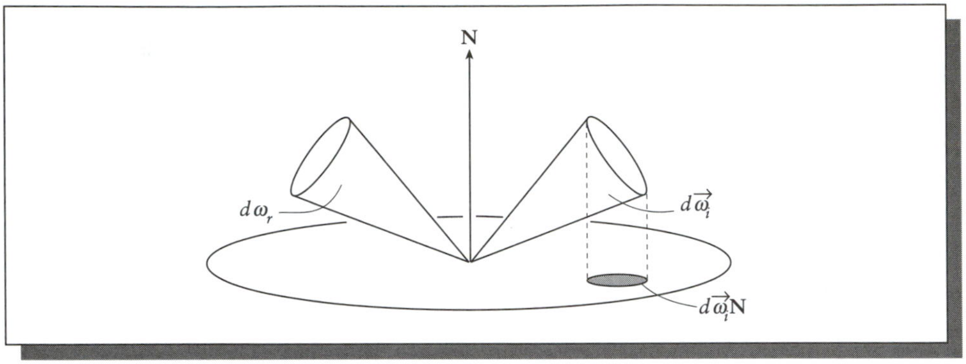

FIGURE 13.8
Geometry for the BRDF.

or, in terms of incident radiance,

$$f_r(d\vec{\omega}_i \to d\vec{\omega}_r) \stackrel{\triangle}{=} \frac{dL^r(d\vec{\omega}_i, d\vec{\omega}_r, E)}{L^i(d\vec{\omega}_i)\, d\vec{\omega}_i^{\mathrm{N}}} \qquad \left[\frac{1}{sr}\right] \tag{13.39}$$

The function f_r defined by Equation 13.39 is called the *bidirectional reflectance distribution function* (BRDF); its geometry is illustrated in Figure 13.8. The BRDF is the fundamental description of how a surface reflects. It characterizes the surface's reflectivity in terms of the incident solid angle, the incident light, and the reflected solid angle. Because the incident radiation can come from a solid angle with no size (that is, just a ray), the BRDF can take on any value from 0 to infinity. We will remedy this problem shortly.

There are two simple but important properties of the BRDF that should be kept in mind when working with these functions.

The first is *reciprocity*, which simply states that if we reverse the roles of the incident and reflected energy, nothing changes. That is, if we send some amount of energy through solid angle Γ_i and measure the energy radiated into solid angle Γ_r, then if we send that same amount *into* solid angle Γ_r, we will measure the same propagated energy coming out of Γ_i. This rule was first stated by Helmholtz and is sometimes known as the *Helmholtz reciprocity rule*.

The second important property of the BRDF is that it must be *normalized*. That is, the total energy propagated in response to some irradiation must be no more than the energy received, and usually will be less. Although one can build mechanical devices that implement arbitrary BRDFs [313], real physical materials never propagate more light than they receive.

In Chapter 12 we saw that volume scattering was linear; that is, multiple independent fluxes passing through a volume summed together. Similarly, in almost all physical materials, surface scattering is linear. This means that the energy arriving from each direction contributes independently to the reflection. In this case, we can find the total reflected radiance in $\vec{\omega}_r$ by simply summing together the contribution from each direction. We do this by integrating over the incident hemisphere Ω_i.

Integrating the incident radiance L^i over the incident hemisphere, we find

$$\begin{aligned} L^r(\vec{\omega}_r) &= \int_{\Omega_i} f_r(\vec{\omega}_i \to \vec{\omega}_r) L^i(\vec{\omega}_i)\, d\vec{\omega}_i^{\mathbf{N}} \\ &= \int_{\phi_i=0}^{2\pi} \int_{\theta_i=0}^{\pi/2} f_r((\theta_i, \psi_i) \to (\theta_r, \psi_r)) L^i(\theta_i, \psi_i) \cos\theta_i \sin\theta_i \, d\theta_i \, d\psi_i \end{aligned} \quad (13.40)$$

using the expanded value of $d\vec{\omega}_i^{\mathbf{N}}$ from Equation 13.1. Equation 13.40 is called the *reflectance equation* [188].

The reflectance equation satisfies the *Helmholtz reciprocity principle*, which states that we can reverse the direction of flow of energy and nothing will change. That is, it doesn't matter in which direction we calculate the transfer. In symbols,

$$f_r(d\vec{\omega}_r \to d\vec{\omega}_i) = f_r(d\vec{\omega}_i \to d\vec{\omega}_r) \quad (13.41)$$

some authors write $f_r(d\vec{\omega}_i \leftrightarrow d\vec{\omega}_r)$ to emphasize this property.

13.7.2 Reflectance ρ

The BRDF is a useful characterization of reflection, but it can take on values from 0 to infinity. A related measure is the ratio of the reflected flux to the incident flux, which due to conservation of energy always lies between 0 and 1 (a patch can never reflect more flux than it receives). This measure is called the *reflectance*, and is denoted ρ. In symbols, we define the reflectance ρ as

$$\rho(\Gamma_i \to \Gamma_r) \triangleq \frac{d\Phi^r(\Gamma_r)}{d\Phi^i(\Gamma_i)} \quad (13.42)$$

for incident and reflected finite solid angles Γ_i and Γ_r.

For a differential solid angle $d\vec{\omega}_i$, we can find the incident flux $d\Phi^i(d\vec{\omega}_i)$ from Equation 13.33:

$$d\Phi^i(d\vec{\omega}_i) = L^i(d\vec{\omega}_i)\, d\vec{\omega}_i^{\mathbf{N}}\, dA \quad (13.43)$$

So for a finite solid angle Γ_i, we need only integrate over all directions in the angle to find the total incident flux:

$$\begin{aligned} d\Phi^i(\Gamma_i) &= \int_{d\vec{\omega}_i \in \Gamma_i} L^i(d\vec{\omega}_i)\, dA\, d\vec{\omega}_i^{\mathbf{N}} \\ &= dA \int_{d\vec{\omega}_i \in \Gamma_i} L^i(d\vec{\omega}_i)\, d\vec{\omega}_i^{\mathbf{N}} \end{aligned} \tag{13.44}$$

We find the reflected flux in the same way, getting

$$d\Phi^r(\Gamma_r) = dA \int_{d\vec{\omega}_r \in \Gamma_r} L^r(d\vec{\omega}_r)\, d\vec{\omega}_r^{\mathbf{N}} \tag{13.45}$$

To evaluate Equation 13.45, we need to find an expression for the reflected radiance L^r. This just requires integrating the differential reflected radiance $dL^r(d\vec{\omega}_i; \vec{\omega}_r; E)$ over all $d\vec{\omega}_i \in \Gamma_i$:

$$\begin{aligned} L^r(d\vec{\omega}_r) &= \int_{d\vec{\omega}_i \in \Gamma_i} dL^r(d\vec{\omega}_i; \vec{\omega}_r; E) \\ &= \int_{d\vec{\omega}_i \in \Gamma_i} f_r(d\vec{\omega}_i \to \vec{\omega}_r)\, dE(d\vec{\omega}_i) \\ &= \int_{d\vec{\omega}_i \in \Gamma_i} f_r(d\vec{\omega}_i \to \vec{\omega}_r) L^i(d\vec{\omega}_i)\, d\vec{\omega}_i^{\mathbf{N}} \end{aligned} \tag{13.46}$$

Where we have used the definitions of the BRDF f_r and irradiance E. Substituting Equation 13.46 into Equation 13.45 gives us the reflected flux:

$$d\Phi^r(\Gamma_r) = dA \int_{d\vec{\omega}_r \in \Gamma_r} \int_{d\vec{\omega}_i \in \Gamma_i} f_r(d\vec{\omega}_i \to \vec{\omega}_r) L^i(d\vec{\omega}_i)\, d\vec{\omega}_i^{\mathbf{N}}\, d\vec{\omega}_r^{\mathbf{N}} \tag{13.47}$$

We can now form the ratio of the fluxes from Equations 13.44 and 13.47:

$$\frac{d\Phi^r(\Gamma_r)}{d\Phi^i(\Gamma_i)} = \frac{\displaystyle\int_{d\vec{\omega}_r \in \Gamma_r} \int_{d\vec{\omega}_i \in \Gamma_i} f_r(d\vec{\omega}_i \to \vec{\omega}_r) L^i(d\vec{\omega}_i)\, d\vec{\omega}_i^{\mathbf{N}}\, d\vec{\omega}_r^{\mathbf{N}}}{\displaystyle\int_{d\vec{\omega}_i \in \Gamma_i} L^i(d\vec{\omega}_i)\, d\vec{\omega}_i^{\mathbf{N}}} \tag{13.48}$$

Notice that the differential areas dA cancel out.

This is still too complicated to work with efficiently for image synthesis. To simplify Equation 13.48, assume (as before) that L^i is constant, so that it doesn't depend on the direction $\vec{\omega}$ at all; that is, $L^i(\vec{\omega}) = L^i$. Then L^i factors out of the numerator and denominator of Equation 13.48, and we get the reflectance formula:

$$\rho(\Gamma_i \to \Gamma_r) = \frac{d\Phi^r(\Gamma_r)}{d\Phi^i(\Gamma_i)} = \frac{\displaystyle\int_{d\vec{\omega}_r \in \Gamma_r} \int_{d\vec{\omega}_i \in \Gamma_i} f_r(d\vec{\omega}_i \to \vec{\omega}_r)\, d\vec{\omega}_i^{\mathbf{N}}\, d\vec{\omega}_r^{\mathbf{N}}}{\displaystyle\int_{d\vec{\omega}_i \in \Gamma_i} d\vec{\omega}_i^{\mathbf{N}}} \quad \text{[dimensionless]} \tag{13.49}$$

This equation was our goal in this section. Equation 13.49 is sometimes written

$$\rho(\Gamma_i \to \Gamma_r) = \frac{1}{\Psi_i} \int_{d\vec{\omega}_r \in \Gamma_r} \int_{d\vec{\omega}_i \in \Gamma_i} f_r(d\vec{\omega}_i \to \vec{\omega}_r)\, d\vec{\omega}_i^{\mathbf{N}}\, d\vec{\omega}_r^{\mathbf{N}} \tag{13.50}$$

where

$$\Psi_i = \int_{d\vec{\omega}_i \in \Gamma_i} d\vec{\omega}_i^{\mathbf{N}} = \int_{d\vec{\omega}_i \in \Gamma_i} \cos\theta_i\, d\vec{\omega}_i \tag{13.51}$$

We note that when the input angle is a hemisphere (that is, $\Psi_i = \Omega_i$), then the integration of Ψ becomes simple:

$$\begin{aligned}\Psi &= \int_{\Omega_i} \vec{\omega}_i^{\mathbf{N}} \\ &= \int_{\Omega_i} \cos\theta\, d\vec{\omega} \\ &= \int_{\psi=0}^{2\pi} \int_{\theta=0}^{\pi/2} \cos\theta \sin\theta\, d\theta\, d\psi \\ &= \pi\end{aligned} \tag{13.52}$$

Types of Reflectance

The reflectance ρ depends on only three things: the BRDF f_r of the surface, and the incident and reflected solid angles Γ_i and Γ_r. Nicodemus et al. [318] have suggested distinguishing three types of solid angles, name *directional*, *conical*, and *hemispherical*. Hanrahan [188] has suggested the more descriptive names *differential*, *finite*, and *hemispherical*. We associate the symbols $d\vec{\omega}$, Γ, and Ω_i with these classes.

Each of the incident and reflected solid angles may take on any of these three values, resulting in a total of nine types of reflectance. The names of the six mixed types are formed by combining the adjective for the incident solid angle type with the reflected solid angle type; the three homogeneous types are preceded with "bi." The symbols and names for all nine reflection types are shown in Table 13.4.

There are three things to note in this table. First, one integral drops out for each differential angle involved, as one would expect. Second, the terms involving a differential incident solid angle are differential factors themselves. Third, the biconical (or bifinite) reflectance subsumes all the others, if we allow the finite angle to become as small as a differential or as large as a hemisphere.

Γ_i	Γ_r: $d\vec{\omega}$	Γ_r: Γ	Γ_r: Ω_o
$d\vec{\omega}$	$d\rho(d\vec{\omega} \to d\vec{\omega})$ $f_r()\,d\vec{\omega}_r^{\mathbf{N}}$ Bidifferential	$\rho(d\vec{\omega} \to \Gamma)$ $\int_{\Gamma_r} f_r()\,d\vec{\omega}_r^{\mathbf{N}}$ Differential-finite	$\rho(d\vec{\omega} \to \Omega_o)$ $\int_{\Omega_o} f_r()\,d\vec{\omega}_r^{\mathbf{N}}$ Differential-hemispherical
Γ	$d\rho(\Gamma \to d\vec{\omega})$ $\frac{d\vec{\omega}_r^{\mathbf{N}}}{d\vec{\omega}_i^{\mathbf{N}}} \int_{\Gamma_i} f_r()\,d\vec{\omega}_i^{\mathbf{N}}$ Finite-differential	$\rho(\Gamma \to \Gamma)$ $\frac{1}{d\vec{\omega}_i^{\mathbf{N}}} \int_{\Gamma_i} \int_{\Gamma_r} f_r()\,d\vec{\omega}_r^{\mathbf{N}}\,d\vec{\omega}_i^{\mathbf{N}}$ Bifinite	$\rho(\Gamma \to \Omega_o)$ $\frac{1}{d\vec{\omega}_i^{\mathbf{N}}} \int_{\Gamma_i} \int_{\Omega_o} f_r()\,d\vec{\omega}_r^{\mathbf{N}}\,d\vec{\omega}_i^{\mathbf{N}}$ Finite-hemispherical
Ω_i	$d\rho(\Omega_i \to d\vec{\omega})$ $\frac{d\vec{\omega}_r^{\mathbf{N}}}{\pi} \int_{\Omega_i} f_r()\,d\vec{\omega}_i^{\mathbf{N}}$ Hemispherical-differential	$\rho(\Omega_i \to \Gamma)$ $\frac{1}{\pi} \int_{\Omega_i} \int_{\Gamma_r} f_r()\,d\vec{\omega}_r^{\mathbf{N}}\,d\vec{\omega}_i^{\mathbf{N}}$ Hemispherical-finite	$\rho(\Omega_i \to \Omega_o)$ $\frac{1}{\pi} \int_{\Omega_i} \int_{\Omega_o} f_r()\,d\vec{\omega}_r^{\mathbf{N}}\,d\vec{\omega}_i^{\mathbf{N}}$ Bihemispherical

TABLE 13.4
The nine types of reflection functions.

13.7.3 Reflectance Factor R

The *reflectance factor* (denoted R) is the ratio of the reflected flux from a surface to the flux that would have been reflected by a perfectly diffuse surface in the same circumstances.

We can form an expression for R by simply finding the ratio of the reflected flux to the flux that would have been reflected by a perfectly diffuse surface; that is, one with a constant BRDF $f_{r,pd} = 1/\pi$ (see Section 13.8.1). Using Equation 13.47 to give us both fluxes, we can easily find their ratio:

$$\frac{\Phi^r}{\Phi_{pd}} = \frac{dA \int_{\Gamma_r} \left[\int_{\Gamma_i} f_r(\vec{\omega}_i \to \vec{\omega}_r) L^i(\vec{\omega}_i)\, d\vec{\omega}_i^{\mathbf{N}} \right] d\vec{\omega}_r^{\mathbf{N}}}{(dA/\pi) \int_{\Gamma_r} \left[\int_{\Gamma_i} L^i(\vec{\omega}_i)\, d\vec{\omega}_i^{\mathbf{N}} \right] d\vec{\omega}_r^{\mathbf{N}}} \tag{13.53}$$

Γ_i	Γ_r: $d\vec{\omega}$	Γ	Ω_o
$d\vec{\omega}$	$R(d\vec{\omega} \to d\vec{\omega})$ $\pi f_r()$ Bidifferential	$R(d\vec{\omega} \to \Gamma)$ $\frac{\pi}{\vec{\omega}_r^{\mathbf{N}}} \int_{\Gamma_r} f_r()\, d\vec{\omega}_r^{\mathbf{N}}$ Differential-finite	$R(d\vec{\omega} \to \Omega_o)$ $\int_{\Omega_o} f_r()\, d\vec{\omega}_r^{\mathbf{N}}$ Differential-hemispherical
Γ	$R(\Gamma \to d\vec{\omega})$ $\frac{\pi}{d\vec{\omega}_i^{\mathbf{N}}} \int_{\Gamma_i} f_r()\, d\vec{\omega}_i^{\mathbf{N}}$ Finite-differential	$R(\Gamma \to \Gamma)$ $\frac{\pi}{\vec{\omega}_i^{\mathbf{N}} \vec{\omega}_r^{\mathbf{N}}} \int_{\Gamma_i} \int_{\Gamma_r} f_r()\, d\vec{\omega}_r^{\mathbf{N}}\, d\vec{\omega}_i^{\mathbf{N}}$ Bifinite	$R(\Gamma \to \Omega_o)$ $\frac{1}{d\vec{\omega}_i^{\mathbf{N}}} \int_{\Gamma_i} \int_{\Omega_o} f_r()\, d\vec{\omega}_r^{\mathbf{N}}\, d\vec{\omega}_i^{\mathbf{N}}$ Finite-hemispherical
Ω_i	$R(\Omega_i \to d\vec{\omega})$ $\int_{\Omega_i} f_r()\, d\vec{\omega}_i^{\mathbf{N}}$ Hemispherical-differential	$R(\Omega_i \to \Gamma)$ $\frac{1}{\vec{\omega}_r^{\mathbf{N}}} \int_{\Omega_i} \int_{\Gamma_r} f_r()\, d\vec{\omega}_r^{\mathbf{N}}\, d\vec{\omega}_i^{\mathbf{N}}$ Hemispherical-finite	$R(\Omega_i \to \Omega_o)$ $\frac{1}{\pi} \int_{\Omega_i} \int_{\Omega_o} f_r()\, d\vec{\omega}_r^{\mathbf{N}}\, d\vec{\omega}_i^{\mathbf{N}}$ Bihemispherical

TABLE 13.5
The nine types of reflection factors.

Again assuming that the incident flux L^i is isotropic, we can pull it out of both integrals and find

$$R(\Gamma_i \to \Gamma_r) \triangleq \frac{\pi}{\left(\int_{\Gamma_i} d\vec{\omega}_i^{\mathbf{N}}\right)\left(\int_{\Gamma_r} d\vec{\omega}_r^{\mathbf{N}}\right)} \int_{\Gamma_r} \int_{\Gamma_i} f_r(\vec{\omega}_i \to \vec{\omega}_r)\, d\vec{\omega}_i^{\mathbf{N}}\, d\vec{\omega}_r^{\mathbf{N}} \quad \text{[dimensionless]} \tag{13.54}$$

There are nine types of reflectance factors, named in the same way as the nine reflectances. Their definitions work out to be slightly different in the normalizing coefficients; the results are summarized in Table 13.5.

13.8 Examples

In this section we will examine the BRDF for two special cases: perfect diffuse, and perfect specular reflection.

13.8.1 Perfect Diffuse

For perfect diffuse reflection, we know that incident light is reflected equally in all directions. The cosine term in the common form of Lambert's law is taken care of automatically in the definition of the reflection equation; it accounts for how much the surface is turned away from the incident light. So the BRDF is simply a constant, often denoted $f_{r,d}$, and takes no arguments:

$$f_r = f_{r,d} \tag{13.55}$$

If we now plug this into the reflectance equation from Equation 13.40, we find

$$\begin{aligned} L_{r,d}(\theta_r, \psi_r) &= \int_{\Omega_i} f_r(\vec{\omega}_i \to \vec{\omega}_r) L^i(\vec{\omega}_i)\, d\vec{\omega}_i^{\mathbf{N}} \\ &= f_{r,d} \int_{\Omega_i} L^i(\vec{\omega}_i)\, d\vec{\omega}_i^{\mathbf{N}} \\ &= f_{r,d} E \end{aligned} \tag{13.56}$$

so that

$$f_{r,d} = L_{r,d}()/E \tag{13.57}$$

Perfect diffuse reflection says that the energy arriving from any direction is completely reflected back into the incident hemisphere with uniform intensity. We can express this in symbols by asserting that the differential-hemispherical reflectance must equal 1:

$$\begin{aligned} 1 = \rho(\vec{\omega}_i \to \Omega_i) &= \frac{d\Phi^r}{d\Phi^i} \\ &= \frac{L_{r,d}\, dA \int_{\Omega_i} d\vec{\omega}_r^{\mathbf{N}}}{E\, dA} \\ &= \frac{f_{r,d}\, E\, dA \int_{\Omega_i} d\vec{\omega}_r^{\mathbf{N}}}{E\, dA} \\ &= f_{r,d}\pi \end{aligned} \tag{13.58}$$

So solving for the BRDF, we find

$$f_{r,d} = \frac{1}{\pi} \tag{13.59}$$

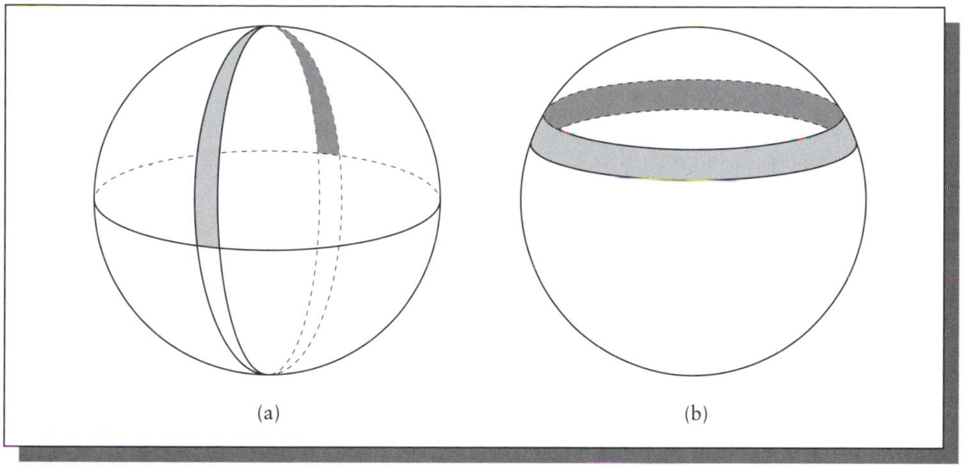

FIGURE 13.9

(a) A hemilune of the sphere. (b) A spherical sector of the sphere.

13.8.2 Perfect Specular

To set up the BRDF, it is helpful to break up the analysis into two sections, geometric and radiometric, as presented in Hanrahan [188].

For perfect specular reflection leaving the surface in the direction (θ_r, ψ_r), the geometry of the situation tells us that the incident light must have come from $\theta_i = \theta_r$, and it must be in the same plane as the reflected light and the normal; that is, $\psi_i = \psi_r \pm \pi$. The radiometric observation is that the radiance that leaves the surface in (θ_r, ψ_r) is the same as the radiance arriving in the incident direction, so $L^r(\theta_r, \psi_r) = L^i(\theta_r, \psi_r \pm \pi)$. Our goal is to find the BRDF f_r that gives this behavior.

We begin with the double-integral form of the reflectance equation from Equation 13.40:

$$L^r(\theta_r, \psi_r) \int_{\psi=0}^{2\pi} \int_{\theta=0}^{\pi/2} f_r((\theta, \psi) \to (\theta_r, \psi_r)) L^i(\theta, \psi) \cos\theta \sin\theta \, d\theta \, d\psi \tag{13.60}$$

Our approach is motivated by separating the integrals in this equation. We can think of it as two nested integrations: the inner one for θ scans hemilunes of width $d\theta$ on the sphere, as in Figure 13.9(a), and the outer integral for ψ scans spherical sectors of height $d\psi$, as in Figure 13.9(b). If we select only the hemilune corresponding to θ_r and the spherical sector corresponding to $\psi_r \pm \pi$, their intersection isolates the direction we seek. So we will first look at the integral for θ, giving us a BRDF $f_{r,\theta}$, and then similarly look for a BRDF $f_{r,\psi}$. Their product will be the BRDF f_r.

We begin by fixing $\psi = \psi_0$, so we need only look at θ. The condition $\theta_i = \theta_r$ implies

$$L^r(\theta_r) = L^i(\theta_r) = \int_{\theta_i=0}^{\pi/2} L^i(\theta_i) f_{r,\theta}(\theta_r \to \theta_i) \cos\theta_i \sin\theta_i \, d\theta_i \tag{13.61}$$

We can make the change of variables

$$u = \cos\theta_i \qquad du = -\sin\theta_i \, d\theta_i \tag{13.62}$$

Equation 13.61 with this substitution gives

$$L^r(\theta_r) = -\int_{u=1}^{0} f_{r,\theta}(u_r \to u) L^i(\cos^{-1} u) u \, du \tag{13.63}$$

Equation 13.63 has a form similar to the one that defines the Dirac delta function. Recall the third definition of the delta function from Equation 4.23:

$$\int_a^b \delta(t-c) g(t) \, dt = g(c), \qquad c \in [a, b] \tag{13.64}$$

If we *guess* that the BRDF $f_{r,\theta}$ is a delta function $f_{r,\theta} = \delta(u - u_r)$, then we can write $g(u) = L^i(\cos^{-1} u)u$ in this definition, giving us

$$L^r(\theta_r) = -\int_{u=1}^{0} \delta(u - u_r) g(u) \, du \tag{13.65}$$

This equation sifts out only $g(u)$ from the integral, leaving us with

$$\begin{aligned} L^r(\theta_r) &= -g(u_r) \\ &= -L^i(\cos^{-1} u_r) u_r \\ &= -L^i(\cos^{-1} \cos\theta_r) \cos\theta_r \\ &= -L^i(\theta_r) \cos\theta_r \end{aligned} \tag{13.66}$$

So the function we guessed for $f_{r,\theta}$ is close, but off by a factor $-1/\cos\theta_r$, which is easily incorporated. So the BRDF for perfect specular reflection is

$$f_{r,\theta}(\theta_i \to \theta_r) = \frac{-\delta(\cos\theta_i - \cos\theta_r)}{\cos\theta_r} \tag{13.67}$$

Now we fix $\theta = \theta_0$, and look at ψ. The integral for ψ has a much simpler form:

$$L^r(\psi_r) = L^i(\psi_i \pm \pi) = \int_{\psi=0}^{2\pi} L^i(\psi) \, d\psi \tag{13.68}$$

We can capture just the values at $\psi_i + \pi$ and $\psi_i - \pi$ by multiplying this equation by the sum of two delta functions, one at each location (note that only one will have a nonzero value for any value of $\psi \in 2\pi$:

$$f_{r,\psi} = \delta(\psi_r - \psi_i - \pi) + \delta(\psi_r - \psi_i + \pi) \tag{13.69}$$

Combining the two BRDFs, we find the composite BRDF $f_{r,s}$ for perfect specular reflection:

$$\begin{aligned} f_{r,s}&((\theta_i, \psi_i) \to (\theta_r, \psi_r)) \\ &= f_{r,\theta} \cdot f_{r,\psi} \\ &= \frac{\delta(\cos\theta_i - \cos\theta_r)}{-\cos\theta_r} \cdot [\delta(\psi_r - \psi_i - \pi) + \delta(\psi_r - \psi_i + \pi)] \end{aligned} \tag{13.70}$$

13.9 Spherical Harmonics

Many of the quantities discussed in this chapter may be parameterized as functions of direction around a particular point. We can think of them as 2D functions defined on a sphere, parameterized by the angles θ and ϕ. But unlike 2D functions in the plane, there are built-in border periodic conditions due to the shape of the sphere.

There exists an infinite family of orthogonal functions called *spherical harmonics*. Like the Fourier transform's complex exponentials, any function on the sphere satisfying some fairly broad conditions may be represented by an infinite sum of scaled spherical harmonics; truncating the infinite expansion gives us a finite approximation to the function.

The real and normalized forms of the spherical harmonics are given by a function $Y_{l,m}$ in two variables, the *order*, l, and the *degree*, m [410]:

$$Y_{l,m}(\theta, \phi) = \begin{cases} N_{l,m} P_{l,m} \cos\theta \cos(m\phi) & \text{if } m > 0 \\ N_{l,0} P_{l,0} \cos\theta / \sqrt{2} & \text{if } m = 0 \\ N_{l,m} P_{l,-m} \cos\theta \sin(-m\phi) & \text{if } m < 0 \end{cases} \tag{13.71}$$

where the normalizing constants $N_{l,m}$ are given by

$$N_{l,m} = \sqrt{\frac{2l+1}{2\pi} \frac{(l-|m|)!}{(l+|m|)!}} \tag{13.72}$$

and the $P_{l,m}(t)$ are *associated Legendre polynomials*, defined by the set of recurrence relations

$$P_{m,m}(t) = (1-2m)\sqrt{1-t^2}P_{m-1,m-1}(t)$$

$$P_{m+1,m}(t) = t(2m+1)P_{m,m}(t)$$

$$P_{l,m}(t) = t\left(\frac{2l-1}{l-m}\right)P_{l-1,m}(t) - \left(\frac{l+m-1}{l-m}\right)P_{l-2,m}(t)$$

$$P_{0,0}(t) = 1 \tag{13.73}$$

The first few spherical harmonics are shown in Figure 13.10.

Because the spherical harmonics as defined above are orthogonal, they are their own duals. Thus for a function $f(\theta, \phi)$, the coefficient $b_{l,m}$ on harmonic $Y_{l,m}$ may be found from the projection of f onto $Y_{l,m}$

$$b_{l,m} = \int_0^{\pi}\int_0^{2\pi} f(\theta,\phi)Y_{l,m}(\theta,\phi)\sin(\theta)\,d\theta\,d\phi \tag{13.74}$$

or, in braket form,

$$b_{l,m} = \langle f|\,Y_{l,m}\rangle_{S^2} \tag{13.75}$$

where we have defined the spherical braket $\langle a|\,b\rangle_{S^2}$ representing integration over a sphere.

One useful property of these functions is that when $l+m$ is even, the corresponding spherical harmonic is symmetrical about the equator $\theta = \pi/2$. So if our function f is antisymmetrical (that is, $f(\theta,\phi) = -f(\pi-\theta,\phi)$), then the total integral against the corresponding spherical harmonic has the same magnitude but opposite sign above and below the equator, sending the coefficient $b_{l,m}$ to zero.

It is sometimes convenient to refer to the spherical harmonics using a single index k. The correspondence between the indices is set up naturally, starting at $l = 0, m = 0$ and then ascending in order through increasing values of m for each increasing value of l. That is,

$$k = m + l(l+1) \tag{13.76}$$

and

$$l = \sqrt{k}$$
$$m = k - (l^2 + l) \tag{13.77}$$

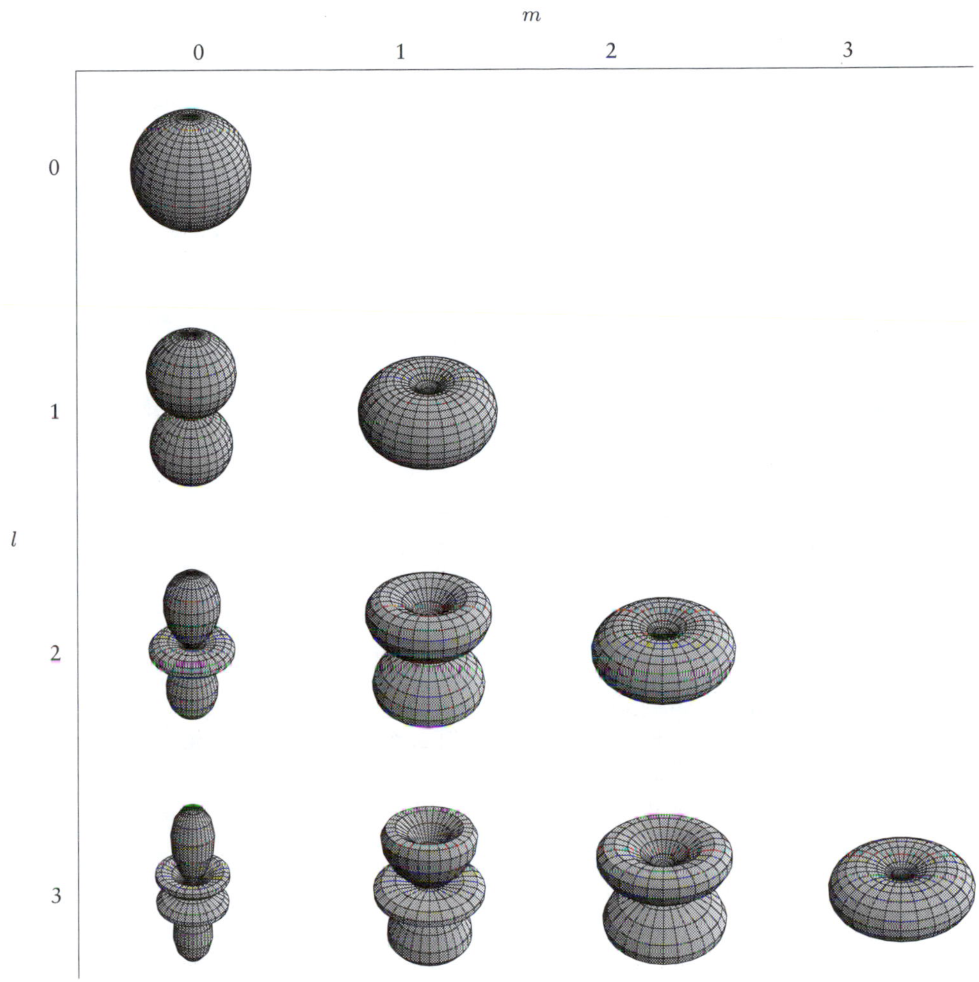

FIGURE 13.10
The first few real spherical harmonics.

13.10 Further Reading

The standard references for radiometric terms and units in the United States are those put forth by the American National Standards Institute (ANSI) [432] and the Illumination Engineering Society of North America (IES) [221]. I have followed their conventions and notation here.

A thorough discussion of reflection is given in the report by Nicodemus et al. [318], who also include a number of alternative naming systems for reflection functions.

Radiometry for computer graphics is discussed by Kajiya [235] and by Shirley [402]. A great deal of practical information for real light sources and principles for lighting design may be found in the early textbook by Moon [312].

13.11 Exercises

Exercise 13.1

(a) Use Equation 13.1 to form a double integral expressing the surface area of the sphere, and evaluate the integral.

(b) Use Equation 13.3 to form a double integral expressing the total projected area of the sphere onto the Z plane. Use domains $\theta \in (0, \pi)$ and $\psi \in (0, 2\pi)$. Briefly explain your result.

(c) Repeat (b) with domains $\theta \in (0, \pi/2)$ and $\psi \in (0, 2\pi)$.

Exercise 13.2

The BRDF for perfect specular reflection in Equation 13.70 is in a form given by Hanrahan in [188]. Nicodemus et al. in [318] give the following, different form:

$$f_r(\theta_i \to \theta_r) = 2\delta(\sin^2\theta_i - \sin^2\theta_r)[\delta(\psi_r - \psi_i + \pi) + \delta(\psi_r - \psi_i - \pi)] \tag{13.78}$$

Derive this form from the definition of the BRDF in Equation 13.39. (Hint: use the substitution $v = \sin^2\theta$.)

Exercise 13.3

A man walked up to the complaints department in a hardware store and stated that he bought two bulbs in that store the previous day. Each bulb had its radiant power in watts printed right on the top of the glass. He bought a 200-watt bulb for reading and a 400-watt bulb for his workshop. He found that the 200-watt bulb was too bright even for the workshop and, surprisingly, the 400-watt bulb was so dim he could hardly see by its light in a dark room. Assuming that the bulbs were correctly labeled and working properly, suggest a reason for these observations.

Exercise 13.4

Consider a conical beam starting a point P with circular cross section and apex angle of θ. Choose two cross sections at distance d_1 and d_2 from P, with radii r_1 and r_2, respectively. Assume the flux in the beam is Φ.

(a) Compute the difference in radiance $L_2 - L_1$ between these cross sections.

(b) When does $L_2 = L_1$?

Exercise 13.5

Show that the intensity I may be interpreted as the flux per unit area at a distance 1 from a point source.

Exercise 13.6

Find an expression for the flux Φ from a differential source S to a large, rectangular patch dR.

Exercise 13.7

Find an expression for the flux Φ from a large finite circular source S to a differential patch dR.

There is an exhilaration about setting up with new materials. It promotes energy, promises a fresh start, and inspires new ideas.

Bet Borgeson
("The Colored Pencil," 1983)

14

MATERIALS

14.1 Introduction

An important issue in image synthesis is why objects appear the way they do. We only see objects because they emit photons. Each emission may be characterized as either *spontaneous* or *responsive*. A spontaneous emission is generated by the material itself in response to its own internal processes. A responsive emission is triggered by an external event, such as the arrival of a beam of particles, physical friction, or agitation.

Both types of emissions are due to the action of subatomic particles within the material. In order to discuss how materials absorb and emit energy, we will first briefly survey some aspects of the nature of atoms and molecules. In Chapter 15, we will consider the large-scale effect of many atomic and molecular interactions with light when we discuss shading. But to understand how such large-scale phenomena arise, it helps to have a basic working knowledge of the underlying physics.

We will develop some of this structural information in detail, particularly by deriving the statistical distribution of electrons and photons in materials. These developments are self-contained and not required for understanding anything else

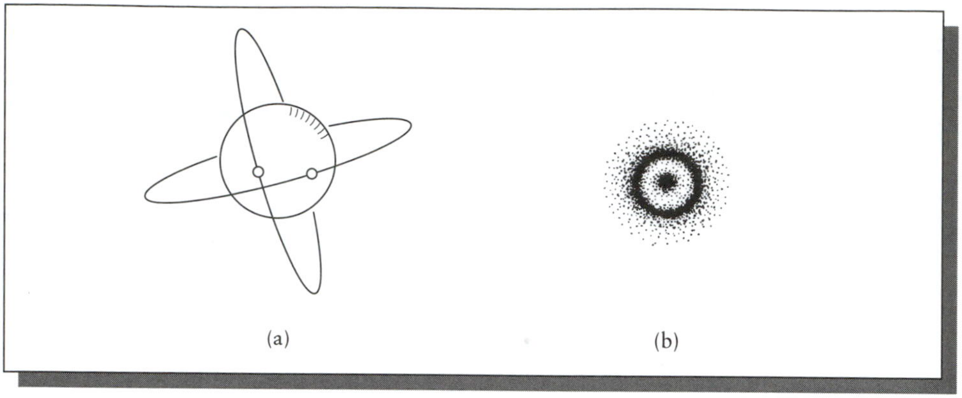

FIGURE 14.1
(a) The classical atom model. (b) A more modern view.

in the book, and may be safely skipped on a first reading. Each of these sections (14.3.1 and 14.6.1) is identified in the first paragraph or two.

14.2 Atomic Structure

The classical model of the atom posits a dense *nucleus* of small particles called *protons* and *neutrons*, which are orbited by a number of *electrons*. Modern quantum-mechanical views of the atom replace these notions of particles and locations with probability functions. This is based on the idea that any given particle cannot be located with precision, but that we can assign a probability of finding the particle in a given place at a given time. When the probability function is large, the particle is likely to be in that place and time. The notion of little billiard balls orbiting around a central clump of balls is then replaced by a cloud of electrons, where the cloud density corresponds to the value of the probability function ψ. These two pictures are contrasted in Figure 14.1.

The center of an atom is called the *nucleus*. A nucleus contains two types of particles (called *nucleons*): the proton and the neutron. The proton is a massive charged particle that is arbitrarily assigned *positive* charge $+e$. The neutron is almost identical to the proton except it has no charge. Protons and neutrons exert a number of attractive and repulsive forces upon each other, which cause them to aggregate and form a nucleus.

The total number of protons in an atom is called the atom's *atomic number*, and is designated Z. A nucleus by itself has an electric charge of $+Z$. Typically there are an equal number of neutrons and protons in the nucleus; when these quantities are different, the atom is called an *isotope*.

An *electron* is a particle that is three orders of magnitude lighter than the nucleons, and has an electric charge $-e$ equal in magnitude but opposite in sign to that of the proton. The complete assembly of nucleus and associated electrons is called an *atom*.

In an electrically neutral atom, Z electrons surround the nucleus, balancing out the nucleus's excess positive charge. When the charge is not 0, the atom is called an *ion*. When there are too few electrons, the atom has a positive charge and is called a *cation*. When there are too many electrons around a nucleus, there is an excessive negative charge; such an atom is called an *anion*.

When an electron is within an atom, it is said to be *bound*. An electron can also exist on its own, independent of any particular atom; this is called a *free* electron.

Nucleons are relatively stable particles and don't typically leave the nucleus or change their internal state under normal conditions. But electrons are very susceptible to external influences, and the way electrons behave is primarily responsible for most of the chemical events that make life possible. Electrons are also responsible for the emission of light by solids.

Electrons are typically in either a *stable* or *unstable* state. A stable state is one in which the electron can exist for a relatively long period of time without change. An unstable state typically has a much shorter lifetime. As an analogy to these states, think of a pencil with a sharp point. If you lay the pencil down on its side on a flat table, it's in a stable state: until something interferes with the system, the pencil won't go anywhere. Now imagine balancing the pencil on its point. You may be able to get it to hold there for a moment, but normal physical pressures (e.g., wind in the room and vibration of the table) will eventually cause the pencil to fall over. The condition of being balanced on its point is an unstable state for the pencil: it can hold it for a while, but not very long compared to the stable states.

The state of an electron at any time is given by a set of four *quantum numbers*. These characterize the electron's energy, momentum, and "spin" (like the other terms, spin is an abstract concept, but it is sometimes convenient to think of a small ball spinning either clockwise or counterclockwise around an axis). One of the great achievements of quantum mechanics was to explain how the periodic table of the elements is constructed in terms of the atomic number. Basically, electrons join the system in a very well-defined way based on their quantum numbers, which we will now summarize [267].

The *principal quantum number*, n, describes the energy of a bound electron. The value of n is drawn from the range of positive integers: $n \in \{1, 2, 3, \ldots\}$. The *angular-momentum quantum number*, l, describes the possible angular momenta of the electron about the nucleus. As the energy of the electron goes up (that is, as n increases), there are more possible angular-momentum states. We capture this fact by drawing the value of l from the range $l \in \{0, 1, 2, \ldots, n-1\}$. The *magnetic-*

I_a	II_a	III_b	IV_b	V_b	VI_b	VII_b	VIII			I_b	II_b	III_a	IV_a	V_a	VI_a	VII_a	O
1 H 1.0079 Hydrogen																	2 He 4.00260 Helium
3 Li 6.941 Lithium	4 Be 9.01218 Beryllium											5 B 10.81 Boron	6 C 12.011 Carbon	7 N 14.0067 Nitrogen	8 O 15.9994 Oxygen	9 F 19.99840 Fluorine	10 Ne 20.179 Neon
11 Na 22.98977 Sodium	12 Mg 24.305 Magnesium											13 Al 26.98154 Aluminum	14 Si 28.086 Silicon	15 P 30.97376 Phosphorus	16 S 32.06 Sulfur	17 Cl 35.453 Chlorine	18 Ar 39.948 Argon

FIGURE 14.2

The first few rows of the periodic table of the elements.

moment quantum number, m_μ, describes the projection of the angular momentum of an electron given by n and l onto an axis defined by an external magnetic field. Its values are $m_\mu \in \{-l, -l+1, \ldots, 0, \ldots, l-1, l\}$. Finally, the *spin-moment quantum number*, s_μ, describes the spin of the electron onto this axis; s_μ only takes on the values $s_\mu \in \{-1/2, 1/2\}$.

We can summarize these rules with a general quantum state rule for electrons:

$$s_\mu = \pm\frac{1}{2} \qquad |m_\mu| \leq l < n = 0, 1, 2, 3, \ldots \tag{14.1}$$

In spectroscopy, the values of $n = 1, 2, 3, \ldots$ are denoted K, L, M, N, and the values for $l = 0, 1, 2, 3, 4, 5, 6$ are denoted s, p, d, f, g, h and are called *orbitals*, or *shells*. The first four letters stand for *sharp*, *principal*, *diffuse*, and *fundamental*, with following letters simply coming alphabetically [295]. These historical names come from the spectral lines observed for atomic sodium. The total angular momentum of all electrons in an atom is assigned the *total angular quantum number*, L, which takes on values $0, 1, 2, 3, 4, 5$ (written S, P, D, F, G, H).

The top few levels of the periodic table of the elements are shown in Figure 14.2 (Table E in Appendix E is the full table). In this table, the horizontal rows are called *periods* and the columns are called *groups*. We can use the rule of Equation 14.1 to build the first few elements. In general, we add electrons to a system in a way very similar to counting in binary: the spin quantum number is the least-significant bit, and the principal quantum number is the most-significant bit. We start with every quantum number at its lowest admissible value and work our way up. We continue to add electrons until we have Z of them, balancing the charge in the nucleus. Table 14.1 summarizes the results we will find, and Figure 14.3 shows how the same quantum numbers describe the first few elements.

One might ask why we should bother changing the quantum numbers at all when accumulating electrons; that is, why not simply use lots of $1s$ electrons? Experiment

Quantum numbers	n	1		2							
	l	0		0		1					
	M_μ	0		0		−1		0		1	
	S_μ	$-\frac{1}{2}$	$+\frac{1}{2}$	$-\frac{1}{2}$	$+\frac{1}{2}$	$-\frac{1}{2}$	$+\frac{1}{2}$	$-\frac{1}{2}$	$+\frac{1}{2}$	$-\frac{1}{2}$	$+\frac{1}{2}$
Element	H	✓									
	He	✓	✓								
	Li	✓	✓	✓							
	Be	✓	✓	✓	✓						
	B	✓	✓	✓	✓	✓					
	C	✓	✓	✓	✓	✓		✓			
	N	✓	✓	✓	✓	✓		✓		✓	
	O	✓	✓	✓	✓	✓	✓	✓		✓	
	F	✓	✓	✓	✓	✓	✓	✓	✓	✓	
	Ne	✓	✓	✓	✓	✓	✓	✓	✓	✓	✓

FIGURE 14.3
The quantum-mechanical distribution of the first few elements.

has shown that electrons in the same *system* (in our case, the same atom) never share the quantum numbers. This is known as the *Pauli exclusion principle*, and it tells us that if two electrons coexist in the same atom, they cannot share the identical set of quantum numbers (actually, this principle holds for all *fermions*, which is a class of particles that includes electrons [427]).

We begin by assigning the smallest value to the principal quantum number: $n = 1$. We can only assign $l = 0$ and $m_\mu = 0$. We now have our choice of spin. We will write $s_\mu = \pm 1/2$ to indicate that this quantum number can have either value (but only one value at a time, of course). This set of four quantum numbers, $\{n, l, m_\mu, s_\mu\} = \{1, 0, 0, \pm 1/2\}$ completely defines one electron (except for the ambiguity in the spin). This describes the electron associated with hydrogen, atomic number $Z = 1$, and the first element on the periodic table. It is common to write the electron configuration by stating the principal quantum number, the letter for the orbital, and a superscript identifying the number of electrons in the orbital. Thus the electron configuration for hydrogen, $n = 1, l = 0 = s$, is written $1s$.

The next element is helium, atomic number $Z = 2$. The second electron is built by fixing a value of s_μ for the first electron, and giving the other value to the

Z	Symbol	Name	Relative configuration	Full electron configuration
1	H	Hydrogen	$1s$	$1s$
2	He	Helium	$1s^2$	$1s^2$
3	Li	Lithium	[He]$2s$	$1s^2, 2s$
4	Be	Beryllium	[He]$2s^2$	$1s^2, 2s^2$
5	B	Boron	[He]$2s^2, 2p$	$1s^2, 2s^2, 2p$
6	C	Carbon	[He]$2s^2, 2p^2$	$1s^2, 2s^2, 2p^2$
7	N	Nitrogen	[He]$2s^2, 2p^3$	$1s^2, 2s^2, 2p^3$
8	O	Oxygen	[He]$2s^2, 2p^4$	$1s^2, 2s^2, 2p^4$
9	F	Fluorine	[He]$2s^2, 2p^5$	$1s^2, 2s^2, 2p^5$
10	Ne	Neon	[He]$2s^2, 2p^6$	$1s^2, 2s^2, 2p^6$
11	Na	Sodium	[Ne]$3s$	$1s^2, 2s^2, 2p^6, 3s$
12	Mg	Magnesium	[Ne]$3s^2$	$1s^2, 2s^2, 2p^6, 3s^2$
13	Al	Aluminum	[Ne]$3s^2, 3p$	$1s^2, 2s^2, 2p^6, 3s^2, 3p$
14	Si	Silicon	[Ne]$3s^2, 3p^2$	$1s^2, 2s^2, 2p^6, 3s^2, 3p^2$
15	P	Phosphorus	[Ne]$3s^2, 3p^3$	$1s^2, 2s^2, 2p^6, 3s^2, 3p^3$
16	S	Sulphur	[Ne]$3s^2, 3p^4$	$1s^2, 2s^2, 2p^6, 3s^2, 3p^4$
17	Cl	Chlorine	[Ne]$3s^2, 3p^5$	$1s^2, 2s^2, 2p^6, 3s^2, 3p^5$
18	Ar	Argon	[Ne]$3s^2, 3p^6$	$1s^2, 2s^2, 2p^6, 3s^2, 3p^6$
19	K	Potassium	[Ar]$4s$	$1s^2, 2s^2, 2p^6, 3s^2, 3p^6, 4s$
20	Ca	Calcium	[Ar]$4s^2$	$1s^2, 2s^2, 2p^6, 3s^2, 3p^6, 4s^2$
21	Sc	Scandium	[Ar]$4s^2, 3d$	$1s^2, 2s^2, 2p^6, 3s^2, 3p^6, 4s^2, 3d$

TABLE 14.1
Building up elements by quantum rules.

second. Thus the two electrons in helium have quantum numbers $\{1, 0, 0, 1/2\}$ and $\{1, 0, 0, -1/2\}$, together written $1s^2$.

We have now exhausted the possibilities for $n = 1$, so we set $n = 2$ and start again with $l = 0$; this again forces $m_\mu = 0$. So we add one electron with arbitrary spin on top of the already full $1s$ shell to make lithium (L), with configuration written $1s^2, 2s$. As before, we can now add another electron, so we have one of each spin, to make beryllium (Be), atomic number $Z = 4$, $1s^2, 2s^2$.

To continue, we notice that $l = 1$ is now a permissible state. In general, Equation 14.1 tells us there will be $2(2l+1)$ electrons associated with any given choice of n and l; the value of $2(2l+1)$ is called the *degeneracy* of the state.

We start with $m_\mu = -1$ and arbitrarily set $s_\mu = -1/2$ to make boron (B), in state $\{2, 1, -1, -1/2\}$. Here we see our first subtlety: electrons filling up this orbital go in with *parallel spins* in order to maximize their mutual repulsion. So from boron $(1s^2, 2s^2, 2p)$, the next electron goes in with a new magnetic moment $m_\mu = 0$ and the same spin $s_\mu = -1/2$, to make carbon (C), in state $\{2, 1, 0, -1/2\}$. We write this as $1s^2, 2s^2, 2p^2$. Similarly, the third electron goes in with magnetic moment $m_\mu = 1$ and spin $s_\mu = -1/2$, to make nitrogen (N), in state $\{2, 1, 1, -1/2\}$. Now we return to the other spins, sequentially adding in electrons in states $\{2, 1, -1, 1/2\}$, $\{2, 1, 0, 1/2\}$, $\{2, 1, 1, 1/2\}$, making sequentially oxygen (O), fluorine (F), and neon (Ne), finally ending up with configuration $1s^2, 2s^2, 2p^6$.

Due to internal energy effects, the orbitals don't fill in exactly sequential order as we might assume from the above. The order is $1s, 2s, 2p, 3s, 3p, 4s, 3d, 4p, 5s, 4d, 5p, 6s, 4f, 5d, 6p, 7s, 5f, 6d$. Note, for example, the transition from calcium ($Z = 20$) to scandium ($Z = 21$) in Table 14.1. When an atom's outermost shell is full, the atom is particularly stable; examples include helium and neon, which form compounds with less readiness than other elements such as carbon and nitrogen.

When there is no magnetic field applied to an atom, the different states distinguished by the quantum number m_μ degenerate into a single state. The spacing between these different levels, when they occur, is typically very small. When a single state splits into three (i.e., when $l = 1$), the resulting set of states is called a *triplet*. The occurrence of *multiplets* of any order when an atom is placed in an external magnetic field is known as the *Zeeman effect*.

The structure of these orbitals influences how atoms link up into molecules. Some orbital diagrams are shown in Figure 14.4. In these figures, the density of the dots at any position indicates the likelihood that the electron will be found at that position; higher density corresponds to higher probability.

All of the s orbitals are spherically symmetric; the others are not so simple [295]. Figure 14.5 shows the three p orbitals, p_x, p_y, and p_z. Actually, these pictures are just the angular parts of the orbital definitions, but they suggest the asymmetry of the orbital's structure.

The quantum numbers associated with an electron also determine its energy. In general, as the principal quantum number n goes up, so does the energy associated with the electron. Figure 14.6 shows some of the energy values associated with the sodium atom. The labels on each line are the wavelengths in angstroms (Å) of the transitions. The vertical lines represent allowable *electronic transitions* by which an electron can gain or lose energy to change states.

In addition to the Z ground states normally inhabited by the electrons of an electrically neutral atom, there are many higher-order *excited-state energy levels*. Above

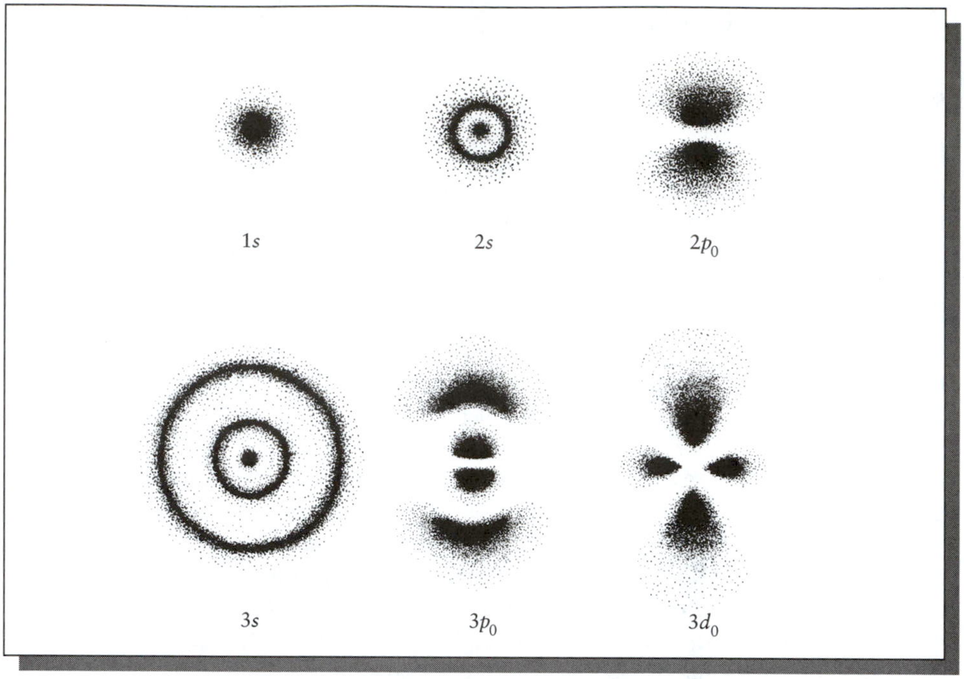

FIGURE 14.4

Probability density plots for some electron orbitals in the hydrogen atom. Redrawn from McQuarrie, *Quantum Chemistry*, fig. 6-12, p. 232.

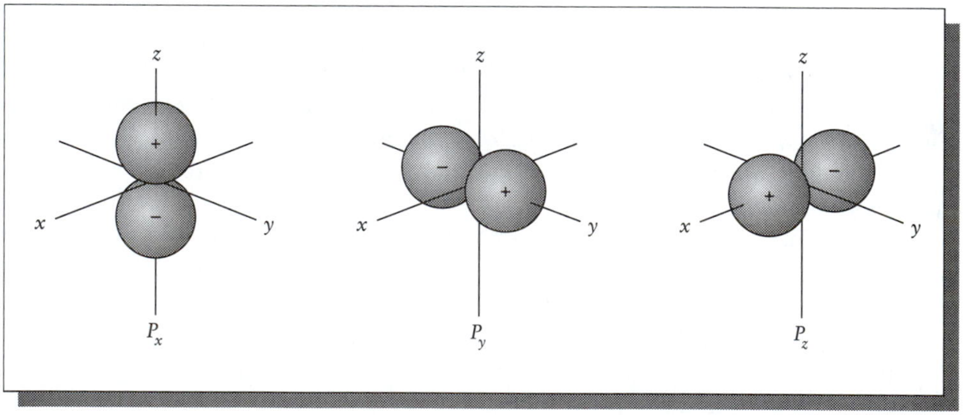

FIGURE 14.5

The p orbitals for $l = 1$. Redrawn from McQuarrie, *Quantum Chemistry*, fig. 6-11, p. 232.

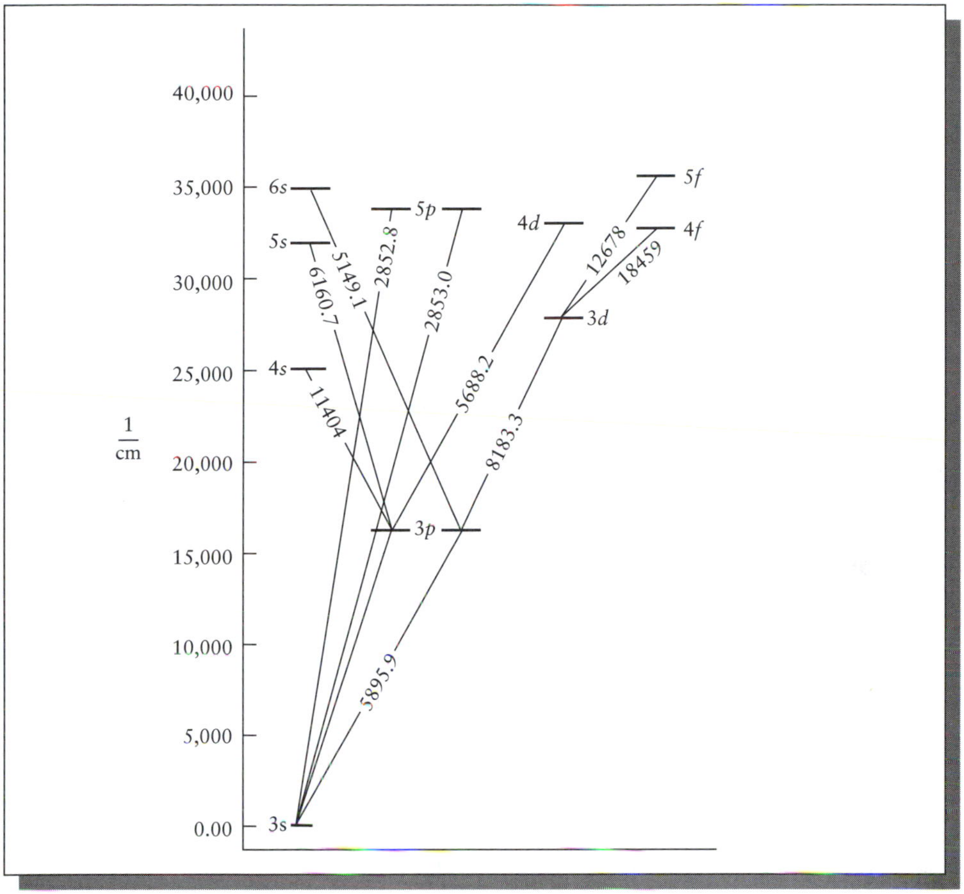

FIGURE 14.6

Some allowed energy levels in the sodium atom. Redrawn from McQuarrie, *Quantum Chemistry*, fig. 8-5, p. 325.

these levels lies the *ionization continuum*, where electrons become disassociated from particular atoms and are free to move away.

The essential point behind Figure 14.6, and the reason this information is useful to us in the first place, is that electrons move between states by absorbing and releasing energy, often in the form of photons. Consider the transition between the 3*p* and 4*d* states. From the diagram, we see that this corresponds to 5688.2 Å. Since the energy E of a photon of wavelength λ is given by $E = hc\lambda$, this corresponds to about 1.13×10^{-31} J. If a photon of this energy arrives at a sodium atom, where there is an electron in the $3p$ state and an opening in the $4d$ state and other conditions are right, then the atom will *absorb* the photon.

In general, absorption means that the photon disappears completely (recall that a photon cannot exist at rest, and cannot transfer only some of its energy), and the atom is now in an *excited state*. The incoming photon is called an *excitant*.

The excited atom may be stable or unstable, depending on its internal structure. Most unstable states have a lifetime no longer than 10^{-8} seconds. By that time, the electron will undergo a *radiative transition* by dropping back to the ground state and *emitting* a new photon to carry away the difference in energy between the two states.

Absorption and radiation have been found to obey certain *transition rules* that specify which electron transitions may happen. These are based on allowable changes in the quantum numbers of the electron and the system. For example, one rule states that the total angular-momentum quantum number L may change by only -1, 0, or $+1$, but in addition the system may never have $L = 0$ both before and after the transition [295].

There are many ways for an electron to absorb energy and reradiate it into the surrounding system. Suppose an electron in a ground state is excited by a photon, and then before it drops back down it is excited again by another photon, raising the electron to yet a higher energy level. If the electron finally drops down to the ground state in one step, it will emit a photon with more energy than either absorbed photon. Even when only one photon is absorbed, typically the radiated photon has less energy. The energy donated to a system by an excitant, and then left in the system after the emission of a photon, is called the *energy deficit*. When an atom responds to an excitant photon by emitting a photon of just the same energy, this is called *resonance radiation*. The ratio of the number of photons emitted for each photon absorbed, multiplied by 100, is called the *quantum efficiency* of the atom.

14.3 Particle Statistics

Large numbers of particles tend to distribute themselves among allowable configurations in predictable ways. This distribution may be characterized by different statistical measures that tell us how many particles we can expect for different ranges of quantum numbers.

The general idea is to consider N particles in s different states and ask for the most likely distribution of those particles among those states. For example, consider a solid that has been heated. The additional heat turns into kinetic energy among the electrons in the solid, and some of these electrons are in excited states. We would like to know how the electrons distribute themselves among these states. A similar question may be asked of the photons emitted by a material that has been exposed to heat or radiation.

The distribution of particles within a material is important to image synthesis because it sets up the phenomena that govern the way the material interacts with light. The appearance (or looks) of a material is dependent on many factors (coating, smoothness, and so on), but the physical properties of the material itself are always relevant. Understanding the distribution of energy states in a material gives us a handle on how the material will interact with light. Similarly, understanding the distribution of generated photons inside a material tells us something about the light that will be radiated by that material. Although we usually don't implement simulations of energy transfer at the subatomic level, it's useful to have a general understanding of the phenomena that we model in the aggregate with shading techniques, such as those in Chapter 15.

When there are a large number of particles in a system, the theoretical prediction for their distribution among the possible energy states is extremely close to what is actually measured [148]. To find this distribution, we will calculate W, the number of ways that the particles may be allocated for a particular distribution, and then find the distribution for which W is a maximum. This is the most likely distribution of particles. The distribution of electrons in particular is governed by *Fermi-Dirac* statistics.

14.3.1 Fermi-Dirac Statistics

Electrons are members of a class of subatomic particles known as *fermions*, which are characterized as being *noninteracting* and *indistinguishable* [465]. Their distribution is given by *Fermi-Dirac statistics*. We derive those statistics in this section. The information here may be skipped on a first reading of the book, since it is not essential to later material.

To develop the Fermi-Dirac statistics, we will follow the presentation in Longini [276]. We begin with Figure 14.7, which shows a pair of electron transitions between energies $E_1 \to E_2$ and $E_4 \to E_3$, where

$$E_1 - E_2 = E_3 - E_4 \tag{14.2}$$

These two events can only occur if energy levels E_1 and E_4 are occupied, and according to the Pauli exclusion principle, levels E_2 and E_3 must be empty. Write p_i for the probability that energy level E_i is occupied; this is called the *occupancy probability*. Then the probability P that the events in Figure 14.7 can occur is given by the product of the probability that E_1 and E_4 are occupied (p_1 and p_4, respectively), and E_2 and E_3 are empty ($1 - p_2$ and $1 - p_3$, respectively). Combined, these form the probability

$$P = p_1 p_4 (1 - p_2)(1 - p_3) F \tag{14.3}$$

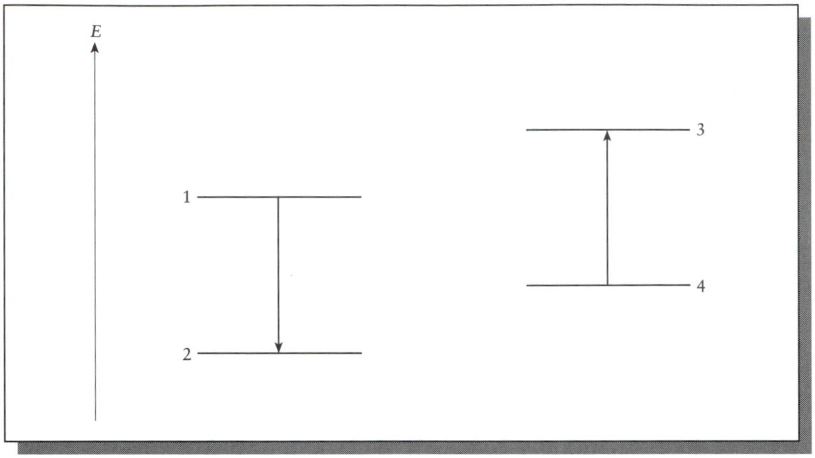

FIGURE 14.7
A pair of electronic transitions.

where we have included a *quantum-mechanical electronic interaction factor*, F.

We can state another condition on the system by using the *principle of detailed balancing*. This quantum-mechanical principle includes some of the notion that in quantum mechanics there is no preferred direction for time; reactions can occur in either direction. The principle of detailed balancing says that in thermal equilibrium, every physical process proceeds on the average at the same rate as its own inverse [276]. This means that the reaction has the same probability of running in the opposite direction, with the appropriate probabilities exchanged:

$$P = p_2 p_3 (1 - p_1)(1 - p_4) F \tag{14.4}$$

where we have used the same factor F.

Since both Equations 14.3 and 14.4 express P, we can combine them to find

$$p_1 p_4 (1 - p_2)(1 - p_3) = p_2 p_3 (1 - p_1)(1 - p_4) \tag{14.5}$$

Dividing through by $p_2 p_4 (1 - p_1)(p - p_3)$, we find

$$\frac{p_1}{1 - p_1} \frac{1 - p_2}{p_2} = \frac{p_3}{1 - p_3} \frac{1 - p_4}{p_4} \tag{14.6}$$

Now from our assumption in Equation 14.2, the left-hand side of Equation 14.6 depends only on the difference of energies $E_2 - E_1$; similarly, the right-hand side

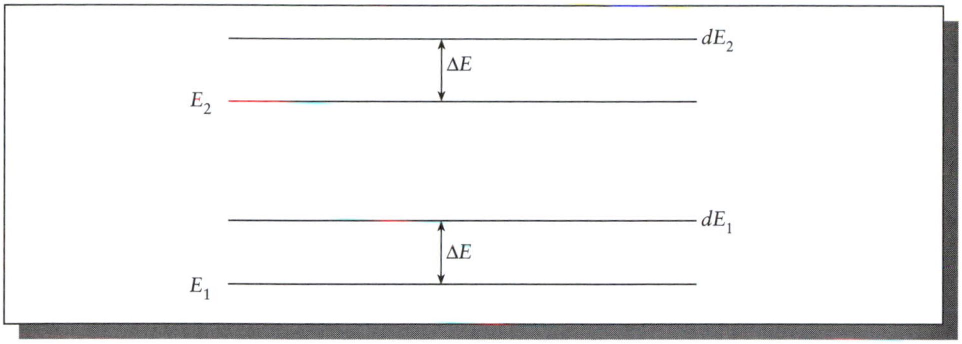

FIGURE 14.8
Energy states dE_1 and dE_2.

depends only on the difference $E_3 - E_4$. To make this product mimic the difference it models, we recast each term as a logarithm:

$$G_1 = \ln \frac{f_1}{1 - f_1} \qquad G_2 = \ln \frac{f_2}{1 - f_2} \tag{14.7}$$

Consider now two new states, $dE_1 = E_1 + \Delta E$ and $dE_2 = E_2 + \Delta E$, as shown in Figure 14.8. Since $G_1 - G_2$ depends only on $E_1 - E_2$,

$$(G_1 + \Delta G) - (G_2 + \Delta G) = (E_1 + \Delta E) - (E_2 + \Delta E) \tag{14.8}$$

Writing dG for ΔG and dE for ΔE, we set

$$\frac{dG_1}{dE_1} = -L_1 \qquad \frac{dG_2}{dE_2} = -L_2 \tag{14.9}$$

So then

$$0 = dG_1 = dG_2 = -L_1\, dE_1 + L_2\, dE_2 = (L_2 - L_1)\, dE_1 \tag{14.10}$$

Since $dE_1 \neq 0$, then $L - 2 - L_1 = 0$, or $L_2 = L_1$. But since the energies E were arbitrary, the values of L must be independent of E.

Suppose we pick a reference energy E_F where $G_F = 0$. This value is called the *Fermi level* of energy; it's the energy where the occupancy probability is $1/2$. Then from Equation 14.9 we can write

$$\int_{G_F}^{G_1} dG = -L \int_{E_F}^{E_1} dE \tag{14.11}$$

Integrating, we find

$$G_1 = L(E_F - E_1) \tag{14.12}$$

Equating this with the definition of G_1 from Equation 14.7, we find

$$\ln \frac{f_1}{1 - f_1} = L(E_F - E_1) \tag{14.13}$$

which we can solve for f_1, finding

$$f_1 = \frac{1}{1 + \exp\left[L(E_1 - E_F)\right]} \tag{14.14}$$

Equation 14.14 is called the *occupancy equation* for energy level E_1. Note that $f_1(E_F) = 1/2$.

Now that we know the likelihood of an electron to be at energy level E_1, we can find the total energy U in the system by summing the products of the number of electrons f_i at each level i with the energy E_i at that level:

$$U = \sum_i E_i f_i \tag{14.15}$$

Comparing this result to experiments, we find that l corresponds to kT, where k is Boltzmann's constant (given in Table E.3). Then we can write the occupancy equation as

$$f_1 = \frac{1}{1 + \exp(E_1 - E_F)/kT} \tag{14.16}$$

which is known as the *Fermi-Dirac distribution*. This distribution is plotted in Figure 14.9.

Note that at absolute zero (that is, $kT = 0$),

$$f_E = \begin{cases} 0 & E > E_F \\ 1 & E < E_F \end{cases} \tag{14.17}$$

This tells us that at absolute zero, all of the electron orbitals below the Fermi energy are filled, and all of the orbitals above it are empty. As energy is introduced into the system, electrons move out of the lower orbitals into the more excited, higher-energy cells.

14.4 Molecular Structure

Understanding the structure of molecules will help us understand some of the aggregate properties of matter, which influence how matter generates energy (or emits

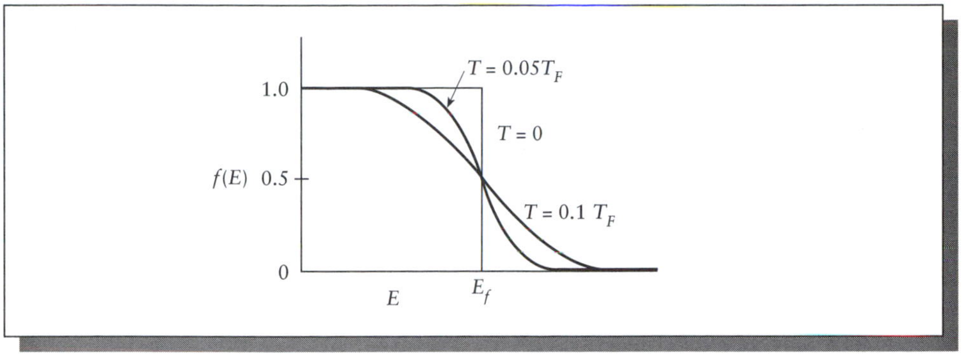

FIGURE 14.9

The Fermi-Dirac distribution. Redrawn from Wang, *Introduction to Solid State Electronics*, fig. 3.5.1, p. 38.

light) and responds to incident energy (or reflects and transmits light). Though we will not be analyzing molecular structures in this book, much of the literature on the appearance and behavior of solids supposes a basic knowledge of molecular structure. That literature is invaluable when writing rendering programs that include real materials. To make that literature accessible, we include here a short survey of molecular structure and bonding. Much of this section is based on material in McQuarrie [295].

A *molecule* is an electrically neutral, stable combination of two or more atoms [267]. These atoms may all be of the same element, or a variety of atoms may be mixed together. Atoms are typically held together by *bonds* that form between their outermost, or *valence*, electrons.

The simplest molecule is probably that formed by joining two hydrogen atoms; it is denoted H_2 (in general, a molecule is named by listing its component elements with a subscript indicating the number of atoms of each type).

There are two general classes of bonds: *ionic* (or *polar*) and *molecular-orbital* (or *covalent*).

14.4.1 Ionic Bonds

Ionic bonding is rather straightforward from a macroscopic viewpoint; this is the sort of bond that forms between two ions, or electrically charged atoms [267]. For example, from Table 14.1 we see that potassium (K) has an atomic structure with a single electron in its outermost shell $4s$. If this single outermost (or *valence*) electron were to be lost by the atom, the atom would become an *ion*, or a charged atom, with a single unit of excess positive charge. This is written K^+.

Similarly, chlorine (Cl) has an outermost shell of $3p^5$. Since the p shell can contain up to six electrons, it's conceivable that chlorine could pick up an extra electron to complete the shell (this electron could come from some other atom in a solid or crystal). Then the outermost shell would be $3p^6$, and the atom would become an ion with a single excessive negative charge, written Cl^-.

If we bring these two ions together, the equal but opposite excess charges will neutralize each other, resulting in an electrically neutral molecule: KCl.

14.4.2 Molecular-Orbital Bonds

Molecular-orbital bonds are not as simple as ionic bonds. We will start with the molecule composed of two hydrogen atoms: H_2.

Recall that the shape of an electron orbital is given by a probability function; the larger the function's value at some point, the more likely the electron is to be there. Suppose we consider the $1s$ orbitals for two hydrogen atoms, initially very far apart but then brought together. At some distance, the probability fields will begin to overlap, and it will become increasingly likely that the electron will be found at some point in a region near a line between the two nuclei. This will cause the total energy in the system to decrease as the atoms approach each other. When the atoms get sufficiently close together, the nuclei will begin to repel one another, sending the energy of the system back up. This dependence of *internuclear potential energy* on distance is plotted in Figure 14.10. The label ΔE_+ shows the energy of the combined system relative to that of two independent hydrogen atoms.

The figure shows that there is some point at which the energy is a minimum, and that this is less than the energy of the two atoms at a great distance; the H_2 atom is in a stable state.

The general idea here is that we can describe the orbitals in a molecule by considering the individual orbitals of the atoms. In fact, we can describe the orbitals of electrons in the molecule as linear combinations of the orbitals of electrons in the component atoms; this is called the *molecular-orbital* method. Mathematically, we sometimes build molecular orbitals from products of linear combinations of atomic orbitals; this is called the LCAO-MO (*linear combination of atomic orbitals–molecular orbital* method).

The mathematics predicts two types of orbitals into which electrons can fit: *bonding orbitals* that represent an attraction between the two nuclei, and *antibonding orbitals* that represent a repulsive force between the nuclei. Typically we subscript an orbital with the letter a or b to identify whether it is antibonding or bonding. The

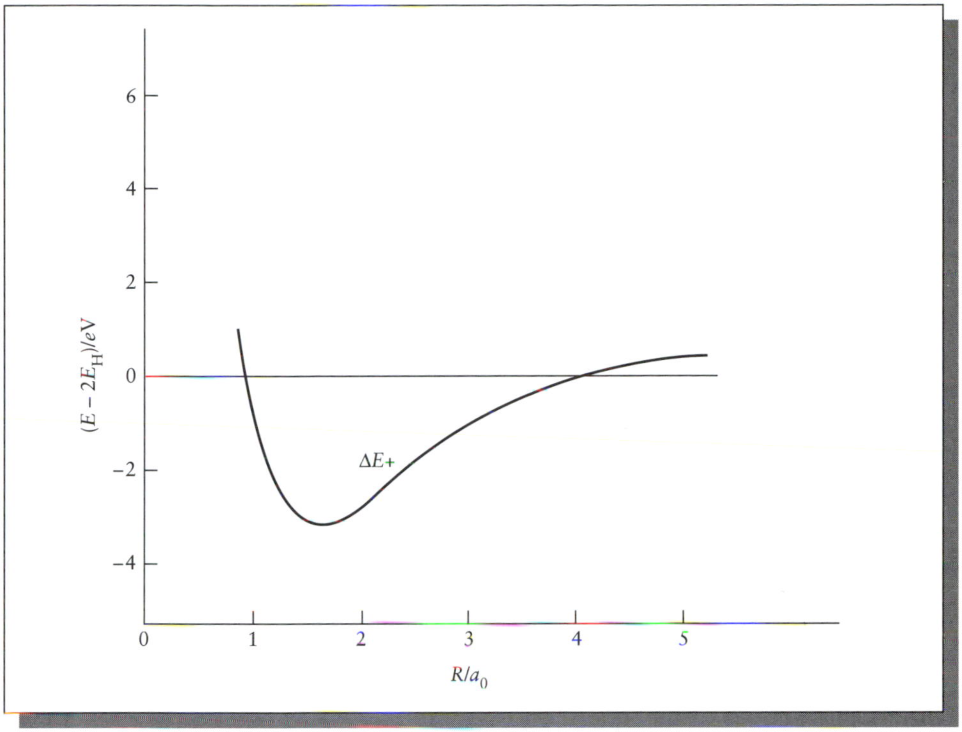

FIGURE 14.10

The internuclear potential energy curves of H_2. Redrawn from McQuarrie, *Quantum Chemistry*, fig. 9-5, p. 352.

bond order, or number of bonds in a molecule, is given by

$$\text{bond order} = \frac{\begin{pmatrix}\text{number of electrons}\\ \text{in bonding orbitals}\end{pmatrix} - \begin{pmatrix}\text{number of electrons}\\ \text{in antibonding orbitals}\end{pmatrix}}{2} \qquad (14.18)$$

Suppose we have two identical hydrogen atoms. Each has an identical single electron, with a wave function ψ defined everywhere in space (the squared value of this complex-valued wave function, $\psi\overline{\psi}$, is the probability of finding the electron at the place and time the function is evaluated). For atoms A and B, we'll call the wave functions for their electrons $1s_A$ and $1s_B$, respectively, reminding us that each one represents an electron in the $1s$ orbital centered around its respective nucleus.

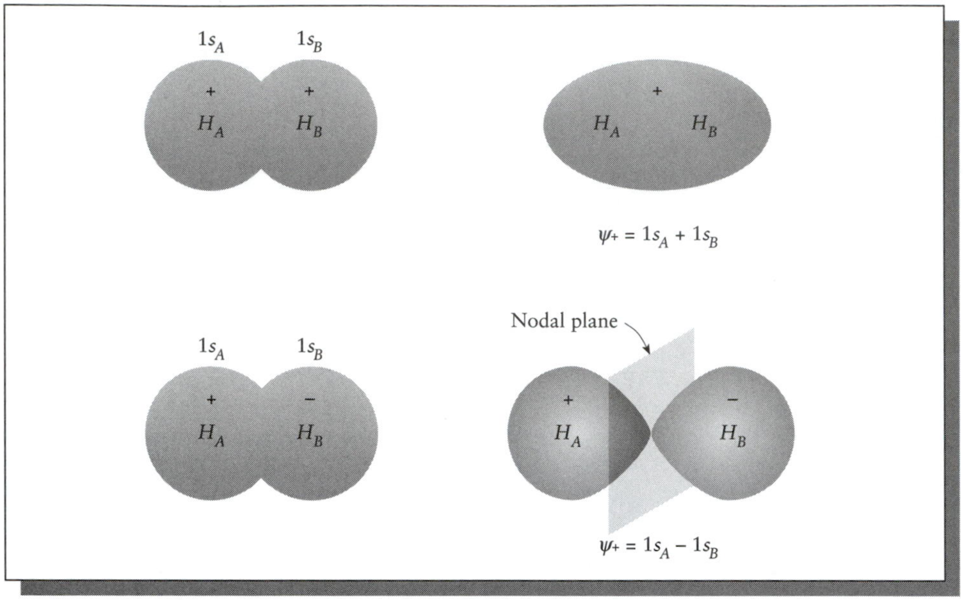

FIGURE 14.11

Linear combinations of two $1s$ orbitals. Redrawn from McQuarrie, *Quantum Chemistry*, fig. 9-8, p. 370.

In the LCAO-MO approach, molecular orbitals are formed from linear combinations of atomic orbitals. For H_2, we'll write the the possible wave functions

$$\begin{aligned} \psi_+ &= 1s_A + 1s_B \\ \psi_- &= 1s_A - 1s_B \end{aligned} \tag{14.19}$$

These two orbitals are shown in Figure 14.11.

The bonding orbital ψ_+ concentrates electron density between the nuclei. The antibonding orbital ψ_- makes the region between the nuclei sparse; in fact there's a plane between the nuclei perpendicular to the axis between them (the *nodal plane*) where the electron density falls to zero.

Note that the electron density in these orbitals is symmetric about the axis between the nuclei, like s orbitals. They have been given the similar name σ orbitals. Because these particular molecular orbitals derive from $1s$ atomic orbitals, they are called the $\sigma 1s$ orbitals. There are two common notational conventions for distinguishing the bonding and antibonding forms of these orbitals [295]. One approach writes

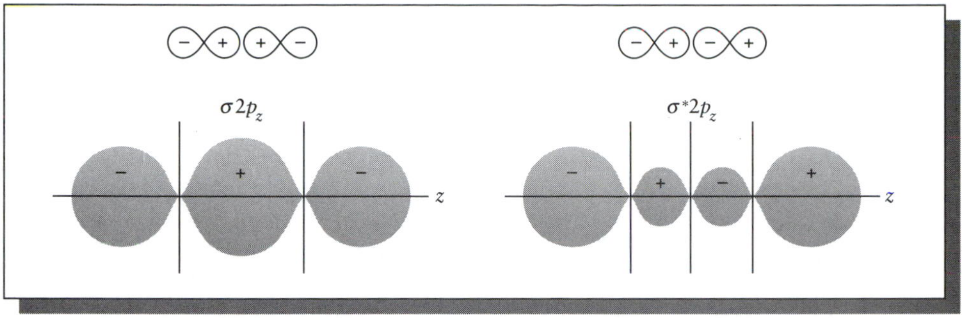

FIGURE 14.12

The $\sigma 2p_z$ and $\sigma^* 2p_z$ molecular orbitals. Redrawn from McQuarrie, *Quantum Chemistry*, fig. 9-9, p. 371.

the bonding form as simply $\sigma 1s$, and the antibonding form as $\sigma^* 1s$. The other approach thinks of the wave function as being either *even* (or symmetrical) or *odd* (or antisymmetrical) about the midpoint between the nuclei, just as cosine and sine are even and odd about the origin. The German word for "even" is *gerade*, so the bonding (even) orbital ψ_+ is sometimes written with the subscript g, as in $\sigma_g 1s$. The German word for "odd" is *ungerade*, so the antibonding (odd) orbital ψ_- is sometimes written with the subscript u, as in $\sigma_u 1s$.

We can continue building molecular orbitals from combinations of atomic orbitals. Usually, only orbitals of similar energies combine, so we can focus our attention on like or nearby combinations of orbitals. The orbitals built from a pair of $2s$ electrons would be written $\sigma_g 2s$ and $\sigma_u 2s$.

Moving to higher energies, we can form combinations of p orbitals. The p orbitals are not radially symmetric; we can identify the three p orbitals, each one looking like a pair of spheres about the origin, located along the x, y, and z axes as in Figure 14.5. Suppose that we place the two hydrogen nuclei some distance apart along the z axis. Adding the $2p_z$ orbitals for the two atoms gives us again a bonding and an antibonding set of orbitals, as shown in Figure 14.12. Because they are symmetric about the internuclear axis, they are classified as σ-type orbitals:

$$\sigma 2p_z = 2p_{zA} + 2s_{zB}$$
$$\sigma^* 2p_z = 2p_{zA} + 2s_{zB} \qquad (14.20)$$

On the other hand, the $2p_x$ and $2p_y$ orbits are not symmetrical about the internuclear axis. In fact, the yz plane forms a nodal plane for the p_x orbitals, and the xz plane is nodal for the p_y orbitals, as shown in Figure 14.13.

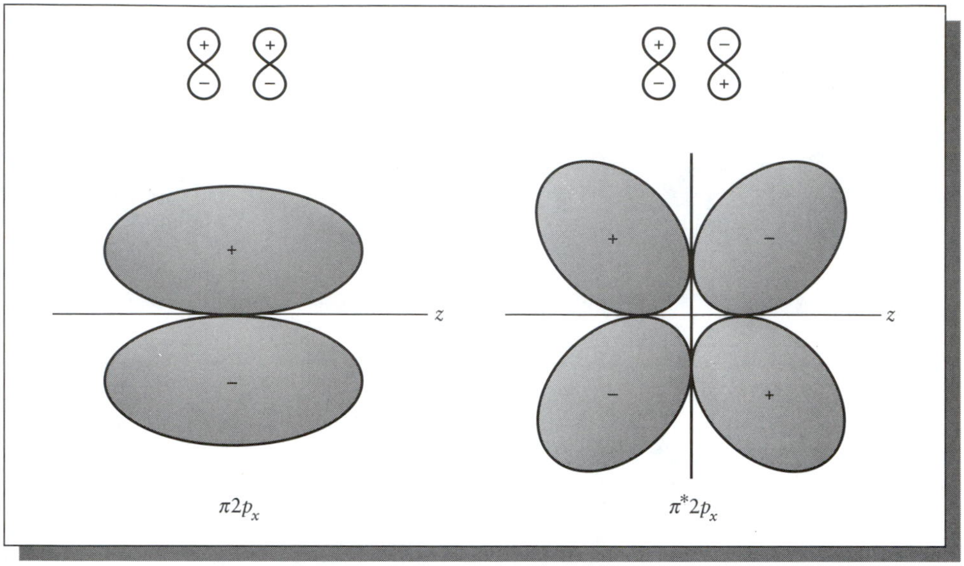

FIGURE 14.13

The $\pi 2p_x$ and $\pi^* 2p_x$ molecular orbitals. Redrawn from McQuarrie, *Quantum Chemistry*, fig. 9-10, p. 372.

Within the atom, an orbital with one nodal plane is called a p orbital, so in the molecular case such orbitals are called π *orbitals*. The bonding $\pi 2p_x$ orbital has one nodal plane; the antibonding $\pi^* 2p_x$ has two nodal planes.

To see how this all works out, we will compute the bond order for H_2 and He_2. We will fill electrons in the system according to the Pauli exclusion principle. In H_2 we have two electrons, so we place one electron of each spin into the $\sigma 1s$ orbital, and the resulting configuration of H_2 is $(\sigma 1s)^2$. The bond order is $(2-0)/2 = 1$, which suggests that there is some net bonding force keeping the atoms together.

Now turn to diatomic helium He_2, which has two electrons in each atom for a total of four. Two of these electrons go into the $\sigma 1s$ orbital, and the other two go into the $\sigma^* 1s$ orbital. The resulting configuration is $(\sigma 1s)^2(\sigma^* 1s)^2$, with a bond order of $(2-2) = 0$. The theory says that there is no net force keeping the atoms together, so this molecule ought not to form. In accordance with this predication, He_2 has never been experimentally observed [295].

The construction of molecular orbitals from electron orbitals can become more complex than the simple examples presented above. As a first example, s and p

orbitals can overlap. This is the case in water (H_2O). The oxygen molecule has an electron configuration of $1s^2 2s^2 2p_x{}^2 2p_y{}^1 2p_z{}^1$ (recall that the p shell fills up so that electrons are as far apart as possible). The unpaired $2p_y$ and $2p_z$ electrons are available to the $1s$ electron in the hydrogen for bonds. We would expect a 90° angle between the two hydrogen molecules, but experiment gives a value of 104°. This is because we're leaving out the mutual ionic repulsion between the two hydrogen atoms, forcing them apart. Including this term brings us closer to 104°.

The full power of the LCAO-MO approach appears when we build up linear combinations of electron orbitals to create new molecular orbitals.

For example, consider the molecule beryllium hydride, BeH_2. There are two Be–H bonds in this molecule, at an angle of 180°. The ground state of beryllium is $1s^2 2s^2$; where could these two hydrogen bonds come from in such a configuration? The answer comes from creating a linear combination of berylliums's $2s$ and $2p_z$ orbitals, creating a new *hybrid orbital*, called sp. The bonds forming from these orbitals are called *bond orbitals*, made of a combination of the newly created sp orbitals on beryllium and the $1s$ orbitals on hydrogen. Figure 14.14 shows the contours associated with one sp orbital; since $2p_z$ has two lobes, there's another orbital just like this at 180° from this one. The complete outer orbital picture for the beryllium atom is shown in Figure 14.15; note that although the $2p_x$ and $2p_y$ orbitals are shown for clarity, they are unoccupied. Finally, the mating of a hydrogen atom with these orbitals is shown in Figure 14.16.

The energy of this hybrid orbital is different from the energy associated with either the $2s$ or $2p$ electron orbitals. This changes the energy transitions that are available to the electrons in the molecule, and hence how that molecule (and substances made of it) will respond to incident energy in the form of light.

This process can be repeated to form an sp^2 hybrid orbital, which forms a molecule such as BH_3.

Carrying it one more step, we can consider forming a compound out of carbon. Compounds containing carbon are called *organic molecules*, because of the importance of carbon to life. Molecules that do not contain carbon are called *inorganic*. The molecule methane, CH_4, is built from one carbon atom and four hydrogen atoms. The molecule forms a regular tetrahedron with the carbon atom at the center.

The carbon forms sp^3 hybrid orbitals, whose contours are shown in Figure 14.17. The resulting sp^3 orbitals link up with hydrogen's $1s$ orbitals to form the tetrahedron that is methane, as shown in Figure 14.18.

More complex hybrid orbitals and more complicated bonding structures can be developed from these principles [295], but these examples are sufficient for our purposes of illustrating the types of structures that form when atoms arrange themselves into molecules.

The essential point is to notice that the basic energy transitions available to electrons change when those electrons are involved in a bonding process that brings

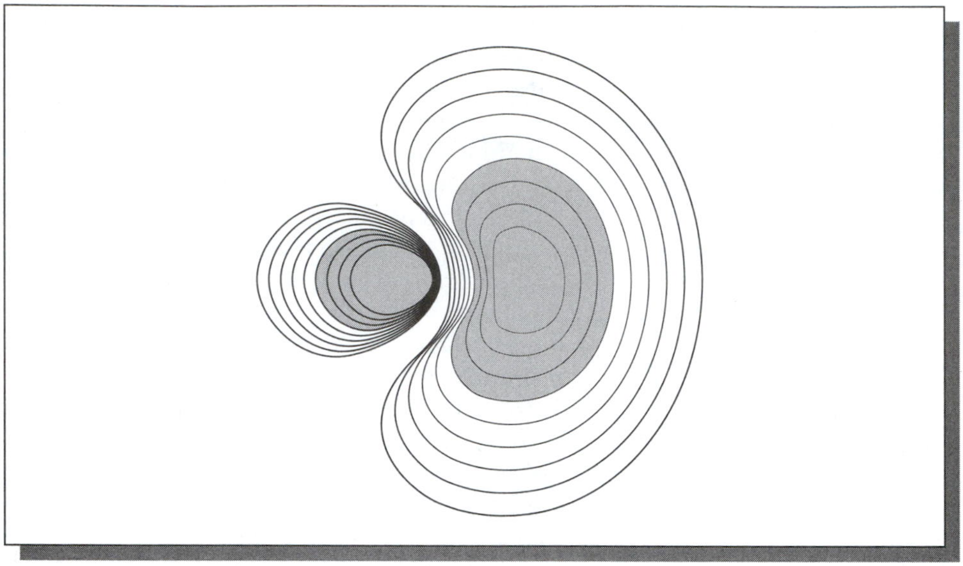

FIGURE 14.14

Contour map for the *sp* hybrid orbital. Redrawn from McQuarrie, *Quantum Chemistry*, fig. 9-18, p. 400.

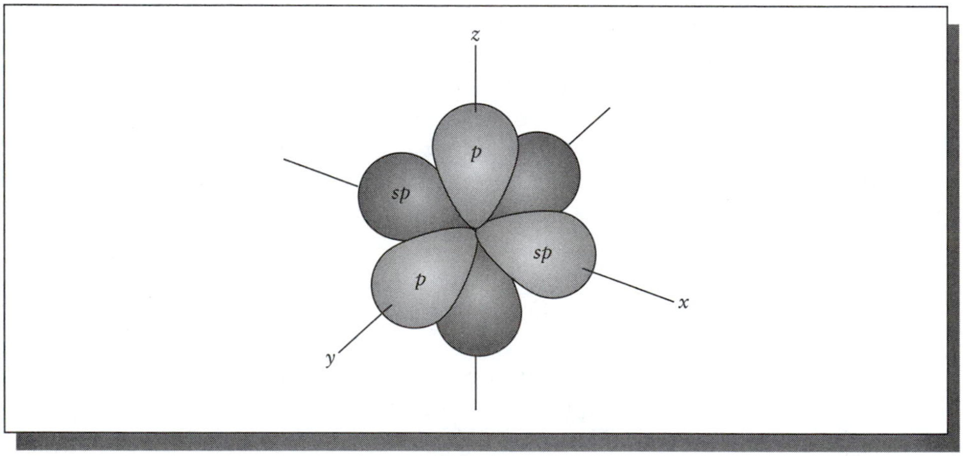

FIGURE 14.15

The *sp* orbitals along p_x. Redrawn from McQuarrie, *Quantum Chemistry*, fig. 9-19, p. 400.

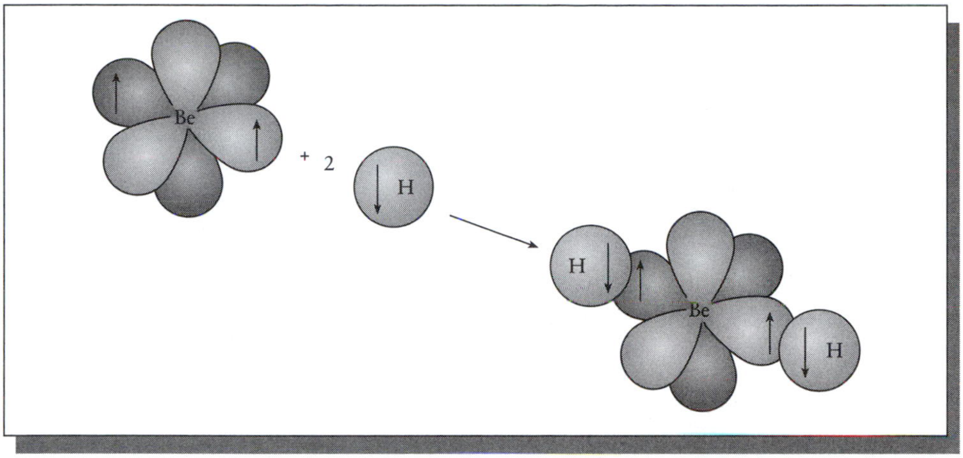

FIGURE 14.16

The formation of BeH_2. The arrows indicate coupled spins. Redrawn from McQuarrie, *Quantum Chemistry*, fig. 9-20, p. 401.

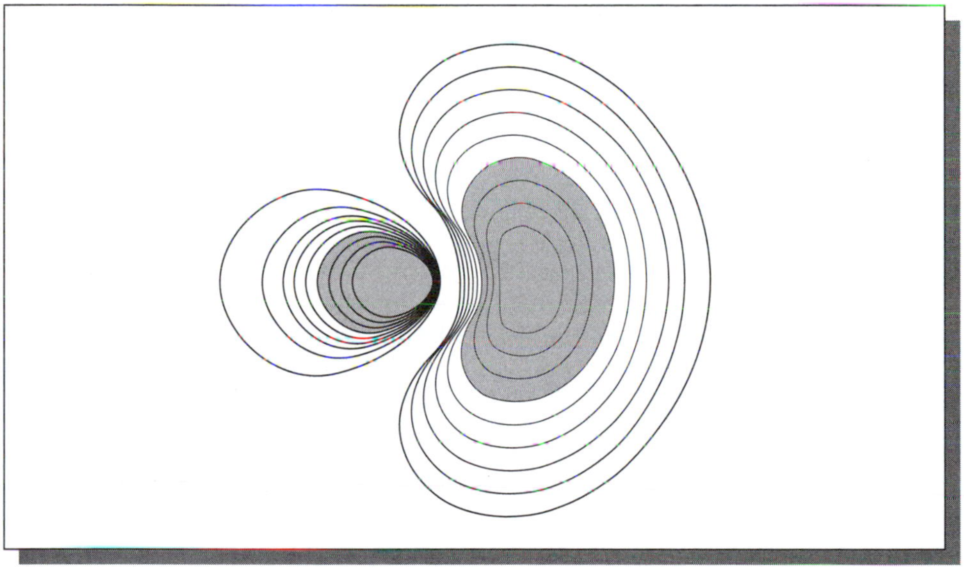

FIGURE 14.17

An electron-density contour map of an sp^3 hybrid orbital. Redrawn from McQuarrie, *Quantum Chemistry*, fig. 9-24, p. 406.

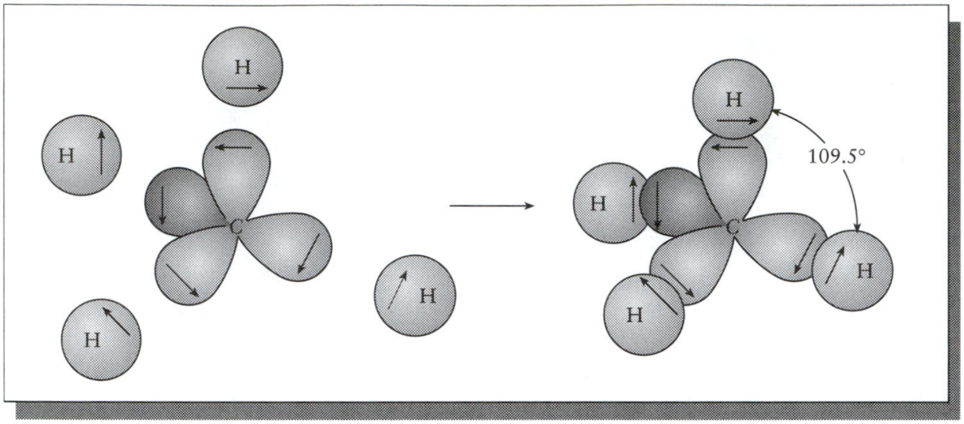

FIGURE 14.18
The structure of methane, illustrating the tetrahedral arrangement of sp^3 hybrid orbitals. Redrawn from McQuarrie, *Quantum Chemistry*, fig. 9-26, p. 407.

atoms together into molecules. In addition, molecules are large compared to atoms, and can contain significant translational and vibrational energy that also affects what energy is absorbed and emitted by a system of atoms.

14.5 Radiation

When we are able to see an object, it is because light is leaving it and arriving at our eye. Such light may be classified into two fundamentally different types: *thermal* and *luminescent* [267].

Thermal emissions are due to the object shedding excess heat energy in the form of light. An incandescent light bulb is a thermal radiator; an electric current is run through the filament to make it hot, and the filament gets rid of the heat by dispersing the energy through the emission of particles in a range of energy. The filaments in simple incandescent bulbs are chosen to maximize the number of particles emitted in the visible band. In a thermal radiator, the amount of light emitted is primarily dependent on the nature of the material and its temperature.

Luminescent emission is due to energy stored (perhaps for a very short time) in the material, and is primarily due to factors other than temperature, though the temperature can affect the material. While thermal energy is generated by the object itself, luminescent light is in response to light energy arriving from elsewhere. We have discussed how an object responds to incident light in a macroscopic way in Chapter 13, where we characterized a material in terms of its bidirectional distribution function.

In the following two sections we will look at thermal radiation and a particularly important class of luminescent materials, the *phosphors*.

14.6 Blackbodies

If we take a piece of almost any common metal and heat it up enough, it will start to glow red. If we raise the temperature still higher, the metal becomes white-hot. This simple observation suggests that there is a link between temperature and radiation, and in fact that is found to be the case.

In general, at least some fraction of the energy emitted by some body at a given wavelength is a function of the material and the temperature. Using the second law of thermodynamics, we can predict the theoretical maximum amount of such light that can be radiated at a wavelength ν given the temperature T for any material. We can posit an imaginary material that satisfies this maximum at every wavelength; such a body is called a *blackbody*.

To find the energy radiated by a blackbody, we first need to find the likely distribution of photons for a system at a given state of energy. Just as electrons distribute themselves according to Fermi-Dirac statistics, photons follow a statistical law as well, called Bose-Einstein statistics, which we derive now.

14.6.1 Bose-Einstein Statistics

To describe the distribution of photons, we turn to *Bose-Einstein statistics*, which are similar in spirit to the Fermi-Dirac statistics but different in detail. The information in this section may be skipped on a first reading of the book, since it is not essential to later material.

Bose-Einstein statistics are appropriate for *bosons*, which are particles that are either spinless or have integral spins (recall that electrons have spins of $\pm 1/2$) [465]. Photons fall in this class because they have no spin. Photons also are not controlled by the Pauli exclusion principle, so multiple photons in a system can share the same quantum numbers.

We will develop Bose-Einstein statistics following Fowles [148]. To begin, we will divide the range of energies that photons may take on into a number of states s. So we will identify each range by the subscript ν, indicating the center frequency corresponding to that region. Within each state s_ν there are g_ν different *quantum modes* in which the photon can exist (these correspond to different internal states

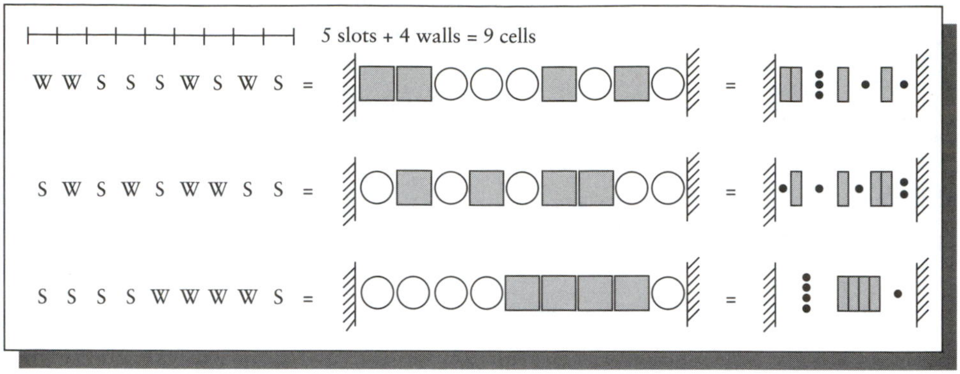

FIGURE 14.19

The $g_\nu = 5$ boxes induce $g_\nu - 1 = 4$ walls for the n_ν photons. We mark the diagram with S for slot (or photon) and W for wall.

of the particle: e.g., polarization). The number of photons n_ν in state i is called the *occupation index* or *occupation number* for that state.

Consider just state i for a moment. It contains n_ν photons, distributed among g_ν different quantum modes. If we think of each mode as a box, then for a given distribution we want to know how many ways the n_ν photons may be allocated among the g_ν boxes.

We can find the answer with a little pictorial construction. If there are g_ν boxes, then there are $g_\nu - 1$ internal walls (walls between boxes). Suppose we make a picture containing $n_\nu + g_\nu - 1$ slots, as in Figure 14.19. Into each slot we can place either a photon or a wall.

To intepret this picture, imagine that there is a horizontal row of g_ν boxes separated by $g_\nu - 1$ walls, and in each box there may be 0 or more photons. We start at the left and count out the number of photons that we see, writing down an S (for slot) for each one. When we have placed an S for every photon we move to the right and encounter a wall, so we write W. Then we repeat the process; if there are no photons, then the next W follows immediately. Each pattern of S's and W's then describes one particular way in which the photons can be distributed among the boxes. We assume that there are walls at the far left and right ends of the boxes that don't need to be explicitly counted.

The total number of such pictures is the number of permutations of $n_\nu + g_\nu - 1$ objects, or $(n_\nu+g_\nu-1)!$. But recall that the photons are indistinguishable; this means that we can permute all the photons and see no difference. So we must divide the number of pictures by the number of permutations of n_ν photons, or $(n_\nu)!$. Similarly, the boxes are all the same, so we must divide by $(g_\nu - 1)!$. The total number of ways W_ν to allocate n_ν photons into g_ν modes is therefore

$$W_\nu = \frac{(n_\nu + g_\nu - 1)!}{n_\nu!\,(g_\nu - 1)!} \tag{14.21}$$

When n_ν is large, $n_\nu - 1 \approx n_\nu$, so we will drop the constant term 1 below for simplicity.

The probability of the system being in some configuration W is then

$$W = \prod_\nu W_\nu = \prod_\nu \frac{(n_\nu + g_\nu)!}{n_\nu!\,(g_\nu)!} \tag{14.22}$$

To simplify this equation, we will replace the factorial with one of *Stirling's approximations*, $\ln x! \approx x \ln x - x$, which is good for large x[1] [41, 184]. So we can write the system probability W as

$$\ln W = \sum_\nu \left[(n_\nu + g_\nu)\ln(n_\nu + g_\nu) - n_\nu \ln(n_\nu) - g_\nu \ln(g_\nu)\right] \tag{14.23}$$

It can be shown that if we differentiate Equation 14.23, we are at a maximum [148]. So differentiating and setting the derivative $d(\ln W)$ to 0, we find

$$d(\ln W) = \sum_\nu \left[\ln(n_\nu + g_\nu) - \ln n_\nu\right] dn_\nu = 0 \tag{14.24}$$

If each of the n_ν were independent, then each term in Equation 14.24 would need to go to zero in order for the whole expression to go to zero. But they are not independent. Recall that we are looking at different distributions for a given, constant energy E. It's that total energy $E = \sum h\nu n_\nu$ that remains constant, so it's this derivative dE that goes to zero:

$$dE \sum_\nu h\nu\, dn_\nu = 0 \tag{14.25}$$

We now want to find n_ν as a function of ν so that Equations 14.24 and 14.25 are simultaneously satisfied. This is easily accomplished by using *Lagrange multipliers*. We multiply Equation 14.25 by an unknown constant $-\beta$, and add the result to Equation 14.24:

$$d(\ln W) - \beta dE = 0 \tag{14.26}$$

---

[1] Stirling also proposed $n! \approx e^{-n} n^n \sqrt{2\pi n}$ [41].

which we can expand to find

$$\sum_{\nu} [\ln(n_\nu + g_\nu) - \ln n_\nu - \beta h\nu]\, dn_\nu = 0 \tag{14.27}$$

We now derive the term in brackets to 0 by choosing β as

$$\beta = \frac{\ln(n_\nu + g_\nu) - \ln n_\nu}{h\nu} \tag{14.28}$$

Solving for n_ν / g_ν, we find the *occupation index* is given by

$$n_\nu = \frac{1}{\exp[\beta h\nu] - 1} \tag{14.29}$$

This distribution maximizes W while holding the total energy E constant. It is known as the *Bose-Einstein distribution law for photons*, or simply *Bose-Einstein statistics*.

14.7 Blackbody Energy Distribution

To derive the blackbody energy distribution, consider an object hung by a thread in the middle of an enclosed cavity, as in Figure 14.20. This object is in *thermal equilibrium* with its environment, which means that it emits energy at the same rate that it absorbs it.

If the object receives irradiance E and has albedo β, then its radiant exitance M is given by

$$M = \beta E \tag{14.30}$$

If there are many objects in the system with different values of β, we find that $E = M/\beta$ is a constant for them all. This statement is *Kirchhoff's law*, and it tells us that the ratio of emitted to absorbed power is the same for all bodies.

A blackbody has a reflectance $\beta = 1$, meaning that it returns to the environment all of the energy it absorbs. Let's look more closely at this energy, following the discussion in Fowles [148] and Möller [311]. The information in this section may be skipped on a first reading of the book since it is not essential to later material. Our goal will be to find a description of how much energy can leave the blackbody at any given frequency. We'll do this by first characterizing the energy that can leave a hole in the surface, and then determining the structure of the energy inside the object. Coupling these two, we will find how much of the internal energy exits through the hole, which is the radiation of the blackbody.

So we begin by imagining a small hole cut into the surface. By integrating the spectral radiant flux density u_ν over all wavelengths we find the radiant flux density u:

$$u = \int_0^\infty u_\nu \tag{14.31}$$

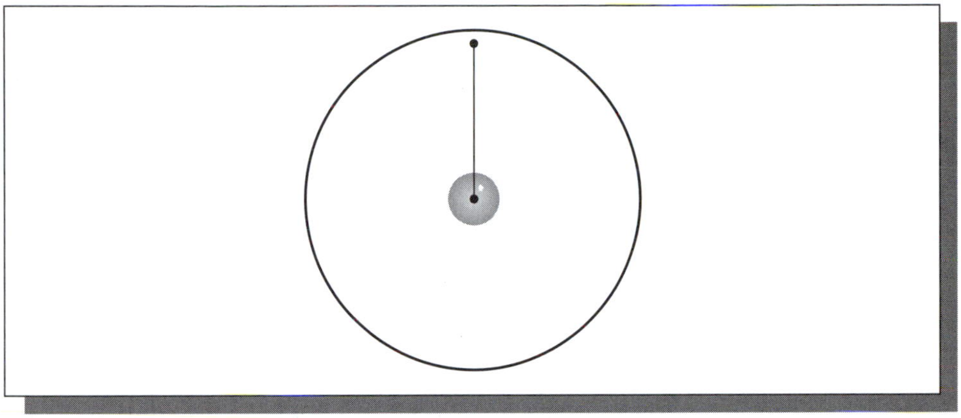

FIGURE 14.20
A blackbody in thermal equilibrium.

We know that the speed of light is c. The fraction of total energy u inside the cavity that can leak out through this hole is then $uc\vec{\omega}/4\pi$, where $\vec{\omega}/4\pi$ represents the amount of the sphere occupied by the solid angle describing the hole. Integrating this over the hemisphere at the hole:

$$M = \int_{\Omega_o} \frac{uc}{4\pi} \vec{\omega}^{\mathbf{N}} = \frac{uc}{4} \tag{14.32}$$

(see Equation 13.52). The spectral radiant exitance M_ν is then $M_\nu = u_\nu c/4$.

Now we want to find the energy u inside the object. To find this, we will simplify the situation by assuming that the object under study is a box with dimensions $A \times B \times C$. We will assume that the system is stable, so that the radiation patterns inside the box are *standing waves*. This means that the radiation will be modeled as a vibrating wave, and we will assume that the wave has a value of 0 at the sides of the box.

One of the simplest waves to model is the plane wave, given by

$$e^{j(\mathbf{k}\cdot\mathbf{r}-\omega t)} \tag{14.33}$$

This sinusoidal wave is traveling in a direction given by the vector $\mathbf{k}$, with a phase at the origin given by ω. If we expand out the vectors, we get

$$e^{j(\mathbf{k}\cdot\mathbf{r}-\omega t)} = e^{j(k_x x)} e^{j(k_y y)} e^{j(k_z z)} e^{-j\omega t} \tag{14.34}$$

As stated above, we want these waves to have a value of zero at the box sides. Sine waves go through zero every π units, so we satisfy our condition in the box if

$$k_x A = \pi n_x \qquad k_y A = \pi n_y \qquad k_z A = \pi n_z \tag{14.35}$$

where n_x, n_y, and n_z are all integers. Each set of values (n_x, n_y, n_z) is called a *mode* of the system, and represents a particular, stable state.

The magnitude of the direction vector $\mathbf{k}$ can now be written

$$k^2 = {k_x}^2 + {k_y}^2 + {k_z}^2 = \pi^2 \left(\frac{{n_x}^2}{A^2} + \frac{{n_y}^2}{B^2} + \frac{{n_z}^2}{C^2} \right) \tag{14.36}$$

Equivalently,

$$\begin{aligned} k^2 &= \left(\frac{2\pi}{\lambda_x}\right)^2 + \left(\frac{2\pi}{\lambda_y}\right)^2 + \left(\frac{2\pi}{\lambda_z}\right)^2 = 4\pi^2 \left(\frac{1}{{\lambda_x}^2}\right) + \left(\frac{1}{{\lambda_y}^2}\right) + \left(\frac{1}{{\lambda_z}^2}\right) \\ &= 4\pi^2 \left(\frac{{\nu_x}^2}{c^2}\right) + \left(\frac{{\nu_y}^2}{c^2}\right) + \left(\frac{{\nu_z}^2}{c^2}\right) = 4\pi^2 \frac{\nu^2}{c^2} \end{aligned} \tag{14.37}$$

Equating these two expressions for k^2, we find

$$\frac{4\nu^2}{c^2} = \frac{{n_x}^2}{A^2} + \frac{{n_y}^2}{B^2} + \frac{{n_z}^2}{C^2} \tag{14.38}$$

The next step makes use of two observations. First, note that Equation 14.38 describes an ellipsoid in space. Then notice that each mode corresponds to a point inside the ellipsoid, with integer multiples of the coordinates $(2\nu_x A/c, 2\nu_y B/c, 2\nu_z C/c)$. Figure 14.21 shows this interpretation. If we label the axes as $2\nu_x A/c$, $2\nu_y B/c$, $2\nu_z C/c$, then the modes correspond to integer points inside the ellipsoid; that is, points on the corners of a lattice of unit cubes.

So the ellipsoid for a frequency ν has volume

$$\frac{1}{8}\,\frac{4\pi}{3}\,\frac{2\nu A}{c}\,\frac{2\nu B}{c}\,\frac{2\nu C}{c} = \frac{4\pi\nu^3 ABC}{3c^3} = \frac{4\pi\nu^3}{3c^3}V \tag{14.39}$$

where $V = ABC$. Because the volume tells us the number of these integer lattice points inside the ellipsoid, this expression tells us the number of modes associated with all frequencies less than or equal to ν.

It turns out that because of polarization there are two photon states that are distinct when counting modes, so we need to double our expression above to account for them [148, 311]. Therefore the total number of modes g per unit volume is

$$g = \frac{8\pi}{3c^3}\nu^3 \tag{14.40}$$

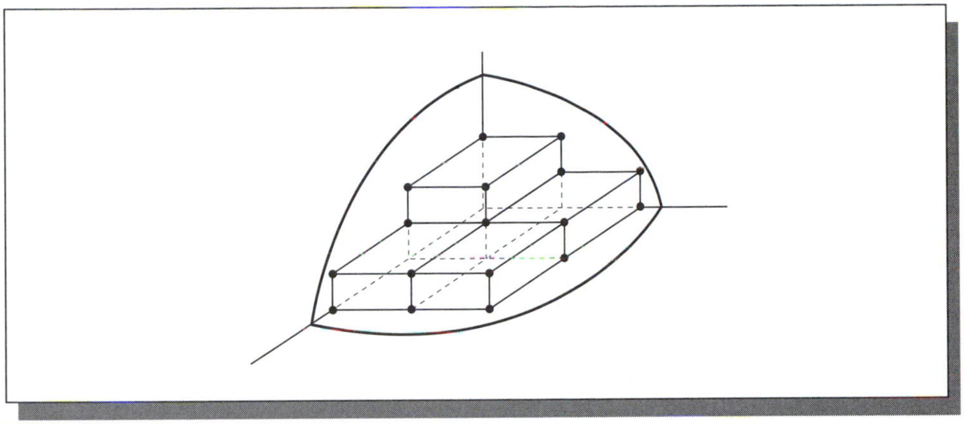

FIGURE 14.21
An octant of the ellipsoid of energy modes.

Within some band of frequencies $d\nu$, we can find the spectral density g_ν of the modes as

$$g_\nu = \frac{dg}{d\nu} = \frac{8\pi}{c^3}\nu^2 \tag{14.41}$$

We're almost there. Now that we know how many modes are associated with each frequency, we can find the total energy in the object by finding the energy associated with each frequency, and by scaling that energy by the total number of modes supported at that frequency. In other words, there are g_ν resonant modes per unit frequency per unit volume. Rayleigh and Jeans supposed that the mean energy per mode is given by kT [148]. Then we can find the spectral radiant flux density $u_\nu = g_\nu kT$ at a wavelength ν:

$$u_\nu = g_\nu kT = \frac{8\pi kT}{c^3}\nu^2 \tag{14.42}$$

Equation 14.42 is called the *Rayleigh-Jeans law of radiation*. From it, we find the spectral exitance is

$$M_\nu = \frac{1}{4}cu_\nu = \frac{2\pi kT}{c^2}\nu^2 \tag{14.43}$$

The Rayleigh-Jeans law has a terrible problem. It tells us that as the frequency ν goes up (that is, as the wavelength λ becomes shorter), the energy in the cavity will grow without bound. We would expect enormous radiation at extremely high frequencies, with more energy all the time as the frequency goes up. Experimentally, we find just the opposite. The Rayleigh-Jeans law matches some of the observed radiation from isolated bodies, but it begins to fail in the region of the ultraviolet, and becomes increasingly inaccurate from there on. This prediction of infinite energy at shorter wavelengths was called *the ultraviolet catastrophe*. The word catastrophe reveals the extent to which physicists were troubled by this result: a seemingly straightforward argument, based on sound classical principles, yielded an answer that was not only at variance with experiment but in fact made a ridiculous prediction. This quandary was resolved only with the development of quantum mechanics.

Planck's idea of the quantum provided a way out of the ultraviolet catastrophe. He supposed, as we have seen above, that energy is only available to a system in integral multiples of a basic quantum h. Then each mode has an integral number of photons, and the energy per mode must be $ih\nu$, where i is some integer. When these ideas were applied to blackbody radiation, the results closely matched experiments. We will derive those results now.

As before, we write n_ν for the occupation index (the number of photons in a given mode). So

$$u_\nu = g_\nu h\nu n_\nu = \frac{8\pi\nu^2}{c^3} h\nu n_\nu = \frac{8\pi h\nu^3}{c^3} n_\nu \tag{14.44}$$

with a corresponding radiant exitance

$$M_\nu = \frac{1}{4} cu\nu = \frac{2\pi h\nu^3}{c^2} n_\nu \tag{14.45}$$

The question now is to find how many photons occupy each mode. If we think of each mode as a possible photon state, then the distribution of photons in the different modes follow the Bose-Einstein statistics developed above. Plugging the statistical distribution Equation 14.29 into Equation 14.45, we find

$$M_\nu = \frac{2\pi h\nu^3}{c^2} \frac{1}{\exp[\beta h\nu] - 1} \tag{14.46}$$

At short wavelengths, we can simplify this expression. When x is small, $e^x - 1 \approx x$. So when the frequency is small ($\beta h\nu \ll 1$), we can write

$$M_\nu = \frac{2\pi\nu^2}{c^2} h\nu \frac{1}{\exp[\beta h\nu] - 1} = \frac{2\pi\nu^2}{c^2} h\nu \frac{h\nu}{\beta h\nu} = \frac{2\pi\nu^2}{c^2} h\nu \frac{1}{\beta} \tag{14.47}$$

This expression matches the Rayleigh-Jeans law if we set $\beta = 1/kT$. This seems reasonable since the Rayleigh-Jeans law is accurate at large wavelengths [148].

Using this value for β, we find

$$e_b(\nu, T) = \frac{2\pi h\nu^3}{c^2} \frac{1}{\exp[h\nu/kT] - 1} \qquad \left[\frac{W}{m^2}\right] \tag{14.48}$$

This is *Planck's law* for the radiation from a blackbody. Because it is so important, the radiant exitance for a blackbody is usually written as e_b, as above. It tells us the theoretical maximum amount of energy that can be radiated from any object as a function of wavelength and temperature. The temperature is measured in degrees kelvin.

In the development of Equation 14.48, we have assumed that the speed of light is c; we made this assumption in Equation 14.32. This is only true in a vacuum; elsewhere the speed of light is scaled by the index of refraction of the medium.

Replacing c with $c/\eta(\lambda)$ gives us the *medium-dependent* form of Planck's law [311]:

$$e_{b\nu}(\nu, T) = \frac{2\pi h\nu^3\eta^2(\nu)}{c^2\left(e^{h\nu/kT} - 1\right)} \qquad \left[\frac{W}{m^2}\right] \tag{14.49}$$

where $\eta(\nu)$ is the index of refraction of the medium surrounding the blackbody at wavelength ν. The other constants in Equation 14.48 are given in Table E.3 in Appendix E.

We can find the total energy e_b radiated from a blackbody over all frequencies by integrating Equation 14.48 with respect to λ from 0 to infinity:

$$e_b(T) = \int_0^\infty e_{b\nu}(\nu, T)\, d\nu \tag{14.50}$$

To ease the integration, we make the substitution $x = \nu(h/kT)$. Then $\nu = (kT/h)x$, so $d\nu = (kT/h)\,dx$. Then, expanding Equation 14.50 and making the substitution for ν,

$$\begin{aligned}
e_b(T) &= \int_0^\infty \frac{2\pi h\nu^3\eta^2(\nu)}{c^2\left(e^{h\nu/kT} - 1\right)} d\nu \\
&= \int_0^\infty \frac{2\pi h\nu^3\eta^2(kTx/h)}{c^2\left(e^x - 1\right)} \frac{kT}{h}\, dx \\
&= \left(\frac{2\pi k^4}{h^3c^2}\right) T^4 \int_0^\infty \frac{x^3}{e^x - 1}\eta^2(kTx/h)\, dx
\end{aligned} \tag{14.51}$$

In Chapter 11 we saw a number of choices for the function $\eta(\nu)$. To use any of these equations in Equation 14.51, we will need to make the substitution $\eta(\nu) = \eta^2(kTx/h)$, and probably integrate numerically. There are two cases in which we can find the integral analytically: when the index of refraction is a constant, and when it is linear with respect to wavelength.

14.7.1 Constant Index of Refraction

If we are willing to assume that $\eta(\nu)$ has a constant value η_k, then we can simplify Equation 14.51 considerably. As we will see, this assumption fails for many materials, but it is perfectly true in a vacuum and close to true for many gases. Pulling the now-constant index of refraction η_k out of the equation gives us

$$\begin{aligned} e_b(T) &= {\eta_k}^2 \left(\frac{2\pi k^4}{h^3 c^2}\right) T^4 \int_0^\infty \frac{x^3}{e^x - 1}\,dx \\ &= {\eta_k}^2 \left(\frac{2\pi k^4}{h^3 c^2}\right) T^4 \frac{\pi^4}{15} \\ &= {\eta_k}^2 \sigma T^4 \end{aligned} \tag{14.52}$$

where σ is the *Stefan-Boltzman* constant,

$$\sigma = \frac{2\pi^5 k^4}{15 c^2 h^3} \tag{14.53}$$

The numerical value for this constant is given in Table E.3. Equation 14.52 is known as the *Stefan-Boltzman law for blackbody radiation.* This law is often simplified further by assuming that the index of refraction $\eta(\nu)$ of the surrounding medium is not simply a constant, but is in fact 1 at all frequencies. This is only true in a perfect vacuum. With this final simplification we find

$$e_b(T) = \sigma T^4 \tag{14.54}$$

14.7.2 Linear Index of Refraction

Equation 14.51 may also be integrated analytically when $\eta(\nu)$ is a linear function of wavelength: $\eta(\nu) = A\nu$. Then we can write

$$\begin{aligned} \int_0^\infty \frac{x^3 \eta^2(\nu)}{e^x - 1}\,dx &= \int_0^\infty \frac{x^3}{e^x - 1} \frac{(AkTx)^2}{h^2}\,dx \\ &= \frac{8(AkT)^2 \pi^2}{63 h^2} \end{aligned} \tag{14.55}$$

giving us a new simplified formula in terms of σ_l, the linear constant:

$$e_b(T) = \sigma_l T^6 \tag{14.56}$$

where

$$\sigma_l = \frac{16\pi^7 k^6 A^2}{63 c^2 h^5} \tag{14.57}$$

14.7.3 Radiators

No physical object reaches the theoretical maximum emission of a blackbody. But it is sometimes convenient to describe the emissive properties of a material by specifying, on a wavelength-by-wavelength basis, the fraction of light it generates with respect to a blackbody. A material described this way is called a *graybody*.

The CIE has defined a number of standard illuminants for use in lighting work. Some of these approximate the sun under certain conditions; others are simple to match with easily manufactured light sources. Tables of these values are given in Appendix G.

14.8 Phosphors

Roughly speaking, a *phosphor* is a material that absorbs energy and then reemits it, generally over some period of time. The lifetime of an excited electron is usually taken to be about 10^{-8} seconds. If a material responds to incident energy by reradiating most of it within 10^{-8} seconds after arrival, we call that *fluorescence*. If the emission persists longer than that interval, it is said to be *phosphorescence*. A material with a strong phosphorescent emission is called a *phosphor*, which means "light-bearer" [267].

Most phosphors are inorganic (that is, carbon-free) crystals that contain structural and impurity defects; that is, the regular crystal lattice is occasionally broken or otherwise distorted, and sometimes atoms that do not belong to the lattice appear, either in addition to the lattice atoms or instead of them.

Figure 14.22 shows different processes whereby materials emit radiation in response to incident energy. In computer graphics we are chiefly interested in *conventional luminescence*, due to the transitions of electrons in the outer shells and incomplete inner shells of electrons.

The photons emitted by a phosphor are generally less energetic than those that are absorbed; the difference appears as heat. This is known as *Stokes' law*, which can be derived from the law of conservation of energy on a quantum level [267]. Stokes' law can be violated but only rarely and in particular circumstances.

Localized transitions in a material, such as a single electron being promoted into a higher energy state within an atom, result in *exponential decays* of phosphorescence, where the energy at time decreases as $e^{-\alpha t}$ with time t. The general idea is that after the electron absorbs energy from the incident photon, it loses a small amount of energy (generally as heat) and then falls into a *metastable state*. A metastable state is an energy level from which the electron is forbidden to make a direct transition back down to the ground state. The electron will reside in the metastable state until it can make it back up to a higher energy state, from which it is able to move back down to the ground state.

Energy of the emitted photon →	Type of emission	Radiation sources	Common types of spectra
	Gamma-ray fluorescence	Transitions of nucleons in atomic nuclei	Gamma-ray line spectra
	X-ray fluorescence	Electronic transitions in inner completed shells of atoms	X-ray line spectra
	Conventional luminescence	Electronic transitions in inner incompleted shells of atoms	Visible and near-visible line spectra
		Electronic transitions in outer (valence) shells of atoms and molecules	Visible and near-visible band spectra
	Thermal radiation	Transitions of atoms and groups of atoms vibrating and rotating; also electrons as in conventional luminescence	Infrared band spectra

FIGURE 14.22
Emissions from luminescent solids. The light we see is due to conventional luminescence. Data from Leverenz, *An Introduction to Luminescence of Solids*, table 7, p. 105.

Conductors are in general not good phosphors, because they have partially filled upper bands. An excited electron can step back down to the ground state through those upper levels in many small transitions, radiating heat at each step rather than a single photon of energy similar to the photon that was absorbed.

When an electron absorbs enough energy, in some materials it can leave the influence of the atom it belonged to and move into the *conducting band*, where it is free to wander throughout the crystal. Such electrons follow a *power-law decay*, losing energy with respect to t^{-n}. This type of decay can last for days even at room temperature.

In fact, some phosphors retain over half their initial stored potential phosphorescence for six months at room temperature, and longer still at colder temperatures [267]. Perhaps the most extreme example involves the illumination of a nonradioactive fluorite crystal to a one-minute burst of ultraviolet light. Using a thousand-hour (or six-week) exposure, a photographic image was made of the crystal from its phosphorescent emission four to five years after excitation [267].

Figure 14.23 gives a schematic view of the radiance emitted by a phosphor in response to illumination, and provides a summary of the relevant terminology commonly used to discuss the process.

Leverenz [267] suggests combining the exponential and power-law phosphorescent decays with the following empirical formula for the radiance L emitted by a phosphor at time t, given an initial radiance L_0 and a material-dependent constant b:

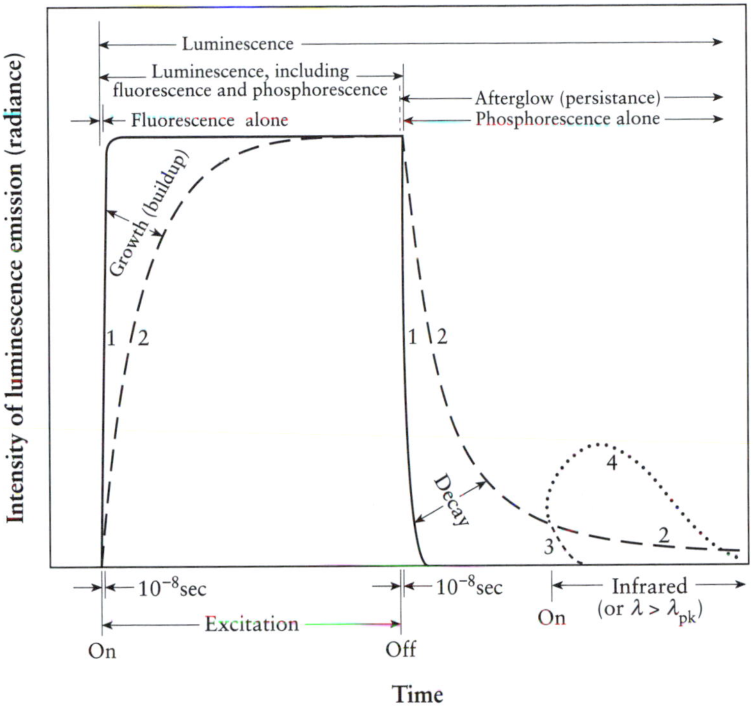

FIGURE 14.23

The radiance of a phosphor over time and the terms used to describe it. 1 = rapid growth and decay; 2 = slow growth and decay. For the effect of irradiation with $\lambda > \lambda_{pk\,(emission)}$ during phosphorescence, 2 = normal decay (no irradiation), 3 = quenching, and 4 = stimulation. Redrawn from Leverenz, *An Introduction to Luminescence of Solids*, fig. 19, p. 150.

$$L = \frac{1}{b\left(\frac{1}{\sqrt{L_0 b}} + t\right)^2} \tag{14.58}$$

It may be surprising that the energy stored in a phosphor may be rapidly depleted by exposing the material to another beam of light. This process is called *quenching*, and usually works best for power-law type phosphors. We irradiate the phosphor with photons whose energies are equal to or slightly above the energy of the emitted photons. The stimulation is able to just raise the stored photons to a point where they can return to their ground state, by virtue of a *nonradiative transition*; that is, the excess energy is dispelled as heat.

The variety of means by which materials radiate energy is summarized in Figure 14.24.

14.9 Further Reading

An excellent introductory text to quantum theory for atoms and molecules is McQuarrie [295], which requires no more mathematics background than this book. Another good introductory quantum mechanics book is Longini [276]. A challenging but accessible and thorough introduction to quantum mechanics and subatomic particles is offered by Sudbery [427]. Many of the optics texts, such as the one by Möller [311] referenced in Chapter 11, also provide good introductions to some of this material, particularly the blackbody developments.

An inexhaustible source of practical and theoretical information on luminescence in general and many phosphors in particular is provided by Leverenz in his book [267].

14.10 Exercises

Exercise 14.1

Research the dispersion of light within crystals, including *asterism* and *chatoyancy* [437, 498, 501]. Describe how you would simulate light within gems and crystals.

Exercise 14.2

Investigate the thirty-two crystallographic point groups [488]. Build a system to model 3D crystals from a stereographic projection.

Exercise 14.3

Study the optical phenomenon of *double refraction*. Distinguish the properties of *uniaxial* and *biaxial* crystals. How would you implement support for such crystals? What input would you require from the user?

Exercise 14.4

How much energy, in watts, is radiated by a perfect blackbody at $T = 5{,}780$ degrees kelvin (the temperature of the Sun [406]) in the visual range $[380, 780]$ nanometers?

Simple absorption and reflection

Dyes and pigments convert incident radiation (photons) into selectively reflected radiation and internal heat.

Tenebrescence

Scotophors are similar to dyes and pigments, except that at least part of their selective absorption of radiation is nonintrinsic. For example, new absorption bands may be *induced* by treatment with X rays or material particles.

Luminescense (physical [electronic] action)

Luminophors, or **lumophors**, convert part of the energy of absorbed photons or material particles into emitted radiation in excess of thermal radiation.

Fluorophors, or **fluors**, exhibit only fluorescence.

Phosphors exhibit phosphorescence (with or without fluorescence).

Designation	*Means used for excitation (***excitant***)*
Photoluminescence	Low-energy photons (visible light, UV)
Roentgenoluminescence	High-energy photons (X rays, gamma rays)
Cathodoluminescence (**electroluminescence**)	Cathode rays, beta rays
Ionoluminescence (**radioluminescence**[1])	Alpha particles, ions
Triboluminescence	Mechanical disruption of crystals

Designation	*Duration of detectable afterglow (***persistence***)*
Fluorescence	Shorter than about 10^{-8} sec for optical photons
Phosphorescence	Longer than about 10^{-8} sec for optical photons
	Effect of irradiation or heating during phosphorescence
Stimulation (Ausleuchtung)	Phosphorescence intensity *increased* during irradiation or heating
Quenching (Tilgung)	Phosphorescence intensity *decreased* during irradiation or heating

Luminescence (chemical action)

Designation	*Excitant*
Chemiluminescence	Energy from chemical reactions
Bioluminescence	Energy from biochemical reactions

Designations that are not recommended

Candoluminescence (non-black-body emissions observed at very high temperatures)

Thermoluminescence (phosphorescence obtained at various temperatures)

[1]Radioluminescence has been used to describe luminescence excited by any or all radioactive-disintegration products. In the case of radium, the alpha-particle excitation predominates.

FIGURE 14.24

Some types of luminescence and related phenomena. Data from Leverenz, *An Introduction to Luminescence of Solids*, table 10, p. 148.

As they made their way along, other familiar landmarks came into view, and they excitedly pointed them out to one another. Within an hour or two they would be down. But then Crean spotted a crevasse off to the right, and looking ahead they saw other crevasses in their path. They stopped—confused. They were on a glacier. Only there were no glaciers surrounding Stromness Bay. They knew then that their own eagerness had cruelly deceived them. The island lying just ahead wasn't Mutton Island, and the landmarks they had seen were the creations of their imagination.

Alfred Lansing
("Endurance: Shackleton's Incredible Voyage," 1959)

15

SHADING

15.1 Introduction

In this chapter we will look at what happens to light as it reflects off a surface or passes through a volume. In contrast to our atomic- and molecular-sized points of view in Chapter 14, here we are interested in macroscopic phenomena, usually on a human scale. In general, we would like to find a description of the scattering distribution function at all points in the environment.

The term *shading* is generally used to describe the process of computing the light that leaves a point either by self-emission or propagation. The point under investigation, which may be on a surface or in space, is called the *shading point*. The function that characterizes the light leaving a shading point as a function of the light arriving upon it is called the *shading model* at that point. Typically we are concerned with the light leaving within some solid angle (which may be as large as a hemisphere or sphere): we call this the *shading exitance solid angle*.

Shading is a field that is still under active development, driven by three forces that are often mutually exclusive: accuracy, expressiveness, and speed. For images that predict and match real scenes we need to have numerical precision when computing how much light is reflected off a surface or transmitted through a volume. For artistic freedom and creativity, we would like shading models that let us make objects look any way we desire them to look, regardless of the difficulty (or impossibility) of achieving that behavior in reality. Finally, any shading model must be fast, since it may be executed many millions of times for a single image; if a model satisfies the other two criteria but is too slow, it will be a theoretical construct only and will not find practical use.

The question of accuracy is important because only sometimes do we really need to match materials with great precision. This is fortunate, because the specific details of how materials reflect light varies greatly even for very similar substances. Different finishes, different densities of mixtures, and different temperatures all affect how a material reflects light. Finding a single practical equation, or set of equations, that will match all materials is probably impossible. To match even a single material with a physical simulation usually requires knowledge of its atomic and molecular composition. When possible, in computer graphics we work with *approximate* shading models. There are a variety of models, each appropriate for a different class of surfaces. All of the shading models in this book make many simplifications regarding the atomic and molecular structure of the material. Those that document all their assumptions carefully are typically called *physically based* models; those that just look good or are useful are called *empirical* models. Although they have a finer pedigree, physically based models can produce less realistic results than an empirical model carefully hand tuned for a particular type of material.

When we care only about opaque surfaces in vacuum (or homogeneous air which we are content to treat as vacuum), then we need only find a description of the bidirectional reflection distribution function (BRDF) f_r at each point on each surface. If the surfaces are partly transparent, then the bidirectional transmission distribution function (BTDF) f_t must also be considered. Together, these functions form the *bidirectional scattering distribution function* (BSDF), which we write as simply f. The BSDF can be applied to points in space as well as points on surfaces.

Because transmission is generally handled very similarly to reflection, when discussing surfaces in this chapter we will concentrate on the BRDF, implicitly including the BTDF by analogy.

Almost all shading models assume that there is no fluorescence, phosphorescence, or significant polarization. Thus, we can speak of each frequency of light independently of all others, and we need not concern ourselves with what light has arrived before the moment of inquiry. So we will write our shading functions without the arguments that encode the wavelength, time, and polarization of the involved light. The general approach for including polarization and color is to run several simultaneous simulations, one for each state of polarization and wavelength. For example, to render a color image, we might calculate the radiance at n different wavelengths, and then convert this sampled-wavelength description to a single indeRGBRGB color appropriate for display on a raster CRT. More efficient methods are sometimes possible, particularly by reusing some geometric information such as visible surfaces and the locations of shadows. However, we must be careful to handle refraction properly, since this characteristic of light can change the path the light takes, and thus the locations of shadows and indirect illumination from different points in the scene.

Even if there are phosphorescent materials in the scene, there will be no problem as long as the image is simulated quickly enough. In other words, if the scene includes a simulated camera, as long as the camera shutter is open for a sufficiently brief interval, phosphorescence doesn't matter. If we start with no radiation and conclude within about 10^{-8} seconds, then even if there are phosphorescent effects, they will not have the time to manifest themselves. Since the speed of light is about 3×10^8 m/s, we can ignore the time factor in this case if the scene can be surrounded within a sphere with a diameter of 3 meters. Note that if another image is generated immediately after this one (say for an animation), then the initial condition that the scene is black will no longer be satisfied. If there are no phosphorescent materials in the scene, then the time interval used for the simulation doesn't matter.

It is often useful to distinguish *direct* and *indirect* illumination upon a shading point. Direct illumination is that light which arrives from a *luminaire*, or light source, without interacting with any other objects along the way. Typical light sources include thermal radiators, such as flames or incandescent filaments, though fluorescent bulbs and even decaying phosphors may be considered sources of direct illumination. In general, light arriving at a point A from some other point B is considered *direct* if it is generated at B by any of these self-emitting mechanisms. If the arriving light was reflected or transmitted before arriving at A, we speak of this as *indirect* illumination. For efficiency, almost all computational methods take special notice of direct illumination. However, they vary in their approach to indirect illumination.

A useful conceptual model of shading is to think of the shading point as surrounded by a set of directional functions, which can be imagined as information painted on spheres. On the surface of each sphere is a scalar function. We can draw the magnitude of the function on the surface of the sphere using black for 0 and white for 1 to create a sphere that is dark in some places and light in others. An alternative is to represent the magnitude of the function in each direction by scaling the radius of the sphere in that direction. If we do this, we don't actually have a hemisphere any more, but rather a radial blob. We will use this convention for drawing the magnitude of these functions, but we'll continue to speak of "spheres" and "hemispheres" rather than "blobs" since we really only want to refer to the function defined on the spheres, and not the way we have chosen to draw them for illustration.

Figure 15.1 shows three spheres around a point: the *illumination sphere*, the *BRDF sphere*, and the *radiance sphere*, respectively describing the incident light, the surface BRDF, and the radiated light. We can also imagine an *emission sphere* for points that generate their own light (say by thermal excitation).

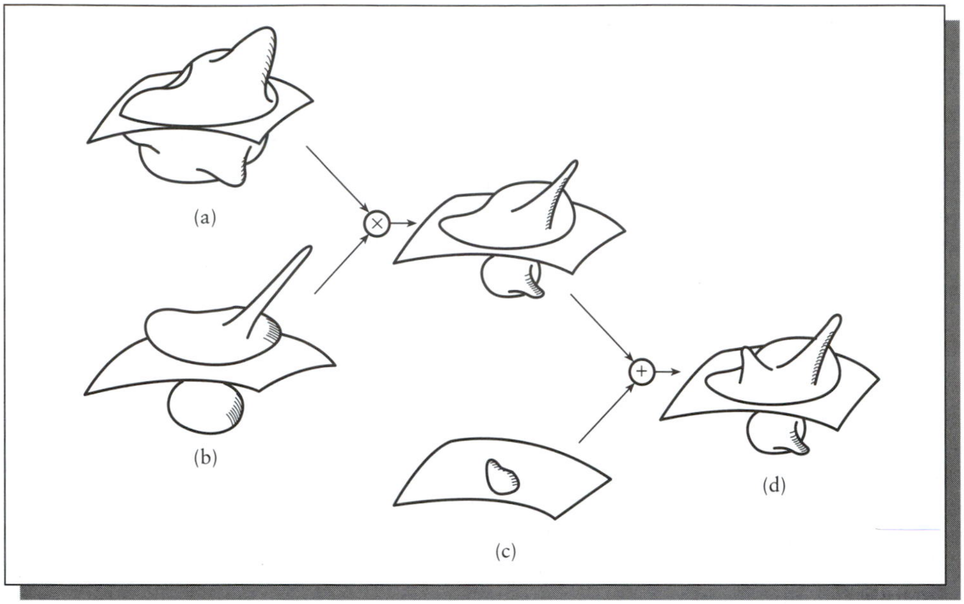

FIGURE 15.1

A set of spheres around a shading point. (a) An illumination sphere. (b) A BRDF sphere for a given direction. (c) An emission sphere. (d) A radiance sphere.

The illumination sphere gives the illumination (typically the incident radiance) of the light arriving from every direction around the shading point (when the point is on the surface of an opaque object, this is just a hemisphere). The BRDF sphere gives the BRDF for light incident from a particular direction. The radiance sphere is the resulting description of the radiance leaving the surface in all directions, either by propagation or self-emission.

For each incident direction, we can create a sphere that gives the magnitude of the reflected radiance in each direction. To compute the complete radiated energy, we can step through each direction in the illumination sphere, compute the correct BRDF sphere, scale it by the magnitude of the incident energy, and add the scaled reflectance function to a running sum of propagated radiance stored in the radiance sphere. When every input direction has been considered, the resulting spherical function describes the propagated light in all directions.

We can use this concept to help organize the shading process. The first step is to find the illuminance sphere, telling us how much light is falling on the point from all directions. When this gathering step has completed, we can then combine the illumination with the BRDF. When that step is finished, we then use the radiance sphere along with the emission sphere to find the energy radiated into any given solid angle.

In practice, we rarely execute these steps completely, and rarely are they so decoupled. Many shading algorithms are composed of a set of interconnected approximations in all three steps. For example, if the surface is a perfect mirror, then when we look at it from a given direction, the only illumination that matters is the radiance coming from the reflected direction with respect to our gaze. Gathering the entire illumination sphere and running it through the complete BRDF for all outgoing directions would be a waste of time if we only need the single sampled direction.

Less drastically, many algorithms sample the illumination sphere carefully in directions from where direct illumination is likely to arrive, since in general it is very difficult to predict from what other directions light might be arriving. The rest of the sphere may be sampled more coarsely, or perhaps not at all and simply approximated. Depending on our needs, we may have to reconstruct and filter the illuminance and radiance spheres before using them to estimate the outgoing light in a particular solid angle.

Those algorithms that explicitly gather illumination information only from the direct light source are called *local illumination* models. Typically these shading models include some form of compensation inside the BRDF for the incomplete illumination sphere. The *ambient light* term found in many hardware implementations of shading is an attempt to use a single value to approximate the total contribution of the unsampled illumination sphere.

Algorithms that estimate indirect lighting information are called *global illumination* models. Some of these models care only about a small number of specific indirect directions. For example, when viewing a nearly perfectly smooth mirror, only a small reflected solid angle needs to be considered. Since the BRDF in this case limits the part of the illumination sphere in which we are interested, we can save ourselves work and not bother with evaluating samples elsewhere.

The two terms *local* and *global* describe the extremes of a continuum; most useful shading models fall somewhere in between.

For simplicity, we will assume that all normal vectors have unit length, and that all derived vectors in this chapter are normalized after they are computed; that is, they have length 1. So when we want to think of finding the average of two vectors $\mathbf{A}$ and $\mathbf{B}$, we might write $\mathbf{C} = (\mathbf{A} + \mathbf{B})/2$, which matches our intuitive idea of averaging, but we actually mean to follow that with a normalization step, so the actual computation would be

$$\mathbf{C} = \frac{\mathbf{A} + \mathbf{B}}{||\mathbf{A} + \mathbf{B}||} \tag{15.1}$$

15.2 Lambert, Phong, and Blinn-Phong Shading Models

The three simplest shading models are named for their developers: the *Lambert* model, the *Phong* model,[1] and the *Blinn-Phong model.* All of these models are usually applied only to simple samplings of the direct illumination, usually from idealized point and directional light sources.

The Lambert model applies to a perfectly diffuse surface; the BRDF is simply a constant for all directions, wavelengths, and polarizations.

The Phong model [69] introduces an ad hoc exponentiated cosine to model specular highlights. Suppose light from a source in direction $\mathbf{S}$ is arriving at a surface point with normal $\mathbf{N}$. The perfect specular reflection of the incident light is along the reflection direction $\mathbf{R}$, as shown in Figure 15.2. The method of *Phong shading* approximates this reflected light as a cone centered around $\mathbf{R}$ with an exponentially decreasing intensity. So the reflected light in any other direction $\mathbf{V}$ can be found by computing the cone angle $\cos\alpha = \mathbf{V}\cdot\mathbf{R}$, and then modulating this by using $(\mathbf{V}\cdot\mathbf{R})^{k_e}$, where k_e is a roughness (or shininess) exponent. Small values of k_e (such as 1 or 2) model rough surfaces; larger values (such as 30 or 40) model smoother, shinier surfaces.

The Phong shading equation for the radiance in direction $\mathbf{V}$ is typically given in the form

$$L(\mathbf{V}) = k_a L_a + k_d \sum_{i=0}^{n-1} L_i(\mathbf{S}_i \cdot \mathbf{N}) + k_s \sum_{i=0}^{n-1} L_i(\mathbf{R}_i \cdot \mathbf{V})^{k_e} \tag{15.2}$$

where L_i is the radiance due to source i arriving along direction $\mathbf{S}_i$, and the reflected vector $\mathbf{R}_i$ is given by

$$\mathbf{R}_i = \mathbf{S}_i + 2(\mathbf{S}_i \cdot \mathbf{N})\mathbf{N} \tag{15.3}$$

The scalars k_d and k_s are used to adjust the overall diffuse and specular reflectivity of the surface; to conserve energy, $k_d + k_s < 1$.

Notice the first term on the right-hand side is $k_a L_a$; this is called the *ambient component* of the shading model. It attempts to account for all the indirect light in the scene, since the remaining two summations only sum contributions over a finite number of infinitely thin solid angles. Since most of the illumination sphere

[1] Bui-Tuong Phong was Vietnamese. In that culture, the first name is a hyphenated construction of the family name (Bui) and a generation name (Tuong) shared by all members of that generation of that family. The last name (Phong) is the individual's unique name. For consistency with the other models, the technique due to Bui-Tuong Phong should probably be called *Bui shading*, but the term *Phong shading* is now firmly established in the literature [107].

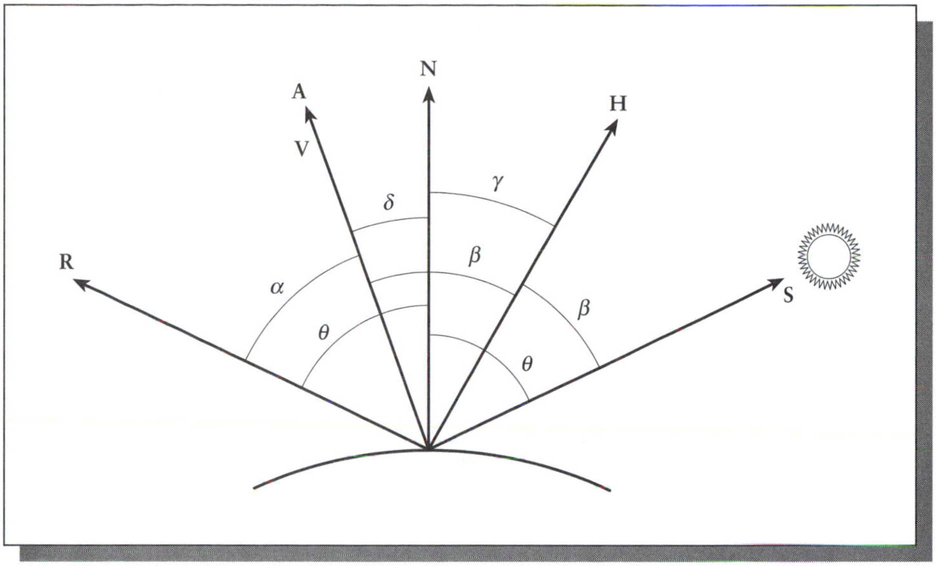

FIGURE 15.2

Some geometry useful for shading.

is completely unsampled, this term is introduced to at least simulate some sort of indirect lighting. The philosophy is that indirect light may be coarsely modeled as a low-level "background" illumination that is constant everywhere in the scene. So we pick a value for this constant and simply add it in.

Although it is certainly ad hoc, ambient light is essential in simple models such as this. If there are only a few (point or directional) light sources in the scene, and if they are not in a position to illuminate some object (perhaps they are behind it, or an intervening object casts a shadow), then the object will be perfectly black. We know from experience that when there's at least enough light in a scene for us to see objects reasonably clearly, then even those parts of the objects that don't receive direct lighting are partly illuminated. For example, consider a table in a small room lit only by a single light bulb directly overhead; the floor under the table receives no direct illumination, but it is not pitch black. Ambient light is an inexpensive way to include at least some approximation of this important light.

A variant of Phong shading was introduced by Blinn [46], which is significant not because it is a more accurate physical simulation (it uses similar empirical approximations), but because it avoids computing the reflection vector $\mathbf{R}_i$ and is thus slightly faster. In *Blinn-Phong shading*, the bisector $\mathbf{H} = (\mathbf{V} + \mathbf{S})/2$ is used instead of the reflected vector $\mathbf{R}$. So the reflection is given by $(\mathbf{H} \cdot \mathbf{N})^{k_e}$. The shading equation is otherwise the same as for the Phong model:

$$L(\mathbf{V}) = k_a L_a + k_d \sum_{i=0}^{n-1} L_i(\mathbf{S}_i \cdot \mathbf{N}) + k_s \sum_{i=0}^{n-1} L_i(\mathbf{H}_i \cdot \mathbf{N})^{k_e} \tag{15.4}$$

where the terms are as in the Phong model, except for the bisector

$$\mathbf{H}_i = (\mathbf{V} + \mathbf{S}_i)/2 \tag{15.5}$$

Neither the Phong model nor the Blinn-Phong model is normalized; we are free to choose coefficients k_a, k_d, k_s, and k_e with almost complete freedom. Often even the minimal energy-conservation condition mentioned above is ignored, and this is entirely reasonable given the simple nature of these models.

15.2.1 Diffuse Plus Specular

The heart of the techniques just described is the separation of the BRDF into diffuse and specular components. Is this justified? Judd and Wyszecki [232] propose that this is an appropriate model for a material that may described as a rough (diffuse) surface upon which there are small specularly reflective patches. As the amount of surface covered by the patches increases, the specular component of the shading model increases. To create such a material, take a piece of glass with a finely ground surface and polish a few spots, and then gradually enlarge those spots until the whole surface is perfectly smooth.

This is a reasonable model for many materials. Figure 15.3 shows the reflectivity for typewriter paper for different angles of incidence. There seems to be a rather circular diffuse component at normal incidence, along with the introduction of a blunt reflection as the incident angle comes down to the horizon. The models discussed above seem to capture this material pretty well over most of its range (though the grazing reflection near the horizon is not accounted for).

On the other hand, one of the most famous exceptions to this rule is Earth's moon. At a full moon the sun, Earth, and moon are almost colinear, as in Figure 15.4. We know that the moon is roughly spherical, so we would expect that a purely diffuse moon would appear bright in the center and fade off to the edges. But during a full moon, except for surface features, the moon looks like a flat disk of uniform brightness.

In fact, Blinn has noted that some parts of the moon may indeed be modeled by a simple combination of a diffuse scattering term and a simple forward scattering term [48]. But this doesn't explain why the entire moon appears equally bright across

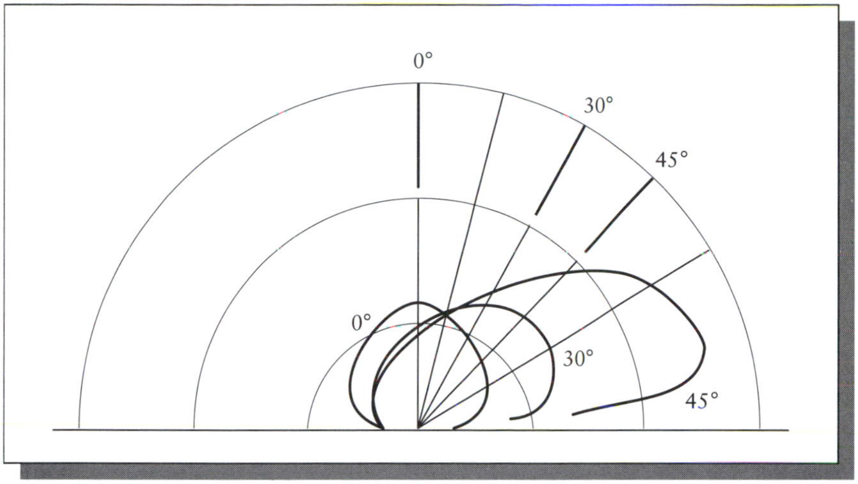

FIGURE 15.3

The reflectivity of a piece of typewriter paper. Redrawn from Siegel and Howell, *Thermal Radiation Heat Transfer*, fig. 5-10, p. 147.

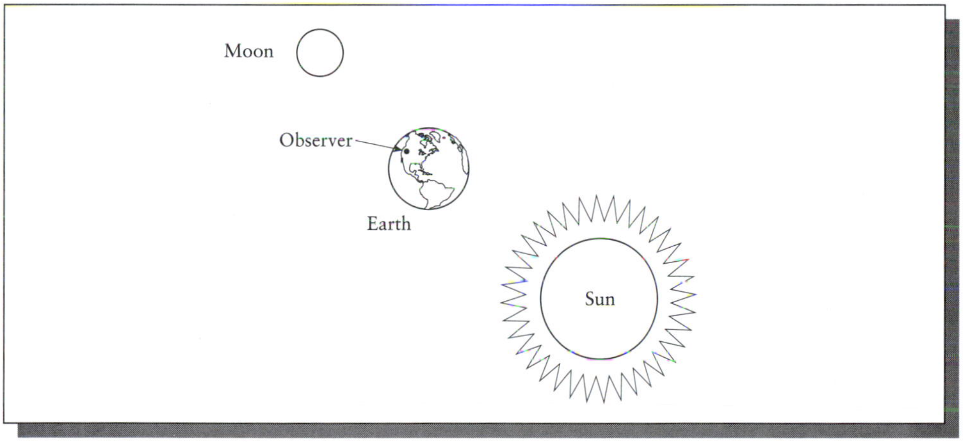

FIGURE 15.4

The geometry of a full moon. Redrawn from Siegel and Howell, *Thermal Radiation Heat Transfer*, fig. 5-12, p. 149.

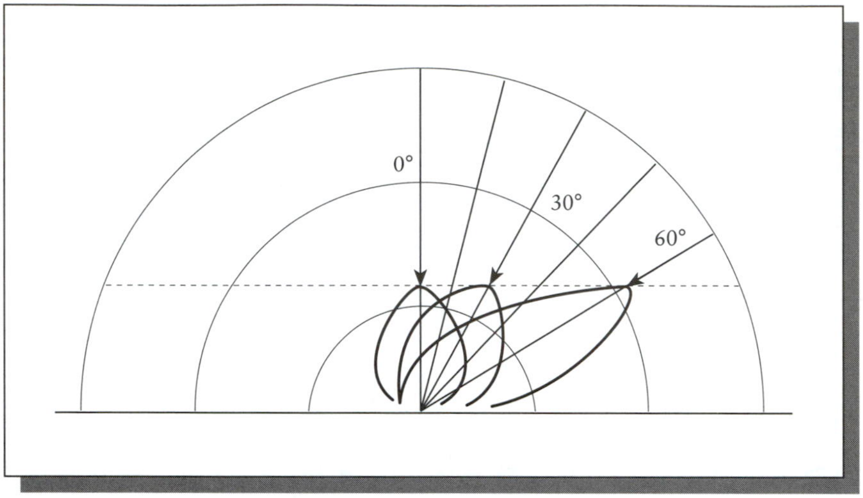

FIGURE 15.5

The reflection function for the moon. The dashed line represents $1/\cos\theta$. Redrawn from Siegel and Howell, *Thermal Radiation Heat Transfer*, fig. 5-11, p. 148.

its surface during a full moon. Because the moon is round, the average normal of its surface makes an angle θ with the sun that increases as we work our way out to the edge. This means that the radiance striking the moon goes down with $\cos\theta$. For the moon to appear equally bright across its face, its reflection function must scale as $1/\cos\theta$, and indeed it does, as shown in Figure 15.5. This is probably a result of a combination of backscattering and the small-scale topology of the moon's surface [406].

Most materials are not described by simple surface models such as a combination of diffuse and specular components, or even the more sophisticated models we'll see below. As mentioned earlier, a material's visual appearance is dependent on how it is applied, the medium through which it is viewed, the density of various other substances in the material, its thickness over some substrate, the properties of the substrate, and so on. Consider some paint applied to a surface [232], as in Figure 15.6.

The gloss (or shininess) of the paint depends on how much pigment is within the vehicle (oil or water). If there is only a bit of pigment, as in a paint enamel, then when the paint dries the outer surface will be smooth and flat, and very glossy. Suppose that the paint particles are larger; then when the paint dries, the surface will reveal

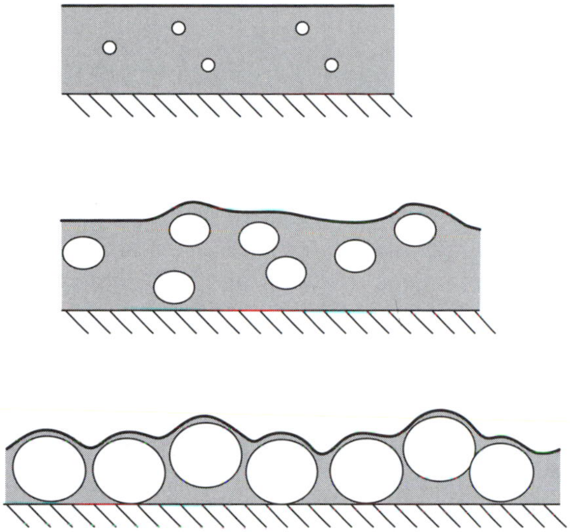

FIGURE 15.6

Three different types of paint. (a) Small particles lead to a glossy finish. (b) Medium particles lead to a semigloss finish. (c) Large particles lead to a diffuse finish.

the presence of the larger bumps by being bumpier itself, so we have a semigloss finish. At the far extreme there is just enough vehicle to hold the particles together, as in a cold-water paint; the final result will be very diffuse. Thus it is not enough to simply specify a paint finish or a color in order to predict how a painted material will look. Closer examination will also reveal brush marks, varying thicknesses, and other phenomena that can affect how a paint appears.

15.3 Cook-Torrance Shading Model

We now turn to *Cook-Torrance* shading, a shading technique that is based on the physics of a surface. It combines work both in applied physics and computer graphics. We will discuss it in some detail to get the flavor for this type of physically based shading model.

The Cook-Torrance model has three main components: a *microfacet model* of the surface, a *Fresnel term* describing reflectance, and a *roughness term* parameterizing the microfacet distribution. We will now discuss these in turn.

15.3.1 Torrance-Sparrow Microfacets

The starting point for Cook-Torrance shading is the geometric description of a surface given by the *Torrance-Sparrow* model [439]. Torrance and Sparrow assumed that a surface is composed of many small V-shaped grooves, which are lined with flat mirrors called *microfacets*, as in Figure 15.7(a). A surface is made up of a sea of these mirrored grooves, where the direction of each groove is randomly oriented with respect to the others.

The complete surface reflects light via two mechanisms: reflections off of the microfacets, and interaction with the substrate below them. Single reflections off the microfacets are responsible for specular reflection, while multiple microfacet reflections and scattering within the substrate cause diffuse reflection.

The geometry of the grooves means that the walls of grooves can block some of the light that would otherwise fall on a facet (called *shadowing*), as in Figure 15.7(b), and that some of the light reflected from a facet can be blocked on its way out (called *masking*), as in Figure 15.7(c).

These geometrical effects influence how much light is specularly reflected by the surface, and in what directions. They are typically gathered together in a *geometry term* denoted G. Blinn [46] gives a detailed description of this term, which may be summarized for a point with normal $\mathbf{N}$, illuminated from a direction $\mathbf{S}$, and viewed from a direction $\mathbf{V}$ as

$$G = \min\left\{1, \frac{2(\mathbf{N}\cdot\mathbf{H})(\mathbf{N}\cdot\mathbf{V})}{(\mathbf{V}\cdot\mathbf{H})}, \frac{2(\mathbf{N}\cdot\mathbf{H})(\mathbf{N}\cdot\mathbf{S})}{(\mathbf{V}\cdot\mathbf{H})}\right\} \tag{15.6}$$

where the bisector $\mathbf{H}$ is given by $\mathbf{H} = (\mathbf{S}+\mathbf{V})/2$, as before.

15.3.2 Fresnel's Formulas

The amount of light reflected and refracted at an interface is a function of the wavelength of the incident light, the geometry of the surface and light, and the angle of incidence. These effects are summarized by a set of formulas known as *Fresnel's formulas*.

Fresnel's formulas may be derived by writing down Maxwell's equations at a surface boundary, and making sure that energy and continuity constraints are satisfied after reflection and refraction. This is a straightforward procedure, but one that would take us on a rather prolonged tangent with few beneficial side effects. A full derivation may be found in any modern optics text, such as Möller [311]. (Others are mentioned in the Further Reading section.)

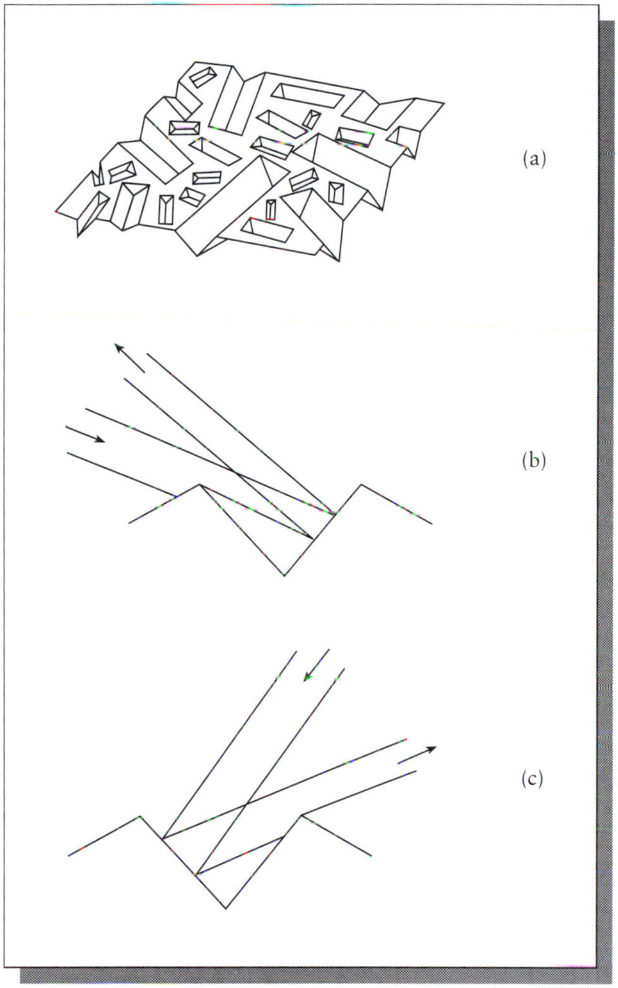

FIGURE 15.7

The grooves of a surface. (a) Microfacets. (b) Shadowing. (c) Masking.

Recall from Chapter 11 that conductors are characterized by a complex index of refraction $N(\nu)$, which is a function of the frequency ν. From Equation 11.15, $N(\nu) = \eta(\nu) + jk(\nu)$, where $\eta(\nu)$ is the *simple index of refraction* and $\kappa(\nu)$ is the *extinction coefficient*. Since we're writing all of our equations for a single frequency in this chapter, we will not write out the explicit dependency on ν; that is, $N = \eta + j\kappa$.

Because of how they are derived, Fresnel's equations are usually written in terms of the polarization of the reflected light. These terms are typically labeled either p or $\|$ for the parallel component and s or $\perp$ for the perpendicular component (s stands for *senkrecht*, the German word for "perpendicular").

At the interface between two materials, we move from a material with complex index of refraction N_1 to a material with complex index of refraction N_2. We can write the *relative* complex index of refraction N as the ratio of these two values:

$$\begin{aligned} N &= \frac{N_2}{N_1} \\ &= \frac{\eta_2 + j\kappa_2}{\eta_1 + j\kappa_1} \end{aligned} \tag{15.7}$$

We can put this into standard complex-number form by multiplying with $\overline{N_1}/\overline{N_1}$:

$$\begin{aligned} N &= \frac{\eta_2 + j\kappa_2}{\eta_1 + j\kappa_1} \frac{\eta_1 - j\kappa_1}{\eta_1 - j\kappa_1} \\ &= \frac{\eta_2\eta_1 + \kappa_2\kappa_1}{{\eta_1}^2 + {\kappa_1}^2} + j\frac{\eta_1\kappa_2 - \eta_2\kappa_1}{{\eta_1}^2 + {\kappa_1}^2} \end{aligned} \tag{15.8}$$

Using this for the relative index of refraction $N = \eta + j\kappa$, the Fresnel formula is

$$\begin{aligned} F_s &= \frac{a^2 + b^2 - 2a\cos\theta + \cos^2\theta}{a^2 + b^2 + 2a\cos\theta + \cos^2\theta} \\ F_p &= F_s \frac{a^2 + b^2 - 2a\sin\theta\tan\theta + \sin^2\theta\tan^2\theta}{a^2 + b^2 + 2a\sin\theta\tan\theta + \sin^2\theta\tan^2\theta} \end{aligned} \tag{15.9}$$

where θ is the angle of incidence, and a and b are given by

$$\begin{aligned} 2a^2 &= \sqrt{(\eta^2 - \kappa^2 - \sin^2\theta)^2 + 4\eta^2\kappa^2} + (\eta^2 - \kappa^2 - \sin^2\theta) \\ 2b^2 &= \sqrt{(\eta^2 - \kappa^2 - \sin^2\theta)^2 + 4\eta^2\kappa^2} - (\eta^2 - \kappa^2 - \sin^2\theta) \end{aligned} \tag{15.10}$$

The Fresnel reflection as a function of the angle of incidence is plotted in Figure 15.8 for an air-glass boundary (the relative simple index of refraction η is about 1.5). Notice that the perpendicular term drops to zero at a particular incident angle θ_f. This angle is given by

$$\tan\theta_f = \frac{\eta_t}{\eta_i} \tag{15.11}$$

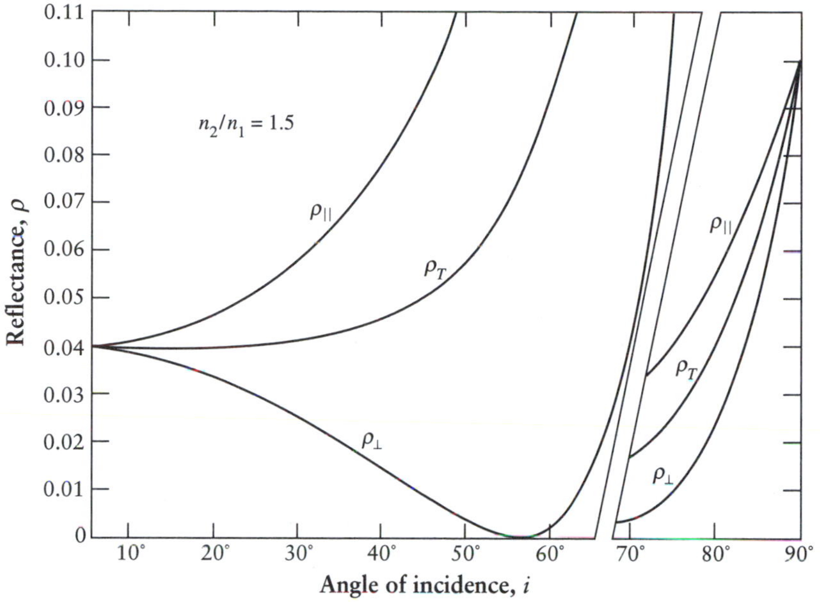

FIGURE 15.8

The Fresnel reflectance for an air-glass boundary with index of refraction 1.5. We show the two polarized components and the term for unpolarized light. Redrawn from Judd and Wyszecki, *Color in Business, Science and Industry*, fig. 3.2, p. 400.

and is known as *Brewster's angle*; Equation 15.11 is known as *Brewster's law*. At Brewster's angle the reflected light is entirely parallel-polarized.

In Figure 15.9 we show the Fresnel reflectance for unpolarized light at a number of different relative indices of refraction.

The reflectance F for polarized light is a weighted sum of the polarized components: $F = sF_s + pF_p$, where $s + p = 1$. Unpolarized light is described by $s = p = 1/2$, so for unpolarized light $F = (F_s + F_p)/2$. The equations for a dielectric-dielectric interface can be found by setting κ to zero and using η as the index of refraction for the second dielectric.

Note that when $\theta = 90°$, then $F_s = F_p = 1$, regardless of the constants η and κ. This is why surfaces such as rough paper appear shiny when we view them at a very shallow, grazing incident angle.

To find the Fresnel coefficients for transmission, we observe that when there is no

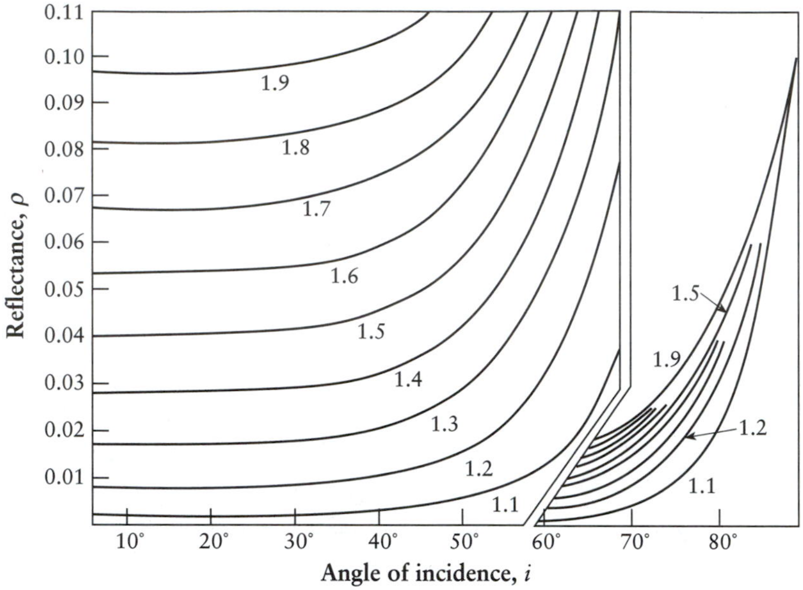

FIGURE 15.9

The Fresnel reflection for unpolarized light for different indices of refraction. Redrawn from Judd and Wyszecki, *Color in Business, Science and Industry*, fig. 3.3, p. 401.

reflection, all the incident flux is either reflected or transmitted: $\Phi_i = F_r\Phi_i + F_t\Phi_i$. If we expand the flux in terms of radiance [181], we find that in terms of the incident radiance L_i, the reflected and transmitted radiances L_r and L_t are as follows:

$$L_r = F_r L_i$$
$$L_t = F_t \left(\frac{\eta_t}{\eta_i}\right)^2 L_i \tag{15.12}$$

The ratio of the simple indices of refraction η_i and η_t of the incident and transmitted materials is necessary because the different solid angles occupied by the incident and transmitted beams.

Computing the Fresnel term requires knowledge of η and κ at the appropriate wavelength. When these terms are not available, but the reflectance at normal incidence is known, Cook and Torrance suggest a practical alternative. For metals and nonmetals alike, they set $\kappa = 0$ to get a value for η at normal incidence. They then use that η and κ for the Fresnel computation.

The Fresnel equation for unpolarized light at normal incidence, with the extinction coefficient $\kappa = 0$, is

$$F = \frac{1}{2}\frac{(g-c)^2}{(g+c)^2}\left\{1 + \frac{[c(g+c)-1]^2}{[c(g+c)+1]^2}\right\} \tag{15.13}$$

where

$$\begin{aligned} c &= \cos\theta = \mathbf{V}\cdot\mathbf{H} \\ g^2 &= \eta^2 + c^2 - 1 \end{aligned} \tag{15.14}$$

At normal incident, $\theta = 0$, so $c = 1$ and $g = \eta$, and the Fresnel coefficient F_0 is

$$F_0 = \left(\frac{\eta - 1}{\eta + 1}\right)^2 \tag{15.15}$$

which we can solve for η:

$$\eta = \frac{1 + \sqrt{F_0}}{1 - \sqrt{F_0}} \tag{15.16}$$

This η may then be used to compute the Fresnel term at other angles of incidence.

15.3.3 Roughness

The last term in the model characterizes the distribution of the slopes of the microfacets. As light arrives at different angles, different distributions of microfacets will cause different patterns of reflection.

We use the term D to describe the facet slope distribution function. Blinn [46] has presented a variety of slope models; one of the simplest is the Gaussian model:

$$D = ce^{-(\alpha/m)^2} \tag{15.17}$$

for an arbitrary constant c. The angle $\alpha = \cos^{-1}(\mathbf{N}\cdot\mathbf{H})$.

The constant m is the RMS slope of the microfacets. A small value of m, such as 0.2, indicates that the surface is smooth and the grooves are shallow, and it produces a sharp highlight. Large values of m, such as 0.8, indicate a rough surface with deep grooves, and produce more spread-out highlights.

Cook and Torrance [103] have pointed out that the Beckmann theory can describe both rough and smooth dielectrics and conductors. For rough surfaces, the Beckmann distribution function is given by

$$D = \frac{\exp[-((\tan\alpha)/m)^2]}{m^2\cos^4\alpha} \tag{15.18}$$

This has the advantage over Equation 15.17 in that it requires only the one parameter m to characterize the surface roughness.

A surface may be characterized as a combination of several different roughnesses at different scales. We can combine the different scales together with simple linear weighting:

$$D = \sum_k w_k D(m_k) \tag{15.19}$$

using a weight w_k on the distribution with RMS slope m_k.

15.3.4 The Cook-Torrance Model

The Cook-Torrance model combines the preceding pieces. We begin by considering an opaque surface, and split its BRDF into two pieces: one to handle the specularly reflected light, the other the diffusely reflected light. This distinction is motivated by our discussion earlier that the BRDF for some surfaces may be described by the sum of a purely diffuse term and a purely specular term, so it seems reasonable to think of writing the two pieces separately. Later on we'll see more complex BRDFs that don't decompose along such intuitive lines, but can be usefully broken down into pieces anyway. In general, it doesn't matter how we decompose the BRDF as long as all the pieces add up to the original.

In this case the diffuse and specular pieces are well understood, and we can write

$$f_r = sf_s + df_d \tag{15.20}$$

where s and d are the specular and diffuse coefficients respectively, and $s + d \leq 1$.

The ambient term is computed as in the previous models, with a hemispherical-reflectance term in the BRDF. Ideally, this should be scaled by the amount of the hemisphere that isn't otherwise accounted for by direct light, but since ambient light is a very crude approximation anyway, there's little additional harm in assuming that the entire hemisphere contributes ambient light.

The total reflected radiance is given by

$$L_r = L_a R_a + \sum_{i=0}^{n-1} L_i (\mathbf{N} \cdot \mathbf{S}_i)(sf_s + df_d)\, d\vec{\omega}_i \tag{15.21}$$

for ambient radiance L_a reflected by R_a, and for a sum over n light sources with radiance L_i in direction $\mathbf{S}_i$ occupying solid angle $d\vec{\omega}_i$ from the shading point.

We have seen the diffuse term f_d in Chapter 13, recalling Equation 13.59,

$$f_d = \frac{1}{\pi} \tag{15.22}$$

The term f_s is found by combining the Fresnel, masking, shadowing, and distribution terms:

$$f_s = \frac{1}{\pi} \frac{F \cdot D \cdot G}{(\mathbf{N} \cdot \mathbf{S})(\mathbf{N} \cdot \mathbf{V})} \tag{15.23}$$

for illumination coming in from direction $\mathbf{S}$.

Recall that Cook and Torrance find η from the reflection at normal incidence, and interpolate from there. The color of the reflected light may also be interpolated. Suppose that for some wavelength λ, we know the reflected flux Φ_0 for normally incident light (that is, $\theta_i = 0$), and also the Fresnel coefficient F_0 at that angle. The reflected flux $\Phi_{\pi/2}$ at perpendicular incidence is the color of the incident light, because the Fresnel coefficient $F_{\pi/2} = 1.0$ at every wavelength, as we saw above. Then we can linearly interpolate between these two fluxes given some incident angle θ_i:

$$\Phi_\theta = \Phi_0 + (\Phi_{\pi/2} - \Phi_0)\frac{\max(0, F_\theta - F_0)}{F_{\pi/2} - F_0} \tag{15.24}$$

where F_θ is the Fresnel coefficient at θ.

A set of vases rendered with the Cook-Torrance model is shown in Figure 15.10 (color plate). These include vases made of carbon, rubber, obsidian, lunar dust, and rust.

The combination of Fresnel reflection and the microfacet distribution means that the peak of the specular reflection function is no longer at the angle of perfect specular reflection. Suppose that the microfacets are equally distributed in all directions, so there are as many facets being struck at small incident angles as at large ones. The Fresnel curves tell us that at a large incident angle the reflectance is greater, so these facets reflect a bit more light. This pushes the peak of the reflection function a bit further from the normal than the perfectly specularly reflected vector [232].

15.3.5 Polarization

Polarization was incorporated into the Torrance-Sparrow model by Wolff and Kurlander [487]. They used Jones matrices (see Section 11.4) to describe the polarization of rays of light, and tracked the changes in polarization when the light was either transmitted or reflected across an interface between media.

They distinguished between the specular and diffuse components of the light during such reflections and transmissions, and accounted for the phase difference that occurs at such transitions, which is important in keeping an accurate record of the polarization state.

In their implementation they followed light of only a certain frequency (or a very narrow range of frequencies), which is necessary since different frequencies undergo different changes in polarization at interfaces.

The tracking of polarization in a geometric-optics simulation can be a tricky business, since as we saw in Chapter 14, photons are part of the class of subatomic particles known as *bosons*, and we cannot distinguish one photon from another. So the state of any particular photon can only be characterized in the sense that the entire beam can be characterized, and individual photons must be accounted for probabilistically [427]. When we treat light beams as containing great numbers of photons, then this distinction becomes less relevant.

15.4 Anisotropy

The previous models have all assumed that the surfaces reflected equally from any direction of view; only the angle made by the incident light with the surface normal mattered. We now turn from these isotropic models to those with explicit *anisotropy*. Recall that a surface that is anisotropic is one for which not only the angle of incidence matters, but also the angle ϕ of the incident light with respect to some distinguished direction. In practice, we can determine if a material is isotropic by locating a small planar piece of the surface in a fixed position with respect to an observer and a light source, and then rotating that piece about an axis defined by its center and its normal, as shown in Figure 15.11. In this case the angle of incidence remains unchanged. If the light reaching the observer is unchanged through a full rotation of the material, it is (at least at that point) isotropic; otherwise it is anisotropic.

Using a *goniometer*, we can measure the reflectivity of a sample, and in particular its isotropy. Figure 15.12 shows a physical apparatus consisting of a piece of material surrounded by an opaque hemisphere. There are two holes in the hemisphere, and through one shines a narrow beam of light. Just outside the other is a detector. If the apparatus is swung around the normal to the surface, then we can measure the reflectance as we swing around the material. The amount by which the reflectance changes is one measure of the anisotropy of the material. We can also independently move the two holes nearer to the pole or the equator to see how the isotropy varies with the angles of incidence and reflection.

Usually an anisotropic surface is considered to possess an intrinsic *grain*, or a distinguished direction lying on the surface in which the surface is particularly smooth, or at least at its smoothest. A good example is satin, which is composed of very fine threads that are are closely woven side by side. As the surface is rotated, we can see a definite preferred position along which light is more strongly reflected than any other; this is the direction when we are looking at the sides of the threads, rather than along their lengths and at the grooves between them. Hair, velvet, and brushed aluminum (such as that found on the front of many stereo systems) are other

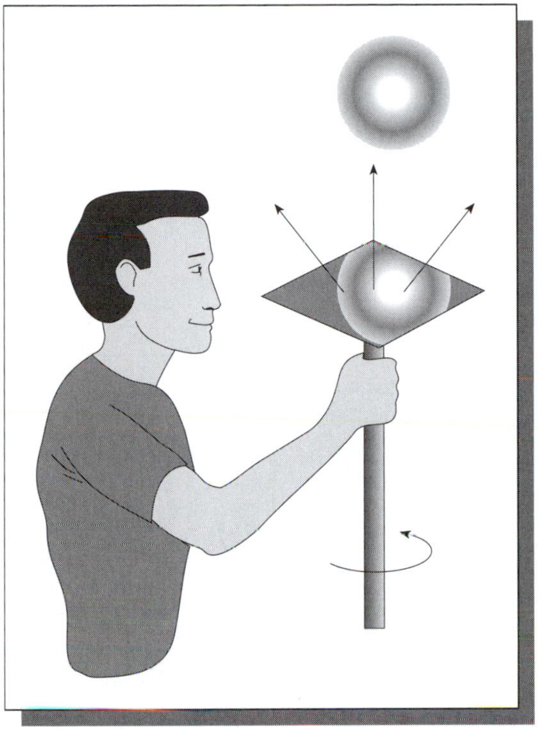

FIGURE 15.11

If the light reaching the detector does not change as the patch is rotated about the vector **V**, the material is isotropic.

common examples of anisotropic materials with obvious grains. It is important to determine this distinguished direction when applying an anisotropic shading model.

15.4.1 The Kajiya Model

The model presented by Kajiya [233] is based on Kirchoff diffraction theory. We will not go into this model in detail because it is based on physical optics (that is, the wave nature of light), rather than the geometrical optics we are using in this book.

The basic idea is that a rough surface is replaced by its local approximate tangent plane. This plane is *oriented*, with one of the directions lying parallel to the surface grain. Kajiya derives an expression for the scattering formula for such a surface,

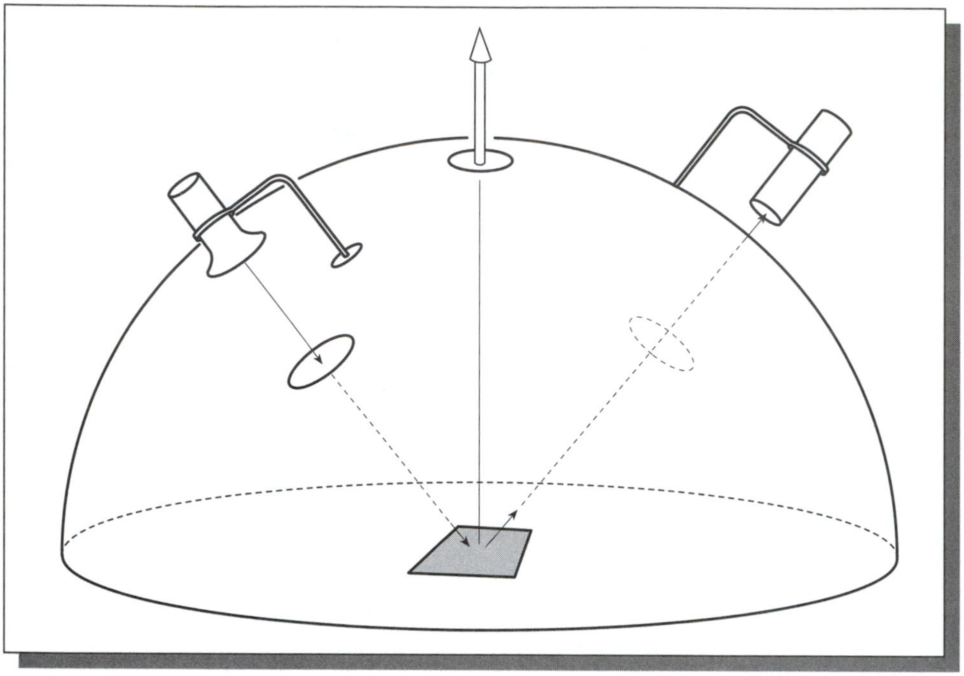

FIGURE 15.12

A goniometer set up to measure isotropy.

including the angle made by the incident light with the preferred direction of the oriented tangent plane. The Kirchoff approximation is valid for surfaces that are relatively smooth, but it breaks down if there is appreciable self-shadowing, or if the surface is rough enough to cause multiple scattering at the surface [344].

15.4.2 The Poulin-Fournier Model

Consider the anisotropic materials of satin and hair; these can be described as long thin cylinders tightly packed parallel to each other. Similarly, brushed aluminum can be described as many tiny locally parallel round scratches inscribed on the metal. We use the term *locally parallel* because though the scratches are close packed and do not overlap, they may not be straight; for example, they may be arranged in concentric circles.

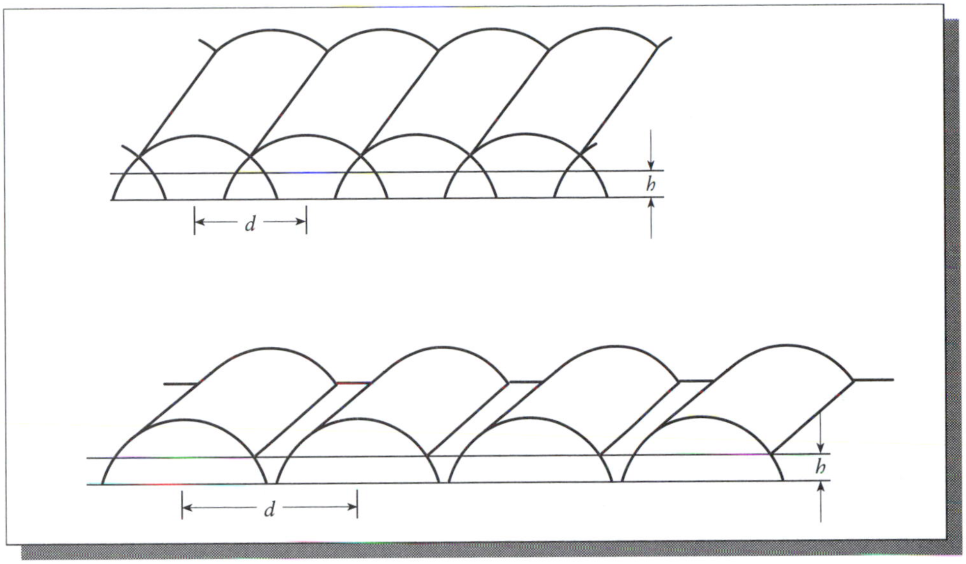

FIGURE 15.13

Cylinders parameterized by the intercylinder distance d and the height h. Redrawn from Poulin and Fournier in *Computer Graphics (Proc. Siggraph '90)*, fig. 2, p. 275.

This model is similar in spirit to the Torrance-Sparrow model, but there are a few important differences: the grooves have a circular rather than V-shaped cross section, they may be both positive (sticking out of the surface) and negative (scratched into the surface), they are not randomly scattered but locally parallel, and they need not be lined with mirrorlike facets but with any material.

The *cylindrical-scratch* model was first used in graphics for anisotropic reflection in special cases by Miller [304]; it was later generalized by Poulin and Fournier [344].

They suggested that a surface made up of many small parallel cylinders may be parameterized by two values: the distance between cylinder centers and the depth to which they are embedded in (or gouged out from) the surface, which they called the *floor*. For positive cylinders, they called the distance from the cylinder's top to the floor the *height*. Figure 15.13 shows these parameters.

They analyzed this geometry and came up with formulas expressing the shadowing and masking effects corresponding to the Torrance-Sparrow geometry term G. They also derived similar formulas for the case where the cylinders are scratched into the surface.

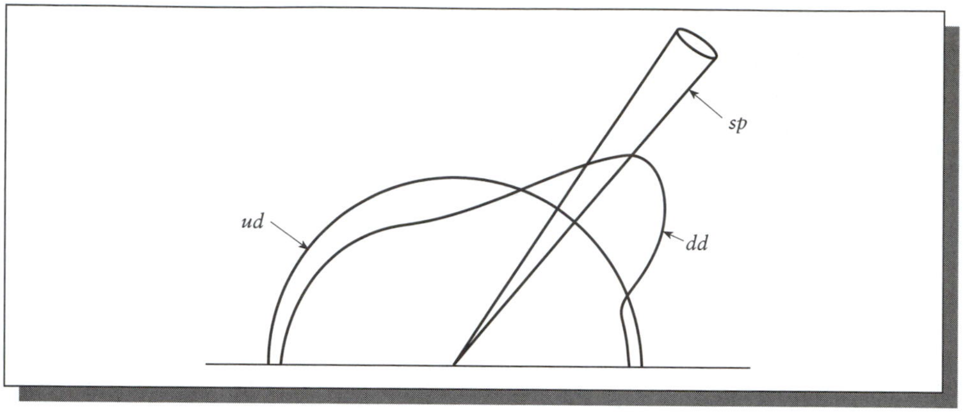

FIGURE 15.14

The three pieces of the BRDF in the HTSG model. Redrawn from He et al. in *Computer Graphics (Proc. Siggraph '91)*, fig. 6, p. 178.

15.5 The HTSG Model

An experimentally verified shading model based on wave optics has been developed by He, Torrance, Sillion, and Greenberg [198], which we call the HTSG model. The derivation is quite complex and is based on Kirchhoff diffraction theory and wave optics, which we have not covered. A careful derivation of the model may be found in their original paper [198].

The model basically distinguishes three types of reflection: *ideal specular* (sp), *uniform diffuse* (ud), and *directional diffuse* (dd), as illustrated in Figure 15.14. These are each accounted for by a different part of the BRDF:

$$f_r = {f_r}^{sp} + {f_r}^{ud} + {f_r}^{dd} \tag{15.25}$$

The complete expression for the BRDF for polarized light is given in their paper. We will content ourselves here with simply stating the formulas for the unpolarized case, which are daunting in their own right. For full details on the model, see [198].

The model is based on two parameters. The first is σ_0, the RMS roughness of the surface, which was symbolized by m in the Cook-Torrance model. The second parameter is τ, the *autocorrelation length*; this is a measure of the distance between peaks on the surface. The ratio σ_0/τ is proportional to the RMS slope of the surface.

Given these parameters, and the geometry in Figure 15.15, the BRDF f_r predicted by the HTSG model is given by the expressions in Equation 15.26. We present these

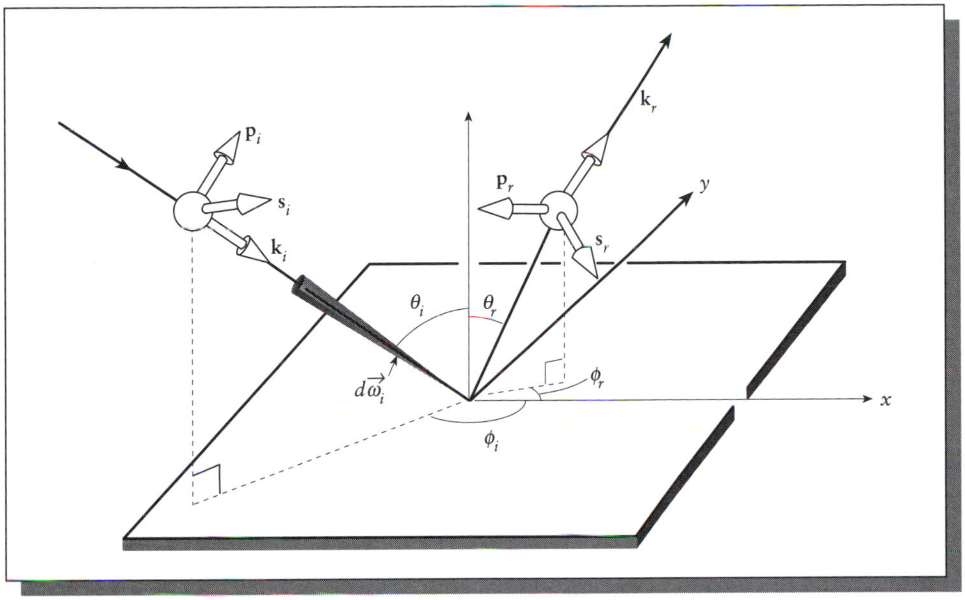

FIGURE 15.15
The geometry for the HTSG model. Redrawn from He et al. in *Computer Graphics (Proc. Siggraph '91)*, fig. 5, p. 178.

equations primarily for reference, not exposition; full details on the derivation of this model and its unpolarized form are available in He et al. [198].

$$
\begin{aligned}
f_r &= f_r{}^{sp} + f_r{}^{ud} + f_r{}^{dd} \\
f_r{}^{sp} &= \frac{\rho_s}{\cos\theta_i \, d\vec{\omega}_i} \times \Delta \\
f_r{}^{dd} &= \frac{|F|^2}{\pi} \times \frac{G \times S \times D}{\cos\theta_i \cos\theta_r} \\
f_r{}^{ud} &= a(\lambda) \\
\rho_s &= |G|^2 \times e^{-g} \times S \\
\Delta &= \begin{cases} 1 & \text{if in specular cone} \\ 0 & \text{otherwise} \end{cases} \\
|F|^2 &= (F_s{}^2 + F_p{}^2)/2
\end{aligned}
$$

$$
\begin{aligned}
G &= \left(\frac{\mathbf{v}\times\mathbf{v}}{v_z}\right)^2 \times \frac{1}{|\mathbf{k}_r\times\mathbf{k}_i|^4} \\
&\quad \times [(\mathbf{s}_r\times\mathbf{k}_i)^2 + (\mathbf{p}_r\times\mathbf{k}_i)^2] \times [(\mathbf{s}_i\times\mathbf{k}_r)^2 + (\mathbf{p}_i\times\mathbf{k}_r)^2] \\
S &= S_i(\theta_i)\times S_r(\theta_r) \\
S_i(\theta_i) &= \frac{1-\frac{1}{2}\mathrm{erfc}(\tau\cot\theta_i/2\sigma_0)}{\Lambda(\cot\theta_i)+1} \\
S_r(\theta_r) &= \frac{1-\frac{1}{2}\mathrm{erfc}(\tau\cot\theta_r/2\sigma_0)}{\Lambda(\cot\theta_r)+1} \\
\Lambda(\cot\theta) &= \frac{1}{2}\left[\frac{2}{\sqrt{\pi}}\times\frac{\sigma_0}{\tau\cot\theta} - \mathrm{erfc}\left(\frac{\tau\cot\theta}{2\sigma_0}\right)\right] \\
D &= \frac{\pi^2\tau^2}{4\lambda^2}\sum_{m=1}^{\infty}\frac{g^m\times e^{-g}}{m!\times m}\exp(-{v_{xy}}^2\tau^2/4m) \\
g &= [(2\pi\sigma/\lambda)(\cos\theta_i+\cos\theta_r)]^2 \\
\sigma &= \frac{\sigma_0}{\sqrt{1+(z_0/\sigma_0)^2}} \\
\sqrt{\frac{\pi}{2}}z_0 &= \frac{\sigma_0}{4}(K_i+K_r)\exp[-{z_0}^2/2{\sigma_0}^2] \\
K_i &= \tan\theta_i\ \mathrm{erfc}\left(\frac{\tau}{2\sigma_0}\cot\theta_i\right) \\
K_r &= \tan\theta_r\ \mathrm{erfc}\left(\frac{\tau}{2\sigma_0}\cot\theta_r\right)
\end{aligned} \tag{15.26}
$$

Equation 15.26 uses a few additional geometric terms not given in Figure 15.15; these are specified in Equation 15.27.

$$
\begin{aligned}
\mathbf{v} &= \mathbf{k}_r - \mathbf{k}_i \\
v_{xy} &= \sqrt{{v_x}^2 + {v_y}^2} \\
\mathbf{s}_i &= \frac{\mathbf{k}_i\times\mathbf{n}}{|\mathbf{k}_i\times\mathbf{n}|} \\
\mathbf{p}_i &= \mathbf{s}_i\times\mathbf{k}_i \\
\mathbf{s}_r &= \frac{\mathbf{k}_r\times\mathbf{n}}{|\mathbf{k}_r\times\mathbf{n}|} \\
\mathbf{p}_r &= \mathbf{s}_r\times\mathbf{k}_r
\end{aligned} \tag{15.27}
$$

The error function erfc is defined by

$$\operatorname{erfc}(x) = 1 - \frac{2}{\sqrt{\pi}} \int_0^x e^{-t^2}\, dt \tag{15.28}$$

although it is usually computed using a series expansion [3].

If we know the spectral reflectivity of a surface, and the values of σ_0 and τ that characterize its roughness, the HTSG model has been shown to predict experimental results on that material fairly well for a wide variety of materials and directions of incident light [198]. This is probably the most complete physically based model in the graphics literature today.

It is important to note that although it has the power to represent a wide variety of anisotropic materials and their interaction with polarized light, the HTSG model is not normalized [469]. We still need to manually select an appropriate diffuse reflectivity component so that energy is conserved.

The HTSG model is very expensive to compute. Precomputation and storage can move the computation into a one-time preprocessing step, but then storage of the data and accurate, efficient reconstruction become serious issues. He et al. report in a follow-up paper to their original presentation that a square table with eighty entries on a side can capture their model to within a relative error of 1%, and that using a spline representation to interpolate this table results in a speedup of two to three orders of magnitude over direct computation [197]. When a model such as this is able to pick up subtle and quickly changing aspects of the BRDF, it is a challenge to sample and reconstruct the function in a way that captures the power of the full formulation.

15.6 Empirical Models

The shading models presented above were based on a physical simulation of the underlying surface structure. Not all shading models require such physical underpinnings. For some applications, the model need only generate an approximation of the right solution. Of course, if accurate simulation is the goal of a particular rendering, then such shading models are inappropriate, but for fast previewing and some applications a fast, approximate, and easily controlled model may be preferable to the physically based ones described above.

15.6.1 The Strauss Model

The Strauss model [424] is an almost entirely approximate model that is intended to give designers an intuitive set of parameters with which to control surface appearance.

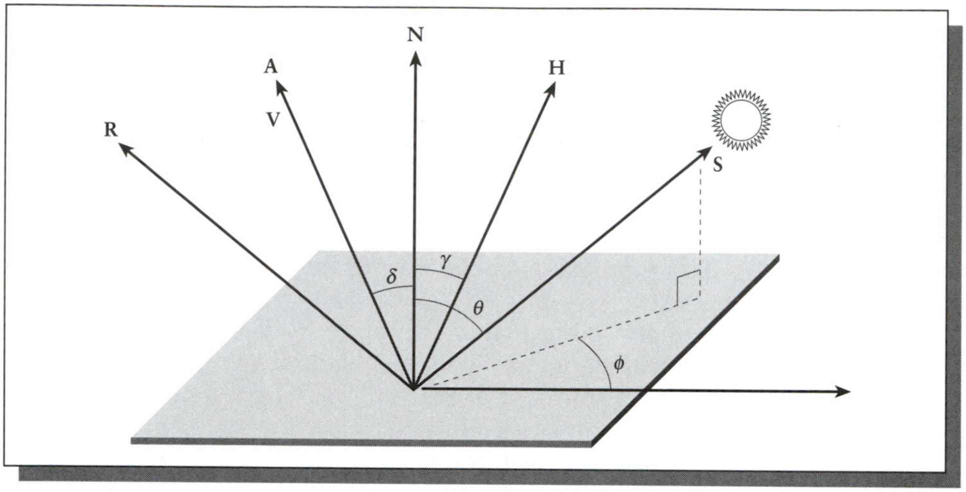

FIGURE 15.16
The geometry for the Strauss model.

The model is based on five surface parameters:

Color specifies the base color C of the object under white illumination at normal incidence.

Smoothness is a scalar $s \in [0, 1]$ sweeping the range from a perfectly diffuse surface at $s = 0$ to one that is perfectly specular at $s = 1$. This controls both the ratio of diffuse to specular reflectance and the size of the specular highlights.

Metalness is a scalar $m \in [0, 1]$ from 0 to 1 that specifies a point in the range from a dielectric at $m = 0$ to a metal at $m = 1$.

Transparency is a scalar $t \in [0, 1]$ that sweeps the range from opaque at $t = 0$ to transparent at $t = 1$.

Index of refraction is a scalar $n \in \mathcal{R}$ specifying the simple index of refraction of the medium.

The Strauss model is based on the geometry shown in Figure 15.16 (the names of vectors and angles have been changed from the original paper for consistency with the other shading models in this chapter). Because the model approximates more complex surfaces with simpler functions, there are several internal parameters that require tuning to get the proper behavior; we will see these below. As always, though each term depends on wavelength, we will not write this explicitly.

The BRDF of the surface is written as the sum of a diffuse term and a specular term:

$$f_r = {f_r}^d + {f_r}^s \tag{15.29}$$

Taking the diffuse term first, it is written as a product of the Lambert diffuse reflection term $\mathbf{N} \cdot \mathbf{S}$, the diffuse reflectivity ρ_d, and a *diffuse adjustment factor* d_a:

$$\begin{aligned} {f_r}^d &= \rho_d(\mathbf{N} \cdot \mathbf{S})d_a \\ \rho_d &= (1 - s^3)(1 - t) \\ d_a &= 1 - ms \end{aligned} \tag{15.30}$$

The diffuse reflectivity ρ_d includes the term $(1 - t)$ to account for diminished diffuse reflectance for increasingly transparent objects, and a term $(1 - s^3)$ to account for less diffuse reflectance as the surface gets smoother. The exponent 3 was chosen empirically so that a linear change in smoothness would cause a linear change in the diffuse reflectivity. The adjustment factor d_m is used to reduce diffuse reflectivity for rough metals.

The specular reflectance is based on a Phong-like exponentiated cosine term, times a *specular adjustment factor* s_a:

$$\begin{aligned} {f_r}^s &= -(\mathbf{R} \cdot \mathbf{V})^h s_a s_c \\ h &= \frac{3}{1 - s} \\ s_a &= \min(1, r_n + (r_n + k_b)b) \\ r_n &= (1 - t) - {f_r}^d \end{aligned} \tag{15.31}$$

The exponent h is determined by an empirical function that produced pleasing and predictable results. The adjustment factor s_a is designed to simulate off-specular peaks and Fresnel reflection. It is based on r_n, which is the fraction of light that is specularly reflected (that is, it is neither transmitted nor diffusely reflected). A bit of light given by k_b is added to this to give the off-specular peak, and then the result is multiplied by b to account for Fresnel and local geometric terms; Strauss reported that $k_b = 0.1$ worked well. The term s_c is discussed below.

The factor b increases the specularity near grazing incidence, except when the angles θ or δ come too close to $\pi/2$, when self-shadowing effects on the surface itself become important and reduce the reflectivity. The value of b is found from two functions, one named F designed to simulate the Fresnel term, and another named G to simulate the geometry term:

$$b = F(\theta)G(\delta)G(\delta) \tag{15.32}$$

These functions are given by

$$F(x) = \frac{\dfrac{1}{(x - k_f)^2} - \dfrac{1}{{k_f}^2}}{\dfrac{1}{(1 - k_f)^2} - \dfrac{1}{{k_f}^2}} \tag{15.33}$$

and

$$G(x) = \frac{\dfrac{1}{(1 - k_g)^2} - \dfrac{1}{(x - k_g)^2}}{\dfrac{1}{(1 - k_g)^2} - \dfrac{1}{{k_g}^2}} \tag{15.34}$$

The argument x in both functions should be from 0 to 1, so input angles are scaled by $1/(\pi/2)$ before computation. The constants k_f and k_g are used to tune the functions to better approximate the Fresnel and geometry terms; Strauss suggests $k_f = 1.12$ and $k_g = 1.01$.

Finally, some color shifting typically occurs on highlights off of metals, a phenomenon that is naturally accounted for in other models through the wavelength dependency in the Fresnel term. In this model, the color at a given wavelength is modulated by the term s_c in Equation 15.31, which is given by

$$c_s = 1 + m(1 - F(\theta))(C(\lambda) - 1) \tag{15.35}$$

where $C(\lambda)$ is the color at the wavelength λ where the model is being evaluated.

This is truly a model that has been seasoned to taste by an experienced cook. There are numerous magical constants that have been chosen empirically to produce a particular type of behavior. But Strauss reports [424] that the final model is intuitive and inexpensive, and because there are only a few user parameters that are relatively decoupled, it is straightforward to design and modify surface behaviors.

15.6.2 The Ward Model

Another simple empirical model with a different spirit was proposed by Ward [469]. He desired a shading model that was both simple enough to be attractive to implementors, and simultaneously accurate for most materials. When discussing how to create such a model, Ward proposed finding "the simplest empirical formula that will do the job" [469].

Ward derived an isotropic reflectance model that leaves out the geometric and Fresnel terms we have seen above. He asserts that these terms are difficult to integrate and tend to cancel each other out, and may be reasonably replaced with a single term that will normalize the BRDF. The geometry for the Ward isotropic model is the same as for the Strauss model. The BRDF generated by this model is given by

$$\rho^{\text{iso}} = \frac{\rho^d}{\pi} + \rho^s \cdot \frac{1}{\sqrt{\cos\theta\cos\delta}} \cdot \frac{\exp[-\tan^2\gamma/\alpha^2]}{2\pi\sigma^2} \tag{15.36}$$

where

ρ^d is the diffuse reflectance,
ρ^s is the specular reflectance,
θ is the angle between **N** and **S**,
δ is the angle between **N** and **V**,
γ is the angle between **N** and **H**, and
σ is the RMS standard deviation of the surface slope.

The terms ρ^d and ρ^s are functions of wavelength, and thus can incorporate Fresnel effects.

Equation 15.36 is very similar to the Phong model, except that it is normalized; inspection of the formula shows that it is symmetric with respect to the incident and reflected angles θ and δ, which is a required symmetry in any BRDF that satisfies reciprocity. The BRDF given in Equation 15.36 is normalized by the term $1/4\pi\alpha^2$. This is accurate as long as $a < 0.2$; beyond that point the surface becomes mostly diffuse and the specular term becomes less important.

The model may be extended in a straightforward way to accommodate two perpendicular and uncorrelated slope distributions, allowing us to describe an anisotropically reflecting surface. The anisotropic form of Ward's model is

$$\rho = \frac{\rho^d}{\pi} + \rho^s \cdot \frac{1}{\sqrt{\cos\theta\cos\delta}} \cdot \frac{\exp[-\tan^2\gamma(\cos^2\phi/{\sigma_x}^2 + \sin^2\phi/{\sigma_y}^2)]}{2\pi\sigma_x\sigma_y} \tag{15.37}$$

where in addition to the terms above,

σ_x is the RMS slope in the x direction,
σ_y is the RMS slope in the y direction, and
ϕ is the azimuth angle of **S** projected into the tangent plane.

Given the importance of efficient evaluation, this formula may be rewritten in a more computationally efficient approximation:

$$\rho = \frac{\rho^d}{\pi} + \rho^s \cdot \frac{1}{\sqrt{\cos\theta\cos\delta}} \cdot \frac{1}{4\pi\alpha_x\alpha_y} \exp\left[-2\frac{[(\mathbf{H}\cdot\mathbf{X})/\sigma_x]^2 + [(\mathbf{H}\cdot\mathbf{Y})/\sigma_y]^2}{1 + (\mathbf{H}\cdot\mathbf{N})}\right] \tag{15.38}$$

As long as $\rho_s + \rho_d < 1$ and $\sigma_x, \sigma_y < 0.2$, this model has been shown to match measured data rather well [469].

This model is described by four parameters that have reasonable physical meaning: ρ_d and ρ_s are the diffuse and directional-diffuse (or rough specular) coefficients, and α_x and α_y represent the RMS slope distribution of the surface in the X and Y directions.

Figure 15.17 (color plate) shows a set of three chairs: one a real photograph, one rendered with the isotropic model, and one rendered with the anisotropic model. Note particularly the highlight on the seat and the reflection of the back wall on the seat.

15.6.3 The Programmable Model

Each of the methods discussed above began with some approximation of a physical surface. Its behavior was characterized by a set of mathematical equations, which could then be implemented in a program. This approach creates a set of *parameterized shading models*, which essentially requires you to choose an appropriate model and then parameters for each material. To be successful, a user must have an intimate knowledge of both the model and the material in order to select the appropriate shading model and properly tune the parameters. Intuitive methods like the Strauss model relieve some of the burden, but the user then has a relatively narrow range of materials from which to choose, compared to all possible shading methods.

Rather than use one single shading model, or even a small set of models, to describe all surfaces, we could instead write a custom shading model, or *shader*, for each surface. Since a shader is just a program, it could in theory implement any of the models above, but also present enough flexibility to support new kinds of models.

To be useful in practice, the shader may be written in a *shading language* that supports the high-level constructs that are useful for this task. Cook presented an architecture [100] for building customized shaders by writing them in the form of tree-shaped networks. A similar language-based approach to shading was presented by Perlin [338], who allowed arbitrary expressions in a simple language to generate pictures from precomputed visibility information.

These ideas were combined by Hanrahan and Lawson [187] into the *RenderMan* shading language, which was intended to be simple enough that many people would write their own shaders, yet powerful enough to produce accurate (or at least accurate-looking) results. The resulting language is described in detail in Upstill [446].

Although they can be powerful enough to include the physically based models described above, the real attraction of shading languages is in their flexibility in creating interesting or complex materials without excessive effort. Often these materials are tuned to appear realistic in some sense, but just as often they are intended instead to create abstract or representational materials.

In some sense all shading is procedural (or programmable), since it always ends up implemented as a computer program. The explicitly programmable approach is based on the idea of taking small building blocks of geometric and environmental primitives and combining them to make a complete surface representation. Often normalization, reciprocity, and other physical criteria that are very important to physically based shaders are ignored when writing a procedural shader. This allows the shader to have an enormous amount of flexibility, including the local simulation of shadows (rather than computing shadows by explicitly interrogating the environment) and the introduction of atmospheric and camera effects.

15.7 Precomputed BRDF

The physically based and procedural reflection functions discussed above can be expensive to evaluate. Even simple scenes can require several million evaluations of the reflection function, so it is important that evaluation be as fast as possible. One way to speed up a slow function is to precompute a range of values and store them in a table, and then interpolate those values at run time.

There is another significant advantage to precomputing the BRDF and storing it in sampled form. Physical models attempt to find a description of the BRDF that is both an accurate representation of the model and mathematically tractable. But if we are sampling the BRDF and storing it, then the underlying physical model can be arbitrary. This is powerful, because it lets us use brute-force techniques to manually construct the underlying small-scale geometry and turn that into a BRDF, even if the mathematical representation would be difficult. For example, the microfacet-distribution equations discussed above use the Gaussian model and characterize the distribution of facets by their RMS slope under this model. But if we are sampling the facets directly, then we can manually orient them any way we want, not necessarily according to a Gaussian distribution. This can make it easier to capture models for which we have some understanding (either intuitive or experimental), but not a precise description, let alone one that is tractable, fast, and easy enough to integrate and normalize.

15.7.1 Sampled Hemispheres

The sample-and-store approach was used by Kajiya [233] to efficiently implement his anisotropic reflectance model. Because this formula contains an integral that is expensive to compute, Kajiya suggested precomputing the reflection for different types of surfaces and storing the results in a set of coarsely sampled hemispheres. The idea is that the BRDF for a given direction is represented by a hemisphere of m cells; if we simply subdivide the hemisphere into a cells by latitude and b by

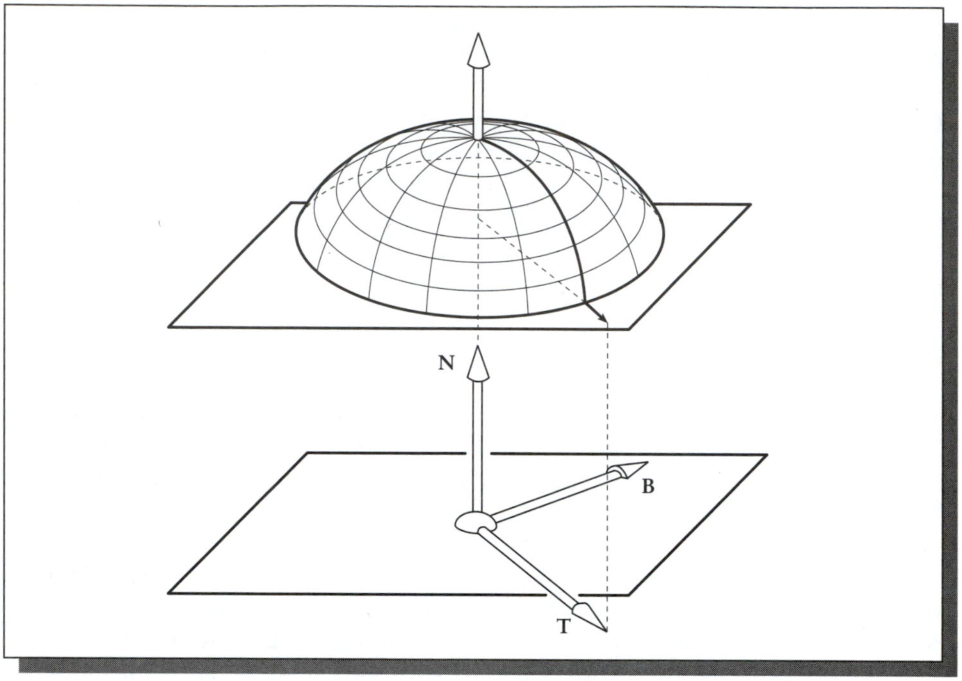

FIGURE 15.18

Lining up a precomputed anisotropic BRDF with a shading point.

longitude, then $m = ab$. We then consider each of these m cells in turn, thinking of it as the source of incident light. For each incoming cell we compute the reflection into every outgoing cell, filling up that outgoing hemisphere for that incident direction. Then the next incident direction cell is considered, and so on; the result is a set of m hemispheres.

To apply the model, we choose the hemisphere closest to the incident angle, and then orient the hemisphere so its north pole lines up with the surface normal. Then the hemisphere is rotated around the normal until the X axis on its base plane is aligned with the grain of the surface, as shown in Figure 15.18.

Given a precomputed set of hemispheres, the rendering step only requires using the incident light and the surface information to select the appropriate hemisphere, line it up, and then perform a set of table look-ups to find the reflected light. The trick then is to determine how to line up the hemisphere. If we can easily find partial derivatives of the surface, then those partials with respect to some reference coordinate system can be used to generate a local tangent plane, and one of the partials can be used as the grain direction. Unfortunately, finding these partials can be difficult or expensive.

Kajiya suggested that just as texture mapping (discussed below) can be used to apply colors and other surface characteristics to a surface, so an entire *frame* can be mapped to a surface. A frame is an origin and a set of three orthogonal vectors: the normal $\mathbf{N}$, the tangent $\mathbf{T}$, and the binormal $\mathbf{B}$. The normal is perpendicular to the surface, and the tangent and binormal span the tangent plane. A frame also needs an origin, but that's simply the shading point itself. So by mapping the frame to the surface, we get a complete 3D coordinate system at each point.

This can be done by computing a three-by-three rotation matrix for the point. We can store a coarsely sampled set of rotations on the surface and interpolate as with a regular texture map (interpolating the rotations as quaternions [404] is probably a good idea), or the rotations can be computed on the fly from other information.

Since the vectors are mutually orthogonal, any one can be computed from the other two. The surface normal can usually be derived directly from the surface information itself. So if the normal can be computed unambiguously, and some deterministic rule generates one of the other vectors, then the third vector can be generated from a cross product producing a complete frame.

One way to produce a second vector is to select one of the principal axes, and find the vector nearest that axis that is perpendicular to the normal. For stability, we can choose the axis that makes the greatest angle with the normal; this is the normal component with the smallest absolute magnitude. Suppose this is the X axis (which corresponds to the vector $\mathbf{X}$). Then we find the perpendicular $\mathbf{T}$ from $\mathbf{T} = \mathbf{X} - (\mathbf{X} \cdot \mathbf{N})\mathbf{N}$, and then $\mathbf{B} = \mathbf{N} \times \mathbf{T}$.

The mapping process then needs only a single number representing the angle by which that frame should be rotated around the normal to line it up with the grain. If the surface is smooth enough to allow a good representation by a uniform sampling (or a nonuniform texture map is used), then only a single scalar texture is needed. However, this technique is not invariant as the surface is moved, because it depends on the local orientation of the normal with respect to the global coordinate system. If we can find the inverse transformation of the canonical object with respect to the global system, this can be applied to the normal before the mapping and then reapplied to the complete frame to find the local transformed frame on the surface. If the object is rigid, then a single matrix will do for the entire surface; if free-form deformations are allowed, then the technique becomes more expensive, and eventually storing enough information to generate the local frame directly becomes more attractive. This time-space trade-off must be settled by the implementor based on practical considerations.

A related sampled-hemisphere approach was described by Becker and Max [35], who stored a BRDF using a *normal distribution*. This is a data structure based on a hemisphere that has been divided into a finite number of bins, and then placed around a small patch of material. Each hemispherical cell contains a count of the number of normals that project into that cell from the material sample; initially all of these counts are set to 0. Points on the material are sampled, and the normal at each point is computed. The value stored in the hemisphere bin corresponding to that normal's direction is then incremented. Becker and Max take care not to count normals from points that would be invisible along the normal direction from outside the hemisphere; that is, they account for a geometric attenuation factor similar to G in the Torrance-Sparrow model by explicit calculation. Becker and Max present an algorithm for transforming the normal table into a pair of BRDFs, one each for the specular and diffuse components. These tables are then interpolated during rendering.

15.7.2 Spherical Harmonics

A different approach using spherical harmonics was developed by Cabral et al. [71]. They wanted to represent the BRDF generated by a surface of explicit microfacets that they created to improve bump mapping. They irradiated a small sample of the opaque surface and counted where the light was reflected for each incident direction, simulating the experimental measurement of a BRDF.

Assuming that the BRDF was isotropic, they realized that it was simply a function defined over a hemisphere, and therefore could be represented in the spherical harmonic basis (recall that spherical harmonics were discussed in Section 13.9). They noted that by truncating the spherical harmonic expansion after some finite number of terms, they could efficiently store and compute with the measured BRDF.

Kajiya and Von Herzen also represented the BRDF around a volumetric scattering point using spherical harmonics [236]. They solved a set of first-order partial differential equations for the coefficients, and saved only the first few terms to store an approximation to the full function.

Spherical harmonics were also used by Sillion et al. [410] to store local illumination information. They noted that this formulation also allowed them to easily accumulate and accurately store light information as it arrived at a surface. Like Cabral et al. [71], they assumed that the BRDF was isotropic. As with practical implementations, they also truncated the expansion after a finite number of terms. To store the BRDF as a function of the incident angle θ, Sillion et al. stored each coefficient in the spherical harmonic expansion in a spline as a function of this angle. Thus for a ray of incident light that makes an angle θ with the normal to the patch, they evaluated the spline for the first coefficient at this angle, then the spline for the second coefficient, and so on, eventually building up a list of all the coefficients. These were then used to weight the spherical harmonic bases to compute the full BRDF.

Sillion et al. noted that this technique allows us to store *smooth* BRDFs with only a finite number of samples (as opposed to the sampled hemispheres mentioned above), but by the same token this method can only represent reasonably smooth functions. A BRDF with a significant specular component has a sharp peak that violates this condition, so they handle that with a separate mechanism.

Spherical harmonics were used to store more complex anisotropic BRDFs by Westin et al. [475]. In this approach, a spherical harmonic expansion was used to store the spherical harmonic coefficients themselves for the BRDF, a process they described colorfully as placing "wheels within wheels."

The idea is based on the multiple projection of a signal (the 4D anisotropic BRDF, which depends on the two scalar angles each of incidence and reflection) onto a set of lower-dimensional bases (the 2D spherical harmonics), and then projecting the resulting coefficients onto the same basis set (the 2D spherical harmonics again). This is an instance of a general technique that allows us to efficiently represent multidimensional data using low-dimensional basis functions; this was discussed in detail in Section 5.3.

The matrix of spherical harmonic coefficients is normally extremely large; Westin et al. say that ten thousand elements are typical. To compress the data, they use a clever observation also used by Sillion et al. [408]: when representing only the top half of the sphere to capture reflection, we are free to choose any signal we want for the lower half (and vice versa when representing transparency). Suppose that we simply mirror the BRDF about the equator; then all the spherical harmonics that are odd with respect to the equator (that is, $f(\theta, \psi) = -f(\theta, -\psi)$) will evaluate to 0. Like the 1D Fourier exponentials about the origin, half of the spherical harmonics are odd about the equator, and since we are forming the products of all the spherical harmonics used, one-fourth of the terms in the matrix are the product of two odd functions and are zero, and one-half of the terms are the product of an even and an odd function and therefore they too are zero. This cuts down on the size of the matrix to one-fourth of its original size. Westin et al. also use a reversible modulation of the BRDF near the equator to reduce high-frequency information, which causes the magnitudes of the spherical harmonics to drop off faster, thereby letting them retain fewer terms.

Westin et al. estimate the coefficients by a Monte Carlo sampling of an explicitly constructed surface patch, similar to the approaches discussed earlier. They then numerically process the matrix to force it to be symmetrical. Results of this approach may be seen in Figures 15.19 and 15.20 (color plates), illustrating the anisotropic surfaces of velvet and nylon.

15.8 Volume Shading

The shaders we discussed above were mostly concerned with *surface shading*, which occurs at the surface of an object, and not with *volume shading*, or the absorption and scattering of light *inside* the object itself. There isn't a firm distinction between these two methods, and often one can be pressed into the service of the other; after all, they're both just scattering functions. In fact, most volumetric models include a surface component to handle the effects at the boundary of the volume where the light passes from one medium to another.

But some shading models have been developed that explicitly represent what occurs inside a material, and we now turn our attention to those methods.

15.8.1 Phase Functions

The core of any shading model is the scattering function. There are a few scattering functions that have been developed for efficient volume rendering that have a solid theoretical basis and span a wide range of materials.

In this section we will survey the most popular of these scattering functions (also called *phase functions* when applied to volumetric scattering). We will not derive these functions, as the theory can be quite lengthy and complex. Derivations may be found in the standard references in optics listed in the section on Further Reading, and in references such as Bohren and Huffman [53], Denman et al. [122], and McCartney [292].

Each scattering function provides the fraction of incident light propagated from a scattering event as a function of the outgoing direction with respect to the incident direction. All of the volume scattering functions we will cover in this section are *isotropic*, and depend only on the angle α between the incident and outgoing directions, as in Figure 15.21. Phase functions are often specified in terms of $a = \cos\alpha$ rather than α itself, and we will use that convention here.

Most scattering functions are based on the idea of a suspension of *particles* in some *medium*; both the particles and the medium are usually assumed to be independently homogeneous. Usually, the particles are also assumed to be of equal size (or distributed in size in some predictable way), and uniformly distributed within the medium. Although the index of refraction of both the particle and the medium of course depends on wavelength, and thus influences the scattering of light, the size of the particles exhibits more of an effect on the phase function than the change in index of refraction [506].

Because of this dependence on particle size, the choice of which type of scattering function to use for a particular problem is usually determined by the ratio of the particle size to the wavelength of the light involved. Rather than switch between models throughout the visible band, we can simply use the scotopic peak wavelength of 555 nm as a characteristic wavelength and select a scattering model using that value. Because the particles also vary in size and shape, we need to choose characteristic values for these particle parameters. Often the particles are assumed to be spherical, with a characteristic radius r given by the average radius. If the wave-

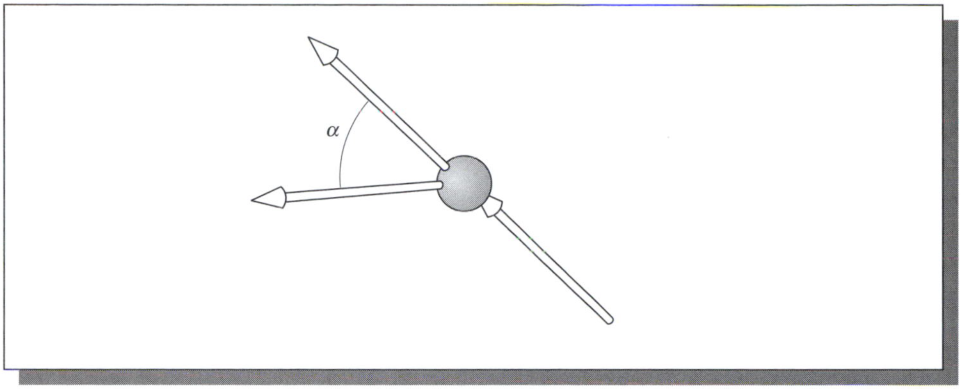

FIGURE 15.21
The angle α at the generic scattering event.

$r \ll \lambda$	Atmospheric absorption
$r < \lambda$	Rayleigh scattering
$r \approx \lambda$	Mie scattering
$r \gg \lambda$	Geometrical optics

TABLE 15.1
Criterion for selecting a phase function, comparing the characteristic particle radius r with the characteristic light wavelength λ.

length or particle characteristic assumptions are violated, the accuracy of the model will be decreased. When this is unacceptable, multiple simulations may be run using different sets of parameters.

Inakage has presented a useful summary of the four principal classes of phase functions and their selection criteria [225]; this summary is listed in Table 15.1.

Table 15.1 tells us that when the particles are far smaller than the wavelength of light, there is no appreciable scattering, and the light is simply absorbed. This is what happens to light passing through the near-vacuum of space. When the particles are much bigger than the wavelength of light, geometrical optics come into play; this is the typical situation when light strikes most solid objects such as wood or metal.

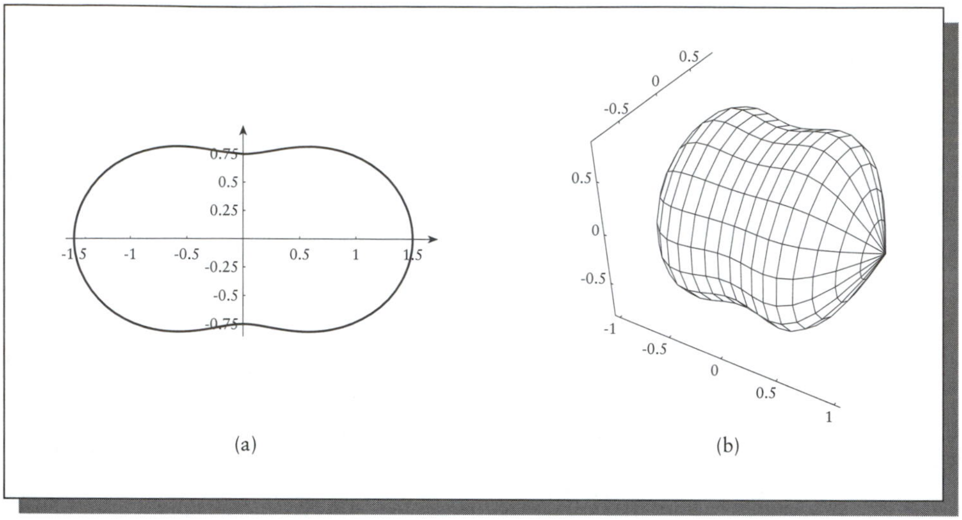

FIGURE 15.22

(a) The Rayleigh phase function. (b) The function in (a) rotated around the incident vector.

The intermediate cases occur when the particle sizes are comparable to the wavelength of light.

When the particles are somewhat smaller than the wavelength of light, we see phenomena described by *Rayleigh scattering*; such particles include cigarette smoke and dust. Klassen suggests that Rayleigh scattering should be initiated when $r/\lambda < 0.05$ [247]. The Rayleigh scattering function is given by

$$P_R(a) = \frac{3}{4}(1 + a^2) \tag{15.39}$$

The Rayleigh scattering function is simple enough that it can be directly implemented and used without approximation. The Rayleigh function is plotted in Figure 15.22(a). Remember that this function is isotropic around the incident direction, so the full 3D function is a surface of revolution found by rotating this curve around the central axis, as in Figure 15.22(b).

When particles are comparable to the wavelength of light, such as for water droplets or fog, the more complex theory of *Mie scattering* becomes applicable. Nishita et al. have reported [320] from the optical literature that the expensive Mie scattering functions may be efficiently approximated for sparse and dense particle densities, called *hazy* and *murky*, respectively. The *hazy Mie* and *murky Mie*

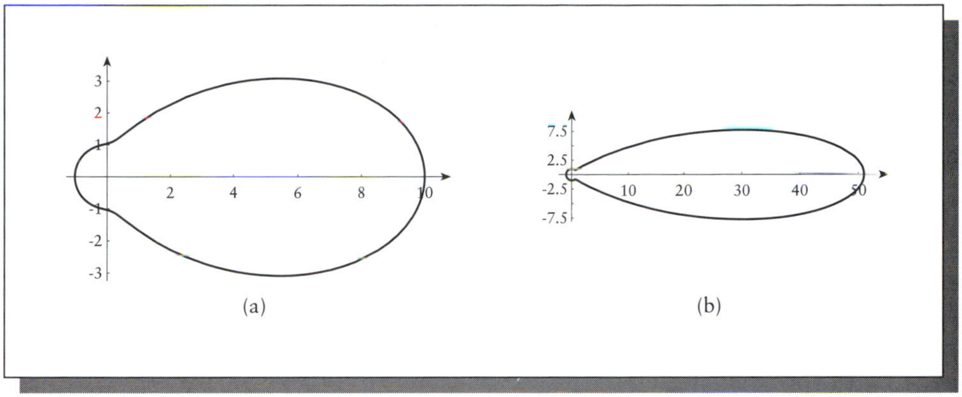

FIGURE 15.23
(a) The hazy Mie phase function. (b) The murky Mie phase function.

approximations are given by

$$P_{HM}(a) = 1 + 9\left(\frac{1+a}{2}\right)^8$$
$$P_{MM}(a) = 1 + 50\left(\frac{1+a}{2}\right)^{32} \tag{15.40}$$

These two phase functions are shown in Figure 15.23.

Note that the scattering functions in Figure 15.23 look like ellipses (albeit with a small blip at one end). Another popular approximation to the Mie functions is given by the *Henyey-Greenstein* phase function [49]:

$$P_{HG}(g, a) = \frac{1 - g^2}{(1 - 2ga + g^2)^{1.5}} \tag{15.41}$$

The Henyey-Greenstein phase function produces an ellipse with eccentricity g, and one focus at the origin. By varying g, we can sweep from predominantly backscattering for $g > 0$, to uniform scattering at $g = 0$, to predominantly forward scattering for $g < 0$. The Henyey-Greenstein phase function is plotted in Figure 15.24 for a few different values of g; compare it to the hazy and murky Mie functions in Figure 15.23.

Observe that the Rayleigh function appears to be two elliptical lobes brought together, and that the small lobe on the hazy and murky Mie functions are also

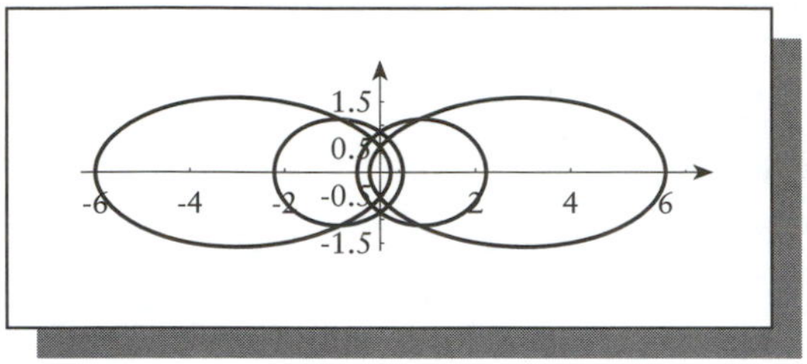

FIGURE 15.24
The Henyey-Greenstein phase function plotted for $g = -0.6, -0.25, 0, 0.25, 0.6$.

elliptical. This suggests that a function that combines two ellipses should be able to match these functions pretty closely.

The two-term Henyey-Greenstein (TTHG) model takes just this approach [506]. It linearly combines two ellipses of different magnitudes and eccentricities:

$$P_{TTHG}(r, g_1, g_2, a) = r\frac{1 - {g_1}^2}{(1 - 2g_1a + {g_1}^2)^{1.5}} + (1 - r)\frac{1 - {g_2}^2}{(1 - 2g_2a + {g_2}^2)^{1.5}} \quad (15.42)$$

Schlick [380] has developed a phase function that approximates the TTHG model, and thus can match both Rayleigh and Mie scattering as well. The model has the important advantage of avoiding the expensive fractional exponentiation in the full TTHG model. Like the TTHG formula, the Schlick phase function depends on a, the cosine of the scattering angle, a blending parameter r, and two eccentricity parameters g_1 and g_2:

$$P_{HG}(g, a) = \frac{1 - g^2}{(1 - 2ga + g^2)^{1.5}} \quad (15.43)$$

Figure 15.25 compares the Schlick phase function with the Rayleigh, hazy Mie, murky Mie, and Henyey-Greenstein functions. The values used for the match to the first three are given in Blasi et al. [45] and summarized in Table 15.2. To match the one-term Henyey-Greenstein function, we set $r = 1$ and $g_2 = 0$.

The Schlick function has the advantage of simplicity (and therefore speed), and the fact that we can invert it to find a probability density function appropriate for sampling the function. Given a uniform real random variable $u \in [0, 1]$, the pdf corresponding to one lobe of the Schlick function is given by Schlick [380]:

$$a = \frac{2u + g - 1}{2gu - g + 1} \quad (15.44)$$

This is very useful when using Monte Carlo methods to simulate scattering events.

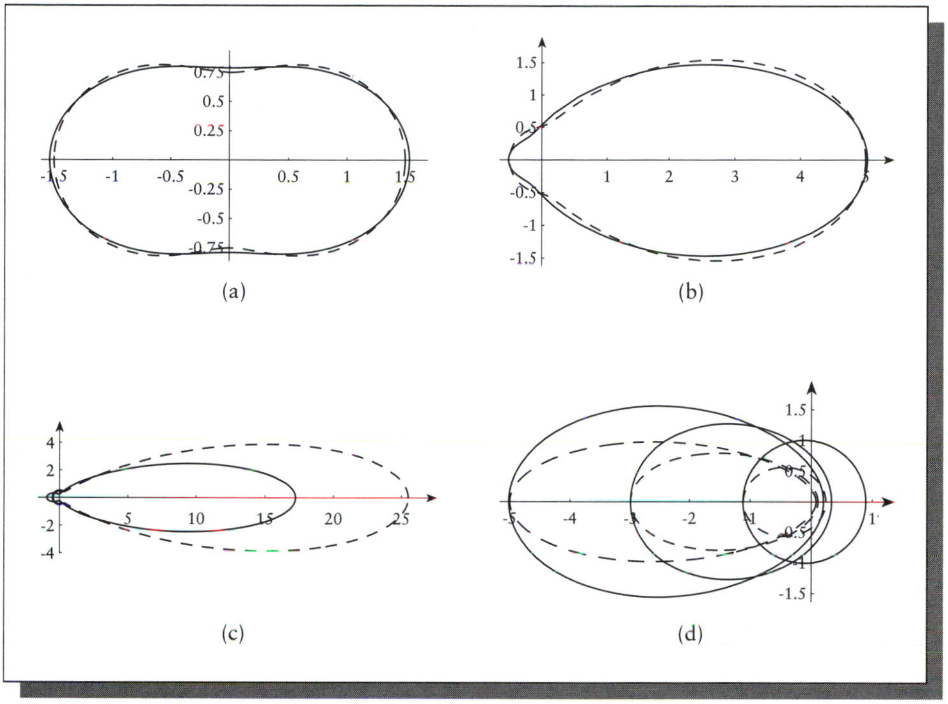

FIGURE 15.25

The Schlick phase function and (a) the Rayleigh function (dashed), (b) the hazy Mie function function (dashed), (c) the murky Mie function (dashed), (d) the Henyey-Greenstein function (dashed). The Henyey-Greenstein function is plotted for $g = -0.6, -0.5, -0.25$, and the Schlick function for $g_1 = -0.667, -0.5\ -0.55$.

Function	r	g_1	g_2
Rayleigh	0.50	−0.46	0.46
Hazy Mie	0.12	−0.50	0.70
Murky Mie	0.19	−0.65	0.91

TABLE 15.2

The values of r, g_1, and g_2 in the Schlick phase function that match the Rayleigh and two Mie functions. *Source:* Data from Blasi et al. in *Proc. Eurographics '93*.

Three other useful scattering functions were discussed by Blinn [48]. The *constant function* P_C is just a single scalar for all angles:

$$P_C = 1 \tag{15.45}$$

The *simple anisotropic function* P_{SI} is a function of the weighted cosine of the angle and a constant term:

$$P_{SI}(w, a) = 1 + wa \tag{15.46}$$

for some real number w. Finally, the *Lambert function* P_L is given by integrating the brightness of a visible disk:

$$P_L(a) = \frac{8}{3\pi}\left[\sin\alpha + (\pi - \alpha)a\right] \tag{15.47}$$

where $\alpha = \cos^{-1} a$.

A summary of how to choose among the different scattering functions in a variety of situations is given in Figure 15.26.

15.8.2 Atmospheric Modeling

An important special case of volume shading is simulation of the atmosphere of Earth. Much work has been done in computer graphics to develop efficient algorithms for rendering Earth's atmosphere and atmospheric effects. Our interest here is primarily in the scattering functions and not in techniques for evaluating them in various situations; references on these important algorithmic methods may be found in the section on Further Reading.

The components of the atmosphere that most strongly affect light from the sun (or *solar radiation*) are four permanent gases—nitrogen, oxygen, carbon dioxide, and argon—along with aerosol, ozone, and water vapor. Explicit formulas may be written for the absorption and scattering of light by each of these components per unit length; a summary of such formulas may be found in Zibordi and Voss [506].

An analysis of light absorption and scattering through atmosphere over the ground has been given by Inakage [225] and is illustrated in Figure 15.27. Of the solar radiation arriving at the outer edge of the atmosphere, 29% of the radiation can be thought of as interacting with the atmosphere, 47% with clouds, and the remaining 24% directly with the ground. Taking these in turn, 17% of the incident radiation is absorbed by the atmosphere itself, primarily by the gases and other components listed above, and 12% of this arriving radiation is scattered. Half of this radiation is backscattered and returns to space, and half is forward scattered and continues on to the ground. Returning to the original solar radiation, we said that 47% interacts with clouds. A total of 3% of the incident radiation is absorbed by clouds, 20% is reflected back into space, and 24% continues downward to the

Body	Physical cross section (cm^2)	Conditions		Type of scattering	Scattering cross section (cm^2)
Photon		Energy of incident photon small			$\sim 2 \times 10^{-56}$
Free electron		Energy of photon $\ll$ electron kinetic energy		Thomson	$\frac{8}{3}\pi r_0^2 = 6.65 \times 10^{-25} \equiv \sigma_T$
		Energy of photon $\gg$ electron kinetic energy		Compton	$\frac{3}{8}\sigma_T \frac{1}{\epsilon_p}\left(\frac{1}{2} + \ln 2\epsilon_p\right)$
Atom or molecule	0.88×10^{-16} (first Bohr electron orbit)	Elastic, $\lambda \gg$ size of molecule or atom	Energy of incident photon $\ll$ electron binding energy	Rayleigh	Proportional to $\sim 6.65 \times 10^{-25}/\lambda^4$
			Energy of incident photon $\gg$ electron binding energy	Rayleigh, approaches Thomson	$\sim 6.65 \times 10^{-25}$
		Inelastic	Energy of incident photon $\ll$ electron binding energy	Raman	$\sim 6.65 \times 10^{-25}$
			Energy of incident photon $\gg$ electron binding energy	Approaches Compton	$\sim \frac{3}{8}\sigma_T \frac{1}{\epsilon_p}\left(\frac{1}{2} + \ln 2\epsilon_p\right)$
Particles of diameter D	$\frac{\pi D^2}{4}$	$\lambda \gg D$, single scattering		Raleigh	Proportional to V^2/λ^4
		$\lambda \approx D$		Mie	Varies widely
		$\lambda \ll D$		Fraunhofer and Fresnel diffraction plus reflection	$\sim 2\left(\frac{\pi D^2}{4}\right)$

FIGURE 15.26

A summary of several different scattering functions. r_0 = classical electron radius, 2.81794×10^{-15} m; $\epsilon_p = hv/m_e c_0^2$, where h is Planck's constant; σ_T = cross section for Thomson scattering; m_e = electron mass, 9.10939×10^{-31} kg. *Source:* Data from Siegel and Howell, *Thermal Radiation Heat Transfer*, table 12-1, p. 530.

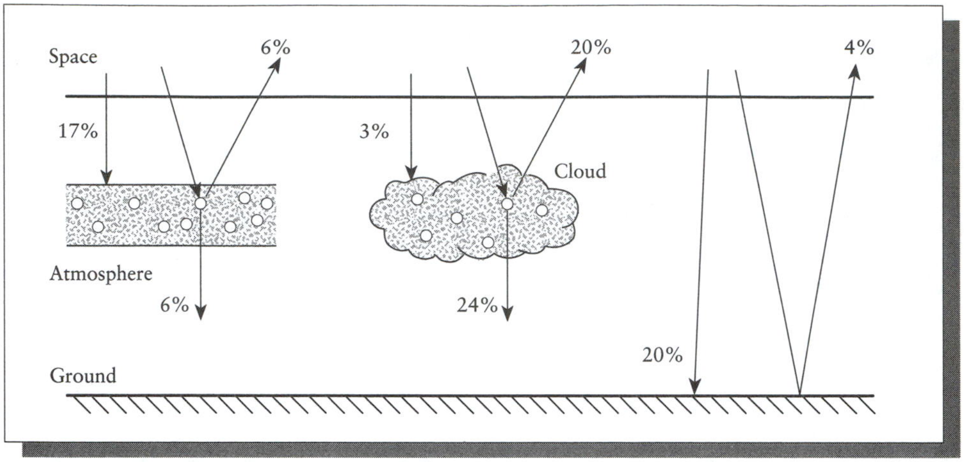

FIGURE 15.27
The distribution of light in the atmosphere over the ground. Redrawn from Inakage, *The Visual Computer*, fig. 1, p. 105.

earth. The third category is the 24% of the solar radiation that makes it directly to the ground without interacting with the atmosphere or clouds; 20% of the incident radiation is directly absorbed by the ground, while 4% is reflected back into space.

The actual distribution of light due to Rayleigh scattering is generally inversely dependent on the fourth power of the wavelength of the light. Two different models have been proposed to simulate this scattering in the atmosphere for graphics.

Inakage [225] has suggested modeling Rayleigh scattering with the equation

$$P_R(a) = \frac{\pi(1 + \cos a)}{\lambda^4} \cdot N \left[\frac{(\eta' - \eta)V}{\eta d} \right]^2 \qquad (15.48)$$

where

η is the simple index of refraction of air,
η' is the simple index of refraction of the scattering particles,
N is the number of particles per cubic centimeter,
V is the volume of each scattering particle in cubic centimeters,
d is the distance from the scattering event to the viewer, and
λ is the wavelength of light.

Note that $\cos a = \cos^2 \alpha$. A similar equation has been suggested by Nishita et al. [323]:

$$P_R(a) = \frac{\pi(1 + \cos a)}{\lambda^4} \cdot \frac{\pi \rho}{N_s} (\eta^2 - 1)^2 \tag{15.49}$$

where in addition to the terms above, N_s is the molecular number density of the standard atmosphere, and ρ is an altitude-dependent function given by

$$\rho = e^{-[h/H_0]} \tag{15.50}$$

where $H_0 = 7{,}994$ meters (at sea level, $\rho = 1$). They model the attenuation of the light as an extinction per unit length β, given by

$$\beta = \frac{8\pi^3 (n^2 - 1)^2}{3 N_s \lambda^4} \tag{15.51}$$

The results obtained by Nishita et al. [323] are shown in Figure 15.28 (color plate). In Figure 15.28(a), we see the atmosphere rendered without a planetary model; in Figure 15.28(b), the Earth and clouds have been added. Notice the change in color near the edges of the shadow.

Nishita et al. have reported [323] on a different approximate Mie phase function that matches experimental data for the atmosphere better than the one-term Henyey-Greenstein function. This better fit comes at a significantly increased evaluation cost. The Cornette function is given by

$$P_C(a, g) = \frac{3(1 - g^2)}{2(2 + g^2)} \frac{1 + a^2}{(1 - 2ga + a^2)^{1.5}} \tag{15.52}$$

where g is given by

$$g = \frac{5}{9}u - \left(\frac{4}{3} - \frac{25}{81}u^2\right) x^{-1/3} + x^{1/3} \tag{15.53}$$

and x is given by

$$x = \frac{5}{9}u + \frac{125}{729}u^3 + \sqrt{\frac{64}{27} - \frac{325}{243}u^2 + \frac{1250}{2187}u^4} \tag{15.54}$$

r	g_1	g_2
0.962	0.713	0.759
0.968	0.836	0.537

TABLE 15.3
Parameters for the two-term Henyey-Greenstein model for Earth atmospheric simulation. *Source:* Data from Zibordi and Voss in *Remote Sensing of the Environment*, p. 357.

where u specifies the atmospheric condition and ranges from 0.7 to 0.85. Unfortunately, this function requires many more operations than the one-term Henyey-Greenstein function, including at least one new cube root.

Zibordi and Voss [506] found that when using the two-term Henyey-Greenstein model to represent atmospheric scattering, the accuracy of an atmospheric shading model is highly sensitive to the eccentricity factors g_1 and g_2. They found good agreement to measured data from a clear sky by using either of the two sets of parameters listed in Table 15.3.

A single-scattering model of a homogeneous volume was used by Max [286] to simulate the glow of illuminated air. He demonstrated the shafts of light visible near the ground as light passes through the leaves of overhead trees.

Other planetary bodies have been studied as well. Blinn [48] noted that the reflectance of the moon may be modeled by combining a Lambert term for the backscattering due to rough particles with a simple anisotropic term for the forward scattering due to glass-like spherical particles:

$$P_{\text{Moon}}(a) = w_1 P_L(a) + w_2 P_{SI}(a) \tag{15.55}$$

Blinn [48] has noted that a two-term Henyey-Greenstein function may be used to model the rings of Saturn as seen from the Earth, with $r = .596$, $g_1 = 0.5$ and $g_2 = -0.5$. For his simulation, Blinn chose a combination of a Lambert terms and a one-term Henyey-Greenstein function, using coefficients that vary with the radius r from the planet's center:

$$P_{\text{Saturn}}(a) = w_1(r) P_L(a) + w_2(r) P_{HG}(-0.5, a) \tag{15.56}$$

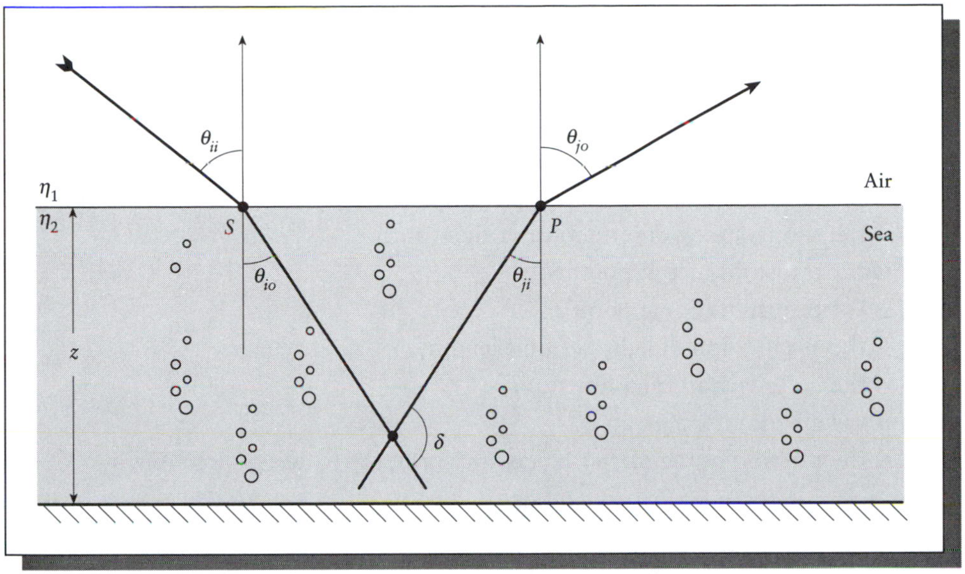

FIGURE 15.29

The two-layer model used to model the ocean. Redrawn from Nishita et al. in *Computer Graphics (Proc. Siggraph '93)*, fig. 5, p. 179.

15.8.3 The Earth's Ocean

Another significant natural object is the ocean that covers much of the Earth. Nishita et al. [323] have developed a shading model tuned for the ocean based on a two-layer model illustrated in Figure 15.29.

The scattering model is based on a combination of the light scattered at the ocean's surface, plus light scattered back up to the surface from inside the water and then transmitted back into the air. This *quasi-single-scattering* model is quite complex and uses several variables we haven't encountered yet; to reduce confusion, we will explicitly write out all of the wavelength dependencies. The light arrives at the water at point S and scattered light departs from point P.

$$\rho(\theta_{ii}, \theta_{io}, z) = \frac{T_i(\theta_{ii}, \theta_{io}) T_o(\theta_{ji}, \theta_{jo}) \beta(\delta, \lambda)}{n^2(\cos\theta_{io} + \cos\theta_{ji}) c(\lambda)[1 - \omega_0(\lambda) F(\lambda)]}$$
$$\times \left(1 - \exp\left[-z c(\lambda)[1 - \omega_0(\lambda) F(\lambda)](\sec\theta_{ji} + \sec\theta_{io})\right]\right) \quad (15.57)$$

where

λ is wavelength,
z is the depth of the sea,
θ_{ii} is the angle between the normal at P and the viewing direction,
θ_{io} is the angle between the direction of the zenith and the incident light,
θ_{jo} is the angle between the reverse direction of the zenith and the refracted light,
n is the simple index of refraction of the water,
T_i is the transmittance at point S,
T_o is the transmittance at point P,
$c(\lambda)$ is the attenuation of light per unit length,
β is the volume scattering function,
ω_0 is the albedo of water, and
F is the fraction of the scattering coefficient in the forward direction.

15.8.4 The Kubelka-Munk Pigment Model

One common type of material used for covering surfaces is *paint*. Paint is physically composed of many small colored particles of *pigment* suspended in some sort of mostly transparent and colorless base such as oil [444].

Materials that exhibit *selective reflection* and *selective absorption* are called *pigments* and *dyes* when there is little luminescence produced due to excitation. The nature of a pigment may vary with absorption. Some materials change their reflective properties in response to strong irradiation, in a process known as *solarization*. For example, the almost-clear compound cubic potassium chloride can be made to *tenebresce*, or darken and bleach from exposure to strong light [267]. Sometimes this effect can be reversed. A material that responds to incident light by getting darker is called a *scotophor* (meaning *dark-bearer*), in contrast to the better-known term *phosphor* (*light-bearer*) [267].

Usually paint is formulated so that it stays wet during storage but dries upon application, either through evaporation of part of the base material, or as a result of a chemical interaction with air. An analysis of the chemistry of paint shows that the color is usually generated by one of a handful of molecular structures attached to some larger carrier molecule [444].

One approach to handling paint is to directly simulate the atomic and molecular interaction of these *chromophores* (meaning *color-bearer*). Alternatively, we can work at a macroscopic level and simply model the aggregate behavior of the paint with respect to incident light. This approach was taken by Kubelka and Munk, who developed a simple relationship between the scattering and absorption coefficients of paint and its overall reflectance [255]. The Kubelka-Munk theory has been discussed

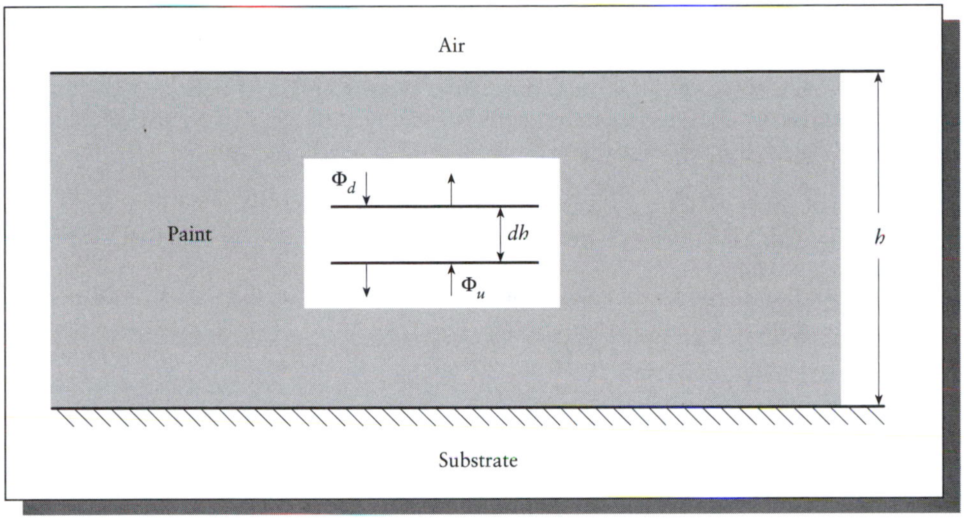

FIGURE 15.30

Paint on a surface. Redrawn from Haase and Meyer in *ACM Transactions on Graphics*, fig. 20, p. 332.

for computer graphics applications in Fishkin [145] and Haase and Meyer [175]. We will rederive this model here because it has good practical value, it's not very complicated and yet provides a very good match with the phenomena it models, and it presents another useful application of the transport theory we developed earlier. Perhaps the most important reason is that this gives us an example of a reasonably complex model that we can derive from first principles and then analyze in some detail.

We start by imagining a surface that has been coated by a layer of paint with thickness x, as in Figure 15.30. We suppose that the paint is homogeneous, has a scattering coefficient of σ_s and an absorption coefficient of σ_a, and has been applied with uniform thickness h. We assume that we know the reflectance ρ_0 of the substrate material to which the paint has been applied. Remember that σ_s, σ_a, and ρ_0 are all functions of wavelength. The Kubelka-Munk literature often uses the letters K and S for σ_a and σ_s.

Consider some differential horizontal slice of thickness dh within the paint. Label the flux that is descending toward the surface as Φ_d, and the upward-moving flux Φ_u (note that these can each be the result of multiple scattering events with the paint material). Then, given the reflectivity ρ_0 of the substrate, we can find the reflectivity

ρ_h of the substrate with a layer of paint of thickness h by solving a transport problem very much like the ones in Chapter 12. This is the approach taken by the Kubelka-Munk theory.

We will follow the derivation in Haase and Meyer [175], which uses arguments similar to those in Chapter 12. We begin by noting that the loss in the descending and ascending fluxes due to a single scattering or absorption event is given by

$$\begin{aligned} \Delta_d{}^- &= (\sigma_a + \sigma_s)\Phi_d \, dh \\ \Delta_u{}^- &= (\sigma_a + \sigma_s)\Phi_u \, dh \end{aligned} \tag{15.58}$$

On the other hand, the gains in each flux come from scattering alone. Assuming a single scattering event in the layer dh, the gains are

$$\begin{aligned} \Delta_d{}^+ &= \sigma_s \Phi_u \, dh \\ \Delta_u{}^+ &= \sigma_s \Phi_d \, dh \end{aligned} \tag{15.59}$$

So the total loss in each direction is found by the loss minus the gain:

$$\begin{aligned} d\Phi_d &= \Delta_d{}^- - \Delta_d{}^+ \\ &= (\sigma_a + \sigma_s)\Phi_d \, dh - \sigma_s \Phi_u \, dh \\ d\Phi_u &= -[\Delta_u{}^- - \Delta_u{}^+] \\ &= -[(\sigma_a + \sigma_s)\Phi_u \, dh - \sigma_s \Phi_d \, dh] \end{aligned} \tag{15.60}$$

(The upward-moving quantity is negated so that we can measure both changes in the same coordinate system, and $d\Phi_u$ is in the opposite direction as $d\Phi_d$.)

Writing $a = 1 + (\sigma_a/\sigma_s)$, we have the pair of differential equations

$$\begin{aligned} \frac{d\Phi_d}{\sigma_s \, dh} &= a\Phi_d - \Phi_u \\ \frac{-d\Phi_u}{\sigma_s \, dh} &= a\Phi_u - \Phi_d \end{aligned} \tag{15.61}$$

Multiplying by Φ_u/Φ_u and Φ_d/Φ_d, respectively, and adding the results, we find

$$\frac{\Phi_u \, d\Phi_d - \Phi_d \, d\Phi_u}{\sigma_s \, dh} = a\Phi_d\Phi_u - \Phi_u{}^2 + a\Phi_d\Phi_u - \Phi_d{}^2 \tag{15.62}$$

and then multiplying both sides by $-\Phi_d/\Phi_d$, we find

$$\frac{\Phi_d \, d\Phi_u - \Phi_u \, d\Phi_d}{\Phi_d{}^2 \sigma_s \, dh} = \frac{-2a\Phi_u}{\Phi_d} + \left(\frac{\Phi_u}{\Phi_d}\right)^2 + 1 \tag{15.63}$$

From the Quotient Rule we can observe that

$$\frac{\Phi_d \, d\Phi_u - \Phi_u \, d\Phi_d}{\Phi_d{}^2 \sigma_s \, dh} = \frac{d(\Phi_u/\Phi_d)}{\sigma_s \, dh} \tag{15.64}$$

Writing $r = \Phi_u/\Phi_d$, we can simplify Equation 15.63 to

$$\frac{dr}{\sigma\, dh} = r^2 - 2ar + 1 \qquad (15.65)$$

or by rearrangement and integration,

$$\int \frac{dr}{r^2 - 2ar + 1} = \sigma_s \int dh = \sigma_s h \qquad (15.66)$$

Since we have assumed the paint is homogeneous, the scattering coefficient σ_s is constant throughout the material and can be brought outside the integral on the right-hand side.

Our goal is to find a value for ρ_h given a paint thickness h. When $h = 0$, the paint is gone, and we are left with the substrate reflectivity ρ_0. So we are interested in evaluating the integral of Equation 15.66 over the range ρ_0 to ρ_h. We cannot directly find the integral, but we note that it is a *rational fraction*, that is, the ratio of two polynomials in r; the numerator is just a constant. To simplify such an integral, we factor the denominator by writing $b = \sqrt{a^2 - 1}$. Then a bit of algebra lets us write the denominator as the product

$$r^2 - 2ar + 1 = [r - (a + b)][r - (a - b)] \qquad (15.67)$$

Using the method of partial fractions, we write

$$\frac{dr}{r^2 - 2ar + 1} = \frac{A_1}{r - (a + b)} + \frac{A_2}{r - (a - b)} \qquad (15.68)$$

By plugging in $r = a - b$ and $r = a + b$ and simplifying, we find that $A_1 = 1/2b$ and $A_2 = (-1/2b)$, so plugging these in and integrating

$$\int_{\rho_0}^{\rho_h} \frac{dr}{r^2 - 2ar + 1} = \int_{\rho_0}^{\rho_h} \frac{1/2b}{r - (a + b)} + \int_{\rho_0}^{\rho_h} \frac{-1/2b}{r - (a - b)} \qquad (15.69)$$

From any table of integrals (such as Beyer [41]), we find

$$\int_u^v \frac{dr}{r - c} = \ln(r - c)\Big|_u^v \qquad (15.70)$$

Applying this to Equation 15.69, we find

$$\frac{1}{2b}\left[\ln[\rho_h - (a+b)] - \ln[\rho_0 - (a+b)] - \ln[\rho_h - (a-b)] + \ln[\rho_0 - (a-b)]\right] = \sigma_s h \qquad (15.71)$$

Multiplying both sides by $2b$ and exponentiating, we find

$$\frac{(\rho_h - a - b)(\rho_0 - a + b)}{(\rho_0 - a - b)(\rho_h - a + b)} = \exp[2b\sigma_s h] \qquad (15.72)$$

Recall that our goal is to find ρ_h, the reflectivity of the substrate seen through a layer of paint of thickness h. Let's assume that the paint is applied so thickly that the substrate is completely invisible. Mathematically, we write the thickness $h \to \infty$, so $\rho_0 \to 0$. We write the reflectance as ρ_∞, or more simply as just ρ. This simplifies Equation 15.72 to

$$(-a-b)(\rho-a+b) = \frac{(\rho-a+b)(-a+b)}{\exp[2b\sigma_s h]} \tag{15.73}$$

If we expand both sides and cancel common factors, we get

$$(a^2-\rho a-b^2)\left(1-\frac{1}{\exp[2b\sigma_s h]}\right) = b\rho\left(1+\frac{1}{\exp[2b\sigma_s h]}\right) \tag{15.74}$$

As $h \to \infty$, both of the fractions go to 0, leaving us with

$$a^2-\rho a-b^2 = b\rho \tag{15.75}$$

Solving for ρ, we find

$$\rho = a-b = \frac{1}{a+b} \tag{15.76}$$

We can show (see Exercise 5) that this may be written in terms of the scattering coefficients as

$$\rho = 1+\sigma_c-\sqrt{{\sigma_c}^2+2\sigma_c} \tag{15.77}$$

where we use the combined coefficient $\sigma_c = \sigma_a/\sigma_s$, or as

$$\sigma_c = \frac{(1-\rho)^2}{2\rho} \tag{15.78}$$

The results of this theory are illustrated in Figure 15.31 (color plate). A real photograph is shown of a canvas painted with fourteen color swatches showing different amounts of combinations of two red paints with white. The spectral reflectances of the paints are shown in Figure 15.32, and the dependencies of the absorption and scattering coefficients are shown in Figure 15.33. Note how much more accurately the pigment model matches the real paints.

Equation 15.77 represents the solution to the basic Kubelka-Munk differential equations as they were originally presented in 1931 [255]. Fishkin has described the evolution of these results through several years of improvements by a series of researchers [145]. We will not follow those developments in detail, but will summarize the main results.

The Kubelka-Munk equations were generalized by Duncan to allow arbitrary mixtures of pigments [132]. He assumed that if there are multiple materials with

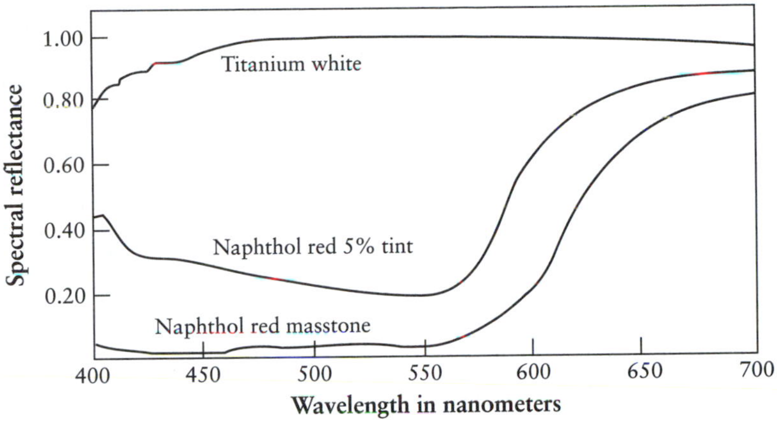

FIGURE 15.32
Spectra of the paints used in the real canvas. Redrawn from Haase and Meyer in *ACM Transactions on Graphics*, fig. 9, p. 318.

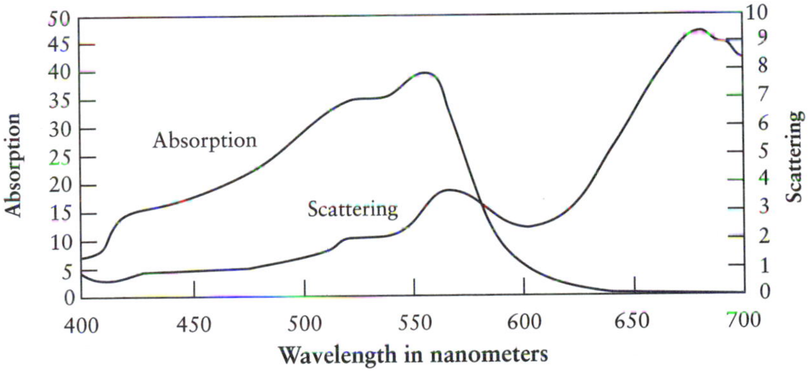

FIGURE 15.33
Scattering coefficients as functions of wavelength of the paints used in the real canvas. Redrawn from Haase and Meyer in *ACM Transactions on Graphics*, fig. 10, p. 319.

different scattering and absorption coefficients, they may be combined by linear weighting:

$$\sigma_s = \sum_{i=1}^{n} w_i \sigma_{s,i}$$
$$\sigma_a = \sum_{i=1}^{n} w_i \sigma_{a,i} \tag{15.79}$$

Remember that these coefficients are both functions of wavelength. This hypothesis was not justified theoretically, but proposed and then confirmed by experiment.

Kubelka [232] later solved the original differential equations of Equation 15.61 for a finite thickness of paint. If the paint has thickness h, then

$$\rho_h = \frac{[p(\rho_0 - \rho)] - \rho(\rho_0 - p)e^{\sigma_s h(p-\rho)}}{\rho_0 - \rho - (\rho_0 - p)e^{\sigma_s h(p-\rho)}} \tag{15.80}$$

where $p = 1/\rho$, and as before ρ is the reflectance of a layer so thick that any increase in thickness doesn't change the reflectance.

A simpler form [145, 256] of this equation can be found using the hyperbolic trig functions sinh, cosh, and coth. Then

$$\rho_h = \frac{1 - \rho_0(a - b \coth b\sigma_s h)}{a - \rho_0 + b \coth b\sigma_s h} \tag{15.81}$$

where

$$a = 1 + \sigma_a/\sigma_s$$
$$b = \sqrt{a^2 - 1} \tag{15.82}$$

as earlier. When the paint becomes thick enough to hide the substrate, $\rho_0 \to 0$, so Equation 15.81 becomes

$$\rho_h = \frac{1}{a + b \coth b\sigma_s h} \tag{15.83}$$

and if the paint is infinitely thick, $h \to \infty$, so $\coth b\sigma_s h \to 1$, reducing Equation 15.83 to

$$\rho_h = \frac{1}{a + b}$$
$$= \frac{\sigma_s}{\sigma_s + \sigma_a + \sqrt{{\sigma_a}^2 + 2\sigma_a\sigma_s}} \tag{15.84}$$

which is exactly Equation 15.76, showing that the infinite-thickness solution is just a special case of the more general finite-thickness solution.

Fishkin points out a number of limitations to this theory of pigment modeling [145]; we list a few of the most significant ones here.

1. The values of σ_a and σ_s are dependent on the combination of pigment and medium; the same pigment in a different medium (say water and oil) will have different coefficients of scattering and absorption.
2. The model completely ignores the chemical and electrical interactions between pigments, the medium in which they are suspended, and the substrate. Such interactions can substantially affect the chemical composition of the materials, and hence the resulting color.
3. The model presented above assumes that the paint is homogeneous; in fact, the particles tend to *flocculate* (or clump), which again changes the color.
4. The scattering assumptions in the transport theory were based on uniformly sized spherical particles. This is rarely the case for real pigment particles, which can take on cylindrical, bulletlike, or teardrop shapes of varying sizes.
5. All of these models have ignored what happens to the light as it enters and exits the particle; this is an interface between two media like any other, which can involve reflection, transmission, and polarization effects.
6. The models all assume that the substrate is planar and the paint is of uniform thickness; this is rarely the case in practice (we can use a texture map to modulate the paint thickness h to compensate for some of this effect).
7. The model assumes that we are viewing the pigment from within a medium of the same index of refraction as the carrier, that is, while both the observer and the paint are immersed in a vat of oil or water. Clearly this is not the usual case on dry land, and some account must be made of reflection and refraction at the paint's surface.

Judd and Wyszecki [232] present a number of alternative solutions to the Kubelka-Munk theory. In addition to Equation 15.81, the most important are probably

$$R_0 = \frac{1}{a + b \coth b\sigma_s h} \tag{15.85}$$

and

$$T_i = \frac{b}{a \sinh b\sigma_s h + b \cosh b\sigma_s h} \tag{15.86}$$

where

R_0 is the reflectance of a layer with an ideal black background
T_i is the transmittance of a layer

An interesting limiting case of these equations is when the scattering coefficient σ_s goes to 0. Then $a = (\sigma_s + \sigma_a)/\sigma_s \rightarrow \sigma_a/\sigma_s$, and $b = (a^2 - 1)^{1/2} \rightarrow a$. Substituting

$a = b = \sigma_a/\sigma_s$ into Equations 15.85 and 15.86 gives us

$$R_0 = \frac{\sigma_s}{\sigma_a(1 + \coth \sigma_s h)} \tag{15.87}$$

and

$$\begin{aligned} T_i &= \frac{1}{\sigma_a(\sinh \sigma_s h + \coth \sigma_s h)} \\ &= \frac{1}{\exp[\sigma_s h]} \end{aligned} \tag{15.88}$$

These equations make the reasonable statements that as the scattering coefficient $\sigma_s \to 0$, the reflectivity R_0 of a layer over a pure black reflector also goes to zero. And the transmittance drops off as an equal percentage per unit layer of colorant.

15.8.5 The Hanrahan-Krueger Multiple-Layer Model

The Hanrahan-Krueger model [190] represents a surface by a series of layers, of different materials, where each layer has a different set of descriptive coefficients, as shown in Figure 15.34. Like the ocean model of Equation 15.57 due to Nishita et al. [323], the Hanrahan-Krueger model explicitly evaluates the reflection and transmission of light at media boundaries, and the volume scattering of light within layers.

According to Judd and Wyszecki [232], a *layer* of material is a thin sheet whose thickness is small compared to its length and width. As we saw for the atmosphere and pigment models above, we assume a layer is homogeneous in all ways.

Multiple-layer models combine surface models with volume models in alternation. A volume model accounts for the structure inside each material, and a surface model represents the interface between each adjacent pair of materials. Each material and interface may use a different model, or the same model with different parameters.

The material descriptors include the index of refraction, absorption and scattering coefficients, depth (or thickness), and the phase function; they use the one-term Henyey-Greenstein phase function.

The algorithm is based on a 1D transport model which is solved with a Monte Carlo sampling scheme. Using the Fresnel formula to find how much light will pass through the outermost surface of the coating, the model then evaluates the scattering and absorption within each layer, including the reflection and transmission effects at each internal boundary. Hanrahan and Krueger assumed that if a material is a mixture of several materials, then the mixture is a uniform and homogeneous combination whose coefficients are given by a sum of the component coefficients weighted by percentage.

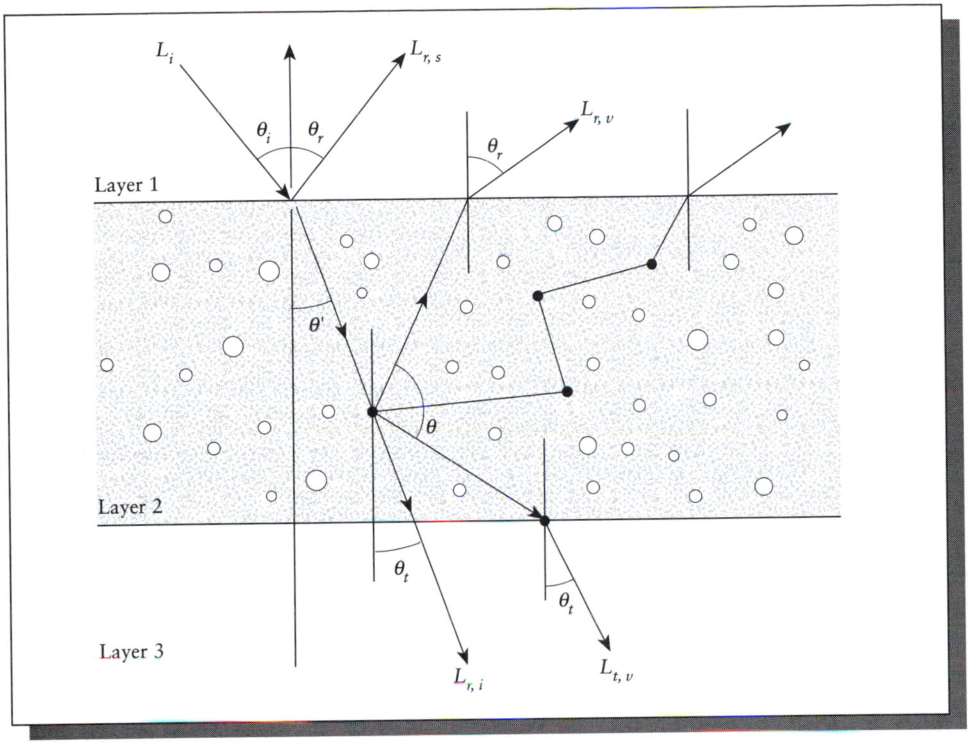

FIGURE 15.34
Several layers of material over a surface, and some light interacting with the materials. Redrawn from Hanrahan and Krueger in *Computer Graphics (Proc. Siggraph '93)*, fig. 1, p. 166.

The BRDF is then described by a combination of the reflection function on the outer surface and the internal subsurface scattering handled by the Monte Carlo evaluation. Figure 15.35 (color plate) shows an example of a head rendered by Lambert shading and by the subsurface model. The skin was assumed to be composed of two layers. The outermost skin layer had tissue and pigment particles containing melanin, which selectively absorbs light, producing a brown-to-black appearance, and scatters strongly in the forward direction. The inner blood-and-tissue layer was assumed to absorb green and blue, and to offer substantial isotropic scattering. The two columns on the left were rendered using Lambert shading, and the two middle columns using the subsurface model. The differences are shown on the right, with red indicating where the subsurface model gave off more light, and blue where it gave less. Figure 15.36 (color plate) shows a head produced by using texture maps to modulate the thickness and density of the layers.

15.9 Texture

The term *texture* has been used in many ways in the image synthesis literature. In its most general sense, anything that is evaluated at a point using only information local to that point is a texture. Such local information can include the point's location in space, its position on a surface, the directions and magnitudes of the partial derivatives of the surface at that point, a surface normal, the gradient of a scalar field evaluated at that point, and so on. The evaluated function often returns a scalar, but it can in theory be any data type, including a vector, a color, or any arbitrary structure. Usually textures are used as parameters to a shading function, but there are notable exceptions. *Texture mapping*, or the application of texture to geometry, represents an important link between geometry and shading.

A *volume texture* can be evaluated at any point in space; a *surface texture* can be evaluated only on the surfaces of points. Textures are typically either *procedural* and evaluated on demand by some program, or *stored* in a table which is accessed to find the texture value. The correspondence between the texture table and a surface or volume is defined by a *texture map*. Textures were originally introduced by Blinn and Newell [51], and a great deal of work has been focused on texturing since then. Much of the work in texturing has been devoted to finding efficient and useful surface parameterizations, useful procedural functions, and efficient methods for sampling and filtering textures. Discussions of modern texture mapping may be found in Heckbert [205] and Watt and Watt [473]. A particularly popular class of procedural textures are generated by the noise functions given in Perlin [338].

The first application of textures was to specify the color of a surface at every point [51]; physically, it was like applying a decal or sticker to a surface.

Textures have been used in several ways to change (or appear to change) the geometry of the surface to which they are applied. The first example is *bump mapping*, introduced by Blinn [47], which perturbs the normal on a surface to create what appear to be small wrinkles or bumps on the surface. This trick breaks down near the silhouette of the object (because the silhouette is unchanged, the bumps implied by the shading are not visible in the geometry), and at near-glancing angles to the surface (because there is no blocking or geometric attenuation due to the bumps). In general, though, as long as the bumps are very small and the object is some distance away, bump mapping is an effective way to imply small deformations to a shape without actually changing the geometry.

The *hypertexture* method due to Perlin and Hoffert [339] allows us to actually change the surfaces of objects. Hypertexture is a volumetric modeling technique that implies surfaces even where explicit surfaces have not been created; it is rendered using volumetric methods. Some examples of hypertexture are shown in Figure 15.37 (color plate).

The *texel-mapping* method of Kajiya and Kay [237] maps not just a scalar or a coordinate system but an entire surface description onto the surface of an object. This bundle of information, called a *texel*, actually carries a complete shading model that may be further parameterized by other values mapped onto the surface. The furry bear of Figure 15.38 (color plate) was produced with this method.

The *displacement texture* method due to Cook provides another way to actually alter the geometry of the surface [100]. Rather than simply perturbing the normal at a surface to simulate a wrinkle or bump, displacement mapping actually moves the surface by a given amount in a given direction. Rendering displacement-mapped surfaces can present a challenge to some systems, particularly when the displacements become large, but the basic idea is straightforward. The results are often much better than with bump mapping, because displacement-mapped objects actually exhibit self-hiding, self-shadowing, and a changed silhouette. Some examples of displacement mapping along with color mapping are shown in Figures 15.39 and 15.40 (color plates).

15.10 Hierarchies of Scale

When we are very far from a surface, we generally need only a coarse representation of its reflectivity and geometric characteristics. As we approach the surface, we begin to see finer detail in both the geometry and the way it scatters light.

The *level-of-detail* problem for geometry was recognized early in computer graphics [110]; to achieve real-time performance, only the minimum number of polygons needed to represent a shape could be displayed. The basic idea is that we ought not to waste time processing detail that is sufficiently small that we could ignore it without introducing significant error. In terms of shading models, we should use the crudest representation of a shading function that will meet our visual or simulation criteria.

Kajiya suggested [233] that the modeling and rendering level-of-detail problems were closely coupled. He suggested that there is a *hierarchy of detail* in geometric models, where increasing levels of detail correspond to the geometry of the model, then texture-mapping, and then shading. Furthermore, these levels overlap, as shown in Figure 15.41. Although we will speak in terms of surfaces in this section, this observation and our discussion are equally applicable to volumes.

The issues raised by Kajiya's hierarchies of scale have to do with the size of an object that is sampled by a rendering algorithm. If the object is observed directly from the viewpoint for an image, then this sample region is directly related to its

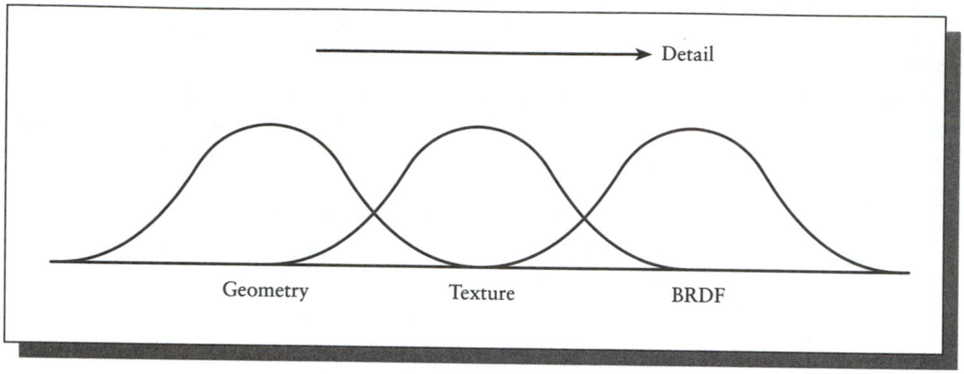

FIGURE 15.41
A hierarchy of detail. Redrawn from Kajiya in *Computer Graphics (Proc. Siggraph '85)*, fig. 2, p. 18.

projection on the screen, and this projection may be used to estimate how much of the surface is being sampled. But within a complex 3D environment, some surfaces that may not be directly visible to the viewer might still be densely sampled; for example, a painting on the wall behind your head could still be visible in the curved wall of a shiny vase. To complicate the issue still further, the same object may be densely sampled from some points in the environment and sparsely sampled from others, even within the same image, or during the rendering of a single pixel!

Even in systems where objects are subdivided and not point-sampled, the correct level of subdivision may vary according to different needs (and viewpoints) during rendering. Figure 15.42 shows two pixels, each sampled with four samples. A small checkerboard is on the right side of the scene, and a mirror is on the left. In Figure 15.42(a) we see that when we look directly at the checkerboard, our four samples land roughly in the four quadrants of the checkerboard, so the region of integration for each sample is roughly a square quadrant, as shown in Figure 15.42(b).

In Figure 15.42(c) we see the world through a different pixel; the samples bounce off of the mirror and land on the checkerboard. The sampling pattern on the checkerboard is quite different, as shown in Figure 15.42(d). Only three pixels hit the board, and the regions over which we integrate the flux from the board are quite different.

Poulin and Fournier [344] discussed the problem in terms of a hierarchy of geometries, as shown in Figure 15.43. At the highest level is the geometric model itself, and below that is a bump-mapped or displacement-mapped version of the geometry;

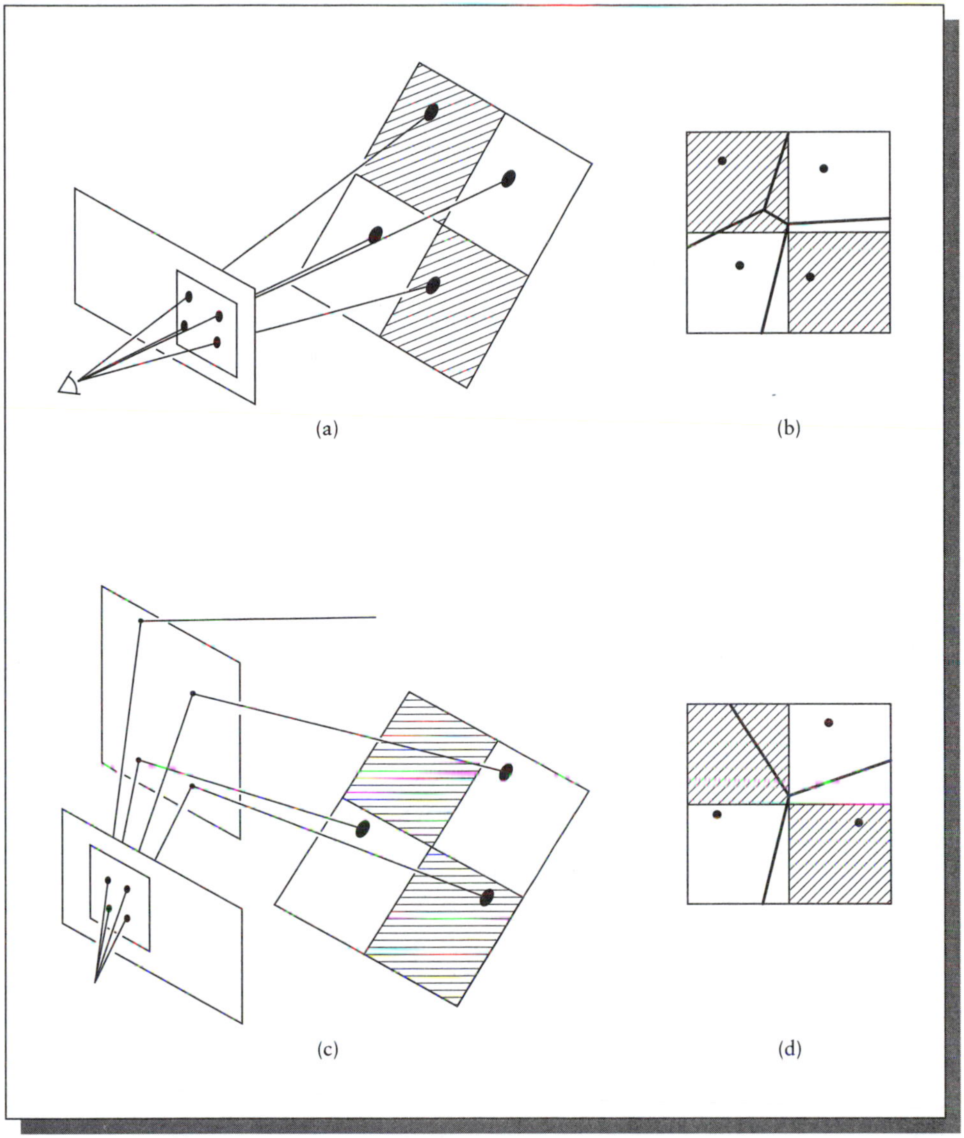

FIGURE 15.42

A scene of a mirror on the left and a checkerboard on the right. (a) A sampling pattern through a pixel. (b) The integration regions induced by (a). (c) A sampling pattern through a different pixel. (d) The integration regions induced by (c).

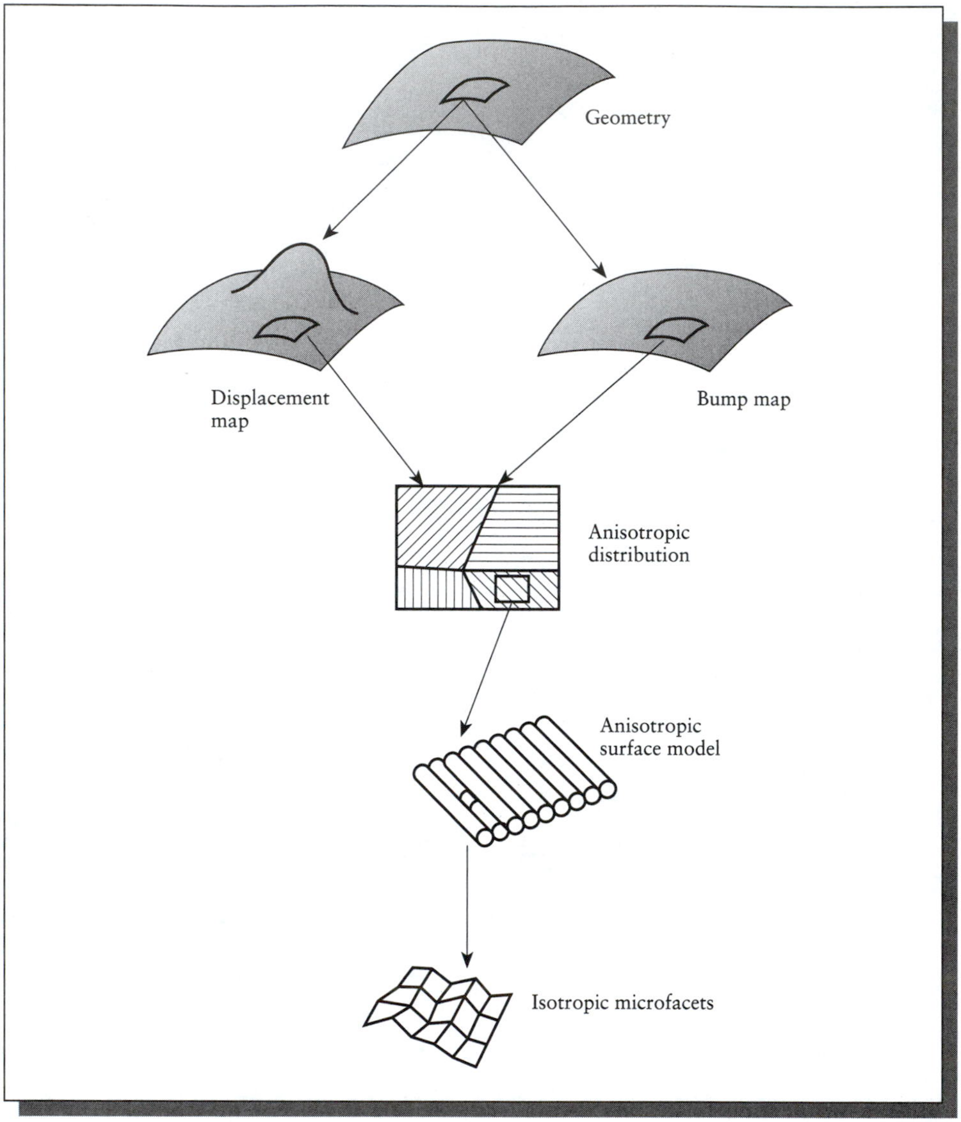

FIGURE 15.43

A hierarchy of geometric models. Reprinted, by permission, from Poulin and Fournier in *Computer Graphics (Proc. Siggraph '90)*, fig. 1, p. 275.

note that only displacement mapping actually moves the underlying geometry. Then comes a texture that parameterizes the underlying fine-scale structure of the surface, which may be based on geometry itself (in their case it was a model of parallel cylinders). Finally comes the BRDF, which can also be represented geometrically as a collection of microfacets.

Westin et al. [475] described the problem in terms of orders of magnitude of scale, as shown in Figure 15.44 (color plate). The largest scale includes phenomena on the size of 1 meter. They call this the *object scale*, and it contains the basic geometry of objects in the scene: polygons, patches, and volumetric functions. Two or three orders of magnitude below that comes 1-millimeter-sized *milliscale* phenomena, which is handled by textures of various sorts, including bump maps and texels. Finally, two or three orders of magnitude smaller one comes to the *microscale*, which is the domain of particle-sized interactions handled by the BRDF.

From this point of view, the size of the sampled region indicates the scale of the phenomena being sampled, and suggests the precision needed to evaluate the sample. If we take a single sample from a house from a distance of 1 kilometer, there is probably no need to carefully integrate the burrowing of the light into the sublayers of paint on the side; if the house is mostly red, then we can just return red and be done with it. But if that sample is near other samples that are only millimeters away, then more careful shading models are called for. Westin et al. presented a model that can move through these scales when the BRDF is used to model the surface geometry [475].

The best way to smoothly move between these scales is still an open problem. One method proposed by Becker and Max [35] is to *redistribute* bump maps so that they have the same overall energy output as a displacement-mapped surface or its underlying BRDF. The Becker-Max algorithm can then use any of the three methods to compute shading based on the size of the interrogated patch, and the overall energy coming from any piece of the surface will match that coming from the rest. Figure 15.45 (color plate) shows a bumpy teapot in extreme close-up, rendered with this method.

The full answer to the hierarchies of scale problem for the reflectance function is not yet in. There seem to be two trends, one that decouples shading from visibility (used by the displacement-mapping method) and another that ties them together intimately (such as the Becker-Max transition method). Some recent developments in the simplification of geometric models [214, 443] offer hope that we can handle the geometry problem in a semiautomatic way, replacing complex models with simpler approximations when appropriate, reducing memory consumption and execution times.

15.11 Color

In Unit I of this book, I discussed color and its perception by the human visual system. We saw that even though the perceptual color space is three-dimensional, an accurate representation of color is not possible when every surface and volume is represented simply by three single-wavelength samples. Although many rendering systems today continue to render a color picture by essentially computing separate red, green, and blue images and then displaying them simultaneously, this model can produce images with severe artifacts even in everyday scenes [181].

One alternative to the *RGB* model is to subdivide the visible band into many smaller pieces, render an image for each band, combine the results, and then transform the combined data into a single picture suitable for display (perhaps on a CRT using an *RGB* color space). Essentially, this is a supersampling approach in the color space; we recognize that sampling only three fixed wavelengths leads to color aliasing, so we sample more densely to capture more high-frequency information. Once the visible band has been stratified, samples may be taken in the center of each band [181], or jittered within the band to trade uniform sampling artifacts for noise [154].

Meyer has observed [300] that this is a very expensive solution: if the visible band is subdivided into relatively coarse 10-nanometer intervals, that still leaves about forty samples that must be evaluated; in effect, forty separate pictures that must be computed. Since many real spectra are rather smooth, Meyer reasoned that perhaps they can be matched by a small number of basis functions. Then we need only track the coefficients on the basis functions rather than the many individual samples across the spectrum.

Meyer describes such an approach in [300]. He first derives a color space called the A, C_1, C_2 space, where the axes pass through the densest regions of the color space defined by the CIE *XYZ* tristimulus curves. This transformation is given by

$$\begin{bmatrix} A \\ C_1 \\ C_2 \end{bmatrix} = \begin{bmatrix} -0.0177 & 1.0090 & 0.0073 \\ -1.5370 & 1.0021 & 0.3209 \\ 0.1946 & -0.2045 & 0.5264 \end{bmatrix} \begin{bmatrix} X \\ Y \\ Z \end{bmatrix} \tag{15.89}$$

A reasonable question to ask now is, if we are committed to sampling the environment with single spectral samples, how many samples should there be and where should they be placed to get the best trade-off of effort to accuracy in evaluating A, C_1, and C_2? Meyer constructed a number of Gaussian quadrature rules using different numbers of points to evaluate the three coefficients. He found that a four-point rule gave good accuracy when evaluating the colors on the Macbeth ColorChecker chart, a standard set of color references [291] (the data for this chart is given in Appendix G). The quadrature rule recommended by Meyer is given in Table 15.4. Note that none of the color parameters uses all four of the spectral samples.

	456.4	490.9	557.7	631.4
A		0.18892	0.67493	0.19253
C_1		0.31824		−0.46008
C_2	0.54640			

TABLE 15.4
Evaluating A, C_1, C_2 from four spectral samples at four values of λ. *Source:* Data from Meyer, *Computer Vision, Graphics, and Image Processing*, table 1a, p. 70.

So we need only sample at four spectral locations in order to evaluate A, C_1, and C_2, and from them find X, Y, and Z using the inverse transformation of Equation 15.89:

$$\begin{bmatrix} X \\ Y \\ Z \end{bmatrix} = \begin{bmatrix} 0.7311 & -0.6130 & 0.3636 \\ 1.0030 & -0.0124 & -0.0064 \\ 0.1194 & 0.2218 & 1.7628 \end{bmatrix} \begin{bmatrix} A \\ C_1 \\ C_2 \end{bmatrix} \tag{15.90}$$

A variation on this idea is described by Raso and Fournier [354]. They divide the visible band into two pieces, split at 555 nm, the peak of the scotopic (night-vision) sensitivity curve. Each subband is represented by a cubic polynomial, so a color is encoded by eight floating-point numbers. They note that when colors are filtered, the order of the polynomial increases, but they then find the best cubic fit using Tchebyshev polynomials and retain that. In essence they are weighting and combining the first four monomials, which serve as basis functions for cubic polynomials.

Another basis-function approach has been described by Peercy [337]. He reasoned that the colors we are most interested in representing in any particular image are those that are combinations of the light source spectra and the surface spectra of the lights and objects in that image (and higher-order combinations of these as well). Peercy started with the spiky spectrum of a fluorescent light, illustrated in Figure 15.46, and combined that with four of the colors on the Macbeth color chart. He then used characteristic vector analysis to extract the principal vectors that best described the spectra produced by combinations of this illuminant and these surface colors, and used the most significant ones as the basis functions for rendering a test scene.

Figure 15.47 (color plate) shows the results of using two, three, four, and then five of the most significant basis functions to render the scene, and also using the

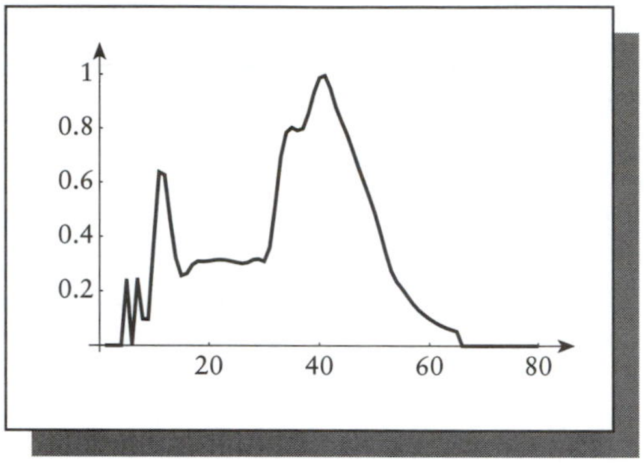

FIGURE 15.46

The spectrum of a fluorescent light. Redrawn from Peercy in *Computer Graphics (Proc. Siggraph '93)*, fig. 1, p. 194.

square of those counts to determine the number of equally spaced point samples in the visible band. In the left column, the two-basis function image is somewhat dark and lacking in green, but the three-basis function image seems indistinguishable from the five-basis image.

But in the right column, the results are not nearly as good; the four-sample image is badly distorted, the nine-sample image has a yellow cast, and the reflections in the cube have a much reduced contrast. The sixteen-sample image still has a bit too much yellow. Finally, the twenty-five–sample image looks very close to the five-basis image.

These images are only test cases and do not tell us the quantitative error, but we can see that for this scene, equal-interval spectral sampling requires at least sixteen samples to do an even approximate job of estimating the color (if the sample locations were not evenly spaced, but instead had been analyzed and optimized for the best locations, the images might have been better).

Point-sampling methods retain the advantage of being able to adaptively sample regions of high-frequency content, and easily support adaptive supersampling, but they are prone to aliasing and other undersampling artifacts. The choice of function used for reconstruction from point samples is also important; we often reconstruct using boxes that extend to the midpoints of adjacent samples, but a smoother filter such as those discussed in Unit II would probably yield better results.

Basis-function methods give continuous results that converge quickly, but they require that we select good basis functions beforehand, which can be difficult.

15.12 Further Reading

General discussions of surfaces and materials may be found in the books by Judd and Wyszecki [232], Wyszecki and Stiles [489], and Siegel and Howell [406]. *RenderMan* is a proposed standard which includes a shading language; Upstill details the language and offers many examples in his book [446]. Discussions of shading models for computer graphics are offered in books by Hall [181], Sillion and Puech [409], and Watt and Watt [473].

Good summaries of what goes on inside materials may be found in Turner's book on paint [444] and Leverenz's book on general luminescence [267].

Physically based shading models are often based on principles of optics. Some of the many good optics books are Möller [311], Born and Wolf [55], and Jenkins and White [230]. The thermal radiation literature surveyed in that field's classic text by Siegel and Howell [406] also contains a wealth of material.

Discussions of scattering in volumes are given in the books by Bohren and Huffman [53], Denman et al. [122], and McCartney [292].

An interactive program for exploring the HTSG model has been written by He et al. [197] and is available on CD–ROM in the Siggraph '92 proceedings.

Finding efficient representations for Earth's atmosphere and atmospheric effects has been a topic of study since the first shading models were developed. Some references to this work include the papers by Blinn [49], Inakage [225], Kajiya [236], Klassen [247], Max [286, 287], Nishita et al. [320, 323], Tadamura [430], and Zibordi [506]. The books by Lenoble [266] and McCartney [292] provide lots of material for this topic.

A good introduction to how light behaves inside many different varieties of crystals may be found in Wood's book [488].

Three very interesting and enjoyable books deserve special mention. Greenler [170] presents the results of numerous ray-tracing experiments designed to simulate complex atmospheric phenomena. Minnaert [305] addresses many fascinating topics on the nature of light in the atmosphere, including a method for observing "with our naked eye, unaided by any instrument, that the light from the sky is polarized!" Meinel and Meinel [296] discuss both rare and common phenomena like twilight colors, the "green flash," the effects of volcanic dust on sunsets and sunrises, and auroras. These books all reward a few evenings' investment with a lifetime of increased awareness and pleasure in the sky above us.

15.13 Exercises

Exercise 15.1

Describe the difference in appearance between objects shaded with the Phong and Blinn-Phong models.

Exercise 15.2

Review the paper by Lewis [273] on adding energy conservation to Phong and Torrance-Sparrow shaders. Do you think that the addition of energy conservation improves these models, or do their assumptions overwhelm the corrections?

Exercise 15.3

Review the empirical shading model proposed by Schlick [381] and compare it against the other empirical models in this chapter. Which would you select for a production rendering system? Why?

Exercise 15.4

Use Equation 15.9 to show that $R_p \to 1$ as $\theta \to 0$.

Exercise 15.5

Use Equation 15.76 and $\sigma_c = \sigma_a / \sigma_s$ to derive Equations 15.77 and 15.78.

Exercise 15.6

Nishita et al. actually state Equation 15.40 in terms of the angle α rather than $\cos \alpha$:

$$P_h(\alpha) = 1 + 9 \cos^{16}(\alpha/2)$$
$$P_h(\alpha) = 1 + 50 \cos^{32}(\alpha/2)$$

Show that these equations are the same as Equation 15.40.

Inversions solve problems.

Gary Marks
("The Gary Marks Piano Method, Book II," 1992)

16

INTEGRAL EQUATIONS

16.1 Introduction

At the end of Chapter 12 we arrived at Equation 12.98, which presented the integral form of the transport equation. This equation describes the flux (or energy) flowing in every direction, everywhere in space. Although the flux $\Phi(\mathbf{r}, \vec{\omega})$ appears on the left-hand side of the equation, it also appears on the right. Thus, rather than providing an *explicit* representation for the flux, this equation gives an *implicit* condition that the flux must satisfy.

As we have seen in Chapter 13, *radiance* is a more useful characterization of the light energy in a scene than the raw flux from which the radiance is derived. Our first goal in Chapter 17 will be to rewrite the transport equation in terms of radiance, giving us the *radiance equation*. The radiance equation is the keystone of image synthesis based on geometrical optics. Our primary job in image synthesis is to find a useful approximation to the radiance function defined by this equation; that function tells us the precise color of every point in an image.

The radiance equation will have the same form as the transport equation; that is, it will specify a function in terms of an integral that contains that function. This type of equation is called an *integral equation*. There are many methods for solving integral equations, and we can look over the history of image synthesis algorithms and categorize nearly all of them as computing different approximations to this equation, even long before it was explicitly realized in graphics that such a unifying equation existed! The most successful (and popular) image synthesis algorithms are so close to the standard integral equation methods that it seems remarkable that they were independently developed.

We will discuss various rendering algorithms in inderadianceUnit IV in terms of how they relate to standard procedures for solving integral equations in general. Therefore we first need to review the theory of integral equations and discuss techniques for their solution.

The central goal of this chapter will be to introduce the relevant theory of integral equations and survey some of the more popular techniques for approximating solutions. Because our goal is not functional or numerical analysis per se, but image synthesis, we will be rather informal when discussing solution algorithms, and we will generally not cover issues of convergence, the existence of inverses, guarantees of continuity and stability, and other important mathematical issues. These topics are discussed with precision in the literature, and we leave the reader who desires such rigor to consult the references for all the details.

Choice of notation is always a difficult issue when alternatives abound, as they do in the integral equations literature. Much of the literature writes the unknown function as $f(s)$, a real-valued function of the real parameter s. In keeping with our notation of Unit II, we write this instead as $x(t)$. Most of the rest of our notation is similar to that of Kanwal [240]. We will discuss integral equations in this chapter in their 1D, one-parameter form for an unknown function $x(t)$. Many of these methods will generalize easily to the multidimensional, multiparametric equations used in image synthesis.

16.2 Types of Integral Equations

Any equation that describes some function in terms of one or more integrals of that function may be called an *integral equation*. In practice, just a few different general structures of integral equations seem to capture most mathematical models of natural phenomena, including the radiance equation.

To help set the stage, consider the following integral equation:

$$x(t) = g(t) + \lambda \int_a^b k(t,u)x(u)\,du \tag{16.1}$$

Equation 16.1 has the general form we will be most interested in for image synthesis. In this equation, we are given everything but the unknown function $x(t)$, which we want to find.

The function $x(t)$ is a real-valued function of the independent real variable t. The real function $g(t)$ is called the *free term* or the *driving function*. The value λ is in general a complex number. The integral involves a real function $k(t, u)$ of two real numbers; this function is called the *kernel* of the integration. In this chapter, we will always use $x(t)$ for our unknown, and letters such as u and v for dummy variables of integration, which are always considered real numbers.

We can now describe the different classes of integral equations based on what characteristics of this general form they share [120, 251]. In general, an integral equation is described by a sequence of adjectives, defined below in a question-and-answer format.

Name: What is the upper bound of the domain of the integral?

Fredholm: Some real number b.

Volterra: The evaluation point t.

Kind: Where does the unknown function appear?

First kind: Inside the integration only.

Second kind: Both inside and outside the integral.

Third kind: Both inside and outside the integral, and weighted on the left-hand side by a function $\mu(t)$, which is zero for at least one t in the domain of integration.

Singularity: Is the integral proper?

Singular: The integral is *singular* (or *improper*), if the domain is infinite, the integrand is unbounded somewhere in the domain, the kernel is discontinuous, or a combination of some or all of these.

Nonsingular: The integral is not improper.

Homogeneity: Is the driving term zero?

Homogeneous: $g(t) = 0$ throughout the domain.

Inhomogeneous: $g(t) \neq 0$ somewhere in domain.

Linearity: Is the unknown function a linear term in the integral?

Linear: The integral is linear in $x(t)$.

Nonlinear: The integral is not linear in $x(t)$.

	Fredholm	Volterra
First kind	$g(t) = \lambda \int_a^b k(t,u)x(u)\,du$	$g(t) = \lambda \int_a^s k(t,u)x(u)\,du$
Second kind	$x(t) = g(t) + \lambda \int_a^b k(t,u)x(u)\,du$	$x(t) = g(t) + \lambda \int_a^s k(t,u)x(u)\,du$
Third kind	$\mu(t)x(t) = g(t) + \lambda \int_a^b k(t,u)x(u)\,du$	$\mu(t)x(t) = g(t) + \lambda \int_a^s k(t,u)x(u)\,du$

TABLE 16.1
Classification of integral equations.

Examples of some of these classes are shown in Table 16.1. A rich taxonomy of integral equations and their various relationships may be found in Golberg [162].

When an equation is homogeneous (the free term is zero), it may have only the trivial solution $x(t) = 0$. However, for some values of λ there may be nontrivial solutions. Such values of λ are called *characteristic values* for the equation, and the corresponding functions are called the *characteristic functions* [93].

In this book, we will focus exclusively on the category occupied by the radiance equation, which is a *linear, inhomogeneous, Fredholm integral of the second kind.* Happily, this is a common form of integral equation, and its study occupies much of the literature. We will refer to this class of integral equations with the notation $\mathcal{F}_2$; e.g., Equation 16.1 is a member of the class $\mathcal{F}_2$.

Singularities arise often in the radiance equation. Unfortunately, the effective treatment of singularities often involves knowing something about the kernel; this is expensive information in computer graphics, since the kernel describes not only the light arriving at a point from every surface in the scene, but the visibility of the entire scene from that point. So for most of this chapter, we will focus on *nonsingular* integral equations. A kernel with a finite number of simple discontinuities can often be replaced by a finite number of continuous kernels; true singularities (such as sharp shadow edges) may require more subtlety. We will discuss methods for dealing with singularities in Section 16.10.

We will be rather informal in this chapter regarding the details of our function spaces. In general, we will make the overly strong assumption that all of our functions live in a *Hilbert space* (a linear space that is *complete*, that is, every

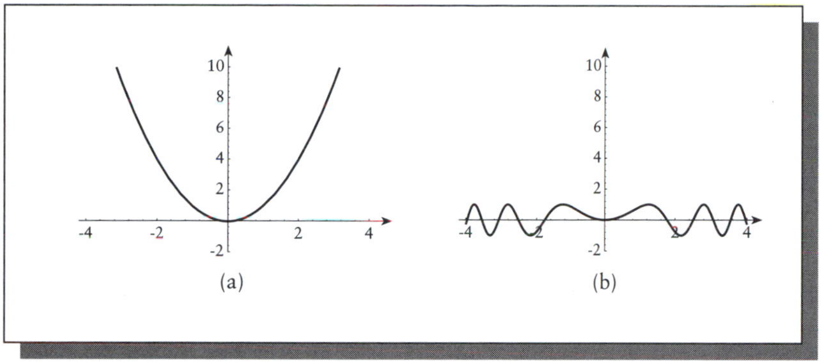

FIGURE 16.1
(a) $x(t) = t^2$. (b) The new function $(\mathcal{F}x)(t) = \sin(t^2)$.

converging sequence of elements converges to something in the space), has a real-valued *norm* $||x||$, and has a norm-derived inner product $\langle x|\, g\rangle$. Appendix A provides some background for these terms.

16.3 Operators

When equations get typographically complex, they can be difficult to understand even if the concepts are straightforward. To keep the notation simple, we will use *operator notation* in this chapter. We saw operators in Unit II, but we didn't do very much with them. Our use here will be much heavier and more varied, so we will review the notation here.

An operator is similar to the idea of a *functional* [251]. Just as a function such as $\sin(t)$ takes a real number and returns a real number, a functional takes a function and returns a new function. For example, a simple functional $\mathcal{F}$ may be defined $(\mathcal{F}x)(t) = \sin(x(t))$, so for $x(t) = t^2$, $(\mathcal{F}x)(t) = \sin(t^2)$, as shown in Figure 16.1.

Note that $(\mathcal{F}x)$ is a *new function* of the parameter t and not simply a composite of two function calls. To see this, note that $x(t) = t^2$ is structurally a quadratic, so we can do things like differentiate it and find its global minimum, but the new function $(\mathcal{F}x)(t)$ has an infinite number of local minima, no global minimum, and is not differentiable at $t = 0$. Another pair of example operators are $\mathcal{D}$, which takes the derivative of a function, and $\mathcal{S}$, the scaling integral operator that integrates a function multiplied by $\cos(x)$ from $[a, b]$. For example, for the function $f(x) = \sin(x)$, differentiation gives $(\mathcal{D}f)(x) = (d/dx)\sin x = \cos(x)$, and scaled integration gives $(\mathcal{S}f)(x) = \int_a^b \sin(x)\cos(x)\,dx = sin^2(x)/2$.

To represent the effect of a functional on a function, we use an *operator*. An operator is written to the left of the function it modifies; the resulting new function uses the original argument. So as above, the operator $\mathcal{F}$ applied to a function $x(t)$ is written $(\mathcal{F}x)(t)$, where the parentheses around $(\mathcal{F}x)$ are intended to remind us that this is a new function.

There exists a notation for defining operators, but it's easier to present them by demonstrating their effect on a generic function $x(t)$. We will initially be concerned with just two operators, the *identity* and *kernel integral* operators.

As its name suggests, the *identity operator* $\mathcal{I}$ does nothing to its argument:

$$(\mathcal{I}x)(t) \triangleq x(t) \tag{16.2}$$

The *kernel integral operator* $\mathcal{K}$ takes a real-valued function $x(t)$ and integrates it over a domain $[a, b]$, as scaled by a real-valued function $k(u, v)$ of two real parameters according to

$$(\mathcal{K}x)(t) \triangleq \int_a^b k(t,u)x(u)\,du \tag{16.3}$$

The function k is called the *kernel* of the integration. Note that $\mathcal{K}$ is linear:

$$\begin{aligned} \mathcal{K}(f+g) &= \mathcal{K}f + \mathcal{K}g \\ \mathcal{K}(\alpha f) &= \alpha\mathcal{K}f \end{aligned} \tag{16.4}$$

This should be no surprise, since we know that integration is linear and $\mathcal{K}$ is simply a notational tool for representing a particular type of integration. Equation 16.4 shows an additional bit of simplification common in operator expressions: the dependent variable is often suppressed. So $\mathcal{K}(f+g)$ is understood to represent the function $(\mathcal{K}(f+g))(t)$, and $\mathcal{K}x$ stands for $(\mathcal{K}x)(t)$.

We can use this notation to rewrite Equation 16.1 in a more compact form:

$$\begin{aligned} x(t) &= g(t) + \lambda \int_a^b k(t,u)x(u)\,du \\ x &= g + \lambda\mathcal{K}x \end{aligned} \tag{16.5}$$

Recalling the identity operator $\mathcal{I}$, we can revise this equation as

$$\begin{aligned} x - \lambda\mathcal{K}x &= g \\ (\mathcal{I} - \lambda\mathcal{K})x &= g \end{aligned} \tag{16.6}$$

Equations 16.5 and 16.6 are the operator forms for equations of type $\mathcal{F}_2$.

We will sometimes find it useful to think of the operator $\mathcal{K}$ as computing the inner product of a constant-t "slice" of the kernel $k(t, u)$ with the function $x(u)$. Writing $k_t(u)$ for the kernel at a particular value of t, we then have

$$(\mathcal{K}x)(t) = \int_a^b k(t, u)x(u)\, du = \langle k_t | x \rangle \tag{16.7}$$

using our definition of the braket from Section 4.3.9. If both k and x are real, as we will suppose throughout this chapter, then the braket is bilinear and symmetric. We will not bother to explicitly conjugate the first term since we know it to be real, and $\langle a | b \rangle = \langle \overline{a} | b \rangle$ for $a \in \mathcal{R}$. So the symmetry condition may be stated

$$\mathcal{K}x = \langle k_t | x \rangle = \langle x | k_t \rangle \tag{16.8}$$

Any operator may have an *inverse*. For example, the operator defined by $\mathcal{F}f = f + 2$ has the inverse $\mathcal{F}^{-1}f = f - 2$. We will suppose in this book that all inverses work both before and after the operator: $\mathcal{F}\mathcal{F}^{-1} = \mathcal{F}^{-1}\mathcal{F} = \mathcal{I}$. Using an inverse, we can "solve" Equation 16.6 for x:

$$x = (\mathcal{I} - \lambda\mathcal{K})^{-1} g \tag{16.9}$$

assuming that such an inverse exists. Right now Equation 16.9 is just a notational device; we don't yet know how to actually find an x to satisfy it.

Because the central equation of study in this chapter is given by $(\mathcal{I} - \lambda\mathcal{K})x = g$, we will find it notationally convenient to represent the composite operator on x by the single operator $\mathcal{L}$:

$$\mathcal{L} \stackrel{\triangle}{=} \mathcal{I} - \lambda\mathcal{K} \tag{16.10}$$

This allows us to write our integral equation in a particularly succinct form:

$$\mathcal{L}x = g \tag{16.11}$$

so that $x = \mathcal{L}^{-1}g$. Our goal will be to find methods for evaluating (or estimating) a function x satisfying this equation.

A pair of operators $\mathcal{A}$ and $\mathcal{A}^*$ are said to be *adjoint* if and only if they satisfy the relationship

$$\langle \mathcal{A}f | g \rangle = \langle f | \mathcal{A}^* g \rangle \tag{16.12}$$

for all f and g. For the integral operator $\mathcal{K}$, this is equivalent to saying

$$\begin{aligned}(\mathcal{K}x)(t) &= \int_a^b k(t, u)x(u)\, du \\ (\mathcal{K}^*x)(t) &= \int_a^b k(u, t)x(u)\, du\end{aligned} \tag{16.13}$$

The kernel $k(u,t)$ is called the *adjoint kernel*, and the second line above is called the *adjoint equation* for the operator $\mathcal{K}$. If the kernel is *symmetric*, then $k(u,t) = k(t,u)$ for all u and t; because such a kernel is its own adjoint, we say its related operator $\mathcal{K}$ is *self-adjoint*: $\mathcal{K} = \mathcal{K}^*$. We will use adjoint equations later in this chapter.

16.3.1 Operator Norms

In general, linear operators map functions from a domain X to a range Y, which may be in different spaces. Because they are linear, the set of all such operators themselves forms a linear space. We can define a norm on this space by finding the largest magnifying effect that an operator $\mathcal{A}$ has on any function x in the domain space X:

$$||\mathcal{A}|| = \sup_{||x|| \neq 0} \frac{||\mathcal{A}x||_Y}{||x||_X} = \sup_{||x||=1} ||\mathcal{A}x||_Y \tag{16.14}$$

where the subscripts indicate the space in which each norm is taken. In words, this tells us to look at every element in the space X, apply the operator to it, and then find the ratio of the norm of the result (in the space of the result) with the norm of the input (in the space of the input). The largest ratio is the norm of the operator. Intuitively, if we place a unit sphere at the origin in space X and apply the operator $\mathcal{A}$ to it, the sphere will in general be turned into some blob, where $||\mathcal{A}||$ is the largest radial distance from the origin to the surface of the blob.

We have defined the operator norm with respect to two spaces: a domain X and a range Y. Often we will only deal with subspaces of X; that is, functions x may come from one subspace X_1 and be mapped into X_2, but both X_1 and X_2 are contained in X.

Because the operator norm is the *largest* stretching that can occur, we can say for any input x:

$$||\mathcal{A}x|| \leq ||\mathcal{A}|| \cdot ||x|| \tag{16.15}$$

From this, we can find an important result describing the combination of two operators $\mathcal{A}$ and $\mathcal{B}$:

$$||\mathcal{AB}|| \leq ||\mathcal{A}|| \cdot ||\mathcal{B}|| \tag{16.16}$$

An operator $\mathcal{A}$ is said to be *bounded* if $||\mathcal{A}|| < \infty$.

The norm of $\mathcal{L}$ is $||\mathcal{L}|| = ||\mathcal{I} - \lambda\mathcal{K}|| = 1 - \lambda||\mathcal{K}||$. The norm of its inverse, $||\mathcal{L}^{-1}||$, is not decomposable in the same way.

16.4 Solution Techniques

Golberg [162] has identified five principal categories of methods for solving integral equations, which we summarize here.

Analytical and semianalytical methods: These techniques rely at least partly on an analytic representation of the solution. This generally requires an analytic representation of all the unknown components in the equation, including the kernel. Unfortunately, practical (that is, nontrivial) image synthesis problems involve kernels that are unlikely to be completely representable analytically.

Kernel approximation methods: We find a sequence of kernels $\mathcal{K}_n(t,u)$ for $n = 1, 2, \ldots$ so that $k_n(t,u)$ converges to $k(t,u)$ as $n \to \infty$. For each kernel, we find an approximate solution x_n. Note that each x_n itself is an *approximation* to the true solution for the kernel $\mathcal{K}_n$, which is in turn an approximation of the ideal kernel $\mathcal{K}$. This method is typically only useful for *degenerate kernels* (discussed below).

Projection methods: These are the most popular methods in practice, and their discussion will occupy the bulk of this chapter. A projection method converts the original equation into another equation in some other, smaller space. For example, we might look for the best solution only among the polynomials, or sums of sines and cosines. Projection methods allow us to restrict the domain of possible solutions to our equation, which can make them easier to find.

Quadrature methods: We replace the integration represented by the kernel with a finite summation. This approximation to an integral by a sum is called *numerical quadrature*. We can view quadrature methods as a subclass of projection methods by thinking of the quadrature operation as the projection of the integral operator into a finite-dimensional subspace represented by the summation operator.

Volterra and initial value methods: Rather than solve the given equation, we can sometimes show that the solution would satisfy some other set of equations, and solve those instead.

The kernel operator $\mathcal{K}$ in Equation 16.9 is usually too complicated for us to solve the original integral equation analytically. In computer graphics, the kernel represents the transfer of energy to a point from potentially everywhere else in the scene; this transfer can be arbitrarily complex and can easily baffle our best analytic techniques. There's no hope of finding a general, analytic solution to the radiance equation in practical situations.

The analytic, semianalytic, Volterra, and initial value methods all require us to know something about the kernel and driving functions. These techniques may be useful in rendering to handle special cases where the functions are tractable, but this has not been explored much except to suppress singularities (discussed later).

So we turn instead to approximate solutions; in this book we focus on the *quadrature* and *projection* methods. We will also, however, discuss two important *analytic* methods that lend key ideas to the approximation techniques. We will call them *symbolic* methods here, because we will not actually evaluate anything analytically, but rather juggle symbolic representations into a variety of useful alternatives. Projection methods usually involve approximating everything in sight by linear equations, resulting in a single big matrix equation.

No matter how we do it, note that if we change the structure of the problem, then even a perfect answer to the new problem may have little relevance to the original problem. That is, starting with the original problem of finding

$$x = (\mathcal{I} - \lambda\mathcal{K})^{-1}g \tag{16.17}$$

we may replace the kernel and the driving function by approximations $\widetilde{\mathcal{K}}$ and $\widetilde{g}$:

$$\widetilde{x} = (\mathcal{I} - \lambda\widetilde{\mathcal{K}})^{-1}\widetilde{g} \tag{16.18}$$

An exact solution $\widetilde{x}$ to this problem may be identical to the original x, or very similar to it, or completely unrelated to it. And if the solution is only an approximation to $\widetilde{x}$, then we're yet another step away from the desired answer.

To properly track the correspondence of our approximations to the ideal solution requires that we carefully monitor the error introduced at every step in the approximation. Usually we can't express the error exactly, and instead settle for an *error bound*, or a guaranteed upper limit on how much error can be introduced. These bounds are often *conservative*, meaning that when there is any uncertainty, we normally use the worst possible error. Alternatively, we may use *probable* bounds, which aren't as pessimistic as conservative bounds, but also don't come with the same assurance. In general, bounds can only be estimated, though we believe in some Platonic *ideal bound*, or *perfect bound*, that would indicate the error if only we had the tools to find it. The *tighter* an error bound is, the more closely it matches this perfect bound; a *loose* bound is generally suspected of being rather far from the ideal value.

Tracking the error at every stage is difficult business; it requires patience and great attention to detail [353]. Furthermore, the error in the realization of any algorithm is also highly dependent on the details of its particular programming and host hardware. Much can be said about the best or expected error properties of these algorithms, but this is only part of our puzzle in image synthesis, where shading, visibility, and other algorithms that we use to solve the rendering equation have their own errors. The interested reader can find detailed error analyses for integral equation methods in the references listed in the Further Reading section.

16.4.1 Residual Minimization

We now turn to looking for solutions of $x = \mathcal{L}^{-1}g$ in general. Methods of finding the "best" version of a function often come down to minimizing the value of some norm over a class of candidates. A common method for describing this approach in general is called *residual minimization*.

We begin by recalling the composite operator $\mathcal{L} = (\mathcal{I} - \lambda\mathcal{K})$, satisfying $\mathcal{L}x = g$. We now introduce the *residual function* r_n and the *error function* e_n for some approximation x_n:

$$\begin{aligned} r_n &= g - \mathcal{L}x_n \\ e_n &= x - x_n \end{aligned} \tag{16.19}$$

To evaluate r_n, we don't need the true solution x. By subtracting $g - \mathcal{L}x = 0$ from r_n, we can derive the identity

$$\begin{aligned} r_n &= (g - \mathcal{L}x_n) - (g - \mathcal{L}x) \\ &= \mathcal{L}(x - x_n) \\ &= \mathcal{L}_n \end{aligned} \tag{16.20}$$

so the residual function is just the error function passed through the composite operator $\mathcal{L}$.

To find the function x_n that comes closest to x, we can try to minimize the norm of the residual error, measuring the distance between g and $\mathcal{L}x$, yielding the "best" approximate function x_n. The choice of norm exerts a great deal of influence on our selection of an approximate solution x_n. We will see that different algorithms may be distinguished on the basis of which norm they attempt to minimize.

16.5 Degenerate Kernels

We mentioned above that some special methods are available for *degenerate* kernels. In fact, methods have been developed for a wide range of specialized kernel forms, of which degenerate kernels are only one example. Degenerate kernels are those that can be defined as the product of a number of one-parameter functions:

$$k(t, u) = \sum_{i=1}^{n} a_i(t) b_i(u) \tag{16.21}$$

A *separable* kernel is composed of only one such pair (that is, $n = 1$):

$$k(t, u) = a(t)b(u) \tag{16.22}$$

A degenerate kernel may be written as a sum of separable kernels.

When an operator applies a kernel of this type to a vector x, we can find the result with an elegant symbolic construction [343]. The basic idea is that in an integral equation $x = g + \lambda\mathcal{K}x$ with a degenerate kernel, we can think of the functions a_i as forming a basis for some function space. It turns out that the solution x may be represented in this space by solving for its coefficients on the functions a_i (it's okay if the a_i are not linearly independent; we discuss the way to handle this below).

We begin by expanding out the operation:

$$\begin{aligned}(\mathcal{K}x)(t) &= \int_a^b k(t,u)x(u)\,du \\ &= \int_a^b \sum_{i=1}^n a_i(t)b_i(u)x(u)\,du \\ &= \sum_{i=1}^n a_i(t)\int_a^b b_i(u)x(u)\,du \\ &= \sum_{i=1}^n a_i(t)\left\langle b_i \middle| x\right\rangle \end{aligned} \tag{16.23}$$

We note that a scaling factor λ applied to $\mathcal{K}x$ can be moved inside the braket, replacing it by a new constant γ_i:

$$\begin{aligned}\lambda(\mathcal{K}x)(t) &= \sum_{i=1}^n a_i(t)\lambda\left\langle b_i \middle| x\right\rangle \\ &= \sum_{i=1}^n a_i(t)\gamma_i \end{aligned} \tag{16.24}$$

Recalling $x = g + \lambda\mathcal{K}x$, we would like to find the values for γ_i that describe x. We begin by writing

$$\begin{aligned}x(t) - g(t) &= (\lambda\mathcal{K}x)(t) \\ \sum_{i=1}^n a_i(t)\gamma_i &= \lambda\sum_{i=1}^n a_i(t)\left\langle b_i \middle| x\right\rangle \\ &= \lambda\sum_{i=1}^n a_i(t)\left\langle b_i \middle| (g+\lambda\mathcal{K}x)\right\rangle \\ &= \lambda\sum_{i=1}^n a_i(t)\left(\left\langle b_i \middle| g\right\rangle + \left\langle b_i \middle| \lambda\mathcal{K}x\right\rangle\right) \end{aligned} \tag{16.25}$$

Now we have an expression for $\lambda(\mathcal{K}x)$ from Equation 16.24, so plugging that into the rightmost term and using linearity, we find

$$\sum_{i=1}^{n} a_i(t)\gamma_i = \lambda \sum_{i=1}^{n} a_i(t)\left(\langle b_i | g \rangle + \left\langle b_i \middle| \sum_{j=1}^{n} a_j \gamma_j \right\rangle \right)$$
$$= \lambda \sum_{i=1}^{n} a_i(t)\left(\langle b_i | g \rangle + \sum_{j=1}^{n} \gamma_j \langle b_i | a_j \rangle \right)$$
$$= \sum_{i=1}^{n} a_i(t)\left(\beta_i + \sum_{j=1}^{n} \gamma_j \alpha_{ij} \right) \tag{16.26}$$

where

$$\beta_i = \lambda \int_a^b b_i(u) g(u)\, du$$
$$\alpha_{ij} = \lambda \int_a^b b_i(u) a_j(u)\, du \tag{16.27}$$

We can find values for each α_{ij} and β_i, so all that remains is to find the γ_i.

For convenience, we will assume that the functions $a_i(t)$ are linearly independent. This isn't a restrictive assumption; if these functions are not linearly independent, we can reexpress the kernel in terms of a smaller number of basis vectors $a_i'(t)$ that span the space of the old $a_i(t)$. Then Equation 16.26 represents n equations in the n unknowns γ_i, each of the form:

$$\gamma_i = \sum_{j=1}^{n} \alpha_{ij}\gamma_j + \beta_i \tag{16.28}$$

In matrix form, we can write $\mathbf{g} = \mathbf{A}\mathbf{g} + \mathbf{b}$, or $(\mathbf{I} - \mathbf{A})\mathbf{g} = \mathbf{b}$. In tableau form,

$$\begin{bmatrix} 1-\alpha_{11} & \alpha_{12} & \cdots & \alpha_{1n} \\ \alpha_{21} & 1-\alpha_{22} & & \vdots \\ \vdots & & \ddots & \vdots \\ \alpha_{n1} & \cdots & \cdots & 1-\alpha_{nn} \end{bmatrix} \begin{bmatrix} \gamma_1 \\ \gamma_2 \\ \vdots \\ \gamma_n \end{bmatrix} = \begin{bmatrix} \beta_1 \\ \beta_2 \\ \vdots \\ \beta_n \end{bmatrix} \tag{16.29}$$

If $(\mathbf{I} - \mathbf{A})$ is nonsingular, it can be inverted, $\mathbf{g} = (\mathbf{I} - \mathbf{A})^{-1}\mathbf{b}$, yielding the unique set of γ_i that describes the function satisfying the original integral equation:

$$x(t) = g(t) + \sum_{i=1}^{n} \gamma_i a_i(t) \tag{16.30}$$

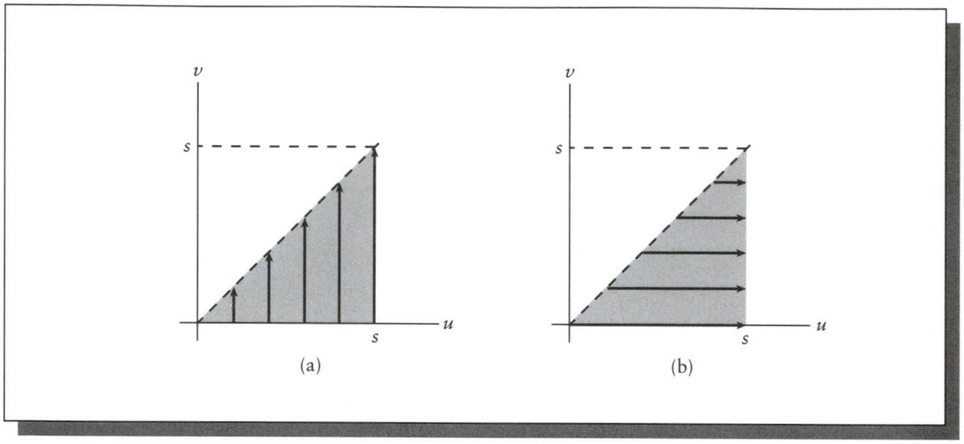

FIGURE 16.2
The Fubini theorem. (a) Scanning across u and sweeping up v. (b) Scanning up v and sweeping across u.

This is our first example of a solution technique for solving an integral equation. We started by assuming something about the problem (here it was the form of the kernel), and then we used that assumption to simplify the problem. This is typical of most solution methods.

16.6 Symbolic Methods

In this section we will consider a number of symbolic manipulations to Equation 16.9 that are intended to make it more tractable for solution.

16.6.1 The Fubini Theorem

We begin with a simple observation that we will find useful in this section. Suppose that we have a continuous, real function $b(u, v)$ of two real parameters, and we want to evaluate the double integral:

$$\int_{u=0}^{s} \int_{v=0}^{u} b(u, v)\, dv\, du \tag{16.31}$$

We can see from Figure 16.2(a) that this is the area of the triangle defined by

$0 \leq u \leq s$, $v \leq u$. In effect, we are moving across the u axis and sweeping upward from $v = 0$ to $v = u$ at each step.

We can reverse the order of integration, as shown in Figure 16.2(b). Now we move up the v axis, sweeping right from $u = v$ to $u = s$ at each step, covering the same territory bottom to top and left to right instead of in the opposite order. Stated symbolically, this is the *Fubini theorem*:

$$\int_{u=0}^{s} \int_{v=0}^{u} b(u, v)\, dv\, du = \int_{v=0}^{s} \int_{u=v}^{s} b(u, v)\, du\, dv \tag{16.32}$$

16.6.2 Successive Substitution

Perhaps the most straightforward method for solving Equation 16.1 for the unknown function x starts with the form in Equation 16.5:

$$x = g + \lambda \mathcal{K} x \tag{16.33}$$

Since we have an expression for x on the left-hand side, we can simply plug that into the right-hand side:

$$\begin{aligned} x &= g + \lambda \mathcal{K} x \\ &= g + \lambda \mathcal{K}(g + \lambda \mathcal{K} x) \\ &= g + \lambda \mathcal{K} g + \lambda^2 \mathcal{K}^2 x \end{aligned} \tag{16.34}$$

we can then repeat the whole process:

$$\begin{aligned} x &= g + \lambda \mathcal{K} g + \lambda^2 \mathcal{K}^2 x \\ &= g + \lambda \mathcal{K} g + \lambda^2 \mathcal{K}^2 (g + \lambda \mathcal{K} x) \\ &= g + \lambda \mathcal{K} g + \lambda^2 \mathcal{K}^2 g + \lambda^3 \mathcal{K}^3 x \end{aligned} \tag{16.35}$$

and so on. If we stop after n steps, then we get a recurrence relation for the *n-step estimate* x_n:

$$\begin{aligned} x_n &= g + \lambda \mathcal{K} x_{n-1} \\ &= \sum_{i=0}^{n-1} (\lambda \mathcal{K})^i g \end{aligned} \tag{16.36}$$

where we have dropped the highest-order term $(\lambda \mathcal{K})^n x$; we will see why this is reasonable in the next section. This relation defines the technique of *successive substitution*. We will look at its error properties in the next section.

16.6.3 Neumann Series

In successive substitution we replaced the estimated solution at each step. Alternatively, we can iterate replacements on the operator. We get the same result, but from a different point of view.

We begin by recalling that for a complex number z, with $|z| < 1$, we can write the infinite series

$$\frac{1}{1-z} = \sum_{i=0}^{\infty} z^i = 1 + z + z^2 + z^3 + \cdots \tag{16.37}$$

Using this series as inspiration, think of z as an operator. It can be shown that under certain reasonable conditions, interpreting Equation 16.37 as an expression for an operator with a norm less than one is valid [343].

Then we can write an expression for x in terms of the operator $(\mathcal{I} - \lambda\mathcal{K})^{-1}$, and use Equation 16.37 as an approximation of that operator:

$$\begin{aligned} x &= (\mathcal{I} - \lambda\mathcal{K})^{-1} g \\ &= \frac{1}{\mathcal{I} - \lambda\mathcal{K}} g \\ &= \sum_{i=0}^{\infty} (\lambda\mathcal{K})^i g \end{aligned} \tag{16.38}$$

Terminating the expansion after n terms gives us an n-step approximation x_n to x:

$$x_n = \sum_{i=0}^{n} (\lambda\mathcal{K})^i g \tag{16.39}$$

This approximation is called the *Neumann series*. This formula is identical to Equation 16.36.

If we continue substituting forever, we get

$$\lim_{n\to\infty} \sum_{i=0}^{n} \mathcal{K}^n = R \tag{16.40}$$

where $x = g + \mathcal{R}x$. The operator $\mathcal{R}$ is called the *resolvent operator*, and it implements the *resolvent kernel*.

For example, after the second step we have $(\mathcal{K}^2 x)(t) = (\mathcal{K}(\mathcal{K}x))(t)$. We can write out this kernel explicitly as

$$\begin{aligned} (\mathcal{K}^2 x)(t) &= (\mathcal{K}(\mathcal{K}x))(t) \\ &= \int_{u=0}^{s} k(t,u)((\mathcal{K}x)(u))\, du \end{aligned}$$

$$= \int_{u=0}^{s} k(t,u) \int_{v=0}^{u} k(u,v)x(v)\,dv\,du$$
$$= \int_{u=0}^{s} \int_{v=0}^{u} k(t,u)k(u,v)x(v)\,dv\,du \tag{16.41}$$

Now we can use the Fubini theorem to switch the order of integration:

$$\begin{aligned}(\mathcal{K}^2 x)(t) &= \int_{v=0}^{s} \int_{u=v}^{s} k(t,u)k(u,v)x(v)\,du\,dv \\ &= \int_{v=0}^{s} \left[\int_{u=v}^{s} k(t,u)k(u,v)\,du\right] x(v)\,dv \\ &= \int_{v=0}^{s} k_2(t,v)x(v)\,dv \\ &= (\mathcal{K}^2 x)(t)\end{aligned} \tag{16.42}$$

where the kernel of $\mathcal{K}^2$ is

$$k_2(t,v) = \int_{u=v}^{s} k(t,u)k(u,v)\,du \tag{16.43}$$

In general, the *iterated kernel of order* n is given by

$$\begin{aligned}k_n(t,v) &= \int_{u=v}^{s} k(t,u)k_{n-1}(u,v)\,du \\ k_0(t,v) &= I\end{aligned} \tag{16.44}$$

Since we're now focusing on iterating the operator rather than the approximate solution, we are tempted to analyze the error from the same point of view. Following Arvo [14], we define the operator $\mathcal{M}_n$ as the result of n steps of this series:

$$\mathcal{M}_n = \sum_{i=0}^{n} \lambda^i K^i \tag{16.45}$$

So the ideal solution is given by $x = \mathcal{M}_\infty g$.

The error in x_n is the error involved from using $\mathcal{M}_n$ instead of $\mathcal{M}_\infty$:

$$\begin{aligned}\|\mathcal{M}_\infty - \mathcal{M}_n\| &= \left\| \sum_{i=0}^{\infty} \lambda^i \mathcal{K}^i - \sum_{i=0}^{n} \lambda^i \mathcal{K}^i \right\| \\ &= \left\| \sum_{i=n+1}^{\infty} \lambda^i \mathcal{K}^i \right\| \le \sum_{i=n+1}^{\infty} \|\lambda^i \mathcal{K}^i\| \le \sum_{i=n+1}^{\infty} \|\lambda \mathcal{K}\|^i\end{aligned} \tag{16.46}$$

using the triangle inequality from the definition of a norm, and Equation 16.16. Since $\|\lambda\mathcal{K}\|$ is a real number, and recalling the series identity

$$\sum_{i=n+1}^{\infty} a^i = \frac{a^{n+1}}{1-a} \tag{16.47}$$

we can write the error in the approximate operator $\mathcal{M}_n$ as

$$\|\mathcal{M}_\infty - \mathcal{M}_n\| = \frac{\|\lambda\mathcal{K}\|^{n+1}}{1-\|\lambda\mathcal{K}\|} \tag{16.48}$$

Returning now to $x_n = \mathcal{M}_n g$, we can find its error $\|x - x_n\|$ as

$$\begin{aligned}\|x - x_n\| = \|\mathcal{M}_\infty g - \mathcal{M}_n g\| &\leq \|\mathcal{M}_\infty - \mathcal{M}_n\| \cdot \|g\| \\ &\leq \frac{\|\lambda\mathcal{K}\|^{n+1}}{1-\|\lambda\mathcal{K}\|}\|g\|\end{aligned} \tag{16.49}$$

So the error depends on the magnitude of $1 - \|\lambda\mathcal{K}\|$. If $\|\lambda\mathcal{K}\| < 1$, we see that the difference between the true solution x and successive iterates x_n from the Neumann series goes to zero as $n \to \infty$.

Note that the kernel of the approximate operator $\mathcal{M}_n$ may be expressed as the sum of the first n iterated kernels:

$$m_n(t, v) = \sum_{i=0}^{n} k_i(t, v) \tag{16.50}$$

16.7 Numerical Approximations

The symbolic methods discussed in the previous section are useful for thinking about the problem of finding the unknown function, but they are not immediately practical in computer graphics. Numerical methods hold much more promise for quantitative solutions, so we now turn to numerical algorithms for finding the unknown function x. Here we simply take the integral equation as given and attempt to replace it with a computable approximation. Development of a good numerical algorithm is not a casual task; we must be scrupulous in every aspect of the design and implementation, including the effects of word size and floating-point resolution in a particular machine. A discussion of some of the pitfalls in designing good numerical algorithms may be found in Press et al. [348] and Ralston and Rabinowitz [353].

In general, each approach will find an approximation to x that best matches a set of conditions; sometimes we will need to search a space of functions to find that best match; other times we need simply solve a matrix equation.

16.7.1 Numerical Integration (Quadrature)

Most of the numerical algorithms that we will discuss for solving integral equations end up computing one or more 1D integrations along the way. The speed and accuracy of different integration routines, when applied to different problems, can vary tremendously. A discussion of different algorithms and their trade-offs may be found in Press et al. [348], Ralston and Rabinowitz [353], and Delves and Mohamed [120]. For completeness, we present here a short introduction to the subject.

Any numerical method for computing an approximation to an integral is called a *quadrature rule*. We can write the perfect integration we desire as the operator $\mathcal{K}$ applied a weighted function $x(t)$:

$$(\mathcal{K}x)(t) = \int_a^b w(u)k(t,u)x(u)\,du \tag{16.51}$$

where $w(t)$ is a *weight function*. Although the operator $\mathcal{K}$ can in principle use any information (given or measured) available about the function to improve the quality of the integration, we will focus on methods that use only the value of x at a set of points given by $\{t_i\}$. (We will label these points as $\{t_i\}$ when they appear outside of an integral, but they will take on the dummy variable—typically u—inside the integral, where they appear as $\{u_i\}$.) We write this quadrature rule as an operator $\mathcal{Q}$:

$$\mathcal{Q}x = \mathcal{K}x - \mathcal{E}_{\mathcal{Q}}x \tag{16.52}$$

where the operator $\mathcal{E}_{\mathcal{Q}}$ measures the error between the estimated integral $\mathcal{Q}x$ and the actual value $\mathcal{K}x$.

This type of quadrature rule may be written

$$(\mathcal{Q}x)(t) = \sum_{i=1}^{N} w_i k(t,u_i)x(u_i) = \langle\, \mathcal{Q} |\, x \rangle \tag{16.53}$$

In words, we measure the value of x at each point u_i, weight each measurement by an associated value w_i, and then add the product into a running sum. The points u_i are called the *quadrature points* or *abscissae*, and the weights w_i are called the *quadrature weights*. The trick in designing a good rule is to choose the u_i and w_i that will make the estimate as good as possible.

There are three general classes for rules of this type [120]:

Automatic rules: Neither the number of points N, nor the points u_i themselves, are determined in advance. Monte Carlo algorithms are examples of this approach.

Optimal rules: Points and weights are chosen in advance so that for some class of functions X_o, the value

$$\sup_{x \in X_o} |\mathcal{K}x - \mathcal{Q}x| \tag{16.54}$$

is minimized over all functions $x \in X_o$.

Error annihilation rules: Points and weights are chosen in advance so that for some class of functions X_a,

$$|\mathcal{K}x - \mathcal{Q}x| = 0 \tag{16.55}$$

for all functions $x \in X_a$. The class X_a is called the *annihilation class* for the rule (an annihilation rule is also an optimal rule, though the optimization class X_o for a given X_a may be difficult to determine).

In this section we will focus exclusively on annihilation rules.

16.7.2 Method of Undetermined Coefficients

We start our study of quadrature rules with a straightforward construction. We will assume that we have a set of N quadrature points $\{s_i\}$, and we want to find the weights w_i for a particular type of rule. We will only look for solutions in a function space of finite dimensions.

In general, we will suppose that the ideal solution x lives in some abstract function space X. Each finite-basis method has access to an n-dimensional subspace $X_n \subset X$, which is spanned by a set of n basis functions $\{h_i\}$. Therefore the n-dimensional approximation function x_n selected by the method may be given by

$$x_n = \sum_{i=1}^{n} \alpha_i h_i \tag{16.56}$$

which suggests interpreting x_n as a point in this n-dimensional function space. We call the vector $\vec{\alpha} = (\alpha_1, \alpha_2, \ldots, \alpha_n)$ the *function vector* in space X. In general, for a given subspace X_n, our goal in identifying an approximating n-dimensional function x_n becomes that of finding the coefficients of its function vector $\vec{\alpha}$.

An expression such as Equation 16.56 is sometimes called an *expansion* for the vector (or function) x. Thus algorithms that result in finding the coefficients α_i are sometimes collectively called *expansion methods*.

Now to create an annihilation rule, we want to choose the u_i and w_i so that $\mathcal{Q}x = \mathcal{K}x$ for all choices of α_i; that is, all functions x in the space X_n:

$$\begin{aligned} \mathcal{Q}x &= \mathcal{K}x \\ \sum_{i=1}^{N} w_i x(u_i) &= \int_a^b w(u)x(u)\,du \end{aligned} \tag{16.57}$$

Since $\mathcal{K}$ is linear, we only need to annihilate the basis functions. That is, if we have chosen our points and weights so we compute the exact integral for each basis function, then linear combinations of the basis functions (that is, all functions in the space spanned by those functions) will also be exactly integrated. So we have p conditions (one for each basis function) that may be written as

$$\sum_{i=1}^{N} w_i h_1(u_i) = m_1 = \int_a^b w(u) h_1(u)\, du$$
$$\sum_{i=1}^{N} w_i h_2(u_i) = m_2 = \int_a^b w(u) h_2(u)\, du$$
$$\vdots$$
$$\sum_{i=1}^{N} w_i h_p(u_i) = m_2 = \int_a^b w(u) h_p(u)\, du \tag{16.58}$$

These are called the *undetermined coefficient* equations, and the m_i are called the *generalized moments* of the weight function $w(t)$ with respect to the bases $\{h_i\}$. This approach is called the *method of undetermined coefficients.*

If $p = N$, then we can write this as a square matrix equation $\mathbf{wH} = \mathbf{m}$, or in tableau form

$$\begin{bmatrix} w_1 \\ w_2 \\ \vdots \\ w_N \end{bmatrix} \begin{bmatrix} h_1(u_1) & h_1(u_2) & \cdots & h_1(u_N) \\ h_2(u_1) & h_2(u_2) & & \vdots \\ \vdots & & \ddots & \vdots \\ h_p(u_1) & \cdots & \cdots & h_p(u_N) \end{bmatrix} = \begin{bmatrix} m_1 \\ m_2 \\ \vdots \\ m_p \end{bmatrix} \tag{16.59}$$

which has a unique solution for the m_i if the matrix $\mathbf{H}$ is nonsingular.

To annihilate a particular space of functions, we need only choose a basis $\{h_i\}$ that spans that space. A particularly common choice is the space of polynomials. These are spanned by the *monomials* $\{m_i\} : m_i(t) = t^{i-1}$, $i \geq 1$ (note that these functions are not orthogonal). Using the monomials, we expect to find an N-point rule that will match all polynomials of degree $N - 1$ or less.

For example, suppose we choose $N = 2$, intended to match all linear functions. Select the interval $[a, b] = [0, h]$, the weight function $w(t) = 1$, and quadrature points $t_1 = 0$ and $t_2 = h$. The first two monomials are $m_1(t) = 1$ and $m_2(t) = t$, so we have

$$\begin{bmatrix} w_1 \\ w_2 \end{bmatrix} \begin{bmatrix} 1 & 1 \\ 0 & h \end{bmatrix} = \begin{bmatrix} \int_0^h 1\, dt \\ \int_0^h t\, dt \end{bmatrix} = \begin{bmatrix} h \\ h^2/2 \end{bmatrix} \tag{16.60}$$

The solution to this matrix equation is $w_1 = w_2 = h/2$, yielding the familiar *trapezoid rule*,

$$\int_0^h x(t)\,ds \approx w_1 x(t_1) + w_2 x(t_2) = \frac{h}{2}[x(0) + x(h)] \tag{16.61}$$

We can easily add more points to the rule, to annihilate increasingly higher-order polynomials. These are called the *closed Newton-Cotes rules of degree* $N - 1$.

We can use any other basis $\{h_i\}$ that we want in order to create other rules that will annihilate other types of functions. Many such rules are covered in Delves and Mohamed [120] and Press et al. [348].

One way to improve the accuracy of an integration with simple low-order rules is to use *repeated rules*. This involves breaking up a domain into pieces and applying a low-order rule to each piece, rather than one large high-order rule. For example, if we have $N = 6$, we could apply three trapezoid rules side by side rather than one rule of order 6 to the entire interval.

16.7.3 Quadrature on Expanded Functions

In the following sections we will often apply a quadrature approximation of the operator $\mathcal{L}$ to the expanded form of x. We will prepare for these operations by developing a shorthand notation for the results of the expansion and approximation now.

We note that in general any function x in an infinite-dimensional linear space spanned by a basis $\{h_i\}$ may be represented as a linear sum of these bases:

$$x(t) = \sum_{i=1}^{\infty} \alpha_i h_i(t) \tag{16.62}$$

Since computing an infinite number of coefficients is impractical, we instead project such a series into a finite-dimensional linear space in order to work with it. The easiest projection operation is *truncation*, where we simply stop the expansion after n terms [26]:

$$x(t) \approx \sum_{i=1}^{n} \alpha_i h_i(t) \tag{16.63}$$

Depending on the situation, we can consider this an n-term approximation of x in an infinite-dimensional space, or an exact representation of a function within an n-dimensional space.

We begin developing our notation by replacing x in $g = \mathcal{L}x$ with this finite expansion in terms of n basis functions $\{h_i\}$:

$$\begin{aligned} g &= \mathcal{L}x \\ &= \mathcal{L}\sum_{i=1}^{n} \alpha_i h_i \\ &= \sum_{i=1}^{n} \alpha_i (\mathcal{L}h_i) \end{aligned} \tag{16.64}$$

where we have used the linearity of summation and the $\mathcal{L}$ operator. So the transformation of x can be accomplished simply by transforming the basis vectors and then recombining them with exactly the same coefficients as in the original expansion.

To find those transformed basis vectors in practice, we will usually need to approximate the result with a quadrature rule $\mathcal{Q}$:

$$\begin{aligned} \mathcal{L}h_i &= (\mathcal{I} - \lambda\mathcal{K})h_i \\ &= h_i - \lambda(\mathcal{K}h_i) \\ &= h_i - \lambda(\mathcal{Q} + \mathcal{E}_{\mathcal{Q}})h_i \end{aligned} \tag{16.65}$$

where the operator $\mathcal{K}$ is replaced by the sum of a quadrature rule $\mathcal{Q}$ and its error $\mathcal{E}_{\mathcal{Q}}$. If we expand this expression and replace $\mathcal{Q}$ with its explicit quadrature formula, we find:

$$\begin{aligned} (\mathcal{L}h_i)(t) &= h_i(t) - \lambda(\mathcal{Q}h_i)(t) - \lambda(\mathcal{E}_{\mathcal{Q}}h_i)(t) \\ &= h_i(t) - \lambda\left[\sum_{m=1}^{q} w_m k(t, u_m) h_i(u_m)\right] - \lambda(\mathcal{E}_{\mathcal{Q}}h_i)(t) \end{aligned} \tag{16.66}$$

Ignoring the error for the moment, the first two terms give us a way to compute an approximation to the transformed basis vector. We call this approximate, transformed basis $p_i(t)$, and define

$$\begin{aligned} p_i &\stackrel{\triangle}{=} (\mathcal{I} - \lambda\mathcal{Q})h_i \\ &= h_i(t) - \lambda\sum_{m=1}^{q} w_m k(t, u_m) h_i(u_m) \end{aligned} \tag{16.67}$$

so including the error, we have

$$\mathcal{L}h_i = p_i - \lambda\mathcal{E}_{\mathcal{Q}}h_i \tag{16.68}$$

We will more often work with the *approximation* $\mathcal{L}h_i \approx (\mathcal{I} - \lambda\mathcal{Q})h_i = p_i$. Notice that to evaluate $(\mathcal{I} - \lambda\mathcal{Q})h_i$, we only need the values of h_i and the kernel $\mathcal{K}$ at the q quadrature points u_m.

In addition to the kernel and the quadrature rule, the functions $p_i(t)$ depend on the set of basis functions $\{h_i\}$ used to represent x_n. We can use the same kernel and rule to compute multiple sets of different p_i for different basis functions, which may span equivalent or different function spaces.

16.7.4 Nyström Method

The *Nyström method* finds an approximation to $x(t)$ by numerical evaluation at a few particular points, and then iterating a guess at the function until it matches those points. The function is then interpolated to get its value elsewhere.

We begin by recalling from the discussion of the Neumann series the basic iteration formula

$$\begin{aligned} x_{n+1} &= g + \lambda\mathcal{K}x_n \\ x_0 &= g \end{aligned} \tag{16.69}$$

If we expand the operators and the independent variable, we get a better idea of what's required to evaluate one step:

$$\begin{aligned} x_{n+1}(t) &= g(t) + \lambda(\mathcal{K}x_n)(t) \\ &= g(t) + \lambda\int_a^b k(t,u)x_n(u)\,du \end{aligned} \tag{16.70}$$

To evaluate this iteration we need to find values for $g(t)$ (which we assume are available upon demand) and the value of the integral on the right-hand side. We can estimate this integral with a quadrature rule $\mathcal{Q}$:

$$\begin{aligned} x_{n+1}(t) &= g(t) + \lambda(\mathcal{K}x_n)(t) \\ &= g(t) + \lambda(\mathcal{Q}x + \mathcal{E}_\mathcal{Q}x)(t) \\ &= g(t) + \lambda\left(\sum_{i=1}^{N} w_i k(t,u_i)x(u_i) + (\mathcal{E}_\mathcal{Q}x)(t)\right) \end{aligned} \tag{16.71}$$

where $\mathcal{E}_\mathcal{Q}$ is the error operator for the rule $\mathcal{Q}$, and the rule is evaluated at N quadrature points u_i in the domain $[a,b]$. We will now become brave and simply ignore the error term $\mathcal{E}_\mathcal{Q}x$. Then we have an iteration rule for an approximation x_{n+1}:

$$x_{n+1}(t) = g(t) + \lambda\sum_{i=1}^{N} w_i k(t,u_i)x_n(u_i) \tag{16.72}$$

Let's look at the first couple of iterations of this formula:

$$\begin{aligned}
x_0(t) &= g(t) \\
x_1(t) &= g(t) + \lambda \sum_{i=1}^{N} w_i k(t, u_i) x_0(u_i) \\
&= g(t) + \lambda \sum_{i=1}^{N} w_i k(t, u_i) g(u_i) \\
x_2(t) &= g(t) + \lambda \sum_{i=1}^{N} w_i k(t, u_i) x_1(u_i) \\
&= g(t) + \lambda \sum_{i=1}^{N} w_i k(t, u_i) \left[g(t) + \lambda \sum_{m=1}^{N} w_m k(u_i, u_m) g(u_m) \right]
\end{aligned} \tag{16.73}$$

The pattern that's developing shows that to evaluate $x_{n+1}(t)$ requires only $g(t)$, the weights w_i, the driving function values $g(u_i)$, and the kernel values $k(t, u_i)$ evaluated at t and the quadrature points u_i. Assuming that we know or can find all of these quantities, we're ready to set up the whole iteration.

The N rules of type Equation 16.72 may be set up simultaneously in a matrix, $\mathbf{x}_{n+1} = \mathbf{g} + \lambda \mathbf{N} \mathbf{x}_n$, or in tableau:

$$\begin{bmatrix} x_{n+1}(t_1) \\ x_{n+1}(t_2) \\ \vdots \\ x_{n+1}(t_N) \end{bmatrix} = \begin{bmatrix} g(t_1) \\ g(t_2) \\ \vdots \\ g(t_N) \end{bmatrix} + \lambda \begin{bmatrix} w_1 k_{11} & w_2 k_{12} & \cdots & w_N k_{1N} \\ w_1 k_{21} & w_2 k_{22} & & \vdots \\ \vdots & & \ddots & \vdots \\ w_1 k_{N1} & \cdots & \cdots & w_N k_{NN} \end{bmatrix} \begin{bmatrix} x_n(t_1) \\ x_n(t_2) \\ \vdots \\ x_n(t_N) \end{bmatrix} \tag{16.74}$$

where $k_{ik} = k(t_i, u_k)$. This matrix defines the *Nyström equations.* If they converge, their limit x_Q is called the *Nyström solution* for quadrature rule $\mathcal{Q}$. The choice of $\mathcal{Q}$ can strongly influence both the speed of convergence and the value of x_Q.

To find $x(t)$ at a value of t that is not a quadrature point ($t \neq u_i$), we can apply a noniterative form of Equation 16.72, where we use the Nyström function x_Q as the interpolated function:

$$x_Q(t) = g(t) + \lambda \sum_{i=1}^{N} w_i k(t, u_i) x_Q(u_i) \tag{16.75}$$

We wrote out the right-hand side of this formula explicitly because we want to emphasize that we can evaluate x_Q at any value of t, depending only on its value at a discrete number of quadrature points u_i.

Now even if Equation 16.74 does converge to a Nyström solution x_Q, this function satisfies the approximate formula $(\mathcal{I} - \lambda\widetilde{\mathcal{K}})x_Q = \widetilde{g}$, which may not necessarily have much to do with the desired solution x of $(\mathcal{I} - \lambda\mathcal{K})x = g$. The question then is whether x_Q is close to x. The answer to this question is not simple, but we can sketch an outline of the error analysis.

Define the error function e_Q in the Nyström solution for rule $\mathcal{Q}$ as

$$e_Q(t) = x(t) - x_Q(t) \tag{16.76}$$

We can express the approximation x_Q with its error from Equation 16.71:

$$x_Q(t) = g(t) + \lambda \int_a^b k(t,u)x_Q(u)\,du - E_u\lambda k(t,u)x_Q(u) \tag{16.77}$$

where E_u is the error from rule $\mathcal{Q}$ on $\lambda k(t,u)x_Q(u)$ as a function of u for a given t. Subtracting this approximate solution from the desired solution $x(t)$, we find

$$\begin{aligned}
e_Q(t) &= x(t) - x_Q(t)\\
&= g(t) + \lambda \int_a^b k(t,u)x(u)\,du - g(t) - \lambda \int_a^b k(t,u)x_Q(u)\,du + E_u\lambda k(t,u)x_Q(u)\\
&= E_u\lambda k(t,u)x_Q(u) + \lambda \int_a^b k(t,u)[x(u) - x_Q(u)]\,du\\
&= E_u\lambda k(t,u)x_Q(u) + \lambda \int_a^b k(t,u)e_Q(u)\,du\\
&= b(t) + \lambda \int_a^b k(t,u)e_Q(u)\,du
\end{aligned} \tag{16.78}$$

This argument has the interesting result that the error $e_Q(t)$ is given by a Fredholm integral of the second kind, with the same kernel as the original equation but a different driving term. In operator notation,

$$(\mathcal{I} - \lambda\mathcal{K})e_Q(t) = b_Q(t) \tag{16.79}$$

which leads to the error term

$$\begin{aligned}
e_Q(t) &= (\mathcal{I} - \lambda\mathcal{K})^{-1}b_Q(t)\\
\|e_Q\| &\leq \left\|(\mathcal{I} - \lambda\mathcal{K})^{-1}\right\| \cdot \|b_Q(t)\|
\end{aligned} \tag{16.80}$$

Unfortunately, the norm of this error term includes $b_Q(t)$, which itself is defined in terms of the original function x and the quadrature rule. But if we can estimate a bound on this term, then we can find a bound on the error e_Q. This tells us that the error in the Nyström approximant x_Q is dependent on the operator norm $\|(\mathcal{I} - \lambda\mathcal{K})^{-1}\|$ and the error in the quadrature rule $\mathcal{Q}$. Given an operator $\mathcal{K}$, we're stuck with its norm, but by choosing the quadrature rule carefully we can get $\|b_Q(t)\|$ to have small magnitude, and thus get good accuracy from this method. Detailed discussion of the numerical performance of the Nyström method on a variety of kernels with respect to a number of different quadrature rules is presented in Delves and Mohamed [120].

16.7.5 Monte Carlo Quadrature

In Chapter 7 we discussed the *Monte Carlo* method for evaluating integrals. This is a form of *automatic* quadrature rule, where we do not choose the quadrature points in advance, but generate them according to some algorithm that is intended to simulate a random process of some kind. This approach has the power of letting us easily sample adaptively, beginning with some initial set of quadrature points and then accumulating additional points as needed. The drawback is that an efficient Monte Carlo method (say one that uses importance sampling) requires us to know (or guess) something about the nature of the underlying signal. The goal of most Monte Carlo methods is to find the parameters that characterize a signal; the family of functions that are thereby parameterized must be chosen in advance. We will see that this situation crops up again below when we discuss projection methods, which also require the solution space to be predefined.

Any method in this chapter may use Monte Carlo methods for evaluating necessary integrals. We will see below that Monte Carlo methods may also be applied to solving complex integral equations like Equation 16.1.

16.8 Projection Methods

In this section we will study a variety of methods for solving integral equations which all share a common feature: they *project* the universe of all possible solutions into some smaller set, so they are called *projection methods*.

The general idea is that when we are faced with an integral equation, we will decide, *before attempting to find a solution*, what kind of function we want to use for a solution. If we think of all functions of a given class as elements of a function space, then any function in that space may be represented by a set of coordinates representing weights on a set of basis functions for that space. For example, we may decide that we want to find a solution in the form of a polynomial; then it would be described by a list of coefficients on the various powers of the independent variable. If we want to find a solution that is a sum of sines, then we need a list of numbers giving the magnitude and phase of each sine wave that is combined to make up the function. The goal of each projection method is to find these numbers, which identify one particular function from a fixed class. If we decide to look for a polynomial solution of order four or less to solve a 1D integral equation, and the real solution is $\sin(x)$, then we will be stuck with a poor approximation; we could re-solve with a trigonometric basis to find a better solution.

In addition to selecting a space of functions, we need to select a set of bases for that space. Different choices of bases can affect the efficiency and accuracy of our algorithms.

Many function spaces are infinite; a polynomial $p(x)$, for example, may be described as an infinite sum of powers of x. To be representable on the computer, we need to stop somewhere. That means that our solution functions will always come from a *finite-dimensional space*. Finite-dimensional spaces have some nice properties, but they have the severe limitation that sometimes the solution we seek lies outside our space (as in the fourth-order polynomial trying to match $\sin(x)$ above). The result of this limitation is that our solutions will almost always be *approximations* to the real solution. The essential question then becomes one of how to find the "best" approximation; this in turn leads us to ask how to measure "best."

There are two parts to this measurement: what is measured and where the measurement is taken. In the integral equation $x = g + \lambda\mathcal{K}x$, it is not x itself that we typically measure, though that is what we are solving for. Rather, since $x - g - \lambda\mathcal{K}x = 0$, we look for an approximate x_n that minimizes this difference, which is itself a function. We can measure the magnitude of this function with any of a variety of norms. But as mentioned earlier, we must decide where to measure the error. Things get tricky because although our function x_n is limited to a particular subspace (say the space of polynomials), the operated function $\mathcal{K}x_n$ in general will not be in that space.

There are several reasonable places to compute the error. Perhaps the most obvious is in the infinite-dimensional space of all functions. Another is in the subspace from which our solution is drawn; after all, since we can't leave this space when looking for an answer, we might as well optimize there. Another approach is to look in the space of transformed functions $\mathcal{K}x$. We will see all of these choices below.

The essential points to keep in mind when thinking about the following projection methods are as follows:

- The solution space is of finite dimension.
- The solution space is chosen in advance.
- The basis for the solution space is chosen in advance.
- The means for measuring the size of the error must be specified.
- The space in which the error is measured must be specified.

We will see that some solution methods (such as Tchebyshev) actually search the solution space looking for the best function, while most of the others are able to find the best function in a single step (usually a matrix inversion).

16.8.1 Projection

The methods called *projection techniques* are based on the idea of finding that function x_n from a finite-dimensional space that "best" approximates the ideal solution x. Each technique has its own definitions for the function space that is considered, and for the meaning of "best."

Recall from Section 16.7.3 that a function x_n living in a finite-dimensional function space may be written as a linear combination of the basis functions $\{h_i\}$ that span that space:

$$x_n = \sum_{i=1}^{n} \alpha_i h_i \tag{16.81}$$

Each of the methods in this section will make use of a *projection operator*. If X is a normed space and $X_n \subset X$ is a nontrivial subspace of dimension n, then a bounded operator $\mathcal{P}_n : X \to X_n$ with the property $\mathcal{P}_n x = x$ for all $x \in X_n$ is a *projection operator* from X to X_n [254]. In other words, a projection operator takes a vector in a space X and turns it into a related vector in a smaller space X_n; if x is already in X_n, nothing happens. A useful example is the *orthographic projection* operator, which simply removes all components of the vector $x \in X$ that are not in the space X_n. If X_n is spanned by a set of bases $\{h_i\}$, then the projection operator $\mathcal{P}_n$ finds a linear combination of just these n bases to represent its input vector x:

$$\mathcal{P}_n x = \sum_{i=1}^{n} \alpha_i h_i \tag{16.82}$$

In particular, when the elements are functions, the result is a function vector $\vec{\alpha}$ that describes the projected function.

For example, suppose we have a space X_2 of linear functions that is spanned by the two monomials $h_1(t) = 1$ and $h_2(t) = t$. An input function $x(t) = 2t^2 + 3t + 4$ would be projected into X_2 by dropping the quadratic term $\mathcal{P}_n x(t) = 3t + 4$, which is a function described by the vector $\vec{\alpha} = (3, 4)$. Since we now have a linear function, repeating the projection will have no effect. Since the result of the projection operator typically has less information than its input, projection is in general not invertible.

16.8.2 Pictures of the Function Space

Since we're working in a Hilbert space, it's natural to think of the various operations on functions in this space as constructions in the familiar Euclidean linear space of

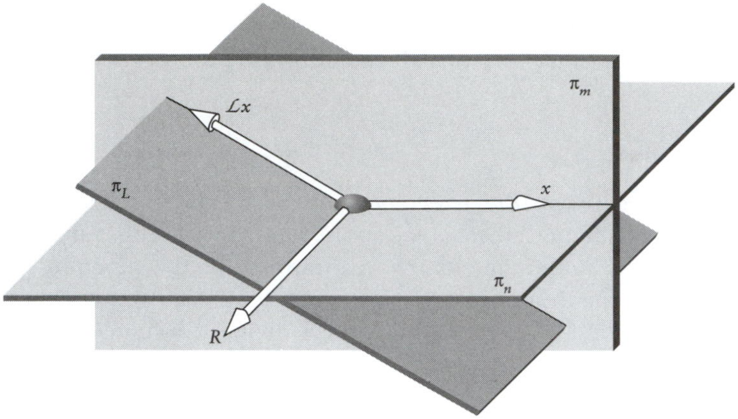

FIGURE 16.3
The vectors x and $\mathcal{L}x$, and the planes π_n, π_L, and π_m.

vectors. Inspired by Arvo [14], in this subsection we will make a pictorial analog to the operations discussed above, which will also help us with some of the methods to come. In this section we will use the words *vector* and *function* interchangeably. Remember that a point in a function space may be interpreted as a function or a traditional Euclidean vector.

We begin by imagining a 3D space X that contains all possible functions in our system. For example, this could be the space of quadratic polynomials, where a point (a, b, c) corresponds to the function $at^2 + bt + c$. We will typically look for functions x that solve an integral equation within a subspace of X. In this case, the subspace will be a plane, which we call π_n, as shown in Figure 16.3. The operator $\mathcal{L}$ is represented in these pictures by a rotation about an axis R; the transformed vector $\mathcal{L}x$ is also shown in the figure. In general, if we find $\mathcal{L}x$ for every $x \in \pi_n$, we will sweep out a new plane which we call π_L. The vectors x and $\mathcal{L}x$ will in general not be colinear, and thus will describe a plane of their own; we call this π_m.

We will make use of two projection operators, $\mathcal{P}_n$ and $\mathcal{P}_L$, which project a vector orthographically onto the planes π_n and π_L, respectively.

An important property of the plane π_m, illustrated in Figure 16.4, is that it contains the vector $x - \mathcal{L}x$. This is always true, even when x and $\mathcal{L}x$ are colinear.

To see how the operators $\mathcal{L}$ and $\mathcal{P}_n$ interact, we begin with the subspace π_n and a rotation axis R for the transformation $\mathcal{L}$, as shown in Figure 16.5. We will illustrate $\mathcal{L}$ on a vector by rotating that vector around R by some fixed amount.

A number of transformed vectors using this axis are shown in Figure 16.6. Note

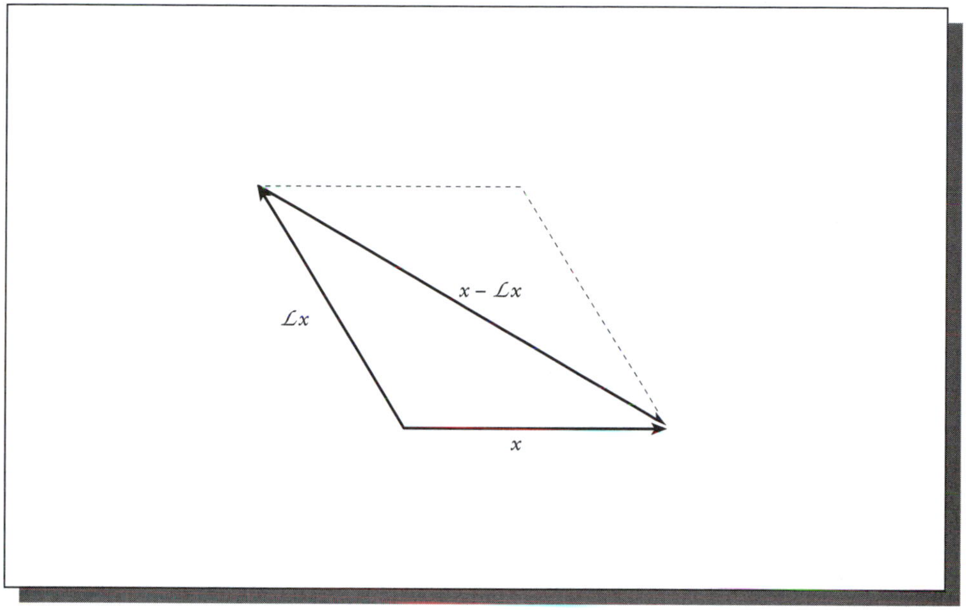

FIGURE 16.4
The parallelogram of x, $\mathcal{L}x$, and $x - \mathcal{L}x$.

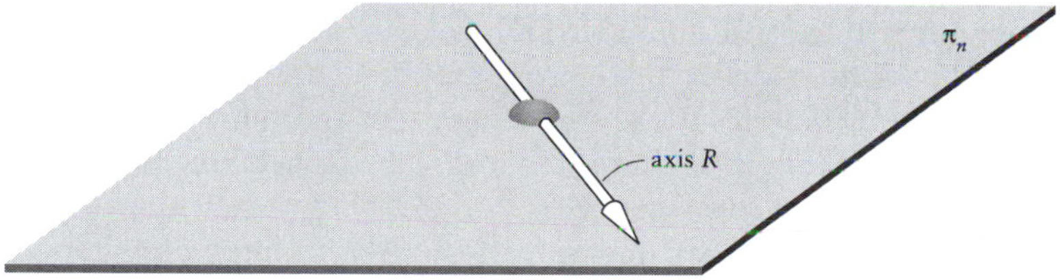

FIGURE 16.5
The plane π_n and rotation axis R.

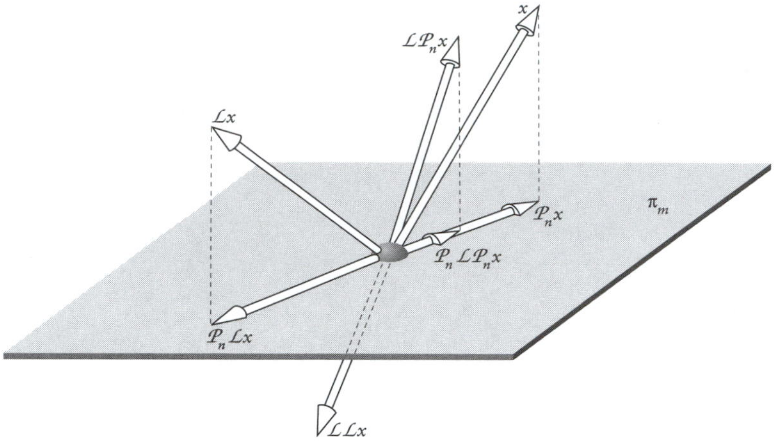

FIGURE 16.6
The effect of different operations on x.

that all the vectors in this diagram lie in the plane π_m. We begin with the vector $x \in X$, and observe that its projection $\mathcal{P}_n x$ is found by erecting a perpendicular to π_n through x. The transformation of x given by $\mathcal{L}x$ is found by rotating x around R, as shown.

Now we can look at multiple operations on x. If we apply $\mathcal{L}$ twice in a row, we get $\mathcal{L}\mathcal{L}x = \mathcal{L}^2x$, which is simply the rotation of $\mathcal{L}x$ around the axis R. The application of $\mathcal{P}_n$ twice gives us $\mathcal{P}_n\mathcal{P}_n x = \mathcal{P}_n x$, since once x has been projected into π_n, further projection operations have no effect.

The more interesting results come from mixed applications. If we transform and then project, the result is $\mathcal{P}_n\mathcal{L}x$. If we project and then transform, we get $\mathcal{L}\mathcal{P}_n x$. As shown in the figure, these results are in general not the same; $\mathcal{P}_n\mathcal{L}x$ by definition lies in π_n, but $\mathcal{L}\mathcal{P}_n x$ rarely will. In other words, the projection and transformation operators $\mathcal{P}$ and $\mathcal{L}$ do not *commute*: $\mathcal{L}\mathcal{P}_n \neq \mathcal{P}_n\mathcal{L}$.

In general, when we look for functions to satisfy an integral equation, we will want to search only within a particular solution space. We can either restrict our search to those functions explicitly, or we can do it implicitly. The former is typically accomplished by writing the unknown function x as a sum of basis functions in the space. The latter approach says that we can search through all $x \in X$, but we immediately apply the projection operator $\mathcal{P}_n$ so that only the part of x in the space π_n is used in the computation. Applying the transformation $\mathcal{L}$ to this projection

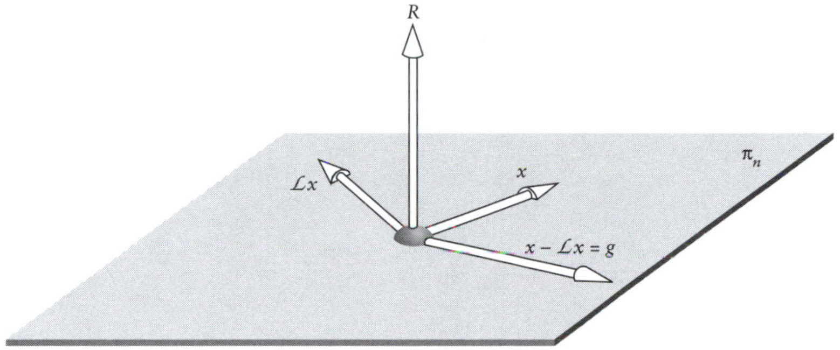

FIGURE 16.7

The transformation $\mathcal{L}$ rotates about a vector $R \perp \pi_n$, and $g \in \pi_n$.

gives us a new, transformed function, but in general this function will not be in π_n anymore, so we have to reproject it to get a result back in π_n. The result of this complete operation is that we end up looking through functions $\mathcal{P}_n \mathcal{L} \mathcal{P}_n x$, that is, projections of transformed functions drawn from the space π_n, themselves the projections of functions $x \in X$.

Recall that we are concerned with solutions to the integral equation $x - \lambda \mathcal{K} x = g$. For convenience we will set $\lambda = 1$ in the following discussion, so we are looking for x that satisfy $x - \mathcal{K}x = g$. To measure the accuracy of a candidate solution for x, we can compute the magnitude of the error vector $d = x - \mathcal{K}x - g$. The smaller this vector, presumably the smaller the error. Of course, the norm that we use for computing the magnitude of d, and the space in which we compute it, will affect our results; we will return to these ideas below.

Suppose we represent the transformation $\mathcal{L}$ as a rotation around an axis R that is normal to the subspace π_n from which we choose our solution functions, as shown in Figure 16.7. In other words, $\pi_n = \pi_m$. If the driving function g is also within the plane π_n, then we can in general find an x such that $x - \mathcal{L}x = g$. This is a perfect solution, with an error vector size $\|d\| = 0$ with any norm.

Now suppose that g is *not* in the plane π_n. Then, since $x - \mathcal{L}x$ is stuck in this plane, we can never match g exactly, as shown in Figure 16.8. The best we can do is try to find a choice for x that minimizes the size of the error d.

We can match a $g \notin \pi_n$ if the transformation $\mathcal{L}$ gives us more freedom. Figure 16.9 shows a different rotation axis R' that is in the plane π_n; now the plane π_m spanned by x and $\mathcal{L}x$ is no longer constrained to π_n, and so the difference $x - \mathcal{L}x$ can move

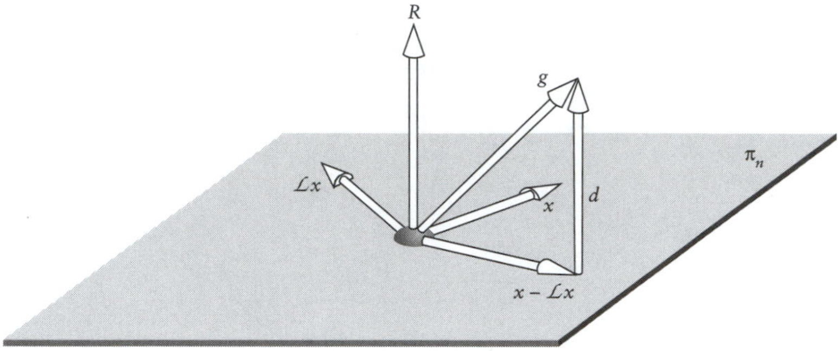

FIGURE 16.8

The transformation $\mathcal{L}$ rotates about a vector $R \perp \pi_n$, and $g \notin \pi_n$.

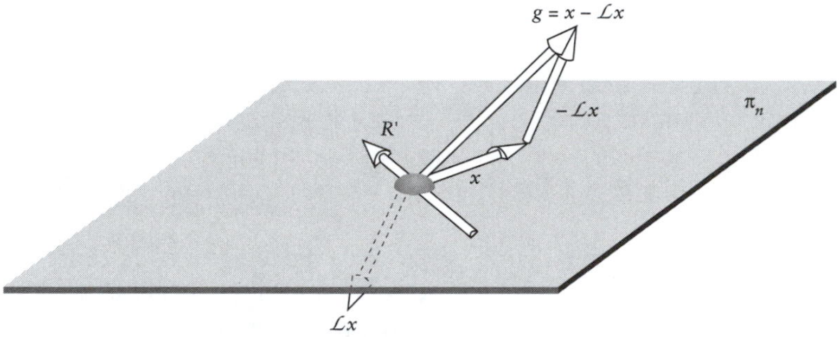

FIGURE 16.9

The transformation $\mathcal{L}$ rotates about a vector $R \in \pi_n$. Now we can match $g \notin \pi_n$.

through the 3D space of functions, eventually matching $x - \mathcal{L}x = g$, again driving $\|d\| = 0$.

This sort of generalization is not usually an option. We are given the subspace π_n in which to search, a transformation $\mathcal{L}$, and a driving function g. There is often no $x - \mathcal{L}x$ that can ever match g for this set of givens. We're then back in the situation of Figure 16.8, where we simply do the best we can. A general construction for d is shown in Figure 16.10, where we have found the error associated with some potential solution function x.

We mentioned above that although we want d to be "small," the definition of

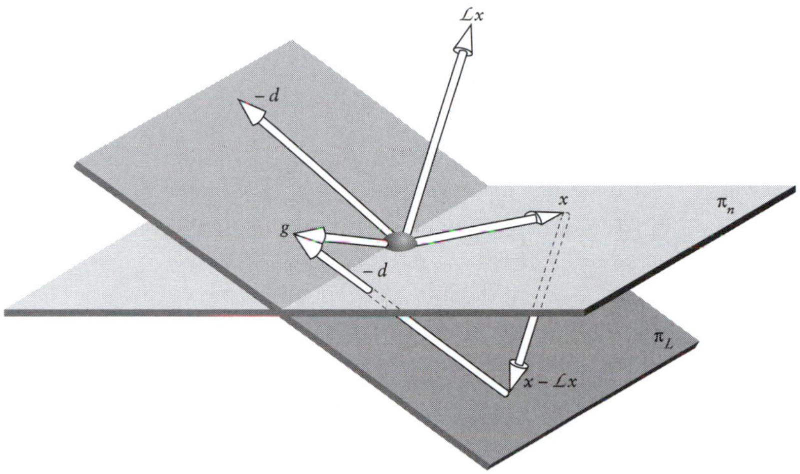

FIGURE 16.10

Constructing $d = x - \mathcal{L}x - g$. (The figure shows $-d$ for clarity.)

"small" depends on the norm we apply to d to measure its length, and the space in which we apply that norm. Figure 16.11 shows three reasonable spaces in which to apply any particular norm.

Perhaps the most straightforward place to compute $\|d\|$ is in the space X of all functions. But we could argue that this is misleading; we aren't after all allowed access to all functions. Perhaps a better place to measure the error is in the plane π_L, by computing its projection $\mathcal{P}_L d$. Carrying this line of reasoning further, we argue that we can only search for functions that are in the space π_n, so perhaps we should measure the norm of $\mathcal{P}_n d$, directing us to the function $\mathcal{P}_n x \in \pi_n$ that minimizes the error in the space of possible functions. Each of these choices is reasonable, and gives rise to its own well-known algorithm discussed below.

16.8.3 Polynomial Collocation

The method of *collocation* is a technique for finding x_n, given values for $g(t)$ and $x_n(t)$ at a number of points t_i. Actually, we find the values of $\vec{\alpha}$ describing x_n such that $(\mathcal{I} - \lambda\mathcal{K})x_n$ matches the constraints; we will return to this distinction in a moment.

The essential observation behind collocation comes from the form of the quadra-

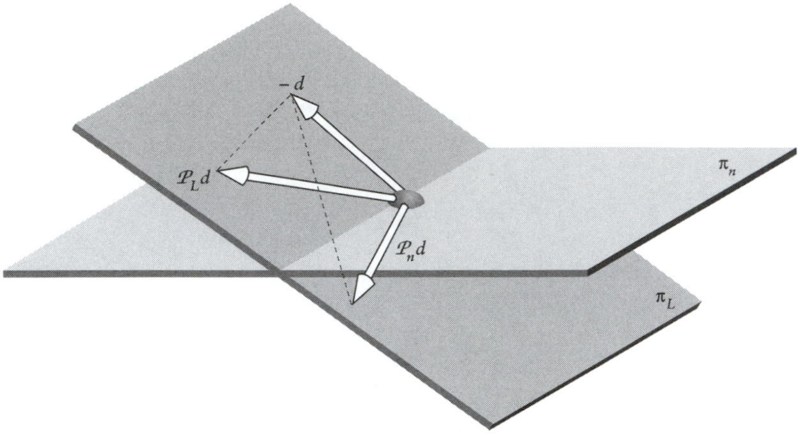

FIGURE 16.11

The error d in X, π_n, and π_L.

ture rule applied to an expanded function. Recall Equations 16.66 and 16.67, which defined this result, repeated here for reference:

$$\begin{aligned}(\mathcal{L}x_n)(t) &= \sum_{i=1}^{n} \alpha_i p_i(t) - (\mathcal{E}_Q x)(t) \\ p_i(t) &= h_i(t) - \lambda \sum_{m=1}^{q} w_m k(t, u_m) h_i(u_m)\end{aligned} \tag{16.83}$$

As mentioned before, we will suppose that we know the value of $g(t) = (\mathcal{L}x_n)(t)$ at the p points u_i. We will also be brave and from here on simply ignore the error term $(\mathcal{E}_Q x)(t)$. Since we're going to find the best solution we can, we know that its error will be the least in that class of functions.

To solve for the values of $\vec{\alpha}$, we start by rewriting the first line of Equation 16.83 to represent the p different known values of x at the points t_k:

$$g_k = g(t_k) = \sum_{i=1}^{n} \alpha_i p_{ik} \tag{16.84}$$

This is just k linear equations (one for each value of t_k) in the n unknowns (the values α_i); each factor p_{ik} is the transformed basis function p_i evaluated at $t = t_k$:

$$p_{ik} = p_i(t_k) = h_i(t_k) - \lambda \sum_{m=1}^{q} w_m k(t_k, u_m) h_i(u_m) \tag{16.85}$$

The p equations may be expressed in matrix form, $\mathbf{g} = \mathbf{P}\vec{\alpha}$. In the finite element literature, the matrix $\mathbf{P}$ is called the *mass matrix* or *stiffness matrix* [203]. In tableau:

$$\begin{bmatrix} g_1 \\ g_2 \\ \vdots \\ g_p \end{bmatrix} = \begin{bmatrix} p_{11} & p_{21} & \cdots & p_{n1} \\ p_{12} & p_{22} & & \vdots \\ \vdots & & \ddots & \vdots \\ p_{1p} & \cdots & \cdots & p_{np} \end{bmatrix} \begin{bmatrix} \alpha_1 \\ \alpha_2 \\ \vdots \\ \alpha_n \end{bmatrix} \tag{16.86}$$

The values of $\vec{\alpha}$ are then simply $\vec{\alpha} = \mathbf{P}^{-1}\mathbf{g}$. If $p = n$, and the matrix $\mathbf{P}$ is square and nonsingular, then we have a unique solution for $\vec{\alpha}$, and hence x_n.

This construction is a great example of the power of linearity. The coefficients $\vec{\alpha}$ that describe x_n may be applied either to the basis functions $\{h_i\}$ in the domain π_n, or to the transformed basis functions $\{p_i\} = \{\mathcal{L}h_i\}$ in the transformed domain π_L. The matrix simply takes us from one space to the other. When we have the right $\vec{\alpha}$ describing x_n, then we satisfy $\mathcal{L}x_n = g$; that is, we simply transform x_n from the space π_n to the space $\mathcal{L}\pi_n = \pi_L$. The same alphas are applied to both spaces.

The most important feature of this algorithm is that it tells us only about the transformed, approximate $(\mathcal{I} - \lambda\mathcal{K})x_n$, and nothing directly of the approximate function x_n. In general, at any point t (including the points $t = t_i$ where we solved for the function), the approximate solution will not match the ideal: $x_n(t) \neq x(t)$. However, as the number of collocation points t_i increases, the approximate solutions x_n will converge to the ideal solution x [22]. As with all other techniques of this type, the choice of the quadrature rule $\mathcal{Q}$ used to evaluate the matrix coefficients can greatly influence the speed and accuracy of the results.

Collocation

The method described above is actually *polynomial collocation*, a special case of a more general method known simply as *collocation* [162]. We will summarize collocation here because it gives us the flexibility to use functions other than polynomials.

Suppose that we have an n-dimensional space X_n of functions, spanned by a basis set $\{h_k\}$, and a projection operator $\mathcal{P}_n$ from some larger function space X onto X_n. Then the projection $(\mathcal{P}_n x)(t)$ of any function $x(t)$ may be expanded out with respect to these functions:

$$(\mathcal{P}_n x) = \sum_{i=1}^{k} \langle x | \, h_k \rangle \, h_k \tag{16.87}$$

Similarly, the projected version of x operated upon by $\mathcal{K}$ is given by

$$\begin{aligned}(\mathcal{P}_n \mathcal{K} x)(t) &= \sum_{i=1}^{k} \langle \mathcal{K} x(t) | \, h_k(t) \rangle \, h_k(t) \\ &= \sum_{i=1}^{k} \left\langle \int_a^b k(t,u) x(u) \, du \, \middle| \, h_k(t) \right\rangle h_k(t)\end{aligned} \tag{16.88}$$

Recalling our basic condition $x - \lambda \mathcal{K} x = g$, we first project our basic equation down onto the subspace X_n:

$$\begin{aligned}\mathcal{P}_n g &= \mathcal{P}_n \left[(\mathcal{I} - \lambda \mathcal{K}) x \right] \\ &= \mathcal{P}_n x - \lambda \mathcal{P}_n \mathcal{K} x \\ &= x_n - \lambda \mathcal{P}_n \mathcal{K} x_n\end{aligned} \tag{16.89}$$

where we have restricted our search of functions x_n to those lying in X_n; thus, $\mathcal{P}_n x_n = x_n$ because x_n is already projected. Now if we know the value of this equation at n known points t_j, we have n equations of the form

$$\begin{aligned}x_n(t_j) - \lambda \mathcal{P}_n \mathcal{K} x_n(t_j) &= \mathcal{P}_n g(t_j) \\ x_n(t_j) - \lambda \sum_{i=1}^{n} \left\langle \int_a^b k(t_j,u) x(u) \, du \middle| h_i \right\rangle h_i &= \sum_{i=1}^{n} \langle g(t_j) | \, h_i \rangle \, h_i\end{aligned} \tag{16.90}$$

This is the general formulation of collocation.

We will now backtrack, find our solution in the space of polynomials, and show that it matches our previous result. We will select as our basis functions $\{h_i\}$ the *Lagrange polynomials* $L_i(t)$, which are a popular set of bases for polynomial interpolation [348]. These functions are given by

$$L_i(t) = \prod_{j=1,\, j \neq i}^{n} \frac{t - t_j}{t_i - t_j} \tag{16.91}$$

The Lagrange polynomials for $i = 4$ are shown in Figure 16.12. Note that each L_i is zero at all t_j except t_i, where it has a value of 1. In symbols,

$$L_i(t_k) = \delta(i - k) \tag{16.92}$$

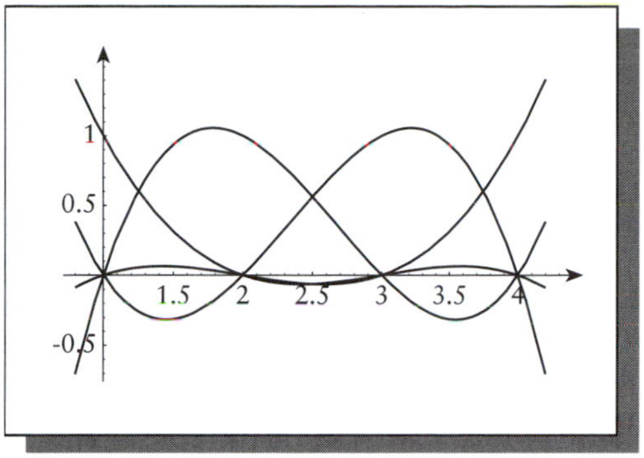

FIGURE 16.12
The Lagrange polynomials for $i = 4$.

To write Equation 16.90 in terms of the Lagrange polynomials, we start by finding the forms of the two relevant projections. Projected functions $\mathcal{P}_n x$ may be expressed

$$
\begin{aligned}
(\mathcal{P}_n x)(t) &= \sum_{i=1}^{n} \left(\sum_{j=1}^{n} x(u_j) L_i(u_j) \right) L_i(t) \\
&= \sum_{i=1}^{n} x(u_i) L_i(t) \qquad (16.93)
\end{aligned}
$$

Using this result, the projected transformed functions $\mathcal{P}_n \mathcal{K} x$ may be similarly simplified:

$$
(\mathcal{P}_n \mathcal{K} x)(t) = \sum_{i=1}^{n} \left(\int_a^b k(t, u) x(u)\, du \right) L_i(t) \qquad (16.94)
$$

so Equation 16.90 may now be written

$$
x_n(t_j) - \lambda \sum_{i=1}^{n} \left(\int_a^b k(t_j, u) x_n(u)\, du \right) L_i(t_j) = \sum_{i=1}^{n} g(u_j) L_i(t_j) \qquad (16.95)
$$

Again noting that $L_i(t_k) = \delta(i - k)$, we can simplify this to the n equations

$$
x_n(t_j) - \lambda \int_a^b k(t_j, u) x_n(u)\, du = g(u_j) \qquad (16.96)
$$

This is the set of *polynomial collocation* equations, and they match our previous result of Equation 16.85.

The advantage of using the general collocation equations is that we need not be restricted to the polynomials $L_i(t)$ for a basis. For example, spline bases are discussed in Atkinson [22] and Baker [26].

16.8.4 Tchebyshev Approximation

When we discussed the residual error function of Equation 16.19, we said that the choice of norm strongly influenced the approximate function found. In this and the following sections we will examine algorithms based on a number of different norms for measuring the approximation error $x - \lambda\mathcal{K}x - g$.

Perhaps the most straightforward norm is the *Tchebyshev* (or *Chebyshev*) norm, which is also called the L_∞ norm. For a function x over an interval $[a, b]$, this is equivalent to

$$\|x\|_\infty = \max_{a\le s\le b} |x(t)| \tag{16.97}$$

To apply this norm to the residual function, we first write the residual in terms of the functions g and x_n. Recalling Equations 16.19 and 16.20, we write

$$r_n = g - (I - \lambda\mathcal{K})x_n \tag{16.98}$$

So the Tchebyshev norm on this error is given by

$$\|r_n\| = \max_{a\le s\le b} |g - (I - \lambda\mathcal{K})x_n| \tag{16.99}$$

The function x_n, which minimizes the norm of the residual, is the one we want. Recalling that x_n is given by a vector of coefficients α_i, the residual $r_{n,o}$ corresponding to the "optimal" $\vec{\alpha}_o$ is then

$$\|r_{n,o}\| = \min_{\vec{\alpha}} \max_{a\le s\le b} |g - (I - \lambda\mathcal{K})x_n| \tag{16.100}$$

We now do the standard procedure of approximating the integral operator $\mathcal{K}$ with a quadrature operator $\mathcal{Q} + \mathcal{E}_\mathcal{Q}$, and then dropping the error:

$$\begin{aligned} \|r_{n,o}\| &= \min_{\vec{\alpha}} \max_{a\le s\le b} |g(t) - [(I - \lambda(\mathcal{Q} + \mathcal{E}_\mathcal{Q}))x_n](t)| \\ &\approx \min_{\vec{\alpha}} \max_{a\le s\le b} |g(t) - [(I - \lambda\mathcal{Q})x_n](t)| \end{aligned} \tag{16.101}$$

Explicitly writing the expansion of x_n over the n bases h_i we have

$$\|r_{n,o}\| = \min_{\vec{\alpha}} \max_{a\le s\le b} \left| g(t) - \sum_{i=1}^{n} \alpha_i p_i(t) \right| \tag{16.102}$$

This type of problem is called a *minimax* problem, since we're trying to minimize a maximum. Typically we evaluate the system at a variety of values for $\vec{\alpha}$, and then, on the basis of those measurements, the search is directed toward what is presumed to be the global minimum. Depending on the shape of the function space, the particular searching strategy chosen can influence to a large or small degree the final function chosen [121]. As always, the choice of quadrature rule $\mathcal{Q}$ will influence the final selection as well.

16.8.5 Least Squares

In the next few methods, we can draw a picture for the goals expressed by minimizing a particular norm.

Recall that the L_2 norm for a continuous function $x(t)$ is defined as

$$\|x(t)\|_2 = \int_a^b |x(t)|^2 \, ds \tag{16.103}$$

We use this norm in the *least-squares* method to find an approximate solution x_n that minimizes the L_2 norm of the residual. We will use this norm to measure any vector by projecting that vector into the space π_L, the space of all transformed functions $\mathcal{L}x$, as shown in Figure 16.13.

The function x we seek is the one that has the smallest projected error vector $\mathcal{P}_L d$. The norm $\|\mathcal{P}_L d\|$ goes to zero when $d \perp \pi_L$; that is, when the vector d is perpendicular to the space of transformed functions $\mathcal{L}x$. As shown in the figure, this can also be interpreted by saying that d is parallel to the normal of plane π_L.

It may be helpful to see quickly how this works in two dimensions before proceeding to the general case. In 2D, the plane π_L is spanned by the two basis functions p_1 and p_2. We get the ball rolling with two simple observations. First, any vector $v = x - \mathcal{L}x$ in π_L may be described by a linear combination of these bases. Second, the vector $d = g - v$ is perpendicular to the plane π_L. We can write these three conditions symbolically:

$$\begin{aligned} \langle d | \, p_1 \rangle &= 0 \\ \langle d | \, p_2 \rangle &= 0 \\ v &= \alpha_1 p_1 + \alpha_2 p_2 \end{aligned} \tag{16.104}$$

Substituting for d in the first line, we find $\langle g - v | \, p_1 \rangle = 0$. Expanding this, we find

$$\begin{aligned} \langle g | \, p_1 \rangle &= \langle v | \, p_1 \rangle \\ &= \langle \alpha_1 p_1 + \alpha_2 p_2 | \, p_1 \rangle \\ &= \alpha_1 \langle p_1 | \, p_1 \rangle + \alpha_2 \langle p_2 | \, p_1 \rangle \end{aligned} \tag{16.105}$$

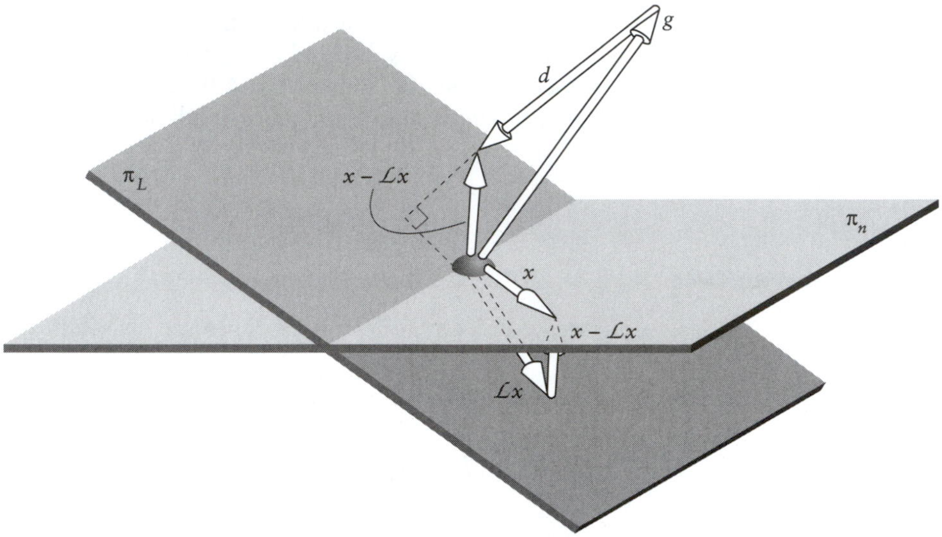

FIGURE 16.13
The vector $d = x - \mathcal{L}x - g$ is projected into π_L. The length of this projection is zero: $\|\mathcal{P}_L d\| = 0$.

Similarly, we find for the second term,

$$\langle g|\, p_2\rangle = \alpha_1 \langle p_1|\, p_2\rangle + \alpha_2 \langle p_2|\, p_2\rangle \tag{16.106}$$

We now have two equations in two unknowns, the coefficients α_1 and α_2. Solving for these, we get the vector $v = x - \mathcal{L}x$ such that $d = g - v$ is perpendicular to π_L.

Using the L_2 norm as a general measure of distance, we can leave behind the 2D imagery of Figure 16.13 and simply observe that the error vector from g to the transformed approximation solution $\mathcal{L}x_n$ must be perpendicular to the transformed space, which is spanned by the n transformed basis vectors $\{\mathcal{L}h_i\} = \{p_i\}$. We can express this statement in symbols by asserting that the inner product of the error vector with every transformed basis vector is zero:

$$\langle \mathcal{L}x_n - g|\, p_i\rangle = 0 \qquad i = 1, 2, \ldots, n \tag{16.107}$$

There are n of these equations, one for each basis function h_i. We can use the linearity of the braket to transform this into a more useful form:

$$\langle \mathcal{L}x_n|\, p_i\rangle = \langle g|\, p_i\rangle \qquad i = 1, 2, \ldots, n \tag{16.108}$$

We can now replace $\mathcal{L}x_n$ with Equations 16.66 and 16.67, which express the transformed function in terms of a quadrature rule applied to the function's expanded form:

$$\begin{aligned}\langle \mathcal{L}x_n | p_i \rangle &= \langle g | p_i \rangle \\ \left\langle \sum_{k=1}^{n} \alpha_k p_k \middle| p_i \right\rangle &= \langle g | p_i \rangle \\ \sum_{k=1}^{n} \alpha_k \langle p_k | p_i \rangle &= \langle g | p_i \rangle \end{aligned} \tag{16.109}$$

So now we again have n equations (one for each basis vector h_i) in the n unknowns of the vector $\vec{\alpha}$. This matrix equation $\vec{\alpha}\mathbf{P}_p = \mathbf{g}$ appears in tableau form as

$$\begin{bmatrix} \alpha_1 \\ \alpha_2 \\ \vdots \\ \alpha_n \end{bmatrix} \begin{bmatrix} \langle p_1 | p_1 \rangle & \langle p_2 | p_1 \rangle & \cdots & \langle p_n | p_1 \rangle \\ \langle p_1 | p_2 \rangle & \langle p_2 | p_2 \rangle & & \vdots \\ \vdots & & \ddots & \vdots \\ \langle p_1 | p_n \rangle & \cdots & \cdots & \langle p_n | p_n \rangle \end{bmatrix} = \begin{bmatrix} \langle g | p_1 \rangle \\ \langle g | p_2 \rangle \\ \vdots \\ \langle g | p_3 \rangle \end{bmatrix} \tag{16.110}$$

If the square matrix $\mathbf{P}_p$ is nonsingular, then it may be inverted to produce a unique result for α, which gives us x_n from $x_n = \sum_{k=1}^{n} \alpha_k h_k$.

16.8.6 Galerkin

The *Galerkin* method, also called the *Ritz-Galerkin method* and the *method of moments*, is similar to the least-squares approach except that it computes the error with respect to a different space.

Recall that the least-squares method found the approximate solution $x_n \in X_n$ such that the transformed function $\mathcal{L}x_n$ was as close as possible to g. In the Galerkin method, we seek a transformed function $\mathcal{L}x_n$ that differs from g only in ways that cannot be represented in X_n. In other words, we imagine that every vector in the system is projected into the subspace X_n, and we ask for the function $\mathcal{L}x_n$ that is closest to the projection of g.

This situation is shown in Figure 16.14, inspired by a similar image in Arvo [14]. The function x_n is chosen so that the error vector between g and $\mathcal{L}x_n$ is perpendicular to the space X_n.

As we did with least-squares, we will take a quick look at the situation in 2D. The plane π_n is spanned by the two basis functions h_1 and h_2, which may be combined to

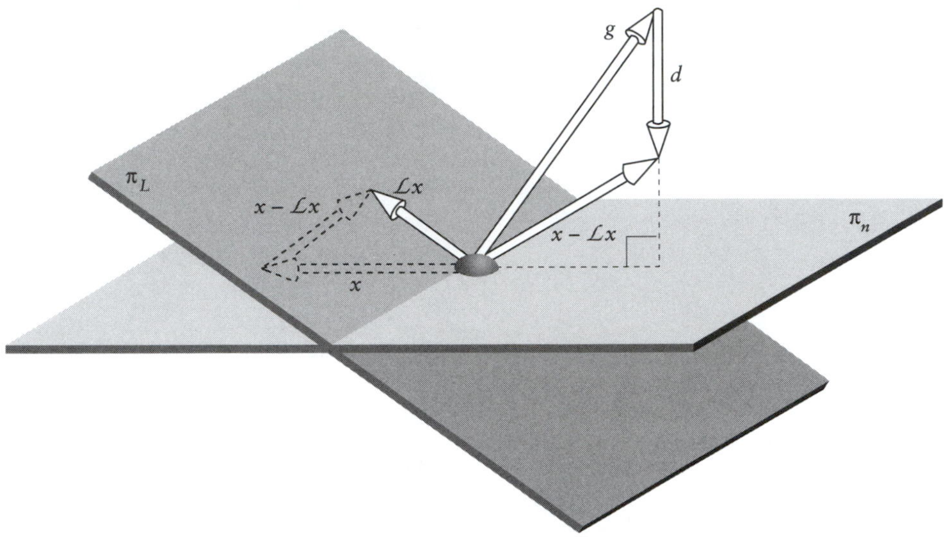

FIGURE 16.14
The error vector from $\mathcal{L}x_n$ to g is perpendicular to the subspace X_n.

form every vector $v = x - \mathcal{L}x$ in π_n. And our constraint is that the vector $d = g - v$ is perpendicular to this plane π_n. Symbolically,

$$\begin{aligned} \langle d|\, h_1\rangle &= 0 \\ \langle d|\, h_2\rangle &= 0 \\ v &= \alpha_1 p_1 + \alpha_2 p_2 \end{aligned} \tag{16.111}$$

We can now go through the same procedure as for the least-squares case, substituting for d, to find $\langle g - v|\, h_1\rangle = 0$. Then, expanding and simplifying, we find

$$\begin{aligned} \langle g|\, h_1\rangle &= \langle v|\, h_1\rangle \\ &= \langle \alpha_1 p_1 + \alpha_2 p_2|\, h_1\rangle \\ &= \alpha_1 \langle p_1|\, h_1\rangle + \alpha_2 \langle p_2|\, h_1\rangle \end{aligned} \tag{16.112}$$

Similarly, we find for the second term,

$$\langle g|\, p_2\rangle = \alpha_1 \langle p_1|\, h_2\rangle + \alpha_2 \langle p_2|\, h_2\rangle \tag{16.113}$$

As before, we now have two equations in two unknowns, the coefficients α_1 and α_2.

To state this approach in general terms, we can use the *projection operator* $\mathcal{P}_n$, which takes any vector $v \in X$ and projects it onto the subspace X_n. Then as we see in the figure, the projections of g and $\mathcal{L}x_n$ are the same:

$$\mathcal{P}_n \mathcal{L} x_n = \mathcal{P}_n g \tag{16.114}$$

Recall that $\mathcal{P}_n$ is not in general invertible; that is, the transformation from X to X_n loses information. In particular, it loses all of the components of the vector that are not in X_n.

The goal then is to make the projected residual zero:

$$\|r_n\| = 0 \tag{16.115}$$

This statement is equivalent to saying that the error vector is perpendicular to the subspace. That is, the inner product of the error vector onto each basis vector of X_n is zero:

$$\langle \mathcal{L}x_n - g | \, h_i \rangle = 0 \qquad i = 1, 2, \ldots, n \tag{16.116}$$

Compare this to Equation 16.107; it only differs in that we are projecting the error vector $\mathcal{L}x_n - g$ onto the basis function h_i rather than the transformed function Lh_i. Following the same procedure as for least squares, we can first open up the expression into two smaller inner products:

$$\langle \mathcal{L}x_n | \, h_i \rangle = \langle g | \, h_i \rangle \qquad i = 1, 2, \ldots, n \tag{16.117}$$

and then use Equations 16.66 and 16.67 once again:

$$\sum_{k=1}^{n} \alpha_k \langle p_k | \, h_i \rangle = \langle g | \, h_i \rangle \qquad i = 1, 2, \ldots, n \tag{16.118}$$

In matrix form, these equations may be expressed as $\vec{\alpha}\mathbf{P}_g = \mathbf{g}$, or in tableau:

$$\begin{bmatrix} \alpha_1 \\ \alpha_2 \\ \vdots \\ \alpha_n \end{bmatrix} \begin{bmatrix} \langle p_1 | \, h_1 \rangle & \langle p_2 | \, h_1 \rangle & \cdots & \langle p_n | \, h_1 \rangle \\ \langle p_1 | \, h_2 \rangle & \langle p_2 | \, h_2 \rangle & & \vdots \\ \vdots & & \ddots & \vdots \\ \langle p_1 | \, h_n \rangle & \cdots & \cdots & \langle p_n | \, h_n \rangle \end{bmatrix} = \begin{bmatrix} \langle g | \, h_1 \rangle \\ \langle g | \, h_2 \rangle \\ \vdots \\ \langle g | \, h_3 \rangle \end{bmatrix} \tag{16.119}$$

As before, if the matrix $\mathbf{P}_g$ is nonsingular, it may be inverted to derive a unique α.

It's not too hard to show that as the space X_n picks up more dimensions, and thus approaches X, the Galerkin method will converge to the correct answer. We start with Equation 16.114 and find

$$\begin{aligned} \mathcal{P}_n g &= \mathcal{P}_n \mathcal{L} x_n \\ g &= \mathcal{P}_n(\mathcal{I} - \lambda\mathcal{K}) x_n \\ g &= \mathcal{P}_n x_n - \lambda \mathcal{P}_n \mathcal{K} x_n \\ g &= (\mathcal{I} - \lambda \mathcal{P}_n \mathcal{K}) x_n \end{aligned} \tag{16.120}$$

or, upon solving for x_n,

$$x_n = (\mathcal{I} - \lambda \mathcal{P}_n \mathcal{K})^{-1} \mathcal{P}_n g \tag{16.121}$$

where we have used the fact that since x_n lies in X_n, its projection into that space is an identity; that is, $\mathcal{P}_n x_n = x_n$.

Now we can find the error between this approximation and the ideal x by simply subtracting the two. By rearranging the difference, we can express it as a factor of a simple term that goes to zero:

$$\begin{aligned} x - x_n &= (\mathcal{I} - \lambda\mathcal{K})^{-1} g - (\mathcal{I} - \lambda \mathcal{P}_n \mathcal{K})^{-1} \mathcal{P}_n g \\ &= \left[(\mathcal{I} - \lambda\mathcal{K})^{-1} - (\mathcal{I} - \lambda \mathcal{P}_n \mathcal{K})^{-1} \mathcal{P}_n\right] g \\ &= \left\{(\mathcal{I} - \lambda \mathcal{P}_n \mathcal{K})^{-1} \left[(\mathcal{I} - \lambda \mathcal{P}_n \mathcal{K}) - \mathcal{P}_n(\mathcal{I} - \lambda\mathcal{K})\right] (\mathcal{I} - \lambda\mathcal{K})^{-1}\right\} g \end{aligned} \tag{16.122}$$

By expanding the internal terms, we can see how they cancel each other and lead to a simpler expression:

$$\begin{aligned} x - x_n &= \left\{(\mathcal{I} - \lambda \mathcal{P}_n \mathcal{K})^{-1} \left[\mathcal{I} - \lambda \mathcal{P}_n \mathcal{K} - \mathcal{P}_n \mathcal{I} + \lambda \mathcal{P}_n \mathcal{K}\right] (\mathcal{I} - \lambda\mathcal{K})^{-1}\right\} g \\ &= \left\{(\mathcal{I} - \lambda \mathcal{P}_n \mathcal{K})^{-1} (\mathcal{I} - \mathcal{P}_n)(\mathcal{I} - \lambda\mathcal{K})^{-1}\right\} g \end{aligned} \tag{16.123}$$

Choosing our spaces so that $X_n \to X$ as $n \to \infty$, the projection operator $\mathcal{P}_n \to \mathcal{I}$, so $(\mathcal{I} - \mathcal{P}_n) \to 0$, and the whole operator goes to zero, so $x_n \to x$ as $n \to 0$ [343]. In other words, as our space X_n enlarges and includes more functions closer to X, the Galerkin method will find those functions and give us a better estimate of x.

The Galerkin method may be enhanced by a single additional step, resulting in the *iterated Galerkin method*. The idea is to pass the estimate x_g derived from the Galerkin method above through one step of successive substitution:

$$x'_g = g + \lambda \mathcal{K} x_g \tag{16.124}$$

Note that the new x'_g is not necessarily in the subspace X_n. Although this one step can refine our approximation, it may be surprising to note that additional steps of iteration will not improve the quality of the approximation [343]. A detailed study of the Galerkin method for integrals of the type $\mathcal{F}_2$ may be found in Ikebe [223].

16.8.7 Wavelets

There are two major sources of computational expense in the techniques presented in the last few subsections. One is the cost of building the matrix, and the other is the cost of inverting the matrix and then evaluating the resulting matrix products.

Recall that in Chapter 6 we saw that a signal projected onto a wavelet basis often had many near-zero coefficients on the wavelet basis functions. If we ignore these near-zero coefficients and treat them as zero, then we can ignore the multiplies and additions that we would otherwise perform. There is some error associated with this operation, but for the moment let's assume that that the error is tolerable. If many of the matrix entries are nearly zero, then the result is a nearly accurate solution at a great savings in time. In fact, the savings are even better, because there are efficient algorithms for computing the coefficients and inverting the resulting matrix.

In other words, rather than solve $x = g+\mathcal{K}x$, we instead solve $\mathcal{W}(x) = \mathcal{W}(g+\mathcal{K}x)$, or $\mathcal{W}x = \mathcal{W}g+(\mathcal{W}\mathcal{K})(\mathcal{W}x)$, where $\mathcal{W}$ is the wavelet transformation. When the kernel k is represented as a matrix, the projected matrix $\mathcal{W}\mathcal{K}$ is often *sparse*, or mostly zero, with only a few nonzero entries. The related operator matrix $\mathcal{W}\mathcal{L} = \mathcal{W}(\mathcal{I} - \lambda\mathcal{K})$ is also sparse.

Several methods for computing the wavelet transform to solve Fredholm integrals of the second kind have appeared recently [7, 8, 42]. The basic idea is to discretize the kernel $k(t, u)$ into a finite matrix, and then take the wavelet transform of that matrix. Where the kernel is smooth, most of the wavelet coefficients will be near zero, since only the lower-order wavelets will be needed to capture the broad, slow undulations of the kernel. In regions where the kernel is discontinuous, or has appreciable high-frequency information, or is otherwise *singular* (a term discussed in Section 16.10), the higher-order wavelet coefficients will become significant. But this is true *in those regions only*. This is the big advantage of the wavelet transform over the Fourier transform. With Fourier, we could dispose of the high-frequency coefficients, but then we would lose all of the high-frequency information everywhere in the matrix. In general, disposing of this high-frequency information will change every element in the matrix, not just those where there is significant local high-frequency information. With wavelets, we have high-frequency information only where we need it, and the corresponding coefficients are near zero where the matrix is smooth.

For a signal of 2^n entries, we will write $\mathcal{P}_i$ to represent projection onto a discretization of size 2^{i-n} [7]. So $\mathcal{P}_0$ is the finest-level resolution that matches the original matrix. Recall that as with any projection method, we're now working in a transformed space, solving not $x = g + \lambda\mathcal{K}x$, but the related problem

$$\mathcal{P}_i x = \mathcal{P}_i g + \lambda \mathcal{P}_i \mathcal{K} \mathcal{P}_i x \tag{16.125}$$

where we have written $\mathcal{P}_i x$ for x_i. Let's look more closely at the composite operator on x at level n, which we write as $\mathcal{K}_n = \mathcal{P}_n \mathcal{K} \mathcal{P}_n$.

We start by finding what $\mathcal{K}_0$ looks like in the *rectangular* (or *standard*) 2D basis.

Defining the resolution-changing operator $\mathcal{Q}_i$ as

$$\mathcal{Q}_i = \mathcal{P}_{i+1} - \mathcal{P}_i \tag{16.126}$$

we can then write

$$\mathcal{P}_n = \mathcal{P}_0 + \sum_{i=1}^{n-1} \mathcal{Q}_i \tag{16.127}$$

In the standard basis, we find

$$\begin{aligned}
\mathcal{K}_n &= \mathcal{P}_n \mathcal{K} \mathcal{P}_n \\
&= (\mathcal{P}_0 + \sum_{i=1}^{n-1} \mathcal{Q}_i)\mathcal{K}(\mathcal{P}_0 + \sum_{i=1}^{n-1} \mathcal{Q}_i) \\
&= \mathcal{P}_0\mathcal{K}\mathcal{P}_0 + \sum_{i=1}^{n-1} \mathcal{P}_0\mathcal{K}\mathcal{Q}_i + \sum_{i=1}^{n-1} \mathcal{Q}_i\mathcal{K}\mathcal{P}_0 + \sum_{i=1}^{n-1}\sum_{k=1}^{n-1} \mathcal{Q}_i\mathcal{K}\mathcal{Q}_k
\end{aligned} \tag{16.128}$$

Schröder et al. have pointed out [384] that this form of representation can lead to inefficient projection of the signal, meaning that we'll have more significantly nonzero coefficients than absolutely required. They note that this is due to the fact that different levels of projection are involved in these terms (e.g., $\mathcal{P}_0$ and $\mathcal{Q}_i$), so that compression at one level does not always completely exploit compression at all others.

These problems are addressed by writing the composite operator in the *square* (or *nonstandard*) basis, in a so-called *telescoping sequence*:

$$\begin{aligned}
\mathcal{K}_n &= \mathcal{P}_n \mathcal{K} \mathcal{P}_n \\
&= \mathcal{P}_0\mathcal{K}\mathcal{P}_0 + \sum_{i=0}^{n-1}(\mathcal{P}_{i+1}\mathcal{K}\mathcal{P}_{i+1} - \mathcal{P}_i\mathcal{K}\mathcal{P}_i) \\
&= \mathcal{P}_0\mathcal{K}\mathcal{P}_0 + \sum_{i=0}^{n-1}((\mathcal{P}_i + \mathcal{Q}_i)\mathcal{K}(\mathcal{P}_i + \mathcal{Q}_i) - \mathcal{P}_i\mathcal{K}\mathcal{P}_i) \\
&= \mathcal{P}_0\mathcal{K}\mathcal{P}_0 + \sum_{i=0}^{n-1}(\mathcal{P}_i\mathcal{K}\mathcal{P}_i + \mathcal{Q}_i\mathcal{K}\mathcal{P}_i + \mathcal{Q}_i\mathcal{K}\mathcal{P}_i + \mathcal{Q}_i\mathcal{K}\mathcal{Q}_i - \mathcal{P}_i\mathcal{K}\mathcal{P}_i) \\
&= \mathcal{P}_0\mathcal{K}\mathcal{P}_0 + \sum_{i=0}^{n-1} \mathcal{Q}_i\mathcal{K}\mathcal{P}_i + \sum_{i=0}^{n-1} \mathcal{P}_i\mathcal{K}\mathcal{Q}_i + \sum_{i=0}^{n-1} \mathcal{Q}_i\mathcal{K}\mathcal{Q}_i
\end{aligned} \tag{16.129}$$

Now we have an equivalent representation, based only on operators at the same level i working together, leading to more efficient compression.

More general wavelet methods applied to the Galerkin technique are reported by Xu and Shann in [493], and efficient quadrature methods are described in Sweldens and Piessens [429].

Method	Matrix element i, k
Nyström	$w_k k(t_i, t_k)$
Collocation	$p_i(t_k)$
Least-squares	$\langle p_k \vert p_i \rangle$
Galerkin	$\langle p_k \vert h_i \rangle$

TABLE 16.2
Matrix elements for Nyström, collocation, least-squares, and Galerkin methods.

16.8.8 Discussion

A review of the integral equation literature quickly reveals that the polynomial collocation, least-squares, and Galerkin methods are overwhelmingly the three most popular and influential algorithms for solving integral equations in general use today. The Nyström method is an important addition to this list because it provides a simple and flexible alternative. The wavelet basis is a recent arrival and is still being developed, primarily to accelerate the performance of these algorithms.

Each of these four methods may be characterized by the matrix it forms to solve a set of linear equations. Table 16.2 summarizes the matrix element m_{ik} for each of these techniques.

Other algorithms do exist; we mention two here as representative examples. *Kantorovich's method* [343] is a projection method. It produces a sequence of integral equations which, when solved by Galerkin methods, will converge to an answer for x more quickly than Galerkin applied to the original equation.

Another technique is in fact a general strategy for improving quadrature-based solution techniques, and is called the *method of iterated deferred correction* [26]. The method begins by creating two estimates for x from the original integral equation: a crude estimate x_0 and a slightly better (and more expensive) estimate f'_0. If both functions are evaluated at n points, then we can construct an n-element error vector $e_0 = f'_0 - x_0$. It turns out that e_0 satisfies a Fredholm equation of the second kind using a kernel derived from the original kernel and the quadrature rule, so we can use any of the methods in this chapter to solve for e_0. We now compute $x_1 = x_0 + e_0$. If we run x_1 through the quadrature rule, it won't in general be exactly equivalent to the $x_0 + e_0$, so we can write $e_1 = x_1 - (x_0 + e_0)$. This gives us a new error function e_1, which we can again solve for and add into x_1 to create an x_2, and so on. We repeat this process until the sequence appears to be converged, the accuracy is good enough, or patience is exhausted.

16.9 Monte Carlo Estimation

We mentioned earlier that we can use Monte Carlo to evaluate the 1D integrals required by most projection methods. In this section we investigate using Monte Carlo to estimate a solution to the full integral equation of Equation 16.1:

$$x(t) = g(t) + \lambda \int_a^b k(t,u)x(u)\,du \tag{16.130}$$

We know from Chapter 7 that in principle we can form a Monte Carlo estimation of the integral of any function that we can evaluate at specific points, but that this estimate is likely to have high variance and converge slowly (proportionally to $\sqrt{n}$ for n samples). When the problem is complicated and the kernel difficult to evaluate (as in our applications), this sort of naïve sampling will prove so time consuming as to be useless in practice. To make Monte Carlo practical for this problem, we need some way to improve the efficiency of our estimates.

Perhaps the most general variance-reduction is *importance sampling*, presented in Section 7.5.2. For convenience, we will review the idea very quickly here before moving on.

Recall that to estimate an integral

$$M = \int m(t)\,dt \tag{16.131}$$

we can rewrite the function m as the product of two functions $m(t) = g(t)f(t)$, giving us the equivalent problem

$$M = \int g(t)f(t)\,dt \tag{16.132}$$

This can always be done; trivially, we can set $g(t) = m(t)$ and $f(t) = 1$. Often by construction $f(t)$ is normalized, that is, $\int f(t)\,dt = 1$. Then we can treat $f(t)$ as a probability distribution function, and draw samples t_i one at a time from that pdf. We evaluate g at each of these sample points, and then average together these samples of $g(t_i)$ to form an estimate of M.

The efficiency of this process (that is, the speed with which our estimates converge to the true value of M) can be improved dramatically by judicious choice of $f(t)$. The basic idea is that the final integral is simply a scalar, made up of a sum of many smaller scalars (the $g(t_i)$). The scalars that make the most contribution to the final figure are those that are largest in size. So if we skew our sampling in such a way that most of the samples are drawn from where the function $g(t)$ has a large magnitude, then we will sample the most important parts of the integral most of the time, speeding us to a reliable answer. We can achieve this by choosing a function

$f(t)$ that is large where the original function $m(t)$ is large; because f tracks the amplitude (or *importance*) of m, we call such an f an *importance function*. So by sampling $\int m(t) f(t)\, dt$, we will tend to preferentially draw samples from m where its magnitude is large. This is called *importance sampling*. There are two big problems with this scheme: the first is that we've now biased our estimate so that the integral is no longer equal to M, because in general $f(t) \neq 1$. The other problem is that in order to design the right f, we need to already know m.

The first problem can be solved by scaling m by $1/f$:

$$M = \int \frac{m(t)}{f(t)} f(t)\, dt \tag{16.133}$$

Now we draw samples t_i as directed by f, evaluate $m_i = m(t_i)/f(t_i)$, and our resulting integral is unchanged. The second problem is much harder; if we knew m well enough to design an ideal f, we wouldn't need to go through this whole process at all. In general, we *guess* at an f based on whatever information we can gather about the function m, and we use that guess as the importance function. We can update our guess over time as we learn more about m to improve our efficiency. If f is close to the ideal importance function, our efficiency will be greatly improved. This does not mean that *any* function f is useful; if f is sufficiently far away from the ideal, our efficiency can be reduced far below that of naïve Monte Carlo.

The beauty of importance sampling is that the importance function f can be almost anything (assuming it satisfies the conditions of a pdf in Section 7.5.2). We can create f based on the function m, or by combining simple analytic functions, or by plotting the daily rainfall in some city; f need not be tied to any other information in the problem. We therefore have tremendous freedom in specifying what is "important" in any given situation.

We will see that importance sampling can be of great abstract and practical use in solving complicated integral equations for rendering. This is because our integral equations describe the distribution of light in an environment, and we usually don't care to compute equally accurate estimates everywhere in the scene: in particular, we don't really care about getting precise results on surfaces we can't see, as long as the results on the surfaces we *can* see are accurate. The result is that we can use importance sampling to direct our attention to find accurate estimates of light energy on the parts of the scene that matter to us for some purpose, and save the work in those regions of the scene that don't matter. Our discussion in this section will be mostly based on Coveyou [105], Hammersley and Handscomb [183], and Kalos and Whitlock [239].

The material in this section has a very natural and compelling geometrical interpretation. Almost all of the equations can be understood in terms of particles moving through an environment, starting at some source and then bouncing off of surfaces until they are finally absorbed (or escape the system), distributing information or energy as they travel. This is, however, only one interpretation of the mathematics, which are quite general and open to other interpretations. The appeal of the geometric interpretation is that it supports our visual imagination, develops intuition, and anticipates our ultimate use of this material. The disadvantage of stressing this one interpretation too hard is that it may suggest that it is the only interpretation; that may make it harder to recognize its applicability in other situations where it is appropriate. Cognizant of this risk, I feel it would be a shame to suppress the evocative geometric interpretation in favor of a more abstract and remote approach. So although the big picture in this section will generally be in abstract terms, the interpretations of the results and steps along the way will be strongly geometric.

16.9.1 Random Walks

Our goal is to find values for the unknown function x as specified by an integral equation such as Equation 16.1:

$$x(t) = g(t) + \lambda \int_a^b k(t, u)x(u)\, du \tag{16.134}$$

We will find it useful to recall Chapter 12 and anticipate Chapter 17 and think of Equation 16.134 as a *transport equation*. That is, it describes the propagation of some unspecified "stuff" throughout an environment. In this section we will assume for the sake of discussion that this stuff is visible light energy. The light is generated by the driving function g, and the kernel k describes how the light is transported by discrete particles from one place in the environment to another.

The most convenient terminology for the following discussion is based on the idea of *particle state* first seen in Chapter 12. The idea is that each particle may be characterized by some vector of attributes; if there are n scalar elements in the vector, then we can think of the particle as a point in an n-dimensional *state space*. We will find it convenient to think of the domain over which we evaluate our integral equation as a bounded interval $\Gamma = [a, b]$, which is tiled into a set of p intervals I_i, which together cover the domain. Since these intervals *tile* the domain, the I_i are *disjoint* (they do not overlap) and *complete* (together, they cover the domain Γ). In a purely 2D world, such as that in Figure 16.15, each interval may be thought of as a piece of surface [202].

A complete state description of a particle can conceptually contain almost any information; a reasonable starting point might be position, direction of travel, energy, and time. To make the discussion below simple, we will eliminate all of these but position. When we say that a particle is "in" some state S_v, we mean that it is just arriving at the surface associated with interval I_v. This arrival can be due to the spontaneous generation of the particle at the surface if it is a source, or as a result of flight from some other surface I_u (or its associated state S_u). The kernel

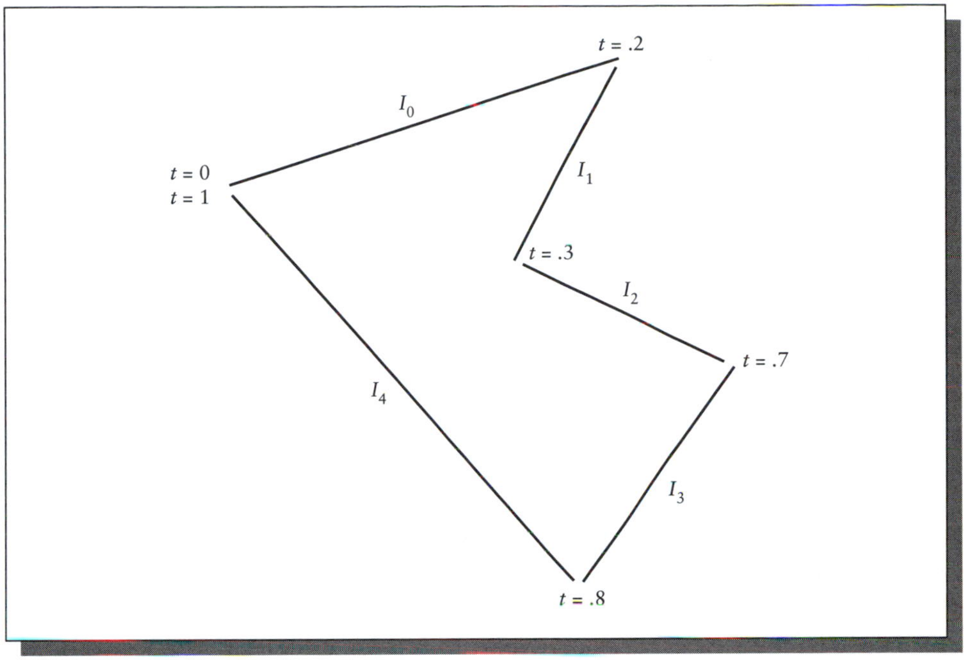

FIGURE 16.15

The domain $[0, 1]$ broken up into five intervals I_0 to I_4 that are complete and disjoint over the domain.

k of the integral equation can then be interpreted as the probability that a particle will travel from state S_u (a point u in interval I_u) to state S_v (a point v in interval I_v). We can write this more explicitly as $k(S_u \to S_v)$. Note that we have placed an explicit arrow between the arguments to indicate the flow of particles. If we only use left-to-right arrows, then the kernel term which has so far appeared as $k(t, u)$ will appear as $k(S_u \to S_t)$; notice the switch in the order in which the states are listed. In physical terms, the kernel represents the source distribution or reflectivity of the surface, giving the likelihood that a particle at one surface will travel toward any other. The value of our unknown $x(t)$ is then the number of particles to be found in state S_t; that is, on the surface p for which $t \in I_p$.

We will find it convenient throughout most of this chapter to refer to states simply as "state t," or even simply t. We will maintain the arrow notation in the kernel to emphasize the direction of transfer (e.g., $k(u \to v)$), but we will often speak of states

t and u rather than S_t and S_u. This convention allows us to discuss the ideas and the math in terms of states, but still use similar notation as in the rest of the book.

This simple definition of the state means that the kernel doesn't have access to the direction from which the incident particle is arriving. The emission (or reflection) distribution may depend on many factors, but the incident angle is not one of them. We make this assumption only to simplify the discussion. The state description could easily include the incident direction, time, and energy of the particle, as well as other information such as all past states. The kernel k could then theoretically make use of all this information. So it is simply for convenience that we will consider the kernel that gives the probability $k(u \to v)$ of transport from state u to state v to be identical for all particles in state u.

We also note that the discretization of the domain into intervals is also simply for convenience. Ultimately, every state S_t can be considered to represent only a single particle vector t rather than a whole range of such vectors; then all of the involved functions will be continuous. We will maintain this idea of continuity in the math because it is conceptually simpler, though in a computer implementation, discretization is an unavoidable fact of life.

By thinking of particles as independent objects that assume a variety of states, we are led to an idea of *particle history*. We say that a particle is described by a series of states, $\{S_0, S_1, \ldots, S_n\}$. The state S_0 is variously described by the adjectives *first*, *initial*, *birth*, *creation*, and *source*. The state S_n is variously described as *last*, *final*, *death*, *termination*, and *absorption*. The complete set of states is called the *path history* (or just *path* or just *history*) of the particle.

16.9.2 Path Tracing

It will be very useful for us to find a way to describe the states through which a particle passes during its history. In general, we can start following states at any point from creation to absorption, and can follow the history either backward or forward. We begin by following the history backward from some state t, which may or may not be the final state.

We start with the integral equation in state transition form:

$$x(t) = g(t) + \int k(s \to t)x(s)\,ds \tag{16.135}$$

We now start following a particle backward from a state t; this will give us a single estimate for $x(t)$. We start by assuming that $g(t)$ is a pdf in the variable t, and that $k(s \to t)$ is a pdf in s for some given value of t. Note that the kernel is being used to compute the transfer *from* state S_s *to* state S_t.

We begin by picking a starting state for the particle: that is, we pick a t from the pdf $g(t)$ to get state S_t. This one data point gives us the estimate

$$x(t) \approx g(t) + \int k(s \to t) x(s)\, ds \tag{16.136}$$

where we have a value for $g(t)$, but the integral term is still just a formal expression for which we have no numerical value.

Now we want to estimate the value of the integral using Monte Carlo:

$$\int k_t(s) x(s)\, ds \tag{16.137}$$

where $k_t(s)$ is the one-parameter function of $k(s \to t)$ for a given t; that is, the probability of a particle successfully arriving at state t from state s. We know how to estimate this type of integral: think of $k_t(s)$ as a pdf, draw a sample value s_s from $k_t(s)$, and estimate $x(s_s)$. Since we have a value of t from the first state S_k, we have $k_t(s)$, and we sample it to find the random variable s_s. We can add this to our estimate from before to get

$$\begin{aligned} x(t) &\approx g(t) + \int k_t(s) x(s)\, ds \\ &= g(t) + x(s_s) \\ &= g(t) + g(s_s) + \int k(r \to s_s) x(r)\, dr \end{aligned} \tag{16.138}$$

where the integral on the right comes from reapplying the definition of x. We are now in state S_{k-1}. Geometrically, we have a particle that has started at t, and has now "bounced" once off of the bit of surface containing s_s, and is now directed toward the previous surface and state S_{k-2}, as in Figure 16.16.

To estimate the integral on the last line of Equation 16.138, we again apply Monte Carlo, now selecting a r_s from the pdf $k_s(r)$ (since we now have a value of s), and evaluating f at that r_s, giving us

$$x(t) \approx g(t) + g(s_s) + g(r_s) + \int k(q \to r_s) x(q)\, dq \tag{16.139}$$

and on it goes.

If the kernel is not normalized, that is,

$$\sigma(t) = \int k(t \to u)\, du < 1 \tag{16.140}$$

then the particle has a probability $\alpha(t) = 1 - \sigma(t)$ of being *absorbed* at any given evaluation. At that point the recursion stops and we have our estimate for x. In

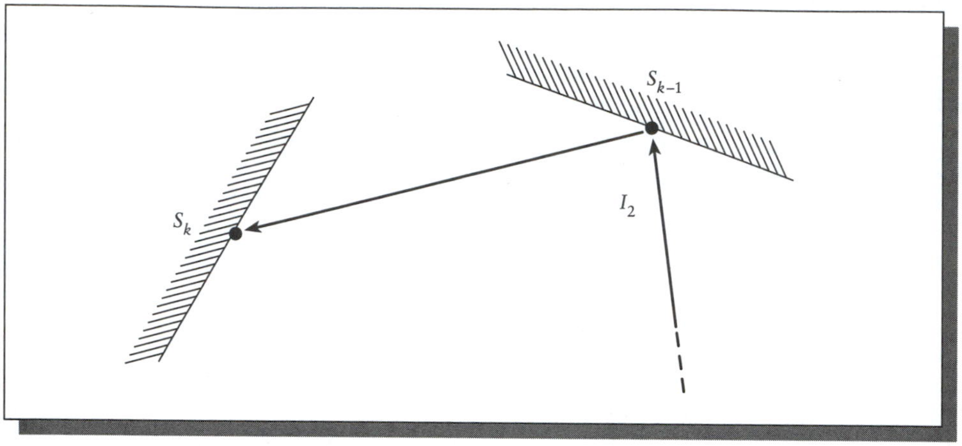

FIGURE 16.16
One bounce off of state S_1.

effect we are following the particle as it bounces through the environment, where each bounce is found by sampling the kernel, using the current state of the particle as the kernel's first argument. This technique is called *path tracing*. Generating the series of states assumed by the particle is called creating a *random walk* for the particle, since it appears to unpredictably "walk" from one state to another. Here we have walked backward; we can in principle walk in either direction.

As mentioned earlier, the kernel has a natural geometric interpretation as the reflectivity of a surface. The value $k(t \to u)$ is the likelihood that a particle currently at the surface including t will be propagated successfully to a surface containing u.

The general idea behind using this approach in practice comes from realizing that one random walk describes the sequence of states taken on by only one particle. If we follow enough walks, then the number of particles that visit each state will begin to approximate the distribution that would be generated by a real set of particles controlled by the probabilities given by the kernel.

This procedure has the advantage of simplicity, but if the absorption probability is small, then it might take a huge number of bounces for each particle to terminate. In rendering, the operations associated with each bounce can be very expensive to compute. Recall that each time a particle enters a state S_i, there is a probability α_i that it will be absorbed. Therefore, out of every N particles entering that state, $\alpha_i N$ will terminate and $(1 - \alpha_i)N$ will continue on to the next state. So the likelihood of a particle making it to state S_n is the combined probability of propagation at every state leading there, or $(1-\alpha_1)(1-\alpha_2)\cdots(1-\alpha_{n-1})$. This can be a small number indeed, but we still pay the same high cost to follow this particle as for some other particle path that might be more likely and more influential on our result.

We can make things more efficient by replacing this swarm of identical particles with *weighted* particles. When a weighted particle moves from one state to another, it carries with it a weight that describes the likelihood that this particle on this path is likely to occur. In other words, suppose that 100 particles enter some state S_i that has an absorption probability of α_i. Then we can absorb $100\alpha_i$ of them and follow the $100(1-\alpha_i)$ others, or simply follow one particle with new weight $1-\alpha_i$.

We may be tempted to make this process even more efficient by terminating a particle when its weight (that is, its probability of continuing on to another state) falls below some threshold τ. This would certainly save us work, but it would introduce a systematic bias in the answer, since all of those low-probability contributions can sum together into a meaningful contribution.

Instead of just stopping our particle history when the probability falls below τ, we stop *probabilistically*, and use a weighting scheme similar to importance sampling. First, we select a number N before starting the simulation: Coveyou et al. suggest $2 < N < 10$ [105]. To start a particle history, we create the particle with a weight $w_0 = 1$. When this weight falls below τ, we generate a uniformly distributed random number $\xi \in [0,1]$. If $\xi > 1/N$, then we say the particle is absorbed. Otherwise, we scale the weight of the particle by the factor N, and generate a next state by sampling the kernel. This procedure is called *Russian roulette*, named after the lethal game. The idea is to cut down on the number of below-threshold particles that we follow by a factor of N at each below-threshold bounce; this prunes our particle count quickly. To compensate, we increase the weight of each surviving particle. When we compute $x(t)$, we don't simply count the number of particles in each state t, but instead sum together their weights.

Figure 16.17 shows an example of this procedure. We assume that each surface has a constant reflectivity of $\rho < 1$ in all directions, and that the threshold kicks in just after the third bounce; to get this behavior, we set $\tau = \rho^2 + \rho/2$. The particle starts in S_0 at the source, with weight $w_0 = 1$, since it is certainly emitted (a different normalization would start the particle with its probability of creation $g(t)$). The particle enters event S_1 with certainty, so it contributes a weight of $w_1 = 1$. Its probability of continuing is given by ρ, so it assumes that weight, $w_2 = \rho$, as it moves out of S_1 and contributes it to S_2. The probability that the particle survives the second bounce is ρ^2, so entering state S_3 we find $w = \rho^2 < \tau$; this triggers a round of Russian roulette in state S_3. Supposing that we have survival, the particle is passed on with weight modulated by ρ but amplified by N; that is, $w_3 = (N\rho)(\rho^2) = N\rho^3$. We suppose the same thing happens at state S_4, so the continuing particle now has weight $w_4 = N^2\rho^4$. Finally, at state S_5 the random number ξ is above $1/N$, so the particle is terminated at that state with the weight it had upon arrival: $w_5 = w_4$. So this particle contributes the weights $\{1, 1, \rho, \rho^2, N\rho^3, N^2\rho^4, N^2\rho^4\}$ to the six states

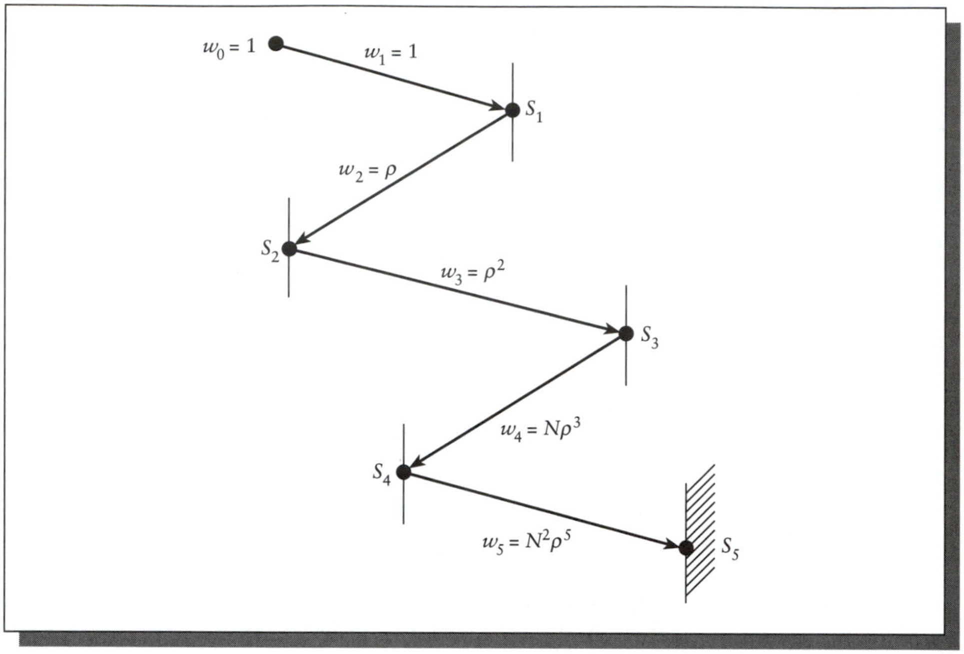

FIGURE 16.17
A five-step random walk.

S_0 through S_5, representing the expected proportions of particles that would occupy those states if we simulated many more particles.

16.9.3 The Importance Function

In some applications, we don't necessarily need the solution $x(t)$ at *all* values of t, but only at some subset. This is often the case in computer graphics. The most obvious example in rendering is that we only need accurate solutions of the radiance equation on those surfaces that are visible; as long as those surfaces are correctly represented, we don't really care what the accuracy is elsewhere. At other times we need to pay close attention to accuracy in shadows, or at shadow boundaries. For example, when simulating the light falling on a garden, we may not care about the illumination within large, well-lit plots, but we might care a lot about how much light falls over the course of a season on the boundaries between crops of different types. In a simulation for an art gallery, we may not care about the light falling anywhere in the scene except on the surfaces of valuable paintings and sculptures. We can use the ideas of importance sampling to direct our solution technique to those locations in the environment where we need accuracy for any reason.

The tricky part of this type of importance sampling in rendering situations is that we typically want to specify *immediate* importance. That is, we want to indicate explicitly only those surfaces where we need accuracy. But since those surfaces receive light from potentially everywhere in the environment, we cannot completely ignore the surfaces that we don't explicitly indicate to be important. To reconcile this problem, we *propagate* importance through the environment, just as light is created from light sources. If a surface is important, then any surface that can contribute a significant amount of illumination to that surface is also important (though perhaps less so), and the surfaces that contribute to that contributor are also (though even less) important, and so on. Finding this *potential* importance everywhere in the domain will occupy our attention here.

To see how to apply these ideas, we begin by considering how the driving function $g(t)$ distributes its effect into the environment via the kernel $\mathcal{K}$ [105]. In the following discussion, we will think of all our functions as *probabilistic* descriptions of the ideal functions. That is, $x(t)$ will represent not the exact $x(t)$, but an estimate that we compute with increasing accuracy. Formally, we might write $E(x(t))$ and $E(g(t))$, but we would soon have more E's than anything else in our formulas. So keep in mind that because we're dealing with random sampling, our solution functions are not exact functions but just probable approximations of varying accuracy.

We therefore solve

$$x(t) = g(t) + \int x(s)k(s \to t)\, ds \tag{16.141}$$

where $x(t)$ is to be interpreted as the *expected value* of t, that is, the probability of finding a particle in state t; $x(t)$ is the probabilistic form of the particle density. The probable number of particles in a volume dt around t is then $x(t)\, dt$. We interpret $g(t)$ similarly as the expected density of creation of particles at t. Note again that we are writing $k(s \to t)$ so the flow of particles is left to right, like the reading of the equation; that is, $x(s)k(s \to t)$ describes particles leaving state s and traveling through $k(s \to t)$ into state t. We're looking backward here; to find the value at $x(t)$, we look around at all the surfaces from which particles may have come to contribute to the density at t.

We define the value $x_p(t)$ as the probability that the pth state of some particle occurs at state S_t. The value $x_0(t)$ is just the probability of creation of a particle at t:

$$x_0(t) = g(t) \tag{16.142}$$

After one bounce, the particle moves from creation state S_s to termination state S_t; the probability $x(t)$ of finding a particle at state t after one bounce from any creation

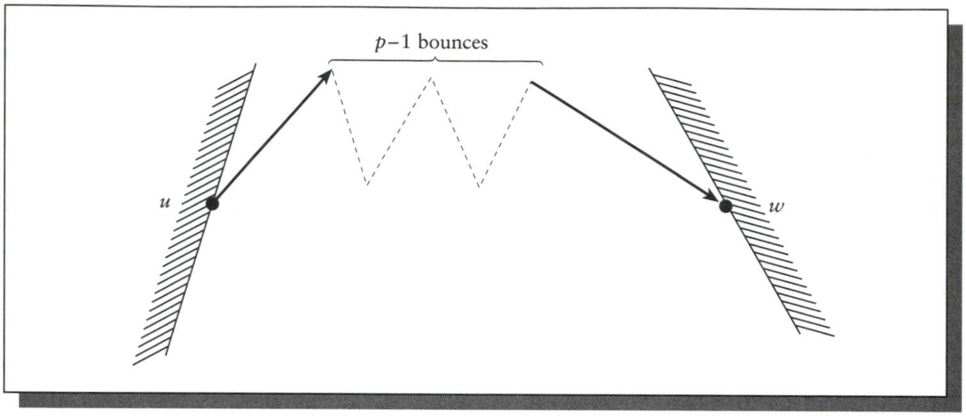

FIGURE 16.18
A particle moving from state u to land at state w after p steps.

state S_s is then the probability of a particle being at state S_s, times its probability of reaching S_t, summed over all such states S_s:

$$x_1(t) = \int x_0(s)k(s \to t)\, ds \tag{16.143}$$

The probability of finding a particle at state t at bounce $p+1$ is then

$$x_{p+1}(t) = \int x_p(s)k(s \to t)\, ds \tag{16.144}$$

So the probability $x(t)$ of finding a particle at t on any bounce is then simply the sum of the probabilities for each bounce:

$$x(t) = \sum_{p=0}^{\infty} x_p(t) \tag{16.145}$$

Now let $k_p(u \to w)$ be the probability that when a particle is in a state u, there will be at least p more steps, and that the pth step will be in state v; that is, this tells us how likely it is that if we start in state u and take p steps, we will end up in state w. We symbolize this in Figure 16.18, which diagrams the path of a particle from state u to state w, where each change in the direction of the path indicates a change of state, weighted by the kernel at that state used as a pdf.

We can write this symbolically as

$$k_p(u \to w) = \underbrace{\int \cdots \int}_{p \text{ times}} k(u \to v_1)k(v_1 \to v_2) \cdots k(v_{p-2} \to v_{p-1})k(v_{p-1} \to w)\, dv_1 \cdots dv_{p-1} \tag{16.146}$$

Note that this is just an iterated kernel, as defined in Equation 16.44.

As before, we can write a few special cases to get a feeling for this probability. We begin with $k_0(u \to w)$, which is simply the probability that state u is the same as state w; this is just the delta function for $S_u = S_w$:

$$k_0(u \to w) = \delta(u \to w) \tag{16.147}$$

where

$$\delta(u \to v) = \begin{cases} 1 & S_u = S_v \\ 0 & \text{otherwise} \end{cases} \tag{16.148}$$

The probability for one bounce k_1 is simply the kernel k itself:

$$k_1(u \to w) = k(u \to w) \tag{16.149}$$

The probability of getting from state u to state w in $p+1$ bounces is just the probability of getting from state u to any state v in p bounces times the probability of moving from that state v to state w. In symbols,

$$k_{p+1}(u \to w) = \int k_p(u \to v)k(v \to w)\, dv \tag{16.150}$$

We integrate because any state v will do; this is illustrated in Figure 16.19 for two different states v.

Finally, we can find the probability of reaching u from w in $p + q$ bounces as the product of reaching some state v from u in p bounces times the probability of reaching w from v in q bounces, as shown in Figure 16.20. Symbolically,

$$k_{p+q}(u \to w) = \int k_p(u \to v)k_q(v \to w)\, dv \tag{16.151}$$

We can combine these ideas of expected density and multibounce probability to give the following equalities:

$$\int x_{p-1}(s)k(s \to t)\, ds = x_p(t) = \int g(v)k_p(v \to t)\, dv \tag{16.152}$$

In words, the left side tells us that $x_p(t)$, the expected number of particles to be found in state t on bounce p, is given by the expected number in some other state

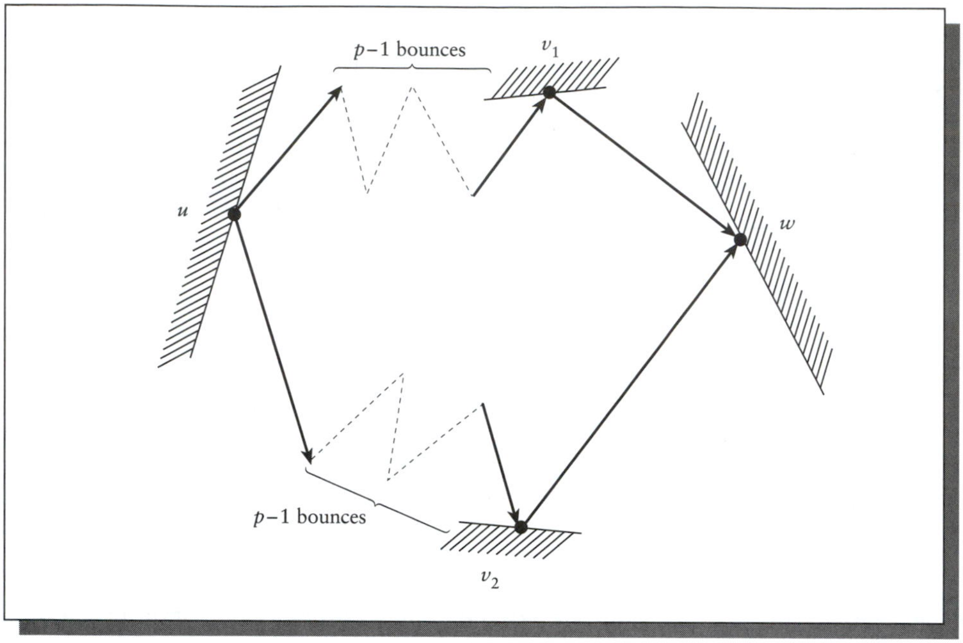

FIGURE 16.19
The transport from u to w via $p - 1$ bounces from u to any v, and then one bounce from v to w.

s times the probability that they will get from s to t in one more bounce, summed over all states s. The right side says that the same quantity can be found by summing the contribution of every source at v, where we determine its contribution at x by finding the probability that a particle starting at v will end at state t after p bounces. This equivalence is diagrammed in Figure 16.21.

It is possible that a particle starting in state u may visit state v many times during the course of its history before it is finally absorbed. The *Green's function* $G(u \to v)$ expresses this probability [105]:

$$G(u \to v) = \sum_{p=0}^{\infty} k_p(u \to v) \tag{16.153}$$

That is, $G(u \to v)$ tells us how many times a particle in state u is likely to visit a state

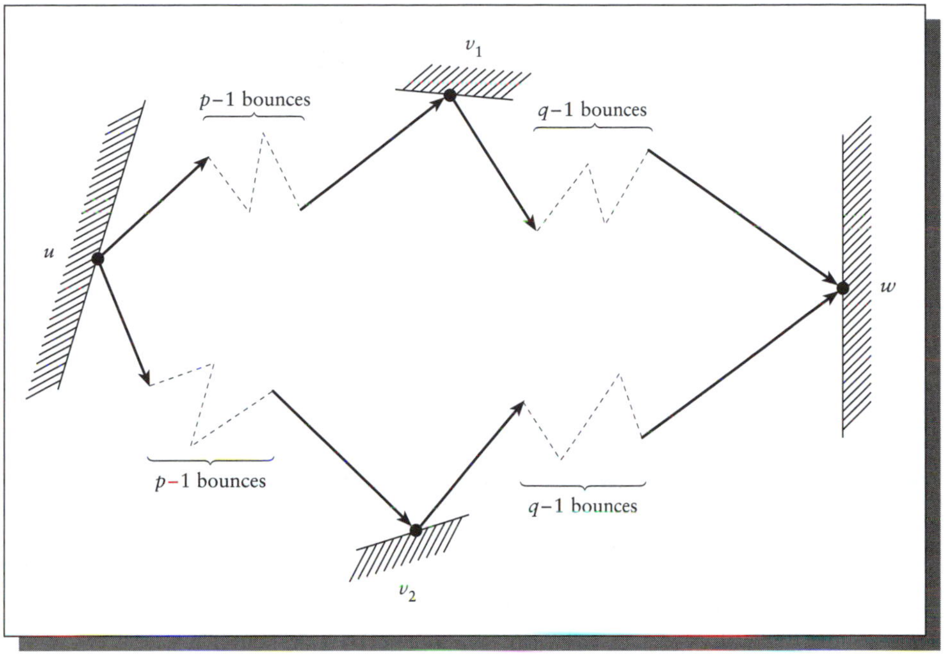

FIGURE 16.20

Traveling from u to v in $p-1$ bounces, and then from v to w in $q-1$ more bounces.

v before it is absorbed. From this, we can write

$$x(t) = \int g(u)G(u \to t)\,du \tag{16.154}$$

That is, the expected number of particles in state t is given by the number of particles leaving a source u times the total number of visits each particle is likely to visit t, summed over all sources u. We note that we can use the Green's function to derive other transitions using the p-bounce kernels; for example,

$$G(u \to w) = \delta(u \to w) + \int G(u \to v)k(v \to w)\,dv \tag{16.155}$$

We can multiply through by dw to get the number of particles in state w rather than

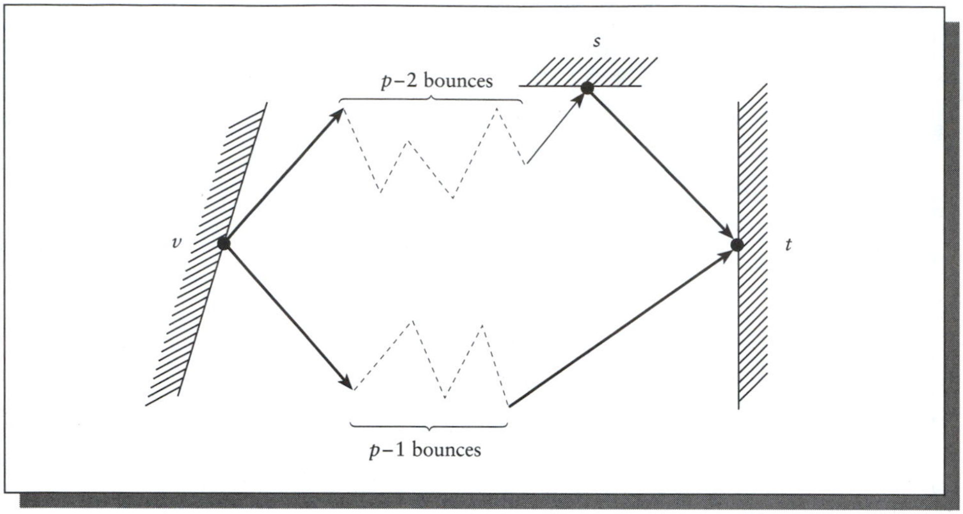

FIGURE 16.21
Two ways of finding the contribution of v to t.

just the density:

$$G(u \to w)\, dw = \delta(u \to w)\, dw + \int G(u \to v)k(v \to w)\, dv\, dw \tag{16.156}$$

In words, this says that the number of particles from state u that will move to a region dw around state w is given by the number of particles already in w (that is, we include the case $u = w$), plus the number of particles from u that will eventually make it to a state v times the probability that those particles will move from v to w in dw, summed over all such intermediate states v.

So far we have only considered the transitions of particles from one state to another, as governed by the kernel k. It's now time to use the importance function to improve the efficiency of this process for some particular purpose.

Suppose that we aren't really interested in the solution function for itself, but rather in some other quantity derived from the solution function. That is, we want to find some scalar value λ defined by the expected density $x(t)$ and some arbitrary $a(t)$:

$$\lambda = \int x(t)a(t)\, dt \tag{16.157}$$

Then as we reviewed earlier, we can normalize a and consider it as a pdf, generate values t from this pdf, sample $x(t)$, and average the samples to make an estimator for λ. This will work no matter what a happens to be, as long as it can be turned into a valid pdf. But things become more interesting when a incorporates some of our *purpose* in evaluating the integral; that is, a is large in regions of the domain which we determine to be *important* based on any arbitrary definition of "important" that we choose.

As mentioned earlier, the "important" parts of a scene in computer graphics can be anything: the visible surfaces from a particular point of view, the paintings on the wall of an art gallery, or the surface of a light-sensitive robot moving through the environment. Our goal in making an image is to compute the scalar values at the pixels; these are just linear functions of the light distribution in the scene. All of these examples may be captured by Equation 16.157. By placing an importance function on the entire environment, and giving it a large magnitude only in the regions where we desire a solution, we can force samples to occur in the regions we care about and thereby get an accurate answer in those regions more quickly. We will now look more carefully at the role of importance functions in solving integrals of the class $\mathcal{F}_2$.

We call the value λ of Equation 16.157 the *score* or the *total payoff* [105, 239]. As a particle travels through states $\{S_0, \ldots, S_n\}$, it contributes some amount $p(S_k)$ at each state; this is called the *payoff* or *contribution* of that state to λ. The payoff function p is where we express our opinion of importance. If a state has a high importance, we assign it a large value of p. The total payoff for some particular particle is then given by the sum of each of these individual scores over the particle's history:

$$\eta = \sum_{k=0}^{n} p(S_k) \tag{16.158}$$

Note that η is not λ; it's only one estimate for λ. If we trace many particles we will get many different values of η, but we are interested in the *expected value* of η; that is, the expected contribution of any particle is our value λ from above:

$$\lambda = \langle \eta \rangle \tag{16.159}$$

so λ is the value of η averaged over all possible histories.

Now consider a particle in state S_k. We can consider the total payoff of this particle over its entire life to be divisible into two segments: the payoff contributed before it reached state S_k, and the payoff at S_k and all states afterward until it is absorbed. We call this latter contribution the *remaining payoff*; note that the payoff at state S_k is included in this definition. The remaining payoff is itself a random variable, which we write as ξ:

$$\xi(S_p) = \sum_{p=k}^{n} p(S_p) \tag{16.160}$$

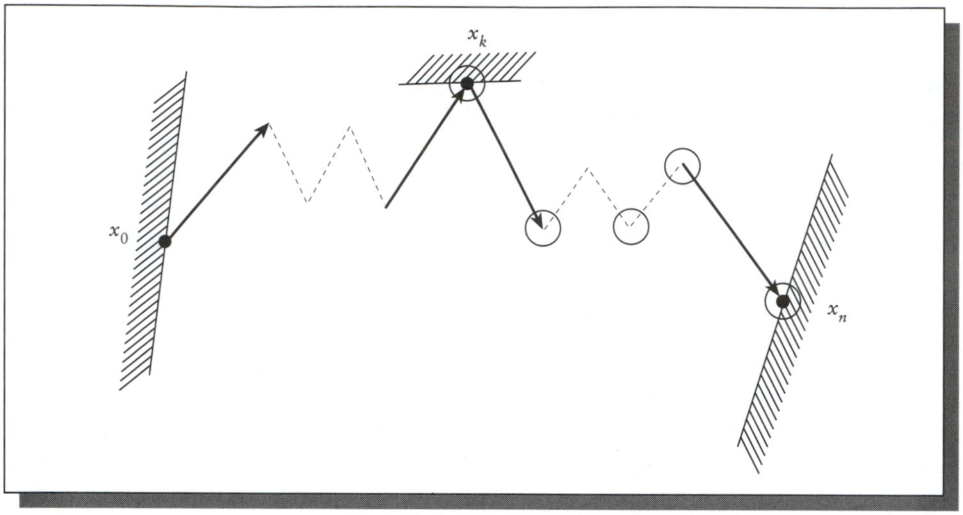

FIGURE 16.22
The remaining payoff ξ of a particle in state S_k; we sum the payoffs of the circled states only.

Figure 16.22 illustrates the idea behind this definition. When the particle is finally absorbed, $k = n$, so $\xi(S_n) = p(S_n)$.

When the particle is in a state $k < n$, that is, before absorption, its remaining payoff may be expressed as the sum of the payoff at the current state plus the payoff yet to come:

$$\begin{aligned} \xi(S_k) &= p(S_k) + \sum_{p=k+1}^{n} p(S_p) \\ &= p(S_k) + \xi(S_{k+1}) \end{aligned} \tag{16.161}$$

The expected value of this remaining payoff will be represented with a function w, which is variously called the *potential function*, the *value function*, or the *potential value function*:

$$w(S_k) = \langle \xi(S_x) \rangle \tag{16.162}$$

The value of $w(S_k)$ tells us the amount of importance to attach to state S_k. That is, it tells us if we have a particle in state S_k, what the remaining payoff of that particle is likely to be in terms of our measuring function. In other words, $w(t)$ is the value that a particle in a state t will eventually contribute to λ if allowed to continue; this payoff waiting to happen is the *potential* of a particle at state t.

We can see this by expanding the formula:

$$\begin{aligned} w(t) &= \langle \xi(t) \rangle \\ &= \alpha(t)p(t) + \int k(t \to u)\,[p(t) + \langle \xi(u) \rangle]\,du \end{aligned} \tag{16.163}$$

The first term is the payoff if the particle is absorbed at state t; it's the payoff at t times the probability of absorption. The second term is the payoff if the particle continues, found by computing the remaining payoff: we start with the payoff at state t, and add to it the payoff at every other state u to which it might go, times the probability that we would actually get a transfer from t to u, summed over all other possible states u.

The most important thing to note here is that we are integrating over all states we might *go to*, rather than all states we might have *come from*, as in previous equations. This is expressed by finding the value at state t by use of the kernel $k(t \to u)$, rather than $k(s \to t)$.

Recall that $\int k(t \to u)\,du = 1 - \alpha(t)$, where $\alpha(t)$ is the probability of absorption at state t. That is, the probability of moving anywhere includes the probability of moving nowhere, or staying in state t without change. Rearranging this equation to pull together the terms on $p(t)$, we find

$$\begin{aligned} w(t) &= \alpha(t)p(t) + \int k(t \to u)\,[p(t) + \langle \xi(u) \rangle]\,du \\ &= \alpha(t)p(t) + \int k(t \to u)p(t)\,du + \int k(t \to u)\langle \xi(u) \rangle\,du \\ &= p(t) + \int k(t \to u)\langle \xi(u) \rangle\,du \\ &= p(t) + \int k(t \to u)w(u)\,du \end{aligned} \tag{16.164}$$

The final line here can be interpreted as saying that the importance of state t is equal to the immediate payoff we get by virtue of being in t, times the remaining payoff from every other state u, times the probability of getting to u from t. This is illustrated in Figure 16.23. This is an important observation; we will return to it in a moment.

We can write down the value of w_p over different numbers of bounces p as we did for E. The importance $w_0(t)$ at t if there are no bounces remaining, as we have seen, is simply the immediate payoff at t:

$$w_0(t) = p(t) \tag{16.165}$$

The payoff after $p + 1$ bounces after t is similarly the p-bounce payoff at each state

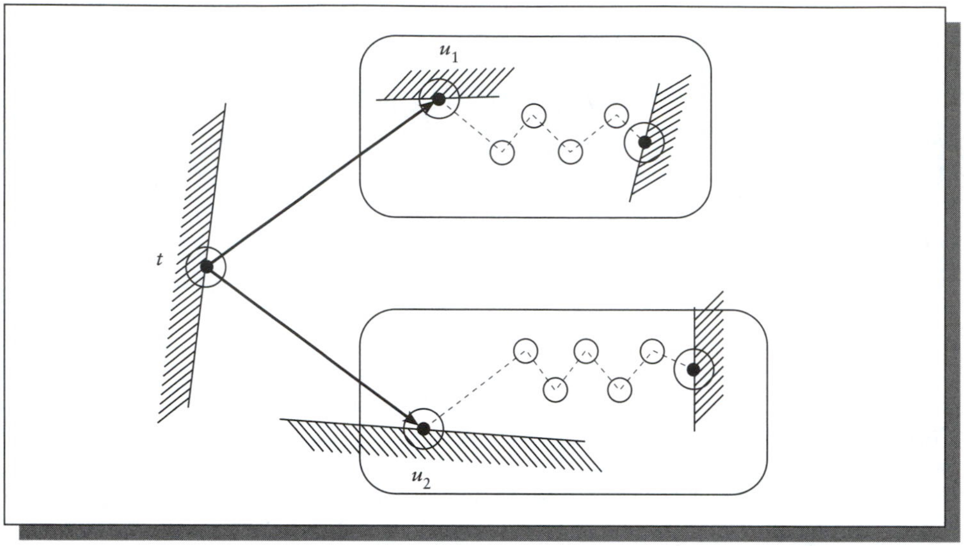

FIGURE 16.23
The importance at t is its immediate payoff, plus the payoff summed over every state u it can reach times the probability of reaching u from t.

v times the probability of reaching v:

$$w_{p+1}(t) = \int k(t \to v) w_p(v)\, dv \tag{16.166}$$

As mentioned earlier, the important difference between this equation for $w_{p+1}(t)$ and Equation 16.144 for $x_{p+1}(t)$ is that for importance we're integrating the importance from all the *future* states where the particle might go, while for x_{p+1} we integrated the probability from all the *past* states from which the particle might have come. In some sense, $w(t)$ tells us how much a particle at state t can still contribute to our result if allowed to continue; $x(t)$ tells us how many particles are in state t to deliver this potential contribution.

The payoff from a particle in state t after p bounces may be written in terms of the chances of getting to each state v times the immediate payoff at v:

$$w_p(t) = \int k_p(t \to v) p(v)\, dv \tag{16.167}$$

So the total payoff from state t is the payoff after all of its bounces:

$$\begin{aligned} w(t) &= \sum_{p=0}^{n} w_p(t) \\ &= G(t \to v)p(v)\, dv \end{aligned} \tag{16.168}$$

Now we return to our comment following Equation 16.164. Compare the interpretation of Equation 16.168 with that of Equation 16.164. Previously, we found the potential at t from the sum of the immediate payoff and the potential payoff everywhere we could go. Here the payoff comes from the chances of getting to state v times the immediate payoff at v.

We see that $w(t)$ is the importance function we referred to earlier. When we decide what domains to make "important" in a problem, we assign importances $p(t)$. Like light sources, these "importance sources" distribute their importance throughout the environment, delivering a potential importance to each surface. In general, this flow of importance is completely unrelated to the flow of "stuff" (e.g., light energy), which is used to find $x(t)$. The paths of particles distributing importance to $w(t)$ and those distributing light to $x(t)$ will be unrelated to each other except for their use of related kernels. Exercise 16.7 looks at this distinction.

Recalling our estimator $\lambda = \langle \eta \rangle$, we find

$$\begin{aligned} \lambda &= \sum_{k=0}^{\infty} p(S_k) \\ &= \int g(t)w(t)\, dt \\ &= \int g(t) \int G(t \to u)p(u)\, du\, dt \\ &= \iint g(t)G(t \to u)p(u)\, du\, dt \end{aligned} \tag{16.169}$$

We now have three equivalent forms for λ, each based on a different expression developed above [105].

1 From the expected density x,

$$x(t) = g(t) + \int x(s)k(s \to t)\, ds \tag{16.170}$$

the expected number of particles at state t is given by the number of particles created at t, plus the number of particles arriving at t from s, summed over all other states s; this arriving count comes from the number of particles at state s times the probability of a transition from s to t. We can then say

$$\lambda = \int x(t)p(t)\, dt \tag{16.171}$$

The total payoff is found by summing over each state t the expected number of particles at t times the immediate payoff per particle at t.

2 From the Green's function G,

$$G(u \to v) = \sum_{p=0}^{\infty} k_p(u \to v) \tag{16.172}$$

we have an expression for the likely number of times that a particle in state u will visit state v. From this we write

$$\lambda = \iint g(u)G(u \to v)p(v)\, du\, dv \tag{16.173}$$

The total contribution is found from the number of particles made at each state u, times the likelihood that each particle will get to state v, times the immediate payoff at state v, summed over all states u and v.

3 From the importance function w,

$$w(t) = p(t) + \int k(t \to u)w(u)\, du \tag{16.174}$$

The total potential of a particle in state t is the sum of its immediate payoff, plus the potential at every state u to which the particle might go times the probability of that transition. Then we can say

$$\lambda = \int g(t)w(t)\, dt \tag{16.175}$$

We can find the total payoff from the number of particles created at state t times the potential payoff of state t.

Recall that an inner product such as λ is just the sort of thing we are looking for in image synthesis; it might be the color of a pixel on the screen, or the amount of light striking a surface in the environment. We now have three different ways of looking at how to compute λ, based on the number of particles in each state and a function that tells us how much each state can contribute to λ.

The most important forms are the first and last in the list above. In the first form, particles are generated from the sources and then propagated throughout the environment. We find the total payoff to our measurement function by first finding this distribution of particles, and then weighting the number of particles at each state times the *immediate* payoff in that state. The third form finds the number of particles created in each state, and then finds the total payoff by weighting these particles by the *potential* payoff in that state.

Gathering these two expressions together,

$$x(t) = g(t) + \int x(s)k(s \to t)\, ds$$
$$w(t) = p(t) + \int k(t \to u)w(u)\, du \qquad (16.176)$$

or in operator notation,

$$x = g + \mathcal{K}x$$
$$w = p + \mathcal{K}^* w \qquad (16.177)$$

where $\mathcal{K}^*$ is the *adjoint* of operator $\mathcal{K}$, so the two equations above are said to be adjoints of each other, or a pair of adjoint equations. As we saw above, these adjoint equations lead to the *source-importance equality*:

$$\langle x|\, p\rangle = \langle g|\, w\rangle \qquad (16.178)$$

This important equality says that we can find our integral by looking at every state t, and *either* multiplying the eventual distribution at the state times the *immediate* payoff per particle, or multiplying the immediate (source) distribution times the *eventual* payoff per particle.

This equality also tells us that if we know w, then we know E, and vice versa, for a given p and g. But both functions x and w come from integral equations in the class $\mathcal{F}_2$ with similar (adjoint) kernels, so it's no easier to find one than the other.

We can now find estimates for the integrals defining λ by using traditional Monte Carlo importance sampling [239]. We start with the linear Boltzmann equation from Equation 16.1:

$$x(t) = g(t) + \int k(s \to t)x(s)\, ds \qquad (16.179)$$

Our goal is to find a new kernel $\acute{\mathcal{K}}$ which will bias our random walk toward the "interesting" or "important" states, as specified originally by p and distributed into the environment as w.

Suppose we have an importance function $I(t)$. For convenience, we will define a normalization constant g_0 over the sources which amplifies each source by its importance:

$$g_0 = \int I(t)g(t)\, dt \qquad (16.180)$$

Now we will define a new function $\acute{x}(t)$ that will be the new, importance-weighted pdf we will sample, but that still has the same integral. That is,

$$\int k(s \to t)x(s)\, ds = \int \frac{k(s \to t)x(s)}{\acute{x}(s)} \acute{x}(s)\, ds \qquad (16.181)$$

We build this new function by multiplying the basic integral equation through by $I(t)/g_0$:

$$\begin{aligned}\acute{x}(t) &= \frac{I(t)}{g_0}x(t)\\ &= \frac{g(t)I(t)}{g_0} + \int k(s \to t)\frac{I(t)}{g_0}\frac{I(s)}{I(s)}x(s)\,ds\\ &= \frac{g(t)I(t)}{g_0} + \int \frac{k(s \to t)I(t)}{I(s)}\frac{I(s)x(s)}{g_0}\,ds\\ &= \acute{g}(t) + \int \acute{k}(s \to t)\acute{x}(s)\,ds \end{aligned} \tag{16.182}$$

By construction, $\int \acute{g}(t)\,dt = 1$. So our desired value λ may then be found from

$$\begin{aligned}\lambda &= \int p(t)x(t)\,dt\\ &= \int p(t)\frac{g_0}{I(t)}\acute{x}(t)\,dt\\ &= g_0 \int \frac{p(t)}{I(t)}\acute{x}(t)\,dt \end{aligned} \tag{16.183}$$

This means that whenever $p(t) \neq 0$, we require $I(t) \neq 0$; that is, we are simply enforcing the reasonable constraint that our importance function I must be nonzero anywhere we have asserted that the immediate importance p is nonzero. Now we find λ by drawing values of t from $\acute{x}(t)$, which is a kernel weighted toward sampling the "important" states more often. We compensate for this distortion in the sampling process with the factor $g_0/I(t)$. But so far we haven't discussed how to find (or create) a good function $I(t)$.

A good $I(t)$ would be big at those states where the contribution to the final integral is big, so it reflects the amount by which particles at state t can contribute to λ. That is exactly the potential importance function $w(x)$ derived above. That is, it's the given importance $p(t)$ propagated into the environment, identifying those states that will affect the integral. From above,

$$w(t) = p(t) + \int k(t \to u)w(u)\,du \tag{16.184}$$

We can derive the adjoint identity from above by multiplying through this importance equation by the expected density $x(t)$, and multiplying through the transport equation by the potential importance $w(t)$, and integrating both equations over all states t:

$$\int w(t)x(t)\,dt = \int p(t)x(t)\,dt + \iint x(t)k(t \to u)w(u)\,dt\,du$$

$$\int x(t)w(t)\,dt = \int g(t)w(t)\,dt + \iint w(t)k(s \to t)x(s)\,ds\,dt \qquad (16.185)$$

The two double integrals on the right are equal, since we are free to rename the dummy variables in the integration. The two left-hand sides are also clearly the same, so the first left-side terms are equal, giving us the source-importance identity Equation 16.178.

Now that we have developed some intuition behind the importance function and how it gets used, we can boil down the entire discussion into just a few basic equations, originally presented to the graphics community by Smits et al. [414], Pattanaik [332], and Pattanaik and Mudur [334]. The main advantage of this step is that it allows us to conveniently summarize our observations, and it makes further manipulations much easier.

We summarize our adjoint equations as

$$\begin{aligned} x &= g + \mathcal{K}x \\ w &= p + \mathcal{K}^* w \end{aligned} \qquad (16.186)$$

We recall from earlier in this chapter that when the operator $\mathcal{K}$ is finite, it may be represented as a matrix K. In computer graphics this will be a matrix of real numbers. Then the adjoint of K is its transpose; that is, $K^* = K^t$. In this case, we can show that $(I - K)^t = I - K^t$ (see Exercise 16.6). So for a matrix $L = I - K$, $L^* = L^t$.

We can rewrite Equation 16.186 in finite dimensions in terms of the matrix L, and column vectors for each of the source and distributed quantities in Equation 16.186:

$$\begin{aligned} L\mathbf{x} &= \mathbf{g} \\ L^t\mathbf{w} &= \mathbf{p} \end{aligned} \qquad (16.187)$$

Equations 16.187 relate the given importance $\mathbf{p}$ to the distributed importance $\mathbf{w}$, and the given source function $\mathbf{g}$ to the distributed information $\mathbf{x}$. These quantities are related through two different uses of the same kernel.

Before leaving this material, we will take a look at the error in λ that comes about from using the finite approximate matrix operator L rather than the exact operator $\mathcal{L}$ [413]. We start with the scalar $\lambda = \mathbf{p}^t\mathbf{x}$ (recall that both $\mathbf{p}$ and $\mathbf{x}$ are column vectors, so we need to transpose one of them to form an inner product):

$$\begin{aligned} \lambda(\mathbf{x}) &= \mathbf{p}^t\mathbf{x} \\ &= (L^t\mathbf{w})^t\mathbf{x} \\ &= \mathbf{w}^t L\mathbf{x} \\ &= \mathbf{w}^t\mathbf{g} \end{aligned} \qquad (16.188)$$

When we replace $\mathcal{L}$ with an approximation L, such as one of the finite-space approximations discussed in this chapter, we can write the approximation as the sum of the exact solution plus an error term: $L = \mathcal{L} + \Delta L$. We might then have an exact solution $\widetilde{\mathbf{x}}$ to the approximation integral equation:

$$L\widetilde{\mathbf{x}} = \mathbf{g} \tag{16.189}$$

or, expanding the approximate operator,

$$\mathcal{L}\widetilde{\mathbf{x}} = \mathbf{g} - \Delta L\widetilde{\mathbf{x}} \tag{16.190}$$

Now, to see what happens to the integral, we find the effect of this change in $\mathcal{L}$ to the value of λ. Since λ is linear,

$$\begin{aligned}\lambda(\mathbf{x} - \widetilde{\mathbf{x}}) &= \lambda(\mathbf{x}) - \lambda(\widetilde{\mathbf{x}}) \\ &= \mathbf{p}^t\mathbf{x} - \mathbf{p}^t\widetilde{\mathbf{x}} \\ &= \mathbf{w}^t\mathbf{g} - \mathbf{w}^t L\widetilde{\mathbf{x}} \\ &= \mathbf{w}^t\mathbf{g} - \mathbf{w}^t(\mathbf{g} - \Delta L\widetilde{\mathbf{x}}) \\ &= \mathbf{w}^t\Delta L\widetilde{\mathbf{x}}\end{aligned} \tag{16.191}$$

So $\mathbf{w}^t\Delta L\widetilde{\mathbf{x}}$ is the error due to using an approximate $\mathcal{L}$ and $\mathbf{x}$. If we knew $\mathbf{w}$, we would know this error, but determining $\mathbf{w}$ means solving an integral equation of the same form required to find $\mathbf{x}$; if we knew one, we would know the other. A useful practical technique is to estimate $\mathbf{w}$ and compute the error $\widetilde{\mathbf{w}}^t\Delta L\widetilde{\mathbf{x}}$.

16.10 Singularities

When the kernel (or free term) in an integral equation is smooth and continuous, the techniques described earlier in this chapter are appropriate. But when these conditions fail, the algorithms may converge slowly or fail altogether. We say that an integral equation is *singular* if one of the following conditions holds [120]:

- The domain of the integral is infinite or semi-infinite.
- The kernel has an infinite or nonexisting derivative.
- The kernel is discontinuous.
- The kernel or free term has discontinuous derivatives.

These conditions are known as *singularities*. In computer graphics we are mostly concerned with singularities of the third and fourth types. For example, consider the integral equation that determines the incident light arriving at some point on a surface. If there is a bright light source blocked by an object with a sharp edge, the illumination function will have a discontinuity at that edge, where the incident light goes from bright to dark. When an integral is not singular, we say it is *regular*.

It is extremely important to handle singularities if we want to get accurate results efficiently. Unfortunately, there is no general method that handles all types of singularities in all situations; generally we must design a technique to suit the particular problem. This is the case in rendering, where singularities have received some focused attention. We will discuss some of these specialized methods in Chapter 17. For now, we will give a brief overview of the general ideas that lie behind most singularity-handling algorithms. Our discussion is mostly based on Delves and Mohamed [120] and Kondo [251].

Singularities can be distinguished into two types: *benign* and *malignant*. Sometimes a singularity in the free term can exactly cancel out a singularity in the kernel, resulting in a smooth solution function. Such cooperative singularities are *benign*. On the other hand, singularities that induce singular solution functions are called *malignant*, since they propagate into our results. In the following discussion we will only address singularities in the kernel.

There is no single best way to handle all forms of singularities. A review of the existing tools suggests that there are six general approaches:

Ignorance: Simply pretend that the singularity doesn't exist. We might never even check for the presence of singularities in the first place.

Removal: Change the kernel so that the singularity no longer exists, typically by subtracting a function that captures the singularity, and then include an error term to correct for the change.

Factorization: Rewrite the kernel as the product of two terms, only one of which is singular. If we're lucky, the singular kernel has a simpler form than the original and is amenable to repair by the other methods on this list.

Avoidance: Change the domain of integration to side-step the singularity.

Divide and conquer: Break up the domain of the integral into several smaller domains. Leave a gap (perhaps of zero measure) between domains where the singularity lurks.

Coexistence: Accept the singularity in the kernel, and rather than try to change the problem, change the quadrature rule so that the singularity doesn't cause the integration error to explode.

These approaches do not all have sharp boundaries; for example, divide and conquer has much in common with coexistence.

To give the flavor of these methods, we will discuss four of them—*removal*, *factorization*, *divide and conquer*, and *coexistence*—below. We will see some of these methods applied to the radiance equation in Chapter 17.

16.10.1 Removal

Suppose the kernel is singular for all values of u for a given value of t; for example, $k(t,u) = 1/(u-q)$ for some value of q. More generally, we can write such a kernel as

$$k(t,u) = \frac{k_0(t,u)}{(u-q)^m} \tag{16.192}$$

for some nonsingular kernel $\mathcal{K}_0$. We say that such a kernel has a *pole of order m* at $u = q$. We can rewrite the kernel to reduce the effect of this singularity by subtracting a term; this operation on the singularity is abbreviated in the list above as *removal*.

We add and subtract a term $\mathcal{K}_0(t,q)$ to the kernel and then rearrange the terms as follows:

$$\begin{aligned}\int_a^b k(t,u)x(u)\,du &= \int_a^b \frac{[k_0(t,u)x(u) - k_0(t,q)x(q) + k_0(t,q)x(q)]\,du}{(u-q)^m} \\ &= \int_a^b \frac{[k_0(t,u)x(u) - k_0(t,q)x(q)]\,du}{(u-q)^m} \\ &\quad + k_0(t,q)x(q) - \int_a^b \frac{du}{(u-q)^m}\end{aligned} \tag{16.193}$$

If $m \leq 1$, then the first term is regular at $t = q$, because the numerator goes to zero faster than the denominator. The second term can be integrated exactly:

$$\int_a^b \frac{du}{(u-q)^m} = \left.\frac{q-u}{(m-1)(u-q)^m}\right|_{u=a}^{b} \tag{16.194}$$

If $m > 1$, then neither integral exists, and we have to resort to other techniques to handle the singularity.

Another common form of singularity is along the line $t = u$. We can *weaken* this type of singularity with a more direct form of subtraction, by simply removing $x(t)$ at $t = t$:

$$\begin{aligned}\int_a^b k(t,u)x(u)\,du &= \int_a^b k(t,u)[x(u) - x(t) + x(t)]\,du \\ &= \int_a^b k(t,u)[x(u) - x(t)]\,du + \int_a^b k(t,u)x(t)\,du \\ &= \int_a^b k(t,u)[x(u) - x(t)]\,du + x(t)r(t)\end{aligned} \tag{16.195}$$

where

$$r(t) = \int_a^b k(t,u)\,du \tag{16.196}$$

is assumed to be known or can be found.

In general, this type of approach works with the function that generalizes Equation 16.192 to the form

$$\frac{b(t)}{\prod_{i=1}^{n}(t-q_i)^{m_i}} = \frac{b(t)}{c(t)} \tag{16.197}$$

which has n poles, each one located at a q_i with order m_i. We want to find a function $x(t) = b(t)c(t)$ to knock out the singularities.

It turns out that for many functions this weakening of the singularity can be done in a straightforward way, but it's algebraically messy and not very illuminating; the details may be found in Delves and Mohamed [120].

16.10.2 Factorization

Sometimes a complicated, singular kernel can be considered the *product* of two simpler kernels, one regular and one singular. The simpler, singular kernel may be easier to work with. On the list we call this approach to a singularity *factorization.*

The goal is to *factorize* the original kernel $k(t, u)$ as the product of two kernels,

$$k(t,u) = p(t,u)k_0(t,u) \tag{16.198}$$

where $p(t, u)$ is an *ill-behaved* function that contains all the singularities in the original kernel, while $k_0(t, u)$ is *well-behaved*, or regular. We will treat $p(t, u)$ exactly, and approximate $k_0(t, u)$ as usual, say with a quadrature rule. A drawback of this approach is that we need to be able to find some information about the function p, say its moments m_{ij} with respect to the monomials:

$$m_{ij} = \int_a^b p(t_i, u)u^j \, du \tag{16.199}$$

If we can find these moments, then we can build a set of rules based on the method of undetermined coefficients [120].

In extreme cases, Equation 16.198 may be extended to represent the sum of many such products:

$$k(t,u) = \sum_{i=1}^{N} p_i(t,u)k_{0,i}(t,u) \tag{16.200}$$

where, thanks to linearity, we can break up the total integral operator $\mathcal{K}$ into a sum of smaller integrals, and attempt to handle each p_i individually.

16.10.3 Divide and Conquer

If the singularity can be handled by splitting up the kernel, then because the kernel operator is linear, we can write the original operation as the sum of two smaller integrals. For example, if the singularity is tightly localized within a disk of radius ϵ around a value $u = q$, then we can write

$$\int_a^b k(t,u)x(u)\,du \approx \int_a^{q-\epsilon} k(t,u)x(u)\,du + \int_{q+\epsilon}^b k(t,u)x(u)\,du \tag{16.201}$$

This approach is listed above as *divide and conquer.* Note that the nature of the kernel over the two domains may be quite different; for example, it may be smooth over the first domain but complicated over the second. We may therefore choose to use different quadrature rules in the two domains.

16.10.4 Coexistence

Rather than try to change the kernel or the original integral equation, we accept it as written and recognize that we will eventually need to use a quadrature rule to evaluate it. This represents another avenue of attack on the problem, since we can tune the rule to the singularity. We might say that by changing the quadrature rule in response to the kernel, we are *coexisting* with the singularity rather than trying to remove it.

This approach has been used with some success in computer graphics. In particular, the calculation of form factors in the radiosity method is particularly sensitive to singularities when two polygons abut. To solve this problem in Galerkin methods, a modified inner product has been used during the quadrature step [503], and a form of divide and conquer has been developed for general bases by adaptively tiling the domain [383].

16.11 Further Reading

Excellent modern surveys of numerical methods for integral equations are offered in the books by Delves and Mohamed [120] and Porter and Stirling [343]; these books are the primary references for this chapter. A good concise summary article is Golberg's dsicussion in [162]. An extensive literature survey to 1976 has been compiled by Atkinson [22]; a survey directed to computer graphics was written in 1993 by Arvo [14].

Good general references to integral equations may be found in the above books. More theoretical developments may be found in books by Kondo [251], Cochran [93], and Kanwal [240]. Many examples of integrals evaluated using a plethora of different methods are given by Baker [26]. Issues of convergence are discussed by Sloan [413]. Error analysis is covered by Baker [26]; a rigorous discussion may be found in the book by Kress [254]. Multigrid methods for solution of integral equations are discussed in a thesis by Schippers [379]; an error analysis appears there and in the article by Hackbusch [176]. Singular integral equations form a subfield of their own. The classic reference on singular integral equations is the book by Muskhelishvili [315]. Another useful book in this area is by Mikhlin [303]. Descriptions of linear integral equation solution systems, complete with code and error analysis, are given by Atkinson [22] (also available in [21]), and Schippers [379], as well as many articles in the high-energy physics journals directed to solving nuclear transport problems.

The literature on integral equations is enormous and expanding. Two comprehensive bibliographies that capture the state of the literature to 1971 are Voigt's [456] and Noble's [324]; I know of no comparable bibliography on the subject since.

16.12 Exercises

Exercise 16.1

Find the iterated kernel of order 2 for the kernel $k(t, u) = su$.

Exercise 16.2

Use the Fubini theorem to show that if k is independent of u,

$$\int_{u=0}^{s} \int_{v=0}^{u} k(v)\, dv\, du = \int_{v=0}^{s} (t - v) k(v)\, dv \tag{16.202}$$

Exercise 16.3

Use a symbolic math program to help you compute the Newton-Cotes rule for $N = 3$. Use the interval $[a, a + 2h]$ and quadrature points $\{a, a + h, a + 2h\}$. Does this rule have a common name?

Exercise 16.4

The Tchebyshev polynomial of degree n is written $T_n(t)$ and is defined by

$$T_n(t) = \cos(n \cos^{-1} s) \tag{16.203}$$

This may be expanded and simplified with trig identities to get the recurrence formula

$$\begin{aligned} T_{n+1}(t) &= 2sT_n(t) - T_{n-1}(t) \qquad n \geq 1 \\ T_0(t) &= 1 \\ T_1(t) &= s \end{aligned} \tag{16.204}$$

(a) Write out expressions for $T_1(t)$ through $T_6(t)$.

(b) Use the method of undetermined coefficients to find the equivalent to the trapezoid rule ($N = 2$) using $\{T_n(t)\}$ as a basis. How do the rules compare?

(c) Use the method of undetermined coefficients to find the equivalent to the $N = 3$ rule you found in Exercise 16.3 for the monomial basis, but use $\{T_n(t)\}$ as a basis. How do the rules compare?

Exercise 16.5

Derive Equation 16.152.

Exercise 16.6

Show that $(I - K)^t = I - K^t$ for a real matrix K.

Exercise 16.7

(a) Suppose we distribute importance exactly along with the driving function; that is, $p(t) = g(t)$. Describe how importance will flow through such a scene with respect to the particles used to find $x(t)$.

(b) Suppose we have a complete solution $x(t)$ and set $p(t) = x(t)$; describe the flow of importance in this situation.

An object known as a camera . . . It pretends to be an ally, but it's not. It's a beckoning come-on for a quick walk around the block—in the Twilight Zone.

Rod Serling
("The Twilight Zone": "A Most Unusual Camera," 1940)

17

THE RADIANCE EQUATION

17.1 Introduction

In this chapter we combine the transport equation with radiometry to arrive at the radiance equation. This is the central equation of image synthesis, because it completely captures the distribution of light in a scene (limited to our built-in restriction to geometric optics). The problem is that the radiance distribution L is described *implicitly*, so we know what conditions it must satisfy, but we don't know what it actually is.

The process of shading in Chapter 15 was based on our being able to find a complete and explicit description of the light falling on a point. The heart of the image synthesis algorithms in this book is to use the radiance equation to find such a description.

17.2 Forming the Radiance Equation

Recall from Chapter 12 the integral form of the transport equation expressed in terms of flux, which we expand here so we can see all the terms:

$$\Phi(\mathbf{r},\vec{\omega}) = \mu(\mathbf{r},\mathbf{s})\left[\epsilon(\mathbf{s},\vec{\omega}) + \int_{\Omega_i} k(\mathbf{s},\vec{\omega}' \to \vec{\omega})\Phi(\mathbf{s},\vec{\omega}')\,d\vec{\omega}'\right] +$$
$$\int_0^h \mu(\mathbf{r},\mathbf{a})\left[\epsilon(\mathbf{a},\vec{\omega}) + \int_{\Theta_i^i} k(\mathbf{a},\vec{\omega}' \to \vec{\omega})\Phi(\mathbf{a},\vec{\omega}')\,d\vec{\omega}'\right] d\alpha \tag{17.1}$$

where here and for the rest of this chapter we write $\mathbf{a} = \mathbf{r} - \alpha\vec{\omega}$.

To find the radiance equation, we follow Arvo [15] and begin by expressing this function in terms of radiance rather than flux. Comparing the definitions of radiance and flux from Equations 13.12 and 13.7, we can see that radiance is just the flux Φ times the energy E of the photons being carried:

$$L = E\Phi \tag{17.2}$$

Each of the terms in Equation 17.1 may be expressed in terms appropriate for radiance by simply multiplying by the energy of the photons involved.

So the big picture is that to find the radiance at a point $\mathbf{r}$ coming from a direction $\vec{\omega}$, we find the nearest surface point $\mathbf{s} = h(\mathbf{r},\vec{\omega})$, compute its outgoing radiance into $\vec{\omega}$, and accumulate all the radiance due to volume emission or inscattering along the way from $\mathbf{s}$. Schematically, we can write this as

$$L(\mathbf{r},\vec{\omega}) = L(\mathbf{s} \to \mathbf{r}) + \int L(\mathbf{a} \to \mathbf{r})\,d\alpha \tag{17.3}$$

where $\mathbf{s}$ is the nearest point on a surface in direction $\vec{\omega}$ as seen from $\mathbf{r}$, and $\mathbf{a}$ is swept by α to generate all the points along the line from $\mathbf{s}$ to $\mathbf{r}$.

We will now make three changes to this basic equation to promote it to the full-fledged radiance equation: we will replace the scattering function k with the *BDF*, and add *phosphorescence* and *fluorescence*.

17.2.1 BDF

The first change we will make to Equation 17.1 is to re-express the scattering function k in terms of the bidirectional functions of Chapter 13. Recall that those functions express outgoing radiance in terms of incident *irradiance*, so each right-hand term $L(\mathbf{p},\vec{\omega})$ gets replaced by $L(\mathbf{p},\vec{\omega})\cos\theta$, where θ is the angle between $\vec{\omega}$ and the normal to the surface at $\mathbf{p}$. When $\mathbf{p}$ is a point in space, the "normal" is the direction in which we're integrating.

We also use the *bidirectional surface-scattering distribution function* (the BSSDF, or simply BDF) f, which is a combination of the *bidirectional reflection distribution function* (or BRDF) f_r, and the *bidirectional transmission distribution function* (or BTDF) f_t. This means that we now integrate over all incident directions Θ_i^i rather than just the hemisphere Ω_i required for reflection.

We will continue to use the scattering term k until Section 17.2.4 when we assemble the radiance-based flux equation.

To satisfy BDFs that depend on polarization, we will also include an ellipsometric vector $\mathbf{e}$ in the description of the radiance $L(\mathbf{r}, \vec{\omega})$.

17.2.2 Phosphorescence

Recall from Chapter 14 that *phosphorescence* is a phenomenon whereby a material traps incident energy for longer than about 10^{-8} seconds before re-emitting it as visible light. Generally this re-emission has no directional character but is radiated uniformly in all directions; that is, it appears as perfect diffuse emission.

To model phosphorescence we will break down the emission term in Equation 17.1 into a *blackbody* (or *thermal* or *incandescent*) term ϵ_b and a *phosphorescent* term ϵ_p:

$$\epsilon(\mathbf{p}, t, \lambda) = \epsilon_b(\mathbf{p}, \vec{\omega}, t, \lambda) + \epsilon_p(\mathbf{p}, \vec{\omega}, t, \lambda) \tag{17.4}$$

The incandescent term comes from Equation 14.49, which gives the light from a blackbody in terms of its temperature T and the surrounding index of refraction $\eta(\nu)$. We will write the temperature as a function of position $\mathbf{p}$ and time t. Normally, incandescent radiation has no preferred direction; it is isotropic. But it is very convenient in computer graphics to associate directional characteristics with light sources; these can be due to low-level geometric and physical properties that we don't want to explicitly include in our models. The easiest way to include these terms is to introduce a modulating function $m_b(\vec{\omega})$ into the expression for the blackbody emission, giving us

$$\epsilon_b(\nu, \vec{\omega}, \mathbf{p}, t) = m_b(\vec{\omega}) \frac{2\pi h \nu^3}{c^2} \frac{1}{\exp\left[h\nu / kT(\mathbf{p}, t)\right] - 1} \tag{17.5}$$

(recall $\nu = c/\lambda$). For convenience, rather than work with the energy given by ϵ_b, we will work with its related radiance L^e.

The phosphorescent term may be derived by simply modeling the behavior of phosphorescent materials. At any given moment, the energy absorbed at a point $\mathbf{p}$ at wavelength λ is determined by the energy arriving from every direction $\vec{\omega} \in \Theta_i^i$ at λ, times a *phosphorescence efficiency* function $P_p(\lambda)$. This energy decays over time as it is radiated according to a decay function $d(t)$. So the radiance at a given moment is the result of all the energy absorbed in the past, times how it's been since that energy was absorbed. We model the absorption term by integrating the irradiance over all directions (giving us the total energy absorbed at that wavelength), and then scaling the result by the efficiency of the material at that wavelength. The total phosphorescent emission at a particular time is given by an integral over all time, which weights the absorption at a given time by the decay function since then. Like the incandescent term, we can add a direction-dependent modulation function m_p into the definition to account for fine surface geometry. In symbols,

$$\epsilon_p(\mathbf{p}, \vec{\omega}, t, \lambda) = m_p(\vec{\omega}) \int_{-\infty}^{t} d(t-\tau) P_p(\mathbf{p}, \lambda) \int_{\Theta_i^i} L(\mathbf{p}, \vec{\omega}', \lambda, \tau) \cos\theta' \, d\vec{\omega}' \, d\tau \quad (17.6)$$

where θ' is the angle made by $\vec{\omega}'$ with respect to the normal at $\mathbf{p}$.

Equation 17.6 is missing a *saturation* component. After a certain point, the material cannot store any more energy at a given wavelength, and the excess is converted to heat or is not absorbed at all. So the scaling factor P_p should actually depend on how much room is left for storing energy at a given wavelength. This would make the expression much more complex; our approximation is designed for low illuminations.

Recall that a good candidate for d is the model in Equation 14.58 proposed by Leverenz [267]:

$$L(t, L_0) = \frac{1}{b\left(\frac{1}{\sqrt{L_0 b}} + t\right)^2} \quad (17.7)$$

A material with no phosphorescence may be modeled with a discrete delta function $d(\tau) = \delta[t - \tau]$; that is,

$$d(\tau) = \begin{cases} 1 & t = \tau \\ 0 & \text{otherwise} \end{cases} \quad (17.8)$$

17.2.3 Fluorescence

Recall from Chapter 14 that *fluorescence* is a phenomenon whereby a material absorbs light at one frequency and then reradiates it at another frequency within about 10^{-8} seconds. Like phosphorescence, this re-emission has no directional character.

To model fluorescence we change the scattering function to account for this transfer of energy from one wavelength to the next. Rather than simply integrating over all incident directions and weighting the energy at each one, we also integrate over all visible wavelengths and scale by a *fluorescence efficiency* $P_f(\lambda' \to \lambda)$ that models the transfer of energy from λ' to λ. In other words, we look in each direction and scatter not just the energy at λ, but the energy at all other λ' that will be absorbed and reradiated at λ. Symbolically, the scattering term becomes

$$\int_{\Theta_i^i} f(\mathbf{p}, \vec{\omega}' \to \vec{\omega}) \int_{\mathcal{R}_\mathcal{V}} P_f(\mathbf{p}, \lambda' \to \lambda) L(\mathbf{p}, \vec{\omega}', \lambda')\, d\lambda'\, d\vec{\omega}' \tag{17.9}$$

If a material has no fluorescence, then P_f may be modeled with a discrete delta function $P_f(\lambda' \to \lambda) = \delta[\lambda - \lambda']$.

17.2.4 FRE

We can now put together the pieces above. We assume that there is no fluorescent-phosphorescent interaction; that is, energy absorbed at a wavelength λ for fluorescent reradiation at λ' does not contribute to later phosphorescent reradiation at λ'. There's no mathematical reason not to model such an effect, but I have not seen it reported in the literature on luminescence [267].

To build the complete radiance equation we can replace the emission and scattering terms in Equation 17.1 with Equations 17.6 and 17.9, respectively. This gives us the following complete (but formidable) result for the radiance at wavelength λ arriving at a point $\mathbf{r}$ from a direction $\vec{\omega}$ at time t:

$$\begin{aligned}
L(\mathbf{r}, \vec{\omega}, \lambda, \mathbf{e}, t) = \mu(\mathbf{r}, \mathbf{s}) \Big[& L^e(\mathbf{s}, \vec{\omega}, t, \lambda) \\
& + m_p(\vec{\omega}) \int_{-\infty}^{t} d(t-\tau) P_p(\mathbf{s}, \lambda) \int_{\Theta_i^i} L(s, \vec{\omega}', \lambda, \mathbf{e}, \tau) \cos\theta'\, d\vec{\omega}'\, d\tau \\
& + \int_{\Theta_i^i} f(\mathbf{s}, \lambda, \vec{\omega}' \to \vec{\omega}) \int_{\mathcal{R}_\mathcal{V}} P_f(\mathbf{s}, \lambda' \to \lambda) L(\mathbf{s}, \vec{\omega}', \lambda', \mathbf{e}, t)\, d\lambda' \, \cos\theta'\, d\vec{\omega}' \Big] \\
+ \int_0^{h(\mathbf{r}, \vec{\omega})} & \mu(\mathbf{r}, \mathbf{a}) \Big[L^e(\mathbf{a}, \vec{\omega}, t, \lambda) \\
& + m_p(\vec{\omega}) \int_{-\infty}^{t} d(t-\tau) P_p(\mathbf{a}, \lambda) \int_{\Theta_i^i} L(s, \vec{\omega}', \lambda, \mathbf{e}, \tau) \cos\theta'\, d\vec{\omega}'\, d\tau \\
& + \int_{\Theta_i^i} f(\mathbf{a}, \lambda, \vec{\omega}' \to \vec{\omega}) \int_{\mathcal{R}_\mathcal{V}} P_f(\mathbf{a}, \lambda' \to \lambda) L(\mathbf{a}, \vec{\omega}', \lambda', \mathbf{e}, t)\, d\lambda' \, \cos\theta'\, d\vec{\omega}' \Big] \, d\alpha
\end{aligned} \tag{17.10}$$

where

$$\mathbf{a} = \mathbf{r} - \alpha\vec{\omega}$$
$$f(\mathbf{s}, \lambda, \vec{\omega}' \to \vec{\omega}) = \text{the surface BDF at } \mathbf{s}$$
$$f(\mathbf{a}, \lambda, \vec{\omega}' \to \vec{\omega}) = \text{the volume BDF at } \mathbf{a}$$

Equation 17.10 is the *Full Radiance Equation*, which we refer to simply as the FRE.[1]

The FRE is frankly a very difficult-looking expression, but it's just a collection of smaller pieces collected into two groups, and a wrapper that combines the groups. The main idea that shows the two groups is in Equation 17.3. All we have done is expand out those groups using the definitions above.

The FRE can be tamed somewhat by putting it into operator notation. This doesn't make it any easier to solve, but it is a bit easier to take in all the steps at once. The definitions of the operators come directly from their use in Equation 17.10. The operator form of the FRE may be written

$$L = (\mathcal{M} + \mathcal{V})[L^e + \mathcal{P}\mathcal{A}L + \mathcal{K}\mathcal{F}L] \tag{17.11}$$

where

$\mathcal{M}$ represents the attenuation of radiance from point $\mathbf{s}$,
$\mathcal{V}$ represents the attenuation of radiance from point $\mathbf{a}$ between $\mathbf{r}$ and $\mathbf{s}$,
$\mathcal{P}$ is the phosphorescence operator,
$\mathcal{F}$ is the fluorescence operator,
$\mathcal{A}$ is the absorption operator, and
$\mathcal{K}$ is the BDF operator.

There is no hope of solving the full radiance equation analytically for the function L, even if we had all of the other functions in a reasonable form. Much of practical image synthesis has been devoted to finding efficient and accurate approximations to solutions of this equation, by approximating either the solution, the equation, or both. That is, since an exact solution to the exact equation is intractable, we instead seek out exact solutions to an approximate equation, approximate solutions to the exact equation, or (most commonly) approximate solutions to an approximate equation.

---

[1] The name *radiance equation* is similar to, but deliberately distinct from, the name *rendering equation* used by Kajiya [234]. Although Equation 17.10 could reasonably be called a "rendering equation," the relationship given that name by Kajiya corresponds to our Equation 17.14, which is derived by a set of additional assumptions. I think that reassigning an existing name to a new equation is likely to cause confusion, so I have chosen a new name.

17.3 TIGRE

The FRE in Equation 17.10 is enough to challenge even the strongest of heart. Since we know that an exact solution to the exact equation is unlikely to be found for a nontrivial environment, we need to start cutting corners somewhere. The most common approximation is to eliminate the terms for polarization, phosphorescence, and fluorescence.

Eliminating polarization means that we are assuming that all light in the image is unpolarized. If we avoid coherent light sources like lasers, we can start without polarized light, but we know from Fresnel's laws that at Brewster's angle (recall Equation 15.11) light will reflect off of a surface linearly polarized. If polarization is important for a particular image, we can run linearly independent simulations and then combine them.

By eliminating fluorescence we are asserting that all wavelengths are *decoupled*. That is, the solution to the radiance at wavelength λ is independent of the solution at some other λ'. This means that we can compute a color image by solving a simplified radiance equation several times at several different wavelengths, and then combining the results. It also makes it much easier to compute color images using basis functions rather than spectral samples, since we don't introduce arbitrary transformations on the bases. We can't leave out the wavelength altogether, since the index of refraction depends upon it, so it remains in the expression for the scattering function. The result is called a *monochromatic* or *gray* equation.

By eliminating phosphorescence we are asserting that every instant of time is the same as every other instant for the system. The underlying 3D model may change at each moment, but when we solve the rendering equation we assume that the model has been frozen in position in an enclosed environment without any illumination, and that only when the simulation begins are the lights turned on. Recalling our terminology from Unit II, this means that the modified radiance equation is *time-invariant*.

The resulting simplified equation is then

$$\begin{aligned} L(\mathbf{r},\vec{\omega}) &= \mu(\mathbf{r},\mathbf{s})\left[L^e(\mathbf{s},\vec{\omega}) + \int_{\Theta_i^i} f(\mathbf{s},\vec{\omega}' \to \vec{\omega},\lambda)L(\mathbf{s},\vec{\omega}')\cos\theta'\,d\vec{\omega}'\right] \\ &+ \int_0^{h(\mathbf{r},\vec{\omega})} \mu(\mathbf{r},\mathbf{a})\left[L^e(\mathbf{a},\vec{\omega}) + \int_{\Theta_i^i} f(\mathbf{a},\vec{\omega}' \to \vec{\omega},\lambda)L(\mathbf{a},\vec{\omega}')\cos\theta'\,d\vec{\omega}'\right] d\alpha \end{aligned} \tag{17.12}$$

Equation 17.12 is the *time-invariant, gray radiance equation*, or TIGRE. Notice that TIGRE contains volumetric terms, so it accommodates *participating media* such

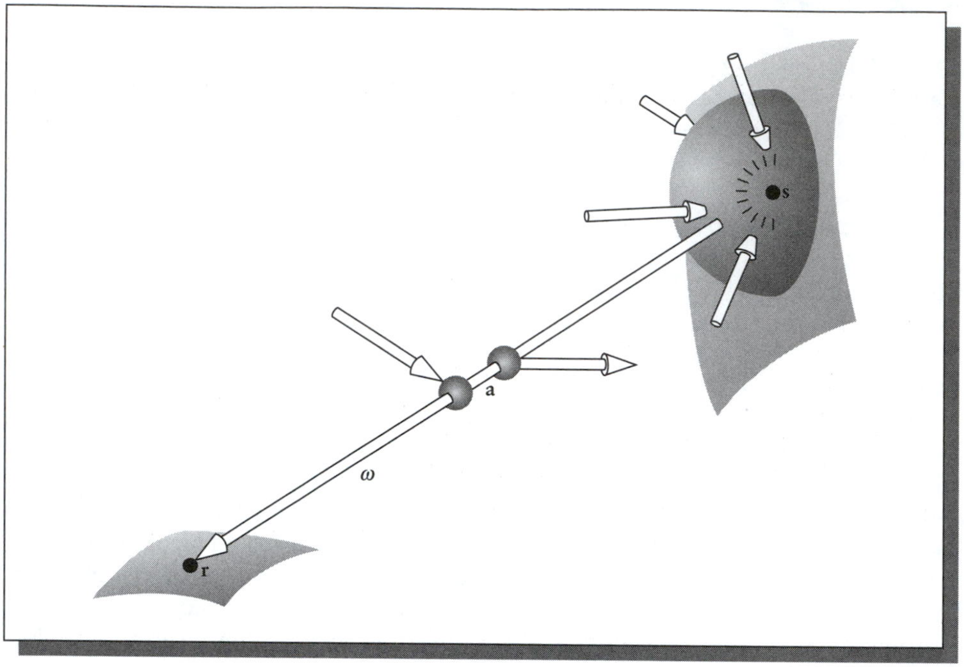

FIGURE 17.1
The geometry of TIGRE.

as smoke and fog, as well as volumetric objects defined not by surfaces but by fields in space. The geometry behind TIGRE is shown in Figure 17.1.

In operator notation, TIGRE may be written

$$L = (\mathcal{M} + \mathcal{V})[L^e + \mathcal{K}L] \tag{17.13}$$

17.4 VTIGRE

The formulation of TIGRE in Equation 17.12 is much simpler than the full radiance equation, but it is often simplified even further by assuming that all synthesis occurs in a vacuum. Under vacuum conditions, the entire right-hand term on the right side of Equation 17.12 goes to zero: there is no volumetric emission, so $L^e(\mathbf{a}, \vec{\omega}) = 0$, and no scattering or absorption, so $f(\mathbf{a}, \vec{\omega}' \to \vec{\omega}, \lambda) = 0$, and $\mu(\mathbf{r}, \mathbf{s}) = \exp\left[\int_0^{||\mathbf{r}-\mathbf{s}||} 0 \, d\tau\right] =$

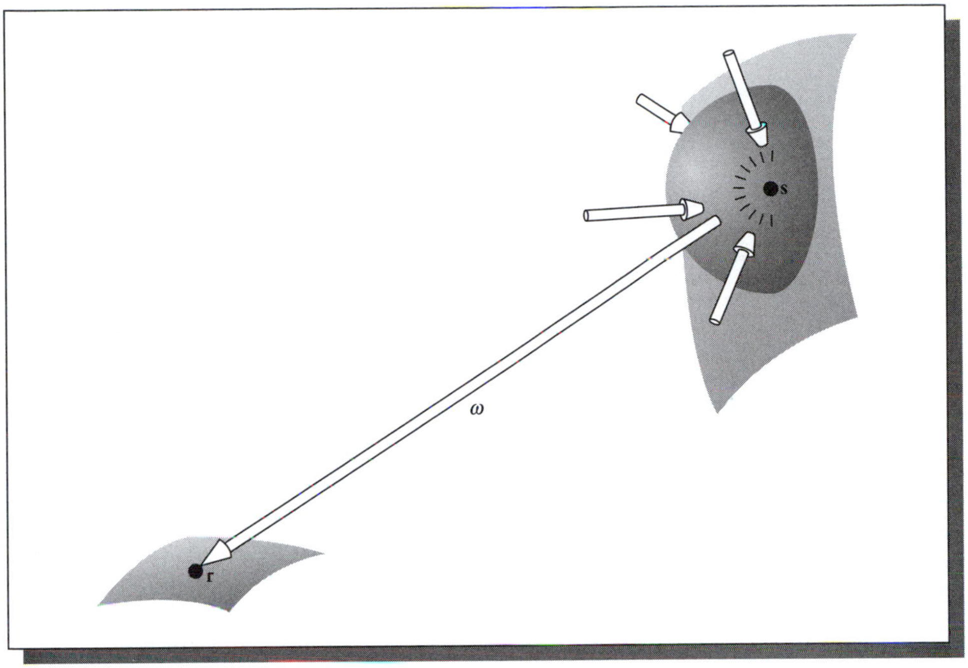

FIGURE 17.2
The geometry of VTIGRE.

$e^0 = 1$. The result is then

$$L(\mathbf{r}, \vec{\omega}) = L^e(\mathbf{s}, \vec{\omega}) + \int_{\Theta_i^i} f(\mathbf{s}, \vec{\omega}' \to \vec{\omega}, \lambda) L(\mathbf{s}, \vec{\omega}') \cos\theta' \, d\vec{\omega}' \tag{17.14}$$

Equation 17.14 is the *vacuum, time-invariant, gray radiance equation*, or VTIGRE. This equation expresses the same physics as the *rendering equation* introduced by Kajiya [234]. We chose not to use that name here because this is a special case of the full radiance equation (see footnote on page 876). The geometry behind VTIGRE is shown in Figure 17.2. In operator notation, VTIGRE may be written

$$L = L^e + \mathcal{K}L \tag{17.15}$$

When we are in a vacuum, we can refer to the radiance at $\mathbf{r}$ coming from s by

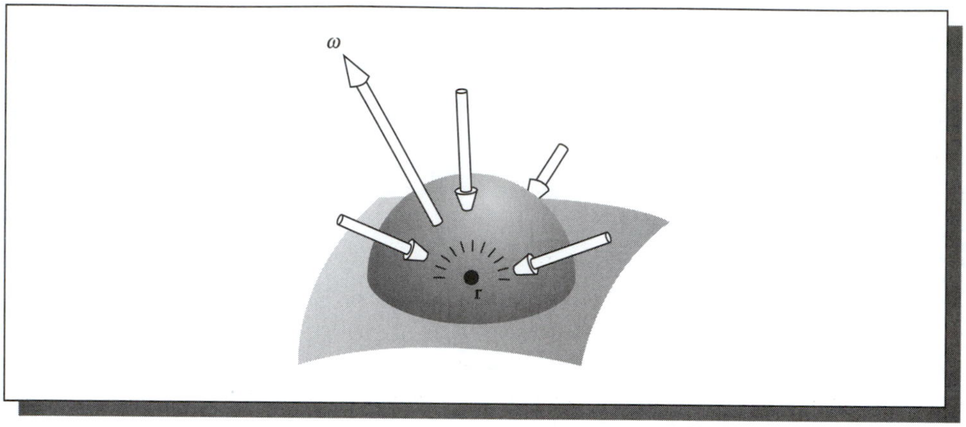

FIGURE 17.3
The geometry of OVTIGRE.

simply indicating the direction vector $\vec{\omega}$ along which light from **s** would arrive. Then we can write VTIGRE in a slightly modified form that describes the light radiated from **r** in an outgoing direction $\vec{\omega}$ in terms of the incident radiance from all directions and the emission at **r** itself.

This modified form is then

$$L(\mathbf{r}, \vec{\omega}^o) = L^e(\mathbf{s}, \vec{\omega}^o) + \int_{\Theta_i^i} f(\mathbf{r}, \vec{\omega} \to \vec{\omega}^o, \lambda) L(\mathbf{r}, \vec{\omega}) \cos\theta_r \, d\vec{\omega} \tag{17.16}$$

where $\vec{\omega}^o \in \Theta_o^o$, and θ_r is the angle between the normal at **r** and $\vec{\omega}$. This form is sometimes a more useful starting place for rendering algorithms. We call this the OVTIGRE form, since it represents the *outgoing* form of the VTIGRE assumptions. The geometry behind OVTIGRE is shown in Figure 17.3.

17.5 Solving for *L*

The goal of image synthesis is to find the function L that satisfies a full or simplified version of the radiance equation. This is called *solving the radiance equation*. Generally this involves positing an *image surface* that is within the scene. The result of the synthesis is an image that represents the light falling upon that image surface. Because most of our viewing devices are roughly planar, we typically imagine the viewing surface to be a *viewing plane*, though there is no restriction forcing that geometry [157, 490].

We must decide whether this image surface is simply a hypothetical one through which light passes, or a real surface within the scene. If the image plane represents the film in a camera, then the camera model surrounding the film can influence the scene (e.g., by casting shadows or reflecting light). On the other hand, if the image plane is a theoretical construct, called a *virtual image plane*, then it is independent of the light distribution in the scene. The virtual image plane is the more common interpretation. This allows us to move the viewing plane throughout the image without the need to compute a new radiance function after each move. If, on the other hand, the image plane is to be considered part of the model, it must be explicitly modeled and included in the 3D scene description.

There are two general approaches to solving the radiance equation, which we call *explicit approximation* and *implicit sampling*.

In explicit approximation we do our best to find an explicit construction for the radiance; that is, we try to find an explicit function $L(\mathbf{p}, \vec{\omega})$ that satisfies the radiance equation. To generate an image, we need merely sample the function on the image plane and use the signal-processing techniques of Unit II to process those samples into image values. This approach is exemplified by the *radiosity* algorithms described in Chapter 18.

The implicit sampling method is directed at finding L only at point samples in phase space (that is, pairs $(\mathbf{p}, \vec{\omega})$) that are known to be necessary for making an image. Typically these are points on the image plane, in directions determined by the viewing geometry. This approach is exemplified by the *ray-tracing* algorithms described in Chapter 19.

Consider a scene with a virtual image plane. Because the explicit approximation describes the radiance function everywhere in the scene, we can move the image plane to any location and evaluate the radiance function over its surface. The solution function L is thus said to be a *view-independent solution*, and the solution method is said to be a *view-independent algorithm*.

On the other hand, the implicit sampling method is often used to gather radiance only over the surface of the viewing plane; therefore, the image is a *view-dependent solution*. If that plane moves, then perhaps some of the old values may be reused in some way, but many new samples must be taken. Therefore this method is said to be a *view-dependent algorithm*.

The names view-dependent and view-independent imply that they are intimately connected with the motion of the image plane in a scene, but that is only one interpretation of the results. If the image plane is modeled as a real part of the scene, then an explicit approximation algorithm will still construct a function that can be evaluated anywhere. Because it includes the image plane as a piece of the scene, when the viewing plane moves, it changes the light distribution in the scene, and thus the radiance function must be recomputed. The solution in this case is not really view-independent.

Therefore we prefer the more descriptive terms *implicit sampling* and *explicit approximation*, implying point sampling to find particular phase-space values of the radiance function, and evaluation of an explicit approximate function, respectively. We will look at these methods in more detail in the following chapters.

17.6 Further Reading

The original presentations of the radiance equation were given by Immel et al. [224] and Kajiya [234]. In particular, Kajiya gives an excellent history of various image synthesis algorithms presented in terms of the VTIGRE form [234]. Another discussion of the reduction of the flux equation to various forms of radiance equation is given by Arvo [15].

17.7 Exercises

Exercise 17.1

A phosphor has a maximum possible amount of energy that it can store at a given wavelength, and any incident energy beyond that is converted into heat. Assume that this cutoff is sharp. Extend Equation 17.6 to account for this saturation. Is the resulting function linear? What does this imply about finding analytic solutions to the full rendering equation using this function?

Exercise 17.2

Derive the form of the radiance equation appropriate for a medium that emits but does not scatter or absorb (this model is used by many volume rendering algorithms).

IV

RENDERING

The surface of every opaque body is affected by the colour of the objects surrounding it. But this effect will be strong or weak in proportion as those objects are more or less remote and more or less strongly [coloured].

Leonardo da Vinci

INTRODUCTION TO UNIT IV

In Unit IV we concentrate on the process of taking a collection of 3D objects, light sources, and a viewpoint, and producing an image from that collection. This is the process of *rendering*.

Our philosophy is that a rendering algorithm is a blend of ideas from vision, signal processing, and physics; each of these has had its own section in the book. We are now ready to draw them together into an interwoven program that produces accurate and good-looking synthetic images.

There are many different types of rendering algorithms; there is no "best." The field of rendering is both theoretical and practical. The theory starts with the *radiance equation*, which was our final achievement in Unit III. From there, we begin compromising and approximating: the full radiance equation is simply too hard to solve analytically for any nontrivial scene. The theory guides our algorithmic development, but we must pay heed to computer engineering and computer science as we go.

This book is not intended as a practical guide to any particular rendering algorithm. Therefore I will not discuss issues that are important to a large-scale software project like a rendering system, including conceptual problems like architecture and implementation, and mechanical problems like reducing page faults. Such discussions may be found in the research papers describing the individual algorithms, which should certainly be consulted before you start programming.

Rather than focus on complete descriptions, this unit emphasizes the big ideas and the major algorithms that are used in modern *physically based* rendering. (The term *physically based* means that the system is based on *some* model of physics, not necessarily the one that describes our world.) We will exclusively discuss *global illumination* algorithms, which take into account the distribution of light in the entire scene when deriving the color for any one surface point or image pixel.

The field of global illumination is dominated by two major algorithms: *radiosity* and *ray tracing*. They are both based on solving the radiance equation, the former by constructing an explicit function that approximates the unknown radiance distribution, and the latter by evaluating point samples of that unknown function. These two algorithms make radically different assumptions about the environment. Classical radiosity assumes that everything in the scene is perfectly diffuse. Classical ray tracing assumes that objects are illuminated only by light coming directly from a light source, or via some intermediate bounces off of perfectly specular surfaces. We are actually fortunate that the two algorithms concentrate on such different phenomena, because they can be combined into a *hybrid* algorithm that uses the best features of both.

The first chapters in this unit discuss the general ideas that make up radiosity, ray tracing, and the hybrid algorithms that combine these two. Our descriptions will generally stay at a descriptive, rather than detailed, level; much more information on all the algorithms discussed may be found in the references listed in the Further Reading sections. We will then discuss some methods for accurately displaying the resulting images and for interacting with those images to influence their design.

This unit demonstrates how the first three units tie together to produce complete rendering algorithms. We need to understand vision so we know how to sample and display the image, we need to understand signal processing so all of our sampling is free from artifacts, and we need to understand physics and materials so we can accurately simulate the interaction of light with the objects in the scene. We have covered all of these ideas in preceding chapters; here we will weave them together to make pictures.

All parts of creation are linked together and interchange their influences. The balanced rhythm of the universe is rooted in reciprocity.

Paramahansa Yogananda
("Autobiography of a Yogi," 1946)

18

RADIOSITY

18.1 Introduction

In this chapter we look at methods for creating explicit approximations to the radiance function L. The most famous of these methods is *radiosity*, which was originally developed for image synthesis by Goral et al. [165] and Nishita and Nakamae [321]. Like many other rendering methods, radiosity in its original form was extremely expensive in both memory and time; practical improvements to the method have greatly enhanced its popularity.

The basic idea of explicit approximation methods is that from a given 3D scene description, we find some sort of explicit equation that expresses the distribution of radiance in the scene. Recall that the various radiance equations in Chapter 17 are all *implicit* expressions; they tell us the conditions that L must satisfy, but they don't tell us how to find such an L.

The development of practical methods for efficient radiosity is an active research area. In this chapter we present the basic ideas that underlie the methods, but we do not attempt to survey the practice in the field at the present time. Thoroughly detailed surveys with plenty of practical information are available in the references in the Further Reading section.

18.2 Classical Radiosity

The method of *classical radiosity* was introduced by Goral et al. [165] and Nishita and Nakamae [321]. The basic approach assumes an environment that is in a vacuum, populated by purely diffuse, opaque surfaces. The first step is to subdivide the surfaces into smaller pieces; this is called *meshing*. Often we speak of a scene as containing some number of *surfaces*, but a larger number of *patches*, where the patches are created when the surfaces are meshed. We will use the terms surface and patch interchangeably. We assume that the reflected, incident, and emitted radiances are all constant in all directions at all points on each surface. Then at a given frequency, a single scalar represents the energy that is leaving each patch: this is a combination of the *emission* created by the surface (e.g., by blackbody radiation), and the *radiosity* B of the surface. The term *radiosity* is a synonym for the *radiant exitance* $M = \Phi/A$, which is defined in Equation 13.10 as the power Φ radiated per unit area A of a surface.

The radiosity algorithm establishes a set of linear equations that relates the fraction of energy leaving one patch to the energy arriving at another, based on the geometry between the two patches. If two patches are close and facing each other, then a large amount of energy will be transferred between them. Two small patches far away from each other exchange little energy. It's not enough to simply transfer power from the luminaires to the reflecting surfaces in the scene. Consider a luminaire A and a few surfaces M_i, as shown in Figure 18.1.

Light is generated at A and travels into the scene. When it strikes M_1, some of the light is reflected off that surface into all directions. Some of that reflected light will strike M_2. In turn, M_2 will reflect some of that light, which will then fall back upon M_1, and so it goes. Eventually the system settles down; we say it reaches *steady state* or *equilibrium*. At that point the system is *balanced*; we find that all the energy leaving the source is eventually absorbed by the surfaces.

In order to establish such an equilibrium condition we need to make sure we can account for all the light. Therefore the environment is usually surrounded by a large surface called the *enclosure*; that way no energy escapes from the system.

The result of the radiosity process is that we know how much light is being reradiated by each surface (remember that the surfaces are uniform and perfectly diffuse, so they give off the same amount of energy per unit area, or radiosity, in each direction from every point). To create an image, we need only determine which object is visible through each screen sample; once we know the object, we can look up its precomputed radiosity and immediately convert that to radiance for display. If we move the image surface, then all we need to do is recompute which objects are visible through which pixels; the distribution of light on each surface is unaffected by our movement of a virtual camera.

We have glossed over many important details in this short description, which we will cover in more detail below. One of the most important problems involves

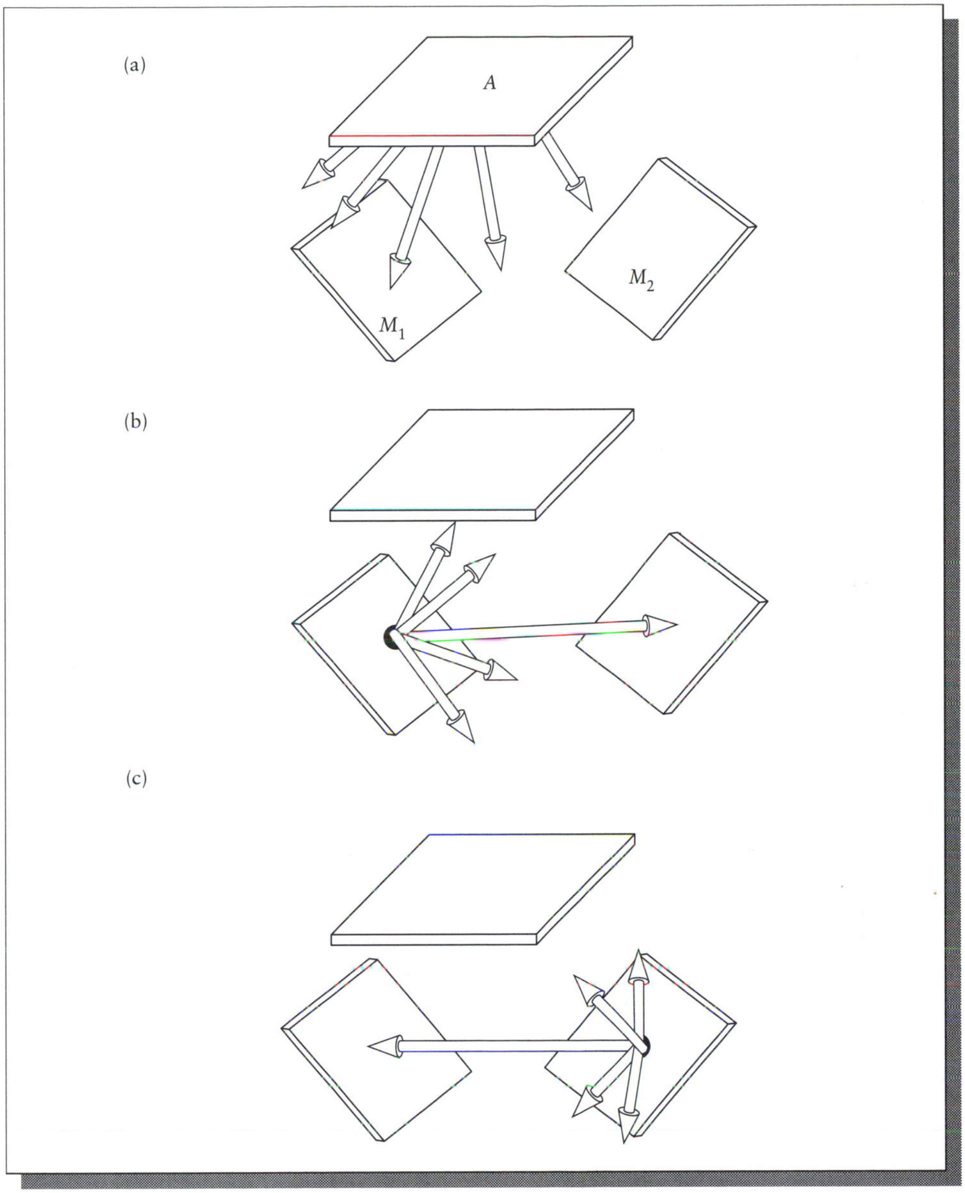

FIGURE 18.1

Surface A is a luminaire, while the others are diffuse reflectors. (a) Light is radiated from the luminaire. (b) Light is reflected from M_1 toward M_2 as well as the luminaire. (c) Light is reflected from M_2 toward M_1 and the luminaire.

converting a solution to make an image. Typically in classical radiosity we will compute the radiosity at the vertices of surface patches, and then blend the vertex radiosities across the surface when displaying using hardware-assisted Gouraud shading. In fact, we can navigate through a radiosity-processed environment very quickly with real-time hardware by associating the color of each surface element with its precomputed radiosity. One way to think about this process is that we have sampled the ideally continuous radiosity function in the scene at a number of points (the model vertices), and we are using a simple linear reconstruction filter (vertex interpolation) to reconstruct the signal. We know from Unit II that such a process is prone to all sorts of problems from aliasing to reconstruction errors, but often these are acceptable in an interactive environment.

The radiosity method has its origins in the finite elements and heat transfer communities [406]. We will present it in its traditional computer graphics form, following the development by Cohen and Wallace [99].

We begin with the OVTIGRE radiance equation (Equation 17.16), which expresses the radiance $L(\mathbf{r}, \vec{\omega})$ leaving from a point $\mathbf{r}$ from the direction $\vec{\omega}$ as a function of the light emitted and propagated:

$$L(\mathbf{r}, \vec{\omega}^o) = L^e(\mathbf{s}, \vec{\omega}^o) + \int_{\Theta_i^i} f(\mathbf{r}, \vec{\omega} \rightarrow \vec{\omega}^o, \lambda) L(\mathbf{r}, \vec{\omega}) \cos\theta_r \, d\vec{\omega} \tag{18.1}$$

where $\vec{\omega}^o \in \Theta_o^o(\mathbf{r})$.

The first thing we want to do is to express the incident light in terms of the light leaving other surfaces; right now we need $L(\mathbf{r}, \vec{\omega})$ arriving at $\mathbf{r}$, but we don't have any way of evaluating it. We will use the same observation we used in deriving the integral form of the transport equation, which is that the point s visible from $\mathbf{r}$ in direction $\vec{\omega}$ is given by the visibility (or nearest-surface or ray-tracing) function ν, such that $\mathbf{s} = \mathbf{r} + \nu(\mathbf{r}, \mathbf{s})\vec{\omega}$. Now we know that when the intercepted surface dS is far away, the solid angle $d\vec{\omega}$ in Equation 18.1 may be written

$$d\vec{\omega} = \frac{dS \ \cos\theta_s}{\|\mathbf{r} - \mathbf{s}\|^2} \tag{18.2}$$

where θ_s is the angle between the normal at dS and the line from s to $\mathbf{r}$.

We can't quite plug this into Equation 18.1, though, because we want to integrate over only the visible surfaces, not all points on all surfaces. There are two ways to limit the integration domain to visible surfaces. One is to explicitly construct a domain that is composed only of the visible surfaces. We can use any analytic visible-surface algorithm for this (such as that in Atherton et al. [20]), but such algorithms are often expensive for very complex scenes. An alternative is to build a *masking function* into the integral that limits the domain implicitly. In our case we want a *visibility-test function* $V(\mathbf{r}, \mathbf{s})$ that has the value 1 when $\mathbf{r}$ and $\mathbf{s}$ are mutually visible, and is otherwise 0. We can build such a function by finding the nearest visible point from $\mathbf{r}$ in the direction of $\mathbf{s}$, and checking to see if that is indeed the test point $\mathbf{s}$:

$$V(\mathbf{r}, \mathbf{s}) = \begin{cases} 1 & \text{if } \mathbf{s} = \mathbf{r} + \nu(\mathbf{r}, (\mathbf{s} - \mathbf{r}))(\mathbf{s} - \mathbf{r}) \\ 0 & \text{otherwise} \end{cases} \tag{18.3}$$

We can now switch domains to all points on all surfaces M, knowing that only the nearest-visible points will actually contribute to the integral:

$$\begin{aligned} L(\mathbf{r}, \vec{\omega}^o) &= L^e(\mathbf{s}, \vec{\omega}^o) + \int_{\Theta_i^i} f(\mathbf{r}, \vec{\omega} \to \vec{\omega}^o, \lambda) L(\mathbf{s}, \vec{\omega}) \cos\theta_r \, d\vec{\omega} \\ &= L^e(\mathbf{s}, \vec{\omega}^o) + \int_M f(\mathbf{r}, \vec{\omega} \to \vec{\omega}^o, \lambda) L(\mathbf{s}, \vec{\omega}) \cos\theta_r \frac{\cos\theta_s}{\|\mathbf{r} - \mathbf{s}\|^2} V(\mathbf{r}, \mathbf{s}) \, ds \\ &= L^e(\mathbf{s}, \vec{\omega}^o) + \int_M f(\mathbf{r}, \vec{\omega} \to \vec{\omega}^o, \lambda) L(\mathbf{s}, \vec{\omega}) G(\mathbf{r}, \mathbf{s}) \, ds \end{aligned} \tag{18.4}$$

where we have introduced the geometry term G to represent the purely geometric part of the computation. Notice that G is completely independent of the energy flowing in the scene.

Equation 18.4 is not an efficient means for computing $L(\mathbf{r}, \vec{\omega}^o)$, since it involves lots of calculations that get weighted by 0 and therefore contribute nothing. We would prefer to integrate over M', a subset of M that contains only those surfaces that are *likely* to be visible from $\mathbf{r}$.

The question now is how we might solve this integral equation. It expresses the radiance at a point and direction potentially in terms of all other radiances at all other points and locations in the scene. What we want is to find an explicit formula for L that satisfies these conditions. Classical radiosity is based on two of the methods that we covered in Chapter 16: polynomial collocation and Galerkin solutions. We will cover their application to Equation 18.4 in turn.

18.2.1 Collocation Solution

Recall from Section 16.8.3 that the collocation method is based on finding a set of *collocation points* for which we can find mutually consistent values of the unknown function. In our case, the collocation points are phase-space points $\mathbf{c}_a = (\mathbf{r}_a, \vec{\omega}_a)$ where a is an integer index. Then for all such points we write the value of L, and then solve the set of simultaneous equations.

To get the ball rolling, we write the value of L at the collocation points $\mathbf{c}_a$. We write Equation 18.4 but we pull all the terms involving L to the left-hand side:

$$L(\mathbf{c}_a) - \int_M f(\mathbf{r}, \vec{\omega} \to \vec{\omega}^o, \lambda) L(\mathbf{s}, \vec{\omega}) G(\mathbf{r}_a, \mathbf{s}) \, ds = L^e(\mathbf{c}_a) \tag{18.5}$$

Notice that one part of the geometry term varies with the integration points across the scene surfaces, but the other part is locked down to the collocation point $\mathbf{r}_a$.

The next step is to expand the radiance with respect to a set of g basis functions $\{\psi_b(\mathbf{r}, \vec{\omega})\}_{b=1}^{g}$. These functions are linearly independent over the phase space $\mathcal{R}^3 \otimes \mathcal{S}^2$, but they are not necessarily orthogonal. An approximatindeione solution $\widehat{L}$ can be written as a weighted sum of these bases:

$$\widehat{L}(\mathbf{r}, \vec{\omega}) = \sum_{b=1}^{g} L_b \psi_b(\mathbf{r}, \vec{\omega}) \tag{18.6}$$

The goal now is to find L_b. The most straightforward solution is to simply project the exact solution L onto the duals of the bases, but if we knew L we wouldn't be bothering with collocation at all! So instead we find values for L_b that hold at the collocation points.

To this end we substitute the approximate L in Equation 18.6 into Equation 18.5, resulting in L at the $\mathbf{c}_a$:

$$\sum_{b=1}^{g} L_b \psi_b(\mathbf{c}_a) - \int_M f(\mathbf{r}, \vec{\omega} \to \vec{\omega}^o, \lambda) \sum_{b=1}^{g} L_b \psi_b(\mathbf{s}, \vec{\omega}) G(\mathbf{c}_a, \mathbf{s})\, d\mathbf{s} = L^e(\mathbf{c}_a) \tag{18.7}$$

$$\sum_{b=1}^{g} L_b \left[\psi_b(\mathbf{c}_a) - \int_M f(\mathbf{r}, \vec{\omega} \to \vec{\omega}^o, \lambda) G(\mathbf{c}_a, \mathbf{s})\, d\mathbf{s} \right] = L^e(\mathbf{c}_a) \tag{18.8}$$

We can write this more succinctly as a matrix relationship

$$\mathbf{KL} = \mathbf{L}^e \tag{18.9}$$

If there are g collocation points, then $\mathbf{K}$ is a square matrix. If $\mathbf{K}$ is nonsingular, then we can find our solution by inversion: $\mathbf{L} = \mathbf{K}^{-1}\mathbf{L}^e$. The expensive part of this method is evaluating the elements of the matrix $\mathbf{K}$, and then inverting it.

18.2.2 Galerkin Solution

Recall from Section 16.8.3 that the Galerkin approach to solving an integral equation starts with the observation that we're going to approximate the solution by a sum of weighted bases. The goal of the method is to find a solution that is orthogonal to each basis function. That is, in terms of Equation 18.6,

$$\langle L | \, \psi_b \rangle = 0 \tag{18.10}$$

for all b, where the braket in this case expands to

$$\langle f | \, g \rangle = \int_M \int_{\Theta_i^i} f(\mathbf{r}, \vec{\omega}) g(\mathbf{r}, \vec{\omega})\, d\vec{\omega}\, d\mathbf{r} \tag{18.11}$$

We will not explicitly conjugate the first argument of the brakets in this unit since all our functions are real.

Writing out Equation 18.4 with the L terms on the left and expanded, we find

$$\left\langle \widehat{L} \middle| \psi_a \right\rangle - \left\langle \int_M f(\mathbf{r}, \vec{\omega} \rightarrow \vec{\omega}^o, \lambda) G(\mathbf{r}, \mathbf{s}) \widehat{L} \middle| \psi_a \right\rangle = \langle L^e | \psi_a \rangle \tag{18.12}$$

for all values of a. Substituting Equation 18.6 for $\widehat{L}$,

$$\left\langle \sum_{b=1}^{g} L_b \psi_b \middle| \psi_a \right\rangle - \left\langle \int_M f(\mathbf{r}, \vec{\omega} \rightarrow \vec{\omega}^o, \lambda) G(\mathbf{r}, \mathbf{s}) \sum_{b=1}^{g} L_b \psi_b \middle| \psi_a \right\rangle = \left\langle L^e \middle| \psi_a \right\rangle \tag{18.13}$$

Grouping the common terms on L_b and moving the summation outside the brakets, we find

$$\sum_{b=1}^{g} L_b \left[\langle \psi_b | \psi_a \rangle - \left\langle \int_M f(\mathbf{r}, \vec{\omega} \rightarrow \vec{\omega}^o, \lambda) G(\mathbf{r}, \mathbf{s}) \psi_b \middle| \psi_a \right\rangle \right] = \langle L^e | \psi_a \rangle \tag{18.14}$$

Once again this may be expressed as a matrix equation $\mathbf{KL} = \mathbf{L}^e$. If we can invert $\mathbf{K}$, then we can find $\mathbf{L} = \mathbf{K}^{-1}\mathbf{L}^e$. As we would expect from the discussion in Chapter 16, the increased accuracy of the Galerkin method over the collocation method comes at the increased cost of computing the Galerkin matrix elements.

18.2.3 Classical Radiosity Solution

The classical radiosity method does not try to solve Equation 18.14. Instead, we make a number of simplifying assumptions that greatly reduces the difficulty of the problem. Some of these assumptions in turn imply other conditions about the radiance function, the surfaces, or both.

In the classical method we assume the following:

1. All surfaces are opaque.
2. All surfaces are perfect diffuse reflectors.
3. Surfaces are small.
4. The radiosity across a surface is constant.
5. The irradiance across a surface is constant.

Because the surfaces are diffuse, we can drop the dependence on $\vec{\omega}$ in the basis functions.

Because we're dealing with purely diffuse surfaces, we can use the relationship $B = L\pi$ to divide through by π and transform the radiances L to the radiosities

B, and the BRDF f to ρ. That means the radiance coefficients L_i become radiosity coefficients B_i.

The classical method uses *box functions* b_i for the basis set. In this formulation, there is one basis function per surface patch in the environment. The function $b_i(\mathbf{r})$ is defined as

$$b_i(\mathbf{r}) = \begin{cases} 1 & \mathbf{r} \in M_i \\ 0 & \text{otherwise} \end{cases} \tag{18.15}$$

so that it has the value 1 everywhere on patch i, and is 0 everywhere else. This means that our number of basis functions g is the same as the number of patches n.

Because the basis functions are disjoint,

$$\langle b_i | \, b_k \rangle = \delta_{ik} A_i \tag{18.16}$$

where δ_{ik} is shorthand for $\delta(i-k)$; that is, it is 1 when $i=k$ and 0 otherwise. Patch i has area A_i, which is the result of integrating the unit function over the patch.

The projection of the emitted terms is similarly

$$\langle E | \, b_i \rangle = \int_{M_i} E(\mathbf{p}) \, d\mathbf{p} = E_i A_i \tag{18.17}$$

where E_i is the emitted power per unit area on patch i.

Finally, we can compute the remaining brakets from

$$\left\langle \int_M f(\mathbf{r}, \vec{\omega} \to \vec{\omega}^o, \lambda) G(\mathbf{r}, \mathbf{s}) b_i \middle| \, b_k \right\rangle = \frac{\rho_i}{\pi} \int_{M_i} \int_{M_k} G(\mathbf{i}, \mathbf{k}) \, d\mathbf{k} \, d\mathbf{i} \tag{18.18}$$

Putting all the pieces of Equation 18.14 back together again with these simplified values, we find

$$\sum_{k=1}^{n} B_k \left(\delta_{ik} A_i - \rho_i \int_{M_i} \int_{M_k} \frac{\cos\theta_i \cos\theta_k}{\pi \|\mathbf{i} - \mathbf{k}\|^2} V(\mathbf{i}, \mathbf{k}) \, d\mathbf{k} \, d\mathbf{i} \right) = E_i A_i \tag{18.19}$$

or by noticing that the first term is simply B_i,

$$B_i A_i = E_i A_i + \rho_i \sum_{k=1}^{n} B_k \int_{M_i} \int_{M_k} \frac{\cos\theta_i \cos\theta_k}{\pi \|\mathbf{i} - \mathbf{k}\|^2} V(\mathbf{i}, \mathbf{k}) \, d\mathbf{k} \, d\mathbf{i} \tag{18.20}$$

The rightmost double-integral term in this equation is pure geometry: it depends only on the relationship between the two patches and not on the energy flowing between them.

This value is called the *form factor* $F_{i,k}$, and is useful because it represents the percentage of the energy radiated into the scene by i that reaches k. The form factor from patch i to patch k, written $F_{i,k}$, is defined as

$$F_{i,k} \triangleq \frac{1}{A_i} \int_{M_i} \int_{M_k} \frac{\cos\theta_i \cos\theta_k}{\pi \|\mathbf{i} - \mathbf{k}\|^2} V(\mathbf{i}, \mathbf{k}) \, d\mathbf{k} \, d\mathbf{i} \tag{18.21}$$

(a)  (b)

FIGURE 18.71
(a) Discontinuity meshing. (b) Hierarchical radiosity. Reprinted, by permission, from Lischinski et al. in *Computer Graphics (Proc. Siggraph '93)*, fig. 9, p. 207.

FIGURE 18.73
Light scattering in a smoky room at sunset. Reprinted, by permission, from Rushmeier and Torrance in *Computer Graphics (Proc. Siggraph '87)*, fig. 12c, p. 302.

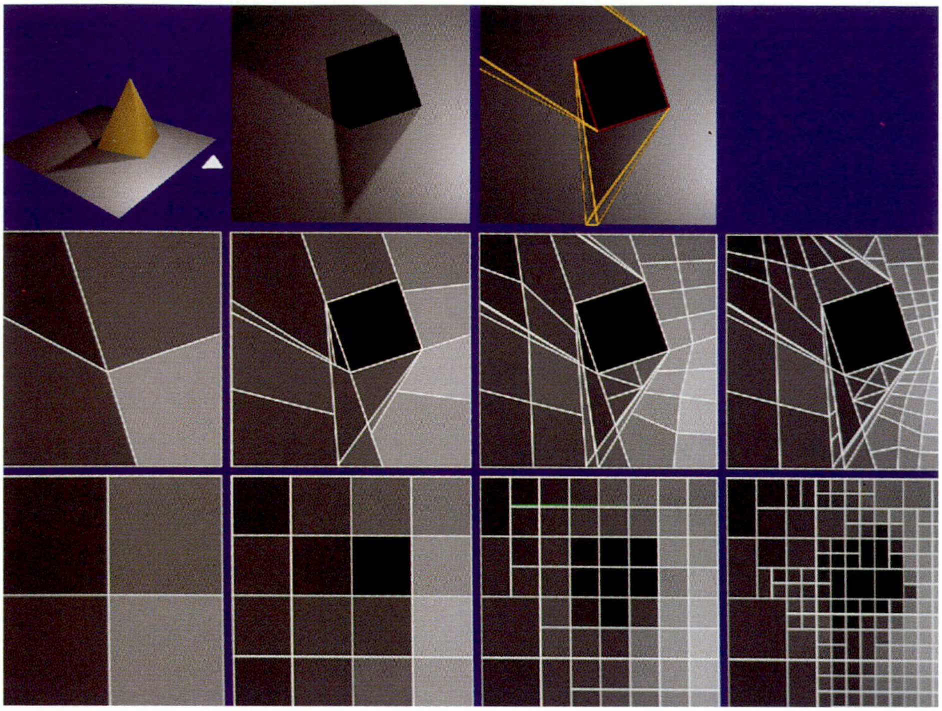

FIGURE 18.69

Discontinuity meshing and regular subdivision. Reprinted, by permission, from Lischinski et al. in *Computer Graphics (Proc. Siggraph '93)*, fig. 4, p. 203.

(a) 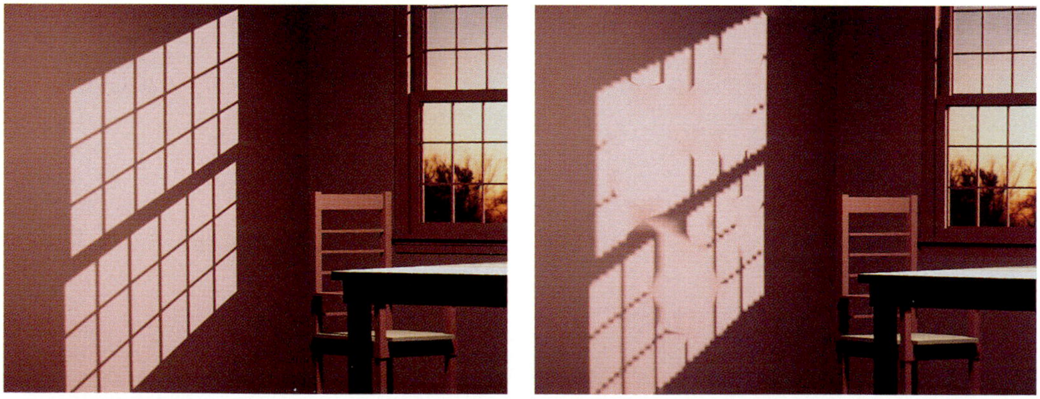 (b)

FIGURE 18.70

(a) A wall produced with discontinuity meshing. (b) A wall produced with standard meshing. Reprinted, by permission, from Lischinski et al. in *IEEE Computer Graphics & Applications*, fig. 14, p. 37. *(©1992 IEEE.)*

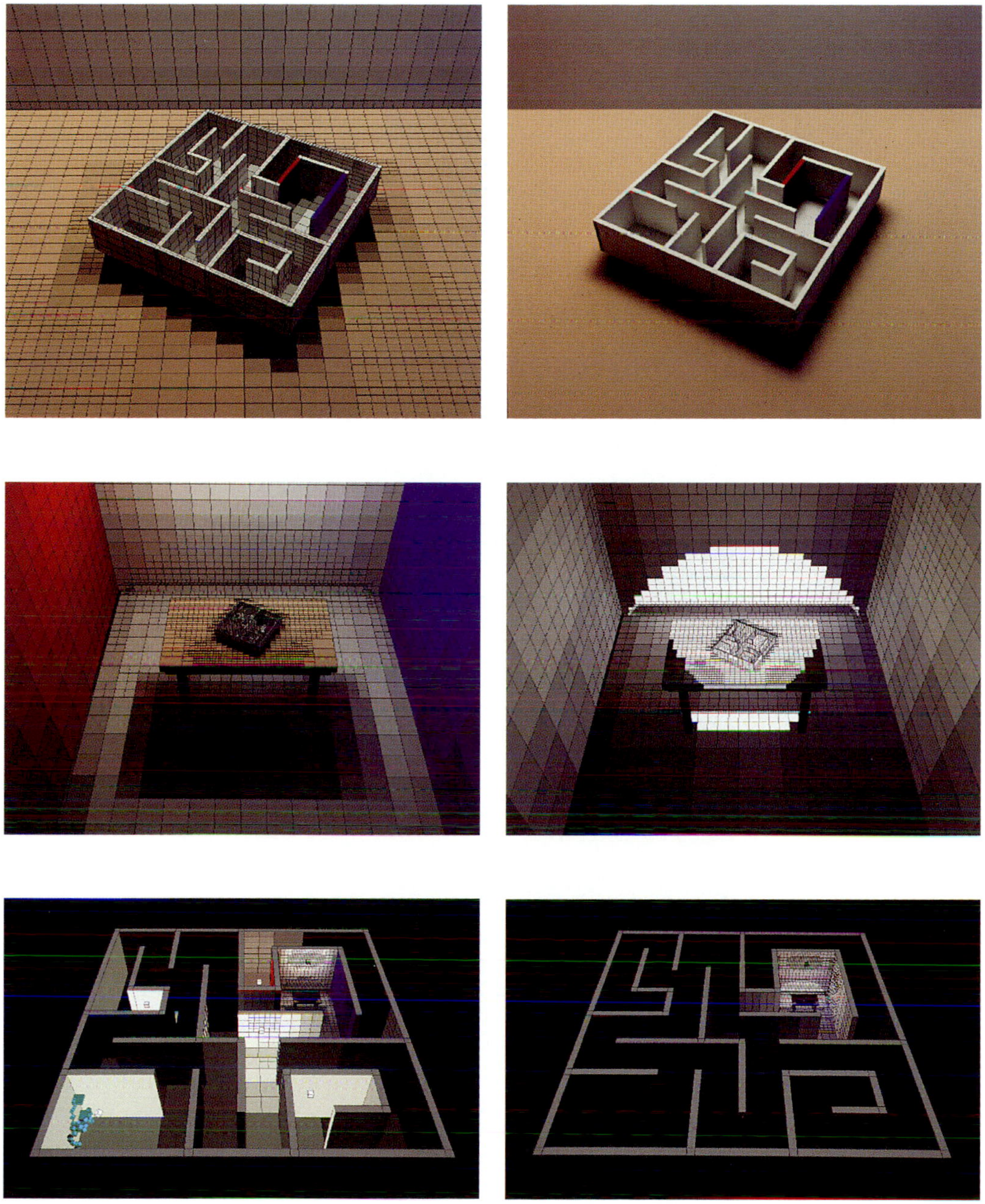

FIGURE 18.68
An importance-driven radiosity solution. These are different images of the same solution. (a) A close-up of the patches generated. (b) A smoothly reconstructed version of (a). (c) The solution for (a) but seen from farther back. (d) The importance solution for (a) from farther back. (e) The solution for the whole environment for (a). (f) The importance of the whole environment for (a). Reprinted, by permission, from Smits et al. in *Computer Graphics (Proc. Siggraph '92)*, figs. 6–11, p. 280.

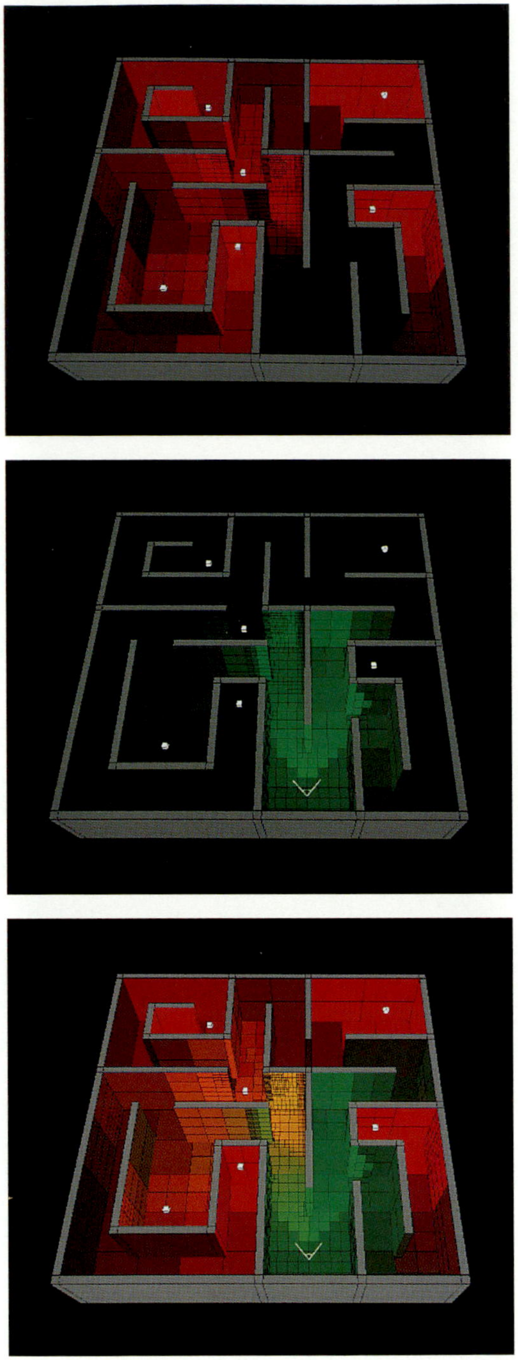

(a)

(b)

(c)

FIGURE 18.60

(a) The radiosity solution. (b) The importance solution. (c) The sum of radiosity and importance. Reprinted, by permission, from Smits et al. in *Computer Graphics (Proc. Siggraph '92)*, figs. 1–3, pp. 274–275.

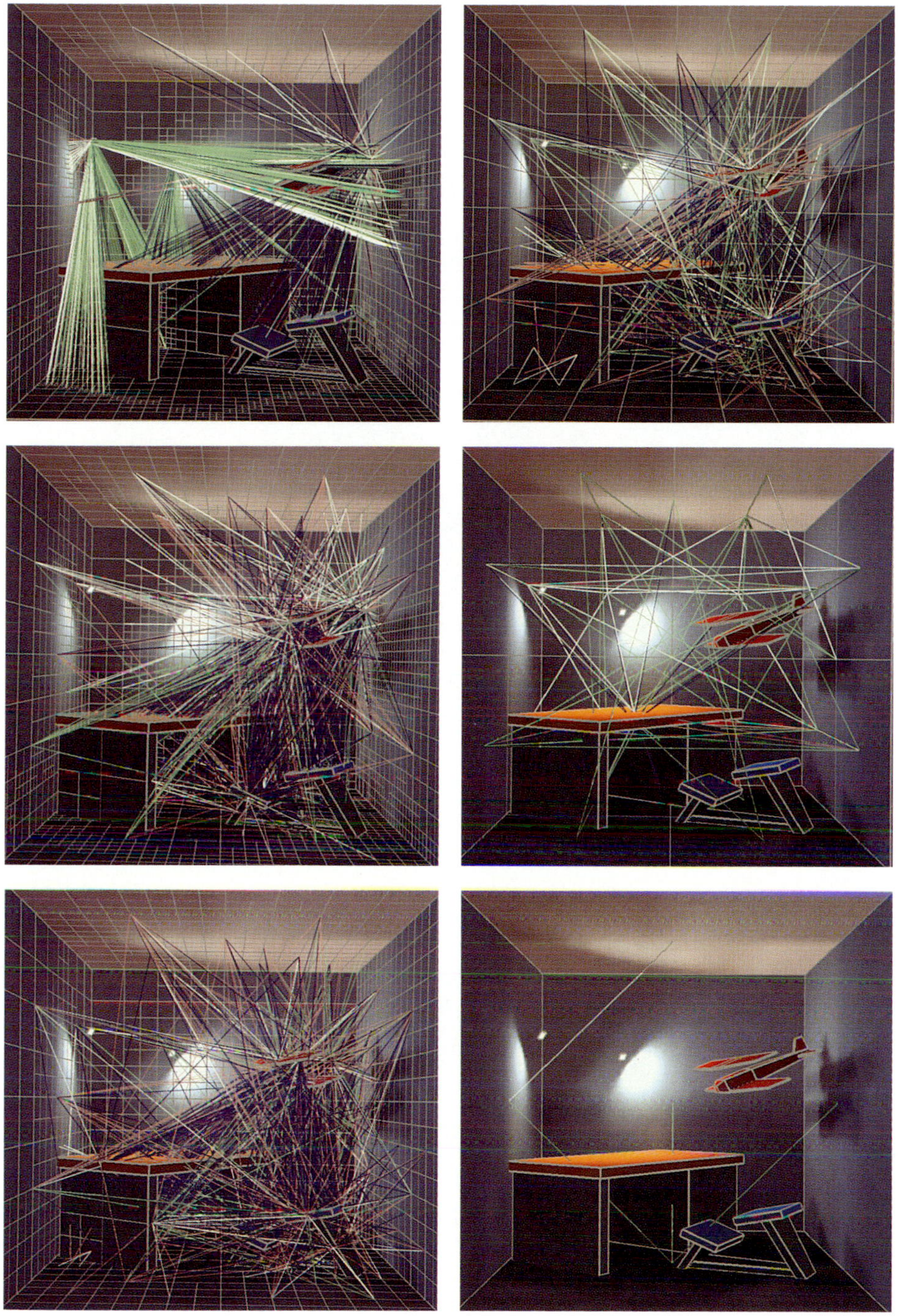

FIGURE 18.59
Results of BF refinement. The images on the left are the solutions corresponding to the refinements on the right. Reprinted, by permission, from Hanrahan et al. in *Computer Graphics (Proc. Siggraph '91)*, fig. 8, p. 205.

FIGURE 18.31
The nave of Chartres Cathedral rendered with ray-traced form factors. Reprinted, by permission, from Wallace et al. in *Computer Graphics (Proc. Siggraph '89)*, fig. 14, p. 323.

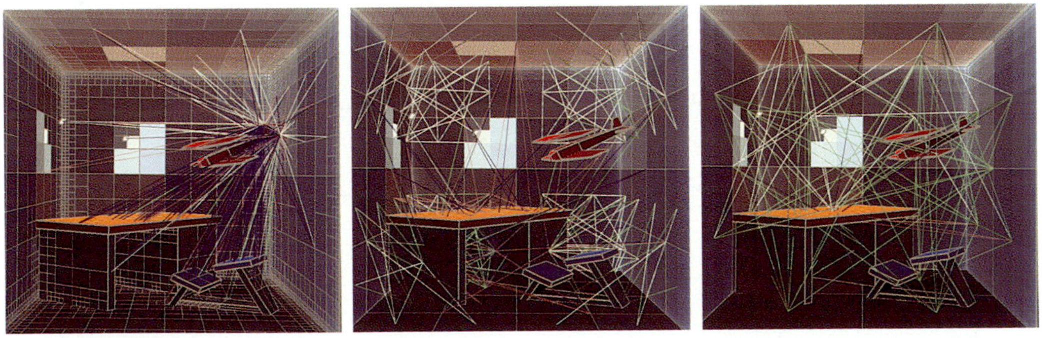

FIGURE 18.54
Results of hierarchical subdivision. The link colors indicate the degree of visibility between the two patches: white is completely visible, green and pink are partly visible, and dark blue is almost invisible. The three images show increasingly larger patches. Reprinted, by permission, from Hanrahan et al. in *Computer Graphics (Proc. Siggraph '91)*, fig. 7, p. 202.

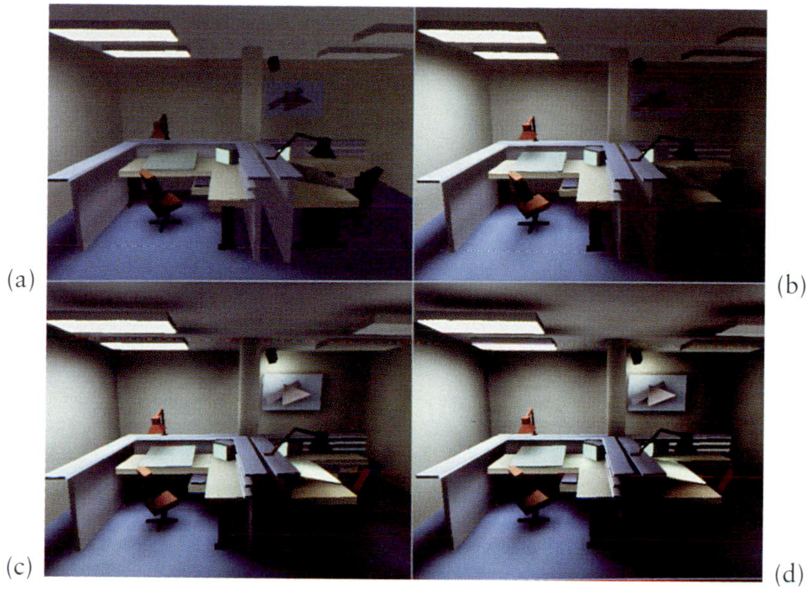

FIGURE 18.13

Progressive refinement after (a) one, (b) two, (c) twenty-four, and (d) 100 steps. Reprinted, by permission, from Cohen et al. in *Computer Graphics (Proc. Siggraph '88)*, fig. 5, p. 81.

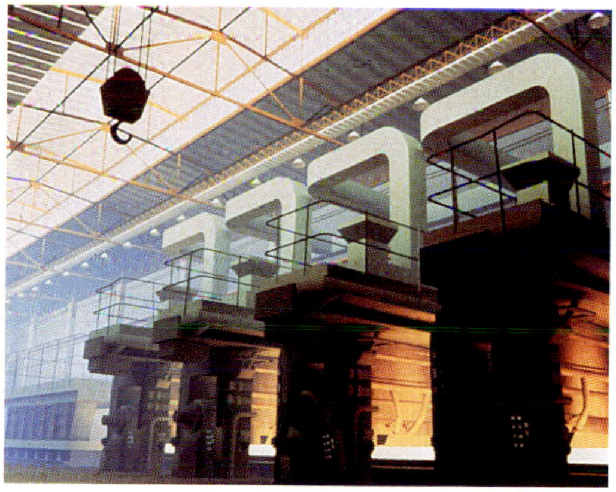

FIGURE 18.14

A scene of 2,000 patches initially computed by progressive refinement. Reprinted, by permission, from Cohen et al. in *Computer Graphics (Proc. Siggraph '88)*, fig. 9, p. 83.

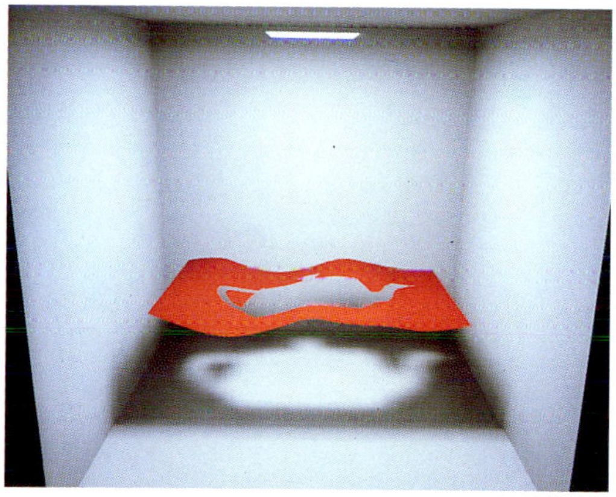

FIGURE 18.30

A quadratic spline teapot. Reprinted, by permission, from Wallace et al. in *Computer Graphics (Proc. Siggraph '89)*, fig. 11, p. 323.

(a) (b) (c) (d)

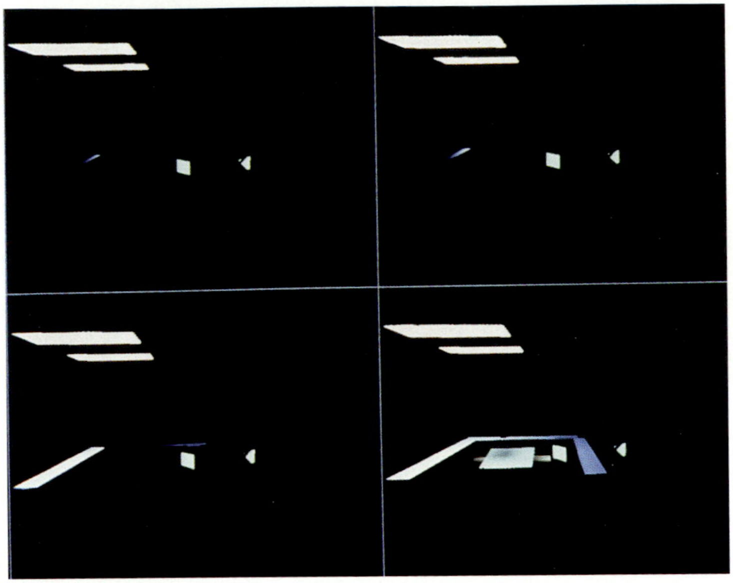

FIGURE 18.10
Gauss-Seidel iteration after (a) one, (b) two, (c) twenty-four, and (d) 100 steps. Reprinted, by permission, from Cohen et al. in *Computer Graphics (Proc. Siggraph '88)*, fig. 2, p. 80.

(a) (b) (c) (d)

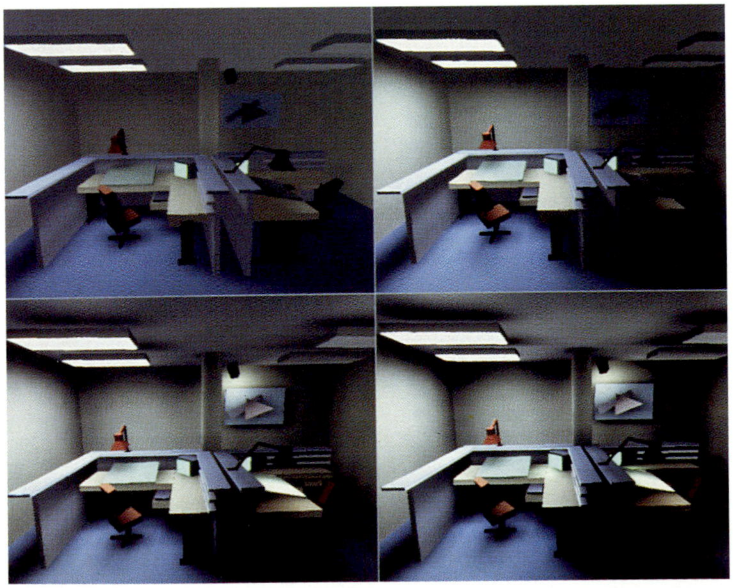

FIGURE 18.12
Southwell iteration after (a) one, (b) two, (c) twenty-four, and (d) 100 steps. Reprinted, by permission, from Cohen et al. in *Computer Graphics (Proc. Siggraph '88)*, fig. 4, p. 81.

FIGURE 15.47
The left column shows (from top to bottom) the result of using two, three, four, and five basis functions to model a scene; on the right are four, nine, sixteen, and twenty-five equally spaced point samples for the same scene. Reprinted, by permission, from Peercy in *Computer Graphics (Proc. Siggraph '93)*, fig. 6, p. 197.

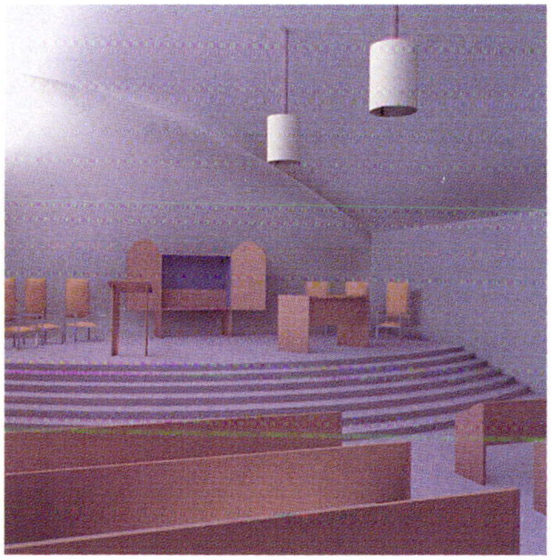

FIGURE 18.4
An indoor scene with 607 surfaces solved by Galerkin methods. Reprinted, by permission, from Zatz in *Computer Graphics (Proc. Siggraph '93)*, fig. 13, p. 220.

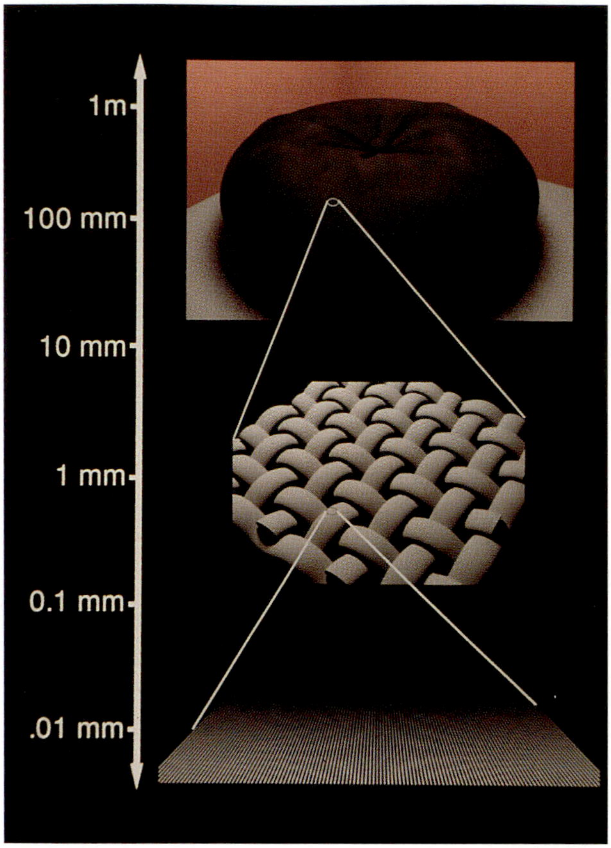

FIGURE 15.44

A hierarchy of scales. *(©1992 Stephen H. Westin/Cornell University Program of Computer Graphics.)*

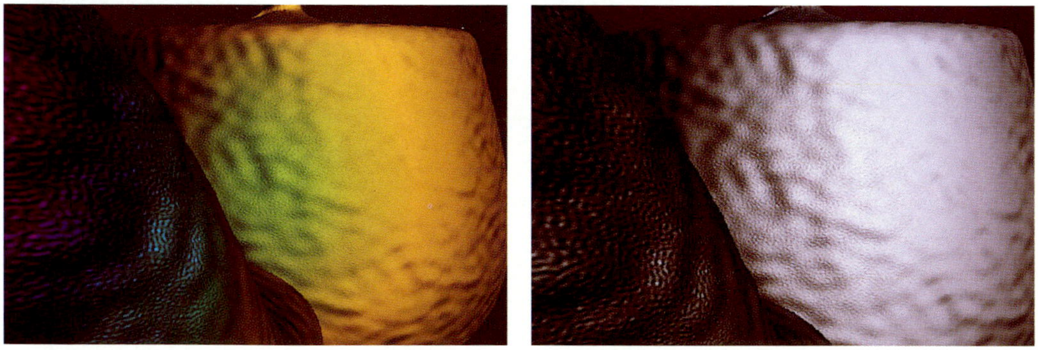

(a) (b)

FIGURE 15.45

A bumpy teapot. (a) The yellow parts of the teapot indicate where the BRDF was used, blue indicates redistribution bump mapping, and red is displacement mapping. (b) The same image without color coding. *(Courtesy of Nelson Max, the University of California, Lawrence Livermore National Laboratory, and the Department of Energy.)*

FIGURE 15.38
A furry bear using Kajiya and Kay's texturing method. *("Herbert the Bear" by J. Kajiya, T. Kay, and J. Snyder. Produced at Caltech and IBM. ©1989 Caltech, IBM.)*

FIGURE 15.39
Some buttons exhibiting displacement and color textures. Reprinted, by permission, from Witkin and Kass in *Computer Graphics (Proc. Siggraph '91)*, fig. 3, p. 307.

FIGURE 15.40
Some mushrooms exhibiting displacement textures. Reprinted, by permission, from Witkin and Kass in *Computer Graphics (Proc. Siggraph '91)*, fig. 5, p. 308.

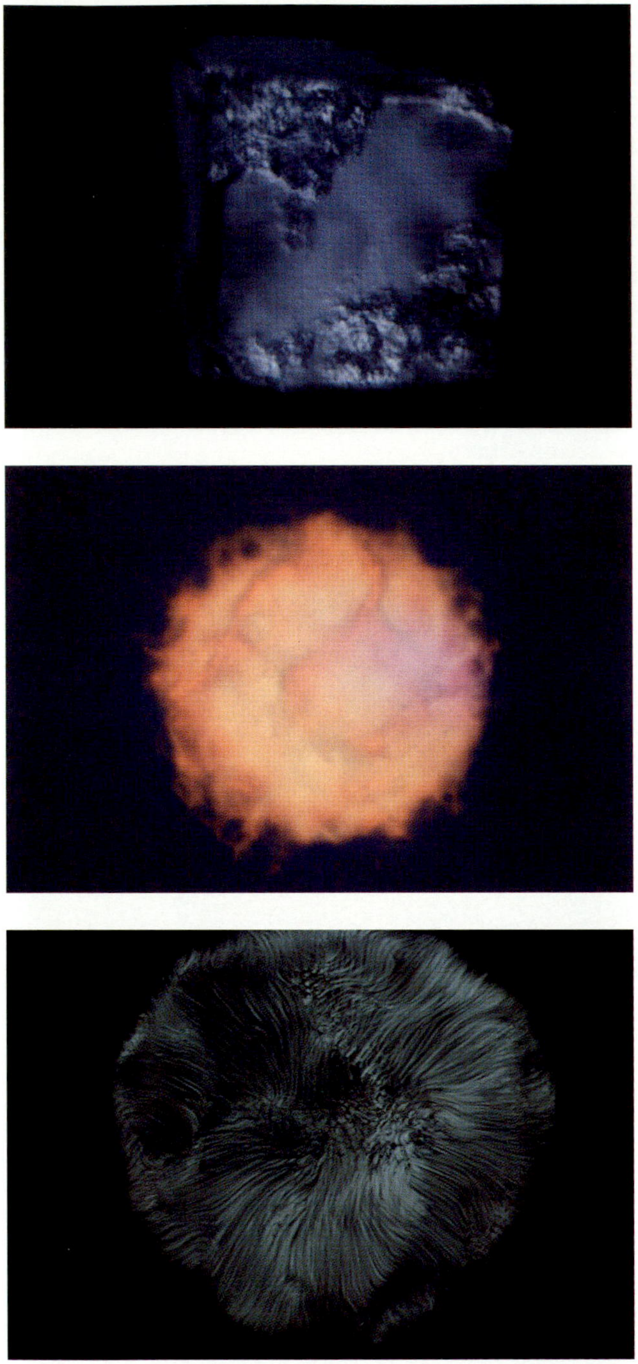

(a)

(b)

(c)

FIGURE 15.37

Three examples of hypertexture. (a) Eroded cube. (b) Fire ball. (c) Tribble. Reprinted, by permission, from Perlin and Hoffert in *Computer Graphics (Proc. Siggraph '89)*, p. 258.

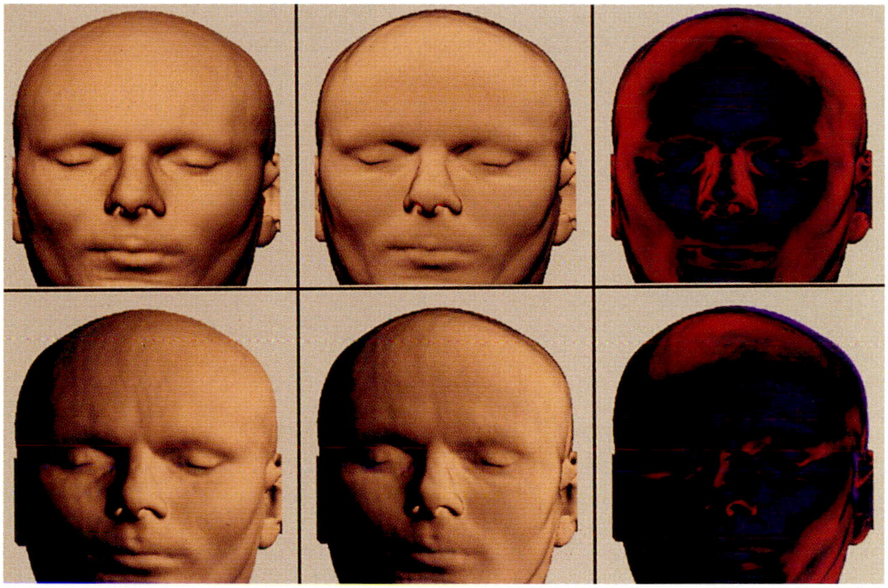

FIGURE 15.35
A head rendered by Lambert shading (left) and subsurface shading (middle). The right column is red where the subsurface model reflected more light, and blue where it reflected less. Reprinted, by permission, from Hanrahan and Krueger in *Computer Graphics (Proc. Siggraph '93)*, plate 2, p. 172.

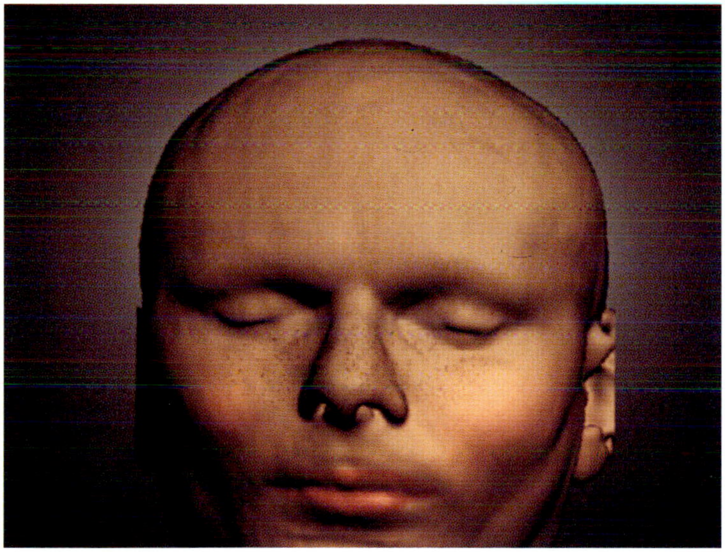

FIGURE 15.36
A head made with the subsurface reflectance model. Reprinted, by permission, from Hanrahan and Krueger in *Computer Graphics (Proc. Siggraph '93)*, plate 4, p. 172.

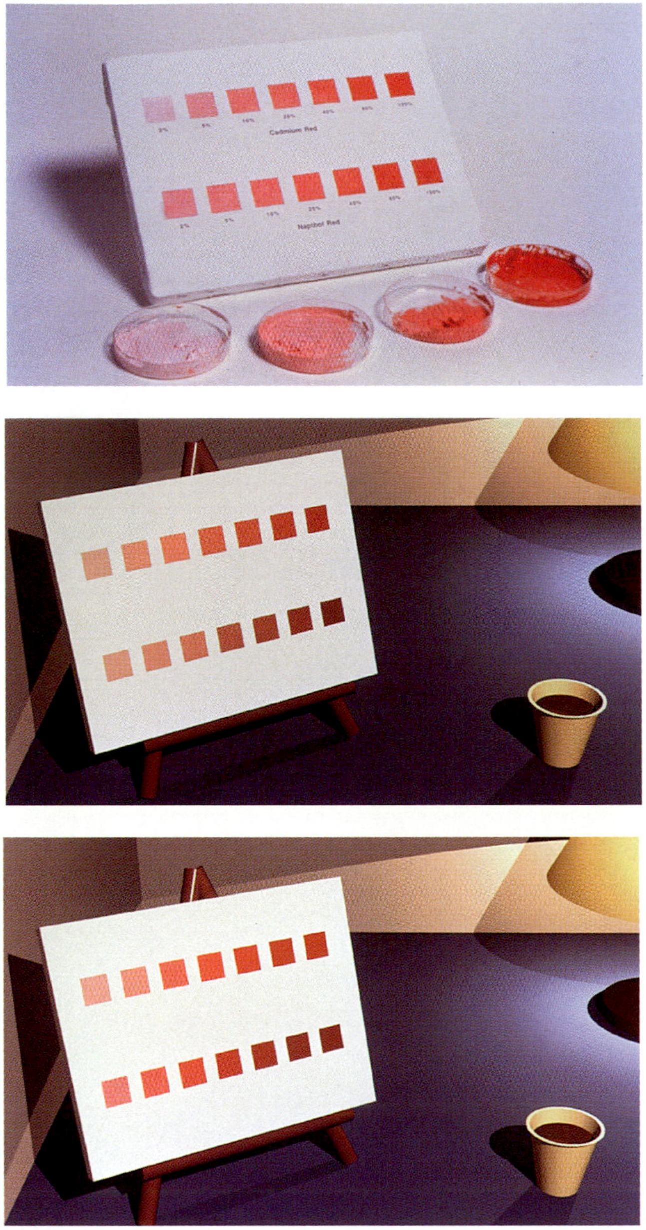

(a)

(b)

(c)

FIGURE 15.31

Results of the Kubelka-Munk theory. (a) A photograph of a real canvas painted with mixtures of cadmium red (top) and naphthol red (bottom). The tint concentrations, from left to right, were 2, 5, 10, 20, 40, 80, and 100% of dry weight by pigment. (b) A simulation of the canvas in (a) using *RGB* values to mix the reds and white. (c) A simulation of the canvas in (a) using the Kubelka-Munk theory. Reprinted, by permission, from Haase and Meyer in *ACM Transactions on Graphics*, figs. 7, 8, and 11, pp. 316–319. (*Courtesy of Chet Haase and Gary Meyer, Department of Computer and Information Science, University of Oregon.*)

FIGURE 15.19
A velvet cushion made with the shading model of Westin et al. (©1992 *Stephen H. Westin/Cornell University Program of Computer Graphics.*)

FIGURE 15.20
A nylon cushion made with the shading model of Westin et al. (©1992 *Stephen H. Westin/Cornell University Program of Computer Graphics.*)

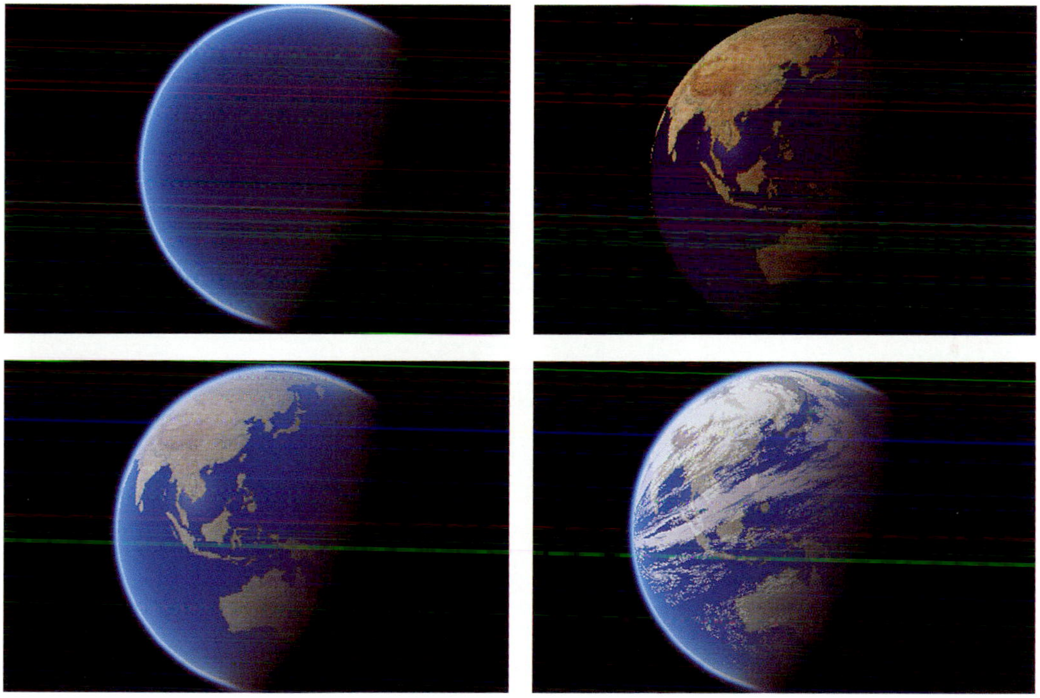

FIGURE 15.28
(a) A model for the atmosphere. (b) Earth. (c) Earth and atmosphere. (d) Earth, atmosphere, and clouds. Reprinted, by permission, from Nishita et al. in *Computer Graphics (Proc. Siggraph '93)*, figs. 6 and 7a–c, p. 181. *(Courtesy of Tomoyuki Nishita, Fukuyama University, and Eihachiro Nakamae, Hiroshima Prefectural University.)*

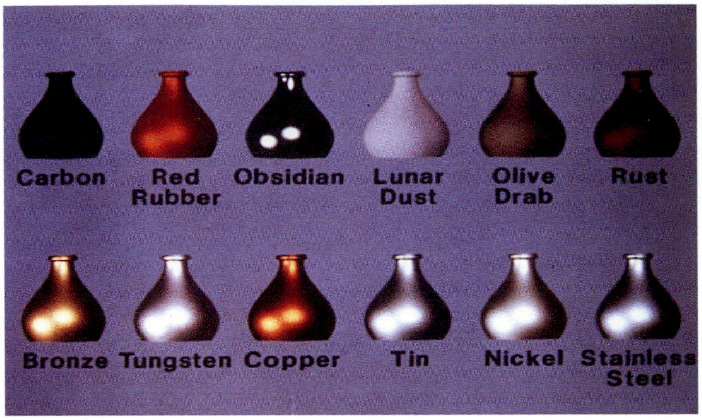

FIGURE 15.10

Vases rendered with the Cook-Torrance model. Reprinted, by permission, from Cook and Torrance in *ACM Transactions on Graphics*, fig. 7, p. 22.

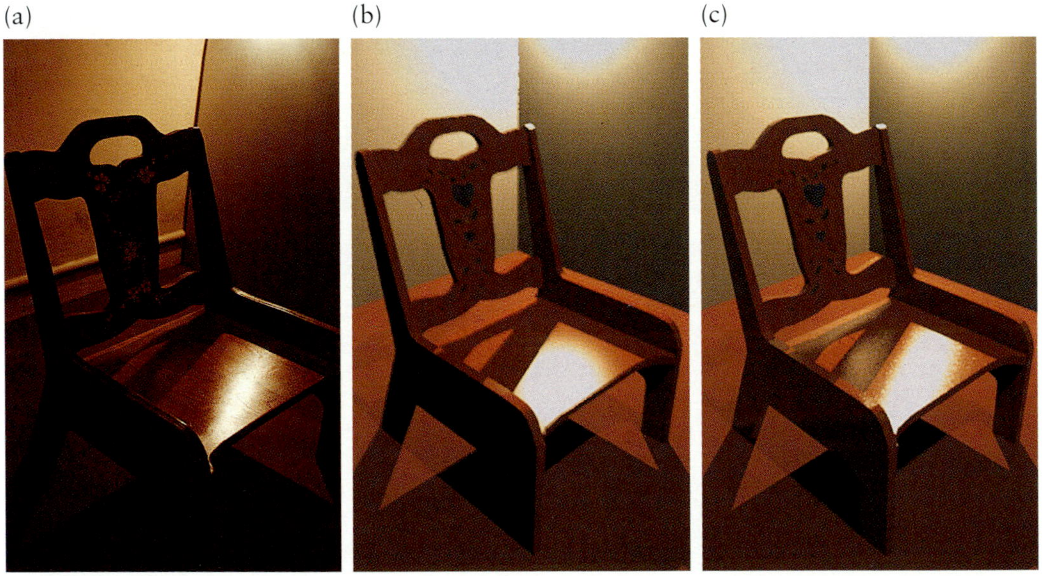

FIGURE 15.17

Three chairs made of varnished wood. The chair in (a) is a photograph. The chair in (b) was rendered with Ward's isotropic reflectance model, that in (c) with Ward's anisotropic reflectance model. Reprinted, by permission, from Ward in *Computer Graphics (Proc. Siggraph '92)*, fig. 8a–c, p. 271.

FIGURE 19.20
An image produced by classical ray tracing. Reprinted, by permission, from Whitted in *Communications of the ACM*, fig. 7, p. 347.

FIGURE 19.41
An image produced by distribution ray tracing. *("1984" by Tom Porter, based on research by Rob Cook. ©1984, Lucasfilm, Ltd.)*

(a) 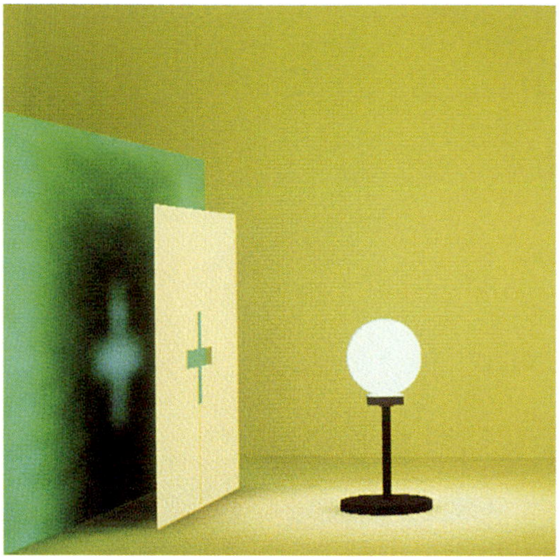 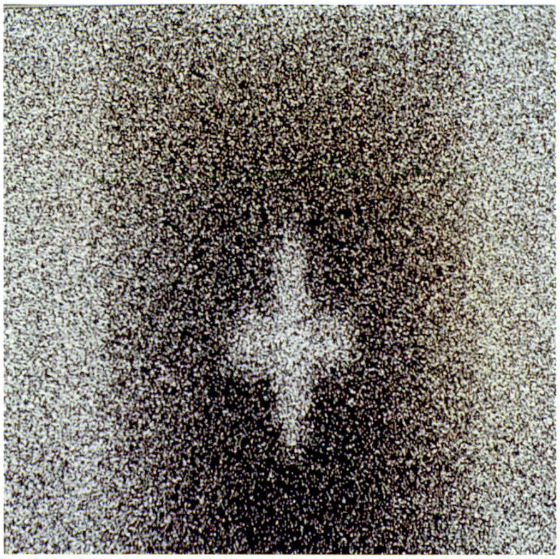 (b)

FIGURE 19.44

(a) A scene to be rendered by photon tracing. (b) The distribution of photon hits on the wall. *(Courtesy of Sumanta Pattanaik.)*

FIGURE 19.47

An image created by a three-pass algorithm. Note the caustic formed by the lens. *(Courtesy of Paul Heckbert.)*

(a) 

 (b)

(c) 

FIGURE 19.48
Hybrid rendering. (a) Direct illumination only. (b) The radiosity solution. (c) The full solution. Reprinted, by permission, from Wallace et al. in *Computer Graphics (Proc. Siggraph '87)*, fig. 10(a)–(c), p. 319.

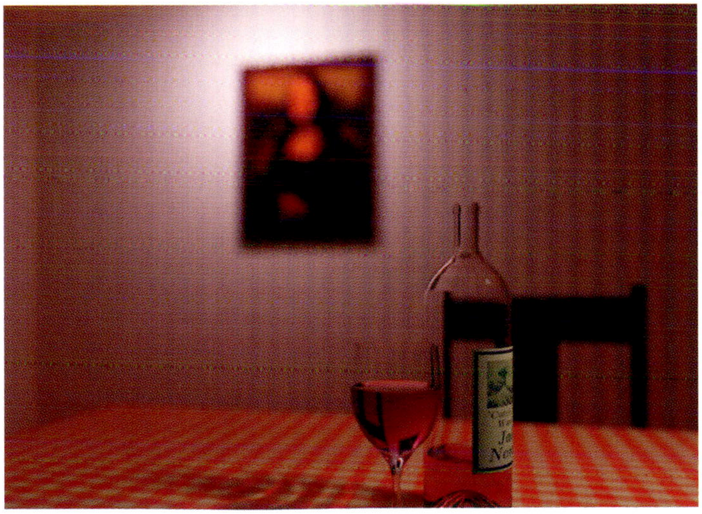

FIGURE 19.49
An image rendered using a three-pass hybrid method. *(Courtesy of Peter Shirley.)*

(a)

(b)

(c)

(d)

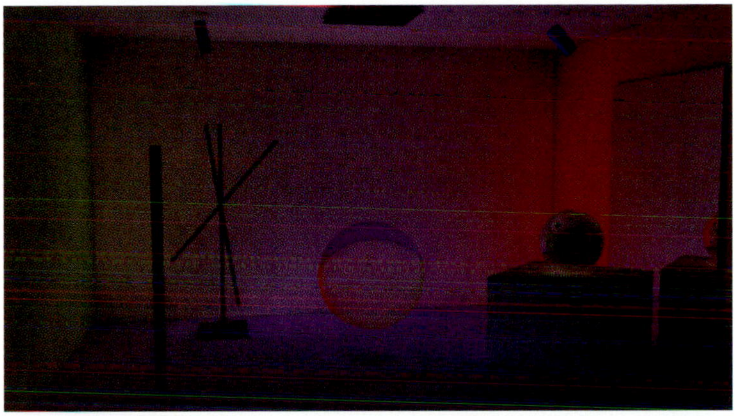

(e)

(f)

FIGURE 19.52

(a) Direct illumination and caustics from radiosity. (b) Interreflections from radiosity. (c) Direct illumination from visibility ray tracing. (d) Caustics from photon ray tracing. (e) Interreflections from visibility ray tracing. (f) The final image. Reprinted, by permission, from Chen et al. in *Computer Graphics (Proc. Siggraph '91)*, figs. 3c and 5a–e, pp. 171–173.

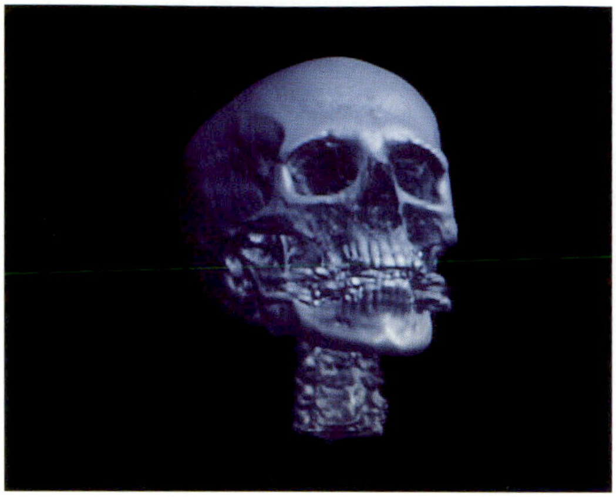

FIGURE 19.53
A volume model rendered with ray tracing. Reprinted, by permission, from Levoy in *ACM Transactions on Graphics*, fig. 8, p. 257.

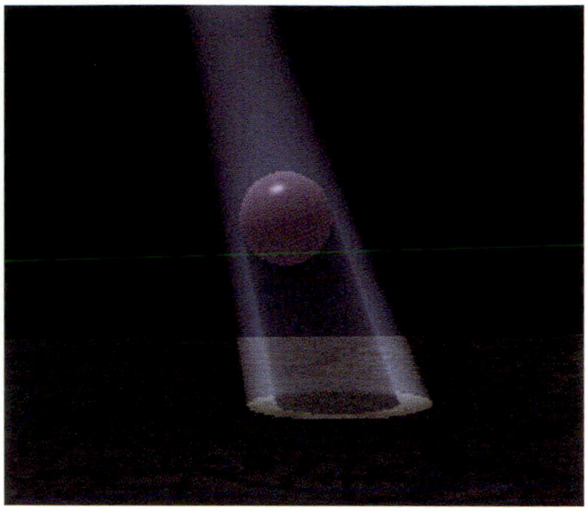

FIGURE 19.54
A volume model including atmospheric media. *(Courtesy of Masa Inakage.)*

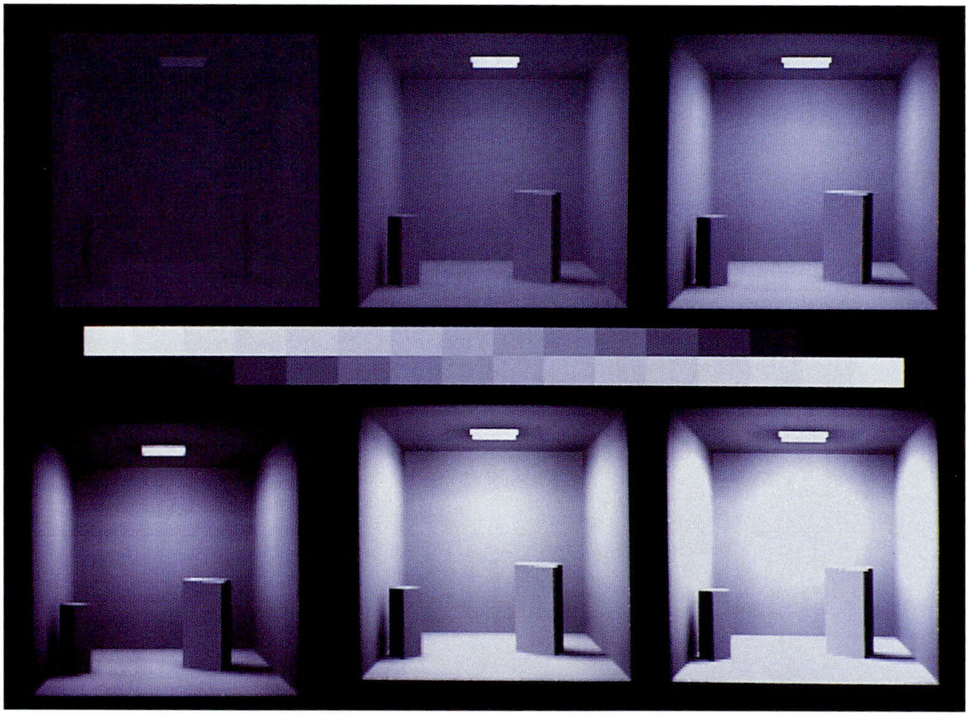

FIGURE 20.3
A room lit by a light source of 1,000, 10, .1, .001, and .00001 lamberts (reading from left to right, top to bottom). The lower left is an unprocessed reference image. *(Courtesy of Jack Tumblin.)*

(a)

(b)

FIGURE 20.4

Color images processed for adaptation. (a) A cabin by day. (b) A cabin by night. *(Courtesy of Greg Ward.)*

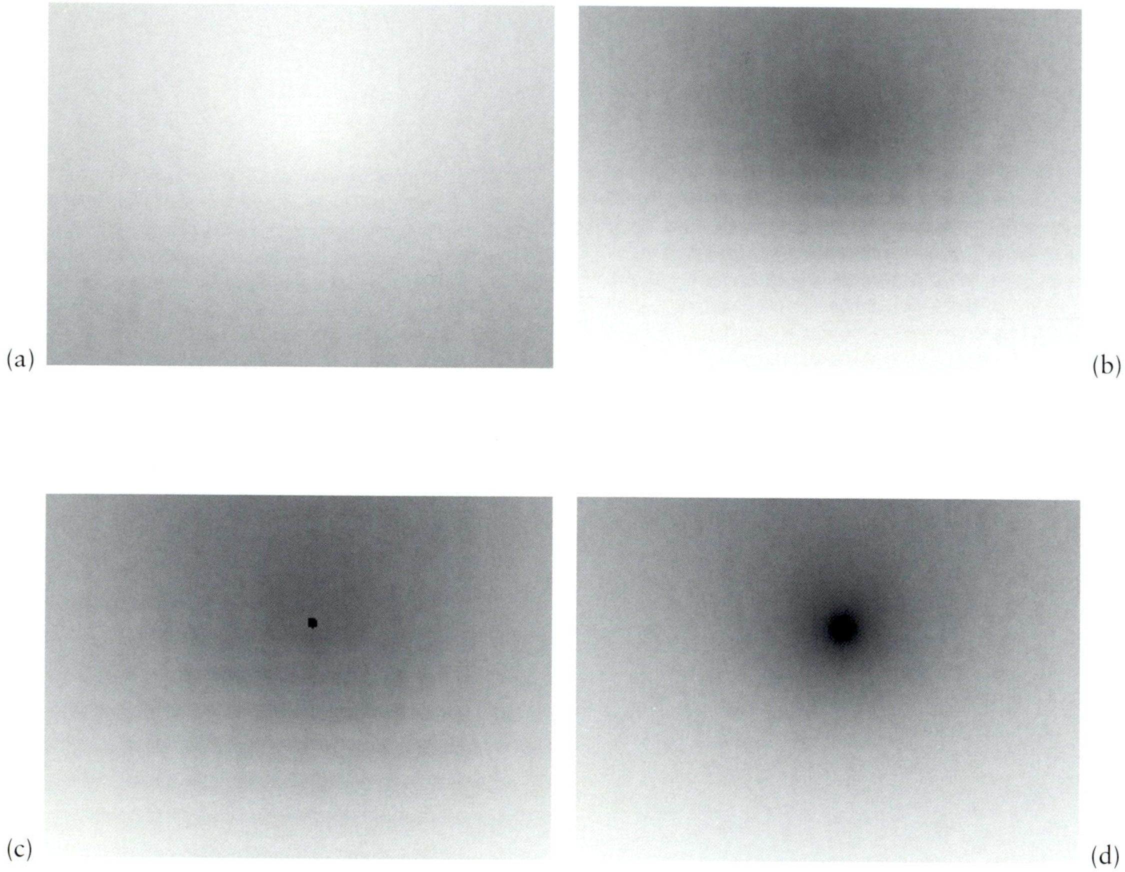

FIGURE 20.5

(a) The blurred image. (b) The scaling function. (c) The clamped scaling function. (d) The smoothed clamped scaling function. *(Courtesy of Kenneth Chiu.)*

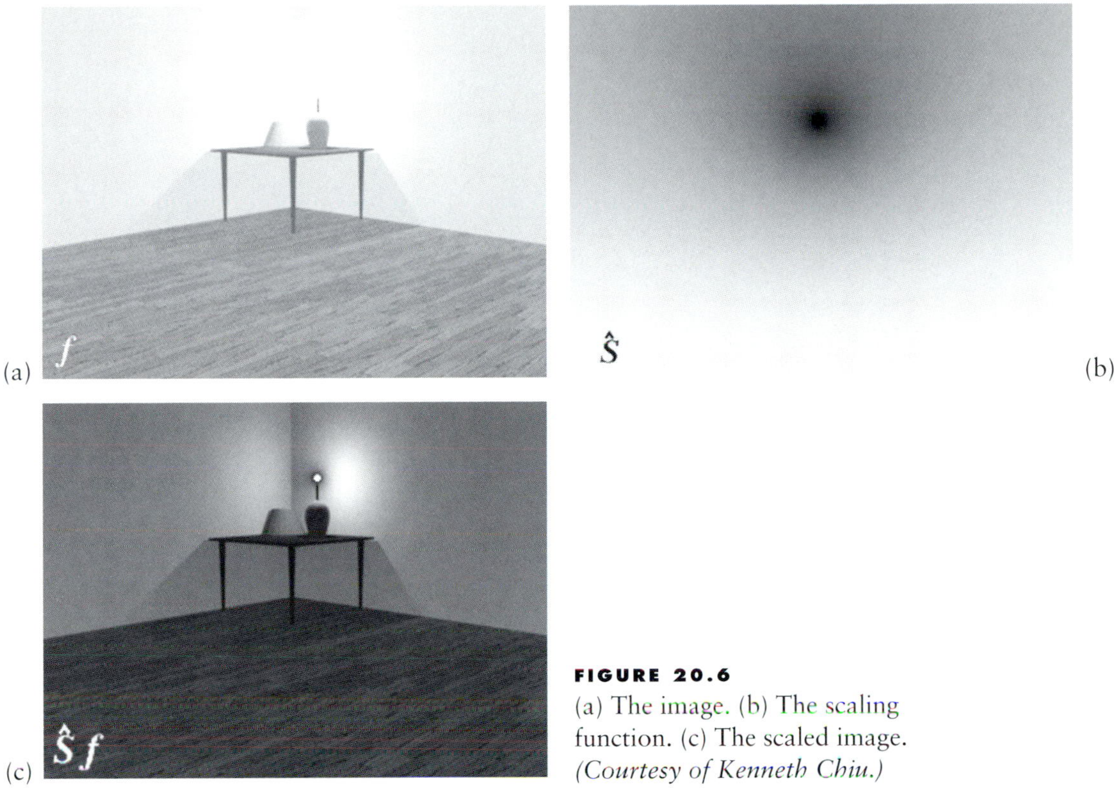

FIGURE 20.6
(a) The image. (b) The scaling function. (c) The scaled image. *(Courtesy of Kenneth Chiu.)*

FIGURE 20.7
An image filtered for scaling and blooming. *(Courtesy of Kenneth Chiu.)*

(a)

(b)

FIGURE 20.8
Images corrected by the Ward scale factor. (a) A cabin by day. (b) A cabin by night. *(Courtesy of Greg Ward.)*

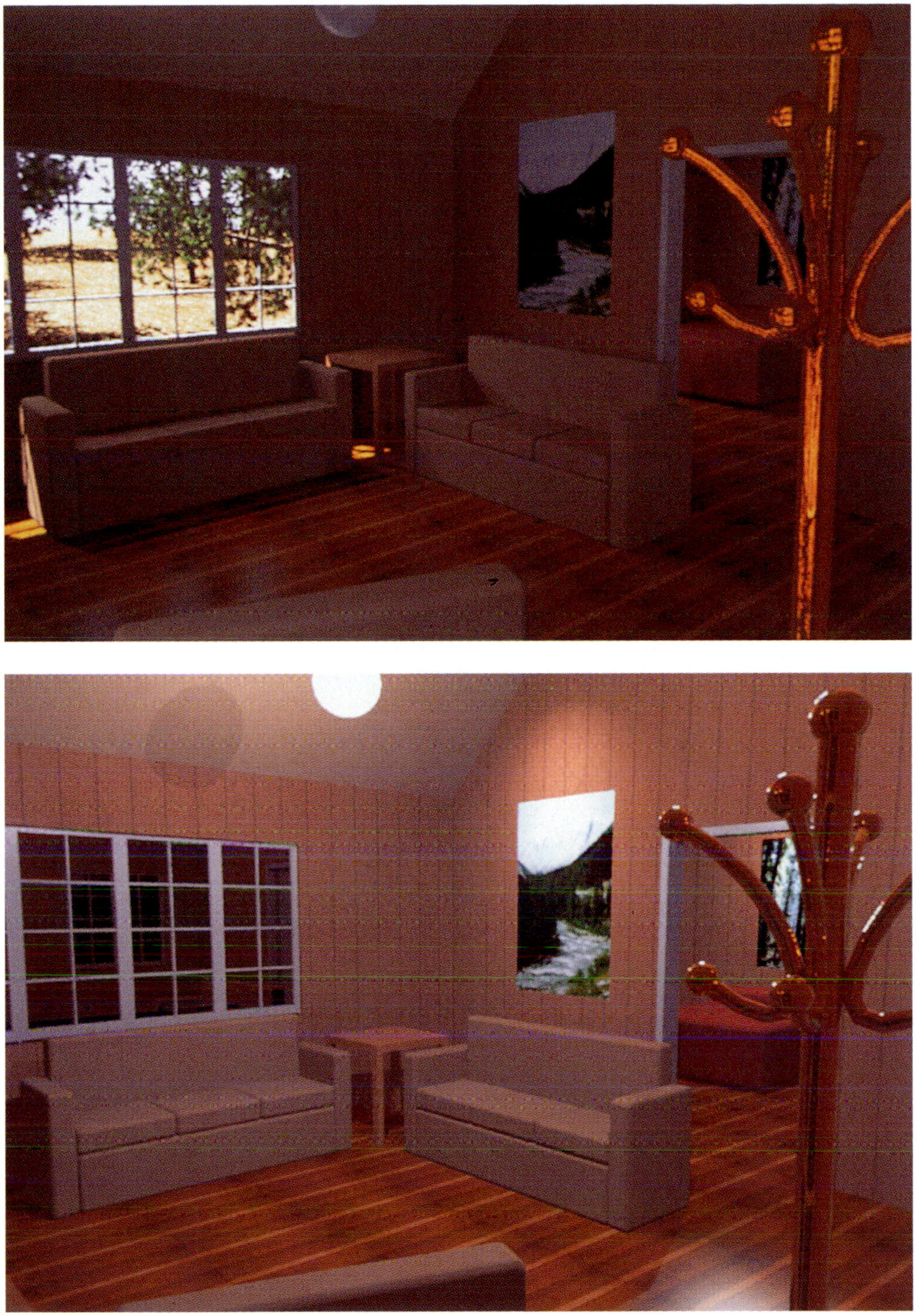

(a)

(b)

FIGURE 20.9

Images corrected by the Ward scale factor, with the adaptation level set at the window. (a) A cabin by day. (b) A cabin by night. *(Courtesy of Greg Ward.)*

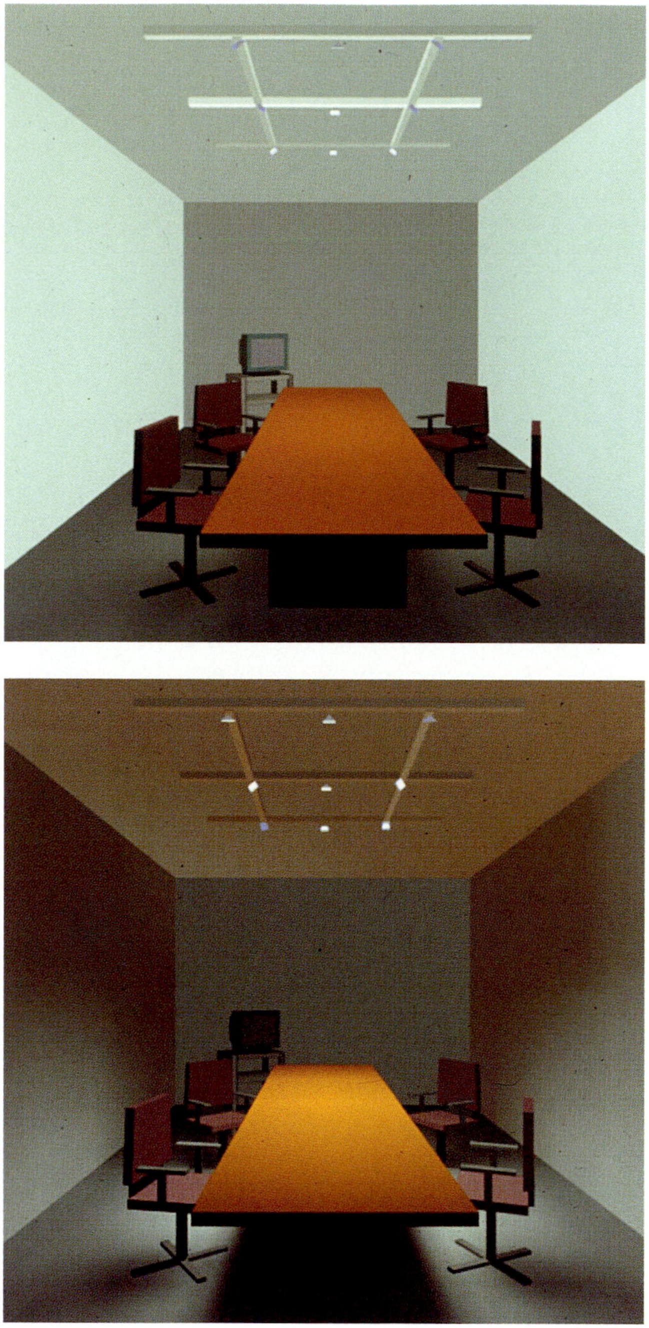

(a)

(b)

FIGURE 20.11

A conference room with optimized lighting. (a) An impression of visual clarity. (b) An impression of privacy. Reprinted, by permission, from Kawai et al. in *Computer Graphics (Proc. Siggraph '93)*, fig. 6, p. 154.

The factor $1/A_i$ is convenient because it means the form factor satisfies a symmetrical *reciprocity rule*:

$$F_{k,i}A_k = F_{i,k}A_i \tag{18.22}$$

which comes straight from the definition. This rule is very useful in computations. The form factor is also called the *radiation factor*, the *angle factor*, and the *configuration factor*.

Writing Equation 18.20 in terms of the form factor gives

$$B_iA_i = E_iA_i + \rho_i \sum_{k=1}^{n} B_kA_iF_{i,k} \tag{18.23}$$

Using the reciprocity of form factors in Equation 18.22, we note that we can re-express this equation as

$$B_iA_i = E_iA_i + \rho_i \sum_{k=1}^{n} B_kA_kF_{k,i} \tag{18.24}$$

Equation 18.24 is the key to developing an intuition for the classical radiosity method. On the left appears B_iA_i, which is the product of the power per unit area leaving patch i times the area of patch i; thus it's the total power radiated by patch i into the universe. This total power is the sum of two terms: the power emitted directly by the patch itself, and the power propagated by the patch by reflection.

Writing out the power explicitly,

$$\Phi_i{}^o = \Phi_i{}^e + \rho_i \sum_{k=1}^{n} \Phi_kF_{k,i} \tag{18.25}$$

we can see at a glance that the form factor describes how much of the energy Φ_k radiated by patch M_k gets to M_i.

The first term on the right of Equation 18.24 is the emitted power per unit area on patch i (e.g., due to incandescent or blackbody processes), times the area of patch i, so this is the total power generated by the patch and sent into the environment.

The right-hand term tells us to look around at every patch k in the environment. We find the power emitted by that patch from B_kA_k. The form factor $F_{k,i}$ tells us how much of this power reaches patch i. The power received from each patch k in the scene is accumulated, and then scaled by the reflectivity ρ_i of the patch. This reflected power is added to the emitted power to represent the total outgoing power.

The value of Equation 18.24 is that it combines both the self-emitted power and the reflected power from every patch to express the total outgoing power. This is the power used by the other $n - 1$ patches. In other words, Equation 18.24 specifies

$B_i A_i$, and there are $n-1$ other equations giving the power of all the other patches. By solving all these equations simultaneously, we get a set of consistent values for B_i that represent the radiosity of every patch in a stable environment.

Equation 18.24 can be made a bit more efficient for practical calculation. As before, we first use the reciprocity of form factors to write $A_i F_{i,k} = A_k F_{k,i}$,

$$B_i A_i = E_i A_i + \rho_i \sum_{k=1}^{n} B_k A_i F_{i,k} \tag{18.26}$$

and then we divide through by A_i:

$$B_i = E_i + \rho_i \sum_{k=1}^{n} B_k F_{i,k} \tag{18.27}$$

Equation 18.27 is the *classical radiosity equation.*

Equation 18.27 expresses a set of n simultaneous equations for the radiosity B for each of the n patches in the scene. We get the classical radiosity system of equations

$$(\mathbf{I} - \mathbf{F})\mathbf{B} = \mathbf{E} \tag{18.28}$$

or in tableau form,

$$\begin{bmatrix} 1-\rho_1 F_{1,1} & -\rho_1 F_{1,2} & \cdots & -\rho_1 F_{1,n} \\ \rho_2 F_{2,1} & 1-\rho_1 F_{1,2} & & \vdots \\ \vdots & & \ddots & \vdots \\ \rho_n F_{n,1} & \cdots & \cdots & 1-\rho_n F_{n,n} \end{bmatrix} \begin{bmatrix} B_1 \\ B_2 \\ \vdots \\ B_3 \end{bmatrix} = \begin{bmatrix} E_1 \\ E_2 \\ \vdots \\ E_3 \end{bmatrix} \tag{18.29}$$

Once the matrix has been built, it may be inverted to find the solution $\mathbf{B} = (\mathbf{I} - \mathbf{F})^{-1}\mathbf{E}$.

The matrix elements in Equation 18.28 are much easier to construct than those in the full collocation or Galerkin cases; it only depends on computing the form factors.

We can demonstrate the classical radiosity technique on a simple example. To make life easy, we will choose a geometric situation where analytic form factors are known and not too complicated. Figure 18.2 shows an infinite shelf made up of three flat pieces: a flat bottom and two walls. The width of the floor B of the shelf is b, and the walls A and C each have height a above them. Defining $g = b/a$, from Appendix D, we can write the six form factors relating each pair of surfaces. Because

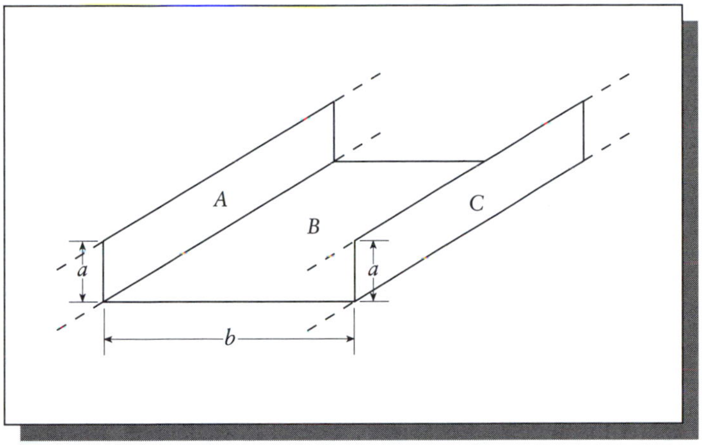

FIGURE 18.2
An infinite shelf.

of symmetry, we need only the three form factors

$$\begin{aligned}F_{A,B} &= \frac{1}{2}\left(1 + g - \sqrt{1+g^2}\right)\\ F_{A,C} &= \sqrt{1+g^2} - g\\ F_{B,C} &= \frac{1}{2}\left(1 + (1/g) - \sqrt{1+(1/g)^2}\right)\end{aligned} \tag{18.30}$$

The others are

$$F_{C,B} = F_{A,B} \qquad F_{C,A} = F_{A,C} \qquad F_{B,A} = F_{B,C} \tag{18.31}$$

The form factor matrix K is

$$K = \begin{bmatrix} 1 & -\rho_A F_{A,B} & -\rho_A F_{A,C} \\ -\rho_B F_{B,A} & 1 & -\rho_B F_{B,C} \\ -\rho_C F_{C,A} & -\rho_C F_{C,B} & 1 \end{bmatrix} \tag{18.32}$$

Figure 18.3 shows four example configurations of the shelf, with results tabulated in Table 18.1. In the first example we turn on emission from wall A only, set its reflectivity to 0, and let the light bounce around. Then we assign a bit of reflectivity to wall A; note that all the radiances go up. This is because of light that leaves A, bounces off of B or C, and then reflects off A to strike B or C again. A bit more

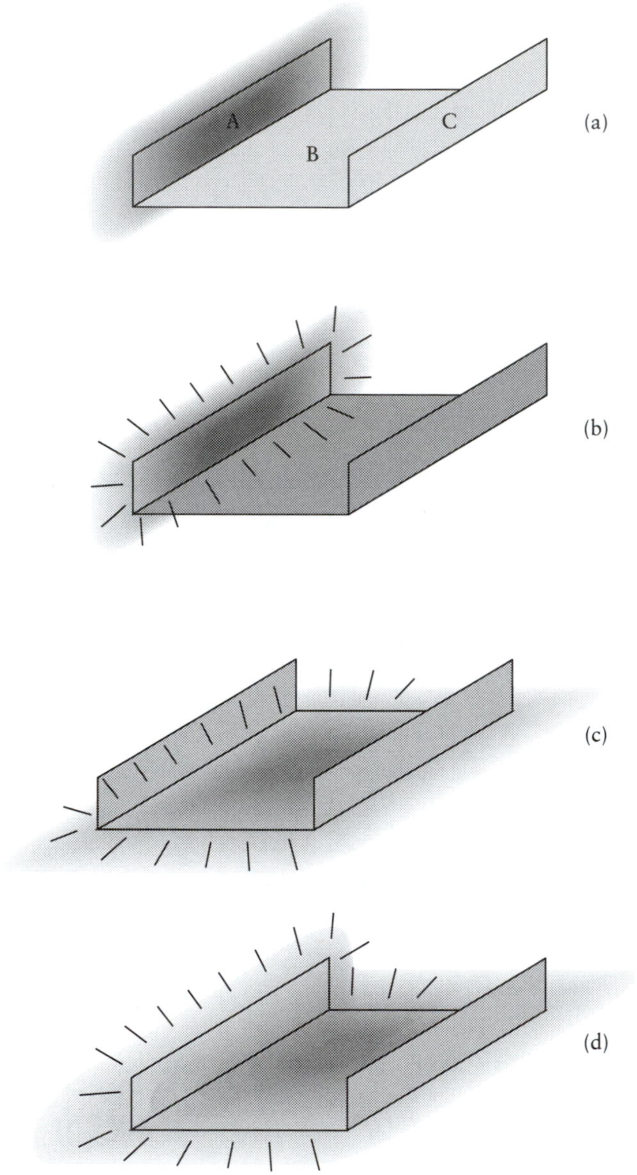

FIGURE 18.3

(a) Wall A radiating, B and C reflecting. (b) Wall A radiating, all walls reflecting. (c) Wall B radiating, B and C reflecting. (d) Walls A and B radiating, all walls reflecting.

Reflectivity	Emissivity	Radiosity
$\begin{bmatrix} \rho_A \\ \rho_B \\ \rho_C \end{bmatrix}$	$\begin{bmatrix} E_A \\ E_B \\ E_C \end{bmatrix}$	$\begin{bmatrix} B_A \\ B_B \\ B_C \end{bmatrix}$
$\begin{bmatrix} 0 \\ 1/2 \\ 1/3 \end{bmatrix}$	$\begin{bmatrix} 1 \\ 0 \\ 0 \end{bmatrix}$	$\begin{bmatrix} 1 \\ 0.11660 \\ 0.10354 \end{bmatrix}$
$\begin{bmatrix} 1/10 \\ 1/2 \\ 1/3 \end{bmatrix}$	$\begin{bmatrix} 1 \\ 0 \\ 0 \end{bmatrix}$	$\begin{bmatrix} 1.00709 \\ 0.11743 \\ 0.10428 \end{bmatrix}$
$\begin{bmatrix} 1/2 \\ 0 \\ 1/2 \end{bmatrix}$	$\begin{bmatrix} 0 \\ 1 \\ 0 \end{bmatrix}$	$\begin{bmatrix} 0.21133 \\ 1 \\ 0.21133 \end{bmatrix}$
$\begin{bmatrix} 1/10 \\ 1/10 \\ 1/2 \end{bmatrix}$	$\begin{bmatrix} 1 \\ 1 \\ 0 \end{bmatrix}$	$\begin{bmatrix} 1.04647 \\ 0.02906 \\ 0.32853 \end{bmatrix}$

TABLE 18.1
Results for the infinite shelf environment.

light therefore comes off of A, and also contributes to B and C. In the third case the only emitter is the floor B; because of symmetry we expect the radiosity on the walls to be equal, and the data shows that it is. Finally, we turn on both the floor and the wall, with a bit of reflectivity for both, and we see that the illumination on the right-hand wall goes up.

18.2.4 Higher-Order Radiosity

We call any radiosity system that uses basis functions other than the constant functions used by classical radiosity an example of *high-order radiosity*. Such systems are appealing because they can relax one or more of the assumptions made by classical radiosity. In particular, the use of nonconstant basis functions means that the environment can be rendered to a given degree of accuracy without requiring the level of fine subdivision required by classical radiosity. This is because higher-order methods are able to describe changing radiosity over a surface, while classical methods rely on subdivision of that surface into constant elements small enough to represent that variation.

A comparative study of collocation and Galerkin methods in 3D has been reported by Troutman and Max [440]. They found that in their implementation the extra cost of the Galerkin method was not justified by its performance with respect to collocation using a discontinuity-based meshing of the environment (discussed below).

Similar results have been reported by Zatz [503] based on his implementation of Galerkin radiosity; he noted that although the Galerkin method required much less memory than collocation, both techniques required about the same amount of time to create an image of about the same quality with respect to a reference image. However, even if the image error metrics are similar, the smooth gradation of radiosity across a curved surface manages to avoid Mach banding and other artifacts that accompany finely meshed radiosity scenes. Figure 18.4 (color plate) shows an interior room containing only 607 surfaces; note the smooth distribution of light in the scene.

One problem with higher-order methods is that they do not easily accommodate sharp shadows (low-order methods have a problem with this, too, but for different reasons). The difficulty is that a single set of basis functions needs to represent the light distribution across a surface, and if that distribution changes suddenly, then it requires some very localized high-frequency changes; these can be difficult to generate with smooth basis functions. Similarly, when a patch P_p sits between two patches P_i and P_k, we need to determine how much of the light from P_i reaches P_k based on the light description over P_i and the geometry of the three patches; this can be difficult. Zatz has developed a *shadow-mask* technique which accounts for partial occlusion, but the method is difficult to control automatically, and scenes including such masks will not converge to a correct solution [503].

Another nonconstant set of basis functions for radiosity are the wavelet bases [384]. These are closely related to the *hierarchical radiosity* technique discussed below.

18.3 Solving the Matrix Equation

In Section 18.2 we wrote matrix equations that defined a set of simultaneous conditions on the radiosity B within an environment. These equations were generally of the form

$$\mathbf{KB} = \mathbf{E} \tag{18.33}$$

for a set of emissivities $\mathbf{E}$ and a matrix $\mathbf{K}$ built from form factors and basis functions. Although formally this equation can be solved for a nonsingular $\mathbf{K}$ by writing $\mathbf{B} = \mathbf{K}^{-1}\mathbf{E}$, this is often impractical.

The problem is twofold: the sheer size of $\mathbf{K}$ presents storage and inversion problems, and the expense of computing each element is usually considerable, so we would prefer not to compute elements that we don't need.

Consider size first. The matrix $\mathbf{K}$ is square, containing n elements on a side when there are n patches in the environment. If we double the number of patches, the size of $\mathbf{K}$ quadruples. The size leads directly to storage problems: we need to put all of these elements somewhere, and when we access them we can begin to find that practical issues like page faults become serious issues. Related to the size is the difficulty of the inversion; Gaussian techniques are $O(n^3)$ in the size of the matrix side n [348]. This can become prohibitively expensive in modern scenes, which can contain tens of thousands of patches.

The other problem with a large matrix is that computation of each element $K_{i,k}$ can be very expensive. Even in the classic radiosity case where we use box functions, we still must calculate the form factor $F_{i,k}$ between each pair of patches i and k. We will see a number of ways of doing this in Section 18.5, but it is generally not an inexpensive operation.

So, rather than explicitly invert the matrix and multiply it with the emission terms, a number of *iterative* methods have been developed that take an initial guess at the solution vector $\mathbf{B}$ and then slowly refine that guess until it contains less than some prescribed amount of error.

The particular form of iterative techniques that are used for solving radiosity problems are called *relaxation methods*. There are many types of relaxation methods described in the numerical methods literature, and efficient and stable programs for implementing them are widely available [348]. In this section we will review four methods that have proven particularly useful for radiosity: *Jacobi iteration*, *Gauss-Seidel iteration*, *Southwell iteration*, and *overrelaxation*.

We will first describe these for a general matrix equation, and then discuss the physical interpretation of the operations in the context of radiosity solutions. Our presentation of these methods follows Gortler and Cohen [166].

We suppose that we are given the linear system

$$\mathbf{K}\mathbf{x} = \mathbf{b} \tag{18.34}$$

where $\mathbf{K}$ is an $n \times n$ matrix, and $\mathbf{x}$ and $\mathbf{b}$ are n-element column vectors. We are given $\mathbf{K}$ and $\mathbf{b}$, and we wish to find $\mathbf{x}$. An element of $\mathbf{x}$ is written x_i for $i \in [1, n]$, and an element of $\mathbf{K}$ is written $K_{i,k}$ for $i, k \in [1, n]$.

We will generate a series of approximate solutions to $\mathbf{x}$ that are intended to converge to the real solution (we will assume that such a solution always exists). The approximation after step g is written $\mathbf{x}^{(g)}$; the parentheses around the superscript are intended to remind us that this doesn't represent an exponent. As in Equation 16.19, we define the *error* $\mathbf{e}^{(g)}$ in the gth approximation by

$$\mathbf{e}^{(g)} \stackrel{\triangle}{=} \mathbf{x} - \mathbf{x}^{(g)} \tag{18.35}$$

and the *residual* $\mathbf{r}^{(g)}$ in the gth approximation by

$$\mathbf{r}^{(g)} \stackrel{\triangle}{=} \mathbf{b} - \mathbf{K}\mathbf{x}^{(g)} \tag{18.36}$$

And as we saw in Equation 16.20,

$$\mathbf{r}^{(g)} = \mathbf{K}\mathbf{e}^{(g)} \tag{18.37}$$

Relaxation methods use the residual to refine the approximation $\mathbf{x}^{(g)}$ and generate its successor $\mathbf{x}^{(g+1)}$. The general plan is to look at some element ${r_i}^{(g)}$ of the residual vector, and apply some transformation to the corresponding element ${x_i}^{(g)}$ so that ${r_i}^{(g)}$ goes to zero. This will probably cause the other elements of $\mathbf{r}$ to change, and perhaps increase, but the hope is that the general trend is toward smaller values for all elements of the residual vector.

Let's find out what we need to do to ${x_i}^{(g)}$ so that the next generation's corresponding residual ${r_i}^{(g+1)}$ will be zero. We begin by writing out the matrix equation for row i:

$$\begin{aligned} \sum_{k=1}^{n} K_{i,k}{x_k}^{(g)} &= b_i \\ K_{i,1}{x_1}^{(g)} + K_{i,2}{x_2}^{(g)} + \cdots + K_{i,i}{x_i}^{(g)} + \cdots + K_{i,n}{x_n}^{(g)} &= b_i \end{aligned} \tag{18.38}$$

Since we want to change ${x_i}^{(g)}$, we can move everything but $K_{i,i}{x_i}^{(g)}$ to the right side of this equation

$$K_{i,i}{x_i}^{(g)} = b_i - \sum_{\substack{k=1\\k\neq i}}^{n} K_{i,k}{x_k}^{(g)} \tag{18.39}$$

and then divide through by $K_{i,i}$:

$$\begin{aligned} K_{i,i}{x_i}^{(g)} &= \frac{b_i}{K_{i,i}} - \sum_{\substack{k=1\\k\neq i}}^{n} \frac{K_{i,k}}{K_{i,i}}{x_k}^{(g)} \\ &= {x_i}^{(g)} + \frac{{r_i}^{(g)}}{K_{i,i}} \end{aligned} \tag{18.40}$$

We call this last quantity $\Delta{x_i}^{(g)}$.

for $i \leftarrow 0$ to n
  $x_i \leftarrow 0$
  endfor
	Initialize the first guess.

while not converged	*Update the unknown vector.*

$\mathbf{r}^{(g)} = \mathbf{b} - \mathbf{K}\mathbf{x}^{(g)}$
  for $i \leftarrow 0$ to n
    $x_i{}^{(g+1)} \leftarrow x_i{}^{(g)} + r_i^{(g)}/K_{i,i}$
    endfor
	Update each element.

endwhile	

FIGURE 18.5

Jacobi iteration.

Adjusting an element so that its residual goes to zero is called *relaxing* the element.

The iteration continues until the *convergence criteria* are met. Typical criteria are that the magnitude of every element of the residual must be less than a threshold, and that the change in an unknown element be less than a threshold:

$$\begin{aligned} \max(|\mathbf{r}|) &< t \\ \left| x_i{}^{(g)} - x_i{}^{(g+1)} \right| &< t \end{aligned} \tag{18.41}$$

18.3.1 Jacobi Iteration

The *Jacobi iteration* method is a straightforward application of the machinery of the previous section. We first create an initial guess of all zeros, and then enter a loop. First we test for convergence; if the error in the solution is low enough, we exit. Otherwise we compute the residual vector $\mathbf{r}^{(g)}$. We now step through each of the n elements of x and add the correction factor required to bring its residual to zero. When we're done, we return to the top and test for convergence. The Jacobi algorithm is summarized in Figure 18.5.

18.3.2 Gauss-Seidel Iteration

The *Gauss-Seidel iteration* method is just like the Jacobi method except for a small change. Recall that the Jacobi loop begins with the calculation of the residual from the current $x^{(g)}$, and then the next generation's elements are computed from that

for $i \leftarrow 0$ to n	
$x_i \leftarrow 0$	*Initialize the first guess.*
endfor	
while not converged	*Update the unknown vector.*
for $i \leftarrow 0$ to n	
$x_i \leftarrow (b_i - \sum_{k=1,k\neq i}^{n} x_k K_{i,k})/K_{i,i}$	*Update each element.*
endfor	
endwhile	

FIGURE 18.6

Gauss-Seidel iteration.

information. This means that we don't actually use the new values in $\mathbf{x}^{(g+1)}$ until they have all been created, and we use them to create the new residual $\mathbf{r}^{(g+1)}$. The Gauss-Seidel method simply updates the elements in place, and calculates the residual anew for each element. This means that when we're updating the $\mathbf{x_3}^{(g)}$, we use the values $\mathbf{x_1}^{(g)}$ and $\mathbf{x_2}^{(g)}$ in the calculation. Rather than explicitly recalculating the entire residual, we use the immediate form in Equation 18.40. The Gauss-Seidel algorithm is summarized in Figure 18.6.

18.3.3 Southwell Iteration

The method of *Southwell iteration* adds another wrinkle to the basic Jacobi algorithm. Like Gauss-Seidel, it uses the most recently computed unknowns to update each element. Notice that Gauss-Seidel always updates each element of the unknown in turn. So if the residual is large for only one element of the unknown and small for the rest, we will only get to process the element with large error every nth step. The Southwell method doesn't bother looping through the elements of the unknown in order, but uses a greedy heuristic to relax the element with the residual of largest magnitude first. Then if we're not converged, it again goes after the largest residual. This means that the same element can be repeatedly adjusted to the exclusion of all others if it's far more out of range.

Since we always want to relax the residual element with the greatest magnitude, we need to make sure that after each adjustment we update the residual vector. This looks expensive, because the residual depends on every unknown. Happily, the new residual can be computed efficiently.

To see how to compute this new residual, start by observing that the change in the unknown vector $\mathbf{x}$ from one step to the next may be written

$$\mathbf{x}^{(g+1)} = \mathbf{x}^{(g)} + \Delta\mathbf{x}^{(g)} \tag{18.42}$$

The new residual is then

$$\begin{aligned} \mathbf{r}^{(g+1)} &= \mathbf{b} - \mathbf{K}\mathbf{x}^{(g+1)} \\ &= \mathbf{b} - \mathbf{K}(\mathbf{x}^{(g)} + \Delta\mathbf{x}^{(g)}) \\ &= \mathbf{b} - \mathbf{K}\mathbf{x}^{(g)} + \mathbf{K}\Delta\mathbf{x}^{(g)} \\ &= \mathbf{r}^{(g)} + \mathbf{K}\Delta\mathbf{x}^{(g)} \end{aligned} \tag{18.43}$$

Now because we only update one element of the unknown at a time, $\Delta\mathbf{x}^g$ is all zero except for component i, which is ${r_i}^{(g)}/K_{i,i}$. Then we can update the residual vector by removing just the amount due to element i from each element k:

$${r_k}^{(g+1)} = {r_k}^{(g)} - \frac{K_{k,i}}{K_{i,i}}{r_k}^{(g)} \tag{18.44}$$

To get the ball rolling we need an initial residual vector $\mathbf{r}^{(0)}$. If as before we use an initial unknown guess of $\mathbf{x} = 0$, then

$$\mathbf{r}^{(0)} = \mathbf{b} - \mathbf{K}\mathbf{x}^{(0)} = \mathbf{b} - 0\mathbf{K} = \mathbf{b} \tag{18.45}$$

The Southwell algorithm is summarized in Figure 18.7.

18.3.4 Overrelaxation

The idea of *overrelaxation* can be used with any of the methods described above. The idea is that instead of subtracting out just the necessary amount from an element to set its residual to zero, we anticipate the need to subtract more later on and subtract it now. This is an aggressive strategy; the degree to which we anticipate the future is determined by a factor ω_i for element i of the unknown. So during any update step:

$${x_i}^{(g+1)} = {x_i}^{(g)} + \Delta{x_i}^{(g)} \tag{18.46}$$

we instead use

$${x_i}^{(g+1)} = {x_i}^{(g)} + \omega_i\Delta{x_i}^{(g)} \tag{18.47}$$

The ith residual is no longer zero, but

$${r_i}^{(g+1)} = (1 - \omega_i){r_i}^{(g)} \tag{18.48}$$

for $i \leftarrow 0$ to n $x_i \leftarrow 0$ $r_i \leftarrow b_i$ endfor	*Initialize the first guess and residual.*
while not converged	*Improve estimate.*
select i so that $r_i = \max(\mathbf{r})$ $x_i \leftarrow x_i + r_i / K_{i,i}$	*Update one element.*
$t \leftarrow r_i$	*Get the residual just relaxed.*
for $k \leftarrow 0$ to n $r_k \leftarrow r_k - t(K_{j,i}/K_{i,i})$ endfor	*Update the residual vector.*
endwhile	

FIGURE 18.7
Southwell iteration.

If $\omega_i > 1$, the technique is called *overrelaxation*, while if $0 < \omega_i < 1$, the technique is called *underrelaxation*. Underrelaxation can be useful for unstable systems.

18.4 Solving Radiosity Matrices

We'll now consider each of the matrix solution methods described above in turn as a method for solving radiosity problems. We will look at the physical interpretation of the mathematics in terms of energy transfer in an environment. We will not focus on issues of convergence and stability. An analysis of convergence may be found in Gortler and Cohen [166], where it is shown that these methods will indeed converge for radiosity problems. Discussions of stability may be found in numerical methods books such as Press et al. [348] and Ralston and Rabinowitz [353].

For the purpose of illustration, we will take a matrix that corresponds to the classical radiosity tableau of Equation 18.29. That is, in the equation

$$\mathbf{KB} = \mathbf{E} \tag{18.49}$$

the n-element vectors $\mathbf{B}$ and $\mathbf{E}$ correspond to the radiosities and emittances of the n patches, and the $n \times n$ matrix $\mathbf{K}$ contains reflectivities and form factors:

$$K_{i,k} = \delta_{ik} - \rho_i F_{i,k} \tag{18.50}$$

We will further assume that all the patches are convex, so the form factor of any patch to itself is zero: $F_{i,i} = 0$.

This matrix is illustrated in schematic form in Figure 18.8 for a simple scene. Here we have only shown the direction of transfer implied by the form factors; the magnitude of the form factors and the coefficient ρ_i aren't shown.

In terms of radiosity, the patch emittances usually form the first guess for the patch radiosities. The residual measures the difference between the emittance and the reflected radiosity; that is, the radiosity that hasn't yet been distributed into the environment. A common metaphor is to think of each patch as having two bins in which radiosity is accumulated. In one bin we have the radiosity of the patch itself; this is the power per unit area we would see if we looked at the patch at that moment. We can think of this as the energy the patch is *shooting* into space. In the other bin is the *undistributed* radiosity; this is some additional energy per unit area that the patch should be distributing into the environment, but we haven't yet gotten around to taking care of computationally; this is also called *unshot* radiosity.

So the residual tells us how much more energy the patch should be distributing into the environment than it already is; by increasing the patch's radiosity, we drive down the residual, and decrease the amount of energy in the undistributed bin.

Many practical algorithms make a time-space trade-off and compute matrix elements only when they are needed. In the case of the simple radiosity system this means that form factors are computed on the fly when a pair of patches exchanges power. We say these elements are computed *on demand*, *dynamically*, or *lazily*. Elements built by lazy evaluation may be cached for a fixed or indefinite period of time in case they are needed again, or disposed of to save on storage.

18.4.1 Jacobi Iteration

In Jacobi iteration we update all the elements of the unknown vector at once. In terms of radiosity, this means that the radiosity of every patch is incremented to represent the undistributed energy.

This method is not widely used because of its great expense. Typically a small number of patches account for most of the radiosity (at least at the beginning of a simulation where we have a dark room and a few luminaires), and it's wasteful to update all the patches at every step when they don't contribute much to the image or the distribution of light in the scene.

18.4.2 Gauss-Seidel Iteration

Gauss-Seidel iteration updates the entire solution one step at a time, but uses the new values as they are computed to increase efficiency. In terms of the classical radiosity

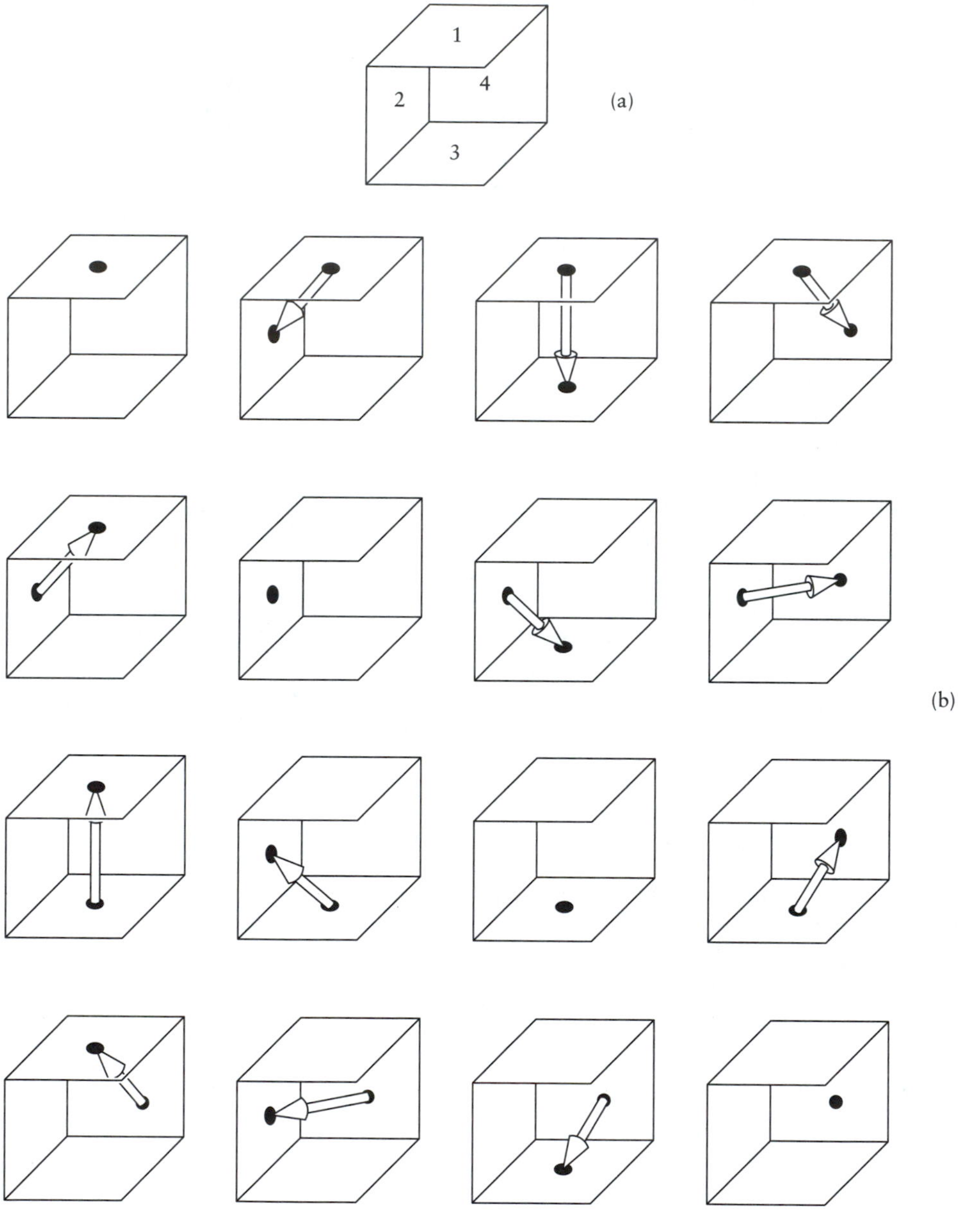

FIGURE 18.8
(a) A scene of four walls. (b) A graphical representation of the form factor matrix for (a).

matrix, the Gauss-Seidel step for patch i takes the form

$$B_i = E_i + \rho_i \sum_{\substack{k=1 \\ k \neq i}}^{n} F_{i,k} B_k \tag{18.51}$$

To see the physical interpretation of this step, we will multiply through by A_i the area of patch i:

$$B_i A_i = E_i A_i + \rho_i \sum_{\substack{k=1 \\ k \neq i}}^{n} B_k A_i F_{i,k} \tag{18.52}$$

and then use the reciprocity relationship of form factors in Equation 18.22 to get the expression in terms of $F_{k,i}$:

$$B_i A_i = E_i A_i + \rho_i \sum_{\substack{k=1 \\ k \neq i}}^{n} B_k A_k F_{k,i} \tag{18.53}$$

We can interpret Equation 18.53 in physical terms. On the left is $B_i A_i$, the power coming out of patch i into the environment. This power is the sum of the emitted power $E_i A_i$ and the reflected power *gathered* from all other patches in the environment. The key here is the loop over all the patches: it visits each patch k, *gathers* the power $B_k A_k$, and then finds the fraction $F_{k,i}$ of that power directly transferred from patch k to patch i. This process is illustrated in Figure 18.9, where we have shown the power transfers involved in updating one patch, and those elements of the matrix involved using the same conventions as Figure 18.8(b).

Notice that what we're doing here is finding the dot product of a vector of radiosities with a column of the matrix (though in the original computational form of Equation 18.51 it's a row of the matrix).

Figure 18.10 (color plate) shows an interior scene after different numbers of steps of the Gauss-Seidel algorithm.

18.4.3 Southwell Iteration

In Southwell iteration we look for the element with the largest residual and relax it. If the solution isn't converged, we repeat the process. In terms of radiosity, this means we're finding the patch with the largest *undistributed* radiosity and sending that into the environment.

In other words, we look for the patch that has the most radiosity that has not yet been accounted for, and we relax that patch by sending this radiosity into the environment. This is called *shooting* the power, as distinguished from the gathering performed by the Gauss-Seidel algorithm. The process begins by selecting the

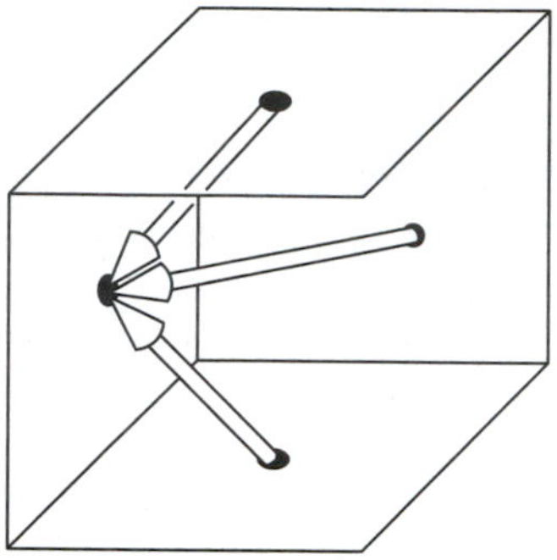

(a)

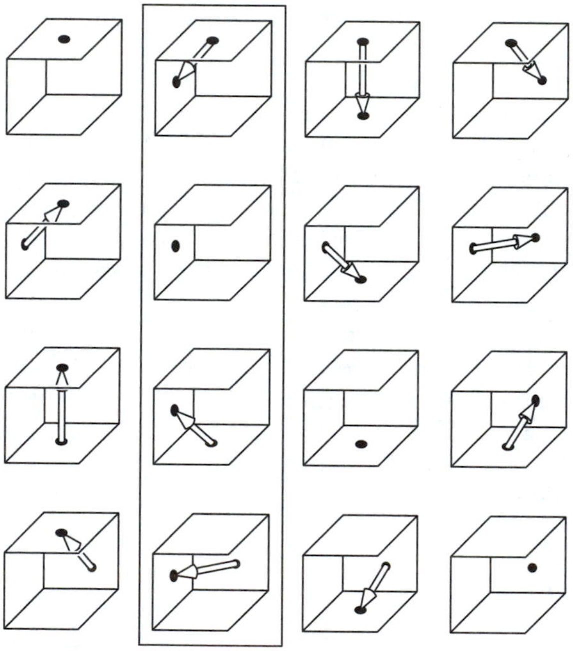

(b)

FIGURE 18.9

(a) A Gauss-Seidel gathering step for surface 2. (b) The column of matrix elements involved in the transfer.

brightest light source in the environment, and distributing the radiosity from that light to all the other surfaces. The next patch chosen might be another light source, or it might be a surface patch if that piece of surface received a lot of energy and had a high reflectivity coefficient.

A step of the Southwell algorithm is shown in Figure 18.11.

Figure 18.12 (color plate) shows an interior scene after different numbers of steps of the Southwell algorithm.

18.4.4 Progressive Refinement

The method of *progressive refinement*, introduced by Cohen et al. [95], uses a variant on Southwell iteration to produce a useful image at each step of the solution process [99]. This is desirable because it allows a designer to see estimates of the final simulation as the computation proceeds.

There are a few important changes introduced in this algorithm beyond straight Southwell iteration. Calling ΔB_i the unshot radiosity at patch i, progressive refinement (PR) selects the next patch to shoot by finding the one with the largest unshot *power* $A_i \Delta B_i$, not just the largest unshot radiosity B_i.

When the Southwell refinement has satisfied the termination criteria, Cohen et al. add a final step of Jacobi iteration to simultaneously distribute the remaining unshot radiosities into the scene.

Because the Southwell approach selects the brightest patch first, progressive radiosity will quickly shoot energy from the bright lights into the environment, and then gradually fill in the subtle details from repeated interreflections. The result of this process was shown in Figure 18.12. Note that it is easier to see the details in the picture and get an overall impression of the final image earlier in the process than with the Gauss-Seidel rule in Figure 18.10. However, in the early iterations, much of the image is still dark. Although Southwell relaxation will eventually find a converged solution, for practical use we would like the intermediate images (particularly the first few) to be closer to the final result.

Cohen et al. have suggested a number of heuristics to improve the *appearance* of the intermediate images. Note that this is effectively *postprocessing* the solution at each step for display; we are not changing the solution process, just how the results are presented after each step. The idea is based on the observation that we can quantify $\overline{\Delta B}$, the average *unshot* radiosity in the scene, by simply adding up all the unshot power and dividing by the total area:

$$\overline{\Delta B} = \frac{\sum_{i=1}^{n} \Delta B_i A_i}{\sum_{i=1}^{n} A_i} \tag{18.54}$$

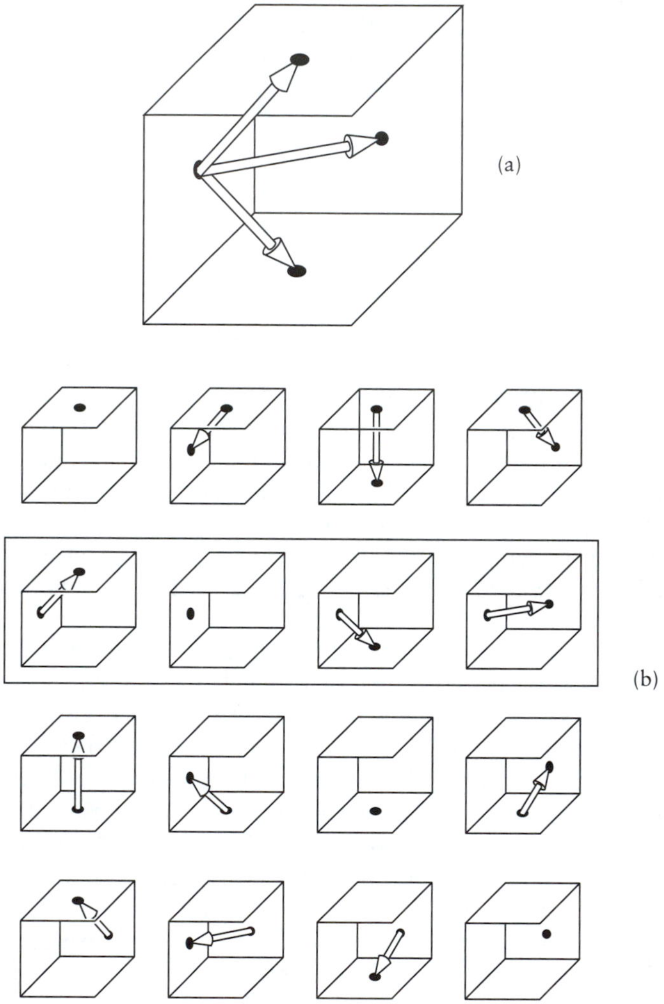

FIGURE 18.11

(a) A Southwell shooting step for surface 2. (b) The row of matrix elements involved in the transfer.

By the same reasoning, we can find the average reflectivity $\overline{\rho}$ from

$$\overline{\rho} = \frac{\sum_{i=1}^{n} \Delta\rho_i A_i}{\sum_{i=1}^{n} A_i} \tag{18.55}$$

Now consider what happens when the unshot radiosity is released into the scene. The initial release of the unshot radiosity adds $\overline{\Delta B}$ to the scene. After one reflection off the surfaces, $\overline{\rho}\overline{\Delta B}$ is reflected back into the environment, where it is reflected again, sending out $\overline{\rho}^2\overline{\Delta B}$, and so on, again and again. The result of all this reflection is B_a, an *ambient* term that estimates the total unshot radiosity after reflecting around the environment:

$$B_a = \overline{\Delta B}(1 + \overline{\rho} + \overline{\rho}^2 + \cdots) = \overline{\Delta B}\frac{1}{1 - \overline{\rho}} \tag{18.56}$$

For the purposes of intermediate images only, each patch i may be displayed with radiosity $B_i + \rho_i B_a$.

As the radiosity estimate improves, the amount of unshot radiosity $\overline{\Delta B}$ drops, reducing the amount of ambient light added to the image. Figure 18.13 (color plate) shows an interior scene after several steps of the progressive refinement algorithm including ambient display. Notice how much better the early pictures appear using this estimate of the ambient light.

Another important practical aspect of the PR approach is that it does not compute and store the entire matrix of form factors before processing. Rather, each time a patch i is selected for shooting, all the form factors $F_{i,k}$ to the environment are computed dynamically, used for a single Southwell step, and then forgotten. This means that the same form factors will likely be created over and over again during a single simulation. This is unfortunate, but when the environment is very large it becomes impractical to store the form factor matrix. In this type of application, an efficient means for computing the form factors is imperative. An example of the PR algorithm in a complex environment is shown in Figure 18.14 (color plate), which contained 2,000 patches (the PR pass was followed by a second pass in which the PR solution was processed to fit a finer mesh).

18.4.5 Overrelaxation

As discussed earlier, overrelaxation may be added to any of the solution methods by scaling up the correction term at each stage. The central question is how much overshooting should be performed at each step.

In an algorithm presented by Feda and Purgathofer [141], the adjusted radiosity $\Delta B_i'$ to shoot is computed as the minimum of two candidates: one is the estimated radiosity produced by the PR algorithm, and the other is this patch's area-weighted share of the average unshot radiosity in the scene.

$$\Delta B_i' = \min(\Delta B_i + \rho_i B_a, \sum_{k=1}^{n} B_k A_k / A_i) \tag{18.57}$$

In fact, the choice of the next patch to be shot in a Southwell-type relaxation algorithm is made based on the overestimated energy $A_i \Delta B_i'$.

Gortler and Cohen [166] have developed an overshooting algorithm that solves a restricted subproblem in the radiosity model. They select a single patch i, and solve for the interaction of this patch with the entire environment, including the reflection of energy back onto the shooting patch.

They report good results in their tests using a relaxation factor of 1.2.

18.4.6 Comparison

All of the algorithms discussed above, plus some variants, were compared by Gortler and Cohen [166]. They constructed a number of test cases, including simple scenes containing cubes, an office environment, and a random matrix with the same general structure as a radiosity matrix (that is, diagonally dominant).

The results are shown in Figure 18.15 for the office environment, and two random matrices with a few emitters (representing light sources) in a dim (low-reflectivity) and bright (high-reflectivity) environment. The error at step g was measured by

$$E^{(g)} = \frac{\sum_{i=1}^{n}(B_i^r - B_i^{(g)})}{\sum_{i=1}^{n}(B_i^r - E_i)} \tag{18.58}$$

where B_i^r is the reference (or correct) value for patch i. Notice that this measure simply estimates accuracy, and not computational cost, speed, or storage requirements.

The algorithms are keyed in the figure by these codes:

GS0 (Gauss-Seidel iteration). The initial guess is 0, and the patches are refined in order.

GSJ (Gauss-Seidel + Jacobi iteration). Like GS0, but the result at each step is the radiosity of each patch plus the unshot radiosity.

S (Southwell iteration). Like GS0, except that the patches are not relaxed in order, but rather the patch with the largest unshot energy is selected at each step.

SJ (Southwell + Jacobi iteration). Similar to S, except that the result at each step is the patch radiosity plus its unshot radiosity.

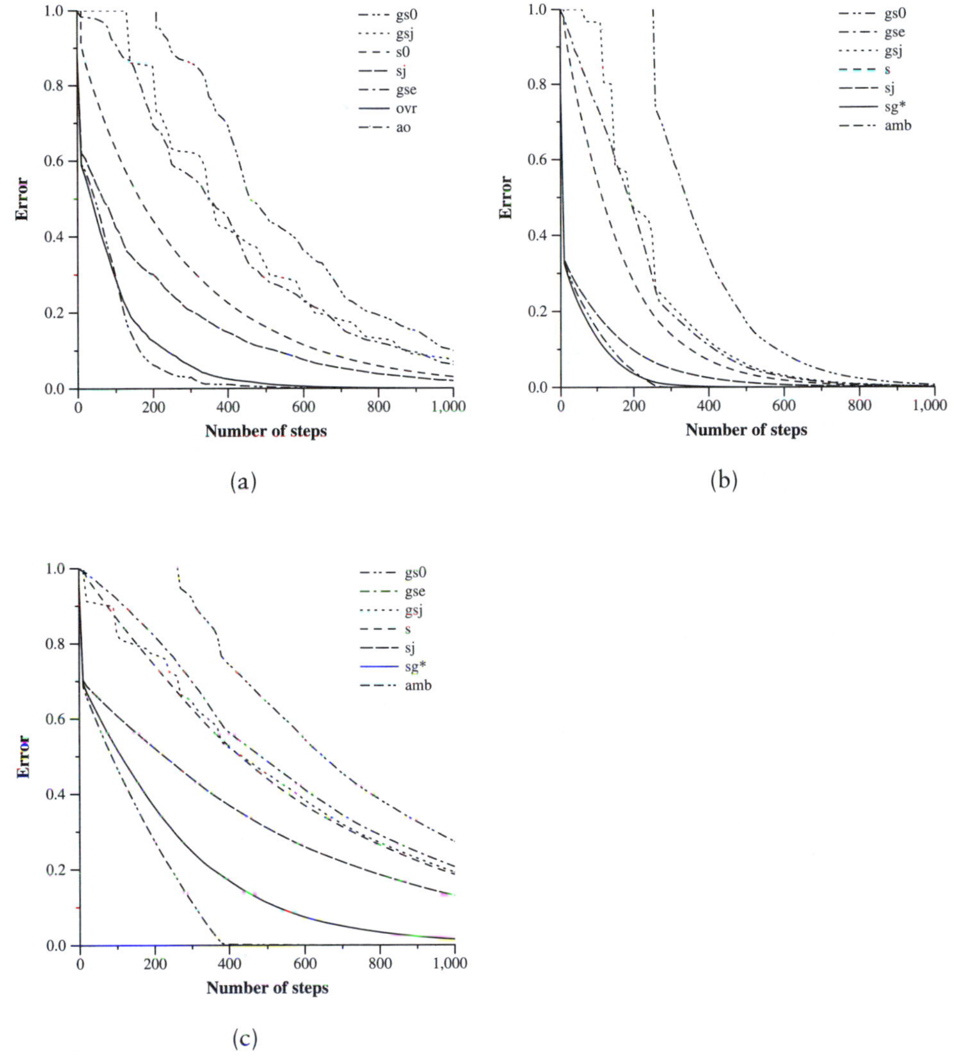

FIGURE 18.15

Performance of radiosity algorithms. (a) An office scene. (b) A random dim matrix with few emitters. (c) A random bright matrix with few emitters. Redrawn from Gortler, Cohen, and Susallek, figs. 3, 6, 7, p. 56.

GSE (Gauss-Seidel-E). Like GS0, but the initial guess is set to the emittances E rather than 0.

Ovr (Overshooting). This is a shooting scheme described by Gortler and Cohen [166], where the energy of each patch is shot into the environment; reflections back onto that patch are immediately accounted for using an overshooting procedure.

As we might expect, the full-fledged Gauss-Seidel iteration (GS0) performed the least well of all methods, because it requires an almost complete pass through the matrix, requiring n steps, before it has visited all the major radiators in the scene. Gauss-Seidel + Jacobi, Gauss-Seidel-E, and Southwell iteration all had roughly the same performance. Simply ordering the computation by selecting the largest unshot energy does not significantly reduce the error. The Southwell + Jacobi method used by progressive radiosity performed very well. Recall that this selects the shooting patches in order by unshot energy, then produces an image that is adjusted to contain an estimate of the unshot radiosity. This produces a better estimate in the early stages of the computation, but the advantages are reduced as the solution converges. The overshooting algorithm performed slightly better than progressive radiosity.

18.5 Form Factors

Recall that the *form factor* $F_{i,k}$ specifies the fraction of energy transferred from patch i to patch k. Because of its intimate link to the propagation of energy throughout an environment, the form factor plays an important role in image synthesis. Unfortunately, the definition of Equation 18.21 cannot usually be analytically integrated as given; we need to either change the definition or compute an approximation.

Form factors are at the heart of any radiosity method. For this reason it is important that we understand how they are defined and used. One of the best ways to develop this understanding is to look at the various methods that have been developed to compute form factors. This section does not present a complete survey of the vast form-factor methods. Rather, I have tried to summarize the most useful methods and ideas and point the way to the rest of the references.

18.5.1 Analytic Methods

We begin by presenting the three basic form factor expressions, which link a pair of differential areas, a pair of finite areas, and a differential and finite area [406].

We start with the form factor linking two differential elements dA_i and dA_k. From the definition of radiance in Equation 13.12, the power Φ leaving dA_i and

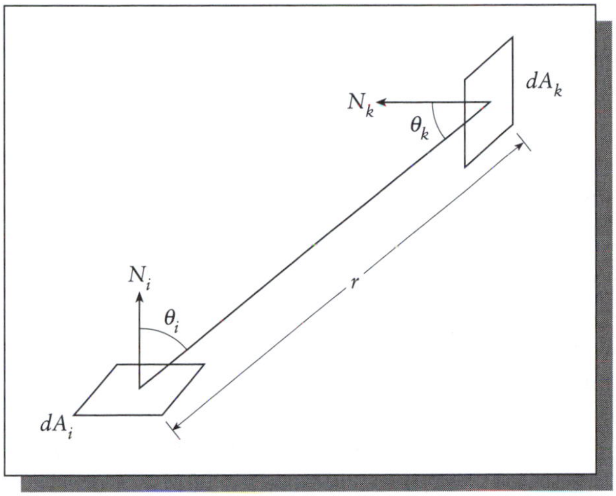

FIGURE 18.16

The geometry for the form factor from dA_i to dA_k.

arriving on dA_k is given by

$$\begin{aligned}\Phi_{i,k} &= L_i \cos\theta_i \, dA_i \, d\vec{\omega}_k \\ &= L_i \cos\theta_i \, dA_i \frac{dA_k \cos\theta_k}{r^2}\end{aligned} \tag{18.59}$$

using the geometry shown in Figure 18.16. Now if A_i is a *purely diffuse* emitter and sends its energy equally in all directions, then from Equation 13.59 its total energy output Φ_i into the hemisphere over it will be

$$\Phi_i = \pi L_i \, dA_i \tag{18.60}$$

The ratio of the energy sent from i to k to the total energy released by i is then

$$\begin{aligned}\frac{\Phi_{i,k}}{\Phi_i} &= \frac{L_i \cos\theta_i \, dA_i \, dA_k \cos\theta_k}{r^2} \frac{1}{\pi L_i \, dA_i} \\ &= \frac{\cos\theta_i \cos\theta_k}{\pi r^2} \, dA_k\end{aligned} \tag{18.61}$$

This ratio is the fraction of the energy emitted by i that arrives at k; that is, it's the form factor F_{dA_i,dA_k}:

$$F_{dA_i,dA_k} = \frac{\cos\theta_i \cos\theta_k}{\pi r^2} \, dA_k \tag{18.62}$$

From inspection, we see that the form factor is completely symmetric except for the area factor dA_k. This means that we can write the form factor for the power transfer in the opposite direction as

$$F_{dA_k,dA_i} = \frac{\cos\theta_i \cos\theta_k}{\pi r^2}\, dA_i \tag{18.63}$$

These two expressions satisfy the *reciprocity relation*

$$dA_i F_{dA_i,dA_k} = dA_k F_{dA_k,dA_i} \tag{18.64}$$

Suppose we now enlarge dA_k so that it becomes a finite element A_k. Then we can integrate the form factor over all points on A_k, but we must be careful: if the point being examined at any moment on A_k is not visible to A_i, then it contributes nothing. Recalling the visibility function $V(\mathbf{r}, \mathbf{p})$ from Equation 18.3, we write it here as $V(i, k)$, indicating the points on the two patches. Then we can integrate over A_k to find

$$F_{dA_i,A_k} = \int_{A_k} \frac{\cos\theta_i \cos\theta_k}{\pi r^2} V(i,k)\, dA_k \tag{18.65}$$

This relationship satisfies the reciprocity relation

$$dA_i F_{dA_i,A_k} = A_k F_{A_k,dA_i} \tag{18.66}$$

Finally, we can enlarge A_i until it is finitely sized as well. The result is a generalization of Equation 18.65, except that we pick up a factor of $1/A_i$. This is because we are measuring the transfer of energy from A_i, which for a constant radiance per unit area is proportional to area. That is,

$$F_{A_i,A_k} = \frac{\displaystyle\int_{A_i}\int_{A_k} \pi L_i \frac{\cos\theta_i \cos\theta_k}{\pi r^2}\, dA_k\, dA_i}{\pi L_i A_i} \tag{18.67}$$

which boils down to

$$F_{A_i,A_k} = \frac{1}{A_i}\int_{A_i}\int_{A_k} \frac{\cos\theta_i \cos\theta_k}{\pi r^2} V(i,k)\, dA_k\, dA_i \tag{18.68}$$

or, in a slightly more comprehensible form,

$$F_{A_i,A_k} = \frac{1}{A_i}\int_{A_i} F_{dA_i,A_k} V(i,k)\, dA_i \tag{18.69}$$

This finite-to-finite transfer satisfies the reciprocity relation

$$A_i F_{A_i,A_k} = A_k F_{A_k,A_i} \tag{18.70}$$

Patches	Form factor	Reciprocity rule
Differential to differential	$F_{dA_i,dA_k} = \frac{\cos\theta_i \cos\theta_k}{\pi r^2}\, dA_k$	$dA_i F_{dA_i,dA_k} = dA_k F_{dA_k,dA_i}$
Differential to finite	$F_{dA_i,A_k} = \int_{A_k} \frac{\cos\theta_i \cos\theta_k}{\pi r^2} V(i,k)\, dA_k$	$dA_i F_{dA_i,A_k} = A_k F_{A_k,dA_i}$
Finite to finite	$F_{A_i,A_k} = \frac{1}{A_i}\int_{A_i}\int_{A_k} \frac{\cos\theta_i \cos\theta_k}{\pi r^2} V(i,k)\, dA_k\, dA_i$	$A_i F_{A_i,A_k} = A_k F_{A_k,A_i}$

TABLE 18.2
Form factors and reciprocity rules.

These three form factors and reciprocity rules are summarized in Table 18.2.

In general, closed-form expressions for form factors are hard to come by. They can be carried out for some of the traditional simple geometries for integration (e.g., spheres, infinite planes, and infinite cylinders), but most practical shapes elude analytical integration. A catalog of some useful form factors collected from the literature is given in Appendix D.

A remarkable exception to this rule is the closed-form relation between two arbitrary (but unoccluded) polygons, recently developed by Schröder and Hanrahan [385, 386]. This is a complex result; details are given in Appendix D.

The problem is not as bad in the restricted world of two dimensions. Analytic expressions for form factors between linear elements in the 2D world of Flatland have been developed by Heckbert [202].

18.5.2 Contour Integration

The form factor integrals of Table 18.2 may be recast into another form that is sometimes more convenient to integrate. Sparrow has noted that Stokes' theorem can be applied to the form factor integrals to change them from area-based integrals to contour-based integrals [416]. An important assumption of all contour-based methods is that the two objects are completely visible to one another; that is, there are no objects anywhere in the space between them.

Suppose that we have an infinitesimal area dA_i located at (x_i, y_i, z_i) with normal (l_i, m_i, n_i), and we wish to find its form factor with respect to a finite patch A_k, where (x_k, y_k, z_k) represents any point on the contour C_k of A_k, and r is the distance from dA_i to that point. Sparrow [416] showed that we can write this form factor as

$$\begin{aligned} F_{dA_i,A_k} = l_i \oint_{C_k} &\frac{(z_k - z_i)\, dy_k - (y_k - y_i)\, dz_k}{2\pi r^2} \\ + m_i \oint_{C_k} &\frac{(x_k - x_i)\, dz_k - (z_k - z_i)\, dx_k}{2\pi r^2} \\ + n_i \oint_{C_k} &\frac{(y_k - y_i)\, dx_k - (x_k - x_i)\, dy_k}{2\pi r^2} \end{aligned} \tag{18.71}$$

For two finite elements A_i and A_k with respective contours C_i and C_k, the result is rather simpler:

$$F_{A_i,A_k} = \frac{1}{2\pi A_i} \left[\oint_{C_i} \oint_{C_k} \ln r\, dx_i\, dx_k + \ln r\, dy_i\, dy_k + \ln r\, dz_i\, dz_k \right] \tag{18.72}$$

where r is the distance between the points on each contour.

Equation 18.72 formed the basis for the form factor calculations used in the original radiosity paper by Goral et al. [165]. More recently, this result has been combined by Sun et al. with the principle of linearity to precompute components of form factors and then construct new form factors on the fly from a table lookup [428].

This method has also been used by Nishita and Nakamae to calculate the illumination due to an area light source [321]. For the transfer from a differential patch to a finite polygon, Equation 18.71 has a particularly simple geometric form. Suppose the polygon has n sides and vertices $V_i, V_k, \ldots, V_n$. Call T_i the triangle formed by $dA_i, V_i, V_{(i+1)\bmod n}$, with normal $\mathbf{S}_i$ (the normal may be calculated from the cross product of two sides of the triangle). The geometry is shown in Figure 18.17.

Define α_i as the angle between $\mathbf{S}_i$ and the plane of dA_i, and β_i as the angle of the triangle nearest to dA_i. Then the form factor may be computed by

$$F_{dA_i,A_k} = \frac{1}{2\pi} \sum_{i=1}^{n} \beta_i \cos \alpha_i \tag{18.73}$$

If there are other polygons between dA_i and A_k, we can use an algorithm like the one in Atherton et al. [20] to clip them to the boundary of this pyramid and then to each other, so that only one polygon is intercepted by any ray from dA_i into the pyramid defined by A_k. The form factor for each of these polygons may then be computed as above and then subtracted from the total found for A_k. If such a clipping algorithm is available, it may be easier to simply clip A_k first, and then compute its proper form factor directly.

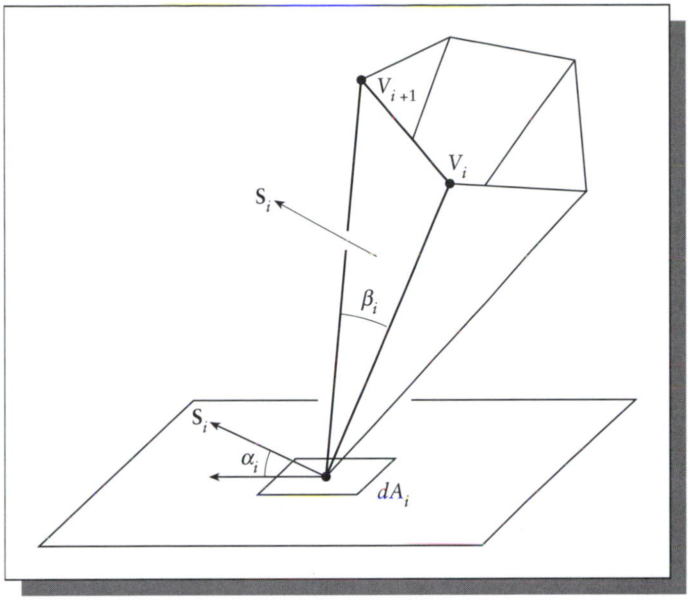

FIGURE 18.17

The geometry for contour integration of a polygon.

18.5.3 Physical Devices

In the engineering literature, we can find descriptions of physical devices that have been built to compute form factors, either directly or indirectly. These devices are interesting in their own right, because they help us improve our intuitive feel for the geometry behind the definitions of form factors.

One device begins with the idea of the *Nusselt analog*, originally described in 1928 [289]. Nusselt observed that the differential-to-finite form factor F_{dA_i,A_k} between a differential element dA_i and an unoccluded finite patch A_k can be computed in the following way, as illustrated in Figure 18.18. We're going to integrate over many small pieces dA_k of A_k. For each piece, find the solid angle $d\vec{\omega}_k = dA_k \cos\theta_k / r^2$; think of this as the projection of dA_k onto a hemisphere of radius 1 above dA_i. Now project that onto the tangent plane at dA_i, which is found from $d\vec{\omega}_k \cos\theta_i$. Now the base of the hemisphere has area $A = \pi r^2 = \pi$, since the hemisphere has radius 1. Finding the ratio of the projected area to the area of the base of the hemisphere, we

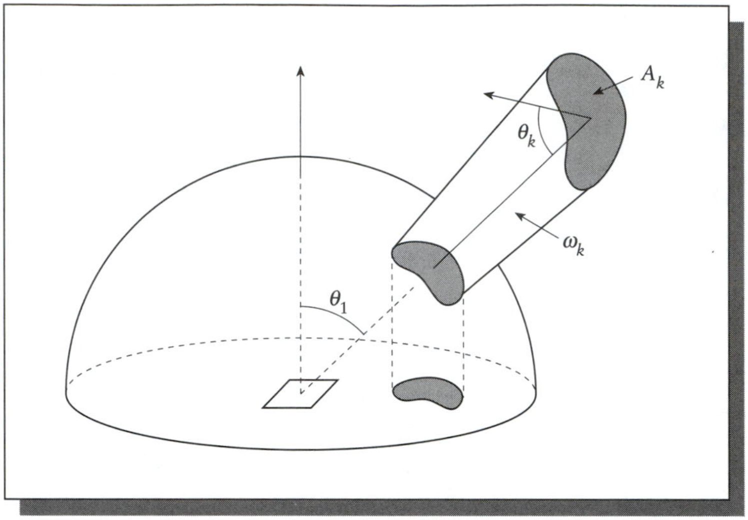

FIGURE 18.18
The Nusselt analog.

find

$$\frac{dA_k \cos\theta_k}{r^2} \cos\theta_i \frac{1}{\pi} \tag{18.74}$$

and integrating this over all of A_k gives us

$$\int_{A_k} \frac{\cos\theta_i \cos\theta_k}{\pi r^2}\, dA_k \tag{18.75}$$

which is just the same as the differential-to-finite form factor defined in Equation 18.65.

The Nusselt analog was employed by Eckert in 1935 to make a form factor computing device, pictured schematically in Figure 18.19 [289]. A small light source was placed at the center of a hemisphere of frosted glass (Eckert used milk glass), and the (opaque) object to be measured was suspended inside the hemisphere in the proper orientation. The lights in the room were turned off, and a camera was placed far from the light source, along a line through the light and perpendicular to the base of the hemisphere.

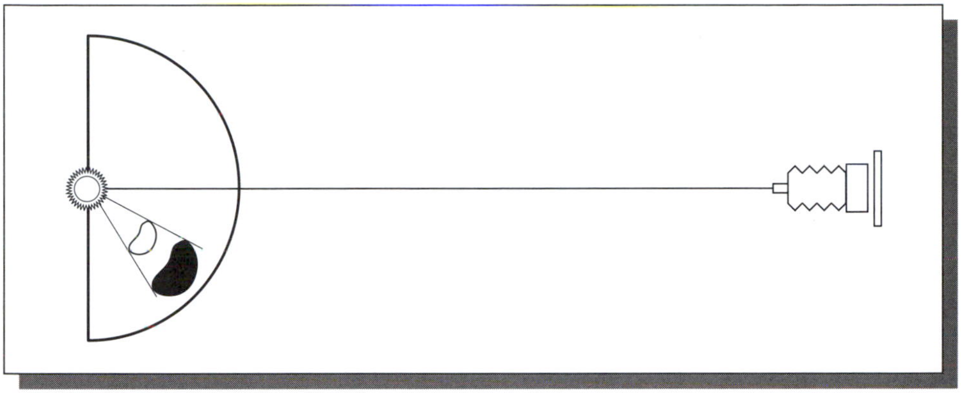

FIGURE 18.19
The Eckert setup for measuring form factors.

Because the only light was coming from the center of the hemisphere, the test object cast a shadow on the glass. The camera was far enough away that a picture of the hemisphere could be considered a parallel projection of the hemisphere onto a plane parallel to its base; that is, the image on the film corresponded to what you would get if you projected the hemisphere onto the base as in the Nusselt analog. Eckert measured the area of the shadow of the object and the area of the base of the hemisphere; the ratio of these two figures was the differential-to-finite form factor for that object.

Another device for measuring form factors was built by Farrell in 1976 [140]. The purpose was to measure the form factors of objects on a drawing with respect to a luminaire; this could be used to help determine the illumination on the floor of a large open building.

Pictured schematically in Figure 18.20, it consisted of a cylindrical light source inside a plastic tube onto which dots were painted. The spacing of the dots was such that when the lamp was directed downward onto the drawing, each dot represented a form factor of 0.001. The form factor of an object in the drawing (say the floor of a room) with respect to the luminaire could be found simply by counting the dots in the room and multiplying by 0.001.

Farrell also provides pointers to other physical devices built to help measure form factors.

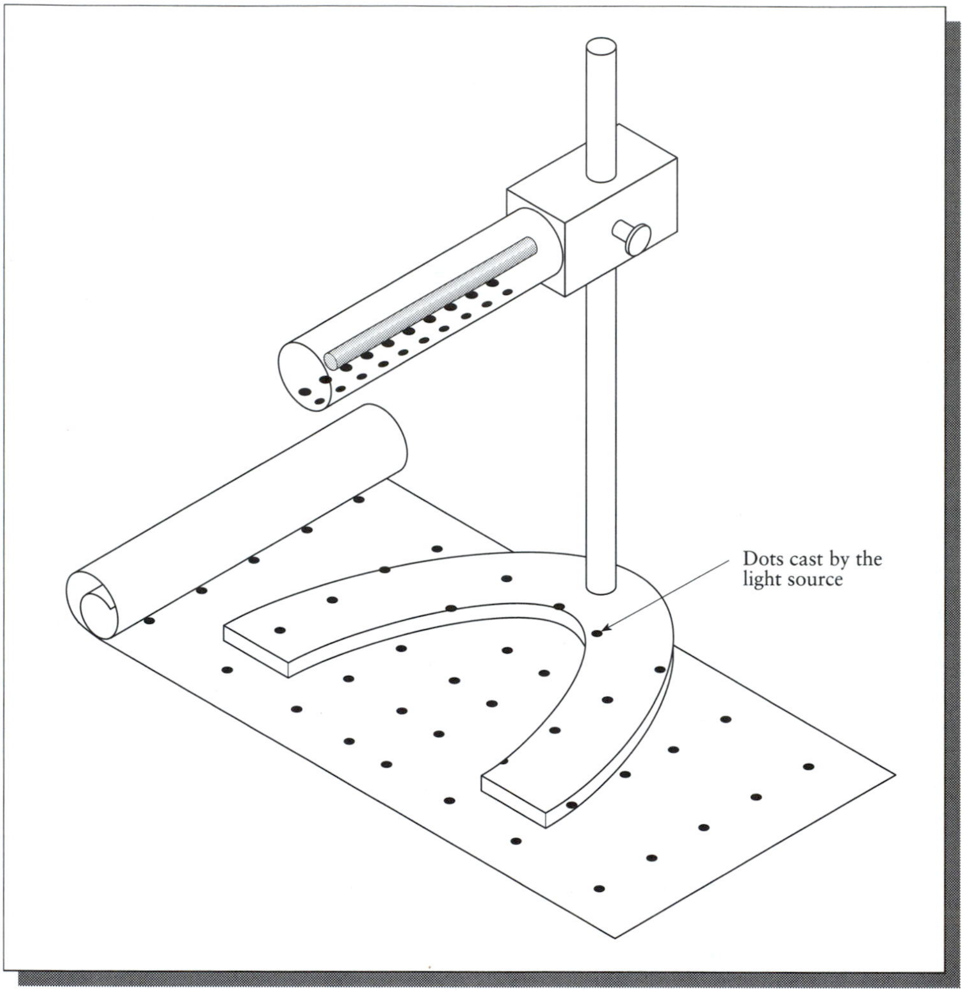

FIGURE 18.20

The Farrell device for measuring form factors.

18.5.4 Projection

As we saw in the last section on Nusselt's analog, form factors between a differential and a finite patch have a lot in common with solid angles. We can imagine building up a library of solid angles Γ_k, and precomputing the form factor F_{dA_i,Γ_k} associated with each solid angle k. For any given patch B, we can approximate its solid angle Γ_B by putting together pieces from the library. Because these solid angles don't overlap, we can simply add together the form factor associated with each one:

$$\begin{aligned} \Gamma_B &\approx \Gamma_1 \cup \Gamma_2 \cup \cdots \cup \Gamma_n \\ F_{dA_i,B} &\approx F_{dA_i,\Gamma_1} + F_{dA_i,\Gamma_2} + \cdots + F_{dA_i,\Gamma_n} \end{aligned} \tag{18.76}$$

This is the basic idea behind *projection* methods. Each of these methods selects a *projection surface*, which is a surface for which efficient project algorithms are known. We'll see that this is usually a hemisphere or plane. The surface is first subdivided into n disjoint (that is, nonoverlapping) cells, and placed over some imaginary differential surface. We then pretend that each cell is the solid angle occupied by an object, and compute the form factor for that object; this is the library of form factors mentioned above.

To use the library to compute a form factor for a particular differential and finite patch, we place the surface over the differential patch and project the finite patch onto it. This determines the *visibility* of the patch, and tells us which solid angles to add to approximate the solid angle of the finite patch. For each occupied solid angle, we include the bit of form factor associated with that angle. The result is an approximate form factor for the cost of a projection step.

The library of form factors are often called *delta form factors*, written ΔF, because to make up a form factor, we accumulate many of these library elements by adding them into a running sum.

The algorithm may be more sophisticated by allowing the library to contain overlapping pieces; this can allow a better fit to the real solid angle at the expense of some extra bookkeeping when computing the form factor.

Hemicubes

The *hemicube* method developed by Cohen and Greenberg was the first projection method used for evaluating form factors in computer graphics [96]. The basic idea is to surround the differential patch with half a cube, as in Figure 18.21. One full face of the cube sits over the patch, parallel to its local tangent plane, and four half-faces surround it. The cube faces are tiled in a regular grid, and a delta form factor is precomputed for each grid cell and stored with that cell.

The big practical benefit of the hemicube method comes from the wide availability of fast hardware for scan-converting polygons into pixels, which form a regular grid on a plane. Thus, the rendering hardware (usually Z-buffer based) in many

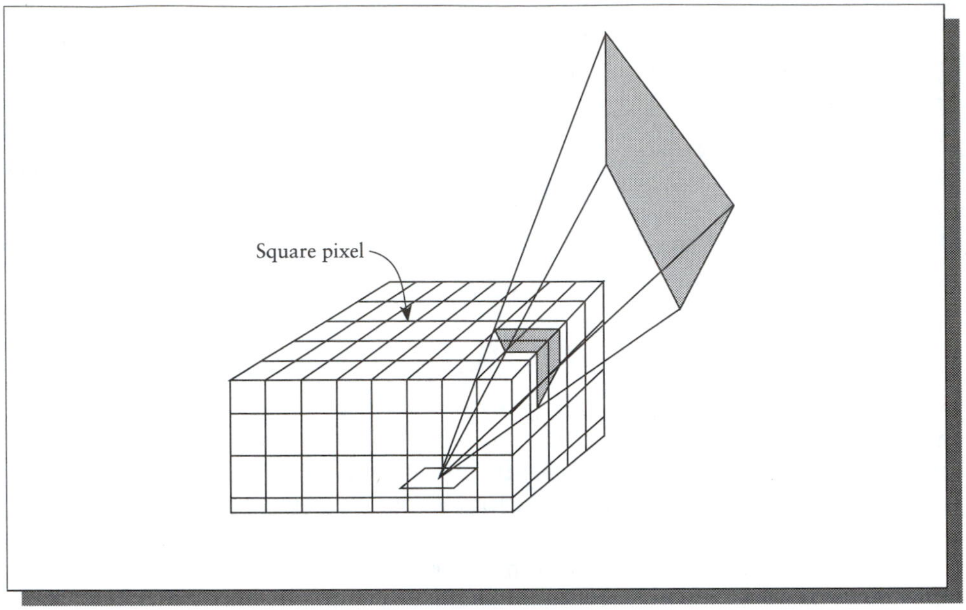

FIGURE 18.21
The hemicube sits over a differential patch. Redrawn from Cohen and Greenberg in *Computer Graphics (Proc. Siggraph '85)*, fig. 6, p. 35.

modern graphics computers may be used to compute the visibility term from a differential area to all the polygons in the environment at once by simply rendering the environment onto the five walls of the hemicube. The only trick is to be able to identify the polygons from the final image, but this may be done easily by simply using a different, constant color for each polygon when rendering; the polygon number is then given by its color. Other methods, such as maintaining the object tag in a separate buffer, are also available on some systems. This approach takes care of occlusion automatically, since it's a natural part of any scan-conversion renderer.

Because it is placed over a point, the hemicube algorithm does not compute the finite-to-finite patch transfers that take place in a real environment. Rather, it simulates these transfers by placing the hemicube at the center of a finite patch and treating the incident radiosity as a constant over the patch.

Although the hardware Z-buffer approach for scan conversion is particularly efficient, software approaches must be used when the hardware is not available. Vilaplana and Pueyo have noted that the visible image of a scene often doesn't change much when we move a small distance. This means that two nearby hemicubes will be very similar, so when evaluating visibility on a hemicube, we may use information from an existing neighbor to speed the process [454].

Additionally, other visibility culling techniques may be used to accelerate the scan-conversion process in the visibility step [169, 178, 368, 435].

The hemicube method is attractive because it is simple to understand and implement, and when the right hardware is available, it is very efficient. But the approach has disadvantages as well.

Baum et al. [33] have identified three major assumptions implicit in the hemicube method. Assuming that the hemicube is centered over a patch A_i, the hemicube algorithm assumes

Proximity: The distance between the patch A_i and all other patches A_k is large compared with the size of A_i.

Visibility: The visibility of A_i does not vary over the surface of A_k.

Aliasing: The periodic sampling pattern of cells on the hemicube faces is sufficient to obtain a high-quality estimate of the projection of A_k.

When any one or more of these assumptions is violated, the accuracy of the method suffers and form factors become less accurate.

The first assumption is violated by the condition in Figure 18.22, because the two patches are adjacent. Baum et al. calculated the analytic form factors for this pair of surfaces to be $F_{k,i} = 0.247$ and $F_{i,k} = 0.0494$. Assuming that a hemicube with infinite resolution was placed in the center of each patch, the computed form factors would be $F'_{k,i} = 0.238$ and $F'_{i,k} = 0.00857$.

The values for $F_{k,i}$ are relatively close because the distance from any interior point on P_k to a particular point on P_i is relatively close to a constant. But if we fix a point on P_k and roam over P_i, the distance will vary quite a bit. In other words, the solid angle subtended by P_i from almost anywhere on P_k is roughly constant, but the solid angle occupied by P_k from points on P_i varies quite a bit, and we have seen that the form factor is closely related to the solid angle. When we calculate the analytic form factor, this change in the solid angle is accounted for, but when we use the hemicube, a single solid angle (taken from the center of the patch) is used to represent them all. Because the solid angle is not linear with distance, the large values up near the common edge and the small values out near the far end of P_i do not cancel out.

The patches do not need to be at right angles to violate the proximity assumption; many other configurations will also fail. For example, consider a patch P_k that is almost coplanar to the patch P_i on which the hemicube sits, but slightly above the plane and tilted slightly inward. There is some small exchange of energy between these two patches, but the hemicube cell pointing toward P_k records either a full form factor related to the size of the cell or nothing at all.

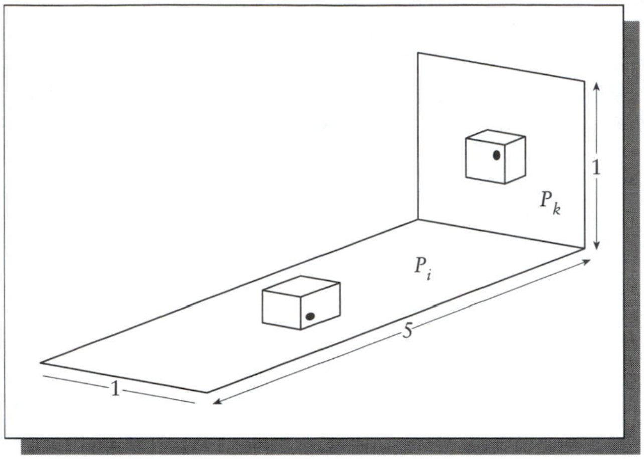

FIGURE 18.22
A violation of the hemicube proximity assumption.

The visibility assumption says that if a patch P_k is visible from the center of P_i, then all of P_i is visible to that point on P_k. After all, the only visibility information we're gathering is where the hemicube is located at the center of the patch, so we are assuming that information is true at all other points. This condition is easily violated by an occluding object between the two patches that does not happen to lie on the line from the hemicube center through the hemicube sample, as in Figure 18.23.

Finally, the aliasing assumption is a natural result of the periodic, finite-resolution grid used by the hemicube as a sampling pattern. The hemicube can fall prey to all the aliasing problems discussed in Unit II, which can result in missed objects and incorrect form factors. Figure 18.24 shows simple examples of over- and underestimates of form factors because of the limited and periodic sampling resolution.

One of the worst effects of the aliasing problem is that the distribution of light in the scene can be splotchy. A large patch in the foreground of an image may be small with respect to a distant but bright light source, and may be missed by the hemicube; that omission will surely be noticed. As with other periodic sampling methods, the hemicube distribution pattern may *beat* with the distribution of polygons in the environment. Figure 18.25 shows a linear mesh of polygons being illuminated by a patch A_i using a hemicube. Notice that only every other patch is illuminated, causing black-and-white stripes on the mesh that should be uniformly illuminated.

Baum et al. suggest that when one of these three assumptions is violated, an

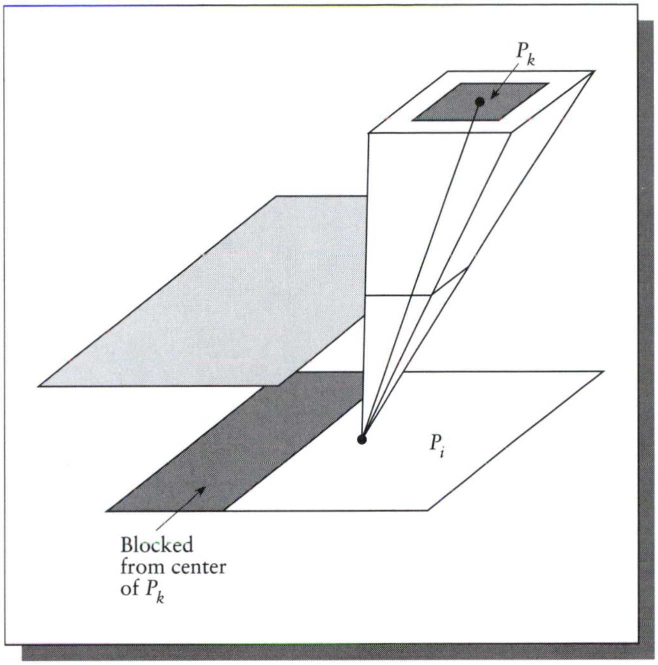

FIGURE 18.23
A violation of the hemicube visibility assumption.

analytic routine (such as a contour-integral method) should be used instead of the hemicube for that form factor.

Wallace et al. [461] note that the hemicube algorithm can only compute form factors to finite patches, but ultimately the radiosity calculation transfers radiosity to the vertices of the environment for display. This is why the hemicube method needs to average the polygon radiosities at each vertex when the system is converged.

Other Surfaces

Other surfaces have been used to generate the library of form factors for projection algorithms. Because they are all based on projection onto a single point, they have many of the same drawbacks as the hemicube method.

Sillion and Puech [408] used a single large plane rather than a five-sided hemicube,

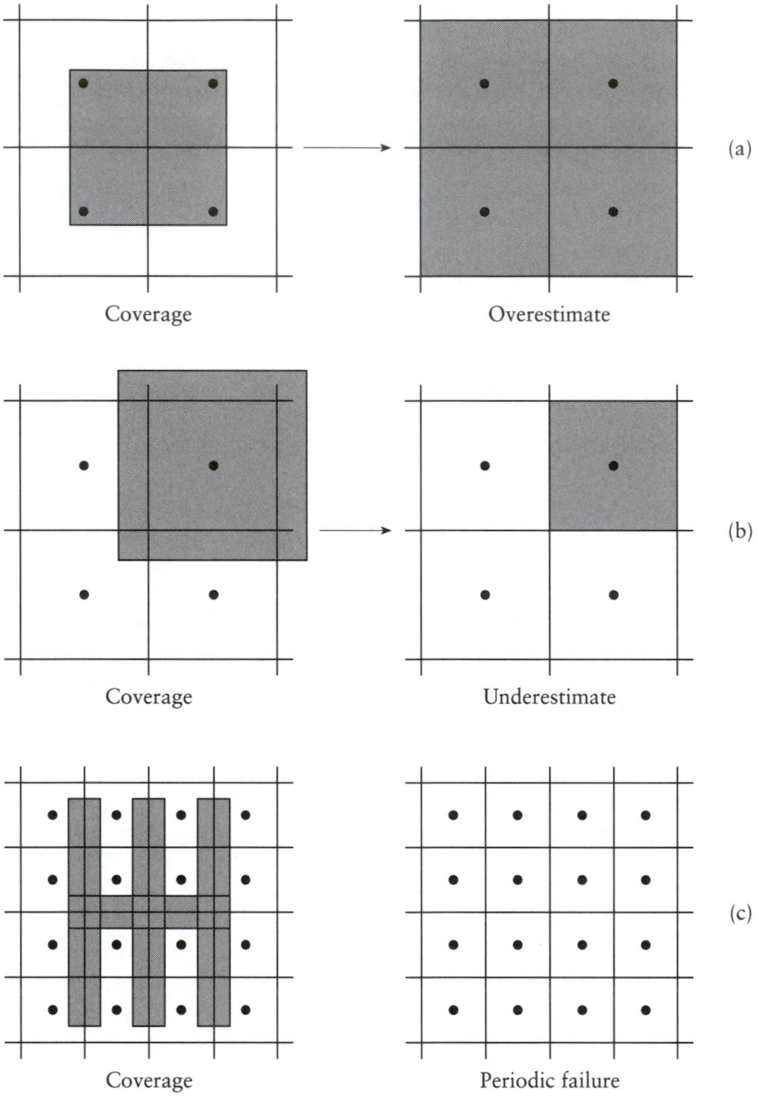

FIGURE 18.24

Violations of the hemicube aliasing assumption. (a) Overestimating. (b) Underestimating. (c) Periodicity failure.

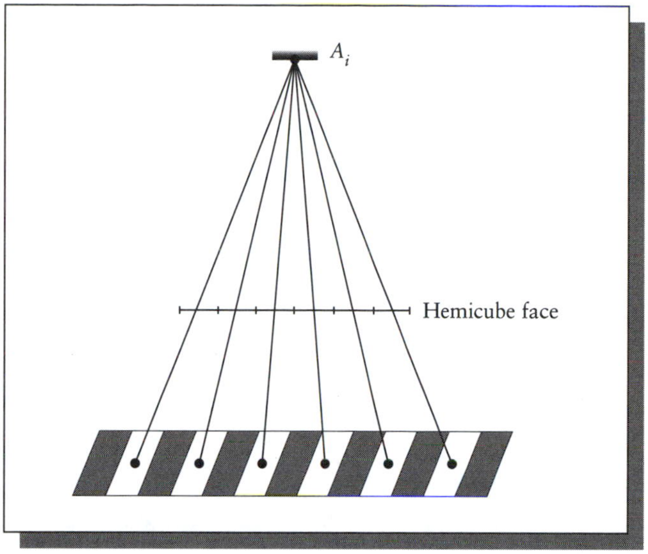

FIGURE 18.25

A polygon mesh beating with the hemicube pattern.

as shown in Figure 18.26. They adaptively subdivided the plane until each cell was empty, fully covered by a single object, or too small to be subdivided further. A single-plane projection method was also used by Recker et al. [356].

The principal advantage of the single-plane projection over the hemicube is that only a single project step is required, not five. A drawback is that the technique will miss objects near the horizon, since there is a gap where the hemicube sides used to sit. We can argue that light arriving along directions that are nearly parallel to the local surface plane are unlikely to contribute much radiosity, so this omission is not much of a loss given all the other approximations inherent in the method.

The single-plane projection method was also used by Zhou and Peng [504], who used two planes to distinguish between visibility information and form factor information.

Hemispheres have been used for projection algorithms by Van Wyk [451] and Spencer [418]. The most direct approach subdivides the surface of the hemisphere using latitude and longitude lines, as shown in Figure 18.27. Unfortunately, coverage and scan-conversion are difficult to perform for this curvilinear grid.

An alternative is inspired by the Nusselt analog: forget about discretizing the surface of the hemisphere, and instead discretize the base [289, 418, 451]. To compute

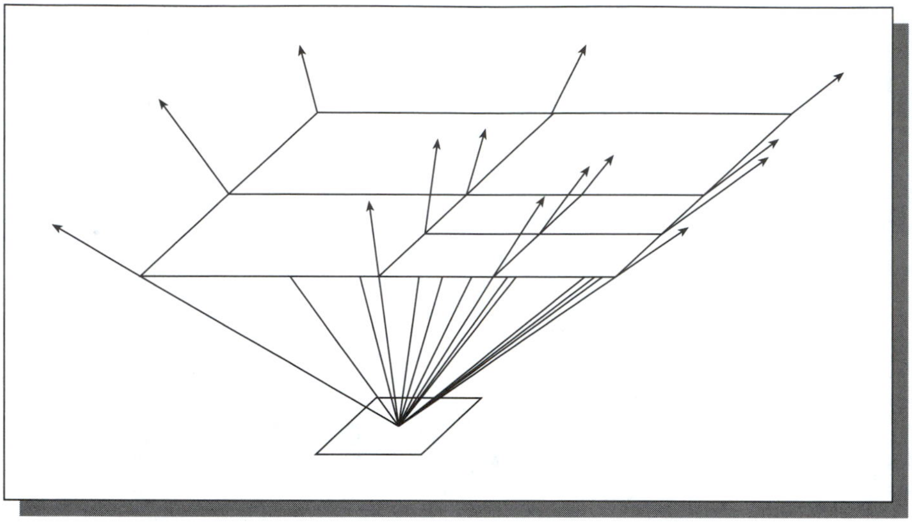

FIGURE 18.26
The single-plane projection method.

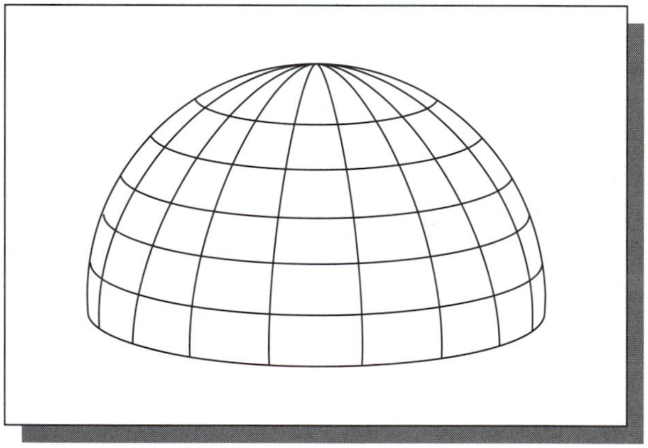

FIGURE 18.27
Subdivision of the hemisphere by latitude and longitude.

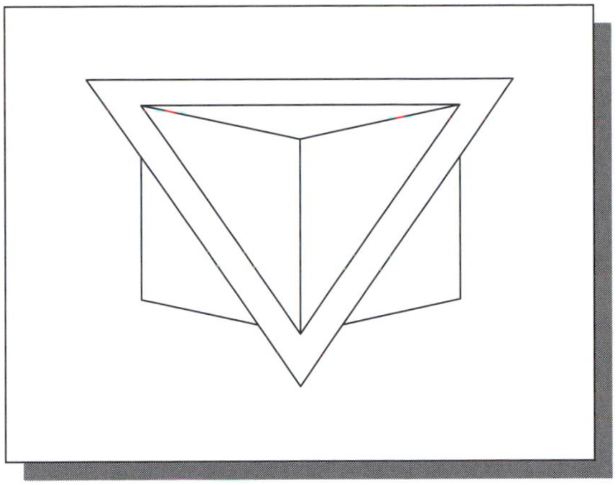

FIGURE 18.28

Positioning the cube for the cubic-tetrahedral projection method.

a form factor, estimate the solid angle on the hemispherical surface and then project it down onto the discretized base, where the number of covered cells can be counted. The ratio of each interior cell to the area of the base is a constant, and the ratios for the cells that are only partly within the hemisphere can be precomputed and saved. This approach can be shown to produce estimates using far fewer cells than required by a comparable hemicube, but the projection onto the sphere must be efficient for the method to be practical.

Projection of a patch onto the hemisphere and then down onto the surface was also investigated by Nishita and Nakamae in their development of form factors for unoccluded Bézier patches [322]. They derived form factors for a patch that was trapped between two latitudinal and two longitudinal great circles. This is like the precomputed subdivision methods above, but has the advantage that the grid cell adapts to fit the projected surface. An analytic equation based on the angles of the great circles gives an approximate form factor. The algorithm becomes more complex if the patch is partially occluded.

Another variation on the hemicube was developed by Beran-Koehn and Pavicic [37]. Rather than embed a subdivided cube into a surface so that its top face is parallel to the surface, as in the hemicube method, they embed the cube so that one corner sticks up above the surface and the three adjacent corners are in the tangent plane, as in Figure 18.28. They call this the *cubic-tetrahedral* method, since they use a single tetrahedral corner of a cube. This has the advantage of surrounding the point like the hemicube, but only requiring three projections. The delta form factors for the three faces are presented in Beran-Koehn and Pavicic [38].

Line Distributions

There is a great body of literature in the computational geometry field that discusses problems involving the intersections of lines and surfaces, and counting those lines in various ways. The theses by de Berg [119] and van Kreveld [449] contain bibliographies that point to much of this literature.

Two general techniques have been used in graphics to compute form factors with clusters of lines: *ray tracing* and *line densities*.

Ray Tracing

Wallace et al. [461] observed that since the radiosity solution is usually reconstructed by interpolating the radiosities at vertices, then we ought to compute the radiosity directly at those vertices. This means that during progressive radiosity we need finite-to-differential form factors from a selected finite patch to all the differential elements (vertices) in the scene. The hemicube algorithm provides just the opposite information: differential-to-finite form factors from a single differential element to all the finite elements.

The approach taken by Wallace et al. was to subdivide the surface of the shooting patch A_i into n of smaller pieces, $\Delta A_i{}^m$, and then compute the form factor to each differential patch dA_j as a sum of the form factors from each piece:

$$F_{A_i,dA_j} \approx \sum_{m=1}^{n} F_{\Delta A_i{}^m,dA_j} V(i^m, j) \tag{18.77}$$

where $V(i^m, j)$ is the visibility term between subpatch $A_i{}^m$ and dA_j.

This method raises three issues: how to test the visibility term V, how to subdivide the surface, and how to compute the individual form factors,

The first issue is easily addressed by tracing a ray from the center dA_j to some point on $\Delta A_i{}^m$. If the ray strikes no other object between these two points, they are mutually visible, and generally we assume that this means the entire finite subpatch is visible to the entire differential patch.

As we saw with the hemicube, this type of visibility assumption is risky. But the risk is lower in the ray-tracing method because the finite patch is smaller than the original patch, and because we can adaptively refine the sampling until we think it is accurate. Wallace et al. [461] derive the adaptive sampling using binary subdivision, as shown in Figure 18.29. They tracked the energy transferred from each cell to the differential receiver, and subdivided the cell if the energy it transferred to the

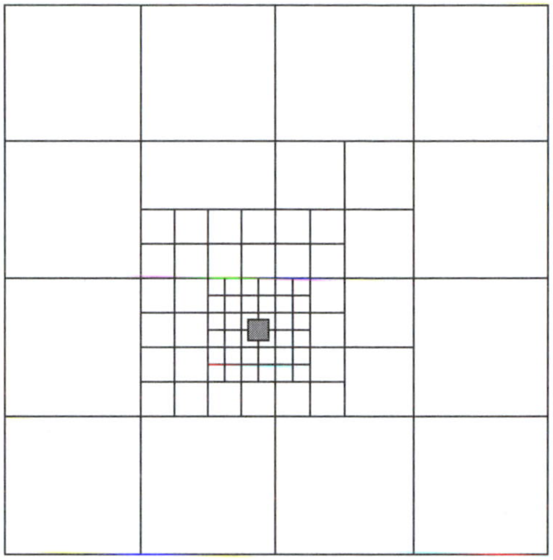

FIGURE 18.29

Subdivision of a large emitter A_i into smaller pieces based on the differential receiver dA_j, shown shaded.

particular receiver via its form factor represented more than a threshold amount of energy.

The individual form factors are computed by imagining that each subpatch $\Delta A_i{}^m$ is replaced by a disk in the same position with the same area. Wallace et al. use an approximate closed-form expression for the form factor from such a disk to a differential element.

A disadvantage of this approach as stated is that it induces a regular sampling grid on the shooting patch A_i. Since we assume that the patch is a pure diffuse radiator, the sampling pattern is unlikely to create artifacts because of its distribution on the source, but it may interact with the other geometry in the scene when shadow testing. Wallace et al. address this problem by jittering the distribution of samples generated on A_i from each vertex.

A feature of this approach is that the geometry used to test visibility may be different than the geometry used for shading and rendering. Suppose that a scene contains some smooth curved surfaces that we have decided to tile into small flat polygons for the purposes of energy balancing. We can retain the original curved surface description of the scene and use it during the visibility tests, intersecting the ray against the original smooth surfaces. This means that curved surfaces may be subdivided to an arbitrary density to get good coverage by many small elements without increasing the cost of determining visibility. Figure 18.30 (color plate) shows a quadratic surface that has been trimmed into a teapot shape with cubic splines. The quadratic surface was subdivided into 28×42 patches. The hemicube algorithm would probably cause severe aliasing in this picture; for example, by alternately finding and missing the small handle of the teapot. Ray-traced form factors were computed at each of the 6,086 vertices for ten steps of progressive radiosity, using five samples per source.

The result of the algorithm on a much more complex database is shown in Figure 18.31 (color plate). Here two bays of the cathedral were modeled and energy-balanced, and then the pair was simply replicated three times to produce the complete nave of six bays. Because the original curved surfaces were retained throughout the process, the final rendering uses the correct surface normal due to the surface at each point, rather than a polygonal approximation. The original two bays contained 9,916 polygons and 74,806 vertices. The solution required 60 steps of progressive radiosity. Shooting patches were not subdivided; only one sample per patch was fired to determine visibility of sources from vertices.

For this method to be efficient, it is essential it be able to quickly determine whether a ray intersects any objects on its way from the vertex to the shooting patch; this requires efficient ray-object intersections on the model. There are many algorithms available for accelerating this process; Arvo and Kirk [17] provide a survey.

Line Densities

All of the algorithms we have seen so far in this section have been demand-driven: when we want a particular form factor, we do the work to compute it. An alternative is to consider an algorithm that might be prohibitively expensive for a small number of form factors, but contains some common piece of work that is repeated for every calculation. Then that step can be moved into a preprocessing step, and then the form factor calculations themselves may prove to be efficient enough to compete with the methods above. If this can be accomplished, then whether or not it pays off depends on the costs of the various steps involved and the number of form factors we wish to compute. In general, the more form factors we need, the more attractive a preprocessing phase becomes.

Such approaches have been considered by Buckalew and Fussell [68] and Sbert [377]. They both generate dense collections of lines in the environment, and then estimate the relationship between pairs of patches by the relative numbers of intersections of those lines. Buckalew and Fussell generate families of parallel lines, while Sbert distributes them randomly in space. To estimate the form factor between two patches, one method offered by Sbert is to form the ratio

$$F_{A_i,A_j} = \frac{N(A_i, A_j)}{N(A_i)} \tag{18.78}$$

where $N(A_i, A_j)$ is the number of lines crossing both patches, and $N(A_i)$ is the number of lines crossing only patch i.

18.5.5 Discussion

All three basic form factors in Table 18.2 contain a term of $1/r^2$. When the radius goes to zero, this becomes a second-order *pole* in the form factor kernel, introducing a singularity into the computation. That is, it is a squared term in the denominator. One approach to handling this singularity is to multiply it with a second-order *zero* in the numerator. This technique was used by Zatz [503] who switched the weight function used in the inner product to a Jacobi polynomial that contained the appropriate r^2 term in the numerator. As pointed out by Schröder [383], this leads to increased work and storage. Schröder has recently investigated singularities in form factor calculations for Galerkin methods in detail [383]. He notes that we do have exact analytic solutions for abutting polygons for box basis functions, but higher-order bases are more difficult to handle. He suggests that a good approach is to switch the quadrature rule being used to carry out the numerical integration to a different rule over a tiled domain, so that the new rule compensates for the singularity.

This section has presented only a survey of some of the more common methods for form factor calculation. There are many more varieties and variations. Figure 18.32 from Cohen and Wallace offers a taxonomy, and in their book they address each of these methods in detail [99].

There is a rich body of material on form factors in the heat transfer literature that has only recently been mined by the computer graphics community; surveys of this literature are identified in the Further Reading section.

18.6 Hierarchical Radiosity

Radiosity programs spend most of their time performing one of two steps: computing form factors and solving the linear system. When using an algorithm like progressive radiosity, the same form factors will be calculated repeatedly every time the same patch is selected as the shooter. Each form factor comes at some cost, and the more form factors there are, the longer it takes to solve the resulting equations. If we could somehow cut down on the number of form factors required to propagate the light through the environment we should see significant savings.

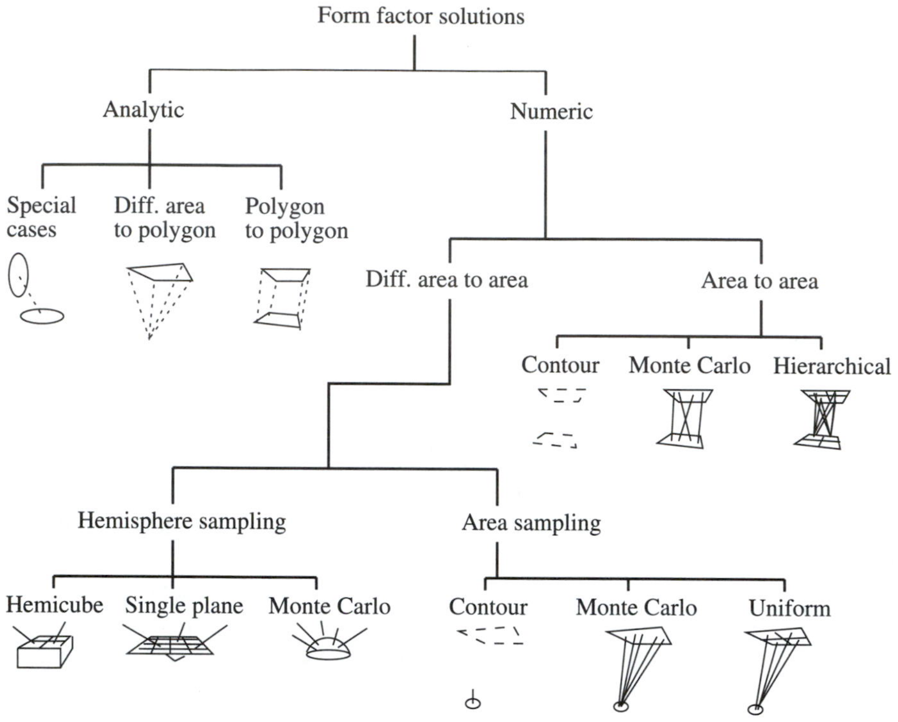

FIGURE 18.32

A taxonomy of form factor methods. Reprinted, by permission, from Cohen and Wallace in *Radiosity and Realistic Image Synthesis*, fig. 4.3, p. 71.

At first this may hardly seem possible; after all, the form factors describe the interaction of light between pairs of surfaces. How could we delete any of them and still hope to get an accurate solution?

One way to avoid computing some form factors is to simply observe that in a complex environment many form factors are zero, because the patches cannot see each other. Geometric processing can help us avoid even consideration of pairs of polygons that are guaranteed not to interact with each other [169, 178, 435].

Another approach is more subtle, and draws on work performed to solve the classic N–body problem in physics. Consider a system of n independent massive objects in space. Each one exerts gravitational force on all the others, so to figure out where each one moves can require explicit evaluation of each of the $n(n-1)/2$

interactions. When we wish to simulate the evolution of a galaxy containing tens of thousands of stars (or even more), the computational costs become prohibitive.

However, we can make a practical observation that dramatically reduces the cost of the problem: we usually do not need perfect accuracy. In other words, the precision of the gravitational field upon one particle due to another is usually limited by the computational hardware and software being used. Consider a test body in space that is separated by a great distance from a cluster of two other bodies that are relatively near each other, as in Figure 18.33. For any given level of desired precision, there is an associated distance where the magnitude and direction of the gravitational fields from the two bodies in the cluster are indistinguishable at the test particle. At that distance we can just replace the two fields by one that is twice as strong in the average direction.

This idea of *clustering interactions* can be applied recursively to ever-larger clusters of bodies. The basic idea is that if the interaction between two bodies decreases with distance and size of the body (smaller objects exert less of a gravitational force than larger ones), then there will always come a distance where a pair of bodies may be considered a single body of larger size, and then this aggregate body may be combined with another body (perhaps itself an aggregate), and so on. It has been proven that this sort of approach can yield an algorithm with running time $O(n)$ rather than $O(n^2)$ [138].

It was noted by Hanrahan and Salzman [191] that the form factor problem has much in common with the N-body problem: both are concerned with the interactions between all pairs of objects, and both the gravitational force and the form factor are proportional to the size of the objects and inversely proportional to the square of the distance between them. The two problems are not identical, since the physics of gravity and light transfer are different, but there is enough similarity that we can apply the general ideas behind the clustering algorithms for the N-body to the form factor problem. The result is the *hierarchical radiosity* (or HR) algorithm [191, 192].

The physical intuition for the hierarchical radiosity algorithm is that small details don't matter when we are far away from something. This is the same observation that guided the development of multiple levels of detail in models and shading algorithms, as discussed in Section 15.10. Suppose that we are rendering an interior scene of a large office containing an overhead lamp, a desk, and chairs, and there are various objects scattered about on the desk. Suppose the desk is in one corner, and consider a patch of the wall near the ceiling in the opposite corner, as in Figure 18.34. The top of the desk and all the objects upon it are visible from the wall, but the illumination from the desk upon the wall patch will probably not change appreciably if we put a pencil on top of the desk. On the other hand, the illumination falling on the patch belonging to the table top directly under the pencil will be significantly affected when the pencil is added to the scene.

From the point of view of the wall, as far as reflected illumination is concerned the entire desk can probably be considered a single big patch; from the point of view

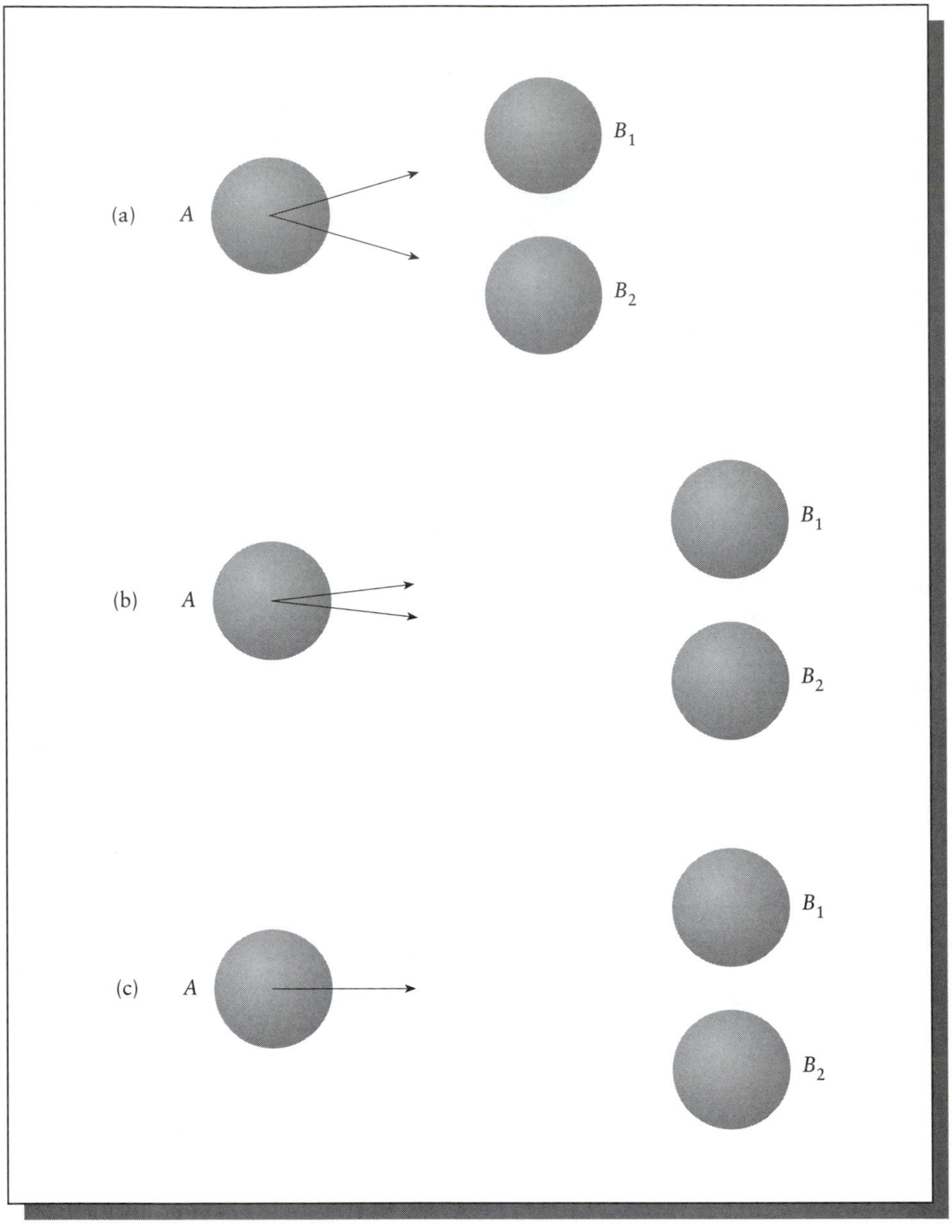

FIGURE 18.33

A test body A and a clump of two other bodies B_1 and B_2. (a) The fields at the test particle are distinguishable. (b) The fields at the test particle identical to within a predefined tolerance. (c) A single force equal to the combination of the two in (b).

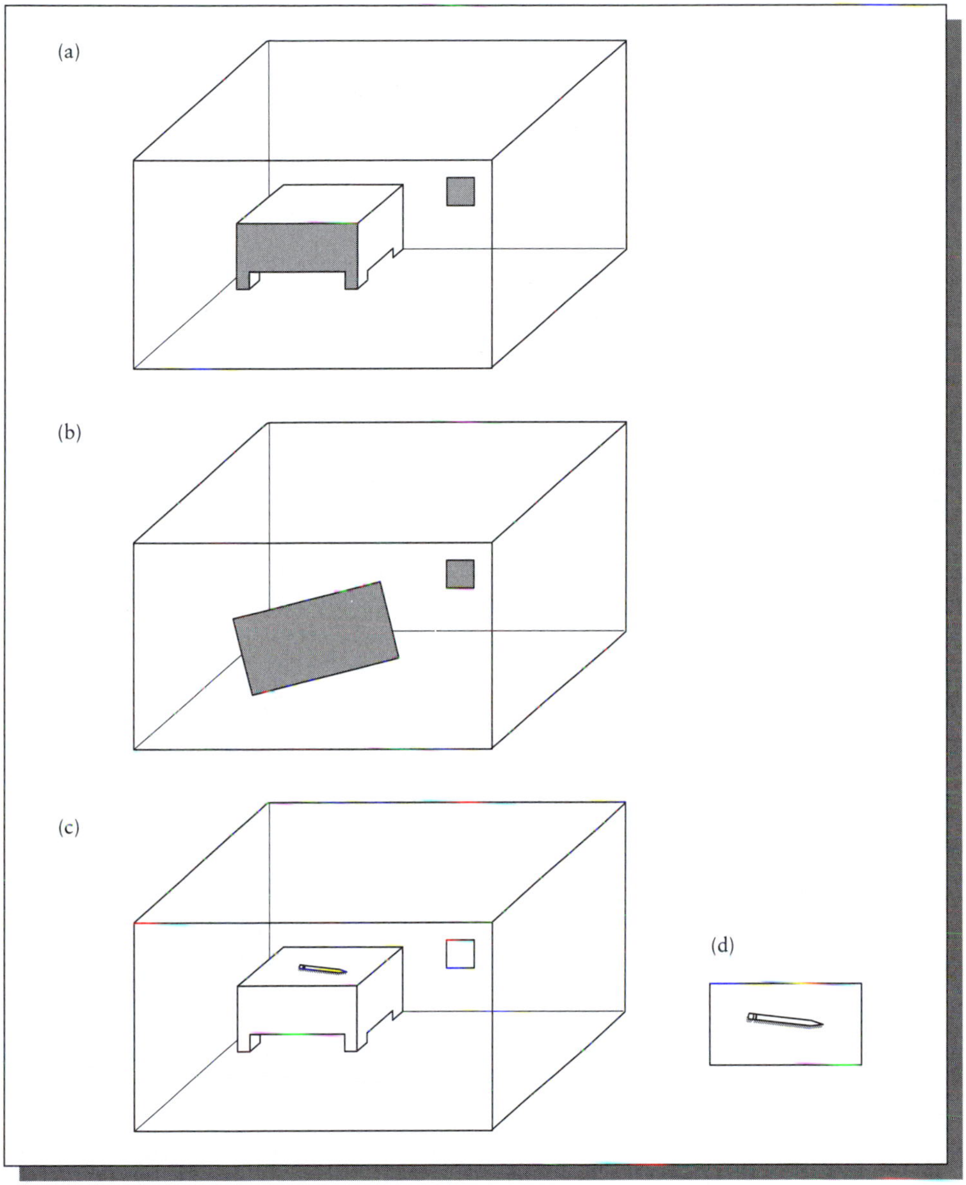

FIGURE 18.34

(a) A patch on the near wall sees a desk. (b) The desk can be considered one polygon. (c) A pencil on the desk top. (d) A close-up of the desktop; it needs to be finely subdivided to capture the pencil's shadow.

of the pencil, however, the specific distribution of illumination on the table matters quite a lot. We need to have a detailed description of the illumination available when it's necessary, but not otherwise.

The result of using the right level of detail at different places in the scene is that we obtain computational savings: we can replace the many wall-desk form factor calculations and balancing operations with a single one. In fact, the wall can probably be considered a single big patch from the point of view of the desk as well, so we also can eliminate the form factors in the other direction. If there are m patches on the desk and n patches on the wall, then we can replace the mn energy interactions between desk and wall with a single one. The interactions between the m patches on the desk with themselves still need to be considered, as we have seen above, but we have managed to eliminate many form factors and energy-balancing calculations.

At the heart of the hierarchical radiosity algorithm is the idea of a *hierarchy* (or tree) of subdivided patches. We begin with some collection of n big patches in our environment, say one for each wall, one for the top of the desk, and so on. Then we compute the form factor between each of these patches. This step requires $n(n-1)/2$ interactions, which we said we wanted to avoid. The essential point is that these are *big* patches, often larger than we would dare use in standard radiosity calculations. For example, usually a wall will be subdivided into a mesh of smaller patches before we start a progressive refinement algorithm, in order to catch the variation of illumination over the wall surface (even when using higher-order basis functions, subdivision is needed to capture shadows and other local variations in radiosity). The hierarchical refinement algorithm starts with just a single patch (or a very coarse grid) for the wall, so although the algorithm starts by computing $O(n^2)$ interactions, this value of n is much lower than for nonhierarchical algorithms.

Each time a pair of patches is examined, the algorithm considers the error that would be introduced if the patches were used at that size. One way of estimating this error is to compute the form factor from one patch to the other and compare it against a threshold. If the form factor is large, the implication is that a lot of the energy radiated by the first patch is transferred from one patch to the other; if too much energy is transferred, then perhaps we would be mistaken in using a single form factor for the entire transfer. However, if the form factor is small, then much less of the energy radiated by the first patch is intercepted by the second patch, and it seems reasonable to use a single form factor to describe the transfer.

For example, consider Figure 18.35(a). The patches share a common border, so they have a large form factor. When the two patches are subdivided (Figure 18.35(b)), we now have eight patches and sixteen form factors, whereas before we had only two of each. The patches farthest away from the common edge transfer relatively little energy back and forth, so they don't need to be subdivided any further. But the patches along the common boundary continue to subdivide until they become smaller than a predefined limit. This is shown in Figure 18.35(c). Note

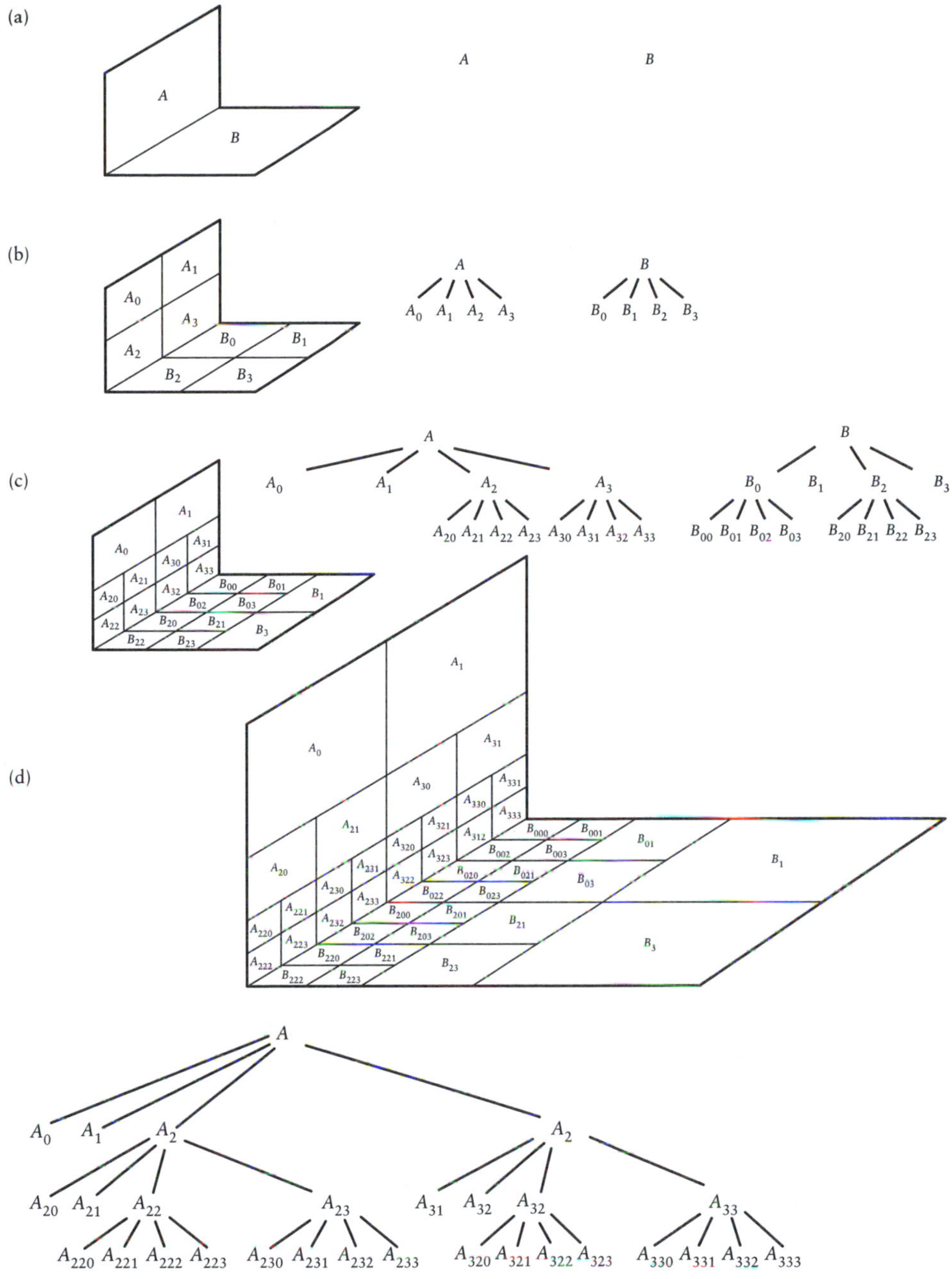

FIGURE 18.35

Two patches undergoing refinement, and their associated hierarchies. (a) The patches before subdivision. (b) After one step of subdivision on both. (c) Refinement of the patches next to the shared edge. (d) After one more step of refinement along the edge.

that the patches aren't simply subdivided without structure; we maintain a hierarchy identifying the parent of every patch created by subdivision.

We can now give specific examples of the sorts of interactions we mentioned earlier. In Figure 18.35(d), patches A_{222} and B_{222} in the near corner need to interact with each other because they exchange a lot of energy. But A_{222} does not share much energy with B_{000} at the opposite corner. In fact A_{222} doesn't really interact with much beyond the two smallest patches of B that are right next to it.

Consider the two patches A_2 and B_0 at the second level of the hierarchy. Their form factor is probably pretty small. As far as these two patches are concerned, there's no reason to subdivide; a single form factor from A_2 to B_0 is probably about as accurate as using the sixteen interactions from A_{2x} to B_{0x} for $x \in [0, 1, 2, 3]$. But we do need to subdivide A_2 further because of its interaction with B_2. The crucial observation is that just because we are subdividing A_2 we don't need to refine its interaction with B_0; that single form factor is fine for that transfer. So when it's time to shoot energy from the patches in that corner, we can do one transfer from A_2 to B_0, and then multiple transfers from A_{2x} to B_{2x}, where more precision is needed.

We say that the hierarchy for a patch contains a *root* (the node at the top representing the original patch), *internal nodes* I within the tree, and *leaves* L at the bottom. The root may be considered an internal node since it has *children*. There are four types of interaction, illustrated in Figure 18.36: IL, LI, LL, and II.

One could represent this structure with a form factor matrix that had an entry for the exchange between each pair of leaf nodes. Consider an LI transfer: one form factor represents the transfer of radiosity from a leaf to all of the leaves below the internal node in the hierarchy. That means that the form factor from the leaf to all of those other leaves would be the same: we would have constructed a *constant block* within the matrix. To see how this works, we can take a simple example in two dimensions (2D radiosity was popularized by Heckbert [202]). In Figure 18.37 we show a pair of perpendicular line segments, each divided into four segments recursively, following the same structure as Figure 18.35 in 3D.

The matrix of form factors corresponding to this fully subdivided pair of lines contains 64 entries, coupling each possible pair of leaves. The AB interactions occupy the upper-right 4×4 submatrix in Figure 18.37(b).

We said above that grouping interactions resulted in blocks of constant value in the form factor matrix. To see this, consider that the hierarchy associated with each line has a root, two interior nodes, and four leaf nodes, for a total of seven nodes. This means that there are forty-nine possible types of interactions from A to B, and forty-nine from B to A.

The forty-nine possible AB transfers are illustrated in Figure 18.38. The rows correspond to the size of the shooting patch, and the columns correspond to the size of the receiving patch. I have organized the rows and columns to correspond to the subdivision tree of the lines. Each colored region represents a block of constant form

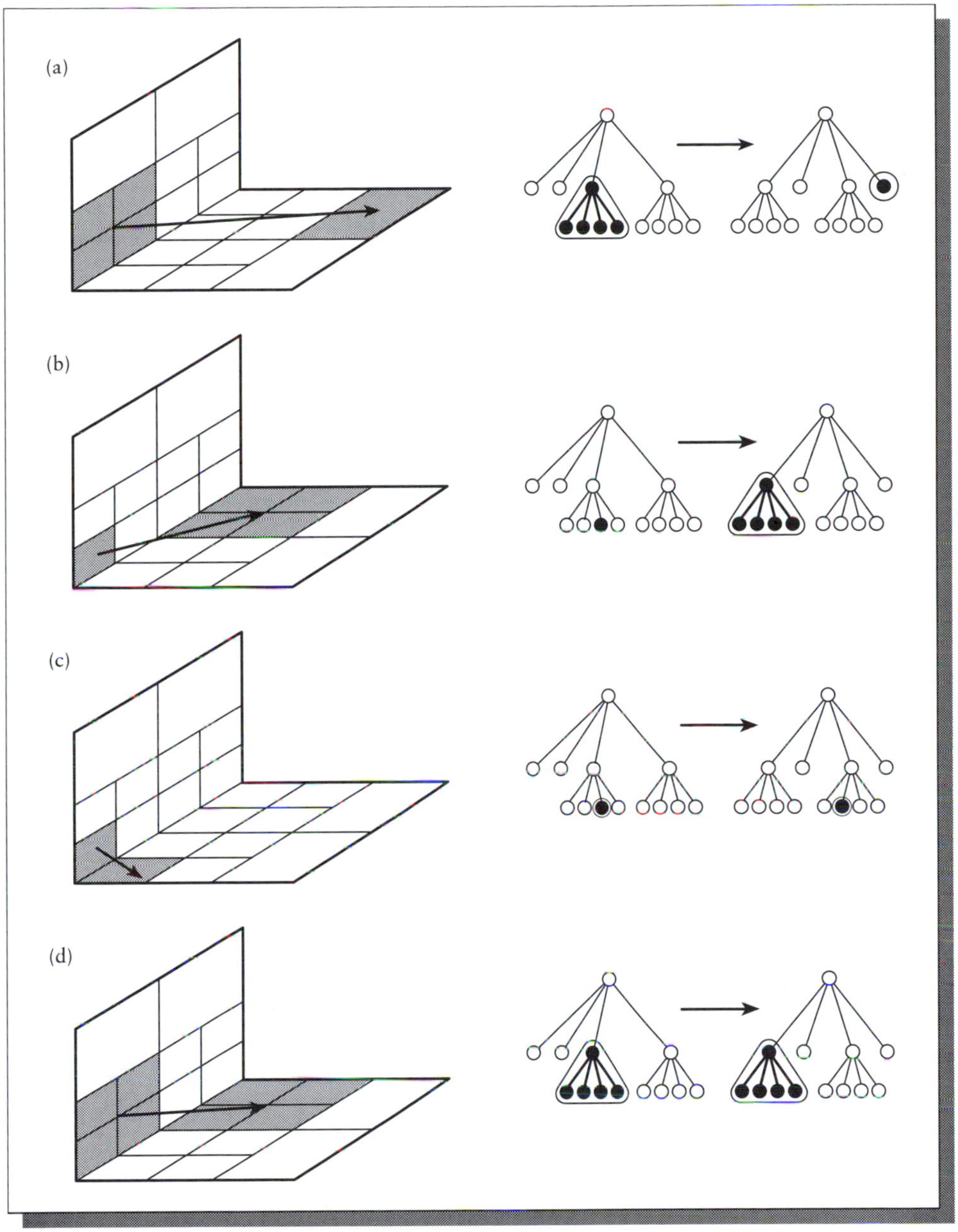

FIGURE 18.36

Interactions between different types of nodes. (a) *IL*. (b) *LI*. (c) *LL*. (d) *II*.

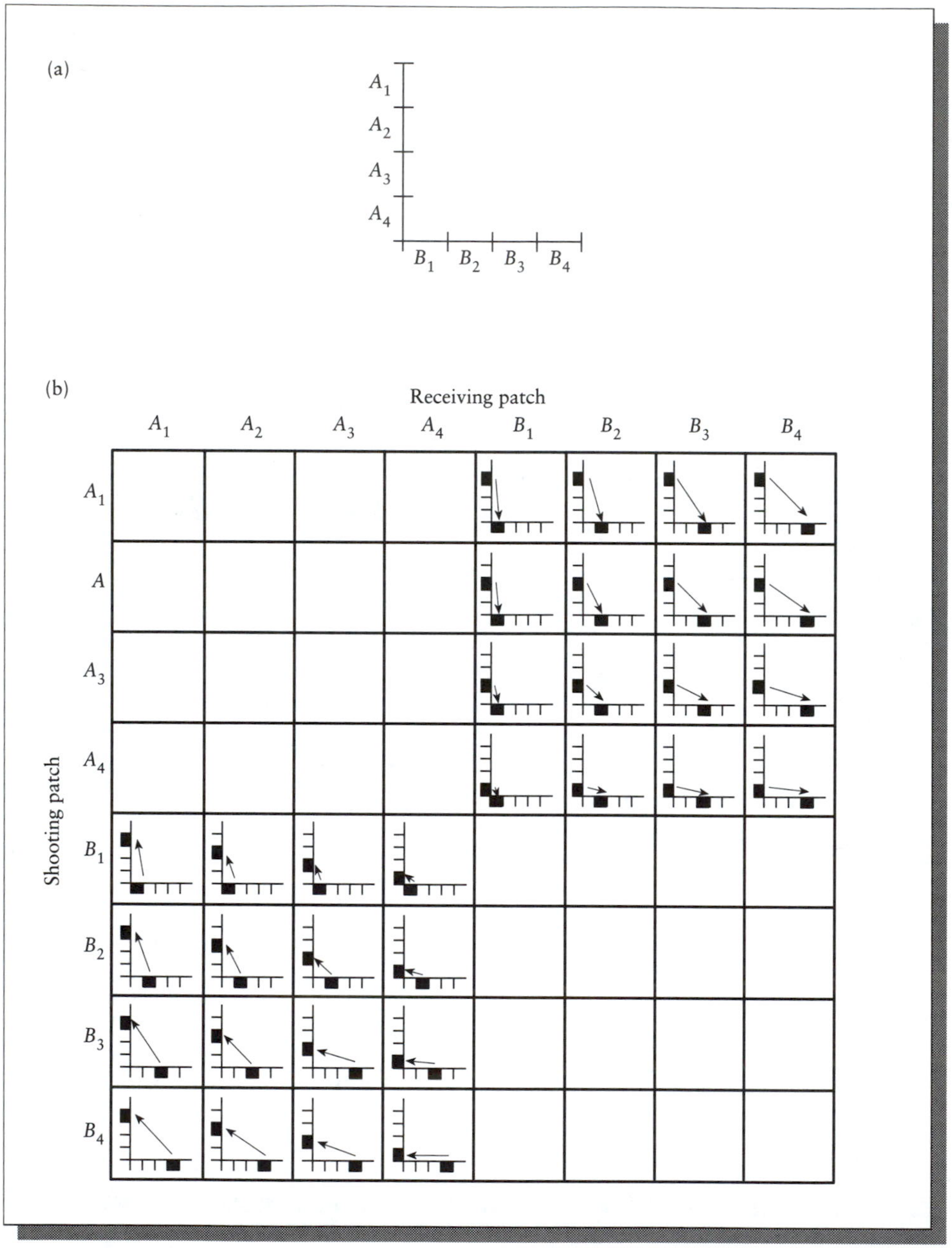

FIGURE 18.37

(a) Two subdivided line surfaces at right angles. (b) The corresponding form factor matrix.

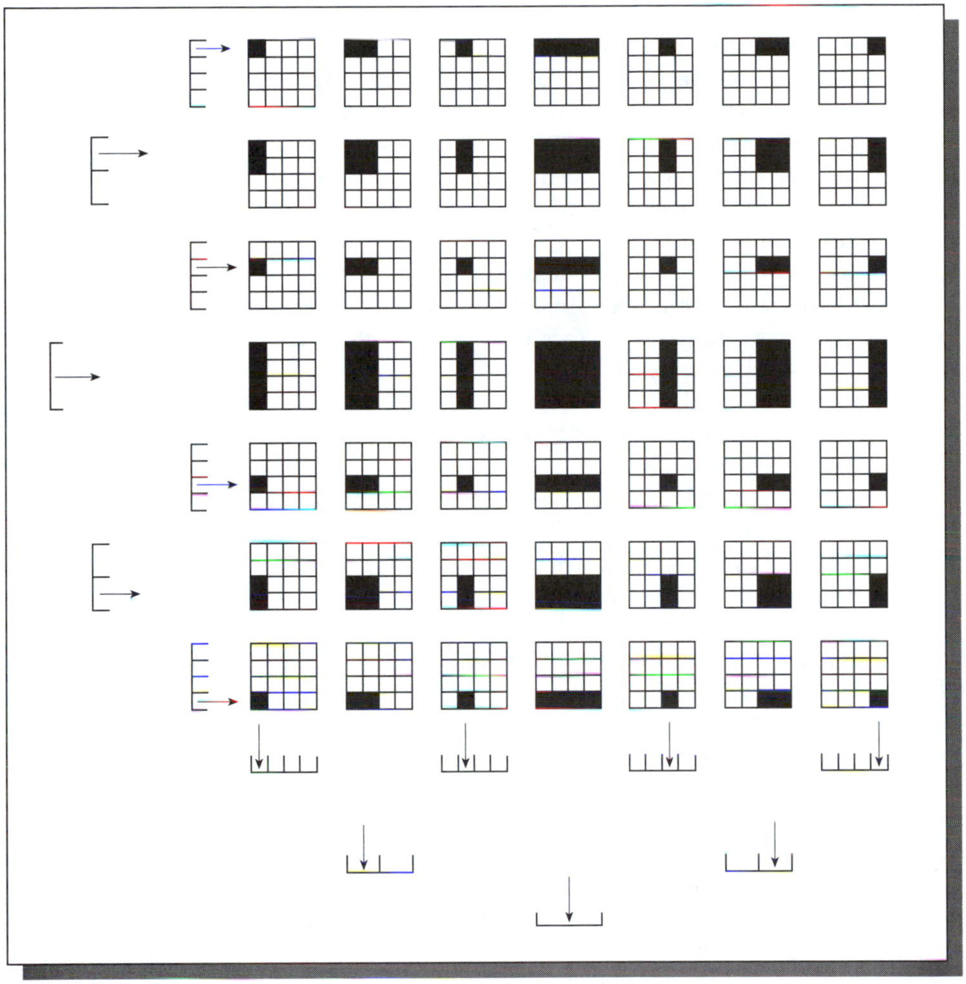

FIGURE 18.38

The various matrix blocks corresponding to the forty-nine possible transfer types.

factors, which could otherwise be replaced by a single form factor representing the complete transfer between leaf and cluster or cluster and cluster.

In general, if there are 2^k leaves for some integer k, then there will be $(2^k)^2 = 2^{2k}$ interactions of type LL within a matrix of $(2^{k+1} - 1)^2$ total interactions. The trick behind HR is that we can use just a few of these nodes; each time we select anything other than an LL node, we eliminate explicitly accounting for all the nodes below the selected ones. Following the same reasoning that led to the subdivision, Figure 18.39 shows the matrix elements that would actually be required by the HR method for AB transfers (the BA transfers, in this case, would be similar). Notice the matrix of all leaves would have sixteen elements, but we have only needed seven. Even in this simple example, we have eliminated over half the form factors, and thus a significant amount of computation.

Although grouped interactions may be represented by constant blocks in a matrix of form factors, that would be an inefficient use of storage, and we would still end up computing with them to balance the energy in the scene. Instead of storing an explicit matrix, HR creates a list of *links*, each of which describes an interaction from one patch to another.

The links are created in order along with the refinement, so that links are built as the subdivision proceeds. Figure 18.40 shows the upper-right corner of the AB hierarchical form factor matrix again, here coded by the level in the hierarchy at which each element is created. The story being told by this picture is that when we are looking at interactions of large clusters, we only need a few links. As the refinement proceeds we start creating more and more links to handle the fine-scale interaction of small patches.

It is instructive to consider how many links will be made in general. Hanrahan et al. have suggested a counting argument that the number of links will be proportional to n, the number of input polygons [192].

Consider Figure 18.41, which shows a linear patch (that is, a line in 2D). We will assume that the subdivision threshold is set so that a patch can interact with another at the same level if they are not adjacent; otherwise both patches must be refined. This means that siblings (two descendants of the same patch) cannot interact because they share the midpoint of the parent patch, and first cousins cannot interact because they share the midpoint of the grandparent patch. In the figure, B_3 and B_4 are siblings, and B_4 and B_5 are first cousins (in the figure we have used letters to designate the generation level, not different patches; e.g., all the C-level patches are descendants of the B-level patches). Leaves must interact if they have not already done so.

Given this structure, how many interactions will there be? At any level of refinement, we need only concern ourselves with links to patches that have not already been linked to by an ancestor. So any patch must connect to the children of its parent's neighbors (the patches its parent couldn't connect to), unless that link is forbidden. Consider patch B_4. Its parent C_2 will interact with C_4, so B_4 need not

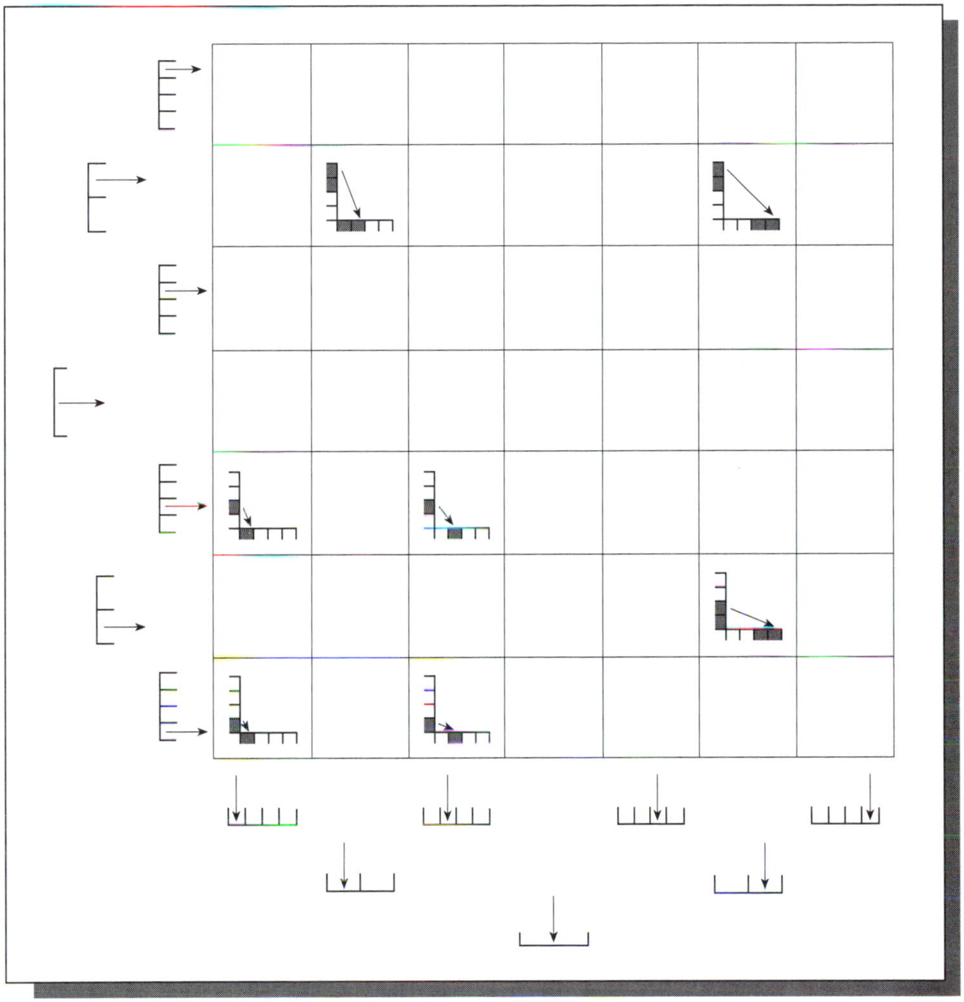

FIGURE 18.39

The seven matrix elements needed by HR in our example.

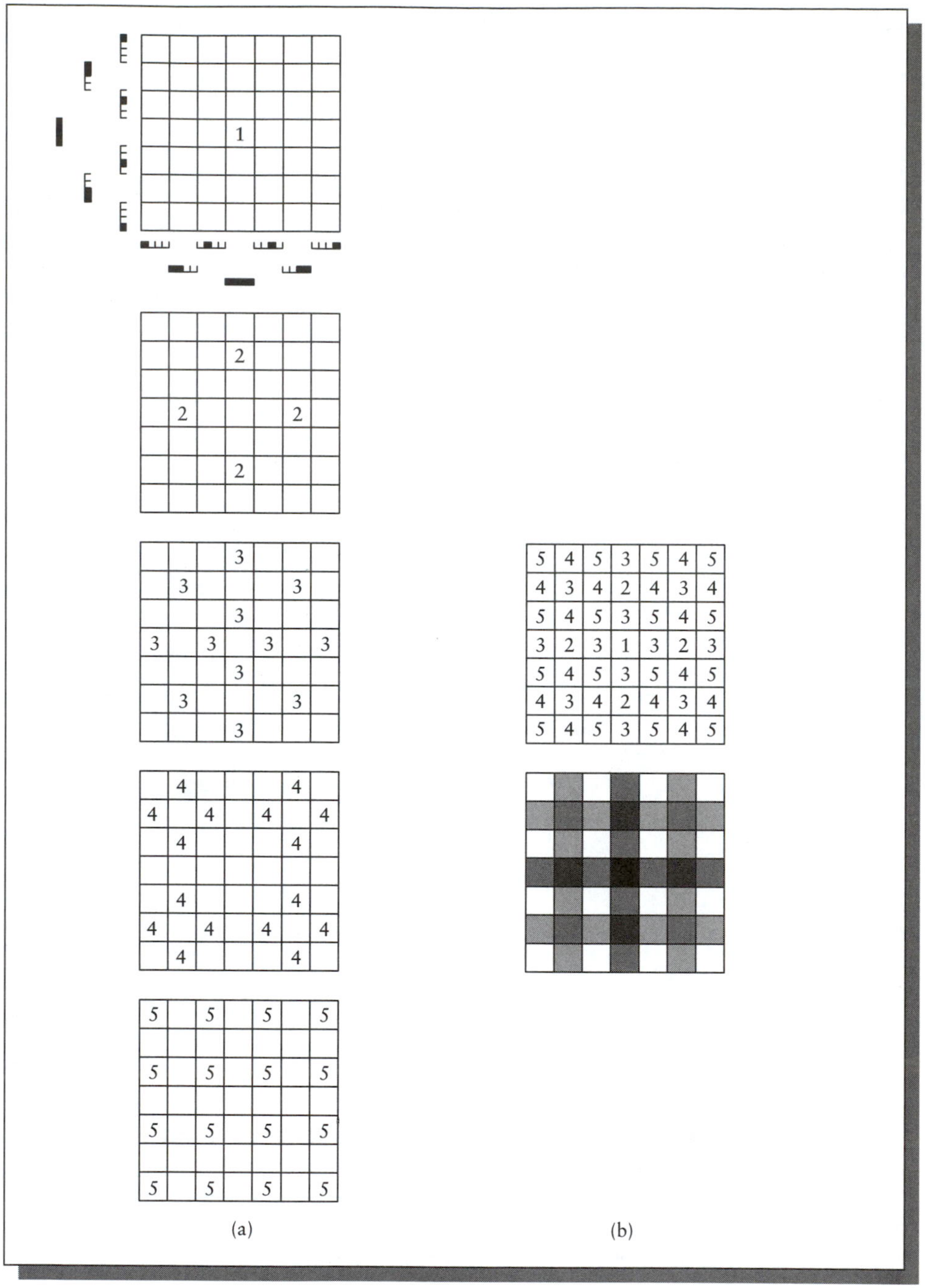

FIGURE 18.40

The order of creating links during refinement. (a) The step number. (b) All the steps at once.

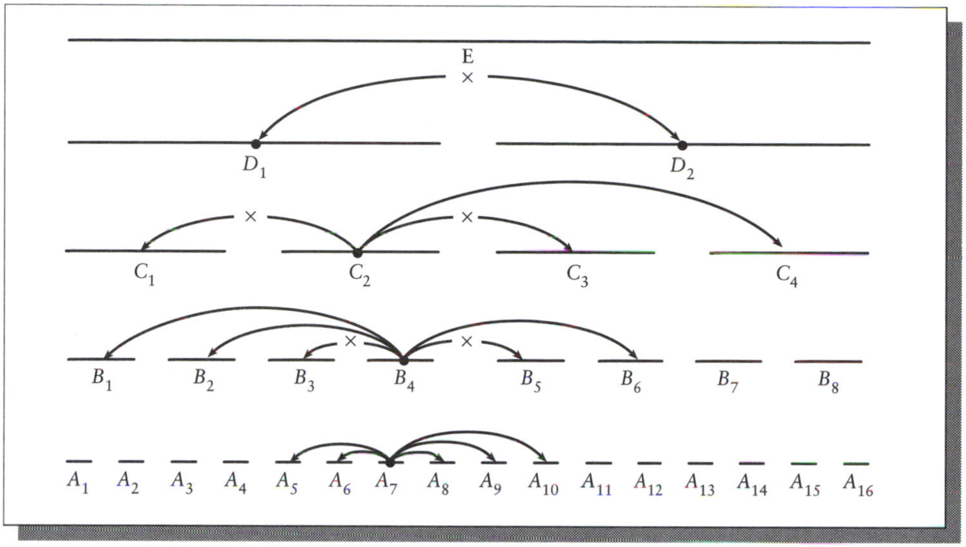

FIGURE 18.41

Determining links for a linear patch.

address any node below C_4 in the tree. But C_2 is prohibited from interacting with C_1 and C_3, so their children are still awaiting interaction with the nodes represented by C_2 (and thus descended from it in the tree). So B_4 can establish links to B_1 and B_2, the children of C_1, and to B_6, a child of C_3. It is prohibited from linking to B_3 or B_5 because it is adjacent to them. There was nothing special about B_4; all the internal nodes (except those on the edge) will go through exactly the same process. So each node connects to a constant number of other nodes, and thus the total number of links is proportional to the number of nodes.

The symmetry of the situation may be a bit easier to see if the nodes are arranged in a circle, as in Figure 18.42(a), so that there are no edge effects. Here we have indicated the groupings with internal lines; these are not meant to indicate new surfaces. The matrix corresponding to this situation is shown in Figure 18.42(b), where the blocks represent constant values.

We can now specify the HR algorithm in a bit more detail. We will present the algorithm as a collection of pseudocode fragments, following the fine organization presented by Cohen and Wallace [99].

We will actually provide quite extensive pseudocode in this section. The purpose of the code is not to suggest actual programming details, but to offer an unambiguous

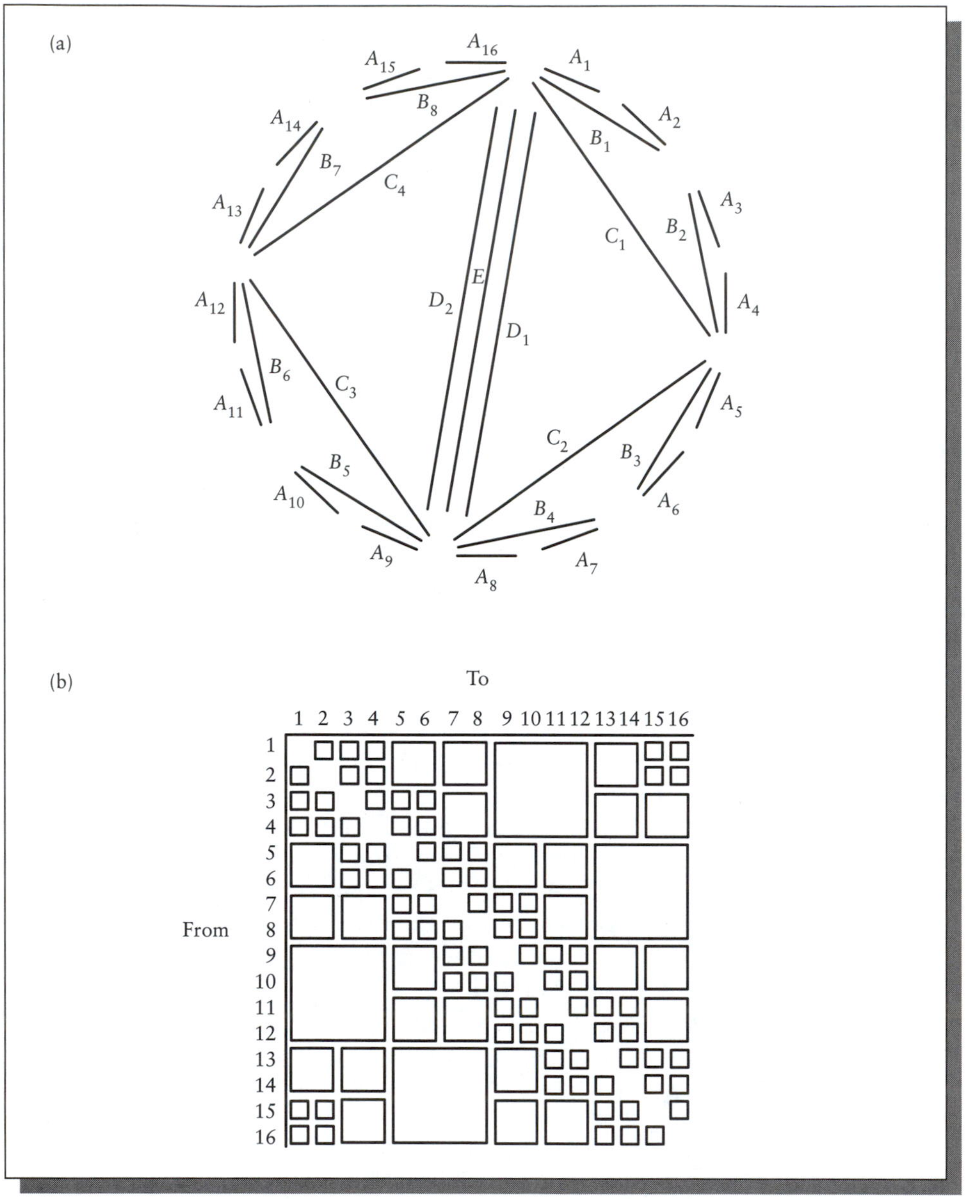

FIGURE 18.42

A refined circular patch. (a) The subdivision. Internal lines represent clustering, not new surfaces. (b) The resulting form factor matrix. Blocks indicate constant values.

struct Node {			
	float	B_g;	*gathering radiosity*
	float	B_s;	*shooting radiosity*
	float	Y_g;	*gathering importance*
	float	Y_s;	*shooting importance*
	float	E;	*emission*
	float	A;	*patch area*
	float	ρ;	*reflectivity*
	struct Node *	N;	*pointer to list of children*
	struct Link *	L;	*pointer to list of links*
	}		

FIGURE 18.43
The Node structure for hierarchical radiosity.

description of the algorithm. Since the HR technique (and the variants we will also discuss) represent the current state of the art in this form of solution process, I feel it is as important to describe the mechanics of these algorithms as it was to describe the derivation of important equations in previous chapters. These code fragments will bear some resemblance to the structure of an actual system, but we will not address any of the critical implementation details that are essential to a working system; the references provide a wealth of information for the implementor.

There are two types of structures in the system: a Link and a Node. A node contains information about a node in the hierarchy, and a link represents a selected transfer of energy between nodes. These two structures are shown in Figures 18.43 and 18.44.

We will indicate an element of a structure with the dot notation; e.g., $p.E$ for the emission field for a node p.

Each Node structure contains a *gathering radiosity* B_g, which is the radiosity it has received but not yet sent into the environment, and a *shooting radiosity* B_s, which is the radiosity it presents to the world at any given moment. A Node also contains an emission term E, an area term A, and a reflectivity ρ. It contains a pointer N to a list of subnodes if this node is subdivided (initially N is set to a default such as NULL), and a pointer L to a list of links connecting this node to other nodes. The fields Y_s and Y_q are used to store importance; these will be discussed in Section 18.6.3.

```
struct Link }
    struct Node*    p;      pointer to shooting node
    struct Node*    q;      pointer to gathering node
    float           Fqp;    form factor
    struct Link *   L;      pointer to next link
    }
```

FIGURE 18.44
The Link structure for hierarchical radiosity.

A Link structure represents a transfer of energy from a shooting patch p to a gathering patch q; the receiving patch q is the patch with which the link is stored. The Link contains the form factor F_{qp} for this transfer, and a pointer L to other links. So to gather radiosity for a node n, we look at each link L and compute $L.p.B_s \times L.F_{qp}$.

The calling dependence of the pseudocode routines is shown in Figure 18.45. We will give explicit listing for all the routines except those in parentheses.

18.6.1 One Step of HR

The general idea for using hierarchical refinement is that we start with the n large patches provided by the designer and run them pairwise into a refinement routine. That routine either builds a link between the two patches if that would be acceptable, or it subdivides one or the other and then calls itself to examine the new patches for possible linking or further refinement. When the links are established, we call a solution program to transfer the energy around on the links until the system is converged.

The driver for the whole operation is called SolveSHR (SHR stands for *simple hierarchical radiosity*) and is listed in Figure 18.46. This is a very simple routine: it just initializes the system and then calls a routine to solve it.

The first step in initialization is to assign the initial patch emittances to the unshot radiosities. We then pass through all the input patches and build the necessary links between them. Since each patch may be refined, we will end up associating a subdivision hierarchy with most of the patches. The root of this hierarchy is called the *root node* for that patch.

To build a complete set of links, we need to check all pairs of nodes in both directions. If one or the other nodes needs subdivision, then it's subdivided and

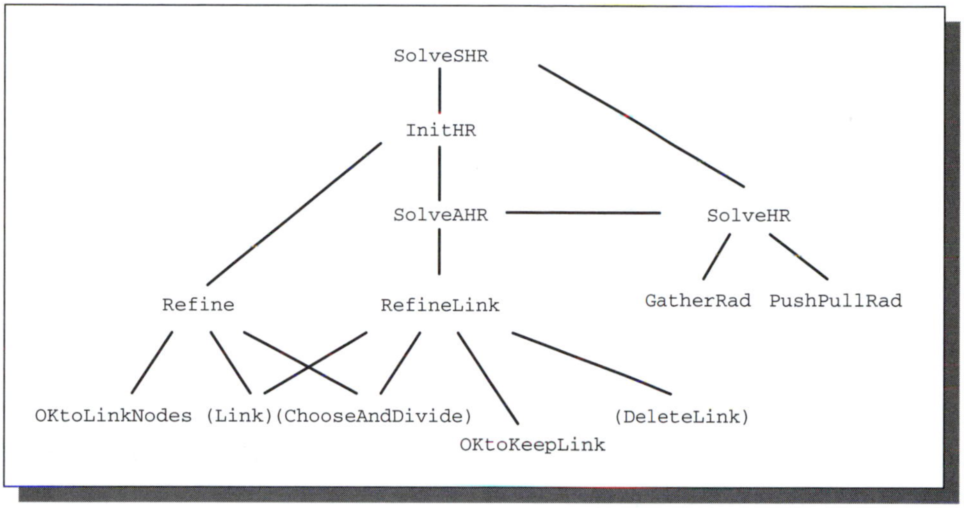

FIGURE 18.45
The calling dependence of HR pseudocode.

`SolveSHR() {`	*Solve simple hierarchical radiosity.*
`InitBg()` `BuildLinks()`	*Create initial link structure.*
`SolveHR()` `}`	*Call the system solver once.*

FIGURE 18.46
Pseudocode for `SolveSHR`.

link-building is tried again. The routine `InitBs` listed in Figure 18.47 initializes the shooting radiosity, and `BuildLinks` in Figure 18.48 builds the links between each pair of polygons.

After initializing the shooting radiosity, the only initialization job left is to call `Refine` with pairs of nodes. Figure 18.49 gives the pseudocode for `Refine`. The first thing that `Refine` does is to see if the two nodes it is given can be linked right away. To determine this, it calls an auxiliary function, `OKtoLinkNodes`, listed in Figure 18.50.

```
InitBs() {                         Initialize shooting radiosity.
  for all nodes n
    n.B_s ← n.E                    Set initial shooting radiosity to emission.
    endfor
}
```

FIGURE 18.47
Pseudocode for `InitBs`.

```
BuildLinks() {                     Build initial set of links.
  for all nodes a
    for all nodes b
      Refine(a,b)                  Build links between each pair of nodes.
      endfor
    endfor
}
```

FIGURE 18.48
Pseudocode for `BuildLinks`.

Hanrahan et al. [192] call `OKtoLinkNodes` an *oracle function*, because to properly do its job, it needs access to more information than we have. The job of this function is to determine if linking these two patches would cause significantly more error than subdividing them and building links between the smaller patches. This is very important, because this single decision controls which links get built.

We would like the oracle to decide on the need for subdivision without going through the expense of actually subdividing the patches. Therefore it is based on a couple of simple heuristics (we will see some more advanced forms of this function later on). As shown in the pseudocode, we allow the link to occur if the two patches are physically smaller than some threshold, or if an estimated form factor is below some threshold. We can use any computationally convenient means for estimating the form factor; Hanrahan et al. used a solid-angle approximation similar to the approaches in Section 18.5.3.

Returning to `Refine`, if the nodes can be linked, then we call the routine `Link` to establish the connection. A call of `Link(`a, b`)` adds a link node to the list at b, indicating that it receives energy from a. This is all that needs to be done, and `Refine` returns.

`Refine(a,b){`	*Establish links between nodes a and b.*
`if OKtoLinkNodes(a,b) then` `Link(a,b)`	*Linking these nodes is fine.*
`else` `node←ChooseAndDivide(a,b)`	*Pick a node to subdivide.*

`if node=a then`
`for each child r of a`
`Refine(r,b)`
`endfor`
	Check links for descendants of a.

`else if node=b then`
`for each child r of b`
`Refine(a,r)`
`endfor`
	Check links for descendants of b.

`else` `Link(a,b)`	*Nodes are not subdividable after all.*

`endif`
`endif`
`}`	

FIGURE 18.49
Pseudocode for `Refine`.

`OKtoLinkNodes(a,b) {`	*Is it okay to link these two nodes?*

if $a.A < \epsilon_A$ and $b.A < \epsilon_A$
`return True`
`endif`
	They're small enough to be okay.

if `EstimateFormFactor(a,b)` $< \epsilon_F$
`return True`
`endif`
	The form factor is small enough.

`return False` `}`	*Subdivide one and try again.*

FIGURE 18.50
Pseudocode for `OKtoLinkNodes`.

```
SolveHR() {                      Balance energy using HR links.
  while not converged
    for every root node r        Gather up energy from all incoming links.
      GatherRad(r)
      endfor
    for every root node r
      PushPullRad(r)             Give energy to children; collect their energy back.
      endfor
  endwhile
}
```

FIGURE 18.51

Pseudocode for `SolveHR`.

But if the nodes cannot be immediately linked, then it must be because the oracle determined that it would create too much error to link them at this level, and one or the other needs to be subdivided. We call a routine called `ChooseAndDivide` that examines the two nodes and chooses one of them to be subdivided. Now, because each root node is tested against all other nodes, the node selected by `ChooseAndDivide` may have already been subdivided; if it isn't, the routine creates the four subdivided children before returning. It is also possible that `ChooseAndDivide` may determine that neither of the nodes can be advantageously subdivided; in this case it returns a value that does not point to either a or b.

When `Refine` resumes after this call, it looks to see which node has been selected and subdivided by `ChooseAndDivide`. `Refine` then calls itself recursively to establish links between the unaffected node and the children of the subdivided node. If neither node was selected for subdivision, they are simply linked together, overruling the oracle.

When the links are finally established, `Refine` returns, and the next pair of nodes are linked. When all pairs have been linked up, control returns to `SolveSHR`, which calls `SolveHR` to actually solve for the radiosity. In a traditional radiosity system this is where a matrix would be inverted. The routine `SolveHR` is given in Figure 18.51.

There's not much to `SolveHR`. It visits every root node and instructs the patch (and hierarchy) associated with that node to gather energy from the other patches in the environment through the routine `GatherRad`. Now comes the tricky part where we need to make sure that the radiosity gathered at different levels of the hierarchy is correctly distributed. We manage this process with the routine `PushPullRad`,

GatherRad(n) {	*Get radiosity into this node.*
$n.B_g \leftarrow 0$	*No radiosity gathered yet.*
for each link L into n $n.B_g \leftarrow n.B_g +$ $n.\rho \times [L.F_{qp} \times L.p.B_s]$ endfor	*Accumulate some radiosity to shoot.*
for each child r of n GatherRad(r) endfor	*Accumulate for each child.*
}	

FIGURE 18.52

Pseudocode for GatherRad.

which is applied to each root node. SolveHR runs through this look again and again until the energy distribution converges, just like every other radiosity algorithm. Let's look at the two routines involved in this process, starting with GatherRad, listed in Figure 18.52.

GatherRad visits each link that transfers energy into the given node and gathers energy from the node at the other end of the link. Since the shooter is node p, the radiosity absorbed and re-radiated at n is over link L simply $n.\rho \times [L.F_{qp} \times L.p.B_s]$, since n is the same as q for this link. If n has any children, they need to gather their energy too, so we call GatherRad recursively. Remember that these child nodes are coincident with n, though they are smaller. They represent energy transfers that were too important in some way (as determined by the oracle) to approximate with just a single big transfer to the parent node.

When all the energy has been gathered, we need to distribute the light gathered at different levels throughout the tree at each node before we can start gathering again. This process is accomplished by the routine PushPullRad, listed in Figure 18.53.

The heart of PushPullRad is how it sends radiosity down the hierarchy (the *push* part) and how it combines the radiosity coming up the hierarchy from a node's children (the *pull* part). Let's look at the pull part first.

Recall that radiosity is power per unit area:

$$B = \frac{\Phi}{A} \tag{18.79}$$

If we take n coplanar, abutting patches, each of which has power Φ_c and area A_c,

`PushPullRad(`n, B_{down}`) {`	*Node n inherits radiosity Bdown.*
`if` n `is a leaf then` $B_{\text{up}} \leftarrow n.E + n.B_g + B_{\text{down}}$	*Send up my emission, reflection, and inheritance.*
`else` $B_{\text{up}} \leftarrow 0$	*Nothing collected yet.*
`for each child` r `of` n	*Get child's radiosity.*
$B_{\text{up}} \leftarrow B_{\text{up}} + (r.A/n.A)\times$ `PushPullRad(`$r,\ n.B_g + B_{\text{down}}$`)`	*Add in child's radiosity scaled by its relative area.*
`endfor` `endif`	
$n.B_s \leftarrow B_{\text{up}}$	*Save what I'm passing up; I want to shoot it.*
`return(`B_{up}`)` `}`	*And pass my radiosity back up.*

FIGURE 18.53

Pseudocode for `PushPullRad`.

then the total radiosity of the aggregate is the total power divided by the total area:

$$\begin{aligned} B &= \frac{\sum_{c=1}^{n} \Phi_c}{\sum_{c=1}^{n} A_c} \\ &= \frac{\sum_{c=1}^{n} B_c A_c}{A} \\ &= \sum_{c=1}^{n} \frac{A_c}{A} B_c \end{aligned} \tag{18.80}$$

where A is the area of the parent. This last expression is just what is computed inside `PushPullRad`. It tells us that the radiosity due to the children of a node is simply the radiosity of each child weighted by the relative area of the child. To find the total radiosity at a given level, we only need to find this contribution from below, and add in the contribution from this level.

The push part is much simpler. Since radiosity is power per unit area, and we assume power output is constant across the node, the radiosity of any subpatch is the same as the radiosity of the parent patch, since the ratio of energy to area remains constant. If the child has an area that is a fraction α of the parent's area A, then

$$B = \frac{\Phi}{A} = \frac{\alpha\Phi}{\alpha A} \tag{18.81}$$

Now we can look at `PushPullRad` as a simple distributor of energy. We start at the top of the hierarchy, and look up the gathered radiosity B_g at that level. That radiosity is inherited by each child, so we recursively call `PushPullRad` passing down this radiosity. If these children are internal nodes, then they add their gathered power to what they inherited and pass the total on downward. Finally we reach a leaf node; it has inherited the sum of the radiosity from every level above it. The leaf adds in its own gathered radiosity plus its emission, and that becomes the new shooting radiosity for the leaf. It stores this locally and then sends the result back up. The parent node now does nothing but combine the shooting radiosities of each of its children (weighted by relative area); the result is that node's own shooting radiosity. It saves it locally and sends it back up the tree, and so on until we reach the root.

At this point the hierarchy for each root node makes sense: each internal node contains the area-weighted radiosities of its children, and each leaf node contains the total radiosity gathered by the entire path of the tree above it. Localized transfers to intermediate nodes stay localized to that node and its descendants, but are included in the averages computed by its ancestors.

Now that all the trees are balanced, control returns to `SolveHR`, which checks for convergence and calls `GatherRad` and `PushPullRad` as many times as necessary until an equilibrium solution has been found.

Figure 18.54 (color plate) shows three images of an office scene at different levels of refinement. The size of each patch is indicated by its image outlined in white.

A summary overview of hierarchical radiosity is shown in Figure 18.55. At the top we come in with two patches and a proposed link from one to the other. First we test each patch to see if it is smaller than a size threshold, and we estimate the form factor to see if it is below threshold. If the patches and the form factor are small enough, then we exit the loop and create the link. Otherwise we subdivide the larger patch, create possible links from each subpatch to the smaller input patch, and run each of these four new pairs of patches through the same process.

18.6.2 Adaptive HR

The routine `SolveSHR` in Figure 18.46 builds a hierarchy and then solves the resulting radiosity relationships. Recall that the oracle function, called `OKtoLinkNodes`, compared two nodes and decided whether or not to link them. We said that this function controlled the structure of the hierarchy because it told us when to subdivide a patch and when we could build a link. The function only had access to

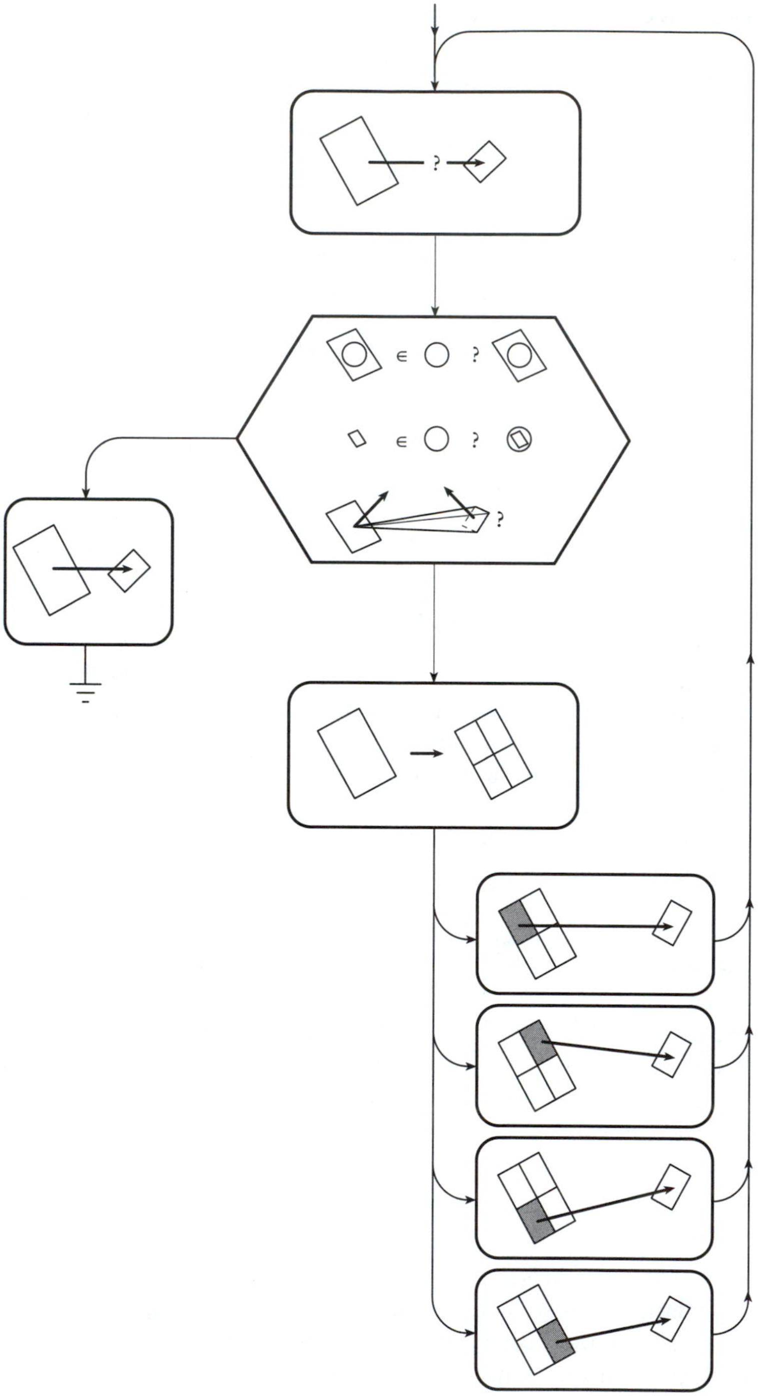

FIGURE 18.55

An overview of hierarchical radiosity.

the geometry of the nodes, so it made a decision based on patch sizes and form factors. Hanrahan et al. [192] called this *F refinement* in reference to the form factor component.

But once the system has been solved from this particular set of links, we have learned something important about the environment that we didn't know before: an estimate for the distribution of energy. What we would really like is for each link in the system to carry the same amount of energy. Once the system has been solved for a particular set of links, we can pass through the structure and make changes, adding links where we were too conservative the first time. When all links carry the same amount of energy, there's no advantage to either shooting or gathering, and nothing to be gained by shooting from the brightest source as in progressive radiosity: every link has just as much effect as every other.

As long as we're moving through the structure again, we can also use a smaller threshold in the form factor test; nodes that were not subdivided before will have to be subdivided in order to get small enough to satisfy this new threshold. This process is an example of a general technique called *multigridding*. The idea behind multigridding is that we can first compute a coarse approximation to the solution using a rough grid, and then slowly refine the grid into smaller and smaller elements. This method will often converge more quickly than starting with the smallest-size cells in the first place, because the coarse solution gets us close to the correct answer at low cost; when the grid is refined, it is usually pretty close to the right answer already.

This combination of geometric and illumination information to control the hierarchy is called *BF refinement*. Implementation of this method requires only two new routines and a replacement for the main control. The main program, now called `SolveAHR` (for *adaptive hierarchical refinement*), is listed in Figure 18.56.

The routine `SolveAHR` is very similar to `SolveSHR`, except that after initialization and one pass through the solver, it runs through all the links in the system looking for any that can be refined. If any links are changed, then the system is re-solved with the new configuration, and the links are scanned again. The process repeats until the system has reached an equilibrium with respect to both the distribution of light and the power carried by the links.

The refinement test for links is called `RefineLink` and is listed in Figure 18.57. As with the patch-based test `Refine`, the routine `RefineLink` calls an oracle to determine if a link needs to be refined. The routine `OKtoKeepLink` provides the BF-refinement version of the oracle, and is listed in Figure 18.58.

The oracle `OKtoKeepLink` checks for one of three conditions that a link must satisfy in order to remain unrefined: the patches involved must be small, the shooter has no power, or not enough radiosity reaches the gatherer. This last step is the key to BF-refinement. As we mentioned earlier, the thresholds for these tests may be large at the start of the process, and then gradually reduced to drive the system

`SolveAHR() {`	*Solve adaptive hierarchical radiosity.*
`InitBg()` `BuildLinks()`	*Initialize and create initial links.*
done`←False`	

`while` *done* `= False`
done`←True`
`SolveHR()`
	Solve current system.

`for all links` *L*
`if RefineLink(`*L*`) = True`
done`←False`
`endif`
`endfor`
	If any link was refined, re-solve later.

`endwhile` `}`	

FIGURE 18.56

Pseudocode for `SolveAHR`.

toward a more accurate solution. A result of applying BF refinement is shown in Figure 18.59 (color plate).

Observe that the hierarchical radiosity algorithm is inherently a *multiresolution* technique: at any given time, different parts of the algorithm are dealing with the same surfaces in differently sized pieces. As we saw in Chapter 6, wavelets are a natural means for discussing multiresolution phenomena. Gortler et al. [167] have shown how to apply wavelet bases to the hierarchical radiosity algorithm, creating a whole family of different higher-order radiosity algorithms based on different wavelet basis sets. This works well because the form factor matrix in radiosity problems (which still exists, though implicitly, in hierarchical methods) is mostly smooth. Wavelets are able to describe this matrix by capturing the large smooth regions with large, smooth functions, and then capturing fast local changes with a few additional localized bases.

18.6.3 Importance HR

Recall the idea of *importance* from our discussion of integral equations in Section 16.9.3. We saw that if we had an *importance function* defined on the same

`RefineLink(`L`) {`	*If link needs refining, do so and return True.*
`  if OKtoKeepLink(`L`)`	
`    return False`	*No refinement needed.*
`    endif`	
$node \leftarrow$ `ChooseAndDivide(`$L.p$, $L.q$`)`	*Pick a node.*
`  if` $node = L.p$	
`    for each child` r `of` $L.p$	*Build new links to L.q.*
`      Link(`$r, L.q$`)`	
`      endfor`	
`  else`	
`    for each child` r `of` $L.q$	*Build new links to L.r.*
`      Link(`$L.p, r$`)`	
`      endfor`	
`  DeleteLink(`L`)`	*Get rid of old link.*
`  return True`	
`}`	

FIGURE 18.57

Pseudocode for `RefineLink`.

`OKtoKeepLink(`L`) {`	*Is it okay to accept this node?*
`  if` $L.p.A < \epsilon_A$ `and` $L.q.A < \epsilon_A$	
`    return True`	*The patches are small enough to be okay.*
`    endif`	
`  if` $L.p.B_s \times L.F_{qp} < \epsilon_{BF}$	
`    return True`	*There's not enough energy to be transferred.*
`    endif`	
`  return False`	*This link needs refinement.*
`}`	

FIGURE 18.58

Pseudocode for `OKtoKeepLink`.

domain as our unknown function, we could use it to guide our process of solving for the unknown.

This idea has been applied to hierarchical radiosity by Smits et al. to create an *importance-driven* hierarchical radiosity algorithm [414]. The algorithm is quite easy to implement and can dramatically improve the efficiency of the solution.

Recall the fundamental identity from Equation 16.178 that relates an unknown function x and its driving function g to the unknown importance w and its driving function p:

$$\langle x|\, p\rangle = \langle g|\, w\rangle \tag{18.82}$$

The importance w and the solution x are unknown in this function, while the given potential p and the driving term g are both known. The product of one known and unknown matches the product of the other known and unknown. Thus we sometimes say that if we knew the importance we would know the solution; the problems are closely related.

In terms of radiosity, the unknown x is the radiosity B, and the driving function is the emittance E. We *define* R to be the driving function for importance, and Y to be the importance. Then we can restate our relation above as

$$\langle B|\, R\rangle = \langle E|\, Y\rangle \tag{18.83}$$

(the notation varies: Smits et al. used $\langle \Phi|\, R\rangle = \langle S|\, \Psi\rangle$ [414], and Cohen and Wallace used $\langle B|\, R\rangle = \langle S|\, \Upsilon\rangle$ [99]). Expanding out this braket into traditional radiosity-style sums over discrete elements gives us the related pair of equations:

$$\begin{aligned} B_i &= E_i + \sum_{k=1}^{n} \rho_i B_k F_{i,k} \\ Y_i &= R_i + \sum_{k=1}^{n} \rho_k B_k F_{k,i} \end{aligned} \tag{18.84}$$

Note the switch in the indices in the two right-hand sides.

We can also write these expressions in matrix notation. For a form factor matrix $\mathbf{K}$, we find

$$\begin{aligned} \mathbf{E} &= \mathbf{K}\mathbf{B} \\ \mathbf{R} &= \mathbf{K}^t\mathbf{Y} \end{aligned} \tag{18.85}$$

The need for the transpose is expected because the importance and the radiosity are adjoint terms, and the adjoint of a real matrix is its transpose. Normally, we are given the emittances $\mathbf{E}$, and we try to find an approximate solution $\widetilde{\mathbf{B}}$ to $\mathbf{B}$ using an approximate form factor matrix $\widetilde{\mathbf{K}} + \mathbf{K} + \Delta\mathbf{K}$. Then the approximate solution satisfies

$$\mathbf{E} = \widetilde{\mathbf{K}}\widetilde{\mathbf{B}} = (\mathbf{K} + \Delta\mathbf{K})\widetilde{\mathbf{B}} = \mathbf{K}\widetilde{\mathbf{B}} + \Delta\mathbf{K}\widetilde{\mathbf{B}} \tag{18.86}$$

which can be rearranged as

$$\mathbf{E} - \Delta\mathbf{K}\widetilde{\mathbf{B}} = \mathbf{K}\widetilde{\mathbf{B}} \tag{18.87}$$

The first part of Equation 18.86 tells us that we can match the exact emittances using an approximation composed of an approximate transport operator $\widetilde{\mathbf{K}}$ and an approximate solution $\widetilde{\mathbf{B}}$. On the other hand, Equation 18.87 says that we can match the approximate emittances $\mathbf{E} - \Delta\mathbf{K}\widetilde{\mathbf{B}}$ by using the approximate solution and an exact transport operator $K\widetilde{B}$.

Our goal in all radiosity algorithms so far has been to minimize the error in our solution; that is, we have tried to make $\mathbf{B} - \widetilde{\mathbf{B}}$ as small as possible. But this is not always necessary. Consider an interior office scene, composed of a room with bookcases, tables, chairs, and so on. If we're standing in the doorway, then we probably cannot see the back of the desk, the insides of the drawers, and many other surfaces. As far as computing an image is concerned, if we can't see these surfaces, then we really don't care what their radiosity is. Of course, the *effect* of their radiated energy onto the surfaces we can see must be present. For example, for the scene just described, the back panel of the desk might be adequately represented by just a single polygon that absorbs and reflects the same energy as a finely subdivided back panel. The difference is that we can't see the back, so we don't care if the approximation is visually acceptable as long as its light propagation is accurate. Going one step further, the interaction of light inside the closed desk drawers is completely irrelevant to us. In F-refinement HR we would compute form factors for all the patches inside the drawers; even in BF-refinement, if a little light was leaking into the drawers, then we might even end up processing it. We would like to focus our attention on getting a good estimate of the radiosity that we can actually see in the environment, and not bother with overwhelming detail in invisible parts of the environment.

We can focus our attention (and computing resources) on the visible parts of the scene by defining an *image function* $v(B)$; think of this function as telling us what linear combination of radiosities must be used to find the radiance at a particular pixel. The importance of each radiosity value to the pixel value is exactly the driving importance term $\mathbf{R}$. This observation allows us to easily derive Equation 18.83 in terms of radiosity and importance [413]:

$$\begin{aligned} v(\mathbf{B}) &= \mathbf{R}^t\mathbf{B} \\ &= \mathbf{Y}^t\mathbf{K}\mathbf{B} \\ &= \mathbf{Y}^t(\mathbf{K}\mathbf{B}) \\ &= \mathbf{Y}^t\mathbf{E} \end{aligned} \tag{18.88}$$

The error we want to minimize is not simply $\mathbf{B} - \widetilde{\mathbf{B}}$, which tries to get a good approximation for the radiosity everywhere in the environment, but rather the *visible* part of that error: $v(\mathbf{B} - \widetilde{\mathbf{B}})$. In other words, it's okay if there are errors in the approximation where we can't see it; as long as the cumulative impact of the invisible part of the environment is accurate, it doesn't matter how the radiosity is distributed. Expanding this error and using the identities derived above, we find

$$\begin{aligned} v(\mathbf{B} - \widetilde{\mathbf{B}}) &= \mathbf{R}^t\mathbf{B} - \mathbf{R}^t\widetilde{\mathbf{B}} \\ &= \mathbf{Y}^t\mathbf{E} - (\mathbf{Y}^t\mathbf{K})\widetilde{\mathbf{B}} \\ &= \mathbf{Y}^t\mathbf{E} - \mathbf{Y}^t(\mathbf{E} - \Delta\mathbf{K}\widetilde{\mathbf{B}}) \\ &= \mathbf{Y}^t\Delta\mathbf{K}\widetilde{\mathbf{B}} \end{aligned} \tag{18.89}$$

So $\mathbf{Y}^t\Delta\mathbf{K}\widetilde{\mathbf{B}}$ is the error in our image due to using the approximations $\widetilde{\mathbf{K}}$ and $\widetilde{\mathbf{B}}$. This is what we want to minimize: the error in the *important radiosity*, not just the error in the radiosity.

These ideas are demonstrated in Figure 18.60 (color plate). Here a maze is illuminated by a number of light sources, and the solution is shown in red in Figure 18.60(a). If an image is rendered from a point of view near the bottom, as indicated by the small eye in Figure 18.60(b), then we can solve for the importance from that view, shown in green. Notice that for this viewpoint there are a lot of unimportant patches in the model. If we superimpose the two solutions as in Figure 18.60(c), we see in yellow that the patches are both important and emit significant radiosity. Those are the patches we care the most about for the given viewpoint.

The problem here is that we don't know $\mathbf{Y}$; in fact, it is just as hard to find as $\mathbf{B}$ itself. So our algorithm will find an estimate $\widetilde{\mathbf{B}}$ for B, and at the same time compute an estimate $\widetilde{\mathbf{Y}}$ for Y. Then we can compute the error

$$\widetilde{\mathbf{Y}}^t\Delta\mathbf{K}\widetilde{\mathbf{B}} \tag{18.90}$$

and use that to refine the solution, improving our guess of both functions at once.

To implement this approach we need to determine how to distribute importance up and down the hierarchy, just as we needed to distribute radiosity after each gathering step. The essential observation comes from the form factors. Suppose that patch P_i is a child of patch P_I, and there is another patch P_k far away, as in Figure 18.61. Then we can observe that P_k will capture about the same fraction of radiated energy from both P_i and P_I:

$$F_{i,k} \approx F_{I,k} \tag{18.91}$$

Similarly, consider power leaving P_k for P_I. The amount of this power caught by P_i is the relative area of the smaller patch to the larger:

$$F_{k,i} \approx \frac{A_i}{A_I} F_{k,I} \tag{18.92}$$

Armed with these approximations we can evaluate the transfer of radiosity and importance downward in the hierarchy from B_I to B_i, and from Y_I to Y_i, using

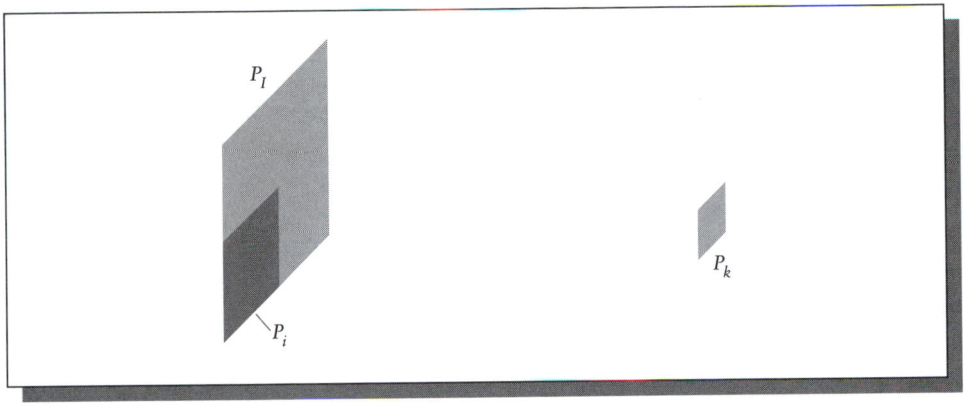

FIGURE 18.61
Parent and child patches I and i viewed from another patch k.

Equation 18.84. Assuming that the assigned importance of P_i is also based on the relative area it occupies on its parent (that is, $P_I(A_i/A_I)$), then we find

$$\begin{aligned} B_i &\approx B_I \\ Y_i &\approx \frac{A_i}{A_I} Y_I \end{aligned} \tag{18.93}$$

This tells us how a subpatch inherits radiosity and importance. The result for radiosity is that the child simply inherits the value from its parent, which is the property we used in `PushPullRad`. On the other hand, importance is area-weighted, so a child has an importance relative to its parent given by the ratio of their areas.

Working now from child to parent, we can observe from the definition of the form factor and reciprocity the following relationships:

$$\begin{aligned} F_{I,j} &= \frac{1}{A_I} \sum i \in I F_{i,j} A_i \\ F_{j,I} &= \sum i \in I F_{j,i} \end{aligned} \tag{18.94}$$

Plugging these into Equation 18.84 gives us

$$\begin{aligned} B_I &= \frac{1}{A_i} \sum_{i \in I} B_i A_i \\ Y_I &= \sum_{i \in I} Y_i \end{aligned} \tag{18.95}$$

`SolveImpHR() {`	*Solve an importance-driven HR problem.*
`InitBg()`	*Initialize gathered radiosity.*
`for all root nodes` r $r.\Gamma_s \leftarrow r.R$ `endfor`	*Set initial shooting importance.*
`BuildLinks()`	*Build initial links.*
$\epsilon_{BFI} \leftarrow \epsilon_{BFI,0}$	*Start with a large error value.*
`while` $\epsilon_{BFI} > \epsilon_t$	*Solve until error is small.*
`SolveDual()`	*Estimate a new solution.*

`for all links` L
`RefineLink(L)`
`endfor`
	See if any links can be improved.

$\epsilon_{BFI} \leftarrow \epsilon_{BFI} - \Delta\epsilon_{BFI}$	*Reduce the permissible error.*
`endwhile` `}`	

FIGURE 18.62

Pseudocode for `SolveImpHR`.

Again we find that radiosities are area-averaged as we work our way up (also used in `PushPullRad`), and that importances are simply summed.

In other words, radiosities and importances are propagated up and down the tree in exactly opposite ways, demonstrating again their adjoint relationship.

Now that we know how to distribute importance after a gathering step, we can create a new oracle that includes the importance of a link into its decision. The result is called *BFI refinement*. The only change required to the data structures is the addition of an importance-shooting element Y_s and an importance-gathering element Y_g to the `Node` data structure. A single link still suffices to relate two patches, but as we can see from Equation 18.84, radiosity and importance travel over the link in opposite directions.

To get the process rolling, we start with a new driving function `SolveImpHR`, listed in Figure 18.62.

`SolveImpRad` initializes not only the element radiosities as in HR, but also the shooting importance from the assigned importance. This brings up the question of what a good value for the assigned importance might be. One reasonable suggestion is to use the magnitude of the solid angle of the visible part of the patch projected onto the viewing surface, as in Figure 18.63. This solid angle can be determined by

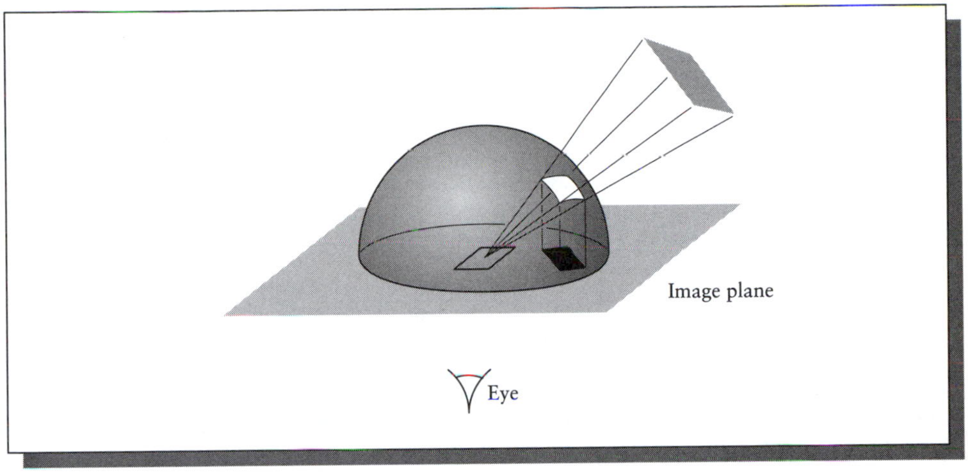

FIGURE 18.63

Assigning importance based on projected solid angle.

any rendering method; effectively, it's the form factor from the patch to the pixel.

Once initial radiosities and importances have been assigned, `SolveImpRad` sets the acceptable error threshold to a large value and calls `SolveDual`, which solves for both the radiosity and the importance as carried by the current links. We then call `RefineImpLink`, which uses a new oracle `OKtoKeepImpLink` that implements *BFI-refinement*. The new oracle is listed in Figure 18.64; it's basically the old oracle with the inclusion of Equation 18.90.

To form estimates for both radiosity and importance, `SolveImpRad` calls `SolveDual`, listed in Figure 18.65.

The operation of the dual solver is similar to that of the basic HR solver. We first pass through all the nodes and gather radiosity, but we also shoot importance across the link at the same time, using `GatherRadShootImp`. Then we balance the radiosities and the importances; for convenience we have left `PushPullRad` alone and added an importance resolver `PushPullImp`. Let's look at these in turn. `GatherRadShootImp` is listed in Figure 18.66.

`GatherRadShootImp` is just about the same as `GatherRad`, except that we also shoot importance over the same link that we're using to gather radiosity.

Finally, `PushPullImp` is listed in Figure 18.67. This routine distributes importance downward by area-weighting, and simply sums importance coming back up, implementing Equations 18.93 and 18.95.

`OKtoKeepImpLink(`L`) {`	*Is it okay to accept this node?*

`if` $L.p.A < \epsilon_A$ `and` $L.q.A < \epsilon_A$
    `return True`
    `endif`
	The patches are small enough to be okay.

`if` $L.p.B_s \times L.F_{qp} \times L.Y_g < \epsilon_{BF}$
    `return True`
    `endif`
	There's not enough energy to be transferred.

`return False`	*This link needs refinement.*
`}`	

FIGURE 18.64

Pseudocode for `OKtoKeepImpLink`.

`SolveDual() {`	*Solve for radiosity and importance.*
`while not converged`	*Repeat until equilibrium.*

`for every root node` r
      $r.Y_g \leftarrow 0$
      `endfor`
	No importance gathered yet in this pass.

`for every root node` r
      `GatherRadShootImp(`r`)`
      `endfor`
	Gather and shoot over all links.

`for every root node` r
      `PushPullRad(`r`)`
      `PushPullImp(`r`)`
      `endfor`
	Share up and down trees.

`endwhile`	
`}`	

FIGURE 18.65

Pseudocode for `SolveDual`.

`GatherRadShootImp(`n`) {`	*Gather radiosity and shoot importance.*
$n.B_g \leftarrow 0$	*No radiosity gathered yet.*
`for each link` L `into` n $n.B_g \leftarrow n.B_g +$ $n.\rho \times [L.F_{pq} \times L.p.B_s]$	*Gather radiosity from p.*
$L.p.Y \leftarrow L.p.Y +$ $n.\rho \times [L.F_{qp} \times n.Y]$	*Shoot importance to p.*
`endfor`	

`for each child` r `of` n
`GatherRadShootImp(`r`)`
`endfor`
	Process my children.

`endwhile` `}`	

FIGURE 18.66

Pseudocode for `GatherRadShootImp`.

`PushPullImp(`n, Y_{down}`) {`	*Node p inherits importance*$_{Ydown}$.
`if` n `is a leaf then` $Y_{\text{up}} \leftarrow n.R + n.Y_g + Y_{\text{down}}$	*Send up my importance, reflection, and inheritance.*
`else` $Y_{\text{up}} \leftarrow 0$	*Nothing collected yet.*
`for each child` r `of` n $Y_t \leftarrow (n.Y_g + Y_{\text{down}}) \times r.A/n.A$	*Get child's importance.*
$Y_{\text{up}} \leftarrow Y_{\text{up}} +$ `PushPullImp(`r, Y_t`)`	*Add it in scaled by that child's relative area.*
`endfor` `endif`	
$n.Y_s \leftarrow Y_{\text{up}}$	*Save what I'm passing up.*
`return(`Y_{up}`)` `}`	

FIGURE 18.67

Pseudocode for `PushPullImp`.

The power of importance-driven refinement is demonstrated by Figure 18.68 (color plate), which is a model of a maze sitting on a table inside a larger maze. In Figure 18.68(a) we see the meshing constructed for the maze from a point somewhat above and behind it, and in Figure 18.68(b) we see a smoothly reconstructed version of the same image. It is informative to view the radiosity and importance solutions from different points, so the remaining images in this figure move the camera back and away from the maze, but they always show the same solution that was generated for Figure 18.68(a). In Figure 18.68(c) and (d) we see the radiosity and importance solutions for the maze from farther away. Note that the meshing where the walls join the floor is much denser in the region where the importance is high. Similarly, the quality of the mesh on the table is very good near the front, where it occupies much of Figure 18.68(a), but the table becomes very coarsely meshed where it is not visible. In Figure 18.68(e) and (f) we see the radiosity and importance solutions for the maze from even farther back, so we can also see the larger maze in which it sits. In the radiosity solution huge, brightly lit walls in the near part of the maze are completely unrefined, because they are unimportant to the image in (a). Notice that the complex block sculpture in the front-left also causes no refinement. The wall facing us just right of center is slightly refined because some of the illumination falling on it eventually makes its way to the maze. The level of subdivision indicates that not much light from the wall contributes to the image in (a). The importance solution in (f) shows us why the block sculpture in the near-left of (e) is unrefined: from the point of view that generates (a), the sculpture is irrelevant.

18.6.4 Discussion

The hierarchical radiosity algorithm and importance-driven refinement are important practical tools for solving energy transport problems in image synthesis. Our goal in this section has been to demonstrate the basic ideas and show how they may be linked to improve the efficiency of finding an equilibrium solution.

Our example for determining importance was based on the direct contribution of a patch to the final image. Although useful, this is only one way to assign importance. We can attach importance to any feature of the model where it is important to have accurate sampling: on the surface of small but aesthetically important objects, on objects that are visible only through reflection, or objects that are completely invisible but contribute significant illumination to surfaces that are visible.

18.7 Meshing

All of the methods we have seen above break down the environment into small patches in order to compute a radiosity solution. This subdivision of the environment is called *meshing*. The problem of meshing is not unique to radiosity: the entire engineering discipline of finite element analysis is intimately concerned with different meshing algorithms.

The quality of a mesh directly affects the quality of the final radiosity solution. Cohen and Wallace offer an excellent analysis of the errors that occur when a scene is not properly meshed. Unfortunately, the definition of "proper" depends on many factors, including not only the scene description itself but particulars of the computing hardware on which the simulation is being run. Visual artifacts caused by insufficient meshing include blocky shadows, Mach bands, and missing features [98].

Surfaces that are too large for the illumination signal falling on them (say a shadow edge in the middle of a patch) must be subdivided. This subdivision may be *regular*, such as the subdivision of a rectangle into four smaller, equally sized rectangles. Some researchers have noted that Delaunay and Voronoi diagrams produce a very uniform mesh, and may be used instead of regular subdivision [387, 426].

An elegant solution to many meshing problems is the technique of *discontinuity meshing* (or DM) [202, 275]. The idea is that if there are easily visible shading features in the environment, then the mesh should adapt to those features. Usually such features are shadows, highlights, and other local phenomena on surfaces that represent *discontinuities* of the radiosity distribution or one of its derivatives. Discontinuity meshing attempts to place the boundaries between mesh elements right at those locations. Figure 18.69 (color plate) shows the basic idea for a small pyramid illuminated by a pair of lights. In the upper row we see the scene from the side and above, and the discontinuities are marked in colored lines. The second row shows the progress of discontinuity meshing the base plane, while the lower row shows the progress of regular adaptive subdivision based on quadrilaterals. Note how much more closely the discontinuity mesh matches the features in the radiosity function.

An example of the difference meshing can make is shown in Figure 18.70 (color plate), which was computed using the algorithm by Lischinski et al. [275]. The figure shows the shadow cast by a window on a wall. Note how the meshing in the standard solution interferes with the pattern of the shadows.

A related set of images are shown in Figure 18.71 (color plate). The picture on the right was computed using hierarchical radiosity; the one on the left with discontinuity meshing. Note how much more crisp the shadows have become, including the fine detail on the table top and under the near chair. Also, note the much stronger presence of a discontinuity along the top of the window and door in the HR solution.

Rather than compute discontinuities implicitly from the geometry of the scene, we can try to construct *isolux contours* on the scene surfaces: like a topographical map, these contours indicate a curve of constant radiance on a surface. If those contours can be found analytically, then it may be easier to find discontinuities. A method for determining the analytic distribution of light in some situations has been described by Drettakis and Fiume [125, 126].

Because most radiosity programs are based on meshing, the results must be smoothed before display to avoid a blocky-looking image. Typically the patch radiosities are averaged at the vertices, and then the vertex radiosities are interpolated using a method like Gouraud shading, which does a simple linear interpolation across pairs of radiances during display. Effectively this is a process of reconstruction of a continuous-time signal from a set of samples, and Gouraud shading is one form of linear interpolation.

We know from Unit II that we can reconstruct a function much better with a sinc function (or even a Gaussian bump) than with linear interpolation, which corresponds to a tent function. A visible drawback of Gouraud interpolation is that we end up smoothing where we don't want to smooth. Suppose we had two adjacent patches, one in bright light and one in dark shadow, sharing an edge generated by discontinuity meshing to follow the edge of a sharp shadow. We certainly don't want to blend colors across this edge. A method for building smooth reconstructions where we want smooth signals, but which also supports abrupt discontinuities, has been offered by Salesin et al. [372]. Hermite interpolation for radiosity has been discussed by Bastos et al. [31].

18.8 Shooting Power

An alternative method to solving a matrix equation (even an implicit one) is to directly simulate the transfer of light throughout a scene. In the terms of progressive refinement, we pick a *shooting* patch and send out rays from that patch into the environment.

Shirley has suggested that the algorithm is simplest if each ray carries power Φ rather than radiance L [398] (recall Equation 18.25).

Such a method requires choosing a number of rays to shoot and a pattern in which to shoot them. Shirley has shown that if we distribute the rays uniformly, then to get the variance of the radiance estimate below some threshold requires only $O(N)$ rays, where N is the number of patches [397].

To show this, we first digress for a moment to summarize some probability that will prove useful (for more information on these terms, see Appendix B). Suppose that we have a set S of N identically distributed random variables X_i, such that each X_i has a value x with probability p, and is 0 otherwise. Then the expected value $E(S)$ of the set is given by

$$E[S] = E\left[\sum_{i=1}^{N} X_i\right] = NE[X_i] = Npx \qquad (18.96)$$

The variance var(S) of the set is given by

$$\text{var}(S) = \text{var}\left(\sum_{i=1}^{N} X_i\right) = N\,\text{var}(X_i) \tag{18.97}$$

The individual variances var(X_i) may be found by direct computation:

$$\text{var}(X_i) = E[{x_i}^2] - E[x_i]^2 = px^2 - p^2x^2 = px^2(1-p) \le px^2 \tag{18.98}$$

Now we can proceed with our radiance argument. We would like to find out how many rays we need to fire from the environment in order for the variance on patch i, given by var(L_i), to be lower than some threshold V_0.

We start by observing that the power reflected Φ_i from patch i is simply the reflectivity of the patch R_i times its total incident power. Suppose that we fire a total of r rays into the environment. We will assume that each ray carries the same amount of power; if the total power to be shot is Φ^t, then each ray carries Φ^t/r.

The power Φ_i^k carried by ray number k to patch i will either be Φ_t/r if the ray makes it to patch i, or else zero.

$$\Phi_i = R_i \sum_{k=1}^{r} \Phi_i^r \tag{18.99}$$

We will assume that the probability of a ray striking patch i is p_i. Because all the rays are generated with the same distribution, this probability is constant for each ray. Then using Equation 18.96, we have $N = r$ rays, a probability $p = p_i$ of intersection, and a value $x = \Phi^t/r$ delivered to the patch upon intersection, giving an expected value power $E[\Phi_i]$ of

$$E[\Phi_i] = R_i\left[\sum_{i=1}^{r} p_i\right] = R_i r p_i \frac{\Phi_t}{r} = R_i p_i \Phi_t \tag{18.100}$$

and an expected radiance $E[L_i]$ of

$$E[L_i] = \frac{E[\Phi_i]}{\pi A_i} = \frac{R_i}{\pi A_i} p_i \Phi_t \tag{18.101}$$

Similarly, we can find the variance in the power and the radiance from

$$\begin{aligned} \text{var}(\Phi_i) &\le R_i r p_i \left(\frac{\Phi_t}{r}\right)^2 = \frac{R_i p_i {\Phi_t}^2}{r} \\ \text{var}(L_i) &\le \frac{R_i p_i {\Phi_t}^2}{r\pi A_i} = \frac{R_i}{\pi A_i} p_i \frac{{\Phi_t}^2}{r} \end{aligned} \tag{18.102}$$

Our goal is to bring $\text{var}(L_i) < V_0$, so we might be tempted to use as large an r as possible; that is, we can drive down the variance by firing a lot of rays. This is reasonable, but not the result we would like. We could also drive the area down, but $\text{var}(L_i)$ in Equation 18.102 blows up as the area A_i gets smaller. Instead, suppose that all areas are bounded by a range $[A_{\text{min}}, A_{\text{max}}]$. Writing A as the total area in the scene, $A = \sum_{i=1}^{N} A_i$, then the average area A_a is given by $A_a = A/N$. For some constant K,

$$\frac{A_i}{A_k} < K \tag{18.103}$$

for all choices of i and k. Equivalently, $A_i < KA_a = KA/N$.

Suppose that the probability of a ray striking a surface with area A_i is given by $p^u < 1$ (this is violated only if the area completely encloses the origin of the ray, since in that situation $p^u = 1$; if the surface is convex, then strict inequality holds). Then using this as our probability for $E[L_i]$ in Equation 18.101,

$$E[L_i] = \frac{R_i}{\pi A_i} p^u \Phi_t \leq L_{\text{max}} \tag{18.104}$$

for some maximum radiance L_{max}. Then solving for this probability,

$$p^u \leq \frac{\pi A_i}{R_i \Phi_t} L_{\text{max}} \tag{18.105}$$

or

$$\text{var}(L_i) \leq \frac{R_i}{\pi A_i} p^u \frac{{\Phi_t}^2}{r} = \frac{R_i}{\pi A_i} \frac{\pi A_i}{R_i \Phi_t} L_{\text{max}} \frac{{\Phi_t}^2}{r} = L_{\text{max}} \frac{{\Phi_t}^2}{r} \tag{18.106}$$

Assuming that the reflectivities R satisfy $0 < R_i \leq R_{\text{max}} = 1$, and recalling $A_i < AK/N$, we can write the variance as

$$\text{var}(L_i) \leq \frac{R_{\text{max}}}{\pi (AK/N)} p^u \frac{{\Phi_t}^2}{r} = \frac{R_{\text{max}} N}{\pi AK} p^u \frac{{\Phi_t}^2}{r} \tag{18.107}$$

or equivalently,

$$\text{var}(L_i) \leq C \frac{N}{r} \tag{18.108}$$

for a constant C defined by

$$C = \frac{R_{\text{max}} p^u {\Phi_t}^2}{\pi AK} \tag{18.109}$$

To set $\text{var}(L_i) < V_0$, we have $C\frac{N}{r} \leq V_0$, or

$$r \geq N \frac{C}{V_0} \tag{18.110}$$

This is the result we sought; it says that to get the variance in the radiance below some threshold V_0, we only need a constant number of rays, given by the product of a constant C/V_0 with N, the number of patches. Note that the constant is inversely proportional to the desired variance, so as we are willing to tolerate more error, we need fewer rays. Shirley has also shown that a similar analysis can be carried out for further levels of interreflection [397]. Kok has noted that groups of patches may be clustered for the purposes of shooting, lowering the required number of power rays even more [249].

So *shooting power* directly from the patches into the environment is a computational alternative to the matrix formulation that has reasonable computational requirements.

18.9 Extensions to Classical Radiosity

The hierarchical and importance-driven radiosity solutions described above are both based on improving the efficiency of the classical radiosity model. At least two of the assumptions behind this model can be relaxed: the limitation to diffuse reflectors, and the limitation to nonparticipating media.

The classical radiosity method may be extended to nondiffuse surfaces by defining other types of form factors. For example, suppose that we have a scene of a room that contains a single flat mirror on a wall. From a point within the room, looking into the mirror is like looking through a window into another, identical room, as shown in Figure 18.72.

Suppose we have two surfaces, P_i and P_k, in the room and we want to compute the form factor from P_i to P_k. In the figure we show two ways light can travel this path: directly from one surface to the next, and via a specular reflection off of the mirror. By constructing an image of the room on the opposite side of the mirror, we can account for this second transfer directly using traditional form factor algorithms, and we can avoid any direct consideration of the patch represented by the mirror [370].

Min-Zhi Shao et al. noticed that this approach to specular surfaces, besides its limitation to flat patches, has an exponential growth with respect to the number of mirrors in the scene [392]. They suggested instead constructing form factors between two patches, which can include light specularly reflected from one to the other. Ping-Ping Shao et al. suggested a different form of specular form factor, called *multipoint form factors* or *extended form factors*, representing the three-point transport of energy from one patch to another by way of an intermediate patch [393].

The basic idea is that we can write a form factor such as F_{P_k,P_l,P_m}, which relates the energy transferred from P_k to P_m *via* reflection at P_l. Since the BDF at P_l is known, we can use the known relative geometry of P_k and P_m with respect to P_l

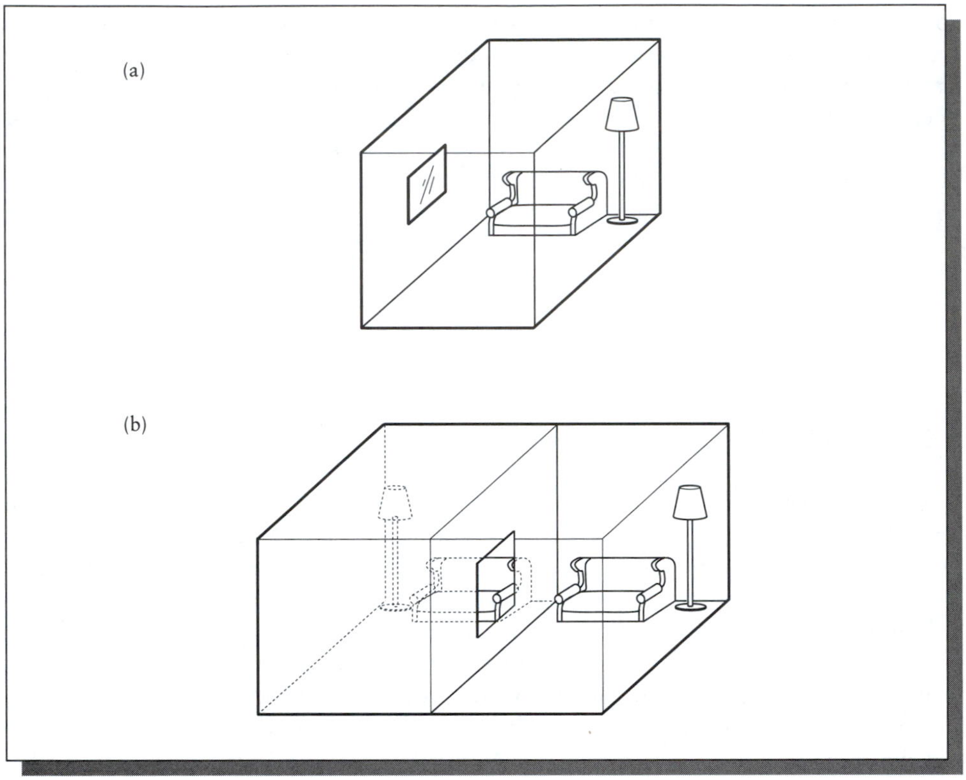

FIGURE 18.72

(a) A room with a mirror on the wall. (b) An equivalent scene with an image of the room and a hole instead of a mirror.

to determine how much energy would be propagated by such a reflection using a general BDF at P_l.

Another way of tracking specular effects is to discretize the outgoing radiance distribution from a point [224]. Rather than simply use a single radiosity value to represent the energy radiated equally in all directions, we can place a *global cube* around a point. Like a hemicube, the global cube faces are subdivided into grids. The light exiting each grid cell may be stored to represent a nonuniform distribution. This approach requires massive amounts of memory to save all the cubes in the scene. It also suffers from aliasing artifacts due to the regular spacing of cells on the cube faces.

A nonuniform propagation function may also be efficiently stored using spherical harmonics [408]. This has the advantage that no a priori discretization is required, and memory is conserved. It also allows the propagation function to be evaluated from a continuous description at any point, rather than interpolated from stored grid elements.

The classical radiosity formulation assumes that the medium between surfaces is a vacuum. If this requirement is relaxed, then we move into the realm of *zonal methods*, developed in the heat transfer literature. Zonal methods were introduced to graphics by Rushmeier and Torrance [369]. The basic idea is that in addition to the *surface-to-surface* form factors we have concentrated on in this chapter, we also develop *surface-to-volume* and *volume-to-volume* form factors. A much larger set of simultaneous equations may then be constructed that relates all of these form factors simultaneously. An example image computed in this way is shown in Figure 18.73 (color plate). An overview of volume methods for radiosity is presented by Rushmeier [367].

Radiosity has been extended to account for furry surfaces [84] and bump-mapped surfaces [83].

Radiosity simulations are closely tied to the geometry of the scene; the form factors are innately geometric and depend on the mutual visibility of points in the environment. Typically if the objects move in a scene, the radiosity solution must be recomputed. However, it can be computationally efficient to *update* a radiosity solution (rather than freshly recompute it) if only a few objects in the scene move. The basic idea is that only the form factors between surfaces whose relative visibility has changed require recomputation. The update takes place in three stages. First, *negative radiosity* is shot between the affected patches; this removes the effect of their interaction. Second, the objects in the scene are moved to their new positions. Third, normal positive radiosity is balanced between the affected pairs of patches. This approach is described by George et al. [152] and Chen [85].

Because classical radiosity algorithms produce $O(N^2)$ form factors for N patches, it is desirable to keep the number of patches as small as possible. Even HR produces an $O(N^2)$ set of form factors, but typically we start with far fewer surfaces than in classical radiosity because they need not be premeshed. One way to simplify the problem is to break it up into two smaller problems. Xu et al. have observed that if we are computing a simulation of two rooms joined by a small doorway, as in Figure 18.74, then we can approximate the transfer through the door as though it was a single polygon [492].

First, solve the right-hand room on its own, as though the door was a perfectly absorbing polygon. Then solve the left-hand room, treating the door as a radiator of the light it absorbed in the first pass. Record the light falling on the door in this solution, and then return to the right-hand room. Iterating this procedure will eventually converge on an approximate solution. This method is attractive because

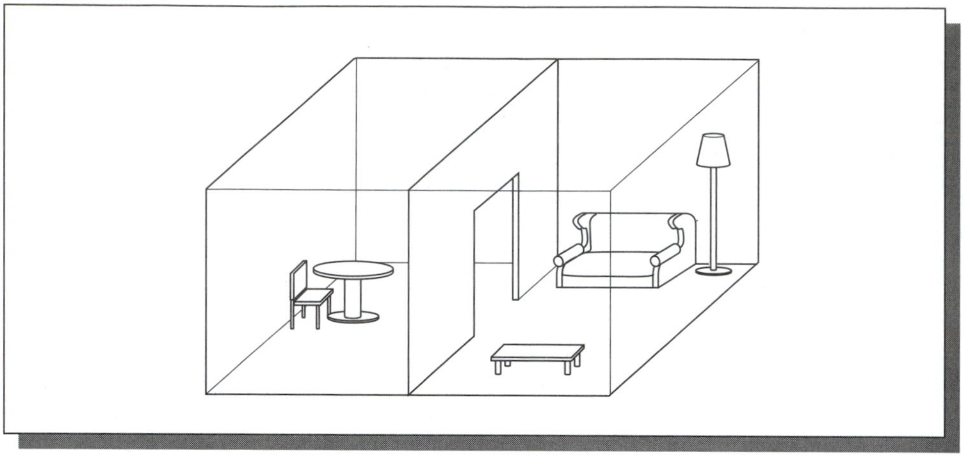

FIGURE 18.74
Two rooms joined by a door.

the cost of performing several solutions on $N/2$ polygons is cheaper than performing one solution on N polygons.

Related approaches have been described by Neumann and Neumann [317] and Rushmeier et al. [366]. They simplify the model to create a radiosity solution on a low-complexity database. This is similar to the multigridding approach used in adaptive hierarchical radiosity. An excellent introduction to multigrid methods is available in the tutorial by Briggs [63].

18.10 Further Reading

This chapter has only surveyed some of the larger issues in radiosity. As a relatively new algorithm of great practical value, radiosity is a subject of intense active research, and there are plenty of important practical issues that should be considered if you are planning to write a radiosity system.

The best places to go for more information are the excellent recent books by Cohen and Wallace [99] and Sillion and Puech [409]. Each offers plenty of theoretical analysis, practical advice, and a substantial bibliography. An extensive analysis of radiosity in the world of two dimensions has been carried out by Heckbert [202]. A nice short retrospective survey has been written by Wallace [459].

The basic ideas behind radiosity have been used in the field of heat transfer for years. The classic texts in that field are the books by Sparrow and Cess [417] and Siegel and Howell [406]; they both offer a wealth of information on topics relevant to radiosity.

In addition to the matrix solution discussion offered by Gortler and Cohen [166], Greiner et al. discuss a variety of methods for reducing the time required to solve the radiosity problem [172], and Shao and Badler offer a survey and comparison [391].

Linear basis functions have been studied by a variety of researchers. Max and Allison have explored the use of linear, tent-shaped basis functions that have a height of 1 at a given vertex and fall off linearly to 0 at all other vertices; they have developed an efficient algorithm for computing images with such functions using the linear interpolation hardware in real-time graphics rendering machines [288]. A similar approach using linear basis functions was described by Bao and Peng [29], who approximated curved surfaces with a triangular polygonal mesh for the storage of radiosity. The radiosity value at any point within the mesh could be derived from linear interpolation of the vertex radiosities. Bian et al. used linear basis functions over quadrilaterals based on bilinear interpolation among the vertices [44]. The use of Galerkin bases was developed by Heckbert for the special case of 2D radiosity [202]. Discussions of the Galerkin solution are offered by Heckbert [202], Troutman and Max [440], and Zatz [503].

The hemicube technique relies on efficient scan-conversion for identifying the cells occupied by each patch in the environment. This scan-conversion may be accelerated with the techniques of Greene et al. [169] and Teller and Hanrahan [435]. Both of these papers provide good bibliographies covering related work. Finding the best distribution of cells on the hemicube face has been studied by Max and Troutman [285].

Surveys of form factor methods for graphics are available in the paper by Pueyo [350] and in the books by Cohen and Wallace and Sillion and Puech mentioned above. Some form factor algorithms that combine several simpler approaches are explored by Pietrek [341]. The heat transfer literature contains a rich body of material on form factors and their computation. The survey by Walton [462] compares form factor calculations in terms of their utility to that community. Emery et al. have compared a number of algorithms in terms of computational efficiency and accuracy; their findings are described in [136]. Their conclusion was that when there was enough computational power to justify the expense, Monte Carlo techniques proved the best method for estimating the form factor in general.

The discussions of hierarchical radiosity and importance-driven refinement left out many details that are important in a practical system. An early form of hierarchical radiosity was the two-tier approach due to Cohen et al. [97]. Implementors are urged to review the original hierarchical refinement paper by Hanrahan et al. [192] and the wavelet radiosity articles by Gortler et al. [167] and Schröder et al. [384]. Importance-driven refinement was introduced by Smits et al. [414]; recent extensions have been described by Aupperle and Hanrahan [24] and Christensen et al. [89].

There is a quickly growing body of literature on meshing for radiosity; much of this growth is being fueled by incorporation of results from finite elements. A good survey of meshing techniques is given by Cohen and Wallace [98]. More recent developments in discontinuity meshing are offered by Asensio [18], Baum et al. [32], Campbell and Fussell [73], Heckbert [202, 210], Lischinski et al. [274, 275], and Sillion [407]. In particular, Lischinski et al. [274] describe the combination of discontinuity meshing with hierarchical radiosity. Rather than mesh a priori, we might attempt to generate a good mesh and then move the mesh points into a better position to adapt to the local illumination; Águas and Müller describe such an approach [4].

These papers also offer pointers into the extensive finite elements and computational geometry literature on meshing. A good starting point for this literature is Ho-Le [212].

Form factors in specular environments have been examined by Eckert and Sparrow for heat and mass transfer [134]; these ideas were applied to radiosity by Rushmeier and Torrance [370]. Extended form factors have also been investigated by Aupperle and Hanrahan [23], Bao and Peng [29], Bouatouch and Tellier [56], Bouville et al. [57], Chen et al. [86], Chen and Wu [82], Hall and Rushmeier [180], Kok et al. [250], Le Saec and Schlick [259], Shirley [396], Sillion et al. [408, 410], and Wallace et al. [460]. In particular, Aupperle and Hanrahan [23] have combined a three-point transport formulation with hierarchical radiosity.

Some hardware and multiprocessor implementations of radiosity algorithms are described by Vilaplana and Pueyo [454, 455], Varshney and Prins [452], Bu and Deprettere [67], Baum and Winget [34], Drucker and Schröder [128], Drettakis et al. [127], Puech et al. [349], and Purgathofer and Zeiller [352].

18.11 Exercises

Exercise 18.1

Suppose that a hemicube is placed over a point with top face $n \times n$ and side faces $n \times n/2$. How many delta form factors do you need to store? What are they?

Exercise 18.2

In Table 18.1, when we increased the reflectivity of patch A from 0 to $1/10$ in the first two lines, the sum of the radiosities increased. Does this mean that there is more power in the environment? Are we getting something for nothing?

Exercise 18.3

Consider Figure 18.75 showing an infinite rectangular tube of dimensions $a \times b$. Write

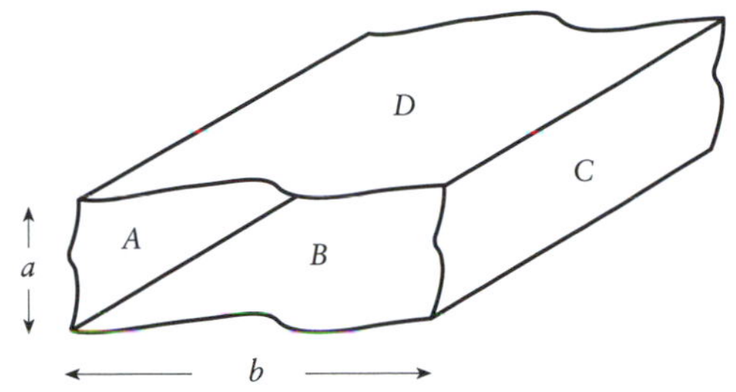

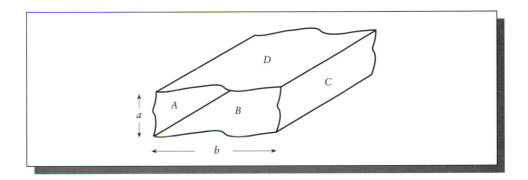

FIGURE 18.75
Geometry for Exercise 18.3.

the eight form factors for this system (use the form factors in Equation 18.30). Write a computer program to evaluate the form factor matrix for different reflectivity and emission values. Determine the radiosities for the conditions in Table 18.3. Interpret your results.

Exercise 18.4

Review the paper by Baum et al. on meshing for radiosity [32]. Can you describe any other problem cases that they did not cover? How hard would it be to write a program that includes both their observations and discontinuity meshing? What do you think would happen to the number of polygons in the system? Is there a way to control the number of polygons?

Exercise 18.5

One problem with hierarchical radiosity is that it starts with large patches and refines them, while sometimes we are given a database consisting of a large number of small polygons. Can you suggest methods for *clustering* these polygons into larger pieces appropriate for refinement with HR?

Exercise 18.6

Consider two spheres with centers A and B, which are each of radius 1 meter and 2 kg in mass, separated by a distance of 5 meters, as in Figure 18.76. The spheres are joined by the line AB with midpoint C. Measured along a line through C and perpendicular to AB, how far away would you have to go in placing a 6-kg mass at T in order for the gravitational force due to the pair to be indistinguishable from a single mass of 4 kg located at C? Assume three digits of precision. The gravitational

Test number	Reflectivity $[\rho_A, \rho_B, \rho_C, \rho_D]^t$	Emissivity $[E_A, E_B, E_C, E_D]^t$
a	$[1, 0, 0, 0]$	$[0, 1/2, 1/2, 1/2]$
b	$[1, 0, 0, 0]$	$[1/2, 1/2, 1/2, 1/2]$
c	$[0, 1, 0, 0]$	$[0, 1, 0, 0]$
d	$[1, 1, 0, 0]$	$[0, 0, 1, 1]$
e	$[1, 0, 1, 0]$	$[3/4, 3/4, 3/4, 3/4]$
f	$[1, 0, 1, 1]$	$[1, 0, 0, 0]$

TABLE 18.3
Conditions for Exercise 18.3.

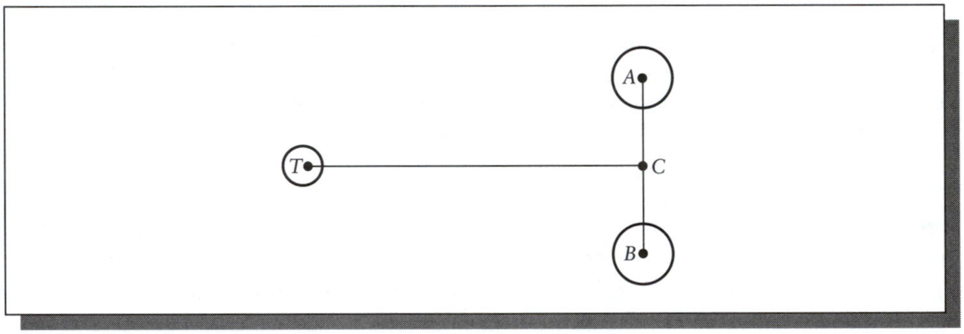

FIGURE 18.76
Two spheres.

force due to an object with mass m_1 at point P experienced by a mass m_2 at point Q at a distance $r = |P - Q|$ is given by

$$F = G\frac{m_1 m_2}{r^2}, \qquad G = 6.6720 \times 10^{-11} N \cdot \mathrm{m}^2/\mathrm{kg}^2 \tag{18.111}$$

in the direction of P, where G is a universal constant for all pairs of particles, and N is the force in newtons.

At the bottom of Mount I, a monk had built a hermitage, and Kyōzan went there and told him what Isan had said, namely: "Most people have the great potentiality, but not the great function." The monk told Kyōzan to ask him concerning the matter, but when Kyōzan was about to do so, the monk kicked him in the chest and knocked him down. Kyōzan went back to Isan and told him, whereupon Isan gave a great laugh.

R. H. Blyth
("Zen and Zen Classics," 1978)

19 RAY TRACING

19.1 Introduction

In Chapter 18 we discussed methods for explicitly constructing a distribution of light in an environment. An alternative solution returns to the original radiance equation and uses Monte Carlo point-sampling techniques to estimate the radiance at particular points $(\mathbf{p}, \vec{\omega})$ in phase space. The approach is generally driven by the desire to find function values over the viewing surface, which in turn requires the generation of radiance values within the environment. The sampling of the viewing plane generally proceeds from the identification of points on the plane, and directions that can influence those points. The goal is to estimate the irradiance signal around each of those points within the necessary solid angle. We know from the radiance law and our construction of the radiance equation that we can find the radiance arriving at a point from a given direction by finding the radiance leaving that surface point that is visible from the shading point in that direction along with the volumetric effects adding and removing light along the way. To find this visible point, we typically use a body of techniques known as *ray tracing*.

In one sense the ray-tracing method is nothing more than an application of the Monte Carlo methods from Unit II to the full radiance equation (or any of its variants in Chapter 17). Theoretically, we can sample the radiance function directly, and as long as bias is avoided (or accounted for), then we can derive an estimator for the function. In practice, however, the costs of ray tracing and the complexity of the function make direct evaluation prohibitively expensive. A large variety of techniques have been developed to explore methods to accelerate the process.

This acceleration has been focused on finding the point of first intersection between a ray and the environment. This is because the ray-tracing process executes this operation many millions of times per image; each execution should be as efficient as possible.

19.2 Photon and Visibility Tracing

The ray-tracing approach is deeply entrenched in classical, geometrical optics: we assume that all objects are much larger than the wavelength of light, and that light travels in straight lines (relaxing the first condition leads to refraction and diffraction, and relaxing the second allows relativistic effects). Suppose that we are simulating a scene composed of two opaque patches, P_1 and P_2, viewed from an eye position E, and that there is a single small (but finite) light source L with uniform illumination in the scene, as in Figure 19.1(a). We suppose that we can see P_1 from E as indicated, and we want to find the light reflected back to the eye.

By examination of the figure, we can see that in addition to any light that P_1 emits on its own, it can only reflect light coming directly from L. The mechanics of the reflection are described completely by the BRDF at P_1, so we need only find the illumination from L. In general, there are two ways to go about finding this illumination.

The first method, illustrated in Figure 19.1(b), is called *photon tracing*. The general idea is that we generate a large number of photons radiated from L and follow them into the scene. Some fraction will strike P_1, and that will represent an estimate of the incident illumination on P_1 for the purposes of applying a shading model.

An alternative method is called *visibility tracing*, illustrated in Figure 19.1(c). The idea here is to look around the shading point and try to find the radiance value at every surface point that can contribute illumination. We do this by sending rays into the environment and determining which object is seen by which ray; the radiance sent from that object toward the shading point contributes to the overall illumination.

We will now look at these two approaches. Because it is a more widely used technique, we will start with visibility tracing.

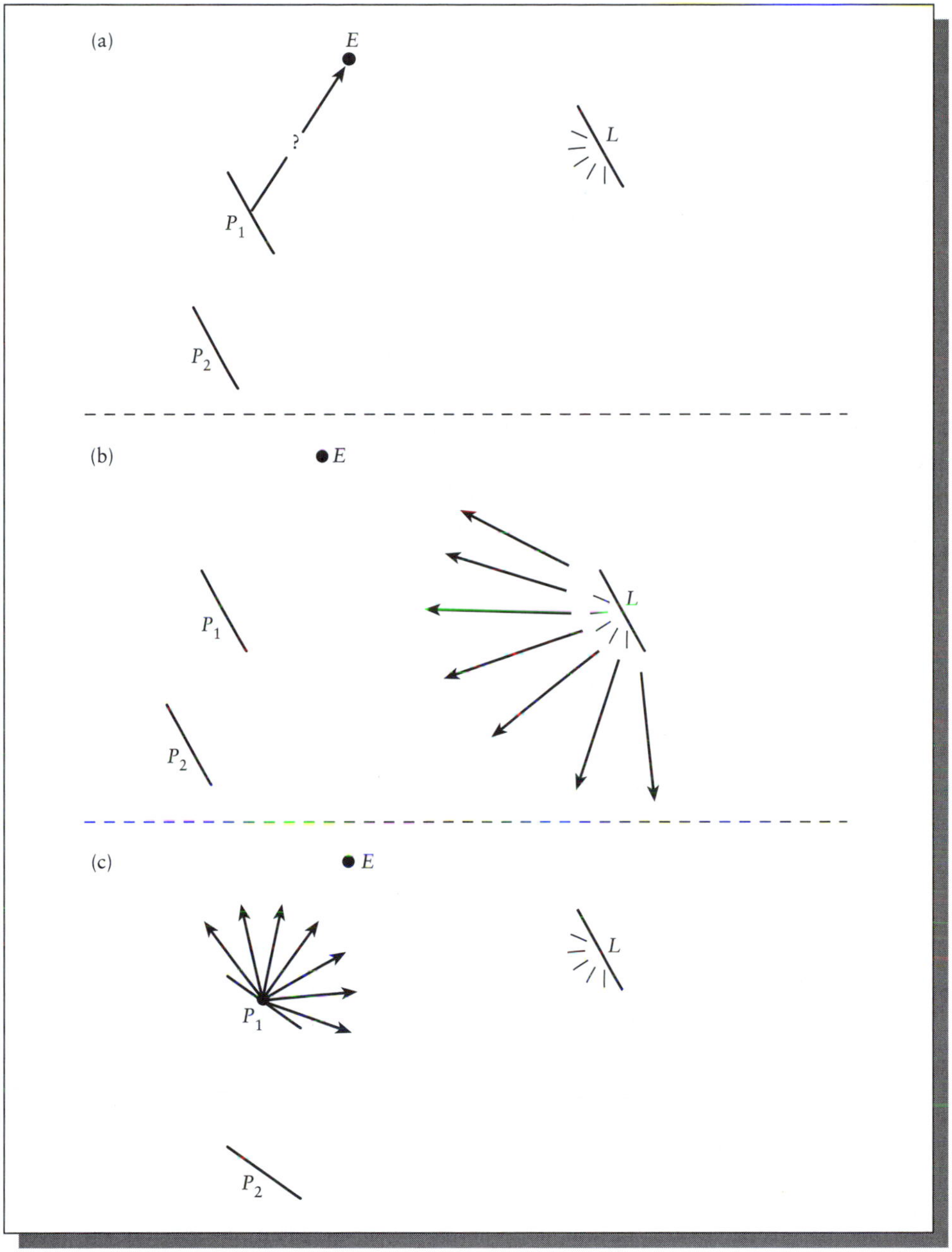

FIGURE 19.1

(a) A simple scene. (b) Sending light from the source. (c) Seeking light from a patch.

19.3 Visibility Tracing

In *visibility tracing* we build up a chain of light-object interactions in reverse, starting with those at the image surface and eventually working our way back to the light sources. Figure 19.2 shows a typical result in a simple scene. In Figure 19.2(a) we show the geometric history of a ray from the eye as it strikes objects and then creates new rays, seeking the illumination at those intersections. In Figure 19.2(b) we have abstracted away the geometry and show just the *tree* of rays.

For visibility tracing in a vacuum, we use the OVTIGRE form of the radiance equation from Equation 17.16:

$$L(\mathbf{r}, \vec{\omega}^o) = L^e(\mathbf{s}, \vec{\omega}^o) + \int_{\Theta_i^i} f(\mathbf{r}, \vec{\omega} \to \vec{\omega}^o, \lambda) L(\mathbf{r}, \vec{\omega}) \cos\theta_r \, d\vec{\omega} \tag{19.1}$$

In image synthesis, the two techniques that have proven most useful to aid in a Monte Carlo evaluation of this integral are stratification and importance sampling. So our first step will be to tile the input domain Θ_i^i of Equation 19.1 into s individual *strata* D_k (recall that these are nonoverlapping subdomains that together match the input domain):

$$\Theta_i^i = \bigcup_{k=1}^{s} D_k \tag{19.2}$$

Within each stratum k we apply *importance sampling*, which means multiplying by a pdf g_k and then dividing by that pdf so we don't introduce bias. The result is

$$\begin{aligned} L(\mathbf{r}, \vec{\omega}^o) &= L^e(\mathbf{s}, \vec{\omega}^o) + \int_{\Theta_i^i} f(\mathbf{r}, \vec{\omega} \to \vec{\omega}^o, \lambda) L(\mathbf{r}, \vec{\omega}) \cos\theta_r \, d\vec{\omega} \\ &= L^e(\mathbf{s}, \vec{\omega}^o) + \sum_{k=1}^{s} \int_{D_k} f(\mathbf{r}, \vec{\omega} \to \vec{\omega}^o, \lambda) \frac{L(\mathbf{r}, \vec{\omega}) \cos\theta_r}{g_k(\mathbf{r}, \vec{\omega})} g_k(\mathbf{r}, \vec{\omega}) \, d\vec{\omega} \end{aligned} \tag{19.3}$$

The stratification of the set of incident directions Θ_i^i on the sphere around s induces a stratification on the set of all surfaces M. To see this, consider Figure 19.3(a), where two strata have been isolated. If we build a cone defined on each stratum with its apex at the origin, then those cones sweep out into the environment, as shown in Figure 19.3(b), and intersect objects. The cone stratifies all points in the environment into two sets: those inside the cone (or on its surface), and those outside the cone. Each time a cone passes through a surface, it divides the surface into those two classes. In other words, the cones induce a stratification of each surface, as shown in Figure 19.3(c).

There is a one-to-one correspondence between strata on the incident hemisphere $\Theta_i^i(\mathbf{s})$ and the strata on the surfaces M_i. It is important to note that the cones in Figure 19.3(b) can be defined using only the apex point s and a cross section.

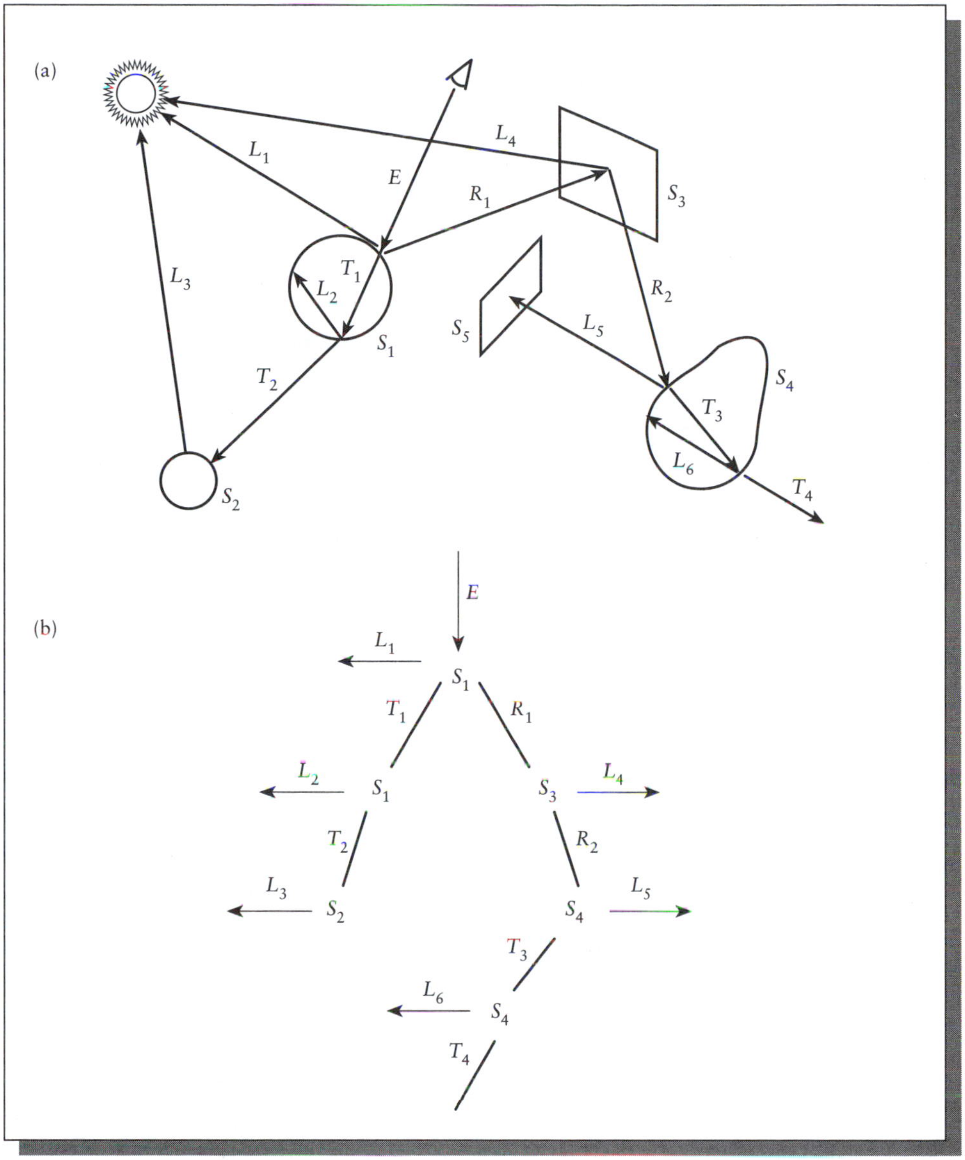

FIGURE 19.2

(a) Using visibility ray tracing in a scene. (b) The tree corresponding to the rays in (a).

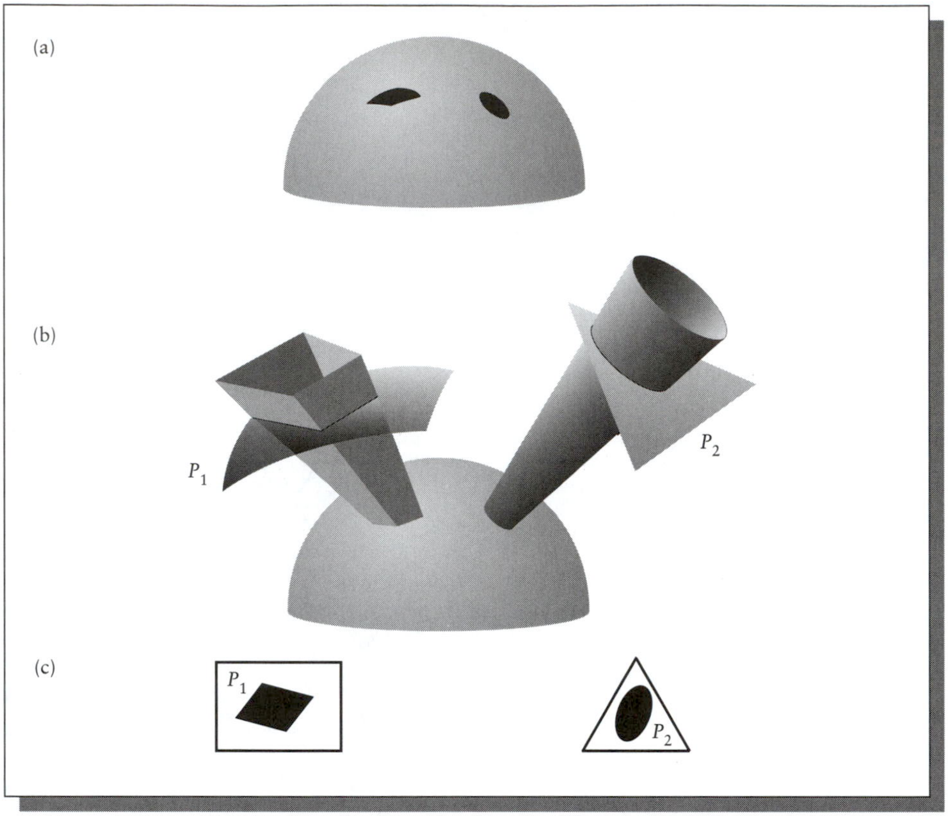

FIGURE 19.3

(a) Two strata on a direction hemisphere. (b) The projection of those strata into the environment. (c) The induced strata on the surfaces.

Whether this cross section is on the hemisphere or on one of the object surfaces doesn't matter. Strata on the hemisphere induce strata on surfaces, and vice versa.

This observation is very important, because it makes explicit the fact that the domains D_i in Equation 19.3 can refer to either sets of directions around s, *or* sets of points on the surfaces M.

The general procedure in visibility ray tracing is to choose some strata in each domain, resolve them so they don't overlap, and then sample the strata. That is, to find the illumination at a point, we choose some directions *and* some surfaces from which we want to gather light. The directions are usually chosen on the basis of the geometry of the shading situation and the object's BDF, while the surfaces are usually chosen on the basis of how much light they emit and propagate.

For example, suppose that we are viewing a shiny surface from a particular angle. We expect that light coming in from near the specularly reflected direction will be important, so we might densely stratify the set of directions near the reflected direction. And if there are some bright light sources in the scene, we will probably want to make sure we pay some attention to them, so we stratify the surfaces of those sources into several domains. In other words, the subdivision of the direction set creates strata through which we *push* visibility to search the world, and subdivision of the surfaces creates strata which *pull* visibility information from the shading point toward the surface.

To make this distinction formally, we will introduce some notation to distinguish different sets of points and directions.

19.3.1 Strata Sets

In this section we will introduce four different types of sets: two sets of directions and two sets of surface points. We will call these different collections *strata sets* since each one is based on elements of a particular stratum.

For convenience we will write a point $\mathbf{p}$ as some point along the ray $\vec{\omega}$ coming *into* $\mathbf{s}$:

$$\mathbf{p} = \mathbf{s} - \alpha\vec{\omega}, \qquad \alpha > 0 \tag{19.4}$$

Notice that $\alpha > 0$ enforces the condition that this is a point that is seen from $\mathbf{s}$ by looking *backward* along the incident vector $\vec{\omega}$. Similarly, we define $N(\mathbf{s}, \vec{\omega})$ to be the point $\mathbf{p}$ with the smallest such α that generates a point on M, as in Figure 19.4. We can use the ray-tracing (or visibility) function $\nu(\mathbf{r}, \vec{\omega})$ defined in Equation 12.94 to define this value:

$$\begin{aligned} N(\mathbf{s}, \vec{\omega}) &\triangleq \mathbf{s} - [\inf\{\alpha > 0 : \mathbf{s} - \alpha\vec{\omega} \in M\}]\,\vec{\omega} \\ &= \mathbf{s} - \nu(\mathbf{s}, \vec{\omega})\vec{\omega} \end{aligned} \tag{19.5}$$

We will relate points in space to directions around $\mathbf{s}$. The directions always come from the set $\Theta_i^i(\mathbf{s})$, so when we say a point is "visible" from $\mathbf{s}$, we mean that we can find a value $\alpha > 0$ that will fit the definition for $\mathbf{p}$. In other words, if we can look *backward* along $\vec{\omega}$ to a point $\mathbf{p}$, we say $\mathbf{p}$ is *visible* to $\mathbf{s}$ along $\vec{\omega}$.

The first strata sets we will consider are the two *direction-driven* sets. Suppose we are given a solid angle Γ_i. Then $P_i = P(\Gamma_i)$ is the set of all surface points that can be reached by a ray passing through that solid angle, as shown in Figure 19.5. We define this set as

$$P_i \triangleq P(\Gamma_i) = \{\mathbf{p} : \mathbf{p} \in M, \vec{\omega} \in \Gamma_i\} \tag{19.6}$$

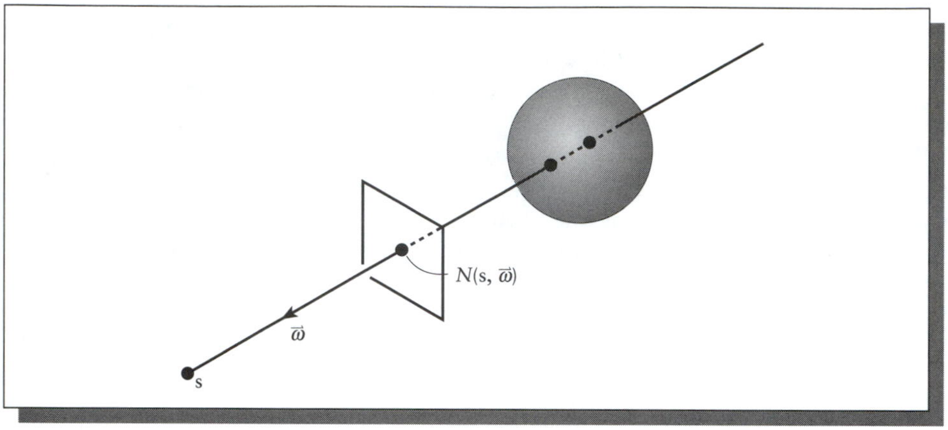

FIGURE 19.4

Determining the first point intersected by a ray.

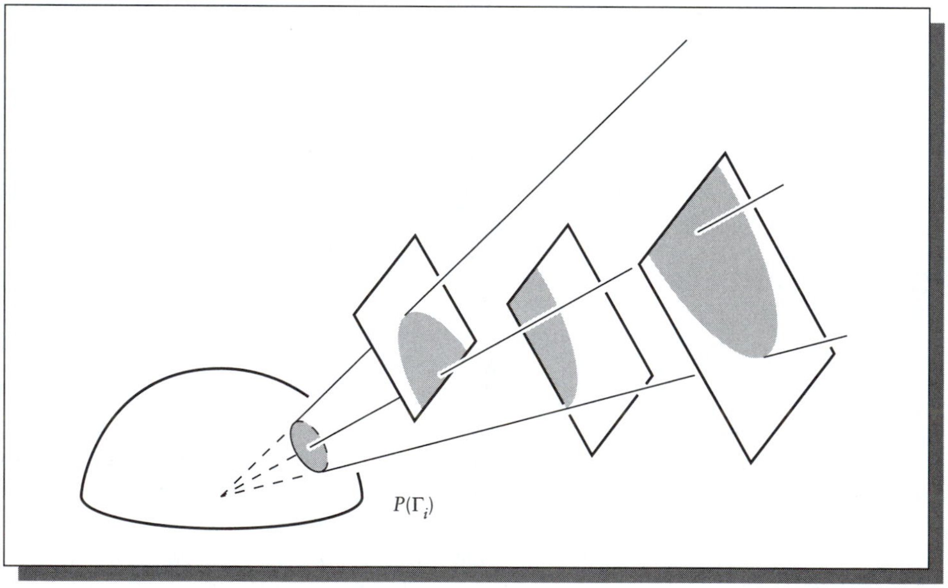

FIGURE 19.5

$P(\Gamma_i)$ is the set of all surface points within Γ_i.

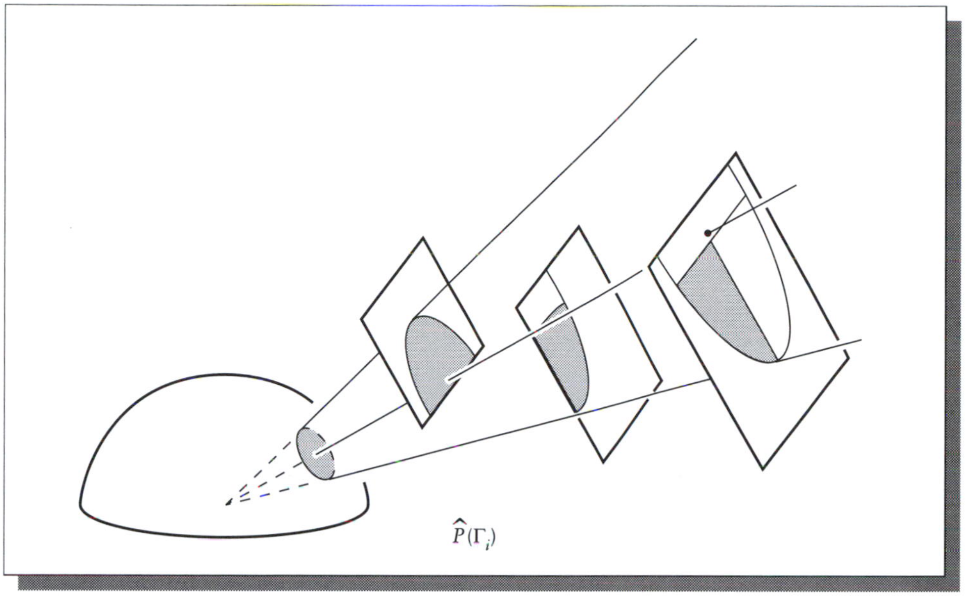

FIGURE 19.6
$\widehat{P}(\Gamma_i)$ is the set of all visible surface points within Γ_i.

Note that the points *need not be visible* from s to be in P_i. This solid angle induces strata on all the surfaces in the scene which are at least partially within it.

A closely related strata set contains only those points in the set P_i that are *directly visible* from s; that is, there is no other surface between that point and s. We write this set $\widehat{P}_i$, and define it:

$$\widehat{P}_i \triangleq \widehat{P}(\Gamma_i) = \{\mathbf{p} : \mathbf{p} = N(\mathbf{s}, \vec{\omega}), \vec{\omega} \in \Gamma_i\} \tag{19.7}$$

Notice that the only difference between P_i and $\widehat{P}_i$ is that the latter includes only points $N(\mathbf{s}, \vec{\omega})$, not all points on M. The set $\widehat{P}_i$ is illustrated in Figure 19.6.

Notice that the sets P_i are not necessarily mutually exclusive, but the sets $\widehat{P}_i$ are. We can express this symbolically by saying that the empty set $\emptyset$ is always the result of intersecting any two $\widehat{P}_i$, but not necessarily any two P_i. For any two $i \neq k$,

$$\begin{aligned} \emptyset &\subseteq P_i \cap P_k \\ \emptyset &= \widehat{P}_i \cap \widehat{P}_k \end{aligned} \tag{19.8}$$

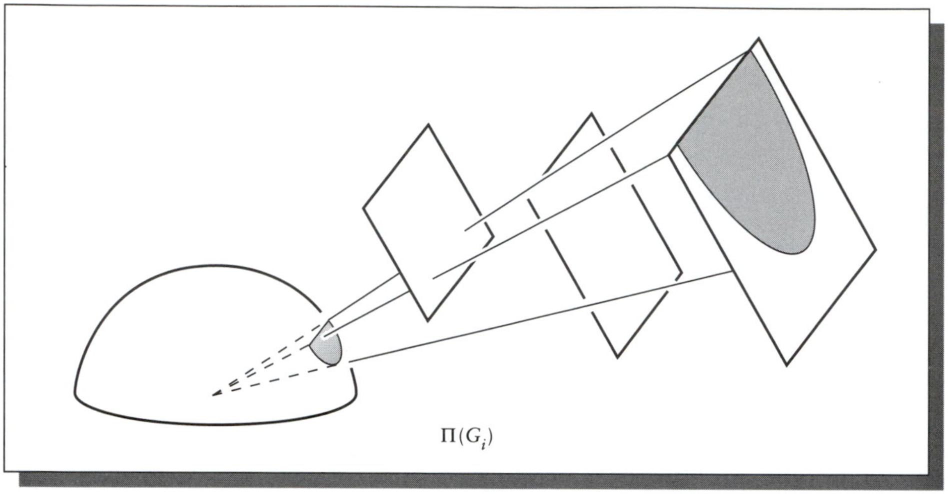

FIGURE 19.7

$\Pi(G_i)$ is the set of all directions leading to a point in G_i.

The sets P_i and $\widehat{P}_i$ defined surface strata in terms of directional strata. The next two sets propagate information in the opposite direction.

Consider a set of points G_i defined over some set of surfaces. The set of all directions in which these points are visible is the set $\Pi_i = \Pi(G_i)$. We define this *point-driven set* as

$$\Pi_i \triangleq \Pi(G_i) = \{\vec{\omega} : \mathbf{p} \in G_i\} \tag{19.9}$$

This definition is illustrated in Figure 19.7. For clarity in the figure, the set G_i is shown on only one surface, though in general it may extend over several surfaces. Taking the natural boundaries of surfaces as the edges of strata, we can always break down G_i into set of smaller point sets that are equivalent to G_i, yet each point set is contained on a single surface.

Not all the elements of G_i are necessarily directly visible to $\mathbf{s}$, due to intervening objects that may block visibility. The set $\widehat{\Pi}_i = \widehat{\Pi}(G_i)$ is the set of directions that see elements of G_i directly, as shown in Figure 19.8. We define $\widehat{\Pi}_i$ as

$$\widehat{\Pi}_i \triangleq \widehat{\Pi}(G_i) = \{\vec{\omega} : N(\mathbf{s}, \vec{\omega}) \in G_i\} \tag{19.10}$$

As with the point sets, the intersection of two different Π_i is not necessarily empty,

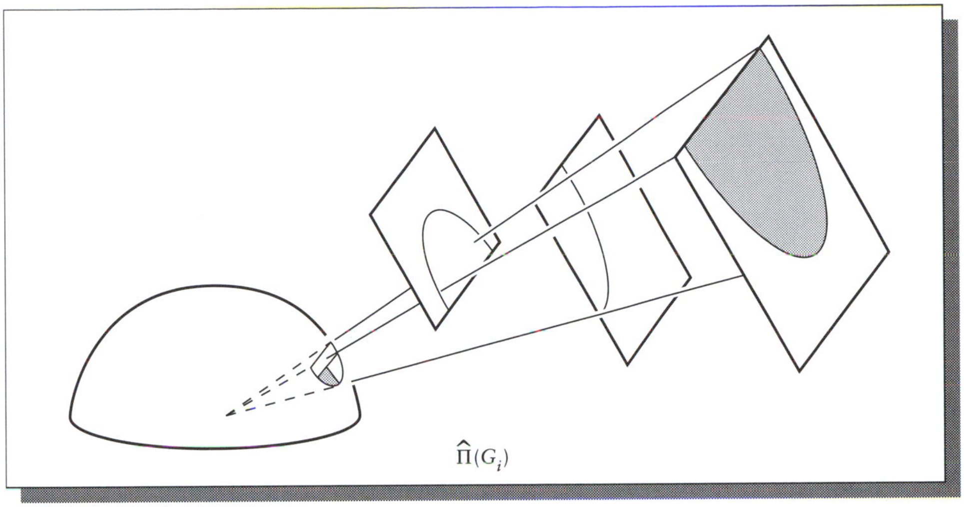

FIGURE 19.8
$\widehat{\Pi}(G_i)$ is the set of all directions that can directly see a point in G_i.

though the intersection of two different $\widehat{\Pi}_i$ will be. In general, for any $i \neq k$,

$$\begin{aligned} \emptyset &\subseteq \Pi_i \cap \Pi_k \\ \emptyset &= \widehat{\Pi}_i \cap \widehat{\Pi}_k \end{aligned} \tag{19.11}$$

These sets allow us to construct strata either on surfaces in space or on the directions around a point, and make sure that we're not counting anything twice. The general plan is to stratify the environment into strata G_i and simultaneously stratify the directions into strata Γ_i. All of the Γ_i are projected into space to further stratify the surfaces, and all the G_i are projected onto the direction sphere to further stratify it. The result is a single, unified set of strata that are consistent in both domains. We call this *resolution* of the strata. At the end of a resolution step, there are as many surface strata as there are solid angle strata.

Figure 19.9 shows an example of this operation. The solid angle Γ_i on the direction sphere includes a circular stratum on each surface, and their edges induce strata on the direction sphere and each other. Figure 19.9(b) shows the view from the point s; the circle and the three rectangles together create eleven different regions in the scene. The stratification on the solid angle and each surface is shown in Figure 19.9(c). The solid angle itself subdivides into five solid angles, and the nearest-to-farthest surfaces are divided into seven, four, and nine regions.

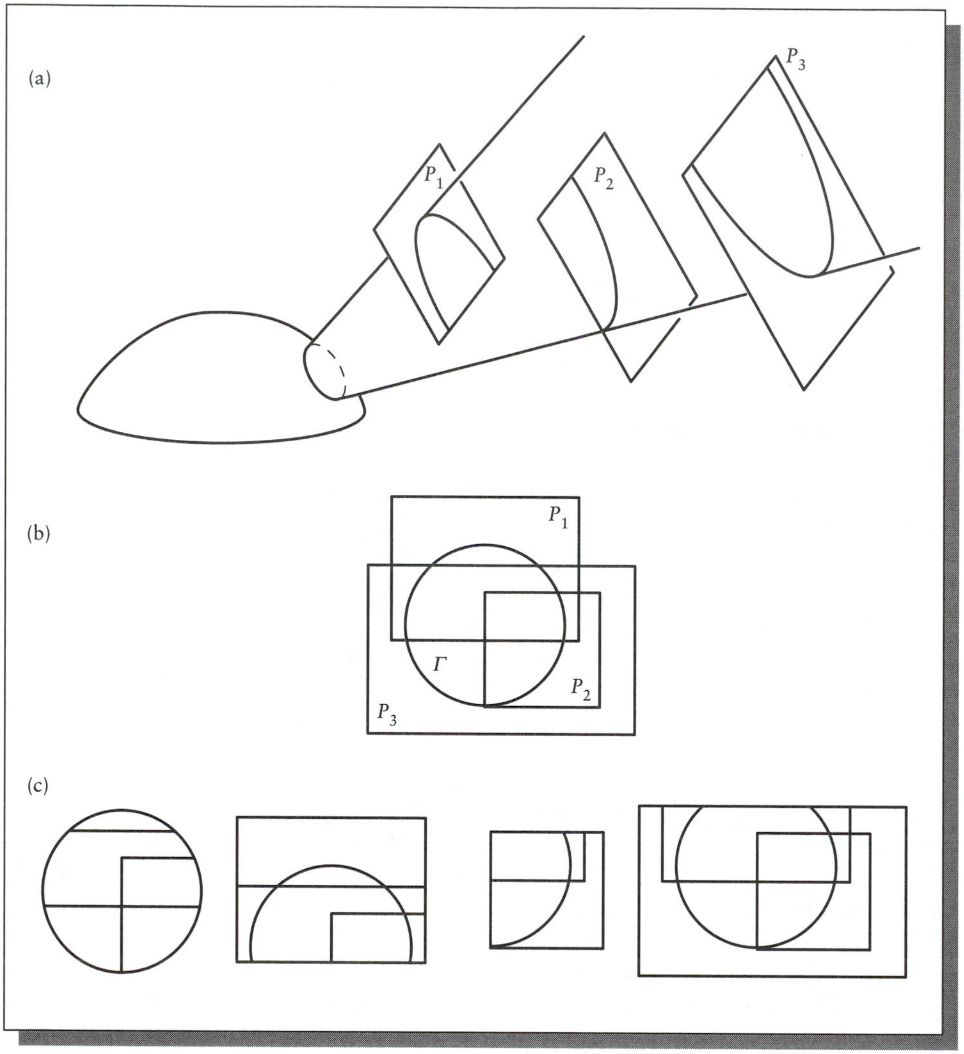

FIGURE 19.9

(a) A solid angle and some intersected objects. (b) The view from the hemisphere. (c) Resolved strata on the hemisphere and each patch.

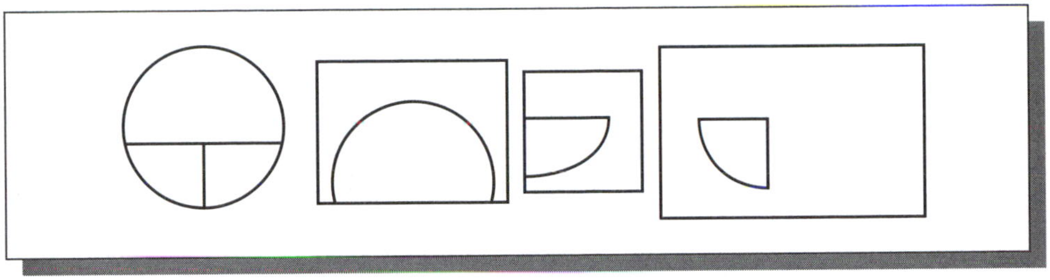

FIGURE 19.10
Visibility-resolved strata.

Recalling Equation 19.3, which wrote the integration over Θ_i^i in terms of smaller domains D_i, each corresponding to a Γ_i, we can now relate a particular region on a particular surface with each solid angle Γ_i.

If we were to actually compute the combination of each surface stratum (including edges) with each solid angle stratum, the result would be a combinatorial explosion. But we don't actually need each individual stratum, since we are really only interested in the nearest-visible surfaces. Figure 19.10 shows that in our example, each surface has only one visible stratum, and the solid angle has only three strata. We call this much smaller set of strata the *visible resolution* of the strata.

19.3.2 Applying Resolved Strata

The heart of the resolved strata method is that each stratum may be represented by *either* its solid angle representation or its surface representation. Recalling our stratified form of OVTIGRE given in Equation 19.3, we have our choice of writing each integration over a domain over either the solid angle or the surface associated with it.

The only remaining step is to find the appropriate integration expression representing the light due to each type of stratum. We will derive these in the same order in which they were presented above.

A stratum P_i is a point set of all points on all objects visible through a solid angle Γ_i. We need only integrate each direction over Γ_i and apply a visibility test at each point. If the point is visible, the visibility test returns 1 and the light is added in to the incident light in that direction; if the test is 0, that light is ignored. Only one

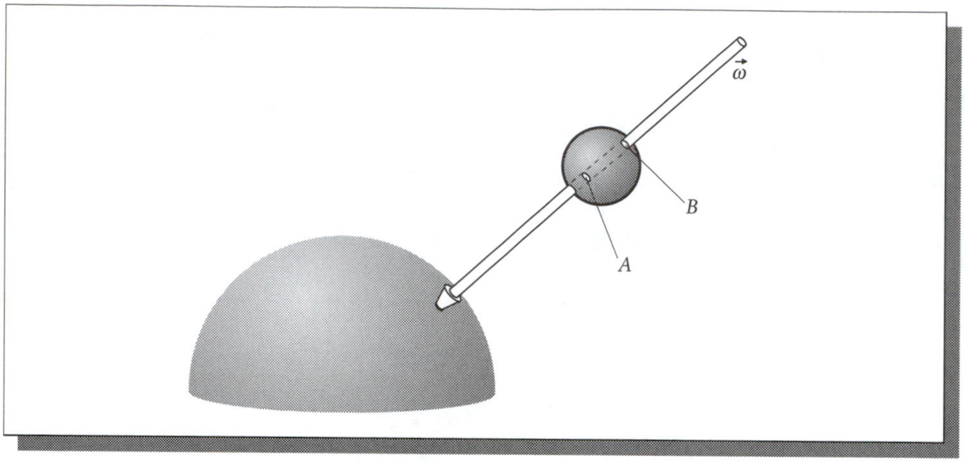

FIGURE 19.11
Points A and B and a direction $\vec{\omega}$.

point for each $\vec{\omega} \in \Gamma_i$ will have a visibility value of 1. The integral is then

$$\int_{D_i} = \int_{\mathbf{p} \in P_i} \rho(\mathbf{s}, \vec{\omega} \rightarrow \vec{\omega}^0) L(\mathbf{p}, \vec{\omega}) V(\mathbf{p}, \mathbf{s}) \cos\theta \, d\mathbf{p} \tag{19.12}$$

The expression for $\widehat{P}_i$ is similar, but because $\widehat{P}_i$ already only contains those points that are directly visible, we can drop the visibility function:

$$\int_{D_i} = \int_{\mathbf{p} \in \widehat{P}_i} \rho(\mathbf{s}, \vec{\omega} \rightarrow \vec{\omega}^0) L(\mathbf{p}, \vec{\omega}) \cos\theta \, d\mathbf{p} \tag{19.13}$$

Now we turn to the direction sets. Things are slightly trickier here than for the point sets. A surface point can be reached from another point s from only a single direction, but a ray from s in that direction may intersect the surface several times. For example, consider Figure 19.11. The point labeled A on the sphere has only a single direction $\vec{\omega}$ associated with it. But a ray in that direction may intersect the sphere not only at A, but at B as well. In general, the number of times a ray may intersect a surface is proportional to the *order* of the surface: a plane has order 1, a sphere has order 2, a cubic patch has order 3, and so on.

When we integrate over a direction set Π_i, we need to identify every intersection of a ray $\vec{\omega} \in \Pi_i$ with every one of the N objects in the environment. If object m has degree d_m, then we can find the point $\mathbf{p}_{m,n}$ corresponding to the nth intersection with object m. Multiplying the radiance there by the visibility function as before gives us the contribution of the radiance leaving that point to s:

$$\int_{D_i} = \int_{\vec{\omega}\in\Pi_i} \rho(\mathbf{s}, \vec{\omega} \to \vec{\omega}^0) \left[\sum_{m=1}^{N} \sum_{n=1}^{d_m} L(\mathbf{p}_{m,n}, \vec{\omega}) V(\mathbf{p}, \mathbf{s}) \right] \cos\theta \, d\mathbf{p} \tag{19.14}$$

Finally we come to the strata represented by $\widehat{\Pi}_i$. This is a set of directions that is guaranteed to lie within one stratum on one surface; we need only find that surface and find the radiance there. So

$$\int_{D_i} = \int_{\vec{\omega}\in\widehat{\Pi}_i} \rho(\mathbf{s}, \vec{\omega} \to \vec{\omega}^0) L(N(\mathbf{s}, \vec{\omega}), \vec{\omega}) \cos\theta \, d\vec{\omega} \tag{19.15}$$

Summarizing the above discussion, there are four ways we can integrate the incident radiance falling on a point $\vec{\omega}$ through a given directional stratum. The *surface-based* methods integrate over all points in the corresponding surface stratum, applying a visibility term if necessary. The *direction-based* methods integrate over all directions in the stratum, finding the corresponding surface points and using their radiance. So for each directional domain D_i in Equation 19.3 (repeated here for reference):

$$L(\mathbf{r}, \vec{\omega}^o) = L^e(\mathbf{s}, \vec{\omega}^o) + \sum_{k=1}^{s} \int_{D_k} f(\mathbf{r}, \vec{\omega} \to \vec{\omega}^o, \lambda) \frac{L(\mathbf{r}, \vec{\omega}) \cos\theta_r}{g_k(\mathbf{r}, \vec{\omega})} g_k(\mathbf{r}, \vec{\omega}) \, d\vec{\omega} \tag{19.16}$$

we have our choice of four equivalent methods, summarized in Equation 19.17.

$$\int_{D_i} = \begin{cases} \displaystyle\int_{\mathbf{p}\in P_i} \rho(\mathbf{s}, \vec{\omega} \to \vec{\omega}^0) L(\mathbf{p}, \vec{\omega}) V(\mathbf{p}, \mathbf{s}) \cos\theta \, d\mathbf{p} \\ \displaystyle\int_{\mathbf{p}\in \widehat{P}_i} \rho(\mathbf{s}, \vec{\omega} \to \vec{\omega}^0) L(\mathbf{p}, \vec{\omega}) \cos\theta \, d\mathbf{p} \\ \displaystyle\int_{\vec{\omega}\in\Pi_i} \rho(\mathbf{s}, \vec{\omega} \to \vec{\omega}^0) \left[\sum_{m=1}^{N} \sum_{n=1}^{d_m} L(\mathbf{p}_{m,n}, \vec{\omega}) V(\mathbf{p}, \mathbf{s}) \right] \cos\theta \, d\vec{\omega} \\ \displaystyle\int_{\vec{\omega}\in\widehat{\Pi}_i} \rho(\mathbf{s}, \vec{\omega} \to \vec{\omega}^0) L(N(\mathbf{s}, \vec{\omega}), \vec{\omega}) \cos\theta \, d\vec{\omega} \end{cases} \tag{19.17}$$

The general procedure for evaluating the propagated radiance at a point may be summarized in six steps:

1. Choose Γ_i based on information at s.

2. Choose G_i based on information on surfaces.
3. Compute the visibility resolution of the strata.
4. For each stratum, choose an integration method.
5. Integrate each stratum.
6. Test each stratum and adaptively subdivide if necessary, returning to step 1.

Most ray-tracing methods published in the literature may be viewed as approximations to this six-step procedure, which either avoid, combine, or approximate different steps. We will review some of these methods below.

An example of this process is shown in Figure 19.12.

Our common departure point is the schematic visibility tracing diagram of Figure 19.13. The diagram shows some patches and solid angles; each has been assigned an arbitrary label for the purposes of discussion. To begin with, suppose we want to find the energy carried back to the apex of solid angle Γ_1. This solid angle has a corresponding domain on patch M_1. To find the light radiated by M_1 back into Γ_1, we need to combine the self-emission of M_1 with the light propagated from there. To find the propagated light from M_1, we need to know the light falling upon it. Suppose we find the light leaving the amount of M_1 within Γ_1 by integrating over every such point. The figure shows one such point.

To compute the illumination on a point within M_1, we can stratify the set of directions around that point, stratify the surfaces in the environment, and resolve the strata. We have labeled by Γ_2 and Γ_3 two of the solid angles round the point on M_1; each of them strikes a surface. To find the light leaving each of those surfaces, we stratify their direction sets and the environment, resolve the strata, and then integrate, illustrated by the solid angles Γ_4 through Γ_7 in the figure.

This idea of *recursive visibility* for computing the radiance at a point was introduced by Whitted [477]. The strength of the method lies in the close coupling of visibility and illumination; a single data structure (the tree of intersections for a ray) can be used to carry both types of information at once. Notice that the stratification of both the direction sets and the environment will in general differ from point to point, even for nearby neighbors on the same patch.

19.3.3 Direct and Indirect Illumination

One way to compute the illumination described by Figure 19.13 is to compute some directional and spatial strata, but not resolve the two sets. This can lead to error when a set of directions or a set of surface points is counted twice; we will return to this later.

The most common approach to constructing strata is to distinguish between *direct* and *indirect* illumination.

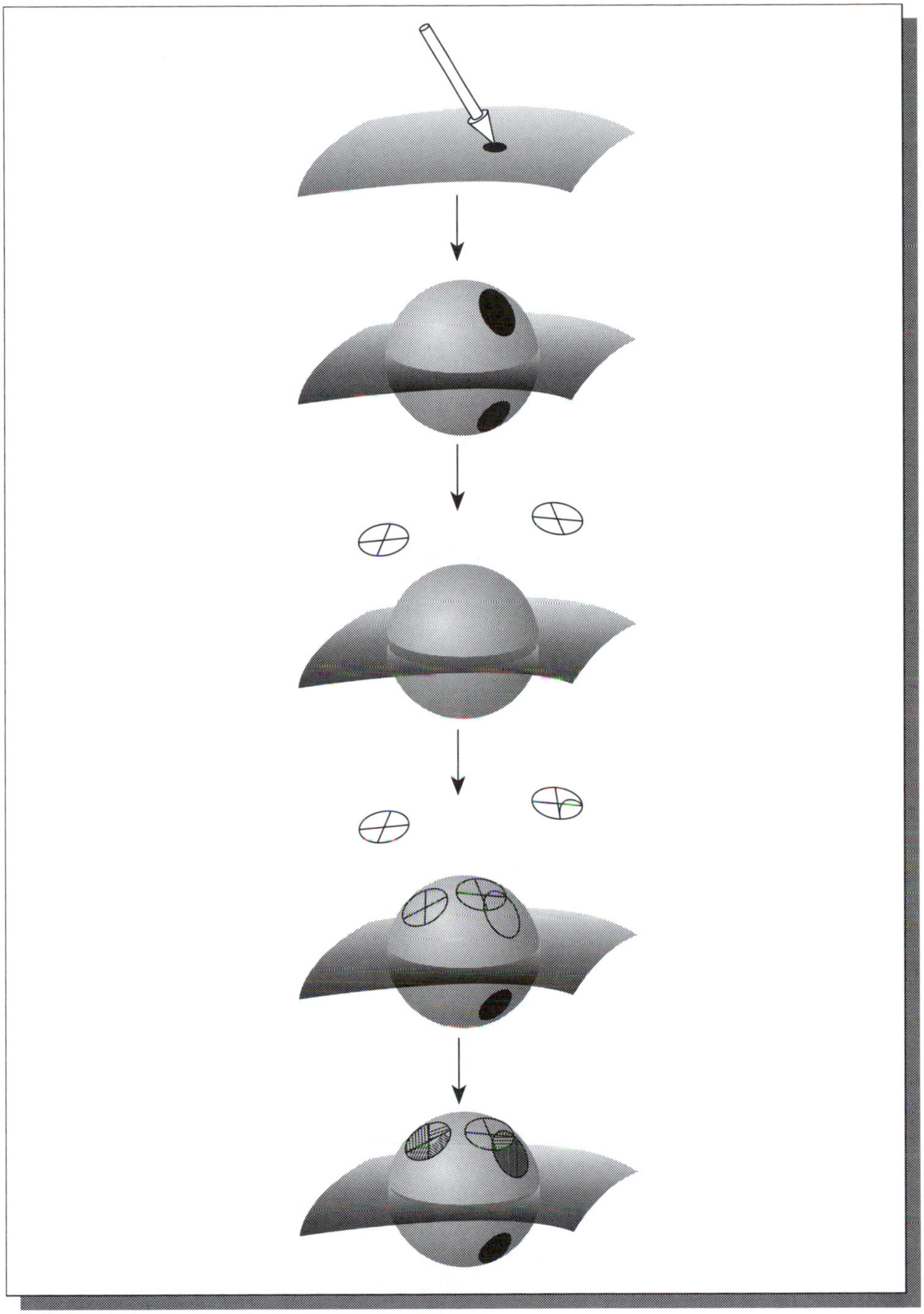

FIGURE 19.12

Visibility ray tracing with different strata.

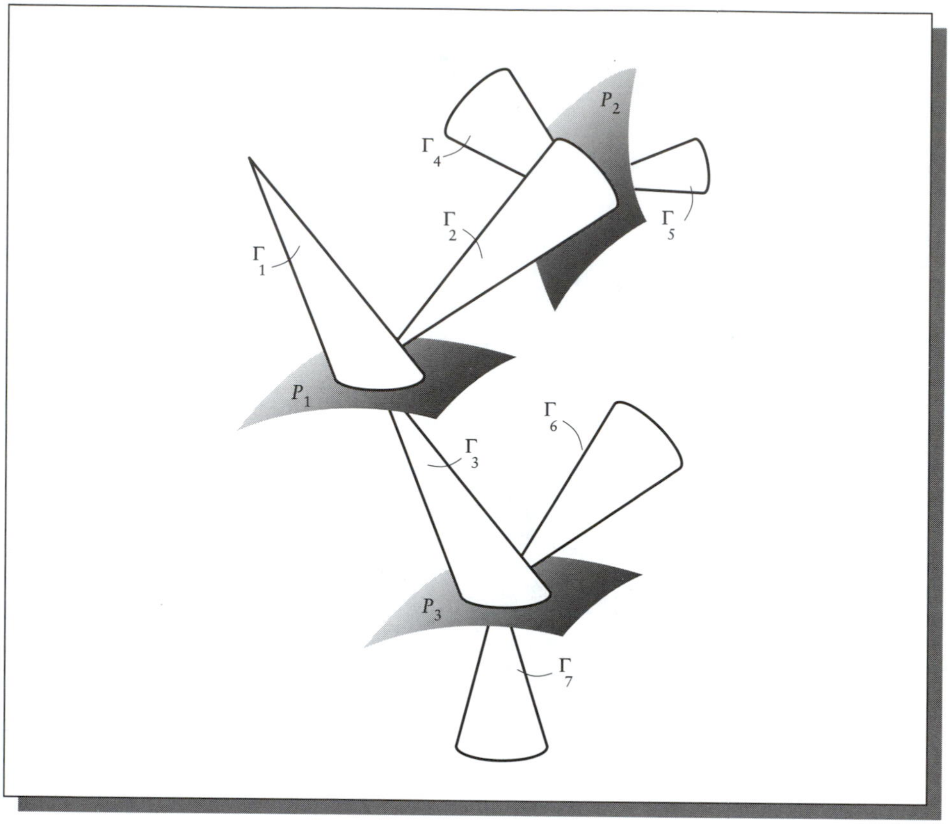

FIGURE 19.13
Visibility tracing.

Direct light at a point is that light which comes from the luminaires without any other interactions along the way, as in Figure 19.14. Since this light is not diminished by reflection or transmission, if the luminaire is bright, then it is likely to make a large impact on the total illumination arriving at the point. To make sure that we include these important sources of illumination in our integral, we determine the light sources in the scene and stratify them. This stratification can be trivial (a single stratum over the source), finely subdivided (e.g., so each stratum carries an equal amount of energy), or aggregate (many luminaires combined into one stratum).

Indirect light accounts for all illumination that does not come directly from a

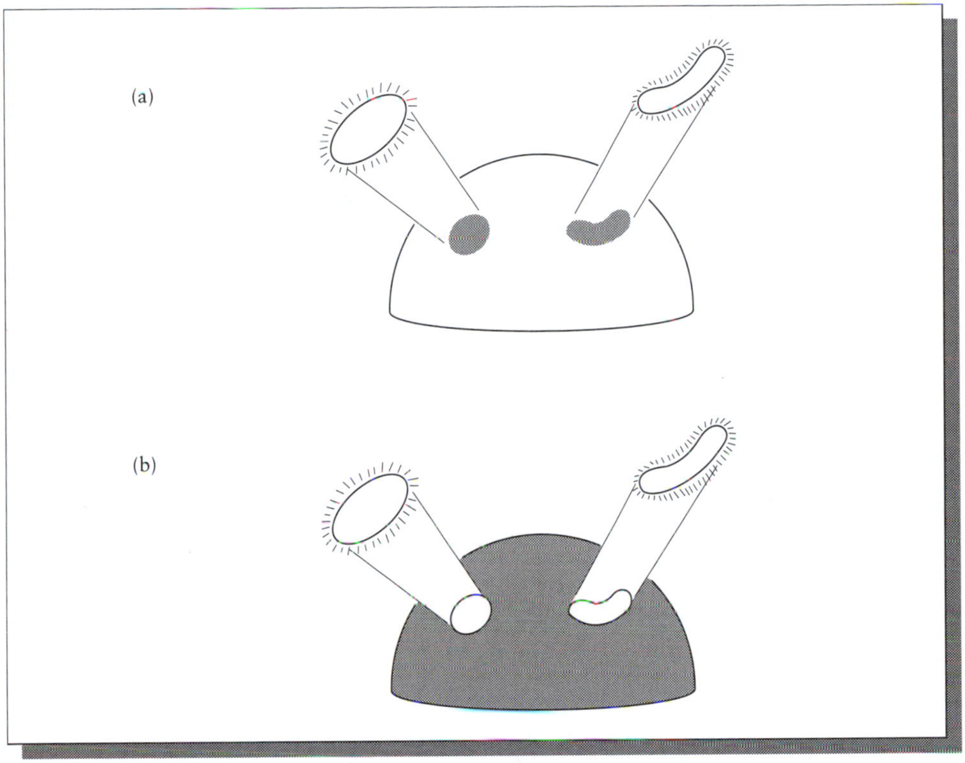

FIGURE 19.14
(a) Direct illumination. (b) Indirect illumination.

luminaire. To model indirect light efficiently, we need to use information about the surface, as well as the environment and the distribution of light within it. For example, a shiny surface will strongly reflect and transmit light by specular reflection, so it is important that we gather a good estimate of light that arrives from the specular directions. This means that to determine the incident light that will significantly contribute to the reflected (or transmitted) light in a particular direction, we place fine strata in the specular solid angles computed with respect to that direction. We can also use any available information about nearby surfaces that are likely to propagate significant quantities of light onto the shading point. For example, we may have determined the energy leaving some nearby surfaces in nearby directions at a previous step; that information can help us identify those surfaces as potential

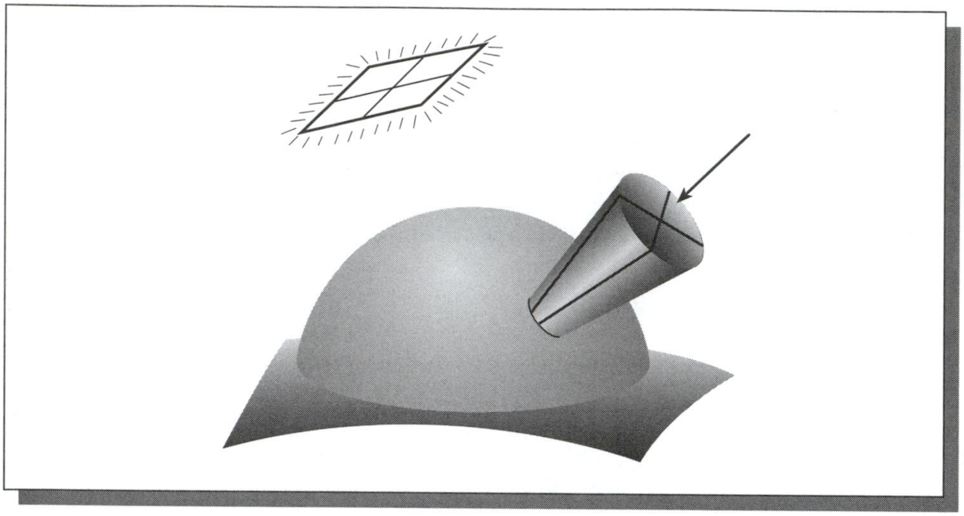

FIGURE 19.15
A simple case of indirect and direct strata.

sources of significant illumination. Then we stratify those surfaces in order to make sure we get their illumination.

Figure 19.15 shows both of these operations in a schematic view. A circular solid angle has been subdivided into four wedge-shaped strata in a specular direction, and a light source overhead has been subdivided into four rectangular strata. If this was where we stopped, then we would estimate the incident illumination by a sum over these eight strata. We would probably use some ad hoc measure (like ambient light, discussed in Chapter 15) to account for the other light not explicitly sampled.

This distinction between direct and indirect illumination is simply a computational convenience; as far as the shading point is concerned, it doesn't really matter whether incident light arrives directly from a luminaire or via propagation by another surface. As long as we resolve the strata before integration, there's no problem.

However, if we don't resolve visibility, then the same region of surface can be accounted for twice: once in a directional stratum and once in a surface stratum. Figure 19.16 shows the same example as in Figure 19.15, only this time the reflected strata overlap with the luminaire strata. If we simply sum together the integral over each stratum, then the luminaire will be accounted for in both places, causing an error.

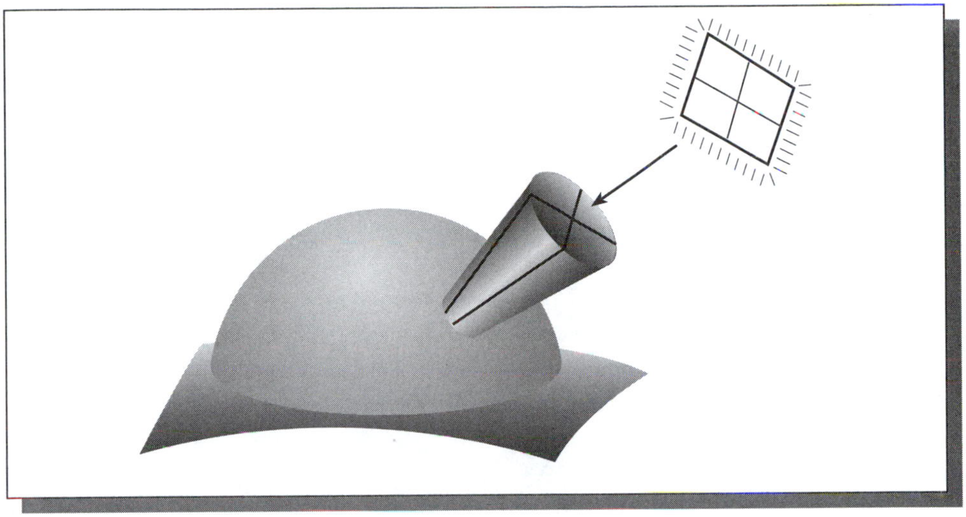

FIGURE 19.16
Overlap of direct and indirect strata.

If we don't wish to resolve visibility before integration, then we can do it dynamically by checking for duplicated regions in pairs of strata. Any region that appears in two places is removed from one. The choice of region may be arbitrary or influenced by the specific algorithm being used.

Most published algorithms generate strata on the fly using a combination of direction-based and surface-based heuristics, and then resolve those strata on the fly simply by checking the surface corresponding to each indirect stratum. If the surface is on a luminaire, then that information is either discarded, or transferred and saved with the appropriate stratum. That way, only indirect surfaces contribute to strata intended to capture indirect illumination.

In all of the examples we will see below, the estimation of illumination is always begun with a set of surface-based strata on direct light sources and direction-based strata representing reflection and transmission. There is no resolution of these strata beforehand; generally the surface strata G_i are converted into direction strata $P_i = \Pi(G_i)$, and direction strata corresponding to specular reflections and transmissions are generated directly at the shading point based on the shading geometry and the BDF.

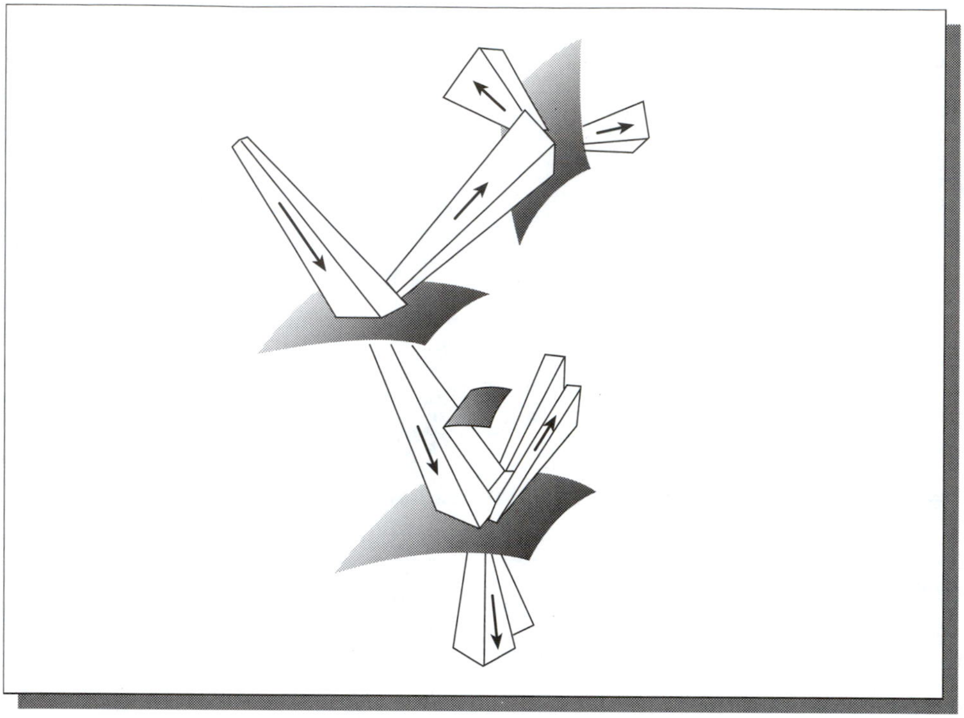

FIGURE 19.17

A schematic form of beam tracing.

Tracing Solid Angles

One method for generating and resolving strata actually projects into space the edges of the cones defined by the direction sets Γ_i and point sets G_i and intersects these cones with the objects in the environment.

The technique of *beam tracing* by Heckbert and Hanrahan [211] is illustrated schematically in Figure 19.17. (In this figure, and all following figures of this type, we draw only two direction-based strata at each shading point; other strata have similar forms.) Each solid angle is approximated with a polygonal cone (called a *beam*); if the environment is all polyhedra, then this solid angle is exact. The beams are clipped against objects in the environment as they are extended from the shading point. At any intersected object a new set of beams is generated to sample direct and indirect illumination.

FIGURE 19.18
A schematic form of cone tracing.

The method of *cone tracing* by Amanatides is similar but uses right circular cones rather than polyhedral cones [9]; it is illustrated schematically in Figure 19.18. Note that a noncircular solid angle may be approximated by a collection of circular cones for a more accurate fit.

An advantage of beam and cone tracing is that they are able to compute surface strata efficiently and dynamically from directional strata. Care must still be taken when a direct light source occupies a stratum intended to collect indirect illumination.

Ray Tracing

If the strata are reduced to the size of a point, then a single ray suffices to sample it, and the correspondence between direction and surface strata becomes trivial: the

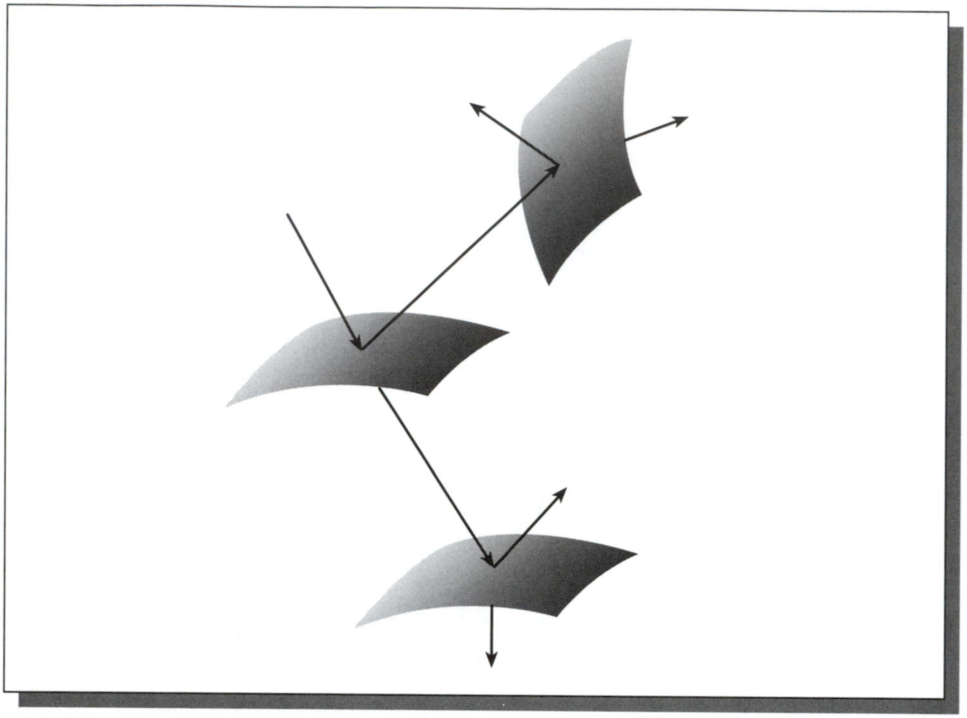

FIGURE 19.19

Classical ray tracing.

point set on each surface induced by a solid angle Γ_i is the single point intersected by the one ray in that solid angle. Similarly, there is only one ray associated with any surface set G_i, since it contains but one point.

This leads us to a structure introduced by Whitted [477], and shown schematically in Figure 19.19. This is the *classical ray tracing method*.

Since all strata have been reduced to point size, then surface strata have only one point as well. Since direct light sources are represented by surface strata, we can only represent point sources.

Figure 19.20 (color plate) shows an example of an image produced by classical ray tracing. Note the sharp shadows due to illumination from point sources, and the sharp images due to perfect reflection and refraction.

Suppose that the strata have not been reduced to point size, but that we have decided to sample the integrals within each stratum using Monte Carlo methods.

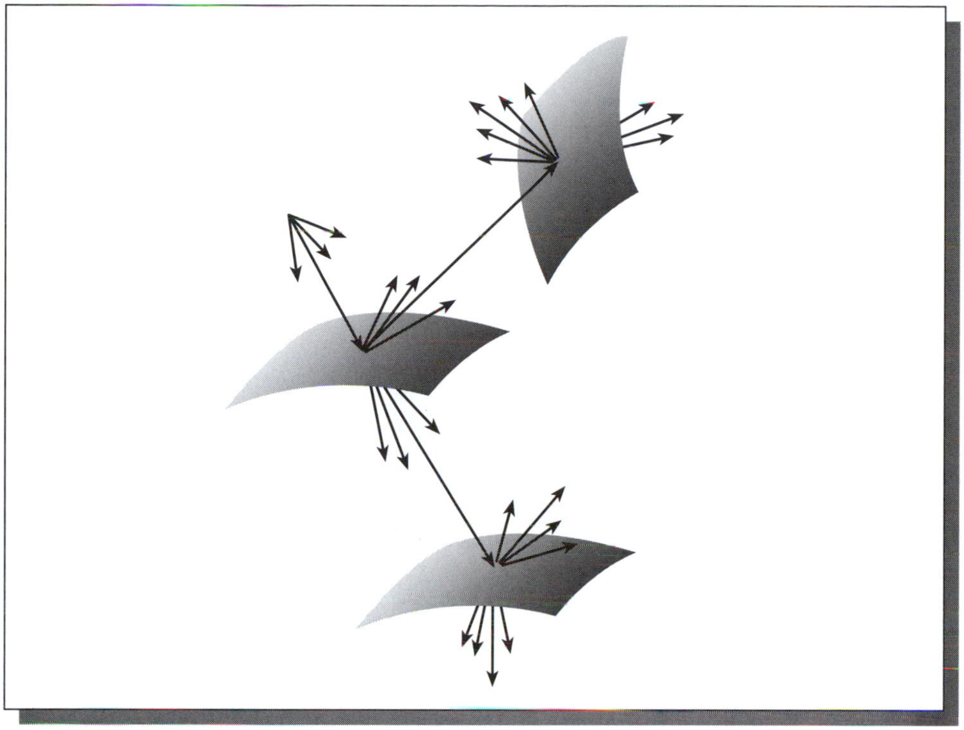

FIGURE 19.21
Distribution ray tracing.

Then we create a number of samples in each stratum, possibly in a nonuniform pattern, to sample the domain. Such a technique was suggested by Cook [101]. The method is called *distribution ray tracing*, and is shown schematically in Figure 19.21 (the names *distributed ray tracing* and *stochastic ray tracing* are also used to describe this algorithm).

This approach may be viewed as a direct use of Monte Carlo methods to sample the signal represented by incident light on the shading point. Stratification is built in by the BDF and the surface strata representing direct illumination, and it's easy to avoid duplication of strata: if an indirect sample lands on a luminaire, either ignore it or use it as a direct contribution (though the stratification on the luminaire must be adjusted to represent this additional piece of sampling).

Another Monte Carlo approach to evaluating the integral was discussed in Chap-

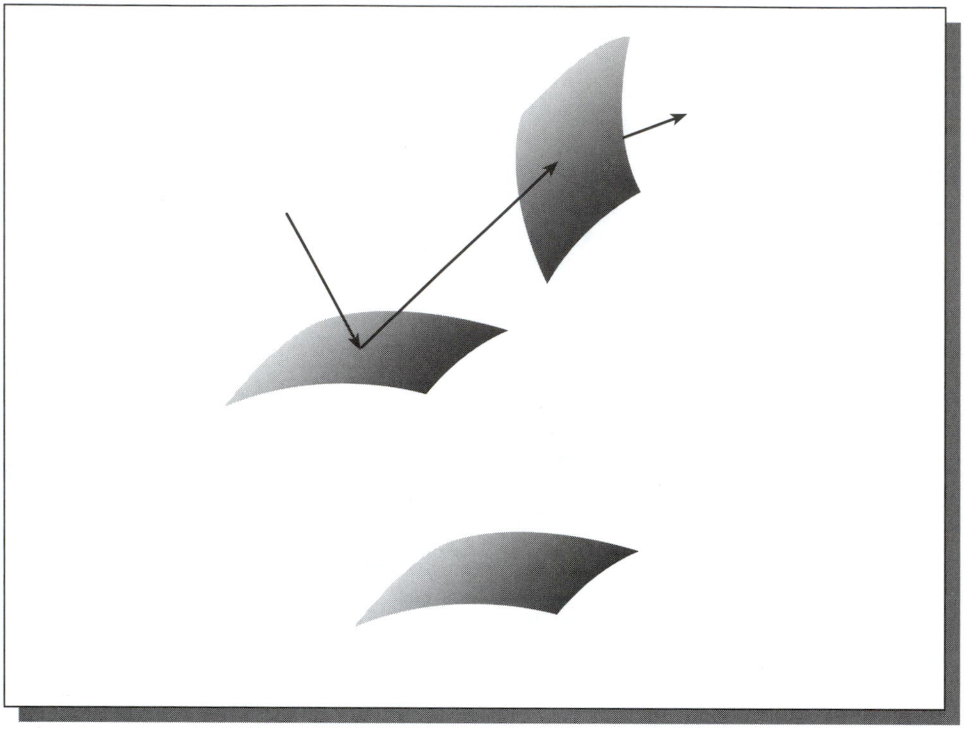

FIGURE 19.22
Path tracing.

ter 16 as *path tracing*. This approach simply creates a path history for a single particle interacting with the environment until absorption. That is, rather than spawn new rays at an intersection, we simply choose a direction for the one ray to follow. Particles are generated and followed until the confidence in the answer is high enough. This method was proposed for image synthesis by Kajiya [234] and is illustrated in Figure 19.22.

Path tracing can be subtle to implement because the distribution of samples needs to follow the desired stratification of the surfaces and directions, yet the stratification is different for each ray cast into the environment from the eyepoint, since the first surface intersection will be different. Some larger-region averaging and history must be maintained in order to preserve the benefits of importance sampling and stratification [234].

Camera Models

Before looking at the details of shading we will first look at the basic ideas for generating the first samples drawn by a visibility tracing algorithm: the samples that make up the image.

Some sort of *imaging model* must be associated with the image surface that defines the image in object space; this limits the light that may strike the surface. Without such a limitation, our simulation would correspond to exposing a piece of photographic film in the real world by simply holding it up in the air. Light from all directions would reach the film, saturating it. Even if our film did not become overexposured, there would be no discernible image. Like our eyes, every image surface needs to be placed within an opaque *enclosure* that has a single *aperture*; light passing through that aperture is the only light that can influence the image surface.

The simplest type of aperture is a small hole. If the hole is of negligible size, then the imaging model is called a *pinhole camera*, after the physical device of the same name. A schematic pinhole camera is shown in Figure 19.23. We have an image plane located so that the normal through the center of the plane goes through the pinhole at point H. For every point P on the image plane, the only light that can contribute to P is that light arriving along the single ray P-H. This model can be used to approximate our own eyes, when the pupil has contracted to its smallest diameter.

Most photographic equipment contains one or more *lenses* to offer broader control over the range of light than the fixed model provided by the pinhole camera. The simplest camera model contains a single, *thin, convex-convex* lens, as shown in Figure 19.24. In this context, *thin* is a technical term that we will discuss in a moment. The lens is said to be convex-convex (or *double-convex*) because both sides create a convex solid when viewed from the center of the lens. The type of lens we will consider here is formed from the intersection of two spheres as shown.

The lens has two *focal points* at equal distances in front of and behind the lens. As shown in Figure 19.25, these points lie on the axis a through the center point C of the lens, at a distance f. Light that comes in from the left parallel to a (e.g., light emitted by an object infinitely far away) will be *focused* so that all its rays pass through the *secondary focal point* F' on the right side of the lens. Similarly, light radiated from the *primary focal point* F on the left side of the lens leaves on the right side in parallel beams [311].

To make it easy to find this focus point, we assume that the lens is thin. Recall that the lens is made up of the intersection of two spheres of radius r_1 and r_2. The lens is said to be thin if the diameter d of the lens is much smaller than either radius: $d \ll r_1$ and $d \ll r_2$. In a *thick* lens, the body of material that the light must pass through is significant. That means that we must account for refraction upon entering the lens, for the distance traveled, and then for refraction upon exiting. When the

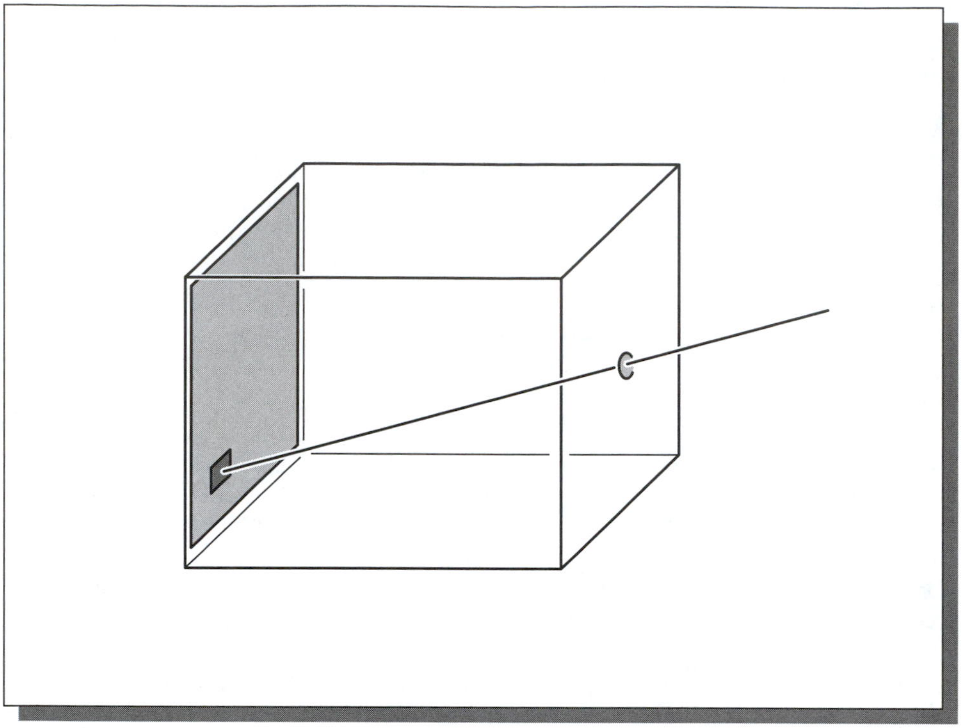

FIGURE 19.23
A pinhole camera.

lens is thin we can consider the distance traveled to be negligible; that means we can combine the two refractions into one, occurring in the plane through the center of the lens. This is called the *thin lens approximation.*

To see how a thin lens focuses light, we can build a small imaging situation and read off the results. Conventionally we use the same labels for corresponding elements on both sides of the lens, distinguishing the elements on the right with a prime. Figure 19.26 shows the geometry for a thin lens.

The lens has a central axis a that passes through the point C in the center of the lens. The primary focal point F is located on this axis at a distance f left of the center, and the secondary focal point F' is similarly at a distance f right of the center. We will suppose that there is a disk of radius y perpendicular to the axis, located M units to the left of C. This distance $|M - C|$ is called s.

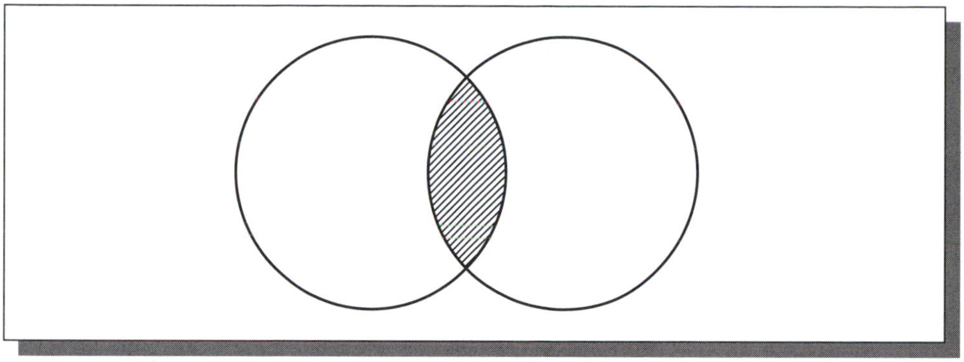

FIGURE 19.24
A thin convex-convex lens formed by two spheres.

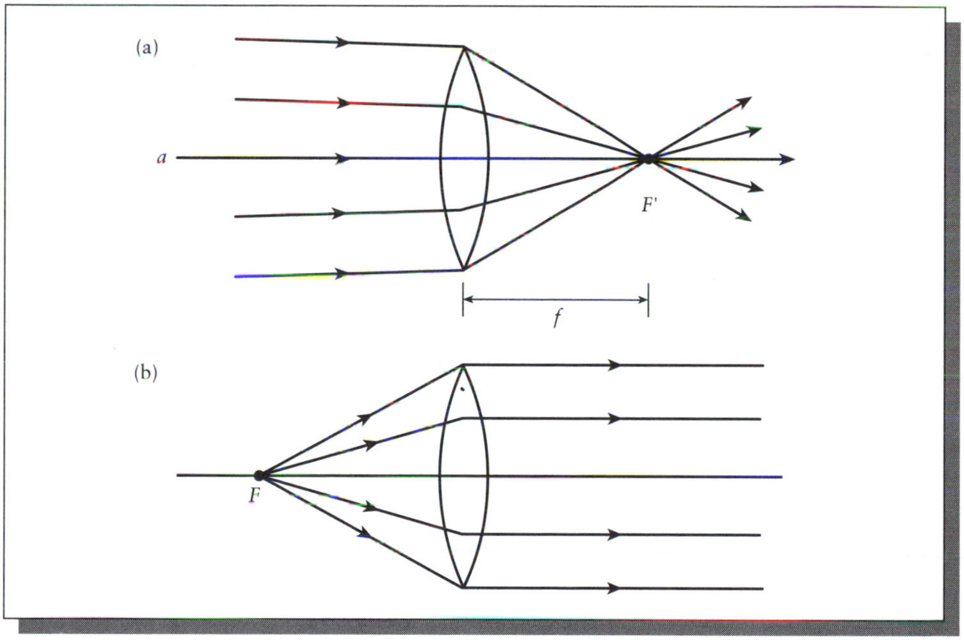

FIGURE 19.25
(a) Incident light parallel to a is focused at F'. (b) Light generated at F leaves parallel to a.

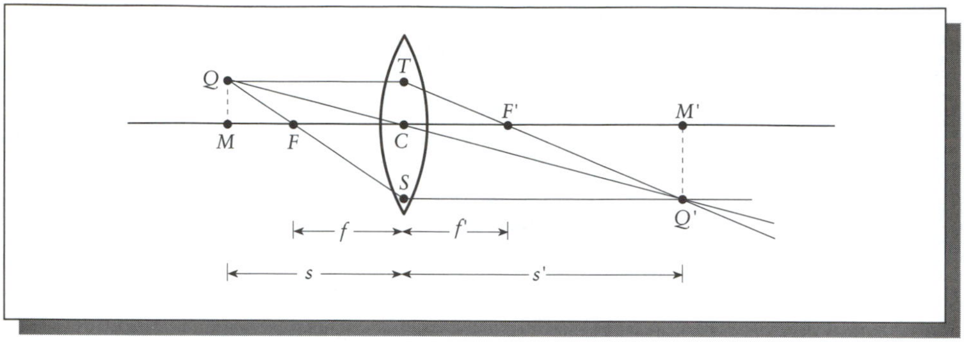

FIGURE 19.26
Geometry for imaging by a thin lens.

We're now ready to find that distance on the right side of the lens where the disk will be in focus; that is, if we built a real model of this situation, this is the distance to the right of C where the image of the disk will be sharp. To find this distance, we begin by selecting a point Q on the perimeter of the disk. As shown in the figure, we trace a line from Q parallel to the axis until it intersects the (thin) lens at T. Now we know by the construction of the lens that all rays coming into the lens parallel to the axis will be refracted to pass through the secondary focal point F', so we can simply draw the line TF'; this line carries some of the light from Q. Now we also know that light rays leaving the lens on the right parallel to the axis must have passed through the primary focal point F on the left side. So we draw another ray from Q that passes through F, and follow it until it strikes the lens at S. According to the construction of the lens, this ray emerges parallel to the axis, so we draw a right-going line parallel to a from S. Eventually this ray will intersect the other ray TF'. The intersection point is Q', and it defines the focused *image* of point Q on the right side at a point M' from the center. The distance $|C - M'|$ is called s'.

We can also trace a ray from Q through the center of the lens C; it will intersect the other lines at Q', so any two of these three lines is sufficient to locate Q. This ray is called the *chief ray* [230]. So to locate Q' we can find either the intersection of two of these lines or the intersection of any of them with the plane perpendicular to the axis located at the distance s'.

The problem now is to find s' for a lens of a given f and an object placed at a given s. The geometry is summarized in Figure 19.27. We have labeled the distances $y = |T - C|$, and $y' = |S - C|$. By convention, y is positive and y' is negative. On the left, we see that $\triangle QTS$ is similar to $\triangle FCS$. Then corresponding sides have the

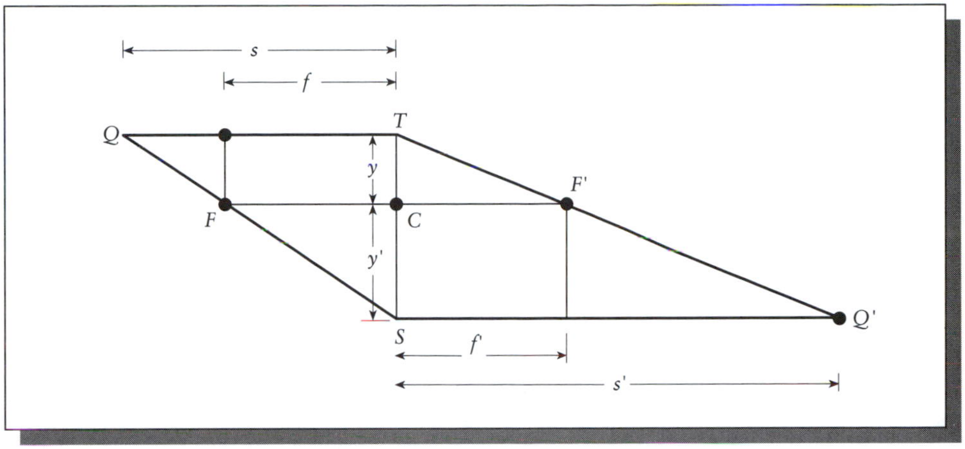

FIGURE 19.27
The triangles for the thin lens model.

same ratio:

$$\frac{y - y'}{s} = \frac{-y'}{f} \tag{19.18}$$

(note that we needed to use $-y'$ rather than y'). We can make the same observation on the right and notice that $\triangle Q'TS$ is similar to $\triangle F'CT$, so

$$\frac{y - y'}{s'} = \frac{y}{f'} \tag{19.19}$$

Adding these two equations, we find

$$\frac{y - y'}{s} + \frac{y - y'}{s'} = \frac{-y'}{f} + \frac{y}{f'} \tag{19.20}$$

Now we know by construction of the lens that $f = f'$, so we can factor out that common term and simplify:

$$(y - y')\left(\frac{1}{s} + \frac{1}{s'}\right) = (y - y')\left(\frac{1}{f}\right)$$

$$\frac{1}{s} + \frac{1}{s'} = \frac{1}{f} \tag{19.21}$$

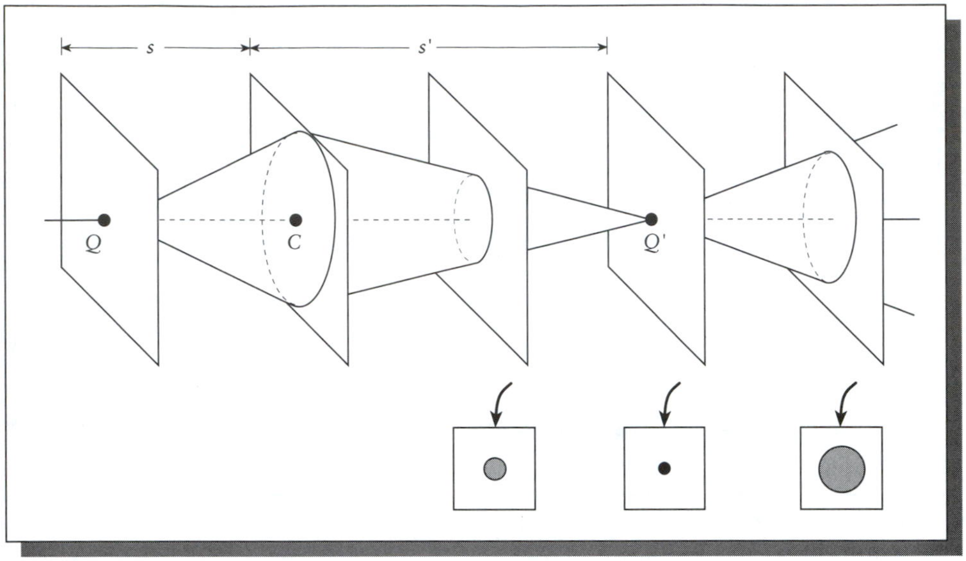

FIGURE 19.28
The cones of light from a point Q.

Equation 19.21 is called the *thin lens formula* [230]. For a lens with a given focal distance f, it tells us the relationship between any object at a distance s and the distance of its image s'.

It's important to observe that no matter where a source is on the left of the lens, we can place a screen anywhere to the right of the lens and receive light from that source. Figure 19.28 shows a cone of light leaving a point Q and impinging on the lens, and then a refracted cone leaving the lens. The apex of the cone is at the distance s, meaning that a sharp point of light at Q will appear as a sharp point of light on a plane perpendicular to a at s'. But as we move that plane along a, it slices the cone so the image of Q becomes a circle; Q thus appears as an out-of-focus little circle of light. This circle is called the *circle of confusion*.

The radius of this circle can be found from Figure 19.29. The cone swept out by Q is as large as the lens at a distance $x = 0$ to the right of the lens, and it has a diameter of 0 at $x = s$. Since a cone is linear, these two measurements are all we need; if the lens has a diameter d, then the diameter $c(x)$ of the cone at distance x is given by

$$c(x) = \frac{-xd}{s} + d \qquad (19.22)$$

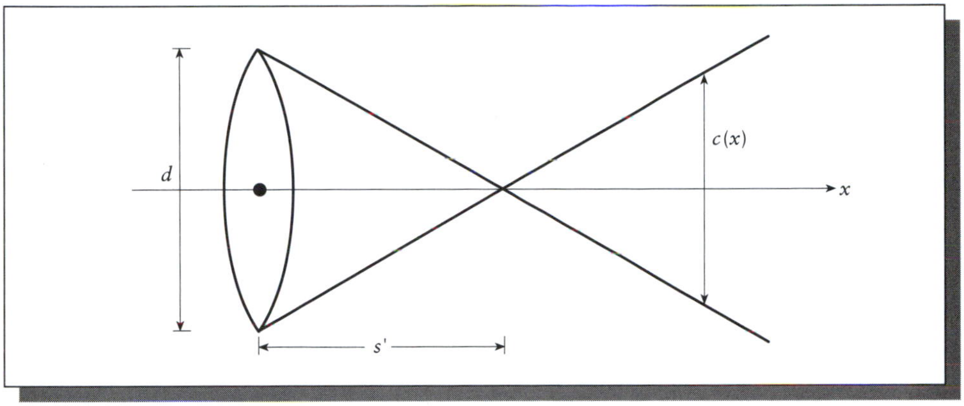

FIGURE 19.29
Computing the diameter of the cone of confusion.

We can solve for s from the lens formula of Equation 19.21:

$$s = \frac{s'f}{s' - f} \tag{19.23}$$

and then plug this into the cone diameter:

$$c(x) = -xd\left(\frac{s' - f}{s'f}\right) + d \tag{19.24}$$

Equation 19.24 tells us that if there is a point at a distance s' from a lens of diameter d, then that point will be blurred into a circle of radius $c(x)$ at a distance of x units to the right of the lens. When $x = s$, the circle has a radius of 0, and thus the object is in focus.

Let's rewrite the circle of confusion equation to isolate the lens diameter d:

$$c(x) = d(1 - xg) \tag{19.25}$$

where we have swept all the geometry terms into a constant g. This tells us that when the lens diameter is small, the growth in the size of the circle as we move away from s will be small. This algebra reflects the geometry of Figure 19.30(a): the lens diameter is small, so the cone diameters are small, and thus the circles of confusion are small. In the limit, the lens diameter goes to 0 and we have a pinhole, where everything is in perfectly sharp focus. When the diameter is large, as in Figure 19.30(b), then the circle of confusion grows quickly with distance from s.

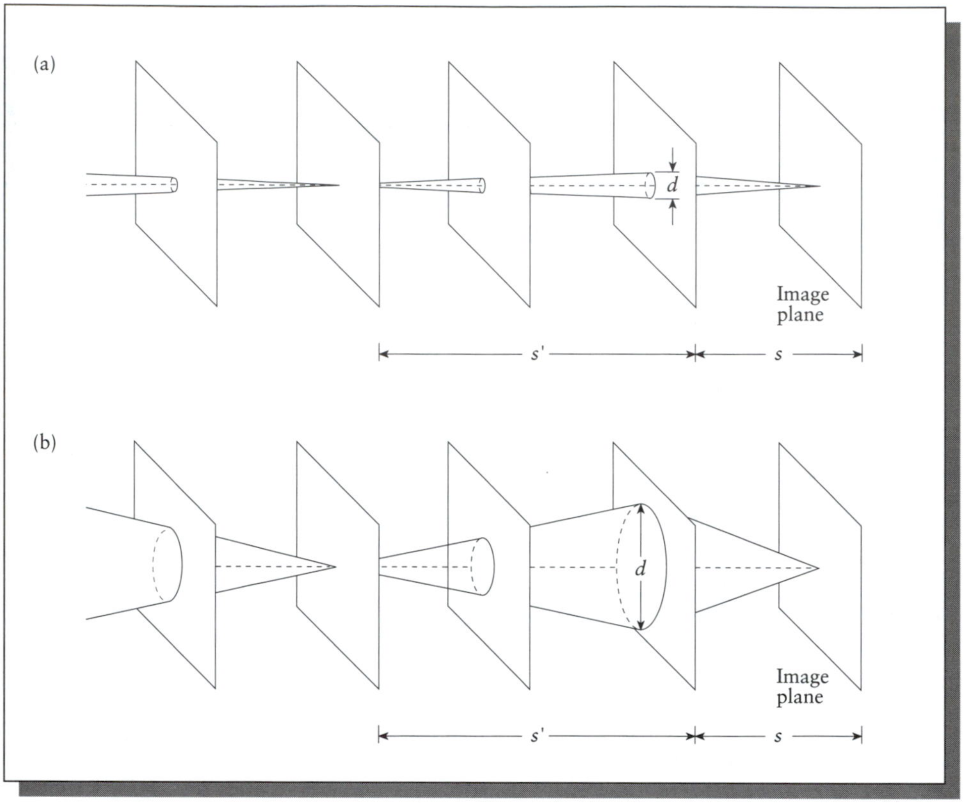

FIGURE 19.30
Cones of confusion. (a) Small lens diameter. (b) Large lens diameter.

Suppose that our image plane (like a piece of film in a camera) is at some given distance s from the center of the lens. Then we know that objects at distance s' will be in focus, and those nearer or farther will be out of focus. When the lens diameter is small, the amount by which objects blur as a function of their distance from s is small; we say that such a lens has a large *depth of field*, meaning that there is a wide range of depths in which objects are nearly focused. When the lens is large, the depth of field is small. The center of the field is determined by the relationship between the lens focal length f and the film distance s', and the depth of the field is determined by these factors and the diameter d of the lens.

This is why photographers move the lens toward and away from the film to focus on different depths, and change the f-stop (or *aperture*), which controls the diameter, to adjust the depth of field. The f-stop numbers are set up on a typical camera so that each increase in setting corresponds to a diameter change that halves the area of the circle. The typical set of f-stop values are $f/1.4$, $f/2$, $f/2.8$, $f/4$, $f/5.6$, $f/8$, $f/11$, $f/16$, $f/22$, $f/32$, $f/45$, and $f/64$. Larger f-stop values correspond to smaller apertures [447].

An algorithm for sampling the environment using the thin-lens model was proposed by Cook [102]. Suppose we have the geometry of Figure 19.31: the film plane is at a distance s' from a thin lens with focal length f and diameter d, and we want to find the light striking a point on the film marked P'. From our construction, we can find the point in the environment that would come into perfect focus at P' by tracing a line from P' through the center of the lens C and finding its point of intersection with the focal plane at a distance s on the other side of the lens. This intersection point is labeled P. We know that all rays that contribute to P' come to it through a cone which has P as an apex and the lens as a cross section.

To find the total contribution of the environment to P', we need to integrate the radiance coming through that cone. We can numerically estimate the radiance by taking points E on the lens, and tracing rays from those points through P. Because the lens is thin, we can generate points on the lens by simply distributing them on a disk of diameter d centered at C. The rays may be written

$$R = P + \alpha(P - E) \tag{19.26}$$

for $0 < \alpha \in \mathcal{R}$. We will call the lens points E since they are effectively the location of an observer's "eye" for that ray.

Distribution Ray Tracing

Distribution ray tracing and path tracing are the most elegant and complete of the ray tracing methods we have seen so far. In this section we will concentrate on distribution ray tracing as an example of how such algorithms work. We'll begin with an algorithm that is inefficient but straightforward, and then add a small twist that will improve the efficiency dramatically.

Before the ray is sent into the environment, we can attach descriptive information to it. For example, we can select a *frequency* for the wavelength of light that the ray is destined to carry; this allows us to sample the visible light spectrum anywhere we want, and thereby carry out *color anti-aliasing*.

We can also choose a *time* for the ray. Suppose that the lens is covered by a shutter which opens momentarily, like the shutter on a camera. Then each part of the lens is only exposed for an interval of time, and each part of the image plane receives illumination over the percent of the interval when it is exposed. To integrate over that interval, we use Monte Carlo methods to attach a time t to the ray.

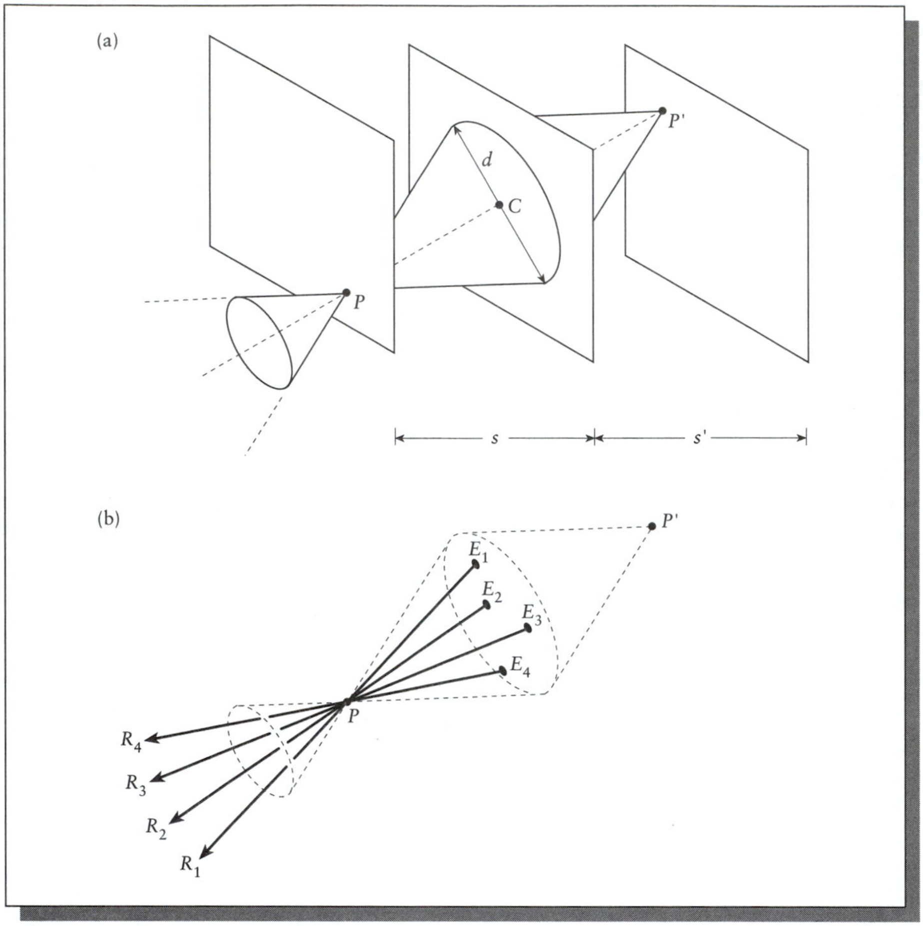

FIGURE 19.31

(a) Viewing the environment through a thin lens. (b) Sampling the view.

The selection of 2D image points, 2D lens locations, frequencies, and times may all be influenced by stratification and importance sampling. If we decide to stratify each dimension into n pieces, then a complete sampling would require n^6 rays for these six dimensions. Happily, such complete sampling is not required, as we will see below.

Once it is constructed, the ray enters the environment. It is common to speak of finding the *first intersection* of the ray with the environment. This is because by construction the ray has its origin in the camera model and is pointed into the environment. In fact, this is just a computational device, since light will travel along the ray from the environment into the camera.

Because of this apparent backward direction of the ray, this type of ray tracing is sometimes called *backward ray tracing*. I do not recommend the use of this term, because historically the same name has been used to describe algorithms that trace rays in the opposite direction, from the light sources into the camera model. The terms *backward* and *forward* have become sufficiently confused that it would be difficult to recommend a single usage here that would be consistent with the literature. I therefore suggest abandoning those adjectives, and instead use *visibility tracing* for this operation. Almost any terms suggested for these two senses of ray tracing can probably be argued as ambiguous under some interpretation, so I will simply use this name for this interpretation consistently in this book.

The most important task associated with this ray is finding the first object it strikes. This involves using a library of *ray-object intersection routines*, which provide the intersection point for a ray with each kind of object that may be in the scene. Many such routines have been developed for primitives ranging from spheres and planes to surfaces of revolution, fractals, and complex aggregate shapes. Such routines range from the simple to the very complex, and we will not review them here. An introduction to ray-object intersection algorithms may be found in Haines [177], and a thorough survey may be found in Hanrahan [186].

As a simple example of a ray-object intersection, consider the intersection of a ray and a sphere, as shown in Figure 19.32. The ray sweeps out points R along a parametric line defined by $P_0 + P_1 s$, where $0 < s \in \mathcal{R}$. Suppose we have a sphere with center C and radius r; all points P on the surface of the sphere satisfy the equation $(P - C) \cdot (P - C) = r^2$. This is a particularly nice pair of equations, because the ray equation is explicit in the parameter s and the sphere equation is implicit for the point P.

Where the ray and the sphere intersect, both equations are satisfied, which means that there is a value of s that can be plugged into the ray equation that generates a point which satisfies the sphere equation. So we can plug the ray equation into the sphere equation: we find

$$\begin{aligned}
0 &= (P - C) \cdot (P - C) - r^2 \\
&= (P \cdot P) - 2(P \cdot C) + (C \cdot C) - r^2 \\
&= (P_0 + P_1 s) \cdot (P_0 + P_1 s) - 2((P_0 + P_1 s) \cdot C) + (C \cdot C) - r^2 \\
&= s^2(P_1 \cdot P_1) + 2s(P_0 \cdot C) + (P_0 - C)^2 - r^2
\end{aligned} \tag{19.27}$$

This last equation forms a quadratic equation for s with the well-known solutions

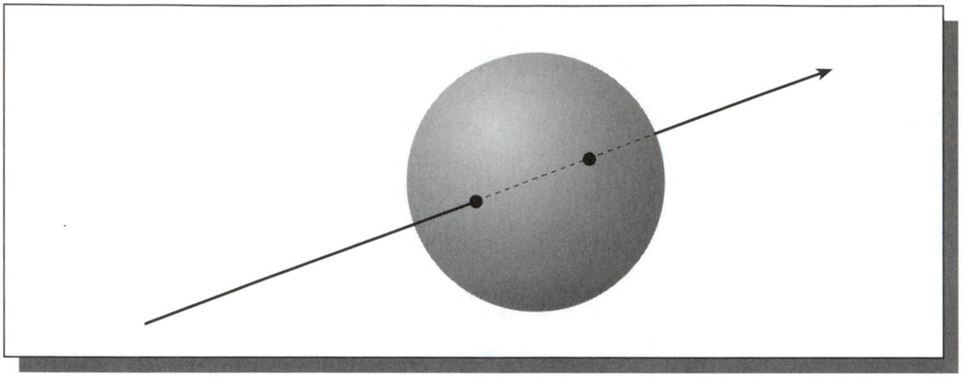

FIGURE 19.32
A ray-sphere intersection.

given by the quadratic formula:

$$s_1 = \frac{-b + d}{2a} \qquad s_2 = \frac{-b - d}{2a} \tag{19.28}$$

where

$$\begin{aligned} a &= (P_1 \cdot P_1) \\ b &= 2(P_0 \cdot C) \\ c &= (P_0 - C)^2 - r^2 \\ d &= \sqrt{b^2 - 4ac} \end{aligned}$$

If the discriminant d is less than zero, then the solutions are imaginary; in geometric terms the ray does not hit the sphere, as shown in Figure 19.33(a). If $d = 0$, then both roots are the same; the ray is tangent to the sphere, as shown in Figure 19.33(b). Finally, if $d > 0$, then there are two real roots, and the ray passes through the sphere, as shown in Figure 19.33(c).

When $d > 0$, we want to select the value of s that is the smallest positive value; this will then give us the point of intersection $P = P_0 + P_1 s$. Note that if the ray starts within the sphere, one value of s will be positive and the other will be negative.

We have presented the simplest algebraic solution to this problem without any concern for efficiency. This method is compared with a more thoughtful approach by Haines [177], who shows that this intersection computation may be significantly optimized by careful analysis.

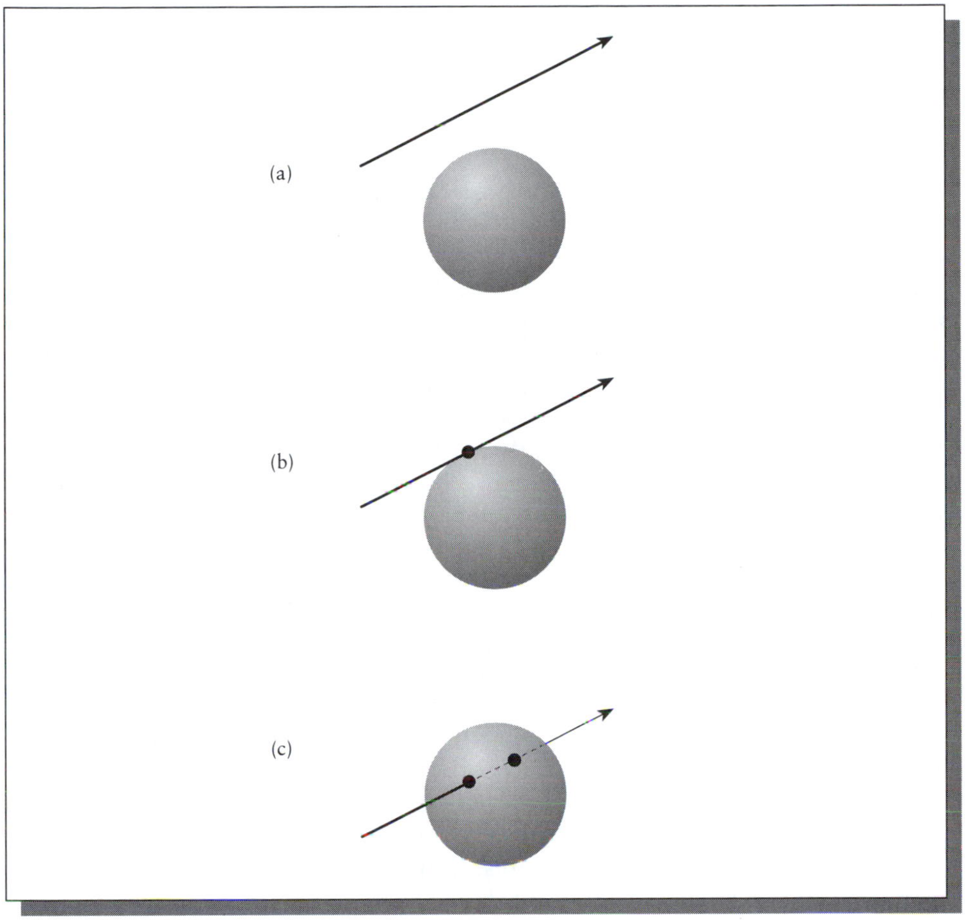

FIGURE 19.33

(a) $d < 0$: The ray misses the sphere. (b) $d = 0$: The ray is tangent to the sphere. (c) $d > 0$: The ray passes through the sphere.

The ray-object intersection routines themselves are notoriously expensive and consume a lot of computer time; a famous statistic due to Whitted is that ray-object intersection calculations occupied 95% of the compute time for images using his original algorithm [477]. As more sophisticated objects are included in scenes and the intersection algorithms grow more complex, the ray-object intersection cost can be expected to grow even larger.

To reduce this expense, a plethora of *acceleration methods* have been designed to speed the process, primarily by eliminating from consideration those objects which certainly cannot be the first intersection object. This exclusion is usually based on the relative geometry of the object and the ray. The methods usually build a data structure which is at least partly in the physical space of the scene, and perhaps also in the phase space of the rays. There are many such acceleration algorithms; a survey is presented by Arvo and Kirk [17].

In general, there are three major approaches to such geometrically based acceleration methods: *bounding volume hierarchies*, *space subdivision*, and *directional subdivision*. Figure 19.34 shows a set of books on a shelf. If we wanted to find the intersection of a ray with these books, the brute-force method would be to compute the intersection of the ray with each book, and then choose the intersection nearest the ray origin. This method would work, but since each intersection test is expensive, then the overall cost could be quite high. Such costs grow surprisingly quickly; a real book has a complicated structure containing many pages, and the front and back cover are generally not perfectly flat polygons but curved in some cases. Intersecting all this geometry can be expensive. And if the bookshelf is replaced by a more complex database, such as the tens of thousands of books on library shelves, then each ray will be prohibitively expensive to trace.

One way to speed up the intersection test is to place a *bounding volume* around the books. For example, suppose we place a single large box around all the books. The test for intersecting a ray with a box is relatively cheap compared to intersecting the ray with a book. So when the ray approaches the books, we test it against the box; if the ray misses the box, it certainly misses everything inside, and we need not test any books at all. We have successfully *culled* this entire set of books from the *candidate list* of objects that might represent the first intersections with this ray.

In fact, we can build a *hierarchy* of these bounding volumes, nesting one inside the other, a strategy originally suggested for ray tracing by Rubin and Whitted [363]. Figure 19.35 shows a couple of levels in this subdivision. When the ray first reaches the box, we can test it against the root of the hierarchy, representing the large enclosing box. If the ray misses the root, then we look no further inside this particular hierarchy. But if the ray does intersect the box, then we must look inside. Rather than plunge immediately into intersecting all the books, however, we can test the ray against the two sub-boxes shown in Figure 19.35(a). The ray will strike one of these boxes before the other, so we can look inside the nearer box first. If we don't

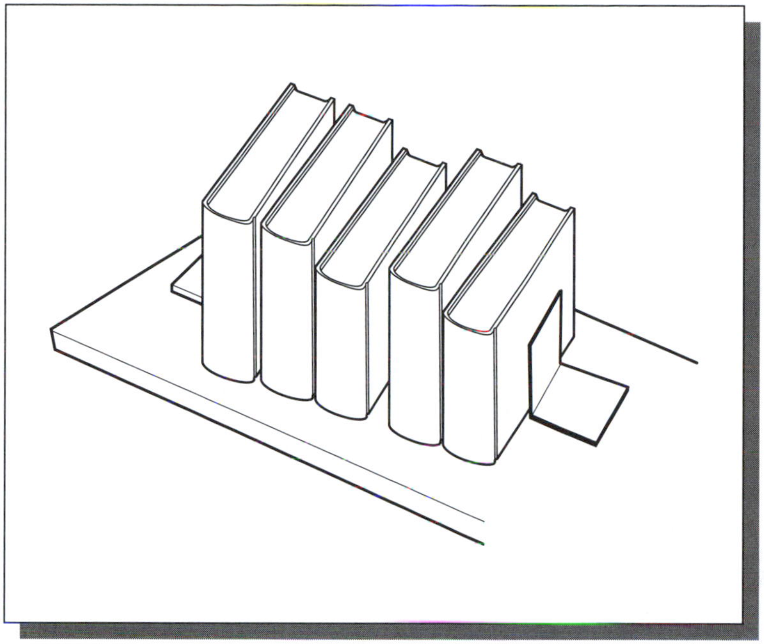

FIGURE 19.34
A set of books on a shelf.

intersect any of the books in this nearer box, then we can look inside the other. This process may be applied recursively; Figure 19.35(b) shows another step.

In general, such methods build the hierarchy from the bottom up, first organizing groups of objects into small clusters, and then clustering the clusters to build a tree. The classical method for this construction is due to Goldsmith and Salmon [163]; a particularly efficient set of bounding volumes are discussed by Kay and Kajiya [243]. A common characteristic of bounding-volume hierarchies is that they tend to keep objects within a single bounding volume.

Another approach to accelerating the first-intersection test is to subdivide the space in which the model is embedded. Figure 19.36 shows the books inside a regular 3D grid of cells. When we build this grid, we attach to each cell a list of all the objects that are inside it. Note that the objects need not be cut up by this process; a single object may reside in multiple cells simultaneously. When a ray strikes the edge of this grid, we determine which cell it enters first, and look for intersections with objects in that cell. If no intersections are found, the ray is *propagated* to the

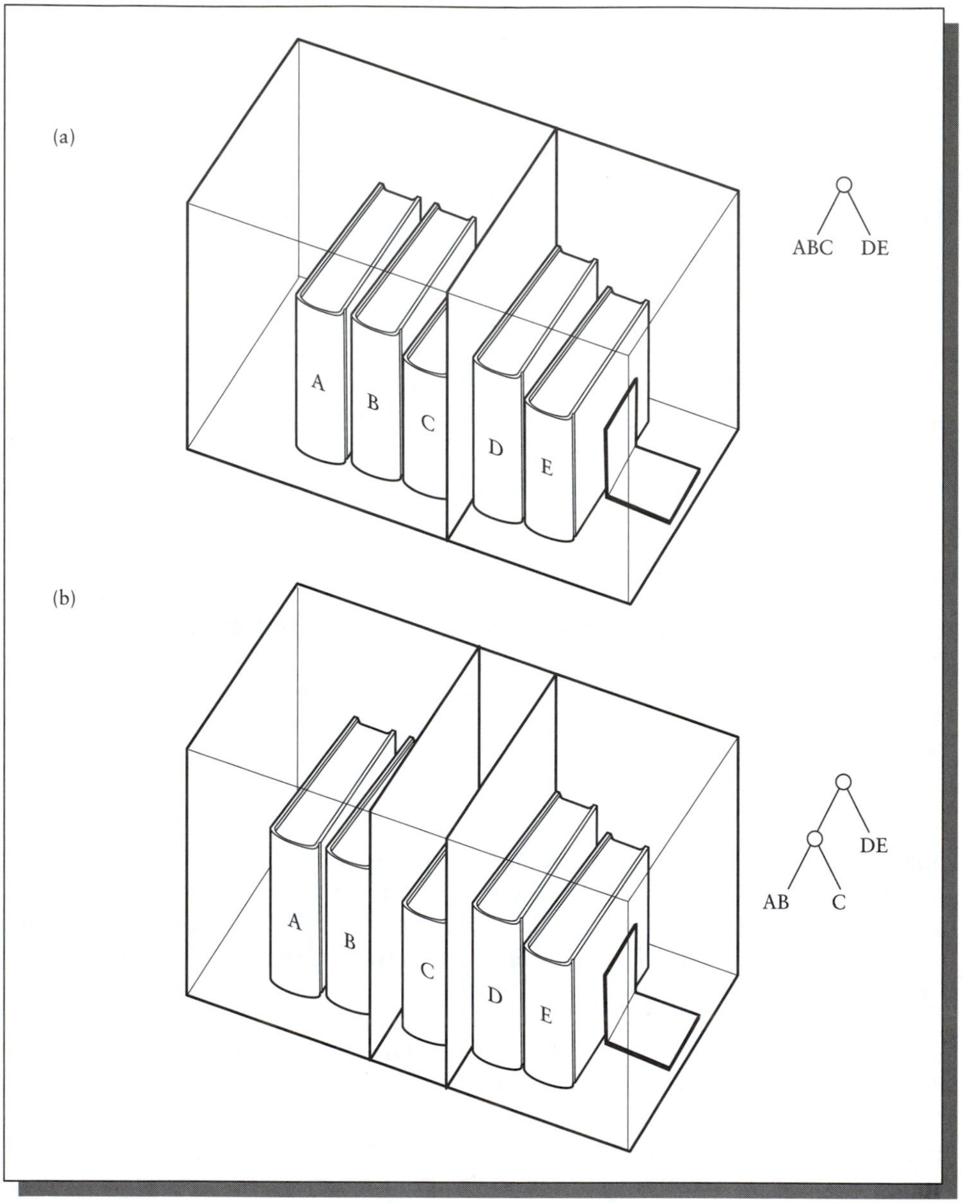

FIGURE 19.35

(a) The second level in the bounding volume hierarchy. (b) The third level.

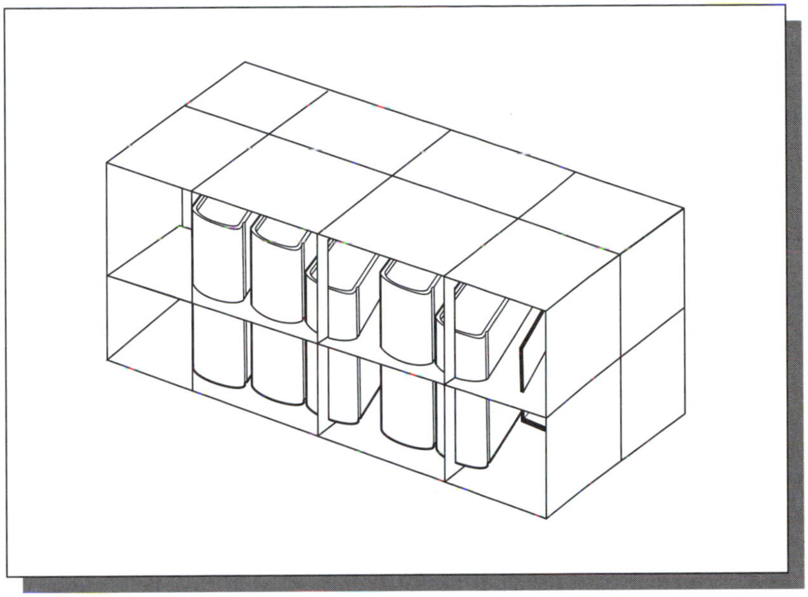

FIGURE 19.36

A space-based subdivision.

next cell and the objects there are tested. If the ray does intersect one or more objects *inside the cell*, the nearest such intersection is easy to find. Because objects can reside in multiple cells, we need to make sure that a ray-object intersection really occurs within the given cell.

This method was introduced for ray tracing by Glassner [153], Kaplan [241], and Fujimoto et al. [150]. Both Glassner and Kaplan subdivided space using an octree, while Fujimoto et al. used a regular grid. A feature of the octree is that it is able to adapt to local variation in object density; where there are many objects in a region of space, there can be many octree cells, so each cell contains only a small number of objects. In large empty areas we can pass through large quantities of space with a single step through a large cell. Unfortunately, this nonuniformity requires some processing in order to advance the ray from one cell to the next, because two consecutive cells visited by the ray may have different sizes. On the other hand, it is easy to advance a ray from one cell to the next in a regular grid; in fact, it can be done with integer arithmetic. But each cell now contains however many objects fall within it, and to traverse empty regions, we must take many steps through empty

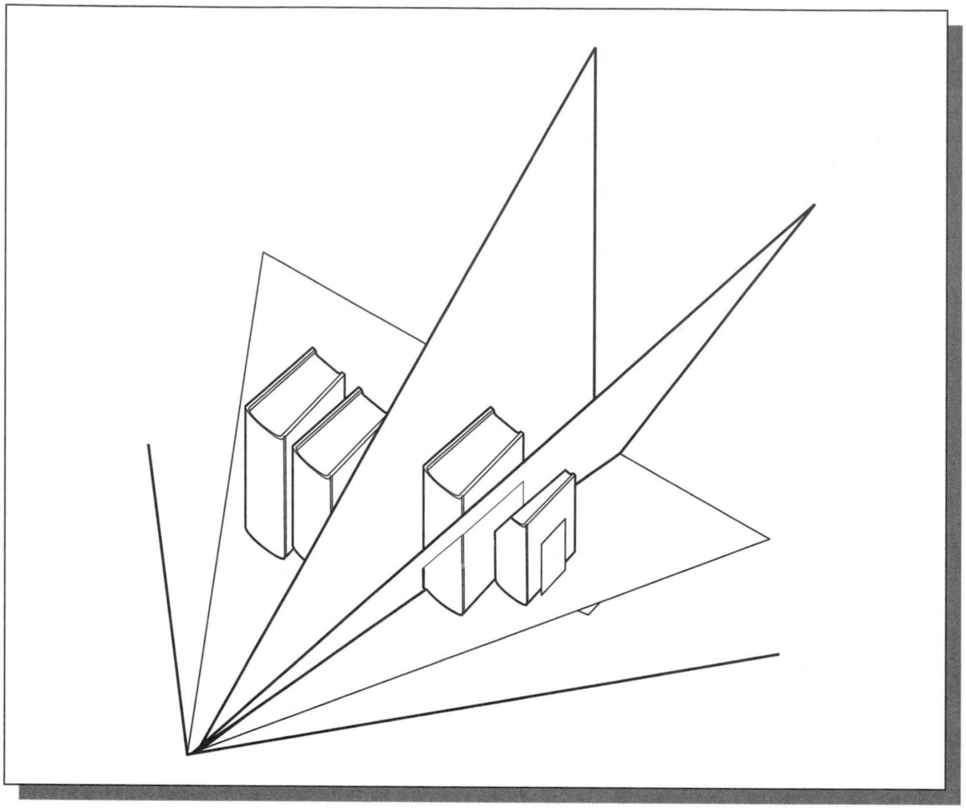

FIGURE 19.37
A direction-based subdivision.

cells. The choice of whether to use adaptive or uniform subdivision must be made based on the scene to be rendered and the characteristics of the implementation and the computer; a comparison of these methods is given by MacDonald [278].

Finally, we can subdivide based not only on the spatial characteristics of the database, but also on the directional distribution of the rays that sample it. This idea was originally used by Arvo and Kirk [16] in an algorithm that combined space subdivision with directional subdivision. Figure 19.37 shows a simple subdivision of the environment into small volumes that correspond to different directions that may be followed by a ray from a common origin. Arvo and Kirk developed a multidimensional subdivision method that built the subdivision cells dynamically as the scene was being rendered.

This brief discussion has only hinted at the wealth of algorithms developed for accelerating ray-object intersections; the interested reader is encouraged to consult the references for much more detail.

Once the first ray-object intersection has been found, we need to determine the light leaving the intersection point s and returning to the eye point E. In general, we assume that the shading point is being queried by a ray that carries light away from the point in an outgoing direction $\vec{\omega}^o$. Note that using our convention, this outgoing direction is opposite to the direction of the ray which struck s; that is, $\vec{\omega}^o = -(P - E)$.

To compute the shading at this point s, we use OVTIGRE from Equation 17.16:

$$\begin{aligned} L(\mathbf{r}, \vec{\omega}^o) &= L^e(\mathbf{s}, \vec{\omega}^o) + L^p(\mathbf{s}, \vec{\omega}^o) \\ &= L^e(\mathbf{s}, \vec{\omega}^o) + \int_{\Theta_i^i} f(\mathbf{r}, \vec{\omega} \to \vec{\omega}^o, \lambda) L(\mathbf{r}, \vec{\omega}) \cos\theta_r \, d\vec{\omega} \end{aligned} \tag{19.29}$$

The emission term $L^e(\mathbf{s}, \vec{\omega}^o)$ we can find directly from the surface definition at s.

Distribution ray tracing uses a particular form of the stratification technique discussed earlier to compute the propagated term $L^p(\vec{\omega}, \vec{\omega}^o)$. We subdivide it into two separate integrals, one over the set of directions representing the luminaires (that is, direct light), and the other over the set of all other directions (that is, the indirect light). Since they combine to make Θ_i^i, the direct set Γ^d and the indirect set Γ^i must together form the set of all incident directions: $\Gamma^d \cup \Gamma^i = \Theta_i^i$. So the propagated term may be written

$$L^p(\mathbf{s}, \vec{\omega}^o) = \int_{\Gamma^d} f(\mathbf{r}, \vec{\omega} \to \vec{\omega}^o, \lambda) L(\mathbf{r}, \vec{\omega}) \cos\theta_r \, d\vec{\omega} + \int_{\Gamma^i} f(\mathbf{r}, \vec{\omega} \to \vec{\omega}^o, \lambda) L(\mathbf{r}, \vec{\omega}) \cos\theta_r \, d\vec{\omega} \tag{19.30}$$

The direct set Γ^d is found by identifying the luminaires and stratifying them into the sets G_d. These surface strata are then converted to direction strata using $\Gamma^d = \Pi(G_d)$, as in Figure 19.14. Then from above, the complement of the direct light with respect to the incident sphere is the indirect light: $\Gamma^i = \Theta_i^i - \Gamma^d$. We can use any integration method to estimate these integrals. Using the ray tracing approach we can find the direct contribution by sending rays from s to each of the strata on the luminaires. Those that are blocked by other objects are added to the indirect component. Notice that this knowledge of a blocking object can be used to help us refine the visible stratum on the luminaire.

To estimate the indirect contribution, we can send out a variety of rays in different directions, using a combination of explicit strata and importance sampling. This is illustrated in Figure 19.38. This sampling may be generated and adaptively refined using any of the uniform or nonuniform methods in Chapter 10; each of those methods yields an algorithm with different performance features.

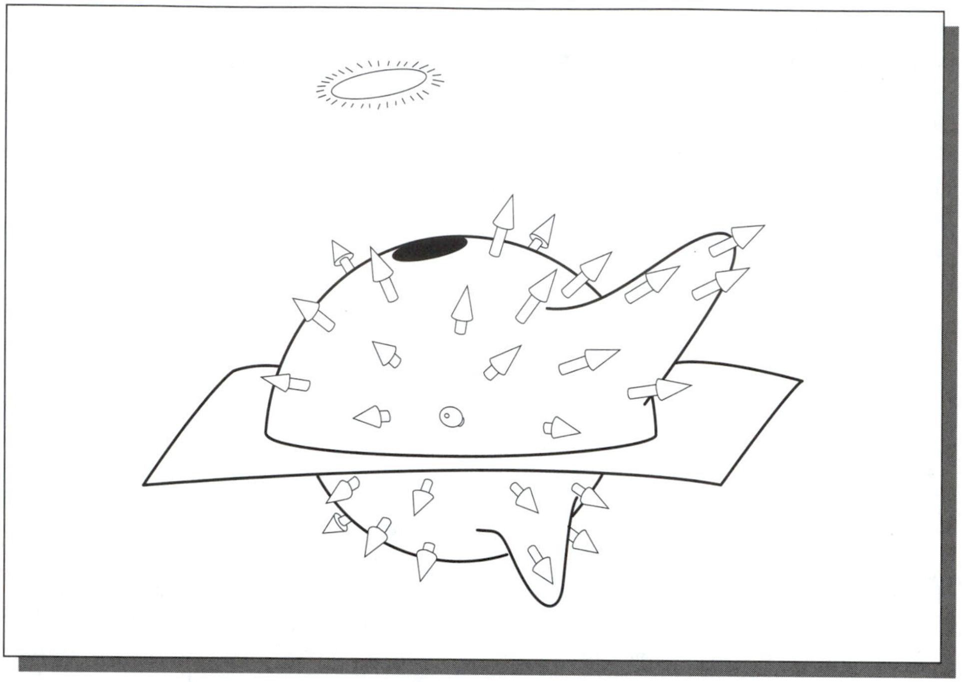

FIGURE 19.38
Sampling the indirect contribution.

The recursive generation of samples continues until it is explicitly stopped. There are many reasons to stop the recursion: the ray may strike a fully absorbing surface, it may escape from the environment (by hitting the enclosure sphere), or it may be terminated. Termination criteria for random walks were discussed in Chapter 16; the important thing to note is that as a sample moves deeper into the environment, it will make less of a contribution with each step, and eventually the contribution to the radiance at L will be so small that the sample can be considered negligible. To avoid introducing bias, we can't simply stop at some cutoff, so a technique such as Russian roulette should be used to determine when to terminate a ray.

Once all the samples have been generated and their intersection points evaluated, the BDF is applied to the irradiance, which is simply the radiance along each sample times the cosine of the angle of incidence of the sample. The resulting propagated light is then added to the emitted light, and that's the radiance that is sent back away from s in the direction $\vec{\omega}^o$, back along the ray that struck s, though in the opposite direction.

An example of this sequence in action is shown in Figure 19.2. The rays form a *ray tree*, with the lens point as the root and each intersection point represented as a node. The arcs in the tree represent the rays themselves. We build the tree from the top down, starting at the lens and determining the intersections with objects as we work our way into the environment. Then we pass shading information back up, starting at the leaves and combining propagated with reflected light until we make it back up to the lens, where the information can be stored as a screen sample.

We need to keep in mind at all steps in this process that we're using samples to represent a continuous signal; the problems of undersampling, and thus aliasing, crop up all along the way and must be addressed through appropriate choice of sampling density, prefiltering of the database, or nonuniform distributions of sample points to trade structured aliasing artifacts for structure-free noise. We want to avoid structured errors even in the illumination estimates (which we normally never see directly) because they are propagated in a nonuniform way by the BDF at the surface. If there is a particularly bad artifact right where the signal has great influence, the effect of that artifact can be greatly multiplied. The best bet is to keep the average error in any region low. So although we noted in Unit II that a noisy signal may have the same overall error as a signal containing structured aliases, it distributes that error more uniformly, and thus is more appropriate for this sort of application.

The explosion of rays in this algorithm is considerable: we said that a complete sampling of a six-dimensional parameter space of rays with a density of n samples required n^6 rays at the screen per pixel, and each of those rays may create many new rays at each ray-object intersection. The whole process can be brought under control by using *incomplete block sampling*. Consider just the two variables (x, y) that describe an image location. If we subdivide each axis into four pieces, this implies that we need sixteen samples to sample the domain, as shown in Figure 19.39(a).

Suppose that rather than require a completely filled block, we only require that the marginal distribution of the block on each axis be filled; that is, there must be one sample in each of the x strata and each of the y strata. We need only four samples to do this job; Figure 19.39(b) gives an example. The pattern in Figure 19.39(b) is highly *correlated*, which can produce errors (recall our discussion of Figure 10.44). As we saw in Chapter 10, there are a variety of ways to distribute samples in this grid that avoid producing correlated patterns. This same idea can be extended to any number of dimensions, so that for an n-dimensional space, where each axis has been subdivided into s pieces, we need only s well-chosen samples.

A summary overview of the entire ray-tracing process is shown in Figure 19.40.

Figure 19.41 (color plate) shows an example of an image produced by distributed ray tracing. Note the soft shadows, produced by numerically integrating over the solid angles occupied by finite light sources, and the motion blur, produced by numerical integration over the time duration of the exposure.

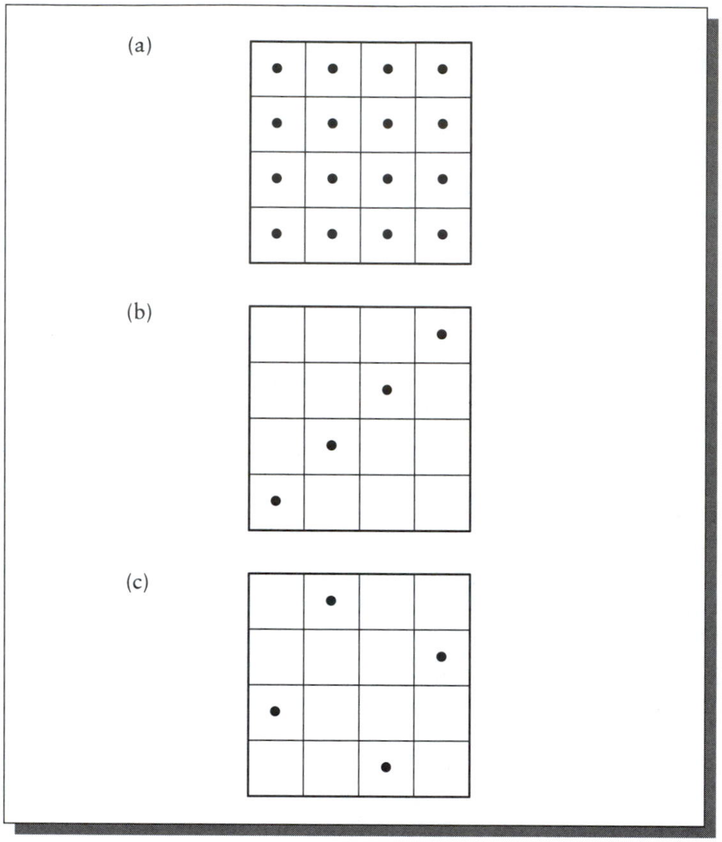

FIGURE 19.39
(a) Complete block sampling. (b) Structured incomplete block sampling. (c) Unstructured incomplete block sampling.

Gathering indirect illumination by distribution ray tracing is very expensive. To cut down on the cost, Ward et al. save this information each time it is computed [470]. When a ray samples a surface, they first look around to see if there are one or more nearby, already computed indirect illumination signals. If so, they are interpolated to produce a signal at the shading point. The assumption is that indirect illumination arrives mostly from diffusely reflecting surfaces, and that the light received from such surfaces changes little as we move about on a receiving surface. Figure 20.4 shows an image generated with this approach.

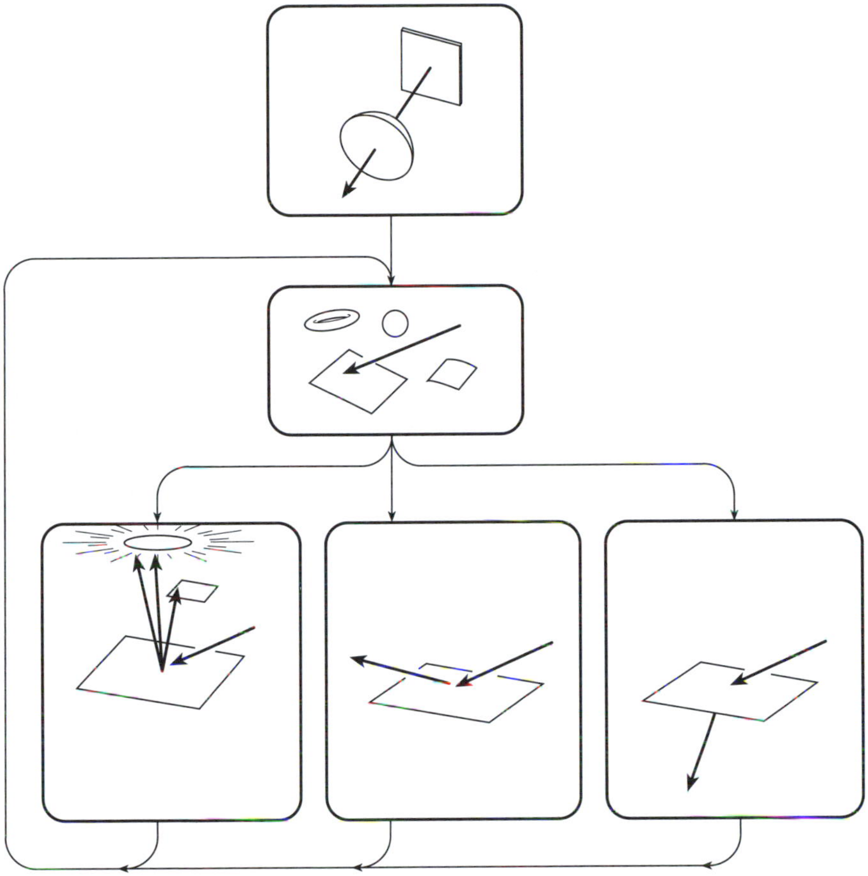

FIGURE 19.40

An overview of distributed ray tracing.

19.3.4 Discussion

The advantages of beam and cone tracing are that they are able to dynamically create and evaluate entire surface strata at once. This can be very efficient, particularly with the use of constant-time filtering methods such as *mip-maps* [480] and *sum tables* [111].

On the other hand, the geometry of reflection and refraction is difficult to model accurately with these methods, and in complex databases the shapes of the strata may become very complex; this can lead to highly fragmented beams and large numbers of cones in order to match oddly shaped solid angles. More discussion of the geometry of beam tracing may be found in Dadoun et al. [114].

The point-sampling methods of classical ray tracing, distribution ray tracing, and path tracing all stratify the environment on the fly, differently for every sample taken. This is sufficiently expensive that the stratification is usually quite coarse: the brightest luminaires generate surface strata, and a few reflection and transmission strata are generated. Resolution is performed on the fly when an indirect sample strikes a luminaire. Path tracing is attractive because it does not produce *bushy trees*. Note that distribution ray tracing (and classical ray tracing) create ray trees that tend to get thicker as they grow deeper, because many rays are generated at each intersection. Kajiya has observed that the rays at the bottom of the tree are the ones that contribute the least to the final image [234], so we're spending the most amount of time and work where it has the least impact on the result. Path tracing places as many rays at the root as it does deeper in the tree, but because the stratification is so sparse (a single point) for each intersection, path tracing typically requires more rays overall than distribution ray tracing for an image of the same error with respect to an ideal reference.

Because the ray-tracing methods discussed here do not explicitly construct strata, they must do so implicitly in order to find the radiance returned by the stratum along the ray that samples it. One common approach is to simply propagate the degenerate strata approach throughout the environment: each sample is a point and all other points may be ignored. We know from signal processing that this method of point sampling can lead to undersampling, and hence aliasing. To reduce structured aliasing, the points can be generated in a nonuniform pattern, but we can still miss large structures. It would be convenient to combine the explicit surface stratification of the solid-angle approaches with the dynamic sampling of the ray-tracing approaches.

Such a combination has been suggested by Glassner [158]. In this approach, any ray-tracing method is used to sample the incident light until the signal is considered acceptable. During this process, the complete ray-object intersection tree of each ray is recorded. When sampling is complete, the illumination information computed in the ray-tracing pass is discarded, and the trees are retraversed (since all the intersections have been stored, this traversal requires no new intersections). At each node, the complete distribution of samples on all objects intersected from that node (including luminaires) is used to induce a stratification on the environment, as shown in Figure 19.42. Notice that the rays that extend into the environment past the first-intersected object help to refine the visible strata on objects farther away, including those on the backs of objects. The radiance sent from each surface stratum to the shading point is then estimated, and this is used as the incident radiance at

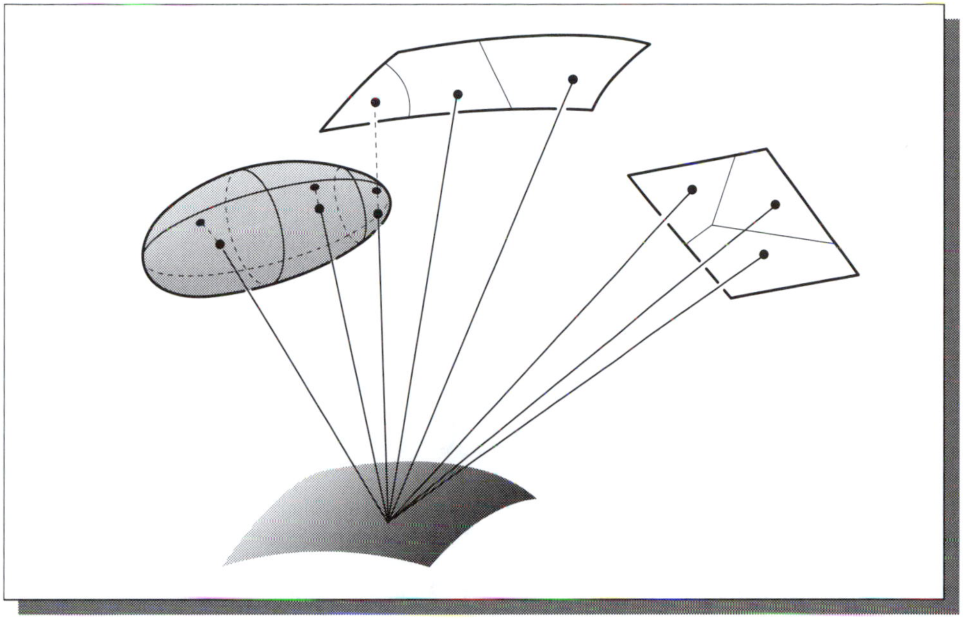

FIGURE 19.42
Dynamic stratification.

that point. To find these propagated radiances may require descending the tree and inducing new, unique sampling patterns on the environment from the subnodes.

19.4 Photon Tracing

Photon tracing involves generating photons at the light sources in a scene and distributing them into the environment. Each photon has an associated frequency ν (and thus energy E, related by $E = h\nu$). If we really traced individual photons in an environment we would never get a picture made in practical time; each photon simply carries far too little energy. Furthermore, in a complex scene many photons will be absorbed before striking a surface that will make a contribution to an image from a given point of view.

In 1968 Appel published an algorithm where random photons were followed from the light source, and the first point intersected by a photon was projected to the virtual screen. Rather than store the image in computer memory, Appel directly

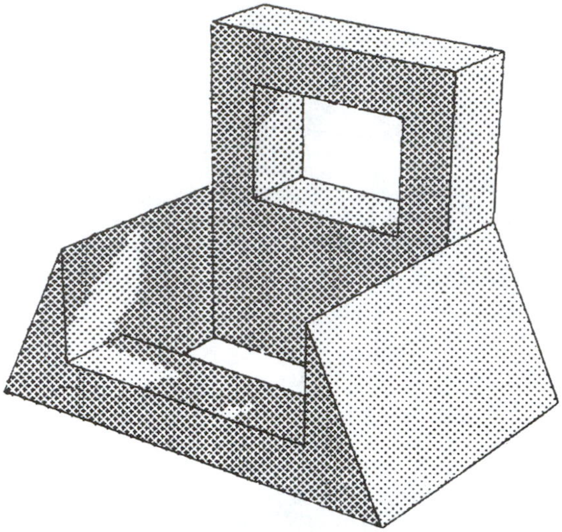

FIGURE 19.43

A shaded drawing of a machine part produced by photon tracing. Reprinted, by permission, from Appel in *AFIPS 1968 Spring Joint Computer Conference*, fig. 14, p. 44.

drew results as they were computed on a plotter [11]. If the point wasn't blocked by any other object between itself and the screen, a dot was placed by the plotter at the appropriate location. After enough dots had been projected, a photonegative of the image would have white areas in regions of high illumination and black areas where illumination levels were low. Figure 19.43 shows an example of this procedure on a machine part, where the rays were generated in a regular pattern, and a plus sign was used instead of a dot. Notice the complex shadows created by light passing through the hole. This method doesn't generalize well for complex scenes, and it fails to take any indirect illumination into account.

A common optimization for this approach is to assume that not just one, but millions of photons or more are produced by the light source in each direction per unit of time. Then, as those photons enter into the environment, we can speak of what happens to the aggregate collection, rather than individual particles.

For example, suppose that 100 photons leave a source in the direction of a receiving patch, and they all arrive. If the patch is a purely diffuse reflector with reflectivity $\rho = 0.6$, then on average six of ten photons will be reflected, and four of ten will be absorbed. If we traced the photons individually, then each time a photon struck the patch, we would either absorb or reflect that photon, with a 40% chance of absorption. The absorbed photons do nothing for us except make the patch a bit warmer (which can influence its thermal emission in the visible band if the heat gets high enough). Except for this possible influence on the heat radiated by the patch, the computationally expensive process of following this absorbed photon has been wasted. It's better to follow a packet of photons, absorb 40% of them, and then follow the path of the remaining 60%.

The direct simulation of photons streaming from the light source into the environment has been studied in detail by Pattanaik [332] and Pattanaik and Mudur [333, 334]. They generate photons at the sources using importance sampling, in order to make sure that the distribution of photons into the environment matches the energy distribution of the luminaire. Each time a photon (or photon packet) strikes a surface, the location of the intersection must be stored, and the amount of energy reflected (and transmitted) at that point must be recorded on an *illumination map* [13]. An example of the simulation is shown in Figure 19.44 (color plate).

In general, every photon-surface intersection will be at a different point, so we have a seemingly impossible storage task. Pattanaik and Mudur instead discretize (or mesh) the environment prior to rendering, just as in radiosity [333]. All of the intersections and reflections within a patch are lumped together, and the re-emission of energy from the patch is determined by this aggregate result. Rather than save samples on a surface, Chattopadhyay and Fujimoto store the values in the nodes of a 3D grid in which the scene is immersed [80].

Deciding how many photons to shoot, where to shoot them from, and where to shoot them to are difficult issues. For example, consider a patch that reflects some of its incident light via diffuse reflection; in which directions should this light be propagated into the environment? Pattanaik uses importance (or potential) to help answer this question; thorough details are presented in [332]. This allows a very natural progressive refinement interpretation of the scene: at any moment during the simulation, we have accounted for some percentage of the photons that are traveling in the environment. We can render an image by simply looking up the number of photons which are radiated from each surface at this moment; waiting a bit longer will allow more photons to distribute, and therefore produce a more accurate simulation. The use of importance helps drive the simulation toward distribution photons where they will make the most impact on an image.

19.5 Bidirectional Ray-Tracing Methods

Visibility tracing and photon tracing may be combined into a *multipass ray-tracing* algorithm.

The inspiration for this combination comes from the observation that visibility tracing is very poor at finding a good estimate for the indirect illumination on a point. Recall that we simply lumped together all the indirect illumination into some solid angle Γ^i, and said that some integration method would be needed to evaluate

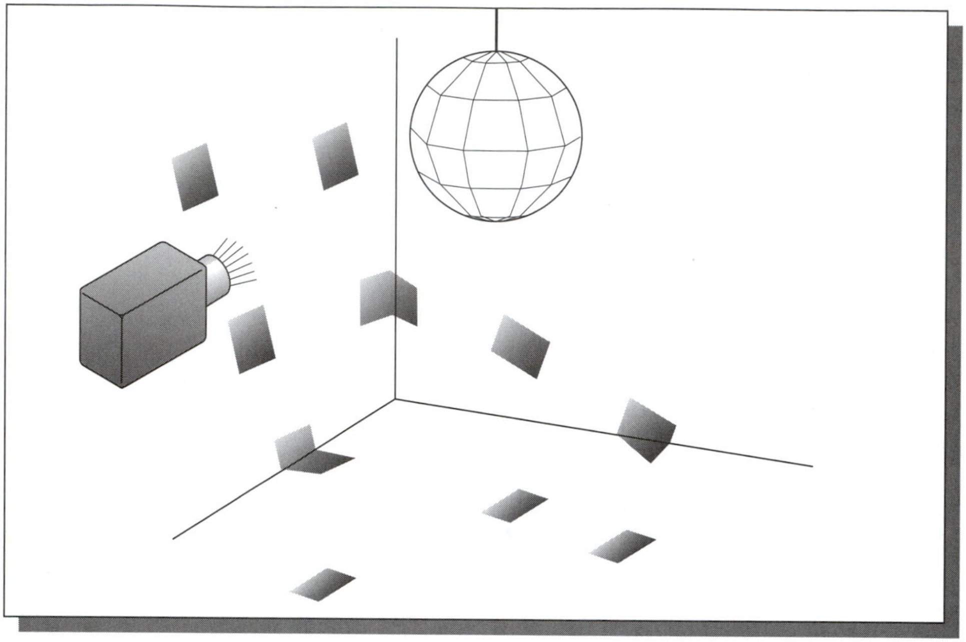

FIGURE 19.45
A mirrored ball in a room.

the illumination in this solid angle. Because potentially every object in the scene is visible to the point, lending it indirect illumination, it would take a great many rays to evaluate this indirect signal accurately. Typically some effort is made, but the error threshold is set very high, so that only a few samples are taken for this term.

A challenging case for visibility ray tracing is a mirrored ball hanging in a room, as shown in Figure 19.45. A bright, tightly directed red spotlight shines on the ball, and the tiny mirrored facets on the ball reflect that light in many different directions. Eventually each mirror creates a small patch of illumination on a wall of the room. Now imagine a person wearing white cotton clothing (that is, primarily diffuse) is standing near the wall, between two of these patches (but not blocking either one from the ball). Suppose that the walls are coated with a diffusely reflecting white paint. We would expect to see the bright red light from the wall partly illuminate the person's white clothing, causing spread-out red regions. This is called *color bleeding*.

Consider trying to render this scene using visibility ray tracing. From the eye (or lens), rays are fired into the scene; suppose one of them struck one of the patches of clothing that we would expect to be red. How is visibility ray tracing going to find that red light? Direct-illumination rays will probably be sent to the light source, but they will be blocked by the light's enclosure. Unless we're coming into the clothing at a very grazing angle, it will not reflect much light via specular reflection, so we're left with estimating the indirect illumination. The problem is that we simply don't know where significant indirect illumination might be arriving from, so we must simply sample randomly and hope to hit something useful.

Of many visibility rays fired in the directions around this spot on the clothing, a few will probably hit the wall. Suppose we are lucky enough to hit one of the red spots. The problem now becomes one of finding the source of the bright red illumination on this patch of the wall; we have the same problem as before, since the wall is a diffuse reflector itself. Since the mirror that is causing this illumination occupies a very small solid angle from this point on the wall, it is unlikely that we will hit it by random sampling of the environment. The chance of getting a complete path from the clothing to the red spot on the wall to the mirror is not zero, but it is small. In practice, visibility tracing will in general fail to find this illumination.

Note that in situations like this we might be able to fix the odds; if there are only a few specular surfaces in the room, then we can try each one as a possible source of illumination. In other words, we create strata on the specular surfaces and then sample those strata as direct sources rather than as part of the overall indirect illumination solid angle. Then we would hit one of the mirrors, and the specular reflection from there would take us to the light source. Following the chain back in the opposite direction, the light will finally make it to the white clothing. But if there are lots of specular surfaces, then this method becomes impractical.

Instead of visibility tracing, we try photon ray tracing. A common use of photon ray tracing is just like classical ray tracing in reverse: we generate photons from the light source and follow them into the scene. If a photon strikes a specular surface, then we reflect it and continue following it. When the photon strikes a diffuse surface, we simply deposit its energy at that point on the surface and stop following that energy bundle.

A convenient way to describe the chain of events experienced by a ray of light is to use a notation introduced by Heckbert [202] which builds a short string of symbols representing creation, absorption, and the various intervening states. Emission of a photon from a light source is written L, and absorption at the eye (or intersection with the image plane) is written E. Along the way from L to E the photon may interact with a volume V, it may be specularly reflected or transmitted S, or it may be diffusely reflected or transmitted D. The sequence is written left to right over time, so when they appear, L is the first character and E is the last. We use standard computer-science regular expression symbology [271] to indicate compound expressions: subexpressions may be grouped in parentheses, an asterisk superscript $*$ represents 0 or more repetitions, and a plus-sign superscript $+$ represents 1 or more repetitions. A term in square brackets is optional; it may be included or not. The vertical bar | represents a selection among members; when a group is repeated, the selection may be different on each repetition. For example, $(S|V)^*$ represents an empty sequence, and the sequences S, V, SSV, $VSSVSVV$, and so on.

Classical ray tracing only models specular reflections and transmissions (both represented by the letter S) in vacuum, so it can be described as modeling $L[D]S^*E$ paths, illustrated in Figure 19.46. We call $L[D]S^*E$ the *characteristic expression* for the classical ray-tracing model. In words, there are four different types of strings that this expression can generate, and hence the same number of different light paths that can be captured by the classical ray-tracing model: LE, LDE, LS^*E, and LDS^*E.

The expression LE corresponds to light that is directly visible from the eye; this represents rays that look directly upon a light source, as shown in Figure 19.46(a). A path of the form LDE represents the light from a source directly striking a diffusely reflecting surface which is immediately visible, as shown in Figure 19.46(b). Strings of the form LSE, $LSSE$, $LSSSE$, and so on, represent light that has been captured at the eye after specular reflection off of a series of surfaces, as shown in Figure 19.46(c). Finally, a string such as $LDSSE$ represents light that has been diffusely reflected and then specularly reflected twice before reaching the eye, as shown in Figure 19.46(d).

The form of the characteristic expression $L[D]S^*E$ is directly related to the classical ray-tracing algorithm. We know that all paths end at the eye, E. As we search into the environment, we may strike a specularly reflecting surface. Direct illumination arriving at that surface and reflected to the eye is represented LSE. Indirect light is of the form $L \cdots SE$, where the dots indicate some series of interactions. Suppose that we strike another specular surface; then the direct light upon that surface is specularly reflected *twice* before reaching the eye, represented by the path $LSSE$, and indirect light follows a path $L \cdots SSE$. Suppose that the next surface is diffuse. In classical ray tracing we simply gather only direct illumination at this point and bring it back to the eye, creating the path $LDSSE$. All of these paths are captured in the characteristic expression for classical ray tracing.

Distribution ray tracing can in theory capture all possible paths; that is, $L(S|D)^*E$. In practice, however, the capturing of diffuse information is sufficiently expensive that it is rarely carried out explicitly. However, near-specular reflection and transmission (gloss and translucency) are well modeled by this method, so we write its characteristic expression as $L[D]G^*E$, where the specular term S has been replaced by the *glossy* term G.

Photon ray tracing, on the other hand, generates paths of the form $LS^*[D][E]$. In words, we start at the light and progress into the environment. If we strike a specular surface, we propagate the light (by reflection or transmission) to the next surface. When we strike a diffusely reflecting surface we stop, since it is unclear where to best propagate the energy. Notice that these paths don't necessarily end at the eye; that's because a ray may be absorbed rather than propagated.

Suppose that we use photon tracing to carry light from the sources to the environment, and visibility tracing to gather radiance from the environment and bring it

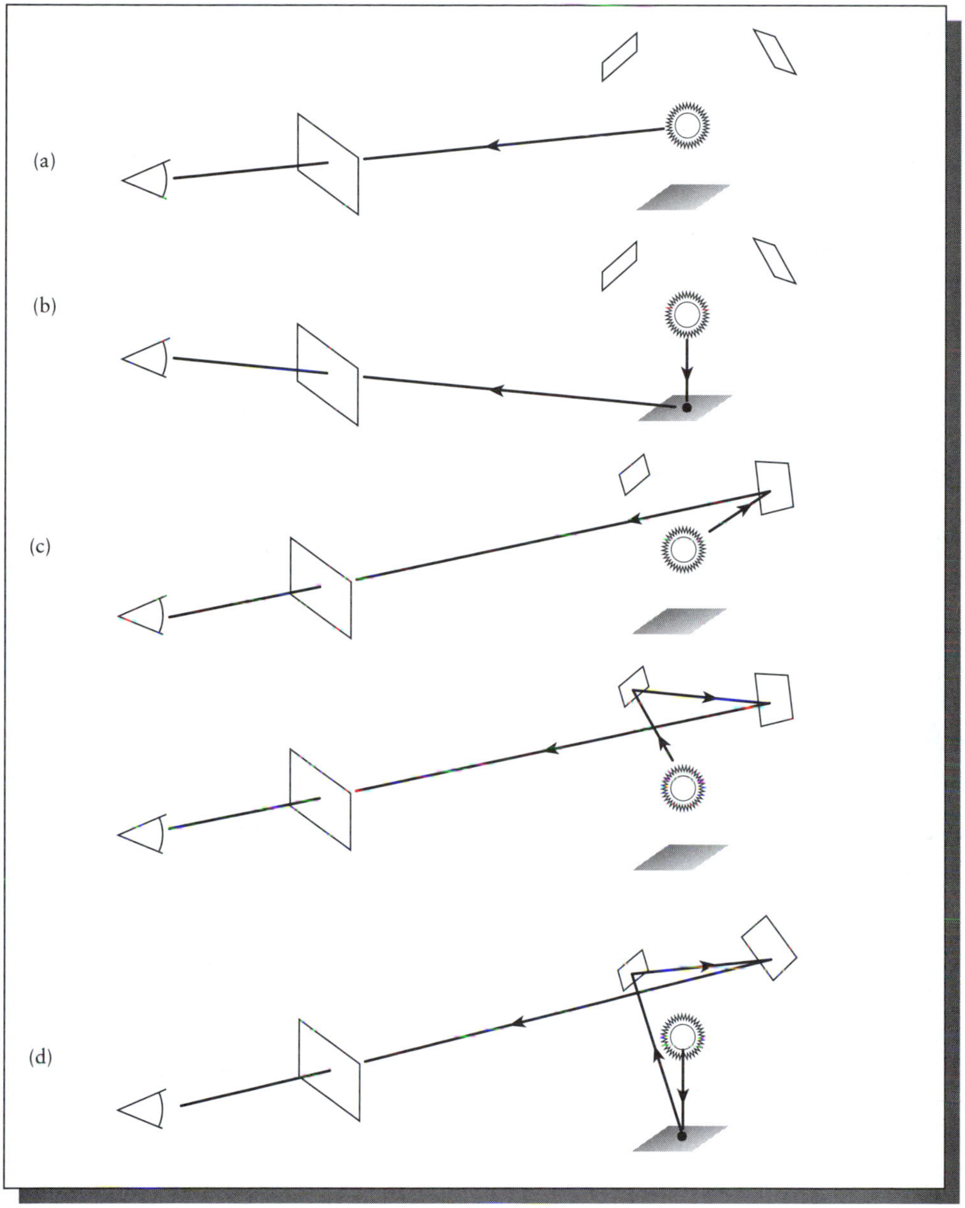

FIGURE 19.46

Paths modeled by classical ray tracing. (a) *LE*. (b) *LDE*. (c) *LSE* and *LSSE*. (d) *LDSSE*.

back to the eye. Then the visibility paths need not start with L, since the distribution of the energy on the diffuse surfaces has already been accounted for; in other words, when striking a diffuse surface, we have already computed the direct illumination. Then the photon tracing paths $LS^*[D][E]$ and the visibility paths $[D]S^*E$ "meet in the middle" [202] to create paths $LS^*[D]S^*E$. This isn't quite the full range of possible expressions, but it's more than either algorithm can produce alone.

This type of combination is called a *bidirectional ray-tracing* algorithm, since rays have been traced in both directions after both algorithms have been executed.

Bidirectional ray-tracing algorithms were introduced by Arvo [13], and further developed by Chattopadhyay and Fujimoto [80], Heckbert [202, 207], Pattanaik [332], Pattanaik and Mudur [333, 334], and Ward et al. [470].

Figure 19.47 (color plate) shows an example result of Heckbert's algorithm. The reflection on the bottom of the ball of the bright highlight on the ground is an example of a $LSDSSE$ path, the richest type of path this algorithm can generate. In this image the meshing on the ground plane has not been smoothed, so the discrete (and nonuniform) nature of the received illumination during the photon tracing pass is easy to see.

19.6 Hybrid Algorithms

Bidirectional ray-tracing algorithms are a member of a larger class of synthesis algorithms called *hybrid algorithms* or *multipass algorithms*. The inspiration behind two-pass techniques is to observe that classical radiosity and classical ray tracing have complementary strengths and weaknesses.

The power of classical ray tracing comes from the fact that the illumination signal is computed anew for each shading point. The direct light sources are stratified and sampled, and the indirect environment is sampled (or approximated from prior evaluations). This means that the method can capture sharp shadows; when a point no longer sees a source, it falls automatically into shadow, and if the source is sufficiently small, the shadow will be sharp. Specular reflections and refractions are also easily captured, since the proper illumination directions are evaluated when needed. All of these components of the illumination signal may be refined adaptively to any level of precision and confidence.

The weak spot in classical ray tracing is that indirect illumination information is very expensive to evaluate accurately. This information comes from everywhere in the environment, and since we can only follow point samples, a complex environment requires many such samples. Significant sources of light can be missed if they aren't luminaires themselves; the brightly focused light or *caustic* created by a lens on a surface can be difficult to find if the shading point doesn't query the lens directly. We can specifically search out the specular surfaces, but illumination from multiple diffuse reflections is prohibitively costly.

On the other hand, classical radiosity algorithms excel at the evaluation of indirect illumination, particularly that produced by multiple diffuse reflection. This gives rise to soft shadows and *color-bleeding*, where the diffuse reflection of one colored patch influences the color of another patch. Each source that radiates energy is considered a first-class light source to the program; each patch is evaluated by the energy it radiates, not its diffuse or specular characteristics.

The weak spot in classical radiosity is the handling of high-frequency detail. This is mostly due to the meshing that is at the heart of the radiosity technique: the resolution of the mesh limits the granularity of the representation of the radiance signal. No incident illumination can be computed with resolution greater than that of the mesh, and no propagated light can be distributed with any more precision than the mesh provides.

The strengths and weaknesses of ray tracing and radiosity are complementary, and it seems reasonable to expect that a single algorithm that employs both methods should be superior to either one individually. This is the philosophy behind *hybrid algorithms*. Typically such algorithms are implemented by a sequence of radiosity and ray-tracing steps, and are therefore called *multipass algorithms*. When only two passes are used, one has a *two-pass algorithm*.

The essence of all hybrid algorithms is that all the different types of light transport paths that will be handled are determined beforehand, and each type of path is handled only once. We must make sure when combining multiple rendering methods that no single type of light transfer is included more than once into the final radiance estimate. This can be tricky because some algorithms do need to follow the same paths multiple times; we must be sure to dispose of the extra copies.

Most hybrid algorithms begin with a *radiosity first pass* to generate the result of multiple diffuse interreflection in the environment. Since radiosity solutions are *view-independent* (at least to within the assumptions discussed in Chapter 17), this solution may be stored with the model and used repeatedly for different views of the scene, as long as nothing changes except the viewpoint. This is then followed by a *ray-tracing second pass*, which adds in the view-dependent features due to specular reflection.

This process is nicely described by Sillion and Puech [409]. Recall the operator form for VTIGRE from Equation 17.15:

$$L = L^e + \mathcal{K}L \tag{19.31}$$

Let's divide the light transport operator $\mathcal{K}$ into the sum of a specular term $\mathcal{K}_S$ and a diffuse term $\mathcal{K}_D$; this is equivalent to breaking down the BDF into two terms. Then

$$L = L^e + (\mathcal{K}_D + \mathcal{K}_S)L \tag{19.32}$$

Now we will *define* the diffuse distribution of light L^d implicitly by the relationship

$$L = L^d + \mathcal{K}_S L \tag{19.33}$$

Comparing this to Equation 19.31, we see that it relates the final radiance distribution L at each point to the sum of the diffusely radiated component at that point plus the result of specular propagation of light throughout the environment. In other words, the diffuse term L^d is the emission term; the diffuse radiation is "painted" onto the surfaces and they radiate it into space. If we propagate this diffusely reflected light into the environment and let it bounce around specularly, the result is the final radiance distribution L.

If we isolate L

$$(\mathcal{I} - \mathcal{K}_S)L = L^d \tag{19.34}$$

and use the Neumann series approximation from Chapter 16, we find

$$\begin{aligned} L &= (\mathcal{I} - \mathcal{K}_S)^{-1} L^d \\ &= \sum_{n=0}^{\infty} (\mathcal{K}_S)^n L^d \\ &= \mathcal{K}_S{}^{\infty} L^d \end{aligned} \tag{19.35}$$

where we have implicitly defined the resolvant operator $\mathcal{K}_S{}^{\infty}$ (recall Equation 16.40 from our discussion of the Neumann series in Section 16.6.3).

Now if we can find the diffuse distribution L^d, then we can find the complete radiance L. First, expand Equation 19.32,

$$L = L^e + \mathcal{K}_D L + \mathcal{K}_S L \tag{19.36}$$

regroup,

$$L - \mathcal{K}_S L = L^e + \mathcal{K}_D L \tag{19.37}$$

and apply the definition of L^d to the left side:

$$L^d = L^e + \mathcal{K}_D L \tag{19.38}$$

Now plugging in Equation 19.35 for L,

$$L^d = L^e + \mathcal{K}_D \mathcal{K}_S{}^{\infty} L^d \tag{19.39}$$

Equation 19.39 is equivalent to Equation 19.31, except that it expresses the radiance in terms of the diffuse component L^d, which is propagated around the environment by specular transfers.

Hybrid algorithms generally compute an approximation to L^d using radiosity, and then compute an approximation to $\mathcal{K}_D \mathcal{K}_S{}^{\infty} L^d$ using ray tracing.

The first hybrid algorithm was presented by Wallace et al. [460]. It used a simple form of extended form factors that could only account for planar mirrors, but the serial staging of radiosity and ray-tracing solutions was presented. We show an example of hybrid rendering using this algorithm in Figure 19.48 (color plate).

The method proposed by Shirley [396] uses three passes, all implemented by ray tracing. Shirley first distributes energy from the light sources using photon tracing, resolves diffuse-diffuse interactions with a version of radiosity that uses ray tracing to shoot power from one patch to another, and then renders the image using visibility ray tracing. A result of this method is shown in Figure 19.49 (color plate); note the bright focused light (a *caustic*) on the tabletop created by the wine glass.

Another three-pass method was developed by Heckbert [207]. The first pass is similar to a traditional visibility ray-tracing algorithm: rays are fired from the eye into the environment. The purpose of this *size pass* is to determine how densely each object in the scene will be sampled when projected to the image plane. This information is collected because in the second pass, called the *light pass*, light is fired from the light sources into the environment, in a distribution pattern initially determined by the results of the size pass: the idea is to make sure that the number of photons visible through each pixel is about the same.

To see the reason for this, suppose that the scene being viewed is just a big flat polygon nearly perpendicular to the screen, viewed in perspective. If we didn't use a size pass, then the samples from the luminaires would fall haphazardly on the polygon; when we integrated over small regions of the polygon to evaluate a pixel's radiance, we would find some pieces of the polygon with no photons, and others with one or more. The result would be a splotchy appearance. So the size pass is used to subdivide the surface into surface strata which we know we will sample; those induce directional strata on the luminaires, and rays are fired outward through each of these directional strata.

Finally an *eye pass* uses ray tracing to render the scene. Figure 19.47 shows a result of this algorithm; note that the ground plane has not been smoothed.

Chen et al. developed a *multipass* method that can be interrupted to show partial results of different types [86]. They considered the broadest light transport path $L(S|D)^*E$, and included extra D and S terms before the eye, creating $L(S|D)^*DS^*DS^*E$. They suggested a very nice visual metaphor for this path, shown in Figure 19.50. The dark polygons represent a diffuse surface, and the white polygons represent one or more specular surfaces.

They considered three types of paths: those containing no diffuse elements, those with one diffuse element, and those with two or more diffuse elements. The first and third cases each have their own algorithm; the case of one diffuse element is distinguished into two classes, depending on whether or not there are specular surfaces between the light and the diffuse element. Together, these classes account for all transport paths.

The case of no diffuse elements corresponds to the path LS^*E. This is shown in Figure 19.51(a). As indicated by the arrows, visibility tracing (that is, rays generated at the eye) is used to evaluate light taking these paths. Note that there might be no specular surfaces involved in this path at all; this would be a path LE indicating that we're looking right into a luminaire. A path of the form LSE indicates that we're

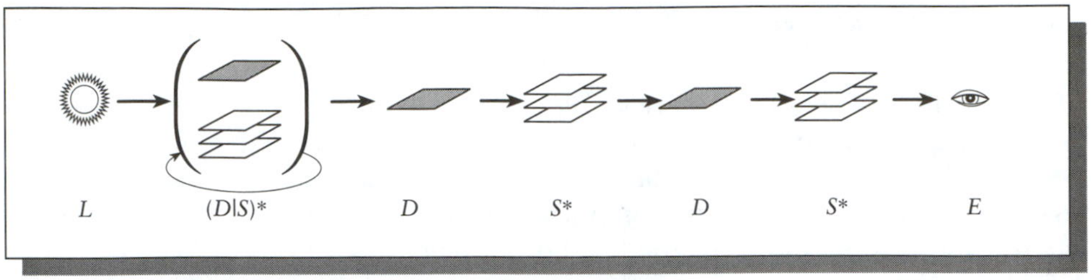

FIGURE 19.50
The general path considered by the multipass algorithm.

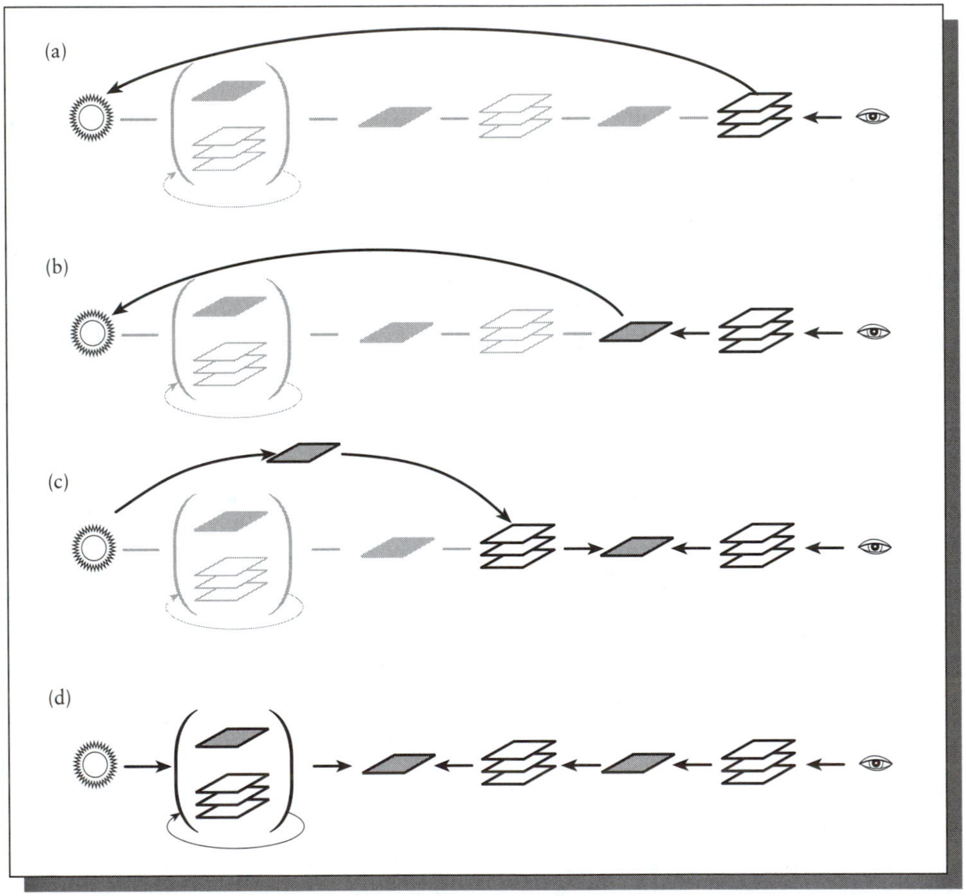

FIGURE 19.51
(a) LS^*E. (b) LDS^*E. (c) LS^+DS^*E. (d) $L(S|D)^*DS^*DS^*E$.

looking at the reflection of a light source in a mirror; a path $LSSE$ is a light source seen in a chain of two mirrors.

The case of a single diffuse element with no specular surfaces between itself and the light corresponds to the path LDS^*E; this is shown in Figure 19.51(b). Note that there may no specular surfaces between the diffuse patch and the eye, or many. Again, we use visibility ray tracing to find these paths.

If there is a specular surface between the light and the diffuse patch, then there may be many paths. Recalling that S^+ means one or more specular surfaces, this path would be written LS^+DS^*E, and is shown in Figure 19.51(c). The arrows in the path show that we use visibility ray tracing to reach the first diffuse patch. Photon tracing is used to generate photons at the light source, and then bounce them off of one or more specular surfaces until they arrive at a diffuse patch, where their power is recorded in an illumination map.

Finally, there's the general case of the path $L(S|D)^*DS^*DS^*E$, as shown in Figure 19.51(d). Visibility tracing is used to find light paths that start at a diffuse surface, bounce off of one or more specular surfaces, strike another diffuse surface, and then bounce off of one or more additional specular surfaces before reaching the eye. Progressive radiosity is used to distribute light from the light source into the environment via multiple specular and diffuse bounces. As mentioned earlier, each type of path is accounted for once and only once.

A result of this approach is shown in Figure 19.52 (color plate). The different light paths are displayed in different images. Notice the high-frequency information in the ray-traced caustics that are not in the radiosity caustics, and the richer variation in diffuse interreflection computed by the radiosity method over the ray-traced interreflections.

The hybrid approach has many other variations. The details involve making different approximations in the two methods, and the mechanics behind coupling them. Some pointers are provided in the Further Reading section.

19.7 Ray-Tracing Volumes

We can use ray tracing to evaluate volume data by using the full form of TIGRE, rather than the vacuum-limited form of VTIGRE. The practical means for efficiently evaluating the integration of scattering and volumetric emission along the ray are closely tied to the nature of the volumetric medium being rendered, and the particulars of its organization in the program.

Some discussions of volume tracing may be found in papers by Bhate and Tokuta [43], Blasi et al. [45], Inakage [225], Kajiya and Von Herzen [236], Levoy [268, 269], Nishita et al. [320], Sakas and Gerth [371], and van der Voort et al. [448].

An example of a ray-traced volume function from Levoy [268] is shown in Figure 19.53 (color plate). An example including atmospheric media from Inakage [225] is shown in Figure 19.54 (color plate).

19.8 Further Reading

The ray-tracing literature is vast. In particular, there has been extensive research into ray-object intersection algorithms and efficiency techniques for locating the first such intersection. There have also been a number of hardware implementations that exploit the natural parallelism in ray tracing (every ray is essentially independent of every other, so they may all be traced simultaneously). Much of this literature is summarized in the book by Glassner et al. [156].

Extensive information on geometrical optics involving lenses may be found in any optics text, such as Born and Wolf [55], Brown [66], Jenkins and White [230], and Möller [311].

Hybrid algorithms combining ray tracing and radiosity in various ways may be found in the papers by Bouatouch and Tellier [56], Bouville et al. [57], Chen et al. [86], Chen and Wu [82], Heckbert [207], Kok et al. [250], Le Saec and Schlick [259], Shirley [395, 396], Sillion et al. [408, 410], Wallace et al. [460], and Zhu, Peng, and Liang [505]. A variety of methods for storing illumination maps have been discussed by Vedel [453].

Efficient Monte Carlo sampling of the BDF for reflection and transmission is discussed by Bouville et al. [58]. The problem of sampling large numbers of light sources is discussed by Wang and Shirley [464].

Many different data structures and algorithms have been explored for accelerating the process of finding the first intersection of a ray with the environment. The seminal survey that organizes this field is by Arvo and Kirk [17]. The acceleration structures may be combined in various ways; some discussions for such combinations may be found in Kirk and Arvo [245] and Glassner [154].

Implementation of a ray tracer and ray-tracing architectures are discussed by Heckbert [209], Shirley [399], and Shirley and Wang [401].

19.9 Exercises

Exercise 19.1

(a) Write equations for picking lens positions assuming a circular shutter on a circular lens that opens at uniform speed over a duration t_0, stays open for a time t_1, and then closes at uniform speed again over an interval t_2, as in Figure 19.55(a).

(b) Repeat the exercise assuming a linear "guillotine" shutter that moves vertically

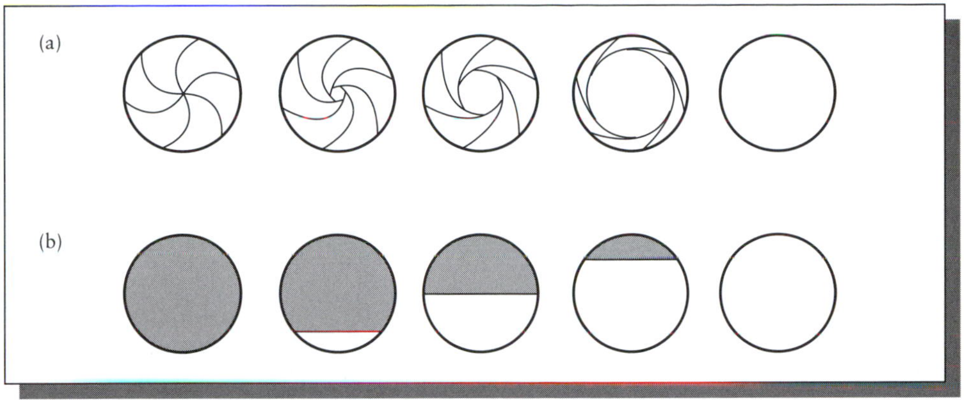

FIGURE 19.55
(a) A circular shutter. (b) A guillotine shutter.

up, revealing the circular lens from bottom to top over time t_0, staying open for time t_1, and then closing over interval t_2, as in Figure 19.55(b).

Exercise 19.2

Use a refraction argument to show that the lens points Q, C, and Q' in Figure 19.56 are colinear accounting for refraction at the surface of the thin lens, even though QGC and CHQ' are not colinear.

Exercise 19.3

Different acceleration methods are best used for different types of databases.

(a) For what sort of scenes are bounding volumes most appropriate?
(b) For what sort of scenes is uniform space subdivision most appropriate?
(c) For what sort of scenes is adaptive space subdivision most appropriate?
(d) Can you suggest a means for automatically selecting and applying the right subdivision strategy for a given model? Would you recommend mixing methods within a scene? How would you choose?

Exercise 19.4

Read the works by Pattanaik [332] and Pattanaik and Mudur [333, 334], and implement an importance- (or potential-) based system for distributing energy from light sources. Is this an expensive algorithm? Can you make it more efficient?

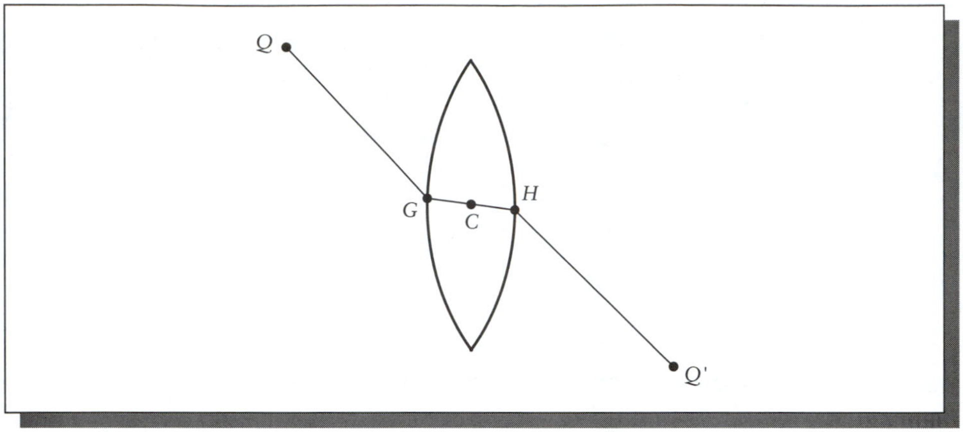

FIGURE 19.56
Lens for Exercise 19.2.

Exercise 19.5

Implement a hybrid radiosity/ray-tracing system using any radiosity and ray-tracing methods. Prove that your method doesn't duplicate any light paths, even if it doesn't capture all types. Demonstrate the range of optical effects you can model.

If we assume . . . that natural signs can simply be copied from nature, the history of art represents a complete puzzle. It has become increasingly clear since the late nineteenth century that primitive art and child art use a language of symbols rather than "natural signs" . . . All art originates in the human mind, in our reactions to the world rather than in the visible world itself, and it is precisely because all art is "conceptual" that all representations are recognizable by their style.

E. H. Gombrich
("Art and Illusion: A Study in the Psychology of Pictorial Representation," 1960)

20 RENDERING AND IMAGES

20.1 Introduction

This chapter is about closing the loop between the rendering program, the display, and the human observer.

We have directed a lot of energy in this book toward evaluating the distribution of radiance in a scene. If the resulting radiance function is intended to be used to represent an image, then we need to understand what happens to our computed radiance values when we display them on a real device, and they are perceived by a real observer.

In this chapter we will look at two quite different topics, which are related through their intimate connection with the displayed image. We will first look at *postprocessing* methods for converting the synthesized color values of an image to a set of displayable color values that will provoke the desired response in an observer. Then we will look at *feedback-rendering* methods, which use accurately displayed images to support the interaction of a designer with the rendered scene.

It is important to know how closely our synthetic images match the reality they simulate. One way to make the match is to compare the results against experiments: this is the approach followed by Ward in his radiance system [469]. Alternatively, you can display a synthetic image side-by-side with a real one, and ask observers if they can tell the difference; this approach was followed by Meyer et al. Meyer86a. This latter approach is a much harder road to follow, because it involves human observers, with all of their idiosyncrasies, biases, and complex visual systems. Both of these approaches have yielded encouraging results, but the match isn't perfect.

Until we are able to confidently assert that our synthetic images contain radiance values that are equivalent to what would be measured, experiments with human observers are premature (Meyer et al. did in fact make these measurements before continuing with the perceptual study). We need to have confidence that our simulation is right, and then we need to understand how to display the results of that computation so that it presents the image we intend.

20.2 Postprocessing

The information in Units II and III is intimately related; we cannot hope to accurately evaluate the radiance without using appropriate signal processing. But it may seem that when the radiance has been computed for every discrete location in the display device (e.g., every pixel in a frame buffer has a color), then our job as image synthesists is complete. This is not the case; in fact, the material in Unit I on the human visual system and displays is as important to image synthesis as the signal processing and physics.

Every display device will affect the picture we intend to show, and that transformation will affect how the picture is perceived. When creating an image for a human observer, our goal is *not* simply to compute the most accurate representation of a physical scene, but rather to give the human viewer a particular perception of the image. If we want the viewer to think that the image on the screen looks like a window into a real scene, then we must account for what happens between the frame buffer and the brain as best we can.

The essence of the argument is that there are physical limits on all display devices: they cannot come near the *dynamic range* of luminance in the physical world. Recall Figure 1.13, which demonstrated a luminance range of 16,000 candelas per square meter from lit snow to .00003 candelas per square meter from the sky on a moonless, overcast night: that's a dynamic range of one hundred million to one! There is no display device that can come close to that range; film has a useful dynamic range of about 1000:1 [441], and CRTs are about 100:1 [467]. And we saw in Unit I that each display has its own color gamut, which is always a subset of the full range of perceptible colors.

This means that except when we happen to make a picture that just fits the natural color and intensity range of the output device it is shown on, we are instead forced to display an approximation. So we will have failed in our goal to present an image that the observer will interpret as a view of a real scene.

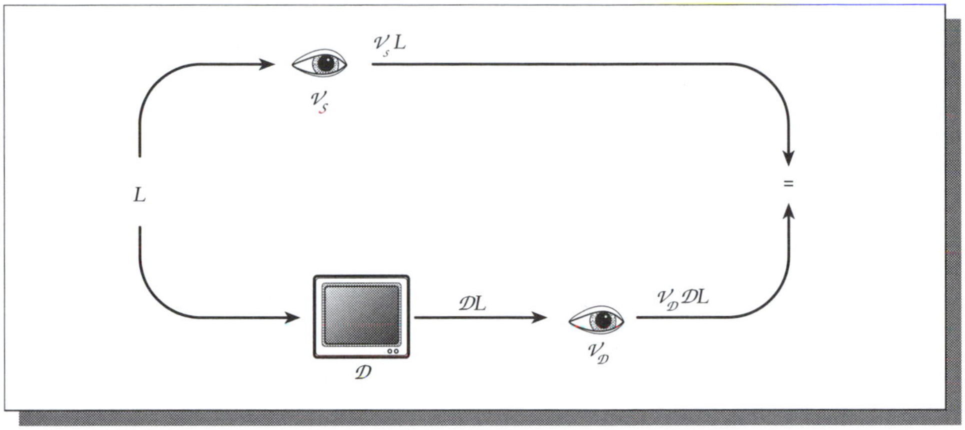

FIGURE 20.1

Radiance values perceived directly and on a CRT.

Or have we? The human visual system is nonlinear in its response. Perhaps if the entire picture is dimmer than a real scene, we will *adapt* to the overall luminance and then in that new state of adaptation the picture will appear correct. This is partly true, but then we have to assume that the colors are entirely within gamut, there is no ambient illumination on the CRT face or glare on the CRT, the phosphors are packed tightly enough together for the viewing distance, and so on.

Even if all the display parameters are perfect, we still have trouble. For example, when the intensity of the light entering the eye becomes bright enough, it begins to scatter appreciably, causing *bloom* and other effects such as star patterns. The presence of bloom is a cue to our perceptual system that the intensity of the light is very high.

The visual system is complex, and all our understanding still leaves us quite ignorant of many important perceptual cues. Still, if we want to provoke the intended response in a viewer, we must understand as well as we can what happens to our radiance values once we dare to display them.

A useful way to think about this has been suggested by Tumblin and Rushmeier [442]. Figure 20.1 shows a set of radiance values (denoted L) that describe a real scene. We'll assume for the moment that they are at frame-buffer resolution and represent the best possible color values for display on an optimal monitor under ideal conditions. The figure shows two paths to perception of these luminances, depending on whether the viewer sees them directly in the real world or on the front

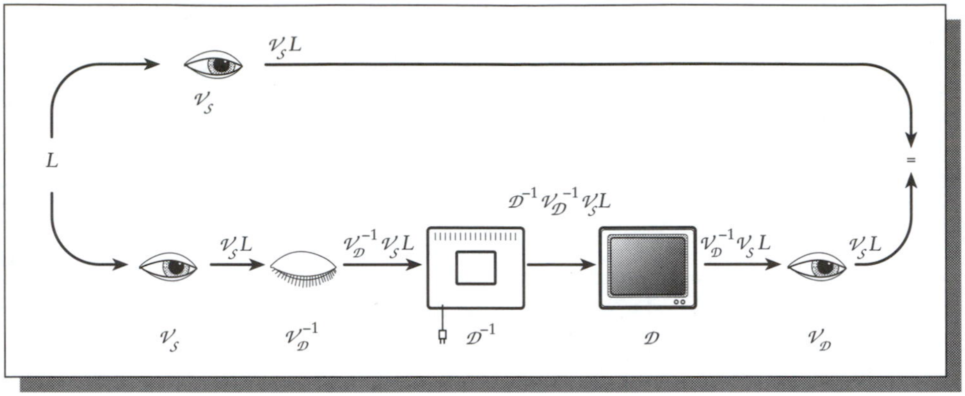

FIGURE 20.2
Compensation for the device.

of a CRT. The top path corresponds to direct perception of the radiance (say by looking at a real scene), and the lower path represents the perception of the scene on a monitor.

The upper path involves the transformation of L by a nonlinear vision operator $\mathcal{V}_S$. When looking at the real scene, the human visual system will adapt in a variety of ways to the incident illumination. The *scene-adapted* state of the vision operator $\mathcal{V}$ is written $\mathcal{V}_S$. This operator (whatever it may be) processes an image and creates a perception of an image in the observer's mind; the result of the operator is the perceived image $\mathcal{V}_S L$.

On the lower path we see the radiance first passes through a display, where it is mapped through an operator $\mathcal{D}$. This operator is intended to capture everything involved in the display of the image, including ambient lighting, gamma correction, color drift over time, and so on. The observer then looks at the display, but because the illumination is different, the adaptation of the visual system is different. We model the *display-adapted* visual system with the operator $\mathcal{V}_\mathcal{D}$, so the perceived image is $\mathcal{V}_\mathcal{D} \mathcal{D} L$.

Unless $\mathcal{V}_\mathcal{D} \mathcal{D} = \mathcal{V}_S$, the image seen on the screen will not produce the same perceptual response as looking at the real scene. We call actions taken to address this problem *display compensation*, and in general it is a *post-processing* method.

The postprocessing approach is illustrated in Figure 20.2. The idea is to insert new operators along the display path so that the final operator result is $\mathcal{V}_S$, not $\mathcal{V}_\mathcal{D} \mathcal{D}$. We do this by inserting three new operators.

Assume for the moment that we understand the visual system well enough that we know just what $\mathcal{V}_\mathcal{S}$ and $\mathcal{V}_\mathcal{D}$ do, and furthermore that both of these operations are invertible. Similarly, assume we know what $\mathcal{D}$ does, and that it too is invertible. All of these assumptions are dubious at best. But if we had these transformations, we could combine them to create the desired perception.

As shown in Figure 20.2, we begin by applying the scene-adapted visual system, creating $\mathcal{V}_\mathcal{S}L$; this creates the image we want to get into the observer's head. But this picture will be seen by the display-adapted observer, so we precorrect for the transformation that will occur in that perception by multiplying with the inverse of that adaptation, creating ${\mathcal{V}_\mathcal{D}}^{-1}\mathcal{V}_\mathcal{S}L$. This is the correct image, but displaying it through the monitor will distort it. So we correct for that distortion by preapplying the inverse of the monitor transformation, creating $\mathcal{D}^{-1}{\mathcal{V}_\mathcal{D}}^{-1}\mathcal{V}_\mathcal{S}L$. Now everything unrolls: we display the picture using the operator $\mathcal{D}$, and it is perceived by the visual system using the display-adapted operator $\mathcal{V}_\mathcal{D}$, creating

$$\mathcal{V}_\mathcal{D}\mathcal{D}\mathcal{D}^{-1}{\mathcal{V}_\mathcal{D}}^{-1}\mathcal{V}_\mathcal{S}L = \mathcal{V}_\mathcal{S}L \tag{20.1}$$

There is a subtlety here. You may have noticed that the $\mathcal{V}_\mathcal{D}$ used in Figure 20.2 is not the same $\mathcal{V}_\mathcal{D}$ used in Figure 20.1. Since the displayed pictures are different (here it's $\mathcal{D}^{-1}{\mathcal{V}_\mathcal{D}}^{-1}\mathcal{V}_\mathcal{S}L$ rather than just L), the visual system will be presented with a different set of stimuli and will thus adapt differently. So ${\mathcal{V}_\mathcal{D}}^{-1}$ is not a constant, but varies with the image being displayed.

A postprocessing approach to display compensation such as this works with a collection of display values: these may be radiances, floating-point color specifications, or even simply integer RGB values for a frame buffer. These methods are appropriate for application after rendering is complete but before display. Thus a single rendered image may be stored with arbitrary color information in a file, and then a different post-processing algorithm may be applied to it for each device on which it is to be shown.

20.2.1 A Nonlinear Observer Model

A general approach to the post-processing problem was taken by Tumblin and Rushmeier [442]. They used a model like that in Figure 20.2, where two different forms of the visual system and an inverse representation of the display device were modeled.

They addressed their work to the correct adjustment of CRT intensity values to compensate for adaptation in different environments. Imagine viewing a simple indoor scene lit by a single firefly. After you had time to *adapt* to the low illumination, a few of the most reflective objects in the room might be barely visible, but there would be little contrast, and most of the room would be shrouded in darkness. Now replace the firefly with an aircraft searchlight. Suddenly the illumination in the room is increased by a factor of 10^{11}. If you could stand to open your eyes, you would find everything washed out in a flood of light. Only the deepest and darkest shadows would interrupt the otherwise bright white visual field.

If we were to render these two images, we would have radiance values that were all well below or well above what could be displayed on a monitor. The dark image would be completely represented by pixels of value 0, and the bright image would be well beyond the luminance put out by the CRT at maximum power. So we would be forced to somehow map both images to the restricted range of the monitor. A reasonable approach would be to scale each image so the darkest pixel went to 0 and the brightest to 1. The result would be that both images would appear exactly the same!

This isn't a desirable result: after all the effort involved in computing an accurate scene simulation, we would hardly like to destroy important information at the very end. If a single room appears the same when lit by a firefly or a searchlight, then we have lost some information.

To compensate for the change in brightness ranges between different devices, printers apply a *tone reproduction operator* $\mathcal{T}$ to the brightness values of the pixels. Typically, this operator implements a *tone reproduction curve* (or TRC), though in general the function may be more complex. Tumblin and Rushmeier have developed such an operator that attempts to capture the effect of adaptation.

The tone reproduction operator $\mathcal{T}$ maps reals to reals, so it doesn't deal with color directly. This is reasonable for a simple algorithm; modeling the human visual system is hard enough when dealing only with brightness. The Tumblin-Rushmeier model creates a composite operator $\mathcal{T} \approx \mathcal{D}^{-1}\mathcal{V}_{\mathcal{D}}{}^{-1}\mathcal{V}_{\mathcal{S}}$.

The starting point for their work was research published by Stevens and Stevens in 1953 and 1963. They gave models for the *perceived brightness* of a target on the basis of the adaptation of the observer and the luminance of the target. The clever idea behind these experiments was to adapt each of a subject's eyes to a different background luminance. The left eye saw only a black field. The right eye saw a panel of some constant luminance L_a and was given enough time to adapt to that luminance.

Then a small spot (the *target*) was displayed in each field, and the subject was asked how bright the target appeared. Brightness is measured in a linear scale of units called *brils*. A single bril is the sensation of brightness from a fully dark-adapted eye viewing a $5°$ target of 1 microlambert for one second. Brils are linear, so $2n$ brils are twice as bright as n brils. Notice that brils quantify subjective *brightness*, not objective luminance or radiance.

Assuming that the eye was shown (and adapted to) a 100% diffuse reflecting white surface with radiance L_a, then a target of radiance L has a brightness of P brils given by

$$\log(P) = \alpha \log(L) + \beta \tag{20.2}$$

where all logarithms are base 10, and

P is the brightness in brils,
L is the target radiance in lamberts, and
L_a is the luminance of the surrounding field.

The experimental constants are given by

$$\begin{aligned} \alpha &= 0.4 \log(L_a) + 2.92 \\ \beta &= -0.4(\log(L_a))^2 - 2.584 \log(L_a) + 2.0208 \end{aligned} \tag{20.3}$$

Often the brightness is denoted B, but that letter would clash with the commonly used letter for radiosity and the two measures would be difficult to distinguish just from context.

Unfortunately, Equation 20.2 doesn't generalize very well for complex scenes. More complex empirical models for brightness perception with respect to adaptation have been developed, but have not yet been explored for graphics [442].

The next step in building the operator $\mathcal{T}$ is to model the display device operator $\mathcal{D}$. Tumblin and Rushmeier used the following model:

$$\left(\frac{L_d}{L_{d,\max}}\right) = v^\gamma + \left(\frac{L_b}{L_{d,\max}}\right) \tag{20.4}$$

where

L_d is the screen display value of a pixel in lamberts.
$L_{d,\max}$ is the maximum screen luminance, typically 0.027 lamberts.
v is the intensity stored in the frame buffer.
γ is 2.8 to 3.0 for uncorrected CRTs, or about 1.2 if the display includes gamma correction.
L_b is the background radiance in lamberts.

The background radiance is the product of the ambient (or surround) radiance L_s and the screen reflectance s, plus the result of internal reflections within the CRT itself, ultimately producing radiance L_c, so $L_b = sL_s + L_c$.

We can solve for the display value v for a desired radiance L_d:

$$v = \left[\frac{L_d}{L_{d,\max}} - \frac{L_b}{L_{d,\max}}\right]^{(1/\gamma)} \tag{20.5}$$

Tumblin and Rushmeier note that the fraction $L_b/L_{d,\max}$ describes the ratio of the darkest to the brightest radiance achievable from the screen; this is the inverse of one definition for the contrast C (using the definition of contrast as brightest to darkest luminances). Typical CRTs have a contrast of about 35 in normal conditions [466].

To find v for a given L_d, we now need only find L_d. We find that value by asserting a brightness match between two observers, one adapted to the real world scene (using the subscript w) and the other to the display (using the subscript d). Then from Equation 20.3 we have the same perceived brightness P for the display pixel radiance L_d and the computed pixel radiance L_w, so

$$\alpha_w \log(L_w) + \beta_w = \alpha_d \log(L_d) + \beta_d \tag{20.6}$$

Solving for $\log(L_d)$, we find

$$\log(L_d) = \frac{\alpha_w \log(L_w) + \beta_w - \beta_d}{\alpha_d} \tag{20.7}$$

or

$$L_d = L_w{}^{(\alpha_w/\alpha_d)} \cdot 10^{(\beta_w - \beta_d)/\alpha_d} \tag{20.8}$$

where we have noted that $10^{a \log(b)} = b^a$.

The only remaining step now is to find values for (α_w, β_w) and (α_d, β_d). These can be computed from Equation 20.3 if we can determine an appropriate value of L_a to use. Tumblin and Rushmeier give a practical solution to determining this constant for both the real-world scene and the display image.

They note from the Stevens and Stevens experiments that the human visual system tends to adapt not to the average luminance in the scene, but to a point where the most of the brightness is a fixed amount *below* the adaptation level L_a. They reason that the logarithm of the adaptation level will be the expected value of the logarithm of the scene luminances, plus 0.84 to account for experimental data. That is,

$$\log(L_{a,w}) = E[\log(L_w)] + 0.84 \tag{20.9}$$

This only holds if we imagine that the eye adapts to the entire scene at once. This generally isn't true. For example, imagine an image of a room interior where you can see both the floor and the lights. If you look at the lights, your eyes will adapt to the bright illumination; if you look at the floor, you'll adapt to the darker illumination. Nevertheless, this single-adaptation idea is a good starting point. The expected value for the image can be computed simply as the log average of all the computed luminances in the scene. This real-world value $L_{a,w}$ can then be used as L_a to compute α_w and β_w.

Now finding the display adaptation level $L_{a,d}$ is a bit trickier. We would like to just average the pixel luminances as in the real-world case, but we don't know them yet. So instead we *assume* that they are evenly distributed, and we estimate the adaptation level as the ratio of the maximum displayable luminance to the square root of the maximum available contrast:

$$L_{a,d} = \frac{L_{d,\max}}{\sqrt{C}} \tag{20.10}$$

This display value $L_{a,d}$ can be used as L_a to compute α_d and β_d.

Now we can put the pieces together. Plugging the value for L_d from Equation 20.8 into the relationship in Equation 20.5, we find the operator $\mathcal{T}$, which maps computed radiances L_w to pixel values v:

$$v = \left[\frac{1}{L_{d,\max}} {L_w}^{\alpha_w/\alpha_d} \cdot 10^{[(\beta_w - \beta_d)/\alpha_d]} - \frac{1}{C} \right]^{(1/\gamma)} \tag{20.11}$$

Although Equation 20.11 looks formidable, most of it is made up of constants that are fixed for a given image. When the values of L_a are known for the image and the display, the values of α and β may be calculated.

Figure 20.3 (color plate) shows a set of five scenes processed by this model. The brightest image contains an overhead lamp with an intensity of 1,000 lamberts; it is mostly washed out. Each successive image shows the result of a decrease in the lamp luminance by a factor of 100. The final image has a 10-microlambert light. No processing has been done to these images except to apply Equation 20.11.

A pair of color figures generated with this method is shown in Figure 20.4 (color plate). Here the three color channels were adjusted independently. Figure 20.4(a) shows a cabin viewed by daytime illumination arriving through the window. Figure 20.4(b) shows the same cabin viewed by artificial nighttime illumination from the overhead lamp; the overall illumination in the room is much lower.

20.2.2 Image-Based Processing

A different approach to constructing a tone reproduction operator for postprocessing has been reported by Chiu et al. [88]. They observed the problem of displaying a typical indoor scene that they rendered. The scene included a bare light bulb. The radiance values for pixels directly displaying the bulb were 500, and those on the floor were about .017, for a dynamic range of about $30,000 : 1$, which is more than we can get from a CRT.

They considered a variety of simple tone reproduction curves, similar to the type of simple choices we discussed for gamut mapping in Section 3.6. As we noted for the gamut-mapping problem, they observed that any TRC that applies uniformly to the entire image is unlikely to produce acceptable results.

Chiu et al. made an interesting observation about the visual system that helped make the problem a bit easier to solve. Recall that the visual system is a poor judge of absolute values; it's *relative* radiances and contrasts that we're optimized to detect. In fact, they note that as long as it's kept within a factor of about four, we can apply a slowly changing scaling factor to the image and it will be undetectable (the precise meaning of "slowly changing" depends on the picture and the adaptation level of the observer). They write the scaling factor as a 2D function $s(i, k)$ for a grid of pixels. The computed pixels themselves are $p(i, k)$, so the displayed image at each pixel (i, k) is given by $s(i, k)p(i, k)$.

One way to achieve a slowly changing scaling function s is to blur the image. Suppose that the blurred image has new pixels $b(i, k)$. Then the scaling function may be written as

$$s(i, k) = \frac{1}{hb(i, k)} \tag{20.12}$$

for some value of h. As the scaling function h pulls the brightest pixels into display range, but the whole picture darkens as well. They found that $h = 8$ was a good compromise for their test images.

To compute the blurred picture, they experimented with several different filters. They discovered that the precise shape of the filter didn't matter much as long as it was smooth and very wide. In fact, the filter had to be about as wide as the picture in order to avoid artifacts. They used the filter $ae^{-0.01r}$, where r is the distance from the filter center and a is the normalization constant for the filter. Applying that filter to the image many times is prohibitively expensive. Such filtering is much easier in Fourier space, where the repeated convolutions become a single multiplication with an exponentiated version of the transformed filter (again a Gaussian). Chiu et al. chose instead to filter a subsampled version of the image and then interpolate to fill in the missing pixels.

The approach still leaves some pixels above 1. Their solution was to *clamp* these pixels. Then the scaling function itself is smoothed several times using a much smaller filter, to round the sharp edges introduced by the clamping process. Figure 20.5 (color plate) shows the blurred original image, the original scaling function, and the scaling function after clamping and smoothing. Pixels that were clamped were not allowed to change as a result of the smoothing.

The result of this operation is shown in Figure 20.6 (color plate), where the image is the one that was blurred for Figure 20.5(a), and the scaling function is the smoothed, clamped version from Figure 20.5(d). Note that in Figure 20.6(a) there is a lot of light coming off the wall near the bulb that is simply clipped, causing a flat, white disk on the wall. This is turned into a nicely shaded glow in Figure 20.6(c), yet the floor is still visible.

One clue that the luminance values in Figure 20.6(c) are not those we would see looking at the real scene is that there is no *bloom* (or *glare*). As mentioned earlier, when light is intense enough it scatters inside the eye, causing a *halo* around the brightest objects in the scene. We can include that halo in the image itself (this is another example of applying the scene-adapted vision operator $\mathcal{V}_S$ to the image).

Chiu et al. modeled blooming with a local function that tends to spread out very bright illumination locally. The image with bloom is found by convolving the image with a *blooming filter* $b(i, k)$, which is a small nonlinear filter that spreads out very bright regions. The blooming filter is given by

$$b(i,k) = \begin{cases} p & \text{if } i = k = 0 \\ f(i,k) & \text{if } \sqrt{i^2+k^2} \le w/2 \\ 0 & \text{otherwise} \end{cases} \tag{20.13}$$

where

w is the width of the filter.

p is the amount of blooming.

$f(i,k) = \frac{1-p}{F}\left|\sqrt{i^2+k^2} - (w/2)\right|^n$

F is the normalization constant for the filter.

n is the bloom spreading factor (> 1).

Figure 20.7 (color plate) shows the same image as in Figure 20.6(a), but after application of the blooming filter.

20.2.3 Linear Processing

As we saw above, the algorithm by Tumblin and Rushmeier [442] estimates the adaptation of the eye to the real-world scene and then shifts the luminances in the image to match the brightness perceived by an observer. For a given image, the transformation involves a scaled exponentiation of the image luminances.

Ward sought a linear transformation that would produce similar results at lower cost [468], transforming the real-world radiance L_w to a display radiance L_d using a scaling factor m:

$$L_d = mL_w \tag{20.14}$$

He noted that the effect of adaptation can be viewed as a shift in the absolute difference in luminance required in order to see a change. In other words, the difference $L_2 - L_1$ might not be visible when adapted to one luminance level, but it might be easily visible when adapted to some other luminance.

Building on the work of Blackwell, Ward began with a relationship that says if the eye is adapted to luminance level L_a, the smallest change in luminance ΔL that can be seen satisfies

$$\Delta L(L_a) = 0.0594(1.219 + {L_a}^{0.4})^{2.5} \tag{20.15}$$

where luminances are measured in candelas per square meter (recall from Table 13.2 that $1\text{cd/m}^2 = \pi \times 10^{-4}$ lamberts).

Now because the world luminances are mapped to the display luminances by Equation 20.14, we can map the smallest discernible changes in luminance as well:

$$\Delta L(L_{a,d}) = m\Delta L(L_{a,w}) \tag{20.16}$$

where, as before, $L_{a,d}$ is the adaptation level of the eye to the display, and $L_{a,w}$ is the adaptation level of the eye to the real-world scene. So the scaling factor m tells us how to map luminances from the world to the display such that a just-noticeable change in world luminance maps to a just-noticeable change in display luminance. Solving Equation 20.16 for m, we find

$$m = \frac{\Delta L(L_{a,d})}{\Delta L(L_{a,w})} = \left[\frac{1.219 + {L_{a,d}}^{0.4}}{1.219 + {L_{a,w}}^{0.4}}\right]^{2.5} \tag{20.17}$$

Now, as with the Tumblin and Rushmeier method, we need to estimate $L_{a,d}$ and $L_{a.w}$. Ward assumed that the display adaptation is at about half of the average radiance of the image, and that the average image is about equally distributed around the mean intensity $(L_{d,\max}+L_b)/2$, where, as before, $L_{d,\max}$ is the maximum displayable luminance and L_b is the background luminance. Ward further assumes that L_b is negligible, so $L_{d,a} = L_{d,\max}/2$. He uses the same approximation as Tumblin and Rushmeier and uses the log average of the scene luminances to estimate $L_{a,w}$.

Plugging these values into Equation 20.17 gives us luminance values from 0 to $L_{d,\max}$, so we divide by the maximum to get values in the range $[0,1]$. The scaling factor is then given by

$$m = \frac{1}{L_{d,\max}}\left[\frac{1.219 + (L_{d,\max}/2)^{0.4}}{1.219 + {L_{a,w}}^{0.4}}\right]^{2.5} \tag{20.18}$$

Ward suggests that a good value for $L_{d,\max}$ is about 100 candelas per square meter for most CRTs; a photograph under indoor lighting can be as high as 120 candelas per square meter.

Figure 20.8 (color plate) shows an indoor cabin scene as viewed by sunlight in the day and by indoor illumination at night, using Equation 20.18. Notice that the nighttime scene is darker.

Figure 20.9 (color plate) was generated assuming that the viewer had fixated on the cabin window and had adapted to the luminance there. In the daytime view in Figure 20.9(a), we can see the outer world through the window with greater clarity because it has been given more dynamic range in the image. The rest of the scene has reduced dynamic range. In the night view in Figure 20.9(b), very little light makes it through the window; at low illumination levels we can't see such dark objects.

20.3 Feedback Rendering

The techniques described in the previous section allow us to display an image that will be perceived in a way similar to the perception of a real scene being directly viewed.

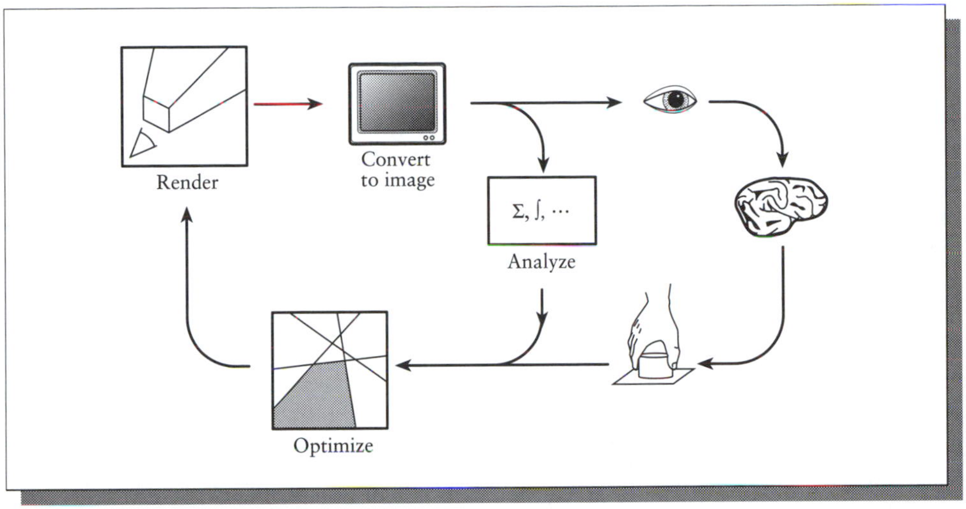

FIGURE 20.10

Feedback rendering.

Given that ability, we can now interact with the resulting image on a higher level, expressing aesthetic judgements about the image that in turn affect the underlying scene and create a new picture. We call this *feedback rendering*.

Feedback rendering is illustrated schematically in Figure 20.10. In this technique the image is rendered, then adjusted and rerendered (perhaps from scratch) until it satisfies some visual criteria. At first glance this looks like the typical interactive cycle of image generation: render, display, judge, change the scene, and repeat. The difference is that at least some fraction of the judging step is taken over by the computer, which makes automatic changes to the underlying scene representation in order to satisfy criteria associated with the displayed image.

The feedback-rendering algorithms presented below use some information derived from an image to change the scene description, and then create a new image. Sometimes the information is in the form of high-level aesthetic judgements by the user, and sometimes it is based on the quality of the displayed image.

The process usually involves expressing the 3D scene in terms of some tractable number of parameters, such as light colors or surface reflectivities. We call these the *scene parameters*. For a given picture, the n scene parameters represent a surface in an n-dimensional *picture space*. All of the possible images that can be generated by that scene may be considered points in that n-dimensional space. Any operations in that space may be thought of as moving around on that surface.

The task now becomes one of finding that point in picture space that has scene parameters that match the desired goals. This can be expressed as an *optimization* problem: given some criteria for the final image, find the set of scene parameters that produce an image that best satisfies those criteria. Optimization is not an easy job, and typically the sorts of problems we need to solve have a large number of dimensions and are very nonlinear. Finding the right optimization method for each task is important.

To support feedback rendering, the renderer needs to save more information about a picture than simply the color values at each pixel. At a minimum, it needs to be able to determine which object is located at a given pixel. This is often accomplished with an *object tag*, which is an integer associated with each pixel that identifies which shape has been drawn into that pixel. The surface parameters for the object at that point are also often stored; means for doing this are discussed by Hanrahan and Haeberli [189]. This approach only works for pixels that have a single sample (and thus are usually full of aliasing artifacts), because if there are multiple samples in a pixel, it can become very difficult to disambiguate a designer's intentions when that pixel is changed. This is acceptable, since interactive design is often carried out at lower resolution and image quality than the final image. When the designer is happy with the scene parameters, then a full (and anti-aliased) rendering may begin.

20.3.1 Illumination Painting

To create an image, we generally design a 3D scene description and then render it. The scene description is often created with a *modeling program*, which is designed to allow the interactive manipulation of the various 3D shapes in the scene. We can usually place cameras and lights as well, but the image is rendered quickly in order to provide rapid feedback; sometimes the modeling program only draws wireframe views of the scene.

Thus when the scene is rendered with a bit more accuracy, the geometry is typically close to what was expected, but the shading can be way off. Often the designer needs to repeatedly adjust the colors, positions, and directions of the lights to achieve a desired result.

Schoeneman et al. [382] noted that the desired illumination can often be expressed by the designer in the form of a sketch, by simply painting in the desired final colors in the scene. Rather than force the designer to manually adjust the lights to find a match to this sketch, the computer could try to automatically find a setting of the lights that does the job.

The scene parameters adopted by Schoeneman et al. are the light intensities and colors. The process begins with an initial rendering of the scene from the designer's starting guess. The result is an image that is displayed.

The designer then uses a *paint program* to interactively draw new colors on top of the rendered image. In effect the designer is telling the system the color of each surface *after* illumination. From the object tag, the system can determine which object is being colored. From the object geometry, the illumination of the object by each light can be determined. From the viewing geometry, the radiance of the object that is displayed on the screen can be determined. The job then becomes one of finding the right intensity and color setting for each light so that each object receives the necessary illumination, such that when it is projected to the screen, it has the color drawn in by the designer.

To find these light colors, Schoeneman et al. use a *constrained least-squares* optimization method to find that set of light colors and intensities that best satisfies the desired combinations of the lights and the surfaces. Surfaces that have been painted receive more weight in this optimization step than others, based on the presumption that the designer has explicitly painted everywhere that matters; by implication, anything left undrawn can change freely.

20.3.2 Subjective Constraints

A related but more ambitious system was built by Kawai et al. [242]. They allowed a richer set of scene parameters, including not just the light intensity, but the direction and focus of spotlights, and the reflectivity of surfaces. Like Schoeneman et al., they restricted their system to diffuse surfaces.

The light sources may be either purely diffuse emitters or Phong-style emitters whose distribution pattern follows a $\cos^n \theta$ distribution around a direction vector $\mathbf{V}$. The overall intensity, the exponent n, and the direction vector $\mathbf{V}$ may all be changed.

The system built by Kawai et al. allowed a user to interactively specify constraints by selecting objects from a rendered image, and then setting values using a set of interactive buttons and sliders. One set of values were derived from subjective criteria based on the work of Flynn, published in the 1970s.

Kawai et al. generated a number of different images of a conference room using different lighting configurations. They asked observers to rate those images with respect to the subjective feelings of *clarity*, *pleasantness*, and *privacy*. They also computed three objective measurements called *brightness*, *nonuniformity*, and *peripheral lighting*. These measurements are based on the brightness P of each surface in the room. Each measurement takes some subset of the patches in the room, computes an area-weighted brightness measure, and then normalizes by the total area in the subset:

Brightness measures the overall energy of the environment by weighting every patch:

$$f_{\text{brightness}} = -\frac{\sum_{i \in M} P_i A_i}{\sum_{i \in M} A_i} \tag{20.19}$$

where M is the set of all surfaces in the scene.

Nonuniformity measures the brightness of the walls with respect to the average surrounding brightness:

$$f_{\text{nonuniform}} = -\sqrt{\frac{\sum_{i \in W} (P_{a,i} - P_i)^2 A_i}{\sum_{i \in W} A_i}} \tag{20.20}$$

where W is the set of all the walls in the scene, and $P_{a,i}$ is the average brightness of all the elements around patch i.

Peripheral brightness measures the difference between the brightness of the horizontal and vertical elements:

$$f_{\text{peripheral}} = \frac{\sum_{i \in H} P_i A_i}{\sum_{i \in H} A_i} - \frac{\sum_{i \in V} P_i A_i}{\sum_{i \in V} A_i} \tag{20.21}$$

where H is the set of all horizontal elements.

The remarkable thing about these objective measures (albeit based on the subjective measurement of brightness) is that they can be correlated to the subjective impressions of clarity, pleasantness, and privacy. This correlation was found despite the fact that the objective measures above don't include perspective and hiding; that is, every surface in the scene is used in the calculation, weighted by its full area. This probably worked in their case because the test images were indoor scenes of a convex room where most of the surface area of the scene was visible. In more complex environments one would probably need to weight the area terms to use the area actually present in the final image.

The amount of clarity, pleasantness, and privacy may be written in terms of the objective measures by the relationship

$$\begin{bmatrix} f_{\text{clarity}} \\ f_{\text{pleasantness}} \\ f_{\text{privacy}} \end{bmatrix} = \begin{bmatrix} 0.90 & -0.38 & 0.58 \\ 0.78 & -0.53 & 0.24 \\ 0.90 & 0.32 & 0.09 \end{bmatrix} \begin{bmatrix} f_{\text{brightness}} \\ f_{\text{nonuniformity}} \\ f_{\text{peripheral}} \end{bmatrix} \tag{20.22}$$

Kawai et al. allow the designer to interactively set weights on these six subjective and objective criteria, and also a weight on the overall energy in the room. They take these as the *design constraints*, which they try to satisfy. The system also includes *barrier constraints* which must be satisfied to produce a physically sensible result; for example, reflectivities must lie in the domain $[0, 1]$. Finally, the renderer imposes its own *physical constraints* in the form of the conservation of energy in the environment.

From the constraints a set of partial differential equations is generated, and a system solver is invoked to walk through the space of images generated by the scene parameters to find one that minimizes the error, computed using the designer's weights.

An example of their results is shown in Figure 20.11 (color plate). In Figure 20.11(a) the table was constrained to have a small amount of illumination, while the overall effect had visual clarity. Figure 20.11(b) uses the same constraints except that an additional privacy constraint was added; notice how the lights have been directed away from the walls and down onto the table.

Optimization processes in high-dimensional spaces can often produce unexpected results. Kawai et al. noted that the system maximized the brightness in the example conference room by pointing the lights at the ceiling. This was aesthetically unacceptable, so they had to manually add a constraint to keep the lights away from the ceiling. This anecdote demonstrates how difficult it is to design completely automatic procedures in situations that involve subjective design criteria; we often find what we want by eliminating what we don't want.

20.3.3 Device-Directed Rendering

The two methods discussed above actually rerender a scene in order to meet aesthetic design goals. A similar approach was taken by Glassner et al. [160] with a system tailored to perform *gamut mapping*. Recall that in Section 3.6 we discussed how the range of displayable colors (or *gamut*) varies considerably between CRTs, film, and print media. Suppose that we have created an image that, when viewed on a CRT, meets our design criteria, including overall brightness levels to simulate adaptation. There's still the problem of getting the image from the screen onto film or paper without ruining the semantic consistency. Glassner et al. noted that if the image is rendered so that it fits the display gamut, then no distortion is needed.

The range of colors of the pixels in an image cannot be predicted; we must actually render the scene. For example, suppose there is a very dark blue chair in an indoor environment; it is unlikely that the chair will lie in the gamut of most printers. Even if the chair isn't directly visible, it may be indirectly visible in a reflection, say off of a tarnished candlestick. The material of the candlestick will influence the color of the reflection; the reflected blue chair might lie within gamut because it is darker or color-shifted. In general, multiple interreflections among objects in a scene will produce colors that are not present in the original objects. In other words, even if the original spectra are all within gamut, their combinations may not be.

We could adjust the image colors on a pixel-by-pixel basis, as in a postproduction method, but then we risk adjusting some reflections and not others. Suppose the blue chair is reflected in two candlesticks, one shiny and one tarnished. Suppose that they also reflect a red chair, where both red reflections are in-gamut, and as a result of gamut mapping we bring the out-of-gamut bluish pixels on one candlestick to the point where they look about the same as on the other candlestick. Then the blue reflections look the same, but the red reflections don't: we are simultaneously being told that the candlesticks reflect light equally (the blues are the same), and that they don't (the reds are different). This is a violation of semantic consistency in the image: the *sense* of what the picture represents has changed as a result of adjusting the colors.

Rather than adjust the image, we can change the colors of the objects and lights so that the computed image is completely within gamut. Then no postproduction would need to be applied to the picture to make it displayable.

In order to track the combination of object (and light) colors that are combined at each pixel, Glassner et al. rendered the image using ray tracing and saved the ray trees (we used one sample per pixel for this phase). From the ray tree we can build a symbolic expression representing how each color in the scene combined [390]. For example, the tree of Figure 20.12(a) corresponds to the expression of Figure 20.12(b).

When the image has been completely rendered, the symbolic expressions are all stored in a text file. Then the actual colors of the scene are used to evaluate the expressions and pixel *RGB* values are calculated. The *RGB* values are compared against the output device gamut, and those pixels that are out of gamut are flagged, along with a real number representing the estimated distance to the nearest point on the gamut.

The symbolic expressions that generated the out-of-gamut pixels are retrieved from the file, and symbolically differentiated with respect to each color. These differential equations tell the system how a given change in each scene color will affect the resulting pixel color. The result is a matrix of differential changes called the Jacobian. It tells us how each *RGB* component of each pixel will change, given a change in the surface properties of objects in the scene.

The goal is to make the picture fit the gamut, so for each pixel we found the nearest point on the gamut, and we computed the difference between these two colors. This becomes the *target* for that pixel: the difference reveals the desired motion of that pixel to bring it into gamut. Recall that the differential equations computed at each pixel describe how the pixel moves with respect to changes in the scene color; this may be written as a matrix equation that relates scene color changes to pixel color changes. Inverting the matrix tells us how to change the scene colors to accomplish the desired changes in pixel colors.

Typically all of the out-of-gamut pixels cannot be brought into gamut at once with the same set of scene color changes, so a best approximate change to the scene colors is computed and a small step is taken. A new image can then be immediately

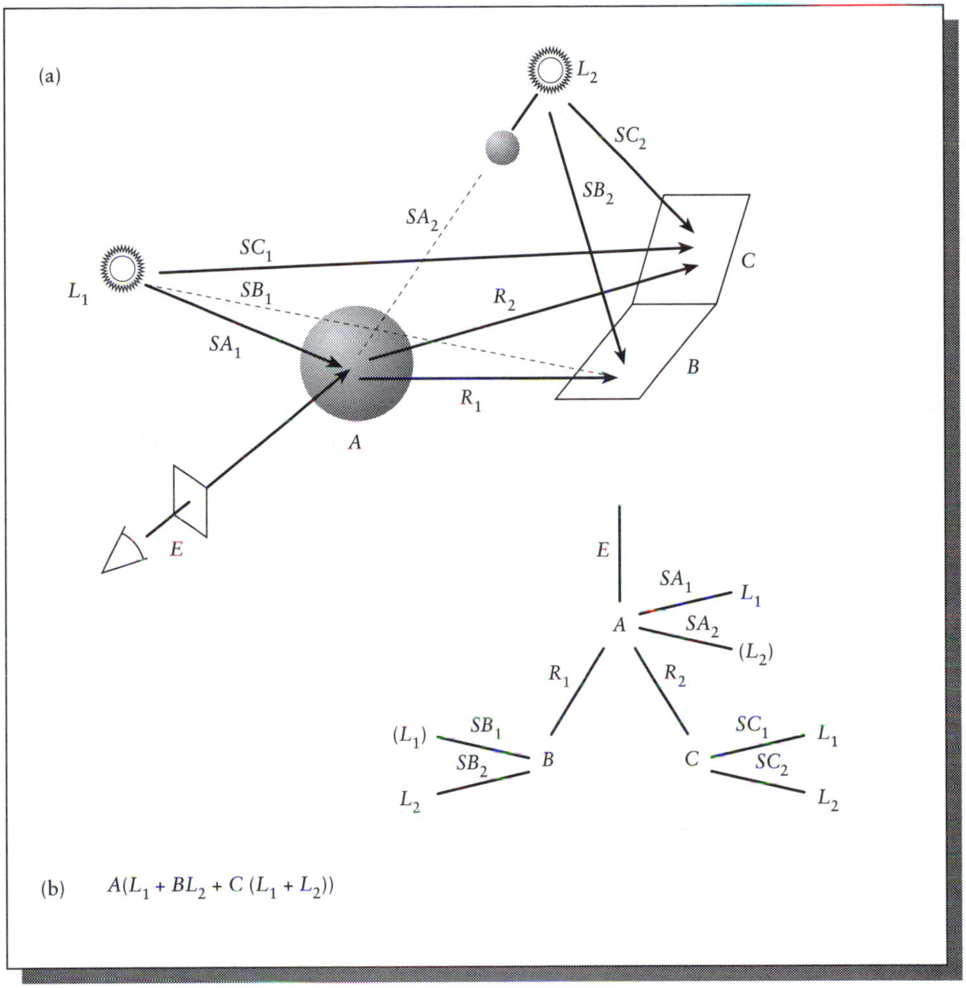

FIGURE 20.12
(a) A ray tree for a pixel. (b) The corresponding symbolic expression.

generated by reevaluating the symbolic expressions; the expensive visibility and shading calculations performed by the ray-tracing step need not be repeated. Then the process repeats.

The result is that we move through picture space coming ever closer to the gamut. It may appear that the method is doomed to produce a bad image, because it is trying to find scene parameters that will match the target image, which was created by simple projection to the gamut (and thus has all the artifacts of that technique). But this is not the case, because no combination of scene parameters can move us out of picture space. So no set of scene parameters will ever reach that projected image and its artifacts; the target is simply a goal that keeps us moving toward the gamut.

As in the system by Kawai et al. [242], the designer may need to supply additional manual constraints to make sure that the automatic solution is aesthetically acceptable.

One interesting property of this method is that the same original scene will create different resulting images for displays with different gamuts: the image destined for a printer will appear different than the image created for CRT viewing. Of course, because their gamuts are different, all gamut-mapping methods will produce different images for different devices, but this method has the advantage that each picture maintains semantic consistency.

20.4 Further Reading

The paper by Tumblin and Rushmeier [442] gives an excellent overview of the tone reproduction problem, and its relationship to the visual system, film, and CRTs. The patent by Statt [419] offers another approach to color image transformation, taking into account viewer adaptation. Kajiya and Ullner have studied the problem of ideal reconstruction on real devices in some detail; their results are reported in a difficult but fascinating paper [238].

20.5 Exercise

Exercise 20.1

We assumed in Section 20.1 that we could build operators ${\mathcal{V}_S}^{-1}$, ${\mathcal{V}_\mathcal{D}}^{-1}$, and $\mathcal{D}^{-1}$. Discuss these operators and what they mean.

If the man who paints only the tree, or flower, or other surface he sees before him were an artist, the king of artists would be the photographer. It is for the artist to do something beyond this: in portrait painting to put on canvas something more than the face the model wears for that one day; to paint the man, in short, as well as his features; in arrangement of colours to treat a flower as his key, not as his model.

James Abbott McNeill Whistler
("The Gentle Art of Making Enemies," 1892)

21 THE FUTURE

To conclude the book I'd like to present my opinion of where the field is headed in the near and more distant future. This chapter is mostly speculative and contains just my opinions, which are not objective, eternal, or universal.

21.1 Technical Progress

There are several directions in which the field can move to greatly increase the power and utility of rendered images. Certainly as computers grow in speed and parallelization, rendering algorithms will benefit. It is a folklore theorem in computer graphics that all research images take a few hours, and all production images take about 10 minutes. This comes about from the fact that every time we invent a new technique to create images more quickly, we compensate by loading the renderer with more work (to take advantage of the freed-up time). So in general people will pick a level of complexity and accuracy that is consistent with the time they're willing to wait for an image, which is the limiting factor. There are certainly important questions to be addressed in terms of exploiting parallelism and analog computation, but I see those as generally responsive moves to changes in the hardware, rather than new directions that will be taken by image synthesists from their own impetus.

21.1.1 Physical Optics

Image synthesis to date has focused on the geometrical optics approximation to light transport that we emphasized in this book. Except for some shading models in Chapter 15, the theory of physical optics has largely been unexplored for graphics. Three notable exceptions are the papers by Bahar and Chakrabarti [25] and Moravec [314], and the thesis by Kochevar [248]. All of these approaches have been computationally expensive, which is probably why physical optics has not been more thoroughly explored for image synthesis. For some applications, it is important that we be able to model diffraction and interference. It would be useful to have the option to include these effects in a scene, even if at a significant increase in cost.

21.1.2 Volume Rendering

The field of the direct rendering of volumes has recently started to achieve more prominence within computer graphics. The annual Visualization and Siggraph conferences routinely contain a multitude of papers on the topic. Generally these papers address practical issues at the border between modeling and rendering: how to convert a 3D vector function into some sort of geometrical or material description that may be rendered. I have not emphasized these methods in this book because they are both very practical (as opposed to theoretical), and developing at a very rapid pace.

The mathematics of volume rendering follow the FRE as described in Equation 17.10. In volume rendering the volumetric absorption and scattering terms dominate, and the boundary conditions are sometimes omitted altogether. Because of the great quantity of data involved, volume rendering algorithms can be very slow; a lot of practical work has been directed toward making such techniques efficient.

For example, volume rendering anti-aliasing methods can combine object-space filtering with screen-space filtering to find approximate but rapid filters. The "splatting" method due to Westover [476] takes such an approach; the method has been extended to hierarchical rendering [258] and texturing [106]. The design of explicit filters for 3D volume rendering has requirements similar to those for the 2D filters we've seen in this book, but some variations as well [74]. We can also explicitly low-pass filter the objects before rendering, creating a scene that is inherently anti-aliased [466].

Important applications of volume rendering are in fields where we physically gather 3D data. Examples include geological exploration, simulated and measured fluid dynamics, and medical imaging.

Medicine is a particularly important field, where results from CAT and MRI scanners are used to make diagnoses and plan treatment. Computer graphics may be used to check the fit of an artificial knee or hip, plan internal surgery, or suggest the results of reconstructive surgery. The use of computer graphics to improve medical science is, I believe, one of its most significant applications.

I believe that volume rendering sits at one of the many crossroads between rendering and modeling. Volume rendering methods must accommodate enormous amounts of data and present it in an intelligible way. I believe that we will find a variety of new methods that are appropriate for all rendering coming from this subfield.

21.1.3 Information Theory

The theory in this book has relied heavily on the ideas and tools of signal processing. A complementary field is that of *information theory*, which examines how well we can communicate a specific sequence of symbols from one place to another (or, when used for storage, from one time to another). The information-theoretic view tries to make sure that any errors introduced into a message can be detected, and perhaps even corrected upon receipt. A large number of *error-correcting codes* and transmission protocols have been developed to accomplish this. An excellent introduction to the subject may be found in the book by Hamming [184]; a more detailed yet still accessible description is provided by Ash [19].

When a photon is emitted from a light source and then strikes an object, that photon has effected the transfer of some *information*. Minimally, it represents that a certain amount of energy of a specific quantity and quality has been transferred from one object to the other. But as we have seen, it also tells us something about the relative visibility of the two points, and the amount of impact that light source will have on the final image. The use of importance to guide the rendering of a scene can be thought of as a first application of information-theoretic ideas to rendering theory. To see this, consider that a point on a surface communicates light information to the image; this communication takes place along a channel (in our case, the physical channel is the air or environment through which the light travels). The importance at the point can be imagined to describe the size of this channel; a point with low importance sends back only a small amount of information, and thus needs only a small channel. The tools of information theory can be applied to this problem to design transmission codes that carry this information effectively and compactly.

This is rather speculative right now, since there has not been much attention paid to applying information theory to image synthesis. I think it holds promise, though, and may help us design new types of efficient rendering algorithms.

21.1.4 Beyond Photo-Realism: Subjective Rendering

Photo-realism has served as a fruitful target for image synthesis research: to produce images that look like photographs, we have had to develop the theory and techniques described in this book. But now that we understand how to make images with computers, we need not be bound to the simulation of everyday reality. The history of art is often described in terms of *movements* or *schools*, in which certain groups of artists have together explored particular ways of representing the world. Impressionism, expressionism, and minimalism are some modern examples of such movements. Photo-realism is a relatively recent newcomer; in fact, the term "photo-realism" was only coined in 1968 [297].

Computer graphics is getting very close to producing photo-realistic images for some simple scenes. An experimental comparison of a real and synthetic image of a very simple environment showed that the match was quite good [301]. As our algorithms become more efficient and include ever more subtle phenomena, and our models more complex and detailed, the match of our simulations to the real world will become better and better.

Three-dimensional image synthesis should extend itself into these other realms. The books by Gombrich [164] and Shlain [403] provide excellent descriptions of art as a captured perception of the world, not always a mirror of it. We should think of the computer not only as a mirror for reality, but as a window into new realities, described by new physical laws and new ways of seeing things.

The emphasis in image synthesis has been to include ever more detail and precision into the image. We can find popular and effective media that have taken exactly the opposite direction; *comics* is one example. The popular art form of comics exploits *simplicity* and *abstraction* to get its message across [293]. Comics has a rich visual language for representing different types of mood and action [135], which in fact can be ruined by too much realism [293].

Complexity, *speed*, and *accuracy* have been the driving forces behind the development of new rendering algorithms; it's time to add *expression*.

Part of the creation of a piece of art involves deciding what will be included and excluded from the work, and how each entity in the work will be presented, both in composition and style. Image synthesis until now has treated everything in a scene as equally important and rendered with equal precision. Now that we understand the general approach to 3D image making with computers, we should begin to consider other styles of rendering and presentation. The accurate presentation of physical phenomena will remain an important application of computer graphics, but there is an entire world of emotional and spiritual visual communication that has so far been largely ignored.

Subjective rendering is the name I use for techniques that allow a designer to create a 3D image that includes not only accuracy and simulation, but also a meaning imposed by the designer that influences how objects are treated and the image is rendered. I believe this subject is a rich and rewarding area for future image synthesis research.

21.2 Other Directions

In addition to the medical and subjective rendering methods mentioned above, there are many directions in which image synthesis can lead, and many places from which it can draw inspiration. In this section I will describe some of the sources and uses that I foresee; there are certainly many others.

With increasingly powerful and inexpensive technology, the portable encyclopedia may make the transition from science fiction to everyday tool. Devices containing complex interactive 3D databases could revolutionize architecture books, allowing us to walk around a building, walk inside at different times of day and see where the shadows fall, and watch the sun rise and set at different times of the year. Engineering and mathematics texts could greatly benefit from animated presentations of dynamic systems. Biology, geology, and the other natural sciences could contain animated developments of complex ideas or time-evolving phenomena. The arts can benefit as well, offering the student captured performances, demonstrations, and instruction in technique, and even simply recording significant examples of artwork from museums and collections of all sorts. Many topics currently illustrated in dictionaries and encyclopedias with drawings and photographs could instead use precomputed animations or interactive simulations. The sheer glitz of such possibilities is likely to overwhelm their utility in the beginning, leading to useless or poorly produced documents, but as they become more common, the standards for quality and information content will rise.

In this book we have considered 3D surfaces in a world governed by classical physics. There's no reason to be restricted to either of these worlds.

The idea of a "fourth dimension" has captured people's imagination since H. G. Wells used it as the basis for his classic story on time travel, *The Time Machine*, in 1895 [474]. The idea of a fourth dimension was given a more scientific basis in the development of the theory of relativity [388]. It is still a fascinating idea to think about, as thoroughly explored by Rucker in his book on the subject [364]. To look into four (or more) dimensions requires a feat of mental visual skill that most people don't seem to have. But we can interpret 3D projections of these objects. In Abbott's classic book *Flatland* [1], residents of a 2D world interpret 3D objects by the projection of those objects onto the plane in which they live. Burger carried this one step further in *Sphereland* [70], where 3D creatures like us interpret 4D objects.

Techniques for actually making these projections in a way that is useful need to be developed. There has been some recent progress in this direction. The book by Banchoff [28] offers an excellent introduction to the subject and a number of methods for looking at 4D objects. More recently, Hanson has developed direct-viewing methods for 4D objects using a careful combination of illumination and transparency [193, 194].

We know from relativity that light deviates from a straight path in the presence of mass; in fact, it follows a geodesic in 4D space-time [306]. Viewed from our 3D space, the light appears to follow a curved path. We would expect this to affect our visual world, in the same way that mirages redirect light from one path to another. Indeed this is the case, and this visual distortion can be modeled. The work of Hsiung and Dunn [216] and Yamashita [495] presented methods for this visualization, which can be extended to include the color shift predicted by the physics [217].

From the early days of television, people have predicted a form of real-time 3D video, rather than the flat screen used today. Usually people imagine a "free-viewing" display, meaning that any number of people can see the image at the same time, all free of any additional viewing technology (such as special glasses).

Such a display continues to elude us, but a variety of alternatives are variously available, plausible, or simply interesting.

One prominent method that is currently available is a number of different *stereo* display technologies. Such systems almost always generate two images, and either directly or indirectly route one image to each eye. Like the random-dot stereograms of Chapter 1, the human visual system manages to combine these two independent views into a single whole. On a very different front, we can use the techniques of *stereolithography* or *computer-directed machining* to actually take a 3D mathematical surface description and turn it into a real 3D object. There are limitations to the types of shapes such machines can make, but geometers have long known that when you have a real object in your hand you can use your tactile and motor-memory skills to augment your visual perception of the shape to improve your understanding of it. Computer-generated holograms are becoming easier to make [179], and a variety of other 3D display technologies are discussed in McAllister's book on the subject [290].

Certainly there are many wild possibilities for display systems if we are willing to consider new technologies. The glow of a firefly can be recreated with manmade chemicals, which can be purchased prepackaged in plastic tubes in automotive supply stores. Inside the tube is a liquid (sold by Kodak under the name *Luminol*) within which is a smaller glass vial containing a second liquid. Bending the glass tube breaks the internal vial, and then shaking the tube mixes the two liquids. The result is a greenish yellow phosphorescent glow that can last for several hours and be used as an emergency light or warning beacon. Similar compounds can be bought at many public gatherings premixed in thin, flexible tubes that may be used as bracelets. Different choices for the activating chemical produce different colors of light, including red, green, and blue.

Imagine a system of airbrushes, where each airbrush is under computer control to specify the atomized liquid it projects, as in Figure 21.1. The computer controls not only the direction of the spray but also the amount of liquid sprayed and its

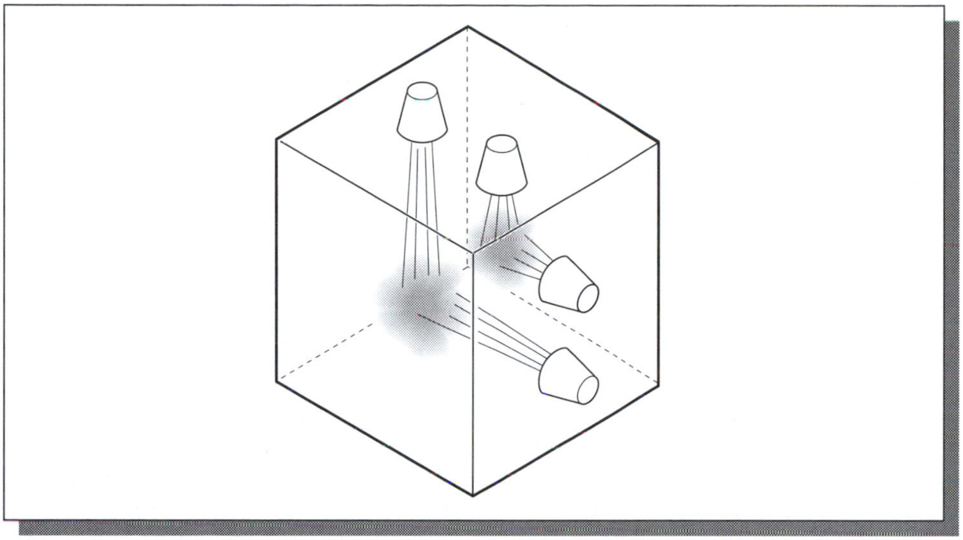

FIGURE 21.1
A schematic view of the color cloud chamber.

spread. Suppose there were several of these atomizers spaced around the inside of an enclosure, each spraying a mist of one chemical. Several other atomizers are distributed in the enclosure, and each one of these emits a spray that upon mixing with the other chemical causes a glowing red, green, or blue cloud. By careful color mixing we can achieve any combination of these colors, just as on a CRT. There are some practical issues to be addressed in such a system, but I particularly like the idea of glowing clouds of light.

There are many exciting applications of synthetic images. As I mentioned before, I believe that some of the most important are in medicine. In addition to the planning and study uses mentioned earlier, synthetic imagery could be used to help those who have poor or no eyesight. Depending on where the problem is located, we can imagine a day when we understand the signal that is conveyed along the optic fiber from the eyes to the brain well enough to predict the signal for a given visual stimulus. Then we could take the visual stimulus, either real or synthetic, convert it into this form, and then directly apply it to the optic fiber. We could in theory work our way ever higher up the visual pathway until we were able to provide direct cortical stimulation to induce the sensation of "seeing" something.

This chain of thought leads to the uses of computer graphics in "virtual reality." Currently two approaches dominate: a user wears a helmet that blocks out all visual (and perhaps aural) stimulation except that provided by the computer, and a partial helmet that superimposes computer-generated imagery between the eye and the world.

The former application may find value for completely imaginary worlds or worlds at a great distance: for example, navigating through a computer file hierarchy or driving a Mars rover from Earth. In a fully controlled environment we can experience *synesthesia*, where senses appear to be cross-coupled, allowing us to feel yellow, taste loudness, or look at the sensation of sour.

The superimposed display can provide some externalization of memory, much as writing extended memory. The computer can provide a *symbolically augmented* world, which enhances our understanding of the natural objects around us. We can simply look around a room and, with the appropriate software, determine how long the lights have been on, or which items in the room were made in a given country, or which were gifts from a particular person. More complex relationships can be established and demonstrated explicitly or symbolically: for example, we could draw connecting lines between all objects that contain information regarding a particular project, or simply highlight them in the visual world.

I believe there is a danger in simply following the technology without considering carefully what impact it has on the person using it and society as a whole. The complete simulation of the natural world may suggest that our bodies can somehow be left behind, and simply maintained at some minimal level while our brains are stimulated by computer-generated information. I believe that a human being is a tightly interconnected system of mind and body, and neither can be ignored without affecting the other. Simulated sensory perception does not replace the direct experience of external reality, metaphysical precision aside. I believe that reducing the importance of our bodies on our experience (or simply paying less attention to them) may take us farther from the important questions of life that have occupied humankind throughout history. I believe that we need both mind and body working together to experience the totality of the human experience, something that cannot be captured by either a remote-controlled robot or a disembodied computer program. Human beings are a combined mind-body system, and I believe both sides of our natures must be honored.

21.3 Summary

I'm happy to say that rendering systems are becoming more of a commodity item. People are now treating rendering systems like calculators: complex systems that can be guided with a few controls to accomplish a task reliably and predictably. We're not yet at the same level of ease that is provided by the calculator, but we're getting there.

I hope image synthesis can be a positive force in the world. I hope people find this another medium for creative self-expression, for sharing ideas and thoughts, for helping bring about more communication between people, and for growing, teaching, learning, and experiencing joy in the remarkable, vibrant universe in which we live.

V

APPENDICES

Abbreviators do harm to knowledge and to love, seeing that the love of any thing is the offspring of this knowledge, the love being the more fervent in proportion as the knowledge is more certain. And this certainty is born of a complete knowledge of all the parts, which, when combined, compose the totality of the thing which ought to be loved.

Leonardo da Vinci

In order to deviate successfully, *one has to have at least a passing acquaintance with whatever* norm *one expects to deviate from.*

Frank Zappa
("The Real Frank Zappa Book," 1989)

A

LINEAR ALGEBRA

A.1 General Notation

A number of typographical conventions are used in this book to simplify formulas and identify algebraic objects and useful phrases. Table A.1 gives a summary.

A.2 Linear Spaces

A *vector space*, or *linear space*, is a combination of a set X and two operators, commonly called *addition* and *scalar multiplication*. Addition of two elements $x, y \in X$ is written $x + y$, and scalar multiplication by some (possibly complex) factor $\alpha \in \mathcal{C}$ is written αx. A vector space is *algebraically closed* under these operators; that is, $(x + y) \in X$ and $\alpha x \in X$ for all $x, y \in X$ and $\alpha \in \mathcal{C}$. The *dimension* of the space is the largest number of linearly independent elements.

A particularly useful linear space is the space of linear functions. Consider the set of all functions $A: \mathcal{R} \rightarrow \mathcal{R}$. Define addition and scalar multiplication pointwise, so that for two functions $f, g \in A$, we write $(f + g)(x) = f(x) + g(x)$ and $(\alpha f)(x) = \alpha f(x)$. If two functions f and g satisfy these equations, they satisfy the requirements

Notation	Meaning
$\mathcal{Z}$	The integers
$\mathcal{C}$	The complex numbers
$\mathcal{R}$	The real numbers
(a, b)	The interval from a to b, excluding both
$[a, b]$	The interval from a to b, including both
Γ	An interval of reals
$\forall$	For all
$\exists$	There exists
$\Leftrightarrow$	If and only if
iff	If and only if

TABLE A.1
Notation for algebraic objects and useful phrases.

for a linear space. In this appendix we will speak variously of *vectors* or *functions* as elements of a linear space, depending on context.

A.2.1 Norms

A *norm* is generally intended to measure the size of some object. A norm for a function $x(t)$, written $\|x\|$, is a function to the reals that satisfies four requirements:

$$\begin{aligned} &\|x\| \geq 0 \\ &\|x\| = 0 \Leftrightarrow x = 0 \\ &\|\alpha x\| = |\alpha| \, \|x\|, \quad \alpha \in \mathcal{C} \\ &\|x + y\| \leq \|x\| + \|y\| \end{aligned} \tag{A.1}$$

The L_p norms are a family of norms that can be defined for functions. The L_p norm for a function $x(t)$ is written $\|x\|_p$; it is given by

$$\|x\|_p = \left[\int_a^b |x(t)|^p \, dt \right]^{1/p} \tag{A.2}$$

The L_1, L_2, and L_∞ norms are the most common, and the only ones used in this book. The L_2 norm is often called the *root-mean-square* (or RMS) norm, and the L_∞

norm is called the *Tchebyshev* norm. They are given by plugging in the appropriate value for p into Equation A.2, giving

$$\begin{aligned}\|x\|_1 &= \int_a^b |x(t)|\,dt \\ \|x\|_2 &= \left[\int_a^b |x(t)|^2\,dt\right]^{1/2} \\ \|x\|_\infty &= \lim_{p\to\infty} \|x\|_p = \max a \le t \le b|x(t)| \end{aligned} \tag{A.3}$$

A linear space together with a norm is called a *normed linear space*.

A.2.2 Inf and Sup

If S is a set or sequence (finite or infinite) of real numbers, then $\inf S$ is the *infimum*, or greatest lower bound, of S: the largest real number r such that $r \le s$ for all $s \in S$ (or $-\infty$ if S is unbounded below). Similarly, $\sup S$ is the *supremum*, or least upper bound: the smallest r such that $r \ge s$ for all $s \in S$.

A related but different pair of terms is *lim inf* and *lim sup*. These apply only to sequences, not to sets. Suppose S is a sequence of elements $s_n : \{s_1, s_2, \ldots\}$. Then $\liminf S$ is the limit of s_n as $n \to \infty$; that is, the largest real number r such that $s_n \ge r$ for all sufficiently large n. Similarly, $\limsup S$ is the smallest real number r such that $r \ge s_n$.

If the sequence S has a limit, the lim sup and lim inf are both equal to the limit. Every sequence has a lim sup and a lim inf whether it has a limit or not. For example, the sequence $\{1, -1, 1, -1, \ldots\}$ has $\liminf S = -1$ and $\limsup = +1$; the sequence and $\{1, 1/2, 1/3, 1/4, \ldots\}$ has $\liminf = 0$ and $\limsup = +\infty$.

If S is a finite set of numbers, then $\inf S = \min(S)$, and $\sup S = \max(S)$. If $S = \mathcal{Z}$ (the set of all integers), then $\inf S = -\infty$, and $\sup S = +\infty$. If S is empty, then by convention $\inf S$ is taken to be $+\infty$.

A.2.3 Metrics

A *metric* is considered some measure of the *distance* between two objects. A metric $d(x, y)$ between two objects x and y must satisfy four requirements:

$$\begin{aligned} &d(x,y) \ge 0 \\ &d(x,y) = 0 \;\Leftrightarrow\; x = y \\ &d(x,y) = d(y,x) \\ &d(x,z) \le d(x,y) + d(y,z), \quad z \in \mathcal{L}^2 \end{aligned} \tag{A.4}$$

The metric may be defined in terms of some norm:

$$d(x, y) = \|x - y\| \tag{A.5}$$

A.2.4 Completeness

Suppose we have some sequence of elements in a space X: $(x_1, x_2, x_3, \ldots)$. We can imagine using a norm in that space to find their distance from some element x. Suppose that in the limit the elements of this sequence get ever closer to x:

$$\lim_{n \to \infty} \|x_n - x\| = 0 \tag{A.6}$$

Then we say that the sequence *converges* to x. A vector space X is *complete* if the limit element for every convergent sequence is also in the space. A complete vector space is called a *Banach space*.

We call a sequence a *Cauchy sequence* if

$$\sup_{m,n>N} \|x_n - x_m\| \to 0 \text{ for } N \to \infty \tag{A.7}$$

which says that as we go further into the sequence, the terms are closer and closer together.

All of these notions of convergence and completeness are based on the norm being used at the time. A sequence in an infinite-dimensional linear space that is convergent under one norm may not be convergent under another. However, *finite*-dimensional linear spaces possess two very useful properties:

1. If a sequence in such a space is convergent under some norm, it is convergent under all norms.

2. Every normed finite-dimensional space is complete.

These properties are of great utility, because although computer graphics deals with problems posed in infinite-dimensional spaces of continuous functions, when represented on a computer all of our algorithms necessarily deal with finite-dimensional spaces of discrete functions.

A.2.5 Inner Products

The *inner product* (or *dot product*) tells us something about how one element *projects* onto another. In this book, we take the inner product of two vectors with the *bra-ket* notation, combining a *bra* $\langle f|$ with a *ket* $|g\rangle$ to form the inner product, $\langle f | g\rangle$.

An inner product must satisfy four requirements:

$$\begin{aligned}
&\langle x|\, y\rangle = \overline{\langle y|\, x\rangle} \\
&\langle ax_1 + bx_2|\, y\rangle = \bar{a}\,\langle x_1|\, y\rangle + \bar{b}\,\langle x_2|\, y\rangle \\
&\langle x|\, x\rangle \geq 0 \\
&\langle x|\, x\rangle = 0 \;\Leftrightarrow\; x = 0
\end{aligned} \tag{A.8}$$

The braket lets us take the inner product of two continuous functions f and g:

$$\langle f|\, g\rangle \triangleq \int \overline{f(t)}g(t)\, dt \tag{A.9}$$

This definition can be easily shown to satisfy the four requirements listed above. When no domain of integration is explicitly listed, the domain of the first function is implied.

It is sometimes useful to generalize this definition with a *weighting function* $w(t)$ that gives different impact to different pieces of the two functions involved. So the full inner product would be written

$$\langle f|\, g\rangle \triangleq \int \overline{f(t)}g(t)w(t)\, dt \tag{A.10}$$

The form we use most often in this book sets $w(t) = 1$.

If we have an inner product for a space, we can always define a norm by

$$\|x\| = \sqrt{\langle x|\, x\rangle} \tag{A.11}$$

We can show that this definition satisfies the requirements of a norm almost immediately from the definition of the inner product.

Not all norms can be written as a function of the inner product in some space. If we indeed have a Banach space with a norm derived from an inner product, we call that a *Hilbert space*. Familiar Euclidean rectilinear space is a Hilbert space.

This cumulative addition of structure to derive a series of spaces is summarized in Table A.2.

The inner product gives rise to the idea of *perpendicular* or *orthogonal* elements. We say two elements $x, y \in X$ are orthogonal, and write $x \perp y$, if and only if $\langle x|\, y\rangle = 0$. By extension, for some set S, $x \perp S$ if $\langle x|\, s\rangle = 0, \forall s \in S$.

A useful result of this property is that we can represent one element in terms of its projections onto other elements. In Euclidean space this is represented by projecting a vector onto the three principal axes, and then adding scaled versions of those axes back together again to retrieve the original vector. In general, we can write an element x in terms of n other suitable elements y_i by

$$x = \sum_{i=1}^{n} \langle x|\, \widehat{y_i}\rangle\, y_i \tag{A.12}$$

Cumulative components	Space name
Set S Addition operator Scalar multiplication operator	Linear space
$x + y \in X \quad \forall x, y \in X$ $\alpha x \in X \quad \forall \alpha \in \mathcal{C}, x \in X$	Complete linear space
Norm $\|\|x\|\|$	Banach space (if not complete, a normed linear space)
Inner product $\langle f \mid g \rangle$ with derived norm	Hilbert space

TABLE A.2
The hierarchy of linear spaces.

where the set of functions $\{\widehat{y}_i\}$ are the algebraic duals of the set of bases $\{y_i\}$.

A.3 Function Spaces

An important class of linear spaces are those occupied by functions.

Classes of functions that satisfy a particular criterion are said to make up a *function space*. The most important function space in this book is called the *function space* $\mathcal{L}^2$; it is made up of all functions $x(t)$ that satisfy

$$\int |x(t)|^2 dt < \infty \tag{A.13}$$

Such a function $x(t)$ is called *square-integrable*. A smaller space is denoted $\mathcal{L}^2(a, b)$, which is the class of functions that are square-integrable on the interval (a, b); that is,

$$\int_a^b |x(t)|^2 dt < \infty \tag{A.14}$$

Two functions $x(t)$ and $y(t)$ in $\mathcal{L}^2$ that are equal for all but a finite number of values of t are said to be *equivalent*, or *equal for almost all values of* t. So if two functions $x(t), y(t) \in \mathcal{L}^2$ are equivalent, they satisfy

$$\int_a^b [x(t) - y(t)]^2 dt = 0 \tag{A.15}$$

A related set of spaces is $\mathcal{L}^1$ and $\mathcal{L}^1(a,b)$, which satisfy

$$\int |x(t)|\, dt < \infty \tag{A.16}$$

for domains $[-\infty, +\infty]$ and (a,b), respectively.

A.4 Further Reading

This appendix barely hints at the rich structure of linear spaces. This is a field of study that has reached great depths and reveals elegant abstract relationships; it rewards careful study. Detailed introductions to this material may be found in most linear algebra texts, such as Strang's book [421]. Good starting points up to and including Hilbert spaces include the books by Young [500] and Berberian [39]. Some discussions intended to set the stage for particular topics are available, for example, integral equations in the books by Hoheisel [213] and Delves and Mohamed [120], and real and functional analysis in the books by Royden [362] and Rudin [365].

A good discussion of states, probabilities, and the linearity of state space in terms of quantum mechanics is given by Sudbery in his book [427].

Each topo map is a mosaic of errors, such as one section drawn 10% too large, while the adjacent one, in compensation, is drawn 10% too small. So, over distances of one to several miles, my figures can be up to 10% off. However, over longer distances, the map's errors balance out, and so do my mileages.

Jeffrey P. Schaffer
("Hiking the Big Sur Country:
The Ventana Wilderness," 1988)

B

PROBABILITY

A full exposition of statistics and probability is beyond the scope of this book. The reader who has not seen this information before or wants more depth should consult one of the many excellent texts on the subject, listed in the Further Reading section. Our survey will follow the work of Papoulis [331], Spanier and Gelbard [415], and Hammersley and Handscomb [183]. We start with events and then discuss total probability, repeated trials, random variables, measures, and distributions.

B.1 Events and Probability

In this section we will define some basic terms from probability theory and statistics. There are many subtleties and variations in the definitions that we will not explore, in favor of a rapid outline of the most relevant ideas. Much more detail on all of these topics may be found in the references.

In probability we often speak of an *experiment*. This is meant to stand for any process that returns a result. Thus an experiment can involve tossing a coin, or running a computer program to determine the first object intersected by a ray. Typically experiments are nondeterministic; that is, they will return one of many (perhaps infinite) answers, where each answer has a particular likelihood of occurring. When discussing outcomes of experiments, we usually group them into *sets* and then use common set operations such as union, intersection, and difference to compare sets and build new ones.

The canonical example of elementary probability is the die-throwing experiment. We suppose we have a *fair die*: a cube with the six integers from 1 to 6 painted on its faces, one number per face. The result of an experiment is the number showing on the top of the die after it has been thrown. Since it's a perfect cube, if we throw the die after sufficient shaking, no face is any more likely to end up on top than any other. When we refer to the "die-throwing experiment" below, we mean one fair throw of one fair die, so that each of the six faces has an equal likelihood of ending up on top.

Another experiment we will use involves bird spotting. Suppose we take a walk in a forest, and we classify the various birds we see in terms of their age and size. We will consider each walk in the woods one experiment, whose outcome may be a description of several birds, only one, or none at all.

We will call each possible set of results of an experiment an *event*, and we will use italic capital letters (A, B, C, or more generally, A_i) to represent events in this appendix. The term "event" should be distinguished from "result"; a single event may include many results. For example, we might speak of "a 9-inch, 3-year-old bird" as an event, or "any 6-month old bird" as an event. An event includes any number of possible results of the experiment: none, one, or many. If the outcome of an experiment matches any element in an event, we say that event has *occurred*. Thus one experiment has only one result, but it could satisfy several events.

We use Ω to denote the set of all possible outcomes of the experiment. Typically Ω is called the *certain event*, meaning that because it contains all possible results, an element of Ω is certain to contain the result of any run of the experiment. The set of no results is the empty set $\emptyset$.

Suppose that in our bird-watching experiment, we have the following events containing (age, size) pairs (the units are arbitrary; years and inches are an example). These events are sets of possible experimental outcomes:

$$\begin{aligned} A_1 &= \{(2,6),(3,1),(1,4)\} \\ A_2 &= \{(1,5),(3,1)\} \\ A_3 &= \{(2,2),(4,3)\} \end{aligned} \tag{B.1}$$

The two sets A_2 and A_3 are said to be *mutually exclusive*, since they share no common elements. Sets A_1 and A_2 are not exclusive. Formally, a list of events is exclusive if for any $i \neq j$, $A_i \cap A_j = \emptyset$.

Turning now to the die-throwing experiment, we might have the following three sets of possible rolls:

$$\begin{aligned} A_1 &= \{1, 2, 4, 5\} \\ A_2 &= \{3\} \\ A_3 &= \{1, 3, 6\} \end{aligned} \tag{B.2}$$

These sets are not exclusive, in pairs or all together. However, taken together they represent all the possible outcomes of the experiment. We call such a collection of events *exhaustive*. Formally, a set of events A_i is exhaustive if $\bigcup_i A_i = \Omega$.

A particular set of events may be exclusive, exhaustive, neither, or both.

A *probability* is a quantitative measure expressing our expectation that a given event will occur. Probability is a number between 0 and 1 inclusive; a value of 0 means that in practice that event will never occur, while a value of 1 means that it will certainly occur. We write the probability of event A as $P(A)$. The probability is defined as a real function that satisfies

$$\begin{aligned} P(\emptyset) &= 0 \\ P(\Omega) &= 1 \\ 0 \leq P(A) &\leq 1 \quad \text{for all } A \end{aligned} \tag{B.3}$$

Several combinations of events will prove useful. The probability of two events *A and B* occurring is written $P(AB)$. The probability of one of two events *A or B* occurring is written $P(A + B)$. Finally, we can write the *conditional probability of A given B*, $P(A|B)$, which is the probability that A will occur given that B has occurred.

Probabilities combine according to two basic laws:

$$\begin{aligned} P(A + B + C + \cdots) &\leq P(A) + P(B) + P(C) + \cdots \\ P(AB) &= P(A|B)P(B) \end{aligned} \tag{B.4}$$

If the events are exclusive, then the inequality in the first equation becomes exact equality.

Two events are called *independent* if

$$P(AB) = P(A)P(B) \tag{B.5}$$

If events A and B are independent, then $P(A|B) = P(A)$.

B.2 Total Probability

Suppose that we have n exclusive and exhaustive events A_i. For example, we might have an experiment that returns points in the unit circle. If we subdivide the circle

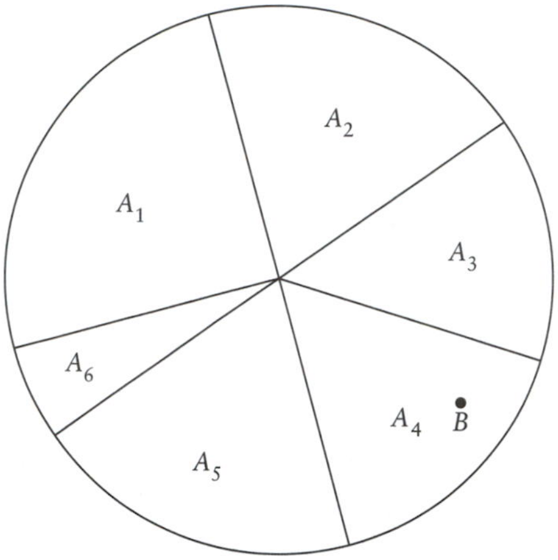

FIGURE B.1

The different wedges W_i tile the circle. Another event B is somewhere in the circle.

into n wedges W_i, as in Figure B.1, then each A_i can correspond to wedge W_i. For any arbitrary event B where $P(B) \neq 0$, we can write the *theorem on total probability*:

$$P(B) = P(B|A_1)P(A_1) + \cdots + P(B|A_n)P(A_n) \tag{B.6}$$

In words, this theorem says that the probability of an event B occurring is equal to the sum of n different probabilities, where n is the number of different events associated with the events A. If the A_n are exhaustive, then we know that in a given experiment exactly one of them must occur. If they are exclusive, then we know that one and only one of them will occur. So $1 = P(A_1) + \cdots + P(A_n)$. The first term on the right-hand side of the theorem is the probability of B occurring given that A_1 has occurred, times the probability that A_1 actually did occur. For any given experiment, only one of the A_i will be satisfied; suppose it's A_q. Then for that experiment (since we already know the outcome), $P(A_i) = 0, i \neq q$, and $P(A_q) = 1$. Thus the right-hand side reduces to $P(B|A_q)P(A_q) = P(B|A_q) = P(B)$. The last simplification comes about because we *know* that A_q actually did occur. The theorem is important because it allows us to express the probability that an event will happen in terms of conditional probabilities for that event and probabilities of other events; often we know this information.

To prove the theorem, think of the different events as exactly corresponding to their regions; thus, the event $A_2 + A_3$ corresponds to the region $W_2 \cup W_3$, and A_2A_3

corresponds to $W_2 \cap W_3$. Then because the A_i are exhaustive, their union is the complete circle, and the intersection of that with B is simply B:

$$B = B(A_1 + \cdots + A_n) = BA_1 + \cdots + BA_n \tag{B.7}$$

Because the A_i are exclusive, then the regions BA_i don't overlap, and from the first line of Equation B.4 we can say

$$P(B) = P(BA_1) + \cdots + P(BA_n) \tag{B.8}$$

Equation B.4 also says that $P(BA_i) = P(B|A_i)P(A_i)$, and combining this with Equation B.8 gives us Equation B.6. The theorem on total probability is useful for finding the $P(B)$ in terms of the $P(B|A_i)$ and the $P(A_i)$.

B.3 Repeated Trials

Suppose we repeat an experiment n times, and we want to know if a particular event occurs k times. For example, in the die-throwing experiment we might want to know how many times the die will come up with an even number. Thus we have two outcomes, represented by the sets $A_{\text{odd}} = \{1, 3, 5\}$ and $A_{\text{even}} = \{2, 4, 6\}$.

We begin by recalling from combinatorial analysis that if we are given n objects, and we are asked to form k distinct sets, then there are $N_n(k)$ sets, where

$$N_n(k) = \binom{n}{k} = \frac{n!}{k!(n-k)!} \tag{B.9}$$

Here a set is an unordered collection of objects, where two sets are distinct if they differ by at least one element. Thus two groups X and Y are different if $(X \cup Y) - (X \cap Y) \neq \emptyset$.

We will use this result to solve a useful problem: suppose we have an experiment with two possible outcomes, a and b, and we know the probabilities for each. What is the probability that we will get k outcomes of type a in n runs of the experiment?

We start by using the result above to answer a simpler question, and then building. Suppose we have an ordered collection of n objects, where each object is one of two types, type a and type b. We could write this ordered collection as a string of n characters, a and b. If there are k objects of type a, then there are $n - k$ objects of type b. How many different n-letter strings of a and b can we write, such that each string contains k instances of a?

Suppose we associate the n positions in the string with the integers 1 through n inclusive, and we make a set of the indices where each a occurs; this will be a set of k integers. For example, for $n = 8$ and $k = 4$, the string *abaabbab* would give us the set $\{1, 3, 4, 7\}$. Our problem now is to count how many subsets of k integers can be formed from a set of n integers. We have transformed our problem into a form that fits our result from above, and we observe that there are exactly $N_n(k)$ different strings of n symbols that contain exactly k instances of a.

We will use this result to find the probability of a certain number of events in repeated trials. Suppose we repeat an experiment n times, and we are looking for an event A that occurs with probability $P(A)$. We want to find $p_n(k)$, the probability that A occurs k times.

Suppose that $P(A) = p$, $P(\overline{A}) = q$, and $p + q = 1$, where $\overline{A}$ is the set of all outcomes that are not A. We write the result of experiment i as B_i, which is either A or $\overline{A}$. The result of the n experiments is then the sequence $\{B_1, \cdots, B_n\}$. The probability of getting k events of type a in a specific order is given by

$$P_1(B_1)P_2(B_2)\cdots P_n(B_n) = p^k q^{n-k} \tag{B.10}$$

where $P_i(B_i)$ is the probability that B_i is of type A. Thus the probability that A will occur k times in a specific order is given by $p^k q^{n-k}$. Now we want to know the probability that k events of type A will occur in any order; this is simply the sum of all the different ways that those k events can occur, which we found above is $N_n(k)$. These $N_n(k)$ different orders are mutually exclusive, so

$$p_n(k) = P(A \text{ occurs } k \text{ times}) = \binom{n}{k} p^k q^{n-k} \tag{B.11}$$

This formula is also known as the result of multiple, independent *Bernoulli trials* for two outcomes.

If there are more than two outcomes, Equation B.11 generalizes directly. Suppose we have m exclusive and exhaustive outcomes A_i, each with a probability p_m (thus $p_1 + \cdots + p_m = 1$). Then the probability that event A_1 occurs k_1 times, *and* event A_2 occurs k_2 times, *and* event A_3 occurs k_3 times, and so on, is given by

$$p_n(k_1, k_2, \ldots, k_{m-1}, k_m) = \frac{n!}{k_1!\, k_2! \cdots k_{m-1}!\, k_m!} {p_1}^{k_1} {p_2}^{k_2} \cdots {p_{m-1}}^{k_{m-1}} {p_m}^{k_m} \tag{B.12}$$

B.4 Random Variables

In the section above we discussed associating a probability with each possible outcome of an experiment. Suppose that we have a set of A_i events that are exhaustive and exclusive, each with an associated value $\eta \geq 0$. Then we say that η is a *random variable* (often abbreviated *r.v.*). Associated with the random variable is a *distribution function* $F(y)$. This function is defined to give the probability that the event that occurs has an associated value which is no greater than y. This function is sometimes called the *cumulative distribution function*. In symbols,

$$F(y) = P(\eta \leq y) \tag{B.13}$$

So this is the probability that *any* event will occur that has an associated value η less than y. If we sort all the events A_i by their associated η, then $F(y)$ is satisfied by all the events A_i for which $\eta < y$. We note that $F(-\infty) = 0$, $F(+\infty) = 1$, and that F is nondecreasing with y.

Associated with each distribution function is a *density function*. Typically the two are notated by the same letter, a capital for the distribution function and lowercase for the density function. When the distribution function is continuous, the density function may be written as its derivative: $f(y) = dF(y)\, dy$. In this situation, the density function $f(y)$ may be thought of as the likelihood that the random variable will take on the value y.

In the die-throwing experiment, we have six outcomes: $\Omega = \{A_1, \ldots, A_6\}$. These six events are exhaustive and exclusive; all six possible results are accounted for, and only one event will describe the result of any experiment. Since there are six possibilities with equal likelihoods, we attach equal probabilities to the events: $p(A_i) = 1/6$, $1 \leq i \leq 6$. The set $A_3 \cup A_4$ corresponds to our throwing *either* a 3 or 4. We will now define a random variable ξ on Ω by creating a real-valued function that associates a number with each event: $\xi(A_i) = i$, $1 \leq i \leq 6$. So for every possible outcome of the experiment, we have an associated number, which is the purpose of creating a random variable.

We will often deal with experiments where two or more random variables are observed simultaneously. For example, we might throw a pair of dice, or we might note the age and size of a bird. Suppose these two random variables are η_1 and η_2, and we are interested in determining if $\eta_1 < s_1$ while simultaneously $\eta_2 < s_2$. We can write the *joint distribution function* F on η_1 and η_2:

$$F(s_1, s_2) = P(\eta_1 < s_1, \eta_2 < s_2) \tag{B.14}$$

Suppose the associated 2D density function f is continuous. Then we can write the joint cumulative distribution function as a sum of all the densities up to a given point (s_1, s_2):

$$F(s_1, s_2) = \int_{-\infty}^{y} \int_{-\infty}^{x} f(u, v)\, du\, dv \tag{B.15}$$

For a given value (s_1, s_2), this tells us the probability that an experiment will have an outcome where the two observed variables satisfy $\eta_1 < s_1$ *and* $\eta_2 < s_2$ simultaneously. For example, this is the probability that we will spot a bird that is less than 2 years old *and* smaller than 8 inches in length. The joint cumulative distribution function is familiar to anyone who has used sum tables [111] to help out with texture mapping.

Suppose we now ask about the distribution of η_1 without regard for the state of η_2. For example, we might simply ask how many birds are less than 2 years old, whatever their size. We could write

$$F_1(s_1) = P(\eta_1 < s_1) = \int_{-\infty}^{x} \left[\int_{-\infty}^{\infty} f(u, v)\, du \right] dv \qquad \text{(B.16)}$$

We call F_1 the *marginal distribution* of F with respect to η_1. Similarly, we can write the *marginal density* of η_1 as

$$f_1(s_1) = F_1'(s_1) = \int_{-\infty}^{\infty} f(s_1, v)\, dv \qquad \text{(B.17)}$$

The marginal distribution (or density) can be thought of as the projection of a distribution (or density) along one or more dimensions.

Let's now posit a function $g(\eta)$, and ask for its *mean value*, also called its *expectation*, written $E[g]$. The *expected value* of g is defined by

$$E[g] = \int g(y)\, dF(y) \qquad \text{(B.18)}$$

There are several interpretations of Equation B.18, depending on how general we want to be about what functions g should be permitted, and what conditions need to be placed on $F(y)$ to create a meaningful definition for $dF(y)$. In practice, two interpretations prove most useful: the continuous and discrete. If we think of $F(y)$ as a function with derivative $f(y)$, then we can write Equation B.18 as

$$E[g] = \int g(y) f(y)\, dy \qquad \text{(B.19)}$$

If $F(y)$ is pieced together from flat segments with heights f_i at y_i, then we can write Equation B.18 as

$$E[g] = \sum_i g(y_i) f(y_i) \qquad \text{(B.20)}$$

Intuitively, the expected value for g is the weighted average of the values g takes on. The weights are given by the probability associated with each value of η. In other words, when a result η_0 is likely to occur, $g(\eta_0)$ will be multiplied by a relatively large value, and when η_0 is unlikely, $g(\eta_0)$ will be scaled down. The sum (or integral) of these weighted values gives us the most likely result to be returned by g over all possible values of η. The values $f(y)$ and f_i in Equations B.19 and B.20 are the *frequency functions* of the random variable η. The function $f(y)$ is called the *probability density function*, or, as mentioned earlier, sometimes simply the *density function* for the random variable η.

The definition of expected value in Equation B.18 has some interesting consequences. For example, we can observe that

$$E[a\eta + b] = a\ E[\eta] + b \tag{B.21}$$

Another result of the definition is that if a set of random variables η_i are independent, then it seems reasonable that the expected value of their mapping through g should be the same as the mapping of their expected value. In symbols,

$$\sum_i E[g_i(\eta_i)] = E\left[\sum_i g_i(\eta_i)\right] \tag{B.22}$$

and indeed this can be proven to be true. The surprise is that this relationship is also true even when the random variables are not independent! Note that this relation does *not* say that $E[g(\eta)] = g(E[\eta])$; this is usually not a true relation.

B.5 Measures

There are several useful measures associated with the expected value of a function; we review some of them here.

The value $E[\eta^r]$ is called the *rth moment of* η. Define $\mu = E[\eta]$. The value $\mu_r = E[(\eta - \mu)^r]$ is called the *rth central moment of* η. The first central moment of η, which is simply μ, is called the *mean* of η. The second central moment of η, written μ_2, is called the *variance* of η, also written $\mathrm{var}(\eta)$ or just V. The mean tells us something about the value of the random variable, while the variance tells us how spread-out the values are around that mean. The *standard deviation* is defined by $\sigma = \sqrt{\mu_2}$. The *coefficient of variation* is defined by σ/μ.

The standard deviation is an important measure of the degree to which observations will cluster about the mean value. To illustrate this, we can state the following theorem [415]: Let η be a random variable with expected value μ and standard deviation σ, and let $k > 0$. Then

$$P(|\eta - \mu| > k\sigma) \leq 1/k^2 \tag{B.23}$$

In words, this says that the probability of getting a result at k standard deviations away from the mean is less than $1/k^2$.

Some definitions tell us how two random variables are associated with each other. Suppose we have two random variables η_1 and η_2 with means μ_1 and μ_2. The *covariance* of these two variables, $\mathrm{cov}(\eta_1, \eta_2)$, is defined by

$$\mathrm{cov}(\eta_1, \eta_1) = E[(\eta_1 - \mu_1)(\eta_2 - \mu_2)] \tag{B.24}$$

The independence of the two random variables is a sufficient (but not necessary) condition for the covariance to be zero.

The *correlation coefficient* ρ is defined by

$$\rho = \frac{\operatorname{cov}(\eta_1, \eta_2)}{\sqrt{\operatorname{var}(\eta_1)\operatorname{var}(\eta_2)}} \tag{B.25}$$

The value of ρ lies in the interval $[-1, 1]$. If $\rho < 0$, then η_1 and η_2 are *negatively correlated*; if $\rho > 0$, then η_1 and η_2 are *positively correlated*; and if $\rho = 0$, then the variables are said to be *uncorrelated*. Another useful formula is given by

$$\operatorname{var}\left(\sum_{i=1}^{k} \eta_i\right) = \sum_{i=1}^{k}\sum_{j=1}^{k} \operatorname{cov}(\eta_i, \eta_j) \tag{B.26}$$

which is a corollary to Equation B.25.

B.6 Distributions

We will be interested in random variables that take on their values according to particular patterns, called *distributions*. A distribution may be thought of as a function that specifies cumulative distribution function for a random variable.

A few distributions are particularly important and are summarized here. The *normal distribution* $F_n(y)$ is specified by the mean and variance of the pattern, as well as a real value t:

$$F_n(y) = \int_{-\infty}^{y} \frac{1}{2\pi\sigma^2} e^{-(t-\mu)^2/(2\sigma^2)}\, dt \tag{B.27}$$

The *exponential distribution* $F_e(y)$ is specified by a single real value λ:

$$F_e(y) = \begin{cases} 0 & y < 0 \\ 1 - e^{\lambda y} & y \geq 0 \end{cases} \tag{B.28}$$

The *rectangular distribution* $F_r(y)$ is specified by an upper and lower bound, given by real numbers a and b:

$$F_r(y) = \begin{cases} 0 & y < a \\ (y-a)/(b-a) & a \leq y \leq b \\ 1 & y > b \end{cases} \tag{B.29}$$

The *binomial distribution* $F_b(y)$ is specified by two non-negative integers n and t, and a real value $p \in [0, 1]$.

$$F_b(y) = \sum_{t \leq y} \frac{n!}{t!\,(n-t)!} p^t (1-p)^{n-t} \tag{B.30}$$

As we saw earlier, this is the distribution of η occurrences of a desired event with probability p out of n trials.

The values associated with each distribution are called the *parameters* of the distribution, and serve to completely characterize it. We will often guess a random variable to have a distribution given by one of the above functions; our job is then to find the appropriate values of the parameters.

B.7 Geometric Series

We will often encounter expressions of the form

$$\sum_{n=0}^{N-1} r^n \tag{B.31}$$

for some real or complex value r. This is called a *geometric series* with *kernel* r. A closed form expression for the the first N terms of such a series can be found in most calculus texts; we provide it here for reference:

$$\sum_{n=0}^{N-1} r^n = \begin{cases} N & r = 1 \\ \dfrac{1 - r^N}{1 - r} & r \neq 1 \end{cases} \tag{B.32}$$

B.8 Further Reading

For more statistical background, any of a number of classic texts may be consulted; I found the book by Papoulis [331] particularly clear and direct. This appendix has presented a classical view of probability. A different approach is advocated by some who work in the field of *fuzzy logic*. A popular introduction to this field is given by Kosko [253]; a textbook approach by the same author may be found in [252].

Science is an attempt to develop a system for the evolution of constructions of reality, and to permit a graceful exit for the dinosaurs.

Walter Truett Anderson
("Reality Isn't What It Used To Be," 1992)

C

HISTORICAL NOTES

In this appendix we briefly review the history of the laws of specular reflection and refraction. They represent one of the most obvious and basic properties of light, and have invited analysis for over 2,000 years.

C.1 Specular Reflection and Transmission

The law of specular reflection states that the angle of incidence equals the angle of reflection ($\theta_i = \theta_r$). The law of specular refraction (or Snell's law) is only slightly more complicated: it states $\eta_i \sin\theta_i = \eta_t \sin\theta_t$, where η_i and η_t are the incident and transmitted indices of reflection. Although both laws are easily verified in everyday situations, it is useful to understand where they come from.

One of the many accessible explanations arises from Fermat's law, which leads to the concept of optical path length. The development of Fermat's law has a beautiful history, which we recapitulate here briefly. This discussion is based on that in Hecht [200].

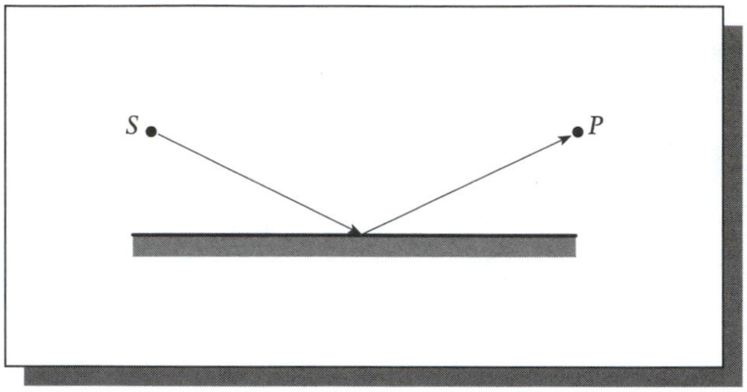

FIGURE C.1
Hero's principle.

Hero of Alexandria was a mathematician and inventor who lived and died somewhere between the second century B.C. and the third century A.D. His findings are as follows.

> **Hero's principle:** A ray of light leaving a point S, reflecting off a mirror and then arriving at some point P, traverses the shortest possible path in space.

Figure C.1 illustrates the geometry of this statement. Although true for reflection in a homogeneous material, we know from experience that when light refracts (e.g., passing from air into water), it bends and therefore does not follow the shortest path in space.

In 1657, Pierre de Fermat, a lawyer and amateur mathematician, generalized the rule:

> **Fermat's law:** A ray of light, in traversing a route from any one point to another, follows the path which takes the least amount of time to negotiate.

Fermat's law is more accurate than Hero's principle, but it is still incomplete. We can generalize it with the idea of the optical path length.

Figure C.2 a shows a ray of light traveling through a liquid of smoothly changing densities. At each point of the liquid the index of refraction is determined by the local density. Thus the *time of flight* required by the ray to travel from point P to point Q is given by

$$t = \int_P^Q \kappa(s)\, ds \tag{C.1}$$

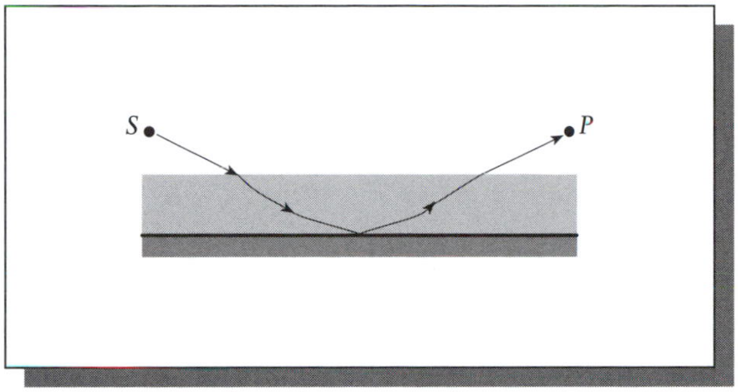

FIGURE C.2
A ray of light traveling through a liquid of smoothly changing densities.

where $\kappa(s)$ represents the index of refraction as a function of position s along the ray. If we replace the continuous medium with a series of thin slabs, each with index of refraction η_j, and the ray travels a distance d_j in each medium, then the time of flight is given by the discrete form

$$t = \frac{1}{c}\sum_{j=1}^{k} d_j \eta_j \tag{C.2}$$

As the slabs become thinner, they approach a medium of smoothly changing density, as in Figure C.2. The time of flight (in either form) is referred to as the *optical path length* (OPL). We may now paraphrase Fermat:

> **Reworded Fermat:** A ray traverses a route that corresponds to the shortest optical path length.

Although this is more succinct, we have not improved the statement. What is wrong with it? Consider light that is leaving a point source P and subsequently being focused by a lens onto another point Q, as in Figure C.3. Clearly there are many paths that light can, and does, take. Fermat's law is too restrictive when specifying *the* shortest optical path length. Correcting this restriction involves the stationary values of the OPL.

A function $f(x)$ has a *stationary value* at $x = x_0$ if $df/dx = 0$ at x_0. Thus a stationary value may correspond to a maximum, minimum, or point of inflection with horizontal tangent, as shown in Figure C.4. One implication of a vanishing derivative is that for a stationary value $f(x_0)$, the value $f(x) \approx f(x_0)$ when $x \approx x_0$.

We can now paraphrase Fermat's law in more general terms:

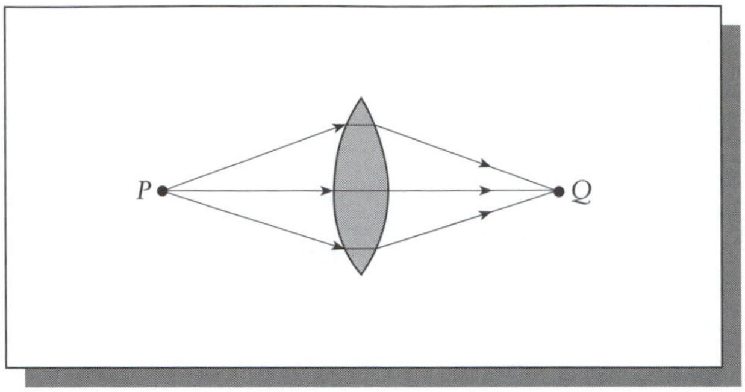

FIGURE C.3
A case where Fermat's law doesn't hold.

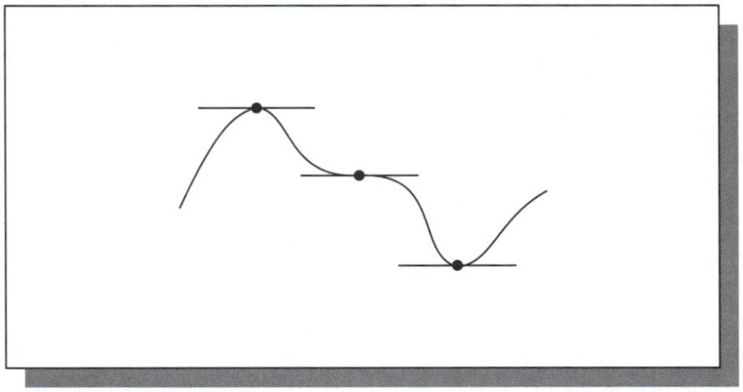

FIGURE C.4
A *stationary value* is a point of zero derivative; that is, a minimum, maximum, or inflection.

> **Fermat's law (modern form):** A ray of light, when traveling from one point to another, follows a path that corresponds to a stationary value of the optical path length.

This agrees with the example of the focused point source, since each of the many paths has the same optical path length. (The light near the edge of the lens travels a longer distance through the air than the light at the center of the lens, but the former travels only a small distance through the glass relative to the latter. Since the light travels more slowly in the glass, the times equal out.)

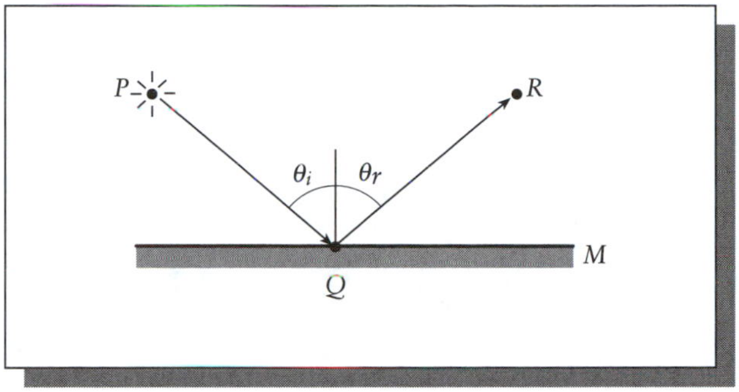

FIGURE C.5
The geometry of specular reflection.

C.1.1 Specular Reflection

We will use now the modern form of Fermat's law to derive the law of reflection. Figure C.5 shows a light source **P**, a mirror **M**, a reflection point Q, and a reflected point R. The angle of incidence is θ_i and the angle of reflection is θ_r; we wish to find their relationship. We will follow the development in Hecht [200]. For convenience and clarity, we will write the index of refraction as a constant, η, rather than explicitly writing the wavelength-dependent form $\eta(\lambda)$.

Assume that the ray travels through a homogeneous material of index of refraction η. The optical path length is thus given by the distances involved:

$$\begin{aligned} OPL &= \eta\overline{PQ} + \eta\overline{QR} \\ &= \eta\sqrt{h^2 + x^2} + \eta\sqrt{b^2 - (a - x)^2} \end{aligned} \tag{C.3}$$

To find the stationary points of this OPL, we find $d(\text{OPL})/dx$ and set the result to 0:

$$0 = \frac{\eta x}{\sqrt{h^2 + x^2}} + \frac{\eta(a - x)}{\sqrt{b^2 + (a - x)^2}} \tag{C.4}$$

Note from the figure that

$$\sin(\theta_i) = \frac{x}{\sqrt{h^2 + x^2}} \tag{C.5}$$

$$\sin(\theta_r) = \frac{a - x}{\sqrt{b^2 + (a - x)^2}} \tag{C.6}$$

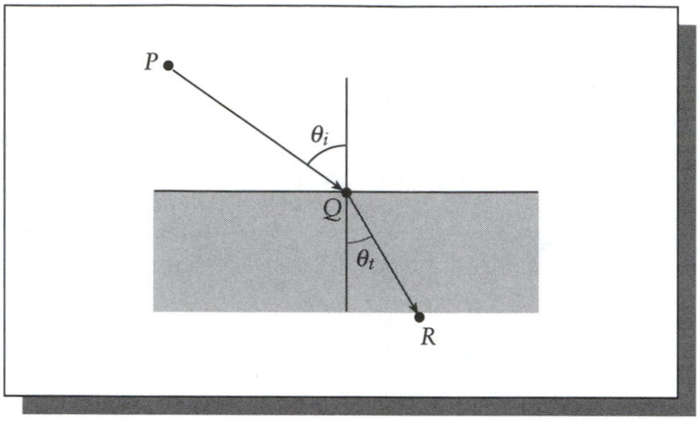

FIGURE C.6
The geometry of specular transmission.

Thus we may rewrite Equation C.4 as

$$0 = \eta \sin(\theta_i) - \eta \sin(\theta_r) \tag{C.7}$$

which brings us to the *law of reflection*:

$$\theta_i = \theta_r \tag{C.8}$$

The law of reflection says that for the light to take a path corresponding to the shortest OPL, it must reflect at a point such that the angle of incidence equals the angle of reflection.

C.1.2 Specular Transmission

We will now use the modern form of Fermat's law to derive the law of specular transmission; the discussion will follow very similar lines to the ones that led to the law of specular reflection.

Figure C.6 shows light leaving a source P, striking an interface at point Q, and arriving at point R. Suppose that the media containing P and Q are distinct, homogeneous media with indices of refraction η_i and η_t. The angle of incidence is θ_i and the angle of refraction (or transmission) is θ_t; we wish to find their relationship.

We proceed as before, first writing the expression for the optical path length:

$$\begin{aligned} OPL &= \eta_i \overline{PQ} + \eta_t \overline{QR} \\ &= \eta_i \sqrt{h^2 + x^2} + \eta_t \sqrt{b^2 - (a - x)^2} \end{aligned} \tag{C.9}$$

We now find the derivative and set it to zero:

$$0 = \frac{\eta_i x}{\sqrt{h^2 + x^2}} + \frac{\eta_t (a - x)}{\sqrt{b^2 + (a - x)^2}} \tag{C.10}$$

Note from the figure that

$$\sin(\theta_i) = \frac{x}{\sqrt{h^2 + x^2}} \tag{C.11}$$

$$\sin(\theta_r) = \frac{a - x}{\sqrt{b^2 + (a - x)^2}} \tag{C.12}$$

Thus we may rewrite Equation C.10 as

$$0 = \eta_i \sin(\theta_i) - \eta_t \sin(\theta_t) \tag{C.13}$$

This brings us to the *law of refraction*:

$$\eta_i \sin(\theta_i) = \eta_t \sin(\theta_t) \tag{C.14}$$

which is Snell's law. This is the relationship between the angles of incidence and refraction, as we desired.

In this section we have derived the relationship between incident, reflected, and transmitted angles by assuming that light took a path governed by the modern form of Fermat's principle. We might wonder how a ray of light "knows" the right path to follow—might it ever take another path only to find that it is not the right one? This and other questions are explored at a conversational level in the context of modern quantum mechanics in Feynman's wonderful little book on quantum electrodynamics [144].

If there exists any one reliable algorithm for finding the roots of transcendental equations it is yet to be found. We have a variety of medicines that work with varying degrees of potency (including zero!), but the state of the art still precludes the confident writing of computational prescriptions without having looked over the patient rather closely.

Forman S. Acton
("Numerical Methods That Work," 1970)

D

ANALYTIC FORM FACTORS

This appendix contains a number of useful analytic form factors for different geometric situations. These form factors are adapted from the catalogs in Siegel and Howell [406] and Howell [215]. These references contain many hundreds of analytic form factors for many general and specialized geometries.

D.1 Differential and Finite Surfaces

This appendix organizes the form factors into three categories, depending on whether the two patches are both differential, both finite, or mixed.

D.1.1 Differential to Differential

DD1: Differential patch to differential patch. See Figure D.1.

$$F_{dA_1,dA_2} = \frac{\cos\theta_1 \cos\theta_2}{\pi r^2}\, dA_2$$

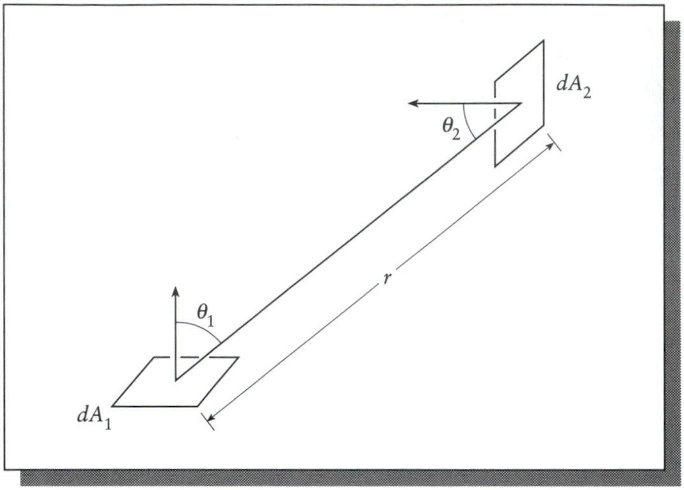

FIGURE D.1

Geometry for DD1: differential patch to differential patch.

D.1.2 Differential to Finite

DF1: Differential patch to finite patch. See Figure D.2.

$$F_{dA_1,A_2} = \int_{A_2} \frac{\cos\theta_1 \cos\theta_2}{\pi r^2} V(P_1, P_2)\, dA_2$$

DF2: Differential plane element to plane parallel rectangle; normal to element passes through corner of rectangle. See Figure D.3.

$$X = a/c, \qquad Y = b/c$$

$$F_{dA_1,A_2} = \frac{1}{2\pi}\left[\frac{X}{\sqrt{1+X^2}}\tan^{-1}\frac{Y}{\sqrt{1+X^2}} + \frac{Y}{\sqrt{1+Y^2}}\tan^{-1}\frac{X}{\sqrt{1+Y^2}}\right]$$

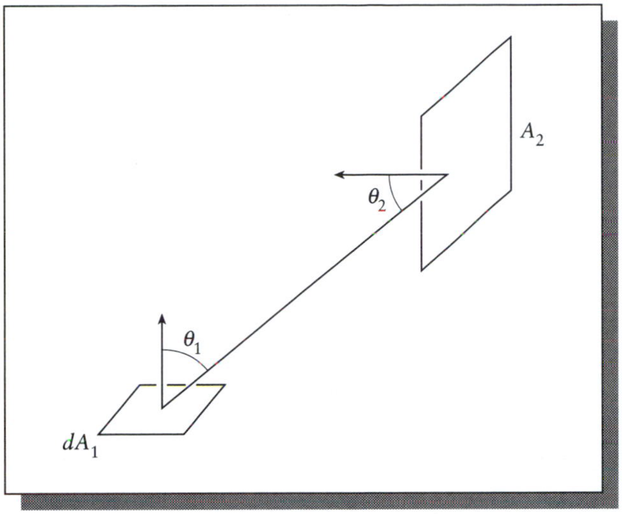

FIGURE D.2
Geometry for DF1: differential patch to finite patch.

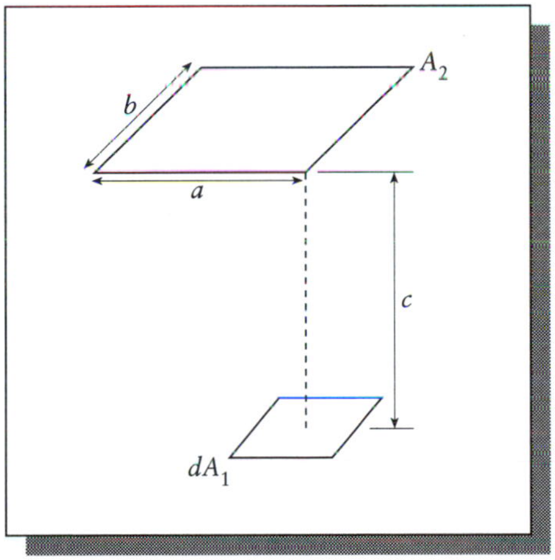

FIGURE D.3
Geometry for DF2: differential plane element to plane parallel rectangle.

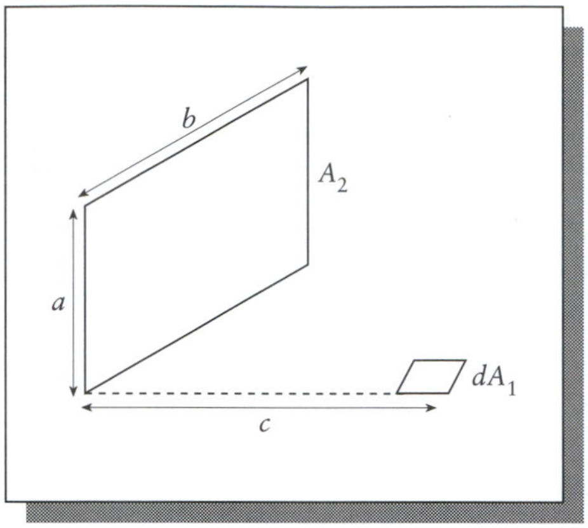

FIGURE D.4

Geometry for DF3: differential plane element to rectangle in plane at right angle to plane of element.

DF3: Differential plane element to rectangle in plane at right angle to plane of element. See Figure D.4.

$$X = a/b, \qquad Y = c/b$$

$$F_{dA_1,A_2} = \frac{1}{2\pi}\left[\tan^{-1}\frac{1}{Y} - \frac{Y}{\sqrt{X^2+Y^2}}\tan^{-1}\frac{1}{\sqrt{X^2+Y^2}}\right]$$

DF4: Plane differential element to circular disk in plane parallel to element; normal to element passes through center of disk. See Figure D.5.

$$F_{dA_1,A_2} = \frac{r^2}{h^2+r^2}$$

DF5: Plane differential element to circular disk in plane parallel to element. See Figure D.6.

$$H = \frac{h}{a} \qquad R = \frac{r}{a} \qquad Z = 1 + H^2 + R^2$$

$$F_{dA_1,A_2} = \frac{1}{2}\left[1 - \frac{1+H^2-R^2}{\sqrt{Z^2-4R^2}}\right]$$

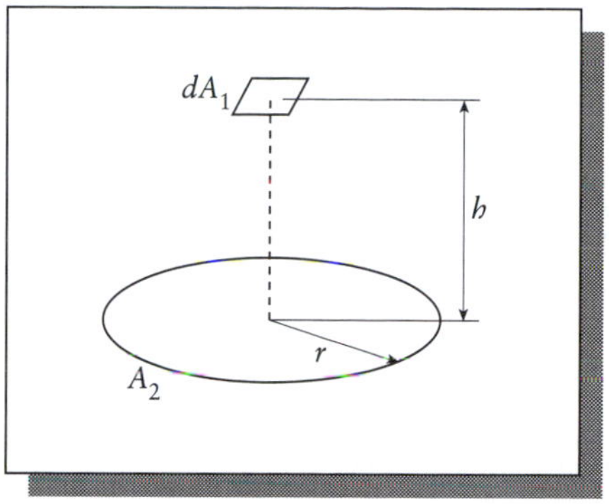

FIGURE D.5

Geometry for DF4: plane differential element to circular disk in plane parallel to element; normal to element passes through center of disk.

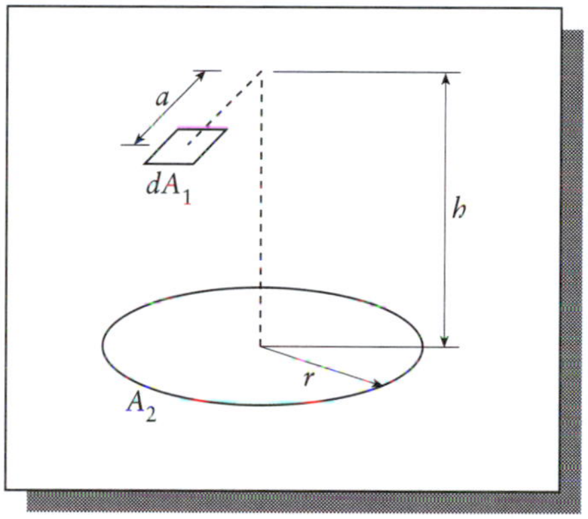

FIGURE D.6

Geometry for DF5: plane differential element to circular disk in plane parallel to element.

DF6: Spherical point source to a sphere of radius r. See Figure D.7.

$$R = \frac{r}{h}$$

$$F_{dA_1,A_2} = \frac{1}{2}\left[1 - \sqrt{1 - R^2}\right]$$

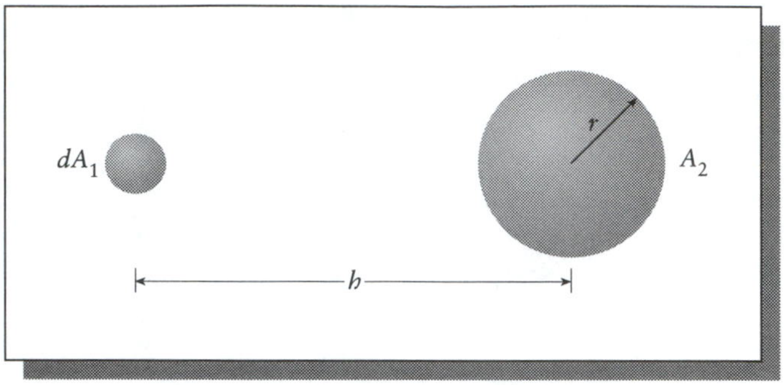

FIGURE D.7

Geometry for DF6: spherical point source to a sphere of radius r.

DF7: Plane differential element to sphere of radius r; normal to center of element passes through center of sphere. See Figure D.8.

$$F_{dA_1,A_2} = \left(\frac{r}{h}\right)^2$$

DF8: Plane differential element to sphere of radius r; tangent to element passes through center of sphere. See Figure D.9.

$$H = \frac{h}{r}$$

$$F_{dA_1,A_2} = \frac{1}{\pi}\left[\tan^{-1}\frac{1}{\sqrt{H^2-1}} - \frac{\sqrt{H^2-1}}{H^2}\right]$$

DF9: Sphere to disk; normal to center of disk passes through center of sphere. See Figure D.10.

$$R_2 = \frac{r_2}{h}$$

$$F_{A_1,A_2} = \frac{1}{2}\left[1 - \frac{1}{\sqrt{1+{R_2}^2}}\right]$$

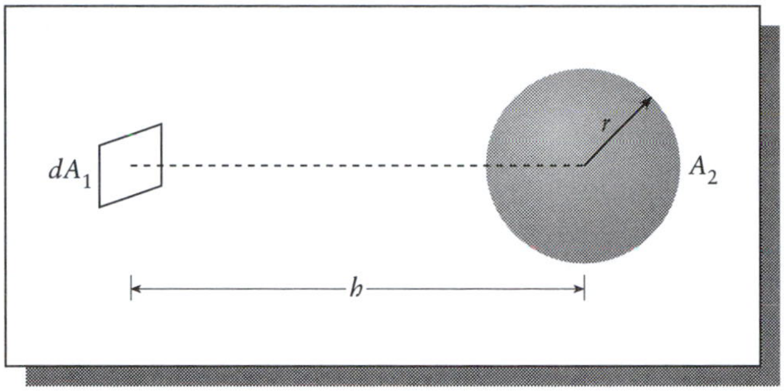

FIGURE D.8

Geometry for DF7: plane differential element to sphere of radius r; normal to center of element passes through center of sphere.

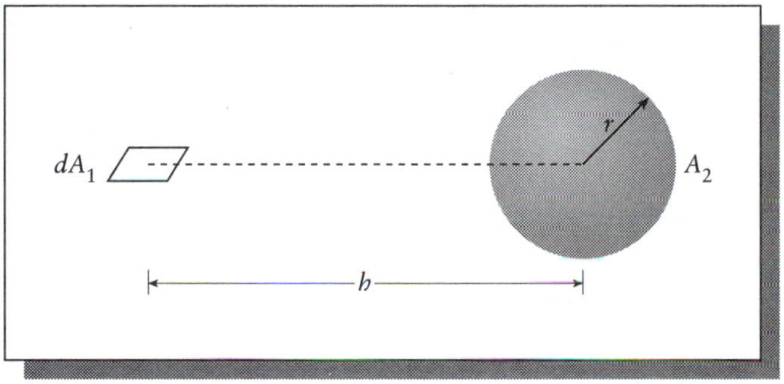

FIGURE D.9

Geometry for DF8: plane differential element to sphere of radius r; tangent to element passes through center of sphere.

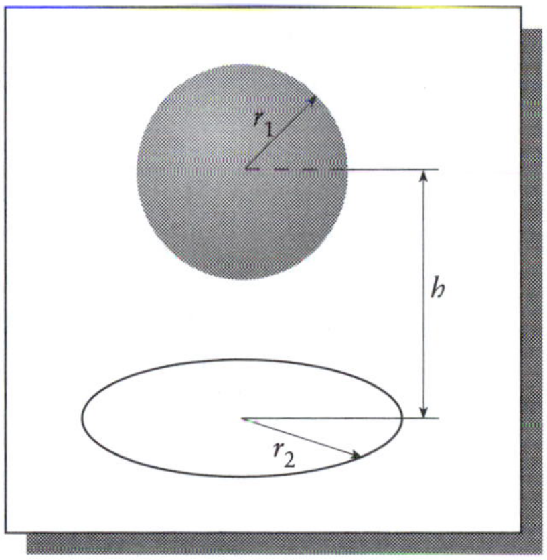

FIGURE D.10

Geometry for DF9: sphere to disk.

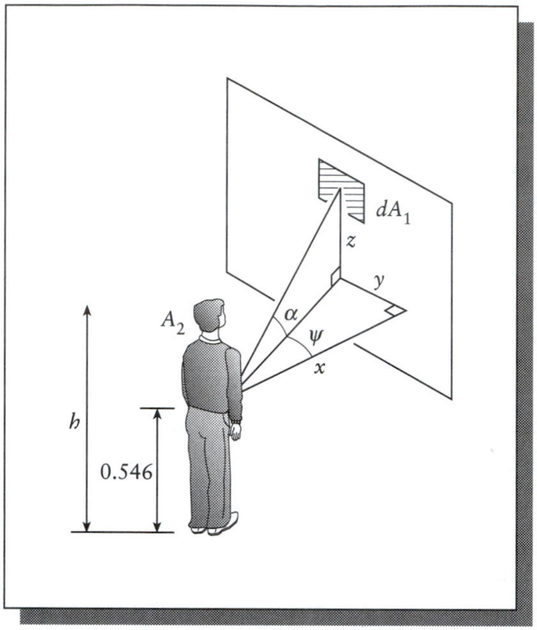

FIGURE D.11

Geometry for DF10: differential element perpendicular to standing person facing it.

DF10: Differential element perpendicular to standing person facing it. Distances are measured in feet, weight in pounds. See Figure D.11.

$$F_{dA_1,A_2} = \frac{x\,[0.65 + \cos\alpha\,(0.715 + 0.52|\cos\psi|)]\,hw^{1/3}}{30.8(x^2 + y^2 + z^2)^{1.5}}$$

DF11: Differential element perpendicular to sitting person facing it. Distances are measured in feet, weight in pounds. See Figure D.12.

$$F_{A_1,A_2} = \frac{x\,[1.365 + (0.2 + 0.673\sin\alpha)\cos\alpha\cos\psi]\,hw^{1/3}}{30.8(x^2 + y^2 + z^2)^{1.5}}$$

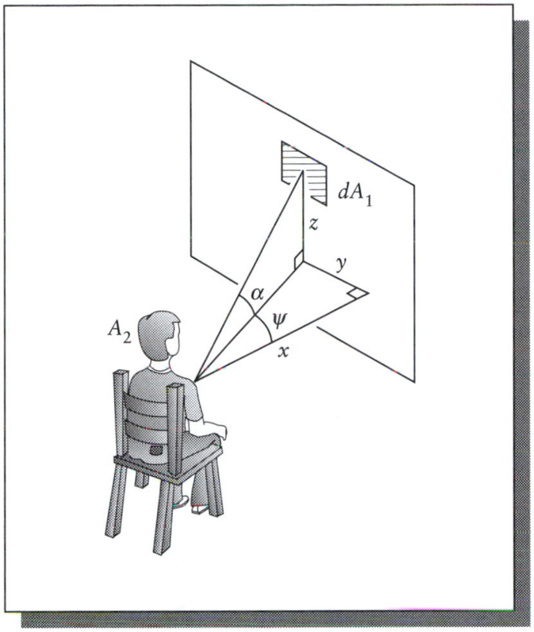

FIGURE D.12

Geometry for DF11: differential element perpendicular to sitting person facing it.

DF12: Differential element to cow. Distances measured in meters. (This is an approximation based on using an ideal spherical cow of radius R.) See Figure D.13.

$$R = \frac{r}{lm} \qquad X = \frac{l}{lm} \qquad Y = \frac{y}{lm}$$

$$F_{dA_1,A_2} = \frac{R^2}{(1 + X^2 + Y^2)^{3/2}}$$

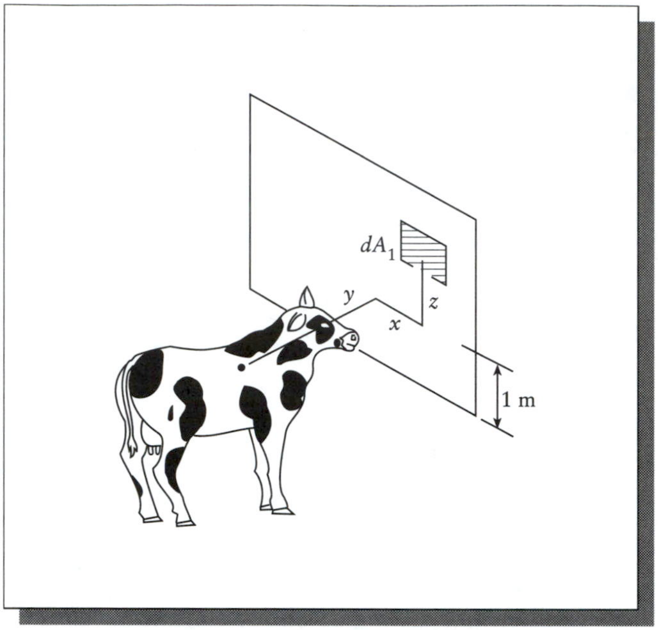

FIGURE D.13
Geometry for DF12: differential element to cow.

D.1.3 Finite to Finite

FF1: Finite patch to finite patch. See Figure D.14.

$$F_{A_1,A_2} = \frac{1}{A_1}\int_{A_1}\int_{A_2}\frac{\cos\theta_1\cos\theta_2}{\pi r^2}V(P_1,P_2)\,dA_2\,dA_1$$

FF2: Strip element to rectangle in plane parallel to strip; strip is opposite one edge of rectangle. See Figure D.15.

$$X = a/c, \qquad Y = b/c$$

$$F_{dA_1,A_2} = \frac{1}{Y\pi}\left[\sqrt{1+Y^2}\tan^{-1}\frac{X}{\sqrt{1+Y^2}} - \tan^{-1}X + \frac{XY}{\sqrt{1+X^2}}\tan^{-1}\frac{Y}{\sqrt{1+X^2}}\right]$$

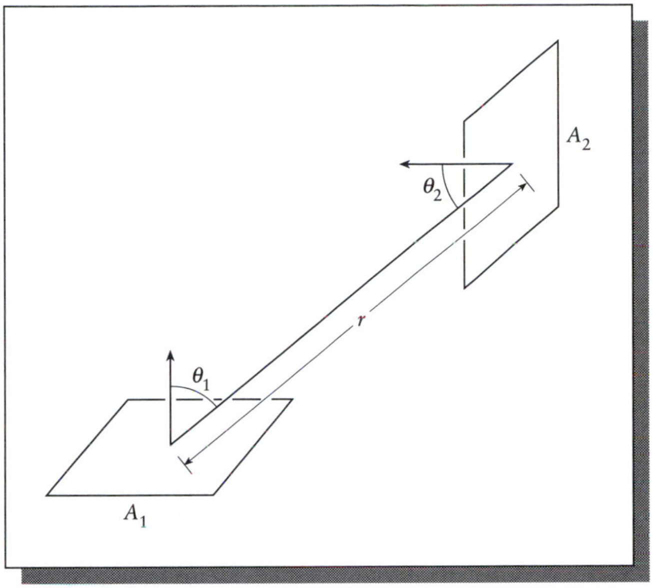

FIGURE D.14
Geometry for FF1: finite patch to finite patch.

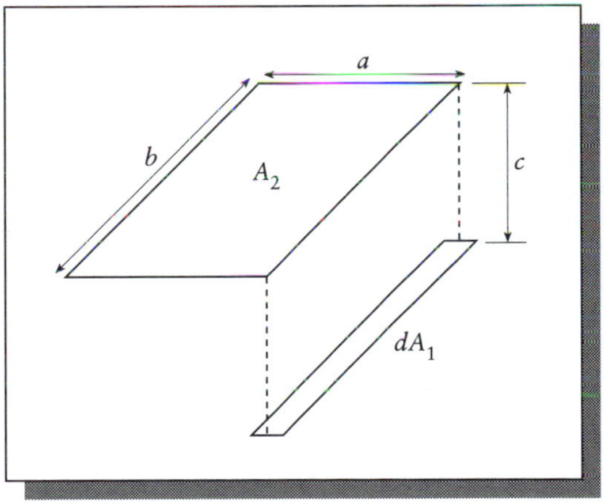

FIGURE D.15
Geometry for FF2: strip element to rectangle in plane parallel to strip.

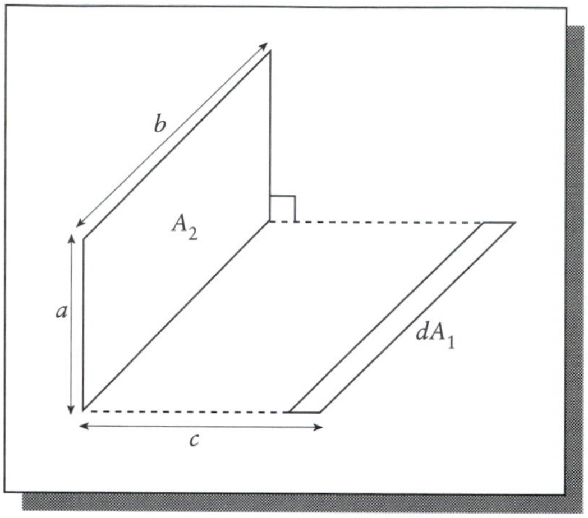

FIGURE D.16
Geometry for FF3: strip element to rectangle in plane at right angles to strip.

FF3: Strip element to rectangle in plane at right angles to strip. See Figure D.16.

$$X = a/b, \qquad Y = c/b$$

$$F_{dA_1,A_2} = \frac{1}{\pi}\left[\tan^{-1}\frac{1}{Y} + \frac{Y}{2}\ln\frac{Y^2(X^2+Y^2+1)}{(Y^2+1)(X^2+Y^2)} - \frac{Y}{\sqrt{X^2+Y^2}}\tan^{-1}\frac{1}{\sqrt{X^2+Y^2}}\right]$$

FF4: Identical parallel directly opposed rectangles. See Figure D.17.

$$X = a/c, \qquad Y = b/c$$

$$F_{A_1,A_2} = \frac{2}{XY\pi}\left[\ln\sqrt{\frac{(1+X^2)(1+Y^2)}{1+X^2+Y^2}} + X\sqrt{1+Y^2}\tan^{-1}\frac{X}{1+Y^2} + Y\sqrt{1+X^2}\tan^{-1}\frac{Y}{1+X^2} - X\tan^{-1}X - Y\tan^{-1}Y\right]$$

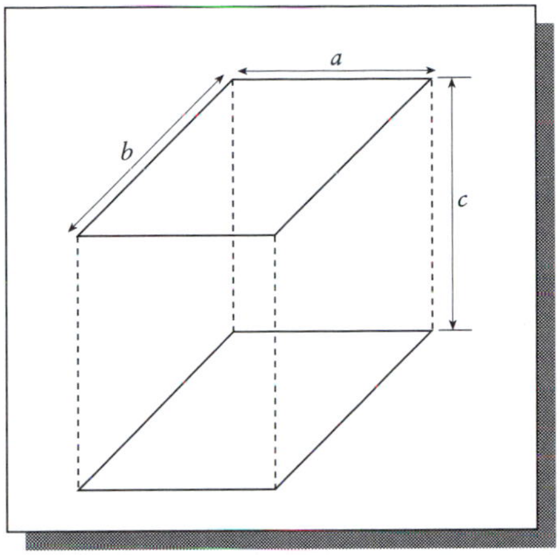

FIGURE D.17
Geometry for FF4: identical parallel directly opposed rectangles.

FF5: Two finite rectangles of same length, with one common edge at right angles to each other. See Figure D.18.

$$H = h/l, \qquad W = w/l$$

$$F_{A_1,A_2} = \frac{1}{W\pi}\left[W\tan^{-1}\frac{1}{W} + H\tan^{-1}\frac{1}{H} - \sqrt{H^2+W^2}\tan^{-1}\frac{1}{\sqrt{H^2+W^2}} + \frac{1}{4}\ln\left\{\frac{(1+W^2)(1+H^2)}{1+W^2+H^2}\left[\frac{W^2(1+W^2+H^2)}{(1+W^2)(W^2+H^2)}\right]^{W^2}\left[\frac{H^2(1+W^2+H^2)}{(1+H^2)(W^2+H^2)}\right]^{H^2}\right\}\right]$$

FF6: Parallel circular disks with centers along the same normal. See Figure D.19.

$$R_1 = \frac{r_1}{h} \qquad R_2 = \frac{r_2}{h} \qquad X = 1 + \frac{1+{R_2}^2}{{R_1}^2}$$

$$F_{dA_1,A_2} = \frac{1}{2}\left[X - \sqrt{X^2 - 4\left(\frac{R_2}{R_1}\right)^2}\right]$$

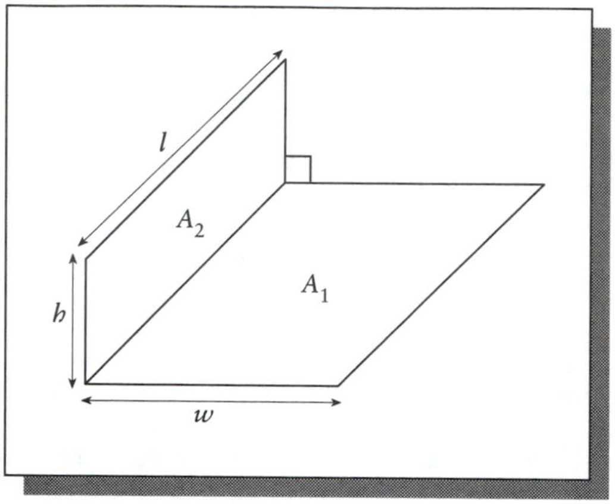

FIGURE D.18

Geometry for FF5: two finite rectangles of same length, with one common edge at right angles to each other.

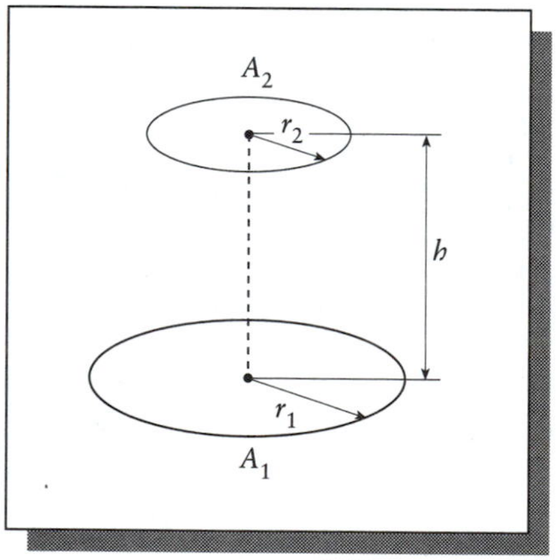

FIGURE D.19

Geometry for FF6: parallel circular disks with centers along the same normal.

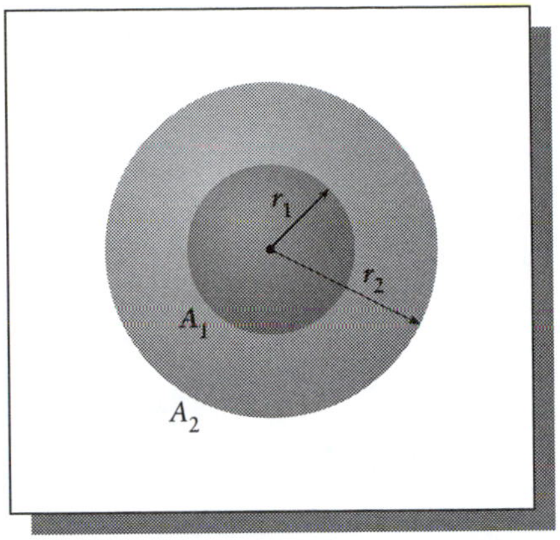

FIGURE D.20
Geometry for FF7: concentric spheres.

FF7: Concentric spheres. See Figure D.20.

$$F_{A_1,A_2} = 1$$
$$F_{A_2,A_1} = \left(\frac{r_1}{r_2}\right)^2$$
$$F_{A_2,A_2} = 1 - \left(\frac{r_1}{r_2}\right)^2$$

FF8: A differential ring on a disk to a sphere whose normal through center passes through sphere center. See Figure D.21.

$$R_1 = r_1/a \qquad R_2 = r_2/a$$

$$F_{dA_1,A_2} = \frac{{R_2}^2}{(1 + {R_1}^2)^{3/2}}$$

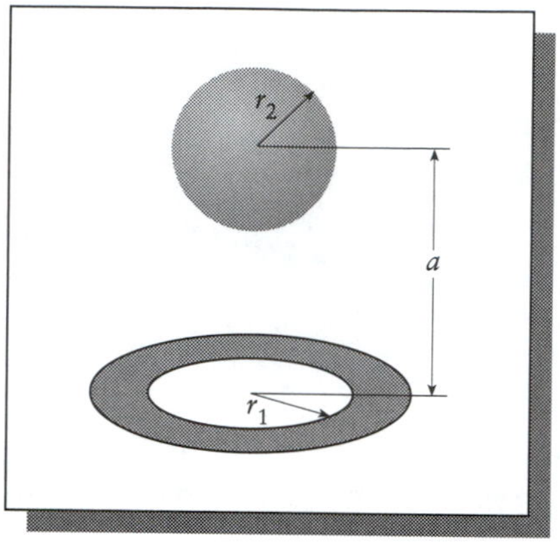

FIGURE D.21

Geometry for FF8: a differential ring on a disk to a sphere whose normal through center passes through sphere center.

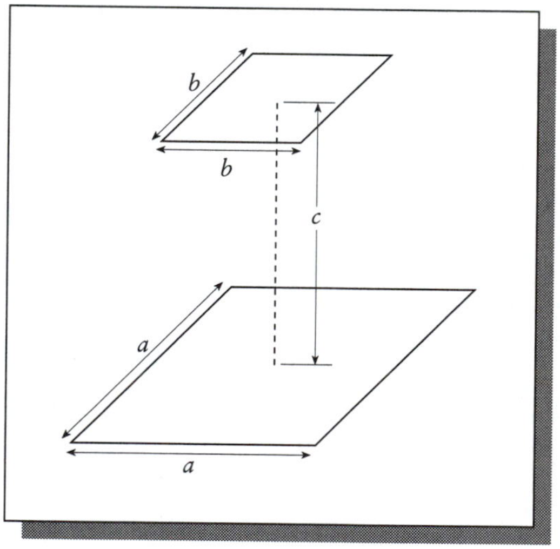

FIGURE D.22

Geometry for FF9: parallel squares of different sizes.

FF9: Parallel squares of different sizes. See Figure D.22.

$$A = a/c \qquad B = b/a \qquad X = A(1+B) \qquad Y = A(1-B)$$

$$A < 0.2 : F_{A_1,A_2} = \frac{(AB)^2}{\pi}$$

$$\begin{aligned} A \geq 0.2 : F_{A_1,A_2} = \frac{1}{\pi A^2} \Bigg\{ & \ln\left(\frac{\left[A^2\left(1+B^2\right)+2\right]^2}{\left(Y^2+2\right)\left(X^2+2\right)}\right) \\ & + \sqrt{Y^2+4}\left[Y \tan^{-1}\left(\frac{Y}{\sqrt{Y^2+4}}\right) - X \tan^{-1}\left(\frac{X}{\sqrt{Y^2+4}}\right)\right] \\ & + \sqrt{X^2+4}\left[X \tan^{-1}\left(\frac{X}{\sqrt{X^2+4}}\right) - Y \tan^{-1}\left(\frac{Y}{\sqrt{X^2+4}}\right)\right]\Bigg\} \end{aligned}$$

FF10: Parallel rectangles with parallel sides. See Figure D.23.

$$X = x/z \qquad N = \eta/z$$

$$Y = y/z \qquad S = \xi/z$$

$$\alpha_{l,i} = S_l - X_i \qquad \beta_{k,j} = N_k - Y_j$$

$$F_{A_1,A_2} = \frac{1}{(X_2 - X_1)(Y_2 - Y_1)} \sum_{l=1}^{2}\sum_{k=1}^{2}\sum_{j=1}^{2}\sum_{i=1}^{2}\left[(-1)^{(i+j+k+l)} G(\alpha_{l,i}, \beta_{k,j})\right]$$

$$\begin{aligned} G(\alpha_{l,i}, \beta_{k,j}) = \frac{1}{2\pi} \Bigg\{ & \alpha_{l,i}\sqrt{1+{\beta_{k,j}}^2}\tan^{-1}\left(\frac{\alpha_{l,i}}{\sqrt{1+{\beta_{k,j}}^2}}\right) \\ & - \beta_{k,j}\tan^{-1}\beta_{k,j} + \sqrt{1+{\alpha_{l,i}}^2}\beta_{k,j}\tan^{-1}\left(\frac{\beta_{k,j}}{\sqrt{1+{\alpha_{l,i}}^2}}\right) \\ & {\alpha_{l,i}}^2 \ln \alpha_{l,i} + (1/2)\ln\left(1+{\beta_{k,j}}^2\right) - (1/2)\ln\left[1+{\alpha_{l,i}}^2+{\beta_{k,j}}^2\right]\Bigg\} \end{aligned}$$

FF11: Infinite concentric cylinders. See Figure D.24.

$$F_{A_1,A_2} = 1$$

$$F_{A_2,A_1} = \frac{r_1}{r_2}$$

$$F_{A_2,A_2} = 1 - \frac{r_1}{r_2}$$

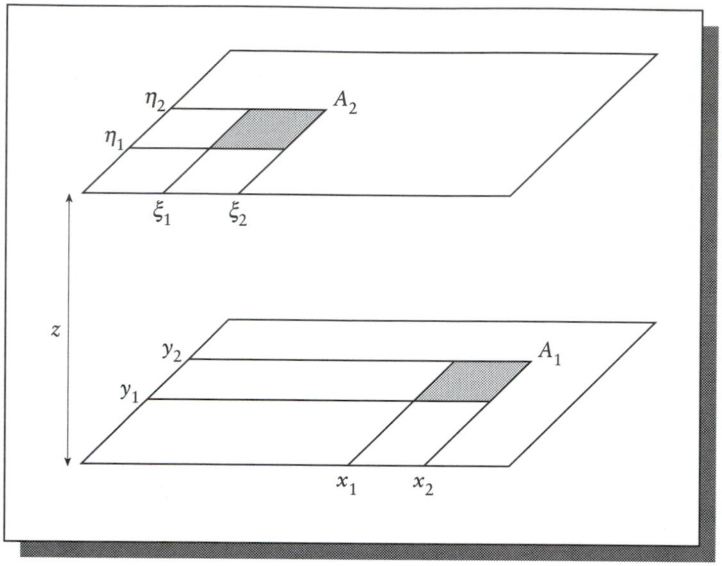

FIGURE D.23
Geometry for FF10: parallel rectangles with parallel sides.

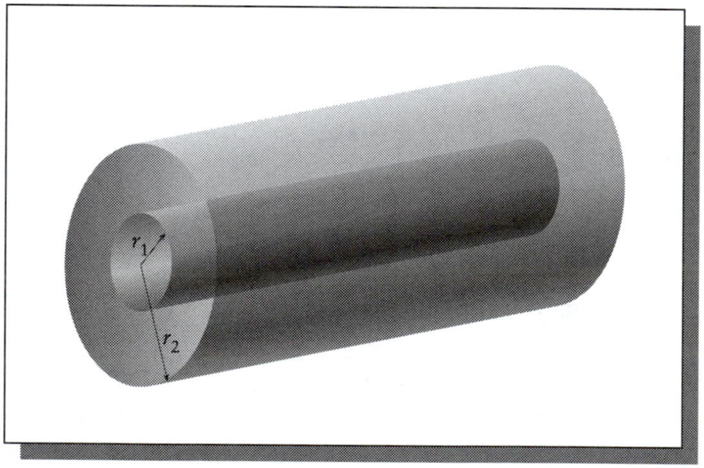

FIGURE D.24
Geometry for FF11: infinite concentric cylinders.

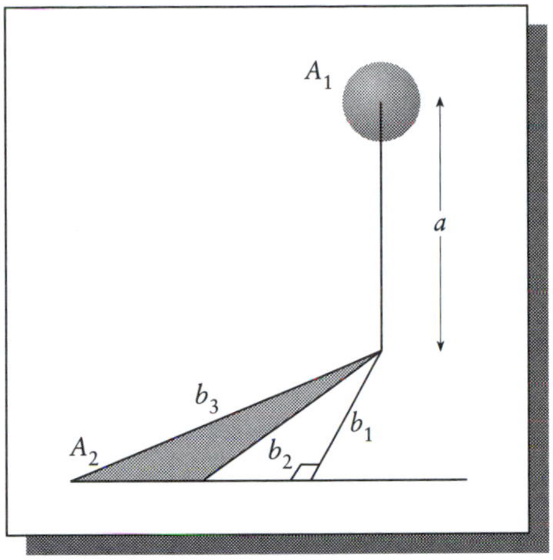

FIGURE D.25

Geometry for FF12: sphere to a scalene triangle.

FF12: Sphere to a scalene triangle. The normal to the triangle through one vertex passes through the center of the sphere. The plane of the triangle does not intersect the sphere. See Figure D.25.

$$B_1 = b_1/a \qquad B_2 = b_2/b_1 \qquad B_3 = b_3/b_1$$

$$F_{dA_1,A_2} = \frac{1}{4\pi}\left[\cos^{-1}\left(\frac{1}{B_3}\right) - \cos^{-1}\left(\frac{1}{B_2}\right)\right] - \frac{1}{8\pi}\left\{\sin^{-1}\left[\frac{(1-B_1{}^2)\,B_3{}^2-2}{(1+B_2{}^2)\,B_3{}^2}\right] - \sin^{-1}\left[\frac{(1-B_1{}^2)\,B_2{}^2-2}{(1+B_1{}^2)\,B_2{}^2}\right]\right\}$$

FF13: Large sphere to a smaller hemisphere, $r \gg r_h$, ignoring base of hemisphere. See Figure D.26.

$$H = h/r$$

$$F_{A_1,A_2} = \frac{1}{4} - \frac{\sqrt{2H+H^2}}{4(1+H)} + \frac{\cos\gamma}{8}\left(\frac{1}{1+H}\right)^2$$

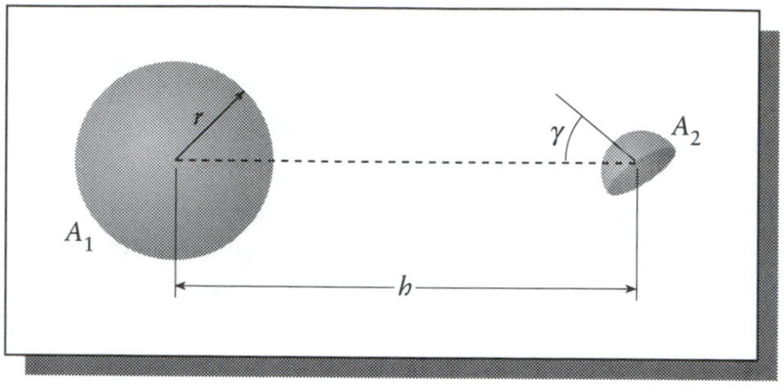

FIGURE D.26
Geometry for FF13: large sphere to a smaller hemisphere, $r \gg r_h$, ignoring base of hemisphere.

D.2 Two Polygons

A closed-form expression for the form factor between two polygons that are completely visible to each other has been developed by Schröder and Hanrahan. They report a summary of their work in [386] and give a more detailed explanation in [385]. The result is quite complex. The following summary of the mathematics is from [385] and appears courtesy of Peter Schröder.

Before listing all the expressions to be computed we first define four auxiliary functions

$$
\begin{aligned}
L(b)(y) = \frac{1}{16}\Bigg(& \frac{-b}{(b+1)^2}\ln(y-1) - \frac{b}{(b-1)^2}\ln(1+y) + \frac{2(b-y)}{(b^2-1)(y^2-1)} \\
& + \left(\frac{2(b+y)(1+by)\left((b-y)^2+(by-1)^2\right)}{(b^2-1)^2(y^2-1)^2} + \ln\frac{(1-y)(1-b)}{(1+y)(1+b)} \right) \ln(b+y) \\
& + Li_2\left(\frac{1-y}{1+b}\right) - Li_2\left(\frac{1+y}{1-b}\right) \Bigg) \\
M(y) = {} & \frac{y}{4(y^2-1)^2} + \frac{y}{8(y^2-1)} + \frac{1}{16}\ln\frac{y-1}{y+1} \\
G(q)(y) = {} & \frac{q'(y)}{2a}\ln q(y) - 2y + \frac{d}{a}\tan^{-1}\frac{q'(y)}{d} \\
H(q)(y) = {} & \left(\frac{y^2}{2} + \frac{c}{2a} - \frac{b^2}{4a^2}\right)\ln q(y) - \frac{y(ay-b)}{2a} - \frac{bd}{2a^2}\tan^{-1}\frac{q'(y)}{d}
\end{aligned}
$$

where $q(x) = ax^2 + bx + c$ is some arbitrary quadratic polynomial, $d = \sqrt{4ac - b^2}$, and

$$Li_2(z) = \sum_1^\infty \frac{z^k}{k^2}$$

is the dilogarithm (see [270]), closely related to the logarithm $\ln \frac{1}{1-z} = \sum_1^\infty \frac{z^k}{k}$. Its series representation is absolutely convergent in the unit disk. Using the functional relationship

$$Li_2(z) = \frac{-\pi^2}{6} - \frac{\ln^2(-z)}{2} - Li_2(z^{-1})$$

the dilogarithm is defined in the entire complex plane. Efficient code for the evaluation of the dilogarithm function can be found in most special function libraries, e.g., *fn* from the mail server at `netlib@research.att.com`.

Given two edges we first compute the bi-quadratic form parameterizing the distance between the two edges as a function of s and t. Let E_i and E_j be parameterized by $\vec{x}_i(t) = \vec{p}_i + t\vec{d}_i$ and $\vec{x}_j(s) = \vec{p}_j + s\vec{d}_j$ with $\|\vec{d}_{i,j}\| = 1$, respectively. We have

$$\begin{aligned}
c_0 &= \|E_j\| \\
c_1 &= -2\vec{d}_i \cdot \vec{d}_j \\
c_2 &= \|E_i\| \\
c_3 &= -2\vec{d}_j \cdot (\vec{p}_i - \vec{p}_j) \\
c_4 &= 2\vec{d}_i \cdot (\vec{p}_i - \vec{p}_j) \\
c_5 &= \|\vec{p}_i - \vec{p}_j\|^2 \\
c_{10} &= 4 - c_1^2 \\
c_{11} &= 4c_4 - c_1 c_3 \\
c_{12} &= 4c_5 - c_3^2 \\
c_{13} &= \frac{c_{11} - \sqrt{c_{11}^2 - 4c_{10}c_{12}}}{2c_{10}} \\
c_{14} &= \frac{\sqrt{c_{11}^2 - 4c_{10}c_{12}}}{c_{10}} \\
c_{15} &= \sqrt{c_{10}c_{14}} \\
c_{16}(s) &= c_1 c_{13} - c_3 - 2s \\
c_{17}(s) &= \frac{-c_{15} + \sqrt{c_{15}^2 - 4|c_{16}(s)|^2}}{-2\bar{i}c_{16}(s)} \\
c_{18}(s) &= \frac{-c_{15} - \sqrt{c_{15}^2 - 4|c_{16}(s)|^2}}{-2\bar{i}c_{16}(s)}
\end{aligned}$$

With these in hand we can compute the integral for a pair of edges

$$\mathcal{I}(E_i, E_j) = \int_0^{c_2} \int_0^{c_0} \ln f(s,t)\, ds\, dt$$

$$= \left[\left(s + \frac{c_3}{2}\right) G(f(s,.))(t) + \frac{c_1}{2} H(f(s,.))(t) \right] \Bigg|_{s=0,t=0}^{s=c_0,t=c_2} - 2c_0c_2$$

$$+ c_{14}c_{15} \Bigg[\pi(2k(s)+1)M(t)$$

$$-i \left\{ L(-c_{17}(s))(t) + L(-c_{18}(s))(t) - L(c_{17}(s))(t) - L(c_{18}(s))(t) \right\} \Bigg] \Bigg|_{s=0,t=\sqrt{\frac{c_{13}}{\bar{c}_{13}}}}^{s=c_0,t=\sqrt{\frac{c_{13}+c_2}{\bar{c}_{13}+c_2}}}$$

in terms of which the form factor for two polygons is given by

$$F_{P_1P_2} = \frac{1}{4\pi A_{P_1}} \sum_{\substack{E_i \in \partial P_1 \\ E_j \in \partial P_2}} c_{1_{ij}}\, \mathcal{I}(E_i, E_j)$$

Converting these equations into running code is difficult; there are many subtleties that must be carefully handled. Peter Schröder has released his implementations in the *Mathematica* and C languages to the public domain. If they are not available to you via some local source, you can obtain them by anonymous ftp transfer from the computer `ftp.cs.princeton.edu` (internet address 128.112.92.1). Some of the files are compressed, so the *binary transfer mode* must be used (give the command `binary` to your ftp server). Under the directory `pub/packages/formfactor` are four files:

`ff.m` An implementation in the *Mathematica* language.

`ffpaper.ps.Z` A compressed version of the *PostScript* for the paper [386].

`fftr.ps.Z` A compressed version of the *PostScript* for the technical report [385].

`libff.tar.Z` A compressed version of an implementation in the C language in Unix-library form.

Files ending in the suffix `.Z` are compressed; under Unix, run the program `uncompress` to expand them. The library is in the `tar` archival tape storage format. To extract the source files, under Unix run `tar xvf libff.tar` in an empty directory.

I give you now Professor Twist,
A conscientious scientist.
Trustees exclaimed, "He never bungles!"
And sent him off to distant jungles.
Camped on a tropic riverside,
One day he missed his loving bride.
She had, the guide informed him later,
Been eaten by an alligator.
Professor Twist could not but smile.
"You mean," he said, "a crocodile."

Ogden Nash
("The Purist," 1935)

E

CONSTANTS AND UNITS

Quantity	Unit name	Symbol	Definition
Unit of length	meter	m	The length of the path traveled by light in a vacuum during a time interval of 1/299,792,458 of a second
Unit of mass	kilogram	kg	A mass equal to the mass of the international prototype of the kilogram (an alloy of platinum with 10% iridium, maintained in the Archives of France)
Unit of time	second	s	The duration of 9,192,631,770 periods of the radiation corresponding to the transition between the two hyperfine levels $F = 4, M = 0$ and $F = 3, M = 0$ of the ground state ${}^2S_{1/2}$ of the cesium-133 atom unperturbed by external fields
Unit of luminous intensity	candela	cd	The luminous intensity, in a given direction, of a source that emits monochromatic radiation of frequency 540×10^{12} hertz and that has a radiant intensity in that direction of 1/683 watt per steradian

TABLE E.1
Definitions of the four basic units from the ANSI standard [432].

Factor	Prefix	Symbol	Factor	Prefix	Symbol
10^{24}	yotta	Y	10^{-1}	deci	d
10^{21}	zetta	Z	10^{-2}	centi	c
10^{18}	exa	E	10^{-3}	milli	m
10^{15}	petta	P	10^{-6}	micro	μ
10^{12}	tera	T	10^{-9}	nano	n
10^{9}	giga	G	10^{-12}	pico	p
10^{6}	mega	M	10^{-15}	femto	f
10^{3}	kilo	k	10^{-18}	atto	a
10^{2}	hecto	h	10^{-21}	zepto	z
10^{1}	deka	da	10^{-24}	yocto	y

TABLE E.2
Basic engineering prefixes for different orders of magnitude. Note: The prefix "deka" is often written "deca." *Source:* Data from the ANSI standard [432].

Constant name	Symbol	Value
Boltzmann's constant	k	$1.38066 \times 10^{-23}\ J/°\mathrm{K}$
Planck's constant	h	$6.62620 \times 10^{-34}\ J \cdot s$
Speed of light	c_0	$299,792,458\ m/s$
Stefan-Boltzmann constant	σ	$5.67032 \times 10^{-8}\ W \cdot m^{-2} \cdot °\mathrm{K}^{-4})$
Solar constant	E_s	$1.35 \times 10^{3}\ W/m^2$
Permittivity of vacuum	ε_0	$4.85 \times 10^{-12}\mathrm{farad}/m = 4.85 \times 10^{-12}(A \cdot s)/(V \cdot m)$
Permeability of vacuum	μ_0	$4\pi \times 10^{7}\mathrm{henry}/m = 4\pi \times 10^{7}(V \cdot s)/(A \cdot m)$

TABLE E.3
Physical constants.

I_a	II_a	III_b	IV_b	V_b	VI_b	VII_b	VIII			I_b	II_b	III_a	IV_a	V_a	VI_a	VII_a	O
1 H 1.0079 Hydrogen																	2 He 4.00260 Helium
3 Li 6.941 Lithium	4 Be 9.01218 Beryllium											5 B 10.81 Boron	6 C 12.011 Carbon	7 N 14.0067 Nitrogen	8 O 15.9994 Oxygen	9 F 19.99840 Fluorine	10 Ne 20.179 Neon
11 Na 22.98977 Sodium	12 Mg 24.305 Magnesium											13 Al 26.98154 Aluminum	14 Si 28.086 Silicon	15 P 30.97376 Phosphorus	16 S 32.06 Sulfur	17 Cl 35.453 Chlorine	18 Ar 39.948 Argon
19 K 39.098 Potassium	20 Ca 40.08 Calcium	21 Sc 44.9559 Scandium	22 Ti 47.90 Titanium	23 V 50.9414 Vanadium	24 Cr 51.996 Chromium	25 Mn 54.9380 Manganese	26 Fe 55.847 Iron	27 Co 58.9332 Cobalt	28 Ni 58.70 Nickel	29 Cu 63.546 Copper	30 Zn 65.38 Zinc	31 Ga 69.72 Gallium	32 Ge 72.59 Germanium	33 As 74.9216 Arsenic	34 Se 78.96 Selenium	35 Br 79.904 Bromine	36 Kr 83.80 Krypton
37 Rb 85.4678 Rubidium	38 Sr 87.62 Strontium	39 Y 88.9059 Yttrium	40 Zr 91.22 Zirconium	41 Nb 92.9064 Niobium	42 Mo 95.94 Molybdenum	43 Tc 98.9062 Technetium	44 Ru 101.07 Ruthenium	45 Rh 102.9055 Rhodium	46 Pd 106.4 Palladium	47 Ag 107.868 Silver	48 Cd 112.40 Cadmium	49 In 114.82 Indium	50 Sn 118.69 Tin	51 Sb 121.75 Antimony	52 Te 127.60 Tellurium	53 I 126.9045 Iodine	54 Xe 131.30 Xenon
55 Cs 132.9054 Cesium	56 Ba 137.34 Barium	57* La 138.9055 Lanthanum	72 Hf 178.49 Hafnium	73 Ta 180.9479 Tantalum	74 W 183.85 Tungsten	75 Re 186.207 Rhenium	76 Os 190.2 Osmium	77 Ir 192.22 Iridium	78 Pt 195.09 Platinum	79 Au 196.9665 Gold	80 Hg 200.59 Mercury	81 Tl 204.37 Thallium	82 Pb 207.2 Lead	83 Bi 208.9804 Bismuth	84 Po 210 Polonium	85 At 211 Astatine	86 Rn 222 Radon
87 Fr 223 Francium	88 Ra 226.0254 Radium	89† Ac 227 Actinium															

Lanthanide series	58* Ce 140.12 Cerium	59 Pr 140.9077 Praseodymium	60 Nd 144.24 Neodymium	61 Pm 147 Promethium	62 Sm 150.4 Samarium	63 Eu 151.96 Europium	64 Gd 157.25 Gadolinium	65 Tb 158.9254 Terbium	66 Dy 162.50 Dysprosium	67 Ho 164.9304 Holmium	68 Er 167.26 Erbium	69 Tm 168.9342 Thulium	70 Yb 173.04 Ytterbium	71 Lu 174.97 Lutetium
Actinide series	90† Th 232.0381 Thorium	91 Pa 231.0359 Protactinium	92 U 238.029 Uranium	93 Np 237.0482 Neptunium	94 Pu 239.11 Plutonium	95 Am 241 Americium	96 Cm 244 Curium	97 Bk 249 Berkelium	98 Cf 252 Californium	99 Es 253 Einsteinium	100 Fm 254 Fermium	101 Md 256 Mendelevium	102 No 254 Nobelium	103 Lr 257 Lawrencium
Transactinide series	104 Rf 257 Rutherfordium	105 Ha 260 Hahnium												

TABLE E.4

The periodic table of the elements.

"If you had high hopes, how would you know how high they were? And did you know that narrow escapes come in different widths? Would you travel the whole wide world without ever knowing how wide it was? And how could you do anything at long last," he concluded, waving his arms over his head, "without knowing how long the last was?"

Norton Juster
("The Phantom Tollbooth," 1961)

F

LUMINAIRE STANDARDS

In this appendix we summarize two standards for representing *luminaires*. In general, a luminaire is a complete physical structure for illumination that is composed of a *lamp*, a *housing*, and associated electrical and electronic support. The lamp is where the light is actually generated, using a variety of methods (e.g., a glowing filament, a carbon arc, or fluorescing gas). The housing is usually a metal container in which the lamp is mounted, and can usually be aimed in a variety of directions. The electrical apparatus supports the needs of the lamp for safety, efficiency, and longevity.

The language of the standards is challenging. Rather than use the precise (and often awkward) language required by a complete standard, in this appendix I will summarize the language and give working descriptions of the standards. The reader thirsty for more detail can obtain copies of the full standards directly from the issuing agencies [222, 434].

F.1 Terminology

The general idea of both formats is to first describe the luminaire and the lamp in physical terms, and then provide a set of photometric measurements of the output

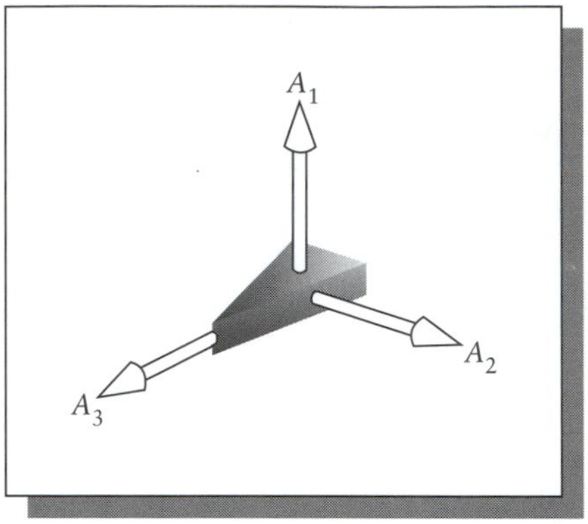

FIGURE F.1
The three axes for a luminaire.

of the luminaire. These measurements are most naturally described using a spherical coordinate system.

We will describe a luminaire by placing it at the center of a Euclidean coordinate system. Using traditional terminology, we call the axes the *first axis*, the *second axis*, and the *third axis*. We will abbreviate these as A_1, A_2, and A_3. They are illustrated in Figure F.1.

There are three ways to position the spherical coordinate system with respect to the luminaire, depending on which axes contain the poles. These are called the three *goniometric configurations*. Each coordinate system is represented by two angles: θ describing a point on a great circle around the sphere (the *equator*), and ψ identifying points on a great hemicircle running from one pole to the other. Traditionally these angles are measured in degrees.

In all systems, the sense of positive angles obeys the *right-hand rule*: wrap your right hand around the axis with thumb extended so that your thumb points away from the origin; the direction in which your fingers curl is the direction of positive rotation.

If the poles are placed along the first axis, then we call this a (C, γ) (or C) type system, illustrated in Figure F.2. This type of arrangement is normally used for indoor and roadway luminaires. The angle $\gamma \in [0°, 180°]$ measures the polar rotation around axis A_3. The angle $C \in [0°, 360°]$ describes the equator rotation around axis A_1.

If the poles are placed along the second axis, then we call this a (B, β) (or B) type system, illustrated in Figure F.3. This configuration is used mostly for adjustable

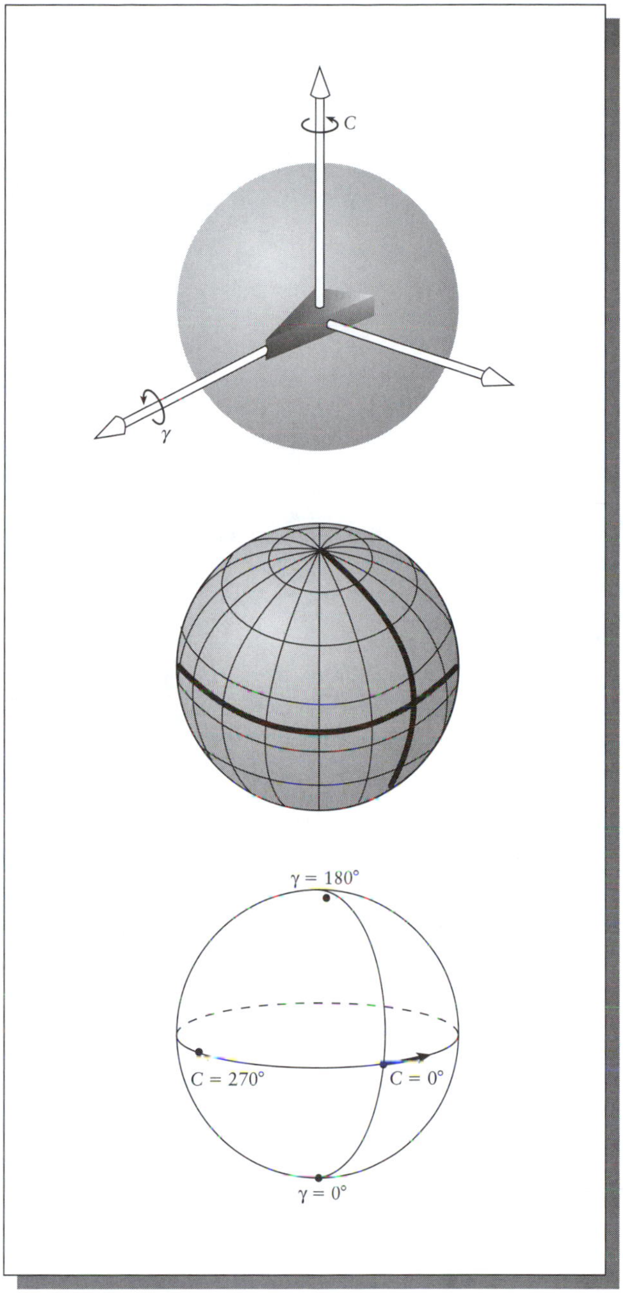

FIGURE F.2

The (C, γ) coordinate system.

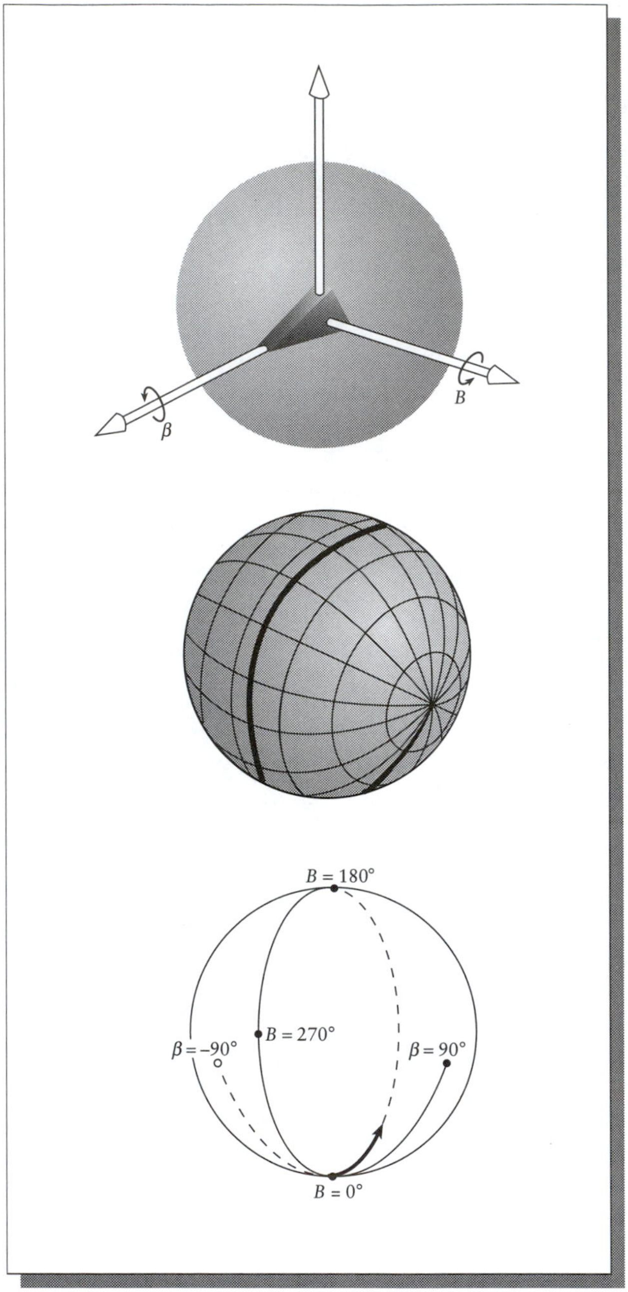

FIGURE F.3

The (B, β) coordinate system.

floodlights and sports lighting. The angle $\beta \in [-90°, 90°]$ measures the polar rotation around axis A_3. The angle $B \in [0°, 360°]$ describes the equator rotation around axis A_2.

If the poles are placed along the third axis, then we call this a (A, α) (or A) type system, illustrated in Figure F.4. This is normally used for headlights and vehicle signal lighting. The angle $\alpha \in [-90°, 90°]$ measures the polar rotation around axis A_2. The angle $A \in [0°, 360°]$ describes the equator rotation around axis A_3.

It is important to observe that these terms, though standardized, are not used consistently. In particular, the (A, α) and (C, γ) systems are often given the other's names and labels [222]. *Caveat emptor*.

F.2 Notation

Both standards are based on human-readable text files of letters, characters, and punctuation. It would be very pleasant to be able to describe the files using the standard grammar notation of computer science [271], but many of our standard metacharacters (such as the asterisk $*$ and the square brackets [and]) are used in the standards documents with different meanings. I think it would be confusing to use those symbols here in a way so different from their use in the reference documents. So instead I have adopted a different, more direct style of representation.

The file formats will be shown by explicit presentation. Strings in a `typewriter font` are required. A field in an *italic font* represents the name of some data. I mark the type of data as integer ($\mathcal{Z}$), floating-point real ($\mathcal{R}$), or alphanumeric ($\mathcal{A}$).

Horizontal bars in the presentation are used just for conceptual grouping and are not part of the file.

Often the standard requires that certain fields must begin new lines. I have found it easier to indicate where previous lines must end. The hook-left arrow $\hookleftarrow$ indicates a *combined* carriage return-line feed; in ASCII that's octal 015 followed by octal 012. I will refer to this combined pair of characters in text with the term "newline."

F.3 The IES Standard

The Illumination Engineering Society of North America (or IESNA, or simply IES) has designed a standard for luminaire description [222]. The standard consists of a file, which contains a *main block*, and a *photometry block*. The two blocks may exist in different files, with the main block providing the name of the file containing the photometry block. There is no explicit symbol that indicates the end of the main block and the start of the photometry block. The photometry block is defined to begin with the first line that begins with the string `TILT`.

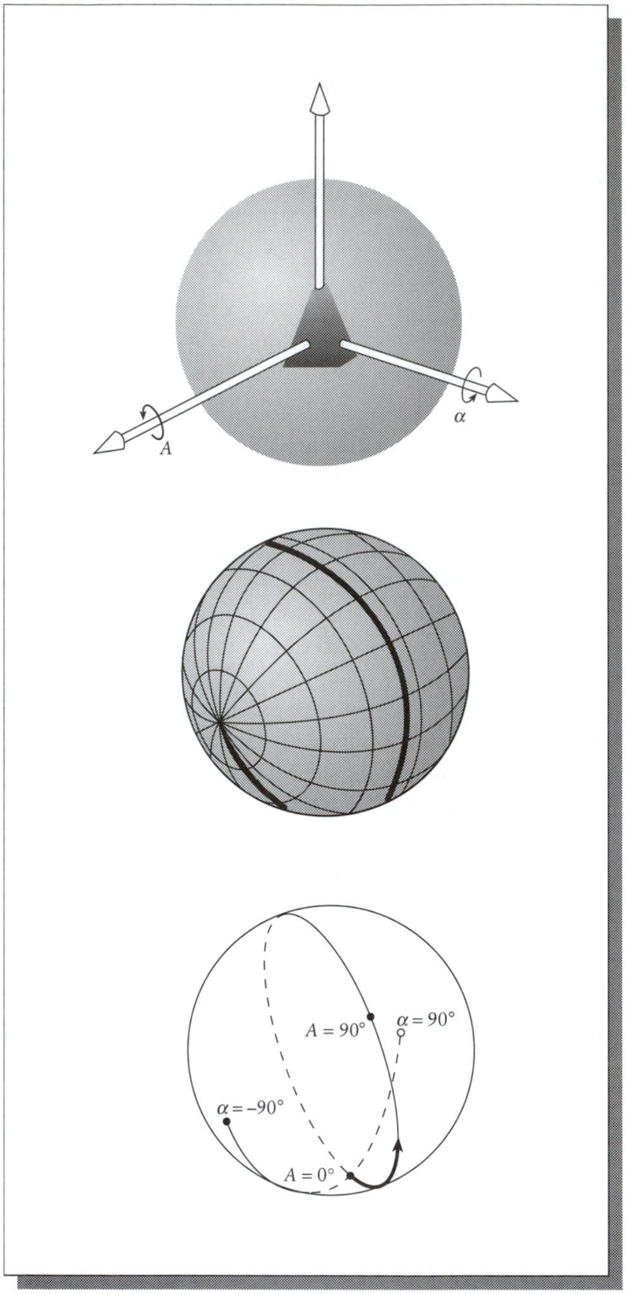

FIGURE F.4

The (A, α) coordinate system.

The main block describes the physical structure of the luminaire. The photometry block describes how it was measured and provides the actual data. A set of measurements is sometimes called a *report*.

F.3.1 The Big Picture

The main and photometry blocks are summarized in Figure F.5. Lines up to the `TILT` line may be no longer than eighty characters; the `TILT` line and all lines after it may be no longer than 132 characters.

The first line of the file must be the seven characters `IESNA91` followed by a newline.

Then comes a number of lines that describe the luminaire. Each line begins with a keyword followed by an equals sign. The rest of the line contains the data that describes that keyword. Other keywords may be used, but they should be in all uppercase and no more than twenty characters long, including the brackets. The standard is somewhat contradictory in its use of square brackets. IES-approved keywords should certainly be surrounded by square brackets; user-invented keywords may or may not require brackets.

As a practical measure, if a string in all capital letters starts a line before the line beginning with `TILT`, I suggest interpreting it as a keyword.

The IES standard requires that the keywords `TEST` and `MANUFAC` be present; the others are optional. They recommend that `LUMCAT`, `LUMINAIRE`, `LAMPCAT`, and `LAMP` also be included, but they aren't mandatory. The list of IES-supported keywords is given in Figure F.6.

The `MORE` keyword can be used to continue the argument from a previous line if it was too long to fit. The `BLOCK` and `ENDBLOCK` keywords allow us to insert an additional set of keywords to attach to the photometry block. That way, one set of photometric data can be associated with a number of different luminaires. Although they don't say so explicitly, by implication `BLOCK` and `ENDBLOCK` nest arbitrarily deep, though there is no advantage to nesting.

F.3.2 The Tilt Block

The *photometry block* begins with the string `TILT`. This is the beginning of a smaller block called the *tilt block*, which may or may not be present. The argument to `TILT` indicates if there is no tilt block at all (`TILT=NONE`), if it is in another file (`TILT=`*filename*), or if the tilt block is included in this file (`TILT=INCLUDE`); the file name may be no more than seventy-five characters long.

If there is a tilt block, then it either comes from another file or appears immediately after the `TILT` line. The format is the same in either case.

IESNA91 $\hookleftarrow$	*Required identifier.*
[TEST] *test-report-information* $(\mathcal{A}) \hookleftarrow$ [MANUFAC] *manufacturer-of-luminaire* $(\mathcal{A}) \hookleftarrow$	*Required key information.*
[*keyword*] *key-information* $(\mathcal{A}) \hookleftarrow$ [*keyword*] *key-information* $(\mathcal{A}) \hookleftarrow$ ⋮ [*keyword*] *key-information* $(\mathcal{A}) \hookleftarrow$	*0 or more keyword lines.*
TILT=*filename* $\hookleftarrow$ TILT=INCLUDE $\hookleftarrow$ TILT=NONE $\hookleftarrow$	*Choose only one.*
Tiltblock $\hookleftarrow$	*Only present if TILT=INCLUDE.*
number-of-lamps $(\mathcal{Z})$ *lumens-per-lamp* $(\mathcal{R})$ *candela-multiplier* $(\mathcal{R})$ *number-of-vertical-angles* $(\mathcal{Z})$ *number-of-horizontal angles* $(\mathcal{Z})$ *photometric-type* $(\mathcal{Z})$ *units* $(\mathcal{Z})$ *width* $(\mathcal{R})$ *length* $(\mathcal{R})$ *height* $(\mathcal{R}) \hookleftarrow$	*Luminaire description.*
ballast-factor $(\mathcal{R})$ *ballast-lamp-factor* $(\mathcal{R})$ *input-watts* $(\mathcal{R}) \hookleftarrow$ *vertical-angles* $(\mathcal{R}) \hookleftarrow$ *horizontal-angles* $(\mathcal{R}) \hookleftarrow$	*Measurement description.*
C1 $(\mathcal{R}) \hookleftarrow$ C2 $(\mathcal{R}) \hookleftarrow$ ⋮ CN $(\mathcal{R})$	*Candela data at each horizontal angle.*

FIGURE F.5
Main block of IES standard.

Keyword	Argument type	Purpose
TEST	($\mathcal{A}$)	Test report and laboratory (**mandatory**).
MANUFAC	($\mathcal{A}$)	Manufacturer of luminaire (**mandatory**).
LUMCAT	($\mathcal{A}$)	Luminaire catalog number (**recommended**).
LUMINAIRE	($\mathcal{A}$)	Luminaire description (**recommended**).
LAMPCAT	($\mathcal{A}$)	Lamp catalog number (**recommended**).
LAMP	($\mathcal{A}$)	Lamp description (**recommended**).
BALLAST	($\mathcal{A}$)	The ballast used in the measurements.
MAINTCAT	($\mathcal{Z} \in [1, 6]$)	An integer from 1 to 6 identifying the maintenance category.
OTHER	($\mathcal{A}$)	Free field for any other information.
SEARCH	($\mathcal{A}$)	For systems without a general text-search facility, we can provide a string here and flag it for an external program.
MORE	($\mathcal{A}$)	Extends the description from the previous line in the file.
BLOCK	none	Allows grouping (see text).
ENDBLOCK	none	End of a block (see text).

FIGURE F.6
Keywords for the IES main block.

The tilt block is used because sometimes the efficiency of the lamp is sensitive to its orientation, so that it is brighter when pointing in some directions than others. The tilt specification allows us to describe how the lamp is mounted in the housing, and how its output depends on the rotation of the housing.

The tilt block has the form given in Figure F.7. Notice that there are no keywords in the block; everything must be of the right type and in the right place.

The first field, labeled *lamp-to-luminaire-geometry*, is an integer with the value 1, 2, or 3, depending on how the lamp is mounted in the housing. Figure F.8 shows the three choices. In each of these three figures, the lamp is in a fixed position with respect to the housing, and the housing is rotated about a mounting axis.

For Type 1 mounting, the luminaire points straight out of the housing, so it always points in the same direction as the luminaire. For Type 2 mounting, the position of the lamp doesn't change as the luminaire is rotated, since it is parallel to the axis of rotation. For Type 3 mounting, the lamp is perpendicular to the axis of rotation, so it moves as the housing moves.

lamp-to-luminaire-geometry $(\mathcal{Z} \in [1, 2, 3]) \hookleftarrow$

number-of-pairs $(\mathcal{Z}) \hookleftarrow$

list of angles $(\mathcal{R}, \mathcal{R}, \mathcal{R}, \ldots) \hookleftarrow$

list of factors $(\mathcal{R}, \mathcal{R}, \mathcal{R}, \ldots) \hookleftarrow$

FIGURE F.7
The IES tilt block.

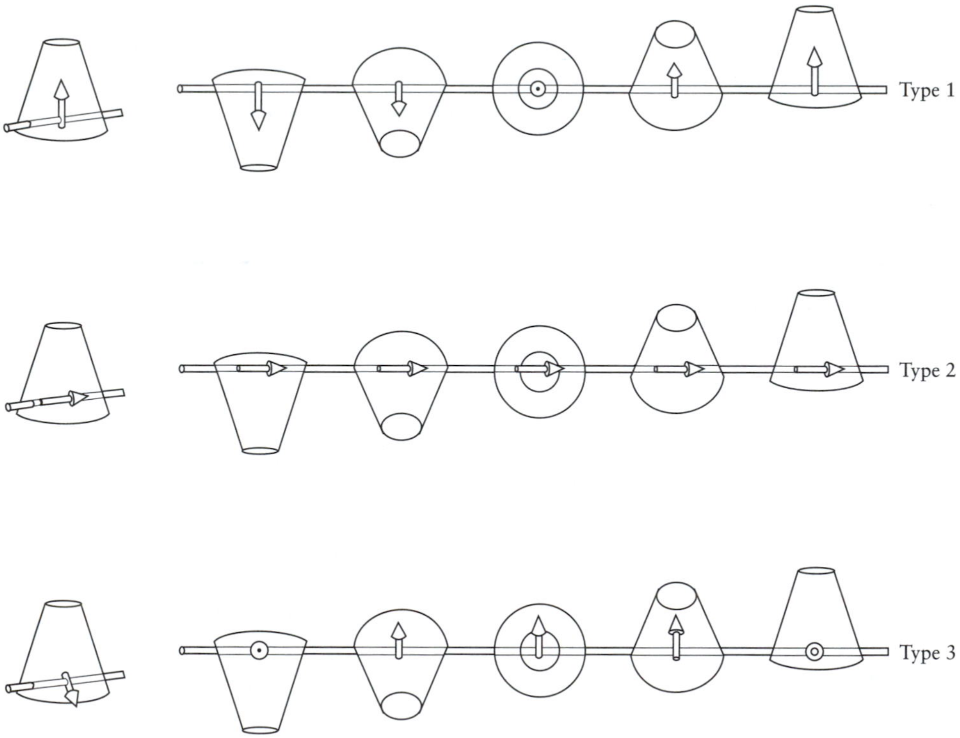

FIGURE F.8
The three choices for *lamp-to-luminaire-geometry*.

2				
5				
0	5	10	20	45
1.0	0.9	0.8	0.6	0.5

FIGURE F.9

The tilt block for a lamp in a Type 2 mounting that had been measured at five different angles: 0, 5, 10, 20, and 45 degrees.

Following the mounting type comes an integer that specifies the number of measurements that have been made of lamp output with respect to rotation. Then comes an ascending list of all the angles (in degrees), and then the relative lamp outputs. An example is shown in Figure F.9.

F.3.3 The Photometry Block

The *photometry block* contains a sequence of unflagged data values. Because there are no keywords in this block, everything must appear with exactly the right type, in exactly the right place, as in Figure F.5. The first set of fields addresses the physical setup of the luminaire and the configuration for measuring its output; we will now discuss those fields sequentially.

number-of-lamps ($\mathcal{Z}$): This is the number of lamps mounted in the luminaire; for example, Figure F.10 shows several bulbs mounted in a single housing.

lumens-per-lamp ($\mathcal{R}$): This is the average number of lumens per lamp in the luminaire.

candela-multiplier ($\mathcal{R}$): The photometric data at the end of the file may be uniformly scaled by this value; it is normally 1.0.

number-of-vertical-angles ($\mathcal{Z}$): This is the number of angles that were measured from pole to pole for this report.

number-of-horizontal-angles ($\mathcal{Z}$): This is the number of angles that were measured around the equator for this report.

photometric-type ($\mathcal{Z}$): This integer identifies which of the three goniometric configurations was used to measure the data. A value of 1 means type C, a value of 2 means type B, and a value of 3 means type A.

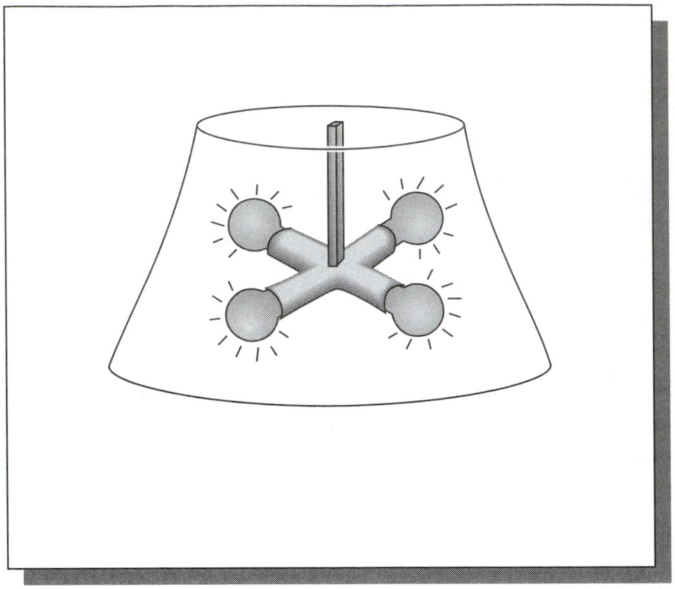

FIGURE F.10
Several lamps in a single luminaire.

units ($\mathcal{Z}$): Identifies the measurement system. A value of 1 means units are in feet, a value of 2 means units are in meters.

width ($\mathcal{R}$): The width of the luminous opening, measured parallel to the A_3 axis; see Figure F.11.

length ($\mathcal{R}$): The length of the luminous opening, measured parallel to the A_2 axis; see Figure F.11.

height ($\mathcal{R}$): The height of the luminous opening, measured parallel to the A_1 axis; see Figure F.11.

When a luminaire is not rectangular, the width, length, and height measurements aren't very useful. Table F.1 indicates how to use these fields to encode circular, elliptical, and point sources.

We now continue through the photometry block to the fields that address the electrical test setup.

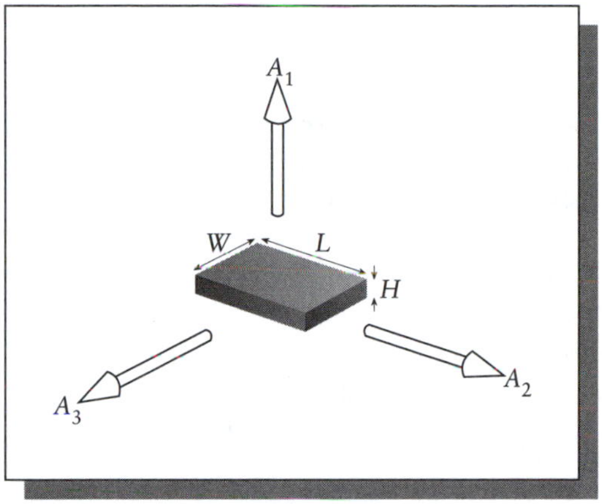

FIGURE F.11
The width, length, and height of a rectangular luminaire with respect to its axes.

Opening shape	Width	Length
Rectangular	width	length
Circular	–diameter	0
Elliptical	–minor axis	major axis
Point	0	0

TABLE F.1
Use of the width and length fields for nonrectangular luminaires.

ballast-factor ($\mathcal{R}$): Some lamps are operated on a *ballast* that can diminish their output. This is the percentage by which the output of the lamp diminishes on a ballast.

ballast-lamp-factor ($\mathcal{R}$): If the measurements in the file used a different ballast than in a standard installation, this factor gives the correction to turn the file data into the installation data.

input-watts ($\mathcal{R}$): This is the total watts applied to the luminaire for the test (including ballast, if any).

vertical-angles ($\mathcal{R}$): This is a list of the vertical angles where measurements were taken, in degrees, in ascending order. For type C measurements, the first value is always 0 or 90, and the last is always 90 or 180.

horizontal-angles ($\mathcal{R}$): This is a list of the horizontal angles where measurements were taken, in degrees, in ascending order. For type C measurements, the first value is always 0. The last value is interpreted as follows:

0: There is only one horizontal angle, and the luminance is assumed to be symmetrical about this angle.

90: Only one quadrant of data is provided; the luminance is symmetric with respect to each quadrant.

180: Only half of the sphere is provided; the luminance is bilaterally symmetric.

Other: This is a value from 180 to 360; the luminance has no lateral symmetry.

For types A and B there are two general cases:

- The luminance is laterally symmetric about a vertical reference plane. Then the first angle is 0 and the last is less than 90.
- The luminance is not laterally symmetric about a vertical reference plane. The first angle is between −90 and 0, and the last is between 0 and 90.

Finally come the measurements themselves, in *candelas*. We start at the first vertical angle and list the candela output of the luminaire at each of the horizontal angles. Then we move to the next vertical angle and start the horizontal list over again, generating a mesh of values. These are simply long lists of floating-point real numbers, separated by white space, commas, or both, and interrupted by mandatory newlines at the end of each set of horizontal measurements. Other newlines are permissible within the data.

Figure F.12 shows an example file in the IES format. This example contains nonsense data that are only intended to demonstrate the format.

F.4 The CIE Standard

The Commission Internationale de L'Éclairage (the CIE) has developed an international standard that is capable of much richer expression than the IES standard. Like the IES, the CIE has chosen a plain-text file format, and has separated the data into blocks. In contrast to the IES, all data in the CIE standard is identified by a keyword. The conventions are somewhat different, though.

```
IESNA91
[TEST]       Luminaire C6567681
[MANUFAC]    Deep 13 Labs
[LUMCAT]     27599-3175
[LUMINAIRE] Portable dry-cell searchlight.  Includes
[MORE]         mounting brackets for vacuum cleaner
[LAMPCAT]    MST-3K
[LAMP]       Gypsy headmount
[OTHER]      Not terribly bright, but reliable
[BLOCK]
[LUMCAT]     94303
[LUMINAIRE] Entertainment spot
[ENDBLOCK]
TILT=INCLUDE
1
5
  0   30   90  120  180
1.0 0.95 0.92 0.75 0.65
1 10000 1.0
3 5 1
2
.4 .8 .5
1.0 1.0 6500
0 45 90
0 20 40 60 90
10000 8000 7000 5500 4000
 9000 6500 4500 4000 3000
 4000 1500  800  500  200
```

FIGURE F.12

An example file in the IES standard.

We will use the same notational conventions as in the section on the IES standard. The main difference is that the CIE standard keywords are four uppercase letters that are not enclosed in square brackets, and may contain arbitrary spaces and lowercase characters. So the keyword `NLPS` may be written as `Number of LamPS` or even as `aaNbbLcc dd eeP Sff`, and it will still be recognized as `NLPS`.

Lines may be no longer than seventy-eight characters each.

	Required identifier.
`CIEF=CIE File Format, Version 1.0 (CIE Publication 102-1993)` ↩	
information line ↩ *information line* ↩ ⋮ *information line* ↩	*0 to 60 free-format information lines.*
IDNM=*identification-number* ($\mathcal{A}$) ↩	*Required identifier.*
keyword=data ↩ *keyword=data* ↩ ⋮ *keyword=data* ↩	*The measurement block.*
PHOT=INCLUDE ↩ PHOT=*filename* ↩	*Choose only one.*
information line ↩ *information line* ↩ ⋮ *information line* ↩	*0 to 60 free-format information lines.*
PTYP=*type* ↩	*Required keyline.*
keyword=data ↩ *keyword=data* ↩ ⋮ *keyword=data* ↩	*The photometry block.*
CONA=*cone angles* ↩	

FIGURE F.13
Main CIE file format.

F.4.1 The Main Block

The general format of the CIE file standard is shown in Figure F.13.

The file must begin with the keyline that identifies the file type, version, and the CIE publication that specifies the standard; this line must appear exactly as shown. Then comes the *information block*, which contain any information at all. This block may contain from zero to sixty free-format text lines. The lines should not begin with anything that might be confused with the first line of the measurement block; simply avoiding any equal signs (=) will make sure that you're safe.

The information block is followed by the *measurement block*. The signal to the system that the measurement block has begun is the appearance of the `IDNM` keyword (possibly including lowercase letters and blanks).

At the end of the measurement block comes the *photometry block*, which may immediately follow in the same file or be included in a different file that is pointed to by name.

F.4.2 The Measurement Block

The measurement block begins with the `IDNM` keyword, but may then contain a variety of other keywords and data. None of them but `IDNM` is mandatory. Each keyword is followed by an equals sign (=) and then its associated data. We list those keywords in Figure F.14 by their four-letter codes and their recommended expansions, including lowercase letters and blanks.

The rotation of the luminaire is given by the `TLME` and `ROME` keywords, illustrated in Figure F.15.

The numeric codes associated with the luminaire shapes used for `LSHP` are the following, illustrated in Figure F.16:

1. A sphere.
2. A half-sphere in the A_1 direction.
3. A cylinder parallel to A_1.
4. A cylinder parallel to A_2.
5. A half-cylinder cylinder parallel to A_2, round half toward A_1.
6. A half-cylinder cylinder parallel to A_3, round half toward A_1.
7. A rectangle with long side perpendicular to A_1.
8. A rectangle with long side parallel to A_1.
9. Anything else.

The measurement block can also provide for the fact that as you look at the luminaire from different angles, different amounts of the luminous opening (through which light escapes) are visible, due to blockages by the housing. This can be encoded by a number of lines that give the area visible in square meters from a variety of angles. Using the keyword `NLAV` provides the number of views, and then the keywords `LA01`, `LA02`, and so on provide the view information. Each line contains the area in square meters, and the angles (θ, ψ) for that view. There is a maximum of ninety-nine views.

Key	Expansion	Argument	Meaning
IDNM	IDentification NuMber	$(\mathcal{A})$	An arbitrary alphanumeric string that identifies the particular test trial or otherwise gives information particular to this file.
LUMN	LUminaire Name	$(\mathcal{A})$	The name of the luminaire.
LAMP	LAMP name	$(\mathcal{A})$	The name of the lamp.
NLPS	Number of LamPS	$(\mathcal{Z})$	The number of lamps in the luminaire.
TOLU	TOtal LUmens	$(\mathcal{R})$	Total lumens generated by the luminaire.
LLGE	Lamp Luminaire GEometry	$(\mathcal{Z}) \in [1,4]$	The relationship of the lamp to the housing, as in Figure F.8. The additional value 4 is defined for a lamp that cannot be replaced.
BLID	BaLlast IDentification	$(\mathcal{A})$	The name of the ballast.
INPW	INput PoWer	$(\mathcal{R})$	The total input power in watts.
INVO	INput VOltage	$(\mathcal{R})$	The voltage for which the luminaire is rated.
INVA	INput Volt Amperes	$(\mathcal{R})$	The total volt ampere requirement of the luminaire.
TLME	TiLt during MEasurement	$(\mathcal{R})$	The degrees of tilt during photometry. This is rotation of the luminaire about the A_2 axis, as in Figure F.15.
TLNM	TiLt NorMal	$(\mathcal{R})$	The amount of tilt around the A_2 axis that is normal when installed.
ROME	ROtation during MEasurement	$(\mathcal{R})$	The degrees of rotation during photometry. This is rotation of the luminaire about the A_3 axis, as in Figure F.15.
LSHP	Luminaire SHaPe	$(\mathcal{Z}) \in [1,9]$	This is one of the nine shape codes illustrated in Figure F.16.
NLAV	Number of Luminous Area Views	$(\mathcal{Z})$	The number of views (see text).
LAnn	Luminous Area view nn	$(\mathcal{R},\mathcal{R},\mathcal{R})$	(A,θ,ψ) (see text)

FIGURE F.14
Keywords for the CIE measurement block.

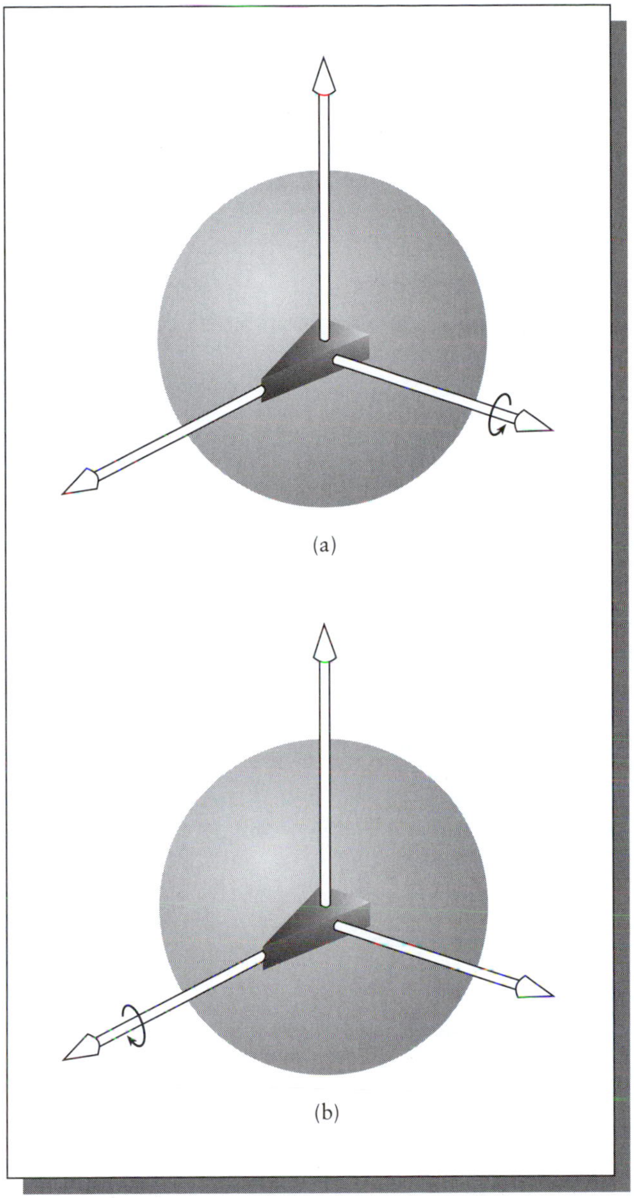

FIGURE F.15

The TLME and ROME tilts measure rotation of the luminaire. (a) The A_2 axis for TLME. (b) The A_3 axis for ROME.

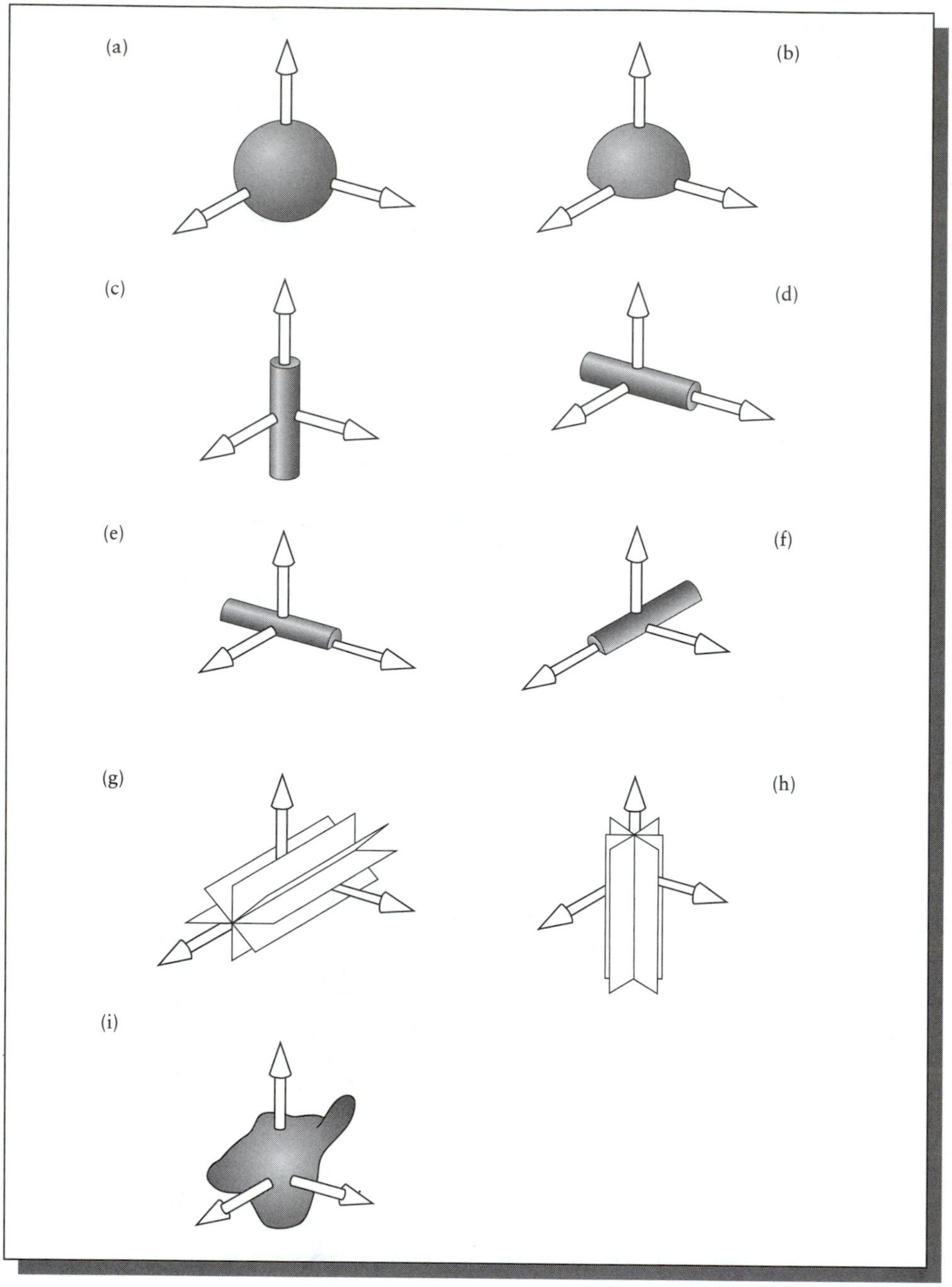

FIGURE F.16

The luminaire shape codes for LSHP. (a) Code 1. (b) Code 2. (c) Code 3. (d) Code 4. (e) Code 5. (f) Code 6. (g) Code 7. (h) Code 8. (i) Code 9.

Key	Expansion	Argument	Meaning
PTYP	Photometric TYPe	$(\mathcal{A}) \in [\mathtt{A}, \mathtt{B}, \mathtt{C}]$	The goniometric configuration.
APOS	Angle POSition	$(\mathcal{A})$	Polar positioning code (see text).
LUBA	LUmen BAsis of photometry	$(\mathcal{R})$	Scale factor for lumens specifications. A value of -1 indicates they are absolute value.
MULT	MULTiplier	$(\mathcal{R})$	A non-negative multiplying factor applied to all intensity values. Normally 1.0.
BAFA	BAllast FActor	$(\mathcal{R})$	A non-negative multiplying factor applied to all intensity values in the file, intended to compensate for changes in ballast. Normally 1.0.
NCON	Number of CONe angles	$(\mathcal{Z})$	Number of cone angles in the data below.
NPLA	Number of PLAne angles	$(\mathcal{Z})$	Number of plane angles in the data below.
CONA	CONe Angles	$(\mathcal{R}, \mathcal{R}, \ldots)$	The cone angles (see text).

FIGURE F.17
Keys for the CIE photometry block.

F.4.3 The Photometry Block

After the measurement block comes the photometry block. It is introduced with the keyword PHOT (or an expansion including spaces and lowercase letters). There are two choices of arguments to PHOT: a filename or the string INCLUDE. If a filename is given, then the photometry block is read from that file. If the string is INCLUDE, then the photometric data starts immediately.

If the photometry block is coming from a file, then that file must begin with the header line:

```
CIEA=CIE-A File Format, Version 1.0 (CIE Publication 102-1993)
```

Then the block follows immediately.

Like the measurement block, the photometry block contains a set of keywords and data. In this block the term *half-plane angle* is used to refer to the angle θ around the equator, and the term *cone angle* is used to refer to the polar angle ψ. The terms for this block are given in Figure F.17.

The photometry block may begin with up to sixty information lines, like the main block. It must begin with the PTYP key to signify the start of the block.

The APOS line serves to orient the equator of the sphere in which the measurements are made. When the luminaire has a set of three well-defined axes as in

Figure F.1, then orientation is no problem in any of the goniometric systems. The right axis is used to select the poles, and the other two span the hemisphere with one of the axes serving to select the 0° origin.

However, even when the luminaire doesn't have such natural axes, the sphere must still be oriented. The CIE has defined a wealth of different geometry codes to cover a variety of special-purpose configurations; they're all listed in the standard [434]. Most luminaires used in computer graphics can be described with respect to one of the three default coordinate systems, and do not need an additional `APOS` specifier.

The photometry block must end with the `CONA` keyline. This lists the values of ψ where measurements were made, in ascending order. For type C configurations the first value must be 0. After the `CONA` key and its arguments come the photometric data. Each line begins with a value of θ, and then lists the candlepower for the luminaire at each value of ψ given on the `CONA` line. Then comes a newline followed by the next value of θ, and so on. The values of θ must be given in ascending order. Notice that this format is rather different than the IES format, though it would not be hard to change one into the other. Values may be separated by commas or any white space, including newlines.

Figure F.18 presents an arbitrary example. This example uses only some of the keywords. Although this is based on a real floodlight, this example contains nonsense data that is only intended to demonstrate the format.

```
CIEF=CIE File Format, Version 1.0 (CIE Publication 102-1993)
Example of the CIE File Format using long names
Floodlight Luminaire based on CIE Example file 2
Luminaire made in Moebius's Garage
IDentification NuMber=Catalog 3141
LUMinaire Name=Floodgate V5
LAMP name = 200 Watt SuperFlood
Number of LamPS = 1
Lamp Luminaire GEometry = 2
BaLlast IDentification = G403
TOtal LUmens = 17500
INput Volt Amperes=190
Luminaire SHaPe = 8
TiLt during MEasurement = 0
Number of Luminous Area Views = 0
PHOTometric file = INCLUDE
Mounting is standard shell WA2YHJ
Used in top half of the Whirlitzer of Wonder
Cabinet finish is walnut
Photometric TYPe = B
Angle POSition Code = B3
LUmen BAsis of photometry = 100
MULTiplier = 1
BAllast FActor=1
Number of CONe angles = 3
Number of PLane Angles = 4

CONe Angles = 0.0    10.0   20.0   25.0
        -15   100     95     50     13
         -5   110    102     63     20
          0    90     80     44      8
         10    70     50     24      3
```

FIGURE F.18

An example file in the CIE Standard.

The first truth is the form. You must put into your drawing most forcefully the facts which you know to be true rather than what you see. What you see, the impression a thing makes on the eye, will take care of itself—in fact, much of the time it is far too insistent. You cannot truthfully portray vision without a knowledge of the facts which underlie it.

Kimon Nicolaïdes
("The Natural Way To Draw," 1941)

G

REFERENCE DATA

This appendix gathers together useful spectral and material data for humans, materials, and light sources. The data has come from a variety of sources, which are indicated in the text for each section. To make the data immediately useful, I have presented it here in 5-nanometer increments from $[380, 775]$ nanometers, for a total of 80 values per curve. Sometimes this has meant interpolating the published data; I reconstructed the data with a hermite cubic spline and point-sampled it to get these values. I didn't extrapolate the data beyond its measured endpoints, since for some of the data such extrapolation would have yielded values that would have dwarfed the rest of the curve. Therefore I instead simply used the endpoint values when out of range.

Morgan Kaufmann Publishers and the creators of this data have agreed to release an electronic form of this appendix to the public domain, so you don't need to type it all in to use it. As of publication, all the data in this appendix is available on the anonymous ftp server `ftp.cs.princeton.edu` (internet address 128.112.92.1), under the directory `pub/people/ps/glassner`. Please feel free to download the data, use it, and share it. You may also repost or redistribute the information in this appendix freely. This release to the public domain applies to this appendix only, and to no other part of this book.

G.1 Material Data

Table G.1 provides some indices of refraction for a variety of materials at normal incidence. The data is from Fowles [148] and Wood [488].

The complex indices of refraction for four different conductors are given in Tables G.2 and G.3. The tables were interpolated from nonuniform data presented in Palik [329]. The data is presented graphically in Figures G.1 and G.2.

Optically isotropic crystals and materials	Simple index η		
Perfect vacuum	1		
Air	1.0003		
Water	1.33		
Isopropyl alcohol	1.38		
Red garnet	1.86		
Zinc sulfide	2.36		
Sodium chloride	1.544		
Diamond	2.417		
Fluorite	1.392		
Uniaxial positive crystals	**Ordinary index η_O**	**Extraordinary index η_E**	
Ice	1.309	1.310	
Quartz	1.544	1.553	
Zircon	1.923	1.968	
Rutile	2.616	2.903	
Uniaxial negative crystals	**Ordinary index η_O**	**Extraordinary index η_E**	
Beryl	1.598	1.590	
Sodium nitrate	1.587	1.336	
Calcite	1.659	1.486	
Tourmaline	1.669	2.638	
Biaxial crystals	η_1	η_2	η_3
Gypsum	1.520	1.523	1.530
Feldspar	1.522	1.526	1.530
Mica	1.552	1.582	1.588
Topaz	1.619	2.620	1.627

TABLE G.1
Some indices of refraction at normal incidence. Frequency of measurement not available. *Source:* Data from Fowles, *Introduction to Modern Optics*, table 6.1, p. 176, and Wood, *Crystals and Light*, table 12-1, p. 114.

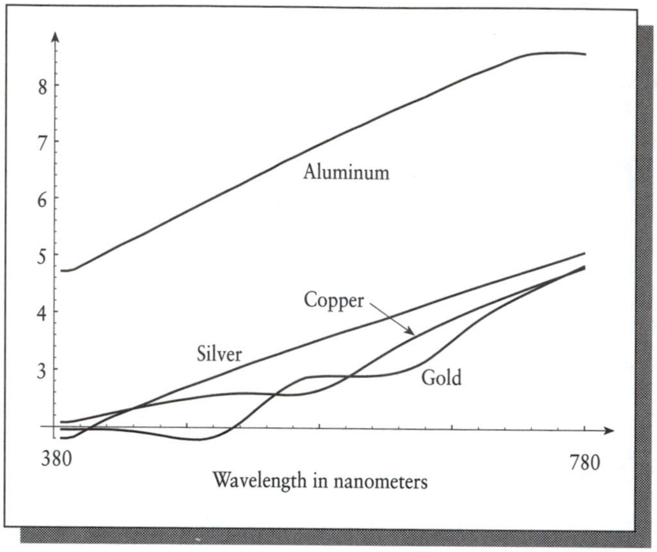

FIGURE G.1
Index of refraction for aluminum, silver, copper, and gold.

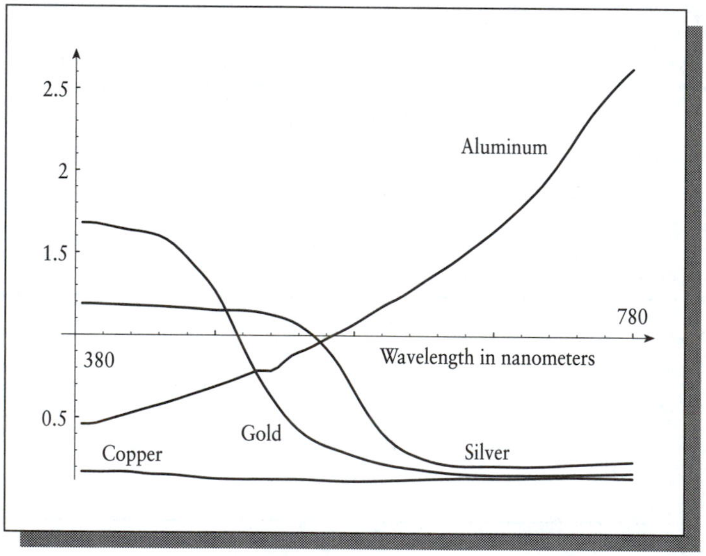

FIGURE G.2
Extinction coefficients for aluminum, silver, copper, and gold.

λ	Aluminum $\eta(\lambda)$	Aluminum $\kappa(\lambda)$	Silver $\eta(\lambda)$	Silver $\kappa(\lambda)$	λ	Aluminum $\eta(\lambda)$	Aluminum $\kappa(\lambda)$	Silver $\eta(\lambda)$	Silver $\kappa(\lambda)$
380	0.459522	4.712543	0.172643	1.801357	580	1.095940	7.034889	0.119176	3.580860
385	0.459522	4.712543	0.172643	1.801357	585	1.123162	7.092927	0.119927	3.620832
390	0.464578	4.737463	0.172179	1.824736	590	1.150000	7.150000	0.121000	3.660000
395	0.477268	4.799026	0.172143	1.886179	595	1.176546	7.206569	0.122437	3.697000
400	0.490000	4.860000	0.173000	1.950000	600	1.200000	7.260000	0.124046	3.733363
405	0.502732	4.920975	0.173857	2.013821	605	1.220000	7.310000	0.125766	3.769467
410	0.515422	4.982537	0.173821	2.075264	610	1.243866	7.364944	0.127538	3.805689
415	0.528027	5.046061	0.171576	2.132024	615	1.271220	7.422566	0.129303	3.842407
420	0.540540	5.111395	0.167032	2.183605	620	1.300000	7.480000	0.131000	3.880000
425	0.553012	5.175306	0.162298	2.231833	625	1.328330	7.535376	0.132869	3.919219
430	0.565131	5.233723	0.159271	2.278383	630	1.356345	7.588417	0.134590	3.959434
435	0.577244	5.288472	0.158423	2.324504	635	1.384367	7.639844	0.136141	4.000389
440	0.589948	5.344414	0.157828	2.371326	640	1.411292	7.690237	0.137502	4.041828
445	0.603591	5.405324	0.155916	2.420021	645	1.439278	7.740152	0.138652	4.083495
450	0.618000	5.470000	0.152160	2.470635	650	1.470000	7.790000	0.139570	4.125135
455	0.632493	5.531815	0.147613	2.520932	655	1.502859	7.841236	0.140110	4.166709
460	0.646781	5.592108	0.143045	2.569545	660	1.534670	7.896558	0.140229	4.208175
465	0.660667	5.653007	0.138757	2.615768	665	1.566741	7.953478	0.140185	4.249203
470	0.674693	5.714261	0.135317	2.660014	670	1.600000	8.010000	0.140050	4.289791
475	0.689087	5.775548	0.132764	2.702999	675	1.634324	8.066238	0.139897	4.329939
480	0.703759	5.836021	0.131138	2.744957	680	1.670565	8.119970	0.139801	4.369645
485	0.718931	5.896012	0.130306	2.786577	685	1.708526	8.171080	0.139833	4.408909
490	0.734853	5.956376	0.130009	2.828568	690	1.747843	8.219450	0.140154	4.447676
495	0.751561	6.017607	0.129992	2.871323	695	1.787991	8.265363	0.141061	4.485809
500	0.769000	6.080000	0.130061	2.916154	700	1.830000	8.310000	0.142139	4.523594
505	0.786605	6.138476	0.130105	2.961894	705	1.872679	8.354383	0.143315	4.561111
510	0.786342	6.196043	0.130103	3.007563	710	1.919912	8.400550	0.144516	4.598441
515	0.784987	6.255528	0.130043	3.052436	715	1.972871	8.452595	0.145667	4.635663
520	0.806091	6.318217	0.130125	3.095771	720	2.030324	8.501185	0.146695	4.672859
525	0.844815	6.382319	0.130219	3.137532	725	2.090685	8.543206	0.147527	4.710108
530	0.878276	6.443884	0.130091	3.178189	730	2.153505	8.575872	0.148028	4.747403
535	0.898602	6.502451	0.129646	3.218184	735	2.220514	8.598589	0.147986	4.784542
540	0.915377	6.563588	0.128675	3.257945	740	2.285233	8.611949	0.147682	4.821890
545	0.934823	6.631030	0.126824	3.297745	745	2.345712	8.618302	0.147174	4.859458
550	0.958000	6.690000	0.124775	3.337667	750	2.400000	8.620000	0.146517	4.897254
555	0.981445	6.743231	0.122763	3.377699	755	2.450850	8.623612	0.145769	4.935289
560	1.002914	6.801953	0.121029	3.417830	760	2.499693	8.625132	0.144987	4.973571
565	1.024224	6.861834	0.119768	3.458226	765	2.545931	8.622376	0.144227	5.012111
570	1.046286	6.919963	0.119005	3.499347	770	2.589417	8.614337	0.143545	5.050918
575	1.070014	6.977149	0.118838	3.540295	775	2.630000	8.600000	0.143000	5.090000

TABLE G.2
Indices of refraction and extinction for aluminum and silver.

λ	Copper η(λ)	Copper κ(λ)	Gold η(λ)	Gold κ(λ)	λ	Copper η(λ)	Copper κ(λ)	Gold η(λ)	Gold κ(λ)
380	1.188280	2.078662	1.678455	1.953596	580	0.595384	2.703188	0.259998	2.909502
385	1.188280	2.078662	1.678455	1.953596	585	0.527793	2.753184	0.247300	2.911371
390	1.187100	2.093040	1.675263	1.953178	590	0.468000	2.810000	0.236000	2.911390
395	1.185312	2.117618	1.666817	1.953892	595	0.415458	2.875556	0.226102	2.910510
400	1.183702	2.142816	1.658000	1.956000	600	0.372648	2.945518	0.217697	2.909684
405	1.182223	2.168463	1.649184	1.958108	605	0.338234	3.018414	0.210535	2.909863
410	1.180822	2.194386	1.640737	1.958822	610	0.310878	3.092775	0.204364	2.912000
415	1.179452	2.220412	1.634183	1.957185	615	0.289246	3.167127	0.198936	2.917045
420	1.178062	2.246369	1.629351	1.952822	620	0.272000	3.240000	0.194000	2.925952
425	1.176602	2.272084	1.622275	1.945549	625	0.256103	3.312184	0.188606	2.939671
430	1.175023	2.297387	1.612759	1.936360	630	0.243055	3.381591	0.183521	2.959155
435	1.173274	2.322103	1.599890	1.925744	635	0.232653	3.448394	0.178812	2.985355
440	1.171306	2.346061	1.579005	1.912865	640	0.224696	3.512766	0.174544	3.019223
445	1.169114	2.369725	1.548932	1.897096	645	0.218982	3.574880	0.170786	3.061712
450	1.166702	2.393291	1.510154	1.878760	650	0.215308	3.634911	0.167605	3.113773
455	1.164034	2.415747	1.464924	1.860113	655	0.213646	3.693233	0.165016	3.179622
460	1.161139	2.437040	1.417717	1.841519	660	0.213653	3.750162	0.163000	3.260394
465	1.158046	2.457114	1.374532	1.821149	665	0.214350	3.805661	0.161554	3.348767
470	1.154787	2.475917	1.325871	1.805653	670	0.215000	3.860000	0.160597	3.442244
475	1.151390	2.493393	1.268297	1.797055	675	0.214749	3.914480	0.160049	3.538330
480	1.150639	2.511981	1.195681	1.790414	680	0.214074	3.967796	0.159829	3.634528
485	1.151381	2.530700	1.110843	1.790218	685	0.213330	4.019675	0.159855	3.728342
490	1.151354	2.547674	1.021396	1.803380	690	0.212720	4.069952	0.160027	3.817474
495	1.150138	2.562687	0.933039	1.832168	695	0.212380	4.118678	0.160222	3.900933
500	1.147313	2.575524	0.846880	1.875281	700	0.212566	4.166057	0.160515	3.978438
505	1.142456	2.585970	0.767504	1.933520	705	0.213295	4.212465	0.160903	4.050759
510	1.135149	2.593811	0.695794	2.004628	710	0.214605	4.258351	0.161383	4.118664
515	1.124970	2.598830	0.631604	2.085559	715	0.216450	4.303980	0.161953	4.182923
520	1.114585	2.599943	0.571663	2.177679	720	0.218648	4.349268	0.162609	4.244306
525	1.102313	2.598045	0.516924	2.276178	725	0.221044	4.394238	0.163349	4.303581
530	1.085276	2.594923	0.469422	2.374557	730	0.223483	4.438778	0.164163	4.361628
535	1.062659	2.591761	0.429107	2.469264	735	0.225852	4.482510	0.165023	4.419346
540	1.034637	2.587950	0.395941	2.557729	740	0.228145	4.525993	0.165954	4.476388
545	1.003658	2.579443	0.369509	2.640573	745	0.230367	4.569252	0.166952	4.532793
550	0.965898	2.575114	0.348463	2.714364	750	0.232522	4.612311	0.168010	4.588597
555	0.921582	2.576699	0.331370	2.779947	755	0.234613	4.655197	0.169122	4.643842
560	0.870931	2.585936	0.316801	2.838163	760	0.236647	4.697934	0.170283	4.698567
565	0.812255	2.603536	0.303023	2.883275	765	0.238625	4.740548	0.171487	4.752808
570	0.740885	2.627422	0.288205	2.896406	770	0.240554	4.783062	0.172728	4.806607
575	0.667504	2.660953	0.273748	2.904831	775	0.242437	4.825503	0.174000	4.860000

TABLE G.3
Indices of refraction and extinction for copper and gold.

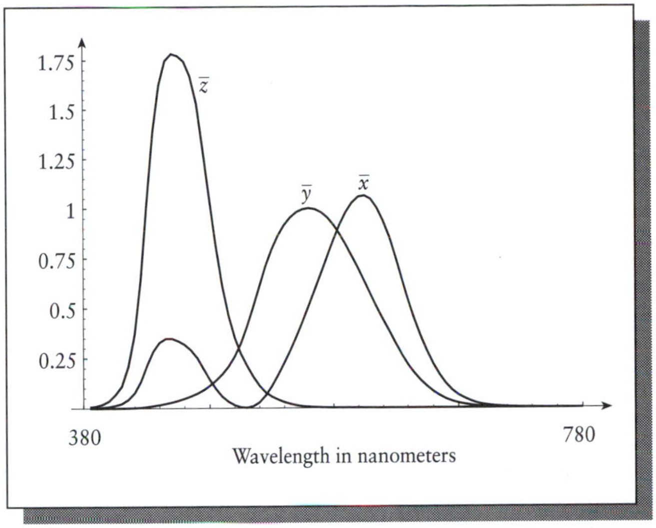

FIGURE G.3
The CIE standard observer matching functions.

G.2 Human Data

Table G.4 tabulates the CIE standard observer matching functions; these functions are plotted in Figure G.3. This data is from Wyszecki and Stiles [489].

Table G.5 tabulates the *SML* cone response curves for a human being. The data in this table was interpolated from data collected from [370, 730] nanometers in 1-nanometer increments in Brian Wandell's laboratory at Stanford University. The data is plotted in Figure G.4.

λ	$\bar{x}(\lambda)$	$\bar{y}(\lambda)$	$\bar{z}(\lambda)$	$V(\lambda)$	λ	$\bar{x}(\lambda)$	$\bar{y}(\lambda)$	$\bar{z}(\lambda)$	$V(\lambda)$
380	0.0014	0.0000	0.0065	0.0000	580	0.9163	0.8700	0.0017	0.8700
385	0.0022	0.0001	0.0105	0.0001	585	0.9786	0.8163	0.0014	0.8163
390	0.0042	0.0001	0.0201	0.0001	590	1.0263	0.7570	0.0011	0.7570
395	0.0076	0.0002	0.0362	0.0002	595	1.0567	0.6949	0.0010	0.6949
400	0.0143	0.0004	0.0679	0.0004	600	1.0622	0.6310	0.0008	0.6310
405	0.0232	0.0006	0.1102	0.0006	605	1.0456	0.5668	0.0006	0.5668
410	0.0435	0.0012	0.2074	0.0012	610	1.0026	0.5030	0.0003	0.5030
415	0.0776	0.0022	0.3713	0.0022	615	0.9384	0.4412	0.0002	0.4412
420	0.1344	0.0040	0.6456	0.0040	620	0.8544	0.3810	0.0002	0.3810
425	0.2148	0.0073	1.0391	0.0073	625	0.7514	0.3210	0.0001	0.3210
430	0.2839	0.0116	1.3856	0.0116	630	0.6424	0.2650	0.0000	0.2650
435	0.3285	0.0168	1.6230	0.0168	635	0.5419	0.2170	0.0000	0.2170
440	0.3483	0.0230	1.7471	0.0230	640	0.4479	0.1750	0.0000	0.1750
445	0.3481	0.0298	1.7826	0.0298	645	0.3608	0.1382	0.0000	0.1382
450	0.3362	0.0380	1.7721	0.0380	650	0.2835	0.1070	0.0000	0.1070
455	0.3187	0.0480	1.7441	0.0480	655	0.2187	0.0816	0.0000	0.0816
460	0.2908	0.0600	1.6692	0.0600	660	0.1649	0.0610	0.0000	0.0610
465	0.2511	0.0739	1.5281	0.0739	665	0.1212	0.0446	0.0000	0.0446
470	0.1954	0.0910	1.2876	0.0910	670	0.0874	0.0320	0.0000	0.0320
475	0.1421	0.1126	1.0419	0.1126	675	0.0636	0.0232	0.0000	0.0232
480	0.0956	0.1390	0.8130	0.1390	680	0.0468	0.0170	0.0000	0.0170
485	0.0580	0.1693	0.6162	0.1693	685	0.0329	0.0119	0.0000	0.0119
490	0.0320	0.2080	0.4652	0.2080	690	0.0227	0.0082	0.0000	0.0082
495	0.0147	0.2586	0.3533	0.2586	695	0.0158	0.0057	0.0000	0.0057
500	0.0049	0.3230	0.2720	0.3230	700	0.0114	0.0041	0.0000	0.0041
505	0.0024	0.4073	0.2123	0.4073	705	0.0081	0.0029	0.0000	0.0029
510	0.0093	0.5030	0.1582	0.5030	710	0.0058	0.0021	0.0000	0.0021
515	0.0291	0.6082	0.1117	0.6082	715	0.0041	0.0015	0.0000	0.0015
520	0.0633	0.7100	0.0782	0.7100	720	0.0029	0.0010	0.0000	0.0010
525	0.1096	0.7932	0.0573	0.7932	725	0.0020	0.0007	0.0000	0.0007
530	0.1655	0.8620	0.0422	0.8620	730	0.0014	0.0005	0.0000	0.0005
535	0.2257	0.9149	0.0298	0.9149	735	0.0010	0.0004	0.0000	0.0004
540	0.2904	0.9540	0.0203	0.9540	740	0.0007	0.0003	0.0000	0.0003
545	0.3597	0.9803	0.0134	0.9803	745	0.0005	0.0002	0.0000	0.0002
550	0.4334	0.9950	0.0087	0.9950	750	0.0003	0.0001	0.0000	0.0001
555	0.5121	1.0002	0.0057	1.0002	755	0.0002	0.0001	0.0000	0.0001
560	0.5945	0.9950	0.0039	0.9950	760	0.0002	0.0001	0.0000	0.0001
565	0.6784	0.9786	0.0027	0.9786	765	0.0001	0.0000	0.0000	0.0000
570	0.7621	0.9520	0.0021	0.9520	770	0.0001	0.0000	0.0000	0.0000
575	0.8425	0.9154	0.0018	0.9154	775	0.0000	0.0000	0.0000	0.0000

TABLE G.4
CIE color-matching and spectral efficiency functions.

λ	$S(\lambda)$	$M(\lambda)$	$L(\lambda)$	λ	$S(\lambda)$	$M(\lambda)$	$L(\lambda)$
380	0.000360	0.000221	0.000179	580	0.000026	0.255411	0.614555
385	0.000729	0.000338	0.000415	585	0.000022	0.221423	0.594825
390	0.001487	0.000606	0.000893	590	0.000018	0.187233	0.569736
395	0.002778	0.001100	0.001690	595	0.000014	0.154635	0.540161
400	0.004501	0.001774	0.002726	600	0.000011	0.124709	0.506265
405	0.006591	0.002605	0.003945	605	0.000008	0.098280	0.468240
410	0.009383	0.003766	0.005533	610	0.000005	0.075870	0.427109
415	0.013095	0.005416	0.007643	615	0.000004	0.057719	0.383763
420	0.017080	0.007449	0.010050	620	0.000003	0.043249	0.337736
425	0.020592	0.009746	0.012488	625	0.000003	0.031762	0.289181
430	0.023358	0.012406	0.014893	630	0.000002	0.022909	0.242081
435	0.025198	0.015492	0.017205	635	0.000001	0.016373	0.200298
440	0.025831	0.018718	0.019180	640	0.000000	0.011623	0.163370
445	0.025129	0.021815	0.020640	645	0.000000	0.008138	0.130186
450	0.023665	0.024936	0.021862	650	0.000000	0.005644	0.101351
455	0.022095	0.028517	0.023380	655	0.000000	0.003927	0.077573
460	0.020711	0.033695	0.026303	660	0.000000	0.002750	0.058247
465	0.019540	0.041407	0.031702	665	0.000000	0.001904	0.042625
470	0.017902	0.051084	0.039913	670	0.000000	0.001308	0.030691
475	0.015234	0.061967	0.051034	675	0.000000	0.000911	0.022336
480	0.012144	0.074044	0.064951	680	0.000000	0.000645	0.016354
485	0.009393	0.087773	0.081841	685	0.000000	0.000450	0.011553
490	0.007173	0.104748	0.103244	690	0.000000	0.000302	0.007898
495	0.005500	0.126791	0.131089	695	0.000000	0.000192	0.005509
500	0.004252	0.155503	0.167484	700	0.000000	0.000120	0.003980
505	0.003281	0.191718	0.213959	705	0.000000	0.000085	0.002859
510	0.002478	0.233411	0.269568	710	0.000000	0.000075	0.002025
515	0.001776	0.277183	0.331625	715	0.000000	0.000075	0.001438
520	0.001227	0.316997	0.392975	720	0.000000	0.000068	0.001032
525	0.000882	0.347571	0.446875	725	0.000000	0.000040	0.000740
530	0.000662	0.369273	0.492693	730	0.000000	0.000000	0.000504
535	0.000476	0.383621	0.531225	735	0.000000	0.000000	0.000504
540	0.000322	0.391089	0.562873	740	0.000000	0.000000	0.000504
545	0.000214	0.392001	0.588075	745	0.000000	0.000000	0.000504
550	0.000142	0.387142	0.607818	750	0.000000	0.000000	0.000504
555	0.000094	0.377206	0.622910	755	0.000000	0.000000	0.000504
560	0.000063	0.362065	0.632895	760	0.000000	0.000000	0.000504
565	0.000043	0.341585	0.637137	765	0.000000	0.000000	0.000504
570	0.000032	0.316419	0.635543	770	0.000000	0.000000	0.000504
575	0.000028	0.287417	0.628100	775	0.000000	0.000000	0.000504

TABLE G.5
SML cone response curves.

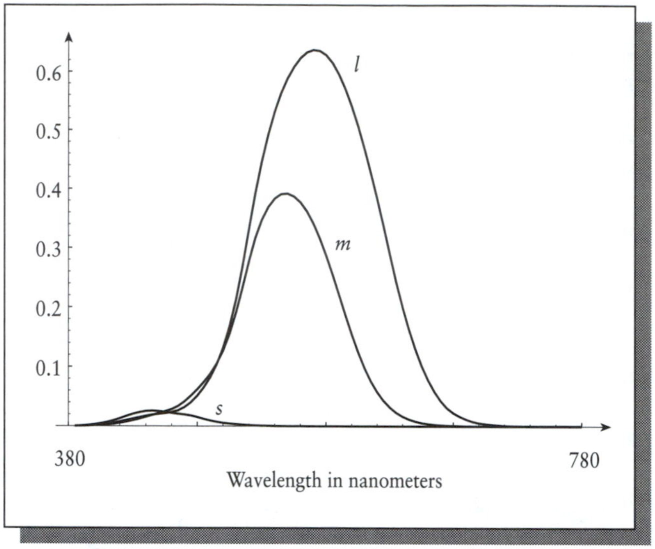

FIGURE G.4

The *SML* cone response curves.

G.3 Light Sources

Table G.6 presents the reference curves for CIE standard illuminants *A*, *B*, and *C*. Table G.7 provides data for a cool-white fluorescent bulb and CIE standard illuminant D65. The values in these figures were interpolated from data collected from [370, 730] nanometers in 1-nanometer increments in Brian Wandell's laboratory at Stanford University. Table G.8 gives the curves for the three CIE standard daylight illuminants. The data for Tables G.6, G.7, and G.8 are plotted in Figures G.5, G.6, and G.7.

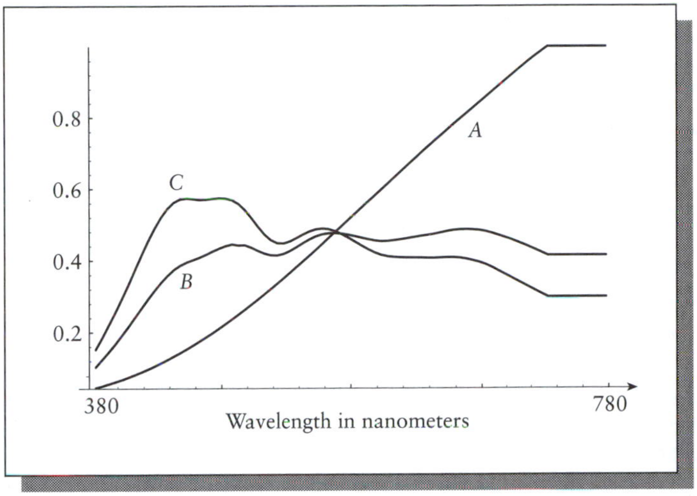

FIGURE G.5
CIE standard illuminants A, B, and C.

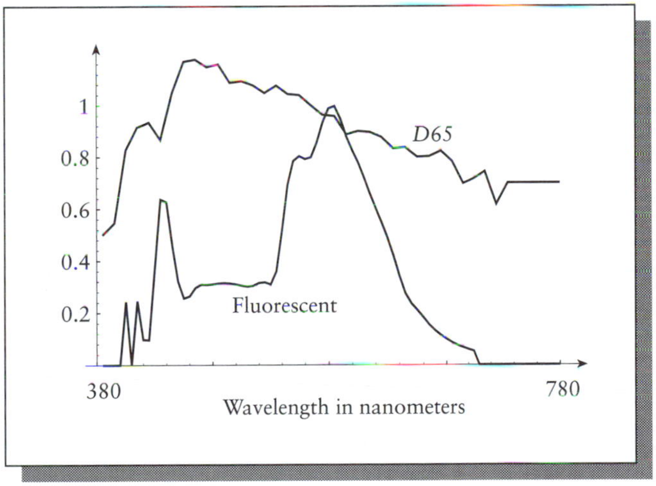

FIGURE G.6
A cool-white fluorescent light bulb and CIE standard illuminant D65.

λ	$A(\lambda)$	$B(\lambda)$	$C(\lambda)$	λ	$A(\lambda)$	$B(\lambda)$	$C(\lambda)$
380	0.045345	0.103646	0.152693	580	0.529521	0.467333	0.452526
385	0.050435	0.124237	0.184712	585	0.546363	0.463030	0.441560
390	0.055941	0.144827	0.219323	590	0.563252	0.459004	0.431242
395	0.061771	0.167407	0.255275	595	0.580187	0.455488	0.422080
400	0.068064	0.191098	0.292893	600	0.597076	0.453452	0.415047
405	0.074727	0.215713	0.332269	605	0.614011	0.453822	0.411022
410	0.081806	0.241070	0.372941	610	0.630900	0.455765	0.409032
415	0.089256	0.266981	0.414261	615	0.647742	0.458356	0.408060
420	0.097122	0.292430	0.453914	620	0.664538	0.461318	0.407644
425	0.105451	0.316352	0.489543	625	0.681288	0.464372	0.407459
430	0.114150	0.338238	0.520081	630	0.697946	0.467333	0.407181
435	0.123265	0.357718	0.544836	635	0.714510	0.469924	0.406533
440	0.132797	0.373866	0.562188	640	0.730983	0.472885	0.406256
445	0.142745	0.386082	0.571210	645	0.747363	0.476818	0.407135
450	0.153109	0.395151	0.573755	650	0.763604	0.480751	0.408107
455	0.163844	0.401999	0.571904	655	0.779706	0.483944	0.408107
460	0.174949	0.408569	0.569591	660	0.795669	0.485841	0.406718
465	0.186470	0.416805	0.570516	665	0.811494	0.486211	0.403572
470	0.198362	0.425689	0.572830	670	0.827179	0.485378	0.399315
475	0.210624	0.433787	0.574172	675	0.842680	0.483759	0.394688
480	0.223209	0.440496	0.573293	680	0.857996	0.480751	0.388673
485	0.236165	0.445262	0.568758	685	0.873126	0.475847	0.380391
490	0.249445	0.442347	0.558486	690	0.888071	0.470109	0.371090
495	0.263048	0.442856	0.540903	695	0.902832	0.464464	0.362021
500	0.276976	0.435869	0.518693	700	0.917361	0.458542	0.353045
505	0.291181	0.427401	0.495003	705	0.931705	0.452064	0.344068
510	0.305664	0.419674	0.473348	710	0.945817	0.445123	0.334999
515	0.320424	0.414816	0.457200	715	0.959698	0.437720	0.325745
520	0.335462	0.414122	0.448362	720	0.973348	0.429854	0.316028
525	0.350685	0.418425	0.447807	725	0.986813	0.421525	0.306774
530	0.366139	0.426615	0.453452	730	1.000000	0.413659	0.297983
535	0.381825	0.437072	0.462428	735	1.000000	0.413659	0.297983
540	0.397696	0.448362	0.472423	740	1.000000	0.413659	0.297983
545	0.413705	0.458819	0.480983	745	1.000000	0.413659	0.297983
550	0.429900	0.467333	0.486767	750	1.000000	0.413659	0.297983
555	0.446234	0.472885	0.488941	755	1.000000	0.413659	0.297983
560	0.462706	0.475662	0.487229	760	1.000000	0.413659	0.297983
565	0.479271	0.476217	0.481723	765	1.000000	0.413659	0.297983
570	0.495928	0.474736	0.473348	770	1.000000	0.413659	0.297983
575	0.512678	0.471497	0.463400	775	1.000000	0.413659	0.297983

TABLE G.6
CIE standard illuminants A, B, and C.

λ	$F(\lambda)$	D65(λ)	λ	$F(\lambda)$	D65(λ)
380	0.000000	50.000000	580	0.996610	95.800003
385	0.000000	52.299999	585	0.948428	92.250000
390	0.000000	54.599998	590	0.879458	88.699997
395	0.000000	68.699997	595	0.826315	89.349998
400	0.243051	82.800003	600	0.778983	90.000000
405	0.000000	87.150002	605	0.721405	89.800003
410	0.246102	91.500000	610	0.660000	89.599998
415	0.097401	92.449997	615	0.603640	88.650002
420	0.096203	93.400002	620	0.548542	87.699997
425	0.368037	90.050003	625	0.488339	85.500000
430	0.637017	86.699997	630	0.418983	83.300003
435	0.626603	95.800003	635	0.341488	83.500000
440	0.459051	104.900002	640	0.274780	83.699997
445	0.320830	110.949997	645	0.234955	81.849998
450	0.256475	117.000000	650	0.208881	80.000000
455	0.263880	117.400002	655	0.180710	80.099998
460	0.296339	117.800003	660	0.152949	80.199997
465	0.308912	116.349998	665	0.131028	81.250000
470	0.308339	114.900002	670	0.113695	82.300003
475	0.310210	115.400002	675	0.098593	80.300003
480	0.313830	115.900002	680	0.085627	78.300003
485	0.315258	112.349998	685	0.075082	74.000000
490	0.313830	108.800003	690	0.066508	69.699997
495	0.309960	109.099998	695	0.059265	70.650002
500	0.305085	109.400002	700	0.052678	71.599998
505	0.301570	108.599998	705	0.000000	72.949997
510	0.304475	107.800003	710	0.000000	74.300003
515	0.315184	106.300003	715	0.000000	67.949997
520	0.317695	104.800003	720	0.000000	61.599998
525	0.309516	106.250000	725	0.000000	65.750000
530	0.359593	107.699997	730	0.000000	69.900002
535	0.518761	106.050003	735	0.000000	69.900002
540	0.693966	104.400002	740	0.000000	69.900002
545	0.784533	104.199997	745	0.000000	69.900002
550	0.803186	104.000000	750	0.000000	69.900002
555	0.792184	102.000000	755	0.000000	69.900002
560	0.798508	100.000000	760	0.000000	69.900002
565	0.854789	98.150002	765	0.000000	69.900002
570	0.931525	96.300003	770	0.000000	69.900002
575	0.987479	96.050003	775	0.000000	69.900002

TABLE G.7
Spectral curves for a cool-white fluorescent light bulb and a CIE standard D65 illuminant.

λ	Day 0(λ)	Day 1(λ)	Day 2(λ)	λ	Day 0(λ)	Day 1(λ)	Day 2(λ)
380	63.4000	38.5000	3.0000	580	95.1000	−3.5000	0.5000
385	64.6000	36.8000	2.1000	585	92.1000	−3.5000	1.3000
390	65.8000	35.0000	1.2000	590	89.1000	−3.5000	2.1000
395	80.3000	39.2000	0.1000	595	89.8000	−4.7000	2.7000
400	94.8000	43.4000	−1.1000	600	90.5000	−5.8000	3.2000
405	99.8000	44.9000	−0.8000	605	90.4000	−6.5000	3.7000
410	104.8000	46.3000	−0.5000	610	90.3000	−7.2000	4.1000
415	105.4000	45.1000	−0.6000	615	89.4000	−7.9000	4.4000
420	105.9000	43.9000	−0.7000	620	88.4000	−8.6000	4.7000
425	101.4000	40.5000	−0.9000	625	86.2000	−9.1000	4.9000
430	96.8000	37.1000	−1.2000	630	84.0000	−9.5000	5.1000
435	105.4000	36.9000	−1.9000	635	84.6000	−10.2000	5.9000
440	113.9000	36.7000	−2.6000	640	85.1000	−10.9000	6.7000
445	119.8000	36.3000	−2.8000	645	83.5000	−10.8000	7.0000
450	125.6000	35.9000	−2.9000	650	81.9000	−10.7000	7.3000
455	125.6000	34.3000	−2.8000	655	82.3000	−11.4000	8.0000
460	125.5000	32.6000	−2.8000	660	82.6000	−12.0000	8.6000
465	123.4000	30.3000	−2.7000	665	83.8000	−13.0000	9.2000
470	121.3000	27.9000	−2.6000	670	84.9000	−14.0000	9.8000
475	121.3000	26.1000	−2.6000	675	83.1000	−13.8000	10.0000
480	121.3000	24.3000	−2.6000	680	81.3000	−13.6000	10.2000
485	117.4000	22.2000	−2.2000	685	76.6000	−12.8000	9.3000
490	113.5000	20.1000	−1.8000	690	71.9000	−12.0000	8.3000
495	113.3000	18.2000	−1.6000	695	73.1000	−12.7000	9.0000
500	113.1000	16.2000	−1.5000	700	74.3000	−13.3000	9.6000
505	112.0000	14.7000	−1.4000	705	75.4000	−13.1000	9.0000
510	110.8000	13.2000	−1.3000	710	76.4000	−12.9000	8.5000
515	108.7000	10.9000	−1.3000	715	69.9000	−11.8000	7.8000
520	106.5000	8.6000	−1.2000	720	63.3000	−10.6000	7.0000
525	107.7000	7.4000	−1.1000	725	67.5000	−11.1000	7.3000
530	108.8000	6.1000	−1.0000	730	71.7000	−11.6000	7.6000
535	107.1000	5.2000	−0.8000	735	74.4000	−11.9000	7.8000
540	105.3000	4.2000	−0.5000	740	77.0000	−12.2000	8.0000
545	104.9000	3.1000	−0.4000	745	71.1000	−11.2000	7.4000
550	104.4000	1.9000	−0.3000	750	65.2000	−10.2000	6.7000
555	102.2000	1.0000	−0.2000	755	56.5000	−9.0000	6.0000
560	100.0000	0.0000	0.0000	760	47.7000	−7.8000	5.2000
565	98.0000	−0.8000	0.1000	765	58.2000	−9.5000	6.3000
570	96.0000	−1.6000	0.2000	770	68.6000	−11.2000	7.4000
575	95.6000	−2.6000	0.4000	775	66.8000	−10.8000	7.1000

TABLE G.8
CIE daylight functions.

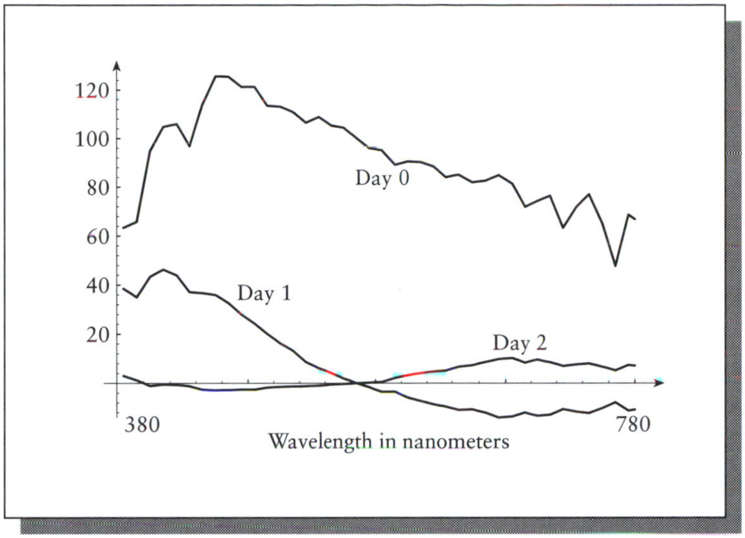

FIGURE G.7
CIE daylight functions.

G.4 Phosphors

Table G.9 presents phosphor intensities measured off of a Hitachi monitor used in a Silicon Graphics workstation. Data represents milliwatts per steradian per square meter. These values were interpolated from data collected from [390, 730] nanometers in 2-nanometer increments by Gary Meyer at the University of Oregon. They are plotted in Figure G.8.

λ	$R(\lambda)$	$G(\lambda)$	$B(\lambda)$	λ	$R(\lambda)$	$G(\lambda)$	$B(\lambda)$
380	0.057931	0.021883	−0.048760	580	0.028820	0.211200	0.004303
385	0.005826	0.003728	0.007903	585	0.100981	0.176914	0.004480
390	0.001204	0.001455	0.021440	590	0.102800	0.150600	0.003878
395	0.000540	0.001771	0.030972	595	0.225702	0.129410	0.004720
400	0.001028	0.001476	0.046450	600	0.051410	0.108400	0.002474
405	0.000649	0.001882	0.067898	605	0.039469	0.090768	0.002581
410	0.000865	0.003481	0.102700	610	0.060840	0.074860	0.002130
415	0.001967	0.004548	0.151278	615	0.330900	0.065217	0.004349
420	0.003545	0.006293	0.212700	620	0.325500	0.053390	0.003388
425	0.005347	0.007975	0.282917	625	1.149734	0.055354	0.010921
430	0.005832	0.010470	0.354000	630	0.645900	0.041820	0.006136
435	0.006674	0.013214	0.418059	635	0.097025	0.026902	0.002018
440	0.007489	0.014730	0.459400	640	0.030390	0.021230	0.001263
445	0.008482	0.017184	0.482813	645	0.022732	0.019673	0.001652
450	0.007565	0.020130	0.502500	650	0.016370	0.011780	0.002494
455	0.007673	0.022908	0.501154	655	0.019276	0.008516	0.000842
460	0.007446	0.027660	0.464300	660	0.015280	0.006605	0.000483
465	0.010566	0.033830	0.421582	665	0.009565	0.004455	0.000729
470	0.016810	0.044000	0.380800	670	0.013110	0.001612	0.000722
475	0.011341	0.059700	0.330554	675	0.012118	0.001597	0.000532
480	0.006619	0.081580	0.277700	680	0.010250	0.001264	0.000576
485	0.007587	0.111515	0.229958	685	0.046663	0.001264	0.002560
490	0.012500	0.149000	0.188900	690	0.023140	0.001264	0.001289
495	0.019539	0.194846	0.152174	695	0.038423	0.001264	0.001632
500	0.011220	0.247200	0.123300	700	0.038330	0.001264	0.001866
505	0.005122	0.299112	0.098008	705	0.750223	0.001264	0.008367
510	0.014670	0.348600	0.076800	710	0.204300	0.001264	0.002788
515	0.027285	0.386872	0.060078	715	0.023084	0.001264	0.001704
520	0.007949	0.422200	0.047210	720	0.011860	0.001264	0.001128
525	0.007450	0.451545	0.037035	725	0.017744	0.001264	0.003022
530	0.009993	0.470300	0.030450	730	0.012540	0.001264	0.002210
535	0.023196	0.468729	0.024329	735	0.012540	0.001264	0.002210
540	0.080380	0.456200	0.020490	740	0.012540	0.001264	0.002210
545	0.021056	0.441443	0.016788	745	0.012540	0.001264	0.002210
550	0.012280	0.427200	0.013200	750	0.012540	0.001264	0.002210
555	0.035867	0.406477	0.011057	755	0.012540	0.001264	0.002210
560	0.012460	0.373000	0.008625	760	0.012540	0.001264	0.002210
565	0.016671	0.334325	0.006725	765	0.012540	0.001264	0.002210
570	0.013910	0.288200	0.006555	770	0.012540	0.001264	0.002210
575	0.011911	0.246348	0.004840	775	0.012540	0.001264	0.002210

TABLE G.9

Phosphor intensities measured off of a Hitachi monitor used in a Silicon Graphics workstation. Data represents milliwatts per steradian per square meter.

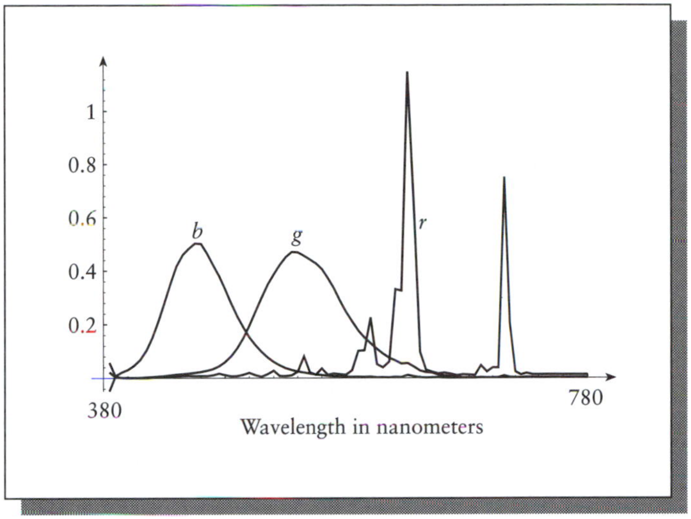

FIGURE G.8
Hitachi monitor phosphor.

G.5 Macbeth ColorChecker

The Macbeth ColorChecker is a printed piece of white board upon which has been printed a 4×6 grid of printed squares of different colors [291]. It is a commercial product manufactured by Macbeth, a division of the Kollmorgen Corporation in New York. The ColorChecker chart is widely available in many art and photo supply stores.

The colors were chosen to represent a variety of different naturally ocurring colors, and provide a convenient and easily accessible standard set of colors. The reasoning and design behind the chart is given in [291].

Table G.10 gives the chromaticity coordinates for the Macbeth ColorChecker squares.

The Macbeth spectra were measured in Brian Wandell's laboratory at Stanford University in the range [380, 720] nanometers in 1-nanometer steps. The 5-nanometer data is presented in Tables G.11 through G.16. The data is plotted in Figures G.9 through G.15.

Name	x	y	Y
Dark skin	0.4002	0.3504	10.05
Light skin	0.3773	0.3446	35.82
Blue sky	0.2470	0.2514	19.33
Foliage	0.3372	0.4220	13.29
Blue flower	0.2651	0.2400	24.27
Bluish green	0.2608	0.3430	43.06
Orange	0.5060	0.4070	30.05
Purplish blue	0.2110	0.1750	12.00
Moderate red	0.4533	0.3058	19.77
Purple	0.2845	0.2020	6.56
Yellow green	0.3800	0.4887	44.29
Orange yellow	0.4729	0.4375	43.06
Blue	0.1866	0.1285	6.11
Green	0.3046	0.4782	23.39
Red	0.5385	0.3129	12.00
Yellow	0.4480	0.4703	59.10
Magenta	0.3635	0.2325	19.77
Cyan	0.1958	0.2519	19.77
White	0.3101	0.3163	90.01
Neutral 8	0.3101	0.3163	59.10
Neutral 6.5	0.3101	0.3163	36.20
Neutral 5	0.3101	0.3163	19.77
Neutral 3.5	0.3101	0.3163	90.00
Black	0.3101	0.3163	3.13

TABLE G.10
1931 CIE chromaticity coordinates for the Macbeth ColorChecker.

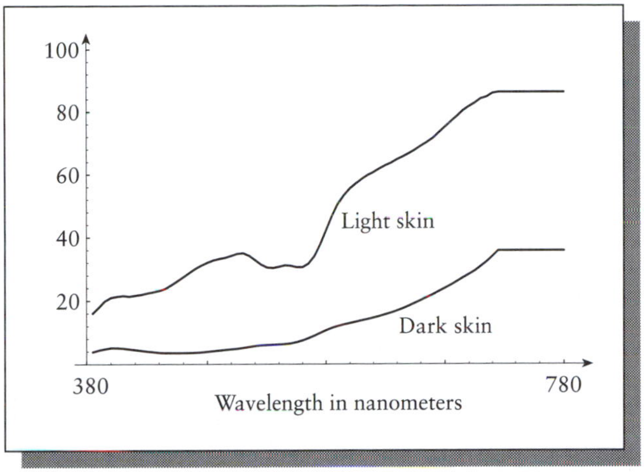

FIGURE G.9

Spectral plots for Macbeth colors light skin and dark skin.

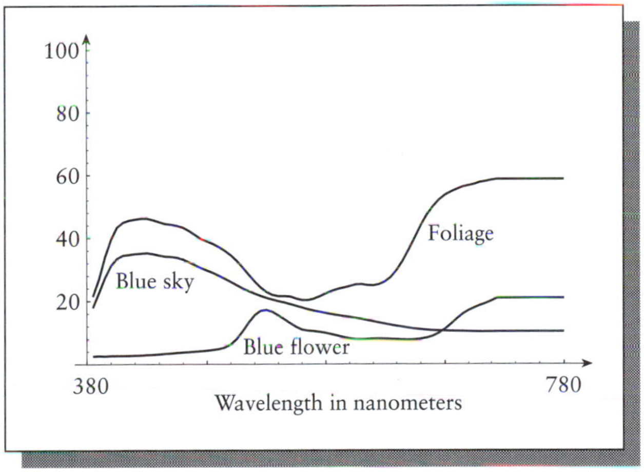

FIGURE G.10

Spectral plots for Macbeth colors blue sky, foliage, and blue flower.

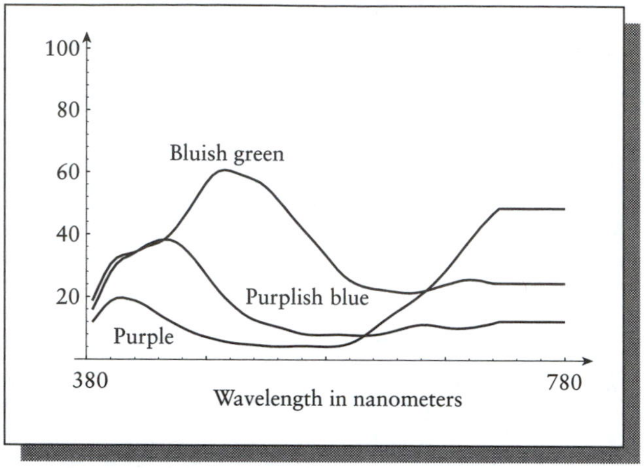

FIGURE G.11
Spectral plots for Macbeth colors purple, purplish blue, and bluish green.

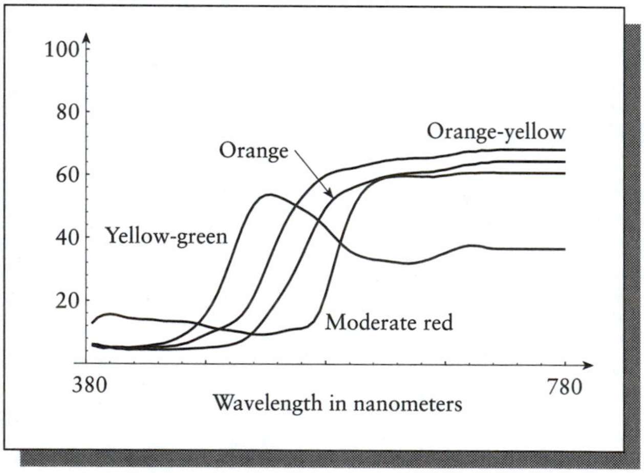

FIGURE G.12
Spectral plots for Macbeth colors orange, orange-yellow, moderate red, and yellow-green.

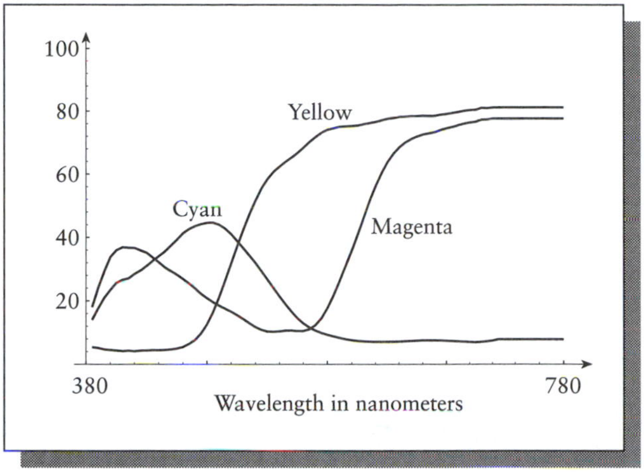

FIGURE G.13

Spectral plots for Macbeth colors yellow, cyan, and magenta.

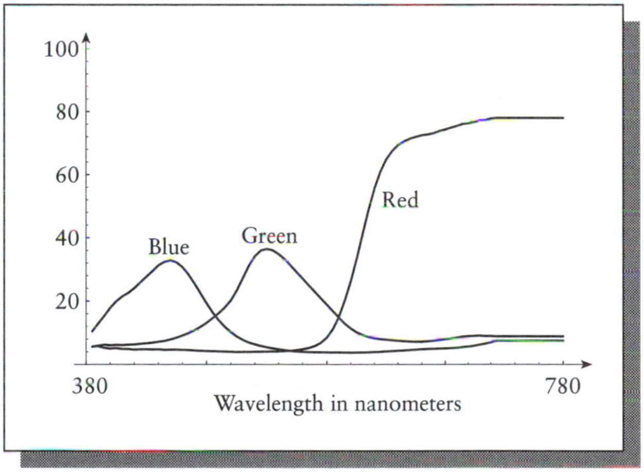

FIGURE G.14

Spectral plots for Macbeth colors red, green, and blue.

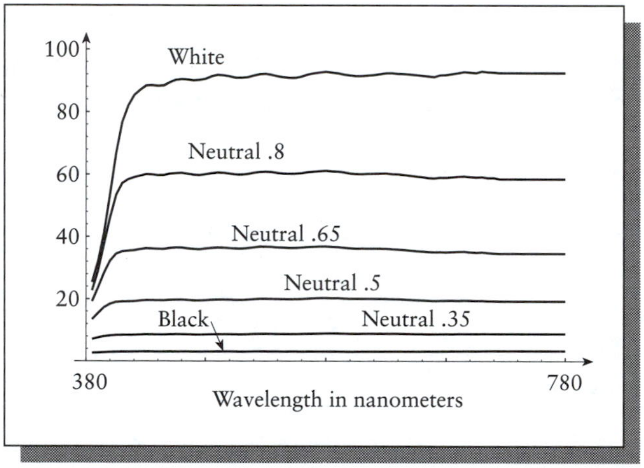

FIGURE G.15

Spectral plots for Macbeth colors black, neutral .35, neutral .5, neutral .65, neutral .8, and white.

λ	Dark skin	Light skin	Blue sky	Foliage	λ	Dark skin	Light skin	Blue sky	Foliage
380	3.885702	16.089849	17.943291	2.546426	580	11.402650	46.825020	15.762640	9.431731
385	4.450390	17.960190	22.671278	2.610934	585	12.016553	50.580948	15.465015	8.970447
390	4.833745	19.966330	27.405220	2.542109	590	12.500280	53.334690	15.172400	8.491978
395	5.165829	21.059692	31.227926	2.640033	595	12.906229	55.485752	14.887200	8.111174
400	5.140137	21.424000	33.491619	2.668386	600	13.344550	57.093788	14.590760	7.881492
405	5.004951	21.630323	34.459782	2.670110	605	13.780877	58.501759	14.266936	7.831820
410	4.745532	21.410021	34.664639	2.679658	610	14.215940	59.758968	13.900530	7.900640
415	4.505754	21.685217	34.934277	2.752025	615	14.655576	60.706512	13.487477	8.019826
420	4.267467	21.972380	35.077499	2.810802	620	15.154200	61.857552	13.114290	8.062486
425	4.049342	22.389822	35.222507	2.941530	625	15.673985	62.866501	12.761962	8.006430
430	3.852713	22.755671	34.938000	3.015812	630	16.227119	63.668449	12.378260	7.889882
435	3.654791	23.196367	34.497162	3.144345	635	16.870535	64.770386	12.054096	7.807934
440	3.559050	23.811920	34.155392	3.318482	640	17.551279	65.642593	11.751030	7.739443
445	3.557104	24.944149	34.030743	3.446844	645	18.364779	66.633049	11.469259	7.723470
450	3.543214	26.212271	33.742401	3.607446	650	19.215750	67.716698	11.184400	7.795821
455	3.553052	27.517824	33.172203	3.751262	655	20.125881	68.979088	10.994964	7.977539
460	3.582899	28.846600	32.299450	3.861416	660	21.052549	70.166290	10.798680	8.310620
465	3.641600	30.132538	31.374500	3.987481	665	21.970407	71.502991	10.651037	8.904679
470	3.750086	31.160351	30.467739	4.128319	670	22.988800	73.308052	10.570910	9.847201
475	3.924307	32.032017	29.688854	4.297079	675	23.967045	75.023354	10.500649	11.135474
480	4.143078	32.780708	28.912260	4.532319	680	24.994640	76.834427	10.429630	12.728550
485	4.340704	33.241966	28.007822	4.811964	685	26.110291	78.500015	10.411583	14.420553
490	4.516574	33.585011	27.065760	5.311668	690	27.267071	80.319321	10.388900	15.916030
495	4.697203	34.209358	26.075449	6.278073	695	28.366152	81.633400	10.317711	17.029913
500	4.884938	34.834000	25.025570	7.983501	700	29.473770	82.811432	10.261740	17.841150
505	5.145301	35.022625	24.017603	10.442900	705	30.904243	84.173866	10.246243	18.574108
510	5.452155	34.222618	23.100170	13.258410	710	32.329899	84.750160	10.232450	19.173149
515	5.723958	32.859192	22.320612	15.591791	715	34.044037	85.906219	10.215766	19.946556
520	5.934415	31.460819	21.590370	16.911671	720	35.786400	86.237663	10.266010	20.861300
525	6.041916	30.508289	20.959642	17.141542	725	35.786400	86.237663	10.266010	20.861300
530	6.115690	30.355829	20.435789	16.550421	730	35.786400	86.237663	10.266010	20.861300
535	6.196870	30.720617	19.948175	15.435068	735	35.786400	86.237663	10.266010	20.861300
540	6.343112	31.166571	19.510401	14.199900	740	35.786400	86.237663	10.266010	20.861300
545	6.560757	31.045612	19.001617	12.963397	745	35.786400	86.237663	10.266010	20.861300
550	6.932740	30.636030	18.471201	11.802250	750	35.786400	86.237663	10.266010	20.861300
555	7.463114	30.617739	17.922029	10.926905	755	35.786400	86.237663	10.266010	20.861300
560	8.179690	31.725121	17.381670	10.582230	760	35.786400	86.237663	10.266010	20.861300
565	8.991974	34.118702	16.938551	10.437484	765	35.786400	86.237663	10.266010	20.861300
570	9.840432	37.883961	16.540689	10.182910	770	35.786400	86.237663	10.266010	20.861300
575	10.683280	42.369698	16.172670	9.858121	775	35.786400	86.237663	10.266010	20.861300

TABLE G.11
Macbeth chart spectra for dark skin, light skin, blue sky, and foliage.

λ	Blue flower	Bluish green	Orange	Purplish blue	λ	Blue flower	Bluish green	Orange	Purplish blue
380	21.504471	18.686119	6.143748	15.799930	580	23.182091	30.971640	51.863571	8.056614
385	26.985552	23.105488	5.192119	19.774714	585	23.787580	28.732615	53.595318	8.098731
390	34.021549	27.136400	4.867970	24.081640	590	24.193159	26.890051	54.809231	8.031386
395	39.510910	30.388052	5.092529	27.756655	595	24.678110	25.456657	55.630657	7.925573
400	43.429729	32.360771	4.717562	30.455971	600	25.161699	24.410139	56.426868	7.856916
405	44.911545	33.244198	4.663087	32.119804	605	25.263716	23.628857	57.159523	7.819657
410	45.581810	33.674278	4.455331	32.956371	610	24.993191	23.123470	57.816502	7.861434
415	45.900398	34.219761	4.562958	34.028576	615	24.918528	22.733202	58.437481	7.986660
420	46.183998	35.044319	4.517197	35.343910	620	25.269529	22.528919	59.110668	8.230119
425	46.186264	36.028893	4.536289	36.495560	625	26.073601	22.263077	59.586777	8.618429
430	45.726070	36.568611	4.454180	37.343262	630	27.443090	21.966181	59.988918	9.067121
435	45.079132	37.241230	4.543101	38.061672	635	29.665966	21.737934	60.345753	9.595715
440	44.509541	38.326118	4.491708	38.233730	640	32.639080	21.489401	60.528080	10.130000
445	44.257874	40.065491	4.528984	38.131840	645	36.210133	21.407528	60.780136	10.664613
450	43.903500	42.215569	4.598219	37.376381	650	40.103359	21.544180	60.880470	11.057190
455	43.277981	44.890938	4.663068	36.047756	655	43.931278	21.870035	61.062321	11.314054
460	42.230179	47.560928	4.753312	34.203388	660	47.289768	22.310350	61.085751	11.284740
465	40.963223	50.571754	4.876582	32.064915	665	49.895874	22.888117	61.250366	11.057791
470	39.665791	53.662781	4.960935	29.636610	670	52.047100	23.528099	61.662369	10.776800
475	38.928234	56.587734	5.130267	27.056273	675	53.572105	24.078556	61.931293	10.465913
480	38.122768	58.940788	5.313134	24.475210	680	54.650139	24.552179	62.382530	10.244980
485	37.096794	60.270790	5.427264	22.069368	685	55.462223	25.144257	62.865440	10.170987
490	35.917110	60.675900	5.687261	19.964800	690	56.214321	25.597771	63.395748	10.256740
495	34.488316	60.404842	6.020061	18.108223	695	56.626854	25.747564	63.531815	10.416534
500	32.753262	59.725731	6.536922	16.407801	700	57.083649	25.676689	63.722641	10.619700
505	30.611862	59.037102	7.313779	14.902749	705	57.652874	25.431557	64.181450	11.001964
510	28.324471	58.389900	8.567378	13.650830	710	57.917110	24.948210	64.155388	11.347610
515	26.148941	57.590084	10.213456	12.728430	715	58.315697	24.583284	64.506691	11.803800
520	24.276060	56.700130	12.347440	12.053160	720	58.571461	24.529430	64.600601	12.386420
525	22.837721	55.223652	14.861832	11.448863	725	58.571461	24.529430	64.600601	12.386420
530	21.911461	53.463741	17.522091	10.954790	730	58.571461	24.529430	64.600601	12.386420
535	21.528542	51.143139	20.319046	10.455321	735	58.571461	24.529430	64.600601	12.386420
540	21.561150	48.929329	23.213921	9.924716	740	58.571461	24.529430	64.600601	12.386420
545	21.424437	46.547081	26.351696	9.342658	745	58.571461	24.529430	64.600601	12.386420
550	20.754511	44.271980	30.008520	8.761171	750	58.571461	24.529430	64.600601	12.386420
555	20.276314	42.037167	34.099560	8.321023	755	58.571461	24.529430	64.600601	12.386420
560	20.258760	39.957352	38.503441	8.052579	760	58.571461	24.529430	64.600601	12.386420
565	20.681358	37.846802	42.740505	7.949393	765	58.571461	24.529430	64.600601	12.386420
570	21.446180	35.616039	46.404800	7.928015	770	58.571461	24.529430	64.600601	12.386420
575	22.377563	33.342571	49.572742	7.994457	775	58.571461	24.529430	64.600601	12.386420

TABLE G.12
Macbeth chart spectra for blue flower, bluish green, orange, and purplish blue.

λ	Moderate red	Purple	Yellow-green	Orange-yellow	λ	Moderate red	Purple	Yellow-green	Orange-yellow
380	12.669950	11.859360	5.699953	6.128503	580	28.888000	4.242651	41.317768	60.767220
385	14.544419	14.397915	5.295924	5.963221	585	35.891396	4.410142	39.298252	61.392555
390	15.348420	16.806971	5.190561	5.502130	590	42.222599	4.726547	37.397831	61.844471
395	15.663042	18.538034	5.193296	5.262633	595	47.389523	5.251801	35.887939	62.124138
400	15.440190	19.507759	5.253389	5.069424	600	51.272831	6.055812	34.859692	62.476151
405	14.938562	19.613047	5.187729	5.262915	605	54.253593	7.160420	34.170391	62.988613
410	14.476950	19.221670	5.058478	5.094549	610	56.294781	8.484931	33.650341	63.419258
415	14.282184	18.745989	5.258210	5.165659	615	57.641983	9.963583	33.258446	63.862713
420	14.062970	17.924740	5.420898	5.269699	620	58.599480	11.448830	33.054859	64.243538
425	14.033772	16.916019	5.601523	5.297654	625	59.279758	12.870117	32.866116	64.701447
430	13.942360	15.635920	5.927870	5.274950	630	59.545589	14.237090	32.563110	64.920761
435	13.707626	14.395824	6.187038	5.308822	635	59.743793	15.569023	32.343559	65.222870
440	13.486230	13.231260	6.503921	5.357237	640	59.785160	16.828690	32.089470	65.231102
445	13.459547	12.166025	7.160728	5.576923	645	59.796532	18.113380	32.033154	65.480751
450	13.427400	11.141210	7.912244	5.758418	650	59.745998	19.487631	32.239601	65.551781
455	13.396607	10.160862	8.914824	6.232115	655	59.640450	20.996145	32.673386	65.568802
460	13.266400	9.231147	10.078100	6.698434	660	59.723228	22.531851	33.203732	65.598961
465	12.960032	8.429399	11.531056	7.507004	665	59.561363	24.294062	33.880280	65.700867
470	12.515480	7.772344	13.340230	8.380088	670	59.904331	26.318970	34.743710	66.116653
475	11.967863	7.196618	15.777214	9.273271	675	60.057800	28.436649	35.445564	66.352913
480	11.482440	6.696550	18.759899	10.123820	680	60.308899	30.740080	36.263580	66.685081
485	11.087990	6.231675	22.517645	10.892391	685	60.629135	33.170681	36.929043	67.072021
490	10.811620	5.775795	27.220400	11.648160	690	60.795078	35.678871	37.536949	67.572678
495	10.615905	5.434763	32.417606	12.608733	695	60.868801	38.061874	37.830456	67.729622
500	10.328200	5.174724	37.850819	13.805800	700	60.864300	40.371368	37.764172	67.714233
505	10.051079	4.984176	42.984535	15.570681	705	61.017906	42.764141	37.608898	68.124062
510	9.664922	4.856252	47.265862	18.120770	710	60.996571	44.761829	37.083248	68.049828
515	9.408811	4.718699	50.485565	21.505651	715	61.058018	46.829060	36.871063	68.218697
520	9.321096	4.556475	52.618839	25.682369	720	60.921082	48.540401	36.803909	68.387672
525	9.370760	4.379337	53.592617	30.245390	725	60.921082	48.540401	36.803909	68.387672
530	9.588202	4.263306	53.714550	34.985229	730	60.921082	48.540401	36.803909	68.387672
535	9.958136	4.217373	53.179836	39.500118	735	60.921082	48.540401	36.803909	68.387672
540	10.435310	4.230328	52.391361	43.667969	740	60.921082	48.540401	36.803909	68.387672
545	10.874439	4.287500	51.413731	47.134743	745	60.921082	48.540401	36.803909	68.387672
550	11.133060	4.372940	50.334900	50.152199	750	60.921082	48.540401	36.803909	68.387672
555	11.316847	4.395883	49.233387	52.729702	755	60.921082	48.540401	36.803909	68.387672
560	11.933180	4.375529	48.121429	55.035461	760	60.921082	48.540401	36.803909	68.387672
565	13.563336	4.314129	46.781601	57.034595	765	60.921082	48.540401	36.803909	68.387672
570	16.881001	4.251691	45.183651	58.611809	770	60.921082	48.540401	36.803909	68.387672
575	22.200445	4.206913	43.403061	59.931717	775	60.921082	48.540401	36.803909	68.387672

TABLE G.13
Macbeth chart spectra for moderate red, purple, yellow-green, and orange-yellow.

λ	Blue	Green	Red	Yellow	λ	Blue	Green	Red	Yellow
380	10.439910	5.613400	5.607345	5.414068	580	3.787635	16.728580	11.225140	74.554909
385	12.886761	5.922082	5.725149	5.137067	585	3.776771	14.735263	15.120548	75.039360
390	15.300090	6.200247	5.218394	4.704292	590	3.750088	12.870290	20.188690	75.159851
395	17.832754	6.012131	4.956743	4.520826	595	3.722865	11.336102	26.293297	75.268250
400	19.873070	6.146746	5.121036	4.344138	600	3.744416	10.124970	33.403919	75.418297
405	21.445684	6.098392	4.849411	4.163425	605	3.774995	9.289590	41.325912	75.863037
410	22.557791	6.206563	4.834329	4.315780	610	3.831947	8.658465	48.992439	76.238503
415	24.002087	6.295394	4.646286	4.125665	615	3.899615	8.251087	55.669144	76.591118
420	25.866680	6.484003	4.741153	4.300586	620	3.970753	7.988280	60.940609	77.154846
425	27.594967	6.663407	4.744888	4.335837	625	4.070755	7.791666	64.768387	77.618408
430	29.415440	6.859391	4.712543	4.441292	630	4.181859	7.609302	67.367477	77.834442
435	31.260592	7.121455	4.758327	4.448205	635	4.297741	7.450396	69.261131	78.160141
440	32.378559	7.413484	4.605003	4.512076	640	4.410157	7.311813	70.503029	78.248161
445	32.824814	7.875336	4.654145	4.661452	645	4.532931	7.222866	71.407242	78.407303
450	32.212132	8.412111	4.639721	4.968147	650	4.670670	7.161132	71.985252	78.438698
455	30.671518	9.119376	4.563574	5.431167	655	4.774706	7.167995	72.515152	78.558060
460	28.334240	9.851811	4.515702	6.415275	660	4.850951	7.324787	72.721283	78.497429
465	25.484060	10.781063	4.380999	7.625481	665	4.924014	7.446044	73.152130	78.523407
470	22.396629	11.853670	4.277033	9.682865	670	4.990421	7.688989	73.842392	78.883820
475	19.292439	13.102253	4.211078	12.573673	675	5.052288	7.914150	74.320816	79.112015
480	16.411600	14.572390	4.135724	16.342621	680	5.141122	8.186454	74.898903	79.429321
485	13.933167	16.115742	4.103681	21.097710	685	5.236134	8.430433	75.451370	79.794380
490	11.879180	17.952681	4.063927	26.350420	690	5.436373	8.752160	76.021973	80.120506
495	10.174302	20.263348	3.998882	31.775793	695	5.612031	8.910556	76.308281	80.328354
500	8.797017	23.403231	3.906034	37.215130	700	5.848758	8.969923	76.621246	80.466164
505	7.712556	27.286863	3.941102	42.412758	705	6.181974	9.050636	77.229218	81.044724
510	6.886145	31.145849	3.924661	47.316730	710	6.504695	8.918600	77.277542	80.947998
515	6.304307	34.160007	3.978011	51.712082	715	6.921960	8.914872	77.749832	81.159058
520	5.817560	35.976002	4.021000	55.590401	720	7.462452	8.840295	77.937653	81.175743
525	5.407475	36.454826	4.037704	58.489658	725	7.462452	8.840295	77.937653	81.175743
530	5.059405	35.995239	4.088925	60.763920	730	7.462452	8.840295	77.937653	81.175743
535	4.751938	34.788082	4.060666	62.378773	735	7.462452	8.840295	77.937653	81.175743
540	4.495099	33.215500	4.200492	63.929630	740	7.462452	8.840295	77.937653	81.175743
545	4.260099	31.219875	4.266126	65.257240	745	7.462452	8.840295	77.937653	81.175743
550	4.095733	29.161699	4.498791	66.725067	750	7.462452	8.840295	77.937653	81.175743
555	3.963588	27.074284	4.790018	68.364166	755	7.462452	8.840295	77.937653	81.175743
560	3.891369	25.007160	5.160057	70.174118	760	7.462452	8.840295	77.937653	81.175743
565	3.841832	22.942715	5.749929	71.759537	765	7.462452	8.840295	77.937653	81.175743
570	3.820277	20.921579	6.728241	73.110298	770	7.462452	8.840295	77.937653	81.175743
575	3.801960	18.823641	8.466923	74.078796	775	7.462452	8.840295	77.937653	81.175743

TABLE G.14
Macbeth chart spectra for blue, green, red, and yellow.

λ	Magenta	Cyan	White	Neutral .8	λ	Magenta	Cyan	White	Neutral .8
380	18.022249	13.999790	25.375759	22.696239	580	21.613300	8.781203	92.538689	60.987720
385	24.141811	17.662146	32.028969	29.054020	585	26.161331	8.340083	92.293861	60.901627
390	29.218670	20.940290	41.140018	37.571621	590	30.903650	7.908925	91.910744	60.653358
395	33.815952	23.452644	53.732193	46.166943	595	35.840412	7.572946	91.650513	60.300995
400	35.977070	25.668360	66.863197	53.429451	600	41.036240	7.351048	91.441002	60.132450
405	36.876205	26.630613	76.693954	57.110985	605	46.447910	7.223466	91.463058	60.118248
410	36.754471	27.105560	81.899612	58.401501	610	51.659920	7.129447	91.623558	60.215561
415	36.671719	28.486927	85.311897	59.024353	615	56.339233	7.113521	91.761253	60.238060
420	35.898029	29.540880	86.954269	59.528542	620	60.391499	7.105100	92.056503	60.303070
425	35.148922	30.971483	88.338806	59.993679	625	63.846664	7.103106	92.346115	60.339325
430	33.675171	32.553398	88.422600	59.915970	630	66.495522	7.099453	92.366142	60.116680
435	32.182053	34.028538	88.229996	59.697506	635	68.510284	7.152534	92.175926	60.058334
440	30.604540	35.484280	88.368492	59.728500	640	70.003822	7.252600	92.107048	59.853298
445	29.404226	37.367111	89.407570	60.187801	645	71.087265	7.349627	91.950233	59.600319
450	28.225990	39.260792	90.160072	60.356602	650	71.911079	7.430556	91.762352	59.369801
455	26.886612	41.293606	90.400452	60.453487	655	72.552330	7.536674	91.552132	59.176750
460	25.465940	42.623539	90.278893	60.163570	660	72.939537	7.535679	91.366997	58.879410
465	23.959021	43.587276	89.992531	59.868294	665	73.311600	7.537577	91.155579	58.789925
470	22.230909	44.182098	90.135948	59.730091	670	74.038681	7.492112	91.727760	58.988022
475	20.828238	44.616940	90.474327	60.002926	675	74.580025	7.411035	91.787041	58.964962
480	19.569361	44.645649	91.306183	60.322170	680	74.964828	7.313859	92.107681	59.136768
485	18.467690	43.998219	91.767899	60.546734	685	75.547630	7.236807	92.397926	59.311607
490	17.499559	42.721741	91.626801	60.466930	690	76.021133	7.118407	92.761703	59.392921
495	16.547125	41.007633	91.293587	60.220291	695	76.412292	7.020689	92.583092	59.202972
500	15.474920	38.825981	90.850433	59.951031	700	76.642761	6.981132	92.438179	59.085461
505	14.258726	36.596691	90.837151	59.914757	705	77.305191	7.056737	92.927948	59.169731
510	12.908480	34.225380	91.037247	60.110161	710	77.348541	7.200351	92.690323	58.877949
515	11.735996	31.868864	91.565384	60.493999	715	77.644272	7.454174	92.630486	58.874104
520	10.841580	29.297951	91.988602	60.780670	720	77.633263	7.847146	92.432678	58.492451
525	10.336895	26.658068	92.111366	60.855427	725	77.633263	7.847146	92.432678	58.492451
530	10.238720	24.025311	91.802696	60.751438	730	77.633263	7.847146	92.432678	58.492451
535	10.372057	21.356544	91.324654	60.423901	735	77.633263	7.847146	92.432678	58.492451
540	10.613430	18.867420	91.041283	60.229000	740	77.633263	7.847146	92.432678	58.492451
545	10.653950	16.573082	90.819458	60.184757	745	77.633263	7.847146	92.432678	58.492451
550	10.483800	14.551340	90.852364	60.230389	750	77.633263	7.847146	92.432678	58.492451
555	10.505778	12.926720	91.282684	60.397083	755	77.633263	7.847146	92.432678	58.492451
560	11.048930	11.628690	91.900436	60.725960	760	77.633263	7.847146	92.432678	58.492451
565	12.309056	10.648726	92.308823	60.882137	765	77.633263	7.847146	92.432678	58.492451
570	14.462500	9.884577	92.568031	61.023682	770	77.633263	7.847146	92.432678	58.492451
575	17.684841	9.296182	92.796066	61.169136	775	77.633263	7.847146	92.432678	58.492451

TABLE G.15
Macbeth chart spectra for magenta, cyan, white, and neutral .8.

λ	Neutral 6.5	Neutral .5	Neutral 3.5	Black	λ	Neutral 6.5	Neutral .5	Neutral 3.5	Black
380	19.224840	13.435700	7.083606	2.632727	580	36.746559	20.266991	8.927324	3.080587
385	23.636890	15.446929	7.548733	2.725736	585	36.652134	20.271544	8.921852	3.083956
390	28.357880	17.290791	8.004693	2.823380	590	36.454571	20.160601	8.878298	3.065194
395	32.256924	18.395866	8.206776	2.909946	595	36.286266	20.079086	8.833010	3.046615
400	34.484650	19.002270	8.360070	2.968467	600	36.186840	20.063580	8.828733	3.057060
405	35.241299	19.151167	8.395691	2.996089	605	36.198948	20.076405	8.845784	3.078887
410	35.403610	19.185089	8.411283	2.988267	610	36.182140	20.069420	8.846595	3.092442
415	35.566936	19.229340	8.430621	3.023094	615	36.176430	20.072975	8.858018	3.102046
420	35.933811	19.443100	8.499412	3.033404	620	36.174900	20.054750	8.873004	3.099842
425	36.208771	19.578882	8.572122	3.046201	625	36.144829	20.051716	8.845028	3.102931
430	36.117641	19.580959	8.547405	3.037941	630	35.990040	19.971340	8.836456	3.111137
435	36.016354	19.543287	8.522265	3.017020	635	35.888779	19.932774	8.839376	3.126484
440	35.987209	19.540529	8.518660	3.015140	640	35.796841	19.851419	8.814060	3.129484
445	36.312756	19.673838	8.606515	3.052497	645	35.573486	19.752970	8.784361	3.123158
450	36.472401	19.738050	8.626643	3.049293	650	35.391460	19.651300	8.743491	3.116263
455	36.458347	19.749012	8.633178	3.060219	655	35.287487	19.577881	8.737347	3.132131
460	36.181461	19.639170	8.579259	3.056880	660	35.124611	19.479120	8.700668	3.135744
465	36.026970	19.496111	8.543505	3.039923	665	35.052013	19.420036	8.690422	3.141036
470	35.905571	19.482559	8.514179	3.035550	670	35.063881	19.458620	8.715772	3.165520
475	36.159534	19.580959	8.561783	3.056961	675	35.013481	19.483587	8.738324	3.171804
480	36.327789	19.708241	8.610093	3.074459	680	35.092709	19.508320	8.728421	3.182123
485	36.461124	19.791525	8.646560	3.088606	685	35.174206	19.473574	8.755197	3.197628
490	36.412868	19.794041	8.645944	3.093020	690	35.228279	19.539480	8.779080	3.213080
495	36.285694	19.767027	8.648259	3.082364	695	35.028103	19.502604	8.756978	3.217463
500	36.178558	19.669411	8.598061	3.053497	700	34.887508	19.432119	8.758911	3.211801
505	36.149555	19.663586	8.584575	3.036846	705	35.003155	19.470539	8.795638	3.251364
510	36.317680	19.771111	8.645377	3.063548	710	34.778690	19.342850	8.789021	3.268996
515	36.559345	19.920492	8.735252	3.104859	715	34.654709	19.343155	8.780120	3.282216
520	36.789268	20.039610	8.780753	3.116698	720	34.568691	19.281151	8.761631	3.286303
525	36.754456	20.045027	8.783650	3.105289	725	34.568691	19.281151	8.761631	3.286303
530	36.714062	20.026381	8.760933	3.090450	730	34.568691	19.281151	8.761631	3.286303
535	36.517780	19.960434	8.725173	3.079003	735	34.568691	19.281151	8.761631	3.286303
540	36.472542	19.936211	8.711111	3.076537	740	34.568691	19.281151	8.761631	3.286303
545	36.370415	19.906458	8.711410	3.078362	745	34.568691	19.281151	8.761631	3.286303
550	36.390388	19.931290	8.727204	3.076893	750	34.568691	19.281151	8.761631	3.286303
555	36.534843	19.997835	8.754922	3.074938	755	34.568691	19.281151	8.761631	3.286303
560	36.681900	20.126101	8.809222	3.084897	760	34.568691	19.281151	8.761631	3.286303
565	36.761192	20.241846	8.855934	3.086724	765	34.568691	19.281151	8.761631	3.286303
570	36.831631	20.304529	8.880202	3.091457	770	34.568691	19.281151	8.761631	3.286303
575	36.870087	20.312584	8.914644	3.087454	775	34.568691	19.281151	8.761631	3.286303

TABLE G.16
Macbeth chart spectra for neutral 6.5, neutral .5, neutral 3.5, and black.

G.6 Real Objects

Tables G.17 through G.26 present spectral information for forty real objects. The data in these tables was interpolated from measurements in the range [390, 730] nanometers at 2-nanometer steps, by Vrhel, Iwan and Gershon [457]. Their work was supported by NCSU and Eastman Kodak. As of publication, the original data, plus data for the Munsell color chips and 130 other real objects is available via anonymous ftp from the server `ftp.eos.ncsu.edu` in the directory `/pub/spectra`. These spectra are plotted in Figures G.16 through G.25.

λ	Pine needles	Silver maple leaf	Dark green maple leaf	Red maple leaf	λ	Pine needles	Silver maple leaf	Dark green maple leaf	Red maple leaf
380	0.029600	0.039800	0.036300	0.018600	580	0.085100	0.071300	0.156900	0.054100
385	0.029600	0.039800	0.036300	0.018600	585	0.079141	0.068097	0.146819	0.049989
390	0.029600	0.039800	0.036300	0.018600	590	0.075200	0.066100	0.139500	0.047400
395	0.028803	0.040595	0.035490	0.018680	595	0.072491	0.065321	0.134735	0.045560
400	0.027800	0.041500	0.034200	0.018300	600	0.070700	0.064500	0.131200	0.044200
405	0.028613	0.040981	0.033669	0.018856	605	0.068064	0.063573	0.126421	0.042232
410	0.029200	0.041400	0.033600	0.019200	610	0.063900	0.061600	0.118800	0.039200
415	0.029513	0.041243	0.033055	0.019189	615	0.059599	0.059510	0.110514	0.036151
420	0.030600	0.041600	0.034000	0.019700	620	0.056400	0.058000	0.104000	0.034000
425	0.031044	0.041406	0.034715	0.019702	625	0.054789	0.057071	0.100686	0.032827
430	0.031200	0.041100	0.035200	0.019800	630	0.054300	0.057000	0.099400	0.032400
435	0.031491	0.041038	0.035971	0.019751	635	0.052772	0.056103	0.095965	0.031496
440	0.031700	0.041000	0.036500	0.019700	640	0.049300	0.054000	0.087200	0.029100
445	0.031994	0.041121	0.037276	0.019789	645	0.045315	0.051874	0.077085	0.026255
450	0.032600	0.041500	0.038400	0.019900	650	0.042600	0.050300	0.069700	0.024400
455	0.032871	0.041761	0.039155	0.020063	655	0.041167	0.049755	0.066340	0.023362
460	0.033100	0.041700	0.039800	0.020000	660	0.039400	0.049000	0.061900	0.022200
465	0.033347	0.043096	0.040400	0.020038	665	0.037525	0.047818	0.056503	0.021029
470	0.033400	0.043500	0.041000	0.020100	670	0.036800	0.047600	0.053800	0.020700
475	0.034198	0.042944	0.041977	0.019992	675	0.036856	0.047899	0.053596	0.021133
480	0.034600	0.043200	0.042500	0.020100	680	0.038000	0.048800	0.055600	0.022100
485	0.035069	0.043571	0.043554	0.020086	685	0.040924	0.051119	0.062490	0.023933
490	0.035500	0.044000	0.044900	0.020300	690	0.049700	0.056600	0.085700	0.030500
495	0.036887	0.044616	0.046992	0.021790	695	0.076329	0.073143	0.141592	0.049319
500	0.038800	0.045200	0.051800	0.022800	700	0.127300	0.110600	0.224300	0.083900
505	0.042594	0.046846	0.060185	0.025527	705	0.191700	0.164531	0.312366	0.129966
510	0.049000	0.050000	0.073900	0.030700	710	0.256600	0.224500	0.391500	0.183600
515	0.059917	0.055638	0.094850	0.039821	715	0.319407	0.286062	0.459499	0.242201
520	0.076500	0.064400	0.124100	0.052200	720	0.378800	0.347500	0.517100	0.304300
525	0.095189	0.074645	0.155038	0.065529	725	0.433914	0.407055	0.563011	0.364725
530	0.111300	0.083900	0.182400	0.075800	730	0.479800	0.460100	0.596300	0.419800
535	0.121705	0.089734	0.201339	0.081755	735	0.479800	0.460100	0.596300	0.419800
540	0.127200	0.092700	0.212400	0.084700	740	0.479800	0.460100	0.596300	0.419800
545	0.130728	0.094851	0.219945	0.086575	745	0.479800	0.460100	0.596300	0.419800
550	0.133200	0.096500	0.225500	0.088100	750	0.479800	0.460100	0.596300	0.419800
555	0.133128	0.097030	0.226116	0.087837	755	0.479800	0.460100	0.596300	0.419800
560	0.128000	0.094400	0.219800	0.084100	760	0.479800	0.460100	0.596300	0.419800
565	0.118589	0.089177	0.207223	0.077073	765	0.479800	0.460100	0.596300	0.419800
570	0.105800	0.082100	0.189400	0.068300	770	0.479800	0.460100	0.596300	0.419800
575	0.093736	0.075570	0.171017	0.059939	775	0.479800	0.460100	0.596300	0.419800

TABLE G.17
Spectra for pine needles and maple leaves (silver, dark green, and red).

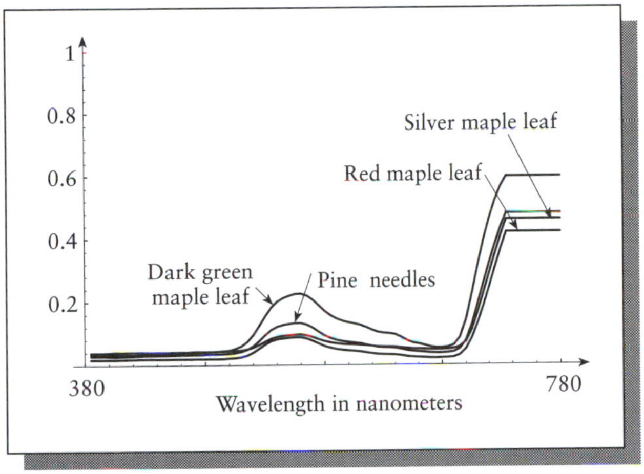

FIGURE G.16
Spectral plots for pine needles and maple leaves (silver, dark green, and red).

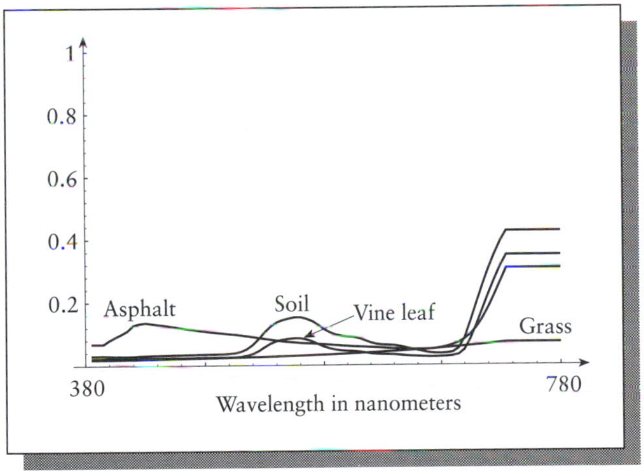

FIGURE G.17
Spectral plots for grass, soil, vine leaf, and asphalt.

λ	Grass	Soil	Vine leaf	Asphalt	λ	Grass	Soil	Vine leaf	Asphalt
380	0.018800	0.030900	0.022000	0.068400	580	0.033800	0.103300	0.052600	0.064900
385	0.018800	0.030900	0.022000	0.068400	585	0.034492	0.096441	0.048718	0.063282
390	0.018800	0.030900	0.022000	0.068400	590	0.035200	0.092100	0.046100	0.061700
395	0.018802	0.030570	0.023131	0.080352	595	0.036003	0.090051	0.044805	0.060297
400	0.019000	0.029700	0.022900	0.090700	600	0.036800	0.088600	0.043800	0.059100
405	0.019211	0.029487	0.022865	0.099929	605	0.037695	0.084619	0.041973	0.058133
410	0.019600	0.029500	0.023400	0.110500	610	0.038500	0.077700	0.039200	0.057200
415	0.019675	0.029776	0.023280	0.128480	615	0.039400	0.070651	0.036258	0.056147
420	0.020300	0.030900	0.023700	0.133500	620	0.040400	0.065800	0.034400	0.055200
425	0.020498	0.031547	0.024150	0.135845	625	0.041303	0.063415	0.033392	0.054103
430	0.020800	0.032000	0.024000	0.133500	630	0.042300	0.062700	0.033100	0.053000
435	0.021082	0.032531	0.024076	0.130632	635	0.043182	0.061868	0.032586	0.051836
440	0.021500	0.033000	0.024200	0.128600	640	0.044400	0.058800	0.031000	0.051000
445	0.021983	0.033474	0.024393	0.125585	645	0.045464	0.054444	0.029281	0.050195
450	0.022200	0.034000	0.024600	0.122700	650	0.046500	0.050000	0.027800	0.049600
455	0.022402	0.034255	0.024548	0.119231	655	0.047588	0.046240	0.027067	0.049407
460	0.022700	0.034400	0.024500	0.116100	660	0.048700	0.041900	0.026100	0.049400
465	0.023049	0.034803	0.024599	0.113976	665	0.049888	0.038002	0.025316	0.050173
470	0.023400	0.035400	0.025200	0.110900	670	0.051300	0.036300	0.025200	0.051700
475	0.023649	0.035487	0.025411	0.108572	675	0.052712	0.036128	0.025691	0.054277
480	0.023900	0.035900	0.025300	0.105900	680	0.054100	0.037000	0.026500	0.058100
485	0.024187	0.036050	0.025407	0.103651	685	0.055643	0.039818	0.028035	0.063422
490	0.024500	0.036400	0.025600	0.102000	690	0.057200	0.052100	0.032500	0.071000
495	0.024909	0.037328	0.025752	0.099743	695	0.058886	0.085055	0.047704	0.081564
500	0.025200	0.039200	0.026300	0.098200	700	0.060600	0.137700	0.081800	0.097000
505	0.025591	0.043587	0.027604	0.095556	705	0.062298	0.195154	0.126645	0.118016
510	0.026100	0.051600	0.030800	0.092900	710	0.063900	0.250400	0.175000	0.146300
515	0.026512	0.065044	0.036376	0.090211	715	0.065747	0.302173	0.223237	0.180895
520	0.026900	0.084400	0.045900	0.087100	720	0.067700	0.349500	0.269700	0.220900
525	0.027338	0.105930	0.057947	0.084199	725	0.069607	0.390741	0.312332	0.263639
530	0.027900	0.123800	0.069100	0.081400	730	0.071400	0.424400	0.347900	0.306600
535	0.028400	0.136531	0.076816	0.078576	735	0.071400	0.424400	0.347900	0.306600
540	0.028900	0.143300	0.081000	0.076000	740	0.071400	0.424400	0.347900	0.306600
545	0.029509	0.148244	0.083776	0.073917	745	0.071400	0.424400	0.347900	0.306600
550	0.030100	0.152300	0.085800	0.072400	750	0.071400	0.424400	0.347900	0.306600
555	0.030648	0.152214	0.085457	0.070747	755	0.071400	0.424400	0.347900	0.306600
560	0.031300	0.147300	0.081800	0.069600	760	0.071400	0.424400	0.347900	0.306600
565	0.031900	0.139512	0.075425	0.068663	765	0.071400	0.424400	0.347900	0.306600
570	0.032600	0.127300	0.066800	0.067600	770	0.071400	0.424400	0.347900	0.306600
575	0.033262	0.113764	0.058398	0.066246	775	0.071400	0.424400	0.347900	0.306600

TABLE G.18

Spectra for grass, soil, vine leaf, and asphalt.

λ	Daisy white petals	Daisy yellow center	Marigold orange	Marigold yellow	λ	Daisy white petals	Daisy yellow center	Marigold orange	Marigold yellow
380	0.028800	0.025700	0.035200	0.058700	580	0.391400	0.411700	0.503200	0.214500
385	0.028800	0.025700	0.035200	0.058700	585	0.395083	0.414181	0.508292	0.251287
390	0.028800	0.025700	0.035200	0.058700	590	0.399300	0.417400	0.513200	0.293600
395	0.022880	0.018409	0.026572	0.058646	595	0.403365	0.421022	0.517930	0.340226
400	0.017900	0.013400	0.021700	0.068000	600	0.406100	0.423600	0.521500	0.386500
405	0.016032	0.012376	0.016391	0.085506	605	0.408193	0.423460	0.524462	0.426925
410	0.014700	0.010200	0.014400	0.111800	610	0.407000	0.420300	0.527500	0.460100
415	0.013631	0.008862	0.011961	0.139686	615	0.404087	0.416098	0.528865	0.484983
420	0.014100	0.008200	0.011900	0.169400	620	0.401800	0.411500	0.530300	0.502800
425	0.013882	0.008100	0.012080	0.194080	625	0.401092	0.409648	0.532011	0.514647
430	0.014800	0.008700	0.012300	0.210600	630	0.402900	0.410600	0.534700	0.524400
435	0.015291	0.008621	0.014122	0.225214	635	0.403656	0.411247	0.536570	0.530300
440	0.015700	0.008300	0.016700	0.227800	640	0.403600	0.411000	0.537000	0.534900
445	0.016063	0.008265	0.019407	0.228770	645	0.400851	0.408202	0.536595	0.537864
450	0.016100	0.008600	0.022200	0.228100	650	0.394500	0.400800	0.535500	0.539600
455	0.016618	0.009442	0.024787	0.224419	655	0.387390	0.389830	0.534526	0.540692
460	0.016900	0.010500	0.028500	0.220500	660	0.374100	0.369100	0.533000	0.541800
465	0.017775	0.011694	0.033288	0.216800	665	0.354589	0.339040	0.527190	0.541834
470	0.018500	0.011700	0.037800	0.210300	670	0.338200	0.312800	0.523100	0.544400
475	0.018538	0.011286	0.038786	0.203693	675	0.329312	0.298273	0.521503	0.544910
480	0.018500	0.011700	0.037500	0.195300	680	0.329600	0.296100	0.524000	0.545800
485	0.018782	0.013526	0.038364	0.186230	685	0.349426	0.321232	0.535810	0.547162
490	0.019800	0.018800	0.043600	0.175600	690	0.389400	0.373600	0.553400	0.548500
495	0.022031	0.029949	0.054371	0.165735	695	0.433821	0.424166	0.568270	0.549694
500	0.027100	0.049900	0.074600	0.156300	700	0.471500	0.460700	0.579100	0.550900
505	0.037496	0.081222	0.100825	0.146827	705	0.500947	0.483861	0.584743	0.550557
510	0.058000	0.120600	0.136800	0.138800	710	0.523400	0.499700	0.590400	0.550000
515	0.092116	0.167515	0.179710	0.131694	715	0.542755	0.510764	0.593858	0.549949
520	0.137400	0.214400	0.225100	0.125100	720	0.557900	0.519600	0.597200	0.548400
525	0.183722	0.257637	0.268897	0.120244	725	0.570330	0.524864	0.598571	0.547954
530	0.226300	0.294900	0.309400	0.117800	730	0.579400	0.528000	0.598300	0.545800
535	0.261351	0.324177	0.345784	0.115398	735	0.579400	0.528000	0.598300	0.545800
540	0.291200	0.347000	0.376900	0.115000	740	0.579400	0.528000	0.598300	0.545800
545	0.314826	0.363243	0.403360	0.115541	745	0.579400	0.528000	0.598300	0.545800
550	0.333000	0.376300	0.424700	0.118700	750	0.579400	0.528000	0.598300	0.545800
555	0.347621	0.386112	0.439731	0.123379	755	0.579400	0.528000	0.598300	0.545800
560	0.359100	0.393600	0.453300	0.131000	760	0.579400	0.528000	0.598300	0.545800
565	0.370424	0.400413	0.467691	0.142828	765	0.579400	0.528000	0.598300	0.545800
570	0.380300	0.405100	0.484600	0.159900	770	0.579400	0.528000	0.598300	0.545800
575	0.386346	0.408152	0.494814	0.183483	775	0.579400	0.528000	0.598300	0.545800

TABLE G.19
Spectra for daisies (white petals and yellow center) and marigolds (orange and yellow).

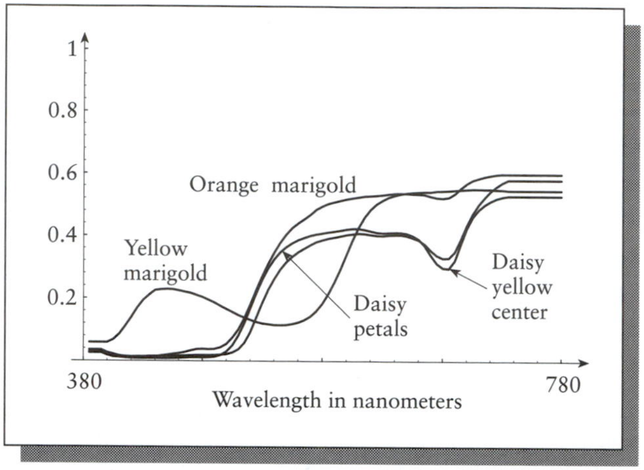

FIGURE G.18

Spectral plots for daisies (white petals and yellow center) and marigolds (orange and yellow).

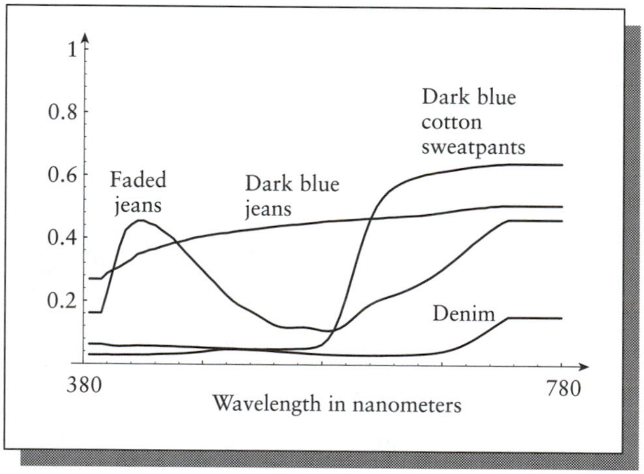

FIGURE G.19

Spectral plots for blue jeans (dark blue and faded), dark blue sweatpants, and denim.

λ	Dark blue jeans	Faded jeans	Dark blue sweat pants	Denim	λ	Dark blue jeans	Faded jeans	Dark blue sweat pants	Denim
380	0.268700	0.161400	0.062500	0.028700	580	0.455900	0.107600	0.081400	0.032400
385	0.268700	0.161400	0.062500	0.028700	585	0.456395	0.109610	0.111418	0.031802
390	0.268700	0.161400	0.062500	0.028700	590	0.458000	0.116800	0.157000	0.031200
395	0.286980	0.226345	0.059801	0.029209	595	0.458866	0.129143	0.215848	0.030958
400	0.297300	0.298700	0.057100	0.028500	600	0.460300	0.145300	0.283100	0.030700
405	0.306263	0.369217	0.056204	0.028691	605	0.461855	0.163165	0.351420	0.030612
410	0.318700	0.423100	0.057000	0.029100	610	0.463600	0.179400	0.412000	0.030600
415	0.330186	0.441091	0.057408	0.029055	615	0.464554	0.192187	0.464012	0.030544
420	0.347600	0.453500	0.058500	0.029500	620	0.465300	0.202200	0.502900	0.030700
425	0.353125	0.453739	0.057932	0.029413	625	0.466899	0.209755	0.530510	0.030841
430	0.360700	0.444900	0.057900	0.029600	630	0.469100	0.216300	0.551300	0.031200
435	0.364644	0.438727	0.057738	0.030913	635	0.469645	0.222692	0.565688	0.031441
440	0.371600	0.423900	0.056900	0.031700	640	0.471400	0.229800	0.577000	0.031900
445	0.377375	0.410957	0.056796	0.032036	645	0.472649	0.237935	0.586149	0.032659
450	0.383700	0.397400	0.056300	0.032600	650	0.473600	0.246300	0.593100	0.033300
455	0.387128	0.375020	0.055206	0.033467	655	0.474737	0.255862	0.598725	0.034343
460	0.391700	0.354700	0.054800	0.034400	660	0.476900	0.266300	0.604800	0.035700
465	0.397751	0.335829	0.054414	0.036025	665	0.478933	0.277449	0.608464	0.037313
470	0.402600	0.315700	0.053900	0.037800	670	0.482000	0.290400	0.612300	0.039800
475	0.405296	0.297177	0.053058	0.039841	675	0.484533	0.303762	0.615180	0.042889
480	0.409200	0.277400	0.052200	0.042400	680	0.487600	0.318800	0.618200	0.047300
485	0.412220	0.259495	0.051811	0.044814	685	0.490451	0.334302	0.621256	0.053033
490	0.415400	0.238300	0.051000	0.046800	690	0.493900	0.350400	0.624600	0.060200
495	0.416431	0.219584	0.050541	0.047834	695	0.496021	0.367197	0.627899	0.069335
500	0.420100	0.202100	0.050200	0.048000	700	0.498600	0.384300	0.630800	0.079700
505	0.423178	0.188678	0.049578	0.047626	705	0.500664	0.398953	0.632980	0.091378
510	0.425300	0.178900	0.048900	0.047100	710	0.501300	0.414200	0.634600	0.103700
515	0.427807	0.169443	0.048345	0.046351	715	0.504693	0.428654	0.636618	0.116187
520	0.429800	0.158900	0.048800	0.045600	720	0.505300	0.441800	0.638500	0.129000
525	0.432536	0.147388	0.048235	0.044664	725	0.507215	0.453581	0.639105	0.141529
530	0.435000	0.136000	0.048800	0.043600	730	0.507200	0.461700	0.640600	0.153600
535	0.437551	0.126196	0.048795	0.042500	735	0.507200	0.461700	0.640600	0.153600
540	0.439800	0.119700	0.048800	0.041200	740	0.507200	0.461700	0.640600	0.153600
545	0.441737	0.117381	0.049468	0.040115	745	0.507200	0.461700	0.640600	0.153600
550	0.443700	0.117500	0.049400	0.038800	750	0.507200	0.461700	0.640600	0.153600
555	0.444670	0.118509	0.050465	0.037499	755	0.507200	0.461700	0.640600	0.153600
560	0.446600	0.118900	0.050900	0.036300	760	0.507200	0.461700	0.640600	0.153600
565	0.449170	0.116871	0.052435	0.035093	765	0.507200	0.461700	0.640600	0.153600
570	0.451000	0.113300	0.056000	0.034100	770	0.507200	0.461700	0.640600	0.153600
575	0.453509	0.109049	0.063744	0.033143	775	0.507200	0.461700	0.640600	0.153600

TABLE G.20
Spectra for blue jeans (dark blue and faded), dark blue sweatpants, and denim.

λ	Wheat bread	Wheat bread crust	Pancake	Swiss army knife	λ	Wheat bread	Wheat bread crust	Pancake	Swiss army knife
380	0.046500	0.036800	0.037600	0.043200	580	0.173500	0.125800	0.066900	0.161300
385	0.046500	0.036800	0.037600	0.043200	585	0.181592	0.131605	0.068629	0.138544
390	0.046500	0.036800	0.037600	0.043200	590	0.190600	0.137700	0.070600	0.117900
395	0.044285	0.037201	0.039479	0.041942	595	0.200123	0.144517	0.072958	0.099273
400	0.044000	0.035700	0.039600	0.039500	600	0.210400	0.151800	0.075300	0.084800
405	0.043415	0.035714	0.039761	0.036937	605	0.220640	0.159311	0.078050	0.074392
410	0.043200	0.036100	0.040100	0.035000	610	0.230600	0.166500	0.080800	0.067700
415	0.043904	0.036506	0.039695	0.032862	615	0.241230	0.174688	0.083613	0.063645
420	0.044400	0.037300	0.040300	0.031200	620	0.251800	0.182700	0.086500	0.061100
425	0.045139	0.038014	0.040289	0.029982	625	0.262158	0.190779	0.089425	0.059752
430	0.046400	0.038600	0.040500	0.028800	630	0.273200	0.199600	0.092700	0.058900
435	0.046735	0.039663	0.040176	0.028481	635	0.283860	0.208138	0.095987	0.057848
440	0.047900	0.040400	0.043400	0.028400	640	0.295200	0.217600	0.099600	0.057300
445	0.049267	0.041363	0.043586	0.028878	645	0.306631	0.227481	0.103325	0.056829
450	0.050700	0.042900	0.043700	0.028600	650	0.317100	0.236400	0.107000	0.057100
455	0.051786	0.043598	0.043974	0.028005	655	0.328214	0.245894	0.111000	0.058483
460	0.053200	0.045100	0.044500	0.029100	660	0.339000	0.255900	0.115000	0.060700
465	0.055323	0.046853	0.044997	0.031929	665	0.350499	0.265646	0.119150	0.063722
470	0.057600	0.049000	0.045300	0.039300	670	0.362400	0.276900	0.123800	0.067100
475	0.059748	0.049963	0.045803	0.057820	675	0.374154	0.287850	0.128239	0.071498
480	0.062200	0.051900	0.045800	0.089900	680	0.386300	0.299700	0.133300	0.077300
485	0.064700	0.053820	0.046117	0.132579	685	0.398272	0.311364	0.138161	0.081875
490	0.067700	0.055800	0.046300	0.186600	690	0.410500	0.323000	0.143100	0.086100
495	0.071126	0.058017	0.047212	0.245520	695	0.422552	0.335264	0.147841	0.089146
500	0.074400	0.060300	0.047900	0.306500	700	0.435000	0.347200	0.152800	0.090800
505	0.079050	0.062978	0.048857	0.363140	705	0.447496	0.358916	0.157440	0.091359
510	0.082300	0.065800	0.049700	0.405000	710	0.458900	0.371100	0.162000	0.091200
515	0.086577	0.068739	0.050541	0.429653	715	0.470512	0.382175	0.167217	0.090185
520	0.092100	0.072300	0.051500	0.435900	720	0.481800	0.394400	0.171600	0.088100
525	0.096983	0.075628	0.052488	0.427653	725	0.493324	0.405722	0.176328	0.086979
530	0.102600	0.079000	0.053500	0.411300	730	0.503700	0.416100	0.180600	0.087900
535	0.108274	0.082690	0.054586	0.390519	735	0.503700	0.416100	0.180600	0.087900
540	0.114000	0.086300	0.055500	0.367400	740	0.503700	0.416100	0.180600	0.087900
545	0.120720	0.090750	0.056771	0.343697	745	0.503700	0.416100	0.180600	0.087900
550	0.127200	0.095000	0.057800	0.317700	750	0.503700	0.416100	0.180600	0.087900
555	0.134153	0.099490	0.059138	0.290481	755	0.503700	0.416100	0.180600	0.087900
560	0.141300	0.104100	0.060400	0.263100	760	0.503700	0.416100	0.180600	0.087900
565	0.149261	0.109333	0.061997	0.236729	765	0.503700	0.416100	0.180600	0.087900
570	0.157300	0.114600	0.063700	0.211200	770	0.503700	0.416100	0.180600	0.087900
575	0.164968	0.119855	0.065260	0.185888	775	0.503700	0.416100	0.180600	0.087900

TABLE G.21
Spectra for wheat bread (bread and crust), pancake, and Swiss army knife.

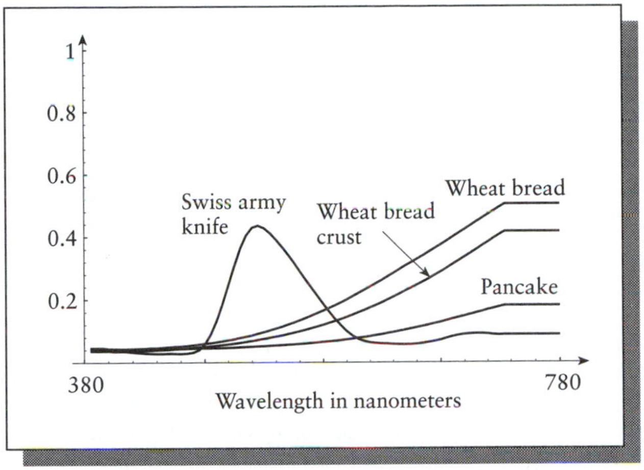

FIGURE G.20
Spectral plots for wheat bread (bread and crust), pancake, and Swiss army knife.

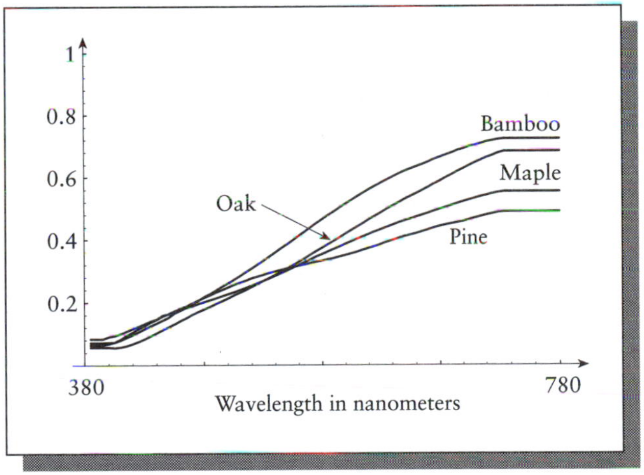

FIGURE G.21
Spectral plots for wood (pine, maple, and oak) and bamboo.

λ	Pine wood	Maple wood	Oak wood	Bamboo	λ	Pine wood	Maple wood	Oak wood	Bamboo
380	0.064500	0.084100	0.057300	0.071900	580	0.337600	0.362500	0.385500	0.479000
385	0.064500	0.084100	0.057300	0.071900	585	0.341304	0.370425	0.396347	0.490194
390	0.064500	0.084100	0.057300	0.071900	590	0.346200	0.378300	0.407400	0.503000
395	0.068718	0.090484	0.057437	0.072583	595	0.350895	0.386917	0.419605	0.515244
400	0.073700	0.094000	0.055600	0.073200	600	0.356100	0.394900	0.430800	0.527100
405	0.082748	0.100325	0.057740	0.079685	605	0.361581	0.403158	0.442333	0.539090
410	0.095200	0.108300	0.061700	0.088400	610	0.367800	0.410700	0.453300	0.550700
415	0.104713	0.116287	0.068096	0.096282	615	0.373057	0.417947	0.464678	0.561204
420	0.116600	0.124200	0.075500	0.106400	620	0.378800	0.425400	0.475200	0.570900
425	0.126632	0.132052	0.083912	0.115930	625	0.384713	0.432113	0.485331	0.580904
430	0.137400	0.140400	0.093600	0.125800	630	0.392000	0.439400	0.496900	0.590500
435	0.145631	0.146844	0.102628	0.133918	635	0.397608	0.446451	0.507248	0.600316
440	0.156400	0.158600	0.112200	0.142900	640	0.404100	0.453700	0.517700	0.609800
445	0.164081	0.163063	0.121981	0.152011	645	0.410208	0.460383	0.528485	0.618494
450	0.173000	0.171000	0.131300	0.166200	650	0.415000	0.466200	0.538000	0.626200
455	0.181318	0.176307	0.141859	0.174713	655	0.419782	0.472380	0.547200	0.633200
460	0.188600	0.183300	0.151000	0.184500	660	0.425800	0.478500	0.557300	0.640400
465	0.198000	0.188929	0.161759	0.195434	665	0.431287	0.484360	0.567096	0.648115
470	0.207100	0.195600	0.170400	0.205600	670	0.437500	0.491200	0.577800	0.656700
475	0.215280	0.201647	0.178030	0.217829	675	0.442778	0.497676	0.587393	0.663958
480	0.223300	0.207500	0.186800	0.227000	680	0.447500	0.503400	0.598700	0.671100
485	0.232423	0.213873	0.195861	0.238774	685	0.451066	0.509587	0.607887	0.677915
490	0.240200	0.220300	0.204300	0.250300	690	0.454500	0.515700	0.618400	0.685800
495	0.248112	0.226527	0.212957	0.260833	695	0.458159	0.521529	0.627128	0.690574
500	0.255800	0.232400	0.222500	0.272000	700	0.463600	0.526600	0.636700	0.697800
505	0.263335	0.239443	0.230962	0.283801	705	0.468595	0.531872	0.645513	0.701852
510	0.269700	0.246500	0.239600	0.296500	710	0.473200	0.537000	0.653700	0.706800
515	0.277259	0.253803	0.249750	0.308582	715	0.477929	0.541029	0.661581	0.712460
520	0.283000	0.261800	0.259300	0.321300	720	0.482300	0.546500	0.668400	0.716200
525	0.288381	0.269478	0.269434	0.333680	725	0.486528	0.550386	0.676647	0.720197
530	0.294700	0.277000	0.278500	0.346900	730	0.488800	0.553200	0.682100	0.722200
535	0.299307	0.285165	0.287866	0.359636	735	0.488800	0.553200	0.682100	0.722200
540	0.304100	0.293400	0.298300	0.373500	740	0.488800	0.553200	0.682100	0.722200
545	0.308641	0.302089	0.308739	0.385863	745	0.488800	0.553200	0.682100	0.722200
550	0.313100	0.311000	0.319000	0.399400	750	0.488800	0.553200	0.682100	0.722200
555	0.317112	0.319455	0.329613	0.412664	755	0.488800	0.553200	0.682100	0.722200
560	0.320900	0.328300	0.340400	0.425900	760	0.488800	0.553200	0.682100	0.722200
565	0.325643	0.337026	0.352314	0.439588	765	0.488800	0.553200	0.682100	0.722200
570	0.329800	0.346600	0.363600	0.453300	770	0.488800	0.553200	0.682100	0.722200
575	0.333401	0.354253	0.374349	0.465823	775	0.488800	0.553200	0.682100	0.722200

TABLE G.22
Spectra for wood (pine, maple, and oak) and bamboo.

λ	Redwood	Walnut wood	Yellow banana	Ripe brown banana	λ	Redwood	Walnut wood	Yellow banana	Ripe brown banana
380	0.061200	0.069900	0.143300	0.168700	580	0.176800	0.141500	0.435800	0.643700
385	0.061200	0.069900	0.143300	0.168700	585	0.181940	0.143904	0.443349	0.624895
390	0.061200	0.069900	0.143300	0.168700	590	0.187300	0.146100	0.451700	0.603900
395	0.066172	0.073110	0.150786	0.190794	595	0.193028	0.148581	0.459972	0.580161
400	0.067900	0.074800	0.155700	0.195000	600	0.198800	0.151200	0.468700	0.557600
405	0.070480	0.075966	0.159610	0.183664	605	0.205169	0.153866	0.478353	0.537136
410	0.073700	0.077900	0.164300	0.169200	610	0.211100	0.156500	0.486400	0.521400
415	0.076424	0.078864	0.167984	0.148548	615	0.216858	0.159086	0.494538	0.511057
420	0.078600	0.080800	0.174700	0.134600	620	0.222700	0.162000	0.502200	0.505100
425	0.082089	0.081801	0.181704	0.119788	625	0.228475	0.164825	0.510005	0.502012
430	0.084100	0.088500	0.189700	0.107700	630	0.234800	0.168000	0.518500	0.499900
435	0.086642	0.090653	0.199238	0.097770	635	0.240596	0.171098	0.526200	0.497272
440	0.089200	0.092000	0.208800	0.090600	640	0.246900	0.174100	0.534400	0.496100
445	0.089773	0.094102	0.216270	0.086080	645	0.253322	0.177629	0.542413	0.497777
450	0.092600	0.094700	0.223100	0.083600	650	0.259300	0.181100	0.549400	0.498900
455	0.094359	0.096410	0.227468	0.082565	655	0.265378	0.184315	0.556135	0.505712
460	0.097100	0.097800	0.235700	0.082800	660	0.272000	0.188000	0.563400	0.512500
465	0.098639	0.099327	0.245483	0.085090	665	0.278704	0.191696	0.570739	0.520993
470	0.101700	0.100300	0.254500	0.091700	670	0.286100	0.196200	0.578800	0.530300
475	0.103200	0.101385	0.259406	0.105027	675	0.293638	0.200470	0.587468	0.543572
480	0.105800	0.102200	0.266000	0.129000	680	0.301500	0.204800	0.596900	0.556800
485	0.107605	0.104301	0.272314	0.164101	685	0.308943	0.209732	0.604826	0.568434
490	0.109300	0.105600	0.280700	0.218400	690	0.316800	0.214400	0.613000	0.577700
495	0.111456	0.107259	0.289338	0.288877	695	0.324036	0.219020	0.621465	0.584393
500	0.114000	0.108700	0.299500	0.378700	700	0.332300	0.223900	0.628800	0.589000
505	0.116402	0.110247	0.309143	0.488499	705	0.339708	0.228504	0.635909	0.590256
510	0.119100	0.111800	0.317800	0.605000	710	0.347300	0.233400	0.643100	0.589800
515	0.121316	0.113665	0.326200	0.712526	715	0.354677	0.238472	0.649656	0.589926
520	0.124500	0.115700	0.333700	0.780500	720	0.363100	0.243300	0.655300	0.588400
525	0.127445	0.117235	0.341678	0.806134	725	0.369773	0.248262	0.660411	0.589531
530	0.130900	0.119300	0.350100	0.802300	730	0.377700	0.252900	0.666100	0.590200
535	0.134559	0.121210	0.358632	0.785143	735	0.377700	0.252900	0.666100	0.590200
540	0.138500	0.123300	0.366900	0.765700	740	0.377700	0.252900	0.666100	0.590200
545	0.142668	0.125380	0.376320	0.748110	745	0.377700	0.252900	0.666100	0.590200
550	0.146700	0.127600	0.384200	0.731600	750	0.377700	0.252900	0.666100	0.590200
555	0.151142	0.129769	0.393096	0.714550	755	0.377700	0.252900	0.666100	0.590200
560	0.155600	0.131900	0.402000	0.699300	760	0.377700	0.252900	0.666100	0.590200
565	0.160788	0.134540	0.410504	0.685223	765	0.377700	0.252900	0.666100	0.590200
570	0.166300	0.137100	0.419300	0.672500	770	0.377700	0.252900	0.666100	0.590200
575	0.171310	0.139224	0.426955	0.658712	775	0.377700	0.252900	0.666100	0.590200

TABLE G.23
Spectra for wood (redwood and walnut) and bananas (yellow and ripe brown).

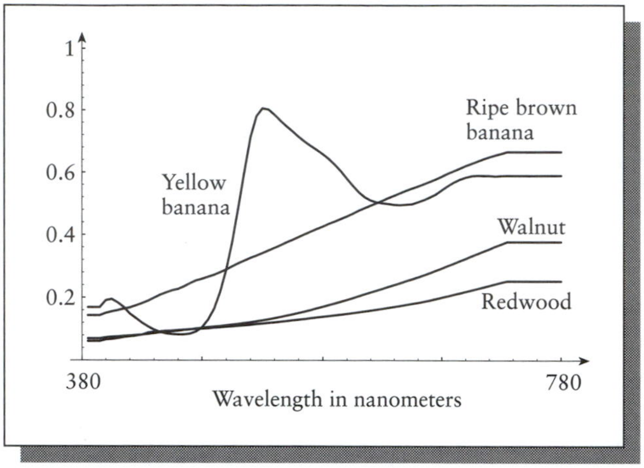

FIGURE G.22

Spectral plots for wood (redwood and walnut) and bananas (yellow and ripe brown).

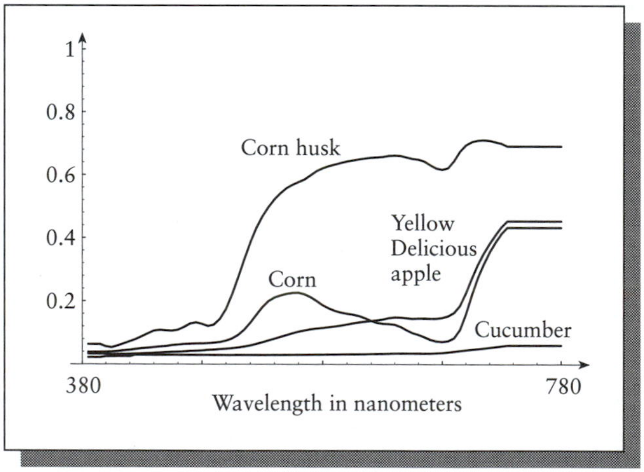

FIGURE G.23

Spectral plots for cucumber, corn (kernel and husk), and yellow Delicious apple.

λ	Cucumber	Corn kernel	Corn husk	Yellow Delicious apple	λ	Cucumber	Corn kernel	Corn husk	Yellow Delicious apple
380	0.021900	0.038300	0.063300	0.033200	580	0.030700	0.176800	0.627600	0.117400
385	0.021900	0.038300	0.063300	0.033200	585	0.031047	0.169011	0.632909	0.119696
390	0.021900	0.038300	0.063300	0.033200	590	0.031300	0.163600	0.638000	0.122700
395	0.024674	0.039030	0.056170	0.032803	595	0.031559	0.160106	0.642686	0.126235
400	0.024600	0.039700	0.053100	0.031400	600	0.031700	0.157200	0.645900	0.129700
405	0.025234	0.041219	0.058641	0.031723	605	0.031939	0.152870	0.649673	0.133033
410	0.025500	0.043500	0.065300	0.032000	610	0.032200	0.145600	0.652300	0.135200
415	0.025080	0.045362	0.072228	0.032260	615	0.032502	0.137547	0.654657	0.137289
420	0.029600	0.048000	0.079200	0.033200	620	0.032800	0.131500	0.655600	0.139400
425	0.029724	0.050382	0.088192	0.033764	625	0.033191	0.128401	0.657084	0.142280
430	0.029600	0.051800	0.097300	0.034700	630	0.033800	0.127800	0.660300	0.146400
435	0.029319	0.053646	0.106038	0.035408	635	0.034258	0.125512	0.661430	0.148518
440	0.029200	0.055500	0.108500	0.036500	640	0.034500	0.118500	0.660500	0.148000
445	0.029092	0.056896	0.106753	0.037562	645	0.034589	0.108264	0.655692	0.146080
450	0.029400	0.060100	0.105900	0.038700	650	0.034600	0.099200	0.651200	0.144300
455	0.029287	0.061714	0.108800	0.039358	655	0.034391	0.093511	0.648822	0.145401
460	0.029300	0.063800	0.117400	0.040300	660	0.034300	0.086000	0.642700	0.145500
465	0.029247	0.064686	0.128304	0.041824	665	0.034495	0.077683	0.630899	0.144514
470	0.029200	0.065300	0.132100	0.042500	670	0.035200	0.072800	0.620800	0.144900
475	0.029123	0.065614	0.127410	0.043368	675	0.036288	0.071492	0.616484	0.147287
480	0.029100	0.066500	0.120800	0.045400	680	0.038100	0.073800	0.621500	0.152500
485	0.029153	0.067963	0.125280	0.046097	685	0.040346	0.082869	0.643807	0.162758
490	0.029200	0.070200	0.143200	0.047900	690	0.042700	0.109100	0.673800	0.185200
495	0.028993	0.074272	0.174151	0.049060	695	0.044845	0.158451	0.694311	0.224842
500	0.029000	0.081300	0.220000	0.050700	700	0.046900	0.219400	0.705000	0.272000
505	0.029109	0.092537	0.273968	0.053039	705	0.048847	0.273197	0.709440	0.315162
510	0.029200	0.109000	0.330800	0.055800	710	0.050900	0.316800	0.710800	0.350800
515	0.029319	0.130748	0.384128	0.059323	715	0.053041	0.353899	0.709191	0.381746
520	0.029200	0.155800	0.430600	0.064100	720	0.055300	0.386000	0.704400	0.409300
525	0.029309	0.180395	0.467646	0.069218	725	0.057767	0.412935	0.700084	0.434222
530	0.029300	0.199400	0.497200	0.075200	730	0.060000	0.432700	0.691400	0.453200
535	0.029409	0.210905	0.521639	0.080795	735	0.060000	0.432700	0.691400	0.453200
540	0.029500	0.217600	0.541000	0.086600	740	0.060000	0.432700	0.691400	0.453200
545	0.029591	0.222459	0.557374	0.092313	745	0.060000	0.432700	0.691400	0.453200
550	0.029800	0.225800	0.568200	0.098000	750	0.060000	0.432700	0.691400	0.453200
555	0.029951	0.226158	0.576834	0.103044	755	0.060000	0.432700	0.691400	0.453200
560	0.030100	0.221200	0.585200	0.107200	760	0.060000	0.432700	0.691400	0.453200
565	0.030199	0.212331	0.598699	0.110777	765	0.060000	0.432700	0.691400	0.453200
570	0.030400	0.200000	0.611900	0.113300	770	0.060000	0.432700	0.691400	0.453200
575	0.030552	0.186925	0.620716	0.114926	775	0.060000	0.432700	0.691400	0.453200

TABLE G.24
Spectra for cucumber, corn (kernel and husk), and yellow Delicious apple.

λ	Green pepper	Lemon skin	Lettuce	Carrot	λ	Green pepper	Lemon skin	Lettuce	Carrot
380	0.094600	0.120000	0.095600	0.061300	580	0.506000	0.320900	0.470200	0.351200
385	0.094600	0.120000	0.095600	0.061300	585	0.519237	0.313389	0.503690	0.344201
390	0.094600	0.120000	0.095600	0.061300	590	0.531400	0.307900	0.534200	0.339500
395	0.093326	0.126553	0.085573	0.059474	595	0.542477	0.304229	0.560528	0.335552
400	0.092600	0.127300	0.079500	0.059700	600	0.551400	0.299600	0.582000	0.333000
405	0.094702	0.123903	0.073264	0.060867	605	0.560581	0.293765	0.599601	0.329360
410	0.099300	0.121700	0.070100	0.065100	610	0.568400	0.285200	0.614500	0.321800
415	0.101202	0.117586	0.066354	0.066726	615	0.574100	0.275822	0.626105	0.311316
420	0.100700	0.117900	0.064200	0.070500	620	0.579000	0.268800	0.634800	0.302500
425	0.101736	0.115284	0.062215	0.072495	625	0.583564	0.265061	0.640823	0.297483
430	0.103200	0.113200	0.060800	0.074000	630	0.590500	0.265100	0.648800	0.297000
435	0.104680	0.111941	0.059053	0.074581	635	0.595442	0.262884	0.654552	0.291332
440	0.105400	0.116700	0.058500	0.076300	640	0.597600	0.251500	0.661600	0.273800
445	0.105773	0.124562	0.058075	0.079578	645	0.597485	0.232761	0.667237	0.248506
450	0.105500	0.135700	0.058100	0.083800	650	0.595600	0.214100	0.669000	0.227800
455	0.105689	0.140357	0.057936	0.089756	655	0.595415	0.202363	0.671217	0.218046
460	0.108300	0.144200	0.058100	0.092400	660	0.591000	0.186700	0.670300	0.200500
465	0.115514	0.146002	0.058914	0.096214	665	0.577792	0.168095	0.668242	0.174213
470	0.120100	0.147200	0.059500	0.098100	670	0.564700	0.155700	0.668200	0.153800
475	0.119231	0.146764	0.059171	0.099076	675	0.557360	0.152540	0.673788	0.145053
480	0.116500	0.146800	0.058200	0.100100	680	0.562900	0.160900	0.684000	0.149800
485	0.118357	0.150648	0.058501	0.103234	685	0.592999	0.197868	0.695115	0.181254
490	0.122900	0.158300	0.059200	0.110700	690	0.635100	0.275000	0.703600	0.252800
495	0.132147	0.171753	0.060497	0.123043	695	0.664002	0.356104	0.707697	0.351446
500	0.146700	0.192900	0.062500	0.141600	700	0.679900	0.407300	0.708100	0.444300
505	0.167334	0.221224	0.064859	0.167188	705	0.688680	0.435447	0.708358	0.513878
510	0.192900	0.253700	0.066300	0.197700	710	0.693400	0.451500	0.706100	0.562800
515	0.223537	0.287602	0.068582	0.232610	715	0.694346	0.460376	0.703404	0.599962
520	0.257700	0.316200	0.070600	0.267600	720	0.693800	0.468000	0.700900	0.629400
525	0.289771	0.337305	0.073698	0.297561	725	0.691971	0.470848	0.696467	0.650883
530	0.320100	0.350100	0.078300	0.321200	730	0.685300	0.472100	0.692000	0.663800
535	0.344889	0.357517	0.086325	0.338013	735	0.685300	0.472100	0.692000	0.663800
540	0.367000	0.361100	0.098700	0.350400	740	0.685300	0.472100	0.692000	0.663800
545	0.386831	0.364681	0.120427	0.360250	745	0.685300	0.472100	0.692000	0.663800
550	0.403200	0.365300	0.154000	0.368500	750	0.685300	0.472100	0.692000	0.663800
555	0.417652	0.363841	0.203076	0.372675	755	0.685300	0.472100	0.692000	0.663800
560	0.433500	0.358100	0.262600	0.372800	760	0.685300	0.472100	0.692000	0.663800
565	0.452520	0.350641	0.325399	0.372553	765	0.685300	0.472100	0.692000	0.663800
570	0.473500	0.341000	0.382000	0.367600	770	0.685300	0.472100	0.692000	0.663800
575	0.490505	0.330396	0.429036	0.358896	775	0.685300	0.472100	0.692000	0.663800

TABLE G.25
Spectra for green pepper, lemon skin, lettuce, and carrot.

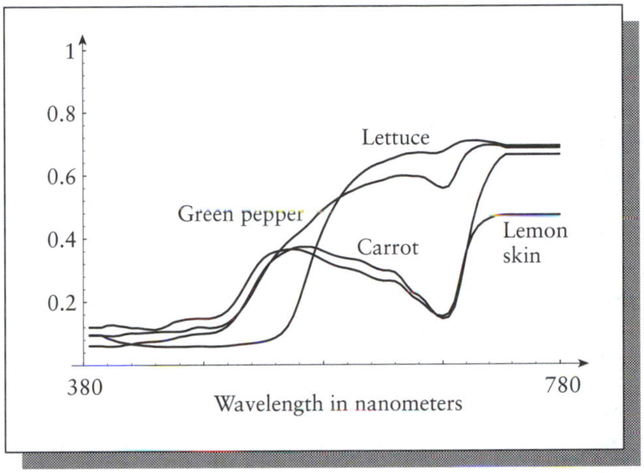

FIGURE G.24

Spectral plots for green pepper, lemon skin, lettuce, and carrot.

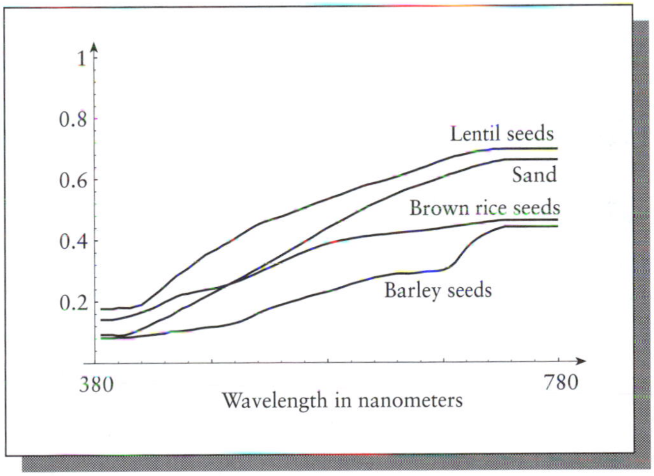

FIGURE G.25

Spectral plots for seeds (barley, lentil, and brown rice) and sand.

	Barley seeds	Lentil seeds	Brown rice seeds	Sand		Barley seeds	Lentil seeds	Brown rice seeds	Sand
380	0.081800	0.177000	0.141700	0.093000	580	0.236000	0.539800	0.392500	0.448700
385	0.081800	0.177000	0.141700	0.093000	585	0.242429	0.545948	0.396736	0.458888
390	0.081800	0.177000	0.141700	0.093000	590	0.249000	0.553400	0.400400	0.469100
395	0.083917	0.181115	0.145423	0.089927	595	0.255451	0.560970	0.404006	0.479434
400	0.083800	0.180300	0.149200	0.091400	600	0.260600	0.567700	0.406800	0.489500
405	0.084282	0.180089	0.153924	0.096172	605	0.265562	0.574773	0.409992	0.499197
410	0.086500	0.185400	0.159100	0.102900	610	0.270600	0.580300	0.411900	0.509500
415	0.088768	0.189811	0.165533	0.111717	615	0.276059	0.584683	0.414605	0.518066
420	0.090300	0.203800	0.171900	0.119400	620	0.279600	0.589100	0.416300	0.526100
425	0.092494	0.218619	0.178945	0.128920	625	0.282683	0.594044	0.417556	0.533944
430	0.094600	0.233500	0.188100	0.138700	630	0.286100	0.600300	0.419800	0.542700
435	0.096399	0.249696	0.198876	0.146069	635	0.288527	0.605476	0.421745	0.550511
440	0.102800	0.267700	0.207600	0.154400	640	0.288900	0.612000	0.423500	0.558900
445	0.103286	0.284197	0.217063	0.166592	645	0.288384	0.618660	0.425350	0.566125
450	0.104500	0.295900	0.223700	0.178300	650	0.289800	0.625000	0.426700	0.572100
455	0.106980	0.308261	0.226014	0.185299	655	0.292516	0.632343	0.428569	0.578473
460	0.109300	0.323300	0.230800	0.195200	660	0.295100	0.638600	0.430700	0.584900
465	0.112907	0.338033	0.234553	0.206107	665	0.295585	0.645523	0.432834	0.590971
470	0.115500	0.352400	0.238000	0.215800	670	0.296700	0.653400	0.434900	0.597800
475	0.117150	0.362057	0.241322	0.225346	675	0.299998	0.659403	0.438065	0.604344
480	0.118200	0.371300	0.244600	0.235600	680	0.307800	0.665400	0.440000	0.612100
485	0.121176	0.383362	0.249995	0.245545	685	0.323354	0.671797	0.442951	0.617125
490	0.124700	0.392900	0.255600	0.255800	690	0.347400	0.674900	0.445300	0.623200
495	0.129341	0.404354	0.262377	0.265608	695	0.370135	0.679349	0.447603	0.628701
500	0.134900	0.416800	0.268900	0.275100	700	0.387700	0.683700	0.450500	0.635300
505	0.142511	0.428654	0.276855	0.285616	705	0.401009	0.687402	0.451710	0.639836
510	0.151200	0.440400	0.284600	0.296700	710	0.411800	0.689600	0.453800	0.644200
515	0.161290	0.450343	0.293104	0.306672	715	0.420478	0.691080	0.457019	0.648103
520	0.169100	0.458500	0.302200	0.316500	720	0.428700	0.694800	0.458300	0.653300
525	0.176810	0.464790	0.310331	0.327847	725	0.434835	0.694626	0.460946	0.656041
530	0.182800	0.470700	0.318800	0.338400	730	0.440400	0.695400	0.461700	0.660000
535	0.188503	0.475985	0.327540	0.348997	735	0.440400	0.695400	0.461700	0.660000
540	0.194100	0.482300	0.336100	0.359800	740	0.440400	0.695400	0.461700	0.660000
545	0.199468	0.490066	0.344323	0.370878	745	0.440400	0.695400	0.461700	0.660000
550	0.204900	0.497300	0.353500	0.381900	750	0.440400	0.695400	0.461700	0.660000
555	0.211328	0.504956	0.360775	0.393087	755	0.440400	0.695400	0.461700	0.660000
560	0.217200	0.512400	0.368300	0.404300	760	0.440400	0.695400	0.461700	0.660000
565	0.221982	0.519839	0.375224	0.415764	765	0.440400	0.695400	0.461700	0.660000
570	0.226300	0.526000	0.381800	0.427800	770	0.440400	0.695400	0.461700	0.660000
575	0.230582	0.532397	0.387436	0.438545	775	0.440400	0.695400	0.461700	0.660000

TABLE G.26
Spectra for seeds (barley, lentil, and brown rice) and sand.

BIBLIOGRAPHY

[1] Edwin A. Abbott. *Flatland*. Dover Publications, Mineola, NY, 1952.

[2] Ralph H. Abraham and Christopher D. Shaw. *Dynamics: The Geometry of Behavior*. Addison-Wesley, Reading, MA, 1992.

[3] Forman S. Acton. *Numerical Methods That Work*. Harper & Row, New York, 1970.

[4] Miguel P. N. Águas and Stefan Müller. Mesh redistribution in radiosity. In Michael Cohen, Claude Puech, and François Sillion, editors, *Fourth Eurographics Workshop on Rendering*, pp. 327–336. Elsevier, Amsterdam, 1993.

[5] Ali N. Akansu and Richard A. Haddad. *Multiresolution Signal Decomposition*. Academic Press, San Diego, 1992.

[6] Taka-aki Akimoto, Kenji Mase, Akihiko Hashimoto, and Yasuhito Suenaga. Pixel selected ray tracing. In W. Hansmann, F. R. A. Hopgood, and W. Straßer, editors, *Proc. Eurographics '89*, pp. 39–50. North-Holland, Amsterdam, 1989.

[7] B. Alpert, G. Beylkin, R. Coifman, and V. Rokhlin. Wavelet-like bases for the fast solution of second-kind integral equations. *SIAM Journal on Scientific Computing*, 14(1):159–184, January 1993.

[8] Bradley K. Alpert. A class of bases in L^2 for the sparse representation of integral operators. *SIAM Journal of Mathematical Analysis*, 24(1):246–262, January 1993.

[9] John Amanatides. Ray tracing with cones. *Computer Graphics (Proc. Siggraph '84)*, 18(3):129–135, July 1984.

[10] Michael A. Andreottola. Color hard-copy devices. In H. John Durrett, editor, *Color and the Computer*, chapter 12, pp. 241–254. Academic Press, San Diego, 1987.

[11] Arthur Appel. Some techniques for shading machine renderings of solids. *AFIPS 1968 Spring Joint Computer Conference*, 32:37–45, 1968.

[12] J. Argence. Antialiasing for ray tracing using CSG modeling. In Tosiyasu Kunii, editor, *New Trends in Computer Graphics (Proc. CG International '88)*, pp. 199–208. Springer-Verlag, New York, 1988.

[13] James Arvo. Backward ray tracing. In Andrew S. Glassner, editor, *Siggraph '86 Developments in Ray Tracing course notes*. ACM Siggraph, New York, August 1986.

[14] James Arvo. Linear operators and integral equations in global illumination. In Paul Heckbert, editor, *Siggraph 1993 Global Illumination course notes*, chapter 2. ACM Siggraph, New York, August 1993.

[15] James Arvo. Transfer equations in global illumination. In Paul Heckbert, editor, *Siggraph 1993 Global Illumination course notes*, chapter 1. ACM Siggraph, New York, August 1993.

[16] James Arvo and David Kirk. Fast ray tracing by ray classification. *Computer Graphics (Proc. Siggraph '87)*, 21(4):55–64, July 1987. Also in *Tutorial: Computer Graphics: Image Synthesis*, pp. 196–205. Computer Society Press, Washington, DC, 1988.

[17] James Arvo and David Kirk. A survey of ray tracing acceleration techniques. In Andrew S. Glassner, editor, *An Introduction to Ray Tracing*, pp. 201–262. Academic Press, San Diego, 1989.

[18] Frédérik Asensio. A hierarchical ray-casting algorithm for radiosity shadows. In Alan Chalmers, Derek Paddon, and François Sillion, editors, *Third Eurographics Workshop on Rendering*, pp. 179–188. Elsevier, Amsterdam, 1992.

[19] Robert B. Ash. *Information Theory*. Dover Publications, Mineola, NY, 1965.

[20] P. R. Atherton, K. Weiler, and D. Greenberg. Polygon shadow generation. *Computer Graphics (Proc. Siggraph '78)*, 12(3):275–281, August 1978.

[21] Kendall Atkinson. An automatic program for linear Fredholm integral equations of the second kind. *ACM Transactions on Mathematical Software*, 2(2):154–171, June 1987.

[22] Kendall E. Atkinson. *A Survey of Numerical Methods for the Solution of Fredholm Integrals of the Second Kind.* SIAM, Philadelphia, 1976.

[23] Larry Aupperle and Pat Hanrahan. A hierarchical illumination algorithm for surfaces with glossy reflection. *Computer Graphics (Proc. Siggraph '93)*, 27(3):155–162, August 1993.

[24] Larry Aupperle and Pat Hanrahan. Importance and discrete three point transport. In Michael Cohen, Claude Puech, and François Sillion, editors, *Fourth Eurographics Workshop on Rendering*, pp. 85–94. Elsevier, Amsterdam, 1993.

[25] Ezekiel Bahar and Swapan Chakrabarti. Full-wave theory applied to computer-aided graphics for 3D objects. *IEEE Computer Graphics & Applications*, 7(7):46–60, July 1987.

[26] Christopher T. H. Baker. *The Numerical Treatment of Integral Equations.* Clarendon Press, Oxford, England, 1977.

[27] A. V. Balakrishnan. On the problem of time jitter in sampling. *IRE Transactions on Information Theory*, IT-8(3):226–236, April 1962.

[28] Thomas F. Banchoff. *Beyond the Third Dimension.* Scientific American Library, New York, 1990.

[29] Hujun Bao and Qunsheng Peng. A progressive radiosity algorithm for scenes containing curved surfaces. In R. J. Hubbold and R. Juan, editors, *Proc. Eurographics '93*, pp. 399–408. North-Holland, Amsterdam, 1993.

[30] Jack Barth, Doug Kirby, Ken Smith, and Mike Wilkins. *Roadside America.* A Fireside Book, New York, 1986.

[31] Rui Manuel Bastos, António Augusto de Sousa, and Fernando Nunes Ferreira. Reconstruction of illumination functions using bicubic hermite interpolation. In Michael Cohen, Claude Puech, and François Sillion, editors, *Fourth Eurographics Workshop on Rendering*, pp. 317–326. Elsevier, Amsterdam, 1993.

[32] Daniel R. Baum, Stephen Mann, Kevin P. Smith, and James M. Winget. Making radiosity usable: Automatic preprocessing and meshing techniques for the generation of accurate radiosity solutions. *Computer Graphics (Proc. Siggraph '91)*, 25(4):51–60, July 1991.

[33] Daniel R. Baum, Holly E. Rushmeier, and James M. Winget. Improving radiosity solutions through the use of analytically determined form-factors. *Computer Graphics (Proc. Siggraph '89)*, 23(3):325–334, July 1989.

[34] Daniel R. Baum and James M. Winget. Real time radiosity through parallel processing and hardware acceleration. *Computer Graphics (Proc. 1990 Symposium on Interactive 3D Graphics)*, 24(2):67–75, March 1990.

[35] Barry G. Becker and Nelson L. Max. Smooth transitions between bump rendering algorithms. *Computer Graphics (Proc. Siggraph '93)*, 27(3):183–190, August 1993.

[36] J. L. Bentley and J. H. Friedman. Data structures for range searching. *ACM Computing Surveys*, 11(4):397–409, April 1979.

[37] Jeffrey C. Beran-Koehn and Mark J. Pavicic. A cubic tetrahedral adaption of the hemi-cube algorithm. In James Arvo, editor, *Graphics Gems II*, pp. 299–302. Academic Press, San Diego, 1991.

[38] Jeffrey C. Beran-Koehn and Mark J. Pavicic. Delta form-factor calculation for the cubic tetrahedral algorithm. In David Kirk, editor, *Graphics Gems III*, pp. 324–328. Academic Press, San Diego, 1992.

[39] Sterling K. Berberian. *Introduction to Hilbert Space*. Oxford University Press, New York, 1961.

[40] G. D. Bergland. A guided tour of the fast Fourier transform. *IEEE Spectrum*, 6:41–52, July 1969.

[41] William H. Beyer. *CRC Standard Mathematical Tables*. CRC Press, Boca Raton, FL, 26th ed., 1984.

[42] G. Beylkin, R. Coifman, and V. Rokhlin. Fast wavelet transforms and numerical algorithms I. *Communications on Pure and Applied Mathematics*, 44:141–183, 1991.

[43] N. Bhate and A. Tokuta. Photorealistic volume rendering of media with directional scattering. In Alan Chalmers, Derek Paddon, and François Sillion, editors, *Third Eurographics Workshop on Rendering*, pp. 227–245. Elsevier, Amsterdam, 1992.

[44] Buming Bian, Norman Wittels, and Donald S. Fussel. Non-uniform patch luminance for global illumination. In Kellogg Booth and Alain Fournier, editors, *Proc. Graphics Interface '92*, pp. 310–318. Canadian Information Processing Society, Toronto, 1992.

[45] Philippe Blasi, Bertran Le Saëc, and Christophe Schlick. A rendering algorithm for discrete volume density objects. In R. J. Hubbold and R. Juan, editors, *Proc. Eurographics '93*, pp. 201–207. North-Holland, Amsterdam, 1993.

[46] James F. Blinn. Models of light reflection for computer synthesized pictures. *Computer Graphics (Proc. Siggraph '77)*, 11(2):192–198, July 1977.

[47] James F. Blinn. Simulation of wrinkled surfaces. *Computer Graphics (Proc. Siggraph '78)*, 12(3):286–292, August 1978.

[48] James F. Blinn. A generalization of algebraic surface drawing. *ACM Transactions on Graphics*, 1(3):235–256, July 1982.

[49] James F. Blinn. Light reflection functions for simulation of clouds and dusty surfaces. *Computer Graphics (Proc. Siggraph '82)*, 16(3):21–29, July 1982.

[50] James F. Blinn. Dirty pixels. *IEEE Computer Graphics & Applications*, 9(4):100–105, July 1989.

[51] James F. Blinn and Martin E. Newell. Texture and reflection in computer generated images. *Communications of the ACM*, 19(10):542–547, October 1976.

[52] Edward A. Boettner and J. Reimer Wolter. Transmission of the ocular media. *Investigative Ophthalmology*, 1(6):776–783, December 1962.

[53] Craig F. Bohren and Donald R. Huffman. *Absorption and Scattering of Light by Small Particles*. John Wiley & Sons, New York, 1983.

[54] A. I. Borisenko and I. E. Tarapov. *Vector and Tensor Analysis with Applications*. Dover Publications, Mineola, NY, 1968. Translated from the Russian by Richard A. Silverman.

[55] Max Born and Emil Wolf. *Principles of Optics*. Pergamon Press, Tarrytown, NY, 2nd rev. ed., 1964.

[56] Kadi Bouatouch and Pierre Tellier. A two-pass physics-based global lighting model. In Kellogg Booth and Alain Fournier, editors, *Proc. Graphics Interface '92*, pp. 319–328. Canadian Information Processing Society, Toronto, 1992.

[57] Christian Bouville, Kadi Bouatouch, Pierre Tellier, and Xavier Pueyo. A theoretical analysis of global illumination models. In K. Bouatouch and C. Bouville, editors, *Eurographics Workshop on Photosimulation, Realism and Physics in Computer Graphics*, pp. 53–66. Elsevier, Amsterdam, 1990.

[58] Christian Bouville, Jean-Luc Dubois, Isabelle Marchal, and M. L. Viaud. Monte Carlo integration applied to an illumination model. In David A. Duce and Pierre Jancene, editors, *Proc. Eurographics '88*, pp. 483–498. North-Holland, Amsterdam, 1988.

[59] Christian Bouville, Pierre Tellier, and Kadi Bouatouch. Low sampling densities using a psychovisual approach. In Frits H. Post and Wilhelm Barth, editors, *Proc. Eurographics '91*, pp. 167–182. North-Holland, Amsterdam, 1991.

[60] William E. Boyce and Richard C. DiPrima. *Elementary Differential Equations*. John Wiley & Sons, New York, 3rd ed., 1977.

[61] Ronald N. Bracewell. *The Fourier Transform and Its Applications*. McGraw-Hill, New York, 2nd rev. ed., 1986.

[62] David H. Brainard. Calibration of a computer controlled monitor. *Color Research and Application*, 14(1):23–34, February 1989.

[63] William L. Briggs. *A Multigrid Tutorial.* SIAM, Philadelphia, 1987.

[64] Willem F. Bronsvoort, Jarke J. van Wijk, and Frederik W. Jansen. Two methods for improving the efficiency of ray casting in solid modeling. *Computer-Aided Design*, 16(1):110–116, January 1984.

[65] Frederick P. Brooks, Jr. Grasping reality through illusion—interactive graphics serving science. In *Proceedings of CHI '88*, pp. 1–11. ACM, New York, 1988. (Special issue of the SIGCHI bulletin).

[66] Earle B. Brown. *Modern Optics.* Reinhold Publishing, New York, 1965.

[67] Jichun Bu and Ed F. Deprettere. A VLSI system architecture for high-speed radiative transfer 3D synthesis. *Visual Computer*, 5(6):121–133, June 1989.

[68] Chris Buckalew and Donald Fussell. Illumination networks: Fast realistic rendering with general reflectance functions. *Computer Graphics (Proc. Siggraph '89)*, 23(3):89–98, July 1989.

[69] Phong Bui-Tuong. Illumination for computer generated pictures. *Communications of the ACM*, 18(6):311–317, June 1975.

[70] Dionys Burger. *Sphereland.* Apollo Editions, New York, 1965. Translated by Cornelie J. Rheinboldt.

[71] Brian Cabral, Nelson Max, and Rebecca Springmeyer. Bidirectional reflection functions from surface bump maps. *Computer Graphics (Proc. Siggraph '87)*, 21(4):273–281, July 1987.

[72] Kathleen Cain. *Luna: Myth & Mystery.* Johnson Books, Boulder, CO, 1991.

[73] A. T. Campbell III and Donald S. Fussell. Adaptive mesh generation for global diffuse illumination. *Computer Graphics (Proc. Siggraph '90)*, 24(4):155–164, August 1990.

[74] Ingrid Carlbom. Filter design for volume reconstruction and visualization. In Gregory M. Nielson and Dan Bergeron, editors, *Proceedings of Visualization '93*, pp. 54–61. IEEE Computer Society Press, Los Alamitos, CA, 1993.

[75] Kenneth M. Case and Paul F. Zweifel. *Linear Transport Theory.* Addison-Wesley, Reading, MA, 1967.

[76] E. D. Cashwell and C. J. Everett. *A Practical Manual on the Monte Carlo Method for Random Walk Problems.* Pergamon Press, Tarrytown, NY, 1959.

[77] Kenneth R. Castleman. *Digital Image Processing.* Prentice-Hall, Englewood Cliffs, NJ, 1979.

[78] Edwin Catmull. A tutorial on compensation tables. *Computer Graphics (Proc. Siggraph '79)*, 13(2):1–13, July 1979.

[79] Zoltan J. Cendes and Steven H. Wong. C^1 quadratic interpolation over arbitrary point sets. *IEEE Computer Graphics & Applications*, 7(11):8–16, November 1987.

[80] Sudeb Chattopadhyay and Akira Fujimoto. Bi-directional ray tracing. In Tosiyasu Kunii, editor, *Computer Graphics 1987 (Proc. CG International '87)*, pp. 335–343. Springer-Verlag, New York, 1987.

[81] David Shi Chen and Jan P. Allebach. Analysis of error in reconstruction of two-dimensional signals from irregularly spaced samples. *IEEE Transactions on Acoustics, Speech, and Signal Processing*, 35(2):173–180, February 1987.

[82] Hong Chen and En-Hua Wu. An adapted solution of progressive radiosity and ray-tracing methods for non-diffuse environments. In T. S. Chua and T. L. Kunii, editors, *Computer Graphics Around the World (Proc. CG International '90)*, pp. 477–490. Springer-Verlag, New York, 1990.

[83] Hong Chen and En-Hua Wu. An efficient radiosity solution for bump texture generation. *Computer Graphics (Proc. Siggraph '90)*, 24(4):125–134, August 1990.

[84] Hong Chen and En-Hua Wu. Radiosity for furry surfaces. In Frits H. Post and Wilhelm Barth, editors, *Proc. Eurographics '91*, pp. 447–457. North-Holland, Amsterdam, 1991.

[85] Shenchang Eric Chen. Incremental radiosity: An extension of progressive radiosity to an interactive image synthesis system. *Computer Graphics (Proc. Siggraph '90)*, 24(4):135–144, August 1990.

[86] Shenchang Eric Chen, Holly E. Rushmeier, Gavin Miller, and Douglass Turner. A progresive multi-pass method for global illumination. *Computer Graphics (Proc. Siggraph '91)*, 25(4):165–174, July 1991.

[87] Kwan F. Cheung and Robert J. Marks II. Imaging sampling below the Nyquist density without aliasing. *Journal of the Optical Society of America*, 7(1):92–104, January 1990.

[88] K. Chiu, M. Herf, P. Shirley, S. Swamy, C. Wang, and K. Zimmerman. Spatially nonuniform scaling functions for high contrast images. *Proc. Graphics Interface '93*, pp. 245–253, Canadian Information Processing Society, Toronto, 1993.

[89] Per Christensen, David Salesin, and Tony DeRose. A continuous adjoint formulation for radiance transport. In Michael Cohen, Claude Puech, and

François Sillion, editors, *Fourth Eurographics Workshop on Rendering*, pp. 95–104. Elsevier, Amsterdam, 1993.

[90] C. K. Chui. *Wavelet Analysis and Its Applications*. Academic Press, San Diego, 1992.

[91] CIE Technical Committee 3.1. An analytic model for describing the influence of lighting parameters upon visual performance. Technical report CIE 19/2.1, International Commission on Illumination, 1981.

[92] James J. Clark, Matthew R. Palmer, and Peter D. Lawrence. A transformation method for the reconstruction of functions from nonuniformly spaced samples. *IEEE Transactions on Acoustics, Speech, and Signal Processing*, 33(4):1151–1165, October 1985.

[93] James Alan Cochran. *The Analysis of Linear Integral Equations*. McGraw-Hill, New York, 1972.

[94] Mac A. Cody. The fast wavelet transform. *Dr. Dobb's Journal*, pp. 16–28, 101–103, April 1992.

[95] Michael Cohen, Shenchang Eric Chen, John R. Wallace, and Donald P. Greenberg. A progressive refinement approach to fast radiosity image generation. *Computer Graphics (Proc. Siggraph '88)*, 22(4):75–84, August 1988.

[96] Michael Cohen and Donald P. Greenberg. The hemi-cube: A radiosity solution for complex environments. *Computer Graphics (Proc. Siggraph '85)*, 19(3):31–40, July 1985. Also in *Tutorial: Computer Graphics: Image Synthesis*, Computer Society Press, Washington, DC, 1988.

[97] Michael Cohen, Donald P. Greenberg, Dave S. Immel, and Philip J. Brock. An efficient radiosity approach for realistic image synthesis. *IEEE Computer Graphics & Applications*, 6(3):26–35, March 1986.

[98] Michael F. Cohen. Is image synthesis a solved problem? In Alan Chalmers, Derek Paddon, and François Sillion, editors, *Third Eurographics Workshop on Rendering*, pp. 161–167. Elsevier, Amsterdam, 1992.

[99] Michael F. Cohen and John R. Wallace. *Radiosity and Realistic Image Synthesis*. Academic Press, San Diego, 1993.

[100] Robert L. Cook. Shade trees. *Computer Graphics (Proc. Siggraph '84)*, 18(4):223–231, July 1984.

[101] Robert L. Cook. Stochastic sampling in computer graphics. *ACM Transactions on Graphics*, 5(1):51–72, January 1986.

[102] Robert L. Cook, Thomas Porter, and Loren Carpenter. Distributed ray tracing. *Computer Graphics (Proc. Siggraph '84)*, 18(3):137–145, July 1984.

[103] Robert L. Cook and Kenneth E. Torrance. A reflectance model for computer graphics. *ACM Transactions on Graphics*, 1(1):7–24, January 1982.

[104] James W. Cooley and John W. Tukey. An algorithm for the machine calculation of complex Fourier series. *Mathematics of Computation*, 19(90):297–301, April 1965.

[105] R. R. Coveyou, V. R. Cain, and K. J. Yost. Adjoint and importance in Monte Carlo application. *Nuclear Science and Engineering*, 27:219–234, 1967.

[106] Roger A. Crawfis and Nelson Max. Texture splats for 3D scalar and vector field visualization. In Gregory M. Nielson and Dan Bergeron, editors, *Proceedings of Visualization '93*, pp. 261–268. IEEE Computer Society Press, Los Alamitos, CA, 1993.

[107] Frank Crow. Personal communication, January 1994.

[108] Franklin C. Crow. The aliasing problem in computer-generated shaded images. *Communications of the ACM*, 20(11):799–805, November 1977.

[109] Franklin C. Crow. A comparison of antialiasing techniques. *IEEE Computer Graphics & Applications*, 1(1):40–48, January 1981.

[110] Franklin C. Crow. A more flexible image generation environment. *Computer Graphics (Proc. Siggraph '82)*, 16(3):9–18, July 1982.

[111] Franklin C. Crow. Summed-area tables for texture mapping. *Computer Graphics (Proc. Siggraph '84)*, 18(3):207–212, July 1984.

[112] Christine A. Curcio, Kenneth R. Sloan, Robert E. Kalina, and Anita E. Hendrickson. Human photoreceptor topography. *The Journal of Comparative Neurology*, 292:497–523, 1990.

[113] Leonardo da Vinci. *The Notebooks of Leonardo da Vinci*. Dover Publications, Mineola, NY, 1970. Reprint of the 1883 edition; translated by Jean Paul Richter.

[114] Norm Dadoun, David G. Kirkpatrick, and John P. Walsh. The geometry of beam tracing. In Joseph O'Rourke, editor, *Proc. of the Symp. on Computational Geometry*, pp. 55–61. ACM Press, New York, 1985.

[115] I. Daubechies. *Ten Lectures on Wavelets*. SIAM, Philadelphia, 1992.

[116] B. Davison and J. B. Sykes. *Neutron Transport Theory*. Oxford University Press, New York, 1957.

[117] Hugh Davson, editor. *The Eye: The Visual Process*, volume 2. Academic Press, San Diego, 1962.

[118] Hugh Davson, editor. *The Eye: Visual Optics and the Optical Space Sense*, volume 4. Academic Press, San Diego, 1962.

[119] Mark de Berg. *Efficient Algorithms for Ray Shooting and Hidden Surface Removal*. Ph.D. thesis, Rijksuniversiteit te Utrecht, The Netherlands, March 1992.

[120] L. M. Delves and J. L. Mohamed. *Computational Methods for Integral Equations*. Cambridge University Press, New York, 1985.

[121] V. F. Dem'yanov and V. N. Molozemov. *Introduction to Minimax*. Dover Publications, Mineola, NY, 1990.

[122] H. H. Denman, W. Heller, and W. J. Pangonis. *Angular Scattering Functions of Spheres*. Wayne State University Press, Detroit, MI, 1966.

[123] Russell L. DeValois and Karen K. DeValois. *Spatial Vision*. Oxford University Press, New York, 1988.

[124] Mark A. Z. Dippé and Erling Henry Wold. Antialiasing through stochastic sampling. *Computer Graphics (Proc. Siggraph '85)*, 19(3):69–78, July 1985.

[125] George Drettakis and Eugene Fiume. Concrete computation of global illumination using structured sampling. In Alan Chalmers, Derek Paddon, and François Sillion, editors, *Third Eurographics Workshop on Rendering*, pp. 189–201. Elsevier, Amsterdam, 1992.

[126] George Drettakis and Eugene Fiume. Accurate and consistent reconstruction of illumination functions using structured sampling. In R. J. Hubbold and R. Juan, editors, *Proc. Eurographics '93*, pp. 385–398. North-Holland, Amsterdam, 1993.

[127] George Drettakis, Eugene Fiume, and Alain Fournier. Tightly-coupled multiprocessing for a global illumination algorithm. In Carlo E. Vandoni and David A. Duce, editors, *Proc. Eurographics '90*, pp. 387–98. North-Holland, Amsterdam, 1990.

[128] Steven M. Drucker and Peter Schröder. Fast radiosity using a data parallel architecture. In Alan Chalmers, Derek Paddon, and François Sillion, editors, *Third Eurographics Workshop on Rendering*, pp. 247–258. Amsterdam, Elsevier, 1992.

[129] James J. Duderstadt and William R. Martin. *Transport Theory*. John Wiley & Sons, New York, 1979.

[130] Dan E. Dudgeon and Russell M. Merserau. *Multidimensional Digital Signal Processing*. Prentice-Hall, Englewood Cliffs, NJ, 1984.

[131] Tom Duff. Splines in animation and modeling. In *Siggraph '86 State of the Art in Image Synthesis course notes*. ACM Siggraph, New York, 1986.

[132] D. R. Duncan. The colour of pigment mixtures. *Proceedings of the Physical Society*, pp. 380–390, 1940.

[133] H. John Durrett. *Color and the Computer*. Academic Press, San Diego, 1987.

[134] E. R. G. Eckert and E. M. Sparrow. Radiative heat exchange between surfaces with specular reflection. *International Journal of Heat and Mass Transfer*, 3:42–54, 1961.

[135] Will Eisner. *Comics & Sequential Art*. Poorhouse Press, Tamarac, FL, 1985.

[136] A. F. Emery, O. Johansson, M. Lobo, and A. Abrous. A comparative study of methods for computing the diffuse radiation viewfactors for complex structures. *Journal of Heat Transfer*, 113:413–422, May 1991.

[137] Bruno Ernst. *Adventures with Impossible Figures*. Tarquin Publications, Norfolk, England, 1986.

[138] E. Esselink. About the order of Appel's algorithm. Technical report computing science note KE5-1, Department of Computer Science, University of Groningen, The Netherlands, 1989.

[139] D. Farnsworth. A temporal factor in colour discrimination. In *Visual Problems in Color, II (National Phys. Lab. Symposium)*, number 8, p. 429. Her Majesty's Stationery Office, London, 1958.

[140] R. Farrell. Determination of configuration factors of irregular shape. *Journal of Heat Transfer*, pp. 311–313, May 1976.

[141] Martin Feda and Werner Purgathofer. Accelerating radiosity by overshooting. In Alan Chalmers, Derek Paddon, and François Sillion, editors, *Third Eurographics Workshop on Rendering*, pp. 21–32. Elsevier, Amsterdam, 1992.

[142] Hans G. Feichtinger and Karlheinz Gröchenig. Iterative reconstruction of multivariate band-limited functions from irregular sampling values. *SIAM J. Math. Anal.*, 23(1):244–261, January 1992.

[143] Hans G. Feichtinger and Karlheinz Gröchenig. Theory and practice of irregular sampling. In John J. Benedetto and Michael W. Frazier, editors, *Wavelets: Mathematics and Applications*, chapter 8. CRC Press, Boca Raton, FL, 1994.

[144] Richard P. Feynman. *QED*. Princeton University Press, Princeton, NJ, 1985.

[145] Kenneth Paul Fishkin. *Applying Color Science to Computer Graphics*. Master's thesis, University of California, Berkeley, December 1983.

[146] Karen Fitzgerald. Don't move that CRT! *IEEE Spectrum*, p. 16, December 1989.

[147] James D. Foley, Andries van Dam, Steven K. Feiner, and John F. Hughes. *Computer Graphics: Principles and Practice*. Addison-Wesley, Reading, MA, 2nd ed., 1990.

[148] Grant R. Fowles. *Introduction to Modern Optics*. Dover Publications, Mineola, NY, 2nd ed., 1975.

[149] R. W. Franke. Smooth interpolation of scattered data by local thin plate splines. *Comp. Math. Appl.*, 8(4):273–181, 1982.

[150] Akira Fujimoto, Takayuki Tanaka, and Kansei Iwata. ARTS: Accelerated ray-tracing system. *IEEE Computer Graphics & Applications*, 6(4):16–26, April 1986. Also in *Tutorial: Computer Graphics: Image Synthesis*, pp. 148–158, Computer Society Press, Washington, DC, 1988.

[151] Robert A. Gabel and Richard A. Roberts. *Signals and Linear Systems*. John Wiley & Sons, New York, 2nd ed., 1980.

[152] David W. George, François X. Sillion, and Donald P. Greenberg. Radiosity redistribution for dynamic environments. *IEEE Computer Graphics & Applications*, 10(7):26–34, July 1990.

[153] Andrew S. Glassner. Space subdivision for fast ray tracing. *IEEE Computer Graphics & Applications*, 4(10):15–22, October 1984. Also in *Tutorial: Computer Graphics: Image Synthesis*, pp. 160–167. Computer Society Press, Washington, DC, 1988.

[154] Andrew S. Glassner. Spacetime ray tracing for animation. *IEEE Computer Graphics & Applications*, 8(3):60–70, March 1988.

[155] Andrew S. Glassner. How to derive a spectrum from an *rgb* triplet. *IEEE Computer Graphics & Applications*, 9(7):95–99, July 1989.

[156] Andrew S. Glassner. An overview of ray tracing. In Andrew S. Glassner, editor, *An Introduction to Ray Tracing*, pp. 1–32. Academic Press, San Diego, 1989.

[157] Andrew S. Glassner. Some ideas for future work. In Andrew S. Glassner, editor, *Siggraph '90 Advanced Topics in Ray Tracing course notes*, chapter 7. ACM Siggraph, New York, 1990.

[158] Andrew S. Glassner. Dynamic stratification. In Michael Cohen, Claude Puech, and François Sillion, editors, *Fourth Eurographics Workshop on Rendering*, pp. 1–14. Elsevier, Amsterdam, 1993.

[159] Andrew S. Glassner. *3D Computer Graphics: A Handbook for Artists and Designers*. Design Books, New York, 2nd ed., 1994.

[160] Andrew S. Glassner, Kenneth P. Fishkin, David H. Marimont, and Maureen C. Stone. Rendering within constraints. Technical report ISTL-CGI-1993-07-01, Information Sciences and Technologies Lab, Xerox PARC, 1993. (To appear in *ACM Transactions on Graphics*).

[161] James Gleick. *Chaos: Making a New Science.* Penguin Books, New York, 1987.

[162] Michael A. Golberg. A survey of numerical methods for integral equations. In Michael A. Golberg, editor, *Solution Methods for Integral Equations*, chapter 1. Plenum Press, New York, 1978.

[163] Jeffrey Goldsmith and John Salmon. Automatic creation of object hierarchies for ray tracing. *IEEE Computer Graphics & Applications*, 7(5):14–20, May 1987.

[164] E. H. Gombrich. *Art and Illusion: A Study in the Psychology of Pictorial Representation.* Pantheon Books, New York, 1960. Bollingen series XXXV 5.

[165] Cindy M. Goral, Kenneth E. Torrance, Donald P. Greenberg, and Bennett Battaile. Modelling the interaction of light between diffuse surfaces. *Computer Graphics (Proc. Siggraph '84)*, 18(3):213–222, July 1984.

[166] Steven Gortler, Michael F. Cohen, and Philipp Slusallek. Radiosity and relaxation methods. *IEEE Computer Graphics & Applications*, 14(6):48–58, November 1994.

[167] Steven J. Gortler, Peter Schröder, Michael Cohen, and Pat Hanrahan. Wavelet radiosity. *Computer Graphics (Proc. Siggraph '93)*, 27(3):221–230, August 1993.

[168] Ned Greene and Paul S. Heckbert. Creating raster Omnimax images from multiple perspective views using the elliptical weighted average filter. *IEEE Computer Graphics & Applications*, 6(6):21–27, June 1986.

[169] Ned Greene, Michael Kass, and Gavin Miller. Hierarchical z-buffer visibility. *Computer Graphics (Proc. Siggraph '93)*, 27(3):231–238, August 1993.

[170] Robert Greenler. *Rainbows, Halos, and Glories.* Cambridge University Press, New York, 1980.

[171] R. L. Gregory. *The Intelligent Eye.* Macmillan, New York, 1970.

[172] Günterh Greiner, Wolfgang Heidrich, and Philipp Slusallek. Blockwise refinement—A new method for solving the radiosity problem. In Michael Cohen, Claude Puech, and François Sillion, editors, *Fourth Eurographics Workshop on Rendering*, pp. 233–245. Elsevier, Amsterdam, 1993.

[173] D. F. Griffiths and G. A. Watson, editors. *Numerical Analysis 1987*, volume 170 of *Pitman Research Notes in Mathematics*. Longman Scientific and Technical, Harlow, Essex, England, 1988.

[174] Branko Grünbaum and G. C. Shephard. *Tilings and Patterns*. W H Freeman, New York, 1987.

[175] Chet S. Haase and Gary W. Meyer. Modeling pigmented materials for realistic image synthesis. *ACM Transactions on Graphics*, 11(4):305–335, October 1992.

[176] Wolfgang Hackbusch. Error analysis of the nonlinear multigrid method of the second kind. *Aplikace Matematiky*, 26(1):18–29, 1981.

[177] Eric Haines. Essential ray tracing algorithms. In Andrew S. Glassner, editor, *An Introduction to Ray Tracing*, pp. 33–78. Academic Press, San Diego, 1989.

[178] Eric Haines. Shaft culling for efficent ray-traced radiosity. In Andrew S. Glassner, editor, *Siggraph 1991 Frontiers in Rendering course notes*, chapter 2. ACM Siggraph, New York, July 1991.

[179] Kenneth Haines and Debby Haines. Computer graphics for holography. *IEEE Computer Graphics & Applications*, 12(1):37–46, January 1992.

[180] David E. Hall and Holly E. Rushmeier. An improved explicit radiosity method for calculating non-lambertian reflections. Technical report GIT-GVU–91–16, Graphics, Visualization & Usability Center, Georgia Institute of Technology, Atlanta, September 1991.

[181] Roy Hall. *Illumination and Color in Computer Generated Imagery*. Springer-Verlag, New York, 1989.

[182] John H. Halton. A retrospective and prospective survey of the Monte Carlo method. *SIAM Review*, 12(1):1–73, January 1970.

[183] J. M. Hammersley and D. C. Handscomb. *Monte Carlo Methods*. Methuen & Co., London, 1964.

[184] R. W. Hamming. *Coding and Information Theory*. Prentice-Hall, Englewood Cliffs, NJ, 2nd ed., 1986.

[185] R. W. Hamming. *Digital Filters*. Prentice-Hall, Englewood Cliffs, NJ, 3rd ed., 1989.

[186] Pat Hanrahan. A survey of ray-surface intersection algorithms. In Andrew S. Glassner, editor, *An Introduction to Ray Tracing*, pp. 79–120. Academic Press, San Diego, 1989.

[187] Pat Hanrahan. Three-pass affine transforms for volume rendering. *Computer Graphics (Proc. San Diego Workshop on Volume Visualization)*, 24(5):71–90, November 1990.

[188] Pat Hanrahan. Rendering concepts. In Michael F. Cohen and John R. Wallace, *Radiosity and Realistic Image Synthesis*. Academic Press, San Diego, 1993.

[189] Pat Hanrahan and Paul Haeberli. Direct WYSIWYG painting and texturing on 3D shapes. *Computer Graphics (Proc. Siggraph '90)*, 24(4):215–223, August 1990.

[190] Pat Hanrahan and Wolfgang Krueger. Reflection from layered surfaces due to subsurface scattering. *Computer Graphics (Proc. Siggraph '93)*, 27(3):165–174, August 1993.

[191] Pat Hanrahan and David Salzman. A rapid hierarchical radiosity algorithm for unoccluded environments. In K. Bouatouch and C. Bouville, editors, *Eurographics Workshop on Photosimulation, Realism and Physics in Computer Graphics*, pp. 151–171. Elsevier, Amsterdam, 1990.

[192] Pat Hanrahan, David Salzman, and Larry Aupperle. A rapid hierarchical radiosity algorithm. *Computer Graphics (Proc. Siggraph '91)*, 25(4):197–206, July 1991.

[193] A. J. Hanson and P. A. Heng. Illuminating the fourth dimension. *IEEE Computer Graphics & Applications*, 12(4):54–62, July 1992.

[194] Andrew J. Hanson and Robert A. Cross. Interactive visualization methods for four dimensions. In Gregory M. Nielson and Dan Bergeron, editors, *Proceedings of Visualization '93*, pp. 196–203. IEEE Computer Society Press, Los Alamitos, CA, 1993.

[195] John C. Hart and Thomas A. DeFanti. Efficient antialiased rendering of 3-D linear fractals. *Computer Graphics (Proc. Siggraph '91)*, 25(4):91–100, July 1991.

[196] Akihiko Hashimoto, Taka aki Akimoto, Kenji Mase, and Yasuhito Suenaga. Vista ray-tracing: High speed ray tracing using perspective projection image. In Rae A. Earnshaw and Brian Wyvill, editors, *New Advances in Computer Graphics (Proc. CG International '89)*, pp. 549–561. Springer-Verlag, New York, 1989.

[197] Xiao D. He, Patrick O. Heynen, Richard L. Phillips, Kenneth E. Torrance, David H. Salesin, and Donald P. Greenberg. A fast and accurate light reflection model. *Computer Graphics (Proc. Siggraph '92)*, 26(2):253–254, July 1992.

[198] Xiao D. He, Kenneth E. Torrance, François X. Sillion, and Donald P. Greenberg. A comprehensive physical model for light reflection. *Computer Graphics (Proc. Siggraph '91)*, 25(4):175–186, July 1991.

[199] Donald Hearn and M. Pauline Baker. *Computer Graphics*. Prentice-Hall, Englewood Cliffs, NJ, 2nd ed., 1986.

[200] Eugene Hecht. *Schaum's Outline of Theory and Problems of Optics*. McGraw-Hill, New York, 1975.

[201] Eugene Hecht and Alfred Zajac. *Optics*. Addison-Wesley, Reading, MA, 1974.

[202] Paul Heckbert. *Simulating Global Illumination Using Adaptive Meshing*. Ph.D. thesis, University of California, Berkeley, January 1991.

[203] Paul Heckbert. Finite element methods for radiosity. In Paul Heckbert, editor, *Siggraph 1993 Global Illumination course notes*, chapter 2. ACM Siggraph, New York, August 1993.

[204] Paul S. Heckbert. Filtering by repeated integration. *Computer Graphics (Proc. Siggraph '86)*, 20(4):315–321, August 1986.

[205] Paul S. Heckbert. Survey of texture mapping. *IEEE Computer Graphics & Applications*, 6(11):56–67, November 1986. Also in *Tutorial: Computer Graphics: Image Synthesis*, pp. 321–332. Computer Society Press, Washington, DC, 1988.

[206] Paul S. Heckbert. *Fundamentals of Texture Mapping and Image Warping*. Master's thesis, Dept. of Electrical Engineering and Computer Science, University of California, Berkeley, June 1989.

[207] Paul S. Heckbert. Adaptive radiosity textures for bidirectional ray tracing. *Computer Graphics (Proc. Siggraph '90)*, 24(4):145–154, August 1990.

[208] Paul S. Heckbert. What are the coordinates of a pixel? In Andrew S. Glassner, editor, *Graphics Gems*, pp. 246–248. Academic Press, San Diego, 1990.

[209] Paul S. Heckbert. Writing a ray tracer. In Andrew S. Glassner, editor, *An Introduction to Ray Tracing*, pp. 263–294. Academic Press, San Diego, 1990.

[210] Paul S. Heckbert. Discontinuity meshing for radiosity. In Alan Chalmers, Derek Paddon, and François Sillion, editors, *Third Eurographics Workshop on Rendering*, pp. 203–216. Elsevier, Amsterdam, 1992.

[211] Paul S. Heckbert and Pat Hanrahan. Beam tracing polygonal objects. *Computer Graphics (Proc. Siggraph '84)*, 18(3):119–127, July 1984.

[212] K. Ho-Le. Finite element mesh generation methods: A review and classification. *Computer-Aided Design*, 20(1):27–38, January/February 1986.

[213] Guido Hoheisel. *Integral Equations*. Frederick Ungar, New York, 1968. Translated by A. Mary Tropper.

[214] Hugues Hoppe, Tony DeRose, Tom Duchamp, John McDonald, and Werner Stuetzle. Mesh optimization. *Computer Graphics (Proc. Siggraph '93)*, 27(3):19–26, August 1993.

[215] John R. Howell. *A Catalog of Radiation Configuration Factors*. McGraw-Hill, New York, 1982.

[216] Ping-Kang Hsiung and Robert H. P. Dunn. Visualizing relativistic effects in spacetime. In *Proc. Supercomputing '89*, pp. 597–606. ACM Press, New York, 1989.

[217] Ping-Kang Hsiung, Robert H. Thibadeau, Christopher B. Cox, Robert H. P. Dunn, Michael Wu, and Paul Andrew Olbrich. Wide-band relativistic doppler effect visualization. In *Visualization '90: Proc. First IEEE Conference on Visualization*, pp. 83–92. IEEE Computer Society Press, Los Alamitos, CA, 1990.

[218] Thomas S. Huang. The subjective effect of two-dimensional pictorial noise. *IEEE Transactions on Information Theory*, pp. 43–53, January 1965.

[219] R. W. G. Hunt. *The Reproduction of Color*. Fountain Press, Surrey, England, 4th ed., 1988.

[220] R. S. Hunter. *The Measurement of Appearance*. John Wiley & Sons, New York, 1975.

[221] IES. Nomenclature and definitions for illuminating engineering. Technical report ANSI/IES RP-16-1986, New York, 1986.

[222] IES Computer Committee. IES standard file format for electronic transfer of photometric data and related information. Technical report IES LM-63-1991, New York, 1991.

[223] Yasuhiko Ikebe. The Galerkin method for the numerical solution of Fredholm integral equations of the second kind. *SIAM Review*, 14(3):465–491, July 1972.

[224] David S. Immel, Michael Cohen, and Donald P. Greenberg. A radiosity method for non-diffuse environments. *Computer Graphics (Proc. Siggraph '86)*, 20(4):133–142, August 1986.

[225] Masa Inakage. Volume tracing of atmospheric environments. *The Visual Computer*, 7:104–113, 1991.

[226] E. Atlee Jackson. *Perspectives of Nonlinear Dynamics I*. Cambridge University Press, Cambridge, England, 1990.

[227] E. Atlee Jackson. *Perspectives of Nonlinear Dynamics II*. Cambridge University Press, Cambridge, England, 1990.

[228] Frederik W. Jansen and Jarke J. van Wijk. Fast previewing techniques in raster graphics. In P. J. W. ten Hagen, editor, *Proc. Eurographics '83*, pp. 195–202. North-Holland, Amsterdam, 1983.

[229] Björn Jawerth and Wim Sweldens. An overview of wavelet based multiresolution analysis. Submitted to *SIAM Review*, January 1993.

[230] Francis A. Jenkins and Harvey E. White. *Fundamentals of Optics*. McGraw-Hill, New York, 1957.

[231] Abdul J. Jerri. The Shannon sampling theorem—its various extensions and applications: A tutorial review. *Proceedings of the IEEE*, 65(11):1565–1596, November 1977.

[232] D. B. Judd and G. Wyszecki. *Color in Business, Science and Industry*. John Wiley & Sons, New York, 3rd ed., 1975.

[233] James T. Kajiya. Anisotropic reflection models. *Computer Graphics (Proc. Siggraph '85)*, 19(3):15–21, July 1985.

[234] James T. Kajiya. The rendering equation. *Computer Graphics (Proc. Siggraph '86)*, 20(4):143–150, August 1986.

[235] James T. Kajiya. Radiometry and photometry for computer graphics. In Andrew S. Glassner, editor, *Siggraph 1990 Advanced Topics in Ray Tracing course notes*, chapter 2. ACM Siggraph, New York, August 1990.

[236] James T. Kajiya and Brian P. Von Herzen. Ray tracing volume densities. *Computer Graphics (Proc. Siggraph '84)*, 18(3):165–174, July 1984.

[237] James T. Kajiya and Timothy L. Kay. Rendering fur with three dimensional textures. *Computer Graphics (Proc. Siggraph '89)*, 23(3):271–280, July 1989.

[238] James T. Kajiya and Michael Ullner. Filtering high quality text for display on raster scan devices. *Computer Graphics (Proc. Siggraph '81)*, 15(3):7–15, August 1981.

[239] Malvin H. Kalos and Paula A. Whitlock. *Monte Carlo Methods: Volume I: Basics*. John Wiley & Sons, New York, 1986.

[240] Ram P. Kanwal. *Linear Integral Equations: Theory and Technique*. Academic Press, San Diego, 1971.

[241] Michael R. Kaplan. Space-tracing, a constant time ray-tracer. In *Siggraph '85 State of the Art in Image Synthesis course notes*. ACM Siggraph, New York, July 1985.

[242] John K. Kawai, James S. Painter, and Michael F. Cohen. Radioptimization—goal based rendering. *Computer Graphics (Proc. Siggraph '93)*, 27(3):147–154, August 1993.

[243] Timothy L. Kay and James T. Kajiya. Ray tracing complex scenes. *Computer Graphics (Proc. Siggraph '84)*, 18(3):269–278, July 1984.

[244] S. P. Kim and N. K. Bose. Reconstruction of 2-D bandlimited discrete signals from nonuniform samples. *IEEE Proceedings*, 137, Pt. F(3):197–204, June 1990.

[245] David Kirk and James Arvo. The ray tracing kernel. In Michael Gigante, editor, *Proc. Ausgraph '88*, pp. 75–82. Australasian Computer Graphics Association, 1988. Also in *Siggraph '90 Advanced Topics in Ray Tracing course notes*. ACM Siggraph, New York, 1990.

[246] David Kirk and James Arvo. Unbiased sampling techniques for image synthesis. *Computer Graphics (Proc. Siggraph '91)*, 25(4), July 1991.

[247] R. Victor Klassen. Modeling the effect of the atmosphere on light. *ACM Transactions on Graphics*, 6(3):215–237, July 1987.

[248] Peter Dale Kochevar. *Computer Graphics on Massively Parallel Machines*. Ph.D. thesis, Cornell University, Ithaca, NY, August 1989.

[249] Arjan J. F. Kok. Grouping of patches in progressive radiosity. In Michael Cohen, Claude Puech, and François Sillion, editors, *Fourth Eurographics Workshop on Rendering*, pp. 221–231. Elsevier, Amsterdam, 1993.

[250] Arjan J. F. Kok, Celal Yilmaz, and Laurens J. J. Bierens. A two-pass radiosity method for Bézier patches. In K. Bouatouch and C. Bouville, editors, *Eurographics Workshop on Photosimulation, Realism and Physics in Computer Graphics*, pp. 117–126. Elsevier, Amsterdam, 1990.

[251] J. Kondo. *Integral Equations*. Clarendon Press, Oxford, England, 1991.

[252] Bart Kosko. *Fuzzy Thinking*. Hyperion Books, New York, 1992.

[253] Bart Kosko. *Neural Networks and Fuzzy Systems*. Prentice-Hall, Englewood Cliffs, NJ, 1992.

[254] Rainer Kress. *Linear Integral Equations*. Springer-Verlag, New York, 1989.

[255] P. Kubelka and F. Munk. Ein beitrag zur optik der farbanstriche. *Zurich Tech. Physik*, 12:543, 1931.

[256] Paul Kubelka. New contributions to the optics of intensely light-scattering materials (Part I). *Journal of the Optical Society of America*, 38:448, 1948.

[257] Edi Lanners. *Illusions*. Holt, Rinehart, and Winston, Orlando, FL, 1977. Translated by Heinz Norden.

[258] David Laur and Pat Hanrahan. Hierarchical splatting: A progressive refinement algorithm for volume rendering. *Computer Graphics (Proc. Siggraph '91)*, 25(4):285–288, July 1991.

[259] Bertrand Le Saec and Christophe Schlick. A progressive ray-tracing-based radiosity with general reflectance functions. In K. Bouatouch and C. Bouville, editors, *Eurographics Workshop on Photosimulation, Realism and Physics in Computer Graphics*, pp. 103–116. Elsevier, Amsterdam, 1990.

[260] Mark E. Lee and Richard A. Redner. A note on the use of nonlinear filtering in computer graphics. *IEEE Computer Graphics & Applications*, 10(5):23–29, May 1990.

[261] Mark E. Lee, Richard A. Redner, and Samuel P. Uselton. Statistically optimized sampling for distributed ray tracing. *Computer Graphics (Proc. Siggraph '85)*, 19(3):61–67, July 1985.

[262] Oscar A. Z. Leneman. Random sampling of random processes: Impulse processes. *Information and Control*, 9:347–363, 1966.

[263] Oscar A. Z. Leneman. Random sampling of random processes: Optimum linear interpolation. *Journal of the Franklin Institute*, 281(4):302–314, April 1966.

[264] Oscar A. Z. Leneman. Statistical properties of random pulse trains. *1966 IEEE International Convention Record*, 6:167–172, March 1966.

[265] Oscar A. Z. Leneman. The spectral analysis of impulse processes. *Information and Control*, 12:236–258, 1968.

[266] Jaquiline Lenoble. *Radiative Transfer in Scattering and Absorbing Atmospheres: Standard Computational Procedures*. A. Deepak Publishing, 1985.

[267] Humboldt W. Leverenz. *An Introduction to Luminescence of Solids*. Dover Publications, Mineola, NY, 1968.

[268] Marc Levoy. Efficient ray tracing of volume data. *ACM Transactions on Graphics*, 9(3):245–261, July 1990.

[269] Marc Levoy. A hybrid ray tracer for rendering polygon and volume data. *IEEE Computer Graphics & Applications*, 10(3):33–40, March 1990.

[270] L. Lewin. *Dilogarithm and Associated Functions*. Macdonald, London, 1958.

[271] Harry R. Lewis and Christos H. Papadimitriou. *Elements of the Theory of Computation*. Prentice-Hall, Englewood Cliffs, NJ, 1981.

[272] J. P. Lewis. Algorithms for solid noise synthesis. *Computer Graphics (Proc. Siggraph '89)*, 23(3):263–270, July 1989.

[273] Robert R. Lewis. Making shaders more physically plausible. In Michael Cohen, Claude Puech, and François Sillion, editors, *Fourth Eurographics Workshop on Rendering*, pp. 47–62. Elsevier, Amsterdam, 1993.

[274] Dani Lischinski, Filippo Tampieri, and Donald P. Greenberg. Combining hierarchical radiosity and discontinuity meshing. *Computer Graphics (Proc. Siggraph '93)*, 27(3):199–208, August 1993.

[275] Dani Lischniski, Filippo Tampieri, and Donald P. Greenberg. Discontinuity meshing for accurate radiosity. *IEEE Computer Graphics & Applications*, 12(6):25–39, November 1992.

[276] Richard L. Longini. *Introductory Quantum Mechanics for the Solid State*. Wiley-Interscience, New York, 1970.

[277] M. Luckiesh. *Visual Illusions*. Dover, Mineola, NY, 1965. (Reprint of the 1922 edition).

[278] David MacDonald. *Space Subdivision Algorithms for Ray Tracing*. Master's thesis, University of Waterloo, Waterloo, Ontario, 1988.

[279] J.-L. Maillot. Personal communication, January 1993.

[280] J.-L. Maillot, L. Carraro, and B. Peroche. Progressive ray tracing. In Alan Chalmers, Derek Paddon, and François Sillion, editors, *Third Eurographics Workshop on Rendering*, pp. 9–20. Elsevier, Amsterdam, 1992.

[281] Farokh Marvasti, Mostafa Analoui, and Mohsen Gamshadzahi. Recovery of signals from nonuniform samples using iterative methods. *IEEE Transactions on Signal Processing*, 39(4):872–878, April 1991.

[282] Farokh Marvasti and Tsung Jen Lee. Analysis and recovery of sample-and-hold and linearly interpolated signals with irregular samples. *IEEE Transactions on Signal Processing*, 40(8):1884–1891, August 1992.

[283] Farokh A. Marvasti. *A Unified Approach to Zero-Crossings and Nonuniform Sampling*. Nonuniform Press, Oak Fork, IL, 1987.

[284] Nelson Max. An optimal filter for image reconstruction. In James Arvo, editor, *Graphics Gems II*, pp. 101–104. Academic Press, San Diego, 1991.

[285] Nelson Max and Roy Troutman. Optimal hemicube sampling. In Michael Cohen, Claude Puech, and François Sillion, editors, *Fourth Eurographics Workshop on Rendering*, pp. 185–200. Elsevier, Amsterdam, 1993.

[286] Nelson L. Max. Atmospheric illumination and shadows. *Computer Graphics (Proc. Siggraph '86)*, 20(4):117–124, August 1986.

[287] Nelson L. Max. Unified sun and sky illumination for shadows under trees. *CGVIP: Graphical Models and Image Processing*, 53(3):223–230, May 1991.

[288] Nelson L. Max and Michael J. Allison. Linear radiosity approximation using vertex-to-vertex form factors. In James Arvo, editor, *Graphics Gems II*, pp. 318–323. Academic Press, San Diego, 1991.

[289] Gregory M. Maxwell, Michael J. Bailey, and Victor W. Goldschmidt. Calculations of the radiation configuration factor using ray casting. *Computer-Aided Design*, 18(9):371–379, September 1986.

[290] David F. McAllister. *Stereo Computer Graphics and Other True 3D Technologies*. Princeton University Press, Princeton, NJ, 1993.

[291] C. S. McCamy, H. Marcus, and J. G. Davidson. A color-rendition chart. *Journal of Applied Photographic Engineering*, 2(3):95–99, summer 1976.

[292] E. J. McCartney. *Optics of the Atmosphere*. John Wiley & Sons, New York, 1976.

[293] Scott McCloud. *Understanding Comics*. Kitchen Sink Press, Princeton, WI, 1993.

[294] Michael McCool and Eugene Fiume. Hierarchical Poisson disk sampling distributions. In Kellogg Booth and Alain Fournier, editors, *Proc. Graphics Interface '92*, pp. 94–105. Canadian Information Processing Society, Toronto, 1992.

[295] Donald A. McQuarrie. *Quantum Chemistry*. University Science Books, Mill Valley, CA, 1983.

[296] Aden Meinel and Marjorie Meinel. *Sunsets, Twilights, and Evening Skies*. Cambridge University Press, New York, 1983.

[297] Louis K. Meisel. *Photo-Realism*. Harry N. Abrams, New York, 1985.

[298] Robin M. Merrifield. Visual parameters for color CRTs. In H. John Durrett, editor, *Color and the Computer*, chapter 4, pp. 63–82. Academic Press, San Diego, 1987.

[299] Dimitris Metaxas and Evangelos Milios. Color image reconstruction from nonuniform sparse samples using a thin plate model. In Carlo E. Vandoni and David A. Duce, editors, *Proc. Eurographics '90*, pp. 75–86. North-Holland, Amsterdam, 1990.

[300] Gary W. Meyer. Wavelength selection for synthetic image generation. *Computer Vision, Graphics, and Image Processing*, 41:57–79, 1988.

[301] Gary W. Meyer, Holly E. Rushmeier, Michael F. Cohen, Donald P. Greenberg, and Kenneth E. Torrance. An experimental evaluation of computer graphics imagery. *ACM Transactions on Graphics*, 5(1):30–50, January 1986.

[302] Yves Meyer. *Wavelets: Algorithms and Applications*. SIAM, Philadelphia, 1993. Translated and revised by Robert D. Ryan.

[303] Solomon Mikhlin. *Multidimensional Singular Equations and Integral Equations*. Pergamon Press, Tarrytown, NY, 1962. Translated by W. J. A. Whyte and edited by I. N. Sneddon.

[304] Gavin Miller. From wire-frames to furry animals. *Proc. Graphics Interface '88*, pp. 138–145, Canadian Information Processing Society, Toronto, 1988.

[305] M. Minnaert. *The Nature of Light & Colour in the Open Air*. Dover Publications, Mineola, NY, 1954.

[306] Charles W. Misner, Kip S. Thorne, and John Archibald Wheeler. *Gravitation*. W H Freeman, New York, 1970.

[307] Don P. Mitchell. Generating antialiased images at low sampling densities. *Computer Graphics (Proc. Siggraph '87)*, 21(4):65–72, July 1987.

[308] Don P. Mitchell. Spectrally optimal sampling for distribution ray tracing. *Computer Graphics (Proc. Siggraph '91)*, 25(4):157–164, July 1991.

[309] Don P. Mitchell. Ray tracing and irregularities of distribution. In Alan Chalmers, Derek Paddon, and François Sillion, editors, *Third Eurographics Workshop on Rendering*, pp. 61–69. Elsevier, Amsterdam, 1992.

[310] Don P. Mitchell and Arun N. Netravali. Reconstruction filters in computer graphics. *Computer Graphics (Proc. Siggraph '88)*, 22(4):221–228, July 1988.

[311] K. D. Möller. *Optics*. University Science Books, Mill Valley, CA, 1988.

[312] Parry Moon. *The Scientific Basis of Illumination Engineering*. McGraw-Hill, New York, 1936.

[313] Parry Moon. On interreflections. *Journal of the Optical Society of America*, 30(5):195–205, May 1940.

[314] Hans P. Moravec. 3D graphics and the wave theory. *Computer Graphics (Proc. Siggraph '81)*, 15(3):289–296, August 1981.

[315] N. I. Muskhelishvili. *Singular Integral Equations*. Wolters-Noordhoff, Groningen, The Netherlands, 1953. Translated by J. R. M. Radok.

[316] S. Hamid Nawab and Thomas F. Quatieri. Short-time Fourier transform. In Jae S. Lim and Alan V. Oppenheim, editors, *Advanced Topics in Signal Processing*, pp. 289–337. Prentice-Hall, Englewood Cliffs, NJ, 1988.

[317] László Neumann and Atilla Neumann. Efficient radiosity methods for non-separable reflectance models. In K. Bouatouch and C. Bouville, editors, *Eurographics Workshop on Photosimulation, Realism and Physics in Computer Graphics*, pp. 83–102. Elsevier, Amsterdam, 1990.

[318] F. E. Nicodemus, J. C. Richmond, J. J. Hsia, I. W. Ginsberg, and T. Limperis. Geometrical considerations and nomenclature for reflectance. Technical report 160, National Bureau of Standards, October 1977. Also in Lawrence B. Wolff, Steven A. Shafer, and Glenn E. Healey, editors, *Physics-Based Vision, Principles and Practice: Radiometry*, pp. 94–145. Jones and Bartlett, Boston, 1992.

[319] Harald Niederreiter. Quasi-Monte Carlo methods and pseudo-random numbers. *Bulletin of the American Mathematical Society*, 84(6), 1978.

[320] Tomoyuki Nishita, Yashuhiro Miyawaki, and Eihachiro Nakamae. A shading model for atmospheric scattering considering luminous intensity distribution of light sources. *Computer Graphics (Proc. Siggraph '87)*, 21(4):303–310, July 1987.

[321] Tomoyuki Nishita and Eihachiro Nakamae. Continuous tone representation of three-dimensional objects taking account of shadows and interreflection. *Computer Graphics (Proc. Siggraph '85)*, 19(3):23–30, July 1985.

[322] Tomoyuki Nishita and Eihachiro Nakamae. A new radiosity approach using area sampling for parametric patches. In R. J. Hubbold and R. Juan, editors, *Proc. Eurographics '93*, pp. 385–398. North-Holland, Amsterdam, 1993.

[323] Tomoyuki Nishita, Takao Sirai, Katsumi Tadamura, and Eihachiro Nakamae. Display of the earth taking into account atmospheric scattering. *Computer Graphics (Proc. Siggraph '93)*, 27(3):175–182, August 1993.

[324] Ben Noble. A bibliography on "Methods for solving integral equations". Technical report 1177, Mathematics Research Center, University of Wisconsin, Madison, September 1971.

[325] Alan Norton, Alyn P. Rockwood, and Philip T. Skolmoski. Clamping: A method of antialiasing textured surfaces by bandwidth limiting in object space. *Computer Graphics (Proc. Siggraph '82)*, 16(3):1–8, July 1982.

[326] Alan V. Oppenheim and Ronald W. Schafer. *Digital Signal Processing*. Prentice-Hall, Englewood Cliffs, NJ, 1975.

[327] Alan V. Oppenheim and Alan S. Willsky with Ian T. Young. *Signals and Systems*. Prentice-Hall, Englewood Cliffs, NJ, 1983.

[328] James Painter and Kenneth Sloan. Antialiased ray tracing by adaptive progressive refinement. *Computer Graphics (Proc. Siggraph '89)*, 23(3):281–288, July 1989.

[329] Edward D. Palik. *Handbook of Optical Constants of Solids*. Academic Press, New York, 1985.

[330] A. Papoulis. A new algorithm in spectral analysis and band-limited extrapolation. *IEEE Trans. Circuits Syst.*, CAS-22:735–742, September 1975.

[331] Athanasios Papoulis. *Probability, Random Variables, and Stochastic Processes*. McGraw-Hill, New York, 1965.

[332] S. N. Pattanaik. *Computational Methods for Global Illumination and Visualisation of Complex 3D Environments*. Ph.D. thesis, Birla Institute of Technology & Science, Pilani, India, February 1993.

[333] S. N. Pattanaik and S. P. Mudur. Computation of global illumination by Monte Carlo simulation of the particle model of light. In Alan Chalmers, Derek Paddon, and François Sillion, editors, *Third Eurographics Workshop on Rendering*, pp. 71–83. Elsevier, Amsterdam, 1992.

[334] S. N. Pattanaik and S. P. Mudur. The potential equation and importance in illumination computations. *Computer Graphics Forum*, 12(2):131–136, 1993.

[335] Mark J. Pavicic. Convenient anti-aliasing filters that minimize "bumpy" sampling. In Andrew S. Glassner, editor, *Graphics Gems*, pp. 144–146. Academic Press, San Diego, 1990.

[336] Theo Pavlidis. Comments on "Stochastic sampling in computer graphics". Letter to the editor, *ACM Transactions on Graphics*, 9(2):233-236, April 1990.

[337] Mark S. Peercy. Linear color representations for full spectral rendering. *Computer Graphics (Proc. Siggraph '93)*, 27(3):191–198, August 1993.

[338] Ken Perlin. An image synthesizer. *Computer Graphics (Proc. Siggraph '85)*, 19(3):287–296, July 1985.

[339] Ken Perlin and Eric M. Hoffert. Hypertexture. *Computer Graphics (Proc. Siggraph '89)*, 23(3):253–262, July 1989.

[340] Roger Tory Peterson. *The Birds*. Time, Inc., Alexandria, VA, 1964. Life Nature Library.

[341] Georg Pietrek. Fast calculation of accurate form factors. In Michael Cohen, Claude Puech, and François Sillion, editors, *Fourth Eurographics Workshop on Rendering*, pp. 201–220. Elsevier, Amsterdam, 1993.

[342] G. C. Pomraning. *The Equations of Radiation Hydrodynamics*. Pergamon Press, Tarrytown, NY, 1973.

[343] David Porter and David G. Stirling. *Integral Equations: A Practical Treatment, from Spectral Theory to Applications*. Cambridge University Press, New York, 1990.

[344] Pierre Poulin and Alain Fournier. A model for anisotropic reflection. *Computer Graphics (Proc. Siggraph '90)*, 24(4):273–282, August 1990.

[345] William K. Pratt. *Digital Image Processing*. John Wiley & Sons, New York, 2nd ed., 1991.

[346] Franco P. Prearata and Michael Ian Shamos. *Computational Geometry: An Introduction*. Springer-Verlag, New York, 1985.

[347] Rudolph W. Preisendorfer. *Radiative Transfer on Discrete Spaces*. Pergamon Press, Tarrytown, NY, 1965.

[348] William H. Press, Saul A. Teukolsky, William T. Vetterling, and Brian P. Flannery. *Numerical Recipes in C, 2nd ed.* Cambridge University Press, New York, 1992.

[349] Claude Puech, François Sillion, and Christophe Vedel. Improving interaction with radiosity-based lighting simulation programs. *Computer Graphics (Proc. 1990 Symposium on Interactive 3D Graphics)*, 24(2):51–57, March 1990.

[350] Xavier Pueyo. Diffuse interreflections. Techniques for form-factor computation: A survey. *Visual Computer*, 7(7):200–201, July 1991.

[351] Werner Purgathofer. A statistical method for adaptive stochastic sampling. In Aristides A. G. Requicha, editor, *Proc. Eurographics '86*, pp. 145–152. North-Holland, Amsterdam, 1986.

[352] Werner Purgathofer and Michael Zeiller. Fast radiosity by parallelization. In K. Bouatouch and C. Bouville, editors, *Eurographics Workshop on Photosimulation, Realism and Physics in Computer Graphics*, pp. 173–183. Elsevier, Amsterdam, 1990.

[353] Anthony Ralston and Philip Rabinowitz. *A First Course in Numerical Analysis*. McGraw-Hill, New York, 2nd ed., 1978.

[354] Maria G. Raso and Alain Fournier. A piecewise polynomial approach to shading using spectral distributions. In Brian Wyvill, editor, *Proc. Graphics*

Interface '91, pp. 40–46. Canadian Information Processing Society, Toronto, 1991.

[355] Mark S. Rea, editor. *Lighting Handbook Reference and Application*. IES, New York, 8th ed., 1993.

[356] Rodney J. Recker, David W. George, and Donald P. Greenberg. Acceleration techniques for progressive refinement radiosity. *Computer Graphics (Proc. 1990 Symposium on Interactive 3D Graphics)*, 24(2):59–66, March 1990.

[357] Christopher E. Reid and Thomas B. Passin. *Signal Processing in C*. John Wiley & Sons, New York, 1992.

[358] Howard L. Resnikoff. *The Illusion of Reality*. Springer-Verlag, New York, 1989.

[359] Olivier Rioul and Martin Vetterli. Wavelets and signal processing. *IEEE SP Magazine*, pp. 14–38, October 1991.

[360] Hazel Rossotti. *Colour: Why the World Isn't Grey*. Princeton University Press, Princeton, NJ, 1983.

[361] Scott D. Roth. Ray casting for modeling solids. *Computer Graphics and Image Processing*, 18(2):109–144, February 1982.

[362] H. L. Royden. *Real Analysis*. Macmillan, New York, 2nd ed., 1968.

[363] Steven M. Rubin and Turner Whitted. A 3-dimensional representation for fast rendering of complex scenes. *Computer Graphics (Proc. Siggraph '80)*, 14(3):110–116, August 1980.

[364] Rudy Rucker. *The Fourth Dimension*. Houghton Mifflin, Boston, 1984.

[365] Walter Rudin. *Real and Complex Analysis*. McGraw-Hill, New York, 2nd ed., 1974.

[366] Holly Rushmeier, Charles Patterson, and Aravindan Veerasamy. Geometric simplification for indirect illumination calculations. In *Proc. Graphics Interface '93*, pp. 227–236. Canadian Information Processing Society, Toronto, 1993.

[367] Holly E. Rushmeier. Radiosity methods for volume rendering. Technical report GIT-GVU–91–01, Graphics, Visualization & Usability Center, Georgia Institute of Technology, Atlanta, 1991.

[368] Holly E. Rushmeier, Daniel R. Baum, and David E. Hall. Accelerating the hemi-cube algorithm for calculating radiation form factors. In *5th AIAA/ASME Themophysics and Heat Transfer Conference*, pp. 1044–1047, 1990.

[369] Holly E. Rushmeier and Kenneth E. Torrance. The zonal method for calculating light intensities in the presence of a participating medium. *Computer Graphics (Proc. Siggraph '87)*, 21(4):293–302, July 1987.

[370] Holly E. Rushmeier and Kenneth E. Torrance. Extending the radiosity method to include specularly reflecting and translucent materials. *ACM Transactions on Graphics*, 9(1):1–27, January 1990.

[371] Georgios Sakas and Mattias Gerth. Sampling and anti-aliasing of discrete 3-D volume density textures. In Frits H. Post and Wilhelm Barth, editors, *Proc. Eurographics '91*, pp. 87–102. North-Holland, Amsterdam, 1991.

[372] David Salesin, Dani Lischinski, and Tony DeRose. Reconstructing illumination functions with selected discontinuities. In Alan Chalmers, Derek Paddon, and François Sillion, editors, *Third Eurographics Workshop on Rendering*, pp. 99–112. Elsevier, Amsterdam, 1992.

[373] Hanen Samet. *Applications of Spatial Data Structures*. Addison-Wesley, Reading, MA, 1990.

[374] Hanen Samet. *Design and Analysis of Spatial Data Structures*. Addison-Wesley, Reading, MA, 1990.

[375] B. Sankur and L. Gerhardt. Reconstruction of signals from nonuniform samples. In *IEEE International Conference on Communications*, pp. 15.13–15.18, June 1973.

[376] Ken D. Sauer and Jan P. Allebach. Iterative reconstruction of band-limited images from nonuniformly spaced samples. *IEEE Transactions on Circuits and Systems*, 34(12):1497–1506, December 1987.

[377] Mateu Sbert. An integral geometry based method for fast form-factor computation. In R. J. Hubbold and R. Juan, editors, *Proc. Eurographics '93*, pp. 409–420. North-Holland, Amsterdam, 1993.

[378] H. M. Schey. *Div, Grad, Curl, and All That*. W. W. Norton, New York, 1973.

[379] H. Schippers. *Multiple Grid Methods for Equations of the Second Kind with Applications in Fluid Mechanics*. Mathematisch Centrum, Amsterdam, 1983. Mathematical Centre tracts 163.

[380] Christophe Schlick. *Divers Éléments pour une synthèse d'images réalistes*. Ph.D. thesis, Université Bordeaux 1, November 1992.

[381] Christophe Schlick. A customizable reflectance model for everyday rendering. In Michael Cohen, Claude Puech, and François Sillion, editors, *Fourth Eurographics Workshop on Rendering*, pp. 73–84. Elsevier, Amsterdam, 1993.

[382] Chris Schoeneman, Julie Dorsey, Brian Smits, James Arvo, and Donald Greenberg. Painting with light. *Computer Graphics (Proc. Siggraph '93)*, 27(3):143–146, August 1993.

[383] Peter Schröder. Numerical integration for radiosity in the presence of singularities. In Michael Cohen, Claude Puech, and François Sillion, editors, *Fourth Eurographics Workshop on Rendering*, pp. 123–134. Elsevier, Amsterdam, 1993.

[384] Peter Schröder, Steven J. Gortler, Michael F. Cohen, and Pat Hanrahan. Wavelet projections for radiosity. In Michael Cohen, Claude Puech, and François Sillion, editors, *Fourth Eurographics Workshop on Rendering*, pp. 105–114. Elsevier, Amsterdam, 1993.

[385] Peter Schröder and Pat Hanrahan. A closed form expression for the form factor between two polygons. Research report CS-TR-404-93, Department of Computer Science, Princeton University, Princeton, NJ, January 1993.

[386] Peter Schröder and Pat Hanrahan. On the form factor between two polygons. *Computer Graphics (Proc. Siggraph '93)*, 27(3):163–164, August 1993.

[387] Sven Schuierer. Delaunay triangulations and the radiosity approach. In W. Hansmann, F. R. A. Hopgood, and W. Straßer, editors, *Proc. Eurographics '89*, pp. 345–353. North-Holland, Amsterdam, 1989.

[388] Bernard F. Schutz. *A First Course in General Relativity*. Cambridge University Press, New York, 1990.

[389] Robert Sekuler and Randolph Blake. *Perception*. Alfred A. Knopf, New York, 1985.

[390] Carlo H. Séquin and Eliot K. Smyrl. Parameterized ray tracing. *Computer Graphics (Proc. Siggraph '89)*, 23(3):307–314, July 1989.

[391] Min-Zhi Shao and Norman I. Badler. Analysis and acceleration of progressive refinement radiosity method. In Michael Cohen, Claude Puech, and François Sillion, editors, *Fourth Eurographics Workshop on Rendering*, pp. 247–258. Elsevier, Amsterdam, 1993.

[392] Min-Zhi Shao, Qun-Sheng Peng, and You-Dong Liang. A new radiosity approach by procedural refinements for realistic image synthesis. *Computer Graphics (Proc. Siggraph '88)*, 22(4):93–101, August 1988.

[393] Ping-Ping Shao, Qun-Sheng Peng, and You-Dong Liang. Form-factors for general environments. In David A. Duce and Pierre Jancene, editors, *Proc. Eurographics '88*, pp. 499–510. North-Holland, Amsterdam, 1988.

[394] Harold R. Shapiro and Richard A. Silverman. Alias-free sampling of random noise. *Journal of the Society for Industrial and Applied Mathematics*, 8(2):225–248, 1960.

[395] Peter Shirley. Physically based lighting calculations for computer graphics: A modern perspective. In K. Bouatouch and C. Bouville, editors, *Eurographics Workshop on Photosimulation, Realism and Physics in Computer Graphics*, pp. 67–81. Elsevier, Amsterdam, 1990.

[396] Peter Shirley. A ray tracing method for illumination calculation in diffuse-specular scenes. In *Proc. Graphics Interface '90*, pp. 205–212. Canadian Information Processing Society, Toronto, 1990.

[397] Peter Shirley. Discrepancy as a quality measure for sample distributions. In Frits H. Post and Wilhelm Barth, editors, *Proc. Eurographics '91*, pp. 183–194. North-Holland, Amsterdam, 1991.

[398] Peter Shirley. Radiosity via ray tracing. In James Arvo, editor, *Graphics Gems II*, pp. 306–310. Academic Press, San Diego, 1991.

[399] Peter Shirley. A ray tracing framework for global illumination systems. In Brian Wyvill, editor, *Proc. Graphics Interface '91*, pp. 117–128. Canadian Information Processing Society, Toronto, 1991.

[400] Peter Shirley. Nonuniform random point sets via warping. In David Kirk, editor, *Graphics Gems III*, pp. 80–83. Academic Press, San Diego, 1992.

[401] Peter Shirley and Changyaw Wang. Distribution ray tracing: Theory and practice. In Alan Chalmers, Derek Paddon, and François Sillion, editors, *Third Eurographics Workshop on Rendering*, pp. 33–43. Elsevier, Amsterdam, 1992.

[402] Peter S. Shirley. *Physically Based Lighting Calculations for Computer Graphics*. Ph.D. thesis, University of Illinois at Urbana-Champaign, 1991.

[403] Leonard Shlain. *Art and Physics*. William Morrow, New York, 1992.

[404] Ken Shoemake. Animating rotations with quaternion curves. *Computer Graphics (Proc. Siggraph '85)*, 19(3):245–254, July 1985.

[405] Renben Shu and Alan Liu. A fast ray casting algorithm using adaptive isotriangular subdivision. In Gregory M. Nielson and Larry Rosenblum, editors, *Proc. Visualization '91*. IEEE Computer Society, Los Alamitos, CA, 1991.

[406] Robert Siegel and John R. Howell. *Thermal Radiation Heat Transfer*. Hemisphere Publishing, Bristol, PA, 3rd ed., 1992.

[407] François Sillion. Detection of shadow boundaries for adaptive meshing in radiosity. In James Arvo, editor, *Graphics Gems II*, pp. 311–315. Academic Press, San Diego, 1991.

[408] François Sillion and Claude Puech. A general two-pass method integrating specular and diffuse reflection. *Computer Graphics (Proc. Siggraph '89)*, 23(3):335–344, July 1989.

[409] François Sillion and Claude Puech. *Radiosity and Global Illumination*. Morgan Kaufmann, San Francisco, 1994.

[410] François X. Sillion, James R. Arvo, Stephen H. Westin, and Donald P. Greenberg. A global illumination solution for general reflectance distributions. *Computer Graphics (Proc. Siggraph '91)*, 25(4):187–196, July 1991.

[411] Louis D. Silverstein. Human factors for color display systems: Concepts, methods, and research. In H. John Durrett, editor, *Color and the Computer*, chapter 2, pp. 27–62. Academic Press, San Diego, 1987.

[412] Sandra Sinclair. *How Animals See*. Croom Helm Ltd., Beckenham, Kent, England, 1985.

[413] I. H. Sloan. Superconvergence. In Michael A. Golberg, editor, *Numerical Solution of Integral Equations*, chapter 2. Plenum Press, New York, 1990.

[414] Brian E. Smits, James R. Arvo, and David H. Salesin. An importance driven radiosity algorithm. *Computer Graphics (Proc. Siggraph '92)*, 26(4):273–282, July 1992.

[415] Jerome Spanier and Ely M. Gelbard. *Monte Carlo Principles and Neutron Transport Problems*. Addison-Wesley, Reading, MA, 1969.

[416] E. M. Sparrow. A new and simpler formulation for radiative angle factors. *Journal of Heat Transfer*, pp. 81–88, May 1963.

[417] E. M. Sparrow and R. D. Cess. *Radiation Heat Transfer*. Wadsworth, Belmont, CA, 1966.

[418] Stephen N. Spencer. The hemisphere radiosity method: A tale of two algorithms. In K. Bouatouch and C. Bouville, editors, *Eurographics Workshop on Photosimulation, Realism and Physics in Computer Graphics*, pp. 127–135. Elsevier, Amsterdam, 1990.

[419] David J. Statt. Method for the reproduction of color images based on viewer adaptation. U.S. patent 5,276,779, January 1994.

[420] Maureen C. Stone, William B. Cowan, and John C. Beatty. Color gamut mapping and the printing of digital color images. *ACM Transactions on Graphics*, 7(3):249–292, October 1988.

[421] Gilbert Strang. *Linear Algebra and Its Applications.* Academic Press, San Diego, 2nd ed., 1980.

[422] Gilbert Strang. Wavelets and dilation equations: A brief introduction. *SIAM Review*, 31(4):614–627, December 1989.

[423] Gilbert Strang. Wavelet transforms versus Fourier transforms. *Bulletin Am. Math. Soc.*, April 1993.

[424] Paul S. Strauss. A realistic lighting model for computer animators. *IEEE Computer Graphics & Applications*, 10(11):56–64, November 1990.

[425] K. R. Stromberg. *An Introduction to Classical Real Analysis.* Wadsworth International, Belmont, CA, 1981.

[426] Wolfgang Stürzlinger. Radiosity with Voronoi diagrams. In Alan Chalmers, Derek Paddon, and François Sillion, editors, *Third Eurographics Workshop on Rendering*, pp. 169–177. Elsevier, Amsterdam, 1992.

[427] Anthony Sudbery. *Quantum Mechanics and the Particles of Nature: An Outline for Mathematicians.* Cambridge University Press, New York, 1986.

[428] Jizhou Sun, L. Q. Zou, and R. L. Grimsdale. The determination of form-factors by lookup table. *Computer Graphics Forum*, 12(4):191–198, 1993.

[429] Wim Sweldens and Robert Piessens. Quadrature formulae for the calculation of the wavelet decomposition. Available via anonymous ftp from Yale wavelet server.

[430] Katsumi Tadamura, Eihachiro Nakamae, Kazufumi Kaneda, Masashi Baba, Hideo Yamashita, and Tomoyuki Nishita. Modeling of skylight and rendering of outdoor scenes. In R. J. Hubbold and R. Juan, editors, *Proc. Eurographics '93*, pp. 189–200. North-Holland, Amsterdam, 1993.

[431] J. H. Tait. *An Introduction to Neutron Transport Theory.* Elsevier, New York, 1964.

[432] Barry N. Taylor. The international system of units (SI). Technical report NIST special publication 330, 1991 edition, U.S. Government Printing Office, Washington, DC, August 1991.

[433] M. M. Taylor. Visual discrimination and orientation. *Journal of the Optical Society of America*, pp. 763–765, June 1963.

[434] Group TC4-16. Recommended file format for electronic transfer of luminaire photometric data. Technical report CIE 102-1003, International Commission on Illumination, 1993. ISBN 3-900-734-40-2.

[435] Seth Teller and Pat Hanrahan. Global visibility algorithms for illumination computations. *Computer Graphics (Proc. Siggraph '93)*, 27(3):239–246, August 1993.

[436] D. Thomas, Arun N. Netravali, and D. S. Fox. Anti-aliased ray tracing with covers. *Computer Graphics Forum*, 8(4):325–336, December 1989.

[437] Spencer Thomas. Dispersive refraction in ray tracing. *Visual Computer*, 2(1):3–8, January 1986.

[438] Georgi P. Tolstov and Richard A. Silverman (translator). *Fourier Series*. Dover, Mineola, NY, 1962.

[439] K. E. Torrance and E. M. Sparrow. Theory for off-specular reflection from roughened surfaces. *Journal of the Optical Society of America*, 57(9):1104–1114, 1967.

[440] Roy Troutman and Nelson L. Max. Radiosity algorithms using higher order finite element methods. *Computer Graphics (Proc. Siggraph '93)*, 27(3):209–212, August 1993.

[441] Jack Tumblin and Holly Rushmeier. Tone reproduction for realistic computer generated images. Technical report GIT-GVU–91–13, Graphics, Visualization & Usability Center, Georgia Institute of Technology, Atlanta, July 1991.

[442] Jack Tumblin and Holly Rushmeier. Tone reproduction for realistic images. *IEEE Computer Graphics & Applications*, 13(6):42–48, November 1993.

[443] Greg Turk. Re-tiling polygonal surfaces. *Computer Graphics (Proc. Siggraph '92)*, 26(4):55–64, July 1992.

[444] G. P. A. Turner. *Introduction to Paint Chemistry*. Chapman and Hall, New York, 1967.

[445] R. Ulichney. *Digital Halftoning*. MIT Press, Cambridge, MA, 1987.

[446] Steve Upstill. *The RenderMan Companion*. Addison-Wesley, Reading, MA, 1989.

[447] Barbara Upton and John Upton. *Photography*. Little, Brown, Boston, 2nd ed., 1981.

[448] H. T. M. van der Voort, H. J. Noordmans, J. M. Messerli, and A. W. M. Smeulders. Physically realistic volume visualization for interactive image analysis. In Michael Cohen, Claude Puech, and François Sillion, editors, *Fourth Eurographics Workshop on Rendering*, pp. 295–306. Elsevier, Amsterdam, 1993.

[449] Marc van Kreveld. *New Results on Data Structures in Computational Geometry*. Ph.D. thesis, Rijksuniversiteit te Utrecht, The Netherlands, June 1992.

[450] Theo van Walsum, Peter R. van Nieuwenhuizen, and Frederik W. Jansen. Refinement criteria for adaptive stochastic ray tracing of textures. In Frits H. Post and Wilhelm Barth, editors, *Proc. Eurographics '91*, pp. 155–166. North-Holland, Amsterdam, 1991.

[451] Christopher G. Van Wyk, Jr. *A Geometry-Based Insulation Model for Computer-Aided Design*. Ph.D. thesis, University of Michigan, Ann Arbor, 1988.

[452] Amitabh Varshney and Jan F. Prins. An environment-projection approach to radiosity for mesh-connected computers. In Alan Chalmers, Derek Paddon, and François Sillion, editors, *Third Eurographics Workshop on Rendering*, pp. 271–281. Elsevier, Amsterdam, 1992.

[453] Christophe Vedel. Improved storage and reconstruction of light intensities on surfaces. In Alan Chalmers, Derek Paddon, and François Sillion, editors, *Third Eurographics Workshop on Rendering*, pp. 113–121. Elsevier, Amsterdam, 1992.

[454] J. Vilaplana and X. Pueyo. Exploiting coherence for clipping and view transformations in radiosity algorithms. In K. Bouatouch and C. Bouville, editors, *Eurographics Workshop on Photosimulation, Realism and Physics in Computer Graphics*, pp. 137–150. Elsevier, Amsterdam, 1990.

[455] Josep Vilaplana. Parallel radiosity solutions based on partial result messages. In Alan Chalmers, Derek Paddon, and François Sillion, editors, *Third Eurographics Workshop on Rendering*, pp. 217–226. Elsevier, Amsterdam, 1992.

[456] Susan J. Voigt. Bibliography on the numerical solution of integral and differential equations and related topics. Technical report 2423, Applied Mathematics Laboratory, Naval Ship Research & Development Center, Washington, DC, November 1967.

[457] Michael J. Vrhel, Ron Gershon, and Lawrence S. Iwan. Measurement and analysis of object reflectance spectra. *Color Research & Applications*, 19(1):4–9, February 1994.

[458] M. Vygodsky. *Mathematical Handbook—Higher Mathematics*. Mir Publishers, Moscow, 1975. Translated by George Yankovsky.

[459] John R. Wallace. Trends in radiosity for image synthesis. In K. Bouatouch and C. Bouville, editors, *Eurographics Workshop on Photosimulation, Realism and Physics in Computer Graphics*, pp. 1–14. Elsevier, Amsterdam, 1990.

[460] John R. Wallace, Michael F. Cohen, and Donald P. Greenberg. A two-pass solution to the rendering equation: A synthesis of ray tracing and radiosity methods. *Computer Graphics (Proc. Siggraph '87)*, 21(4):311–320, July 1987.

[461] John R. Wallace, Kells A. Elmquist, and Eric A. Haines. A ray tracing algorithm for progressive radiosity. *Computer Graphics (Proc. Siggraph '89)*, 23(3):315–324, July 1989.

[462] George N. Walton. Algorithms for calculating radiation view factors between plane convex polygons with obstructions. *Fundamentals and Applications of Radiation Heat Transfer*, *HTD* Vol. 72:45–52, August 1987.

[463] Brian Wandell. *Foundations of Vision: Behavior, Neuroscience, and Computation*. Sinauer Press, Sutherland, MA, 1994.

[464] Changyaw Wang, Peter Shirley, and Kurt Zimmerman. Monte Carlo techniques for direct lighting calculations. *ACM Transactions on Graphics*. In press.

[465] Franklin F. Y. Wang. *Introduction to Solid State Electronics*. North-Holland, Amsterdam, 1980.

[466] Sidney W. Wang and Arie E. Kaufman. Volume sampled voxelization of geometric primitives. In Gregory M. Nielson and Dan Bergeron, editors, *Proceedings of Visualization '93*, pp. 78–84. IEEE Computer Society Press, Los Alamitos, CA, 1993.

[467] Greg Ward. Personal communication, 1994.

[468] Greg Ward. A contrast-based scalefactor for luminance display. In Paul Heckbert, editor, *Graphics Gems IV*, pp. 391–397. Academic Press, San Diego, 1994.

[469] Gregory J. Ward. Measuring and modeling anisotropic reflection. *Computer Graphics (Proc. Siggraph '92)*, 26(4):265–272, July 1992.

[470] Gregory J. Ward, Francis M. Rubinstein, and Robert D. Clear. A ray tracing solution for diffuse interreflection. *Computer Graphics (Proc. Siggraph '88)*, 22(4):85–92, August 1988.

[471] Tony T. Warnock. Computational investigation of low-discrepancy point sets. In S. K. Zaremba, editor, *Applications of Number Theory to Numerical Analysis*, pp. 319–343. Academic Press, San Diego, 1972.

[472] G. S. Wasserman. *Color Vision: An Historical Perspective*. John Wiley & Sons, New York, 1978.

[473] Alan Watt and Mark Watt. *Advanced Animation and Rendering Techniques: Theory and Practice*. Addison-Wesley and ACM Press, Reading, MA, 1992.

[474] H. G. Wells. The time machine. In *Seven Science Fiction Novels of H. G. Wells*. Dover Publications, Mineola, NY, 1955.

[475] Stephen H. Westin, James R. Arvo, and Kenneth E. Torrance. Predicting reflectance functions from complex surfaces. *Computer Graphics (Proc. Siggraph '92)*, 26(4):255–264, July 1992.

[476] Lee Westover. Footprint evaluation for volume rendering. *Computer Graphics (Proc. Siggraph '90)*, 24(4):367–376, August 1990.

[477] Turner Whitted. An improved illumination model for shaded display. *Communications of the ACM*, 23(6):343–349, June 1980. Also in *Tutorial: Computer Graphics: Image Synthesis*. Computer Society Press, Washington, DC, 1988. Abstract in *Computer Graphics (Proc. Siggraph '79)*, no. 2, p. 14.

[478] Charles S. Williams and Orville A. Becklund. *Optics: A Short Course for Scientists & Engineers*. Wiley-Interscience, New York, 1972.

[479] David R. Williams and Robert Collier. Consequences of spatial sampling by a human photoreceptor mosaic. *Science*, 221:385–387, July 1983.

[480] Lance Williams. Pyramidal parametrics. *Computer Graphics (Proc. Siggraph '83)*, 17(3):1–11, July 1983.

[481] M. M. R. Williams. *Mathematical Methods in Particle Transport Theory*. Butterworth-Heinemann, Stoneham, MA, 1971.

[482] G. Milton Wing. *An Introduction to Transport Theory*. John Wiley & Sons, New York, 1962.

[483] Duncan J. Wingham. The reconstruction of a band-limited function and its Fourier transform from a finite number of samples at arbitrary locations by singular value decomposition. *IEEE Transactions on Signal Processing*, 40(3):559–570, March 1992.

[484] Andrew Witkin and Michael Kass. Reaction-diffusion textures. *Computer Graphics (Proc. Siggraph '91)*, 25(4):299–308, July 1991.

[485] George Wolberg. *Digital Image Warping*. IEEE Computer Society Press, Los Alamitos, CA, 1990.

[486] Erling Wold and Kim Pépard. Comments on "Stochastic sampling in computer graphics". Letter to the editor, *ACM Transactions on Graphics*, 9(2):237-243, April 1990.

[487] Lawrence B. Wolff and David J. Kurlander. Ray tracing with polarization parameters. *IEEE Computer Graphics & Applications*, 10(11):44–55, November 1990.

[488] Elizabeth A. Wood. *Crystals and Light: An Introduction to Optical Crystallography*. Dover Publications., Mineola, NY, 2nd rev. ed., 1964.

[489] Günter Wyszecki and W. S. Stiles. *Color Science: Concepts and Methods, Quantitative Data and Formulae.* John Wiley & Sons, New York, 2nd ed., 1982.

[490] Geoff Wyvill and Craig McNaughton. Optical models. In T. S. Chua and T. L. Kunii, editors, *Computer Graphics Around the World (Proc. CG International '90)*, pp. 83–93. Springer-Verlag, New York, 1990.

[491] Geoff Wyvill and P. Sharp. Fast antialiasing of ray traced images. In Tosiyasu Kunii, editor, *New Trends in Computer Graphics (Proc. CG International '88)*, pp. 579–587. Springer-Verlag, New York, 1988.

[492] H. P. Xu, Q. S. Peng, and Y. D. Liang. Accelerated radiosity method for complex environments. *Computers and Graphics*, 11(1):65–71, 1990.

[493] Jin-Chao Xu and Wei-Chang Shann. Galerkin-wavelet methods for two-point boundary value problems. Submitted to *Bulletin Am. Math. Soc.*, July 1993.

[494] S. Yakowitz, J. E. Krimmel, and F. Szidarovszky. Weighted Monte Carlo integration. *SIAM Journal of Numerical Analysis*, 15(6):1289–1300, December 1978.

[495] Yoshiyuki Yamashita. Computer graphics of black holes: The extension of ray-tracings to 4-dimensional curved space-time. *Transactions of the Information Processing Society of Japan*, 30(5):642–651, 1989. (In Japanese).

[496] John I. Yellot, Jr. Spectral consequences of photoreceptor sampling in the rhesus retina. *Science*, 221:382–385, July 1983.

[497] J. L. Yen. On nonuniform sampling of bandwidth-limited signals. *IRE Transactions on Circuit Theory*, CT-3:251–257, December 1956.

[498] Shigeki Yokoi, Kosuke Kurashige, and Junichiro Toriwaki. Rendering gems with asterism or chatoyancy. *Visual Computer*, 2(9):307–312, September 1986.

[499] D. C. Youla and H. Webb. Generalized image restoration by the method of alternating orthogonal projections. *IEEE Transactions on Circuits and Systems*, CAS-25:694–702, September 1978.

[500] Nicholas Young. *An Introduction to Hilbert Space.* Cambridge University Press, New York, 1988.

[501] Ying Yuan, Tosiyasu L. Kunii, Naota Inamato, and Lining Sun. Gemstone fire: Adaptive dispersive ray tracing of polyhedrons. *Visual Computer*, 4(11):259–270, November 1988.

[502] S. Zaremba. The mathematical basis of Monte Carlo and quasi-Monte Carlo methods. *SIAM Review*, 10:303–314, 1968.

[503] Harold R. Zatz. Galerkin radiosity: A higher order solution method for global illumination. In *Computer Graphics, Annual Conference Series, 1003*, pp. 213–220. ACM Siggraph, New York, 1993.

[504] Yong Zhou and Qunsheng Peng. The super-plane buffer: An efficient form-factor evaluation algorithm for progressive radiosity. *Computers and Graphics*, 16(2):151–158, 1992.

[505] Yining Zhu, Qunsheng Peng, and Youdong Liang. PERIS: A programming environment for realistic image synthesis. *Computers and Graphics*, 12(3/4):299–307, 1988.

[506] Giuseppe Zibordi and Kenneth J. Voss. Geometrical and spectral distribution of sky radiance: Comparison between simulations and field measurements. *Remote Sensing of the Environment*, 27:343–358, 1989.

INDEX

NUMBERS

1D box filtering
  in frequency space, 357
  in signal space, 356
1D Nonuniform Sampling Theorem, 500–501
1D Uniform Sampling Theorem, 340, 342
2D aliasing, 351
2D brakets, 166
2D continuous box, 235–238
  illustrated, 237
2D convolution, 167
2D discrepancies, 458
  for circular regions, 461
  disk, 460
  for edges, 460, 461
  illustrated, 459
2D discrete box, 239
2D distributions, 407–408
2D Fourier transforms, 234–239
  continuous-time, 234–238
  discrete-time, 238–239
  magnitude of, 236
  phase of, 236
2D impulse response, 168
2D lattice, 415
2D linear systems, 165–166
2D reconstruction, 352–354
  filter, 353
2D reptiles, 253
2D sampling theory, 347–352
2D signal, 165–169, 407
  Fourier transform of, 125
  in image rendering, 165
  impulse, 165
2D spherical harmonics, 757
2D Uniform Sampling Theorem, 351, 354
2D wavelets, 291–296
3D
  flux in, 614
  particle transport in, 596–618
  scattering in, 619–621
3D energy transport, 591–596
  components of, 621–630
3D image synthesis, 408, 1076
4D objects, 1077–1078
4D space-time, 1078

A

absence of bloom, 566
absolute integrable function, 194
absolutely summable function, 227
absorption, 592–593, 623
  curve, 57
  explicit flux, 594
  flux, 623
  illustrated, 622
acceleration methods, 1026
accommodation, 9
achromatic channel, 44

active interval, 130
adaptation, 18
  range of, 19
  rod and cone, 21
adaptive hierarchical integration, 495
adaptive HR, 961–964
adaptive refinement, 376
  biased, 377
  defined, 409
  sampling density and, 487
  unbiased, 380
  See also refinement; refinement algorithm; refinement geometry
adaptive sampling, 327, 371, 376–381, 391, 466
  defined, 371
  implementation of, 376
  intuitive nature of, 375
  methods, 376
  point, 466
  See also sampling
adaptive supersampling, 243
  reptiles for, 420
  See also sampling
adjoint equations, 861, 863
adjoint kernel, 798
adjoint operators, 797, 861
aerial perspective, 40
albedo, 592
aliases, 193, 340, 343
aliasing, 28, 174, 343, 1033
  2D, 351
  anti, 193
  coherent, 381
  controlling, 118
  defined, 117, 497
  effects, 118, 380
  hemicube assumption, 927, 928, 930
  high frequencies and, 380
  high-frequency foldover, 381
  noise and, 398–404
  reason for, 118
  from regular sampling, 414
  structured, 1036
    artifacts, 375
  structures, 412
  trading for noise, 369, 371–375
  unstructured, 381
  See also anti-aliasing
alpha filters, 520
alpha measures, 305
alpha-trimmed mean, 521
alternating nonlinear projections onto convex sets, 504
ambient component, 726
ambient light, 725, 727, 738
ambient term, 913
American National Standards Institute (ANSI), 649, 678
  standard definitions, 1135
Ames room, 40
amplitude
  of electric field, 550
  surfaces of constant, 550
  wavelet, 265
analysis equation, 200, 214, 224
  See also Fourier transform; synthesis equation
analysis window, 247
analytic form factors, 1113–1134
  See also form factors
analytic signals. *See* continuous-time (CT) signals
angle factor. *See* form factor
angle-restrictive filters, 75
angular-momentum quantum number, 683
anion, 683
anisotropic effects, 518
anisotropic function, 764
anisotropic shading models, 740–743
anisotropy, 740–744
ANLAB color system, 63
anomalous dispersion, 568
anti-aliasing, 193
  analytic, 333
  color, 1021
  in pixels, 332–333
  See also aliasing
antibonding orbitals, 696
antithetic variates, 326
  defined, 326
  estimand, 328
  estimator, 328
  variance for, 326
aperiodic box, 206
aperiodic sampling, 373, 381–385
  characteristics, 381
  See also sampling

aperiodic signals, 131, 197
with active interval, 197, 198
Fourier series coefficients for, 199
Fourier transform of, 204
See also periodic signals; signals
aperture, 1013, 1021
approximations
constructing, 225
discrete Fourier series, 225
error function for, 801
error monitoring, 800
finite-space, 863
flux, 659
hazy Mie, 760–761
integral, 227
jittered hexagon, 443
Kirchoff, 742
murky Mie, 760–761
Neumann series, 1046
numerical, 808–817
Riemann sum, 312
solid angle, 602, 956
Stirling's, 707
Tchebyshev, 830–831, 869
thin lens, 1014
two-coefficient, 276
area bisection, 485–490
Argand diagram, 138–139
atmospheric modeling, 764–769
Cornette function for, 767
TTHG for, 768
atomic number, 682
atomic structure, 682–690
atom model, 682
atoms, 683
bonds, 695
excited state of, 690
See also specific elements
autocorrelation, 382
Fourier transform of, 382
See also power spectral density (PSD)
autocorrelation function, 402, 403
measure of support for, 403
autocorrelation length, 744
automatic rules, 809
"average observer," 660
avoidance singularity method, 865
azimuth angle, 554

B

backward ray tracing, 1023
Banach space, 1088
bandlimited, 337, 340–341
reconstruction formula, 342
signal, 340–341, 363
band-pass filters, 219–220
bandwidth, 411
high, 409, 543
local, 376, 463
bar chart functions, 177
basis, 178
barrier constraints, 1068–1069
base pattern. *See* initial sampling pattern
bases
1D, 188, 189
representation, in lower dimension, 186–191
base samples, 376
basis functions, 175–186, 814
1D, 186, 187
bar chart, 178
in column vectors, 190
complex exponential basis, 184–186
discrete, 238
dual basis, 182–184
linear, 983
orthogonal families of, 179–182
projections of, 176–179
points in space, 175–176
rectangular, 837
for rectangular wavelet decomposition, 292
scaled, 188
for square wavelet decomposition, 293, 295
STFT, 251
summed, 188
two-parameter family of, 251
weighted, 182
basis representation, 176
basis vectors, 176
linearly independent, 179
orthogonal, 179
transformed, 813, 832
BDFs, 872–873
beams, 108
blanked, 97
at scan line, 97
beam tracing, 1008
See also ray tracing; tracing
Becker-Max algorithm, 785
Beckmann distribution function, 737

Beckmann theory, 737
benign singularities, 865
Bernoulli trials, 378
best candidate algorithm, 430–431
  decreasing radius algorithm vs., 435–437
  examples, 433
  Fourier transform and, 432, 433
  pseudocode, 431
  two-stage, 454
BFI refinement, 970
  implementation, 971
BF refinement, 963
bias, 302, 377, 379
  correcting for, 380
  geometry for analyzing, 378
  isolating, 377
  removing, 379
bias adjustment, 99
bidirectional ray-tracing algorithm, 1044
bidirectional ray-tracing methods, 1039–1044
bidirectional reflectance distribution function. *See* BRDF
bidirectional scattering distribution function. *See* BSDF
bidirectional scattering-surface reflectance-distribution function. *See* BSSRDF
bidirectional transmission distribution function. *See* BTDF
binary transfer mode, 1134
binocular depth, 35–37
binomial distribution, 1102
binomial theorem, 570, 571
blackbodies, 705–708
blackbody emission, 873
blackbody energy distribution, 708–715
blackbody term, 873
black field. *See* uniform black field
black matrix CRT, 75
blind Monte Carlo methods, 207–219
  crude, 307–308, 328
  multidimensional weighted, 315–319
  quasi, 310–312, 328
  rejection, 308–309, 328
  stratified sampling, 309–310, 328
  types of, 307
  weighted, 312–315, 328
  See also Monte Carlo methods
blind spot
  defined, 9
  demonstrating, 11
  diagram, 12
blind stratified sampling, 309–310
  efficiency of, 310
  estimand, 328
  estimator, 328
  problem with, 310
  variance for, 310
  See also stratified sampling
Blinn-Phong shading model, 726–731
  defined, 728
bloom, 1055, 1062
  absence of, 565–566
blooming filter, 1062–1063
blue-yellow chromatic channel, 44
blurring, 518, 1062
Boltzmann equation, 628, 642, 861
bonding orbitals, 696, 698
bond orbitals, 701
bond order, 697
bonds, 695
  ionic, 695–696
  molecular-orbital, 696–704
  types of, 695
Boolean function, 415
Bose-Einstein distribution law for photons, 708
Bose-Einstein statistics, 705–708
  developing, 705–706
  function of, 705
  See also blackbodies
bosons, 705, 740
bounces, 849–850
  illustrated, 850, 852, 853
  multiple, 851
  numbers of, 857
  particle moving after, 850
  probability of, 851
  remaining, 856
boundary conditions, 589, 630–635
  differential equations and, 630
  explicit, 633–634
  finding, 630
  free, 633
  implicit, 634–635
  mixed, 635
  periodic, 633
  reflecting, 634
  specifying, 631, 632
  types of, 632–635
bounding vectors, 318

bounding volume hierarchies, 1026–1027
  illustrated, 1027, 1028
bounds
  conservative, 800
  error, 800
  ideal, 800
  probable, 800
"bow tie," 490
boxes, 365
  1D filtering, 356–357
  dilation equation applied to, 256
  discrepancy calculation for, 457
  enlarging, 351
  frequency-space, 505
  half-integer-sized, 293
  half-width, 254, 255
  multiplying in time domain with, 249
  transform of, 355
box filter, 534
box functions, 153–154, 256, 364, 894
box reconstruction filters, 354–358
box signals, 153–154
  2D, 235–238
  continuous, 153
  discrete, 153
  Fourier series for, 203–204
  Fourier transform for, 204–206
  See also signals
box spectrum, 206–208
  Fourier transform of, 207, 342
  illustrated, 207
  width, 208
box window, 247
braket notation, 1088–1089
  2D, 166
  arguments, 144
  properties, 145
  in signal processing, 145
BRDF, 662, 663–667, 722, 873
  anisotropic, 757
  around volumetric scattering point, 756
  combining, 675
  composite, 675
  decomposing, 738
  as function of incident angle, 756
  geometry, 666
  in Hanrahan-Krueger multiple-layer model, 779
  in HTSG model, 744
  with normal distribution, 755
  normalized, 666–667
  precomputed, 753–757
  properties, 666–667
  reciprocity and, 666
  smooth, 756
  with specular component, 757
  sphere, 723, 724
  splitting, 738
  Ward shading model, 751
breadth-first refinement, 494
Brewster's angle, 735, 877
Brewster's law, 735
brightness, 1059, 1067
  defined, 1068
  monitor control, 98, 99
  perceived, 1058
  peripheral, 1068
  pixel values, 1058
  subjective, 1058
  See also contrast; CRT display
brils, 1058
BSDF, 722
BSSRDF, 664, 873
BTDF, 722, 873
bump mapping, 780
  redistribution and, 785

C

camera models, 1013–1021
candelas, 19
candidate list, 1026
carbon, 687, 701
Cartesian product, 293–294, 614
  operator, 137
  space, 137
Cartesian sum, 137
  combining spaces by, 282
cathode, 560
cation, 683
Catmull-Rom spline, 531
Cauchy-Schwarz inequality, 400
Cauchy sequence, 1088
Cauchy's formula, 570–572
  coefficients for, 572
cells, 484
  regions in, 483, 484
  See also regions; samples
centered variance, 399

central-star reconstruction, 511
  notation for, 512
centroid, 399
certain event, 1094
channels, 43–44
  achromatic, 44
  blue-yellow, 44
  red-green, 44
characteristic equation, 589–590
characteristic expression, 1042
characteristic functions, 794
child nodes, 959, 960, 961
  See also nodes
chroma, 66
chromatic aberration, 14
chromaticity diagram, 49
  illustrated, 50
chromophores, 770
CIE color matching, 44–51
  chroma, 66
  experiment, 46
  functions, 1170
  hue-angle, 65
  phosphors, 102
  r, g, b curves, 46
  XYZ tristimulus curves, 786
  See also colors
CIE standard, 1152–1161
  daylight functions, 1176–1177
  file format, 1154
  illuminants, 1173–1174
  notation, 1153
  observer matching functions, 1169
  See also IES standard
ciliary body, 8–9
  relaxing/tensing, 34
circle of confusion, 1018, 1019
circularly birefringent, 557
circularly dichroic, 557
circular shutter, 1051
classical radiosity, 886, 888–900
  assumptions, 893
  box functions, 894
  collocation solution, 891–892
  extensions to, 979–982
  Galerkin solution, 892–893
  Gauss-Seidel iteration and, 907–909
  higher-order radiosity, 899–900
  intuition for, 895
  solution, 893–899
  strength of, 1045
  weakness of, 1045
  See also radiosity; radiosity algorithms
classical radiosity equation, 896
classical ray tracing, 986, 1010
  characteristic expression for, 1042
  defined, 1010
  illustrated, 1010
  paths modeled by, 1043
  power of, 1044
  strata in, 1011–1011
  weakness of, 1044
  See also ray tracing
clipping, abrupt, 524
closed Newton-Cotes rules, 812
clustering interactions, 939
clusters of four, 85–89
clusters of two, 89–94
coarse-to-fine operator, 269
coefficient of variation, 1101
coexistence singularity method, 865, 868
collisions
  probability of, 584
  types of, 621
collocation, 825
  classical radiosity and, 891–892
  general formulation of, 828
  matrix elements for, 839
  points, 827, 891
  polynomial, 825–830
  quadrature rule and, 825–826
color anti-aliasing, 1021
color bleeding, 1040, 1045
color cloud chamber, 1079
color computation, 66
color contrast, 42, 44
colored reflectivities, 110
color grid, 163
colormap correction, 112
color matching, 44–51
  experiments, 47
  r, g, b curves, 46
  x, y, z, 48
  See also CIE color matching
color opponency, 42–44
  defined, 43
  schematic, 43
color picking system, 68

colors
  3D linear space of, 49
  advancing, 14
  calculation of, 106
  corner, 513
  Euclidean distance between, 65
  interpolating, 69
  with same distance metric, 65
  shading and, 786–788
  See also Macbeth ColorChecker
color shifting, 750
color spaces, 59–68
  HSL , 67, 68
  HSV , 67, 68
  $L^*a^*b^*$, 63–66
  $L^*u^*v^*$, 59–66
  reference white defined, 60
  RGB, 66, 67, 100–106
  RGB color cube, 66, 67
  shift in, 60
  uniform, 60
  XYZ, 59–60
comb function. *See* impulse train
compact support, 130, 131
completeness, 176, 1088
completion phenomena, 11
complex conjugate, 139
complex exponentials, 140–143
  as basis, 184–186
  discrete, 222
  eigenfunction, 143
  Gaussian and, 209
  LTI systems and, 164
  matrix of, 223
  properties of, 141
  shorthand, 143
complex functions
  complex-valued, 139
  real-valued, 139
complex-linear systems, 134
complex numbers, 138–139
  defined, 138
  magnitude of, 139
  on Argand diagram, 138–139
  See also real numbers
complex refractive index, 553
complex scaling factor, 169, 215
component vectors, 175
composite operator, 1058
compression, 191
  lossy, 191
  representation, 193
  wavelet, 274–276
    function of, 275
    illustrated, 274–275
    methods of, 275–276
computer-directed machining, 1078
computer graphics
  aliasing in, 341, 537–538
  color computation in, 66
  filters and, 537
  importance sampling in, 395
  interval analysis and, 372–373
  mathematically continuous signals in, 331
  model surfaces, 567
  singularities and, 864, 868
  warping and, 503
  wavelets in, 245
  See also image synthesis; synthetic images
conditional probability, 1095
conducting band, 716
cone of confusion, 1019–1020
cones, 9, 15
  adaptation, 21
  contrast sensitivity and, 24
  in daylight, 19–20
  of light from a point, 1018
  photopigment in, 16
  polyhedral, 1009
  response curves for, 16
  response of, 22
  types of, 16
cone tracing, 1009
  advantages of, 1035
  illustrated, 1009
confidence interval, 476
confidence refinement test, 476–479
configuration factor. *See* form factor
constant function, 764
constant index of refraction, 713–714
  See also index of refraction
constant Q resonant filter, 287
constants and units, 1135–1137
constant-time filtering methods, 1035
constrained least-squares optimization, 1067
constraints, 1067–1069
  barrier, 1068–1069
  design, 1068
  physical, 1069

continuous signals, 128–129
  Fourier series coefficients for, 198
continuous-time (CT) signals, 128–129
  arguments, 129
  defined, 128–129
  Fourier transform, 231
  reconstructing, 363
  scan line image modeled by, 360
  See also discrete-time (DT) signals
continuous-time Fourier representations, 191–192
continuous-time Fourier transform (CTFT), 197–203
  2D, 234–238
  defined, 200
  pairs, 231, 232
  See also discrete-time Fourier transform (DTFT); Fourier transforms
contour integration, 919–921
  geometry, 921
contrast, 79
  for cluster of four, 91
  for cluster of two, 95
  computing, 89, 92
  CRTs, 79, 1059
  gloss, 565, 566
  lightness, 31–32
  maximum available, 1060
  monitor control, 98, 99
  refinement test, 467
  relative, 1061
  spot spacing and, 89, 92
  test patterns, 86
  for white field, 96
  See also brightness; CRT display
contrast sensitivity, 23–28
  experiment, 24
  rods and cones and, 24
contrast sensitivity function (CSF), 24
  for adult, 25, 27
  for different species, 45
  for infant, 25, 27
  with respect to orientation, 28
  in response to frequency adaptation, 25, 26
  for scotopic/photopic vision, 24, 26
contribution, 855
  finding, 860
control variates, 325–326
  defined, 325
  estimand, 328
  estimator, 328
  variance for, 326
convergence, 194–197
  condition, 506
  criteria, 903
  increased speed of, 318
convolution, 119, 155–165
  2D, 167
  algorithm implementation, 160
  of discrete signals, 161
  discrete-time, 164–165
  example, 158
  filtering operation as, 250
  Fourier transform of, 216
  in frequency domain, 337, 383
  frequency-space equivalent of, 219
  of Gaussian bump, 170
  importance of, 160
  as integration, 123
  intuitive interpretation, 218
  manual evaluation, 161
  multiplication and, 123
  operator, 156
  physical example, 160–161
  properties, 161–162
  results, 159
  signal, 120, 122
  for three functions, 162
  transform pair, 233
  with triangles, 515
  See also impulse response
Cook's filter, 524–526
  See also reconstruction filters
Cook-Torrance shading model, 731–740
  See also shading; shading models
cornea, 6–8
corner refinement, 483
Cornette function, 768
correlation coefficient, 1102
coupled fields, 549
covariance, 1101
critical angle, 575
critical flicker frequency (CFF), 18
cross-correlation, 382
CRT displays, 4, 71–76, 344
  black matrix, 75
  contrast, 79, 1059
  display spot interaction, 76–97
  electron guns, 71–72
  filters, 75–76

CRT displays (*continued*)
  gamma correction, 100
  gamut mapping, 106–111
  guard band and, 75
  image creation, 73
  monochromatic, 76
  phosphors in, 72–73, 101
  radiance values perceived on, 1055
  RGB color space, 100–106
  schematic, 72
  shadow mask pitch and, 74
  subset of colors on, 49
  tension of, 97
  See also displays; monitors
crude Monte Carlo, 307–308
  box width, 313
  convergence properties, 314
  estimand error, 328
  estimator, 308, 328
  See also Monte Carlo methods
crystalline lens, 8
  accommodation, 9
  thickness of, 34
crystals, 579
cubic B-spline, 531
cubic-tetrahedral projection method, 933–934
  cube positioning for, 933
cumulatively compatible, 492
cutoff frequency, 337, 342, 363
cylindrical-scratch model, 743

D

dart-throwing, 429
  2D discrepancies, 458
  drawbacks to, 429–430
  illustrated, 430
  patterns, 459–462
  pixel errors, 462
Daubechies first-order wavelets, 279–280
daylight functions, 1176–1177
DC component, 210
decibels (dB), 235
decomposition, 272
  filters, 267
deconstructions
  rectangular, 291
  square, 291
decreasing radius algorithm, 432–435
  best candidate algorithm vs., 435–437
  geometry of, 435
  pseudocode, 434
definition symbol, 139
degenerate interval, 136
degenerate kernels, 801–804
  defined, 801
  See also kernels
del operator, 627
delta form factors, 925, 934
delta functions
  Dirac, 148, 150–151, 674
  discrete, 874, 875
    2D, 166
  jitter transform and, 384
density function, 322, 1099, 1100
  perfect, 325
depth of field, 1020
depth perception, 33–42
  binocular depth, 35–37
  defined, 33
  monocular depth, 37–41
  motion parallax, 41–42
  oculomotor depth, 34–35
  types of, 34
design constraints, 1068
destructive interference, 549
device-directed rendering, 1069–1072
diamond lattice, 420
  defined, 420
  over set of pixels, 422
diamond pattern sampling, 489
didymium glass spectrum, 76
differential equations, 544, 590, 635
  boundary conditions and, 630
  Kubelka-Munk, 774–776
differential radiance, 663
differential solid angle, 651
diffraction, 563
  defined, 545
  effects of, 563
  See also interference; light
diffuse adjustment factor, 749
diffuse distribution, 1045, 1046
diffuse plus specular, 728–731
diffuse reflection, 564
  directional, 744
  perfect, 672
  uniform, 744
  See also reflection
diffuse reflectors, 889
diffuse transmission, 566, 567

digital signal processing, 117–118
dilation equation, 253–255
  application of, 253
  applied to box, 256
  coefficients, 254, 267
    conditions from, 278
    inverse square of, 286–287
  in Fourier domain, 285
  functions and, 255
  See also wavelets; wavelet transforms
dilogarithm, 1133
diopter, 6
  defined, 6
Dippé filter, 527, 528
  See also reconstruction filters
Dirac delta function, 148, 674
  behavior, 151
  plotted, 150–151
direct current transmission, 210
direct illumination, 723, 1002–1007
  illustrated, 1005
  indirect illumination vs., 1006
  See also illumination
directional stratum, 1001
directional subdivision, 1026, 1030–1031
  illustrated, 1030
direction-based methods, 1001
direction-driven strata sets, 993–996
direction hemisphere, strata on, 992
direction of propagation, 550
directions, 598–599, 993
  around points, 607
  front outgoing, 631
  incident, 724
  locating, 599
  set of, 996, 997
direction sets, 606–613
  hemispherical, 608
    combinations of, 609, 611
    combining, 610
    interpretation of, 610–612
    orientations of, 612
  incoming, 608, 631
  outgoing, 608, 631
  See also directions
direction vectors, 710
direct parameters, 450
direct strata, 1006
  overlap of, 1007
Dirichlet criteria, 194
  in digital domain, 227
discontinuity, 195–197, 975
  detecting, 517, 975
  Fourier series, 195
  meshing, 975
  radiosity and, 975
  signals bouncing into/out of, 196
discrepancy, 456
  2D, 458
    for circular regions, 461
    disk, 460
    for edges, 460, 461
    illustrated, 459
  calculating, from boxes, 457
  circular regions and, 459
  definition, 456
  for different patterns, 458
  generalized, 456
  measurement, 456
  pixel errors and, 462
discrete-time (DT) signals, 129–130
  convolution of, 161, 164–165
    sum, 165
  defined, 130
  sampled, 130
  See also continuous-time (CT) signals
discrete-time Fourier representatives, 222–229
discrete-time Fourier series, 222–225
  pair, 224
discrete-time Fourier transform (DTFT), 225–229
  2D, 238–239
  of convolution sum, 231
  example, 228–229
  See also continuous-time Fourier transform (CTFT); Fourier transforms
displacement texture method, 781
display-adapted operator, 1057
display-adapted visual system, 1056
display compensation, 1056, 1057
display device operator, 1059
display reconstruction filters, 120
  anomalous, 568
  See also reconstruction filters
displays, 71–111
  adaption level, 1060
  light-emitting, 71
  light-propagating, 71
  physical limits on, 1054
  RGB color space, 100–106

displays (*continued*)
technology of, 4
See also CRT displays; monitors
display spot interaction, 76–97
centered spot, 80, 81
clusters of four, 85–89
clusters of two, 89–94
discussion, 97
display measurement, 79–82
interspot spacing, 78
pattern description, 82–84
profile, 76–78
spot brightness, 80
spot patterns, 80
two-spot, 78–79
uniform black field, 85
uniform white field, 94–96
See also phosphors; spots
distinctness of image, 566
illustrated, 565
distribution functions, 306, 307, 447, 1098–1099
Beckmann, 737
cumulative, 1099
joint, 1099
See also BRDF; BSDF; BTDF
distribution ray tracing, 492, 1011, 1021–1035
defined, 1011
illustrated, 1011
for indirect illumination gathering, 1034
overview, 1034, 1035
path capture and, 1042
stratification and, 1031
See also ray tracing
distributions, 148
2D, 407–408
binomial, 1102
blackbody energy, 708–715
defined, 1102
diffuse, 1045, 1046
estimand, 302
exponential, 1102
Fermi-Dirac, 694, 695
Gaussian, 753
indirect parameter, 454
jitter, 426–427
joint, 455
line, 934
normal, 1102
normality of, 307
parent, 302, 307
probability, 1102–1103
radiance, 871, 886
rectangular, 1102
sampling, 302
Student's, 305–306
dithering, 17
divergence theorem, 627–628
divide and conquer singularity method, 865, 868
dodecahedron, 600
domain, 135, 148
defined, 148
See also spaces
dot product. *See* inner products
double-slit experiment, 545–549
defined, 546
illustrated, 547
downsampling, 271
driving function, 636, 793, 966
radiosity and, 966
dual basis, 182–184
defined, 182
for function analysis, 183
for function synthesis, 183
projection coefficients, 182
See also basis functions
duality, 213–214
defined, 213
importance of, 214
dyadic points, 260, 281
dyes, 770
See also pigments
dynamic equilibrium, 626
dynamic Poisson-disk patterns, 440–443
defined, 440
hexagonal jittering, 441–443
point-diffusion, 440–441
dynamic stratification, 496
illustrated, 1037
See also stratification

E

edges
clumping at, 534
intercepts of, 513
linear, 510
eigenfunctions, 143
of 2D systems, 168–169
of LTI systems, 163–164
eigenvalues, 143

eigenvectors, 281
electric fields, 549
  amplitude of, 550
  illustrated, 553
electromagnetic, 549
electron guns, 71–72
  arrangement of, 73
  blue, 73
  dedication of, 73
  green, 73
  magnetic fields and, 100
  red, 73
electronic transitions, 687, 692
electrons, 682, 683–687
  bound, 683
  free, 683
  ground state of, 690
  in parallel spins, 687
  stable, 683
  unstable, 683
  See also photons; quantum numbers
elements
  building, by quantum rules, 686
  computed on demand, 907
  importance-gathering, 970
  importance-shooting, 970
  orthogonal, 1089
  periodic table of, 1137
  perpendicular, 1089
  relaxing, 903
  residual, 904
  See also specific elements
ellipses
  description of, 554
  vibration, 556
ellipsoid
  of energy modes, 711
  frequency, 710
ellipsometric parameters, 556, 558
emission, 623
  blackbody, 873
  BRDF, 723
  explicit flux, 594
  illustrated, 622
  luminescent, 704–705, 716
  phosphorescent, 874
  radiance, 723
  responsive, 681
  sphere, 723, 724
  spontaneous, 681
  thermal, 704
  volume, 621
emmetropic eyes, 13
empirical shading models, 747–753
  programmable, 752–753
  Strauss, 747–750
  Ward, 750–752
enclosure, 888
energy
  absorption, 873–874
  arriving, 652
  blackbody, 708–715
  definition, 654
  distribution of, 691
  Fermi level of, 693
  internuclear potential, 696
  luminous, 660, 661
  modes, 711
  moving, 652
  radiant, 651, 652
  states, 693
energy deficit, 690
energy transport, 581–644
  3D, 591–596
    components of, 621–630
  boundary conditions and, 630–635
  integral form, 635–643
  light transport equation and, 643–644
  model, 626–629
  particle density and, 583–584
  particle flux and, 583–584
  rod model and, 582–583
  scattering and, 584–587
  scattering-only particle distribution equations, 587–591
  from source to receiver, 657
  See also energy
ensemble, 382
equations
  adjoint, 861, 863
  Boltzmann, 628, 642, 861
  classical radiosity, 896
  for dielectric-dielectric interface, 735
  differential, 544, 590, 630, 635, 774–776
  dilation, 253–255, 256, 267, 278, 285–287
  Fredholm, 839
  Fresnel's, 732–737
  gray, 877
  homogeneous, 636
  inhomogeneous, 636

equations (*continued*)
integral, 543, 635, 636, 791–869
integro-differential, 635, 636
light transport, 643–644
matrix, 833, 900–906
Maxwell's, 549, 551–552
occupancy, 694
particle distribution, 587–591
particle transport, 628, 630
Phong shading, 726
polynomial collocation, 829–830
radiance, 543, 544, 791, 794, 871–882, 885
ray, 1023
reflectance, 667, 669, 672
rendering, 879
Snell's law, 576
source-importance identity, 863
sphere, 1023
synthesis, 193, 198, 200, 202, 206, 224, 226
transport, 582, 637–643, 842
undetermined coefficient, 811
equilibrium, 622, 626
dynamic, 626
flux change and, 626
equivalence classes, 176
error annihilation rules, 810
error bound, 800
tightness, 800
error-correcting codes, 1075
error diffusion, 440
error function, 801
error vectors, 832
illustrated, 834
estimand, 300
distribution, 302
value of, 300
variance, 302
See also Monte Carlo methods
estimand error, 303, 304
antithetic variates, 328
blind stratification, 328
control variates, 328
crude Monte Carlo, 328
formula for, 304
halving, 305
importance sampling, 328
informed stratification, 328
quasi Monte Carlo, 312, 328
rejection Monte Carlo, 328
weighted Monte Carlo, 314, 328
estimated value, 302
estimator, 303
antithetic, 328
blind stratification, 328
control variates, 328
crude Monte Carlo, 308, 328
importance sampling, 328
informed stratification, 328
linear, 303
minimum-variance, 303
linear, 303
quasi Monte Carlo, 328
rejection Monte Carlo, 328
unbiased, 303
variance of, 304
weighted Monte Carlo, 328
See also Monte Carlo methods
Euler's identity, 140
Euler's relation, 142
excitant, 690
excited-state energy levels, 687
exitance, 652, 653
expansion, 191
methods, 810
expected density, 583
expected value, 1100
explicit approximation, 881, 882
function of, 887
explicit boundary condition, 633–634
explicit expressions, 595
explicit flux, 593–595, 791
exponential decays, 715
exponential distribution, 1102
extended form factors, 979
external variance, 497
extinction coefficients, 554, 734
for aluminum, silver, 1166, 1167
for copper, gold, 1166, 1168
eye. *See* human eye
eye pass, 1047

F

factorization singularity method, 865, 867
Farrell device, 923–924
illustrated, 924
pointers, 923
See also form factors
farsighted, 14
fast Fourier transform (FFT), 240

features
  correspondence of, 35
  extraction of, 35
  matching, 35
  shifting of, 37
feedback rendering, 1053, 1064–1072
  See also rendering
feedback-rendering algorithms, 1065
Fermat's law, 1105, 1106, 1107, 1108
Fermi-Dirac distribution, 694
  illustrated, 695
Fermi-Dirac statistics, 691–694
Fermi level, 693
fermions, 685, 691
  distribution of, 691
fields
  coupled, 549
  electric, 549, 550, 553
  magnetic, 549, 553
  out of phase, 554, 555
  in phase, 554, 555
  polarization of, 556
  time-harmonic, 549–550
filter bank, 287
  illustrated, 289
filter criteria, 517, 518
  anisotropic effects, 518
  blurring, 518
  reconstruction error, 518
  ringing, 518
  sample-frequency ripple, 518
filter function, 395
  points conforming to, 397
filtering, 155, 411, 1062
  as convolution, 250
  defined, 216
  example, 216
  image box, 358
  local, 517–521
  low-pass, 516
  techniques survey, 537
filters, 119, 445
  alpha, 520
  alpha-trimmed mean, 521
  angle-restrictive, 75
  band-pass, 219–220
  blooming, 1062–1063
  box, 534
  common, 219–221
  computer graphics and, 537
  constant Q resonant, 287
  Cook's, 524–526
  decomposition, 267
  defined, 155
  designing, 299, 358
  Dippé, 527, 528
  display reconstruction, 120
  dividing, 395
    by equal-sized regions, 447
    by equal volume, 446
  fine-to-coarse, 267
  FIR, 220, 359
  flat-field response of, 519
  Gaussian, 359
  high-pass, 219, 267, 270
  ideal, 219, 221
  IIR, 220, 359
  importance of, 216
  low-pass, 120, 123, 219, 263, 267, 363
  Max's, 527–529, 530, 531
  Mitchell and Netravali, 529–532
  multistage, 535
  neutral-density, 76
  noise sensitivity of, 520–521
  nonuniform cubic B-spline, 524
  normalization of, 519–520
  over domain tiled with rectangles, 514
  Pavicic, 525
  piecewise cubic, 535
  reconstruction, 120, 122–123, 342, 353, 354, 363, 394, 526–527
  rings, 221
  scaled, 396
  selective, 76
  separable, 514
  shapes of, 358–359
  space-invariant, 517
  space-variant, 517
  system, 155
  weighted-average filter, 532
  windowed, 220
  See also filter criteria; filtering
fine-to-coarse filters, 267
finite-dimensional space, 818
finite discontinuity, 194
  illustrated, 195
finite-elements approach, 516–517
finite impulse response (FIR) filters, 220, 359
  with good frequency selectivity, 359

finite-support signal, 158–159
  illustrated, 159
finite-to-finite transfer, 918
first-order matching, 278
fission, 585
fixation point, 34
fixed points, 281
flat-field response, 519
  noise spectrum (FFRNS), 456
flicker, 18
  rate, 18
  reduction, 98
  sensitivity, 19
  See also CRT displays
flip() function, 415
flocculate, 777
fluorescence, 715, 872
  defined, 874
  efficiency, 874
  light spectrum, 788
  modeling, 874
  scattering term, 875
  See also phosphorescence
fluorine, 687
flux, 591, 614–618
  in 3D, 614
  absorbed, 623
  approximation, 659
  arriving, 652
  components of, 588
  cosine term in, 616
  defined, 583, 652
  derivation, 618
  equilibrium and, 626
  explicit, 593–595, 791
  falling on patch, 658
  falling on surface, 617
  implicit, 595–596, 791
  incident, 631, 662
  input, 620
  inscattered, 625, 643
  leaving, 652
  left-moving, 587–588
  linear properties, 617
  magnitude, 615
  outscattered, 624
  particle flow and, 618
  percentage of, 623
  radiance vs., 872
  radiant, 652
  radiant, density, 708
  ratio of, 652, 653
  reflected, 662, 668
  right-moving, 587
  solution, 629
  from streaming, 623
  surface, 592
  time derivative, 596
  traveling through space, 637
  as vector quantity, 616
  volumetric emission, 623
  See also rod model
flux-radiance relations, 655
focal points, 1013
  primary, 1013
  secondary, 1013
  See also lenses
folded radical-inverse function, 311
forcing function, 636
form factor integrals, 919
form factor matrix, 897, 907
  illustrated, 908
form factors, 894, 916–937
  analytic, 1113–1134
  analytic methods and, 916–919
  calculation methods, 937, 938
  computation of, 916
  contour integration and, 919–921
  defined, 916
  delta, 925, 934
  discussion, 937
  Eckert setup for measuring, 923
  energy ratio, 917
  estimating between two patches, 936
  estimation methods, 983
  extended, 979
  finite-to-differential, 934
  Galerkin method and, 937
  geometry, 917
  image synthesis and, 916
  library of, 925, 929
  matrix of, 944, 946, 966
  measuring, 921–924
  multipoint, 979
  patches, 942
  physical devices and, 921–924
  polygon, 920–921
  projection, 925–937
    hemicubes, 925–929
    line densities, 936–937

projection (*continued*)
    line distributions, 934
    ray tracing, 934–936
    surfaces, 929–934
  ray-traced, 936
  reciprocity of, 895, 896
  reciprocity rules and, 919
  in specular environments, 984
  surface-to-surface, 981
  surface-to-volume, 981
  volume-to-volume, 981
  See also radiosity
formulas. *See* equations
fourth dimension, 1077–1078
forward Fourier transform, 200
forward ray tracing, 1023
forward scattering. *See* inscatter
Fourier basis functions, 243
Fourier domain
  dilation equation in, 285
  wavelets in, 285–291
Fourier pairs, 200, 214
  CT, 231, 232
  discrete-time Fourier series, 224
  of Gaussians with cutoff points, 360
  reference of, 231
  See also Fourier transforms
Fourier series, 192–197
  for box signal, 203–204
  discontinuity and, 195
  discrete approximation, 225
  discrete-time, 222–225
  examples, 203–213
  of periodic signal, 204
  synthesis equation for, 198, 202
  time-shifting property, 231
Fourier series coefficients, 193
  for aperiodic signal, 199
  for continuous function, 198
  impulse train, 211–212
  for periodic signal, 197
Fourier series expansion, 192–193
  defined, 192
  relations definition for, 193
Fourier transforms, 148, 173–240
  2D, 234–239
  amplitude of, 210
  analysis equation, 200, 210, 224
  of aperiodic box, 206
  of aperiodic function, 204
  of autocorrelation, 382
  basis functions, 175–186
  best candidate algorithm and, 432, 433
  for box signals, 204–206
  of box spectrum, 207, 342
  of continuous signal, 195
  continuous-time, 197–203
  continuous-time Fourier representations and, 191–192
  of convolution, 216
  defined, 174
  definition of, 200
  differentiation property of, 399
  discrete properties, 233
  of discrete signal, 349
  discrete-time, 225–229, 231
  duality, 213–214
  essence of, 191
  examples, 203–213
  fast (FFT), 240
  forward, 200
  frequency content and, 244
  function of, 174
  of Gaussian, 208–209
  high-order, 239
  history of, 191
  of impulse signal, 210–211
  impulse train, 212
  inverse, 200, 201, 202, 352
  magnitude of, 427, 430
  N-dimensional, 239
  Parseval's theorem and, 203
  of periodic signals, 201–202
  properties of, 217
  representation of bases in lower dimension, 186–191
  short-term, 244, 246–252
  of signals, 123
    1D, 124
    2D, 125
  spectrum of, 201
  summary of, 230
  synthesis equation, 193, 198, 200, 202, 206, 224, 226
  table, 221
  of wavelet functions, 262
  of wavelets, 255
  See also Fourier pairs

four-level refinement test, 468–470
  Argence test, 470
  criteria, 469
  for small objects, 469
  "small object test," 470
fovea, 9
  cone density in, 10
  fixation point on, 34
  rod-free zone, 11
frames, reference, 175
Fredholm equation, 839
Fredholm integral of the second kind, 794, 816, 837
free boundary condition, 633
free interval, 136
free term, 793
F refinement, 963
frequency, 142, 252
  cutoff, 337, 342, 363
  ellipsoid for, 710
  functions, 1100
  global estimation of content, 409
  of light beam, 549
  natural, 569
  Nyquist, 340, 361, 362
  resampling, 429
  resolution, 289
  sampling, 339, 344, 361
  of wavelength, 1021
frequency domain, 286
  convolution in, 337, 383
  multiplication in, 341
frequency response, 164, 171, 214
  of 2D systems, 168–169
  of band-pass filter, 220
  of high-pass filter, 219
  of ideal low-pass filter, 219
  of LTI system, 215
frequency space, 174, 364
  1D box filtering in, 357
  advantage of, 174
  box, 505
  equivalent of convolution, 219
  operator, 505, 506
  properties, 516
  sinc function in, 358
Fresnel coefficients, 735
Fresnel reflection, 734
  for air-glass boundary, 735
  for unpolarized light, 736
Fresnel's formulas, 732–737
  deriving, 732
  for unpolarized light, 737
Fresnel's laws, 877
Fubini theorem, 804–805
  illustrated, 804
  symbolic statement of, 805
  using, 807
Full Radiance Equation (FRE), 875–876
  defined, 876
  operator notation, 876
functional techniques, 499
functions, 820
  2D projection, 188, 189
  absolute integrable, 194
  absolutely summable, 227
  analysis of, 183
  anisotropic, 764
  autocorrelation, 402, 403
  bar chart, 177–178
  basis, 175–186, 188, 190, 238, 251, 814
  Boolean, 415
  box, 153–154, 256, 364, 894
  BSSRDF, 664
  centroid of, 399
  characteristic, 794
  CIE color-matching, 1170
  complex, 139
  constant, 764
  Cornette, 767
  cumulative distribution, 1099
  daylight, 1176–1177
  delta, 166, 384, 874, 875
  density, 322, 325, 1099, 1100
  dilating, 253
  dilation equation and, 255
  Dirac delta, 148, 150, 151
  distribution, 306, 307, 447, 737, 1098–1099
  domain, 135
  driving, 636, 792, 966
  energy in, 194
  error, 801
  filter, 395, 397
  folded radical-inverse, 311
  forcing, 636
  frequency, 1100
  gain, 639
  Gamma, 306
  Gaussian, 208–209
  Green's, 852, 853, 860

functions (*continued*)
  hat, 258, 259
  Henyey-Greenstein, 761–762, 767–768
  Hermite, 139
  illumination, 864
  image, 967
  importance, 321, 322, 841, 848–864, 964–966
  infinite discontinuity, 194–195
  input, 636
  integral equation solutions and, 817
  integrating, 606
  integrating factor, 640
  joint distribution, 1099
  Lambert, 764
  mapping, 500
  masking, 890
  Mie, 760–761, 766
  moments of, 260–261, 399
  nearest-surface, 641
  nonflat, 445
  Nyström, 815
  observer matching, 1169
  oracle, 956, 961
  orthogonal, 179–182
  phase, 758–764, 765
  phase space density, 614
  phosphorescence efficiency, 873
  potential, 856
  potential value, 856
  projection of, 176–179
  radical-inverse, 311
  ramp, 149, 150
  Rayleigh, 760
  ray-tracing, 641
  real, 139
  refinement, 377
  reflectance, 662, 724
  reflection, 334–336, 670, 730
  residual, 801
  sampling, 361
  scaling, 244, 253, 279, 282, 284, 1062
  scattering, 758–764
  Schlick, 762–763
  separable, 234
  shifting, 253
  sinc, 155, 204, 341, 355, 358, 365, 384, 387
  spectral efficiency, 1170
  square, 253
  square integrable, 194, 1090
  surface emission, 634
  surface-scattering, 634
  surface-scattering distribution, 634
  synthesis of, 183
  unit step, 149
  value, 856
  visibility, 993, 1000, 1001
  visibility-test, 890
  visible-surface, 641, 642
  volume inscattering probability, 625
  volume outscattering probability, 624
  Walsh, 170
  warped, 500, 502
  wavelet, 260–263
  weight, 809, 1089
  window, 246–247
  See also signals
function spaces, 1090–1091
function vector, 810
fuzzy logic, 1103

G

Gabor transform, 247
gain function, 639
Galerkin bases, 983
Galerkin matrix elements, 893
Galerkin method, 833–836, 891
  3D, 900
  classical radiosity and, 692–693
  form factors and, 937
  iterated, 836
  projection operators in, 835–836
Galerkin radiosity, 900
gamma correction, 100
  coordinate shift due to, 101
Gamma function, 306
gamut, 1069
  defined, 106
  monitor, 106
  printer, 111
gamut mapping, 106–111, 1069
  defined, 106
  difficulty of, 106
  global, 107–110
  local, 107, 110
  methods, 106–107
  rendering information and, 111
gathering radiosity, 953

Gaussian bump, 114, 345, 359, 365
  convolution of, 171
  Fourier pair of, 360
  illustrated, 209
  limit of, 195
  shifted downward, 524
Gaussian distribution, 753
Gaussian filter, 359
Gaussian function, 208–209
  area under, 208
  complex exponentials and, 209
  defined, 208
  Fourier transform of, 208–209
  standard deviation, 208
  variance, 208
Gaussian window, 249
Gauss-Seidel + Jacobi iteration, 914, 915
Gauss-Seidel iteration, 901
  classical radiosity and, 907–909
  defined, 903
  element updating, 904
  gathering step, 910
  illustrated, 904
  performance, 915
Gauss's theorem, 627
generalized discrepancy, 456
generating wavelet. *See* mother wavelet
generations, 422
  number of samples in, 422
geometrical optics, 562
  advantage of, 563
geometric models, 784
geometric series, 1103
geometry, 76, 82–84, 412
  for analyzing bias, 378
  BRDF, 666
  contour integration, 921
  form factors, 917
  of full moon, 729
  hierarchy of, 782
  HTSG shading model, 745
  for imaging by thin lens, 1016
  level of detail problem, 781
  new sampling, 411
  node, 963
  nonuniform, 490
  OVTIGRE, 880
  patch, 654
  of plane waves, 551
  "predictable," 480
  refinement, 480–481
  refinement test, 411
  reflection, 663
  sample selection, 485, 488
  sampling, 412
  shading, 727, 1007
  of specular reflection, 573
  of specular transmission, 577
  Strauss shading model, 748
  of test pattern, 414
  TIGRE, 878
  VTIGRE, 879
  Ward shading model, 750–751
  of zones, 601
  See also patterns
geometry term, 732
Gibbs phenomenon, 197
global cube, 980
global gamut mapping, 107–110
  drawbacks, 108
  methods, 107–108
  See also gamut mapping
global illumination algorithms, 885
global illumination models, 725
gloss, 564–565
  absence of bloom, 566
  contrast, 566
  distinctness of image, 566
  illustrated, 565
  of paint, 730
  sheen, 566
  specular, 566
  types of, 564
  See also surfaces
goniometer, 740
  set up to measure isotropy, 742
goniometric configurations, 1140
Gouraud interpolation, 976
Gouraud shading, 59, 66, 976
grains, 740–741
  size of, 173
Gram-Schmidt orthogonalization, 183, 184
graphic equalizers, 216
grating, 24
graybody, 715
gray equation, 877
Green's function, 852, 860
  using, 853
groups, 684
group velocity, 568

guard band, 75
guillotine shutters, 1051

H

Haar basis, 245, 260
  See also wavelets
Haar wavelets, 252, 257, 258–262
  building up, 257
  coefficients for, 280
  defined, 258
  matrix, 271
  mother, 260
  operator input average, 271
  space combinations and, 282, 283
  transform, 263
  zero-order matching properties, 278
  See also wavelets
halo, 1062
Halton sequence, 311
Hammersley sequence, 311
Hanrahan-Krueger multiple-layer model, 778–780
  BRDF in, 779
hat functions, 258
  illustrated, 259
hazy Mie approximation, 760–761
head-motion parallax, 41–42
heat transfer, 982–983
Heckbert's algorithm, 1044
Heisenberg uncertainty principle, 398–399
  deriving, 399
  testing, 402
  for time and energy, 402
  unitless form, 401
helium, 685–686
  diatomic, 700
Helmholz reciprocity rule, 666, 667
hemicube algorithm, 926, 929
hemicube method, 925–929, 983
  assumptions, 927–929, 930
    aliasing violation, 930
    proximity violation, 928
    violations of, 927
    visibility violation, 929
  benefit of, 925–926, 927
  distribution pattern, 928
  over differential path, 926
hemispheres
  precomputed set of, 754
  as projection algorithms, 831
  sampled, 753–756
  subdivision, 932
hemispherical direction sets, 608
  combinations of, 609, 611
  combining, 610
  interpretations of, 610–612
  orientations of, 612
  surface points with, 631
  See also direction sets
Henyey-Greenstein phase function, 761–762
  defined, 761
  experiential data for, 767
  plotted, 762
  Schlick function vs., 763
  two-term (TTHG), 762, 768
Hermite function, 139
Hermite interpolation, 976
Hero's principle, 1106
hexagonal jittering, 441–443
  example of, 444
  pseudocode, 443
  See also jittered patterns
hexagonal lattice, 417–420
  code for, 417
  defined, 417
  density of, 418–420
  drawbacks, 420
  illustrated, 419, 423
  isotropic nature of, 420
  jittered, 426, 428, 444
  qualities, 418
  subdivided, 420–424
hexagonal sampling, 419
hidden-surface removal techniques, 37
hierarchical integration, 495
  adaptive, 495
hierarchical radiosity (HR), 900, 937–974
  children, 944
  importance HR, 964–974
  internal nodes, 944
  leaves, 944
  links, 948, 950, 951, 953–955
  link structure for, 954
  matrix elements needed by, 949
  node structure for, 953
  one step, 954
  pseudocode, 954, 955
  root, 944
  simple (SHE), 954

hierarchical radiosity (HR) (*continued*)
- summary overview of, 961, 962
- *See also* nodes; radiosity

hierarchical radiosity (HR) algorithm, 939, 951, 974
- importance-driven, 966
- multiresolution analysis and, 964
- physical intuition of, 939
- wavelet bases to, 964
- *See also* hierarchical radiosity (HR); radiosity algorithms

hierarchical refinement algorithm, 942
hierarchy of detail, 781
- illustrated, 782

hierarchy of scale, 781–785
- microscale, 785
- milliscale, 785
- object scale, 785

high-frequency foldover, 381
high-frequency noise, 373, 381
high-order radiosity, 899–900
- problem with, 900
- *See also* radiosity

high-pass filters, 219
- coefficients, 270
- operators as, 267
- *See also* filters

Hilbert space, 819, 1089, 794
homogeneous signals, 479
horizontal retrace, 97
horizontal sweep, 97
HSL (hue, saturation, lightness), 68
- illustrated, 67

HSV (hue, saturation, value) hexcone, 68
- illustrated, 67

HTSG shading model, 744–747
- BRDF in, 744
- computing, 747
- geometry, 745
- reflection types and, 744
- *See also* shading; shading models

hue-angle, 65
human data, 1169–1172
human eye, 5–14
- ciliary body, 8
- cones, 9, 15, 16, 19–20, 21, 22, 24
- converging, 34
- cornea, 6–8
- crystalline lens, 8–9
- depth perception and, 33
- eccentricity, 11–13
- emmetropic, 13
- Gullstrand's schematic, 7, 8
- hyperopic, 14
- iris, 8
- myopic, 13
- nodal point, 6
- optical power, 11
- physiology, 6
- pupil, 8
- retina, 9, 15, 55
- rods, 9, 11, 15, 21, 22, 24
- shape variation, 11–13
- structure and optics, 6–14
- transmissive characteristics of, 22, 23

human visual system, 3, 5–55, 174
- color opponency, 42–44
- components, 5
- depth perception, 33–42
- illusions, 51–54
- perceptual color matching, 44–51
- spectral and temporal aspects of, 14–23
- understanding of, 4
- visual phenomena, 23–33

hybrid algorithms, 886, 1044–1049
- approximation computation, 1046
- general path of, 1048
- light transport paths and, 1045
- radiosity first pass and, 1045
- three-pass method, 1047
- variations of, 1049

hybrid orbitals, 701
- contour map, 702
- electron-density contour map, 703

hydrogen, 685
- atom, 688, 701

hyperbolic trig function, 776
hyperopic eyes, 14
hypertexture method, 780–781

I

iconic bonds, 695–696
identity matrix, 388
identity operator, 270, 796
IES (Illumination Engineering Society of North America), 649, 678
IES standard, 1143–1152
- example file in, 1153
- keywords, 1145, 1147
- lamp-to-luminaire geometry, 1147, 1148

IES standard (*continued*)
main block, 147, 1143, 1145
photometry block, 1143, 1145, 1149–1152
tilt block, 1145–1149
See also CIE standard
ignorance singularity method, 865
IIR sinc function, 359
See also infinite impulse response (IIR) filters
illumination
background, 727
calculating, 920, 1002
direct, 723, 1002–1007
estimation of, 1007
function, 864
global, 885
models, 725
indirect, 723, 1002–1007, 1034, 1039
local, models, 725
map, 1039
painting, 1066–1067
See also light
Illumination Engineering Society of North America. *See* IES
illumination sphere, 723–724
sampling, 725
unsampled, 726–727
illusions. *See* optical illusions
image-based processing, 1061–1063
image box filtering, 358
in frequency space, 357
in signal space, 356
See also filtering; filters
image function, 967
image plane, 881
virtual, 881
image-plane sampling, 395
image surface, 880–881
hypothetical, 881
image synthesis, 4
3D, 408, 1076
algorithms, 792
colored dots and, 117
emphasis of, 1076
form factors and, 916
goal of, 880
inner product and, 860
light and material and, 543
positive force of, 1081
See also synthetic images
imaging models, 1013
immediate payoff, 858, 860
per particle, 861
implicit boundary condition, 634–635
illustrated, 633
implicit expressions, 595
implicit flux, 595–596, 791
implicit sampling, 881, 882
importance-driven refinement, 974
importance function, 321, 841
defined on same domain as unknown function, 964–966
illustrated, 322
important domains and, 859
Monte Carlo estimation and, 848–864
importance-gathering element, 970
importance hierarchical radiosity, 964–974
attaching importance and, 974
importance determination, 974
importance distribution, 968, 970
radiosity distribution, 968
shoot importance, 971
See also hierarchical radiosity (HR)
importance sampling, 320–325, 392–398, 840, 990
by dividing filters into regions, 446
defined, 320, 388, 392, 444, 841
developing, 321
disadvantages, 446
distribution function, 447
estimand, 328
estimator, 328
function of, 321, 444–445
for generating photons, 1039
implementing, 395, 446
importance function and, 841
integral equations and, 841
Monte Carlo, 861
multiple-scale patterns, 448
patterns, 443–448
propagating, 849
rendering situations and, 849
stratified sampling and, 395–398
of variable-scale patterns, 449
zero-variance estimation, 320–321
See also importance function; sampling
importance-shooting element, 970
important radiosity, 968
impulse process, 381

impulse response, 156
  2D, 168
  analytic expression for, 218
  arbitrary system, 168
  finding, 218
  with finite support, 169
  illustrated, 157, 158
  reversed copy, 158
  using, 157
  See also convolution
impulse signals, 148–153
  2D, 165
  continuous, 151
  defined, 148
  discrete, 151
  Fourier transform of, 210–211
  scalogram for, 290
  sifting property of, 156
  spectrogram for, 290
  unit step as, 149
impulse train, 154, 354
  2D, 247
  Fourier series coefficients, 211–212
  Fourier transform, 212
  frequency-space of convolution with, 219
  illustrated, 211
  jittered, 384
  supersampling, 362
incident light
  description of, 336
  evaluating at points, 334–336
incomplete block sampling, 1033
  illustrated, 1034
  unstructured, 1033, 1034
  See also sampling
index of refraction, 567–572, 1164–1165
  for aluminum, silver, 1166, 1167
  Cauchy's formula, 570–572
  constant, 713–714
  for copper, gold, 1166, 1168
  as function of wavelength, 568
  at normal incidence, 1165
  Sellmeier's formula, 569–570
  simple, 567
  Strauss model, 748
  in visible band, 571
  See also refraction
indirect contribution
  estimating, 1031
  sampling, 1032
indirect illumination, 723, 1002–1007
  direct illumination vs., 1006
  estimating, 1039
  gathering, through distribution ray tracing, 1034
  illustrated, 1005
  See also illumination
indirect parameters, 450
  distribution of, 454
  multiple, 453
  See also parameters
indirect strata, 1006
  overlap of, 1007
  See also strata
infimum (inf), 1087
infinite impulse response (IIR) filters, 220, 359
infinite shelf, 897
  environment results, 899
infinite support, 243
infix operator, 156, 165
information block, CIE, 1154–1155
information theory, 1075
informed Monte Carlo, 319–326
  antithetic variates, 326, 328
  control variates, 325–326, 328
  defined, 319
  importance sampling, 320–325, 328
  stratified sampling, 319–320, 328
  See also Monte Carlo methods
informed sampling, 388
informed stratified sampling, 319–320, 329
  estimand, 328
  estimator, 328
inhomogeneous signals, 479
initial sampling patterns, 409–411, 415–462, 492
  creation approaches, 415
  density of, 409
  diamond lattice, 420
  discussion of, 455–462
  frequency content and, 409
  hexagonal lattice, 417–420
  importance sampling, 443–448
  jitter distribution, 426–427
  multidimensional, 448–455
  nonuniform sampling, 424
  N-rooks sampling, 424–426

initial sampling patterns (*continued*)
  Poisson-disk, 427
    dynamic, 440–443
    multiple-scale, 430–437
    precomputed, 427–430
  Poisson sampling, 424
  sampling tiles, 437–440
  square lattices, 420–424
  subdivided hexagonal lattices, 420–424
  subdivision, 487
  triangular lattice, 420
  uniform sampling, 415–417
  See also sampling
inner products, 1088–1090
  of continuous functions, 1089
  defined, 1088
  norms as function of, 1089
  requirements, 1089
inorganic molecules, 701
input function, 636
inscattering, 593, 625–626
  defined, 625
  explicit flux, 594
  flux, 625
  illustrated, 625
  volume, probability function, 625
  See also outscattering; scattering
integers, 136
integral equations, 543, 635, 791–869
  1D, 818
  characteristic functions, 794
  characteristic values of, 794
  classes of, 793
    examples, 794
  common feature of, 817
  converting into, 636
  defined, 636, 792
  degenerate kernels and, 801–804
  driving function, 793
  function of, 791
  general form of, 792
  homogeneity, 793
  importance sampling and, 841
  kind, 793
  linearity, 793
  methods for solving, 791–792
  Monte Carlo estimation, 840–864
  name, 793
  nonsingular, 794
  notation, 792
  numerical approximations and, 808–817
  operation effect on, 822
  operators, 795–798
    identity, 796
    kernel integral, 796
    norms, 798
  projection methods, 817–839
  regular, 864
  singular, 864, 869
  singularities, 793, 864–868
  solutions to, 798–801
    functions for, 817
    methods, 799
  in state transition form, 844
  symbolic methods for, 804–808
  types of, 792–795
integral form, 635–643
  of transport equation, 637–643
integrating factor, 640
integration, 140
  circular regions of, 505
  double, 348
  hierarchical, 495
  kernel of, 793
  methods, 280
  Monte Carlo, 299–329
  numerical, 300
  over solid angles, 605–606
  rule, 280
integro-differential equation, 635
  transforming to integral equation, 636
  with unknown function, 636
intensities, 653
  of α points, 90
  of β points, 90
  of γ points, 90
  computing, 89
  different, 465
  sample, 464–465
  similar, 465
  white field, 96
intensity comparison refinement test, 465–467
  intensity difference, 466
  intensity groups, 466–467
  summary of, 474
  See also refinement tests
intensity statistics refinement test, 473–480
  confidence test, 476–479
  sequential analysis test, 479–480
  SNR test, 474

intensity statistics refinement test (*continued*)
- summary of, 480
- *t* test, 479
- variance test, 475–476
- *See also* refinement tests

interactions
- clustering, 939
- between different types of nodes, 945

interface, 574, 577

interference, 549
- constructive, 549
- destructive, 549
- effects of, 563
- fringes, 549
- *See also* diffraction; light

interlaced monitor, 98–99

internal variance, 497

internuclear potential energy, 696
- curves for hydrogen, 697

interpolation, 497–537
- formula, 342
- Gouraud, 976
- Hermite, 976
- linear, hardware, 983
- spline, 523

interposition cue, 37

interreflection, 979

intersection
- photon-surface, 1039
- point, 1021
- ray-object, 1023, 1026, 1031
- of rays, 1023, 1029
- ray-sphere, 1023–1024

interspot
- distance, 78
- spacing, 78, 80
  - apparent, 97
  - contrast and, 89
- *See also* display spot interaction

intervals, 136–137
- analysis of, 372–373
- confidence, 476
- sifting property for, 152
- subrods in, 592
- time, 451

invariant embedding, 644

inverse Fourier transform, 200, 201, 202
- to central square, 352
- of spectrum, 206, 229

ionization continuum, 687

ions, 683

iris, 8

irradiance, 652
- definition, 654
- incident, 872

irradiance-radiance relation, 655

isolux contours, 975

isosceles triangular lattice, 420

isosceles triangular subdivision, 485

isotope, 683

isotropic materials, 629–630, 664
- absorption coefficient, 630
- illustrated, 629
- incident/scattered directions and, 629
- outscattering coefficient, 630
- *See also* materials

isotropy, measuring, 742

iterated Galerkin method, 836

iterated kernel of order, 807

iteration, 503–506
- methods, 505–506

iterative methods, 901
- Gauss-Seidel iteration, 903–904
- Jacobi iteration, 903
- overrelaxation, 905–906
- Southwell iteration, 904–905
- types of, 901

J

Jacobi iteration, 901
- defined, 903
- illustrated, 903
- radiosity and, 907
- use of, 907

Jacobi loop, 903

jitter distribution, 426–427
- pseudocode, 428

jittered hexagonal lattice, 426, 428
- illustrated, 444

jittered impulse train, 384

jittered patterns, 459–462
- 2D discrepancies, 458
- pixel errors, 452

jittered sampling, 384, 385

jittering, hexagonal, 441–443

joint distribution function, 1099

joint distributions, 455

Jones matrices, 558
- defined, 559
- examples of, 560

Jones vectors, 558
    defined, 559
joules, 651
just noticeable difference (jnd), 24

K

Kajiya shading model, 741–742
Kantorovich's method, 839
kernel approximation methods, 799
kernel integral operators, 796
kernels, 793
    adjoint, 798
    of approximate operator, 808
    arrow notation in, 843
    bounce probability and, 851
    degenerate, 801–804
    discontinuous, 837
    factorizing, 867
    iterated, of order, 807
    pole of order, 866
    product, 867
    resolvent, 806
    separable, 234, 801
    weighted, 863
kets, 143–144
    defined, 144
    into numbers, 144
Kirchhoff's law, 708
Kirchoff approximation, 742
Kirchoff diffraction theory, 741
Kubelka-Munk differential equations, 774–776
Kubelka-Munk pigment model, 770–778
    solutions, 777–778
    theory, 772
    See also paint; pigments

L

$L^*a^*b^*$ color space, 63–66
    recovering XYZ coordinates of color from, 64–65
    sketch of, 64
$L^*u^*v^*$ color space, 59–66
    recovering XYZ coordinates of color from, 64–65
    sketch of, 63
    XYZ color space conversion, 61
Lagrange multipliers, 323, 707
Lagrange polynomials, 828
    illustrated, 829
Lambert function, 764
Lambert shading model, 726–731
    See also shading; shading models
lamp-to-luminaire geometry, 1147
    choices for, 1148
lateral inhibition, 29
lateral separation, 37
lattice, 415
    2D, 415
    densities, 423
    diamond, 420, 421
    hexagonal, 417–424, 426, 428
    points, 418
    rectangular, 416, 417, 427
    regular, 417
    sampling, 417
    square, 420–424
    triangular, 415, 420, 421
law of reflection, 1110
law of refraction, 574, 1111
LCAO-MO (linear combination of atomic orbitals-molecular orbital), 696, 698
    power of, 701
LCD panels, 71
L cones, 16, 17
least-square projection method, 831–832
LED displays, 71, 345
Legendre polynomials, 675–676
lenses
    convex-convex, 1013, 1015
    double-convex, 1013
    focal points, 1013
    shutters, 1051
    thick, 103
    thin, 1013, 1015
    See also crystalline lens; focal points
light, 545–578
    ambient, 725, 727, 738
    arriving at Earth, 613
    atmospheric distribution of, 766
    behavior of, 545
    circularly polarized, 556
    cones of, from a point, 1018
    direct, 1004
    double-slit experiment, 545–549
    elliptically polarized, 554–556
    fluorescent spectrum of, 788
    frequency, 549
    incident
        description of, 336
        evaluating, 334–336

light (*continued*)
- from incident direction, 335–336
- index of refraction, 567–572
- indirect, 726, 1004–1006
- linearly polarized, 556
- luminescent, 704–705
- material and, 543
- mixing, 68
- particle-wave duality, 563
- paths, 1048–1049
- peripheral, 1067, 1068
- photoelectric effect, 560–562
- polarization, 549, 554–560, 735
- propagation of, 408
- propagation speed, 549
- reflection, 563–567
- sources, 1172–1177
- striking a point, 335
- striking particles, 612
- thermal, 704
- transmission, 563–567, 663
- unpolarized, 558, 737
- wavelength, 549
- wave nature of, 549–554

lightness constancy, 32–33
- defined, 32

lightness contrast, 31–32
- defined, 31
- example, 31–32
- illustrated, 31

light pass, 1047

light transport equation, 643–644

limit errors, 107
- preventing, 111

linear algebra, 1085–1091

linear bisection, 481–485

linear estimators, 303
- minimum-variance, 303

linear index of refraction, 714

linearity, 134, 145

linearly birefringent, 557

linearly dichroic, 557

linear perspective, 40

linear processing, 1063–1064

linear spaces, 1085–1090
- *See also* spaces

linear systems, 132
- 2D, 165–166
- complex-linear, 134
- definition of, 134
- real-linear, 134
- time-invariant, 132–135
- *See also* systems

line density projection method, 936–937

line distributions, 934

links, 948
- building set of, 954–955
- creation order, 950
- defined, 953
- for linear patches, 951
- refinement test for, 963
- *See also* hierarchical radiosity (HR)

link structure, 954

lithium, 686

local bandwidth, 376
- establishing, 376
- estimation of, 463

local filtering, 517–521
- criteria, 517, 518
- flat-field response, 519
- noise sensitivity, 520–521
- normalization, 519–520
- *See also* filtering; filters

local gamut mapping, 107, 110
- clipped profile, 107, 108
- illustrated, 108
- methods, 107
- *See also* gamut mapping

local illumination models, 725

locally parallel, 742

local sampling rate, 376

log-linear scale, 478

long-persistence phosphor, 72

low-pass filters, 120
- choosing, 123
- ideal, 219
- illustrated, 364
- operators as, 267
- reconstruction, 363
- wavelets and, 263
- *See also* filters

LTI systems
- 2D, 168
- complex exponentials and, 164
- eigenfunctions of, 163–164
- frequency response of, 164, 215

lumen, 661

luminaire, 634, 723, 1005
  axis, 1140
  bright, 1004
  components, 1139
  defined, 1139
  goniometric configurations, 1140
  housing, 1139
  identifying, 1031
  illustrated, 889
  lamps, 1139
    illustrated, 1150
  nonrectangular, 1151
  output measurements, 1139–1140
  rectangular, 1151
  rotation, 1155, 1157
  shape codes, 1155, 1158
  spherical coordinates, 1140
    system illustration, 1141, 1142
  stratifying, 1031
  terminology, 1139–1143
luminaire standards, 1139–1161
  CIE standard, 1152–1161
  IES standard, 1143–1152
  notation for, 1143
luminance
  adapting to, 1060
  dynamic range of, 1054
  of everyday backgrounds, 20
  mapping, 1064
  measured in candelas per square meter, 1063
  ratio of maximum displayable, 1060
  world, 1063
luminescence, 648
  conventional, 715
  types of, 719
luminescent emission, 704–705, 716
luminous efficiency curves, 21, 22
luminous energy, 660
  transport of, 661

M

MacAdam ellipses, 59
  in Farnsworth's nonlinear transformation, 62
  illustrated, 60
  in perceptually linear space, 61
Macbeth ColorChecker, 1179–1190
  chart, 786, 1170
  chromaticity coordinates for, 1179, 1180
  colors, 1179
Mach bands, 29–31
  defined, 29
  illustrated, 30
  neural analysis of, 31
  origin of, 29
magnetic fields, 549
  illustrated, 553
magnetic-moment quantum number, 683–684
magnification, 260
main block, CIE, 1154–1155
main block, IES, 143, 1145
malignant singularities, 865
mapping
  bump, 780
  function, 500
  gamut, 106–111, 1069
  one-to-one, 502
  texel, 781
  texture, 755, 780
marginal density, 1100
marginal distribution, 1100
masking
  defined, 732
  expressing, effects, 743
  function, 890
  illustrated, 733
mass matrix, 827
material data, 1164–1169
material descriptors, 778
materials, 543, 681–718
  atomic structure of, 682–690
  blackbodies, 705–708
  blackbody energy distribution and, 708–715
  isotropic, 629–630, 664
  layers of, 778
  light interacting with, 779
  localized transitions in, 715
  molecular structure of, 694
  particle statistics of, 690–694
  phosphorescent, 723
  phosphors and, 715–718
  radiation of, 704–705
  selective absorption, 770
  selective reflection, 770
  uniform, 664
  visual appearance, 730
matrix
  blocks, 947
  collocation elements, 839
  constant block within, 944

matrix (*continued*)
finite approximate, operator, 863
of form factors, 897, 907, 908, 944, 946, 966
Galerkin elements, 893
HR elements, 949
identity, 388
inversion, 223
Jones, 558–560
mass, 827
notation, 966
stiffness, 827
wavelet transform of, 837
matrix equation, 833
error, 902
general, 901
residual, 902
solving, 900–906
Max's filter, 527–529
See also reconstruction filters
Maxwell's equations, 549
for electromagnetic energy, 551–552
list of, 552
parameters, 552
for plane waves, 552
M cones, 16, 17
mean-distance refinement test, 471–472
distance criterion, 472
filter criterion, 472
illustrated, 471
uniformity criterian, 472
See also refinement tests
mean squared error (MSE), 180–181
defined in symbols, 181
minimizing, 181–182
mean value, 1100
measurement block, CIE, 1155–1158
measure theory, 639
meshing, 888, 984
defined, 974–975
discontinuity, 975
on ground plane, 1044
problem of, 975
techniques, 984
metastable state, 715
methane, 704
method of iterated deferred correction, 839
method of moments. *See* Galerkin method
metrics, 1087–1088
defined, 1087
in terms of norms, 1088
microfacets, 732
illustrated, 733
RMS slopes of, 737
microscale, 785
Mie phase function, 760–761
approximate, 767
defined, 760
illustrated, 761
Schlick function vs., 763
Mie scattering, 760
milliscale phenomena, 785
minimal bounding spheres, 469
minimax argument, 387
minimax problem, 831
minimum-distance constraint, 383, 429
minimum-variance estimator, 303
linear, 303
mip-maps, 1035
Mitchell and Netravali filter, 529–532
See also reconstruction filters
mixed reflection, 564
mixed transmission, 566
illustrated, 567
modeling methods, 408
modeling program, 1066
modes, 710
energy, 711
molecular-orbital bonds, 696–704
molecular orbitals, 699, 700
construction of, 700–701
molecular structures, 694–704
molecules, 695
inorganic, 701
organic, 701
moments, 260–261
first two, 399
method of, 833
rth, 1101
rth central, 1101
vanishing, 261
monitors, 97–100
brightness control, 98, 99
chromaticity diagram, 106
colors displayed on, 100
contrast control, 98, 99
defined, 97
flicker of, 98
gamma correction, 100
gamut, 106

monitors (*continued*)
  interlaced, 98
  noninterlaced, 97
  raster screen patterns, 98
  RGB, 103
  See also CRT displays; displays
monocular depth, 37–41
  cues, 37
  defined, 37
  interposition, 37
  perspective, 39–41
  size, 38–39
monomials, 811
Monte Carlo estimation, 840–864
  importance function, 848–864
  path tracing, 444–448
  random walks, 442–444
Monte Carlo importance sampling, 861
Monte Carlo methods, 123, 299–329, 1010–1011
  adaptive sampling, 327
  antithetic variates, 326, 328
  for attaching time to rays, 1021
  basic ideas, 300–305
  bias, 302
  blind, 307–319
  blind stratified sampling, 309–310, 328
  confidence in, 305–307
  control variates, 325–326, 328
  crude, 307–308, 328
  defined, 300
  estimand, 300
  estimand distribution, 302
  estimand error, 303, 304, 305, 312, 314, 328
  estimand variance, 302
  expected value, 302
  fundamental result of, 304
  importance sampling, 320–325, 328
  informed, 319–326
  informed stratified sampling, 319–320, 328
  integral equations and, 817
  multidimensional weighted, 315–319
  observation set, 301
    size, 301
  parent distribution, 302
  problems with, 305
  quasi, 310–312, 328
  rejection, 308–309, 328
  research, 305
  sample set, 300
  sample size, 300
  sampling distribution, 302
  sampling variance, 302
  summary of, 328
  weighted, 312–315, 328
  weighted averages, 301
  zero-variance, 320–321
  See also estimator
Monte Carlo quadrature, 817
moon illusion, 38–39
  defined, 38
  explanation, 38–39
  illustrated, 39
mother wavelet, 244, 258
motion, 412
motion parallax, 41–42
  defined, 41
  head-motion, 41, 42
  object-motion, 41
  usefulness of, 42
Mueller matrices, 558
Müller-Lyer illusion, 52–53
  illustrated, 53
multidimensional patterns, 448–455
multidimensional reconstruction, 365
multidimensional sampling, 365
multidimensional subdivision method, 1031
multidimensional weighted Monte Carlo, 315–319
  nearest-neighbor approach, 315
  trapezoid approach, 315
multigridding, 963, 982
multipass algorithms. *See* hybrid algorithms
multi-pass ray-tracing algorithm, 1039
multiple-level sampling algorithm, 490–492
  cumulatively compatible templates and, 492
  defined, 490
  n-level strategy, 490
  two-level, 492
multiple-scale Poisson-disk patterns, 430–437
  best candidate algorithm, 430–431
  building methods, 430
  decreasing radius algorithm, 432–435
multiple-scale templates, 447
  refinement of, 497
multiplets, 687
multiplication
  convolution and, 123
  in frequency domain, 341
  linear systems and, 134

multiplication (*continued*)
  matrix, 245
  in one domain, 355
  property, 217
  scalar, 1085
  in time domain, 383
  transform pair, 233
  vector, 245
multipoint form factors, 979
multiresolution analysis, 282–285, 297
  defined, 282
  framework for, 284
  HR algorithm and, 964
  properties of, 285
  See also resolution; wavelets
multistage filters, 534–536
  defined, 534
  sampling rate and, 535
  spectrum, 535
  summary, 536
  See also reconstruction filters
multistep reconstruction, 532–535
  spectrum, 535
murky Mie approximation, 760–761
myopic eyes, 13

N

natural frequency, 569
nearest-neighbor approach, 315
nearest-surface function, 641
nearsighted, 13
negative radiosity, 981
neon, 687
nested spaces, 284
Neumann series, 806–808
  approximation, 1046
  defined, 806
  resolvent operator, 806
neutral-density filter, 76
neutrons, 682
new sampling geometry, 411
Newton-Cotes rules, 812, 869
nitrogen, 687
nodal plane, 698
node refinement, 494
nodes
  children of, 959, 960, 961
  data structure, 970
  defined, 953
  delayed linking of, 958
  emission field for, 953
  geometry of, 963
  for hierarchical radiosity, 953
  intermediate, 961
  linking, 955–956
  parent, 961
  root, 954, 958, 959, 961
  structures of, 953
  See also hierarchical radiosity (HR)
noise, 28, 538
  aliasing and, 398–404
  artifacts, 374
  filter, sensitivity, 520–521
  high-frequency, 373, 381, 520
  shot, 520
  white, 402
  See also signal-to-noise ratio (SNR)
noninterlaced monitor, 97–98
nonlinear observer model, 1057–1061
  scenes processed by, 1061
nonradiative transition, 718
nonuniform cubic B-spline filter, 524
nonuniform geometry, 490
nonuniformity, 1067
  defined, 1068
nonuniform reconstruction, 371, 404
  algorithms for, 404
  difficulties in, 404
  See also reconstruction
nonuniform sampling, 369–404, 411–415
  1D Nonuniform Sampling Theorem, 500–501
  2D Nonuniform Sampling Theorem, 503
  adaptive, 327, 371, 375, 376–381
  aperiodic, 373, 381–385
  defined, 369
  patterned, 424
  random, 411, 424
  recurrent, 522, 523
  types of, 375
  See also stochastic sampling; uniform sampling
normal dispersion, 568
normal distribution, 1102
normalization, 519–520
  BRDF, 666–667
norms, 1086–1087
  metrics defined in terms of, 1088
  RMS, 1086
  Tchebyshev, 430, 1087

notation, 135–138
  2D signal, 165
  for algebraic objects, 1086
  assignment and equality, 139–140
  braket notation, 143–146
  central-star reconstruction, 512
  CIE standard, 1153
  complex exponentials, 140–143
  complex numbers, 138–139
  FRE, 876
  integers, 136
  integral equation, 792
  intervals, 136–137
  linear algebra, 1085
  luminaire standard, 1143
  matrix, 966
  operator, 265–267, 795, 876, 878, 879
  orbital, 698
  product spaces, 137–138
  radiometry, 648–649
  real numbers, 135
  solid angle, 603–605
  spaces, 146–148
  summation and integration, 140
  TIGRE, 878
  transport equation, 639
  VTIGRE, 879
N-rooks sampling, 424–426
  d-dimensional form of, 451, 453
  pattern, 425
  pseudocode, 426
  See also sampling
nucleons, 682
nucleus, 682
number-theoretic Monte Carlo. *See* quasi Monte Carlo
numerical approximations, 808–817
  Monte Carlo quadrature, 817
  numerical integration, 809–810
  Nyström method, 814–816
  quadrature on expanded functions, 812–814
  undetermined coefficient method, 810–812
numerical integration, 809–810
Nusselt analog, 921–923
  defined, 921
  Eckert setup with, 923
  function of, 922
  illustrated, 922
  See also form factors
Nyquist frequency, 340, 362
  for sampling density, 361
Nyquist limit, 343–344, 371
  leaking into central copy, 343
  sampling frequency at, 344
  of sampling grid, 371
Nyquist rate, 340, 372, 403, 408
  of resampled pulses, 498
Nyström method, 814–817
  defined, 814

O

object-based refinement test, 468–472
  Cook's test, 472
  four-level test, 468–470
  mean-distance test, 471–472
  object-count test, 470–471
  object-difference test, 468
  See also refinement tests
object-motion parallax, 41
objects
  4D, 1077–1078
  algebraic, 1086
  basis representations for, 176
  candidate list of, 1026
  convex, 601, 602
  halo around, 1062
  important, 974
  intersected, 998
  occupying same solid angle, 605
  radially projected, 604
  scale of, 785
  spectral information for, 1191–1206
object scale, 785
object tags, 1066
observation set, 301
  size, 301
occupancy equation, 694
occupancy probability, 691
occupation index, 706, 712
ocean, 769–770
  two-layer model for, 769
oculomotor depth, 34–35
  defined, 34
on-demand patterns. *See* dynamic Poisson-disk patterns
operation mapping, 176
operator notation, 265–267, 795

operators, 132
  adjoint, 797, 861
  building, 267–274
  coarse-to-fine, 269
  composite, 1058
  convolution, 156
  del, 627
  display-adapted, 1057
  display device, 1059
  frequency-space, 505, 506
  as high-pass filters, 267
  identity, 270, 796
  infix, 156, 165
  integral equation, 795–798
  kernel integral, 796
  as low-pass filters, 267
  norms of, 798
  projection, 144, 812, 819, 820, 835
  resolution-changing, 838
  resolvent, 806
  restriction, 267
  self-adjoint, 798
  tone reproduction, 1058
  vision, 1056
optical illusions, 51–54
  found by Roger Penrose, 54
  "impossible figures," 55
  Müller-Lyer, 52–53
  subjective contours, 52
  two inner circles, 53, 54
optical path length (OPL), 1107
optimal rules, 809–810
optimization, 1066
  constrained least-squares, 1067
oracle function, 956, 961
orbitals, 684
  antibonding, 696
  bond, 701
  bonding, 696, 698
  combination of, 699
  hybrid, 701, 702, 703
  molecular, 699, 700
  notation convention for, 698
  probability density plots for, 688
  shapes, 696
  spherically symmetric, 687
  structure of, 687
ordinary integro-differential equation, 635
organic molecules, 701
orthogonal constraint, 179
  normalized, 180
orthogonal functions, 179–182
  complete, 180
  family of, 180
outlyers, 520
out of phase, 554
  illustrated, 555
outscattering, 593, 624–625
  explicit flux, 595
  flux, 624
  illustrated, 624
  isotropic, 630
  methods, 624
  volume, probability function, 624
  See also inscattering; scattering
overrelaxation, 901, 905–906
  defined, 906
  solution methods and, 913
oversampling, 340
overshooting, 915, 916
OVTIGRE, 880, 890
oxygen, 687

P

paint, 730, 770
  handling, 770
  horizontal slice of thickness within, 771
  on surfaces, 771
  reflectance of, 774
  scattering coefficients of, 775, 777–778
  spectra, 775
  types of, 731
  See also pigments
Painter and Sloan's method, 512–515
  advantage of, 513
painter's algorithm, 37
paint programs, 1067
parallel axis, 557
parallel network, 162
  illustrated, 163
parallelogram, 821
parameterized shading models, 752
parameters
  arguments of, 128
  direct, 450
  ellipsometric, 556, 558

parameters (*continued*)
  indirect, 450, 453, 454
  phenomenological material, 552
  Stokes, 558
  Strauss shading model, 748
parent distribution, 302, 307
parent node, 961
Parseval relation, 287
  for wavelet transform, 286
Parseval's theorem, 203
  Fourier transform differentiation property and, 399
particle distribution equations, 587–591
particle history, 844
  stopping, 847
particle phase space, 613
particles, 613–614
  absorbed, 584, 845
  bounce, 849–850
  collision of, 584
  counting, 585–587
  density of, 583–584, 614
  distribution of, 587, 691
  flowing over surface element, 615
  flow of, 618
    net, 622, 623
  flux of, 583–584
  interaction of, 613
  left-moving, 586
  light striking, 612
  outscattering of, 624
  path history, 844
  properties of, 582
  right-moving, 585–586
  saturation of, 591
  scattered, 584
    space-time diagram, 586
  size of, 758
  speed, 613, 617
  state visits, 852
  statistics of, 690–694
  steady state flow, 595
  streaming, 594
  suspension of, 758
  transport in 3D, 596–618
  weighted, 847
  See also particle state
particle state, 842
  absorption, 844
  birth, 844
  bounce off of, 846
  creation, 844
  first, 844
  initial, 844
  particle description by, 844
  path history, 844
  payoff, 858
  potential, 860
  state space, 842
  transfer from, 844
  See also particles
particle-wave duality, 563
pass band, 220–221
patches, 888
  big, 942
  child, 969
  circular, 952
  differential, 653
    receiving, 651
    source, 656
  diffuse, 1049
  flux falling on, 658
  form factor, 942
  geometry, 654
  hierarchy, 944
  linear, 951
  links for, 951
  parent, 948, 969
  perpendicular, 656
  projected onto source point, 658
  rays striking, 977
  reflected power from, 909
  shooting, 936, 976
  source, 653
  spherical, 649–651
  subdivided, 936
    hierarchy of, 942
  undergoing refinement, 943
  visibility of, 925
path tracing, 844–848, 1012, 1036
  advantage of, 846–847
  defined, 846, 1012
  illustrated, 1012
patterned nonuniform sampling, 424
patterns
  for associating time intervals with spatial regions, 451
  dart-throwing, 459–462
  diamond, 489
  discrepancies for, 458

patterns (*continued*)
    discrepancy of, 311
    equidistibuted, 311
    initial sampling, 409–411, 415–462
    jittered, 459–462
    judging, 455–456
    multidimensional, 448–455
    multiple-scale, 448, 497
    N-rooks sampling, 425
    Poisson-disk, 427–437
    regular, 412
    space-time, 452
    test, geometry, 414
    variable-scale, 449
    Yen's study of, 522
    Zaremba, 459
    See also geometry; tiles
Pauli exclusion principle, 685
Pavicic filter, 523–524
    See also reconstruction filters
payoff, 855
    eventual, 861
    immediate, 858, 860, 861
    from particle in state, 858
    potential, 860
    remaining, 855, 856
    total, 855, 860
perceived brightness, 1058
perception
    altering, 50–51
    depth, 33–42
perfect diffuse reflection, 672
perfect specular reflection, 673–675
periodic boundary condition, 633
periodic box, 204–206
periodic signals, 130–132, 197
    analyzing, 201
    approximate, 199
    building, 225
    defined, 130
    formation of, 131
    Fourier series coefficients for, 197
    Fourier series of, 204
    Fourier transform of, 201–202
    input, 199, 201
    with interval, 131
    See also aperiodic signals; signals
periodic table of elements, 1137
periodic waves, 549
periods, 684
peripheral lighting, 1067, 1068
perpendicular axis, 557
perpendicular patch, 656
persistence, 72
perspective
    aerial, 40
    cue, 39–41
    forced, illusion, 40
    linear, 40
    projection, 39
    texture gradient, 40, 41
phase, 252
phase functions, 758–764
    classes of, 759
    constant, 763
    criterion for selecting, 759
    defined, 758
    Henyey-Greenstein, 761–762
    isotropic nature, 758
    Lambert, 764
    Mie, 760–761
    Rayleigh, 760
    Schlick, 762–763
    simple anisotropic, 764
    summary of, 765
phase space, 613
    density function, 614
    illustrated, 614
phase velocity, 551
Phong shading, 59
    equation, 726
    model, 726–731
phosphorescence, 112, 648, 715, 872
    defined, 873
    efficiency function, 873
    modeling, 873
    power-law, 716
    See also fluorescence
phosphorescent emission, 874
phosphorescent materials, 723
phosphorescent term, 873
phosphors, 72–73, 705, 715–718
    arrangement of, 73
    beam spread and, 74
    chromaticities of, 103
    conductors as, 716
    in CRTs, 101
    defined, 72, 715, 770

phosphors (*continued*)
    geometry, 76
        β-type points, 83
        γ-type points, 83
        patterns, 82–84
        triangular, 76, 77
    Hitachi monitor, 1178–1179
    intensities, 1178
    light emission, 99
    long-persistence, 72
    on-and-off, 82
    photons emitted by, 715
    radiance of, 716, 717
    reference data, 1177–1179
    shadow mask and, 73
    short-persistence, 72
    standard, 102
        coordinates for, 102
    See also display spot interaction; spots
photoelectric effect, 560–562
    apparatus for observing, 561
    defined, 561
    photons and, 562
photometric terms, 660
    list of, 650
photometry, 647, 660–661
    defined, 660
photometry block, CIE, 1159–1160
photometry block, IES, 1143, 1145, 1149–1152
photons, 562
    absorbed, 1038–1039
    apparent mass of, 562
    Bose-Einstein distribution law for, 708
    emitted by phosphor, 715
    generating, 1039
    occupation index, 706
    points intersected, 1037
    striking surfaces, 1039
    See also electrons
photon tracing, 988–989, 1037–1039
    defined, 988
    illustrated, 989
    machine produced by, 1038
    path generation and, 1042
    process of, 1037
    See also ray tracing; visibility tracing
photopic spectral luminous efficiency, 660
photopic vision, 19–20
    CSF for, 24, 26
    luminous efficiency functions, 21, 22
photopigment, 15
photoreceptors, 9–10
    cells on top of, 17
    density change, 11
    density of, 10, 117
    function of, 117
    in invertebrates, 18
    packing patterns, 55
physical constants, 1136
physical constraints, 1069
physical devices, 921–924
    Farrell device, 923–924
    Nusselt analog, 921–923
physically based rendering, 885
physical optics, 549, 1074
    as image formation model, 563
picture space, 1065
piecewise-continuous reconstruction, 507–517
    Painter and Sloan's method, 512–515
    thin-plate splines, 515–517
    for triangles, 514
    Whitted's method, 507–509
    Wyvill and Sharp's method, 509–512
    See also reconstruction
piecewise cubic filter, 535
pigments, 730, 770
    defined, 770
    modeling limitation, 776–777
    See also paint
pinhole camera, 1013
    illustrated, 1014
pitch, 74
pixel centers, 360
    resampling at, 483
pixel errors, 462
pixel grid
    sampling function and, 361
    supersampling impulse train and, 362
pixel level, 496
pixels, 407
    anti-aliasing in, 332–333
    average color of, 332
    clamped, 1062
    diamond lattice over, 422
    out-of-gamut, 1070
    ray tree for, 1071
    sampling, 361, 414, 476
    sampling pattern through, 783
    split, 477
    target for, 1070

Planck's constant, 562
Planck's law, 713
  medium-dependent, 713
Planck's relation, 401
plane waves, 550
  geometry of, 551
  Maxwell's equations for, 552
point-diffusion algorithm, 440–441
  example of, 442
  pseudocode, 442
point driven strata sets, 996–999
points
  collocation, 827
  directions around, 607
  direct light at, 1104
  intersection, 1021
  particle transport in 3D, 596–597
  quadrature, 809
  radiance leaving, 656
  surface, 993
point samples, 119
point-sampling approach, 333, 372, 412, 1036
  adaptive, 466
  See also sampling
point set matrix, 387
point sets, 386
Poisson-disk criterion, 427
Poisson-disk patterns, 427–437
  building by dart throwing, 429
  defined, 427
  dynamic, 440–443
  jittered hexagon approximation to, 443
  multiple-scale, 430–437
  precomputed, 427–430
  pseudocode, 429
  sampling tiles and, 437–440
  weighted, 449
Poisson sampling, 424
  pseudocode, 425
polarization, 554–560
  Torrance-Sparrow model, 739
  tracking of, 740
polarized light, 558
polygons
  clustering, 985
  form factor between, 1132–1134
  mesh beating, 931
  rendering systems, 408
polynomial collocation, 825–830
  defined, 827
  equations, 829–830
  See also collocation
polynomial interpolation, 828
post-aliasing, 518
postprocessing, 911, 1054–1064
  defined, 1056–1057
  image-based processing, 1061–1063
  linear processing, 1063–1064
  methods, 1053, 1056
  nonlinear observation model, 1057–1061
potential function, 856
potential payoff, 860
potential value function, 856
Poulin-Fournier shading model, 742–743
power
  shooting the, 909
  unshot, 911
power-law decay, 716
power SNR, 456
power spectral density (PSD), 382, 384
  computing, 386
  defined, 382
  flat, 402
  single copy of, 383
precomputed BRDF, 753–757
  advantages, 753
  lining up, 754
  sampled hemispheres, 753
  spherical harmonics, 756–757
precomputed Poisson-disk patterns, 427–430
primary focal points, 1013
principle of detailed balancing, 692
principle of reciprocity of transfer volume, 655
principle of univariance, 17
principle quantum number, 683, 685
printers
  chromaticity diagram, 106
  gamut, 111
probability, 1093–1103
  certain event, 1094
  conditional, 1095
  defined, 1095
  distributions, 1102–1103
  events and, 1093–1095
  experiment, 1093
  further reading, 1103
  geometric series and, 1103
  measures, 1101–1102
  random variables and, 1098–1101

probability (*continued*)
- repeated trials and, 1097–1098
- total, 1095–1097

processes
- impulse, 381
- skip, 381
- weighted, 381

processing
- image-based, 1061
- linear, 1063–1064
- *See also* postprocessing

product spaces, 137–138
- Cartesian, 137

progressive radiosity, 934, 963, 1049
- *See also* radiosity

progressive refinement, 911–913
- defined, 911
- *See also* refinement

progressive refinement algorithm, 942

projected areas, 597–598
- defined, 597
- illustrated, 598
- radiometry and, 649

projected solid angles, 603
- radiometry and, 649

projection methods, 799, 817–839, 925
- cubic-tetrahedral, 933–934
- discussion, 839
- essential points about, 818
- Galerkin, 833–836
- Kantorovich, 839
- least square, 831–833
- line density, 936–937
- method of iterated deferred correction, 839
- pictures of function space, 819–825
- polynomial collocation, 825–830
- ray tracing, 934–936
- single-plane, 931, 932
- Tchebyshev approximation, 819, 830–831
- wavelets, 837–838

projection operators, 144, 819, 820
- in Galerkin method, 835–836
- orthographic, 819
- truncation, 812

projections, 504
- alternating nonlinear, 504
- form factors, 925–937
- length of, 832
- vector, 832

projection surface, 925

projection techniques, 819

propagation
- direction of, 550
- speed of, 549

protons, 682
- absorption of, 690

pseudocode
- best candidate algorithm, 431
- `BuildLinks`, 956
- decreasing radius algorithm, 434
- `GatherRad`, 959
- `GatherRadShootImp`, 973
- hexagonal jittering, 443
- HR, calling dependence, 954, 955
- `InitBs`, 956
- jitter distribution, 428
- N-rooks sampling, 426
- `OKtoKeepImpLink`, 972
- `OKtoKeepLink`, 965
- `OKtoLinkNodes`, 957
- point-diffusion algorithm, 442
- Poisson-disk patterns, 429
- Poisson sampling, 425
- `PushPullImp`, 973
- `PushPullRad`, 960
- `Refine`, 957
- `RefineLink`, 965
- `SolveAHR`, 964
- `SolveDual`, 972
- `SolveHR`, 958
- `SolveImpHR`, 970
- `SolveSHR`, 955

pupil, 8

pure DC, 210

Purkinje shift, 21

pyramid algorithm, 273

Q

quadratic formula, 400

quadrature
- methods, 799
- Monte Carlo, 817
- on expanded functions, 812–814
- points, 809
- weights, 809

quadrature rules, 809
- automatic, 817
- classes of, 809–810
- collocation and, 825–826

quanta, 401

quantum efficiency, 690
quantum-mechanical distribution, 685
quantum-mechanical electronic interaction factor, 691
quantum modes, 705–706
quantum numbers, 683
  angular-momentum, 683
  magnetic-moment, 683–684
  principle, 683, 685
  spin-moment, 684
  total angular, 684
  See also electrons
quantum optics, 563
quasi Monte Carlo, 310–312
  defined, 311–312
  estimand, 328
  estimand error for, 312
  estimator, 328
  See also Monte Carlo methods
quasi-single-scattering model, 769
quenching, 717
quincunx lattice. *See* diamond lattice

R

radiance, 643, 653, 791
  argument, 977
  computing, 659
  definition, 654, 656
  differential, 663
    reflected, 668
  discussion of, 656–659
  distribution, 871, 886
  flux vs., 872
  incidence, 667
  leaving points, 656
  moon, 730
  perceived values, 1055
  of phosphors, 716, 717
  reflected, 738
  relative, 1061
  sphere, 723, 724
radiance equation, 543, 544, 791, 871–882, 885
  absorption term, 874
  BDF and, 872–873
  blackbody term, 873
  fluorescence and, 874–875
  forming, 872–876
  FRE and, 875–876
  full, 876
  importance of, 871
  OVTIGRE, 880, 890
  phosphorescence and, 873–874
  singularities in, 794
  solutions to, 544
  solving, 880
  TIGRE, 877–878
  time-invariant, 877
  VTIGRE, 878–880
  See also radiance
radiance exitance, 652, 653
radiant energy, 651
  definition, 654
  density, 652
radiant exitance, 888
radiant flux, 652
  area density, 652
  definition, 654
  lumen, 661
  watt, 652
  See also flux
radiation, 704–705
  of blackbodies, 708, 713
  solar, 764, 766
radiation factor. *See* form factor
radiators, 715
radical-inverse function, 311
  folded, 311
radiometric conversions, 648
radiometric relations, 653–661
radiometric terms, 649, 651–653
  list of, 650, 662
  spectral, 649–650
radiometry, 543, 643, 647–677
  defined, 547
  definitions, 654
  examples, 672–675
  notation, 648–649
  projected areas and, 649
  projected solid angles and, 649
  reflectance and, 661–671
  spectral, 659
  spherical harmonics and, 675–677
  spherical patches and, 649–651
radiosity, 885, 887–982
  adaptive, 961–964
  classical, 886, 888–900, 979–982, 1045
  defined, 887
  discontinuities of, 975
  distribution, 968
  driving function and, 966

radiosity (*continued*)
  due to children of a node, 960
  estimate, 913
  finding, 960
  Galerkin, 900
  gathering, 953
  heat transfer and, 982–983
  hierarchical, 900, 937–974
  higher-order, 899–900
  important, 968
  meshing, 974–976
  negative, 981
  power per unit area, 959, 960
  progressive, 934, 963, 1049
  reflected, 907
  result of, 888
  shooting, 953, 955
  shooting power, 976–979
  simulations, 981
  steps, 937
  strengths/weaknesses of, 1045
  of surfaces, 888
  transfer of, 968
  undistributed, 907, 909
  unshot, 907, 911
  view-independent solutions, 1045
  See also form factors; radiosity matrices
radiosity algorithms, 881, 888, 967
  hardware implementations of, 984
  See also hierarchical radiosity (HR) algorithm
radiosity matrices
  Gauss-Seidel iteration and, 907–909
  Jacobi iteration and, 907
  overrelaxation and, 913–914
  progressive refinement and, 911–913
  solving, 906–916
  Southwell iteration and, 909–911
  See also radiosity
ramp function, 149
  derivative of, 150
  illustrated, 150
random-dot stereogram, 35
  illustrated, 36
  single-image (SIRD), 35–37
random nonuniform sampling, 411, 424
random order breadth-first refinement, 494
random variables, 300
  average, 301
  covariance of, 1101
  cumulative distribution function, 1099
  distribution function, 1098–1099
  negatively correlated, 1102
  normal, 301
  positively correlated, 1102
  probability and, 1098–1101
  transformations from uniform, 398
  uncorrelated, 1102
  uniformly distributed, 397
random walks, 442–444
  creating, 846
  five-step, 848
range, 148
range compression, 107
  partial, 109
  six possibilities for, 109
rasterization, 497
rational fraction, 773
ray equation, 1023
ray law, 659
Rayleigh-Jeans Law of Radiation, 711–712
Rayleigh phase function, 760
  Schlick function vs., 763
Rayleigh scattering, 760
  light distribution due to, 766
  modeling, 766
ray-object intersection, 1023, 1026, 1031
  routines, 1023
rays
  chief, 1016
  constructing, 1022–1023
  intersection of, 1029
    first, 994, 1023
  missing sphere, 1025
  passing through sphere, 1025
  propagated, 1027–1029
  tangent to sphere, 1025
  time for, 1021
  tree of, 990, 991, 1033, 1071
ray-sphere intersection, 103
  illustrated, 1024
ray-traced form factors, 936
ray-tracer, 119, 122
ray tracing, 372, 659, 885, 934–936, 987–1050
  architectures, 1050
  backward, 1023
  bidirectional, 1039–1044
  classical, 886, 1010–1011, 1042–1043, 1044
  defined, 987–988
  distribution, 492, 1011, 1021–1035, 1042

ray tracing (*continued*)
forward, 1023
hybrid algorithms, 1044–1049
implementation of, 1050
overview, 1033, 1035
strengths/weaknesses of, 1044
See also photon tracing; rays; visibility tracing
ray-tracing algorithms, 881
ray-tracing function, 641
ray-tracing projection method, 934–936
disadvantage of, 935
efficiency of, 936
ray-tracing volumes, 1049–1050
ray-tree comparison refinement test, 472–473
Akimoto test, 472, 473
refinement levels for, 473
real functions
complex-valued, 139
real-valued, 139
real index of refraction, 554
real interval, 137
real-linear systems, 134
real numbers, 135
complex conjugate of, 139
See also complex numbers
real object spectral information, 1191–1206
reciprocal basis. *See* dual basis
reciprocity, 666
reciprocity relation, 918
reciprocity rules, 895
form factors and, 919
reconstruction, 174, 341–346, 371, 411
1D continuous signal, 336–340
2D, 352–354
after sampling with shah functions, 345
bandlimited, formula, 342
central-star, 511–512
defined, 331, 341
evaluating incident light at point, 334–336
in image space, 354–359
interpolation and, 497–537
low-pass, 363
mechanics of, 352
multidimensional, 365
multistep, 532–535
nonuniform, 371, 404
piecewise-continuous, 507–517
Painter and Sloan's method, 512–515
thin-plate splines, 515–517
Whitted's method, 507–509
signal, 336
from sum of sinc function, 343
spectrum, 358
star, 483
target, density, 496
of uniformly sampled signals, 498
zero-order hold, 344–346
reconstruction errors, 344, 415, 518
defined, 497
reconstruction filters, 120, 342
2D, 353
box, 354–358
choosing, 122–123, 343
coefficients of, 526, 527
Cook, 524–526
Dippé and Wold, 527, 528
Max, 527–529
Mitchell and Netravali, 529–532
multiplying, 354
multistage, 534–536
Pavicic, 523–524, 525
pixel-based, 394
selecting, 537
summary of, 536
reconstruction points, 498
location of, 498
rectangular 2D basis, 837
rectangular deconstruction, 291
rectangular distribution, 1102
rectangular lattice, 417
defined, 417
illustrated, 416
jittered, 327
rectangular wavelet decomposition, 291–293
basis functions for, 292
example, 293
recurrent nonuniform sampling, 523
illustrated, 522
recursive visibility, 1002
red-green chromatic channel, 44
reference data, 1163–1206
human data, 1169–1172
light sources, 1172–1177
Macbeth ColorChecker, 1179–1190
material data, 1164–1169
phosphors, 1177–1179
real objects, 1191–1206
reference frames, 175
3D, 176

reference white, 60
refiltering, 408
refinement, 371
  adaptive, 376, 377, 379, 409, 487
  Akimoto process, 491
  BF, 963
  BFI, 970, 971
  breadth-first, 494
  corner, 483
  criteria for higher-density sampling, 380
  F, 963
  function, 377
  importance-driven, 974
  initial sampling and, 463–465
  multiple-scale template, 497
  node, 494
  optimistic approach, 463
  patches undergoing, 943
  pessimistic approach, 463
  sample intensities and, 464–465
  straightforward, 376
  tree, 493
refinement algorithm
  hierarchical, 942
  progressive, 942
refinement criteria, 376
  implementing, 463
refinement geometry, 480–497
  area bisection, 485–490
  linear bisection, 481–485
  multiple-level sampling and, 490–492
  nonuniform, 490
  sample, 480–481
  tree-based sampling and, 492–497
refinement strategy, 376
  two-stage, 376
refinement tests, 411, 463, 465–480
  acceptance, 463
  Akimoto, 472, 473
  Argence, 470
  contrast, 467
  geometry, 411
  Hashimoto, 471
  intensity comparison, 465–467
    intensity difference, 466
    intensity groups, 466–467
    summary of, 474
  intensity statistics, 473–480
    confidence test, 476–479
    sequential analysis test, 479–480
    SNR test, 474
    summary of, 480
    t test, 479
    variance test, 475–476
  Jansen and van Wijk's test, 467
  for links, 963
  object-based, 468–472
    Cook's test, 472
    four-level test, 468–470
    mean-distance, 471–472
    object-count, 470–471
    object-difference test, 468
  ray-tree comparison, 472–473
  Roth test, 468
  samples in, 465
  types of, 465
  See also refinement
reflectance, 661–671
  of blackbodies, 708
  defined, 661
  functions, 662, 724
  paint, 774
  for polarized light, 735
  types of, 669–670
reflectance equation, 667, 669, 672
  double-integral form, 673
reflectance factors, 662
  defined, 670
  types of, 671
reflectance ρ, 662, 667–669
  defined, 667
reflected radiosity, 907
reflected vector, 573–574
reflecting boundary condition, 634
reflection, 594
  anisotropic, 566
  defined, 563, 661
  diffuse, 564
    directional, 744
    uniform, 744
  energy transport and, 592
  forms of, 563–564
  Fresnel, 734, 735
  geometry, 663
  gloss, 564–565
  interreflection, 979
  isotropic, 566
  law of, 1110
  mixed, 564
  from normal incidence, 739

reflection (*continued*)
  perfect diffuse, 672
  perfect specular, 673–675
  retro, 564
  specular, 563, 564, 1105–1110
    geometry of, 573
    ideal, 744
  total internal (TIR), 574–576
reflection functions, 334–336
  for moon, 730
  types of, 670
reflectors, 889
refraction, 14
  constant index of, 713–714
  defined, 574
  illustrated, 576
  index of, 567–572, 713, 1164–1165
  law of, 574, 1111
  linear index of, 714
  relative index of, 734
  simple index of, 734
region of support, 130
regions, 483–484
  Voronoi, 508
  See also cells; samples
rejection Monte Carlo, 308–309
  defined, 308
  error due to, 309
  estimand, 328
  estimator, 328
  See also Monte Carlo methods
relaxation algorithm, Southwell-type, 914
relaxation methods, 901
  overrelaxation, 901, 905–906
  residual and, 902
  underrelaxation, 906
remaining payoff, 855
  illustrated, 856
removal singularity method, 865, 866–867
rendering, 1053–1072
  defined, 885
  device-directed rendering, 1069–1072
  feedback, 1064–1072
  house painter example of, 544
  importance sampling and, 849
  physically based, 885
  subjective, 1076–1077
  systems, 408
  volume, 1074–1075
rendering algorithms, 885
  development of, 1076
rendering equation, 879
rendering methods, 408, 544
  solid angles and, 970–971
  See also radiosity
RenderMan shading language, 752, 789
repeated rules, 812
repeated trials, 1097–1098
reptiles, 253
  adaptive supersampling and, 420
  defined, 253, 420
  illustrated, 254
resampling, 429
  frequency, 429
  grid, 418
  locations, 408, 464
  at pixel center, 483
  points, 498
  See also sampling
residual, 902
  element, 904
residual function, 801
residual minimization, 800–801
  defined, 800
resolution
  frequency, 289
  limit, 173
  signal, 244
  spatial, 173
  of strata, 997
  visible, 999, 1002
  wavelets and, 252
    multiple resolutions, 282–285
resolution-changing operator, 838
resolution of identity, 286
resolved strata, 998
  applying, 999–1002
resolvent kernel, 806
resolvent operator, 806
responsive emissions, 681
restriction operator, 267
retina, 9
  packing patterns on, 55
  photosensitive cells, 15
retinal disparity, 35, 37
retinal ganglion cells, 29
retro-reflection, 564
RGB coefficients, 66

RGB color cube, 66
  illustrated, 67
RGB color space, 66, 100–106, 786
  interpolation of two colors in, 67
  XYZ conversion to, 104
RGB monitors, 103
rhodopsin, 15–16
Riemann sum approximation, 312
right-hand rule, 1140
ringing, 518
Ritz-Galerkin method. *See* Galerkin method
rod model, 582–583
  illustrated, 583
  particle properties, 582
  scattering rule, 585
  See also flux
rod ring, 11
rods, 9
  adaptation, 21
  contrast sensitivity and, 24
  hyper-polarized, 19
  outside fovea, 11
  photopigment in, 15–16
  response of, 22
  See also rod model
rogues, 520
  eliminating, 520
root-mean-square (RMS)
  error, 519
  for microfacets, 737
  norm, 186
  roughness, 744
  SNR, 474
root nodes, 954, 958, 959
  hierarchy for, 961
roughness, 737–738
  RMS, 744
  surface, 738
Russian roulette, 847, 1032

S

sampled signals. *See* discrete-time (DT) signals
sample-frequency ripple, 518
samples, 119, 174
  aperiodic, 373
  base, 376
  clumping at edge, 534
  concentric rings, 413
  direct parameters of, 450
  distributing, 451
  distribution of, 445
  indirect parameters of, 450
  intensities of, 464–465
  light, 334–336
  modeled by loose/stiff springs, 515
  per pixel, 414
  "pilot" set of, 379
  point, 119, 334
  preciousness of, 122, 408
  refinement geometry, 480–481
  in refinement tests, 465
    with same value, 471
  rogue, 520
  See also cells; regions
sample selection geometry, 485
  recursion and, 488
sample set, 300
sample size, 300
sampling, 119
  in 2D, 347–352
  adaptive, 327, 371, 375, 376–381, 466
  aliasing caused by, 414
  anti-aliasing in pixel, 332–334
  aperiodic, 373, 381–385
  blind stratified, 309–310
  complete block, 1034
  continuous signal, 331
  credo, 122, 408
  diamond pattern, 489
  distribution, 302
  downsampling, 271
  error, 412
  geometry, 412
  hexagonal, 419
  image-plane, 395
  implicit, 881, 882
  importance, 320–325, 392–398, 840, 841, 990, 1039
  incomplete block, 1033
  with incomplete block designs, 450
  informed, 388
  informed stratified, 319–320, 329
  jittered, 384, 385
  multidimensional, 365
  multiple-level, 490–492
  new, geometry, 411
  nonuniform, 369–404, 411–415, 424
  N-rooks, 424–426, 451, 453
  oversampling, 340
  pixel, 361, 414, 476

sampling (*continued*)
  point, 333, 372, 412, 1036
  Poisson, 424, 425
  rate, 343
    instantaneous, 501
    local, 376
    low, 415
    multistage filter and, 535
  recurrent nonuniform, 522, 523
  sequential uniform, 492–495
  signal, 120, 336, 361
  space-time pattern, 452
  square pattern, 489–490
  stochastic, 373, 375, 411
  stratified, 310, 388–392, 395–398, 479
  supersampling, 359–365, 416
  system, 338
  tree-based, 492–497
  undersampling, 340, 398, 1033
  uniform, 332, 336–340, 411–415, 415–417
  upsampling, 271
  variance, 302
  of viewing plane, 987
  See also initial sampling patterns
sampling density, 361
  high, 370, 379, 380
  proportional to intensity, 370
  uniform, 532
  uniform sampling and, 370
  variable, 369–371
  variant, 532
sampling frequency, 339, 361
  at Nyquist limit, 344
sampling lattice, 417
sampling patterns
  comparison of, 386–388
  initial, 409–411
  See also initial sampling patterns
sampling theorem, 336
  for uniformly spaced samples, 341
  See also uniform sampling
sampling tiles, 437–440
  2D, 437
  continuous transformation to, 439–440
  nonuniform, 437, 438
  square, 439, 440
saturation, 874
scalar multiplication, 1085
scalars, 440
  elements in vectors, 842
scale, wavelet, 252
scaled filter, 396
scaled impulses, 202
scaling coefficients, 253
scaling factor, 1061–1062, 1063, 1064
scaling function, 244, 253, 255, 282, 284
  regularity of, 279
  slowly changing, 1062
  wavelet construction from, 255
scalogram, 287, 289
scan conversion, 122, 926–927, 983
scan lines, 97
scanning algorithm, 453
scattering, 584–587
  in 3D, 619–621
  approaches to, 593
  Mie, 760
  particles, 584
    space-time diagram, 586
  probability, 584
  quasi-single, 769
  Rayleigh, 760, 766
  rod model, 585
  rule results, 585
  volume, 619
  See also inscattering; outscattering
scattering coefficients, 775, 777–778
scattering functions, 758–764
scene parameters, 1065
Schauder basis, 258
Schlick phase function, 762–763
  comparisons, 763
  defined, 762
  illustrated, 763
  values in, 763
S cones, 16, 17
score, 855
scotophor, 770
scotopic vision, 19
  CSF for, 24, 26
  luminous efficiency functions, 21, 22
secondary focal points, 1013
selective filter, 76
Sellmeier's formula, 569–570
  simplifying, 570
  square root, 570
  as summation of resonance terms, 569
  using, 569–570
semantic inconsistency errors, 108
  preventing, 111

semi-major axis length, 554
semi-minor axis length, 554
senkrecht, 734
sequential analysis, 479
 refinement test, 479–480
sequential probability ratio test (SPRT), 479
sequential uniform sampling, 492–495
series network, 162
set of measure zero, 639
shaders, 752–753
shading, 381, 412, 543, 721–788
 accuracy and, 722
 anisotropy and, 740–743
 Blinn-Phong, 728
 color and, 786–788
 defined, 721
 directional functions and, 723
 geometry, 727, 1007
 Gouraud, 59, 66, 976
 hierarchies of scale, 781–785
 language, 752
 Phong, 726
 precomputed BRDF and, 753–757
 programmable, 752–753
 surface, 757
 texture and, 780–781
 volume, 757–780
shading exitance solid angle, 721
shading models, 549, 721
 anisotropic, 740–743
 approximate, 722
 assumptions of, 722
 Blinn-Phong, 726–731
 Cook-Torrance, 731–740
 criteria for, 721–722
 empirical, 722, 747–753
 HTSG, 744–747
 Kajiya, 741–742
 Lambert, 726–731
 multiple-layer, 778
 parameterized, 752
 Phong, 726–731
 physically based, 722
 Poulin-Fournier, 742–744
 programmable, 752–753
 Strauss, 747–753
 Ward, 750–752
 See also shading
shading point, 738
 lining up BRDF with, 754
shadow boundaries, 848
shadowing
 defined, 732
 expressing, effects, 743
 illustrated, 733
shadow mask, 73
 dot spacing on, 74
 pitch, 74
shadow-mask technique, 900
shadows, accuracy in, 848
shah function. *See* impulse train
sheen, 566
shells, 684
shifting functions, 253
shift-invariant systems, 135, 164
shoot importance, 971
shooting patches, 936, 976
shooting power, 909, 976–979
 directly from patches, 979
shooting radiosity, 953, 963
 initializing, 955
short-persistence phosphor, 72
short-term Fourier transform (STFT), 244, 246–252
 basis functions, 251
 defined, 246
 dot spacing, 287
 lattice, 288
 See also Fourier transforms
shot noise, 520
shutters, 1051
sifting property, 152
 of impulse function, 156
 for intervals, 152
 for points, 152
signal(s)
 1D, 120
 2D, 121, 165–169, 407
 aperiodic, 131, 197, 198, 199, 204
 autocorrelation of, 382
 bandlimited, 340–341, 363
 box, 153–154, 203–204, 235–238
 continuous, 128–129
 continuous-time (CT), 128–129, 363
 convolving, 120, 122
 cross-correlation of, 382
 DC component, 210
 decomposition of, 272
 defined, 127–128
 difference, 270

signal(s) (*continued*)
  discontinuous, 195
  discrete-time (DT), 129–130, 161, 164–165
  dividing, 393
  downsampling, 271
  even, 129
  finite support, 158–159
  finite width of, 341
  flat, 210
  Fourier space representation of, 355
  Fourier transform of, 123
  frequency content of, 246
  frequency-space, 148
  half-flat, 394
  half-ramp, 394
  high-resolution, 269
  homogeneous, 479
  impulse, 148–153, 165
  impulse train, 154
  inhomogeneous, 479
  low-resolution, 269
  multidimensional, 127
  odd, 129
  oversampled, 340
  periodic, 130–132, 199, 201–202, 204
  period of, 130
  product, 120
  quantized, 130
  reconstructing, 336
  resolution of, 244
  sampling, 120, 336, 361
  sinc, 155, 204, 341
  smoothed, 268–269
  subsampling, 265
  systems and, 127–169
  time, 213
  types of, 127–132
  uncertainties in, 400
  undersampled, 340
  upsampling, 271
  windowing, 247–249
  See also systems
signal estimation, 409
  block diagram, 410
signal processing
  braket notation in, 145
  digital, 169, 174
  for filter design, 299–300
  multidimensional, 169
  nonuniform, 369
  operations, 169
  theory, 299
  trick of, 122
signal space, 364
  1D box filtering in, 356
signal-to-noise ratio (SNR)
  power, 456
  refinement test, 474
  RMS, 474
  See also noise
simple hierarchical radiosity (SHE), 954
simple index of refraction, 734
simulations, 543
sinc function, 155, 204, 341, 355, 384
  2D separable, 387
  clipped, 365
  in frequency space, 358
  IIR, 359
single-image random-dot stereogram (SIRD), 35–37
single-plane projection method, 931
  advantage of, 931
  illustrated, 932
singular integral equations, 864, 869
singularities, 864–868
  benign, 865
  computer graphics and, 864, 868
  defined, 864
  handling methods, 865
    avoidance, 865
    coexistence, 865, 868
    divide and conquer, 865, 868
    factorization, 865, 867
    ignorance, 865
    removal, 865, 866–867
  ill-behaved, 867
  malignant, 865
  weakening, 866, 867
  well-behaved, 867
size cue, 38–39
  illustrated example, 38
size pass, 1047
skip process, 381
slits
  as cylindrical point source, 547
  distances of, 549
  experiments, 579
  two parallel, 546
  See also double slit experiment
SML cone response curves, 1169, 1172, 1173

smoothed signals, 268
  illustrated, 269
Snell's law, 575–576, 578, 1111
  equation, 576
  illustrated, 575
sodium, 689
solarization, 770
solar radiation, 764, 766
solid angles, 598, 599–605, 617
  2D, 599–600
  approximation, 602, 956
  defined, 599
  differential, 651
  hemispherical, 603
  illustrated, 618
  incident, 669
  integrating over, 605–606
  intersected objects and, 998
  inverse-square term in, 658
  multiple objects occupying, 605
  notation for, 603–605
  projected, 603, 649
    importance assignment and, 971
  properties of, 603
  ratio of flux and, 653
  reflected, 669
  rendering methods and, 970–971
  resolved strata method and, 999
  shading exitance, 721
  splitting, 621
  steradian, 600
  stratification on, 997
  tracing, 1008–1009
  types of, 669
  to zero size, 617
source-importance equality, 861
source-importance identity equation, 863
source patch, 653
Southwell + Jacobi iteration, 914, 915
Southwell iteration, 901
  defined, 904
  illustrated, 906
  performance, 915
  radiosity and, 909
  shooting step, 912
space-invariant filters, 517
spaces, 127, 146–148
  chord, 146–147
  combining, 282
  defined, 146
  frequency, 146, 148
  function, 1090–1091
  linear, 1085–1090
  nested, 284
  product, 137–138
  signal, 146, 148
space subdivision, 1026, 1027–1030
  illustrated, 1029
spatial resolution, 173
spectral coefficients. *See* Fourier series
  coefficients
spectral efficiency functions, 1170
spectral locus, 51
spectral radiometric terms, 649
  defined, 659
  list of, 650
  See also radiometric terms
spectral radiometry, 659
spectrogram
  frequency resolution, 289
  illustrated, 289
  for impulse function, 290
  STFT, 289
    for computing, 287
  for sum of three sines, 290
  wavelet, 287
spectrum, 15
  box, 206–208
  containing infinite grid of replications, 350
  flat, 210
  inverse Fourier transform of, 206, 229
  not within limiting square, 351
  reconstructed, 358
  within limiting square, 351
specular adjustment factor, 749
specular gloss, 565, 566
specular reflection, 563, 564, 573, 744,
  1105–1110
  geometry, 1109
specular surface, 1049
specular transmission, 566, 567, 577,
  1105–1108, 1110–1111
  geometry, 1110
specular vectors
  computing, 572–578
  geometry, 573
  reflected vector, 573–574
  total internal reflection, 574–576
  transmitted vector, 576–578
sphere equation, 1023

spheres
around shading point, 724
BRDF, 723, 724
emission, 723, 724
hemilune of, 673
illumination, 723–724
radiance, 723, 724
spherical sector of, 673
spherical harmonics, 675–677
2D, 757
defined, 675
illustrated, 677
precomputed BRDF and, 756–757
with single index, 676
for storing local illumination info, 756
spherical patches, 649–651
differential patch, 651
spin-moment quantum number, 683
spline interpolation, 523
splitting
input face, 621
solid angle, 621
spontaneous emissions, 681
spots
brightness of, 80
Gaussian analysis, 112
patterns of, 80
spacing, 89
apparent, 97
See also display spot interaction; phosphors
square basis, 838
square deconstruction, 291
square function, 253
square-integrable function, 194, 1090
square lattice, 420–424
illustrated, 423
subdivided, 423
squares
of isolation, 349, 350
limiting, 351
stratification of, 390, 391
square tiles, 439
circumscribing circles in, 440
square wavelet decomposition, 293–296
basis functions, 293, 295
defined, 293
example, 296
See also wavelets
standard deviation, 1101
Gaussian, 208
standard observer, 45, 49
standard one-speed particle transport equation, 628, 630
standard phosphors, 102
coordinates for, 102
standing waves, 709
star patterns, 1055
star reconstruction, 483
central, 511–512
See also reconstruction
stationary value, 1107
finding, 1109
illustrated, 1108
steady state, 595, 888
Stefan-Boltzman constant, 714
Stefan-Boltzman law for blackbody radiation, 714
steradian, 600
stereoblind, 37
stereolithography, 1078
stereopsis, 35, 37
Stevens and Stevens experiments, 1060
stiffness matrix, 827
Stiles-Crawford effect, 15
Stirling's approximations, 707
stochastic ray tracing. *See* distribution ray tracing
stochastic sampling, 373, 375, 411
defined, 373
illustrated, 373
trading aliasing and, 375
See also nonuniform sampling
Stokes' law, 715
Stokes parameters, 558
stop band, 221
strata, 389
choosing, 391
in classical ray tracing, 1010–1011
constructing, 1002
direct, 1006, 1007
directional, 1002
equal-energy portion, 395
illustrated, 389
indirect, 1006, 1007
induced, on surfaces, 992
on direction hemisphere, 992
poor choice of, 390
projection, 992
resolution of, 997
resolved, 998, 999–1002

strata (*continued*)
  signal broken into four, 390
  spatial, 1002
  splitting, 392
  visibility-resolved, 999
  See also stratification
strata sets, 993–999
  direction-driven, 993–996
  directly visible points, 995
  point-driven, 996–999
  types of, 993
stratification, 990, 1004
  for circular domain, 391
  distributed ray tracing and, 1031
  dynamic, 496, 1037
  on solid angle, 997
  of square, 390, 391
  See also strata
stratified sampling, 310, 479
  adaptive, 391
  advantage of, 391
  blind, 309–310
  defined, 388
  importance sampling and, 395–398
  informed, 319–320, 329
  method of, 388–389
Strauss shading model, 747–750
  color shifting, 750
  diffuse adjustment factor, 749
  geometry, 748
  specular adjustment factor, 749
  surface parameters, 748
stream, particle, 594
streaming, 621, 622–623
  defined, 622
  explicit flux, 594
  flux due to, 623
  illustration, 622
Student's distribution, 305–306
Student's ratio, 306
subdivided patches, 936
  hierarchy of, 942
subdivisions, 483
  directional, 1026, 1030–1031
  initial sampling and, 487
  isosceles triangular, 485
    centered, 486
  levels, 508
  multidimensional method of, 1031
  right triangular, 486
  space, 1026, 1027–1030
  in Whitted's method, 507
subjective constraints, 1067–1069
subjective contours
  defined, 52
  illustrated, 52
subjective rendering, 1076–1077
subsampling, 265
successive substitution, 805
  defined, 805
summations, 140, 222
  distinct terms in, 223
  infinite, 140
  reversing, 223–224
  switching order of, 231
sum tables, 1035
supersampling, 359–365
  adaptive, 243, 420
  cells, 416
  defined, 359
  impulse train, 362
  methods, 359–360
  model of, 362
support interval, 130
supremum (sup), 1087
surface-based methods, 1001
surface emission, 592, 593–594
  function, 634
surface flux, 592
surface points, 993
  set of, 994
  visible, 995
surfaces, 888
  of constant amplitude, 550
  of constant phase, 550
  enclosure, 888
  hemisphere above, 608
  illustrated, 618
  paint on, 771
  projection, 925
  radiosity of, 888
  subdividing, 888, 975
  viewing, 881
surface-scattering distribution function, 634
surface-scattering function, 634
surface shading, 757
  volume shading vs., 757–758
surface texture, 780
surface-to-surface form factors, 981
surface-to-volume form factors, 981

symbolic expression, 111
symbolic methods, 799, 804–808
  Fubini theorem, 804–805
  Neumann series, 806–808
  successive substitution, 805
synesthesia, 1080
synthesis equation, 193, 200, 224
  coefficients in, 226
  definition of, 206
  Fourier series, 198, 202
  See also analysis equation; Fourier transform
synthetic images
  applications for, 1079
  computed on digital computer, 117
  matching to reality, 1053–1054
  as multidimensional signals, 127
  reasons for creating, 3
  See also image synthesis
systems
  2D, 165–169
  avalanche, 591
  balanced, 888
  defined, 132
  in equilibrium, 595–596, 888
  as filters, 155
  frequency response, 164
  impulse response, 156
  linear
    2D, 165–166
    time-invariant, 132–135
  LTI, 163–164, 168, 215
  maps of, 132
  self-sustaining, 591
  shift-invariant, 135, 164
  signals and, 127–169
  steady state, 888
  subcritical, 591
  supercritical, 591
  types of, 132–135
  See also signals
system transfer function. *See* frequency response

T

talbots, 660
target reconstruction density, 496
Tchebyshev approximation, 819, 830–831, 869
Tchebyshev norm, 430, 1087
Tchebyshev polynomials, 787
telescoping sequence, 838
templates
  cumulatively compatible, 492
  multiple-scale, 447, 497
temporal smoothing, 18
tensor products, 291
  for basis functions, 293
  sixteen, 292
test body, 939
texel, 781
texel-mapping, 781
texture
  defined, 780
  displacement, 781
  procedural, 780
  shading and, 780–781
  stored, 780
  surface, 780
  volume, 780
texture gradient, 40
  example of, 41
texture map, 780
texture mapping, 755
  defined, 780
texturing, 412
thermal emission, 704
thermal equilibrium, 708
  blackbody in, 709
thin convex-convex lens, 1013
  formed by two spheres, 1015
thin lens, 1013
  approximation, 1014
  formula, 1018
  geometry for imaging by, 1016
  triangles for model, 1017
  viewing environment through, 1022
  See also lenses
thin-plate splines, 515–517
  disadvantage of, 516
  illustrated, 515
  utility of, 517
three-dimensions. *See* 3D
three-pass method, 1047
TIGRE, 877–878, 1049
  defined, 877
  geometry, 878
  operator notation, 878
  See also VTIGRE
tiles, 427
  2D, 437
  defined, 375

tiles (*continued*)
- minimum-distance criterion and, 429
- sampling, 437–440
- unit parameterization, 427
- *See also* patterns

tiling, 348
tilt block, IES, 1145–1149
time-harmonic fields, 549–550
time-invariant gray radiance equation. *See* TIGRE
time-invariant systems, 134–135
- *See also* linear systems

time of flight, 1106
time signal, 213
tone reproduction curve (TRC), 1058
- applied uniformly, 1061

tone reproduction operator, 1058
Torrance-Sparrow microfacets, 732
total angular quantum number, 684
total internal reflection (TIR), 574–576
- defined, 575

total payoff, 855
- calculating, 860

total probability, 1095–1097
- theorem on, 1096

tracing
- beam, 1008, 1035
- cone, 1009, 1035
- path, 844–848, 1012, 1036
- solid angles, 1008–1009
- *See also* photon tracing; ray tracing; visibility tracing

transition band, 220
transition rules, 690
transmission, 563–567
- defined, 566, 663
- diffuse, 566, 567
- mixed, 566, 567
- specular, 566, 567, 1105–1108, 1110–1111
  - geometry of, 577, 1110

transmitted vectors, 576–578
transparencies, 71
transport equation, 442, 582, 842
- basic, 637
- integral form of, 637–643
- light, 643–644
- notation for, 639
- solution to, 582

transport theory, 543, 581
transverse waves, 552
trapezoid approach, 315
trapezoid rule, 812
tree-based sampling, 492–497
- adaptive hierarchical integration, 495
- dynamic stratification, 496–497
- hierarchical integration, 495
- sequential uniform sampling, 492–495
- *See also* sampling

tree of rays, 990, 1033
- building, 1033
- illustrated, 991
- for pixels, 1071
- *See also* rays; ray tracing

t refinement test, 479
triangles
- convolution with, 515
- for thin lens model, 1017

triangular lattice, 420
- illustrated, 417, 421
- isosceles, 420

triangular phosphor geometry, 76
- illustrated, 77

triangular subdivision
- isosceles, 485
  - centered, 486
- right, 486

triple integral, 597
triplet, 687
Tumblin-Rushmeier model, 1058, 1059, 1060
two dimensions. *See* 2D
two-pass algorithm, 1045
two-spot interaction, 78–79
two-stage best candidate algorithm, 454
- generalization of, 454
- illustrated, 455

two-stage refinement strategy, 376
two-term Henyey-Greenstein (TTHG) phase function, 762
- for atmospheric scattering, 768
- for modeling Saturn rings, 768
- parameters for, 768

U

ultraviolet catastrophe, 712
uncertainties, 400
underrelaxation, 906
undersampling, 340, 1033
- aliasing and noise and, 398

undetermined coefficient equations, 811
undetermined coefficients method, 810–812

uniform black field, 85
  illustrated, 86
uniform sampling, 332, 411–415
  1D continuous signal, 336–340
  1D Uniform Sampling Theorem, 340, 342
  2D Uniform Sampling Theorem, 351, 354
  attraction of, 411
  patterns, 415–417
  sampling density and, 370
  sequential, 492–495
  See also nonuniform sampling
uniform white field, 94–96
  contrast for, 96
  illustrated, 86
  intensity, 96
  min, max for, 96
  point position, 94–95
unit step function, 149
upsampling, 271

V

vacuum time-invariant gray radiance equation. *See* VTIGRE
valence, 695
value function, 856
vanishing moments, 258, 261
variables, random, 301, 397–398, 1098–1101
variable sampling density, 369–371
variance
  centered, 399
  external, 497
  Gaussian, 208
  internal, 497
  probability, 475
  refinement test, 475–476
vectors, 820
  antiparallel, 638
  basis, 176, 179, 813, 832
  bounding, 318
  column, 190
  component, 175
  direction, 598–599, 710
  error, 832, 834
  expansion for, 810
  function, 810
  Jones, 558, 559
  projection, 832
  reflected, 573–574
  span of, 179
  transformation rotating about, 823, 824
  transmitted, 576–578
  wave, 550, 553
  wavelet-transformed, 245
vector space. *See* linear spaces
vertical retrace, 97
vibration ellipse, 556
view-dependent algorithm, 881
view-dependent solution, 881
view-independent algorithm, 881
view-independent solution, 881
viewing plane, 881
virtual image plane, 881
virtual reality, 1079–1080
visibility, recursive, 1002
visibility function, 993, 1000, 1001
visibility-test function, 890
visibility tracing, 988–989, 990–1037
  in a vacuum, 990
  beam tracing, 1008–1009
  camera models, 1013–1021
  cone tracing, 1009
  defined, 988
  with different strata, 1003
  distribution tracing, 1011
  illustrated, 989, 1004
  light-object interactions, 990
  mirrored ball in a room and, 1040–1041
  path tracing, 1012
  pulling visibility and, 993
  pushing visibility and, 993
  strata sets, 993–999
  using, 1047, 1049
    in scenes, 991
  See also photon tracing; ray tracing
visible resolution, 999
  computing, 1002
  See also resolution
visible-surface function, 641
  illustrated, 642
vision operator, 1056
visual angle, 6
  defined, 6
  measurement of, 7
visual band, 14, 660
visual phenomena, 23–33
  contrast sensitivity, 23–28
  lightness constancy, 32–33
  lightness contrast, 31–32
  Mach bands, 29–31
  noise, 28

visual range, 14
visual system. *See* human visual system
volume emission, 621
  flux, 623
volume inscattering probability function, 625
volume methods, 981
volume outscattering probability function, 624
volume rendering, 1074–1075
  anti-aliasing methods, 1074
  applications, 1074–1075
  importance of, 1075
  mathematics of, 1074
  See also rendering
volume shading, 757–780
  atmospheric modeling and, 764–769
  defined, 757
  Hanrahan-Krueger multiple-layer model and, 778–780
  Kubelka-Munk pigment model and, 770–778
  multiple-layer models, 778
  ocean and, 769
  phase functions and, 758–764
  surface shading vs., 757–758
  See also shading
volume texture, 780
volume-to-volume form factors, 981
volumetric emission, 593
Voronoi diagram, 315
  illustrated, 316
VTIGRE, 878–880, 1049
  defined, 879
  geometry, 879
  operator notation, 879
  outgoing (OVTIGRE), 880
  See also TIGRE

W

Walsh functions, 170
Ward shading model, 750–752
  anisotropic form, 751
  BRDF, 751
  chair photos and, 752
  geometry, 750–751
  parameters, 751–752
warped function, 500, 502
warping, 499–503
  computer graphics and, 503
  defined, 499
wavefront, 550
wavelength, 14
  decoupled, 877
  decoupled energy, 648
  defined, 549
  frequency of, 1021
  index of refraction as function of, 568
  power vs., 15
wavelet basis, 243
  to HR algorithm, 964
wavelet coefficients, 263, 265
  computing, 265
  conditions, 277–282
  finding, 270
  inner product computation with, 280
  nonzero, 277
  for real-world signals, 276
wavelet functions
  basis, 263
  evaluating, 281
  Fourier transforms of, 262
  moment of, 260–261
  shape of, 281
  two-parameter family of, 261
  values at dyadic points, 281
wavelets, 243
  2D, 291–296
  amplitude of, 265
  analysis property of, 244
  applications of, 297
  bandwidth ratio and, 287
  compression of, 274–276
    function of, 275
    illustrated, 274–275
    methods, 275–276
  in computer graphics, 245
  creating, 255
  Daubechies first-order wavelets, 279
  defined, 244
  development of, 244
  dilation equation and, 253–255, 267
  dilation parameter, 260
  first two generations of, 264
  four-coefficient, 279
  in Fourier domain, 285–291
  Fourier transform of, 255
  frequency adaption, 289
  Haar, 252, 257, 258–262
    2D, 125
    building up, 257
    defined, 258
    matrix, 271

Haar (*continued*)
mother, 260
space combinations and, 282, 283
zero-order matching properties, 278
hat functions and, 258
higher-order, 255
high-frequency information and, 837
introduction to, 297
level of, 263
moments and, 260–261
mother, 244, 258
multiresolution analysis, 282–285
multiresolution framework for, 284
normalization term, 267
order of, 279, 280
orthogonal, 260
orthonormal basis and, 244
position of, 263
as projection method, 837–838
reason for studying, 244–245
rectangular decomposition, 291–293
resolution and, 252
at same scale, 262
scale and, 252
from scaling function, 255
series of, stacked together, 266
square decomposition, 293–296
stretched in time, 286
translation parameter, 260
See also Haar basis
wavelet spectrogram, 287
wavelet transforms, 243–296
computing, 263, 297, 837
defined, 243
function of, 244
Haar, 263
inverting, 277
Parseval relation for, 286
pattern for, 287
principles of, 263
See also wavelets
wave packet, 563
waves
cylindrical point source of, 547
homogeneous, 550
inhomogeneous, 550
interference between, 549
periodic, 549
plane, 550, 551
spherical point source of, 546
standing, 709
transverse, 552
wave theory, 562
wave vectors, 550
illustrated, 553
Weber fraction, 24
weighted-average filter, 532
weighted averages, 301
weighted Monte Carlo, 312–315
convergence properties, 314
defined, 312
estimand, 328
estimand error, 314
estimator, 328
multidimensional, 315–319
See also Monte Carlo methods
weighted particles, 847
weighted process, 381
weight function, 809, 1089
weights
kernel, 862
quadrature, 809
white field. *See* uniform white field
white noise, 402
Whitted's method, 507–509
subdivision in, 507
weight assignment and, 509
windowed filters, 220–221
window function, 246–247
windows
analysis, 247
box, 247
Gaussian, 249
Wyvill and Sharpe's method, 509–512
assumption, 512
illustrated, 510

X

XYZ color space, 59–60
$L^*u^*v^*$ conversion, 61
recovering, 64
RGB conversion, 104
spectra conversion, 104–106
See also color spaces

Y

Yen's method, 522–532
Bouville, 526–527
Cook's filter, 524–526
Dippé and Wold, 527

Yen's method (*continued*)
Max, 527–529
Mitchell and Netravali, 529–532
Pavicic, 523–524
sample patterns, 522

Z

Zaremba sequence, 311
discrepancy due to, 456, 458
pattern, 459
z-buffer, 163
approach, 926
scan converter, 119
Zeeman effect, 687
zero-order hold reconstruction, 344–346
illustrated, 346
model of, 346
zero-order matching, 278
zero-variance estimation, 320–321
zonal methods, 981
zones, 601
geometry of, 601

When you want to know a thing you have studied in your memory proceed in this way: When you have drawn the same thing so many times that you think you know it by heart, test it by drawing it without the model; but have the model traced on flat thin glass and lay this on the drawing you have made without the model, and note carefully where the tracing does not coincide with your drawing, and where you find you have gone wrong; and bear in mind not to repeat the same mistakes. Then return to the model, and draw the part in which you were wrong again and again till you have it well in your mind.

Leonardo da Vinci

. . . there ain't nothing more to write about, and I am rotten glad of it, because if I'd a knowed what a trouble it was to make a book I wouldn't a tackled it and ain't agoing to no more.

Mark Twain
("The Adventures of Huckleberry Finn," 1884)